Why World Band Radio?

The urge to seek turns restlessly within us. What is the news from beyond the mountain, the other side of the big water? How do people there work, play and celebrate? Does their music move the heart as does ours? What of warring factions? The answers, we hope, will make us feel connected.

World band radio allows us to wander the globe from the comfort of our familiar fire, revealing fresh perspectives from distant cultures. Unwrapping valuables of song and human tales. We voyage upon the airwaves to seek the other side of the hill . . . only to find we have discovered the world and, in so doing, ourselves.

1993 Passport To

Egyptian Tourist Authority

Page 147

World Band Radio

Page 95

Glossary

Page 37

ISSN 0897-0157

 **International Broadcasting Services, Ltd.**

1993

Passport To World Band Radio™

Our reader is the most important person in the world

EDITORIAL

Editor-in-Chief	Lawrence Magne
Editor	Tony Jones
Features Editor	Rick Booth
Contributing Editors	Jock Elliott • Craig Tyson
Consulting Editors	John Campbell • Don Jensen
Editorial Contributors	James Conrad (U.S.) • Gordon Darling (Papua New Guinea) • Antonio Ribeiro da Motta (Brazil) • Anatoly Klepov (Russia) • Marie Lamb (U.S.) • *Número Uno*/John Herkimer (U.S.) • Toshimichi Ohtake (Japan) • *Radio Nuevo Mundo*/Tetsuya Hirahara (Japan) • Jairo Salazar (Venezuela) • Don Swampo (Uruguay) • David Walcutt (U.S.)
Worldscan™ Software	Richard Mayell
Laboratory	Sherwood Engineering Inc.
Graphic Arts	Mike Wright, CCI
Cover Artwork	Gahan Wilson

ADMINISTRATION & OPERATIONS

Publisher	Lawrence Magne
Associate Publisher	Jane Brinker
Advertising & Production	Mary Kroszner, MWK
Order Fulfillment	Konrad Kroszner • Mary Kroszner, MWK
Media Communications	Consultech Communications, Inc. • Fax: +1 (518) 283 0830

OFFICES

IBS - North America	Box 300, Penn's Park PA 18943 USA • Fax: (Advertising & Distribution) +1 (215) 794 3396; (Editorial) +1 (215) 598 3794
IBS - Latin America	Casilla 1844, Asunción, Paraguay • Fax: +595 (21) 446 373
IBS - Australia	Box 2145, Malaga WA 6062 • Fax: +61 (9) 342 9158
IBS - Japan	5-31-6 Tamanawa, Kamakura 247 • Fax: +81 (467) 43 2167

Library of Congress Cataloging-in-Publication Data

Passport to World Band Radio.
   1. Radio, Short wave—Amateurs' manuals.   2. Radio Stations, Short wave—Directories.
I. Magne, Lawrence, 1941–
TK9956.P27   1992   384.54'5   91-22739
ISBN 0-914941-40-2

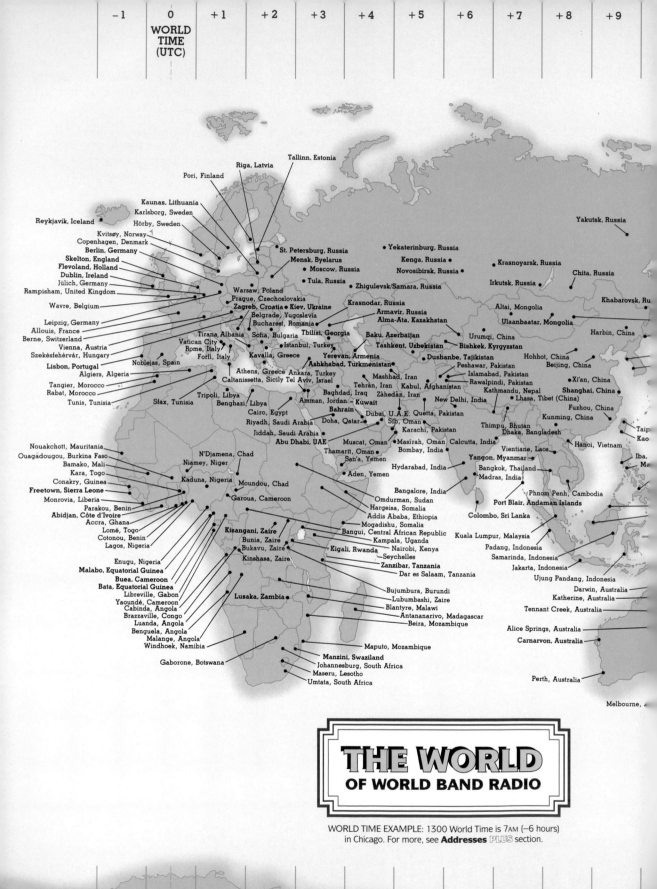

| −1 | 0 | +1 | +2 | +3 | +4 | +5 | +6 | +7 | +8 | +9 |

WORLD
TIME
(UTC)

Reykjavik, Iceland
Yakutsk, Russia

Pori, Finland
Riga, Latvia
Tallinn, Estonia

Kaunas, Lithuania
Karlsborg, Sweden
Hörby, Sweden
Kvitsøy, Norway
Copenhagen, Denmark
Berlin, Germany
Skelton, England
Flevoland, Holland
Dublin, Ireland
Rampisham, United Kingdom
Wavre, Belgium

St. Petersburg, Russia
Mensk, Byelarus
Moscow, Russia
Tula, Russia
Zhigulevsk/Samara, Russia

Yekaterinburg, Russia
Kenga, Russia
Novosibirsk, Russia

Krasnoyarsk, Russia
Chita, Russia
Irkutsk, Russia
Khabarovsk, Ru

Warsaw, Poland
Prague, Czechoslovakia
Zagreb, Croatia • Kiev, Ukraine
Belgrade, Yugoslavia
Bucharest, Romania
Krasnodar, Russia
Armavir, Russia
Alma-Ata, Kazakhstan
Altai, Mongolia
Ulaanbaatar, Mongolia
Harbin, China

Leipzig, Germany
Allouis, France
Berne, Switzerland
Vienna, Austria
Székésfehérvár, Hungary
Noblejas, Spain
Tirana, Albania
Sofia, Bulgaria
Tbilisi, Georgia
Baku, Azerbaijan
Urumqi, China
Hohhot, China
Beijing, China
Xi'an, China

Lisbon, Portugal
Vatican City
Rome, Italy
Forlì, Italy
Istanbul, Turkey
Yerevan, Armenia
Tashkent, Uzbekistan
Bishkek, Kyrgyzstan
Shanghai, China

Algiers, Algeria
Athens, Greece
Kaválla, Greece
Ankara, Turkey
Ashkhabad, Turkmenistan
Dushanbe, Tajikistan
Kathmandu, Nepal
Lhasa, Tibet (China)
Fuzhou, China

Tangier, Morocco
Caltanissetta, Sicily
Tel Aviv, Israel
Mashhad, Iran
Peshawar, Pakistan
Islamabad, Pakistan
Thimpu, Bhutan
Kunming, China

Rabat, Morocco
Tehrãn, Iran
Kabul, Afghanistan
Rawalpindi, Pakistan
New Delhi, India
Taip
Kao

Tunis, Tunisia
Sfax, Tunisia
Tripoli, Libya
Benghazi, Libya
Baghdad, Iraq
Zähedãn, Iran
Quetta, Pakistan
Dhaka, Bangladesh
Hanoi, Vietnam
Iba,
Ma

Cairo, Egypt
Amman, Jordan
Kuwait
Dubai, U.A.E.
Sib, Oman
Karachi, Pakistan
Calcutta, India

Riyadh, Saudi Arabia
Bahrain
Doha, Qatar
Muscat, Oman
Masïrah, Oman

Jiddah, Saudi Arabia
Abu Dhabi, UAE
Thamarit, Oman
Bombay, India
Kunming, China

Nouakchott, Mauritania
N'Djamena, Chad
San'a, Yemen
Hyderabad, India
Vientiane, Laos

Ouagadougou, Burkina Faso
Niamey, Niger
Aden, Yemen
Yangon, Myanmar
Bangkok, Thailand

Bamako, Mali
Madras, India
Phnom Penh, Cambodia

Kara, Togo
Kaduna, Nigeria
Moundou, Chad
Bangalore, India
Port Blair, Andaman Islands

Conakry, Guinea
Garoua, Cameroon
Omdurman, Sudan

Freetown, Sierra Leone
Hargeisa, Somalia
Colombo, Sri Lanka

Monrovia, Liberia
Addis Ababa, Ethiopia
Kuala Lumpur, Malaysia

Parakou, Benin
Mogadishu, Somalia
Padang, Indonesia

Abidjan, Côte d'Ivoire
Kisangani, Zaire
Bangui, Central African Republic
Samarinda, Indonesia

Accra, Ghana
Bunia, Zaire
Kampala, Uganda
Jakarta, Indonesia

Lomé, Togo
Bukavu, Zaire
Kigali, Rwanda
Nairobi, Kenya

Cotonou, Benin
Kinshasa, Zaire
Seychelles
Ujung Pandang, Indonesia

Lagos, Nigeria
Zanzibar, Tanzania
Darwin, Australia

Enugu, Nigeria
Dar es Salaam, Tanzania
Katherine, Australia

Malabo, Equatorial Guinea
Tennant Creek, Australia

Buea, Cameroon
Bujumbura, Burundi

Bata, Equatorial Guinea
Lubumbashi, Zaire

Libreville, Gabon
Blantyre, Malawi
Alice Springs, Australia

Yaoundé, Cameroon
Antananarivo, Madagascar
Carnarvon, Australia

Cabinda, Angola
Beira, Mozambique

Brazzaville, Congo
Lusaka, Zambia

Luanda, Angola

Benguela, Angola

Malange, Angola
Maputo, Mozambique

Windhoek, Namibia
Perth, Australia

Gaborone, Botswana
Manzini, Swaziland
Johannesburg, South Africa
Maseru, Lesotho
Umtata, South Africa

Melbourne,

THE WORLD
OF WORLD BAND RADIO

WORLD TIME EXAMPLE: 1300 World Time is 7AM (−6 hours)
in Chicago. For more, see **Addresses** PLUS section.

WORLD
TIME
(GMT)

| −1 | 0 | +1 | +2 | +3 | +4 | +5 | +6 | +7 | +8 | +9 |

TO HEAR THE NEWS FASTER, YOU'D HAVE

Imagine travelling from London to Moscow
to Tokyo. All in the time it takes to push
a button. With Sony's World Band Receiver,™
radio, you can. Our preprogrammed Station
Name Tuning lets you change stations as effort-
lessly as time zones. So for a local perspective
on global events, call 1-800-833-6302. And
get your current events
while they're still current.

TO BE THERE.

SONY

Ten of the Best: Top Shows for 1993

One man's meat is another man's poison, and the aleph to ziganka of world band programs drives this home. Anything goes, from the weird to the wonderful. You won't experience anything like it on 94.1 or channel 10.

With so much being offered, this year's *Ten of the Best* (and *of* is the operative word) represent only a nibble from hundreds of juicy choices. As in previous years, we have tapped ten varied programs, this time with a special nod to music. These shows are among the best of their breed. Several contain material difficult for most of us to find anywhere—except on world band.

"Folk Box"
Radio Moscow World Service

A marriage of the exotic and the exquisite. A musical treasure chest of unequalled proportions anywhere on the airwaves. Style, quality, originality, talent and—best of all—entertainment. Karelian wedding dances, Kyzylian guttural singing. You name it.

Jew's harp to balalaika, cimbalom to Russian bagpipes, the range of instruments is vast. More vast still is the variety of musical styles, covering virtually every form of musical expression to be found in the former Soviet Union.

Programs of folk music—"roots music" to some cognoscenti—are not uncommon on the international airwaves. Indeed, there are a number of very good ones. But it is exceptional to come across a presentation that offers such a fine combination of excellence and authenticity.

Folk Box has that "something" which sets it apart from other programs of its kind, akin to the beautiful object forever unobtainable, but nevertheless admired from afar.

The program is broadcast several times a week, and there is no excuse for anyone to miss it, anywhere in the world. It's available to all continents and is broadcast one hour earlier in summer.

> Moscow's musical treasure chest is of proportions unequalled anywhere on the airwaves.

For North America winters, try 0031 World Time Saturday (Friday evening, local time) on 7105, 7115, 7150, 11920, 12010, 12050, 15425, 17665, 17690, 17700 and 17720 kHz. In summer, listeners in Eastern North America can tune to frequencies such as 11780 and 15355 kHz, while those farther west still have access to a number of 15 and 17 MHz channels.

Many of the frequencies used for the 0031 Saturday edition are also available at

---

The Jizo guardian deity is believed to cure those who rub his head. One of the many aspects of traditional and modern Japanese culture explained over *Hello from Tokyo*.

Radio Moscow's *Folk Box* staff. With paper, Olga Fedorova, plus Marina Skalkina, host Kate Starkova, and two more Olgas—Nesterova and Shapovalova.

0231 Tuesday and Sunday. If Radio Moscow's Cuban relay continues operating (which is far from certain), try the winter channels of 6000 and 6045 kHz, and 9720 (or 11850) and 11710 kHz in summer.

There is another opportunity at 0431 Thursday, but mainly for Western North America. For the time being, listeners should dial around the 7, 9, 15 and 17 MHz segments; but should the separate North American service be terminated, try the following frequencies (some of which are seasonal): 7150, 7270, 7310, 9635, 9895, 12010, 12050, 13605, 13645, 15180, 15425, 15455, 17700 and 17720 kHz.

In Europe, tune in at 0931 Wednesday and Saturday, 1231 Tuesday and 1531 Monday on (among others) 13705 (or 13710), 15345 and 17660 kHz. Many of the former channels aimed at Europe were via transmitters in Ukraine, transmitters now used for other purposes, and it is difficult to forecast frequency usage for the coming months.

Europeans have a further opportunity at 1831 Friday. Winters, try frequencies in the 7 and 9 MHz bands, with 9765 and 9795 kHz reasonable bets. Best summer reception can generally be found in the 11,

15 and 17 MHz segments—tune around to find a suitable channel.

There are so many channels available to East and Southeast Asia that it is probably easier, in some cases, to give the Megahertz segments rather than the individual frequencies. At 0031 Saturday and 0231 Tuesday and Sunday try 7170, 7390, 9480 and 9745 kHz (winter only); and 11675, 11730, 15340, 17890, 21690 and 21790 kHz (year-round). At 0431 Thursday the principal Asian targets are in the south and southeast of the continent. Fortunately, many of these channels are also widely heard in other parts of Asia. Workhorse channels include 15295, 15420, 15530, 17610, 17890, 21690 and 21790 kHz.

For the 0931 Wednesday and Saturday broadcasts, try the same channels as at 0431 Thursday, although listeners in the northeast of the continent can try the 7 and 9 MHz segments (e.g., 7245 and 9855 kHz) during the winter months.

Most of the 15, 17 and 21 MHz channels are still available for the 1231 Tuesday version but, again, listeners in the northeast should try the lower frequencies. In winter, try 4810, 5940, 5950, 5960, 7245 and 7260 kHz; while 7175, 7315, 7370 and 9885 kHz are good bets during the summer months.

THE WORLD SERVICE OF THE CHRISTIAN SCIENCE MONITOR SPECIAL OFFER

We are offering the compact, easy-to-use ATS-803A World Band Receiver at the exceptional price of $189. You can enjoy everything from Radio Beijing to the BBC. Plus round-the-clock hourly news from The World Service of The Christian Science Monitor. The portable, multi-function ATS-803A gives you quick, push-button access to your favorite AM and FM stations, plus easy digital tuning, a 14-station memory, a built-in clock and alarm, lighted dial and more. This model carries the logo of The World Service and you also get a carrying strap, stereo headphones and the Introduction to International Radio Listening guide at no extra cost.

Order your ATS-803A World Band Receiver today and tune into world news as it happens. Simply complete the order form below.

WHO SAYS YOU CAN'T TAKE IT WITH YOU WHEN YOU GO.

Sangean Portables.
Get away from it all and still
stay in touch.

Whether traveling around the world or across town, Sangean portables keep you informed. Tune into international broadcasters or wake up to your favorite morning DJ, wherever

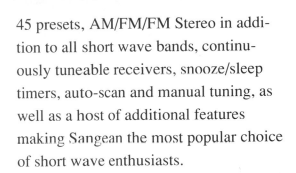

you are. There's no need to leave it all behind, because Sangean goes where you go. . .and further.

Multiple Band. Multiple Choice.

From the full featured ATS-818CS Digital Receiver with programmable built-in cassette recorder, to the world's most popular digital receiver, our highly acclaimed ATS-803A, Sangean's complete line of full featured analog and digital receivers offer the utmost in reliability and performance at a price just right for your budget.

To fully understand the
difference between us and them. . .
just listen.

Only Sangean offers you the features and advanced technology of a high priced communication receiver at a portable price. Features like; PLL Tuning for rock steady short wave listening, tuneable BFO for single sideband reception, dual displayed time systems, up to

45 presets, AM/FM/FM Stereo in addition to all short wave bands, continuously tuneable receivers, snooze/sleep timers, auto-scan and manual tuning, as well as a host of additional features making Sangean the most popular choice of short wave enthusiasts.

All models carry the standard Sangean 1 full year warranty of quality and workmanship; the signature of a company recognized throughout the world as a pioneer and leader in the design and development of multi-band portable radios.

Sangean portables, somehow with them the world seems a little bit smaller.

Call or write for more information.

SANGEAN
A M E R I C A ,   I N C .
A World Of Listening

2651 Troy Avenue, South El Monte, California 91733
(818) 579-1600   FAX: (818) 579-6806

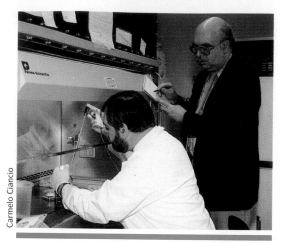

For a first-rate peek into the world of science and medicine, try the Voice of America's *New Horizons*. Here, Producer Brian Cislak interviews George Washington University dermatologist Edward De Fabo concerning the effect of sunlight on the immune system.

For Australia and the South Pacific, try 0031 Saturday, 0231 Sunday and Tuesday, and 0431 Thursday on 15420, 21690 and 21790 kHz, plus frequencies between 17550 and 17720 kHz. Many of these channels are still available for the repeat editions at 1231 Tuesday, and 0931 Wednesday and Saturday.

"New Horizons"
Voice of America

That bland title hides a program of remarkable quality. Each 20-minute broadcast is devoted to a topic of current interest from the fields of medicine, science or technology.

New Horizons is at its best when discussing medicine, and past programs dealing with diseases such as lupus and panic disorder have been exceptional.

This is not to say that nonmedical subjects are uninteresting. Topics such as the work of U.S. weapons laboratories are both pertinent and well-presented; and if you prefer something more exotic, how about zoopharmacognacy?

World band listeners who are keen to discover a whole new world, or those who just wish to be better informed, should give this show a try.

It can be heard in Europe Sunday at 1510 on 15205 and 15255 (or 15260) kHz, and again at 2110 on 6040, 9760, 11710 and 15205 kHz. Listeners in the Middle East

should tune in at these same times, but on 9700 and 15205 kHz.

For East Asia and the Pacific there is just one opportunity: 1110 Sunday. East Asia is served by 9760 and 15155 kHz, with 5985, 11720 and 15425 kHz available for the Pacific.

The VOA is prohibited by its charter from broadcasting to the United States, but it is still widely heard within its home country. North American listeners who wish to enjoy *New Horizons* should try 0110 Monday (Sunday evening, local date), when the program is broadcast to the rest of the Americas on 5995, 6130, 7405, 9455, 9775, 11580, 15120 and 15205 kHz.

"Blues, Rags, Jazz"
HCJB—Voice of the Andes

It doesn't really matter if you are into jazz or not; *Blues, Rags, Jazz* is a delight by any yardstick. Produced by Bill Rapley in religious station HCJB's United Kingdom office, this is a program to cheer even the most miserable curmudgeon. No need to feel uneasy about the religious content—it's a gentle part of the program's landscape.

The program contains not only classic performances by some of the greatest names in jazz, but also more recent compositions from European artists such as Chris Barber, Terry Lightfoot and the Dutch Swing College Band. Where else is it possible to hear the likes of Louis Armstrong's Hot Five, Kid Ory, Bix Beiderbecke, Sidney Bechet and Humphrey Lyttleton—all in one fell swoop?

Bill Rapley, producer of *Blues, Rags, Jazz*, is heard each Sunday with the best of classic jazz and blues.

IT'S AMAZING WHAT YOU CAN PICK UP FROM THE BBC WORLD SERVICE.

To get the very best out of the BBC World Service, you need new BBC Worldwide magazine.

Published monthly, it contains comprehensive details of all World Service radio and TV programmes broadcast in English, together with information on the best frequencies to use around the world.

But it's much more than just a programme guide.

It's also a lively and well written blend of in-depth previews and special features, reflecting all the many facets of the BBC's world – including sport, comedy, drama and music.

And if you take out a subscription now, you'll pick up one of three very special World Service gifts: a sturdy travel bag, a sport umbrella, or a handsome tie.

It only costs £24 sterling or $40 for a year's subscription, so complete the coupon now – indicating what you'd like to receive from the BBC World Service.

BBC WORLD SERVICE

Even better, you won't hear a single note from Wailin' Willie Clinton.

Now the sad part: For some inexplicable reason, *Blues, Rags, Jazz* is only available in HCJB's broadcasts to Europe, not to other parts of the world. Those fortunate enough to be able to hear the program should listen at 2130 Sunday on 15270 (or 21480) and 17790 kHz. For listeners outside Europe, there is 21455 kHz in the upper-sideband mode. Alas, most world band radios are ill-equipped to receive such signals.

"Monitor Radio"
World Service of the Christian
Science Monitor

A simple title that covers an all-embracing program of news, news features and interviews. Preferred by some even to the BBC World Service's comprehensive output of news and news analysis.

Indeed, the two stations complement each other, even though both are internationally oriented. The BBC World Service is inclined to devote more time to Europe and Asia, while the Christian Science Monitor tends to give more time to events in North America. True news hounds won't want to miss either.

The *Monitor* scores heavily over its fellow U.S. giant, the Voice of America, in both quality and quantity. The VOA, strong on news analysis, is surprisingly weak on news itself. The Christian Science Monitor, with a full hour at its disposal, provides worthy coverage of not only the United

States, but also the world in general. *Monitor Radio* also trumps both the BBC and the VOA with its presentation, which is almost conversational.

The program is available around the clock to different parts of the globe, alternating hourly with the Christian Science Monitor's features and mailbag programs, which are also worth hearing. All transmissions aimed at areas outside the Americas are weekdays (Monday through Friday) only. Weekend programming is devoted to the teachings and experiences of the Christian Science faith.

> **Monitor Radio is preferred by some even to the BBC World Service's comprehensive news and news analysis.**

Monitor Radio is beamed to Europe at 0600 on 9840 kHz, at 0800 on 9840 or 11705 kHz, at 1400 on 15665 kHz, at 1800 on 15665 or 17510 kHz, at 2000 on 15665 and 13770 (or 17510) kHz, and at 2200 on 13770 or 15665 kHz. Where alternative channels are listed, the higher frequencies are used in summer, lower ones in winter. Listeners in the Middle East can tune in at 0200 on 9350 kHz, at 1800 on 9495 or 15665 kHz, and at 2000 on 13770 or 15665 kHz.

East Asia is the best-served of all areas, with eight times from which to choose— 0400 and 0600 on 17780 kHz, 0800 and 1000 on 17555 kHz, 1400 on 9530 kHz, 1600 on 11580 kHz, 2000 on 9455 kHz, and 2200 on 15405 kHz. Pacific listeners, try 0800 on 13615 and 15665 kHz, 1200 on 9430 or 15665 kHz, 1800 on 9430 or 13840 kHz, and 2000 on 13840 (or 13625) kHz.

A number of these broadcasts are audible in North America, but there are additional transmissions specifically beamed to the United States and Canada. *Monitor Radio* is targeted at Eastern North America Monday through Friday at 1000 and 1200 on 9495 kHz, at 1800 and 2000 on 15665 kHz (replaced summers by 17510 kHz), and at 2200 on 9465 kHz. There is a fifth opportunity at 0000 Tuesday through Saturday (Monday through Friday, local American evenings) on 7395 kHz. Listeners farther west can tune in at 0200, 0400 and 0600 on

Monitor Radio co-hosts Rod MacLeish and Pat Bodnar bring depth and analysis to the day's news.

(continued on page 60)

BECOME WELL TRAVELED

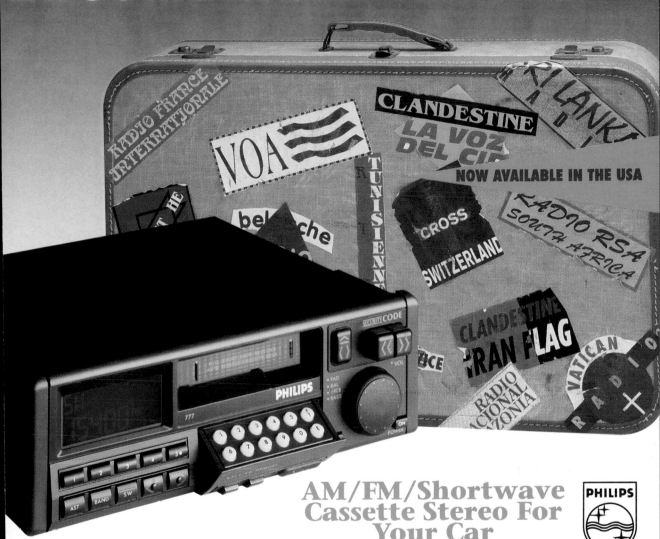

NOW AVAILABLE IN THE USA

AM/FM/Shortwave Cassette Stereo For Your Car

PHILIPS

YOU'VE ALWAYS WANTED SW BUILT INTO YOUR CAR

The Philips DC-777 packs a sophisticated AM/FM/Shortwave (SW) tuner, cassette player and powerful amplifier into a single compact car stereo unit. The DC-777 can be fitted into cars, trucks, mobile homes or boats, providing access to the world of shortwave from almost any location. The DC-777 covers the shortwave frequencies from 3170 kHz to 21910 kHz (13 to 90 meter bands). The commercial shortwave bands are just part of the frequency range covered by the DC-777. By means of the manual search function, any frequency between the commercial bands can be selected. Some shortwave transmitters may be less accurate; so the Philips DC-777 allows manually or 'search' tuning of the frequency adjustable in 1 kHz steps to optimize reception.

WITH 20 SOFT TOUCH DIGITAL PRESETS & A NARROW IF BAND

Since a SW station often transmits at different times, on different frequencies, to different continents, depending on the weather conditions, one frequency may give better reception than the other. The DC-777 lets you take advantage of this by offering the possibility to program up to 5 frequency settings on each of the four presets. You can then run through the frequencies to select the best reception.

Philips also incorporates a narrow IF Band to counter transmitter problems. When the treble control is set to its lowest level, shortwave sound quality is optimized and the IF Band is automatically switched to a higher selectivity level.

YOU'LL GET GREAT SOUND

The Philips DC-777 features 50 Watts RMS for superb quality sound with low distortion and extended frequency response. It also has an Audio Super Control (ASC), which makes it possible to compensate for the variation in sound between different radio wavebands and the radio and cassette sections.

AND A HIGH-END CASSETTE DECK TO BOOT

The DC-777 features an autoreverse cassette deck that gives you the convenience of non-stop cassette play, avoiding the necessity of flipping the cassette over when one side is finished. Autostart sets the tape running as soon as it's inserted and radio reception automatically CUTS IN whenever a tape is being rewound or forwarded.

THE DC-777 IS THE CAR STEREO WITH SHORTWAVE RECEIVER THAT WILL MAKE YOU WELL TRAVELED AND WELL RECEIVED.

For more information about the Philips DC-777 and the names of dealers near you, call toll-free;

1-800-524-6638

©1992 ASC IMPORTED AND DISTRIBUTED BY ASC.

THE GRUNDIG SATELLIT 700

World Receiver

FEATURES

- FM, AM (MW), LW and "gapless" (continuous) SW range from 1.6 – 30 MHz. FM stereo operation via headphones or additional external speaker.
- ROM table: 12 or 15 AM stations with 120 frequencies can be tuned from internal memory.
- 64 memories with 8 alternate frequencies.
- Illuminated multifunction display with indication of frequency, wave band, memory position, m-band, stereo, field strength, battery check, station name (8 digits), RDS, USB/LSB, bandwidth, MGC, LOC, ext.ant., ROM table, automatic memory, synchronis detector, clock time, timer setting, time zone, "sleep".
- Alphanumeric indication of station name by programmable letter/digits, for RDS stations automatically.

- Store compare function with indication of station number and station name in the display.
- Ferrite aerial for AM (MW)/LW, multi-match telescopic aerial for FM/SW reception, switchable.
- Direct frequency input. Direct input of SW-bands.
- RDS (Radio Data System): For FM, staion names (PS code) and alternative frequencies can be tuned and memorized (PI/AF code).
- AM: Genuine double superset with band with selector, gain control and preselection tuning. Built-in SSB/BFO section (switchable to USB/LSB) for receiving single-sideband and unmodulated telegraph transmitters.

- 2 x 3 watts peak power. Powerful wideband speaker. Individual bass and treble control.
- Timer: The built-in 24-hour quartz clock timer can be used to pre-program 2 switch-on and switch-off times per day. 2 time zones. Switch-on automatically.
- Connections: Outdoor/ external aerial (75Ω coaxial socket for all bands), Line-out (CINCH), external loud-speaker, stereo headphones (3.5 mm jack plug), external power supply 9 – 12 V.
- PLL frequency synthesizer.

Automatic or manual search.
- 3 additional memory elements with a total of 2048 frequencies can be built-in.
- Accu/mains operation.
- Battery operation.
- Dimensions: approx. 30.4 x 17.8 x 6.6 cm (12 x 7½ x 3").
- Weight: approx. 1.8 kg (without batteries).
- Finish: black metallic.

Satellit® 700

The new definition of top class.
The Satellit® 700 is a modern
world receiver which also sets
standards for FM reception.

3 further chips ensure up to 2048 memory possibilities

3 easy to build-in chips (not included in delivery) extend the memory possibilities to 256 stations with 8 alternative frequencies. Overall, you have then up to 2048 memory positions.

Radio Data System for FM

First class reception convenience with RDS for FM, e.g. the station names are displayed. Connection possibility for stereo headphones and external loudspeakers.

Series-equipped with 512 memories

64 memories on 8 frequencies extend the memory capacity to 512 memory positions. Digits and letters can be recalled.

Code	Station	Display
0.1	Deutsche Welle	DW.....D
0.2	Deutsche Welle	DW.....D
0.3	Radio Austria International	ROEI . AUT
0.4	Swiss Radio International	SRI .. SUI
0.5	Radio Nederland	RNED. HOL
0.6	Radio France International	R F I ....F
0.7	Radio Televisione Italiana	RAI I
0.8	BBC / London	BBC .WS. G
0.9	BBC / London	BBC .WS. G
0.10	Radio Moscow World Service	RMWS.URS
0.11	Radio Moscow World Service	RMWS.URS
0.12	Radio Japan	NHK ....J

Easy operation with the ROM table for SW

12 of the worldwide most important stations with 96 frequencies can be recalled via code from the internal memory.

GRUNDIG

P.O. Box 2307, Menlo Park, CA 94026
Local 415 361-1611
US 1 800 872-2228
Canada 1 800 637-1648

Welcome to World Band Radio!

How to Get Started

Welcome to the wild side, the Twilight Zone of broadcasting. Come cruise the exotic world of international radio, an auditory adventure that's one part *Newsweek*, another *National Geographic*.

You'll be eavesdropping on news from the Orient, drama from Europe, propaganda from the Caribbean, sports from Down Under, music from the Andes and the whirl of social change from the erstwhile Soviet Union. Nearly 150 countries fill the air from hundreds of stations, broadcasting thousands of hours a week. English is the most commonly heard language—and most of the programming is commercial-free!

World band radio is your direct connection to the world, no intermediaries. When you tune into world band, it's as though you are editor-in-chief of your own international wire service. You're in charge. You alone decide what's important. What you hear is no longer filtered through the news desks of ABC, CBS, NBC or even CNN or ITV.

Here are some things you need to know to become an Indiana Jones of the airwaves . . .

It's About Time

World band radio is a global enterprise, with nations broadcasting around the clock from virtually every time zone. Imagine the chaos if each broadcaster used local time for scheduling. In England, 9 PM is different from nine in the evening in Japan or Canada. How could anybody know when to tune in?

To eliminate confusion, international broadcasters use World Time, or UTC, as a standard reference. Formerly and in some circles still known as Greenwich Mean Time (GMT), it is keyed to the Greenwich meridian in England and is announced in 24-hour format, like military time So 2 PM, say, is 1400 hours.

There are three easy ways to know World Time. First, you can tune in one of the standard time stations, such as WWV or WWVH in the United States. WWV in Colorado and WWVH in Hawaii are on 5000, 10000, 15000 and 20000 kHz 24 hours a day. There you will hear a series of time "pips" every minute, followed by an announcement of the exact World Time. Boring, yes, but very handy when you need it.

Second, you can tune in one of the major international broadcasters, such as Britain's BBC or the Voice of America. Most announce World Time at the top of the hour.

Third, there's a quick calculation. If you live on the East Coast of the United States, you *add* five hours winter (four hours summer) to your local time to get World Time. So, if it is 8 PM EST (the 20th hour of the day) in New York, it is 0100 hours World Time. On the U.S. West Coast, add eight hours winter (seven hours summer).

Thomas Cicippio, brother of freed hostage Joseph Cicippio, unpacks his new Sangean radio, while his wife, Frances, studies *Passport*. Standing: AP's George Widman and Amy Hostetler.

The President of the United States is fed more international information than any other person on earth. Yet, he still relies on his Sony ICF-2003 world band radio (shelf, right) to keep abreast of world news and opinion.

In Britain, it's easy—World Time (oops, better call that Greenwich Mean Time) is local winter time. But you have to subtract one hour from your local time summer to get World Time. Elsewhere in the European Community, subtract one hour winter (two hours summer) from your local time. In *Passport's* "Addresses PLUS" section you will find information for calculating World Time in all parts of the world.

Once you find the correct World Time, set the clock on your radio so that you'll have World Time handy whenever you want to listen. Your radio doesn't have a 24-hour clock? You might consider buying a 24-hour clock, setting it to World Time, and parking it next to your radio. You'll find an exhaustive review of timepieces especially suited to world band radio on page 37. Among other things, this report shows how a no-frills World Time clock can cost less than $10.

Hit a snag? Margaret Girard (front left) of the Christian Science Monitor World Service's "Shortwave Helpline" may be able to help. Also pictured: Tina Hammers, Trudy Brasure, Dave Cananave, John Lauritzen, Fred Telschow and Jay Jostyn.

What Day Is Today?

There's a trick to World Time that can occasionally catch even the most experienced listener. What happens at midnight? A new day arrives as well. Remember: midnight World Time means a new day, too. So if it is 9 PM Wednesday in New York City, it is 0200 hours *Thursday* World Time. Don't forget to "wind your calendar."

(continued on page 64)

1993's Winners: 20+ Big Signals

To get out a powerful, clear signal, wise world band broadcasters mimic real estate investors: Look first for a good location. That's not as hard as it used to be, either—the advent of satellite communications means world band transmissions need no longer emanate from native soil. Instead, satellites can be used to send signals from the studio to a world band transmitter halfway across the globe. That's one reason reception is improving, even while the cost of broadcasting is being reduced.

A leader in the use of this relay technique is forward-looking Radio Japan, not surprising given that it is the official station of the world's most electronically oriented country. Radio Japan now has relay agreements with countries on all five continents—Canada, French Guiana, Gabon, Sri Lanka and the United Kingdom.

> One great advantage of world band is there's no external hand controlling what's heard.

One great advantage of world band is the absence of any external hand controlling what's heard. Once a signal is out, it's there for all who care to grab it. While airings over local radio stations and cable systems are fine for every day, come conflict or controversy it's the world band signal that gets through unfettered.

So that you can take advantage of all this, here are 20-odd world band outlets that are among the most likely to give you reliable day-to-day reception.

All times used by international broadcasters, and in this book, are World Time. For more information, look elsewhere in this *Passport*. You won't understand much about world band radio until you become familiar with this uncommonly straightforward way of keeping track of time worldwide.

EUROPE
Austria

A favorite with many listeners, **Radio Austria International** continues to be heard worldwide with its refreshingly enjoyable half-hour blocks in English. Informative programs, friendly presentation and a more-than-adequate signal ensure a regular audience for this strategically placed Central European broadcaster.

Austria is heard in English to North America at 0130-0200 on 9875 and 13730 kHz; 0330-0400 on 9870 and 13730 kHz; 0530-0600 and 0630-0700 via the Canadian relay on 6015 kHz; and 1130-1200 on

---

The BBC World Service is staffed by people from myriad lands, including these women from the Eastern Service.

ORF

War may be brewing nearby, but Austrians still find no end of ways to enjoy life. Radio Austria International airs it all.

13730 kHz. Europeans can listen at 0530 and 0830 (winter), 1130 (year-round), 1430 (summer) and 1530 (winter) on 6155 and 13730 kHz; and at 1830 and 2130 (year-round) on 5945 and 6155 kHz. Listeners in Australia should try 0830 (year-round) and 1030 (summers) on 15450 and 21490 kHz. If you're in Asia, best bets are 1130 and 1330 on 15450 and 11780 or 17730 kHz. For the Middle East, there's 0530 (winters) on 15410 kHz and 1830 (year-round) on 12010 kHz.

Belgium

Belgische Radio en Televisie, the voice of Belgium's restive Dutch-speaking population, is another station that reaches a surprisingly large audience despite limited transmitting resources. Well-heard in Europe and Eastern North America, its signal often reaches well beyond. The 25-minute English broadcasts, like their longer Dutch counterparts, are a tasteful and highly enjoyable potpourri of Belgian news and features.

In North America, BRT is heard at 1230 Sundays on 17555 or 21810 kHz; plus daily at 0030 on 9930 (or 9925) and 13655 kHz. In Europe there are daily broadcasts at 0730 on 5910 (or 6035) and 11695 kHz; 1900 on 5910 (winters) and 9905 kHz; and again at 2200 on 5910 and 9905 kHz. The frequency of 9905 kHz is also audible in parts of Eastern North America. There is an additional transmission at 1000, Monday through Saturday, on 9905 (or 9855) and 13675 kHz.

The 0730 broadcast is also directed to the Pacific on 11695 kHz, and there is a transmission to Southeast Asia, Monday through Saturday, at 1400 on 21810 kHz.

All broadcasts are one hour earlier during the summer.

Czechoslovakia

Radio Czechoslovakia, despite its name change from Radio Prague International, maintains the lively and interesting format that has made it such a popular choice. Short and varied features provide a pleasant alternative to the heavily news-oriented fare of some of the major broadcasters.

The approximately 30-minute broadcasts can be heard in North America at 0000 on 7345, 9540 (or 9580) and 11990 kHz; 0100 on 5930, 7345 and 9540 (or 9580) kHz; 0300 on 5930 (or 9810), 7345 and 9540 (or 9580/11990) kHz; and 0400, winters on 5930, 7345 and 9540 (or 9580) kHz; summers on 7345, 9810, 11990, 13715 and 15355 kHz.

English is beamed to Europe (one hour earlier in summer) at 0700 and 1130 on 6055, 7345, 9505 and 11990 kHz; 1800, 2100 and 2200 on 5930, 6055, 7345 and 9605 kHz; and 1930 on 6055 and 7345 kHz. Listeners in Asia and the Pacific can listen at 0730-0800 on 17725 and 21705 kHz.

Radio Czechoslovakia

While the fate of its country hangs in the balance, Radio Czechoslovakia continues to grace the airwaves. English Section staffers, front, include studio managers Zuzana Suchánková (in green) and Daniela Cerná (in yellow). Listeners' letters are handled by Markéta Albrechtová (left rear, in red).

JRC NRD-535D

"Best Communications Receiver"
World Radio TV Handbook 1992

"Unsurpassed DX Performance"
Passport to World Band Radio 1992

Setting the industry standard once again for shortwave receivers, the NRD-535D is the most advanced HF communications receiver ever designed for the serious DXer and shortwave listener. Its unparalleled performance in all modes makes it the ultimate receiver for diversified monitoring applications.

Designed for DXers by DXers! The NRD-535D (shown above with optional NVA-319 speaker) strikes the perfect balance between form and function with its professional-grade design and critically acclaimed ergonomics. The NRD-535D is the recipient of the prestigious World Radio TV Handbook Industry Award for "Best Communications Receiver."

- Phase-lock ECSS system for selectable-sideband AM reception.
- Maximum IF bandwidth flexibility! The Variable Bandwidth Control (BWC) adjusts the wide and intermediate IF filter bandwidths from 5.5 to 2.0 kHz and 2.0 to 0.5 kHz—continuously.
- Stock fixed-width IF filters include a 5.5 kHz (wide), a 2.0 kHz (intermediate), and a 1.0 kHz (narrow). Optional JRC filters include 2.4 kHz, 300 Hz, and 500 Hz crystal type.
- All mode 100 kHz – 30 MHz coverage. Tuning accuracy to 1 Hz, using JRC's advanced Direct Digital Synthesis (DDS) PLL system and a high-precision magnetic rotary encoder. The tuning is so smooth you will swear it's analog! An optional high-stability crystal oscillator kit is also available for ±0.5 ppm stability.
- A superior front-end variable double tuning circuit is continuously controlled by the CPU to vary with the receive frequency automatically. The result: Outstanding 106 dB Dynamic Range and +20 dBm Third-Order Intercept Point.
- Memory capacity of 200 channels, each storing frequency, mode, filter, AGC and ATT settings. Scan and sweep functions built in. All memory channels are tunable, making "MEM to VFO" switching unnecessary.
- A state-of-the-art RS-232C computer interface is built into every NRD-535D receiver.
- Fully modular design, featuring plug-in circuit boards and high-quality surface-mount components. No other manufacturer can offer such professional-quality design and construction at so affordable a price.

JRC Japan Radio Co., Ltd.

Japan Radio Company, Ltd., New York Branch Office – 430 Park Avenue (2nd Floor), New York, NY 10022, USA Tel: (212) 355-1180 / Fax: (212) 319-5227

Japan Radio Company, Ltd. – Akasaka Twin Tower (Main), 17-22, Akasaka 2-chome, Minato-ku, Tokyo 107, JAPAN Tel: (03) 3584-8836 / Fax: (03) 3584-8878

Radio France Internationale is one of the few world band stations to devote major resources to African news and culture.

Eastern North America than the one at 1230 nominally beamed there.

At 1230-1300, Europeans can tune in on 9805, 11670, 15155 and 15195 kHz; for North America, try 15365 (or 21635) and 21645 kHz. The 1600-1700 African program is audible in Europe on 6175 kHz, while North American listeners can eavesdrop on 15360, 15530, 17620, 17795 and 17850 kHz. These channels are all aimed at Africa (with 15530 also available for the Middle East), but several of the frequencies also provide reasonable reception in parts of North America.

There is a separate one-hour broadcast to the Middle East and Asia at 1400-1500 on 17650 kHz, with 11910 (or 7125) and 17695 (or 21770) kHz also available for Asia.

Holland

A longtime world band favorite, **Radio Nederland**, which announces in English as **Radio Netherlands** and in Dutch as **Radio Nederland Wereldomroep**, recently introduced a number of changes to its English-language programming. Although more adjustments are in the pipeline, early indications are for a wider choice without sacrificing the accustomed-to high quality.

This is good news indeed for the station's many faithful listeners, spread as they are right across the globe. Thanks to two strategically located relay sites, in Madagascar and the Netherlands Antilles, the station's signal is reliably received in most of the intended areas.

Radio Nederland is one of the most listener-oriented world band broadcasters, as is amply demonstrated by the ever-

France

Radio France Internationale, though heavily oriented toward disseminating all things French, still manages a first-rate English service. Professionally produced features are presented in that inimitable French style which is so pleasing to many. A class act!

The 60-minute English broadcast for Africa at 1600 has justifiably claimed its place as one of the foremost sources of news and information about a continent often relegated to the basement of world reporting.

> ## RFI's features are in that inimitable French style which is so pleasing to many.

RFI is also in the process of upgrading all its transmitters in continental France to an impressive 500 kilowatts each, and installing and improving relays overseas. In the meantime, RFI is still easily audible, notably in French, throughout Europe and much of North America—especially on the latter's eastern seaboard.

There is a daily English program to Europe and North America at 1230. That's a tough hour for good reception, so it doesn't come in very well in either the United States or Canada. The transmission for Africa and Europe at 1600 is actually better heard in

Ginger da Silva and Luc Lucas prepare another edition of Radio Nederland's timely *Newsline* program.

Innovation, Ingenuity, Intelligence.

Seeker 500E™ Wideband Receiver

SASI engineering innovation enabled the production of the Seeker 500E™ — an ultra-miniaturized wideband receiver with frequency coverage from 2-950 MHz. It represents the cutting edge in advanced receiver technology with stealth-style portability. Contact SASI for more information on the Seeker 500E™.

Remote Control Scanning System

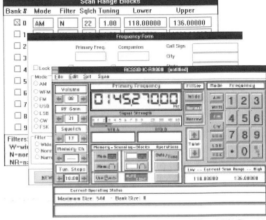

SASI's RCSS™ provides computer control over Seeker 500E™ and ICOM™ models R7000, R7100, R71 and R9000 receivers. RCSS™ simplifies receiver operation while providing feature-rich, enhanced control over all receiver functions. Contact SASI for more information on RCSS™. Both PC and Mac versions available.

You only find the innovation and ingenuity required to produce intelligent products like the Seeker 500E™ and RCSS™ in a small engineering firm where the engineers are encouraged to explore the unexplored and push the envelope of technology. Systems and Software International developed these and other advanced products by making quality paramount and encouraging individual thinking.

Fundamental to SASI's mission is the commitment to develop and produce real products that meet real needs and to support these products over their full life cycle. This philosophy has enabled SASI to create products such as the stealth-like Seeker 500E™ ultra-miniaturized wideband receiver and the RCSS™ remote control scanning system.

SASI doesn't rest on todays accomplishments, however. To gain the advantage over tomorrows technologies SASI aggressively pursues projects identified by its customers in the fields of communications engineering, computer and software engineering, and systems engineering. SASI offers a variety of services including requirements analysis, system design, system installation, and "special projects".

SASI's clients include private industry, government organizations, military groups, and entrepreneurs. The one thing they all have in common is a belief in SASI's dedication to quality and commitment to excellence.

For more information on SASI, RCSS™ or the Seeker 500E™, contact SASI by calling **(703) 680-3559**.

SYSTEMS & SOFTWARE
INTERNATIONAL • LTD

Systems & Software International is a small business and manufactures all equipment in the USA. Please contact us at:
4639 Timber Ridge Drive, Dumfries, Virginia, 22026-1059, USA; (703) 680-3559; Fax (703) 878-1460; Compuserve 74065,1140

Listen In With the Pros

Did you know ICOM receivers are used by local, state and federal government agencies? The professionals in these critical positions require the utmost in signal clarity, performance and reliability. ICOM's R7100 ultra high-tech receiver meets, and even exceeds, these stringent demands.

Listen To Them All ...on ICOM's R7100. Capture lowband, marine, aircraft, amateur, emergency— or relax with FM and television! Cover the entire 25 MHz to 2 gHz bands in 8 tuning steps: 100 Hz, 1-, 5-, 10-, 12.5-, 20-, 25- and 100-kHz, and 1 MHz.

900 Memory Channels. 9 bands of 100 channels each let you group and access all your favorite frequencies automatically.

All Mode Scan. Super fast scanning in Programmed Scan, Selected Memory and Window Scan— flexibility never before realized.

Auto Memory Write Scan automatically records busy frequencies for later monitoring.

Loud and Clear With DDS. Direct Digital Synthesis means an extremely low carrier-to-noise ratio for the ultimate in receiver performance. Compare it and hear the difference!

Dual Windows. Scan in one window, tune in the other— like two receivers in one!

The Most Important Feature. Designed and backed by ICOM. Our reputation for quality, reliability and service is unsurpassed in the communications industry. The pros don't settle for anything less. Neither should you.

For more information, see your ICOM dealer or call our Brochure Hotline 1-800-999-9877.
ICOM America, Inc., 2380-116th Ave. N.E. Bellevue, Washington 98004
Customer Service Hotline (206) 454-7619
All stated specifications are subject to change without notice or obligation. All ICOM radios significantly exceed FCC regulations limiting spurious emissions. R7100392

IC-R1
Put the whole world in your pocket.
Only 4″ high!

BUY ANY R7100, GET A TINY R1 AT A TINY PRICE!
Special limited time offer.
See Icom Dealer for details.

ICOM
Simply the Best®

popular *Happy Station*, a weekly get-together now in its 65th successful year.

The station is well heard throughout much of North America at 0030-0125 on 6020, 6165 and 11835 kHz; 0330-0425 on 6165 and 9590 kHz; 1730-1925 on 21515 and 21590 kHz; and 1930-2025 on 17605 and 21515 kHz. The 1730 and 1930 transmissions are beamed to Africa, and contain some programming different from what North America hears.

For Europe, Radio Nederland broadcasts just once daily, at 1230-1325 on 5955 kHz. Asian listeners should tune in between 1330 and 1625, but since not all frequencies are available for the entire broadcast period, they will have to pick and choose a little. Try 9890 (or 13770), 15150, 17575 (or 17580), 17605 and 21665 kHz. For Australia and the Pacific, it's 0730-0825 on 9630 kHz, 0930-1025 on 9720 kHz, and 0730-1025 on 11895 kHz.

Germany

The official German station, radio **Deutsche Welle**, is one of the few international broadcasters that can rightly claim a worldwide audience. An exceptionally well-run station, with relay facilities as far afield as Russia, Rwanda and the Caribbean, could hardly be otherwise.

Technically, it is possibly the best of all world band stations, with most of the program output also of the highest standard. Its outlook is similar to that of the BBC World Service: to reach an ever-increasing number of listeners, regardless of cultural or national frontiers.

Broadcasts to North and Central America can be heard at 0100-0150, winters on 6040, 6055, 6085, 6145, 9565, 9610, 9640 and 11865 kHz; summers on 6040, 6145, 9565, 11810, 11865, 13610, 13770 and 15105 kHz. The first repeat is at 0300-0350, winters on 6055, 6085, 6120, 9535, 9545, 9640, 9705 and 9770 kHz; summers on 6085, 9700, 11810, 11890, 13610, 13770 and 15205 kHz. The third and final broadcast goes out at 0500-0550, winters on 5960, 6045, 6055, 6120, 6130, 9670 and 9690 kHz; summers on 5960, 6130, 9515, 11705, 11925, 13610 and 13790 kHz. This last slot is best for Western North America.

(continued on page 68)

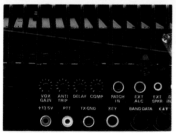

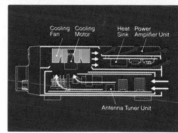

Clocks for World Band Listeners

by Jock Elliott

Crouched by the edge of his field, a subsistence farmer crumbles soil between his fingers and wonders if the monsoon will arrive on time. Halfway around the world, an executive glances at her watch, anticipating the commuter train that will whisk her home in darkness. In a quiet California hill town, a movie buff programs his VCR for *The Voice of Terror* that airs at two the following morning.

There's no avoiding it: All of us—from the wandering bedouin trying to reach an oasis before dark to the international stock trader pouncing at the opening market bell—keep track of time in ways relevant to our needs.

World band listeners also have a specialized time requirement: Coordinated Universal Time (UTC, or World Time), and international broadcasting is synchronized to it. "Welcome to World Band Radio," elsewhere in this *Passport*, explains the hows and whys of World Time. Another section, "Addresses PLUS," tells how each country's time differs from World Time.

But to observe World Time you need a suitable timepiece. An increasing number of world band radios come with built-in 24-hour clocks, and these usually suffice. But many clocks are visible only if the all-important frequency display is switched off. A full-time clock is handier.

Handier still may be a clock that tells you, "What time is it in the place I am listening to?" or, "Is it light or dark there?" Dedicated DXers, who hunt exotic stations, may also want to know exactly where the "grayline" is, the line between sunlight and darkness. Knowing where it is creeping across the globe at a given moment lets them take advantage of the enhanced reception it sometimes offers.

Even more basic to understanding World Time is to know what day of the week it is in World Time—*World Day*. If it's Thursday, 9 PM EST in New York, it's the next day, Friday World Day, 0200 World Time. After midnight, the day changes for any time standard. VCRs have this, but for some odd reason most international clocks don't, a glaring omission. The absence of World Day on clocks is a leading cause of confusion for world band listeners trying to figure which day a desired program is "really" on.

We've ferreted out and tested more than a dozen clocks that seem particularly useful to world band listeners. These range in price in the United States from just under $10 to more than $1,000. Some display world maps; one talks; another listens to the radio and sets itself (really!). None goes "cuckoo."

Clocks With Maps

Clocks with maps go with world band radio like brandy with cigars. True, most people

London's Big Ben chimes in World Time over the BBC World Service. Lucia Woods reports on this most famous of timepieces.

BBC

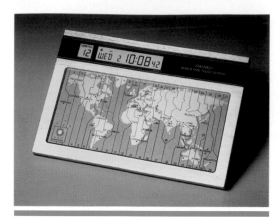

Seiko's World Time Touch Sensor, which includes World Day and date, is the best clock tested for world band listening.

★ ★ ★ ★ ½ **Seiko World Time Touch Sensor.** 2¼" H × 7¾" W × 5" D (57 × 197 × 127 mm), two "AA" batteries, shows World Day, compensates for daylight saving (summer) time, 3.5 seconds slow after one week, $110.00.

At last, a normal digital clock that shows not only time and day, but date! At the touch of a finger, this clock displays the time to the second in 12- or 24-hour format, plus date and day of the week in 27 different time zones. A 6¾" × 3⅛" (171 × 79 mm) map dominates the face of this clock. Just touch the time zone you want, and the time, day and date pop to the display window. Another button in the lower left of the display compensates for daylight saving time. A perpetual calendar keeps track of days and dates through the year 2035.

While Seiko's clocks are the most accurate after the Heath offering, they still gain or lose a few seconds every week. This means periodic resetting, and this clock is easier than most to adjust, thanks to a third button for zeroing seconds. While you can't rely on it as the definitive word on the world's time zones, it does a good job of displaying World Time, including seconds, at a glance, plus World Day. There is, however, no backlighting for nighttime reading.

For world band listening purposes, the Seiko World Time Touch Sensor is the best overall choice among the various clocks we tested. Even though it has no World Time readout that's constant year-round, by not using the daylight saving (summer) time feature you can use London Time as World Time year-round. Very highly recommended.

don't drink brandy and even fewer smoke cigars. But those who do delight in the combination.

Unlike most clocks, those with maps usually do more than show ordinary time. Some display time in various parts of the world, whereas others show exactly where it's light and where it's dark. Not only can this information be helpful, such a clock in your room can make a powerful visual statement about your international perspective and special listening interests.

The only clocks we unearthed for testing that show World Day are those with maps. Incredibly, that day is not labeled as such. Instead, to determine World Day— and, indeed, World Time—you have to look at the day in London, which except for summer happens to correspond to World Time. The omission of a dedicated World Time/ World Day display is a silly one, as we shall see, but one you can overcome.

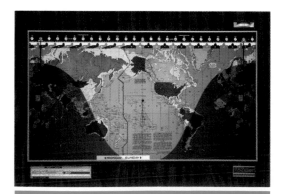

If you want to know where it's light and where it's dark, nothing quite equals the Geochron World Time Indicator.

★ ★ ★ ★ **Original Kilburg Geochron World Time Indicator.** 34¼" W × 22½" H × 4¾" D (870 × 570 × 120 mm), shows World Day year-round, does not display World Time in proper 24-hour format, compensates for daylight saving (summer) time, 120V AC (220V AC optional), approximately correct to the minute after two weeks if no power outages, $1,365.00.

To compare the Geochron to other clocks is a bit unfair to the other clocks and not quite fair to Geochron, either. This is not a device that will give you the time spot-on to the second; instead, it is a hybrid—somewhere between a clock and a map—that displays the time accurate roughly to the minute, along

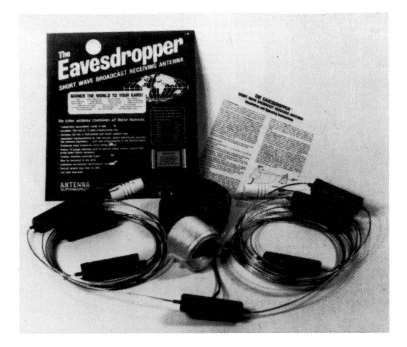

with a bellyful of other information that world band listeners may find useful. Company literature calls the Geochron the "world's first global time indicator." And so it is.

At the heart of the Geochron is a large (26½" × 13¼" or 673 × 337 mm) backlit Mercator projection that moves slowly across the expansive display at one inch (25 mm) per hour. It is always high noon along the red longitude line at the center of the map. The map shows countries, some cities and mountain ranges. At the top of the map, time-zone arrows point to a ribbon displaying the time in 12-hour format with five-minute intervals. Daylight saving (summer) time is also shown. On our model, a separate display shows time in minutes. Less expensive models omit the minutes.

Sections of the map are keyed to the time-zone arrows with letters and additional information. Iran, for example, shows "C +30." That means Iran's local time is the same as the "C" time zone, plus 30 minutes. Geochron updates the map every year to reflect any changes in political boundaries and alterations in time-zone information. They work hard at getting the most accurate information. Company officials tell us that the U.S. Department of Defense calls Geochron when the Government is updating its time-zone information. When things change in the world, Geochron owners can get an updated map for $150.

The Geochron also displays the date and position of the sun. But its biggest pay-off to world banders is that it displays the grayline—the twilight zone between sunlight and dark—as it moves across the face of the earth. Not only that, the Geochron

automatically adjusts the grayline as seasons change. In summer, the grayline curves like a sine wave so that the arctic circle is in perpetual sunlight. In winter, the antarctic enjoys 24-hour sun, and the grayline curve reverses itself. Grayline adjustment is continuous and automatic throughout the year, a great boon to serious DXers.

Beyond that, the Geochron provides a spectacular display, a real head-turner that doesn't tire. Geochrons pop up all the time in movies that involve spies and international tensions. Sink one of these into the wall above your favorite receiver, and you've created your own "situation room." Mumble something about "government work," and you should keep the neighborhood buzzing for weeks. The Geochron has that kind of potential, right along with its practical virtues—but you pay for the privilege.

A complicated device, the Geochron is not new. Early versions had a reputation for acting up, and there were management problems to boot. However, management has been upgraded and the clock reportedly now is much more reliable.

Recommended if you have deep pockets, a desire to have real-time grayline information and the urge to create *The Twilight Zone* in your own situation room. A good separate 24-hour clock for displaying World Time will still be needed, however.

Footnote: Those close to their money who want grayline information and are willing to fiddle with a straightforward mechanical device can obtain it with "The DX Edge," available from world band specialty outlets for only $20 or so. More hassle and zero sex appeal, but the price can't be beat.

World weather averages are what make the Seiko World Time Clock stand out. No World Day, though.

★ ★ ★ ★ Seiko World Time Clock. 8″ W × 2¾″ H × 6¼″ D (23 × 70 × 159 mm), two "D" batteries, shows date but not World Day, compensates for daylight saving (summer) time, 2 seconds fast after one week, $295.00.

This, the biggest and most expensive of the Seiko clocks we evaluated, displays the time to the second (12- or 24-hour format), date—but not World Day—calendar (good until 2099) and weather and time data in 20 cities throughout the world. Even though it has no World Time readout that's constant year-round, by not using the daylight saving

(continued on page 80)

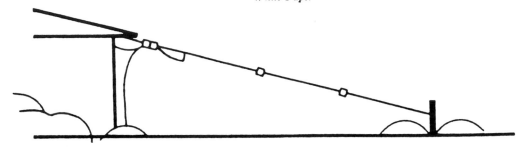

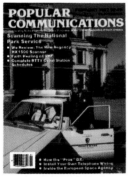

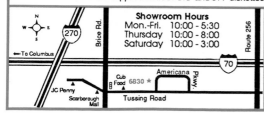

See the World Tonight

Pictures and good reads from around the world
by Fred Osterman

Just when you were getting comfortable with over-the-radio news and entertainment, along come those ingenious Swiss with a new idea: radio newspapers.

Yes, newspapers, except they are generated off a printer in your home or office, not at some distant plant. And they don't have pictures, at least not yet. Nevertheless, those with the right equipment—radioteletype, or *RTTY*—find their "electronic dog" bringing Switzerland's latest digital technology newspaper right to their homes, to be read at leisure.

Swiss "Radio Newspaper" Reaches Worldwide

Although Swiss Radio International's newspaper of the air is aimed primarily at Swiss citizens living abroad, it's enjoyed by the intellectually curious everywhere. It includes all manner of news and features about Switzerland, as well as the various ways Swiss view the world. These transmissions are aired daily in English, French and German in the RTTY-standard Baudot mode, so they can be handled by even the simplest radioteletype decoder.

As if having their own on-air newspaper isn't novel enough, the Swiss have added yet another twist. Most world band radio stations reply with verification cards to confirm signal reports from DXers. But Swiss Radio International alone returns a card telling listeners when their personal verification will be sent—over the air!

> The Swiss may be on the leading edge of an exciting trend.

Where all this is headed is anybody's guess, but SRI may well be on the leading edge of an exciting trend in which international broadcasters routinely offer both voice and text programming. For one thing, teletype transmitting is remarkably easy and inexpensive, requiring only antennas and a modest-power shortwave transmitter—Switzerland's reaches worldwide with a mere ten kilowatts—plus data handling equipment. Even the poorest developing country should be able to afford at least some sort of radioteletype "newspaper transmissions" for foreign audiences, and if it catches on private stations would likely follow.

Pictures via Radiofax

Even better, broadcasters could transmit illustrated "news magazines" via facsimile (fax) in concert with, or instead of, radioteletype. Modern decoders increasingly

With the proper hardware, your eyes and ears can explore the world.

Swiss Radio International's newsroom prepares its reports in digital form suitable for radioteletype transmission.

handle both, and shortly will be able to switch automatically between them.

Although radioteletype punches through mediocre reception conditions better than fax, fax has the enormous advantage of pictures along with text. That makes it an excellent compromise between world band radio, oriented to newsworthiness in the way only a words-only medium can be, and television, which although entertaining is driven primarily by the availability of exciting visuals.

> ## Fax by radio has the enormous advantage of pictures along with text.

Actually, technology to receive text and pictures over the air has been around for years, but until recently was the little-known purview of news services and intelligence agencies. Nothing secret, really; it just took arcane technical knowledge and a fat wallet to pick up these signals and turn them into something you could fold and read. Now, with advanced digital technology, that's fast changing.

Fax and radioteletype are among the chirps, gurgles, buzzes and whines you occasionally hear tuning around the world bands. Just as you need a special machine to convert fax signals over phone lines, so you need special equipment to turn these odd radio sounds into material you can see and use. That means a tabletop world band radio, which you may already have, and a special decoder—and let's not forget the learning curve. Baudot, which the Swiss use, is the oldest and most popular form of radioteletype, but better new flavors are continuously appearing.

Though the Swiss have the only true newspaper of the air, there's lots else on—private stuff not intended for you and me. Much of it is as dull as reading other people's mail, junk and all, but some is downright handy.

Take fax and radioteletype weather stations, which transmit weather maps and text from nearly every corner of the globe. Special books exist to help you sort them out.

Intercepted: Secret Peace Plan

Embassy traffic can be interesting, too, if occasionally puzzling. Embassy officers will occasionally break from official business to discuss the day's political gossip or last night's steamy date. Problem is, this clear embassy traffic can turn into gibberish, as it

UNIVERSAL RADIO & GRUNDIG

ALLOW YOU TO EXPERIENCE 45 YEARS OF LEGENDARY GERMAN ENGINEERING!

GRUNDIG

The Satellit 500

Selected by Larry Magne as Editor's Choice in Passport '91

Already a classic! The **Satellit 500** offers advanced features for the beginner or serious shortwave listener such as: direct keypad tuning, alpha-numeric station ID, 42 station presets, synchronous detector, switchable LSB/USB, and two scanning modes. Sound quality, sensitivity and construction are to exacting German standards for excellence! An 18 minute VHS video training manual and the new *Grundig Shortwave Listening Guide for North America* are included. New low price!

The Traveller II

- ✓ Compact AM/FM/SW radio with world timer/humane alarm
- ✓ Five shortwave frequency bands: 49, 41, 31, 25 and 19 meters covering 5.8-15.6 MHz.
- ✓ A "Must Have" for any traveller!

The Cosmopolit

- ✓ Seven shortwave bands plus FM stereo, and AM.
- ✓ Cassette player-recorder with timer function.
- ✓ Digital "talking" clock with alarm.
- ✓ The ideal "All In One" solution.

The Traveller III

- ✓ Twelve band with 3.9-21.8 MHz shortwave, stereo FM/AM/LW.
- ✓ Digital clock with a humane wake-up alarm and sleep timer.
- ✓ Liquid crystal display of world clock and calendar.
- ✓ Great for short or long trips!

The Yachtboy 206

- ✓ Twelve shortwave bands plus LW, AM and FM.
- ✓ Multifunction 24 hour digital LCD clock.
- ✓ Repeat alarm feature with sleep function.
- ✓ Great for the person who wants to hear the world!

universal radio inc.

Universal Radio, Inc.
6830 Americana Pkwy.
Reynoldsburg, OH 43068
➤ 800 431-3939 Orders
➤ 614 866-4267 Information

- ◆ We are happy to ship worldwide.
- ◆ In business since 1942!
- ◆ Visa, Mastercard and Discover cards.
- ◆ Prices & specifications subject to change.
- ◆ Free catalog on request.
- ◆ Used equipment list available.

MFJ ACCESSORIES

Here's an economical desktop tuned active antenna with performace that rivals or exceeds outside long wires hundreds of feet long!

MFJ-1020A

$79⁹⁵

Receive strong clear signals from all over the world with this indoor **tuned** active antenna that rivals the reception of long wires hundreds of feet long!

"**World Radio TV Handbook**" says MFJ-1020 is a "fine value...fair price...**performs very well indeed!!**" Set it on your desktop and listen to the world!

No need to go through the hassle of putting up an outside antenna you have to disconnect when it storms.

Covers 300 kHz to 30 MHz so you can pick up all of your favorite stations. And discover new ones you couldn't get before. Tuned circuitry minimizes inter-modulation, improves selectivity and reduces noise from phantom signals, images and out-of-band signals.

Adjustable telescoping whip gives you maximum signal with minimum noise. Full set of controls for tuning, band selection, gain and On-Off/Bypass.

Also, functions as preselector with external antenna connected to MFJ-1020A.

Measures a compact 5'' x 2'' x 6''. Use 9 volt battery (not included) 9-18 VDC or 110 VAC with MFJ-1312, $12.95. Get yours today.

MFJ Antenna Matcher

MFJ-959B

$89⁹⁵

Don't miss rare DX because of signal power loss between receiver and antenna!

The MFJ-959B provides proper impedance matching so you transfer maximum signal from antenna to receiver.

Covers 1.6-30 MHz. 20 dB preamp with gain control boosts weak stations. 20 dB attenuator prevents overload. Select from 2 antennas, 2 receivers (SO-239 connectors). Measures 9'' x 2'' x 6''. Use 9-18 VDC or 110 VAC with MFJ-1312, $12.95.

MFJ LW/MW/SW Preselector/Tuner

MFJ-956

$39⁹⁵

MFJ-956 lets you boost your favorite stations while rejecting images, intermod and other phantom signals. It improves reception from 1.5-30 MHz with most dramatic results below 2 MHz. Has tuner bypass and ground receiver postition. Measures 2'' x 3'' x 4''.

Outdoor Active Antenna

"**World Radio TV Handbook**" says MFJ-1024 is a "first rate easy-to-operate...quiet...excellent dynamic range...good gain...low noise...broad coverage...excellent choice."

Mount it outdoors away from electrical noise for maximum signal, minimum noise. Covers 0.5-30 MHz.

Receives strong, clear signals from all over the world. 20 dB attenuator, gain control. On LED. Switch two receivers and aux. or active antenna. 6 x 3 x 5 in. Remote unit has 54 inch whip, 50 ft. coax and connector. 3 x 2 x 4 in. Use 12-VDC or 110 VAC with MFJ-1312,$12.95.

MFJ-1024 **$129⁹⁵**

MFJ DXers' World Map Clock

MFJ-112
$24⁹⁵ *NEW*

New MFJ DXers' World Map Clock from MFJ shows you the time at any place in the world and lets you see the place the signal comes from on the world map clock face. Also shows day of week, month, date and year. Push buttons let you move the display to a place in every time zone. Recall feature instantly moves the display back to local time. Alarm. Day light savings time feature. Map on gold background. User selectable 12/24 hour. Great display gift! Measures 51/8''W x 3½''H x2¼''D.

SWL's Guide for Apartment/Condo Dwellers

MFJ-36
$9⁹⁵ *NEW*

Even if you're in an apartment in the middle of a crowded city and you can't pick anything up, world reknowned SWL expert Ed Noll's newest book gives you the key to hearing news as it's happening, concerts from Vienna and soccer games from Germany!

You learn what shortwave bands to listen to, the best times to tune in, how to DX and successfully QSL. This antenna guide shows you how to make the most of a small space. Much more.

MFJ-1278 Multimode

MFJ-1278
$279⁹⁰

MFJ's famous top-of-the-line computer interface lets you receive FAX, RTTY, Amtor, Morse code, packet radio, Navtex, SSTV and ASCII on your computer screen. Zillions of features ... Automatic Signal Analysis™ analyzes RTTY, ASCII, AMTOR and HF Packet. Optional starter packet **MFJ-1289**, **$59.95; MFJ-1282B, $39.95; MFJ-1290, $49.95.** Gives you multi-gray news photos and weather maps. Full color SSTV.

MFJ Dual Tunable Filter

MFJ-752C

$99⁹⁵

This all mode **dual** tunable filter lets you zero in and pull out your favorite stations and notch out interference at the same time. Two independently tunable filters let you peak, notch, low or high pass signals to eliminate heterodynes and interference— even on the most crowded shortwave bands. Tune both filters from 300 Hz to 3000 Hz. Vary bandwidth from 40 Hz to almost flat. Notch depth to 70 dB.

Headphone and speaker jacks with 2 watts audio provided let you monitor stations through filter. Inputs for 2 radios (switch selectable). Switchable noise limiter from impulse noise through clipper removes background noise. OFF bypasses filter. Use 9-18 VDC or 110 VAC with MFJ-1312, $12.95. 10'' x 2'' x 6''.

All Band Transceiver/Preselector

MFJ-1040B

$99⁹⁵

Lets you copy weak signals. Rejects out-of-band signals, images. Covers 1.8 to 54 MHz. Up to 20 dB gain. Gain control. Dual gate MOSFET, bipolar transistors for low noise, high gain. 20 dB attenuator. Connect 2 antennas, 2 receivers. Coax and phone jacks. Automatic bypass when transmitting to 350 watts. Delay. Jack for PTT. Use 9-18 VDC or 110 VAC with MFJ-1312, $12.95.

MFJ-1045B, $69.95. Like MFJ-1040B without attenuator, auto transceiver bypass, delay control or PTT.

<figcaption>Radiofax photos help flesh out world band news coverage.</figcaption>

Fred Osterman

Sometimes, you get lucky. Not often, but once in a while, they don't switch on the scrambler or it doesn't function right. When that happens, you can find yourself eavesdropping on people making history. Several radioteletype listeners, for example, copied startling messages between the Egyptian embassies in Washington and Cairo during the Persian Gulf war. One intercept even provided confidential details of a Soviet peace proposal to settle the conflict.

> ## You can find yourself eavesdropping on people making history.

Monitoring military radioteletype traffic can be revealing, whether in war or peace. The French, for instance, have an extensive communications web centered in Paris, one that reaches the most remote ends of their former colonial empire. Using an advanced mode called ARQ-M2, these "Action Jacqueson" channels are continuously linked to bases in Martinique, Djibouti, Senegal, Tahiti, Reunion Island, Gabon and French Guiana.

Maritime traffic can be copied daily from commercial ships. If you've ever heard what sounds like crickets on your radio, chances are you've stumbled onto a form of radioteletype called SITOR-A, the mode of choice for ships and coastal stations. Maritime traffic is often routine, nothing more startling than a cruise ship's huge liquor requisition. Yet, at the right time maritime radioteletype can make for adventurous listening.

Unfiltered News From Wire Services

Swiss aside, much of radioteletype's appeal lies in intercepting the world's lesser-known wire services, otherwise available only to elite news professionals. This gets the news to you unfettered by the hidden hands of newspaper or network editors. With the right equipment and conditions, you can read English teletype press transmissions from such capitals as Ankara, Baghdad, Beijing, Bucharest, Budapest, Cairo, Lagos, Pyongyang, Taipei, Tirana, Tokyo, Warsaw and Tripoli.

is typically sent "scrambled." So don't panic—your radioteletype decoder hasn't suffered a nervous breakdown. Rather, it's receiving sensitive communications which, understandably, are often "encrypted," as James Bond would say.

THE GRUNDIG DIFFERENCE

Tuning In to the World, via Shortwave

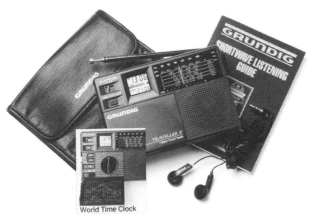

Traveller II

F*rom Traveller to serious short-wave radio listener, Lentini Communications has the Grundig radio that is right for you. Call and talk to one of our experts about Grundig Shortwave Radios*

YB 206

Satellit 500

Cosmopolit

How to Do It

Fax and radioteletype reception equipment has become surprisingly affordable. If you already own a tabletop world band radio, you're halfway there; add a personal computer and you're in the home stretch.

You can turn your radio into your private eye on the earth.

The two basic approaches are to either add a decoder to your personal computer or buy a dedicated decoder. External computer interfaces start at $150 in the United States, typically more elsewhere. With these, radioteletype and fax can be displayed on your computer's monitor or printer. The more sophisticated, high-performance units, such as the internally mounted Universal M-1000, start at $400 Stateside. Make sure, though, that your computer doesn't emit digital radio noise—"hash"—that can blot out weak signals. If you're in the United States, a good starting point is to ensure that all your computer hardware is rated Class B by the FCC

Passport's Top Video Frequencies

World Time	Frequency (kHz)	Location	Service
Radioteletype—Swiss Radio International "Newspaper" (one hour daily)			
0030	10515	Bern, Switzerland	German to South America
0200	10515	Bern, Switzerland	German to North America
1700	15835	Bern, Switzerland	English to Australasia, but also received in North America
1830	17530	Bern, Switzerland	French to Africa
2000	10515	Bern, Switzerland	French to Asia
Radioteletype—Press ("Wire") Services			
0000	6848	Warsaw, Poland	PAP; also 11497 kHz
0115	7996	Belgrade, Yugoslavia	TANJUG, English from 1700-0400 World Time; also 5240 and 7658 kHz
0300	7428	Buenos Aires, Argentina	TELAM; also 4004 kHz
0400	11478	Pyongyang, Korea (DPR)	KCNA, English
0600	17468	Budapest, Hungary	MTI, English
0700	9830	Phnom Penh, Cambodia	SPK, English
1120	17470	Beijing, China	XINHUA, English
1340	14800	Tunis, Tunisia	TAP, French
1400	14373	Baghdad, Iraq	INA, English
1400	9090	Taipei, China (Taiwan)	CNA; also 7695 kHz
1400	8175	Tokyo, Japan	KYODO; also 5097 kHz
1430	16117	Dakar, Senegal	PANA, English
1500	9430	Tirana, Albania	ATA, English
1500	10599	Hanoi, Vietnam	VNA; also 9331 kHz
1500	19980	Tehran, Iran	IRNA, English
1540	14764	Manama, Bahrain	GNA, English
1545	20085	Rome, Italy	ANSA, English
1600	20560	Tripoli, Libya	JANA, English
1700	11080	Damascus, Syria	SANA, English
1900	14928	Havana, Cuba	PRENSA LATINA

and proper cables are used. Avoid Class A, which is noisier.

If you don't wish to use a computer or simply want better performance, consider a dedicated decoder. It requires only a video monitor and, if you want hard copy, a parallel printer. The Universal M-900, at under $500, copies all standard modes of teletype, plus fax, and works with all types of printers except laser. For most purposes, including optimum reception of Swiss Radio International's daily transmissions, that's more than enough. For the perfectionist who wants to be able to see it all, including such esoterica as Indonesian diplomatic communications, the Universal M-8000 defines the high end at $1,299, plus VGA color monitor and printer.

Remember, though, that although today's decoders are remarkably automated, it still takes patience to sift through the thousands of coded signals on the air. A good frequency directory, such as the *Guide to Utility Stations* or *Guide to Facsimile Stations*, is an absolute must.

Whether you like your news straight and unfiltered, or just want to scratch your knowledge itch, you can turn your world band radio into your private eye on the earth. It's knowledge you'll scarcely find elsewhere.

Fred Osterman is President of Universal Radio, Inc. He has prepared several books and articles over the years, including a number specializing in international radioteletype and facsimile reception. He is also keenly involved in the development of world band radioteletype and fax equipment.

Fax—Weather and Press Services

World Time	Frequency (kHz)	Location	Service
Various	6900	Norrköping, Sweden	Weather
Evenings	6944	Vancouver BC, Canada	Weather
Various	7475	Khabarovsk, Russia	Weather
Various	7530	Boston MA, USA	Weather
24 hours	8080	Norfolk VA, USA	Weather; also 3357, 10863 and 16410 kHz
Evenings	8459	Kodiak AK, USA	Weather; also 4296 kHz
Various	9060	Novosibirsk, Russia	Weather
Various	9157	Mobile AL, USA	Weather; also 6850 kHz
Various	9438	Tokyo, Japan	Weather
Various	10535	Halifax NS, Canada	Weather; also 6496 kHz
Various	12728	San Francisco CA, USA	Weather; also 8682 and 17151 kHz
Various	13947	Tashkent, Uzbekistan	Weather
Various	14828	Pearl Harbor HI, USA	Weather; also 4853, 7993, 8492 and 9395 kHz
Various	17069	Tokyo, Japan	TOKYO RADIO press; also 5768, 8467 and 22542 kHz
Various	17585	Rota, Spain	Weather
Various	18060	Darwin, Australia	Weather; also 10555 kHz
Various	18093	Buenos Aires, Argentina	Weather
Mornings	19862	Apra Harbor, Guam	Weather; also 9383 kHz

Credits: *World Press Service Frequencies*, *The RTTY Listener* and Fred Osterman.

Canada's Best Stocked S.W.L. Store

ALLOWS YOU TO EXPERIENCE 48 YEARS OF LEGENDARY GERMAN ENGINEERING !

Satellit 650

The world's best sounding shortwave for hour after hour listening. A powerful 30 watt audio system with full, independent bass and treble control provides for the best audio quality available in a shortwave receiver. 60 user programmable memories. Giant liquid crystal digital display. Three programmable turn on/off timers. Built-in preselector for enhanced SW reception. Built-in Ni-cad battery charger. Power from built in 120/220V supply.

Satellit®500

Already a Classic! Advanced features such as: direct keypad tuning, 42 station preset with alphanumeric station ID, synchronous detector, switchable LSB/USB, two scanning modes, and built in nicad charger. Sound quality, sensitivity and construction are to exacting German standards for Excellence!

GRUNDIG Traveller II

Imagine a feature packed world band radio that sits comfortably in the palm of your hand. Powerful enough to reach the far corners of the globe, you have the choice of 5 shortwave bands (49, 41, 31, 25 and 19M), plus FM and AM reception. Grundig's Humane Wake System alarm gently alerts you.

GRUNDIG Cosmopolit

Three-in-one unit featuring stereo (when headphones are used) cassette player with monaural recording. FM stereo receiver, AM, 7 shortwave bands, digital clock, talking clock, full alarm clock features and wake-up timer. Powered by 3 "AA" batteries (not included).

We Stock all GRUNDIG *Shortwave Radios!*

Ten of the Best

(continued from page 18)

9455 kHz, but the first two times are Tuesday through Friday only, with the 0600 broadcast also available on Monday.

"Omnibus"
BBC World Service

Omnibus, to quote the BBC World Service's own publication, is "a half-hour program on almost any topic under the sun," with a "tradition of delving into all things rich and strange." Embellished, perhaps, but not by much.

Topics have ranged from Mennonites in Belize to Rasputin, the Russian monk; from chocolate to Barbie dolls; and from Good King Wenceslas to the challenges facing war correspondents.

Each week sees a well-produced 30-minute program devoted to a single subject, although the central theme varies wildly from one week to the next. Whatever the topic, the ubiquitous BBC professionalism shines throughout.

Omnibus is targeted to Europe at 1001 Wednesday on 9750, 9760, 12095 and 15070 kHz; and again later the same day at 1930 on 6195 (winter), 7325 (winter), 12095 (summer) and 9410 kHz. It is also available to the Middle East at these same times, at 1001 on 11760, 15575, 17640 and 21470 kHz; and at 1930 on 9410, 9740, 12095 and 15070 kHz.

> BBC professionalism shines throughout *Omnibus*.

Listeners in East Asia have only one shot, 1001 Wednesday on 9740, 17830 and 21715 kHz; while listeners in Australia and the Pacific must try for 1930 Wednesday on 11955 kHz.

North Americans also have just one opportunity, 0030 Wednesday (Tuesday evening, local date) on 5975, 6175, 7325, 9590, 9915 and 12095 kHz.

"Hello from Tokyo"
Radio Japan

Many listener response programs are little more than thinly-disguised forums for acknowledging listeners' mail, with very little substance to be found therein. Not so, *Hello from Tokyo*, Radio Japan's successful attempt at providing a balanced, interesting and enjoyable weekly encounter with its audience. It's also pleasant evidence that Radio Japan's English programs, once among the world's most boring, are beginning to shine. Indeed, Radio Japan hopes to expand its programming during 1993.

This program is something of a hybrid, combining listener contact with magazine-like programming. Unlike many other shows of its type, listeners' questions are often answered in the form of a feature, sometimes recorded on location. Topics can include virtually anything, from Shintoism to "walking advertising."

There are also special guests, telephone conversations with listeners, highlights of upcoming programs and interludes of Japanese music. This is a fully packed 39 minutes of entertainment with plenty of mass appeal.

Interested? If you live in North America, try Sundays at 0315 (0115 Monday in summer) on 5960 kHz; 0515 on 11870 (or 15230)

Andrew Ward

The BBC's *Omnibus* covers just about anything, including human skin. Producer Roy Hanes looks on while tattooist Lal Hardy needles a client.

and 17825 kHz; and 1415 and 1715 on 9505 or 11865 kHz. Europeans are best served Sunday at 0715 on 9670, 9770, 15170 and 21575 kHz. Listeners in the Middle East can tune in that same day at 0715 on 21575 kHz and at 1715 on 15210 (or 15345) kHz.

Best bets for East Asia are Sunday at 1115 on 11840 kHz and 1715 on 7140 kHz. Listeners in the Pacific can hear the program several hours earlier, at 0515 and 0715 on 17860 (or 17890) kHz.

"The Jive Zone"
BBC World Service for Africa

Like poi, not for every taste. Yet, as fans of African popular music know, this is, to lift from Little Richard, "the healing music that makes the blind see, the lame walk." If your limbs are limber and your heart beats strong, grab a partner and dance to the rhythms.

Besides the music, there are short interviews with celebrated African musicians, who provide *Rolling-Stone*-type insight into the African musical scene.

The Jive Zone is tailored to an African audience, and so is not available on mainstream BBC World Service English programming. However, since more than one transmitter is sometimes used on the same frequency, it is possible to hear the program in a number of regions outside the African continent.

The first airing is at 1930 Thursday on 6005, 6190 and 15400 kHz; repeated at 0730 Sunday on 11860 and 15105 kHz.

"American Stories"
Voice of America

What's this doing here, drama with no pictures? In "special" slow-speed English? From Government employees in Washington?

If you like classic American fiction, unplug the TV, gather the family around the radio and check it out. *American Stories* is a weekly 15-minute slot which is part of a VOA service for those who speak English as a second language. The title says it all—readings of short stories written by American authors.

Stories selected for the program vary considerably from week to week, ranging from the first American detective story to classics from the likes of O. Henry and Jack London. Also included are American versions of centuries-old international favorites.

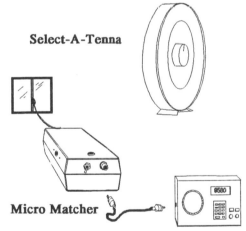

It's no mean trick nowadays to dig up anthologies of American short stories which, lest we forget, are among the best the world has to offer. Even tougher is to be able to hear them being read. For those who fancy this genre, *American Stories* should not be missed. The slow-speed English is not unduly irritating and, on occasion, actually enhances.

The program is aimed to Europe Saturday at 1645 on 9760, 11710, 15205 and 15245 kHz; and at 1845 on 6040, 9760 and 15205 kHz. It can also be heard the same day in the Middle East at 1045 on 11735, 15160, 15195, 21455 and 21570 kHz; at 1645 on 6180 and 15205 kHz; and at 2245 on 9530, 11905, 11960, 15225, 15445 and 17885 kHz.

Listeners in Australasia have two Saturday slots at their disposal: at 1045 on 5985, 11720 and 15425 kHz; and at 1345 on 15425 kHz. East Asia is less lucky, having to make do at 1345 on 9760 and 15155 kHz.

North Americans are not officially served by the VOA, but can still hear the broadcasts without much difficulty. *American Stories* is heard in the United States and Canada at 0045 Sunday (Saturday evening, local date) on 5995, 7405, 9775, 11580, 15120 and 15205 kHz. Well, those are the official frequencies. The computer that controls the transmitters in Greenville, North Carolina, was wrongly programmed some time back, so you may find that the actual frequencies are 6130, 9455, 11695 and 15120 kHz.

"Health Matters"
BBC World Service

World band radio has quite a number of quality programs dealing with scientific topics, but few directly touching on people's health and fitness.

Full marks, then, to the BBC World Service for its regular weekly 15-minute spot devoted to aches, pains and other ills that affect the human mind and body.

Obesity, brittle bones, coughs and chills, backache. These and many more miseries are covered in international radio's clinic of the air, as well as more serious ailments such as cystic fibrosis and multiple sclerosis. Occasionally there is even a touch of exoticism, when part or all of the quarter-hour is given over to discussion of some little-known tropical disease.

Health Matters is a wide-ranging pro-

gram that deals with virtually all aspects of modern medicine: prevention, diagnosis, symptoms, pain relief, new developments in medical science, care of terminally ill patients, nutritional education, personal hygiene and just about anything else one could ask for from a program like this.

There are interviews and expert opinions, as well as information on books and other relevant publications; not to mention a wide range of "fact sheets" available—at no cost—by writing to the program.

A word of warning, though: this is not a show for hypochondriacs!

Europeans can hear the program Monday at 0815 on 5975, 7325, 9410, 12095 or 15070 kHz; later the same day at 1945 on 6195 (winter), 7325 (winter), 12095 (summer) and 9410 kHz; and Tuesday (for early risers) at 0415 on 3955, 6195, 7230 or 9410 kHz. In the Middle East, try Monday at 0815 on 17640 kHz; at 1945 on 9410, 9740, 12095 and 15070 kHz; and Tuesday at 0415 on 11760, 11955, 12095, 15070 and 15575 kHz.

Listeners in East Asia can choose from 0815 Monday on 15280, 15360, 17830 and 21715 kHz; 0145 Tuesday on 17790 kHz; and 0415 Tuesday on 15280 and 21715 kHz. Those in the Pacific area have just two opportunities—0815 Monday on 11955 and 17830 kHz; and almost 12 hours later, at 1945, on 11955 kHz.

For North America and the Caribbean, it's a case of Tuesday only (Monday evening, local date). Easterners can listen in at 0145 on 5975, 6175, 7325, and (summer only) 9915 and 12095 kHz; while those farther west can try some of these very same frequencies, plus 9590 kHz. In winter, the 0415 broadcast is also available to Eastern North America on 5975, 6175 and 7325 kHz; and to western parts on 5975, 7325 or 9915 kHz. During summer, there is no frequency available at this time for Eastern North America, but listeners on the West Coast can try 5975 or 12095 kHz—East Coast listeners can often hear these, too.

"Music from Ukraine"
Radio Ukraine

True to its title, the program covers all forms of Ukrainian music, some of which may not appeal to non-Ukrainian speakers. A case in point is modern Ukrainian folk—"bardic"—music, which loses some of its enchantment if you don't understand the lyrics. But what would Ukrainians think of early recordings by the likes of Leonard Cohen?

At their best, though, the contents of this weekly window on Ukrainian music are stupendous. The choral performances for which Ukrainians are justifiably famous will please even the most discerning ear.

Between the extremes of bardic ballads and chesty choirs, Radio Ukraine broadcasts a nifty potpourri of musical offerings, from the celebrated Nina Patienkov to symphony music based on centuries-old folk melodies.

Now that Ukraine (between me and thee, there is no more "the" in "Ukraine") has full control of the many shortwave transmitters on its newly independent territory, there's not much difficulty in tuning in the station, especially in Europe and Eastern North America. For western North America, the use of relay facilities in the Russian Far East ensures a signal that is more than adequate.

Music from Ukraine is aimed to Europe at 2230 Sundays on a number of frequencies. Winters, choose from 5960, 6010, 6020, 7240, 7340, 7380, 9680 and 9785 kHz; summers, try 5960, 7250, 9785, 9865, 15135 and 15570 kHz.

The repeat broadcast at 0130 is intended not only for North America, but also for European insomniacs. Winter, listeners in Western Europe and Eastern North America can try 4825, 7240, 7400, 9640, 9685 or 9860 kHz; summer, 7195, 7250, 9785, 12000, 12040, 12060 and 15570 kHz. For Western North America, there is a relay of the 0130 broadcast via Russian transmitters, winter on 17605 and 17690 kHz, and summer on 13645 and 15580 kHz.

All transmissions are one hour earlier in summer.

As a footnote, if you want to obtain first-rate recordings of Ukrainian music, try Apon Records, Box 3082, Steinway Station, Long Island City NY 11103 USA.

Prepared by the staff of Passport to World Band Radio.

Welcome to World Band Radio

(continued from page 24)

The Great International Radio Bazaar

Even if you have never listened to world band radio before, you are accustomed to turning on your radio and hearing local AM or FM stations at the same place on the dial day and night. Things are very different when you roam the international airwaves.

World band radio is like a great international bazaar, where merchants come and go at different times: stations enter and leave the same spot on the dial throughout the day and night. Where you once tuned in a British station, hours later you will find a Russian or Chinese broadcaster roosting on that same spot.

Or on a nearby perch. If you suddenly hear interference from a station on an adjacent channel, it doesn't mean something is wrong with your radio; it means another station has begun broadcasting on a nearby frequency. These stations sometimes try to outshout each other, like merchants in a bazaar: "Listen to me! Listen to me!"

You can find world band broadcasters by looking them up in *Passport's* by-country or "What's On Tonight" sections, or by using *Passport's* vast Blue Pages to cruise within the several "segments" or "bands"—neighborhoods in the electronic spectrum—where they can be found. Incidentally, frequencies may be given as kilohertz, kHz, or Megahertz, MHz. The only difference is decimal places (three). So 6175 kHz is exactly the same as 6.175 MHz. All you really need to know is that 6175 refers to a spot on your radio's dial.

Here are the main "neighborhoods" where you can find world band broadcasters and when they're most active. Except for the 4700-5100 kHz segment, which has mainly Latin American and African stations, you'll discover a great variety of types of stations on all the other bands.

4700 - 5100 kHz	Early morning and night, mainly during winter
5850 - 6250 kHz	Night
7100 - 7600 kHz	Night
9300 - 10000 kHz	Early morning, late afternoon and night
11500 - 12160 kHz	Night and, to some degree, day
13600 - 13900 kHz	Day and, to some degree, night
15000 - 15700 kHz	Day and, to some degree, night
17500 - 17900 kHz	Day and, to a slight degree, night
21450 - 21850 kHz	Day

A Stroll in the Bazaar

One of the most enjoyable things you can do with world band radio is to cruise up and down the different bands. Daytime, you'll get best results above 11500 kHz; night, below 10000 kHz.

Tune slowly, savor the sound of foreign tongues (there's lots of English-language programming, too), enjoy the music, listen to the opinions of other peoples.

If the broadcast seems to fade out and in, there is nothing wrong with your radio. Signals travel a long way to get to your ears, sometimes bouncing off layers of the atmosphere many times. The result is "fading," an ordinary world band occurrence. That same

---

The Passport Five-Minute Ultra-Fast Start

In a hurry? Here's how to get off and running right away:

1. Make sure it is evening, preferably before midnight, and dark outside.
2. Ensure your radio is plugged into the wall or has fresh batteries. Extend the telescopic antenna straight up and fully. The DX/local switch (if there is one) should be set to "DX."
3. Turn your radio on. Tune it to 5900 kHz and begin tuning slowly toward 6200 kHz. You will now begin to encounter a number of stations from around the world. Adjust the volume to a level that is comfortable for you. Voilà! You are now an initiate of world band radio.

Where do Japanese listeners go to buy receivers or *Passport to World Band Radio*? Why, Tokyo's glitzy Akihabara district, of course! Surprisingly, prices are sometimes higher than in the United States.

changeability can also work in your favor. Sometimes faint stations from exotic locales —stations you would not ordinarily hear— arrive at your radio with surprising strength. Reception changes hour to hour, day to day, always presenting something new.

By the way, there is a new type of high-tech radio circuit, synchronous detection, to help reduce the effects of fading. See the "Buyer's Guide" to find out which receivers have this and how well it works.

You and Your Radio

If you haven't yet purchased a world band radio, here's some good news: although cheap radios should be avoided, you don't need an expensive set to enjoy exploring the world's airwaves. With a decent portable, you'll be able to hear much of what world band has to offer. And you won't need an outside antenna, either, unless you're using a tabletop model. All portables are designed to work off the built-in telescopic antenna. Try, though, to purchase a radio with digital frequency display; its accuracy will make tuning around the bands much easier than with old-fashioned slide-rule tuning.

In *Passport's* award-winning "Buyer's Guide" you'll find much more information about radios: independent tests of the currently available radios, as well as expert recommendations for a best starter radio. It's all there to help you make an informed, cost-effective choice.

Radio in hand, read the owner's manual carefully. You'll quickly discover that, despite a few unfamiliar controls, your new world band set isn't all that much different from the radios you have used all your life. Experiment with the controls so you'll become comfortable with them. You can't harm your radio twiddling switches and knobs.

Bon Voyage

Elsewhere in *Passport*, you'll find information on English-language broadcasts, the easiest stations to hear and other "must" information. You're now ready to embark. Welcome to world band radio, an adventure that lasts a lifetime!

Prepared by Jock Elliott and the staff of Passport to World Band Radio.

20 + Big Signals

(continued from page 34)

Surprisingly, there is no specific broadcast in English to Europe, but Deutsche Welle can still be heard by Europeans. In the United Kingdom, reception of 6120 kHz (winters) and of 9515 and 11705 kHz (summers) at 0500-0550 is usually excellent. At 0600-0650 try 11765, 13610, 13790 or 15185 kHz; and in the evening tune in at 1900-1950, winters on 9765, 11765 and 13790 kHz; summers on 11810, 13790, 15350 and 15390 kHz. This broadcast is also available to the Middle East, winters on 11905 kHz, and summers on 13780 kHz. Listeners in Asia and the Pacific are catered to at 0900-0950 on 6160, 11915, 17780, 17820, 21465, 21650 and 21680 kHz; and again at 2100-2150 on 6185 (or 13780), 9670, 9765 and 11785 kHz.

Dieter Brauer, Head of Deutsche Welle's English Service, interviews German President Dr. Richard von Seizäcker.

Russia

Despite losing a sizable part of its transmitting facilities to newly independent countries and the ravages of hyperinflation, **Radio Moscow's** 24-hour World Service is still among the most frequently heard stations.

How long this will continue is anyone's guess, as not even the station's personnel can tell for sure. The fate of Radio Moscow is closely linked to the state of the Russian economy, and it would take a brave—or foolish—man to forecast what the future holds.

Broadcasts to Europe and North America are virtually continuous, and consist of the (West Coast) North American Service, which operates from 0400 to 0800 (one hour earlier in summer), and the World Service, which operates the rest of the time.

There is ample programming choice, covering everything from the Russian parliament to jazz in Vladivostok. While news-related programs may occasionally be a little uneven as journalists leave for juicier jobs at the newer independent stations, Moscow's musical offerings remain among the best.

There's a can-do spirit among Radio Moscow's staff that allows it to air first-class programs under trying circumstances. Make it a point to tune in this station regularly. It's bringing you history in the making—from where it's happening, and from whom it's happening to.

Where and when to listen? Some gaps exist, most notably Western Europe and Eastern North America. Nevertheless, it is expected that Radio Moscow will do its best to fill these gaps and continue to broadcast in the same portions of the world band spectrum as before.

Roll over Tchaikovsky! The bells of freedom ring loud and clear over Radio Moscow International.

> Radio Moscow brings history in the making—from where it's happening, from whom it's happening to.

Winter, listeners in these areas should dial around the 6, 7, 9 and 11 MHz bands; with 9, 11, 13, 15 and 17 MHz being better bets for summer. The future of the Cuban relay for North America remains uncertain, but while it lasts try 11840 kHz during the day, and 6000, 6045 or 11850 kHz evenings.

Reception in Western North America

should continue very much unchanged. Try the lower bands during the night, and the higher ones during the day. Dial around to see which channel sounds best.

If you're in the Middle East or East Asia, try frequencies in the 6, 7, 9 and 11 MHz bands. Listeners in the Middle East can also try frequencies higher up the spectrum, where they can eavesdrop on broadcasts targeted farther afield.

For Southeast Asia and Australasia, the best channels are likely to be found in the 15, 17 and 21 MHz bands, with several being year-round frequencies.

Switzerland

One of the most popular news-oriented stations, **Swiss Radio International** has drastically restructured its transmission schedule and also added a radioteletype "newspaper of the air," explained elsewhere in this *Passport*. Fortunately, the English-language broadcasts have retained all the virtues of the former program format.

The weekday lineup of news and news

analysis was given a further boost in April 1992 by a program cooperation agreement with the International Committee of the Red Cross. This gives SRI a clear advantage over other news gathering sources when it comes to virtually inaccessible war-torn regions.

> Cooperation with the Red Cross gives SRI a clear advantage in war-torn regions.

On weekends, the 30-minute broadcasts are lighter in nature, with news and entertainment providing more balance. Whatever the day of the week, this is a station well worth a segment of your time.

North American listeners can tune in at 0000 on 6135, 9650, 9885, 12035 and 17730 kHz; 0200 on 6135, 9650, 9885 and 12035 kHz; and again at 0400 on 6135, 9885, 12035 and 13635 kHz. In Europe—one hour earlier summers—hear SRI at 0500 and 0700 on 3985, 6165 and 9535 kHz; and at 1200 on 6165, 9535 and 12030 kHz.

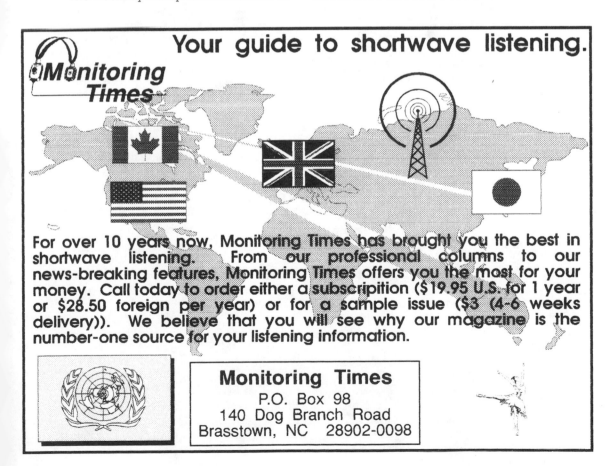

BBC

Elizabeth Robson and Olexiy Solohubenko of the BBC World Service interview Prime Minister John Major during the inauguration of the Ukrainian Service.

Best bets for Asia and the Pacific are 0900 on 9560, 13685, 17670 and 21770 kHz; plus 1100 and 1330 on 13635, 15505, 17670 and 21770 kHz. There is also a relay via Radio Beijing at 1300 on 7480 and 11690 kHz. A further broadcast (also available to the Middle East) can be heard at 1500 on 13635, 15505, 17670 and 21770 kHz; with a repeat at 1700 on 13635, 15430, 17635 and 21770 kHz. For the Middle East and Africa there is a broadcast at 2000 on 9885, 12035, 13635 and 15505 kHz.

Ukraine

When it comes to shortwave transmitters, Russia's loss has been Ukraine's gain. Radio Moscow relied heavily in the past on major Ukrainian facilities at such places as Kiev, Lvov and Simferopol for its broadcasts to Western Europe and Eastern North America. Now, these transmitters carry **Radio Ukraine International**.

Formerly Radio Kiev, Radio Ukraine International does an excellent job of reporting on everyday events in the newly independent Ukrainian homeland, covering political, cultural, sporting and all other aspects of Ukrainian life. Good stuff.

European listeners can tune in at 2200-2300 winters on a variety of channels from 5960, 6010, 6020, 7240, 7340, 7380, 9680 and 9785 kHz; summers on 5960, 7250, 9785, 9865, 15135 and 15570 kHz. The repeat at 0100 is available not only for Eastern North America, but also for European night owls. Winters try 4825, 7240, 7400,

9640, 9685 or 9860 kHz; summers, on 7195, 7250, 9785, 11520, 11790, 12000, 12040, 12060 and 15570 kHz.

For Western North America there is a relay of the 0100 transmission via the Russian Far East, winters on 17605 and 17690 kHz, and summers on 13645 and 15580 kHz.

All transmissions are one hour earlier summer.

United Kingdom

If there were to be a gold medal given for world band broadcasting, the **BBC World Service** would surely earn it. Technical excellence coupled with 24-karat programming is a guaranteed formula for success. And there are over 120 million listeners worldwide to prove it.

A roster of BBC transmitter relays reads like a school geography book: Cyprus, Oman, Singapore, Hong Kong, Lesotho, Seychelles, Ascension, Antigua, Canada and the United States. No wonder the "Beeb" is so widely heard and enjoyed.

Although the programming is exceptionally varied, even by world band standards, the BBC World Service is best known for its news and expert news analysis—a daily 24-hour service relied upon by well over a hundred million listeners, from peasants to presidents.

Expect it to continue. The BBC's plans are for further expansion, continued broadening of dissemination vehicles, plus improved coverage in key areas. In short, a better signal for a larger audience.

> **The BBC World Service is relied upon by over a hundred million, from peasants to presidents.**

Mornings, the BBC World Service is best heard in Eastern North America at 1100-1400 on 5965, 9515 or 15220 kHz; at 1400-1615 on 9515 and 17840 kHz; and at 1615-1745 on 9515 kHz. In Western North America, try 1100-1400 on 15220 kHz, 1200-1400 and 1500-1600 (1200-1600 Saturday and Sunday) on 9740 kHz, and 1600-1745 (weekends from 1500) on 15260 kHz. Listeners in the Caribbean can tune in at 1100-1400 on 15220 kHz, 1100-1430 on 6195 kHz, and at 1430-1615 on 15205 kHz.

Early evenings in Eastern North

Canada's Best Shortwave Store

ICOM R-71A 100 kHz to 30 MHz general coverage receiver with SSB/CW/RTTY/AM modes, FM optional. Dual VFO's and direct keyboard entry; 32 tunable mode and frequency memories. RIT, passband tuning, notch, selectable AGC, noise blanker, tone, squelch, recording jack, built-in speaker. Selectivity: 500 Hz, 2.3 kHz, 6 kHz, 15 kHz bandwidth.

SONY ICF-SW7600 Covers 153 kHz to 29.995 MHz and 76 to 108 MHz; AM/SSB/CW/FM. FM stereo with supplied headphones. Tunes manually, by keyboard entry, memory scan or 10 memory presets. LCD readout, fine tuning, 12/24-hour clock with timer.

YAESU FRG-8800 Covers 150 kHz to 29.99 MHz and 118 to 173.99 MHz with optional VHF converter. Manual tuning and 21-button keyboard for direct entry and programming of 12 memories. LCD with 100 Hz resolution, bargraph S/SINPO indicator. Three scanning modes, dual 24-hour clock/timer.

KENWOOD R-5000 Covers 100 kHz to 30 MHz and 108 to 174 MHz with optional VHF converter; SSB/CW/AM/FM. Dual VFO's, direct keyboard frequency entry. 100 memories store mode, frequency and antenna selection. Scanning, dual noise blankers, selectable AGC, attenuator, dual 24-hour clocks and timer.

KENWOOD

Panasonic

ICOM

Bearcat

YAESU

DRAKE

SONY.

JRC *Japan Radio Co.*

uniden

SANGEAN

Whether you require advice or are ready to purchase, you can always count on us!

- Experienced Advice
- Competitive Pricing
- Wide Selection
- Customer Satisfaction

NORHAM RADIO INC.

4373 Steeles Ave. W., North York, Ontario MN3 1V7

Mail Order
(416) 667-1000, FAX 24 hours/day: (416) 667-9995

Visit Our Retail Store
Monday: 10–7
Tuesday– Friday: 10–6
Saturday: 10–3
Closed Sunday

America, you can tune in at 2000-2200 on a wealth of frequencies, including 5975 or 15260 kHz. An additional plum is *Caribbean Report*, aired at 2115-2130 (Monday through Friday only) on 6110, 15140 and 17715 kHz—one of the few ways you can get regular news about that part of the Western Hemisphere.

Throughout the evening, North Americans can listen in at 2200-0815 on a number of frequencies. Best bets are 5975 (to 0730), 6175 (to 0330 or 0430), 9640 (0500-0815) and 9915 (to 0330 or 0430).

In Europe, try 6195, 7325, 9410, 9750, 9760, 12095 or 15070 kHz at various times between 0300 and 2315. For special programs on the European continent, listen in at 0430-0500 on 3955, 3975, 6010, 6180 and 6195 kHz; and at 2030-2100 on 3955 (winters), 5975 (summers), 6180 and 6195 kHz. Both programs are one hour earlier during summer.

Listeners in the Middle East should tune in at 0200-0330 on 6195 (or 9670) and 7135 kHz; 0230-0430 on 11955 kHz; 0300-0430 on 9410 (or 12095) kHz; 0300-0815 and 0900-1400 on 11760 kHz; 0400-0730 and 0900-1515 (0400-1515, weekends) on 15575 kHz; 0800-1515 on 17640 kHz; 0430-0730 and 0900-1615 (0430-1615, weekends) on 21470 kHz; and on 7160, 9410, 9740, 12095 or 15070 kHz thereafter.

In East Asia, good choices are 0100-0330 on 17790 kHz; 0300-0915 (weekends, from 0100) on 15280 and 21715 kHz; 0600-0915 on 15360 kHz; 0915-1030 on 17830 and 21715 kHz; 1000-1400 on 9740 kHz; 1300-1400 on 7180 and 11820 kHz; 1500-1600 on 7180 and 9740 kHz; 2100-2200 on 7180, 9570 and 11955 kHz; 2200-2300 on 9570 and 11955 kHz; and 2300-0030 on 11945, 11955 and 17830 kHz.

In Australia and New Zealand, tune to 7150, 9640, 9740, 11750, 11955, 15340 and 17830 kHz at various prime-time hours. For further details, see the "Worldscan" section later in this book.

MIDDLE EAST
Israel

A curse of international broadcasting is that those who listen and appreciate it are abroad and out of sight, while those who foot the bill are relatively close and visible. For politically minded administrators, there always exists the temptation to divert funds from international to domestic operations, which are more apparent to those who vote and rule.

1992 was when **Kol Israel** almost disappeared from the air, a near-victim of funds being diverted to just such a domestic Israeli broadcasting project. Not only has the international station survived, it has also managed an increase, albeit small, in the number of hours it is on the air—although no longer at times convenient to the vast and growing North American world band audience.

If ever an international broadcaster was hard done by, Kol Israel must be it. A highly respected reputation and a sizable and faithful audience are apparently of little account when it comes to internal Israeli politics, which can be fully as parochial as those of any other country.

Fortunately for world band listeners, not to mention the Israeli state and friends worldwide, Kol Israel continues to broadcast a commendable combination of news, commentary and entertainment. Although the greater part of its audience is, by necessity, located in Europe, listeners in Eastern North America also have the opportunity—though not at prime-time hours—to hear a reliable source of news from and about the Middle East and Israel.

English-language broadcasts beamed to Western Europe and Eastern North America are transmitted at 0500-0515 on 11588 kHz; 1100-1130 on 17545 kHz; 1400-1425 on 11587, 11605, 15640 and 17575 kHz; 1800-1815 on 11587 and 15590 (or 15640) kHz; 2000-2030 on 9435 (or 15640), 11587, 11605 and 17575 kHz; and 2230-2300 on 7465 (or 15590), 9435 (or 15640), 11587 and 11605 kHz. Listeners in Western North America can try at 1400 on 17590 kHz, 1800 and 2000 on 11675 kHz, and 2230 on 15100 (or 11675) kHz, but they shouldn't be over-optimistic—Kol Israel uses no relay facilities, and thus reception there is touch and go. For Australasia, there's just the one slot, 1400-1425 on 15650 kHz.

All transmissions are one hour earlier during summer.

Turkey

The Turkish Radio and Television Corporation's **Voice of Turkey** continues with its ongoing transmitter expansion program, and the installation of several new 500-kilowatt units should allow its broadcasts to be heard over a wider area than at present. In the meantime, English-language broadcasts are targeted only at Europe, Eastern North America and the Middle East.

A valuable perspective on the Near and Middle East, the Voice of Turkey additionally broadcasts some delightfully exotic Turkish music. The station also has some of the most esoteric features ever to hit the international airwaves.

If you're looking for something different, this may be just the ticket. The station's 50-minute English broadcast is beamed to Europe at 2100 on 9445 kHz, and at 2300 on 11710 or 11895 kHz. There are also two opportunities for Eastern North America, at 2300 and 0400 on 9445 kHz. If you're in the Middle East and an insomniac, try 2300 on 7185 kHz or, at a more convenient hour, there is a reduced version at 1330-1400 on 9675 kHz.

All transmissions are one hour earlier summer.

United Arab Emirates

Technically excellent, and just about as friendly as any station could be, **UAE Radio** in Dubai is one of several smaller world band broadcasters to have a regular and faithful following. Although the station is not all that big, its transmitters pump out an impressive 300 to 500 kilowatts each, so it is well heard.

All English broadcasts either start or finish with a news bulletin, with the rest of the time dedicated to features on Arab and Islamic life and culture, including readings from Arab literature.

UAE Radio can be heard in North America at 0330-0355 on 11945, 13675, 15400 and 15435 (or 17890) kHz. English is beamed to Europe at 1030-1055 and 1330-1355 on 15320, 15435 (or 17890) and 21605; and at 1600-1640 on 11795, 15320, 15435 (or 17890) and 21605 kHz—some of these signals can also be heard in North America. East Asian and Pacific listeners can tune in at 0530-0555 on 15435, 17830 and 21700 kHz.

ASIA
China (People's Republic)

Radio Beijing continues to provide some of the most varied and interesting programming from the Asian continent, and thanks to arrangements with stations in other coun-

tries reception is now adequate in most listening areas.

Its news-oriented and cultural programs provide a valuable insight into a country and people still not fully understood by the world outside, while many of the musical offerings are a pleasure to the ear.

In North America, reception is usually better to the west than it is farther east, although most Canadian and U.S. listeners have a decent opportunity to hear the English broadcasts. Even when reception is so-so, the quality of the programming justifies an extra effort.

Radio Beijing broadcasts English six or seven times a day to North America, depending on the season. News is updated for each 55-minute broadcast, but the feature programs remain the same in all transmissions. Try at 0000 on 9770 and 11715 kHz; 0300 on 9690, 9770 and 11715 kHz; 0400 winter on 11695 kHz; 0400 summer on 11680 and 11840 kHz; 0500 winter on 11840 kHz; 1200 on 9665 or 15210 kHz; 1300 summer on 11855 kHz; 1400 on 7405 (winter) and 11855 (summer) kHz; and 1500 winter on 7405 kHz.

Radio Beijing's News Center processes news from China and the world. Note world band radio under clocks.

Europeans can hear Radio Beijing at 2000-2055 and 2100-2155 on 9920 and 11500 kHz; 2200-2225 (2100-2125 summers) via Switzerland on 3985 kHz; and via their Russian relay at 2200-2255, winters on 7170, and summers on 9740 kHz.

In much of Asia, you can hear it at 1200-1255 and 1300-1355 on 9715 and 11660 kHz. In Australia and New Zealand, one-hour broadcasts can be heard at 0900 and 1000 on 11755, 15440 and 17710 kHz; at 1200 on 11600 and 15450 kHz; and 1300 on 11600 kHz.

China (Taiwan)

In order to increase the availability of world band relays of Taiwanese domestic programs, there are plans in the pipeline for a reduction in foreign-language broadcasts from the **Voice of Free China**. It is not yet known whether these will affect the English service in any way, but for now you can enjoy a daily mix of Taiwanese news and entertainment.

Reception is good throughout North America, thanks to a relay via the transmitters of religious broadcaster Family Radio (WYFR) in Okeechobee, Florida. In Europe, however, the signal quality is far more uncertain.

North American listeners are further favored in that if they happen to miss a

favorite program, there's no need to worry—the 0200 broadcast is repeated at 0300 the following evening. If you're in North America, you can take in a full two-hour show, as both one-hour broadcasts, today's and the repeat of yesterday's, are carried back-to-back on the same channels—5950 and 9680 kHz.

The Voice of Free China also broadcasts to Asia and the Pacific at 0200 on 9765, 11860 and 15345 kHz; and at 0300 on 9765, 11745 and 15345 kHz. The transmission for Europe is at 2200, winters on 7355 (or 11580/11915) and 9850 (or 9852.5) kHz, summers on 17750 and 21720 kHz.

Japan

At a time when many international broadcasters are wondering where to spend what money they have, a few go-getters are investing where they believe it will yield the greatest long-term benefit. Among these is **Radio Japan**, arguably the number-one broadcaster in the Asia-Pacific region.

Already in the process of upgrading its facilities on home soil, and not content with a virtual 24-hour service in English and Japanese, Radio Japan is adding to its hours and improving its signal overseas by increasing its relay agreements. In the Japanese tradition, it is getting a little better each day.

Technically sound and with program production to match, Radio Japan is on a path to the 21st century. There is no better source of news about the countries on the Pacific Rim.

Eastern North America is now amply served by the relay from Radio Canada International's Sackville site. The General Service can be heard at 1100 on 6120 kHz, and again at 0300 (0100 summers) on 5960 kHz. Listeners on the western side of the continent receive their signals direct from Tokyo at 0300 on 11870 (or 15230), 17825 and 21610 kHz; and at 1400, 1700 and 1900 on 11865 kHz.

> There is no better source of news about the Pacific Rim than Radio Japan.

Europeans can tune in at 0700 on 9670, 9770, 15170 (or 15250) and 21575 kHz, and again at 2300 on 6025 and 6160 kHz. For the Middle East, try listening at

0700 on 21575 kHz, and 1700 on 15210 (or 15345) kHz.

If you're in Australasia, try Radio Japan's Regional Service at 0900 on 15270 and 17860 (or 17890) kHz; the General Service is available at 0500 and 0700 on 17860 (or 17890) kHz; 1900 on 9640 and 11850 kHz; and 2100 on 15280 and 17890 kHz.

AUSTRALASIA
Australia

Radio Australia, although on the air around the clock, is officially targeted only at Asia and the Pacific. Fortunately for those who live elsewhere, the station's signal reaches well beyond. Popular wherever it is heard, Radio Australia is also one of the most widely listened-to stations in North America.

There's no secret to its success—good news coverage and entertaining programs, presented in an easily digestible package. There is also a certain uniqueness to many of the programs. Where else can you hear *in situ* recordings of gruesome murder ballads?

In Eastern North America, try in the morning between 0800 and 1300 on 9580 kHz. On the Pacific coast, tune 17795 kHz at 0200-0400, 21740 kHz at 0030-0400,

and 5995, 6060, 9580 and 11800 kHz from 1400 onward.

For Europe, best bets are 13755 kHz at 1530-1800; and 15240 and 21775 kHz at 0700-0900. In the Middle East, try 13755 kHz between 1430 and 1800; 21720 kHz at 1100-1300; and 21775 kHz up to 0900.

If you live in East Asia, the best frequencies are 17750 kHz at 0000-0400, 21525 kHz at 0200-0800, and 13605 and 15170 kHz at 0900-1000 and 1100-1200.

LATIN AMERICA
Brazil

The English broadcasts of **Radio Nacional do Brasil**, also known as **Radiobras**, are well heard in Europe and North Africa, but less so in North America, despite being aimed there. A pity, because the 80-minute programs are packed with highly enjoyable chunks of exotic Brazilian music, especially on weekends. This station has the potential, realized in the past, of operating at times and on frequencies where reception is excellent throughout North America.

Radiobras is beamed to North America at 1200-1320 on one of two channels: either 15445 kHz, which is fair, or 11745 kHz,

South America's best-known world band station, HCJB, has the microwave link to its Pifo transmitter site located atop Mount Pichincha, overlooking Ecuador's capital city, Quito.

Charles Chan

which is hopeless. Listeners in Europe and North Africa, where reception is better, can enjoy the broadcasts by tuning in at 1800-1920 on 15265 kHz.

Cuba

The programs of **Radio Habana Cuba** are probably better now than they have been for decades, so it is ironic that the station has now had to reduce its output. Following the breakup of the former Soviet Union and the resulting drastic cuts in economic aid, Cuba—Radio Habana Cuba included—has been forced to rationalize and reorganize in virtually every department.

Yet, broadcasts in the English language have not suffered unduly. There have been cuts, but there is still ample opportunity to enjoy entertaining programs, including excellent Cuban music.

The revolutionary message has long since mellowed (would the last real Marxist please shut off the light?), but the station's political slant may still deter some listeners. A pity, since the broadcasts are a good listen, even if you don't agree with them one iota.

Broadcasts in English to North America

evenings are at 0000-0200 on 11970 (or 11950) kHz; 0200-0400 on 11970 (or 11950) and 13700 kHz; 0400-0500 on 6180, 11760, 11970 (or 11950) and 13700 kHz; and 0600-0800 on 11760 kHz. The initial hour-long broadcast at 0000-0100 repeats at 0200 and 0400, and the 0100-0200 broadcast airs again at 0300. Europeans can try their luck at 2000-2100 on 17705 kHz; and 2200-2300 winters on 7215 kHz, summers on 11705 (or 11930) kHz. In the Middle East, try 2000-2100 on 9760 or 17815 kHz.

Ecuador

Undoubtedly the most widely heard of all South American broadcasters, the friendly evangelical station, **HCJB**, in Quito, Ecuador, is the granddaddy of shortwave broadcasters. Many world band listeners cut their teeth on it.

Essentially religious, the station also carries several largely secular programs of interest to the general listener. And for an evangelical station, much of the locally produced religious fare is surprisingly palatable, even for nonbelievers. HCJB's powerful voice doesn't shout.

HCJB broadcasts mornings to North America at 1130-1600 on 11925 and 17890 kHz, and 1130-1430 on 15115 kHz. The evening broadcast is at 0030-0430 on 9745 and 15155 kHz, and 0500-0700 on 9745 and 11925 (or 6230) kHz. The station also beams to Europe, where it is less clear, at 0700-0830 on 9585 or 9695 (winter), 15270 (summer) and 11730 kHz; plus 1900-2000 and 2130-2200 on 15270 (or 21480) and 17790 kHz. The evening frequencies are also valid for the broadcast to the Middle East at 1630-1745 (extended to 1800, Monday through Friday). Programs for the South Pacific are broadcast at 0730-1130 on 9745 and 11925 kHz.

If your world band radio operates in upper sideband, you can also listen to many of HCJB's programs on 21455 kHz, which is scheduled to be replaced by 17895 kHz.

NORTH AMERICA
Canada

Radio Canada International is only now beginning to recover slowly from the almost mortal blow it received in 1991, when it was reduced to relaying programs of the domestic Canadian Broadcasting Corporation. World band listeners lost some of their best-loved programs overnight.

The CBC produces some excellent material, most of it of interest mainly to Canadians—less so to the world at large. A few RCI-produced programs are now inching their way back into the schedule, and there is encouraging talk of more money being made available.

But that's in the future. In the meantime, much programming is still a relay of domestic fare, some of it of an exceptionally high caliber. Gems like *The World at Six* and *As It Happens* are news programs that should be on everybody's list.

Reception of RCI is much better in Eastern North America than out west, but the station can still be heard in most of the United States. English is broadcast Monday through Friday at 1300-1400 on 9635, 11855 and 17820 kHz; and 1400-1700 Sunday on 11955 and 17820 kHz; with both transmissions being one hour earlier in summer. During winter, evening broadcasts air at 0000-0130 daily, plus 0130-0200 Sunday and Monday, on 5960 and 9755 kHz. Summer broadcasts are carried on the same frequencies, but with different scheduling:

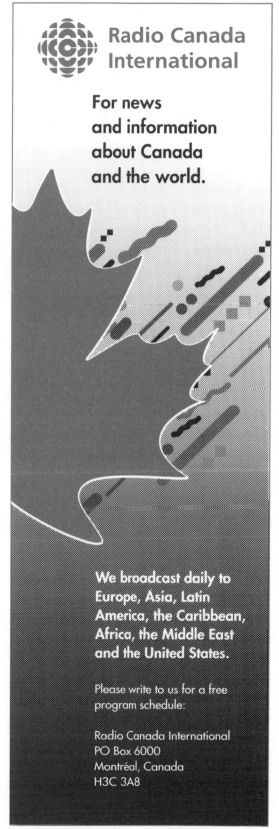

daily at 2200-2230 and 2330-0030, plus Sunday and Monday at 0030-0100.

The afternoon transmission to Africa, heard fairly well in North America and sometimes even in Europe, begins at 1800 on 13670, 15260 and 17820 kHz, and follows a slightly different format: 1800-1830 and 1900-1930 Monday through Friday, and 1800-1900 Saturday and Sunday.

For Europeans who are *really* early risers, the first transmission of the day goes out at 0400-0430, winters on 6150 and 9670 kHz, and summers on 9650 and 11905 kHz. The second broadcast (Monday through Friday only) can be heard at 0618-0700 on 6050, 6150, 7155 and 9760 kHz (winters), and 6050, 6150, 7295 and 9750 kHz (summers).

Early evenings, there is a 15-minute news bulletin at 1515 on a variety of frequencies, including year-round channels of 11935, 15315, 15325, 17820 and 21545 kHz. Later, try 1700-1730 and 2000-2100, choosing from frequencies such as 5995, 7235, 9555, 11935, 13650, 15325, 17820, 17875, 21545 or 21675 kHz. The 2000-2030 segment is sometimes superseded by 30 minutes of bilingual programming for Canadian military personnel in Europe. The final broadcast is at 2200-2300 on 9760 and 11945 kHz (summers on 15325 and 17875 kHz), with the first half-hour also available on 5995, 7180 (or 7235) and 13650 kHz.

With the exception of the 0400 broadcast, all transmissions are one hour earlier in summer.

Listeners in the Middle East are restricted to one 30-minute slot at 0400-0430, winters on 9505 and 11925 kHz, and summers on 15275 and 15445 kHz.

There is a broadcast for East Asia at 1330-1400 on 6095, 6150, 9535 and 9700 kHz (summers on just two channels: 9535 and 11795 kHz); and to Southeast Asia at 2200-2230 on 11705 kHz.

United States

One of the best known and best heard of all international broadcasters, the **Voice of America** is not without its critics. That being said, the VOA is still—for many—a highly valued, even crucial, source of news and entertainment.

No other world band station has so many regional variations in its worldwide programming. The service for Africa, especially, commands an audience no other broadcaster can match, while those for the Caribbean and Pacific are also very popular in their respective areas.

The two best times to listen in North America are at 0000-0200 (to 0230 Tuesday through Saturday) on 5995, 6130, 7405, 9455, 9775, 11580, 15120 and 15205 kHz; and 1000-1200 on 6030 (or 15120), 9590 and 11915 kHz; when the VOA broadcasts to South America and the Caribbean. The African Service is also audible in North America—try at 0300-0700 on 6035, 7405 and 9575 kHz; and again at 1600-2200 on 15410, 15580, 17800 and 21485 kHz.

European listeners can hear the VOA at 0400-0700 on 5995, 6040, 6140, 7170 and 11965 kHz; 0400-0600 on 7200 and 15205 kHz; 1400-1500 on 15205 kHz; 1500-1800 on 15255 (or 15260) kHz; and 1700-2200 on 6040, 9760 and 15205 kHz. For the Middle East there is a half-hour block at 0300-0330 on 5965, 15160, 15195, 17705 and 17865 kHz. Longer broadcasts can be heard at 0800-1100 on 11740, 15160, 15195, 21455 and 21570 kHz; 1500-1700 on 9700 and 15205 kHz, and 1700-2200 on 9700 kHz.

English is available to the Pacific at 1000-1200 on 5985, 11720 and 15425 kHz; 1200-1330 on 11715 and 15425 kHz, 1330-1500 on 15425 kHz; 1900-2000 on 9525, 11870 and 15180 kHz; 2100-2200 on 11870, 15185 and 17735 kHz; and 2200-0100 on 15185 and 17735 kHz. In East Asia, good bets include 1100-1400 on 9760 and 15155 kHz; 1400-1500 on 9760 and 15160 kHz; 2200-2400 on 15290, 15305, 17735 and 17820 kHz; and 0000-0100 on 15290, 17735 and 17820 kHz.

> **The Christian Science Monitor World Service is one the foremost sources of news on the air.**

For decades, the name "Voice of America" was more or less synonymous with U.S. international broadcasting. Then, in early 1987, the **World Service of the Christian Science Monitor** started test transmissions from a site in the northeastern state of Maine. Few suspected at the time that this one-transmitter fledgling would later contest the VOA's mantle as North America's major international news station.

Today, using transmitters as massive as 500 kW, it is one of the exalted few, right up there with the BBC World Service as one of the foremost sources of in-depth news on the air. The only drawback for its news audience is that most of this secular fare is replaced weekends by religious programming. Not that this isn't appropriate. The World Service of the Christian Science Monitor is, after all, owned by a religious organization, albeit one that is sometimes misunderstood. Yet, it would be a boon to have at least some news-oriented programs to rely on throughout the week.

The station broadcasts around the clock from two sites in the United States, Maine and South Carolina, plus a third on the Pacific island of Saipan. Each weekday broadcast is almost two hours long, the first hour consisting of news and news analysis, then 30 minutes of features, with the final 25 minutes devoted to a listener-response program.

In Eastern North America, try tuning in at 0000 on 7395 kHz; 1000 and 1200 on 9495 kHz; 1800 and 2000 on 15665 or 15710 kHz; and 2200 on 9465 kHz. Farther west, you can listen at 0200, 0400 and 0600 on 9455 kHz; and again at 1400 on 13760 kHz. Although beamed elsewhere, 13760 kHz also provides good reception in much of North America at 0000-0555. Note that Friday through Monday some of these channels carry a certain amount of Spanish programming.

Transmissions for Europe are at 0600 on 9840 kHz, 0800 on 9840 or 11705 kHz, 1400 and 1800 on 15665 or 17510 kHz, 2000 on 13770 (or 17510) and 15665 kHz, and 2200 on 13770 or 15665 kHz. The Middle East is best served at 0200 on 9350 kHz, 1800 on 9430 or 13840 kHz, and 2000 on 13770 or 15665 kHz.

East Asia is the most fortunate of all, with virtually 16 hours daily. Choose from 0400 and 0600 on 17780 kHz, 0800 and 1000 on 17555 kHz, 1400 on 9530 kHz, 1600 on 11580 kHz, 2000 on 9455 kHz, and 2200 on 15405 kHz. Listeners in Australasia can tune in at 0800 on 13615 and 15665 kHz, 1200 on 9430 or 15665 kHz, 1800 on 9430 or 13840 kHz, and 2000 on 13840 kHz.

Prepared by the staff of Passport to World Band Radio.

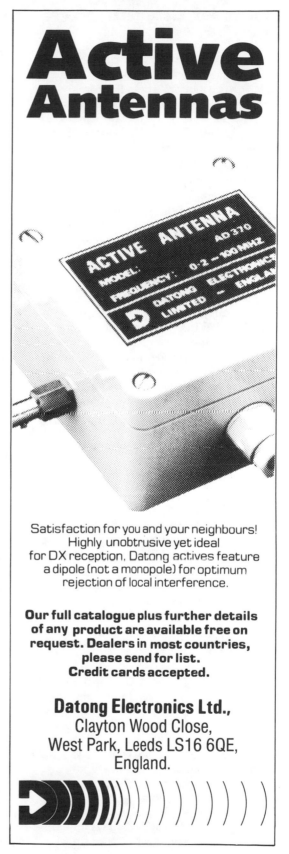

Clocks for Listeners

(continued from page 42)

(summer) time adjustment you can use London time as World Time year-round.

Press a button, and a fluorescent blue band shows which portion of the globe is in daylight. However, the display does not show the true, curved path of the demarcation between daylight and dark. As a result, this display will be of no help to the DXer who wishes to take advantage of grayline propagation. Press the Monitor button, and that blue band marches across the world map. This feature really doesn't give the user any information, but the display is impressive. An alarm can be engaged to show the time from another city of the user's choice.

Press the Weather button, and the average temperature for a particular month and the average number of rainy days pop to the display. Keep pressing the Weather button and the month advances, displaying the corresponding information. In all, this clock seems designed for the international executive who might be wondering what the weather will be like in Tokyo when he flies there next month.

Lots of glitz and beaucoup bucks. Yet, not a lot more—and in some important ways less—information than the far-less-costly World Time Touch Sensor. Recommended if you crave international weather averages.

★ ★ **Howard Miller 612-371 World Time Clock. 18″ H × 26″ W × 5¼″ D (457 × 660 × 133 mm), 120V AC (220V AC optional), does not show World Day, does not display World Time in proper 24-hour format, compensates for daylight saving (summer) time in North America only, accuracy limited by lack of visual precision and power outages, $315.00.**

Passport's headquarters office, located in a historically preserved 200-year-old building, for some time has had this unusual offering from Howard Miller hanging in a place of prominence.

This tastefully attractive wall clock features a large antique-looking world map, decorated with likenesses of ancient sea creatures and Santa-Maria-type sailing ships. It is set in a stained oak frame with likewise aged appearance, right down to cornice moulding, and displays time on a moving background scroll through windows

in the map's face. As such, it is a clock really designed, like analog gauges on a car, for a general feel of the time rather than up-to-the-second or even up-to-the-minute accuracy. It's something like the World Time equivalent of a grandfather clock.

A glance at the top right window will reveal that it is, say, somewhere between 6:00 and 6:30 PM Eastern Daylight Time, but it is hard to get much more accurate than to the nearest quarter hour or so. Through windows at appropriate locations in the face of the map, this clock also gives the time in 70 cities around the world. All features are set with a single concealed knob.

The Geochron, though costly, keeps local time variants with fanatical accuracy, and right up to date. This Howard Miller clock, however, is not always spot-on. Displays for Israel and New Zealand, for instance, are each an hour off. And times, including World (i.e., London) Time, are in 12-hour format only. Having local times in AM and PM is fine, but displaying World Time in 12-hour format defeats one of the primary reasons for having a dedicated clock for world band listening.

The time scroll behind the map is coded black for PM and white for AM, so a glance reveals roughly where across the globe is it is day or night. A fluorescent bulb illuminates the windows, albeit unevenly—the Americas are most brightly lit—for easier reading.

This venerable clock, which has been on the market more or less unchanged since

Far from the realm of advanced technology is Howard Miller's traditionalist World Time Clock, complete with sea serpents and ancient sailing ships.

1959, is without equal for antique buffs and other traditionalists who value a tasteful conversation piece above to-the-minute precision. But it has severely limited utility for world band listeners, with the possible exception of those who want a quick, general feel for the grayline and time in foreign cities.

★ ★ **Seiko World Time Voice Alarm.** 8″ W × 2¼″ H × 5⅜″ D (203 × 57 × 137 mm), two "AA" batteries, shows date but not World Day, does not display World Time in proper 24-hour format, compensates for daylight saving (summer) time, 1 second slow after one week, $125.00.

The World Time Voice Alarm displays 12-hour format only, a significant disadvantage. Neither does it display seconds or World Time. It, too, has a map (6⅝″ × 3″, or 168 × 71 mm) that shows the World Time zones, but they are activated by pressing one of 20 touch pads at the bottom of the display, labeled with city names. There is no backlighting of the display, but an alarm may be set.

This clock's maker admits that it is not the final authority on the world's time zones. Indeed, there is a section in the manual

entitled, "Places which are not included in the proper time zones."

Why, then, include this clock in these tests? Because, by throwing a switch the user can choose to have the city and time there announced by a woman's voice when the appropriate city touch pad is pressed.

Recommended for anyone who needs to have the time announced, such as the visually impaired or preschoolers.

With the Seiko World Time Voice Alarm, you don't have to turn on your radio to hear the time throughout the world.

MFJ's DXers' World Map Clock. Nice idea, no cigar.

and features an alarm. East and West buttons allow the user to display time at various cities shown on the map.

Unfortunately, the 12-hour format is useless for World Time, which makes the otherwise-welcome World Day feature beside the point. Too, seconds are not displayed—although a cursor blinks to indicate their passage. In addition, the map is so small as to be virtually useless. The city names are barely readable, and the cursor that indicates which city is activated is positively microscopic.

Not worth your time.

★ ½ **MFJ-110 DXers' World Map-Clock. 5¼" W × 3¼" H × ¾" D (133 × 82 × 19 mm), lithium battery (included), does not display World Time/Day in proper 24-hour format, does not compensate for daylight saving (summer) time, 7 seconds slow after one week, $24.95.**

This clock, which features a small world map (1¾" × 3", or 45 × 75 mm) with cities, displays time in 12-hour format only, shows World Day and date, has a local time switch,

★ **Howard Miller World Time Traveler Alarm Clock 621-258. 4¼" W × 5½" H × 1⅝" D (108 × 140 × 41 mm), "AA" battery, approximately correct to the minute after two weeks, does not show World Day, does not display World Time in proper 24-hour format, does not compensate for daylight saving (summer) time, $31.95.**

Here's another 12-hour-only special, but without the voice feature. This analog desk clock/alarm has a tiny (2", or 50 mm, diam-

eter) but attractive blue-and-gold world map that rotates inside the outer numerals to line up World Time zones with a fixed 24-hour scale. As a result, with a little effort the user can figure out roughly what time it is in another part of the world. There is no provision for nighttime lighting.

Despite its overall attractiveness, this clock gets a goose egg for World Time applications.

24-Hour Digital Clocks Without Maps

No two ways about it: for world band radio, digital clocks make sense. They're precise, and in broadcasting that's important, especially for catching news headlines.

The catch: None displays World Day.

★ ★ ★ ★ **Heath GCW-1000-H. 8¾" W × 6⅛" D × 4" H (222 × 155 × 102 mm), telescopic antenna, when extended, adds another 43" (1092 mm), 120V AC, doesn't show World Day, exactly on time after one week except during power outages, $399.95.**

Much improved over the original version we tested some years back, this clock incorporates a scanning world band receiver. It searches for the WWV or WWVH time stations on 5000, 10000 and 15000 kHz, locks onto the time signal, then automatically sets itself to the correct time using digitally encoded information from the time station. The time is then displayed on red LEDs, which show everything from hours through tenths of a second. The time can be displayed in 12- or 24-hour format. There is also a local/World Time switch, and any of 23 time zones can be selected via dip switch. The clock even corrects automatically for daylight saving (summer) time.

Heath calls this the "most accurate clock," and claims accuracy of plus or minus one-hundredth of a second. As such, it would seem a nearly perfect solution if you want up-to-the-split-second accuracy. Our tests revealed that after one week this clock was exactly synchronized with WWV, making it, hands down, the accuracy champion of the clocks we evaluated.

This self-setting feature can be handy, too. Recently I returned from a day trip to find all the AC-powered digital clocks in the house blinking madly. There had obviously been a power outage. The Heath clock,

Howard Miller's World Time traveler alarm clock looks great, but is nigh useless for world band needs.

For split-second timing, you can't beat Heath's "Most Accurate Clock." That's just what it is, too.

however, had already reset itself and was displaying the correct World Time.

But what happens when Heath's nifty clock is unable to receive WWV or WWVH? To find out, I collapsed the telescoping antenna and waited three days. The clock was still exactly on time. Suspicious that the clock still may have been able to lock onto the WWV signals even with a very short antenna, I unscrewed the antenna entirely and waited three more days. With no reception of WWV possible, the time at the end of those three days was correct to within 1/10th of a second! This is a substantial improvement over the original version of the clock, which had trouble receiving WWV and which was less than accurate without that signal from WWV.

Aside from price and the lack of a date display, the Heath's greatest shortcoming is that it operates properly only where it can hear American time stations WWV (Colorado) and WWVH (Hawaii). If you live well beyond North America or the Pacific island region, this clock isn't for you. North Americans beware as well: if you live within the "skip zone"—the doughnut-shaped "dead zone" that surrounds every shortwave station—around Boulder, Colorado, you may find the Heath clock to be inappropriate, as well. You can check by tuning your radio to WWV or WWVH throughout the day to ensure you get reasonable reception for at least an hour.

Another problem—ironically, given Heath's long experience preparing first-rate manuals back when it made kits—is the operating manual. It is clearly written for technonerds. Instead of opening with a section on "How To Get Your Clock Operating," it begins, after an introduction that reiterates the clock's features and specifications, with a section on "Theory of Operation." Nor are other sections user-oriented. For example, the part on "Operation" opens with, "Install either the telescoping antenna, if not already done, or an external antenna . . ." However, the manual tells neither how nor where to install the antenna.

We found out just how much of a drawback this can be. After hunting around, I found a plastic plug in the top of the case, but couldn't budge it. I took the case apart and was able to remove the plug by pushing from the inside. As I started to install the telescoping antenna, I discovered that a nut and lock washer were missing from the assembly that connects the antenna to the clock's radio circuitry. I found the nut and washer in the bottom of the case, but re-attaching them required yet more disassembly of the clock innards. It took nearly an hour of toil just to get the clock working.

Still, very highly recommended if you can afford it and want to keep molecular track of World Time—and with the provisos about both its manual and quality control. Remember that for all this clock's virtues, it lacks important features found on other, less costly models.

The following three clocks performed essentially identically. Listed by price.

★ ★ ★ **MFJ-24-107B. 2″ H × 2¼″ W × 1″ D (50 × 57 × 25 mm), 1.5V button battery, doesn't show World Day, 6.5 seconds slow after one week, $9.95.**

Here's the one I use. This small, simple and inexpensive LCD clock displays 24-hour time in large, 5/8-inch (16 mm) numerals that are exceptionally easy to read, even for

MFJ's Scotsman's Special, the 24-107B, $9.95 in the United States, somewhat more elsewhere.

"over 40" eyes. The small plastic LCD movement slides into a silver aluminum frame, and the overall package is small enough to perch on a tabletop radio.

Seconds are not displayed, although a cursor blinks to indicate their passage. DXers, those who lust for hard-to-hear

stations, appreciate seeing seconds displayed numerically so they can be ready to hear a station identification when it is given exactly at the top of the hour.

There is no backlighting for reading the display in darkness. In order to synchronize this clock exactly to World Time, the "set" and "minutes" buttons must be pressed so that the minutes' display advances to the correct numeral exactly when the time signal sounds, such as by station WWV. The setting buttons are tiny; using a ballpoint pen make them easier to push. As a result, it is easy to miss exact synchronization with the time signal. There is no way to go back. If you overshoot the time, you have to "go around the horn" for the next attempt.

Despite its numerous shortcomings, this clock is highly recommended if you're looking for a bargain.

★ ★ ★ NI8F LCD. 2⅜″ H × 2⅜″ W × 1⅛″ D (60 × 60 × 28 mm), 1.5V button battery, doesn't show World Day, 12 seconds slow after one week, $14.95.

This is exactly the same movement as the MFJ-24-107, with the same advantages and shortcomings. The only difference is that NI8F, a ham radio operator who works for Universal Radio, has created a solid walnut frame to replace the aluminum in the MFJ model. The result is a very handsome small clock that less likely to scratch the surface it sits on.

Very highly recommended for those who prefer wood over metal.

A bargain with looks is the NI8F LCD digital clock.

Two time zones? The MFJ-108 does a nice job on the cheap.

★ ★ ★ MFJ-108. 4½″ W × 2″ H × 1″ D (114 × 50 × 25 mm), two 1.5V button batteries, doesn't show World Day, 9 seconds slow after one week, $19.95.

This diminutive unit features two LCD clocks —a 24-hour clock for World Time and a 12-hour clock for local time—side by side in the same aluminum frame. The numerals are 5/8 inch (16 mm) tall and very easy to read. These are completely separate clocks, with separate batteries, displays and setting systems akin to those of the MFJ-107.

One virtue of this separateness is that the World Time clock is in 24-hour format, while the local clock is set to the 12-hour scheme we're comfortable with. This is a welcome improvement over World/local time clocks built into radios, virtually all of which force the user to adopt the same standard for both World and local times.

Neither clock displays seconds or has backlighting for night reading. Also, the elongated aluminum frame is more difficult to handle when setting the clocks.

Highly recommended if you want 24-hour World Time and 12-hour local time in the same unit sitting next to the radio.

24-Hour Analog Clocks

If you've wearied of modern car dashboards and their ultra-tech digital displays, you know there are times where analog is better. Unfortunately, World Time isn't one of those.

The inherent difficulty with analog clocks is that most of us have been taught, "When the big hand is straight up and the little hand is straight down, it's six o'clock." Problem is, 24-hour analog clocks violate the rules. When the hands are straight up and down, it's 1200 World Time! As a result, a quick glance at a 24-hour analog clock is more likely to confuse than inform.

Best analog is the NI8F Wood.

NI8F Black is reasonably priced.

★ ★ **NI8F 6" Wood. 9¼" W × 9" H × 2" D (235 × 228 × 50 mm), "AA" battery, does not show World Day, approximately correct to the minute after two weeks, $59.95.**

This is a wall clock with a second hand and a gorgeous hand-rubbed walnut frame.

Short of trying to remove the battery at the top of the minute, there is no sensible way to set this clock to World Time with to-the-second accuracy. All other reservations about 24-hour analog clocks apply.

Recommended if you value beauty over utility.

★ ★ **NI8F 6" Black. 7¾" diameter by 2" D (197 × 50 mm), "AA" battery, approximately correct to the minute after two weeks, does not show World Day, $29.95.**

This is a handsome black-plastic-framed round wall clock that's essentially identical to the clock above, but without a second hand.

Recommended for those who are experienced with this type of clock format, like veterans of military situation rooms.

The Clock We Didn't Find

What world band listeners need is a simple digital 24-hour clock that displays World Day, date and seconds, offers high accuracy and visibility, can be illuminated, is easy to set—backward and forward arrows for adjusting time, like on any VCR, would be welcome—and costs less than, say, $30. We didn't find such a model as a stand-alone device, and it's not found built into any radios, either.

The Bottom Line

Years ago, many plug-in analog electrical clocks with second hands were synchronized with the line frequency (50 or 60 Hz) of the electrical power. As this frequency is exceptionally accurate, those clocks also tended to be spot-on—so long as the power didn't fail.

Now, clocks have high-tech circuits and digital displays that imply greater accuracy. Alas, we've found all, with one exception, to be less accurate than ordinary household clocks from the Korean War era. Progress, this isn't.

For those whose finances allow them to afford the very best in clocks with geopolitical glitz, the snazzy Geochron provides the ultimate in grayline accuracy and time-standard authority, while the Heath offers split-second precision day after day. Indeed, if you want to-the-second accuracy without having to reset your clock every few days, only the Heath fits the bill.

Yet, at less than a tenth of the cost, the Seiko World Time Touch Sensor displays seconds, day and date, offers relatively high accuracy—and shows some time zones, too. For world band listening, it's the best bet.

If you simply wish to keep track of World Time sans seconds or day, the bare-bones MFJ 107B or NI8F 24-hour digital clocks offer a simple solution at bargain-basement prices.

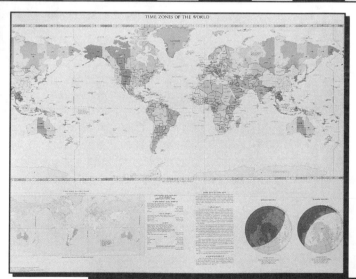

The best new portable introduced this year is Grundig's Satellit 700.

1993 Buyer's Guide to World Band Radio

How to Choose a World Band Radio

World band radios, unlike TVs, differ greatly from model to model. Some use old technology and barely function. Others, more advanced, perform superbly. As usual, money talks—but even that's a fickle barometer in this exceptional field.

Exceptional? Think of world band as a jungle, for that's what it is: 1,100 channels, with stations scrunched cheek-by-jowl. This crowding is far greater than on AM or FM, and to make matters worse signals are made weak and quivery by long-haul travel. Coping with all this calls for your radio to perform some extraordinary electronic gymnastics.

> ## Money talks, but even that's a fickle barometer.

The good news? There's no need to put up with mediocrity. The selection of available radios is vast, dozens upon dozens of models, and many perform very well, indeed.

Which ones? Since 1977 we've tested all sorts of world band products. These independent evaluations, which have nothing to do with advertising, include both rigorous hands-on use by veteran listeners and highly specialized laboratory tests. These form the basis of this Buyer's Guide, and are thoroughly detailed in our unabridged *Radio Database International*™ *White Papers*.™

Key Points to Consider

First: How much do you want to spend? Don't fool yourself— world band radios are sophisticated electronic devices. Unless you want a small radio for the road, recognize that an acceptable world band radio costs only slightly less a video cassette recorder.

Yes, a VCR could sell for $99.95 or £60—stripped of counter, timer, clock, channel indicator, and remote control, and susceptible to adjacent-channel interference. But you wouldn't buy something like that, and few others would, either. That's why VCRs don't sell cheap. Use the same reasoning for world band, and avoid disappointment.

Radios as low as $30 or £20 can give a coarse idea of what world band's like. But when the novelty wears thin, most people wind up hiding them in the closet. After all, there are good cigars, and there are nickel cigars—but there are no good nickel cigars.

Second: Determine what you feel the minimum performance is that you are looking for, then choose a model that surpasses that by a notch or two. This helps ensure against disappointment without wasting money.

If world band is new to you, but you

Indoors or out, the new Lowe HF-150 "portatop" combines worthy overall performance with superior audio quality.

think you'll take it seriously, try a mid-sized or compact portable selling in the $160-$280 or £100-175 range, street price. Most of those are snug enough to take on trips, yet big enough to be daily home companions.

> ## Choose a model that surpasses what you are looking for by a notch or two.

If you just want to gain a nodding acquaintance with world band, the two-star sets around $100 or £60 can give a taste, of sorts, of what the fuss is about. Still, you're better off making your first radio something good—$180 or £120, perhaps more, and another star.

Even if you're experienced with world band, you need to weigh your needs. Do you want a few powerful stations? Or do you hanker for softer voices from more exotic lands? Three stars will do nicely for the former, and street prices on some of these start under $200 or £125. For the latter, think four stars—perhaps five—and more money.

Third: Consider your location. Signals tend to be strongest in and around Europe, different but almost as good in Eastern North

Features to Look For on Better Models

You can't tell by looking at a world band radio in a store whether it will work better than another model, or how long it will hold up.

But features are another story. That's why sales folks love features: They are relatively free from mystery. If the customer's attention can be focused on "bells and whistles," then performance and reliability usually slide to the back burner. And as if this weren't enough, people pay extra for features whether they do any good or not.

Still, certain performance features can be genuinely useful, and are alluded to under "Advantages" and "Disadvantages" in the Buyer's Guide. For example, a very important performance feature is *multiple conversion*, essential to rejecting spurious signals—unwanted growls, whistles, dih-dah sounds and the like. A power lock also borders on a "must" if you travel frequently with your radio.

Also look for two or more *bandwidths* for superior rejection of stations on adjacent channels; properly functioning *synchronous selectable sideband* for yet greater adjacent-channel rejection, and also to reduce distortion from fading; and continuously tuned bass and treble. For world band reception, *single-sideband* (SSB) reception capability is of only minor use, but it's essential if you want to tune in shortwave utility or "ham" signals.

On heavy-hitting tabletop models, designed to flush out virtually the most stubborn signal, you pay more so you expect more. Additional features to look for include a tunable *notch filter* to zap howls and squeals; *passband offset*, also known as *IF shift*, for superior adjacent-channel rejection and audio contouring; an attenuator, preferably multi-step, to curb overloading; and multiple *AGC decay* rates with selectable *AGC off*. A *noise blanker* sounds like a better idea than it really is, given existing technology—but it doesn't hurt, either.

Highly recommended operating (nonperformance) features, for portables and tabletops alike, include digital frequency readout, a virtual *must*; a 24-hour World Time clock, especially one that always shows; and such tuning aids as a keypad, tuning knob, presets (channel memories) and perhaps up/down slewing controls. Useful, but less important, are on/off timing, especially if it can control a tape recorder; illuminated display and controls; a dedicated separate button for each preset (single-keystroke call up), rather than having to call up presets via the keypad (multiple-keystroke call up); numerically displayed seconds on the 24-hour clock; and a good signal-strength indicator.

Outdoor Antennas: Do You Need One?

If you're wondering what antenna you'll need for your new radio, the answer for portables is simple: none. All portables come with built-in telescopic antennas.

Indeed, for use in Eastern North America or Europe nearly all portables perform *less* well during evenings with sophisticated outboard antennas than with their built-in ones. But if you listen during the day, or live in the North American Midwest or West, for example, your portable may need more oomph.

For portables, the best solution in the United States is also the cheapest: $8.49 for Radio Shack's 75' (23 m) "SW Antenna Kit" (#278-758), which comes with insulators and other goodies, plus $1.99 for a claw clip (Radio Shack #270-349 or #270-345). The antenna itself may be a bit too long for your circumstances, but you can always trim it. Alternatively, many electronics and world band specialty firms, such as Universal in North America and other firms in Europe and Australasia, sell the necessary parts and wire for you to make your own. An appendix in *Passport's* publication, the RDI™ White Paper™ *Popular Outdoor Antennas*, gives minutely detailed step-by-step instructions on making and erecting such an antenna.

Basically, you attach the claw clip onto your radio's rod antenna (not the set's external antenna input socket, which may have a desensitizing circuit) and run it out your window as high as is safe and practical to something like a tree. *Keep it clear of any hazardous wiring—the electrical service to your house, in particular—and respect heights.* If you live in an apartment, run it to your balcony or window—as close to the fresh outdoors as possible.

For portables, this "volksantenna" will probably help with most signals. But if it occasionally makes a station sound worse, disconnect the claw clip.

It's a different story with tabletop receivers. They require an external antenna, either electrically amplified (so-called "active") or passive. Active antennas use small wire or rod elements that aren't very efficient, but make up for it with electronic circuitry. For apartment dwellers, they're a godsend—provided they work right.

Choosing a suitable active antenna for your tabletop receiver takes some care. Certain models—notably, those made by California's McKay Dymek and Britain's Datong—are designed better than others, as you'd expect. But sometimes other models perform better in specific locations, which you might not expect, so buy with care. Most sell for under $200 or £125; few are more.

If you have space, an outdoor passive wire antenna is better, especially when it's designed for world band frequencies. Besides not needing problematic electronic circuits, good passive antennas also tend to reduce interference from the likes of fluorescent lights and electric shavers—noises which active antennas amplify, right along with the signal. As the *cognoscenti* say, the "signal-to-noise ratio" with passive antennas tends to be better.

With any outdoor antenna, especially if it is high up and out in the open, disconnect it and affix it to something like an outdoor ground rod if there is lightning nearby. Handier, and equally effective except for a direct strike, is a "gas-pill" type lightning protector, such as is made by Alpha Delta. Otherwise, sooner or later the odds are that you will be facing a very expensive repair bill.

Many firms—some large, some tiny—offer world band antennas. Among the best passive models—all under $100 or £60—are those made by the Antenna Supermarket and Alpha Delta Communications. Two separate, detailed reports on passive outdoor and active indoor antennas are available as Radio Database International™ White Papers™, described elsewhere in this book.

America. If you live in either place, you might get by with less radio. But if you're in Western North America, Australia or New Zealand, you're better off digging deeper: You'll need an unusually sensitive receiver—mentioned under "Advantages" in the Buyer's Guide—and maybe an outdoor antenna, too. Central North America and the Caribbean are better, but think twice.

Your first receiver? A good portable will do all but the toughest work. If you decide on a tabletop later, save the portable for trips, even if only to the balcony or backyard.

But if you're an experienced hand and want to play high-stakes games, go for the five-star tabletops. The ante is high, though: Figure at least $800 or £600, and the antenna is extra.

Fourth: What features make sense to you? Separate these into two categories: those that affect performance, and those that don't (see box). Don't rely on performance features alone, though. As our Buyer's Guide tests show, a great deal more besides features goes into performance.

Fifth: Unlike TVs and ordinary radios, world band sets rarely test well in stores, except perhaps in specialty showrooms with the right outdoor antennas at the right time of the day. Even so, given the fluctuations in world band reception, long-term satisfaction is hard to gauge from a spot test. The exceptions are audio quality and ergonomics. Even if a radio can't pick up any world band stations in the store, you can get a thumb-nail idea of fidelity by catching some mediumwave AM stations. And by playing with the radio you can get a feel for handiness of operation. Otherwise, whether you buy in the neighborhood or through the mail makes little difference. Use the same horse sense you would for any other significant appliance.

> ## Long-term satisfaction is hard to gauge from a spot test.

Repair? Judging from both our experience and reports from *Passport* readers, this tends to correlate with price. At one extreme, some off-brand portables from such places as Hong Kong and the People's Republic of China seem essentially unserviceable, although most outlets will replace a defective unit within warranty. On the other hand, for high-priced tabletop models, factory-authorized service is usually available to keep them purring for many years to come. Of course, nothing else quite equals service at the factory itself. So if repair is especially important to you, bend a little toward the home team: Drake in the United States, Grundig in Germany, Lowe in the United Kingdom, and so on.

Finally: A good way to judge a store is by bringing *Passport* when you shop. Reputable dealers welcome it as a sign you are serious and knowledgeable. The rest react accordingly.

READING LAST WEEK'S TV GUIDE?

Probably not, and world band changes more—much more— than TV. There are **thousands** of new schedules and programs on the air each year.

If you want your next **Passport** fresh off the press, drop us a line at New Passport, Box 300, Penn's Park, PA 18943 USA—or fax 215/598-3794. When the new edition is being readied for shipment to dealers, we'll notify you by first-class mail.

World Band in Your Car

...or RV ...or Truck ...or Boat

We've all been there—burrowing into the night, hands steady on the wheel, determined to put a couple of hundred miles behind us before we rest.

Then it happens: we crest a rise, round a bend or simply go too far, and the AM or FM station that's been keeping us company fades into oblivion. Then comes the frantic search for another station that suits the mood. The interruption disturbs the mantra of the road.

Long-Haul Radio for Long-Haul Driving

Well, there's good news for the long-haul driver who wants uninterrupted listening—or the motorist who wants radio with something different from droid synthesound, "Done Me Wrong" twangs, or endless chatter and ads. World band signals, by dint of their very nature as long-distance radio, blanket large portions of land mass. As a result, they can offer hour upon hour of unbroken programming as you cover long distances, particularly at night. And the meaty choices are unmatched: news with varied and fresh perspectives, music, commentary, sports—even original radio dramas, which are something like public-TV shows without video. Here, indeed, is food for the ear that keeps the mind stimulated while your eyes soak up the unwinding ribbons of asphalt.

> There's hour upon hour of unbroken programming as you cover long distances.

This is no mere pipe dream. Philips has built first-class world band capability into its model DC777, a car stereo designed for in-dash installation. It offers mediumwave AM, FM stereo, longwave, auto-reverse cassette

Best sound on the road: Philips DC777 world band auto stereo.

player and 50 watts of power to drive four speakers. Once you've used it, you'll never want to go back to an ordinary car stereo.

The '777, which displays the frequency digitally, covers shortwave from 3170 to 21910 kHz continuously in the AM mode only. There is no tuning knob, but a pair of slewing buttons allows you to traverse the spectrum in 1 kHz increments. Another button causes a small drawer to slide out at a 45-degree angle, revealing a six-over-six keypad for direct frequency entry. Although that keypad layout is unorthodox, it's straightforward enough to operate properly. If you want, say, the BBC World Service on 6175 kHz, press 6, 1, 7, 5, Enter, and there it is. The horizontal layout of the keypad and the relatively small size of the keys make direct frequency entry something that is best done while you're stopped at a light, parked, or on a long, clear straightaway.

Ease of Use

Where the '777 really shines is in its ease of use for the driver on the move. Press the SW button, and you can step through the world band spectrum—90 meters, 75 meters, right on up to 13 meters. Then poke the up or down SEARCH button, and the '777 mutes itself, scans the band in 5 kHz steps, finds the next powerful station in that band, then un-mutes so you can hear it. If you want a different station, press SEARCH again, and the '777 trots off on its quest. If you wish to return to a station previously uncovered in the search process, just press the opposite SEARCH button to reverse the search. It's a scheme that is very handy and works well.

For convenience on the road, the '777 is equipped with 20 world band presets for favorite stations. There are four preset buttons, each of which stores up to five frequencies. Select one preset, and a fifth button allows you to step through the presets, carousel-style. This, too, works quite well and allows you to punch up world band broadcasters while keeping your eyes where they should be—on the road.

The '777 is reasonably sensitive to weak stations, yet is not a receiver for chasing faint signals. The radio isn't up to it, ignition noise limits reception, and in any event DX bandscanning demands attention that drivers shouldn't divert from the task at hand. Indeed, the limitation on what you can hear has more to do with your particular car's level of ignition, wiper and related electrical noises than the radio's quality of performance.

Ignitions Cause Noise

On strong signals, however, the DC777 sounds great. The audio is exactly what you would expect from a high-quality car stereo, and coming through the '777's single bandwidth is some of the best world band audio we've ever heard. And that brings us back to an important caveat: ignition noise is frequently the spoiler when it comes to hearing world band on the road.

> **Coming through is some of the best world band audio we've ever heard.**

Because of that, unless you drive a diesel you may want to arrange with your dealer to purchase it on some sort of money-back trial basis, pending your satisfaction. Alternatively, try driving around the block with a colleague carefully holding a world band portable up high with its telescopic antenna sticking out a window, away from the car's metal. This will give you a rough idea of what to expect with the '777.

The Philips DC777 is one of the better things to happen to world band radio in recent years. It sets the standard for what an over-the-road world band receiver ought to be: good-sounding, easy to use, a companion to shorten the lonesome hours.

And think of the eyebrows you'll raise when you say, "I drove to Baghdad last night."

Prepared by Jock Elliott and the staff of Passport to World Band Radio.

World Band Portables for 1993

Portable or tabletop?

If you eat, breathe and dream world band radio, stop right now and go to the tabletop section of this Buyer's Guide. Indeed, for 1993 there is an excellent new tabletop model—the Lowe HF-150—that also serves as a portable of sorts.

Otherwise, this section on portables is the place to start. The best rated among these affordable portables will meet the needs of all but the most exacting listener.

Analog or digital tuning?

Analog, or slide-rule, tuning goes back to the earliest days of radio. It's fading from the marketplace, and can't vanish a day too soon. With analog, finding the one station you want from the hundreds on the air is a hit-and-miss proposition that chews up time and patience. With digital models as little as $50 or £40, there's no reason to go any other route.

Here are the results of this year's hands-on and laboratory testing—evaluations of nearly every widely distributed world band portable currently produced that meets minimum standards. Thus, we exclude such models as the Icom IC-R1 and Kenwood RZ-1 that lack bandwidths narrow enough to qualify for acceptable world band reception.

Models are listed by size; and, within size, in order of world band listening suitability. Unless otherwise indicated:

- Each radio covers the usual 88.7-107.9 MHz FM band.
- AM band (mediumwave) coverage in models with *digital* frequency display includes the forthcoming 1600-1705 kHz segment for the Americas; AM band coverage in models with *analog* frequency display stops short of 1705 kHz.

The longwave band is used for domestic broadcasts in Europe, North Africa and Russia. If you live in these parts of the world, or plan to travel there, longwave coverage is a plus. Otherwise, forget it. Keep in mind, though, that when a model is available with and without longwave coverage, the version with longwave may include that at the expense of some world band coverage.

For the United States, suggested retail ("list") prices are given. Discounts for most models are common, although those sold under the "Realistic" brand name are usually discounted only during special Radio Shack sales. Elsewhere, observed selling prices (including VAT) are usually given.

Duty-free shopping? In some parts of the EC, such as France and Switzerland, it may save you 10 percent or more, *provided* you don't have to declare the radio at your destination. Check on warranty coverage, though. In the United States, where prices are already among the world's lowest, you're better off buying from regular stores. Canada, too, and to an increasing extent even the United Kingdom and Germany.

Naturally, all prices are as we go to press and may fluctuate. Some will probably have changed before the ink dries.

We try to stick to plain English, but some specialized terms have to be used. If you come across something you don't understand, check it out in the Glossary at the back of the book.

What *Passport's* Ratings Mean

Star ratings: ★ ★ ★ ★ ★ is best. We award stars solely for overall performance and meaningful features, both here and in our tabletop model reviews elsewhere in this *Passport* Buyer's Guide. The same star-rating standard applies regardless of price, size or whathaveyou. So you can cross-compare any radio—little or big, portable or tabletop—with any other radio evaluated in this edition of *Passport*. A star is a star.

For 1993, in order to reflect industry advances in technology and performance, we've stiffened our star-rating criteria, with many models having been dropped by one-half star over what they were or would have been in prior years. Too, starting this year we consider the quality of bandscan tuning—freedom from excessive chugging and muting—in the ratings assignment. We feel this better reflects the realities of today's improved marketplace.

A portable rating of three stars should please most day-to-day listeners. However, for occasional use on trips a small portable with as little as one-and-a-half stars may suffice.

Editor's Choice models are our test team's personal picks of the litter—what we would buy ourselves.

¢ : denotes a price-for-performance bargain. It may or may not be a great set, but gives uncommon value for your money.

Models in **(parentheses)** have not been tested by us, but appear to be essentially identical to model(s) tested.

MINI-PORTABLES

Great for Travel, Poor for Home

Mini-portables weigh under a pound, or half-kilogram, and are about the size of a hand-held calculator or a bit larger than an audio cassette case. They operate off two to four ordinary little "AA" (UM-3 penlite) batteries. These tiny models do one job well: provide news and entertainment when you're traveling, especially abroad by air. A few will do for day-to-day listening, but only through good headphones—not an attractive prospect, given that none has the full array of Walkman-type features, such as a hidden antenna. Listening to these radios' tiny speakers can be downright tiring.

Best bet? Sony's ICF-SW1S or ICF-SW1E, if you can stand the sticker shock. No other minis come close, although Sangean's forthcoming digital ATS-606, while a bit larger, looks very interesting at roughly one-third the cost. Also, look over the large selection of compact models, just after the minis in this Buyer's Guide. They're not much larger than minis, but have more sizable speakers and so tend to sound better.

★ ★ ★   *Editor's Choice*

Sony ICF-SW1S
Portable Receiving System

Price: $359.95 in the United States, CAN$450 in Canada, under £250 in the United Kingdom, $370-480 elsewhere in Europe (EC), AUS$599.00 in Australia.

Advantages: Superior overall world band performance for size. High-quality audio when earpieces (supplied) are used. Various helpful tuning features. Unusually straightforward to operate for advanced-tech model. World Time clock. Alarm/sleep features. Travel power lock also disables alarm and display illumination. FM stereo through earpieces. Receives longwave and Japanese FM bands. Amplified outboard antenna (supplied), in addition to usual built-in antenna, enhances weak-signal reception below about 15 MHz. Self-regulating AC power supply, with American and European plugs, adjusts automatically to all local current worldwide. Rugged travel case for radio and accessories.

Disadvantages: Tiny speaker, mediocre audio. No tuning knob. Tunes only in coarse 5 kHz increments. World Time clock readable only when radio is switched off. Volume control at

Sony's ICF-SW1S, complete with a case full of goodies, is the best mini. Too much to carry? Leave the accessories behind.

Best of the low-tech, low-cost mini-portables is the Sony ICF-SW20.

rear, vulnerable to accidental change. For price class, substandard rejection of certain spurious signals ("images"). No meaningful signal-strength indicator. Earpieces less comfortable than foam-padded headphones. Amplified antenna does not switch on and off with radio.

Bottom Line: Although pricey, the Sony ICF-SW1S—the closest thing to a world band Walkman-type radio—is easily the best mini-portable on the market.

★ ★ ★ *Editor's Choice*

Sony ICF-SW1E

Price: £149.95 in the United Kingdom, $260-340 elsewhere in Europe (EC), AUS$499.00 in Australia.

Identical to Sony ICF-SW1S, except minus carrying case and most accessories. Not available in North America.

Sony ICF-SW1E: Same radio as the Sony ICF-SW1S, but cheaper and sans accessories. Not available in all countries.

★ ★   ¢

Sony ICF-SW20

Price: $99.95 in the United States, CAN$149 in Canada, around £70 in the United Kingdom, $110-150 elsewhere in Europe (EC), AUS$169.00 in Australia.

Advantages: Superior adjacent-channel rejection, similar to pricier ICF-SW1S and ICF-SW1E siblings, for size. Travel power lock.

Disadvantages: No digital frequency display. Limited world band spectrum coverage, omits important 13 MHz segment. Tiny speaker, mediocre audio. No longwave band reception. No meaningful signal-strength indicator. Dial not illuminated. No AC power supply.

Bottom Line: Although its circuitry is getting long in the tooth, the ICF-SW20 remains the best low-cost teeny travel radio.

★ ½

Sangean MS-103 (Sangean MS-103L)

Price: *MS-103:* $99.95 in the United States; *MS-103L:* $75-150 in Europe (EC).

Advantages: Better world band coverage than otherwise-identical MS-101 ($85.95 in the United States). Travel power lock. FM stereo through headphones. *MS-103L:* Receives longwave band.

Disadvantages: No digital frequency display. Slightly limited world band coverage. Mediocre adjacent-channel and spurious-signal ("image") rejection. Inferior audio. Dial not illuminated. No meaningful signal-strength

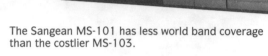

The Sangean MS-103 has mediocre spurious-signal rejection, but good world band coverage.

The Sangean MS-101 has less world band coverage than the costlier MS-103.

indicator. No AC power supply. *MS-103:* Does not receive longwave band. *MS-103L:* Lacks coverage of world band from 2.3-5.2 MHz.

Bottom Line: Preferable to the cheaper MS-101, but interesting only to the weight- and price-conscious traveler. Also sold under other names, including Goodmans and Siemens.

Bottom Line: A low-priced, plain-vanilla portable of interest almost exclusively to the weight- and price-conscious traveler. Also sold under other names, including Curry's, Dixons, Goodmans and Siemens.

★ ½

Sangean SG-789
(Sangean SG-789L)

Price: *SG-789:* $69.95 in the United States, CAN$149.95 in Canada, AUS$79.95 in Australia; *SG-789L:* $60-95 in Europe (EC).

Advantages: Inexpensive. FM stereo through headphones. *SG-789L:* Receives longwave band.

Disadvantages: No digital frequency display. Somewhat limited coverage, omits important 13 MHz band. Mediocre adjacent-channel and spurious-signal ("image") rejection. Inferior audio. No meaningful signal-strength indicator. Dial not illuminated. No AC power supply. *SG-789:* Does not receive longwave band. *SG-789L:* Lacks 2.3-5.2 MHz world band coverage.

Bottom Line: Similar to the Sangean MS-101, but with less complete coverage. If this isn't cheap enough for you, try the Sangean SG-796, which lists in the United States for $59.95—same play, fewer acts.

★ ½

Sangean MS-101
(Aiwa WR-A100)
(Roberts R101)

Price: *Sangean:* $84.00 in the United States, CAN$99.95 in Canada, $65-125 in Europe (EC), AUS$99.95 in Australia; *Aiwa:* $109.95 in the United States.

Advantages: Inexpensive. Travel power lock. FM stereo through headphones.

Disadvantages: No digital frequency display. Limited world band coverage. Mediocre adjacent-channel and spurious-signal ("image") rejection. Inferior audio. Dial not illuminated. No meaningful signal-strength indicator. No AC power supply.

Comment: Aiwa styled differently from other versions of this model.

Low-Profile Radios for Globetrotting

Customs inspectors and airport security officials, even in totalitarian countries, rarely give a second glance at everyday small world band portables. But larger, more exotic-looking radios—world band or otherwise—can invite unwelcome attention, even theft, especially if they contain tape recorders.

When you're flying internationally, take along a mini or compact portable that doesn't have a built-in tape recorder. There are lots of models to choose from, and some are cheap enough that you can shrug off their loss, should it come to that.

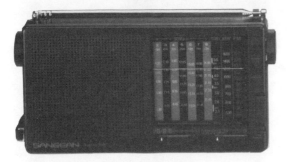

One of Sangean's cheapest models, the lightweight SG-789.

COMPACT PORTABLES

Good for Travel, Fair for Home

Compacts weigh in at 1.0-1.5 pounds, or 0.5-0.7 kg, and are typically sized 8 × 5 × 1.5", or 20 × 13 × 4 cm. Like minis, they feed off "AA" (UM-3 penlite) batteries—but more of them. They travel almost as well as minis, but sound better and usually receive better, too. For some travelers, they also suffice as home sets—something minis can't really do. However, if you don't travel so frequently by air that every ounce or gram counts, you will probably find much better value and performance in a mid-sized portable.

Which stand out? Any of the five Editor's Choice models performs well for world band, with the main differences being in what you have to do to operate them. Of these five, the lowest-cost Panasonic RF-B45 stands out as an excellent buy, whereas the Sangean ATS-808 is refreshingly uncomplicated to operate. Both are top choices if you've never owned a world band radio before or simply don't like to fuss about with controls. Sony's new ICF-SW55 is a worthy performer—best by a skootch—and has arguably the clearest audio, but is unusually complicated to operate.

Sony ICF-SW55

Price: $429.95 in the United States, CAN$599 in Canada, £249.00 in the United Kingdom.
Advantages: By a small margin, best overall performance in a compact portable. Among the best in audio quality for size class. Dual bandwidths, unusual in this size radio, make for unusually pleasant listening. Controls neatly and logically laid out. Innovative tuning system, including factory prestored presets and displayed alphabetic identifiers for groups ("pages") of stations. Good single-sideband reception, although reader reports suggest some BFO "pulling" (not found in our unit). Comes complete with carrying case containing reel-in wire antenna, AC power supply, DC power cord and in-the-ear earpieces. Signal/battery strength indicator. Local and World Time clocks, either (but not both) of which is displayed separately from frequency. Summer time adjustment for local time clock. Sleep/alarm features. Five-event (daily only) timer nominally can automatically turn on/off certain models of Sony cassette recorders, a plus for VCR-type multiple-event recording. Illuminated display. Receives longwave and Japanese FM bands.
Disadvantages: Tuning system unusually difficult for most people, except radiophiles, to grasp. Operation sometimes unnecessarily complicated by any yardstick, but especially for listeners in the Americas. Wide bandwidth somewhat broad for world band reception. Display illumination dim and uneven. Costly to operate from batteries. Local clock in non-standard 24-hour format.
Evaluation of New Model: Like the mini ICF-SW1S, this is another one of Sony's "packaged" receivers. A gray plastic travel case stashes the receiver itself, plus in-the-ear earpieces, an AC power supply, a DC power cord and a "tape measure" outboard antenna. All useful, although true headphones would be more comfortable than the supplied earpieces. The AC power supply is conventional,

Sony's latest with superior performance, the ICF-SW55. Innovative, but relatively complicated.

not the automated worldwide version that comes with the 'SW1S. Beware the polarity, though—it's center-pin positive, the opposite of most.

All this is a bit much for most people to lug along on trips, but the receiver itself is nicely sized for travel, and there's a power lock to keep it from turning on accidentally.

Controls are logically and neatly laid out. The large, helpful LCD, dimly and unevenly backlit, includes a map of the world with time zones, local and World Time clocks, signal and battery-strength indicator, digital fre-quency readout to the nearest kHz, and a tuning-rate indicator. Instead of the usual speaker grille, there are two speaker openings—round perforations on the back of the set and a narrow rectangular port above the LCD. This novel arrangement sounds quite clean, especially for a compact, even though there's little bass response and only a switch for perfunctory tone adjustment. Too, the lack of a speaker grille frees up front-panel space for other purposes.

What really makes the '55 unusual is its operating system, in particular the presets

Sony's ICF-SW77: "Macintosh-Windows" for World Band

Sony is one of the world's most successful high-technology organizations, turning out a stream of resourceful engineering coups year after year. World band is no exception. Its innovative ICF-2010/ICF-2001D was introduced in 1985, and to this day continues to outclass any other manufacturer's product for sheer technological wizardry.

New Ideas for Easier Operation

More recently, Sony has focused on inventive ways to demystify the operation of a world band radio. They've tried making digital radios look like old-fashioned needle-and-dial models, and there are even models that operate off preprogrammed "credit cards."

These attempts, noble but flawed in their fundamental logic, pale when compared with what appeared in 1991 with the ICF-SW77, which was soon withdrawn from the market because of problems and thus didn't appear in last year's *Passport* Buyer's Guide. A slightly improved version appeared more recently. We've tested both.

The '77 performs similarly to the venerable '2010/'2001D, but with a variety of small but nice improvements—better wide bandwidth and easier synchronous-detector operation, for example—and some steps backward, such as disconcertingly loud synthesizer chugging during tuning. But none of this really gets to the point of what makes the '77 so exceptional: its operating system.

Computer-Type Operating System Debuts

Yes, "operating system." Radios are now so full of computer-type circuitry that it was a matter of time before some bright bulb decided that they ought to be operated like computers. Enter the '77, which with its software and compact video display is world band's answer to the "see and choose" operating environment of a Macintosh computer or Microsoft Windows software.

Nice idea, no cigar. Advanced technology is supposed to make things perform better and easier, not the other way around—that's why a "windows" operating environment was devised for Apple computers in the first place. With the circa 1985 '2010/'2001D, one poke at a button brings up a station. With the new '77, not only are more button-pushes required, you have to figure out which buttons to push in what sequence—and there's no mouse to help out. Initial operation without the manual in hand is virtually impossible, although once you get the hang of it you can do as with your unfavorite computer software: learn to adjust to its requirements.

scheme. Presets, some prestored at the factory with world band stations, rest within "pages," with up to five frequencies per page. Each page can be assigned a name, so on page three, for example, you could store the frequencies for up to five Arab stations, then title that page "ARABS." Every time you access page three, "ARABS" would appear—a plus over the Sony ICF-2010/ICF-2001D's system, which requires a written notation or human memory.

The factory prestored presets should give the newcomer a taste of what world band radio has to offer. It may reduce the chances of a newcomer's buying his or her first world band radio and saying, "I can't hear anything." In principle, at any rate.

Unfortunately, this system comes at a stiff price in convenience. Unlike the '2010/'2001D, which brings up a station with the mere tap of one key, it takes from two to several keystrokes to call up a desired preset station on the '55. While the '55's system is novel and innovative, with some handy

Simpler is Better

The tide of technology is towards simpler operation. Most folks don't have the time to take the square root and cube it when a simple two-plus-two will do. The objective of technical innovation in world band operating systems is to help make radios adapt to people's needs, the reverse of what the '77, which lacks so much as prompts or a help menu, does.

Rating? Give the $624.95—CAN$750 in Canada, £349 as the ICF-SW77E in the U.K.—'SW77 three-and-a-half stars, mainly because of its generally commendable performance. If you enjoy the technical challenges of computers, go for it—at least one journalist colleague we loaned the radio to very much liked its operating system, even if not the loud chugging. Otherwise, look to the ICF-2010/ICF-2001D for very nearly the same end result with much less bother, chugging and cost.

As to the future, computer concepts will increasingly be used, by receiver manufacturers and broadcasters alike, to better effect than in the '77. This will make world band operation simpler, and thus more accessible to the general public. The basic concept of the pioneering '77 is probably valid, but at this point is, as the Chinese proverb puts it, only the first step in a march of 1,000 li. Or, lifting from the ruminations of Robert Samuelson in *Newsweek*, it just might be "technology in reverse."

New Version in The Wings?

Footnote: In 1992, Sony discussed with us certain improvements, including proper (non-muting) solutions to chugging, they would like to see in the ICF-SW77 in due course. These have not been incorporated in the current version, released too early to have been covered by those comments. In principle, this should mean that yet another version is due out. Whether this will actually happen is anybody's guess, as Sony has not replied to our inquiries. However, we will continue to monitor the situation to see if a truly finalized version will be available. If so, we will delve into it in the 1994 *Passport*—and hopefully have good news.

Sony's ICF-SW77: window on the future?

labeling, presets are above all supposed to be a convenience. The bottom line is that those on the '55 are, in terms of keystrokes, far less convenient to operate than those of the '2010. They also take some figuring out, which can be a pain if you're not a habitual listener.

Fortunately, there is a conventional tuning knob—two speeds, at that—and up/down slewing buttons that double as "signal-seeking" scan controls. Both are a snap to operate.

Another pain on the '55 is a hard-wired spectrum memory which "knows" that certain frequencies and modes have been assigned to particular services. So, if you punch up 6175 kHz, the '55 will automatically select the AM mode and wide bandwidth because that is a frequency within a segment set aside for international broadcasting. So far, so good— but there's more.

The radio "knows" if you are in the Americas, as you would have set mediumwave AM channel spacing at 10 kHz, rather than the 9 kHz used in other parts of the world. In the Americas, 7000-7300 kHz is used by hams, who operate in the lower-sideband mode; whereas in other parts of the world 7100-7300 kHz is used for world band stations, which operate in the AM mode. So if you select 7155 kHz, for example, the '55 will automatically select lower sideband with the narrow bandwidth, appropriate for hearing hams but wrong for world band stations.

Similarly, in the Americas the band-select control skips the 7 MHz band altogether. A simple solution is set the mediumwave channel setting to 9 kHz, tricking the radio into thinking you're not in the Americas. Of course, this, in turn, disrupts mediumwave AM reception. Another is to preset your favorite 7 MHz channels into memory in the AM mode. However, this is clunky and doesn't do much good for bandscanning.

Above 7300 kHz in any part of the world, the radio "knows" this is official turf for utility stations, not world band. There, it selects upper sideband with narrow bandwidth— again, wrong for world band reception.

Problem is, textbook theory and the realities of 7 MHz transmissions are far apart. Americans can and do listen frequently to world band stations between 7100-7300, and throughout the world people listen between 7300-7600 kHz. The '55 assumes otherwise, forcing the listener to go through gyrations for the set to receive in the proper AM mode used by world band stations. It's confusing and a bother, all caused by a system naively designed to make operation "simpler." There are a lot of these sorts of well-meaning attempts coming out of Sony these days, unfortunately.

To get a real-world handle on this, we passed the '55 around to a variety of bright,

educated folks to see how long it would take them to figure out how to use the radio without having to refer to the operating manual. Normally, this sort of exercise is successfully concluded in a matter of minutes. This time, however, not a single individual could figure out the basics of operation—even how to hear the factory prestored frequencies designed to get the beginner off and running—without thumbing through the manual. Even after having done that, operation was perceived as being user-unfriendly, although radiophiles accepted the operating quirks in short order and with good grace.

Performance is another matter—in general, it's quite good. The '55's wide bandwidth measures 8 kHz, adequate but somewhat wide for many world band stations. However, the 4 kHz narrow bandwidth provides reasonable audio quality, including low distortion, while rejecting adjacent-channel interference. Switching between the two bandwidths can be complicated. The narrow single-sideband bandwidth measures 3.2 kHz, which is adequate. All three bandwidths have good shape factors and ultimate rejection is excellent.

Front-end selectivity, dynamic range and image rejection are only fair, which is pretty much par for portables. Yet, numerous low-level spurious signals sometimes appear in some spectrum segments. Sensitivity to weak signals with the built-in telescopic antenna is adequate for most parts of the world, although on mediumwave AM and longwave sensitivity is more pedestrian.

Astonishingly, considering that the '55 costs about the same as a '2010/'2001D, there is no synchronous detection. This important high-tech feature, which reduces adjacent-channel interference and selective fading distortion, is a key plus of the '2010.

If you can afford the likes of a '55, you shouldn't have to worry about the cost of batteries. Still, an estimated cost of $0.25-0.50 per hour can make anybody think twice about leaving the radio on with batteries hour after hour.

For the vast majority of world band listeners, the '55's operating quirks are probably not worth the bother—there are too many other, handier models from which to choose. For radiophiles who want fade-resistance and superior adjacent-channel rejection, there's the bulkier Sony ICF-2010/ICF-2001D, which is also freer from spurious signals.

Yet, if the ICF-SW55's operating scheme meets with your approval—say, you are comfortable utilizing the more sophisticated features of a typical VCR—and you're looking for a small, worthy-performance portable with good audio, this radio is a superior performer in its size class.

The Panasonic RF-B65 combines advanced technology with ease of operation and superior performance.

Sony's ICF-SW7600, the result of a product evolution beginning in 1983 with the ICF-2002.

★ ★ ★   *Editor's Choice*

Panasonic RF-B65 (Panasonic RF-B65D) (Panasonic RF-B65L) (National B65)

Price: *RF-B65:* $269.95-279.95 in the United States, CAN$399 in Canada, AUS$499.00 in Australia; *RF-B65 and RF-B65D:* £169.95 in the United Kingdom, $290-450 elsewhere in Europe (EC). RP-65 120V AC power supply $6.95 in the United States; RP-38 120/220V AC worldwide power supply $14.95 in the United States. (Power supply prices are as provided by Panasonic; actual selling prices in stores are much higher.)

Advantages: Superior overall world band performance for size. Very easy to operate for advanced-technology radio. Pleasant audio. Various helpful tuning features. Signal-strength indicator. World Time clock, plus second time-zone clock. Alarm/sleep features. Demodulates single-sideband signals, used by hams and utility stations. Receives longwave band. Travel power lock. AC power supply comes standard (outside North America).

Disadvantages: Cumbersome tuning knob inhibits speed. With built-in antenna, weak-signal sensitivity slightly low. Adjacent-channel rejection (selectivity) slightly broad. Clocks not displayed separately from frequency. Display and keypad not illuminated. Keypad not in telephone format. AC power supply extra (North America).

Bottom Line: A very nice, easy-to-use portable, especially if you live in Europe or Eastern North America, where world band signals tend to be fairly strong.

★ ★ ★   *Editor's Choice*

Sony ICF-SW7600

Price: $249.95 in the United States, CAN$399 in Canada, £149.95 in the United Kingdom, $250-400 elsewhere in Europe (EC), AUS$399.00 in Australia.

Advantages: Superior overall for size. High-quality audio with supplied earpieces. Easy to operate for level of technology. Helpful tuning features. World Time clock with timer that controls certain tape recorders. Alarm/sleep features. Demodulates single sideband, used by hams and utility stations. Illuminated display. Travel power lock also disables display light. Comes with reel-in portable wire antenna, besides built-in telescopic one. Stereo FM, through earpieces, also covers Japanese FM band. Receives longwave band. Comes with AC power supply.

Disadvantages: No tuning knob. No meaningful signal-strength indicator. Earpieces less comfortable than foam-padded headphones.

Bottom Line: Excellent all-around performer for globetrotting.

★ ★ ★   *Editor's Choice*

Panasonic RF-B45 (Panasonic RF-B45DL) (National B45)

Price: *RF-B45:* $189.95-199.95 in the United States, CAN$299 in Canada, AUS$329.00 in Australia; *RF-B45DL:* £129.95 in the United Kingdom, $220-320 in Europe (EC). RP-65 120V AC power supply $6.95 in the United

Here's value for your money: Panasonic's RF-B45, excellent for newcomers and experienced listeners, alike.

States; RP-38 120/220V AC worldwide power supply $14.95 in the United States.

Advantages: Best performance for price/size category. Easy to operate for advanced-technology radio. A number of helpful tuning features. Signal-strength indicator. World Time clock. Alarm/sleep features. Demodulates single-sideband signals, used by hams and utility stations. Has longwave band.

Disadvantages: No tuning knob. Weak-signal sensitivity a bit lacking. Adjacent-channel rejection (selectivity) a bit broad. Clock not displayed separately from frequency. No display or keypad illumination. AC power supply extra.

Bottom Line: The best buy on the market in a compact portable under $200. Excellent for newcomers and travelers.

Retested for 1993
★ ★ ★   *Editor's Choice*

Sangean ATS-808
(Aiwa WR-D1000)
(Realistic DX-380)
(Roberts R808)
(Siemens RK 661)

Price: *Sangean:* $259.00 in the United States, CAN$279.95 in Canada, AUS$299.00 in Australia; *Aiwa:* $259.95 in the United States; *Realistic:* CAN$299.95 in Canada, AUS$299.95 in Australia; *Roberts:* around £120 in the United Kingdom; *Siemens:* 399.00 DM in Germany. ADP-808 120V AC power supply $9.95 in the United States, CAN$14.95 in Canada.

Advantages: Exceptional simplicity of operation for technology class. Dual bandwidths, unusual in this size radio (see Disadvantages). Already-pleasant speaker audio improves with

supplied earpieces. Various helpful features. Weak-signal sensitivity at least average for size. Keypad has exceptional feel and tactile response. Receives longwave band. 24-hour World Time clock, displayed separately from frequency, and local clock. Alarm/sleep features. Signal strength indicator. Travel power lock. Stereo FM via earpieces. Superior FM performance. *Realistic:* 30-day money-back trial period.

Disadvantages: Fast tuning mutes receiver. Narrow bandwidth performance only fair. Spurious-signal ("image") rejection very slightly substandard for class. Display and keypad not illuminated. Keypad not in telephone format. No carrying strap or handle. Supplied earpieces inferior to comparable foam-padded headphones. AC power supply extra.

Comments: The only Editor's Choice compact that doesn't demodulate single-sideband signals—a disadvantage for some radiophiles, but an advantage for world band listening in that it makes operation less confusing. *Aiwa:* Cabinet styled differently from the other versions of this model.

Bottom Line: Exceptional simplicity of operation and solid overall performance make this the top choice among compact models for most newcomers and others seeking simplicity of operation. However, an unworthy choice for bandscanning.

Supplementary Findings—Retest: Our original unit, tested in 1990, was exceptionally sensitive to reception of weak signals. However, it also had modest spurious-signal ("image") rejection. This made it unusually appropriate for use in Western North America, Hawai'i, Australia and New Zealand, where signals tend to be relatively weak. Equally, it made it less appropriate for use in Europe, North Africa and the Near East, where signals tend to be strong.

Sangean's ATS-808 is among the easiest to operate advanced-technology portables.

The unit tested for this year's *Passport* is slightly less sensitive, but also has less trouble with spurious-signal rejection. While this is likely to be the result of a circuit change at the factory, it could also result from sample-to-sample variation in performance.

Otherwise, the '808 continues, as before, to be a top-class compact . . . with some reservations. Muting during bandscanning continues to be a major drawback—all traces of audio vanish completely when the knob is turned even at moderate speed. And the narrow bandwidth doesn't slice off adjacent-channel interference as well as it should.

Overall, the changes, although minor, make the Sangean ATS-808 less attractive than before for use in weak-signal regions. This was the '808's high card, as no other model in its class could equal its sensitivity. While the most recent unit is also more attractive for use in Europe and certain other parts of the world, it performs no better there than do a number of other compact models.

★ ★ ★

Sony ICF-PRO80
(Sony ICF-PRO70)

Price: $499.95 in the United States, CAN$499 in Canada, £295.00 in the United Kingdom, $550-700 elsewhere in Europe (EC), AUS$799.00 in Australia.

Advantages: Superior overall performance for size. Above average at bringing in weak world band stations. Helpful tuning features, includ-

Need a scanner and world band radio in one package? Sony's ICF-PRO80 will do the trick. Deplorable ergonomics, though.

ing scanning, and comes with versatile VHF scanner (reduced coverage in some versions). Demodulates single-sideband signals, used by utility and ham signals. Receives Japanese FM band, longwave band, VHF-TV audio. Illuminated display.

Disadvantages: Awkward to operate—especially outboard scanner module, which requires removal and replacement of antenna and battery pack. Mediocre audio. No tuning knob. Few travel features. No signal-strength indicator. No AC power supply.

Bottom Line: Great for puzzle lovers. Otherwise, of value mainly to weak-signal chasers who need a small world band portable with a VHF scanner.

Note: According to unconfirmed reports, this model may be discontinued before long in some countries.

★ ★ ½   ¢

Sony ICF-SW800
(Sony ICF-SW700)

Price: *ICF-SW800:* $199.95 in the United States; *ICF-SW700:* ¥13,000 (around $100) in Japan. AC-D3M 120V AC/4.5V DC power supply $12.95 in the United States.

Advantages: Innovative card-type tuning system helps newcomers get started. Incorporates a number of other helpful tuning features, too. Refreshingly obvious how to operate for level of technology. World Time clock. Alarm feature. Highly effective travel power lock. Comes with reel-in portable wire antenna. *ICF-SW700:* Relatively inexpensive for level of technology provided.

The novel Sony ICF-SW800 and ICF-SW700 are tuned using what look like credit cards.

Disadvantages: No tuning knob. Slightly limited world band coverage, including omission of important 21 MHz segment. No longwave band. Adjacent-channel rejection (selectivity) only fair. Tunes only in coarse 5 kHz increments. Keypad uses unorthodox two-row configuration and offers no tactile feedback. Clock not displayed separately from frequency. No display or keypad illumination. No signal-strength indicator. AC power supply extra. Not widely distributed outside Japan at present, but this could change. *ICF-SW800:* No mediumwave AM. *ICF-SW700:* No FM.

Bottom Line: Innovative tuning that's a snap to grasp, plus respectable performance—but once you become familiar with world band, the ICF-SW800's tuning innovation fades into novelty.

★ ★ ½   ¢

Magnavox AE 3805
(Philips AE 3805)

Price: *Magnavox:* $119.95 in the United States; *Philips:* equivalent of US$100-125 in China.

Disadvantages: *Magnavox:* FM and mediumwave AM tuning steps do not conform to channel spacing in much of the world outside the Americas. *Philips:* Mediumwave AM tuning steps do not conform to channel spacing within the Americas.

Bottom Line: Similar, except for layout and lack of stereo earphone output, to Sangean ATS 800. Although still available in stores, this model is not in the 1993 catalog, so it may shortly be replaced by the forthcoming AE 3625.

The Magnavox AE 3805, also sold by Philips, may be replaced shortly by the AE 3625.

The Sangean ATS 800, also sold as the Realistic DX-370 and Siemens RP 647G4, provides some advanced technology at low cost.

★ ★ ½   ¢

Realistic DX-370
Sangean ATS 800
(Siemens RP 647G4)

Price: *Realistic:* $119.95 in the United States, AUS$199.95 in Australia. *Sangean:* $139.00 in the United States, CAN$149.95 in Canada. ADP-808 120V AC power supply $7.99 in the United States, CAN$14.95 in Canada. *Siemens:* About $90 in Europe (EC).

Advantages: Not expensive for model with digital frequency display and presets. Already-pleasant speaker audio improves with headphones. Five preset buttons retrieve up to ten world band and ten AM/FM stations. Relatively selective for price class. Relatively sensitive, a plus for listeners in Central and Western North America, as well as Australia and New Zealand. Simple to operate for radio at this technology level. World Time clock. Timer/sleep/alarm features. Travel power lock. Low-battery indicator, unusual in price class. Stereo FM via earpieces (supplied in Sangean version). *Realistic:* 30-day money-back trial period.

Disadvantages: Mediocre spurious-signal ("image") rejection. Inferior dynamic range, a drawback for listeners in Europe, North Africa and the Near East. Does not tune 2300-2500, 7300-7600, 9300-9500, 21750-21850 and 25600-26100 kHz world band segments—some of which are important. Tunes world band only in coarse 5 kHz steps. No tuning knob; tunes only via multi-speed up/down slewing buttons. No longwave band. Signal-strength indicator nigh useless. No display or keypad illumination. Clock not displayed separately from frequency. No carrying strap or handle. AC power supply extra. *Sangean:* Supplied earpieces inferior to comparable foam-padded earphones. *Realistic:* No earpieces. *Sangean and Realistic:* FM and mediumwave AM tuning steps do not conform to channel spacing in much of the world outside the Americas. *Siemens:* Mediumwave AM tuning steps do not conform to channel spacing within the Americas. *Sangean and Siemens:* Do not receive 1635-1705 kHz portion of forthcoming expanded AM band in Americas, although this could change.

Bottom Line: A popular starter set that's okay for the price.

★ ★

Sony ICF-7700 (Sony ICF-7600DA)

Price: *ICF-7700:* $229.95 in the United States, CAN$339.95 in Canada; *ICF-7600DA:* under £150 in the United Kingdom, $230-300 elsewhere in Europe (EC), AUS$399.00 in Australia.

Advantages: Very easy to use. World Time clock. Alarm/sleep features. Only model featuring digital frequency display complemented by unusual digitalized "analog" tuning scale. Helpful tuning aids include 15 presets—five for world band—and a tuning knob. Travel power lock. Covers longwave and Japanese FM bands.

Disadvantages: Poor adjacent-channel rejection (selectivity). Slightly limited world band coverage. Mediocre unwanted-signal rejection. Coarse 5 kHz tuning increments. No display or "dial" illumination. No meaningful signal-strength indicator. No AC power supply.

Bottom Line: In today's marketplace of rich choices, there's no longer any reason to put up with this overpriced model's utter lack of adjacent-channel rejection. In this size and price class, a much better bet for the technically timid is the Sangean ATS-808 or Panasonic RF-B45.

Sony's ICF-7700 is digital, but tries to come off as an old-fashioned needle-and-dial set. It's also sold as the ICF-7600DA.

Sony's ICF-7601, the Volkswagen Beetle of world band radio. Although its circuitry is dated, it remains the best nondigital small portable around.

★ ★ ¢

Sony ICF-7601

Price: $139.95 in the United States, CAN$199 in Canada, $125-170 in Europe (EC), AUS$199.00 in Australia.

Advantages: Weak-signal sensitivity above average for size. Travel power lock. Covers Japanese FM band.

Disadvantages: No digital frequency display. Dial not illuminated. Slightly limited world band coverage. Adjacent-channel rejection only fair. Some crosstalk among adjacent world band segments. No longwave band coverage. No meaningful signal-strength indicator. No AC power supply.

Bottom Line: Honest, basic performance at an attractive price, but technology is long in the tooth.

★ ★ ¢

DAK MR-101s

Price: *DAK:* $39.90 by mail order in the United States, about the equivalent of US$45 in China.

Advantages: Least costly portable tested with digital frequency display and presets (ten for world band, ten for AM/FM). Slightly more selective than usual for price category. Relatively simple to operate for technology class. World Time clock. Alarm/sleep timer. Illuminated display. Available on 30-day money-back basis. FM stereo via optional headphones.

Disadvantages: Relatively lacking in weak-signal sensitivity. No tuning knob; tunes only via presets and multi-speed up/down slewing.

Pricebuster: DAK's MR-101s.

Tunes world band only in coarse 5 kHz steps. Mediumwave AM tuning steps do not conform to channel spacing in much of the world outside the Americas. Frequency display in confusing XX.XX/XX.XX5 MHz format. Poor spurious-signal ("image") rejection. Mediocre dynamic range. Does not tune relatively unimportant 6200-7100 and 25600-26100 kHz world band segments. Does not receive longwave band or 1615-1705 kHz portion of forthcoming expanded AM band in the Americas. No signal-strength indicator. No travel power lock switch. No AC power supply. Reportedly prone to malfunction; flimsy antenna, especially swivel, prone to breakage. Antenna swivels, but does not rotate. Limited dealer network.

Bottom Line: Audi cockpit, moped engine. Nevertheless, in Eastern North America a better choice than cheap analog-tuned alternatives. This radio may be discontinued shortly.

Note: DAK, "King of the Closeouts," went into Chapter 11 creditor-protection proceedings in 1992. Both our most recent ordering experience and other such experiences reported to us indicate this firm sometimes takes orders for items it claims are in stock, charges the customer's card, then weeks later sends not the product, but rather a notice indicating the product is not in stock. *Caveat emptor!*

Advantages: Relatively inexpensive for a model with digital frequency display and presets (ten for world band, ten for AM/FM). Relatively simple to operate for technology class. Alarm/sleep timer with clock. Illuminated display. FM stereo via optional headphones.

Disadvantages: Mediocre sensitivity to weak signals. No tuning knob; tunes only via presets and multi-speed up/down slewing. Tunes world band only in coarse 5 kHz steps. Frequency display in confusing XX.XX/XX.XX5 format. Poor spurious-signal ("image") rejection. Mediocre dynamic range. Does not tune important 7300-9500 and 21750-21850 kHz segments. Does not receive longwave broadcasts or 1635-1705 kHz portion of forthcoming expanded AM band in the Americas. No signal-strength indicator. Clock in 12-hour format. No travel power lock. No AC power supply. Quality of construction appears to be below average. FM and mediumwave AM tuning increments not switchable, which may make for inexact tuning in some parts of the world other than where the radio was purchased.

Note: The Amsonic is available in at least five versions: AS-138 for China, AS-138-0 for Europe, AS-138-3 for USA/Canada, AS-138-4 for Japan, and AS-138-6 for other countries and Europe. Each version has FM and mediumwave AM ranges and channel spacing appropriate to the market region, plus the Japanese version replaces coverage of the 21 MHz band with TV audio.

Bottom Line: No bargain in the United States, where the slightly better DAK MR-101s is available for much less, but more attractively priced elsewhere.

★★

Rodelsonic Digital World Band
Rodelvox Digital World Band
(Amsonic AS-138)
(Dick Smith A-4338)
(Shimasu PLL Digital)

Price: *Rodelvox and Rodelsonic:* $99.95 plus $6.95 shipping in United States. *Amsonic:* Y265 (about US$48) in China. *Dick Smith:* AUS$99.95 in Australia.

Rodelvox is but one of a number of names, including the Dick Smith A-4338, under which this digital compact is sold.

Lowe's SRX-50, just introduced, is exceptionally low-priced.

★ ★

(Amsonic AS-908)
(Lowe SRX-50)
(Morphy Richards R191)

Price: *Lowe:* £39.95 in the United Kingdom; *Morphy Richards:* £37.00 in the United Kingdom.

Comment: Not yet tested, and until this is done the two-star rating should be considered provisional. Reportedly similar, except for styling, to the Rodelvox Digital World Band, preceding, save that they tune longwave 153-281 kHz, mediumwave AM 531-1602 kHz, shortwave 5900-15500 kHz and FM 87.5-107.9 MHz, using increments appropriate to European channel-spacing norms. Too, the Lowe, at any rate, includes stereo earphones. Attractively priced for European market.

★ ★

(Pulser)
(SEG SED ECL88)

Comment: Not tested, but reportedly very similar to certain of the above three groups of low-cost digital models from China.

Price: *Pulser:* CAN$59.99 in Canada; *SEG:* equivalent to US$40-50 in China.

New for 1993
★ ★

DAK DMR-3000 Global Interceptor

Price: $69.90 plus $6.00 shipping in the United States.

Advantages: Least costly portable tested with digital frequency display and keypad. Least

costly portable tested with presets (18 for world band, 18 for AM/FM). Up/down slew tuning with "signal-seek" scanning. Slightly better adjacent-channel rejection (selectivity) than usual for price category. Relatively simple to operate for technology class. World Time and local clocks. Alarm/sleep timer. Illuminated display. Nominally available on 30-day money-back basis. FM stereo via optional headphones. Selectable 9/10 kHz mediumwave AM increments, unusual in price class.

Disadvantages: Insensitive to weak—or even moderate—signals on 9 and 11 MHz segments of the world band spectrum, and DAK's optional "Station Stalker" active antenna doesn't help much. Mediocre sensitivity to signals in other parts of the world band spectrum. No tuning knob. Tunes world band only in coarse 5 kHz steps. Mediocre dynamic range and spurious-signal rejection. Does not tune important 9350-9495, 13600-13800 and 15000-15095 kHz portions of world band spectrum. Does not receive longwave band. No signal-strength indicator. No travel power lock, but power switch not easy to turn on accidentally. No AC power supply. Clocks do not display independent of frequency. Local clock in nonstandard 24-hour format.

Bottom Line: Excellent features, many carefully thought out and heretofore unheard of at this price. Yet, on some world band segments stations hardly come in. Were it not for this failing, the DMR-3000 would rank at the top of the two-star category.

Note: DAK went into Chapter 11 creditor-protection proceedings in 1992. Both our most recent ordering experience and other such experiences reported to us indicate this firm sometimes takes orders for items it claims are in stock, charges the customer's card, then weeks later sends not the product, but rather a notice indicating the product is not in stock. *Caveat emptor!*

DAK's new DMR-3000 lacks weak-signal reception even with the optional DAK "Station Stalker."

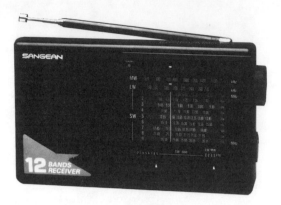

Designed for taking on trips is the new Realistic DX-350, also sold as the Sangean SG-700L.

★ ½

Realistic DX-350
Sangean SG-700L

Price: *Realistic:* AUS$99.95 in Australia. Realistic #273-1454 120V AC/6V DC power supply $7.95. *Sangean:* $69.95 in the United States, CAN$79.95 in Canada;

Advantages: Inexpensive. Receives longwave band. *Realistic:* 30-day money-back trial period.

Disadvantages: No digital frequency display. Slightly limited world band coverage. Mediocre spurious-signal ("image") rejection. Adjacent-channel rejection (selectivity) only fair. Modest sensitivity to weak signals. Mediocre audio quality. Antenna swivels, but does not rotate. No meaningful signal-strength indicator. Dial not illuminated. AC power supply optional.

Bottom Line: Adequate for use on trips, but a dubious choice for day-to-day listening.

★ ½

Panasonic RF-B20L
(National B20)
(Panasonic RF-B20)

Price: CAN$189.95 in Canada, around £70 in the United Kingdom, $120-195 elsewhere. No longer offered in the United States.

Advantages: Good audio for size; continuous tone control. Weak-signal sensitivity slightly above average for class.

Disadvantages: No digital frequency display. Limited world band coverage, omits important 13 and 21 MHz segments. Mediocre adjacent-channel rejection. No meaningful signal-strength indicator. No AC power supply.

Bottom Line: Lacks complete world band coverage and ability to sort stations out more successfully.

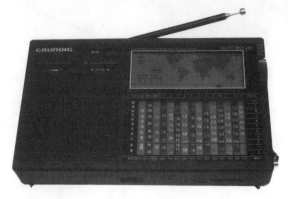

Grundig's Yacht Boy 230 is also available in a travel kit version with pocket knife, alarm clock, pen/pencil set, and flashlight.

★ ½

Grundig Yacht Boy 230
(Amsonic AS-912)
(Grundig Travel Kit 230)
(Panopus Yacht Boy 230)

Price: *Grundig Yacht Boy 230:* $199.95 in the United States, CAN$259.95 in Canada, £79.00 in the United Kingdom, AUS$139.00 in Australia. *Grundig Travel Kit 230:* $279.95 in the United States, CAN$399.95 in Canada. *Panopus Yacht Boy 230:* AUS$169.00 in Australia.

Advantages: Includes World Time and worldwide multi-country clock/alarm/sleep timer with electronic map. Illuminated dial. Receives longwave band. Stereo FM through earphones. Extra-cost Grundig Travel Kit version, apparently available only in North America, comes with zippered carrying case, pocket knife, alarm clock, pen/pencil set and flashlight.

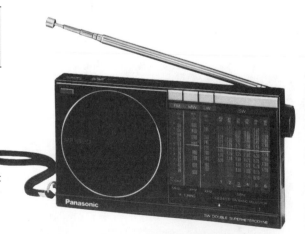

Panasonic's RF-B20 is no longer competitive—and no longer available in the United States.

Disadvantages: No digital frequency display. Slightly limited world band coverage. Mediocre spurious-signal ("image") and adjacent-channel rejection (selectivity). Tricky on-off switch. Pushbutton volume control increases or decreases sound in sizable bites, compromising adjustability. Annoying tuner backlash at lower end of each band. No meaningful signal-strength indicator. No AC power supply.

Bottom Line: An undistinguished and over-priced radio of interest mainly for its world map clock.

★ ½

Sangean SG 621
(Sangean SG 631)
(Siemens RK 710)
(Roberts R621)

Price: *SG 621:* $119.00 in the United States, not available in Canada; *SG 631:* $139.00 in the United States, not available in Canada; *RK 710:* DM149.00 in Germany.

Advantages: World Time clock, plus second time-zone clock. Alarm/sleep features. Self-extinguishing clock light. Stereo FM through earpieces (supplied). Superior FM capture ratio helps in selecting desired station. Smaller than most models in compact category, a plus for traveling. *SG 631:* Clock programmed with local time and date for 260 different cities around the world.

Disadvantages: No digital frequency display. Frequency dial not illuminated. Limited world band coverage. Mediocre spurious-signal and adjacent-channel rejection. Antenna swivels, but does not rotate. No meaningful signal-strength indicator. FM reception sometimes compromised by SCA interference. Does not receive longwave broadcasts. No AC power supply. Lacks carrying strap or handle.

Bottom Line: No surprises, except perhaps the clock, in this latest outdated-technology offering from Sangean. Somewhat overpriced for what it does, which isn't much.

Sangean makes a variety of small, low-cost portables. The SG 621 uses digital readout only for its clock—not frequencies.

The Magnavox OD1875BK, also sold as the Philips OD1875BK, is a pedestrian performer.

★ ½

Magnavox OD1875BK
Philips OD1875BK

Price: *Magnavox:* $79.95 in the United States, not available in Canada; *Philips:* £49.95 in the United Kingdom, $75-125 elsewhere in Europe.

Advantages: Receives longwave band.

Disadvantages: No digital frequency display. Limited world band coverage. Mediocre adjacent-channel and spurious-signal ("image") rejection. No meaningful signal-strength indicator. No dial illumination. No AC power supply.

Bottom Line: So-so performer.

New for 1993
★ ½ ¢

International AC 100

Price: $34.95, including shipping, in the United States. Availability elsewhere not yet established, but almost certainly found in Asia and parts of Europe.

Advantages: Cheapest radio tested. Sensitivity to weak signals at least average for size. Audio quality slightly above average for price class. Receives longwave band.

Disadvantages: No digital frequency display. Adjacent-channel rejection (selectivity) poor. Mediocre spurious-signal ("image") rejection. Limited world band coverage, omits important 13 MHz segment and 11990-12095 kHz portion of 11 MHz segment. Tested sample also lacks coverage of 2.3-5.1 MHz tropical stations; however, other versions may receive

Low tech, low performance. Yet, the International AC 100 is 1993's "King of the Throwaways" for travelers who need something cheap for occasional listening.

2.3-5.1 MHz in lieu of longwave. Antenna swivels, but does not rotate. Quality of construction appears to be below average. Dial not illuminated. No meaningful signal-strength indicator. Mediumwave AM coverage stops at roughly 1650 kHz, five channels shy of American AM band's forthcoming upper limit. Tuning knob "mushy."

Bottom Line: Performs similarly to the Pomtrex, but with greater frequency coverage and a clearer dial. A good buy for occasional listening on trips.

★ ½ ¢

Pomtrex 120-00300 (MCE-7760) (Pace) (TEC 235TR)

Price: $29.95 plus $4.00 shipping in the United States; availability and prices elsewhere not yet established.

Advantages: Inexpensive. Sensitivity to weak signals at least average for size. Audio quality slightly above average for price class. Receives longwave band (tested sample).

Disadvantages: No digital frequency display. Adjacent-channel rejection (selectivity) poor. Mediocre spurious-signal ("image") rejection. Limited world band coverage, omits important 13 and 21 MHz segments and 11970-12095 kHz portion of 11 MHz segment. Tested sample also lacks coverage of 2.3-5.1 MHz tropical stations; however, some other Pomtrex samples with the same model number receive 2.3-5.1 MHz in lieu of longwave. Antenna swivels, but does not rotate. Quality of construction appears to be below average, including flimsy battery clips. Batteries awkward to install. Dial not illuminated. Some dial numbering difficult to read. No meaningful

The Pomtrex 120-00300, available under a number of ever-changing names, is nearly equal to the new International AC 100.

signal-strength indicator. Mediumwave AM coverage stops at roughly 1650 kHz, five channels shy of American AM band's forthcoming upper limit. No AC power supply. Warranty, only 90 days, written such that it is next to useless.

Bottom Line: Not noted for sale in the United States under the "Pomtrex" label for several months, but likely to be sold under one name or another in various parts of the world. Not easy on the ears, but its extremely low price makes it worth considering if you're traveling to where it may be lost, damaged or stolen.

New for 1993
★ ½

Jäger PL-440

Price: $79.95 plus $6.00 shipping in the United States.

Advantages: Digital frequency display, a rarity in price class. Tuning aids include up/down slewing buttons with "signal-seek" scanning, and 20 presets (five for world band). 24-hour World Time clock. Sleep/timer features. Receives longwave band. Antenna rotates and swivels, a rarity in price class. Travel power lock.

Disadvantages: Limited coverage of world band spectrum omits important 5800-5945, 7305-9495, 9905-10000, 11550-11645, 12055-12160, 17500-17900 and 21450-21850 kHz segments. Tortoise-slow band-to-band tuning, remediable by using presets as band selectors. Slightly insensitive to weak signals. Poor adjacent-channel rejection (selectivity). Apparently mediocre quality

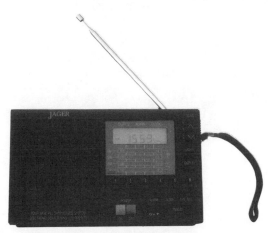

"Jäger PL-440" may sound European, but it's really just another mediocre performer from China.

Giros R918—basic performance in a small digital portable.

control. Even frequencies displayed with final zero omitted; e.g., 5.75 rather than conventional 5.750. No signal-strength indicator. Dial not illuminated. Not offered with AC power supply. Lacks selector for 9/10 kHz medium-wave AM steps.

Bottom Line: This apparent improvement on the Giros, below, has reasonable audio and nice features for the money, with presets and digital readout to make tuning easier than with analog models.

New for 1993
★ ½

Giros R918

Price: CAN$64.50 plus shipping in Canada; about $60, including shipping, shipped from Metragen Ltd. in Downsview, Ontario, to the United States. Almost certainly available in parts of Asia and Europe.

Advantages: Digital frequency display, a rarity in price class. Unusually small size for a compact—close to a mini, thus useful for travels. Tuning aids include up/down slewing buttons with "signal-seek" scanning, and 20 presets (five for world band). 24-hour World Time clock. Sleep/timer features. Battery strength indicator. Receives longwave band. Antenna rotates and swivels, a rarity in price class. Selector for 9/10 kHz mediumwave AM steps, a rarity in cheap digital radios.

Disadvantages: Limited coverage of world band spectrum omits important 5800-5945, 7305-9495, 9905-10000, 11550-11645, 12055-12160, 17500-17900 and 21450-21850 kHz segments. Tortoise-slow band-to-band tuning, remediable by using presets as band selectors. Insensitive to weak signals. Audio quality mediocre, tinny and distorted.

Poor adjacent-channel rejection (selectivity). Mediocre quality control—our unit arrived with a balky on-off control, for example. Even frequencies displayed with final zero omitted; e.g., 5.75 rather than conventional 5.750. No signal-strength indicator. Dial not illuminated. Hums badly if AC power supply used. Not offered with AC power supply.

Bottom Line: Lots of nice features for the money, and presets/digital readout make tuning easier than with analog models. Still, this is a pretty marginal performer.

New for 1993
★ ½   ¢

SEG Precision World SED 110

Price: $33.50, including shipping, in the United States; Y142, about $26, in China.

Advantages: Unusually small for a compact. Inexpensive. Receives longwave band. Comes with twin earpieces.

Disadvantages: No digital frequency display. Limited coverage of world band spectrum. Mediocre sensitivity to weak signals, adjacent-channel rejection (selectivity) and spurious-signal (image) rejection. Coarse frequency readout. Lacks power lock, a drawback for traveling. No dial illumination. No AC power supply. No meaningful signal-strength indicator.

Bottom Line: Okay for now-and-then listening on trips, especially if you travel ultra-light.

Evaluation of New Model: The SEG Precision World SED 110 is nearly a mini, making it appropriate for those who travel with as little luggage as possible. World band coverage is

The SEG Precision World SED 110 is small enough to be attractive for traveling.

reasonably complete between 5.88-21.85 MHz, albeit with major "holes" in the important 9.4 to 9.5, 12.0-12.1 and 15.6-15.7 MHz ranges. Too, it doesn't cover much of the forthcoming new 1605-1705 kHz AM band

extension for the Americas. However, it does cover FM and longwave.

Frequency readout is coarse, indeed, being off by as much as 50 kHz—ten channels. There's no power lock, a drawback for traveling. The telescopic antenna, like all those on cheap portables, swivels, but does not rotate, which is unhandy. However, the radio does come equipped with a pair of "in-the-ear" earpieces—even though FM is monaural only, not stereo as such earpieces might suggest.

Performance is elementary: mediocre everything, from sensitivity to selectivity to image rejection. Audio quality, while tough to endure over long periods, is at least equal to that on a number of mini-portables tested over the years.

The SEG Precision World SED 110 won't hack it at home. Yet, it makes one of the best throwaway portables for taking on trips for casual listening, especially if you plan to tune the 13 MHz band. If it's lost or stolen, who cares? And it makes a nice gift if you don't care to bring it back home. The biggest drawback for traveling DXers is that it doesn't pick up tropical stations, those found between 2.3-5.1 MHz.

World Band Flashlight

Here's something that seems aimed right at the Boy Scout who has everything: the Grundig Explorer II, $54.50 in the United States. It's a world band radio, cassette player, FM, mediumwave AM . . . and flashlight and siren.

The flashlight lights, and the electronic siren shrieks loud enough to be of some use in the woods. FM and mediumwave AM performance are reasonable, and the cassette, although it lacks reverse, works okay.

Tuning world band, though, is akin to playing on a Ouija board. The analog readout shows only meter bands—from 49 to 16. There's no fine tuning, so a segment with dozens of stations has to be tuned over a mere quarter-inch range—a few millimeters. It's like threading needles to tune in a station, and as there's no real readout you have to listen patiently to divine which station you've got. When you take your hand off the case, the radio tends to drift off-channel. Poof! The station you labored so long to tune in is gone.

World band performance isn't much better. Sensitivity to weak signals is poor, adjacent-channel rejection (selectivity) awful. Yet, powerful stations in the clear can sound pleasant. Unfortunately, there aren't many such stations to be found.

As a toy for outdoor-loving kids? Sure. Otherwise, forget it.

Grundig's Explorer flashlight/radio offers everything but performance.

New for 1993
★ ½

(Precision World)

Price: Y138, about $25, in China.
Comment: Not tested, but appears to be essentially identical to the tested SEG Precision World SED 110 except that it lacks coverage of 22 meters and longwave. This model has no designation on the box or radio itself other than "Precision World," so don't confuse it with other products sold under that name.

Magnavox AE 3205 GY (Philips AE 3205 GY)

Price: $69.95 in the United States.
Advantages: Receives longwave band.
Disadvantages: No digital frequency display. Adjacent-channel rejection (selectivity) poor. Mediocre spurious-signal ("image") rejection. Limited world band coverage, omits important 13 and 21 MHz segments. Antenna swivels, but does not rotate. Dial not illuminated. No meaningful signal-strength indicator. Mediumwave AM coverage stops at roughly 1620 kHz, eight channels shy of American AM band's forthcoming upper limit. No AC power supply.
Bottom Line: Okay for taking on trips, but there are clearly better choices for the price.

The Panashiba FX-928, one to avoid.

★

Panashiba FX-928 (Shiba Electronics FX-928)

Price: $29.95-39.95 plus around $5.00 shipping when it was available in the United States.
Advantages: Cheap. Receives longwave band.
Disadvantages: No digital frequency display. Adjacent-channel rejection (selectivity) poor. Mediocre spurious-signal ("image") rejection. Lackluster sensitivity to weak signals. Limited world band coverage, omits important 13 MHz segment and 12010-12095 kHz portion of 11 MHz segment. Mediocre automatic-gain control (AGC) causes wide disparity in volume from signal-to-signal. Volume slider control touchy to adjust. Antenna swivels, but does not rotate. Quality of construction appears to be below average. Batteries awkward to install. Dial not illuminated. Dial calibration off as much as 85 kHz. No meaningful signal-strength indicator. Mediumwave AM coverage stops at roughly 1620 kHz, eight channels shy of American AM band's forthcoming upper limit. No AC power supply.
Bottom Line: You can't find it and you don't want it. Not seen for sale anywhere in recent months, but possibly still being offered here and there under who-knows-what brand designation.

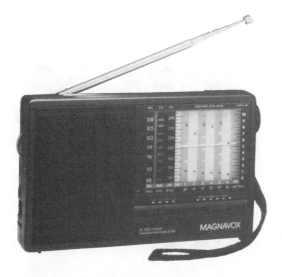

Magnavox's AE 3205 GY, also sold under the Philips label, is priced and sized for the budget traveler.

★

Cougar H-88 (Precision World SED 901)

Price: *Cougar:* $49.95 in the United States, $40-70 in Europe (EC); *Precision World:* Y140 (about $25) in China.

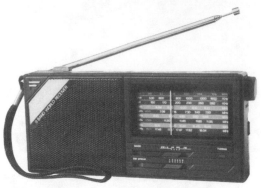

The Cougar H-88, also sold as the Precision World SED 901, isn't worth the money.

Advantages: Inexpensive. Receives longwave band.

Disadvantages: No digital frequency display. Limited world band coverage. Mediocre adjacent-channel and spurious-signal ("image") rejection. Modest sensitivity to weak signals. Tuning knob somewhat stiff. Power switch easily activated by accident, as when radio packed on trips. No dial illumination. No meaningful signal-strength indicator. No AC power supply. Not known to be widely distributed in any country.

Bottom Line: Tinker's toy. Possibly available under other brand designations.

Opal OP-35
(Grundig Traveller II)
(Siemens RK 702)

Price: *Opal:* Under $70 in the United States; *Grundig:* $99.95, but has sold for up to $119.95, CAN$99.95 in Canada; *Siemens:* $75-160 in Europe (EC).

Advantages: Includes novel World Time and worldwide multi-country clock/timer, what Opal calls the "World Time Handy Humane Wake System." *Opal:* Relatively inexpensive. *Grundig:* Comes with stereo earpieces, even though radio is not stereo.

Disadvantages: No digital frequency display. World band coverage limited to 6, 7, 9, 11 and 15 MHz segments. Inferior adjacent-channel rejection (selectivity) makes for unpleasant listening. Poor spurious-signal ("image") rejection in both in world band and mediumwave AM band. Modest weak-signal sensitivity. Can drift off frequency when held. No signal-strength indicator. Does not receive longwave band. No AC power supply.

Bottom Line: Clock in drag.

Dog of the Year: Windsor 2138, also sold as the Silver International MT-798. Torture for the ears.

New for 1993
★

Windsor 2138
(Silver International MT-798)

Price: *Windsor:* $34.99, including shipping, in the United States; *Silver:* SIN$19-22 (about $11.50-13.50) in Singapore. Aspirin extra.

Advantages: Cheap.

Disadvantages: Everything—no digital frequency display, rank distortion, horribly tinny audio, awful adjacent-channel rejection (selectivity), poor rejection of spurious signals ("images"), mediocre sensitivity to weak signals.

Bottom Line: Great gift for your worst enemy.

Evaluation of New Model: The Windsor 2138 covers longwave, mediumwave AM and FM, plus world band from roughly 5.83-6.25, 7.07-7.55, 9.44-9.94, 11.35-11.96, 15.1-15.56 and 17.45-18 MHz (49, 41, 31, 25, 19 and 16 meters). Omitted are 22, 13 and 11 meters; tropical segments below 5.1 MHz;

Grundig's Traveller II is the latest incarnation of the Opal OP-35, but with twin earpieces added. No stereo, though.

and such useful world-band ranges as 9.39-9.44 and 11.96-12.1 MHz.

This mediocre roster is nothing compared to performance—or lack of it. Sensitivity to weak signals is mediocre, while image rejection and adjacent-channel rejection are downright awful. More ghastly yet is the audio. It's arguably the tinniest, most-distorted sound we've ever encountered in 16 years of testing world band radios.

Worst of the worst.

MID-SIZED PORTABLES

Good for Home, Fair for Travel

If you're looking for a home set, but also one that can be taken out in the backyard and on the occasional trip, here's where to look. These are large enough to perform well and can sound pretty good, yet are compact enough to tote in your suitcase now and then. Most take 3-4 "D" (UM-1) cells, plus a couple of "AA" (UM-3) cells for their fancy computer circuits.

How large? Typically just under a foot wide—that's 30 cm—and weighing in around 3-4 pounds, or 1.3-1.8 kg. For air travel, that's okay if you are a dedicated listener, but a bit much otherwise. Too, larger sets with snazzy controls occasionally attract unwanted attention from suspicious customs and airport-security personnel.

Three stand out: the high-tech Sony ICF-2010, also sold as the ICF-2001D; Grundig's sleek new Satellit 700; and the much cheaper Sangean ATS-803A, also sold under other names. The mid-priced Sony is the obvious choice for radio enthusiasts, whereas the costlier Grundig should appeal to the larger body of regular listeners to world band, FM and mediumwave AM stations. The Sangean is the best buy if you feel the others are outside your financial bounds.

★ ★ ★ ½   *Editor's Choice*

| Sony ICF-2010 |
| Sony ICF-2001D |
| (Sony ICF-2001DS) |

Price: *ICF-2010:* $449.95 in the United States, CAN$499 in Canada; *ICF-2001D:* £279.95 in the United Kingdom, $500-950 elsewhere in Europe (EC), AUS$899.00 in Australia.

Advantages: High-tech synchronous selectable sideband reduces adjacent-channel interference and fading distortion on world band, longwave and mediumwave AM signals; it also provides superior reception of reduced-carrier single-sideband signals. Use of 32 separate preset buttons in neat rows and columns is ergonomically the best to be found—simply pushing one button brings in your station. Numerous other helpful tuning features. Two bandwidths offer superior tradeoff between audio fidelity and adjacent-channel rejection (selectivity). Tunes in precise 0.1 kHz increments. Separately displayed World Time clock. Alarm/sleep features, with superior four-event timer. Illuminated LCD. Travel power lock. Signal-strength indicator. Covers Japanese FM band. Some reception of air band signals (most versions). AC power supply. In Europe (EC), available for £319.95 in a special "ICF-2001DS" or "kit" version supplied with Sony AN-1 amplified antenna. Elsewhere, the AN-1 may be purchased separately for around $90.

Disadvantages: Controls and high-tech features, although exceptionally handy once you get the hang of them, initially may intimidate or confuse. Presets and clock/timer features sometimes erase when set is jostled. Wide bandwidth somewhat broad for world band reception. Audio quality only average, with mediocre tone control. Chugs a bit when tuned. First RF transistor (Q-303) reportedly prone to damage by static electricity, as from nearby lightning strikes, when used with external wire antenna (such antennas should be disconnected with the approach of snow, sand, dry-wind or thunder storms); or when amplified (active) antennas other than Sony AN-1 are used. Telescopic antenna swivel gets slack with use, as do those of most less-costly models, requiring periodic adjustment of tension screw. Keypad not in telephone format.

World's best affordable portable: Sony's exceptional ICF-2010, also sold as the ICF-2001D.

The Present and Promise of World Band Cassette Recorders

Many do it daily: record television programs on VCRs so they can be enjoyed at a more convenient time. You'd think that with world band radio sales rising for several years now, history would repeat itself, and there would be a number of world band cassette recorders—WCRs—from which to choose.

Not so. There are a number of "boom box" recorders and the like with some crude coverage of the shortwave spectrum. But there are few worthy world band radios available with recorders built in.

Best Bet: Sangean ATS-818CS

Sangean has helped ameliorate matters with its new digitally tuned $329.00 ATS-818CS WCR—$329.00 in the United States, CAN$429.95 in Canada and AUS$399.00 in Australia. It's one-event, so you can't record more than one time automatically, and even then it can be programmed for only one given day. Too, while you can set the recording "on" time, it shuts off automatically only when the tape runs out.

The '818CS is the same as the new two-and-a-half-star ATS-818—for performance details, see the review of the '818 elsewhere in this section—but with a cassette deck added and a smaller speaker cavity. Recording features are bare-bones (no level indicator, no counter, no stereo) but there is a condenser microphone. The fast-forward and rewind controls are inverted from the customary positions, so the indicator arrows are backwards—fast forward points left, rewind points right. Still, recording quality is acceptable, and the limited timing facility works as it should.

Sangean's ATS-818CS is no high-tech wonder, but it is, hands down, the best WCR on the market. It's also available for £199.00 in the United Kingdom as the Roberts RC818, and in Germany with factory preprogrammed stations as the Siemens RK 670.

Sangean's ATS-818CS is easily the best world band cassette recorder on the market.

Pedestrian Offerings from Sony

Other, lesser, choices include Sony's pricey WA-8000MKII and WA-8800, £199 in the United Kingdom, ¥50,000 in Japan—that is, about $325-375. (Prices within Continental Europe are, as usual, higher.) Each comes with an auto-reverse stereo cassette recorder and microphone, FM stereo, and stereo speakers. There's also a World Time clock with alarm, sleep and timer features.

Performance? Two stars, at best, with superior sensitivity to weak signals and spurious-signal ("image") rejection. However, adjacent-channel rejection (selectivity) is only average, and there's no digital frequency display or presets. Without presets, the ability to record different stations automatically at different times—multi-event recording—is unrealized.

The rub for Americans: No Sony WCR is available in the United States or Canada, except perhaps on the gray market. Yanks and Canadians thus have to ferret them out at electronic and airport shops abroad.

Bottom Line: Still the Big Enchilada for radiophiles, and fairly priced for all it does so well. Except for pedestrian audio quality and FM, plus the learning curve, Sony's high-tech offering remains, by a bit, the best performing travel-weight portable—regardless of where you are—and its use of separate pushbuttons for each preset makes station call-up easier than with virtually any other radio tested. Its synchronous selectable sideband, which works as it should, not only reduces distortion but also, as one reader aptly puts it, offers the adjacent-channel rejection (selectivity) of a narrow filter with the fidelity of a wide filter.

Note: This model reportedly has been scheduled to be dropped from the Sony line for some time now. Yet—thankfully—it continues to be produced for at least some markets, including North America. Sony of America has not responded to our inquiries, so there is no way of knowing what the future is for this receiver.

 An *RDI WHITE PAPER* is available for this model.

Grundig's Mediocre Cosmopolit Features Clever Design

In a lesser league, yet, of performance is the $249.95 Grundig Cosmopolit—£95.00 in the United Kingdom, CAN$299.95 in Canada. It's cleverly constructed to be as small as possible, with the radio's dial serving as the cover for the cassette cavity.

The Cosmo, made in Indonesia, comes with a digital clock that operates from either the 24- or 12-hour standard. But for tuning, there's only an analog needle-and-dial with one-event recording. World band coverage, reasonably adequate, is from about 5850-6300, 7000-7500, 9400-10000, 11500-12150, 13450-13950, 15050-15700 and 17400-18100 kHz.

The Cosmo doesn't offer keypad tuning, presets or any other advanced tuning aids. Its lone tuning device, a thumbwheel, is stiff. There's no travel power lock switch, and—incredible at this price—the telescopic antenna doesn't rotate at its swivel.

World band performance is mediocre. Sensitivity, adjacent-channel rejection (selectivity) and audio quality are only fair, and spurious-signal ("image") rejection is downright poor. In all, this comes across as a $90 radio, which is hardly surprising: Except for the recorder and clock/timer, that's just about what it is. Give Grundig's overpriced Cosmo one cheer, or one-and-a-half stars.

The Cosmopolit is imaginatively designed, but lacks much in the way of recent technology.

Sony's Uninspiring WA-6000 Passes Muster . . . If You Can Find It

Something cheaper? Most other available choices are dreadful. An uninspiring, but passable, alternative is the Sony WA-6000. Its coverage of the world band spectrum is limited, as is its performance. For world band, it barely musters one-and-a-half stars.

The WA-6000, not offered in North America and not often found elsewhere, either, sells for just under half as much as the Sony WA-8000 and WA-8800.

Sony's ICF-SW55—Another Solution

Sony's new ICF-SW55, reviewed in this section, nominally can turn certain models of Sony recorders on and off. The '55 has five-event timing features, albeit daily only, making it a more useful performer than any single-package WCR currently on the market. Still, two devices are more cumbersome than one, and the cost of both is a further deterrent. Grundig's new Satellit 700 nominally has similar capabilities, but an even stiffer price tag.

Grundig Satellit 700, one of the very best for 1993.

New for 1993

★ ★ ★ ½   *Editor's Choice*

Grundig Satellit 700

Price: $799.00 in the United States, CAN$799.00 in Canada, £349.99 in the United Kingdom.

Advantages: Superior audio quality, aided by separate continuous bass and treble controls. High-tech synchronous detector circuit with selectable sideband reduces adjacent-channel interference and fading distortion on world band, longwave and mediumwave AM signals; it also provides superior reception of reduced-carrier single-sideband signals. Two bandwidths offer superior tradeoff between audio fidelity and adjacent-channel rejection. 512 presets standard; up to 2048 presets optionally available. Schedules for 22 stations stored by factory in memory. Stored station names appear on LCD. Numerous other helpful tuning features. Tunes in precise 0.1 kHz increments in synchronous and single-sideband modes; this, along with a fine-tuning clarifier, produce the best tuning configuration for single sideband in a conventional travel-weight portable. Separately displayed World Time clock. Alarm/sleep features with superior timer. Superb FM reception. Stereo FM through headphones. Superior mediumwave AM reception. Illuminated LCD, which is clearly visible from a variety of angles. Travel power lock. Runs off AC power worldwide. RDS circuitry for European FM station selection—eventually North America, too—by program format. Excellent operator's manuals.

Disadvantages: Chugs annoyingly when tuned slowly by knob; mutes completely when tuned quickly. Relatively complex memory operation. Synchronous selectable sideband circuit produces rumble and has relatively little sideband separation. Excessive overall distortion except in AM mode. Wide bandwidth slightly broad for world band reception. Keypad lacks feel and is not in telephone format. Antenna keels over in certain settings.

Bottom Line: Right up there with the very best in portables, and for many regular program listeners simply the very best. Withal, especially for bandscanning, not all it could be.

Evaluation of New Model: The regular version of the 700 covers longwave, mediumwave AM and world band from 150 kHz to 30 MHz, as well as FM from 87.5-108 MHz. (The "Italia" version skips 1612-3949 and 26101-30000 kHz.) AM, LSB, USB and synchronous sideband selectable modes are included, as well as FM mono and stereo. The 700 operates from four "D" cells or an outboard worldwide 110-127/220-240V AC power supply that is shipped with the radio. A charging circuit for NiCd cells is built in. The owner's manual claims 90-110 hours' battery life with alkaline cells, or around 25 hours per NiCd charge.

On the face of the 700 is a helpful LCD that, unlike those on most other models, is clearly visible from a variety of angles. It shows various items of information, including both the frequency and World Time simultaneously, plus station name for stored frequencies. The keypad software works nicely, but the keys are not in the standard telephone configuration. There are some 18 other keys, many of which are multifunction.

On the right end of the case is a tuning knob with dimple, a nigh-useless automatic gain control adjustment, an external 50-ohm antenna connector, a clarifier for fine tuning single-sideband signals, a signal-strength attenuator (LOCAL/DX), and a switch for choosing between internal and external antennas. That coaxial external antenna connector, by the way, conforms to a European standard. Other connectors don't appear to fit, so North Americans wanting an external antenna will have to search about to find a suitable European plug.

Mortised neatly into the left end of the case are separate knobs for treble, bass and the volume control. There's also a lock switch to prevent the power from coming on accidentally during trips, and a series of external connectors: left and right line out, external power supply, headphones, loudspeaker and a useful switched output for controlling a tape recorder. Since the tuning knob is on one side and the volume control on the other, operating the 700 is a two-handed affair that keeps you unnecessarily "glued" to your receiver.

On the back is a flip-down prop, which "unflips" too easily, for holding the 700 at a convenient angle on a tabletop, and a hatch for inserting batteries. Atop the receiver is a handy flip-up carrying handle and a commendably robust telescopic antenna. That antenna, if not set to one of four 90-degree rotational detent positions, tends to keel over, like falling timber. On the bottom of the case are metric screw mounts for mobile or maritime operation, and a hatch that opens to reveal removable read-only memory (ROM) chips . . . but more about this later.

The kilobuck Grundig Satellit 650 and predecessor 600, both now discontinued, produced the best audio quality of any world band receiver in their time or since. The 700 is not really in that same league, but its audio, although a bit bassy, is definitely above par both through the built-in speaker and headphones. FM stereo is also available through the headphones—the 700 has only one speaker—and a pair of "line out" sockets can feed an external audio system or speakers. Too, there's Radio Data System (RDS) circuitry to allow European, and eventually American, FM listeners to choose stations by program format.

Even weak world band, as well as FM and mediumwave AM, stations tend to be more readable and sound better on the 700 than on the vast majority of other models, including costly tabletops. This is true both within the international band segments, where the BBC and such reign, and the static-plagued tropical segments that are home to myriad little stations in Latin America and beyond. It's this important aural plus, more than anything else, that can make the 700 preferable to such alternatives as Sony's ICF-2010/ICF-2001D.

Yet, in one way the 700's audio is not quite up to what it sounds like at first. In the AM mode, *Passport's* laboratory tests reveal overall distortion of 6% at 100 Hz, a mediocre showing. Other measurements at 200, 400, 1000 and 2500 Hz produce excellent-to-superb results which, along with the 700's continuous bass and treble controls, pretty much rescue the situation.

However, overall distortion does not drop when synchronous selectable sideband is used, even though reduction of distortion is one of the primary purposes of that feature. Rather, it gets *worse*: 15% at 100 and 200 Hz, and 8% at 400 Hz.

Conventional single-sideband reception shows a whopping 30% overall distortion at 100 Hz and 15% at 200 Hz. This is virtually the worst we've encountered on any radio. From Grundig, which has earned a reputation for outstanding audio quality, this comes as quite a surprise.

Distortion, even that which is virtually undetectable to the human ear, results in

Coming Up in Passport/94 . . .

Here are some of the forthcoming portables you can expect to see reviewed in the 1994 edition of *Passport to World Band Radio* . . .

Grundig, which heretofore has had its main strength in the high-end market, plans to enter the mid-priced digitally tuned market in 1993 with the Satellit 303 (around $199) and Satellit 404 (about $299). With those Peugeot-like model numbers, is a Satellit 505 in the offing, too?

Philips, often sold in North America as Magnavox, adds the analog AE 3405GY ($89.95), digital AE 3625 ($119.95) and digital AE 3905 ($349.95).

Sangean, often also sold under other brand names, expects to have its ATS-606 ready for introduction at the American Consumer Electronics Show in Las Vegas. It's billed by the manufacturer as being a smaller version of the current ATS-808, but with more advanced timer functions and a backlight for the LCD. Price? Likely $119-129, incredibly low if it's all it is made out to be.

Radio Shack plans to expand its Realistic line of world band radios with two small analog units: the DX-342 ($69.95) and the DX-343 ($89.95).

The clock and watch firm of Casio is poised to be initiated into the world band market with a compact portable having—what else?—a digital clock.

Finally, "For the People," a populist program aired over U.S. station WWCR (see "Addresses PLUS"), hopes to introduce a Pennsylvania-made world band radio before early 1993. Price is targeted at under $150.

Sangean ATS-606.

premature listening fatigue. It's a bit like sitting in an over-padded recliner chair. At first it may seem billowy and comfortable, but after several hours, you feel achy. Radios with low levels of distortion tend to offer hour-after-hour listening pleasure. Radios with high levels of distortion do not.

Fortunately, relatively few world band listeners care about the single-sideband mode, used by hams and such. For them, especially if they make little use of the synchronous mode, the distortion issue is essentially moot.

In our other lab tests, the 700 generally fares relatively well. Sensitivity, image rejection, blocking and phase noise measurements are all good, with first IF rejection being excellent. All of these point to a quality receiver, which is hardly surprising. Dynamic range is only fair, sometimes even poor—again, hardly surprising in a portable, where circuits to increase dynamic range also tend to increase battery consumption. This is why portables tend to "overload" under certain conditions, such as if a substantial external antenna is used.

The 700 has two bandwidths to help in selecting the right tradeoff of audio fidelity and rejection of interfering stations. The 700's "wide" bandwidth is somewhat broad, although less so than that of, say, the Sony ICF-2010/2001D. Both the narrow and wide bandwidths have excellent skirt selectivity.

In the AM mode, the receiver tunes only in 1 kHz steps, which cause it to chug annoyingly. If you are trying to tune about to hear what's on, you'll find bandscanning in-CHUG-ter-CHUG-rup-CHUG-ted by the synthesizer. Tuning is in more precise 100 Hz increments in the sideband and synchronous modes, but it still chugs.

Worse, if you turn the dial more briskly the entire tuning circuit mutes so that you hear nary a station. In all, for dialing around to see what's on—bandscanning—the 700 earns a goose egg.

Better news is that tuning with the keypad, which lacks "feel," is almost the soul of simplicity. If you want 6175 kHz, just enter 6, 1, 7, 5, press the Frequency/M-band button, and there you are. Operating the rest of the 700 is not always that simple. Pressing the MENU button invokes a series of commands, which may be selected using the SEARCH/SELECT up/down button. Items controlled include two handy timers, a memory copy function, dim backlight for the LCD (the keypad backlight, found on the recently discontinued Satellit 500, is gone, however), beep and 9/10 kHz mediumwave AM tuning. The relative complexity of operating this receiver is implied by the fully 17 different error messages which can appear on the LCD.

To Grundig's credit, the 700's operating manual is one of the best, and is supplemented by a helpful "get going quickly" mini-manual. Both are clearly written, well illustrated and never leave the user in doubt about what to do next. That's important, because there are functions of the 700 that even seasoned veterans of world band are unlikely to divine offhand. To ensure there's no confusion, for Americans there's a special pamphlet that explains European terms and norms used in the manuals, which are prepared in Germany.

For example, the North American version of the 700 has 120 frequencies for 22 radio stations prestored in ROM chips. To access them, you have to enter one of a series of codes, such as 0.1, then press the MEMORY/FILE button. This brings up a memory file with preset frequencies for, say, Deutsche Welle, with "DW" appearing in the alphanumeric display. Pressing the MEMO-AF button accesses the various frequencies that appear in the DW file. Press the MEMORY SCAN up/down button, and the memory files for other world band stations appear. Because these memory files are not likely to be discovered without a manual, the 700 comes with a wallet-sized card listing prestored memory files and their codes.

Because world band stations come and go

Converter Plug for Most Countries

When traveling abroad, most of us simply use batteries to fire up our radios. Yet, larger portables can gobble up batteries, making wall sockets look tempting, indeed. But first, you need a plug that fits, or a suitable converter plug. Franzus, Radio Shack and others sell these, but when you travel widely you have to take along several types.

Now there's a single "do-it-all" plug converter, the Globetrotter International Adaptor. It works as it should, provided it is used *only* with nongrounded appliances. Fortunately, virtually no world band radio requires electrical grounding.

We purchased ours for $32.95, including shipping, from Markline, Box 1058, Elmira NY 14902 USA. The Globetrotter is also available direct from the manufacturer, Traveller International Products Ltd., 51 Haysmews, London W1, United Kingdom.

on the same frequency at different times of the day, the stations preset at the factory present a problem—any given frequency at any one time may not be what it is labeled. For example, when we paged through the frequencies for Radio Nederland, none was active. Later, there was a "live" one which turned out to be not Radio Nederland, but Radio Moscow International. The only way around this potential confusion is to tie each frequency into the active times for each individual station on a frequency. However, schedules change often enough to make this approach impractical beyond a certain point.

If you are not satisfied with the prestored station information, the 700's user manual includes more than six pages of instructions on how to create your own alphanumeric memory files, right down to how to copy information from one memory chip to another. The 700 is packed with numerous sophisticated memory functions, so you really need this manual to access them to full effect.

The 700 is one of a handful of world band portable and tabletop receivers equipped with synchronous selectable sideband. This high-tech feature, when it works properly, improves listening by doing away with most distortion caused by fading. It strips away the station's carrier, weary and knock-kneed from its long journey to your radio, and inserts a substitute carrier of relatively steady local quality generated within the receiver itself. Further, to fight interference from adjacent channels, synchronous selectable sideband allows you to choose either the lower or upper sideband for whichever sounds better.

The 700's synchronous circuit is operated similarly to that on the Sony ICF-2010/2001D. Pressing the SYNCH button on the 700 brings up the upper sideband. To get to the lower sideband, turn the tuning knob toward a slightly lower frequency until the LSB indicator appears. This arrangement is okay, but not quite so handy as that of the new Sony ICF-SW77.

Although the 700's "sync" circuit operates similarly to that of the ICF-2010/2001D, it doesn't perform in the same league. To begin with, when the 700's sync circuit is switched in, the station begins to "gurgle" or "rumble," and no amount of fine tuning gets rid of it. Too, unwanted sideband rejection is only 16 dB. Sony's equivalent circuit produces virtually no such audible degradation, and has sideband suppression of a more respectable 24 dB—about as good as can be expected from phase cancellation.

Although most world band listeners rarely tune single-sideband signals, hams and others who do will find the 700's single-sideband tuning system to be superior to anything else on the conventional portable market. To complement the receiver's 100 Hz tuning increments, there is an analog clarifier to make tuning spot-on. That clarifier even has a center detent to make operation handier.

Overall, the Grundig Satellit 700 is a top-of-the-line portable having superior world band audio, packed with sophisticated features and promising great potential. In many ways it succeeds, and it's certainly a healthy step forward over the earlier Satellit 500. Yet, certain imperfections prevent the 700 from being all that it could have been.

★ ★ ★   *Editor's Choice*

Sangean ATS-803A
(Clairtone PR-291)
(Eska RX 33)
(Matsui MR-4099)
(Quelle Universum)
(Siemens RK 651)
(TMR 7602 Hitech Tatung)

Price: *Sangean:* $249.00 in the United States, CAN$299.95 in Canada, £109.95 in the United Kingdom, $150-330 in Europe (EC), AUS$269.00 in Australia; *Clairtone:* CAN$229.95 in Canada; *Eska:* Dkr. 1995 (about $315) in Denmark; *Matsui:* $160-220 in Europe (EC); *Quelle Universum:* $180-250 in Europe(EC); *Siemens:* $180-250 in Europe(EC); *Tatung:* under £110 in the United Kingdom.

Advantages: Superior overall world band performance. Numerous tuning features. Two bandwidths for good fidelity/interference tradeoff. Superior spurious-signal ("image") rejection. Superior reception of utility signals for price class. Illuminated display. Signal-strength indicator. World Time clock. Alarm/

An outstanding buy is the Sangean ATS-803A, sold under various names. Large enough for home, small enough for most travel.

sleep/timer. Travel power lock. FM stereo through headphones (usually supplied). Separate bass and treble controls. Receives longwave band. Sangean ATS-803A and most other versions supplied with AC adapter.

Disadvantages: Synthesizer chugs a little. Audio only slightly above average. Clock not displayed separately from frequency, disables keypad when displayed. Keypad not in telephone format.

Bottom Line: A dollar cigar for 75 cents. An excellent model for getting started, provided all the features don't intimidate. If they do, look over the simpler Panasonic RF-B45.

New for 1993
★ ★ ½

Realistic DX-390
Sangean ATS-818

Price: *Realistic:* $239.95 plus #273-1454 AC power supply at Radio Shack stores in the United States, CAN$299.95 plus #273-1454 AC power supply in Canada, AUS$399.95 plus #273-1454 AC power supply in Australia; *Sangean:* $299.00 in the United States, CAN$399.95 in Canada.

Advantages: Superior overall world band performance. Numerous tuning features. Two bandwidths for good fidelity/interference tradeoff. Superior spurious-signal ("image") rejection. Illuminated display. Signal-strength indicator. World Time clock displayed separately from frequency. Alarm/sleep/timer. Travel power lock. FM stereo through headphones. Receives longwave band. Sangean version supplied with AC adapter. *Realistic:* 30-day money-back trial period.

Disadvantages: Mutes when tuning knob turned, making bandscanning difficult. Key-

Realistic's new DX-390 is Radio Shack's top model.

pad not in telephone format. Does not come with tape-recorder jack. *Realistic:* AC power supply extra.

Bottom Line: A decent, predictable radio—performance and features, alike—but mediocre for bandscanning.

Evaluation of New Model: Sangean's new ATS-818, also sold as the Realistic DX-390, covers FM stereo (via earphones only, although earphones aren't supplied), plus longwave, AM and all world band through 29999 kHz. Tuning and frequency readout can be as fine as in 1 kHz increments. Helpful tuning features include a knob, keypad (excellent feel, but not in standard telephone format), up/down slewing and some scanning—plus 45 presets, of which 18 are for world band.

Withal, there is a fly in the tuning ointment. In order to cope with the tendency of synthesized tuning circuits to chug, a muting circuit has been included. Yes, it gets rid of the chug-a-chug noise when the tuning knob is turned, but it also gets rid of the stations you're trying to hear as you tune along. Turn the tuning knob to dial up or down, and the set goes utterly silent until you stop turning. For bandscanning, this is extremely frustrating.

Single-sideband reception is by a BFO switch and variable-pitch potentiometer—no separate LSB or USB controls. That potentiometer tunes so broadly that it requires a surgeon's skill to adjust, but the result, although clumsy and archaic, is satisfactory.

There is a signal-strength/battery indicator on the LCD, which is backlit. There's also a power lock switch to keep batteries from running down accidentally on trips. Tone is adjusted by a lone control, a step backwards from the separate bass and treble controls found on the venerable and in many other ways similar Sangean ATS-803A portable.

There are also dual bandwidths, sleep-off and a 24-hour clock/timer with two time zones. World Time can be displayed regardless of whether the radio is on or off, a helpful touch.

The '818 is a typical performer for its price class. Sensitivity to weak signals, an important variable in the central and western parts of North America, as well as Australia and New Zealand, is good but not outstanding. Audio quality, not quite what you might expect from a set of this size, is adequate—even though it can be a bit "hissy" at times.

Adjacent-channel rejection (selectivity) in the wide position is rather broad, but adequate for receiving a good many signals without undue interference. The narrow position fares much better—it's well-chosen for when interference rears its head.

In all, this is a well-rounded, if noninnovative, performer. Bandscanners, though, should look to the sibling Sangean ATS-803A.

FULL-SIZED PORTABLES

Very Good for Home,
Poor for Travel

Let's call big portables tabletop-type models that run off batteries—usually several "D" (UM-1) cells, plus some "AA" (UM-3) cells for their computer circuitry. Real tabletop models, however, have the advantage of lying flat, and thus are better suited for everyday home use. Real tabletop models also provide more performance for the money.

Some full-sized portables weigh as much as a stuffed suitcase, and are almost as large. Take one on a worldwide air excursion and you should have your head examined. The first customs or security inspector that sees your radio will probably do it for you.

None of the present full-sized portable crop really excites. However, the Sony CRF-V21 is full of techy goodies.

Sony's beefy CRF-V21 is the best portable, overall, but five-star tabletop models perform better for far less money.

★ ★ ★ ½

Sony CRF-V21

Price: $6,500.00 in the United States, £2,699 in the United Kingdom, $4,500-6,500 elsewhere in Europe (EC).

Advantages: Superior overall world band performance. High-tech synchronous detector circuit with selectable sideband cuts adjacent-channel interference and fading distortion on world band, longwave band and mediumwave AM band. Two bandwidths mean superior tradeoff between audio fidelity and adjacent-channel rejection. Helpful tuning features, including 350 presets. Unusually straightforward keypad. Processes off-the-air narrow-band FM, RTTY (radio teletype) and fax. Covers longwave down to 9 kHz, as well as four satellite fax frequencies. Liquid-crystal video display for various functions, including frequency, station name (in preset mode), separately displayed World Time/Day, and RTTY. Display doubles as spectrum monitor. Built-in thermal printer allows print-screen and fax hard-copy with very high resolution. World Time/Day clock displays seconds numerically. Alarm/sleep/timer/scanner/activity-search can also do hands-off spectrum surveys. Tunes and displays in precise 10 Hz increments. World's best tuning knob, a

pure delight. Best portable, barely, for ham and utility signals. Superior weak-signal sensitivity, plus blocking, AGC threshold, dynamic range, ultimate rejection, skirt selectivity, phase noise, spurious-signal ("image") rejection, IF rejection and stability. Very low audio distortion in the AM and synchronous-detection modes. Illuminated display. Precise signal-strength indicator. Amplified antenna, which may be placed up to 15 feet, or 4.5 meters, away. Receives Japanese FM broadcasts. Worldwide AC power supply and rechargeable NiCd battery pack. Except for U.S. version, comes with RS-232C port for computer interface.

Disadvantages: Expensive. Complex and generally not user-friendly. Mediocre ergonomics. Video display lacks contrast, very hard to read. Size, weight and no fixed telescopic antenna seriously mar portable operation. Wide bandwidth setting a bit broad for world band. Audio only average. Tuning knob rates are either too slow or too fast. Flip-over night light ineffective—and easily mistaken for carrying handle, and thus broken. Slow-sweep spectrum-occupancy display not real-time. Two of three spectrum-occupancy slices too wide for shortwave use, and the other so narrow it's barely of any use at all. AGC decay much too fast for single sideband. For premium device, only so-so unwanted-sideband suppression. Mediocre front-end selectivity. Does not decode 50 wpm RTTY, AMTOR or CW.

RS-232C port not supplied with U.S. version, as it does not meet FCC Part 15 spurious-emission requirements; contrary to Sony's earlier suggestion, the missing port cannot be retrofitted.

Bottom Line: A fax-oriented "portable" with more goodies than Dolly Parton. On world band, however, the CRF-V21 in most respects doesn't equal some tabletops costing a fifth as much, and only modestly exceeds the performance of some portables that are cheaper yet. According to one *Passport* reader, Sony's customer technical support for this model is abysmal.

 An *RDI WHITE PAPER* is available for this model.

★ ½

Marc II NR-108F1 (Pan Crusader)

Price: $300-550 worldwide.
Advantages: Unusually broad coverage, from 150 kHz longwave to 520 MHz UHF, plus 850-910 MHz UHF (North American/Japanese version). Many helpful tuning features. World Time clock, displayed separately from frequency. Sleep/timer. Signal-strength indicator. Illuminated display.
Disadvantages: Marginal overall performance within certain portions of world band, including hissing, buzzing, and serious overloading.

Oldies, Some Goodies

The following models reportedly have been discontinued, yet may still be available new at some retail outlets. Cited are typical sale prices in the United States ($) and United Kingdom (£) as *Passport/93* goes to press. Prices elsewhere may differ.

★ ★ ★ ½   *Editor's Choice*
Grundig Satellit 650

World band audio just doesn't get any better than that found on this recently discontinued full-sized, feature-laden model. Great FM and mediumwave AM, too. Should be available from at least some dealers for months to come for under $1,000 or £460.

★ ★ ★ ½   *Editor's Choice*
Grundig Satellit 500

Superior audio quality, FM and mediumwave AM, along with a host of advanced-tuning features, make this a pleasant mid-sized set for listening hour after hour. Should be available from at least some dealers for months to come for under $400, £300 or its equivalent in North America and Europe.

★ ★ ★   *Editor's Choice*
Magnavox D2999 Philips D2999

A fine-sounding receiver that works equally well as a large portable and tabletop. Virtually impossible to find, but a delightful receiver with superior audio quality, FM and world band performance, among other virtues. A few units turn up new here and there, such as in dusty boxes in one Beijing store for Y2,200 (about $400).

★ ★ ★   *Editor's Choice*
Magnavox D2935 Philips D2935

One of the very best affordable portables ever—a junior version of the D2999. Virtually impossible to find, but under $200 when it's available. Grab it—you'll love the audio quality!

★ ★ ★
Sony ICF-2003 (Sony ICF-7600DS) Sony ICF-2002 (Sony ICF-7600D)

George Bush's receiver. Precursors to the current compact Sony ICF-SW7600, they all perform similarly. Under $260, under £140.

The Marc II, also sold as the Pan Crusader, is the worst buy in a world band radio. Priced as a premium model, it performs more poorly than many low-cost radios.

Poor adjacent-channel rejection. Poor spurious-signal ("image") rejection. Poorly performing preselector tuning complicates operation. Excessive battery drain. Mediocre construction quality, including casual alignment. Not widely available.

Bottom Line: Rabbit fur at mink prices.

★

Venturer Multiband (Alconic Series 2959) (Dick Smith D-2832) (Rhapsody Multiband) (Shimasu Multiband) (Steepletone MRB7)

Price: *Basic model:* $79.95-99.95 in the United States, £69.95 in the United Kingdom, AUS$129.00 in Australia; *With cassette player:* $129.95; *With cassette player, stereo audio and digital clock:* $159.00.

★★ ½

Panasonic RF-B40 (Panasonic RF-B40DL) (National B40)

Precursors to the RF-B45 *et al.*, which perform noticeably better. Under $170, around £125.

★★

Sony ICF-7600A (Sony ICF-7600AW)

Similar to the current compact Sony ICF-7601, but 13 MHz coverage omitted. No digital frequency display. Under $100, under £110.

★★   ¢

Sony ICF-4920 (Sony ICF-4900II) (Sony ICF-5100)

Identical in all but styling to the current mini Sony ICF-SW20. No digital frequency display. Under $100, under £80.

★ ½   ¢

Magnavox D1835 (Philips D1835)

Performance nigh identical to current compact Magnavox OD1875BK and Philips OD1875BK. No digital frequency display. Still available occasionally for under $70 or £40, but not in Canada.

★

Panasonic RF-B10 (National B10)

Mini with third-rate performance, no digital frequency display, no 13 MHz coverage. Around $70 or £60; also, AUS$199.00.

★

Philips D2615

Pleasant audio, but miserable performance and you can't tell tuned frequency. Under £60.

The Passport *portable radio review team includes Lawrence Magne, along with Jock Elliott and Tony Jones, with laboratory measurements by Robert Sherwood. Additional research by Lars Rydén, Harlan Seyfer and Craig Tyson, with a tip of the hat to George Ellenberger, J. Michael Graves, Jon Klinedinst and Hugh Waters.*

Thanks to heavy advertising, the Alconic Series 2959 is widely sold under various names. It's a miserable performer.

Advantages: Inexpensive. Covers VHF-TV channels and air/weather bands. Audio at least average. Built-in cassette player (two versions only). Stereo audio (one version only). Digital clock (one version only), displayed separately from frequency. Signal-strength indicator. Rotating ferrite-bar direction finder for mediumwave AM. Built-in AC power supply.

Disadvantages: No acceptable frequency display, so finding a station is a hit-and-miss exercise. World band coverage omits the 2, 3, 13, 15, 17, 21 and 26 MHz segments. Performance inferior in nearly every respect. Does not receive longwave band.

Bottom Line: Pink flamingo. Sold widely throughout North America, Europe (EC) and beyond under various names—or even no advertised name. Assembled in Hong Kong from Chinese-made components.

With radios such as the Electro Brand 2971, you have to hunt and peck to find the station you want—and when you finally find it you may wish you hadn't.

 ★

Electro Brand 2971

Price: $149.95, including cassette player, stereo audio, NiCd batter charger, and digital clock/calendar.

Bottom Line: The Big Radio That Can't. Essentially identical in performance and features to Alconic Series 2959 except for appearance and that Electro Brand is made *and assembled* in the People's Republic of China.

Tabletop Receivers for 1993

For most, a good portable is more than adequate to enjoy the offerings found on world band radio. Others, though, seek something better.

That "better" is a tabletop receiver. Many excel at flushing out the really tough game— faint stations, or those swamped by interference from competing signals. The very best now also provide enhanced-fidelity reception, welcome relief from the aural demerits of shortwave. Still, world band is far from a high-fidelity medium, even with the best of radios. International stations beam over great distances, and you can tell it with your ears.

Tabletop models can be especially useful if you live in a part of the world, such as Central and Western North America, where signals tend to be weak and choppy— a common problem when world band signals have to follow high-latitude paths, paths close to or over the North Pole. To get an idea how much this phenomenon might affect your listening, place a string on a globe (an ordinary map won't do) between where you live and where various signals you like come from. If the string passes near or above latitude 60° N, beware.

Tabletop radios also excel for daytime listening, when signals tend to be weaker, and for listening to stations not beamed to your part of the world. Thanks to the scattering properties of shortwave, you can eavesdrop on some "off-beam" signals, but it's harder.

A good tabletop won't guarantee hearing a favorite daytime or off-beam station, but it will almost certainly help. Tabletops also do unusually well with nonbroadcasting signals, such as ham and utility stations— many of which use single sideband and other specialized transmission modes.

Tabletop models are easily found in certain countries, such as the United States, Canada, the United Kingdom, Germany and Japan, and almost as easily in such places as Australia. At the other extreme, a few countries, such as Saudi Arabia and Singapore, frown upon the importation of tabletop models. That's because tabletops often look like transceivers, which can be used by terrorists and spies. However, when tabletop models are brought in as part of a household's goods, problems are unlikely to arise.

For the most part, tabletop receivers are pricier than portables, and for that extra money you tend to get not only better performance, but also a better-made device. However, what you rarely find in a tabletop is FM, much less FM stereo. This is especially annoying with "portatop" models, as it means if you wish to listen to FM you have to tote a second radio.

Most tabletop models also require, and should have, an outboard antenna. Indeed, *tabletop performance is substantially determined by antenna quality and placement*. A first-rate world band outdoor wire antenna, such as the various models manufactured by Antenna Supermarket and Alpha Delta, usually runs from $60 to $80 in the United

States—a bit more elsewhere. These wire antennas are best, and should be used if at all possible. If not, a short amplified antenna suitable for indoors, and sometimes outdoors when space is at a premium, is the next-best choice. Leading models, such as those made by McKay Dymek and Britain's Datong, go for $130-180 Stateside. Check with the two *RDI White Papers* on antennas for details on performance and installation.

Models new for 1993 are covered at length in this year's Buyer's Guide. Every model, regardless of its introduction year, has taken the various testing hurdles we established and have honed since 1977, when we first started evaluating world band equipment.

Each model is thoroughly tested in the laboratory, using criteria developed especially for the strenuous requirements of world band reception. The receiver then undergoes hands-on evaluation, usually for months, before we begin preparing our detailed internal report. That report, in turn, forms the basis for our findings, summarized in this *Passport* Buyer's Guide.

Our unabridged laboratory and hands-on test results are far too exhaustive to reproduce here. However, for many tabletop models they are available as *Passport's* Radio Database International White Papers—details on price and availability are elsewhere in this book.

When shopping, remember that most tabletop models, unlike portables, are available only from electronics and world band specialty outlets. Most firms that sell, distribute or manufacture world band tabletops support them with service that is incomparably superior to that for portables, and often continues well after the model has been discontinued. Drake, Lowe, Kenwood and Japan Radio have particularly good track records in this regard.

With tabletop receivers, "list" prices are sometimes available, sometimes not, but in any event the spread between "list" and actual selling prices is almost always small. Prices given in this section thus reflect the higher end of actual selling prices. World band tabletop models are virtually unavailable at duty-free shops.

Prices are as of when we go to press and are subject to fluctuation. During the past couple of years prices for tabletop models have tended to hold steady, although Icom prices have moved up.

Receivers are listed in order of suitability for listening to difficult-to-hear world band radio broadcasts, with important secondary consideration being given to audio fidelity and ergonomics.

Unless otherwise stated, all tabletop models have:
- digital frequency synthesis and illuminated display;
- a wide variety of helpful tuning features;
- meaningful signal-strength indication;
- the ability to properly demodulate single-sideband and CW (Morse code); also, with suitable ancillary devices, radioteletype and radiofax; and
- full coverage of at least the 155-29999 kHz (155-26099 kHz within Central Europe) longwave, mediumwave AM and shortwave spectra—including all world band segments.

Unless otherwise stated, all tabletop models do *not*:
- tune the FM broadcast band (87.5-107.9 MHz); and
- come equipped with synchronous selectable sideband.

What *Passport's* Ratings Mean

Star ratings: ★ ★ ★ ★ ★ is best. We award stars solely for overall performance and meaningful features; price, appearance and the like are not taken into account. To facilitate comparison, the same rating system is used for portable models, reviewed elsewhere in this *Passport*. Whether a radio is portable or a tabletop model, a given rating—three stars, say—means essentially the same thing. A star is a star.

For 1993, in order to reflect industry advances in technology and performance, we've stiffened our star-rating criteria, with some models having been dropped by one-half star over what they were or would have been in prior years. We feel this better reflects the realities of today's improved marketplace.

Editor's Choice models are our test team's personal picks of the litter—what we would buy ourselves.

¢ : Denotes a model that costs appreciably less than usual for the level of performance provided.

Models in **(parentheses)** have not been tested by us, but appear to be essentially identical to the model(s) tested.

PROFESSIONAL MONITOR RECEIVERS

Professional shortwave receivers are made, of course, for professional applications, which usually have only some things in common with the needs of world band listening. Realistically, for world band listening there is precious little difference—sometimes none of import—between these pricey receivers and regular tabletop models costing a fraction as much.

Nevertheless, if money is no object you may wish at least to consider these models, along with regular tabletop models, when weighing a purchase decision.

★ ★ ★ ★ ★   *Editor's Choice*

Icom IC-R9000

Price: $5,851.00 in the United States, CAN$6,965.00 in Canada, £4,080.00 in the United Kingdom, AUS$6,399 in Australia.

Advantages: Unusually appropriate for hour-after-hour world band listening. Exceptional tough-signal performance. Flexible, above-average audio for a tabletop model, when used with suitable outboard speaker. Three AM-mode bandwidths. Tunes and displays frequency in precise 0.01 kHz increments. Video display of radio spectrum occupancy. Sophisticated scanner/timer. Extraordinarily broad coverage of radio spectrum. Exceptional assortment of flexible operating controls and sockets. Very good ergonomics. Superb reception of utility and ham signals. Two 24-hour clocks.

Disadvantages: Very expensive. Power supply runs hot. Both AM-mode bandwidths too broad for most world band applications. Both single-sideband bandwidths almost identical. Dynamic range merely adequate. Reliability, especially when roughly handled, may be wanting. Front-panel controls of only average construction quality.

Top performer, by a hair, for catching rare signals is the costly Icom IC-R9000.

Bottom Line: The Icom IC-R9000, with at least one changed AM-mode bandwidth filter—available from world band specialty firms—is right up there with the best-performing models for DX reception of faint, tough signals.

 An *RDI WHITE PAPER* is available for this model.

★ ★ ★ ★ ★   *Editor's Choice*

Japan Radio NRD-93

Price: $6,850.00 in the United States, $6,000 to $10,000 elsewhere.

Advantages: Professional-quality construction with legendary durability to survive around-the-clock use in punishing environments. Uncommonly easy to repair on the spot. Unusually appropriate for hour-after-hour world band listening. Superb all-around performance. Excellent ergonomics and unsurpassed control feel. Above-average audio. Sophisticated optional scanner, tested. Superb reception of utility and ham signals.

Disadvantages: Very expensive. Designed several years ago, so lacks some advanced-technology tuning aids. Distribution limited to Japan Radio offices and a few specialty organizations, such as shipyards.

Bottom Line: Crafted like a watch, but tough as a tank, the Japan Radio NRD-93 is a breed apart. It is a pleasure to operate for band-scanning hour after hour, but its overall performance is not appreciably different from that of some cheaper tabletop models, and because its technology is getting a bit long in the tooth it lacks certain advanced-technology features.

 An *RDI WHITE PAPER* is available for this model.

For ruggedness and quality of construction, nothing approaches the Japan Radio NRD-93.

Lowe's HF-235 is designed for the professional user, but is also purchased by radio enthusiasts.

★ ★ ★ ★

Lowe HF-235/R
(Lowe HF-235/F)
(Lowe HF-235/H)
(Lowe HF-235)

Editor's Note: As the Lowe HF-235 in its various configurations is based on, and in most performance respects is very similar to, the HF-225, the following writeup concentrates on how the '235 differs from the '225.

Price: Up to $2,700.00 in the United States, depending on configuration; CAN$2,995.00 in Canada in some configurations; £1,116.00-1,509.95, depending on configuration, in the United Kingdom.

Advantages over HF-225: Physically and electrically more rugged, including enhanced capability to handle high-voltage signal input. AGC may be switched off. Rack mounting, preferred for most professional applications. Power supply inboard and dual-voltage (110/220V). IF gain. *HF-235/R:* Scan/search and other remote control via personal computer using RS-232C interface. Allows for computer display of receiver data. *HF-235/F:* Fax capability. *HF-235/H:* Enhanced stability.

Disadvantages over HF-225: Larger footprint. Lacks tone control and optional mouse-type remote keypad. Built-in AC power supply nominally not suited to voltages in 120-129V range commonly found in the United States (in practice, however, this may not be a problem). *HF-235/F:* Does not receive lower-sideband signals.

Change for 1993: This and other Lowe receivers are now also available in the United States and Canada, as well as Europe.

Bottom Line: This radio is essentially the highly rated Lowe HF-225 reconfigured for selected professional applications; it's essentially a thrifty, bare-bones surveillance receiver. As such, it offers features some professionals require, but lacks certain niceties for home use and bandscanning. World band listeners and manual-bandscanning professionals are better served by the cheaper Lowe HF-225 and HF-150.

 An *RDI WHITE PAPER* is available for the Lowe HF-225/HF-235.

If you want a top performer, here is where your money stretches farthest. Five-star models should satisfy even the fussiest, and four-star models are no slouches, either.

The best tabletop models are the Ferraris and Mercedes of the radio world. As with their automotive counterparts, like-ranked receivers may come out of the curve at the same speed, though how they do it can differ greatly from model to model. So, if you're thinking of choosing from the top end, study each contender in detail.

The most interesting news for 1993 concerns the introduction of the Lowe HF-150, a one-of-a-kind tabletop that can also serve as a portable. Too, the top-rated Drake R8 and Japan Radio NRD-535 have both undergone a number of improvements, as has the Icom IC-R71.

Improved for 1993
★ ★ ★ ★ ★   *Editor's Choice*

Drake R8
Drake R8E

Price: $979.00 in the United States, CAN$1,199.00 in Canada, £965.00 in the United Kingdom, AUS$2,400 in Australia.

Advantages: Unparalleled all-around listening performance. Most appropriate model available for hour-after-hour reception of world band programs. Superior audio quality, especially with suitable outboard speaker. Synchronous selectable sideband for reduced fading and easier rejection of interference. Five bandwidths, four suitable for world band—among the best of any model tested. Highly flexible operating controls, including

The Drake R8 has been improved for 1993. It's unsurpassed for serious enhanced-fidelity listening, but needs a good outboard speaker.

100 superb presets, variable notch filter and excellent passband offset. Superior reception of utility, ham and mediumwave AM signals. Tunes in precise 0.01 kHz increments. Displays frequency for some modes in those same 0.01 kHz increments. Superior blocking performance. Slow/fast/off AGC. Sophisticated scan functions. Can access all presets quickly via tuning knob and slew buttons. Built-in preamplifier. Accepts two antennas. Two 24-hour clocks, with seconds displayed numerically and timer features.

Disadvantages: Ergonomics, now noticeably improved, still mediocre. Notch filter extremely fussy to adjust. Most pushbuttons rock on their centers. XX.XXXXX MHz frequency display format lacks decimal for integers finer than kHz. Neither clock displays for more than three seconds when radio on. Individual presets not tunable. Flimsy front feet. Matching optional MS8 outboard speaker not equal to receiver's fidelity potential.

Bottom Line: Improved performance, ergonomics and quality control for 1993. Now clearly the best of the best for pleasant listening to news, music and entertainment from afar. Superb for DX reception of faint, tough signals, too. Downside: Ergonomics, although definitely improved over the version tested last year, could be much better. A good small outboard hi-fi speaker is needed for the R8 to really shine—but don't bother with Drake's MS8 offering.

 An *RDI WHITE PAPER* is available for this model, including latest improvements.

Japan Radio's NRD-535D, upgraded for 1993, is a gem. Superior optional outboard speaker, too.

Advantages: One of the best DX receivers ever tested. Very good ergonomics. Construction quality slightly above average, likely to be unusually reliable. Computer-type modular plug-in circuit boards ease repair. Highly flexible operating controls, including 200 superb presets, tunable notch filter and passband offset. Superior reception of utility and ham signals. The only receiver tested that tunes frequency in exacting 0.001 kHz increments. Displays frequency in precise 0.01 kHz increments. Slow/fast/off AGC. Superior front-end selectivity. Sophisticated scan functions. World Time clock with timer features; displays seconds, albeit only if a wire inside the receiver is cut. Excellent optional NVA-319 outboard speaker. *NRD-535D:* Synchronous selectable sideband for reduced fading and easier rejection of interference. Continuously variable bandwidth in single-sideband mode (narrow bandwidth). Continuously variable bandwidth also in AM mode (wide bandwidth).

Disadvantages: Audio quality, although improved over some earlier Japan Radio offerings, still somewhat muddy. Dynamic range and blocking performance adequate, but not fully equal to price class. Excessive beats and birdies. AGC sometimes causes "pop" sounds. Clock shares display with frequency readout. Clock not visible when receiver off. Front feet do not tilt receiver upwards. *NRD-535D:* Synchronous selectable sideband circuit locking performance suboptimal, notably with passband offset in use. Variable bandwidth comes at the expense of deep-skirt selectivity.

Bottom Line: A variety of improvements over the past year have combined to make this an exceptional receiver, especially in the "D" version. Best ergonomics we've ever come across in a tabletop model. Outstanding reception of tough DX signals, plus superior quality of construction.

 An *RDI WHITE PAPER* is available for both versions of this model.

Kenwood's R-5000 performs superbly. Sounds good, too.

Japan Radio's proven NRD-525 is a superb performer, except for audio quality.

★ ★ ★ ★ ½   *Editor's Choice*

Kenwood R-5000

Price: $1,099.95 in the United States, CAN$1,349.95 in Canada, £925.00 in the United Kingdom, $1,000-1,500 elsewhere in Europe, AUS$1,500.00 in Australia.

Advantages: Unusually appropriate for hour-after-hour world band listening. Superb all-around performance. Unusually good audio for a tabletop, provided a suitable outboard speaker is used. Exceptionally flexible operating controls, including tunable notch filter and passband offset. Tunes and displays frequency in precise 0.01 kHz increments. Excellent reception of utility and ham signals. Superior frequency-of-repair record.

Disadvantages: Ergonomics only fair, especially keypad, which uses an offbeat horizontal format. Mediocre wide bandwidth filter supplied with set; replacement with high-quality YK-88A-1 substitute adds $88.95 to cost. Audio significantly distorted at tape-recording output.

Bottom Line: The Kenwood R-5000's combination of superior tough-signal performance and above-average audio quality makes it an excellent choice for those who need a receiver for tough-signal DXing, as well as reasonable fidelity for listening to world band programs.

An *RDI WHITE PAPER* is available for this model.

★ ★ ★ ★ ½   *Editor's Choice*

Japan Radio NRD-525U
Japan Radio NRD-525E
Japan Radio NRD-525J
Japan Radio NRD-525G

Price: $1,275.00 in the United States, CAN$1,395.00 in Canada, under £1,100 in the United Kingdom, $1,300-2,000 elsewhere in Europe, AUS$2,150.00 in Australia.

Advantages: Superb all-around performance. Highly flexible operating controls, including tunable notch filter and passband offset. Very good ergonomics. Construction quality slightly above average. Computer-type modular plug-in circuit boards ease repair. Sophisticated scan features. Superior reception of utility and ham signals. Slow/fast/off AGC. Tunes and displays frequency in precise 0.01 kHz increments. Two 24-hour clocks with timer features.

Disadvantages: Woolly audio, a major drawback for program listening. Dynamic range below par for genre.

Note: This model is being discontinued, but should be available from some dealers for many months to come.

Bottom Line: A superb performer that's well put together, but lacks audio fidelity.

Comment: When tested with Sherwood SE-3 synchronous selectable sideband device fitted to a Realistic Minimus 7 speaker, audio quality improved to excellent.

An *RDI WHITE PAPER* will continue to be available for this model until the supply of copies is exhausted.

Improved for 1993
★ ★ ★ ★

Icom IC-R71A
Icom IC-R71E
Icom IC-R71D

Price: *IC-R71A:* $1,204.00 in the United States, CAN$1,559.00 in Canada, AUS$1,599.00 in Australia; *IC-R71E:* £875.00 in the United Kingdom; *IC-R71E and IC-R71D:* $1,000-1,800 in continental Europe.

Advantages: Variable bandwidth (reactivated for 1993). Superb reception of weak, hard-to-hear signals. Reception of faint signals alongside powerful competing ones aided by superb ultimate selectivity, as well as excellent dynamic range. Flexible operating controls,

Icom's venerable IC-R71 once again has variable bandwidth, found on few other receivers.

including tunable notch filter. Excellent reception of utility and ham signals. Tunes in precise 0.01 kHz increments (reads in 0.1 kHz increments).

Disadvantages: Mediocre audio. Diminutive controls, and otherwise generally substandard ergonomics. Should backup battery die, operating system software erases, requiring reprogramming by Icom service center (expected battery life is in excess of 10 years).

Change for 1993: Variable bandwidth, a useful feature, appeared in the original version, but was dropped in a revised version sold between early 1989 and late 1991. Since then, that variable bandwidth, marketed under the confusing rubric "passband tuning," has once again been included in all production units—a welcome revival, indeed.

Bottom Line: The venerable Icom IC-R71 has long been one of the favorite choices among those seeking faint, hard-to-hear signals, as well as official agencies seeking compact, low-cost radio surveillance gear. However, the 'R71 is not fully competitive with some other tabletops for hour-on-hour program listening, nor is it quite equal to the very best newer models for chasing faint DX signals. According to Icom, although the 'R71 is costly to produce, so long as the set continues to sell well it will be kept in production.

 An *RDI WHITE PAPER* is available for this model.

New for 1993
★ ★ ★ ★   *Editor's Choice*

Lowe HF-150

Price (including optional mouse keypad):
$689.90 in the United States, CAN$1,014.95 in Canada, £368.95 in the United Kingdom. AK-150 accessory kit $99.95 in the United States, CAN$119.95 in Canada, £39.99 in the United Kingdom. XLS1 monitor speaker £59.95 in the United Kingdom.

Advantages: With AK-150 option, "portatop" design combines virtual tabletop performance with the convenience of a portable. Exceptional audio quality with external speaker or headphones. Synchronous detection allows for selectable sideband or double sideband, the only receiver tested that does this. Exceptionally rugged housing. Mouse keypad, a *de rigeur* option, performs superbly for tuning and presets. 60 presets store frequency and mode. Outstanding mediumwave AM performance. Tunes in precise 8 Hz increments. Small footprint. Optional accessory kit provides telescopic antenna, rechargeable nickel-cadmium batteries and shoulder strap with built-in antenna. Excellent operating manual.

Disadvantages: Bereft of certain features—among them notch filter, adjustable noise blanker, passband tuning and signal-strength indicator—found on premium-priced tabletop models. Wide filter a touch too broad. Inferior front-end selectivity limits performance quality near mediumwave AM transmitters. Frequency readout no finer than 1 kHz resolution. Lacks lock indicator for synchronous detector. No tone control. No elevation feet. Erratic contact on outboard-speaker socket. *Portable operation:* Comes with no convenient way to attach keypad to cabinet (remediable, see story). Lacks FM broadcast reception, normally found on portables. Telescopic antenna swivels properly, but is clumsy to rotate.

Bottom Line: Superb world band and mediumwave AM program listener's radio which also provides respectable tough-signal ("DX") performance and excellent single-sideband reception. With the AK-150 option, it sets a new standard in combining full-fidelity tabletop performance with portability. This makes it unnecessary to own two receivers or to have to choose between a portable and a tabletop. An outstanding buy, provided you don't need the specialized features found on costlier models, or the FM reception found on portables.

Evaluation of New Model: Two roads diverge in a forest. One leads to the Bali Ha'i of premium tabletop receivers; the other, to a shiny Valhalla of easy-to-use portables. England's Lowe says nay, and proceeds to carve out a fresh path—one that leads to a diminutive receiver as easy to use and carry as a portable, yet with performance comparable to that of a worthy tabletop.

This welcome new genre of "portatop" receiver is now here in the Lowe HF-150, available in Europe, the United States and Canada. With only two knobs and three buttons, it is positively Zen-like in its simplicity. Outwardly, it looks like a designer brick with knobs. Brick-like, too, is the tough aluminum frame that envelops this little receiver like tank armor.

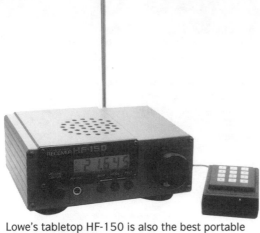

Lowe's tabletop HF-150 is also the best portable tested.

The '150 offers reception in LSB, USB, AM and synchronous AM modes from 30 kHz to 30 MHz in precise 8 Hz increments. The synchronous mode, unlike that of other models, works either when both sidebands are being received, or with any one sideband at a time—a first among tested receivers. The '150 runs off outboard AC power or eight "AA" batteries that drop into two slide-out trays in the back of the set. A charging circuit is supplied for NiCd cells, which nominally operate the '150 for four hours per charge.

At slightly over three inches in height, the '150 is significantly thicker than most portables. Yet, its small footprint (7¼" W × 7" D, or 184 × 178 mm, including knobs and other projections) produces an overall cubic volume roughly equivalent to that of the Sony ICF-2010/ICF-2001D. As a result, the '150 can easily be popped into a suitcase, briefcase or knapsack—but not into even the roomiest of jacket pockets. It also fits nicely into most people's palms.

Here's what all this means, and why it is so exciting. With the batteries charged and the telescopic antenna attached, you can simply grab the '150 one-handed, like the family cat, and take it around the house or yard to keep you company wherever you go. You just can't do that with other highly rated tabletop receivers.

The optional accessory kit which contains the telescopic antenna also includes a short carrying handle and a shoulder strap with a built-in wire antenna. The shoulder-strap-cum-antenna works reasonably well, so long as it rests on your shoulder and the antenna is roughly vertical. Lay the strap down on a horizontal surface and performance degrades. This makes the strap a mediocre substitute for the telescopic antenna. Fortunately, that telescopic antenna can be used while the shoulder strap is still attached. Although the telescopic antenna does not rotate or fold away without

first being loosened up, then tightened back, it does swivel conventionally.

The tuning knob—metal, with a shallow "speed" dimple—is a bit stiff to turn. Because the radio is light, some find it easy to push the '150 around the desk during operation. In addition, the three pushbuttons are mounted low on the cabinet, which can make them awkward to use when the radio is sitting flat on its four squat rubber feet.

Propping up the front of the '150 with a stick or book helps all around: The receiver tends to stay put when tuning; controls are easier to use; the display is easier to read. Clearly what is needed is a pair of elevated front feet or, better, a carrying handle that swivels to become an elevation rod, such as is found on the discontinued Philips/Magnavox D2999. Whomever you are considering buying the radio from may be able to provide longer feet as part of the deal. Otherwise, you can concoct your own solution.

The '150 sounds genuinely delightful when used with headphones or a first-rate external speaker, although the internal speaker produces only okay results and there is no tone control whatsoever. Too, the mini-socket for an external speaker tends to lose contact with the speaker plug—a problem encountered with other models of Lowe receivers.

Not only is audio quality superior, our lab measurements show low overall distortion and circuit noise. These characteristics, plus fade-reducing synchronous detection, produce aural quality comparable to that of the costlier Lowe HF-225, and even approaching that of the top-rated Drake R8.

Our lab tests show sensitivity to weak signals that is good to excellent; ditto dynamic range. Image rejection is excellent, as is the receiver's stability. The AGC threshold is superb. Front-end selectivity, though, is clearly inferior—only a low-pass filter is used—which could cause problems for those living close to mediumwave AM transmitters. In short, for the most part the '150 acquits itself very well on the test bench—far better than portables and, for the most part, close, but not quite equal, to tabletop supersets.

The '150, as measured in our laboratory, is equipped with a 6.5 kHz "wide" bandwidth having an excellent shape factor, and a 2.6 kHz "narrow" bandwidth with a good shape factor. The narrow bandwidth works very well for selectable-sideband or single-sideband listening, but is too constricted for regular world band reception in the AM mode. The wide bandwidth, on the other hand, works well for much AM-mode listening, but occasionally lets through interference from adjacent stations that would be lessened by a slightly narrower bandwidth.

Lowe has taken a novel approach to the operating scheme for the '150, in which bandwidth is usually not selectable independent of mode. The middle button on the receiver's front panel is marked "MODE." Press that, and you can then use the buttons on either side to move forward and backward through a carousel of mode and filter combinations—LSB/2.6 kHz, USB/2.6 kHz, AM/6.5 kHz, AM/2.6 kHz, AM synchronous/double-sideband/6.5 kHz, AMS/hi-fi/6.5 kHz, AMS/LSB/2.6 kHz, AMS/USB/2.6 kHz.

Because the buttons operate both forward and backward, much of the curse is taken off having these selections on a rotary—you're never more than four button pokes away from the selection you want. One ergonomic drawback: the menu of mode options is not displayed, requiring you to keep the sequence of choices in your head or to push a button until what you want appears.

The presets—programmable channel memories—are easy to use. Press the left-hand "MEM" button, then a presets indicator appears in the display. You can then preview visually, but not aurally, any of the presets while still listening to a station you have previously selected. When you get to a preset you want, press the middle button and you can listen to the channel. The only rub is that this visual scan is slowed by about one second per preset channel because the LCD sequentially displays first the preset number (pause), then the preset frequency.

Going from band to band is equally easy. If you press the extreme right-hand ("FAST") button, the two right-most digits of the frequency display are blanked and the receiver mutes. Spin the tuning knob and the remaining three digits change with warp speed. Press that "FAST" button again, and the receiver goes to the new portion of the spectrum you have selected.

Thankfully, Lowe also offers as an option its excellent outboard keypad, laid out in the familiar three-by-three-over-one format like a telephone. This optional keypad, the same that's used on the '225, is, hands down, the world's best. It sits on the table, much like a computer mouse, on the end of a 22-inch (55 cm) wire. To enter any frequency between 3 and 30 MHz, just tap in the numbers—no decimals, no leading zeros—and the station appears. This keypad sets the standard by which all others are judged. Don't buy the '150 without it.

There's more. You can access directly any of the receiver's 60 presets which, unlike those on the '225, store not just frequency, but also mode. Tap in any number between 1 and 60, press the # button, and up comes the desired preset.

In fact, the keypad is so handy that you'll want to use it for portable operation as well, which raises the issue: How do you deal with a dangling outboard keypad on a portable? Answer: with a bit of sticky-backed Velcro, available at local stores.

Tougher is having full-fidelity performance during portable operation. Toting about a separate speaker is cumbersome, and the built-in speaker is pedestrian. Best bet is a set of cheap foam-padded walkaround-type headphones, such as the $5.95 Realistic Nova-34. Fancy headphones can provide a bit too much fidelity for world band or mediumwave AM.

Fading can also make listening less pleasant than it might otherwise be. As world band signals travel around the world by bouncing off a continually changing ionosphere, they tend to fade and produce annoying distortion. Even fringe-area mediumwave AM stations can distort badly around twilight and at night.

The '150 is one of a small but growing number of tabletop and portable receivers that can fight this by using high-technology "synchronous detection" circuitry. Synchronous detection removes the transmitted carrier from the signal and replaces it with one of local quality generated by the receiver. The result: world band stations sound better, more like local stations.

That's not all that properly designed synchronous detectors can do. World band and mediumwave AM stations alike have two

---

Surge Protection That Works

Have costly electronic equipment to be protected? The Zero Surge Eliminator (103 Claremont Rd., Bernardsville NJ 07924 USA; fax +1 908/766-4144) line of 120V surge arresters, which we have been testing for nearly two years, performs so well it's hard to go into sticker shock: $149–199 apiece. Originally developed to protect computers in local area networks, they are also the ne plus ultra for protecting communications gear.

"sidebands"—those parts of the signal containing the words and music you hear. Only one needs to be heard, as both are essentially identical. The '150's synchronous detection circuit allows you to listen to both sidebands when the signal is in the clear, but more important it also allows you to select either the lower or upper sideband to shift away from interference from an adjacent channel. This, too, can make for more pleasant reception.

In practice, if you select any of the synchronous modes and don't tune the receiver exactly onto the correct frequency, the '150 will growl softly until you adjust the tuning knob and the circuit "locks on." Similarly, in our unit the keypad consistently lands the receiver about 200 Hz away from the proper lock frequency, making it necessary to fine tune the receiver each time the keypad is used with the synchronous detector. Compounding this minor nuisance, which may be related to circuit alignment at the factory, is the lack of precise frequency resolution or a lock indicator to help in tuning the receiver to lock. This is especially surprising, in that other Lowe models have a just such a lock indicator on the LCD.

Regular single-sideband reception is excellent, with even independent-sideband feeder transmissions being received with no perceptible crosstalk. While none of this is surprising in the world of tabletop receivers, in its role as a portable the '150's performance in these matters is clearly superior to that of any conventional portable around.

All the synchronous modes work quite well—including the hi-fi mode, labeled "ASF," which offers greater treble response. This works to excellent effect with powerful mediumwave AM stations free from interference. While the National Association of Broadcasters, an American group, forks out research money trying to figure out how to develop advanced-fidelity AM receivers, the Brits have produced one on their own. So if you're tired of hearing mediumwave AM radio sound as though it were being transmitted through a bathtub drainpipe, the '150 will come as a delightful surprise—nigh full fidelity, with no selective-fading distortion.

Most receivers with synchronous detection will growl, howl and whine if you turn the tuning knob. Or they will switch out of synchronous mode until you select it again. Not necessarily so with the '150. Turn the tuning knob quickly, and the receiver automatically switches into AM (nonsynchronous) "wide" so you can travel up or down the band without aural complaint. After you have found a station to stay with for a while, the receiver automatically reverts to the original synchronous mode when the tuning knob has not been

moved rapidly for about a second. It works well, save when you bandscan too slowly for the synchronous circuitry to switch out.

The '150 also features variable-rate incremental tuning—tune slowly, one speed; quicker, the radio tunes at a rate several times faster. Our test panel was split on whether the '150 would have been better off without this feature.

No split in opinion, though on the frequency readout, which is only to the nearest kilohertz. In principle this makes some sense, but most of us found the lack of finer visual resolution thoroughly annoying.

Other niceties are absent, as well. For example, the '150 lacks many of the controls that DXers—who struggle to tweak every last erg out of a faint signal—have come to cherish: passband tuning, notch filter, AGC decay, adjustable noise blankers and the like. There isn't even a signal-strength indicator. So if chasing hard-to-hear stations is your passion, other tabletop receivers will better suit your needs.

When the '150 is placed on a normal waist-level table, the vertical face and non-elevated front of the receiver make that LCD harder to read than it needs to be. Too, that display is not illuminated for nighttime use—say, outdoors.

Yet, for the program listener the Lowe HF-150 outperforms "real" portables, while offering performance for hour-after-hour listening that is comparable to that of the best tabletop models. Price is hundreds less, and you can take it with you just about anywhere you go. It sounds great, and it's made to last.

 An *RDI WHITE PAPER* will be issued shortly for this model.

★ ★ ★ ★   *Editor's Choice*

Lowe HF-225

Price (including optional keypad): $839.90 in the United States; CAN$1,314.95 in Canada, £468.95 in the United Kingdom. Synchronous detector and other accessories additional.

Advantages: Among the best for listening to world band programs hour after hour. Superior audio with outboard speaker. Straightforward to operate. Generally excellent ergonomics, especially with keypad. Four bandwidths. Tunes in precise, if unusual, 8 Hz increments. Physically rugged. Optional synchronous detector, tested, reduces distortion. Optional field-portable configuration, tested. Small footprint. Attractively priced.

Sturdy design and quality audio are among the hallmarks of the Lowe HF-225, shown in its quasi-portable configuration.

Disadvantages: Limited operational flexibility, including AGC. Two of four bandwidths too wide for most world band applications. Front-end selectivity only fair. In tabletop use, less sensitive to weak signals than top-rated models. Optional portable configuration relatively insensitive to weak signals. Frequency reads in relatively coarse 1 kHz increments. Optional

synchronous detector works only on double sideband, not selectable sideband.
Change for 1993: This and other Lowe receivers are now also available in the United States and Canada, as well as Europe.
Bottom Line: A hardy, easy-to-operate set with superior audio quality. Reasonably priced.

 An *RDI WHITE PAPER* is available for this model and the Lowe HF-235.

★ ★ ★ ½

Icom IC-R72
Icom IC-R72E

Price: $1,103.00 in the United States, CAN$1,239.00 in Canada, £669.00 in United Kingdom, AUS$1,199.00 in Australia.
Advantages: Pleasant audio with outboard speaker or headphones. Generally superior ergonomics. Tunes and displays frequency in precise 0.01 kHz increments. World clock/timer. Operates for about one hour off built-in rechargeable battery—useful during power failure. Novel center-tuning LED for world band and certain other signals. Superb image and IF rejection. Small footprint. Smoothly operating tuning knob. Preamplifier.

Coming Up In Passport/94 . . .

Here are some of the forthcoming tabletop models you can expect to see reviewed in the 1994 edition of *Passport to World Band Radio* . . .

By early 1993, Lowe expects to have introduced its new HF-250. This is billed as a fidelity-oriented model complete with sophisticated features, such as those currently found on high-end Japanese and American communications receivers. Look for a price in the vicinity of $1,000 or £600.

Too, the long-awaited Grove SW-100, another feature-laden model, is now scheduled to appear before the beginning of 1993 at a price of $899. We will analyze both these receivers in complete detail in new RDI White Papers to be issued within three months or so of the receivers' introductions.

Grove and Lowe aren't the only manufacturers beavering away. Yaesu and one other firm are busy preparing something mid-priced for mid-1993 or thereabouts.

Wildcards: Britain's innovative Phase Track Ltd. is actively seeking working arrangements with other world band firms that, if consummated, could lead to new enhanced-fidelity models in the mid-Nineties. And Asian manufacturers of portables have been batting around the idea of $500-700 plastic "portatop" models, similar in concept to the AM/FM/world band Philips/Magnavox D2999 that was manufactured in Hong Kong until manufacturing costs became excessive.

Bottom line: Choices should increase slightly, but nothing technologically uncommon appears to be on the horizon.

Icom's IC-R72, shown, and IC-R71 have similar prices, but are very different from each other.

Disadvantages: Wide bandwidth too broad. Dreadful audio from built-in speaker. Noisy synthesizer. Noise blanker reduces dynamic range. Relatively few features, compared to better models. In our unit, poor low-frequency audio reproduction in upper-sideband.

Bottom Line: Nice, but nothing special—especially considering the price. A number of other models offer much better value.

★ ★ ★ ½

Yaesu FRG-8800

Price: $784.00 in the United States, CAN$1,229.00 in Canada, £639.00 in the United Kingdom, $800-1,100 elsewhere in Europe, AUS$1,295.00 in Australia.

Advantages: Flexible controls. Slightly above-average audio for tabletop model. Superior sensitivity and related blocking measurements help weak signal reception. Fairly good ergonomics. Two 24-hour clocks. Established circuit design, going back many years, is by now thoroughly proven.

Disadvantages: "Wide" bandwidth too broad for most world band receiving applications. "Narrow" bandwidth somewhat wide for a "narrow," yet rather narrow for a "wide." Spurious-signal ("image") rejection only fair. Front-end selectivity only fair. Utility and ham signal reception, though acceptable, below average for tabletop model. Some control settings difficult to see, and a couple of controls are unhandy to reach. Keypad not in

telephone format. Microprocessor reportedly sometimes tends to malfunction.

Bottom Line: The only world band receiver sold by Yaesu, the FRG-8800, by now well past its technological prime, is a proven, well-balanced performer very much in need of tighter selectivity.

 An *RDI WHITE PAPER* is available for this model.

★ ★ ★

Kenwood R-2000

Price: $799.95 in the United States, CAN$1,049.95 in Canada, £549.00 in the United Kingdom, $750-1,250 elsewhere in Europe.

Advantages: Straightforward to operate, with fairly good ergonomics. Audio slightly above average for tabletop model. Superior sensitivity makes model relevant to needs of listeners in such places as Western North America and Australasia, where world band signals tend to be relatively weak. Two 24-hour clocks.

Disadvantages: Mediocre dynamic range materially compromises performance by allowing overloading to take place in many parts of the world, such as Europe and even Eastern North America—especially with high-gain antennas. "Wide" bandwidth too broad for most world band applications. Keypad uses nonstandard, unhandy layout.

Bottom Line: This model, which came on the market years ago, can be quite pleasurable for listening to the major world band stations—especially if you live in Western North America or Australasia. But for other, more demanding applications, it is in need of tighter selectivity and better dynamic range. Why bother, when better alternatives are to be had?

The Passport tabletop-model *review team: Lawrence Magne, along with Jock Elliott and Tony Jones, with laboratory measurements by Robert Sherwood.*

The only model offered by Japan's Yaesu is the FRG-8800, priceed less than most others.

Kenwood's R-2000 is cheaper than its R-5000 brand mate, but the R-5000 is well worth the extra money.

Where to Find It:

Index to Tested Radios—1985–1993

Has *Passport* tested it? When? Is more detailed information available?

To find out, here is *Passport's* Buyer's Guide menu, going right back to our earliest reviews. Our most concise findings are published each year, and appear so long as a model is still being sold by the manufacturer. Some of these reviews are longer, appearing only the year the model was introduced. These are in **bold** below.

Not enough? For premium receivers and antennas there are comprehensive *Passport* RDI White Papers (indicated below with an asterisk). These usually run 15-30 pages in length, with one report thoroughly covering a single model or topic. Each RDI White Paper—$5.95 in North America, $7.95 airmail in most other regions—contains virtually all our panel's findings and comments during hands-on testing, as well as laboratory measurements and what these mean to you. They're available from key world band dealers, or write us or call our 24-hour automated order line (+1 215/794-8252).

1987 and earlier editions were called *Radio Database International*, the forerunner of today's *Passport to World Band Radio*. Sorry, we don't have any back editions, but libraries sometimes do.

Model	Passport Edition	Passport/93 Page No.	Model	Passport Edition	Passport/93 Page No.
Aiwa WR-A100	1993	100	Grundig Travel Kit 230	1991	112
Aiwa WR-D1000	**1993**	106	Grundig Yacht Boy 210	1989	
Alconic Series 2959	1990	129	Grundig Yacht Boy 215	1989	
Amsonic AS-138	1993	110	Grundig Yacht Boy 220	1990	
Amsonic AS-908	1993	111	Grundig Yacht Boy 230	1991	112
Amsonic AS-912	1993	112	Grundig Yacht Boy 650	1987	
Antennas, Indoor (various models)*			Grundig Yacht Boy 700	1987	
Antennas, Outdoor (various models)*			Heathkit/Zenith SW-7800	**1985**	
Bearcat/Uniden DX1000	**1985**		Heathkit/Zenith SW-7800		
Clairtone PR-291	1992	125	(revised version)	1987	
Cougar H-88	1990	117	Icom IC-R100	1991	
DAK DMR-3000 Global Interceptor	1993	111	Icom IC-R71 (all versions)*	**1985/1988**	136
DAK MR-101	**1991**		Icom IC-R72	**1991**	141
DAK MR-101s	**1992**	110	"Icom IC-R7000HF"	1991	
Dick Smith A-4338	1993	110	Icom IC-R9000*	**1990**	133
Dick Smith D-2832	1993	129	International AC 100	1993	113
Drake R7/R7A	1987		Jäger PL-440	1993	114
Drake R8*	**1992**		Japan Radio NRD-93*	1987	133
Drake R8/R8E (revised version)*	1993	134	Japan Radio NRD-515	**1985**	
Drake R4245	1987		Japan Radio NRD-525		
EEB 4950	1988		(all versions)	**1987/1988**	136
Electro Brand 2971	1991	130	Japan Radio NRD-535/535D*	**1992**	
Embassy Ambassador 2020	**1988**		Japan Radio NRD-535/535D		
Embassy Diplomat 4950	1987		(revised version)*	1993	135
Emerson ATS-803A	1990		Kenwood R-11	1987	
Emerson PSW4010	1990		Kenwood R-600	1987	
Eska RX99PL	**1985**		Kenwood R-1000	1987	
Eska RX 33	**1988**	125	Kenwood R-2000	1987	142
General Electric World Monitor	**1987**		Kenwood R-5000*	**1988**	136
Giros R918	1993	115	Linaplex F1	**1985**	
Goodmans ATS-803	1989		Lowe HF-125	**1988**	
Grundig Cosmopolit	1992	121	Lowe HF-150*	**1993**	137
Grundig Explorer II	1993	116	Lowe HF-225*	**1990**	140
Grundig Satellit 300	1987		Lowe HF-235 (all versions)*	**1992**	134
Grundig Satellit 400	**1988**		Lowe SRX-50	1993	111
Grundig Satellit 500	**1990**	128	Magnavox AE 3205/AE 3205 GY	**1992/1993**	117
Grundig Satellit 500 (revised version)	**1991**		Magnavox AE 3805	**1991**	108
Grundig Satellit 600	**1985**		Magnavox D1835	1988	129
Grundig Satellit 650	**1988**	128	Magnavox D1875/OD1875BK	1990/1992/1993	113
Grundig Satellit 700	**1993**	122	Magnavox D2935	**1987**	128
Grundig Traveller II	1992	118	Magnavox D2999	**1987/1988**	128
Grundig Travel Kit 220	1991		Marc II NR-108F1	1989	128

Model	Passport Edition	Passport/93 Page No.	Model	Passport Edition	Passport/93 Page No.
Matsui MR-4099	1989	125	Sangean ATS-803	**1987/1988**	
MBR Mark II	1991		Sangean ATS-803 (revised)/803A	1988	125
MCE-7760	1993	114	Sangean ATS-808	**1991/1993**	106
McKay Dymek DR 33-C	1987		Sangean ATS-818	**1993**	126
McKay Dymek DR 101-6	1987		Sangean ATS-818CS	1993	120
Morphy Richards R191	1993	1110	Sangean MS-101	1989	100
National B10	1989	129	Sangean MS-103/MS-103L	1990	99
National B20	1989	112	Sangean SG 621	**1992**	113
National B40	1990	129	Sangean SG-631	**1992**	113
National B45	**1992**	105	Sangean SG-700L	**1992**	112
National B50	1989		Sangean SG-789/SG-789L	1987	100
National B60	**1989**		SEG Precision World SED 110	**1993**	115
National B65	1990	105	SEG SED ECL88	1993	111
National B300	1989		Sharp FV-310GB	1987	
National B600	1989		Sharp FV-610GB	1987	
National DR-22	1987		Shiba Electronics FX-928	1993	117
National DR-29	1987		Shimasu Multiband	1993	129
National DR-31	1987		Shimasu PLL Digital	1993	110
National DR-49/RF-4900	1987		Siemens RK 641	1989	
National DR-63	1987		Siemens RP 647G4	1992	108
National DR-90	1987		Siemens RK 651	1990	125
National Micro 00	1987		Siemens RK 661	**1993**	106
Opal OP-35	1989	118	Siemens RK 702	1989	128
Pace	1993	114	Siemens RK 710	1993	113
Panashiba FX-928	**1992**	117	Silver XF1900	1987	
Panasonic RF-9/RF-9L	1987		Silver International MT-798	**1993**	118
Panasonic RF-799	1987		Sony CRF-1	1987	
Panasonic RF-2200	1987		Sony CRF-V21*	**1990**	127
Panasonic RF-2900	1987		Sony ICF-2001	1987	
Panasonic RF-3100	1987		Sony ICF-2001D/ICF-2001DS*	**1985/1988**	119
Panasonic RF-4900	1987		Sony ICF-2002	1988	128
Panasonic RF-6300	1987		Sony ICF-2003	**1988**	128
Panasonic RF-9000	1987		Sony ICF-2010*	**1985/1988**	119
Panasonic RF-B10	1989	129	Sony ICF-4900	1987	
Panasonic RF-B20/B20L	1989	112	Sony ICF-4900 II	1989	129
Panasonic RF-B40/RF-B40DL	1989	129	Sony ICF-4910	1987	
Panasonic RF-B45/B45DL	**1992**	105	Sony ICF-4920	1989	129
Panasonic RF-B50	1987		Sony ICF-5100	1989	129
Panasonic RF-B60/B60L	**1988**		Sony ICF-6800W	**1987**	
Panasonic RF-B65/B65D/B65L	1990	105	Sony ICF-7600A	1987	129
Panasonic RF-B300	1989		Sony ICF-7600AW	1987	129
Panasonic RF-B600	1989		Sony ICF-7600D	1988	128
Pan Crusader	1989	128	Sony ICF-7600DA	**1988**	109
Panopus Yacht Boy 230	1993	112	Sony ICF-7600DS	**1988**	128
Philips AE 3205/AE 3205 GY	**1992**/1993	117	Sony ICF-7601	1989	109
Philips AE 3805	**1991**	108	Sony ICF-7700	**1988**	109
Philips D1835	1987	129	Sony ICF-PRO70	**1988**	107
Philips D1875/OD1875BK	1990/1992/1993	113	Sony ICF-PRO80	**1988**	107
Philips D2615	1990	129	"Sony ICF-SW1"	1991	
Philips D2935	**1987/1988**	128	Sony ICF-SW1E	1990	99
Philips D2999	**1987**	128	Sony ICF-SW1S	1989	98
Philips D7476	1989		Sony ICF-SW20	1990	99
Philips DC777 automobile radio	1991/1993	95	Sony ICF-SW55	**1993**	101
Pomtrex 120-00300	**1992**	114	Sony ICF-SW77	1993	102
Precision World	1993	117	Sony ICF-SW700	**1992**	107
Precision World SED 901	1993	117	Sony ICF-SW800	**1992**	107
Pulser	**1992**	111	Sony ICF-SW7600	**1991**	105
Quelle Universum	1990	125	Sony WA-6000	1990	121
Racal RA6790/GM	1987		Sony WA-8000MKII	1991	
Realistic DX-350	**1992**	112	Sony WA-8800	1990	
Realistic DX-360	1987		Steepletone MRB7	1993	129
Realistic DX-370	**1991**	108	Supertech SR-16H	1987	
Realistic DX-380	**1991/1993**	106	TEC 235TR	1993	114
Realistic DX-390	**1993**	126	Ten-Tec RX-325	**1988**	
Realistic DX-440	**1988**		TMR 7602 Hitech Tatung	1991	125
Rhapsody Multiband	1989	129	Toshiba RP-F11	1987	
Roberts R101	1993	100	Trio R-11	1987	
Roberts R621	1993	113	Trio R-600	1987	
Roberts R808	1992/**1993**	106	Trio R-1000	1987	
Rodelsonic Digital World Band	**1992**	110	Trio R-2000	1987	
Rodelvox Digital World Band	**1992**	110	Tunemaster Classic Radio	**1990**	
Saisho SW5000	1989		Venturer Multiband	1989	129
Sangean ATS 800	**1991**	108	Windsor 2138	**1993**	118
Sangean ATS-801	1987		Yaesu FRG-7700	1987	
Sangean ATS-802	1990		Yaesu FRG-8800*	**1985/1988**	142

Leo Sarkisian

The Voice of America's Leo Sarkisian is acclaimed worldwide not only as a knowledgeable broadcaster, but also as a talented musician and artist. Shown is his drawing of a nomad in Niger.

Worldscan

What's On Tonight?

Passport's Hour-by-Hour Guide to World Band Shows

World band offers everything from giants like the BBC to emerging lilliputians like Croatian Radio. No cables, satellite dishes or fancy equipment are needed, and you can tune in nearly anywhere, anytime.

There's unparalleled access to news and news analysis. No domestic radio or TV offers as much first-rate news reporting, nor such a variety of perspectives. The listener becomes his own editor, unaffected by the dictates of media managers and special interest groups.

Nobody can prevent reception, either, as they can with, say, regular TV. French TV's Antenne 2 newscast, for example, is shown nightly in New York over WNYE, channel 25. It was partially blanked out there throughout the 1992 Winter Olympics because CBS claimed exclusive rights to news about the Olympics. Such manipulation can't happen over world band. It's direct, not filtered through media gatekeepers or official regulators.

When we think of world band, news—the real stuff—springs to mind. Yet, there are more types of non-news shows on world band than on ordinary radio or TV. Where else is it possible to hear the likes of Bedouin music from Morocco, or learn Japanese direct from Tokyo?

World band is no network cookie cutter, either, with umpteen channels of the same old tea in new bags. Not just the program names are different, the *types* of programs cover just about every facet of human activity. *Passport's* seasoned listeners worldwide keep track of these thousands of shows all year long so you can know what to hear, when, using this "What's On Tonight."

Times are given in World Time, days as World Day. See this *Passport's* Glossary, as well as "Welcome to World Band Radio," for details. Many stations announce World Time at the beginning of each broadcast, on the hour, or both. Use these to set your 24-hour clock—see "Clocks for World Band Listeners" in this edition—so you'll be in sync with the world.

Schedules include not only observed activity, but also that which we have creatively opined will take place throughout 1993. This latter information is original from *Passport*, and since world band radio is a dynamic medium, the data will not be so exact as real-time factual information. Key channels are given for North America, Western Europe, East Asia and the Pacific (including Australasia), plus general coverage of the Middle East. Information on secondary and seasonal channels, as well as channels for other parts of the world, may be found in the "Worldwide Broadcasts in

---

BBC's Katty Kay goes to any heights to research stories for *The World Today*, heard three times each weekday.

English" and Blue Pages portions of this Worldscan section.

Unless otherwise noted, "summer" and "winter" refer to seasons in the Northern Hemisphere.

Many stations supplement their programs with printed material—newsletters, tourist brochures, magazines, books and the like. See this *Passport's* "Addresses PLUS" section for full details.

0000-0559
EVENING PRIME TIME—
NORTH AMERICA

00:00

BBC World Service. Britannia may no longer rule the sea waves, but she is still very much the queen of the international airwaves. First, there's the half-hour *Newsdesk*, which includes both international and British news. This is followed by any one of a wide variety of programs, including *The Ken Bruce Show* (Sunday), *From the Weeklies* and *Recording of the Week* (Saturday) and *Comedy Show* (Thursday). On other days you can hear such offerings as *In Praise of God* (Monday), *Omnibus* (Wednesday), or music programs (Tuesday and Friday). Continuous to North America on 5975, 6175, 7325, 9590, 9915 and 12095 kHz; to East Asia until 0030 on 11945, 11955 and 17830 kHz; and to the Pacific until 0030 on 11955 kHz.

Christian Science Monitor World Service, USA. Considered by many to be North America's best station for news and reasoned analysis. *News*, then *Monitor Radio*—news analysis and news-related features with emphasis on international developments. The first part of a two-hour cyclical broadcast repeated throughout the day to different parts of the globe. To Eastern North America and the Caribbean Tuesday through Saturday (Monday through Friday, local American date) on 7395 kHz, and heard throughout much of North America on 13760 kHz although targeted elsewhere. Also to Europe Tuesday through Friday on 9850 kHz, and to Southeast Asia Monday through Friday on 17555 kHz. On other days, the broadcasts feature Herald of Christian Science religious programming (all of it not necessarily in English) or transmissions of the Sunday Service from the Mother Church in Boston.

Radio Sofia, Bulgaria. Winters only, the final quarter-hour of a 90-minute broadcast (see 2245). To North America on 9700, 11660, 11720 and 11950 kHz. For a separate summer service, see the next item.

Radio Sofia, Bulgaria. Summers only, the start of a 45-minute potpourri of news, commentary, interviews and features, liberally garnished with lively Bulgarian music. To North America on 11660, 11720 and 15330 kHz.

Spanish Foreign Radio. *News*, followed most days by *Panorama*, which features commentary, a review of the Spanish press, weather and foreign press comment on matters affecting Spain. The remainder of the program is a mixture of literature, science, music and general programming. Each day's programming has a special emphasis; for instance, the arts on Friday. On weekends the format is varied somewhat, including *Who's Visiting Spain?* and *Radio Club*. Sixty minutes to Eastern North America on 9530 kHz.

Radio Norway International. Sunday and Monday only. Repeat of the 2300 transmission. Thirty minutes of friendly programming to North and Central America, winters on 9645 kHz, summers on 15165 kHz.

Radio Canada International. On weekdays during winter, relays the excellent CBC domestic service *news* programs *World at Six* and *As It Happens*, which feature international stories, Canadian news and general human interest features. On the remaining days, relays other CBC domestic programs. Summer programming is also a relay of CBC domestic fare, but not of quite the same high quality as that heard in winter. To North America on 5960 and 9755 kHz (summer weekdays, to 0030 only).

Radio Moscow World Service. Beamed to various parts of the world at this hour. Winter programming is aimed at a general audience, with some excellent musical fare during the second half-hour. Summers, it's *News*, followed Tuesday through Saturday by *Focus on Asia and the Pacific* and a music program. Monday features the 45-minute *Music and Musicians*, with *Audio Book Club* occupying part of the Sunday slot. Available on more than 20 channels, so tune around. Listeners in Eastern North America are best served winters by channels—dial about for the latest, as these change often—in the 7, 9 and 11 MHz segments, while those farther west are best advised to try frequencies in the 11, 15, 17 and 21 MHz segments of the world band spectrum. These latter segments are also valid for summer reception throughout North America. Additional options are via the Cuba relay, if operating—6000 or 6045 kHz (winters), and 11710 or 11850 kHz (summers). Listeners in East Asia should look to outlets in the 7 and 9 MHz segments in winter, and 11 and 15 MHz in summer (though 9480 kHz should be a good all-year channel). For Southeast Asia and the Pacific, try year-round frequencies in the 17 and 21 MHz segments; channels like 17890, 21690 and 21790 kHz are established favorites.

Radio Czechoslovakia. Well, at least that is the station's name as we go to press. *News*, followed by a lively magazine-style program covering a variety of topics. A half-hour to North America on 7345, 9540 (or 9580) and 11990 kHz.

Radio Vilnius, Lithuania. Winters only at this time. *News* about events in Lithuania, short features about the country's history and culture, and a small amount of Lithuanian music. Thirty agreeable minutes to North America on 7400, 17605 and 17690 kHz. One hour earlier in summer.

Swiss Radio International. Tuesday through Saturday, it's *News* and *Dateline*, a thoroughly workmanlike compilation of news and background reports on world and Swiss events. On the remaining days there's a shorter version of *Dateline*, complemented Sunday by *The Grapevine* and *Swiss Shortwave Merry-Go-Round* (which answers technical questions sent in by listeners), and Monday by *Supplement*, *Roundabout Switzerland* or *The Name Game*—features which alternate on a regular basis. A half-hour to North America on 6135, 9650, 9885, 12035 and 17730 kHz.

Croatian Radio. A special relay via religious station WHRI in Noblesville, Indiana. Mostly in Croatian, but with approximately 15 minutes of English *news* and commentary, usually the first quarter-hour of the broadcast. To North America on 7315 kHz.

Radio Pyongyang, North Korea. See 1100 for program details. Fifty minutes to the Americas on 11335, 13760 and 15115 kHz.

Radio Ukraine International. Summers only at this time. An hour of just about anything Ukrainian—news, sports, politics, culture—and ample coverage, at that. Not to be missed is *Music from Ukraine*, aired Mondays (Sunday evenings in the Americas) on the half-hour. Sixty minutes to Europe and North America on a variety of channels, including 7195, 7250, 9640, 11790, 12000, 12040, 12060, 13645, 15355 and 15570 kHz. One hour later in winter.

Voice of America. First hour of VOA's two-hour broadcasts to the Caribbean and Latin America. *News*, followed by split programming Tuesday through Saturday (Monday through Friday evenings in the Americas). Listeners in the Caribbean can tune in to *Report to the Caribbean* followed by *Music USA*. For Latin America there is *Newsline* and Special English news and features. On Sunday both services carry *On the Line* before splitting into separate programs for the last half-hour. Monday's programming is common to both services, consisting of two highly recommended programs—*Encounter* and *Spotlight*. An excellent way to keep in touch with events in the western hemisphere. The service to

the Caribbean is on 6130, 9455 and 11695 kHz; and the one to the Americas is on 5995, 7405, 9775, 11580, 15120 and 15205 kHz. The final hour of a separate service to East and Southeast Asia and the Pacific (see 2200) can be heard on 7120, 9770, 11760, 15185, 15290, 17735 and 17820 kHz.

Radio Beijing, China. *News,* then *News About China* and *Current Affairs.* These are followed by various feature programs, such as *Culture in China* (Friday), *Listeners' Letterbox* (Monday/Wednesday), *Travel Talk* (Sunday), *Cooking Show* (Sunday) or *In the Third World* (Saturday). The highly recommended *Music from China* is aired Sunday (local Saturday evening in the Americas). One hour to Eastern North America on 9770 and 11715 kHz.

Radio Habana Cuba. The start of a two-hour cyclical broadcast to North America. *News,* followed by feature programs such as *Newsbreak, Spotlight on Latin America, DXers Unlimited, Dateline Havana,* or *The Jazz Place.* Interspersed with some good Cuban music. The station, which emanates from one of the world's few remaining countries that jams foreign broadcasts—"La Voz de la Fundación" and Radio Martí, for example—claims that it, too, is now being jammed. Consequently, as we go to press Radio Habana's channel of 11970 kHz to Eastern North America has been changed to 11950 kHz.

WJCR, Upton, Kentucky. Twenty-four hours of gospel music targeted at North America on 7490 kHz. Also heard elsewhere, mainly during darkness hours. For more religious broadcasting at this hour, try **WYFR-Family Radio** on 5985 kHz, **KTBN** on 7510 kHz, **WINB** on 15145 kHz, or **KVOH-Voice of Hope** Tuesday through Saturday (Monday through Friday, local American date) on 17775 kHz. For those who like something a little more controversial, tune to Dr. Gene Scott's University Network, via **WWCR,** on 12160 kHz.

"For the People," WWCR, Nashville, Tennessee. Summers, the show starts at this time, but winters it doesn't start until 0100. Populism is currently a significant topic in the United States, and here is the most celebrated program on the air that promotes classic populism—an American political tradition going back to 1891 which, in more recent times, has been led by Huey "Redistribute the Wealth" Long and the more moderate Ross "Adios" Perot. Suspicious of concentrated wealth and power, *For the People* promotes economic nationalism ("buying foreign amounts to treason"), little-reported health concepts and a sharply progressive income tax, while opposing the "New World Order" and international banking. Taped in Florida five hours earlier, this two-hour talk show, hosted by former deejay Chuck Carter, may be heard Tuesday–Saturday (Monday through Friday local days) on 7435 kHz. Targeted at North America, but heard far beyond.

00:30

Radio Nederland. *News,* followed Tuesday through Sunday by *Newsline,* a current affairs program. Then there's a different feature each night, including the excellent *Research File* (Tuesday; science), *Mirror Images* (Wednesday; arts in Holland), *Rembrandt Express* (Saturday; various topics), the communications program *Media Network* (Friday), and a feature documentary (Thursday). Monday (Sunday evening local time in North America) is devoted to *The Happy Station,* an ever popular program of chat, greetings and light music. Fifty-five minutes to Eastern North America on 6020, 6165 and 11835 kHz.

Belgische Radio en Televisie, Belgium. Winters only at this time; see 1900 for program details, although they're one day later, World Day. Twenty-five minutes to Eastern North America on 9930 kHz; also audible on 13655 kHz though beamed elsewhere. One hour earlier in summer.

Radio Yugoslavia. Summers only at this time. *News,* followed by short features (see 0130). Thirty minutes to Eastern North America on 11870 kHz.

Radio Korea, South Korea. See 0600 for specifics, although programs are a day later, World Day. Sixty minutes to Eastern North America on 15575 kHz.

Voice of the Islamic Republic of Iran. Winters only at this time. One hour of *news,* commentary and religion, with the accent on the Islamic viewpoint. Targeted at North America on 9022, 9720 (or 9765) and 15260 kHz. One hour earlier in summer.

HCJB, Ecuador. *Studio 9,* featuring eight minutes of world and Latin American *news,* followed Tuesday through Saturday (Monday through Friday, local American date) by 20 minutes of in-depth reporting on Latin America. The final portion of *Studio 9* is given over to one of a variety of 30-minute features—including *Dateline 90* (Tuesday), *Happiness Is* (Wednesday and Friday) and the excellent *Música del Ecuador* (Saturday). On Sunday (Saturday evening in the Americas) news is followed by *DX Partyline,* which in turn is replaced Monday by *Saludos Amigos*—HCJB's international friendship program. To North America on 9745 and 15155 kHz, also available on 21455 (or 17895) kHz, upper sideband.

01:00

BBC World Service. Tuesday through Saturday (weekday evenings in North America) it's *News,* followed by *Outlook,* a program of news and human-interest stories. This is succeeded by a variety of features, including *Health Matters* (Tuesday), *Waveguide, Book Choice* and *The*

Farming World (Thursday), *Global Concerns* (Friday), and *Short Story* (Saturday). There are also 15-minute jazz, folk or country music programs on several of these days. On Sunday and Monday, weekends in North America, look for a summary of *news* and longer drama and classical music programs. Continuous to North America on 5975, 6175, 9590, 9915 and 7325 or 12095 kHz; and to East Asia on 17790 kHz, plus—Sunday only—15280 and 21715 kHz.

Christian Science Monitor World Service, USA. Continuation of the 0000 broadcast to Eastern North America and the Caribbean. *News*, then *Monitor Radio Features* which, as the name suggests, places less emphasis on news, and more on general interest stories. The final 25 minutes include *Letterbox* (listener response program) and a religious article from the *Christian Science Monitor*. Tuesday through Saturday on 7395 kHz; also widely heard on 13760 kHz. Additionally, available to Europe Tuesday through Friday on 9850 kHz, and to Southeast Asia Monday through Friday on 17555 kHz. On other days, programming is of a religious nature.

Radio Canada International. Winters only. Weekday programming (Tuesday through Saturday World Day) consists of the final 30 minutes of *As It Happens* (see 0000). The broadcasts are extended to one hour over the weekend, and include additional CBC domestic programming. To North America on 5960 and 9755 kHz.

Radio Czechoslovakia formerly **Radio Prague.** *News*, then features, including *Sports Roundup* (Tuesday), *Mailbag* (Thursday), *Ecology* (Friday), *Tip for a Trip* (Saturday) and *Czechoslovakia This Week* (Sunday). Monday (Sunday evening in North America) features the popular *Scrapbook*. Thirty minutes to North America on 5930, 7345 and 9540 (or 9580) kHz.

Radio Norway International. Sunday and Monday only. Repeat of the 2300 broadcast. Thirty minutes of *news* and chat from and about Norway. To North and Central America on 9605 or 9615 kHz.

Radio Argentina al Exterior - R.A.E. Tuesday through Saturday only. Lots of mini-features dealing with aspects of life in Argentina, interspersed with examples of the country's various musical styles, from tango to zamba. Fifty-five minutes to North America on 11710 kHz. Broadcast an hour later during winter in Argentina (summer in the northern hemisphere).

Radio Sweden. *News* and features of mainly Nordic content. Thirty minutes to Asia and the Pacific on 9695 and 11730 kHz.

Radio Japan. One hour to Eastern North America summers only on 5960 kHz via the powerful relay facilities of Radio Canada International in Sackville, New Brunswick. See 0300 for program details, except that all programs are one day later, and *Hello From Tokyo* replaces

Media Roundup and the Japanese language lesson local Sunday evening in North America.

Spanish Foreign Radio. Repeat of the 0000 transmission. To Eastern North America on 9530 kHz.

Radio For Peace International, Costa Rica. Where have the love, peace and peoplehood ideals of the Sixties gone? Why, they're alive and kicking over RFPI, an enthusiastic American-cum-internationalist station located in army-less Costa Rica. This hour is the start of English programming—the initial hour being in Spanish. *FIRE* (Feminist International Radio Endeavour) is one of the finer offerings from the mélange of programs that make up RFPI's eighthour cyclical blocks of predominantly counterculture and New Wave programming. Sixty minutes audible, with strength varying from hopeless to good, in Europe and throughout the Americas on 7375, 13630, 15030 and, irregularly, 21465 kHz. Some transmissions are in the single-sideband mode, which can be processed properly only on certain radios.

"Radio Free Croatia," WHRI. A Chicago-produced 30-minute program aired over this religious station in Noblesville, Indiana. Brief news-oriented tidbits in English are haphazardly sprinkled within a predominantly Croatian broadcast. To North America Tuesday, Thursday and Saturday (one day earlier, local American date) on 7315 kHz.

Radio Moscow World Service. *News*, features and music on a multitude of frequencies. Tuesday through Saturday, winters, it's *Focus on Asia and the Pacific*, replaced summers by *Update*. The second half-hour contains mainly musical fare. In North America, try 6000 or 6045 kHz winters, 11710 or 11850 kHz summers; as well as dialing about for new channels that might spring up in the 7, 9, 11, 15 and 17 MHz segments. Reception is generally better on lower segments winter, higher frequencies summer. Moscow's frequencies can change as often as every two months, so tune around with gusto. Listeners in East Asia should try the 7 and 9 MHz segments winter, 11 and 15 MHz summer (though 9480 kHz is available throughout the year). For Southeast Asia and the Pacific, dial around the 15, 17 and 21 MHz segments—prime choices are 15295, 17655, 17890, 21690 and 21790 kHz.

Radio Habana Cuba. See 0000 for program details. Continues to North America on 11950 or 11970 kHz.

HCJB, Ecuador. The second part of *Studio 9* (different programs at the weekend—see 0030), followed Wednesday through Sunday by *Focus on the Family*. At the same time Monday (Sunday evening in the Americas) there's religious fare, with a telephone talk program—*Open Line*—being aired on Tuesday. To North America on 9745 and 15155 kHz, also available on 21455 (or 17895) kHz, upper sideband.

Voice of America. *News*, then *Report to the Americas*, a series of news features about the United States and other countries in the Americas. This is replaced Sunday by *Communications World* and *Press Conference USA*, and Monday by the highly recommended *New Horizons* and *Issues in the News*. To the Americas on 5995, 6130, 7405, 9455, 9775, 11580, 15120 and 15205 kHz.

Radio Ukraine International. Winters only at this time; see 0000 for program details. Sixty minutes of informative programming targeted at European insomniacs and North Americans who keep more normal hours. Try 4825, 7240, 9860, 9870, 17605 and 17690 kHz. One hour earlier in summer.

Radio Tashkent, Uzbekistan. *News* and features reflecting local and regional issues. Thirty minutes to South Asia, occasionally heard in North America; winters on 5930, 5955, 7190 and 7265 kHz; summers on 7325, 7335, 9740 and 11975 kHz. This last frequency is sometimes replaced by 9755 kHz.

Deutsche Welle, Germany. *News*, followed Tuesday through Saturday by the comprehensive *European Journal*, which includes commentary, interviews, background reports and analysis. The Saturday edition is followed by *Through German Eyes*, while Sunday (Saturday night in North America) is given over to *Commentary*, *Mailbag* (or *Nickelodeon*) and *German by Radio*. Monday brings *Living in Germany* and the popular *Larry's Random Selection*. Very good reception in North America on 6040, 6145, 9565 and 11865 kHz; plus seasonal channels of 6085, 9610, 9640, 13610, 13770 and 15105 kHz.

"For the People," WWCR. Starts at this time winters only; is halfway through its two-hour broadcast summers. See 0000 for specifics. Targeted weeknights to North America on 7435 kHz, but also heard elsewhere.

"National Vanguard Radio," WRNO. This time summers only. Metairie, Louisiana is not only the home of world band station WRNO, but also that of the well-known former Klan chief David Duke and this tedious neo-Nazi skinhead program. If you're pale, male and have made so little of your life that you have only your ancestors to crow about, perhaps this yawner is for you. For virtually everyone else, it serves mainly as a case study in the banality of evil. Thirty minutes Sunday (Saturday local day) on 7355 kHz. Targeted at North America, but reaches beyond.

WJCR, Upton, Kentucky. Continues with gospel music to North America on 7490 kHz. Also with religious programs to North America at this hour are **WYFR-Family Radio** on 5985 and 9505 kHz, **WWCR** on 12160 kHz, **KTBN** on 7510 kHz, **WINB** on 15145 kHz, and Tuesday through Saturday, **KVOH-Voice of Hope** on 17775 kHz.

01:30

Radio Austria International. *Report from Austria*, which includes a brief bulletin of *news* followed by a series of current events and human interest stories. Ample coverage of national and regional issues, and an excellent source for news of Central and Eastern Europe. Thirty minutes to North America on 9875 and 13730 kHz.

Radio Finland. Summers only at this time. Tuesday through Saturday it's *Northern Report* and *Press Review*, followed by a five-minute feature. On Sundays there's *Perspectives* and a Finnish language lesson, while *Business Monday* and *Airmail* are the featured programs on the remaining day. Twenty minutes to North America on 11755 and 15185 kHz.

Voice of Greece. Preceded and followed by lots of delightful Greek music, plus news and features in Greek. There's a ten-minute English *newscast*, more or less at 0130, heard daily except Sunday (Saturday evening local North American date). To Eastern North America on 7430 or 11645 kHz, plus 9395 and 9420 kHz.

Radio Yugoslavia. Fifteen minutes of *News*, concentrating mainly on events in the Balkans, then items of general interest (science, medicine, ecology, sports, etc.). A half-hour to Eastern North America, winters on 9580 kHz, and summers on 11870 kHz.

01:45

BBC World Service for Asia. *South Asia Survey*, 15 minutes of in-depth analysis of political and other developments in the region (Tuesday through Saturday only). Also audible in parts of North America and the Pacific on 9580, 11955 and 5965 (or 15310) kHz.

02:00

BBC World Service. Thirty minutes of *Newsdesk*, followed on different days of the week by a variety of features, including a documentary (Sunday), *Composer of the Month* (Monday), *People and Politics* (Saturday), drama (Friday), a quiz (Tuesday) and *Sports International* (Thursday). Continuous to North America on 5975, 6175, 9590 (to 0230), 9915, and 7325 or 12095 kHz; and to East and Southeast Asia on 17790 kHz. For East Asia there are two additional Sunday frequencies—15280 and 21715 kHz. Also available to the Middle East on 7135 and 6195 or 9670 kHz.

Christian Science Monitor World Service, USA. See 0000 for program details. To the Middle East Monday through Friday on 9350 kHz, and to Western North America Tuesday through Friday (Monday through Thursday, local American days) on 9455 kHz. Also audible throughout much of North America on 13760 kHz, although not beamed there. Programming on the remaining days relates to the teachings and experiences of the Christian Science Church.

Radio Cairo. The first hour of a 90-minute potpourri of exotic Arab music and features reflecting Egyptian life and culture, with *news* and commentary about events in Egypt and the Arab world. There are also quizzes, mailbag shows, and answers to listeners' questions. Fair reception in North America on 9475 and 11865 kHz.

Voice of America. *News*, then *Focus*—an examination of the major issues of the day. Thirty minutes to the Americas, Tuesday through Saturday, on 5995, 7405, 9775, 11580, 15120 and 15205 kHz.

Radio Argentina al Exterior - R.A.E. Broadcast at this time only during the Argentinean winter (summer in the northern hemisphere). See 0100 for program details. To North America Tuesday through Saturday (Monday through Friday, local American days) on 11710 kHz.

Radio Budapest, Hungary. This time summers only. Repeat of the 2100 transmission, but all features are one day later World Day. Sixty minutes to North America on 6110 (or 15220), 9835 and 11910 kHz. One hour later in winter.

Radio Norway International. Sunday and Monday only. Repeat of the 2300 transmission. *News* and features from one of the friendliest stations on the international airwaves. Thirty minutes to North America on 9605 or 11930 kHz.

HCJB, Ecuador. Thirty minutes of religious programming, then a repeat of the first half of *Studio 9* or special weekend programs (see 0030). To North America on 9745 and 15155 kHz; also widely available on 21455 kHz upper sideband.

Voice of Free China, Taiwan. *News*, followed by three different features. The last is *Let's Learn Chinese*, which has a series of segments for beginners, intermediate and advanced learners. Other features include *Focus, Jade Bells and Bamboo Pipes, Journey into Chinese Culture* and *Kaleidoscope*—a potpourri of business, science, interviews and just about anything else. One hour to North and Central America on 5950, 9680 and 11740 kHz; to East Asia on 15345 kHz; and to the Pacific on 9765 kHz.

Radio Sweden. Repeat of the 1500 transmission. Thirty minutes to North America on 9695 and 11705 kHz.

Radio Moscow World Service. Continuous to Asia, the Pacific and North America. *News*, features and music to suit all tastes. Targeted at North America via the Cuba relay (if operating), winters on 6000 and 6045 kHz, summers on 9720 (or 11850) and 11710 kHz; also dial around for the latest frequencies in the 7, 9 11, 15 and 17 MHz segments. In winter, best recep-

tion is usually found on the lower frequencies, while the higher segments perform better in summer. Best winter frequencies for East Asia are in the 9 and 11 MHz segments; try 15 MHz and higher in summer. Listeners in Southeast Asia and the Pacific have several year-round frequencies in the 15, 17 and 21 MHz bands, such as 15295, 17890, 21690 and 21790 kHz.

Radio Habana Cuba. Repeat of the 0000 transmission. To North America on 11950 (or 11970) and 13710 (or 13700) kHz.

Swiss Radio International. Repeat of the 0000 broadcast to North America. Thirty minutes on 6135, 9650, 9885 and 12035 kHz.

"For the People," WWCR. Winters only at this time; see 0000 for specifics. The last half of a two-hour broadcast targeted weeknights at North America on 7435 kHz, but also well beyond.

Radio For Peace International, Costa Rica. Part of an eight-hour cyclical block of counterculture and New Wave programming audible in Europe and the Americas on 7375, 13630, 15030 and (irregularly) 21465 kHz. Some transmissions are in the single-sideband mode, which can be properly processed on only some radios.

Radio Romania International. *News*, commentary, press review and features on Romania, not to mention some charming selections of Romanian folk music. Recommended listening includes *Romanian Musicians* (Thursday) and *Skylark* (Friday). Other features include *Youth Club* (Tuesday), *Friendship and Cooperation* (Thursday) and *Cultural Survey* (Saturday). To North America on 5990, 6155, 9510, 9570, 11830 and 11940 kHz.

WJCR, Upton, Kentucky. Continues with gospel music to North America on 7490 kHz. Also with religious programs to North America at this hour are **WYFR-Family Radio** on 5985 and 9505 kHz, **WWCR** on 5920 kHz, **KTBN** on 7510 kHz, **WINB** on 15145 kHz, and Tuesday through Saturday, **KVOH-Voice of Hope** on 17775 kHz.

"National Vanguard Radio," WRNO. Only winter Sundays (Saturday evenings, local American date) at this time. See 0100 for program details. Thirty tiresome minutes to North America and beyond on 7355 kHz.

"Radio Free America," WWCR, Nashville, Tennessee. This time summers only, see 0300 for details. For two hours—they're hoping for three sometime in the future—to North America and well beyond on 7435 kHz.

02:30

Radio Finland. Winters only at this time. See 0130 for program details. Twenty minutes to North America on 9560 and 11755 kHz.

Radio Yugoslavia. Winters only at this time. See 0130 for specifics. Thirty minutes to North America on 9580 kHz.

Herald of Christian Science is heard each weekend, presented by (front left) Suzanne Smedley, Rosalie Dunbar, Enrique Smeke, Cornelia Muller-Landau; (rear) Michael Pabst, Cyril Rakhmanoff, Rita Polatin and Ed Thomas.

Radyo Pilipinas, Philippines. Unlike most other stations, this one opens with features and closes with *news*. Monday's themes are business and authentic Filipino music; sports are featured Tuesday and Thursday; Friday fare includes *Listeners and Friends* and *Welcome to the Philippines*; Saturday airs *The Week that Passed*; and Sunday there's *Issues and Opinions*. Approximately one hour to South and East Asia on 17760, 17840 and 21580 kHz.

Radio Portugal. *News*—which usually takes up at least half the broadcast—followed by feature programs: *Welcome to Portugal* (Tuesday), *Music Time* (Wednesday), *Challenge of '92* (Thursday), *Portugal Past and Present* (Friday), and either *Mailbag* or *DX Program* and *Collectors' Corner* (Saturday). Incredibly, there are no broadcasts on Sunday or Monday (Saturday and Sunday evenings local North American dates). Only fair reception in Eastern North America—worse to the west—on 9570, 9600, 9705 and 11840 kHz.

Radio Tirana, Albania. Twenty-five minutes of things Albanian. Veridical accounts of events in this beleaguered country, complemented by some delightful Albanian music. No longer the Tiranasaurian station of yesteryear. To North America on 9580 and 11820 (or 11825) kHz.

02:45

Radio Yerevan, Armenia. Summers only at this time. Approximately ten minutes of *news* about Armenia, mainly of interest to Armenians abroad. To North America on 11675, 13645 and 15580 kHz.

02:50

Vatican Radio. While concentrating mainly on issues affecting Catholics around the world, this station also features some secularly oriented items, such as ecology and the search for peace in areas of armed conflict. Weekend programming is of a less secular nature. Twenty minutes to Eastern North America, winters on 6095 and 7305 kHz, and summers on 9605 and 11620 kHz.

03:00

BBC World Service. *News*, then *Words of Faith* and *Sports Roundup*. On Monday, Tuesday and Saturday the next half-hour is taken up by music programs, while the remaining days are given over to some of the BBC's best: *Discovery* (Wednesday), *Assignment* (Thursday), *Focus on Faith* (Friday), and *From Our Own Correspondent* (Sunday). Continuous to North America on 5975, 6175 and 9915 kHz; also available to early risers in parts of Europe on 6195, 9410 and 3955 or 12095 kHz; to the Middle East on 11760 and 11955 kHz; and to East Asia on 15280 and 21715 kHz.

Christian Science Monitor World Service, USA. See 0100 for program details. Continuation of transmission to the Middle East Monday through Friday on 9350 kHz; and to Western North America, Tuesday through Friday (Monday through Thursday, local American days) on 9455 kHz. Also audible in much of North America on 13760 kHz, despite being targeted elsewhere. Programs on other days are religious in nature.

Voice of Free China, Taiwan. Similar to the 0200 transmission, but with the same programs broadcast on different days of the week. To North and Central America on 5950 and 9680 kHz; to East Asia on 15345 kHz; and to the Pacific on 9765 kHz.

Radio Beijing, China. Repeat of the 0000 transmission. One hour to North America on 9690, 9770 and 11715 kHz.

Deutsche Welle, Germany. Repeat of the 0100 broadcast. To North America and the Caribbean winters on 6085, 6120, 9535, 9545, 9640 9705 and 9770 kHz; and summers on 6085, 9545, 9700, 11810, 13610, 13770 and 15205 kHz.

Radio Budapest, Hungary. Winters only at this time; see 2100 for program details, with all features being one day later World Day. Sixty minutes to North America on 6110, 9835 and 11910 kHz. One hour earlier in summer.

Voice of America. Four hours of continuous programming aimed at an African audience. Opens with *News*, followed Monday through

Friday by the excellent *Daybreak Africa*. Weekends, there's *VOA Morning*, a mixed bag of sports, science, business and other features. Although beamed to Africa, this service is widely heard elsewhere, including many parts of the United States. Try 6035, 6090, 7265, 7405, 9575, 9885 or 11835 kHz.

Radio Norway International. Sunday and Monday, winters only. Repeat of the 2300 transmission. Thirty minutes to North America on 9645 kHz.

Radio Moscow World Service. Continuous to North America, the Middle East, Asia and the Pacific. Worth a listen are *Audio Book Club* (0330 winters on Tuesday, Thursday, Saturday); *Music and Musicians* (0311 winter Sundays); *Jazz Show* (0330 summer Mondays) and *Folk Box* (0330 summer Thursdays). On more than 50 ever-changing channels, so tune around and find it. For North America, there is also the relay via Cuba—if on—winters on 6000 and 6045 kHz, summers on 11710 and 9720 or 11850 kHz.

Radio Moscow—North American Service. Summers only at this time. The first of four hours of separate programming for the West Coast, consisting of programs heard on the World Service at other times. To Western North America and Hawai'i on 12050, 13645, 15405 and 15425 kHz. One hour later during winter.

Radio Sofia, Bulgaria. Summers only at this time; see 0400 for more specifics. The first hour of a 90-minute early morning package targeted at Europe, also audible in North America, on 9850, 11720 and 15160 kHz.

Radio Habana Cuba. Repeat of the 0100 transmission; see 0000 for program details. To North America on 11950 (or 11970) and 13710 (or 13700) kHz.

HCJB, Ecuador. Continues with *Studio 9* until 0330 (see 0030 for program details) , then switches to religious programs (except for Sunday, when *Musical Mailbag* is aired). To the United States and Canada on 9745 and 15155 kHz; also available to many parts of the world on 21455 kHz, upper sideband (scheduled to be changed to 17895 kHz).

Radio Cairo. The final half-hour of a 90-minute broadcast to North America on 9475 and 11865 kHz.

Radio Japan. On most days, *News*, followed by *Radio Japan Magazine Hour*, an umbrella for features like *Asian Hotline* (Tuesday), *Business Today* (Thursday) and *A Glimpse of Japan* (Friday). Saturday, it's an hour of *This Week*, with *Let's Learn Japanese*, *Media Roundup* and *Viewpoint* on Sunday. One hour winters to Eastern North America on 5960 kHz. There is also a separate year-round broadcast to the Americas, consisting of *News*, followed by *Let's Learn Japanese* or a feature program. Thirty minutes on 15325, 17825 and 21610 kHz.

Voice of Turkey. Summers only at this time. Repeat of the 2200 broadcast. See 2300 for specifics. Fifty minutes to Eastern North America on 9445 kHz. One hour later in winter.

Radio Czechoslovakia. Repeat of the 0100 broadcast. A half-hour's pleasant listening targeted at North America on 5930 (winter), 7345 (all-year), 9540 or 9580 (winter), and the summer frequencies of 9810 and 11990 kHz.

WJCR, Upton, Kentucky. Continues with gospel music to North America on 7490 kHz. Also with religious programs to North America at this hour are **WYFR-Family Radio** on 5985 and 9505 kHz, **WWCR** on 5920 kHz, **WINB** on 15145 kHz, **KTBN** on 7510 kHz, and Tuesday through Saturday, **KVOH-Voice of Hope**, winters on 17775 kHz and summers on 9785 kHz.

Radio For Peace International, Costa Rica. Continues with counterculture and New Wave programming. Audible in Europe and the Americas on 7375, 13630 and 15030 kHz. Some transmissions are in the single-sideband mode, which can be properly processed on only some radios.

"Radio Free America," WWCR, Nashville, Tennessee. Winters, starts at this time; summers, it is already at its halfway point. Sponsored by the Liberty Lobby, this live call-in show's populist features focus on what it perceives as conspiracies by the American medical establishment, as well as the Bilderberg meetings (which it tries to infiltrate), Trilateral Commission and similar internationalist organizations otherwise seldom reported upon. What most distinguishes this program from other current populist agendas is hostility towards Israel and conservative Arab states, and warmth towards radical Arab governments and the German people during World War II. Hosted by Tom Valentine for two hours Tuesday through Saturday (Monday through Friday local days). Well heard in North America and beyond via the Sun Radio Network and WWCR on 7435 kHz.

03:30

United Arab Emirates Radio, Dubai. *News*, then a feature devoted to Arab and Islamic history or culture. Twenty-five minutes to North America on 11945, 13675, 15400 and 15435 (or 17890) kHz, and heard best during the warm-weather months.

Radio Nederland. Repeat of the 0030 transmission, except Sunday (Saturday evening in North America), when most of the broadcast is taken up by the off-beat *East of Edam*. Fifty-five minutes to North America on 6165 and 9590 kHz.

BBC World Service for Africa provides separate programs for and about that continent, which otherwise tends to be poorly covered by the international media. Although this special service is beamed only to Africa, it can sometimes be heard in other parts of the world, as well. There is a daily five-minute bulletin of African *news*, followed Monday through Friday by *Network Africa*, a fast-moving breakfast show. On Saturday it's *Quiz of the Week*, replaced Sunday by *Postmark Africa*. If you are interested in what's happening in this fascinating continent, tune in to 3255, 6005, 6190, 9600, 11730 or 15420 kHz—you won't be disappointed!

Radio Austria International. Repeat of the 0130 broadcast. A half-hour to North and Central America on 9870 kHz.

Radio Tirana, Albania. *News*, commentary and interviews from and about the country, with enjoyable Albanian music filling in the remainder of the broadcast. Twenty-five minutes to North America on 9580 and 11820 (or 11825) kHz.

Voice of Greece. Repeat of the 0130 transmission. Ten minutes of English, surrounded by long periods of Greek music and programming, to North America, except Sunday (Saturday evening local American date), on 9395, 9420, and 11645 kHz.

03:45

Radio Yerevan, Armenia. Winters only at this time. Approximately ten minutes of *news* about Armenia, mainly of interest to Armenians abroad. To North America on 7400, 9750, 17605 and 17690 kHz.

04:00

BBC World Service. *News*, followed on the quarter-hour by one or more short features. Pick of the bunch is Tuesday's *Health Matters*. At 0430, Monday through Friday, it's *Off the Shelf*, readings from the best of world literature. Weekends are devoted to music, with Saturday featuring the excellent *Jazz Now and Then*. The final quarter-hour features a variety of offerings, including *Andy Kershaw's World of Music* (Monday), *Country Style* (Wednesday), and *Folk in Britain* (Friday). Continuous to North America on 5975 kHz; to Europe on 3955, 6195, 7230, 9410 and 12095 kHz (some of which are only available for the initial half-hour); to the Middle East on 11760, 11955 (till 0430), 12095 and 15575 kHz; and to East Asia on 15280 and 21715 kHz.

Christian Science Monitor World Service, USA. See 0000 for program details. Monday through Friday to Africa (but also heard in parts of Europe and North America) on 9840 kHz, and to East Asia on 17780 kHz. Tuesday through Friday, the broadcast is also targeted at Western North America on 9455 kHz, with 9870 kHz (winter) or 13760 kHz (summer) also available to parts of the United States. Programming on the remaining days relates to the beliefs and teachings of the Christian Science Church.

Radio Habana Cuba. Repeat of the 0000 broadcast. To North America and the Caribbean on 6180, 11760, 11950 (or 11970) and 13710 (or 13700) kHz.

Swiss Radio International. Repeat of the 0000 broadcast to North America on 6135, 9885, 12035 and 13635 kHz. There is also a separate transmission to Europe, summers only, on 3985, 6165 and 9535 kHz—see 0500 for specifics.

Radio Czechoslovakia. Repeat of the 0000 broadcast. To North America on a variety of frequencies (depending on the time of year). Try 5930, 7345, 9540, 9580, 9810, 11990, 13715 or 15355 kHz.

Radio Norway International. Sunday and Monday, summer only at this time. Repeat of the 2300 transmission. A half-hour of *news* and features targeted at North America on 9560 and 11865 kHz.

HCJB, Ecuador. Thirty minutes of religious programming to North America on 9745 and 15155 kHz; also heard elsewhere on 21455 (or 17895) kHz, upper sideband.

Radio Sofia, Bulgaria. Winters, the start of a 90-minute transmission; summers, the final half-hour of the same. A potpourri of news, commentary, interviews and features, plus a fair amount of music. Targeted at European early risers, but also audible in North America; winters on 9850, 11720 and 11765 kHz; and summers on 9850, 11720 and 15160 kHz.

Deutsche Welle, Germany. *News*, followed Monday through Friday by the informative and in-depth *European Journal* and the equally good *Africa Report* (replaced Monday by *Africa in the German Press*). Saturday features *Commentary*, *Panorama* and *Man and Environment*; substituted Sunday by *Sports Report* (or *Commentary*), *International Talking Point* and *People and Places*. Aimed primarily at Africa, this transmission is also available to the Middle East on 13770 kHz.

Radio Canada International. *News*, followed Tuesday through Saturday by *Spectrum*. On Sunday and Monday this is replaced by domestic programming from the Canadian Broadcasting Corporation. Thirty minutes to Europe and the Middle East, winters on 6150, 9505, 9670 and 11925 kHz; summers on 9650, 11905, 15275 and 15445 kHz.

Radio Beijing, China. Repeat of the 0000 transmission; to North America winters on 11685 kHz, and summers on 11680 and 11840 kHz.

Voice of America. Directed at Europe, North Africa and the Middle East 0400-0700, but widely heard elsewhere. *News*, followed Monday through Friday by *Newsline*, and *VOA Morning*—a conglomeration of popular music, interviews, human interest stories, science digest, sports news, and so on, with news summaries on the half-hour. On 5995, 6040, 6140, 7170 and 7200 kHz. In the meantime, the popular African service also carries the same programs on 6035, 7265,

7405, 9575 and 11850 khz. Reception of some of these channels is also good in North America.

Radio Romania International. An abbreviated version of the 0200 transmission, beginning with national and international *news* and commentary, then the feature program from the first half-hour of the 0200 broadcast. To North America on 5990, 6155, 9510, 9570, 11830 and 11940 kHz.

Voice of Turkey. Winters only at this time. Repeat of the 2300 broadcast; see there for program details. Fifty minutes to Eastern North America on 9445 kHz. One hour earlier in summer.

WJCR, Upton, Kentucky. Continues with gospel music to North America on 7490 kHz. Also with religious programs to North America at this hour are **WYFR-Family Radio** on 5985 and 9505 kHz, **WWCR** on 5920 kHz, **KTBN** on 7510 kHz, and **KVOH-Voice of Hope** on 9785 kHz.

Kol Israel. Summers only at this time. *News* for 15 minutes from Israel Radio's domestic network. To Europe and North America on 11588 kHz.

Radio For Peace International, Costa Rica. Part of an eight-hour cyclical block of counterculture and New Wave programming audible in Europe and the Americas on 7375, 13630 and 15030 kHz. Some transmissions are in the single-sideband mode, which can be properly processed on only some radios.

Radio Moscow World Service. Continuous to Europe, the Middle East, Asia the Pacific on scads of frequencies. Winters, it's *News and Views* followed by some of Radio Moscow's finest musical output, while summer programming includes the timely *Update* (Tuesday through Saturday). Listeners in Europe and the Middle East should dial about for the latest frequencies within the 7, 9 and 11 MHz segments, with 15, 17 and 21 MHz being more suitable for Asia and the Pacific.

Radio Moscow—North American Service. The only separate regional service still produced by Radio Moscow International. Beamed to the West Coast on several channels, including year-round 12050 kHz. Additional winter frequencies include 7270, 9505, 9895, 12010, 17605, 17700 and 17720 kHz; summers, try 13645, 15405 and 15425 kHz. Continues to just about every other part of the globe on more than 50 channels. Tune around for the channel which comes in best.

"Radio Free America," WWCR, Nashville, Tennessee. This time winters only. See 0300 for details. The second half of a broadcast targeted at North America on 7435 kHz, but which is also heard well beyond.

04:30

BBC World Service for Europe. Summers only at this time. Monday through Saturday, it's *Europe Today*, 30 minutes of the latest news,

comment and analysis. This is replaced Sunday by *Europe This Weekend*—a compendium of news, features and profiles presented in a magazine-like format. To Europe on 3955, 3975, 6010, 6180 and 6195 kHz. One hour later during winter.

BBC World Service for Africa. Monday through Saturday, it's a repeat of the 0330 broadcast, while Sunday's offering is *African Perspective*. Thirty minutes targeted at African listeners, but also heard elsewhere, on 3255, 6005, 6190, 9600, 15400, 15420 and 17885 kHz.

05:00

BBC World Service. *Newshour*—just about the most comprehensive and up-to-date news program to be heard anywhere. Sixty minutes of excellence, heard in North America on 5975 kHz; in Europe on 3955, 6195 and 9410 kHz (though not all channels may be available winter for the second half-hour); in the Middle East on 11760, 12095 (or 15070) and 15575 kHz; and in East Asia on 15280 and 21715 kHz.

Christian Science Monitor World Service, USA. See 0100 for program details. Monday through Friday to Africa (also heard in parts of Europe and North America) on 9840 kHz, and to East Asia on 17780 kHz. Tuesday through Friday, the broadcast is targeted at Western North America on 9455 kHz, with 9870 or 13760 kHz being additionally available to parts of the United States. On other days, programs are of a religious nature.

Deutsche Welle, Germany. Repeat of the 0100 transmission to North America, winters on 5960, 6045, 6120 and 9670 kHz; and summers on 5960, 9515, 9670, 11705, 11925, 13610 and 13790 kHz. This slot is by far the best for Western North America.

Spanish Foreign Radio. Repeat of the 0000 and 0100 transmissions to North America, on 9530 kHz.

Croatian Radio. See 0000 for specifics. A special relay via religious station WHRI in Noblesville, Indiana. To North America on 7315 kHz.

Swiss Radio International. Winters only at this time. Monday through Friday, it's *News* and *Dateline*, a well produced résumé of world and Swiss events. On weekends there's a change of pace, with a shorter *Dateline* being complemented by one or more features. Saturday brings *The Grapevine* and the technically oriented *Swiss Shortwave Merry-go-Round*, while Sunday is given over to *Supplement, Roundabout Switzerland* or *The Name Game*, features which alternate on a regular basis. Thirty minutes to Europe on 3985, 6165 and 9535 kHz. One hour earlier in summer.

Radio Beijing, China. This time winters only. Repeat of the 0000 broadcast; to North America on 11840 kHz.

Radio Sofia, Bulgaria. Winters only at this time. The final half-hour of a 90-minute broadcast (see 0400). Targeted at Europe on 9850, 11720 and 11765 kHz; also audible in North America.

HCJB, Ecuador. Repeat of 0030 transmission. To North America on any two of the following: 6230, 9745 or 15155 kHz; also audible in many areas on 21455 (or 17895) kHz, upper sideband.

Voice of America. Continues with the morning broadcast to Europe and the Middle East on the same frequencies as at 0400. The same programming is beamed to Africa on 6035, 7405, 9575, 9885, 11850 and 15600 kHz, with several of these channels providing good reception in North America.

Voice of Nigeria. Targeted at West Africa, but also audible in parts of Europe and North America, especially during winter. Opens with *Morning Flight* followed by *VON-Scope*, a half-hour of *news* and press comment. The first 60 minutes of a daily two-hour broadcast on 7255 kHz.

Radio Moscow—North American Service. Continuation of the transmission beamed to Western North America (see 0400); winters on 7270, 9505, 9895, 12010, 12050 and 17720 kHz; summers on 12050, 13645, 15405 and 15425 kHz.

Radio Moscow World Service. Continues to many parts of the world on more than 30 channels. Tuesday through Saturday, the first half-hour features *Update* (winters) or *Focus on Asia and the Pacific* (summers). Best heard in Europe on various and changing frequencies within the 7, 9 or 11 MHz segments; with 15, 17 and 21 MHz more appropriate for Asia and the Pacific. Dial around and take your pick.

WJCR, Upton, Kentucky. Continues with gospel music to North America on 7490 kHz. Also with religious programs at this hour are **WYFR-Family Radio** on 5985 kHz, **WWCR** on 5920 kHz, **KTBN** on 7510 kHz, and **KVOH-Voice of Hope** on 9785 kHz.

Radio For Peace International, Costa Rica. Continues with a mixture of United Nations, counterculture and New Wave programming, including *Sound Currents of the Earth* (Monday) and *Outlaw for Peace* (Willie Nelson and Friends, 0530 Tuesday and Saturday). Audible in Europe and North America on 7375, 13630 and 15030 kHz. Some transmissions are in the single-sideband mode, which can be properly processed on only some radios.

Kol Israel. Winters only at this time. *News* for 15 minutes from Israel Radio's domestic network. To Western Europe and North America on 11588 kHz.

05:20

Radio Canada International. Summers only at this time, and actual start is 0518. See 0615 for

program details. To Europe and Africa on 6050, 6150, 7295, 9750, 11775 and 17840 kHz.

Radio Finland. Summers only at this time. A brief ten-minute broadcast with the accent on Finnish and Nordic news. To Europe on 6120 and 9665 kHz, and to the Middle East on 11755 and 15440 kHz. One hour later in winter.

05:30

BBC World Service for Europe. Winters only at this time. See 0430 for program details. Thirty minutes on 3955, 3975, 6180 and 6195 kHz.

Radio Austria International. *Report from Austria*; see 0130 for more details. To North America (year-round) on 6015 kHz, and to Europe (winters only) on 6155 and 13730 kHz.

United Arab Emirates Radio, Dubai. See 0330 for program details. To East Asia and the Pacific on 15435, 17830 and 21700 kHz.

0600-1159
EVENING PRIME TIME—
EAST ASIA AND THE PACIFIC

06:00

BBC World Service. *News*, *News about Britain* and (Tuesday through Saturday) *The World Today* (replaced Sunday by *Letter from America* and Monday by *Recording of the Week*). The second half-hour includes offerings such as *Meridian*, an arts show (Wednesday, Friday and Saturday); *Jazz for the Asking* (Sunday); and *Sports International* (Thursday) Continuous to North America on 5975 and 9640 kHz; to Europe on 3955, 6195, 9410, 12095 and 15575 kHz; to the Middle East on 11760, 12095, 15575 and 21570 kHz; to East Asia on 15280, 15360, 17830 and 21715 kHz; and to the Pacific on 7150, 9640, 11955 and 17830 kHz.

Christian Science Monitor World Service, USA. See 0000 for program details. Monday through Friday to Europe on 9840 kHz, to Western North America on 9455 kHz and 9870 kHz, to East Asia on 17780 kHz, and to Southeast Asia on 17755 kHz. Weekend programs deal with various aspects of the Christian Science faith.

Radio Habana Cuba. Repeat of the 0000 transmission. To Western North America on 11760 kHz.

Croatian Radio. Monday through Saturday, summers only at this time; actually starts at 0603. Ten minutes of on-the-spot *news* from one of Europe's most troubled areas. Intended mainly for Europe at this hour, but also heard elsewhere—try 6210, 7240, 9830, 13640, 13830 or 21480 kHz. Although not available at this time Sunday, there is a short summary of news at

0703 for those who have an interest in what's happening in the region. One hour later during winter.

Swiss Radio International. See 0500 for specifics. Thirty minutes to the Middle East and Africa on 15430, 17565 and 21770 kHz; also to Europe, summers only, on 3985, 6165 and 9535 kHz.

BBC World Service for Africa. Repeat of the 0330 broadcast, and only available at weekends. Thirty minutes on 15400, 15420 and 17885 kHz.

Voice of America. Final hour of the transmission to Europe, North Africa and the Middle East. See 0400 for program details. On 5995, 6040, 6060, 7170, 7325 and 15205 kHz. Meanwhile, the mainstream program for the African continent continues with *News* and *Daybreak Africa* (replaced weekends by *VOA Morning*). Good reception in regions other than the target area (including North America) on 6035, 7405, 9530, 9575, 9885, 11850 and 15600 kHz.

Voice of Nigeria. The second (and final) hour of a daily broadcast targeted at West Africa, but also heard in parts on Europe and North America (especially during winter). This segment includes a 25-minute bulletin of *news*, starting on the half-hour. To 0700 on 7255 kHz.

Radio Moscow World Service. Continuous and varied programming targeted at virtually all countries between the United Kingdom to the west and Japan to the east. "Fish" for frequencies—they change often—within the 15, 17 and 21 MHz segments, although in Europe (winters) 7 and 9 MHz channels tend to be best.

Radio For Peace International, Costa Rica. Continues with counterculture and New Wave programming ranging from *Sound Currents of the Earth* (Thursday) to *World Goodwill Forum* (Monday). Audible in Europe and the Americas on 7375, 13630 and 15030 kHz. Some transmissions are in the single-sideband mode, which can be properly processed on only some radios.

Radio Moscow—North American Service. Another hour of programming to Western North America. Available on a variety of frequencies—winters, try 5905, 7270, 9505, 9795, 9825 and 17720 kHz; summers, on 12050, 13645, 15405 and 15425 kHz.

Radio Czechoslovakia. Summers only at this time. *News* and features with a distinct Central European flavor. Thirty minutes to Europe on 6055, 7345, 9505 and 11990 kHz. One hour later in winter.

Deutsche Welle, Germany. Repeat of the 0400 broadcast. Targeted at Africa, but one of the better opportunities for listeners in Western Europe. Heard winters on 11765, 13610, 13790, 15185, 15435 and 17875 kHz; and summers on 11780, 13610, 13790, 15185, 15205 and 17875 kHz.

Radio Korea, South Korea. The hour-long broadcast opens with *news*, followed on most days by commentary, *Seoul Calling* (various topics), *Let's Learn Korean!*, and features like *Korean Cultural Variety* (Tuesday) and *Pulse of Korea* (Wednesday). On other days, the news is followed by features such as *Sites and Sounds* (Saturday) and *Echoes of Korean Music* (Sunday). To North America on 11810 and 15170 kHz, and to East Asia on 7275 kHz.

WJCR, Upton, Kentucky. Continues with gospel music to North America on 7490 kHz. Also with religious programs for North American listeners at this hour are **WYFR-Family Radio** on 5985 kHz, **WWCR** on 5920 and 7435 kHz, **KTBN** on 7510 kHz, **WHRI-World Harvest Radio** on 7315 and 9495 kHz, and **KVOH-Voice of Hope** on 9785 kHz.

Voice of Malaysia. Actually starts at 0555 with opening announcements and program summary, followed by *News*. Then comes *This is the Voice of Malaysia*, a potpourri of news, interviews, reports and music. The hour is rounded off with *Personality Column*. Part of a 150-minute broadcast to Southeast Asia and Australia on 6175, 9750 and 15295 kHz.

HCJB, Ecuador. An hour of predominantly religious programming. Popular features include *Music from the Mountains* (0630 Thursday) and *Musical Mailbag* (0600 Sunday). To North America on at least one of the following: 6230, 9745, or 11925 kHz. Listeners in other areas can try 21455 (or 17895) kHz, provided their receiver is equipped to receive broadcasts in the upper sideband mode.

06:20

Radio Canada International. Winters only, and actual start is 0618. Forty minutes of programming targeted at Canadians overseas. *News*, then a feature: *The Inside Track* (Monday; sports), *Double Exposure* (Tuesday), *Open House* (Wednesday), or *Arts Tonight* (Thursday and Friday). To Western Europe and Africa, Monday through Friday, on 6050, 6150, 7155, 9760, 9740 and 11905 kHz.

Radio Finland. Winters only at this time. A brief ten-minute broadcast concentrating mainly on Finnish and other Nordic news. To Europe on 6120 kHz, and to the Middle East on 11755 and 15440 kHz. One hour earlier in summer.

06:30

BBC World Service for Africa. Repeat of the 0430 broadcast, except for Saturday (when the full half-hour is dedicated to *Spice Taxi*—a sideways look at African culture). Thirty minutes intended for Africa, but also audible in other parts of the world. Well worth the effort if you can hear it—try 15400 and 17885 kHz.

Radio Austria International. Tuesday through Saturday, it's *Report from Austria* (see 0130), replaced Sunday by the entertainment program *Austrian Coffeetable*, and Monday by the technically oriented *Austrian Shortwave Panorama*. A half-hour via the Canadian relay to Western North America on 6015 kHz.

Belgische Radio en Televisie, Belgium. Summers only at this time. Weekdays, there's *News* and *Press Review*, followed Tuesday through Friday by *Belgium Today* (various topics) and features like *Focus on Europe* (Tuesday), *Around the Arts* (Wednesday), *Living in Belgium* and *Green Society* (Thursday) and *North-South* (Friday). Weekend features include *Record of the Week* and *Radio World* (Saturday) and *Musical Roundabout* (Sunday), while Monday's *Press Review* is followed by a repeat of *Radio World*, which in turn gives way to *Tourism in Flanders*. Twenty-five minutes to Europe on 5910 and 11695 kHz; and to the Pacific on 11695 kHz. One hour later in winter.

06:45

Radio Finland. Summers only at this time. See 0745 winter transmission for program details. Fifteen minutes to Europe on 6120, 9560 and 11755 kHz.

Radio Romania International. *News*, commentary, press review and a short feature, with interludes of lively Romanian folk music. A half-hour to Australasia and the Pacific on 11810, 11940, 15335, 17720, 17805 and 21665 kHz.

Ghana Broadcasting Corporation. Intended for listeners in neighboring countries, so reception is marginal outside the target area—especially during the summer months. The broadcast begins with West African music, followed by *news*, then a further serving of lively African rhythms. On 6130 kHz.

07:00

BBC World Service. *Newsdesk*, followed by pretty much a mixed bag, depending on the day of the week. Of the regular year-round programs, try Thursday's *Network UK*, a valuable insight into the British way of life. Continuous to Eastern North America (till 0730) on 5975 kHz, and for the full hour to Western parts on 9640 kHz; to Europe on 7325, 9410, 12095 and 15070 kHz; to the Middle East on 11760, 15575 and 21470 kHz (the last two frequencies are available only till 0730 from Monday through Friday, and for the full hour on weekends); to East Asia on 15280, 15360 and 21715 kHz; and to the Pacific on 7150, 9640, 11955 and 17830 kHz.

Christian Science Monitor World Service, USA. See 0100 for program details. Monday through Friday to Europe (and parts of North America) on 9840 kHz, to Western North America on 9455 and 13760 kHz, to East Asia on 17780 kHz, and to Southeast Asia on 17555 kHz. Weekends are given over to nonsecular programming, mainly of interest to members of, and others interested in, the Christian Science Church.

Radio Habana Cuba. Repeat of the 0100 transmission; see 0000 for program details. To Western North America on 11760 kHz.

Voice of Malaysia. First, there is a daily feature with a Malaysian theme (except for Thursday, when *Talk on Islam* is aired), then comes a half-hour of *This is the Voice of Malaysia* (see 0600), followed by 15 minutes of *Beautiful Malaysia*. Continuous to Southeast Asia and Australia on 6175, 9750 and 15295 kHz.

Swiss Radio International. Winters only at this time. Repeat of the 0500 broadcast. Thirty minutes to Europe on 3985, 6165 and 9535 kHz. One hour earlier in summer.

Radio Czechoslovakia. This time winters only. Thirty minutes of *news* and features, with a strong emphasis on all things Czech and Slovak. A good way to start the European day. Available on 6055, 7345, 9505 and 11990 kHz. One hour earlier in summer.

Radio For Peace International, Costa Rica. Part of an eight-hour cyclical block of counterculture and New Wave programming audible in Europe and the Americas on 7375, 13630 and 15030 kHz. Some transmissions are in the single-sideband mode, which can be properly processed on only some radios.

Radio Moscow—North American Service. Winters only at this time. The final hour of separate programming for West Coast North America on a variety of frequencies. Try 5905, 7175, 7260, 7270, 7345, 9795 and 9825 kHz.

Radio Moscow World Service. Continuous programming beamed to most parts of the world. Tuesday through Saturday, summers, there's the informative *Update*. For Europe winters, dial about for frequencies in the 9, 11 and 15 MHz segments; at other times and in other areas tune around 15, 17 and 21 MHz. There are over 40 ever-changing channels from which to choose.

WJCR, Upton, Kentucky. Continues with gospel music to North America on 7490 kHz. Also with religious programs to North America at this hour are **WYFR-Family Radio** on 5985 kHz, **WWCR** on 5920 and 7435 kHz, **KTBN** on 7510 kHz, **WHRI-World Harvest Radio** on 7315 and 9495 kHz, and **KVOH-Voice of Hope** (winters only) on 9785 kHz.

Croatian Radio. Monday through Saturday, winters only at this time; actually starts at 0703 (Sunday, there is a brief summary at 0803). Ten minutes of English *news* from one of

Croatian Radio's domestic networks. In times of crisis, one of the few sources of up-to-date news on what is actually happening in the region. On at least three frequencies from 6210, 7240, 9830, 13640, 13830 and 21480 kHz. One hour earlier in summer.

Voice of Free China, Taiwan. Repeat of the 0200 transmission. Targeted at Central America, but audible in southern and western parts of the United States on 5950 kHz.

HCJB, Ecuador. Opens with 30 minutes of religious programming—except for Saturday, when *Musical Mailbag* is on the air. Then comes *Studio 9* (see 0030 for more details, except that all features are one day earlier), replaced Saturday by *DX Partyline*. Sunday is given over to *Saludos Amigos*—the HCJB international friendship program. To Europe on 9695 (or 15270) and 11730 kHz; and to the Pacific (from 0730) on 9745 and 11925 kHz. Also widely available on 21455 kHz, upper sideband.

07:30

Radio Czechoslovakia. *News*, generally followed by short features. These include *Czechoslovakia This Week* (Monday and Saturday), *Economic Report* and *Tip For a Trip* (Thursday), *Sports Roundup* and *The Arts* (Monday), *Scrapbook* and *Encore!!!* (Sunday), and *Opinion* and an ecological feature on Thursday. Thirty minutes to the Pacific on 17725 and 21705 kHz.

Radio Nederland. The first 60 minutes of a three-hour block of programming targeted at the South Pacific. See 0030 for specifics, except that all features are one day earlier. Heard on 9630 and 11895 kHz, and well worth a listen.

BBC World Service for Africa. See 0330 for details, the only difference being on Sunday, when the entire broadcast is taken up by *The Jive Zone*—a program of contemporary African music. Thirty minutes targeted at Africa (but also heard elsewhere) on 11860 and 15105 kHz.

Belgische Radio en Televisie, Belgium. Winters only at this time. See 0630 for program details. To Europe on 5910 and 11695 kHz; and to the Pacific on 11695 kHz. One hour earlier in summer.

07:45

Radio Finland. Winters only at this time. Monday through Friday it's *Northern Report* (except for *Business Monday* on the day of that name), then *Press Review*. Saturday's broadcast is reduced to ten minutes of *Northern Report* (which is followed by five minutes of Latin!), while Sunday is given over to *Perspectives*. Fifteen minutes (except for Saturday) targeted at Europe on 6120, 9560 and 11755 kHz.

08:00

BBC World Service. *News*, then the religious *Words of Faith*, followed by a wide variety of programming depending on the day of the week. Choice programs include a selection of classical music (Sunday and Tuesday), *Health Matters* and *Anything Goes* (Monday), *Good Books* and *John Peel* (Thursday), and *Music Review* (Friday). Continuous to Europe on 7325, 9410, 12095 and 15070 kHz; to the Middle East on 17640 kHz (plus 15575 and 21470 kHz on weekends); to East Asia on 15280, 15360 and 21715 kHz; and to the Pacific on 11955 and 17830 kHz.

Christian Science Monitor World Service, USA. See 0000 for program details. Monday through Friday to Europe and parts of North America on 9840 or 11705 kHz, with 9455 kHz available to the Americas. Listeners in East Asia can tune to 17555 kHz, while those in the Pacific region can choose from 13615 and 15665 kHz. Weekend programs are devoted to the teachings and beliefs of the Christian Science Church.

HCJB, Ecuador. Continuous programming to Europe and the Pacific. The final half-hour of *Studio 9* (or weekend variations), followed (for the Pacific, only) by 30 minutes of religious fare. To Europe (until 0830) on 9695 (or 15270) and 11730 kHz; and to the Pacific on 9745 and 11925 kHz. Listeners in other areas, whose receivers are capable of receiving signals in the single-sideband mode, can try tuning 21455 (or 17895) kHz.

Voice of Malaysia. *News* and commentary, followed Monday through Friday by *Instrumentalia*, which is replaced weekends by *This is the Voice of Malaysia* (see 0600). The final 25 minutes of a much longer transmission targeted at Southeast Asia and Australia on 6175, 9750 and 15295 kHz.

Croatian Radio. Monday through Saturday, summers only at this time; actually starts at 0803. Ten minutes of English *news* from one of the domestic networks (replaced Sunday by a brief summary at 0903). A good way to keep abreast of events in one of Europe's most unstable regions. Frequency usage varies, but try 6210, 7240, 9830, 13640, 13830 or 21480 kHz. One hour later in winter.

Radio Pakistan. Opens with a brief bulletin of *news* followed by recitations from the Koran (with English translation). This in turn is followed by a press review and a ten-minute interlude of Pakistani music. On the half-hour there's a feature on Pakistan or Islam, which then gives way to extracts from Pakistani concert recordings. Fifty minutes to Europe on 17900 and 21520 kHz.

Radio Australia. Part of a 24-hour service to Asia and the Pacific, but which can also be heard at this time throughout much of North America, as well as in parts of Western Europe. Begins with *International Report*, followed

Monday through Friday by *Stock Exchange Report*, then the daily *Sports Report*. Not very original titles, but the program content makes up for it. To southern parts of Asia and the Pacific on a variety of channels, and audible year-round in Europe on 15240 and 21725 kHz, with the latter frequency also available for the Middle East. Listeners in North America can tune in on 5995 and 9580 kHz.

WJCR, Upton, Kentucky. Continues with gospel music to North America on 7490 kHz. Other U.S. religious broadcasters operating at this hour include **WWCR** on 5920 and 7435 kHz, **KTBN** on 7510 kHz, and **WHRI-World Harvest Radio** on 7315 and 7355 kHz.

Radio Finland. Summers only at this time; see 0900 for program details. To East Asia and the Pacific on 17800 and 21550 kHz.

Radio Moscow World Service. *News*, then Tuesday through Saturday, winters, it's *Update* followed by *Audio Book Club* or *Russian by Radio*, with *Music and Musicians* the featured program on Sunday. In summer, *News* is followed Tuesday through Saturday by *Focus on Asia and the Pacific*. This in turn is followed, on the half-hour, by some excellent musical fare—try the top-rated *Folk Box* (Wednesday and Saturday), *Yours for the Asking* (Monday), or Friday's interesting *Jazz Show*. Listeners in Europe and the Middle East can try dialing around the segments from 9 MHz upwards. These segments are also suitable for East Asia, while listeners in Southeast Asia and the Pacific have year-round channels at their disposal in the 15, 17 and 21 MHz segments of the spectrum.

Radio New Zealand International. *News*, then features, music or special programs for the South Sea Islands, all with a distinctly Pacific flavor. Weekend programming features *Saturday Scrapbook* and relays from the domestic National Radio. Part of a much longer broadcast for the South Pacific, but well heard in North America on 9700 kHz.

Radio Korea, South Korea. See 0600 for program details. To Europe on 7550 and 13670 kHz.

08:30

Radio Austria International. The comprehensive *Report from Austria*; see 0130 for more details. To Australia and the Pacific (year-round) on 15450 and 21490 kHz, and to Europe (winters only) on 6155 and 13730 kHz.

Radio Finland. Summers only at this time; see 0900 for program details. To East Asia and Australia on 15355 and 17800 kHz.

Radio Nederland. The second of three hours aimed at Australasia. *News*, followed Monday through Saturday by *Newsline*, then a feature program. Well worth an ear are Thursday's

Research File and Wednesday's and Friday's documentaries. Sunday features the undefinable *East of Edam*, a well-produced hodgepodge of a program. One edition started off with an account of Dutch herring-eating habits, and then moved on to a lengthy feature on Indian film music. If you believe variety's the spice of life, tune in on 11895 kHz.

09:00

BBC World Service. Starts with *News* and business information, and ends with *Sports Roundup*. The remaining time is taken up by a series of short features, the pick of which are *Short Story* and *Folk in Britain* (Sunday), *Andy Kershaw's World of Music* (Monday), *The Farming World* (Thursday), and *Global Concerns* (Friday). To Europe on 5975, 9750, 9760, 12095, 15070 and 17640 kHz; to the Middle East on 11760, 15575 and 21470 kHz; to East Asia on 17830 and 21715 kHz, and to the Pacific on 11750 and 17830 kHz.

Christian Science Monitor World Service, USA. See 0100 for program details. Monday through Friday to Europe on 9840 or 11705 kHz, to East Asia on 17555 kHz, and to the Pacific on 13615 and 15665 kHz. Also audible in parts of North America on 9455 and 9840 kHz. Weekend programs are of a religious nature and are mainly of interest to members of, and others interested in, the Christian Science faith.

Deutsche Welle, Germany. *News*, followed Monday through Friday by *Newsline Cologne* and *Asia-Pacific Report* (substituted Monday by *Through German Eyes*). These are replaced Saturday by *International Talking Point, Development Forum* and *Religion and Society*; and Sunday by *Arts on the Air* and *German By Radio*. To Asia and the Pacific on 6160, 11915, 17780, 17820, 21465, 21650 and 21680 kHz.

Radio New Zealand International. Mostly relays programs from the domestic National Radio at this time, but some days has special programming for the islands of the South Pacific, where the broadcasts are targeted. Continuous on 9700 kHz, and audible in much of North America.

Belgische Radio en Televisie, Belgium. Monday through Saturday, summers only at this time. See 0630 for program details. Twenty-five minutes to Europe on 9905 and 13675 kHz. One hour later in winter.

Croatian Radio. Monday through Saturday, winters only at this time; actually starts at 0903 (Sunday, there is only a brief summary at 1003). Ten minutes of on-the-spot *news* from one of Europe's most unstable regions. Frequencies vary, but try 6210, 7240, 9830, 13640, 13830 or 21480 kHz. One hour earlier during summer.

HCJB, Ecuador. Sixty minutes of religious programming to the Pacific on 9745 and 11925

kHz, also available on 21455 (or 17895) kHz, upper sideband.

Swiss Radio International. Repeat of the 0500 transmission. Thirty minutes to East Asia and the Pacific on 9560, 13685, 17670 and 21770 (or 21695) kHz.

Radio Moscow World Service. Tuesday through Saturday, winters, *News* is followed by *Focus on Asia and the Pacific*, replaced summers by a variety of features. Year-round, the second half-hour features some highly enjoyable musical fare. Sixty minutes of continuous programming targeted just about everywhere. Dial around from 9 to 21 MHz and choose a frequency—there are plenty available.

Radio Australia. World and Australian *news*, followed most days by music and information. Then, on the half-hour, comes any one of a wide variety of features. These change on a seasonal basis (sometimes more often). Hardly the best way to keep the listeners happy, but to a certain extent this is made up for with some interesting program content. Heard in North America on 5995 and 9580 kHz, in Europe on 15240 and 21725 kHz (the latter frequency is also available for the Middle East), and in East Asia on 13605 and 15170 kHz.

Radio For Peace International, Costa Rica. *FIRE* (Feminist International Radio Endeavour). Repeat of the 0100 broadcast. Audible in Europe and the Americas on 7375, 13630 and 15030 kHz. Some of the transmissions are in the single-sideband mode, which can only be received on superior world band radios.

WJCR, Upton, Kentucky. Continues with gospel music to North America on 7490 kHz. Other U.S. religious broadcasters operating at this hour include **WWCR** on 5920 and 7435 kHz, **KTBN** on 7510 kHz, and **WHRI-World Harvest Radio** on 7315 and 7355 kHz.

Radio Finland. Winters only at this time. The regular programs are *News Update* and *Press Review* (Monday through Friday) and *Northern Report* (Tuesday through Saturday). These are complemented by short features such as *Airmail* (Tuesday), *Sports Fare* (Wednesday) and *Names in the News* (Friday). The Saturday broadcast (five minutes shorter) includes *Finnish History* and *Starting Finnish*, while Sunday features *Forum Helsinki*. To East Asia and the Pacific on 17800 and 21550 kHz.

09:30

Radio Finland. Winters only at this time; virtually the same features as 0900, but not necessarily in the same order. To East Asia and Australia on 15245 and 17800 kHz.

Radio Nederland. Repeat of the 0730 broadcast. Fifty-five minutes to Australasia on 9720 and 11895 kHz.

10:00

BBC World Service. *News Summary*, followed by some of the classiest programming on the international airwaves (some of which starts at 1030). The list includes *Jazz Now and Then*, *Letter from America* and *From the Weeklies* (Saturday), *Science in Action* (Sunday),*The Vintage Chart Show* (Monday), *Discovery* (Tuesday), *Omnibus* and *Jazz for the Asking* (Wednesday), *Assignment* and comedy (Thursday), and *Focus on Faith* (Friday). Tune in any day of the week for some high-quality programming. Continuous to Western Europe on 5975, 9750, 9760, 12095, 15070 and 17640 kHz; to the Middle East on 11760, 15575 and 21470 kHz; and to East Asia and the Pacific on 17830 kHz. 11750 kHz (for Australia) and 21715 kHz (for East Asia) are available until 1030.

Christian Science Monitor World Service, USA. See 0000 for program details. Monday through Friday to Eastern North America on 9495 kHz (also audible farther west on 9455 kHz). Listeners in East Asia can tune to 17555 kHz, while those in the southeast of the continent can try 13625 kHz. Weekend programming is nonsecular, and is devoted to the teachings and beliefs of the Christian Science Church.

Radio Australia. *International Report*, followed Monday through Friday by *Stock Exchange Report*, then one of several feature programs, some of which are subject to seasonal rescheduling. Heard well in North America on 5995 and 9580 kHz, and in Europe and the Middle East on 21725 kHz.

Radio New Zealand International. A mixed bag of Pacific regional *news*, features, and relays of the domestic National Radio network. Continuous to the Pacific on 9700 kHz, and easily audible in much of North America.

Voice of Vietnam. Much better heard in Europe than in North America. Begins with *News*, then political commentary, interviews, short features, and some very pleasant Vietnamese music. Omnidirectional on 9840 and 12019 or 15009 kHz. Repeats of this transmission can be heard on the same frequencies at 1230, 1330, 1600, 1800, 1900, 2030 and 2330 World Time.

Belgische Radio en Televisie, Belgium. Monday through Saturday, winters only at this time. See 0630 for program details. Twenty-five minutes to Europe on 9855 (or 9905) and 11695 (or 13675) kHz. One hour earlier in summer.

Kol Israel. Summers only at this time. *News* from Israel Radio's domestic network, followed by various features: *You're on the Air* (phone-in program, Sunday), *Israel Mosaic* (a variety of topics, Monday), *Letter from Jerusalem* and *Thank Goodness It's Friday* (yes, Friday), *Talking Point* (discussion, Tuesday), *Studio Three* (arts in Israel, Thursday), *This Land* (travel show, Wednesday), and *Spotlight* (issues in the news,

Saturday). A half-hour to Europe—occasionally audible in Eastern North America—on 17545 kHz. One hour later during winter.

Voice of America. The start of VOA's daily broadcasts to the Caribbean. *News*, *Newsline* and *VOA Morning*—a compendium of sports, science, business and features—on 9590, 11915 and 6030 or 15120 kHz. For a separate service to the Pacific, see the next item.

Voice of America. *News*, followed weekdays by *Newsline* and *Magazine Show*. On the remaining days there are features such as *Weekend Magazine* (Saturday) and *Critic's Choice* (Sunday). To the Pacific on 5985, 11720, and 15425 kHz.

Radio For Peace International, Costa Rica. Another hour of counterculture programming, audible in Europe and the Americas on 7375, 13630 and 15030 kHz. Some transmissions are in the single-sideband mode, which can be properly processed on only some radios.

All India Radio. *News*, then a composite program of commentary, press review and features—accompanied by ample servings of highly enjoyable Subcontinental music. To East Asia on 15050 and 17895 kHz; and to the Pacific on 15050, 17387 and 21735 kHz.

WJCR, Upton, Kentucky. Continues with gospel music to North America on 7490 kHz. Other U.S. religious broadcasters operating at this hour include **WWCR** on 5920 and 7435 kHz, **KTBN** on 7510 kHz, **WYFR-Family Radio** on 5950 kHz, and **WHRI-World Harvest Radio** on 7315 kHz.

Radio Moscow World Service. *News*, followed winters by a variety of features, and summers by *Update* (Tuesday through Saturday), *Culture and the Arts* (Sunday), and *Science and Engineering* (Saturday). The second half-hour is given over to *Audio Book Club*, *Russian by Radio* or music, with the first two being summers only. A truly worldwide broadcast, beamed to all continents at this time. Dial around above 9 MHz and find yourself a channel. If operating, the Cuban relay is available to North America on 6000 kHz winters and 11840 kHz summers.

HCJB, Ecuador. Monday through Friday it's *Studio 9*. As 0030, but one day earlier. Saturdays, you can hear *DX Partyline*, while Sundays are given over to *Saludos Amigos*. To the Pacific on 9745 and 11925 kHz; also broadcast on 21455 (or 17895) kHz, upper sideband.

10:30

Radio Korea, South Korea. Summers only at this time. Monday through Saturday, *News*, followed by *Seoul Calling* Monday and Tuesday, music Wednesday through Friday, and *From Us to You* Saturday. *Shortwave Feedback* follows *Weekly News in Review* on Sunday. On 11715 kHz via

Canadian relay, so this is the best chance for North Americans to tune in the station.

Radio Czechoslovakia. This time summers only. A pleasant mix of news and features from a genuinely friendly station. A half-hour to Europe on 6055, 7345, 9505 and 11990 kHz.

Radio Austria International. Summers only. *Report from Austria* (see 0130), replaced Saturday by *Austrian Coffeetable*, and Sunday by *Shortwave Panorama*. Thirty minutes to Australasia on 15450 and 21490 kHz.

United Arab Emirates Radio, Dubai. *News*, then a feature dealing with aspects of Arab life and culture. Weekends, there are replies to listeners' letters. To Europe on 15320, 15435 (or 17890), 17775 and 21605 kHz.

Voice of the Islamic Republic of Iran. This time summers only. Sixty minutes of *news*, commentary and features, with the accent on the Islamic viewpoint. Targeted at the Middle East on 9525, 11715 and 11930 kHz; and to South and East Asia on 9685, 11790 and 11910 kHz. One hour earlier in summer.

11:00

BBC World Service. *Newsdesk*, followed 30 minutes later by the arts program *Meridian* (Wednesday, Friday and Saturday), *The Ken Bruce Show* (Sunday), *Composer of the Month* (Monday), *Megamix* (Tuesday), and drama (Thursday). Continuous to North America on 5965, 6195, 9515 and 15220 kHz; to Western Europe on 5975, 9750, 9760, 12095, 15070 and 17640 kHz; to the Middle East on 11760, 15575 and 21470 kHz; and to East Asia and the Pacific on 9740 kHz.

Christian Science Monitor World Service, USA. See 0100 for program details. Audible Monday through Friday in North America on 9455 and 9495 kHz, in East Asia on 17555 kHz, and in Southeast Asia on 13625 kHz. Weekends are given over to programming of a religious nature.

Radio Australia. World and Australian news, then music, followed on the half-hour by a 30-minute feature. A popular choice with many listeners, and rightly so. Heard clearly in North America on 5995 and 9580 kHz; in East Asia on 6080, 9710, 13605 and 15170 kHz; and also audible in Europe and the Middle East on 21725 khz.

Voice of Vietnam. Repeat of the 1000 transmission. To Asia on 7420 and 9730 kHz.

Radio Korea, South Korea. See 0600 for program details. Sixty minutes to the Middle East and beyond on 15575 kHz.

HCJB, Ecuador. Thirty minutes of religious programming to the Pacific on 9745 and 11925 kHz; also available on 21455 (or 17895) kHz, upper sideband.

Voice of America. The second—and final—hour of the morning broadcast to the Caribbean. *News*, followed weekdays by *Focus* and *VOA Morning*. On Saturday there's *Agriculture Today* and *Music USA*, while Sunday features *Critic's Choice* and *Studio One*. On 6030 (or 15120), 9590 and 11915 kHz. For a separate service to Asia and the Pacific, see the next item.

Voice of America. These programs are different from those to the Caribbean. *News*, followed Saturday by *Agriculture Today* and *Press Conference, USA*, Sunday by *New Horizons* and *Issues in the News*, and weekdays by special features and *Music USA*. To East Asia on 6110, 9760 and 15155 kHz, and to the Pacific on 5985, 11720 and 15425 kHz.

Kol Israel. Winters only at this time. *News* from Israel Radio's domestic network, followed by various features (see 1000). A half-hour to Europe—sometimes heard in Eastern North America—on 17545 kHz.

Trans World Radio, Netherlands Antilles. The first hour of a transmission which lasts until 1330, and which is predominantly of religious content from 1200 onwards. Monday through Friday it's *Morning Sounds*, 60 minutes of world and Caribbean *news*, weather reports, temperature forecasts for U.S. cities, sports results, currency exchange rates, chat and gospel music. There is also a small amount of religiously oriented talk, but this is kept to a minimum. Weekends, the programming is totally nonsecular. To Eastern North America on 11815 and 15345 kHz.

Radio Sofia, Bulgaria. Summers only at this time. The first hour of a 90-minute compendium of *news* and entertainment, including some highly enjoyable Bulgarian folk tunes. Targeted at Europe on 11630 kHz.

Radio Moscow World Service. Continuous programming to virtually all parts of the globe. Tuesday through Saturday, winters, it's the highly informative *Update*, a potpourri of news and comment. Summers at this time there's the daily *News and Views*. The second half-hour is given over to a variety of musical styles, alternating summers with *Audio Book Club* and *Russian by Radio*. Forty available channels—just tune around until you find one. North Americans can try the Cuban relay (if operating) on 6000 kHz (winters) or 11840 kHz (summers).

Swiss Radio International. See 0500 for specifics. Thirty minutes to Asia and the Pacific on 13635, 15505, 17670 and 21770 kHz; also to Europe, summers only, on 6165, 9535 and 12030 kHz.

Radio Japan. On weekdays, opens with *Radio Japan News-Round*, with news oriented to Japanese and Asian affairs. *Radio Japan Magazine Hour* follows, with more feature content, including *Crosscurrents* (Monday), *Environment Update* (Tuesday) and *A Glimpse of Japan* (Friday). *Commentary* and *News* round off the hour.

On Saturday, there's *This Week*, and Sunday features *News*, *Hello from Tokyo*, and *Viewpoint*. One hour to North America on 6120 kHz, and to East Asia on 11815 and 11840 kHz.

Radio For Peace International, Costa Rica. Part of an eight-hour cyclical block of counterculture and New Wave programming audible in North America on 7375, 13630 and 15030 kHz. Some transmissions are in the single-sideband mode, which can be properly processed on only some radios.

Radio Pyongyang, North Korea. Lots of patriotic songs and an abundance of political commentary are hardly enough to enthuse most listeners. Each broadcast starts with *News*; then come features with titles like "The Happiness of Living under a Great Leader," accompanied by children's choirs praising the eternal beneficence of Comrade Kim. Monolithic mediocrity at its very worst. Hear it while you can—and then forget about it. Fifty minutes to North America on 6576, 9977 and 11335 kHz.

WJCR, Upton, Kentucky. Continues with gospel music to North America on 7490 kHz. Other U.S. religious broadcasters operating at this hour include **WWCR** on 5920 (or 12160) and 7435 (or 15690) kHz, **KTBN** on 7510 kHz, **WYFR-Family Radio** on 5950 and 6105 (or 11830) kHz, and **WHRI-World Harvest Radio** on 7315 kHz.

Voice of Asia, Taiwan. Broadcasts open with features like *Asian Culture* (Monday) and *Touring Asia* (Tuesday), followed by *News*, *Festival Asia*, and *Let's Learn Chinese*. Heard in East Asia and the Pacific—but only occasionally in North America—on 7445 kHz.

11:30

Radio Finland. Monday through Friday, summers only at this time. Actually starts at 1125. Twenty-five minutes of features dealing almost exclusively with Nordic culture and events. To North America on 15400 kHz. One hour later in winter.

Radio Korea, South Korea. Winters only at this time. See 1030 for program details. On 9700 kHz via their Canadian relay, so a good chance for North Americans to tune in the station.

Belgische Radio en Televisie, Belgium. Summer Sundays only at this time. *News*, followed by *P.O. Box 26* (a mailbag program) and *Musical Roundabout*. Twenty-five minutes to North America on 17555 kHz, and to Southeast Asia on 21810 kHz. One hour later in winter.

Radio Austria International. Monday through Friday features *Report from Austria* (see 0130 for further details). On Saturday there's *Austrian Coffeetable*, which consists of light chat and musical entertainment; and Sunday it's *Shortwave Panorama* for radio enthusiasts. Thirty minutes to North America on 13730 kHz; to Europe on 6155 and 13730 kHz; and to East Asia on 11780 (or 17730) and 15450 kHz.

Radio Czechoslovakia. Winters only at this time. A midday potpourri of news and entertainment targeted at European listeners on 6055, 7345, 9505 and 11990 kHz. One hour earlier in summer.

HCJB, Ecuador. First 30 minutes of a four-and-a-half-hour block of religious programming to North America on 11925, 15115 and 17890 kHz; also widely heard on 21455 (or 17895) kHz, upper sideband.

Voice of the Islamic Republic of Iran. Winters only at this time. Sixty minutes of *News*, commentary and features, much of it with an Islamic slant. Targeted at the Middle East on 7215 and 9525 kHz, and to South and East Asia on 9685, 11790 and 11930 kHz. One hour earlier in summer.

1200-1759
EVENING PRIME TIME—ASIA AND WESTERN AUSTRALIA

12:00

BBC World Service. Except for Sunday, the hour starts with *News* and *News about Britain*, then *Multitrack* (Tuesday, Thursday, Saturday), a quiz, or a special feature. *Sports Roundup* follows at 45 minutes past the hour. This time Sunday there's a *News Summary* followed by *Play of the Week*—the best in radio theater. Continuous to North America on 5965, 6195, 9515, 9740 and 15220 kHz; to Europe on 5975, 9750, 9760, 12095, 15070, and 17640 kHz; to the Middle East on 11760, 15575 and 21470 kHz; and to East Asia and the Pacific on 9740 kHz.

Christian Science Monitor World Service, USA. See 0000 for program details. Monday through Friday to North America on 9495 and 13760 kHz, to the Pacific on 9425 or 15665 kHz, and audible in Southeast Asia on 13625 kHz. Weekends, the news-oriented fare gives way to religious programming.

Radio Canada International. Summers only at this time; see 1300 for program details. Monday through Friday to North and Central America on 9635, 11855 and 17820 kHz.

Radio Tashkent, Uzbekistan. *News* and commentary, followed by features such as *Life in the Village*, *Youth Program*, and *On the Asian Continent*. Heard better in Asia, the Pacific and Europe than in North America. Thirty minutes winters on 5945, 9540, 15470 and 17745 kHz; and summers on 7325, 9715, 15460 and 17815 kHz.

Polish Radio Warsaw, Poland. This time summers only. *News*, commentary and features on Poland past and present. Fifty-five minutes of interesting fare to Europe on 6135, 7145, 9525 and 11815 kHz. One hour later in winter.

Radio Australia. *International Report*, followed 30 minutes later, Sunday through Thursday, by *Soundabout*—a program of contemporary popular music. On the remaining days, there is a special feature program. Although targeted elsewhere, is well heard in North America on 5995 and 9580 kHz, and often audible in Europe and the Middle East on 21725 kHz.

Croatian Radio. Summers only at this time; actually starts at 1203. Ten minutes of English *news* from one of the domestic networks. A valuable source of up-to-the-minute information from a region renowned for its volatility. Heard best in Europe at this hour—try 6210, 7240, 9830, 13640, 13830 or 21480 kHz. One hour later in winter.

HCJB, Ecuador. Continuous religious programming to North America on 11925, 15115 and 17890 kHz, also heard on 21455 (or 17895) kHz, upper sideband.

Radio Norway International. Saturday and Sunday only. A well-packaged half-hour of *news* and features targeted at Asia and the Pacific on any two channels from 17860, 21695, 21705 and 25730 kHz.

Voice of America. *News*, then—weekdays—*Newsline* and *Magazine Show*. End-of-week programming consists of features like Saturday's *Weekend Magazine* or Sunday's *Encounter* and *Studio One*. To East Asia on 6110, 9760 and 15155 kHz; and to the Pacific on 15425 kHz.

Swiss Radio International. This time winters only. Repeat of the 0500 broadcast. Thirty minutes to Europe on 6165, 9535 and 12030 kHz. One hour earlier in summer.

Radio Beijing, China. *News* and various features—see 0000 for specifics, although programs are one day earlier. To Eastern North America winters on 9665 kHz, and summers on 15210 kHz; to East Asia on 9715 and 11660 kHz; and to the Pacific on 11600 (or 15440) and 15450 kHz.

Radio Sofia, Bulgaria. Winters, the first hour of a 90-minute program of *news*, commentary, features and Bulgarian music; summers, the final half-hour of the same. To Europe on 11630 kHz.

Radio Nacional do Brasil (Radiobras), Brazil. Variously titled *Life in Brazil* or *Brazilian Panorama*, Monday through Saturday you can hear a mix of Brazilian music and news, facts and figures about South America's largest and most fascinating country. The *Sunday Special*, on the other hand, is devoted to one particular theme, and often contains lots of stupendous Brazilian music. Eighty minutes to North America on 11745 or 15445 kHz.

Radio For Peace International, Costa Rica. Part of an eight-hour cyclical block of counterculture and New Wave programming audible in North America on 7375, 13630 and 15030 kHz. Some transmissions are in the single-sideband mode, which can be properly processed on only some radios.

Radio Moscow World Service. Winters, it's *News and Views*; Tuesday through Saturday, summers, there's *Focus on Asia and the Pacific*; and outside these programs, it's music, *Audio Book Club* or *Russian by Radio*. Continuous programming worldwide. Tune around from 11 MHz upwards and choose a channel, although the 7 and 9 MHz segments are likely to be best for East Asia during winter. Listeners in North America can try the Cuban relay (if operating), winters on 6000 and summers on 11840 kHz.

WJCR, Upton, Kentucky. Continues with gospel music to North America on 7490 kHz. Other U.S. religious broadcasters operating at this hour include **WWCR** on 5920 (or 12160) and 15690 kHz, **KTBN** on 7510 kHz, **WYFR-Family Radio** on 5950, 6015 (or 7355) and 11830 kHz, and **WHRI-World Harvest Radio** on 7315 kHz.

12:15

Radio Cairo. The start of a 75-minute package of news, religion, culture and entertainment. The initial quarter-hour consists of virtually anything, from quizzes to Islamic religious talks, then there's *news* and commentary, which in turn give way to political and cultural items. To Asia on 17595 kHz.

Radio Korea, South Korea. Repeat of the 0800 transmission, but to Eastern North America on 9750 kHz.

12:30

Radio France Internationale. *News*, which gives ample coverage of French politics and international events, usually followed by one or more short features such as *Land of France* (Tuesday), *Books* (Wednesday), *Arts in France* (Thursday), or *Science* (Saturday); and if you are interested, tune in Monday for the weekend's sports results. A half-hour to North America, usually received with a so-so signal on 15365 (or 21635) and 21645 kHz; and to Europe on 9805, 11670, 15195 and 15425 kHz.

Radio Bangladesh. *News*, followed by Islamic and general interest features, not to mention some very pleasant Bengali music. Thirty minutes to Europe (sometimes heard in North America) on 15200 kHz.

Radio Nederland. *News*, followed Monday through Saturday by *Newsline*, a current affairs program. Then there's a different feature each day, including the excellent *Research File* (Monday; science), *Mirror Images* (Tuesday; arts

in Holland), *Rembrandt Express* (Friday; various topics), Thursday's *Media Network* (communications), and a feature documentary (Wednesday). Fifty-five minutes to Europe on 5955 kHz.

Radio Finland. Monday through Friday only; summers from 1230, winters from 1225. Twenty-five minutes of predominantly Nordic fare targeted at North America on 15400 kHz, with 17880 kHz also available in summer.

Voice of Turkey. This time summers only. Thirty minutes of *News*, features and Turkish music targeted at the Middle East and Southwest Asia on 9675 kHz. One hour later in winter.

Radio Sweden. Summers only at this time. See 1500 for program details. To Asia and the Pacific on 15170 and 17740 kHz. One hour later in winter.

Belgische Radio en Televisie, Belgium. Winter Sundays only at this time. See 1130 for program details. Twenty-five minutes to North America on 17555 kHz, and to Southeast Asia on 21810 kHz. One hour earlier in summer.

13:00

BBC World Service. *Newshour*—international radio's 60-minute showpiece of news and in-depth analysis. To North America on 5965, 6195, 9515, 9740 or 15220 kHz. Continuous to Europe on 5975, 9410, 9750, 9760, 12095, 15070 and 17640 kHz; to the Middle East on 11760, 15575 and 21470 kHz; to East Asia on 7180, 9740 and 11820 kHz; and to the Pacific on 9740 kHz.

Christian Science Monitor World Service, USA. See 0100 for program details. Monday through Friday to North America on 9495 and 13760 kHz, to the Pacific on 9425 or 15665 kHz, and audible in Southeast Asia on 13625 khz. Weekends are given over to religious offerings from and about the Christian Science Church.

Radio Canada International. Winter weekdays only at this time. Relay of CBC domestic network programming. One hour Monday through Friday to North and Central America on 9635, 11855 and 17820 kHz. For an additional service, see next item.

Radio Canada International. Summers only at this time; see 1400 for program details. Sunday only to North and Central America on 11955 and 17820 kHz.

Radio Pyongyang, North Korea. Repeat of the 1100 transmission. To Europe on 9325 and 9345 kHz; and to North America and East Asia on 9640, 13650, and 15230 kHz.

Swiss Radio International. See 0500 for specifics. Thirty minutes to Asia and the Pacific on 7480, 11690, 13635, 15505, 17670 and 21770 kHz.

Radio Sofia, Bulgaria. Winters only at this time. The final half-hour of a 90-minute broadcast (see 1200). To Europe on 11630 kHz.

Radio Norway International. Saturday and Sunday only. Repeat of the 1200 transmission. A half-hour of *News* and features targeted at Europe on 9590 and 15270 (or 25730) kHz.

Radio Nacional do Brasil (Radiobras), Brazil. The final 20 minutes of the broadcast beamed to North America on 11745 or 15445 kHz.

Belgische Radio en Televisie, Belgium. Summers only at this time, Monday through Saturday. See 0630 for program details. Twenty-five minutes to North America on 17555 kHz, and to Southeast Asia on 21810 kHz. One hour later in winter.

Radio Beijing, China. See 0000 for program details, but one day earlier at this hour. To Western North America summers on 11855 kHz, year-round to East Asia on 9715 and 11660 kHz, and to the Pacific on 11600 or 15440 kHz.

Polish Radio Warsaw, Poland. This time winters only. *News* and commentary, followed by a variety of features. Fifty-five minutes of interesting fare to Europe on 6135, 7145, 9525 and 11815 kHz. One hour earlier during summer.

Radio Cairo. The final half-hour of the 1215 broadcast, consisting of listener participation programs, Arabic language lessons and a summary of the latest news. To Asia on 17595 kHz.

Radio Finland. Saturday and Sunday, summers only at this time. Saturday programming consists of *Northern Report*, *Finnish History* and *Airmail*; replaced Sunday by *Perspectives* and *Forum Helsinki*. Thirty minutes to North America on 15400 and 17880 kHz. One hour later in winter.

Radio Romania International. First daily broadcast for European listeners. *News*, commentary, press review and features about Romanian life and culture. Relax to some delightful Romanian folk music—Bucharestful 60 minutes on 11940, 15365, 17720 and 17850 kHz.

Croatian Radio. Winters only at this time; actually starts at 1303. Ten minutes of on-the-spot *news* from one of Europe's hot-spots. Best heard in Europe at this hour; frequency usage varies, but try 6210, 7240, 9830, 13640, 13830 or 21480 kHz. One hour earlier during summer.

Radio Australia. World and Australian *news*, followed by *Sports Report* and a half-hour of music. Beamed elsewhere, but tends to be easily audible in North America on 5995 and 9580 kHz.

Radio For Peace International, Costa Rica. Most days, starts off with United Nations features, with the remainder of the time being given over to counterculture or New Wave programming. Audible in North America on 7375, 13630 and 15030 kHz. Some transmissions are in the single-sideband mode, which can be properly processed on only some radios.

Kol Israel. Sunday through Thursday, summers only at this time. World and Israeli *News*, then one or more features—*Israel Sound* and *Postmark* (Sunday), *Calling All Listeners* and *DX Corner* (Monday), *Israel Mosaic* and *New from Israel* (Tuesday), *Jewish News* and *This Land* (Thursday), and *Talking Point* (Wednesday). Twenty-five minutes targeted at Europe and Eastern North America on 11587, 11605, 15640 and 17575 kHz; and to Southeast Asia and the Pacific on 15650 kHz.

WJCR, Upton, Kentucky. Continues with gospel music to North America on 7490 kHz. Other U.S. religious broadcasters operating at this hour include **WWCR** on 12160 and 15690 kHz, **KTBN** on 7510 kHz, **WYFR-Family Radio** on 5950, 6015 (or 9705) and 11830 kHz, and **WHRI-World Harvest Radio** on 9465 and 11790 kHz.

Radio Moscow World Service. *News*, then very much a mixed bag depending on the day and season. Continuous to virtually everywhere; tune around and find a channel that suits you. Listeners in East Asia should try the 7 and 9 MHz segments during winter, otherwise the best place to look is in the 11, 15, 17 and 21 MHz segments of the spectrum.

HCJB, Ecuador. Sixty minutes of religious broadcasting. Continuous to North America on 11925, 15115 and 17890 kHz; plus 21455 (or 17895) kHz, upper sideband.

Voice of America. *News*, followed by *Focus* (weekdays), *On the Line* (Saturday) or *Critic's Choice* (Sunday). The last half-hour includes special features. To East Asia on 9760 and 15155 kHz; and to the Pacific on 15425 kHz.

13:30

United Arab Emirates Radio, Dubai. *News*, then a feature devoted to Arab and Islamic history and culture. Twenty-five minutes to Europe on 15320, 15435 (or 17890), 17775 and 21605 kHz.

Radio Austria International. *Report from Austria*; see 0130 for more details. A half-hour to South and East Asia on 11780 (or 17730) and 15450 kHz.

Voice of Turkey. This time winters only. A reduced version of the normal 50-minute broadcast (see 2000). A half-hour of *news* and features targeted at the Middle East and Southwest Asia on 9675 kHz. One hour earlier in summer.

Radio Finland. Twenty minutes, Monday through Friday, winters; and a daily half-hour during summer. Heavily slanted in favor of Finnish and other Nordic fare. To North America on 15400 and 17880 kHz.

Radio Canada International. *News*, followed Monday through Friday by *Spectrum*, and weekends by CBC domestic programming. Targeted at East Asia, summers on 9535 and 11795 kHz, and winters on 6095, 6150, 9535 and 9700 kHz.

Radio Sweden. Winters only at this time; see 1500 for program details. To Asia and the Pacific on 15170 and 17740 kHz. One hour earlier in summer.

Radio Tashkent, Uzbekistan. Repeat of the 1200 transmission. Heard in Asia, the Pacific, Europe and parts of North America winters on 5945, 9540, 15470 and 17745 kHz; and summers on 7325, 9715, 15460 and 17815 kHz.

13:45

Vatican Radio. Twenty minutes of religious and secular programming to Asia and the Pacific on 11640, 15090, 17525 and 21515 kHz.

14:00

BBC World Service. Weekdays, it's *World News,* followed by *Outlook.* On the half-hour you can hear *Off the Shelf,* readings from some of the best of world literature. The final 15 minutes are mainly devoted to cultural themes. Saturday features *Sportsworld* (winters from 1430), and Sunday is given over to a documentary or phone-in program, followed by *Anything Goes.* Continuous to North America on 6195 (till 1430), 9515, 15205 (1430 onwards) and 17840 kHz; to Europe on 5975, 9410, 9750, 9760, 12095, 15070 and 17640 kHz; and to the Middle East on 15575 and 21470 khz.

BBC World Service for Asia. Monday through Friday, the BBC World Service airs a special program for the Eastern part of that continent—the highly informative *Dateline East Asia.* Fifteen minutes on 7180, 9740 and 11820 kHz, 9740 also being available for Australia and the Pacific.

Christian Science Monitor World Service, USA. See 0000 for program details. Monday through Friday to Europe on 15665 or 17510 kHz, to Western North America on 13760 kHz, and to East and Southeast Asia on 9530 and 13625 kHz. All weekend programs are nonsecular.

Radio France Internationale. *News,* press review and a variety of short features, including *Club 9516* (Sunday), *North/South* or *Look East* (Monday), *Land of France* (Tuesday), *Press on Asia* (Thursday) and *Made in France* (Friday). Fifty-five minutes to Southeast Asia and the Pacific on 11910, 17650 and 17695 (or 21770) kHz.

Radio Moscow World Service. Winters, it's *News* and a variety of features, followed on the half-hour by music, *Audio Book Club* or *Russian by Radio.* Summer offerings include *News and Views* followed by some of the cream of Radio Moscow's musical output. Continuous worldwide. Best channels are in the 11, 15 and 17 MHz segments of the spectrum, except for East Asia winters, when 7 and 9 MHz frequencies are likely to be more suitable.

Radio Finland. Winter weekends only at this time; see 1330 for program details. Thirty minutes to North America on 15400 and 17880 kHz. For a separate summer service, see the next item.

Radio Finland. Summers only at this time. Actually starts at 1405; see 1500 for program details. Twenty-five minutes to Europe on 6120, 11755 and 11820 kHz. Also available to the Middle East (and heard elsewhere) on 15440 and 21550 kHz.

Radio Australia. *International Report,* followed Monday through Friday by *Stock Exchange Report* and, on the half-hour, special feature programs. Audible in North America on 5995 and 9580 kHz, despite being targeted elsewhere.

Radio Beijing, China. See 0000 for program details, but one day earlier at this hour. To Western North America winters on 7405 kHz, and summers on 11855 kHz.

Belgische Radio en Televisie, Belgium. Monday through Saturday, winters only, at this time. See 0630 for program details, including *News* and *Press Review,* followed by features such as *Belgium Today, Focus on Europe* and *Around the Arts.* Twenty-five minutes to North America on 17555 kHz, and to Southeast Asia on 21810 kHz.

Radio Canada International. *News* and the Canadian Broadcasting Corporation's excellent *Sunday Morning.* A three-hour broadcast starting at 1400 winters, and 1300 summers. Sunday only to North and Central America on 11955 and 17820 kHz.

Radio Korea, South Korea. Repeat of the 0600 broadcast. Sixty minutes to Southeast Asia (also audible in Australia) on 9570 kHz.

HCJB, Ecuador. Another hour of religious fare to North America on 11925, 15115 (till 1430) and 17890 kHz. Also available in the upper sideband mode on 21455 (or 17895) kHz.

Kol Israel. Sunday through Thursday, winters only at this time; see 1300 for specifics. Twenty-five minutes to Europe and Eastern North America on 11587, 11605, 15640 and 17575 kHz; and to Southeast Asia and the Pacific on 15650 kHz.

Radio For Peace International, Costa Rica. Continues with counterculture programming to North America on 7375, 13630 and 15030 kHz. Some transmissions are in the single-sideband mode, which can be properly processed on only some radios.

Voice of America. *News.* This is followed weekdays by *Asia Report.* On Saturday there's jazz, and Sunday is given over to classical music. At 1455, there's a daily editorial. To East Asia on 9760 and 15160 kHz; and to the Pacific on 15425 kHz.

WJCR, Upton, Kentucky. Continues with gospel music to North America on 7490 kHz. Other U.S. religious broadcasters operating at this hour include **WWCR** on 12160 (or 17535) and 15690 kHz, **KTBN** on 7510 kHz, **WYFR-Family Radio** on 6015 (or 9705) and 11830 kHz, and **WHRI-World Harvest Radio** on 9465 and 115105 kHz.

CFRX-CFRB, Toronto, Canada. Audible throughout much of the northeastern United States and southeastern Canada during the hours of daylight with a modest, but clear, signal on 6070 kHz. With programs for an Ontario audience, this pleasant, friendly station carries news, sports, weather, traffic reports—and, at times, music. Arguably most interesting are talk-show discussions concerning such topics as the status of neighboring Quebec. Call in if you'd like at +1 (514) 790-0600—comments from outside Ontario are welcomed.

14:15

Radio Canada International. Summers only at this time. Fifteen minutes of *news* targeted at Europe daily on 11935, 15315, 15325, 17820 and 21545 kHz; and Monday through Saturday on 15305 and 17795 kHz. One hour later during winter.

14:30

Radio Nederland. Basically a repeat of the 0830 transmission, and targeted at South and East Asia on 9890, 15150, 17605 and 21665 kHz.

Radio Tirana, Albania. *News,* press review and interviews, with interludes of delightful Albanian music. Twenty-five minutes to Europe on 7155 and 9760 kHz.

Radio Romania International. Fifty-five minutes of *news,* commentary, features and thoroughly enjoyable Romanian folk music. Targeted at Asia on 11775, 15335 and 17720 kHz.

Radio Finland. Winters only at this time. Main features include *Press Review, Closeup* and *News Update* (Monday through Friday); and *Northern Report* (Tuesday through Friday). There is a five-minute Latin feature weekends at 1455. Thirty minutes to North America on 15400 and 17880 kHz. One hour earlier in summer.

Radio Austria International. Summers only at this time. Repeat of the 1130 transmission. To Europe on 6155 and 13730 kHz; to Asia on 11780 kHz; and to West Africa (also heard in parts of Europe) on 21490 kHz.

15:00

BBC World Service. *World News,* followed Saturday by *Sportsworld* and Sunday by *Concert Hall* (or its substitute). Weekday programming includes a documentary feature (Monday), *A Jolly Good Show* (Tuesday), comedy (Wednesday) and classical music (Thursday and Friday). Continuous to North America on 9515, 9740, 15205, 15260 (weekends only) and 17840 kHz; to Europe on 6195, 9410, 12095, 15070 and 17640 kHz; to the Middle East on 9740, 15070 and 21470 kHz; and to East Asia on 7180 and 9740 kHz.

BBC World Service for Africa. Monday through Friday, starts at 1515 with *Focus on Africa,* a quarter-hour of up-to-the-minute reports from all over the continent. Extended to 30 minutes (from 1500) on weekends—Saturday, it's *Spice Taxi,* replaced Sunday by *Postmark Africa* and five minutes of African news. Targeted at Africa, but heard well beyond, on 11860, 15420, 17860 and 21490 kHz.

Christian Science Monitor World Service, USA. See 0100 for program details. Monday through Friday to Europe on 15665 or 17510 kHz, to Western North America on 13760 kHz, and to East and Southeast Asia on 9530 and 13625 kHz. Weekend programs are devoted to the beliefs and teachings of the Christian Science Church.

Radio Sweden. *News* and features, with the accent strongly on the Nordic countries. Thirty minutes to North America on 17870 and 21500 kHz, and to the Middle East on 15270 kHz.

Polish Radio Warsaw, Poland. This time summers only. *News,* commentary and features covering everything from politics to culture. Fifty-five minutes to Europe on 7285, 9525 and 11840 kHz. One hour later in winter.

Radio Beijing, China. See 0000 for program details, but one day earlier at this hour. To Western North America winters on 7405 kHz. One hour earlier during summer.

Swiss Radio International. See 0500 for specifics. Thirty minutes to the Middle East, Asia and Australia on 13635 (or 13685), 15505 (or 15430), 17670 and 21770 kHz.

Radio Norway International. Saturday and Sunday, winter only at this time. Repeat of the 1200 transmission. Thirty minutes of friendly programming to North America on 11870 kHz.

Radio Canada International. Continuation of the CBC domestic program *Sunday Morning.* Sunday only to North and Central America on 11955 and 17820 kHz.

Deutsche Welle, Germany. *News,* followed Monday through Friday by *Newsline Cologne, African News* and a feature. Weekends, the news is followed by features such as *Development Forum* and *Science and Technology* (Saturday), and *Religion and Society* (Sunday). Primarily aimed at Africa, but also beamed to the Middle East on 17735 kHz.

Radio Moscow World Service. Predominantly news-related fare for the first half-hour, then a mixed bag, depending on the day and season. Continuous to most areas, and audible on over 40 channels—try from 11 MHz upwards, except for East Asia winters, when the 7 and 9 MHz segments are likely to provide better quality reception.

Radio Finland. Winters only at this time. Actually starts at 1505. *News Update* is followed Tuesday through Saturday by *Northern Report*, with *Perspectives* on Sunday, and *Business Monday* (guess when!). Monday through Friday, there is then a daily *Press Review*, replaced Saturday by *Finnish History*, and Sunday by *Starting Finnish*. Other features include such titles as *Airmail* (Monday), *Sports Fare* (Wednesday), *Roots in Finland* (Thursday), and *Names in the News* (Friday). Twenty-five minutes to Europe on 6120, 9730 and 11755 kHz, with 15440 and 21550 kHz also available for the Middle East and beyond. One hour earlier in summer.

WJCR, Upton, Kentucky. Continues with gospel music to North America on 7490 kHz. Other U.S. religious broadcasters operating at this hour include **WWCR** on 12160 (or 17535) and 15690 kHz, **KTBN** on 7510 kHz, and **WYFR-Family Radio** on 11705 (or 15215) and 11830 kHz.

Radio Japan. *News* and various features. See 0300 for details. One hour to North America on 9505 or 11865 kHz.

Radio For Peace International, Costa Rica. Continuous to North America with counter-culture programs such as *The Great Atlantic Radio Conspiracy* (Friday) and *Living Enrichment Center* (Sunday). Not for every taste, but one of the very few world band stations to provide this type of programming. Audible in North America on 7375, 13630 and 15030 kHz. Some transmissions are in the single-sideband mode, which can be properly processed on only some radios.

HCJB, Ecuador. Continues with religious programming to North America on 11925 and 17890 kHz; also widely heard elsewhere on 21455 (or 17895) kHz.

CFRX-CFRB, Toronto, Canada. See 1400.

15:15

Radio Canada International. Winters only at this time. Fifteen minutes of *news* for European listeners on 9555, 11915, 11935, 15325, and 21545 kHz; plus, Monday through Saturday only, 13650, 15315 and 17820 kHz. One hour earlier in summer.

15:30

Radio Nederland. A repeat of the 0730 broadcast (except for Tuesday, when the arts program *Mirror Images* is replaced by another feature).

See 0030 for specifics, with all features one day earlier. Fifty-five minutes to South and East Asia on 9890, 15150, 17580 and 17605 kHz.

Radio Austria International. Repeat of the 1130 broadcast. A half-hour to Europe (winters only) on 6155, 13730 and 21490 kHz; and to Asia (year-round) on 11780 kHz. Includes a brief bulletin of *news* followed by a series of current events and human interest stories. Ample coverage of national and regional issues, and an excellent source for news of Central and Eastern Europe. Thirty minutes to North America on 9875 and 13730 kHz.

16:00

BBC World Service. *World News*, followed by *News About Britain*. Feature programs that follow include sports, drama, science or music. Particularly worthwhile are *Network UK* (Thursday), *Science in Action* (Friday) and *Megamix* (Tuesday). Saturday sees a continuation of *Sportsworld*, and at 1645 Sunday there's Alistair Cooke's popular *Letter from America*. On weekdays at the same time you can hear a news analysis program, *The World Today*. Continuous to North America on 9515 and 15260 kHz; to Europe on 6195, 9410, 12095 and 15070 kHz; and to the Middle East on 9740, 12095 and 15070 kHz.

Christian Science Monitor World Service, USA. *News* and *Monitor Radio*—60 minutes of news, analysis and news-related features, with emphasis on international developments. Available Monday through Friday to parts of Europe and the Middle East (though not beamed there) on 17510 or 21640 kHz; and to East and Southeast Asia on 11580 and 13625 kHz. Weekends at this and other times, this news-oriented programming is replaced by religious offerings from and about the Christian Science Church, not necessarily all in English.

Radio France Internationale. This program, formerly called *Paris Calling Africa*, is heard quite well in North America and Europe. Begins with world and African *news*, followed by feature programs, including the *Land of France* (Tuesday), *Arts in France* (Thursday), *Club 9516* (Sunday), *Counterpoint* (Wednesday), and *Spotlight on Africa* (Saturday). Fifty-five minutes (essentially to Africa, but also audible in Europe and North America) on 6175, 11705, 12015, 15530, 17620, 17795 and 17850 kHz. 15530 kHz is also available for listeners in the Middle East.

United Arab Emirates Radio, Dubai. Starts with a feature on Arab history or culture, then music, and a bulletin of *news* at 1630. Answers listeners' letters at weekends. Forty minutes to Europe on 11795, 15320, 15435 and 21605 kHz.

Radio Korea, South Korea. See 0600 for program details. To Asia, the Middle East and beyond on 5975 and 9870 kHz.

Polish Radio Warsaw, Poland. Winters only at this time. Fifty-five minutes of *news*, commentary and features targeted at Europe on 7285, 9525 and 11840 kHz.

Radio Pakistan. Fifteen minutes of *news* from the Pakistan Broadcasting Corporation's domestic service, followed by a similar period at dictation speed. Intended for the Middle East and Africa, but heard well beyond on 11570, 13665, 15060, 15550, 17555 and 17725 kHz.

Radio Norway International. Saturday and Sunday only. Repeat of the 1200 transmission. Thirty minutes of Norwegian hospitality targeted at the Middle East on 15230 and 17720 kHz.

Radio Moscow World Service. *News*, then very much a mixed bag, depending on the day and season. Recommended listening is *Music and Musicians*, heard on summer Saturdays. Continuous programming, heard on an ample range of frequencies. In Europe and the Middle East try the 7, 9 and 11 MHz segments in winter; 11, 15 and 17 MHz in summer. North Americans should dial around the 11, 15 and 17 MHz segments of the spectrum, although there isn't much beamed their way at this hour.

Radio Canada International. Winters only. Final hour of CBC's *Sunday Morning*; Sunday only to North and Central America on 11955 and 17820 kHz. For a separate service to Europe, see the next item.

Radio Canada International. This time summers only. *News* and *Spectrum*, replaced

weekends by CBC domestic programming. Thirty minutes targeted at Europe on 11935, 15305, 15325, 17820 and 21545 kHz. One hour later during winter.

Voice of America. *News*, followed by *Nightline Africa*—special news and features on African affairs. Heard beyond Africa—including North America—on a number of frequencies, including 13675, 15410, 15445, 15580 and 17800 kHz.

WJCR, Upton, Kentucky. Continues with gospel music to North America on 7490 kHz. Other U.S. religious broadcasters operating at this hour include **WWCR** on 15690 and 17535 kHz, **KTBN** on 15590 kHz, and **WYFR-Family Radio** on 11705 (or 15215) and 11830 kHz.

CFRX-CFRB, Toronto, Canada. See 1400.

16:30

HCJB, Ecuador. The first half-hour of a 90-minute broadcast to the Middle East. Monday through Friday, it's *Studio 9* (see 0030, except that all features are one day earlier), replaced weekends by religious programming. On 15270 (or 21480) and 17790 kHz; plus 21455 (or 17895) kHz, upper sideband.

17:00

BBC World Service. *World News*, followed by *World Business Report/Review* (Sunday–Friday) or *Personal Choice* (Saturday), then a quiz show, drama, music, sports or religion. There is a daily summary of world sporting news at 1745, in *Sports Roundup*. Until 1745 to North America on 9515 and 15260 kHz. Continuous to Western Europe on 6195, 9410, 12095 and 15070 kHz; and to the Middle East on 9410, 9740, 12095 and 15070 kHz.

BBC World Service for Africa. Forty-five minutes of alternative programming from and about the African continent. A bulletin of world *news* is followed by *Focus on Africa* (see 1500), with five minutes of African *news* closing the broadcast. Targeted at Africa on 3255, 6005, 6190, 9630, 15400, 15420, 17860 and 17880 kHz, but heard well beyond (especially on the higher frequencies).

Christian Science Monitor World Service, USA. *News*, then *Monitor Radio Features*, followed by *Letterbox* (a listener response program) and a religious article from the Christian Science Monitor. Available Monday through Friday to parts of Europe and the Middle East (though not beamed there) on 17510 or 21640 kHz, and to East and Southeast Asia on 11580 and 13625 kHz. Weekend programming at this and other times is of a religious nature, and may be in languages other than English.

Radio Pakistan. Opens with 15 minutes of *news* and commentary. The remainder of the broadcast is taken up by a repeat of the features from the 0800 transmission (see there for specifics). One hour to Europe on 11570 and 15550 kHz.

Radio Czechoslovakia—at least that is the station's name as we go to press. Summers only at this time. *News*, then a variety of features with a Czechoslovak slant. Thirty minutes to Europe on 5930, 6055, 7345, and 9605 kHz. Pleasant listening.

Swiss Radio International. See 0500 for specifics. Thirty minutes to the Middle East on 13635, 15430 (or 15525), 17635 and 21770 kHz. Summers only, there is also a separate 15-minute news-oriented broadcast for Eastern Europe on 9885 kHz.

Polish Radio Warsaw, Poland. This time summers only. *News* and commentary, followed by a variety of features from and about Poland. Fifty-five minutes to Europe on 7270 and 9525 kHz. One hour later during winter.

Radio Moscow World Service. The initial half-hour is taken up winters by *News* and features; summers by *News and Views*. The final 30 minutes are given over to a variety of musical styles, and include some of the best of Moscow's output. In Europe and the Middle East, try the 7, 9 and 11 MHz segments in winter, and 11, 15 and 17 MHz in summer. For North America, best bets are in the 11, 15 and 17 MHz segments, especially in summer, when channels such as 17565 and 17695 kHz are well heard in eastern parts of the U.S. Dial around to find the channel that best suits your location.

Radio Canada International. Winters only at this time. *News* and *Spectrum*, replaced weekends by CBC domestic programming. Thirty minutes to Europe on 5995, 7235, 13650, 15325, 17820 and 21545 kHz. One hour earlier in summer.

Radio For Peace International, Costa Rica. The first daily edition of *FIRE* (Feminist International Radio Endeavour), and the start of the English portion of an eight-hour cyclical block of predominantly counterculture and New Wave programming. Audible in North America on 7375, 13630 and 15030 kHz. Some transmissions are in the single-sideband mode, which can be properly processed on only some radios.

Radio Norway International. Saturday and Sunday only. Repeat of the 1200 broadcast. Thirty minutes to Europe on 9655 kHz.

HCJB, Ecuador. The final hour of programming targeted at the Middle East. Monday through Friday, it's the second half of *Studio 9* followed by 30 minutes of religious fare. The popular *Music from the Mountains* is aired at 1715 weekends, and continues until 1745, when programs in Arabic replace the usual English

ones. On 15270 (or 21480) and 17790 kHz, as well as 21455 (or 17895) kHz in the upper sideband mode.

Voice of America. *News*, followed Monday through Friday by *Newsline* and *Magazine Show*. Saturday, it's *Communications World* and *Weekend Magazine*, and Sunday features *Critic's Choice* and *Issues in the News*. To Europe on 6040, 9760 and 15205 kHz; and to the Middle East on 9700 kHz. For a separate service to Africa, see the next item.

Voice of America. Programs for Africa. *News*, followed Monday through Friday by *African Panorama*—interviews, current affairs, music and human interest features. Weekend offerings include the excellent *Music Time in Africa* at 1730 Sunday. Audible in many parts of the world on 13675, 15410, 15445, 15580, and 17800 kHz.

Kol Israel. Summers only at this time. *News* from Israel Radio's domestic network. Fifteen minutes to Western Europe on 11587 and 15590 kHz, the latter frequency also audible in parts of Eastern North America.

WJCR, Upton, Kentucky. Continues with gospel music to North America on 7490 kHz. Other U.S. religious broadcasters operating at this hour include **WWCR** on 15690 and 17535 kHz, **KTBN** on 15590 kHz, and **WHRI-World Harvest Radio** on 13760 and 15105 kHz.

CFRX-CFRB, Toronto, Canada. See 1400.

17:30

Radio Nederland. Targeted at Africa, but well heard in parts of North America. *News*, followed by *Newsline* and a feature (both replaced Sunday by the aptly named *Happy Station*). Choice plums include *Research File* (Monday), *Airtime Africa* (Friday), and Wednesday's documentary. For listeners in North America, best bets are 21515 and 21590 kHz, via the relay in the Netherlands Antilles.

Radio Sofia, Bulgaria. Summers only at this time. The first half-hour of a 90-minute broadcast. Mostly *news* and news-related items, but includes a fair amount of lively Bulgarian folk music later in the transmission. To Europe, Africa and beyond on 9700, 11720, 11765, 15330, 17780 and 17825 kHz.

17:45

All India Radio. The first 15 minutes of a two-hour broadcast to Western Europe, the Middle East and Africa; consisting of regional and international *news*, commentary, a variety of talks and features, press review and enjoyably exotic Subcontinental music. Continuous till 1945. To Europe on 7412, 9950 and 11620 kHz; and on 11860, 11935 and 15080 to the remaining areas.

1800-2359
EVENING PRIME TIME—
EUROPE

18:00

BBC World Service. Thirty minutes of *Newsdesk*, followed most days by pop, jazz, or classical music. Notable exceptions are the quality science program *Discovery*, broadcast Tuesday at 1830, and the excellent *Focus on Faith*, heard at 1830 Thursday. Continuous to Western Europe on 6195, 9410, 12095 and 15070 kHz; to the Middle East on 7160 (1745-1830 only), 9410, 9740, 12095 and 15070 kHz; and to the Pacific on 11955 kHz.

Christian Science Monitor World Service, USA. See 1600 for program details. Monday through Friday to Europe and the Middle East on 9495 or 15665 kHz, to Eastern North America and Europe on 15665 or 17510 kHz, to South Africa (and heard in parts of North America) on 21545 or 21640 kHz, and to the Pacific on 9430 or 13840 kHz. Weekends are given over to Christian Science religious programming.

Radio Canada International. Targeted at Africa, but heard quite well in North America. Weekdays, there's a bulletin of *news* from the CBC domestic service, then *Spectrum*. This is replaced weekends by a relay of CBC domestic programming, mainly of interest to Canadians. A half-hour weekdays, one hour weekends on 13670, 15260 and 17820 kHz.

Radio Kuwait. The start of a three-hour idiosyncratic package of Islamic-oriented features and western popular music. Don't be put off—some of the historical talks border on the fascinating. To Europe and Eastern North America on 13620 kHz.

Radio For Peace International, Costa Rica. Continues to North America with mainly counterculture programming. An exception is the communications program *World of Radio*, heard Saturday at this time. Also heard outside North America—try 7375, 13630, 15030 or 21465 kHz. Some transmissions are in the single-sideband mode, which can be properly processed on only some radios.

Belgische Radio en Televisie, Belgium. Summers only at this time. See 1900 for program details. Twenty-five minutes to Europe on 9905 kHz, and to Africa and beyond on 17550 kHz. One hour later in winter.

All India Radio. Continuation of the transmission to Europe, the Middle East and beyond (see 1745). *News* and commentary, followed by programming of a more general nature. To Western Europe on 7412, 9950 and 11620; and heard in the Middle East and Africa on 11860, 11935 and 15080 kHz.

Radio Czechoslovakia. Winters only at this time. *News* and a variety of features dealing with Czechoslovak topics. Friendly and interesting. Thirty minutes to Europe on 5930, 6055, 7345 and 9605 kHz. One hour earlier in summer.

Radio Nacional do Brasil (Radiobras), Brazil. A repeat of the 1200 broadcast. Eighty minutes to Europe on 15265 kHz.

Polish Radio Warsaw, Poland. This time winters only. *News*, commentary and features, covering multiple aspects of Polish life and culture. Fifty-five minutes to Europe on 7145 and 9525 kHz. One hour earlier during summer.

Swiss Radio International. Winters only at this time. A brief 15-minute news-oriented broadcast for Eastern Europe on 9885 kHz. One hour earlier in summer.

Radio Moscow World Service. Predominantly news-related fare during the initial half-hour, with some excellent musical offering at 1830 winters. Continuous to Europe and the Middle East on an ample range of frequencies. Winters, try the 7, 9 and 11 MHz segments; summer channels are more likely to be found in the 11, 15 and 17 MHz segments of the spectrum. In North America winters, try the 9, 11 and 15 MHz segments; summer reception is best on 15 and 17 MHz frequencies.

Voice of America. *News*, followed by *Focus* (weekdays), *On the Line* (Saturday), and *Encounter* (Sunday). The second half-hour is devoted to news and features in "special English"—that is, simplified talk in the American language for those whose mother tongue is other than English. To Europe on 6040, 9760 and 15205 kHz; to the Middle East on 9700 kHz; and to Africa, but often heard elsewhere, on 13710, 15410, 15580 and 17800 kHz.

Radio Argentina al Exterior - R.A.E. Winters only at this time. See 1900 broadcast for program details. Fifty-five minutes to Europe on 15345 kHz.

Radio Sofia, Bulgaria. Summers, from 1800; winters, from 1830. Part of a 90-minute transmission targeted at Europe and Africa (but heard well beyond), containing a mixture of news, features, interviews and music. Audible winters on 6035, 9560, 9700, 11680, 11720 and 11735 kHz; and summers on 9700, 11720, 11765, 15330, 17780 and 17825 kHz.

Kol Israel. Winters only at this time. *News* from Israel Radio's domestic network. Fifteen minutes to Europe, often audible in Eastern North America, on 11587 and 15640 kHz.

WJCR, Upton, Kentucky. Continues with gospel music to North America on 7490 kHz. Other U.S. religious broadcasters operating at this time include **WWCR** on 15690 and 17535 kHz, **KTBN** on 15590 kHz, and **WHRI-World Harvest Radio** on 13760 and 17830 (or 17835) kHz.

CFRX-CFRB, Toronto, Canada. See 1400.

18:30

Radio Nederland. Well heard in parts of North America, despite being targeted at Africa. *News*, followed Monday through Saturday by *Newsline* and a feature. Recommended listening includes *Research File* (Tuesday) and *Airtime Africa* (Friday), not to mention Sunday's *East of Edam*—a mixed bag, if ever there was one. Listeners in North America should try 21515 and 21590 kHz, from the relay in the Netherlands Antilles.

Radio Czechoslovakia. Summers only at this time. *News* and features, dealing mainly with Czech and Slovak life and culture, and presented in a magazine-type format. Thirty minutes to Europe on 6055 and 7345 kHz.

Radio Austria International. *Report from Austria.* See 0130 for complete details. A half-hour to Europe and Africa on 5945, 6155 and 13730 kHz; and to the Middle East on 12010 kHz.

Radio Alma-Ata, Kazakhstan. Summers only at this time. See 1930 for further details.

Polish Radio Warsaw, Poland. This time summers only. Repeat of the 1700 broadcast. Fifty five minutes to Europe on 7145 and 9525 kHz. One hour later during winter.

Radio Yugoslavia. Summers only at this time. *News* and a variety of features, most of which have a regular weekly slot. Thirty minutes to Europe on 6100 and 7200 kHz. One hour later during winter.

Radio Finland. Summers only at this time; see 1930 for specifics. Twenty-five minutes to Europe and West Africa on 6120, 9550, 11755 and 15440 kHz.

Voice of the Islamic Republic of Iran. Summers only; see 1930 for program details. One hour to Europe on 6035, 9022 and 15260 kHz.

BBC World Service for Africa. Monday through Friday it's *Focus on Africa* (see 1500), followed by a five-minute bulletin of African *news*. These are replaced Saturday by *Spice Taxi*, a somewhat off-beat look at African culture, with Sunday featuring the discussion program *African Perspective*. To the African continent (and heard elsewhere) on 6005, 6190, 9630 and 15400 kHz.

19:00

BBC World Service. Begins on weekdays with *World News*, then the magazine program *Outlook*. These are followed by just about anything, depending on the day of the week. Choice plums include *Health Matters* (1945 Monday) and *Omnibus* (1930 Wednesday). The excellent *Play of the Week* can be heard Sunday at this time. Continuous to Europe on 6195 (not available at 1930-2000 summers—see separate item), 9410 and 12095 kHz; to the Middle East on 7160, 9410, 9740, 12095 and 15070 kHz; and to the Pacific on 11955 kHz.

Christian Science Monitor World Service, USA. See 1700 for program details. Monday through Friday to Europe and the Middle East on 9495 or 15665 kHz, to Eastern North America and Europe on 15665 or 17510 kHz, to Africa (and audible in parts of North America) on 21545 or 21640 kHz, and to Australasia on 9430 or 13840 kHz. This news-oriented programming is replaced weekends by nonsecular offerings from and about Christian Scientists.

Radio Nacional do Brasil (Radiobras), Brazil. Final 20 minutes of the 1800 broadcast to Europe on 15265 kHz.

Radio Algiers, Algeria. *News*, then rock and popular music. There are occasional brief features, such as *Algiers in a Week*, which covers the main events in Algeria during the past seven days. One hour of so-so reception in Europe, where the broadcast is targeted. Nominally on 11715 kHz, but sometimes pops up on channels like 7245 and 15315 kHz. Also known to have used 9509, 9535, 9640, 9685, 15215 and 17745 kHz in the past.

Belgische Radio en Televisie, Belgium. Winters only at this time. Weekdays, there's *News*, *Press Review* and *Belgium Today*, followed by features like *Focus on Europe* (Monday), *Around the Arts* (Tuesday and Friday), *Living in Belgium* (Wednesday) and *North-South* (Thursday). Weekends include features like *Radio World* (Saturday) and *Musical Roundabout* (Sunday). Twenty-five minutes to Europe on 5910 and 9905 kHz; also to Africa (and heard elsewhere) on 15515 kHz. One hour earlier in summer.

Radio Kuwait. See 1800; continuous to Europe and Eastern North America on 13620 kHz

Radio Norway International. Saturday and Sunday only. Repeat of the 1200 broadcast.

The BBC World Service's *Outlook* mixes conversation, controversy and color to produce a fresh perspective on the latest developments. Barbara Myers interviews freed hostage Terry Waite.

Thirty minutes to Australasia on 17730 or 17860 kHz.

Kol Israel. Summers only at this time. *News* and features, concentrating heavily on things Israeli. The week begins with *Calling All Listeners* and *DX Corner*, then *New from Israel* (science and technology, Monday), *Talking Point* (discussion, Tuesday), *Jewish News* and the travel show *This Land* (Wednesday), *Studio Three* (Israeli arts, Thursday), *Letter from Jerusalem* and *Thank Goodness It's Friday* (on the day of the same name), and *Spotlight* (issues in the news, Saturday). A half-hour to Europe—also audible in Eastern North America—on 11587, 15640 and 17575 kHz. Winters, is one hour later.

All India Radio. The final 45 minutes of a two-hour broadcast to Europe, the Middle East and Africa (see 1745). Starts off with *news*, then continues with a mixed bag of features and Subcontinental music. To Western Europe on 7412, 9950 and 11620; and to the Middle East and Africa on 11860, 11935 and 15080 kHz.

Radio Sofia, Bulgaria. Winters only at this time. Final hour of a 90-minute broadcast (see 1800) targeted at Europe and Africa. Try 6035, 9560, 9700, 11680, 11720 and 11735 kHz.

HCJB, Ecuador. The first evening transmission for Europe. Repeat of the 1000 broadcast to the Pacific. Weekdays it's *Studio 9*, with *DX Partyline* on Saturday, and *Saludos Amigos* on Sunday. Sixty minutes of popular programming on 15270 (or 21480) and 17790 kHz, plus 21455 (or 17895) kHz, upper sideband.

Deutsche Welle, Germany. Repeat of the 1500 broadcast. Intended primarily for African listeners, the program is also carried to the Middle East winters on 11905 kHz and summers on 13780 kHz.

Radio Romania International. *News*, commentary, press review and features, including *Tourist News* and *Favorite Tunes* (Monday), *Romanian Musicians* (Wednesday), *Listeners' Letterbox* and *Skylark* (Thursday), *Pages of Romanian Literature* (Saturday) and *Sunday Studio* the following day. Sixty minutes to Europe;

winters on 5990, 7195 and 9690 kHz; and summers on 7145, 9690, 9750 and 11940 kHz.

Radio Moscow World Service. Thirty minutes of news-oriented fare, followed by a half-hour of flexible programming. To Europe winters in the 7, 9 and 11 MHz segments; summers in the 9, 11, 15 and 17 MHz segments. For Eastern North America, try 9 MHz channels in winter, and 15 and 17 MHz frequencies in summer.

Radio Canada International. Monday through Friday only; a repeat of the 1800 transmission. Targeted at Africa—but heard well in parts of North America—on 13670, 15260 and 17820 kHz. For a separate service for European listeners, see the next item.

Radio Canada International. This time summers only. Monday through Friday there's *news* from the Canadian Broadcasting Corporation's domestic service, followed by the RCI-produced *Spectrum*. This is replaced weekends by CBC domestic programming. Thirty minutes to Europe on 5995, 7235, 13650, 15325, 17875 and 21675 kHz. The weekday broadcast is sometimes replaced by bilingual programming for Canadian military personnel who form part of the United Nations peace-keeping force in Europe.

Radio Portugal. Summers only at this time, Monday through Friday. See 0230 for program details, although programs in this time slot are one day earlier. Thirty minutes to Europe on 11740 kHz.

Radio For Peace International, Costa Rica. Part of an eight-hour cyclical block of counterculture and New Wave programming audible in Europe and North America on 7375, 13630, 15030 and 21465 kHz. Some transmissions are in the single-sideband mode, which can be properly processed on only some radios.

Spanish Foreign Radio. *News*, followed by features and Spanish music; see 0000 for program details. To Europe, Africa and the Middle East on 9530, 9675, 9685 and 9875 kHz.

Voice of America. *News*. For Europe and the Pacific there then follows *Newsline* until 1930, when Europeans get *Magazine Show* (Monday–Friday); *Press Conference USA* (Saturday), and Sunday's *Music USA*. For the Pacific it's *Music USA* Sunday through Friday, replaced Saturday by *Press Conference USA*. For listeners in Africa—weekdays—there are *African Panorama* and *World of Music*. Weekend offerings on this service include the second part of the highly entertaining *Music Time in Africa* Sunday at 1930. The European transmission is on 6040, 9760 and 15205 kHz (also available for the Middle East on 9700 kHz); the broadcast to the Pacific is on 9525, 11870 and 15180 kHz; and the African service (also heard in North America) on 13710, 15410, 15495, 15580 and 17800 kHz.

Radio Argentina al Exterior - R.A.E. Monday through Friday only. Lots of mini-features dealing with aspects of life in Argentina, liberally interspersed with examples of the country's various musical styles, from tango to milongo. Fifty-five minutes to Europe on 15345 kHz. Broadcast an hour earlier during summer in Argentina (winter in the northern hemisphere).

WJCR, Upton, Kentucky. Continues with gospel music to North America on 7490 kHz. Other U.S. religious broadcasters operating at this time include **WWCR** on 15690 and 17535 kHz, **KTBN** on 15590 kHz, and **WHRI-World Harvest Radio** on 13760 and 17830 (or 17835) kHz.

CFRX-CFRB, Toronto, Canada. See 1400.

19:30

BBC World Service for Europe. Summers only at this time. Sunday through Friday, it's *Europe Tonight*, 30 minutes of the latest news, comment and analysis. This is replaced Saturday by *Europe This Weekend*—a compendium of news, features and profiles presented in a magazine-like format. To Europe on 5975, 6180 and 6195 kHz. One hour later during winter.

BBC World Service for Africa. A series of features aimed at the African continent, but well worth a listen if you live farther afield and have an interest in what's going on there. The list includes *Fast Track* (sports, Monday), *Spice Taxi* (culture, Tuesday), *Midweek* (discussion, Wednesday), *The Jive Zone* (music and musicians, Thursday), *African Perspective* (Saturday), and *Postmark Africa* (Sunday). Best heard where it is targeted, but often reaches well beyond. Worth the effort if you can hear it—try 6005, 6190 and 15420 kHz.

Polish Radio Warsaw, Poland. *News,* commentary and features, dealing with multiple aspects of Polish life and culture. Fifty-five minutes of interesting fare to Europe, winters on 7145 and 9525 kHz, and summers on 6095, 6135, 7145, 7270 and 9525 kHz.

Voice of the Islamic Republic of Iran. Sixty minutes of *news*, commentary and religion—much of it with an Islamic slant. The programming is possibly a little on the heavy side for some listeners, but worth a listen even if not entirely to one's taste. The station has come a long way from the days of Ayatollah Khomeini, and sometimes has valid points of view, easily overlooked by westerners. To Europe, winters only, on 6030 (or 6140), 9022 and 15260 kHz. One hour earlier in summer.

Radio Canada International. This time summers only. Thirty minutes of RCI's feature program *Spectrum*. Heard in Europe (and parts of North America) on 5995, 9670, 13650, 15325, 17875 and 21675 kHz. One hour later during winter.

Radio Yugoslavia. Winters only at this time. See 1930 for specifics. Thirty minutes to Europe on 6100 and 7200 kHz.

Radio Alma-Ata, Kazakhstan. Thirty minutes of *news* and features, consisting of a wide variety of topics, depending on which day you listen. Offerings include programs with an Islamic slant, readings from Kazakh literature, features on the country's history and people, and a mailbag program. Saturdays and Sundays are given over to recordings of the country's music, ranging from rarely heard folk songs to even rarer Kazakh opera. One of the most exotic stations to be found on world band radio, so give it a try. These broadcasts are not targeted at any particular part of the world, since the transmitters only use a modest 20 to 50 kilowatts, and the antennas are, in the main, omnidirectional. No matter where you are, try 3955, 5035, 5260, 5960, 5970, 9505, 11825, 15215, 15250, 15270, 15315, 15360, 15385, 17605, 17715, 17730, 17765 and 21490 kHz. One hour earlier in summer.

Radio Nederland. Repeat of the 1730 transmission, and targeted at Africa. That being said, the broadcast is also well heard in parts of North America. Fifty-five minutes on 17605 and 21590 kHz.

Radio Czechoslovakia. This time winters only. A half-hour of *news* and features, concentrating heavily on Czechoslovak issues. To Europe on 6055 and 7345 kHz.

Radio Finland. Winters only. Monday through Friday, it's *Northern Report* and *Press Review*, followed by a ten-minute feature. On weekends there's a bulletin of *news*, preceded Saturday by *Perspectives*, *Starting Finnish* and *Closeup*; and Sunday (somewhat paradoxically) by *Business Monday*, *Airmail* and *Nuntii Latini*—one of the more scholarly of curiosities to grace the international airwaves. Thirty minutes to Europe and West Africa on 6120, 9730 and 11755 kHz. One hour earlier in summer.

19:45

Radio Sofia, Bulgaria. Summers only at this time; see 2045. Forty-five minutes to Europe, Africa and beyond on 11765, 17780 and 17825 kHz. One hour later during winter.

20:00

BBC World Service. *World News*, then news analysis weekdays on *The World Today*. Saturday, there's *Personal View*, replaced Sunday by *Folk in Britain*. These are followed by *Words of Faith*, then a quiz or feature program. Recommended at this time are *Meridian* (Tuesday, Thursday, Saturday), *The Vintage Chart Show* (Monday), *Science in Action* (Friday) and *Assignment* (Wednesday). Continuous to most of Eastern North America on 5975 and 15260 kHz; to Europe on 3955, 6195, 9410 and 12095 kHz (3955 and 6195 kHz are not available at 2030-2100 winters—see later for separate item); to the Middle East till 2030 on 7160, 9410, 9740,

12095 and 15070 kHz, then on 9410 and 12095 kHz only; and to the Pacific on 11955 and 15340 kHz.

Christian Science Monitor World Service, USA. See 1600 for program details. Monday through Friday to Europe and the Middle East on 13770 or 15665 kHz, to Eastern North America and Europe on 15665 or 17510 kHz, to South America (and well heard in much of North America) on 17555 kHz, to East Asia on 9455 kHz, and to Australia and the Pacific on 13840 kHz. Replaced weekends by programs devoted to the beliefs and teachings of the Christian Science Church.

Radio Habana Cuba. One hour of *news*, features and Latin music—much of it Cuban, and thoroughly enjoyable, at that. Long gone is the anti-imperialist, anti-colonialist rhetoric, but many of the views expressed are still at odds with those of the giant neighbor to the north. Not that this detracts unduly from some pleasant and inoffensive programming. To Europe on 17705 kHz; and to the Middle East winters on 9760 kHz, summers on 17815 kHz.

Radio Damascus, Syria. Actually starts at 2005. *News*, a daily press review, and different features for each day of the week. These include *Arab Profile* and *Palestine Talk* (Monday), *Syria and the World* (Tuesday), *Selected Readings* (Wednesday), *From the World Press* (Thursday), *Arab Newsweek* and *Cultural Magazine* (Friday), *Arab Civilization* (Saturday), and *From Our Literature* (Sunday). Most of the transmission, however, is given over to Syrian and some western popular music. One hour to Europe, often audible in Eastern North America, on 12085 and 15095 kHz.

Swiss Radio International. See 0500 for specifics. Thirty minutes to the Middle East and Africa on 9885, 12035, 13635 and 15505 kHz.

Radio Moscow World Service. The initial 30 minutes are oriented to *news* and commentary. The next half-hour may contain Radio Moscow general features or paid programming from other sources. To Europe, Eastern North America and the Pacific on more than 20 channels, most of them in the 7, 9 and 11 MHz segments in winter; and 9, 11, 15 and 17 MHz in summer.

Radio Kuwait. See 1800; the final hour to Europe and Eastern North America on 13620 kHz.

Radio Canada International. This time winters only. See 1900 for specifics. Thirty minutes to Europe (also audible in parts of North America) on 5995, 7235, 11945, 13650, 15325 and 17875 kHz.

Voice of Greece. Fifteen minutes of *news* from and about Greece. To Europe, Monday through Saturday, on 7450 and 9395 kHz.

Radio Beijing, China. *News*, then various feature programs; see 0000 for details, although all programs are one day earlier. To Europe on 9920 and 11500 (or 7315) khz.

Voice of Turkey. Summers only at this time. *News*, followed by *Review of the Turkish Press*, then features on Turkish history, culture and international relations, interspersed with enjoyable selections of the country's popular and classical music. Fifty minutes to Western Europe on 9445 kHz. An hour later in winter.

Radio Pyongyang, North Korea. Repeat of the 1100 broadcast. To Europe, the Middle East and beyond on 6576, 9345, 9640 and 9977 kHz.

Radio Portugal. Winters only at this time. *News*, followed by a feature about Portugal; see 1900 for program details. A half-hour to Europe Monday through Friday on 11740 kHz.

Kol Israel. Winters only at this time. *News*, followed by various features (see 1900). A half-hour to Europe—often also audible in Eastern North America—on 7465, 9435, 11587 and 11605 kHz.

Voice of America. *News*. Listeners in Europe can then hear *Music USA* (jazz on Saturday)—replaced Sunday by *The Concert Hall*—on 6040, 9760 and 15205 kHz (with 9700 kHz also available for the Middle East). For African listeners there is the daily *Nightline Africa*—with news, interviews and background reports—on 13710, 15410, 15495, 15580, 17800 and 21625 kHz. Both transmissions are also audible elsewhere, including parts of North America.

Radio For Peace International, Costa Rica. Continues with counterculture programming to North America and Europe on 7375, 13630, 15030 and 21465 kHz. Some transmissions are in the single-sideband mode, which can be properly processed on only some radios.

WJCR, Upton, Kentucky. Continues with gospel music to North America on 7490 kHz. Other U.S. religious broadcasters which operate at this time include **WWCR** on 15690 and 17535 kHz, **KTBN** on 15590 kHz, and **WHRI-World Harvest Radio** on 13760 and 17830 (or 17835) kHz.

Radio Czechoslovakia. This time summers only. *News*, followed by a variety of features, including politics, economy, ecology, sport and cultural affairs (to name but some). Thirty full minutes to Europe on 5930, 6055, 7345, and 9605 kHz.

CFRX-CFRB, Toronto, Canada. See 1400.

20:30

BBC World Service for Europe. This time winters only. See 1930 for program details. Thirty minutes of quality programming for Europe on 3955, 6180 and 6195 kHz.

Radio Sweden. Summers only at this time. Sixty minutes of news and features, with the accent on Scandinavia. To Europe on 6065 and 9655 kHz, and to Asia and the Pacific on 11730 kHz. One hour later in winter.

Radio Canada International. This time winters only. Monday through Friday there's a half-hour of features in the RCI-produced *Spectrum*, replaced weekends by domestic programming from the Canadian Broadcasting Corporation. To Europe (also audible in parts of North America) on 6010, 7230, 11945, 13650, 15325 and 17875 kHz. One hour earlier in summer.

Polish Radio Warsaw, Poland. Winters only at this time. Fifty-five minutes of *news*, interviews and features, providing a composite picture of Poland past and present. To Europe on 6095, 6135, 7145, 7270 and 9525 kHz. One hour earlier during summer.

Radio Alma-Ata, Kazakhstan. Summers only at this time. Repeat of the 1830 broadcast; see 1930 for more details.

20:45

All India Radio. Press review, Indian music, regional and international *news*, commentary, and a variety of talks and features of general interest. Continuous till 2230; to Europe on 7412, 9950 and 11620 kHz; and to the Pacific on 9910, 11715 and 15265 kHz.

Radio Sofia, Bulgaria. This time winters only. Forty-five minutes of *news* and entertainment, including lively Bulgarian folk rhythms. To Europe and Africa on 9560, 11680 and 11735 kHz.

21:00

BBC World Service. *Newshour*, the gold standard for all in-depth news shows from international broadcasters. A 60-minute class act. For the uninitiated, it's available to Europe on 3955, 6195, 9410 and 12095 kHz; to the Middle East on 9410 and 12095 kHz; to most of Eastern North America on 5975, 9590, 15070 (possibly summers only) and 15260 kHz; to East Asia on 11955 kHz; and to the Pacific on 11955 and 15340 kHz.

Christian Science Monitor World Service, USA. See 1700 for program details. Monday through Friday to Europe and the Middle East on 13770 or 15665 kHz, to Eastern North America and Europe on 15665 or 17510 kHz, to the Americas on 17555 kHz, to East Asia on 9455 kHz, and to Australasia on 13840 kHz. Weekend programming is nonsecular, and mainly of interest to Christian Scientists.

Radio Yugoslavia. Summers only at this time. *News* and short features with a strong regional slant. A valuable source of news about the area. Thirty minutes to Europe on 7200 kHz.

Spanish Foreign Radio. Repeat of the 1900 broadcast (see 0000 for specifics). One hour to Europe on 9875 kHz.

Radio Ukraine International. Summers only at this time. *News*, commentary, reports, interviews and music—reflecting virtually every aspect of Ukrainian life. Sixty minutes to Europe on 5960, 7250, 7340, 9600, 9635, 9865, 15135 and 15570 kHz. One hour later in winter.

Belgische Radio en Televisie, Belgium. Summers only at this time. Repeat of the 1800 transmission; 25 minutes daily to Europe on 5910 and 9905 kHz. One hour later in winter.

Radio Czechoslovakia. *News*, then a variety of features dealing with Czechoslovak life and culture. Summer features may differ from those heard at the same time in winter. A half-hour to Europe on 5930, 6055, 7345 and 9605 kHz.

Radio Beijing, China. Repeat of the 2000 transmission; see 0000 for details, though programs are one day earlier at this time. To Europe on 9920 and 11500 (or 7315) kHz.

Croatian Radio. Summers only at this time; actually starts at 2103. Ten minutes of on-the-spot news from one of Europe's hot-spots. Best heard in Europe and Eastern North America at this hour. Channel usage varies, but try 6210, 7240, 9830, 13640, 13830 or 21480 kHz. One hour later during winter.

Radio Moscow World Service. Thirty minutes of *news* and comment, followed by music, Radio Moscow general features or paid programming from other sources. Continuous to Europe, North America, East Asia and the Pacific on a wide variety of frequencies. Winters, try the 7, 9 and 11 MHz segments; 15 and 17 MHz are better bets in summer.

Radio Budapest, Hungary. Summers only at this time. *News*, followed by a variety of features, including *Update* (Monday through Saturday), *The Business of Music* or *Music and ...!* (Monday), and *168 Hours* (the pick of the previous week's news stories, Monday). Other regular spots include *Letter from Budapest*, *Talk Back*, *Magazine 90* and *What You Say*. These and a number of other features are aired on a regular basis, albeit in a somewhat haphazard fashion. Sixty minutes to Europe and the Middle East on 6110, 9835 and 11910 kHz. One hour later in winter.

Radio Norway International. Saturday and Sunday only. Repeat of the 1200 transmission. A pleasant half-hour's listening; winters to North America on 9590 kHz, and summers to Australasia on 17735 (or 17845) and 21705 kHz.

Deutsche Welle, Germany. *News*, followed Sunday through Thursday by *European Journal* and such features as *Man and Environment* (Monday), *Science and Technology* (Sunday), *Insight* (Tuesday), *Living in Germany* (Wednesday) and *Spotlight on Sport* (Thursday). Friday and Saturday programs include *Panorama* and *Economic Notebook* (Friday), and *Commentary* and *Mailbag Asia* (Saturday). To Asia and the Pacific on 6185 (winter), 9670, 9765, 11785, 13780 (summer) and 15350 kHz.

Radio Japan. Repeat of the 0300 transmission. An hour to Europe on 11735 kHz, and to

Roundtable discussion over Germany's popular radio Deutsche Welle.

East Asia and the Pacific on 11815, 11840, 15430, 17810 and 17890 kHz.

Radio Canada International. Summers only at this time. CBC domestic programs for European listeners. Thirty minutes on 5995, 7235 and 13650 kHz; and a full hour on 15325 and 17875 kHz. One hour later during winter.

Radio Romania International. *News*, commentary and features (see 1900), interspersed with some thoroughly enjoyable Romanian folk music. One hour to Europe; winters on 5990, 6105, 7105, 7195 and 9690 kHz; summers on 5955, 7145, 9690, 9750 and 11940 kHz.

Radio For Peace International, Costa Rica. A mix of United Nations features, counter-culture programs (such as *World Citizen's Hour*, Saturday) and New Wave music (*Sound Currents of the Earth*, Sunday). Continuous to North America and Europe on 7375, 13630, 15030 and 21465 kHz. Some transmissions are in the single-sideband mode, which can be properly processed on only some radios.

Voice of Turkey. Winters only at this time. See 2000 for program details. Some arcane features coupled with friendly presentation make for interesting listening. To Western Europe on 9445 kHz. One hour earlier in summer.

Voice of America. *News*, followed Monday through Friday by *World Report* and weekends by a variety of features. These depend on the area being served, and include the excellent *New Horizons* (Africa and Europe; Sunday), *VOA Pacific* (Sunday), and *Issues in the News* (Africa; Sunday). To Europe on 6040, 9760 and 15205 kHz; to the Middle East on 9700 kHz; to Africa, but often heard elsewhere, on 13710, 15410, 15495, 15580, 17800 and 21485 kHz; and to Southeast Asia and the Pacific on 11870, 15185 and 17735 kHz.

All India Radio. Continues to Europe on 7412, 9950 and 11620 kHz; and to the Pacific on 9910, 11715 and 15265 kHz. Look for some authentic Indian music from 2115 onwards.

CFRX-CFRB, Toronto, Canada. See 1400. Summers at this time, you can hear the excellent *The World Today*, 90 minutes of news, interviews, sports and commentary. On 6070 kHz.

21:15

Radio Damascus, Syria. Actually starts at 2110. *News*, a daily press review, and a variety of features (depending on the day of the week). These include *Arab Profile* (Sunday), *Palestine Talk* (Monday), *Listeners Overseas* and *Selected Readings* (Wednesday), *Arab women in Focus*, (Thursday), *From Our Literature* (Friday), and *Human Rights* (Saturday). Much of the transmission, however, is given over to Syrian and some western popular music. Sixty minutes to North America and the Pacific on 12085 and 15095 kHz.

BBC World Service for the Caribbean. *Caribbean Report*, although intended for listeners in the area, can also be clearly heard throughout much of Eastern North America. This brief, 15-minute program provides comprehensive coverage of Caribbean economic and political affairs, both within and outside the region. Monday through Friday only, on 6110, 15140 and 17715 kHz.

Radio Cairo, Egypt. The start of a 90-minute broadcast devoted to Arab and Egyptian life and culture. The initial quarter-hour of general programming is followed by *news*, commentary and political items. This in turn is followed by a cultural program until 2215, when the station again reverts to more general fare. A Middle Eastern cocktail liberally laced with exotic Arab music. To Europe on 9900 kHz.

WJCR, Upton, Kentucky. Continuous gospel music to North America on 7490 kHz. Other U.S. religious broadcasters operating at this hour include **WWCR** on 15690 and 17535 kHz, **KTBN** on 15590 kHz, and **WHRI-World Harvest Radio** on 13760 kHz.

21:30

BBC World Service for the Falkland Islands. *Calling the Falklands* is one of the curiosities of international broadcasting. Chatty and personal, there's no other program quite like it on the international airwaves. Tuesdays and Fridays on 13660 kHz—easily heard in North America.

Kol Israel. Summers only at this time. Sunday through Thursday, a repeat of the 1300 broadcast. Friday, the news is followed by *Press Review* and *Letter from Jerusalem*; and Saturday, it's *Spotlight*. A half-hour beamed to Europe and Eastern North America on 11587, 11605, 15590 and 15640 kHz. One hour later during winter.

Radio Finland. Summers only at this time.

See 2230 for program details. Twenty-five minutes to Europe on 6120 and 11755 kHz, and to East Asia on 15440 kHz.

Radio Alma-Ata, Kazakhstan. Winters only at this time. Repeat of the 1930 broadcast, and on the same channels. Thirty minutes of exotica.

HCJB, Ecuador. Saturday brings *Musical Mailbag,* Sunday has the highly recommended *Blues, Rags, Jazz,* and the rest of the week is devoted to religious offerings. Thirty minutes to Europe on 15270 (or 21480) and 17790 kHz; also available on 21455 (or 17895) kHz, upper sideband.

Radio Austria International. *Report from Austria.* See 0130 for more details. A half-hour to Europe and Africa on 5945, 6155 and 9870 kHz; and to the Middle East on 12010 kHz.

Radio Sweden. Winters only at this time. Sixty minutes of predominantly Nordic fare. To Europe on 6065 kHz, and to the Pacific on 11730 kHz. One hour earlier in summer.

21:45

Radio Sofia, Bulgaria. Summers only at this time. The first quarter-hour of a 90-minute broadcast, see 2200 for specifics. To North America on 11660, 11720 and 15330 kHz.

Radio Yerevan, Armenia. Summers only at this time. Approximately ten minutes of *news* about Armenia, mainly of interest to Armenians abroad. To Europe (and sometimes audible in Eastern North America) on 9450 and 11920 kHz. One hour later in winter.

Radio Korea, South Korea. See 0600 for program details. One hour to Europe and beyond on 6480, 7550 and 15575 kHz.

22:00

BBC World Service. *World News* and *News About Britain,* then some of the best of the BBC's output. Worthy of note are *Sports International* (Wednesday), *Jazz for the Asking* (Saturday), *Network UK* (Thursday), *Short Story* and *Letter from America* (Sunday), *People and Politics* (Friday) and *Megamix* (Tuesday). The hour is rounded off with 15 minutes of *Sports Roundup.* To Eastern North America on 5975, 7350 (or 15070), 9590, and 15260 kHz; to Europe on 6195, 7325 and 12095 kHz; to East Asia on 9570 and 11955 kHz; and to the Pacific on 11955 and 15340 kHz.

Christian Science Monitor World Service, USA. See 1600 for program details. Monday through Friday to Europe on 13770 or 15665 kHz, to North America on 9465 and 17555 kHz; and to East and Southeast Asia on 13625 (or 13840) and 15405 kHz. Weekend programming concentrates on Christian Science beliefs and teachings.

Radio Sofia, Bulgaria. Summers, continuation of 2145 broadcast; winters, does not start until 2245. Ninety minutes of *news,* interviews and features, interspersed with sizable portions of lively Bulgarian folk music—it's not often you can hear so many pleasantly sounding bagpipes. To North America winters on 9700, 11660, 11720 and 11950 kHz; and summers on 11660, 11720 and 15330 kHz.

Radio Cairo. The second half of a 90-minute broadcast to Europe on 9900 kHz; see 2115 for program details.

Radio Czechoslovakia. This time winters only. *News* and features in a magazine-style format. Thirty enjoyable minutes to Europe on 5930, 6055, 7345 and 9605 kHz.

Voice of America. The beginning of a three-hour block of *News,* sports, science, business, music, and features. To East and Southeast Asia and the Pacific on 7120, 9770, 11760, 15185, 15290, 15305, 17735 and 17820 kHz. For listeners in the Middle East there is a separate service consisting of 30 minutes of news-oriented fare, followed by a half-hour feature in "special" or slow-speed English, available winters on 6160, 9530, 11895, 11905, 11960 and 15445 kHz; and winters on 6095, 9745, 15215, 15255 and 17885 kHz.

Radio Moscow World Service. *News,* then Monday through Friday winters, it's *Focus on Asia and the Pacific* followed by music or features; Saturday's spot is given over to the interesting *Music and Musicians;* and Sunday has flexible programming. Summers at this time there's *Update,* followed by music or features. Beamed to North America, Asia and the Pacific on more than 20 channels, most of them for Asia and the Pacific. In Eastern North America try the 7 and 9 MHz segments in winter, 11 and 15 MHz in summer. For Western North America, best year-round bets are channels in the 17 MHz segment of the spectrum, with the area around 12050 kHz also worth a try in winter. East Asia is best served by the 7 and 9 MHz segments in winter; 9, 11 and 15 MHz in summer. Best for Southeast Asia and the Pacific are frequencies in the 15, 17 and 21 MHz segments.

Voice of Free China, Taiwan. See 0200. For Western Europe, winters on 9850 (or 9852.5) and 11805 (or 7355) kHz, and summers on 17750 and 21720 kHz.

Croatian Radio. Winters only at this time; actually starts at 2203. Ten minutes of on-the-spot *news* from Croatian Radio's Zagreb studio. Best heard in Europe and Eastern North America—try 6210, 7240, 9830, 13640 or 13830 kHz. One hour earlier in summer.

Radio Habana Cuba. Sixty minutes of *news* and entertainment, including some thoroughly enjoyable Cuban music. Targeted at Europe, winters on 7215 kHz, summers on 11705 kHz; also to the Caribbean (and audible in parts of North America) on 9620 kHz. The future of the European broadcast is uncertain, and it may be terminated.

Radio Budapest, Hungary. Winters only at this time; see 2100 for program details. Sixty minutes to Europe and the Middle East on 6110, 9835 and 11910 kHz. One hour earlier in summer.

Voice of Turkey. Summers only at this time. See 2000 for program details. Fifty minutes to Europe on 11895 kHz, to Eastern North America on 9445 kHz, and for late-night listeners in the Middle East on 7185 kHz. One hour later in winter.

Radio Yugoslavia. This time winters only. *News* and features, providing useful coverage of events in one of the most volatile areas of the world. To Europe on 7200 kHz, and one hour earlier in summer.

Radio Beijing, China. Repeat of the 2000 broadcast. To Europe winters on 7170 kHz, summers on 9740 kHz.

Belgische Radio en Televisie, Belgium. Winters only at this time; see 1900 for program details. Twenty-five minutes to Europe on 5910 and 9905 kHz, with the latter frequency also being audible in parts of Eastern North America. One hour earlier in summer.

Radio Canada International. Winters only at this time. A relay of CBC domestic fare to Europe. Thirty minutes on 5995, 7135 and 13650 kHz; and one hour on 9760 and 11945 kHz. For a separate summer service to North America, see the next item.

Radio Canada International. Summers only. Monday through Friday, there's CBC's *World at Six*, replaced weekends by other CBC domestic programming. To North America on 5960, 9755, 11905 and 13670 kHz.

Radio Tirana, Albania. The second, and final, transmission of the day for European listeners. Twenty-five minutes of *news*, press review, interviews and music, all of it from or about Albania. Try 7215, 9725 or 9760 kHz.

Radio Ukraine International. Winters only at this time. A potpourri of all things Ukrainian. Sixty minutes to Europe on 5960, 6020, 7380 and 9785 kHz. One hour earlier in summer.

United Arab Emirates Radio, Abu Dhabi. Begins with *Readings from the Holy Koran*, in which verses are chanted in Arabic, then translated into English. This is followed by a dramatized serialized version of an Arab literary work. The last half-hour is a relay of Capital Radio in Abu Dhabi, complete with pop music and local contests. To Eastern North America winters on 7215, 9605 and 11965 kHz, and summers on 13605, 15305 and 17855 kHz.

Radio For Peace International, Costa Rica. Programs heavily oriented towards peace and goodwill, with Tuesday's spot being given over to New Wave music—*Sound Currents of the Earth*. Continuous to North America and Europe on 7375, 13630, 15030 and 21465 kHz. Some transmissions are in the single-sideband mode, which can be properly processed on only some radios.

All India Radio. Final half-hour of transmission to Europe and the Pacific, consisting mainly of news-related fare. To Europe on 7412, 9950 and 11620 kHz; and to the Pacific on 9910, 11715 and 15265 kHz. Also sometimes audible in Eastern North America on 11620 kHz.

WJCR, Upton, Kentucky. Continues with gospel music to North America on 7490 kHz. Other U.S. religious broadcasters heard at this hour include **WWCR** on 12160 and 15690 kHz, **KTBN** on 15590 kHz, and **WHRI-World Harvest Radio** on 13760 kHz.

CFRX-CFRB, Toronto, Canada. If you live in the northeastern United States or southeastern Canada, try this pleasant little local station, usually audible for hundreds of miles/kilometers during daylight hours on 6070 kHz. At this time, you can hear the excellent *The World Today* (summers, starts at 2100)—90 minutes of news, sport and interviews.

22:30

Radio Finland. Winters only at this time. Monday through Friday it's *Northern Report* and *Press Review* followed by a short feature. On Saturdays there's *Perspectives* and a Finnish language lesson, with *Business Monday* and *Airmail* the featured programs on the remaining day. To Europe on 6120 and 9730 kHz, and to East Asia on 11755 kHz.

Kol Israel. Winters only at this time. *News*, followed by a variety of features, depending on which day it is (see 2130 for program details). A half-hour to Eastern North America and Europe on 7465, 9435, 11585 and 11605 kHz.

Radio Sweden. Summers only. Thirty minutes of *News* and features, mainly concerning Nordic life and culture. To Europe on 6065 kHz.

22:45

Vatican Radio. Twenty-five minutes of religious and secular programming to Asia and the Pacific on 7310 (or 15090), 9600 and 11830 kHz.

Radio Yerevan, Armenia. Approximately ten minutes of *news* about Armenia, mainly of interest to Armenians abroad. To Europe winters on 7440 and 9480 kHz, and to South America summers on 11920, 12050 and 17660 kHz. Both transmissions are sometimes audible in Eastern North America.

23:00

BBC World Service. *News*, then *World Business Report* (Monday–Friday), *World Business Review*

(Sunday), or *Words of Faith* (Saturday). The remainder of the broadcast is mainly taken up by music programs like *Multitrack*, *Concert Hall*, *Music Review* or *A Jolly Good Show*. Continuous to North America on 5975, 6175, 7325, 9590, 9915, 12095 and 15070 kHz (some of which are seasonal channels); to East Asia on 11945, 11955 and 17830 kHz; and to the Pacific on 11955 kHz.

Christian Science Monitor World Service, USA. See 1700 for program details. Monday through Friday to Europe on 13770 or 15665 kHz, to North and South America on 9465 and 17555 kHz, and to East and Southeast Asia on 13625 (or 13840) and 15405 kHz. Weekends, news-oriented fare is replaced by Christian Science religious programming.

Voice of Turkey. Winters only. See 2000 for program details. Fifty minutes to Europe on 11895 kHz, to Eastern North America on 9445 kHz, and to Middle Eastern night-owls on 7185 kHz. One hour earlier in summer.

Radio Vilnius, Lithuania. Summers only at this time. See 0000 for program details. A reliable source of news about the Baltic states, even at the most critical of times. To Europe and North America on 9710, 11780, 13645 and 15580 kHz.

Radio Norway International. Saturday and Sunday only. *News* and features from and about Norway, with the accent often on the lighter side of life. A pleasant 30 minutes to North America on 11795 or 11925 kHz.

Radio Japan. Similar to the 0300 broadcast, but with *Hello from Tokyo* on Sunday instead of *Media Roundup*. One hour to Europe on 6025 and 6160 kHz; and to East Asia on 11815, 15195 and 17810 kHz.

Radio Sofia, Bulgaria. Continuous programming to North America (see 2200); summers till 2315 on 11660, 11720 and 15330 kHz; and winters till 0015 on 9700, 11660, 11720 and 11950 kHz.

Radio Pyongyang, North Korea. See 1100 for program details. Fifty minutes to the Americas on 11700 and 13650 kHz.

Radio For Peace International, Costa Rica. The final hour of a cyclical eight-hour block devoted mainly to counterculture and New Wave programming. An exception at this hour is Sunday's communications program *World of Radio*. Audible in Europe and North America on 7375, 13630, 15030 and 21465 kHz. Some transmissions are in the single-sideband mode, which can be properly processed on only some radios.

Radio Moscow World Service. The initial 30 minutes consist of mainly news-oriented fare, followed on the half-hour by features or music. The musical shows at this time summers are among the best that Moscow offers. For Eastern North America and East Asia winters, tune

around the 7 and 9 MHz segments; 11 and 15 MHz are best in summer. In Southeast Asia and the Pacific, try 15 and 17 MHz channels plus the year-round 21690 kHz.

United Arab Emirates Radio, Abu Dhabi. The first quarter-hour is a review of articles and editorials from the Arab press, which is then followed by a feature with an Islamic slant. The final part of the broadcast is devoted to recordings of Arab music. Heard in Eastern North America winters on 7215, 9605 and 11965 kHz, and summers on 13605, 15305 and 17855 kHz.

Voice of America. *News* and *VOA Morning*. Continuous programming to the Middle East, East Asia and the Pacific on the same frequencies as at 2200.

WJCR, Upton, Kentucky. Continuous gospel music to North America on 7490 kHz. Other U.S. religious broadcasters heard at this time include **WWCR** on 12160 kHz, **KTBN** on 15590 kHz, and **WHRI-World Harvest Radio** on 13760 kHz.

CFRX-CFRB, Toronto, Canada. See 2200.

23:30

Belgische Radio en Televisie, Belgium. Summers only at this time. See 1900 for program details. Twenty-five minutes to Eastern North America on 9930 kHz; also audible on 13655 kHz, targeted at South America.

Voice of the Islamic Republic of Iran. This time summers only. Sixty minutes of *News*, commentary, features and religion, with the accent on the Islamic viewpoint. An interesting source of news about the Middle East. Targeted at North America on 9022, 9720 (or 9765) and 15260 kHz. One hour later in summer.

Radio Canada International. Summers only at this time. A relay of CBC's excellent weekday *news* program *As It Happens*, with weekends being given over to alternative programs from the CBC domestic network. To Eastern North America on 5960 and 9755 kHz; also on 13670 kHz Monday through Friday.

23:45

Radio Yerevan, Armenia. Winters only at this time. Approximately ten minutes of *news* about Armenia, mainly of interest to Armenians abroad. To South America (and sometimes audible in Eastern North America) on 9480, 11980 and 12060 kHz. One hour earlier in summer.

Prepared by Don Swampo and the staff of Passport to World Band Radio.

CHOOSING A PREMIUM RECEIVER?

Get premium advice before you buy!

If you could, you'd spend weeks with each receiver. Learning its charms and foibles. Checking the specs. Seeing for yourself how it handles — *before* you spend.

Now, you can do the next best thing — better, some readers insist. *Radio Database International™ White Papers*, from the *Passport to World Band Radio™* library of in-depth test reports, put the facts right into your hands.

We run each receiver for you. We put it through comprehensive laboratory and bench tests to find out where it shines. And where it doesn't.

Then our panel takes over: DXers, professional monitors, program listeners — experts all. They're mean, grumpy, hyper-critical ... and take lots of notes. They spend weeks with each receiver, checking ergonomics and long-run listening quality with all kinds of stations. Living with it day and night.

With *Passport™ RDI White Papers™*, these findings — the good, the bad and the ugly — are yours, along with valuable tips on how to operate your radio to best advantage. Each report covers one model in depth, and is $5.95 postpaid in the United States; CAN $7.95 in Canada; US $7.95 airmail in

the EC, Scandinavia, Australia, New Zealand and Japan; US $12.35 registered air elsewhere. Separate reports are available for each of the following premium radios:

> **Drake R8/R8E**
> **Icom IC-R71**
> **Icom IC-R9000**
> **Japan Radio NRD-93**
> **Japan Radio NRD-535/NRD-535D**
> **Kenwood R-5000**
> **Lowe HF-150***
> **Lowe HF-225 and HF-235**
> **Sony CRF-V21**
> **Sony ICF-2010/ICF-2001D**
> **Yaesu FRG-8800**

*Available as of 12/92

Other *Passport RDI White Papers* available:

> **How to Interpret Receiver**
> **Specifications and Lab Tests**
> **Popular Indoor Antennas**
> **Popular Outdoor Antennas**

Available from world band radio dealers or direct. For Visa/MasterCard orders call our 24-hour automated order line: +1 (215) 794-8252. Or send your check or money order (Pennsylvania add 6%), specifying which report or reports you want, to:

US: DX Radio, EEB, Universal • **Canada:** PIF • **UK:** Lowe
Japan: IBS-Japan • **Latin America:** IBS-Latin America

 Passport RDI White Papers
Box 300
Penn's Park, PA 18943 USA

Worldwide Broadcasts in English

Country-by-Country Guide to Best-Heard Stations

Dozens of countries, large and small, reach out to us in English over world band radio. Here are the times and frequencies (channels) where you're most likely to hear them.

Four Helpful Tips

- Best time to listen, in general, is during the late afternoon and evening. This is when most programs are targeted at your location. An exception for North Americans: Some Asian and Pacific stations are strongest around dawn.
- Best times to listen in North America in bold—for example, **2200-0430**. Best times for Europe are underlined—<u>1900-2100</u>.
- Best late-afternoon and evening frequencies are usually 5850-12100 kHz, sometimes even 3900-17900 kHz. Earlier in the day, try 9250-21785 kHz, sometimes even 5850-26100 kHz. See *World Band Spectrum* in the glossary at the back of the book for how to tune for best results.
- Best frequencies are often those in bold— say, **6175**—as they are from transmitters that may be located near you.

World Time Simplifies Listening

Times and days of the week are given in World Time, explained in the *Passport* Glossary. Midyear, many programs are heard an hour earlier, whereas some in the southern hemisphere are heard an hour later.

World Time—a handy concept also known as Universal Time, UTC and GMT— is used to eliminate the potential complication of so many time zones throughout the world. It treats the entire planet as a single zone and is announced regularly on the hour by many world band stations.

For example, if you're in New York and it's 6:00 AM EST, you will hear World Time announced as "11 hours." A glance at your clock shows that this is five hours ahead of your local time. You can either keep this figure in your head or use a separate clock for World Time. A growing number of world band radios come with World Time clocks built in, and separate 24-hour clocks are also widely available.

Special Times for Programs

Some stations, particularly those targeted at a domestic audience, shift times of transmission by one hour midyear. Countries with these time shifts are cited in *Passport's* "Addresses PLUS."

Stations also may extend their hours of transmission or air special programs during national holidays. These holidays are detailed in UPS's quarterly *International Update* newsletter, as well as Federal Express' monthly *International Newsletter*—both free. Either may be available at your place of work but, if not, Americans may request being put on the *International Update* mailing list by writing UPS, International Update,

Rockefeller Center Station, P.O. Box 1588, New York NY 10124-0243. Enclose your name, title, firm's name and mailing address.

Schedules Prepared for Entire Year

To be as helpful as possible throughout the year, *Passport's* schedules consist not just of observed activity, but also that which we have creatively opined will take place during the entire year. This latter information is original from us, and therefore, of course, will not be so exact as factual information.

Broadcasts in other than English? Turn to the next section—"Voices from Home." Also, the Blue Pages give detailed information on broadcasts in all languages, including English.

ALBANIA
RADIO TIRANA
0230-0300	9580 & 11825 (**E North Am**)
0330-0400	9580 & 11825 (**E North Am**)
1430-1500	7155 & 9760 (W Europe)
1730-1800	9480 (W Europe)
2200-2230	9760 & 11825 (W Europe)

ALGERIA
RTV ALGERIENNE
2000-2100	7245 (Europe & N Africa), 11715 (Europe)

ARGENTINA
RADIO ARGENTINA-RAE
0100-0200	Tu-Sa 11710 (**Americas**)
1800-1900	M-F 15345 (Europe & N Africa)

ARMENIA
RADIO YEREVAN
0250-0300	**11675** (**E North Am**), **13645** & **15580** (**W North Am**)
0350-0400	**7400** & **9750** (**E North Am**), **10344** (E Asia), **17605** & **17690** (**W North Am**)
2145-2200	9450 (Europe), 11920 (Europe & C America)
2245-2300	**7440** (W Europe), 9480 (Europe), 11920 (Europe & C America)
2345-2400	11980 (C America)

AUSTRALIA
ABC/CAAMA RADIO—(Australasia)
2130-0830	4835, 4910

ABC/RADIO RUM JUNGLE
2130-0830	5025 (Australasia)

AUSTRALIAN BROADCASTING CORP—
(Australasia)
24h	9610
0900-0100	6140
1800-1300	9660
1900-1400	4920
2245-0915	15425

RADIO AUSTRALIA
0000-0100	15240 (E Asia)
0000-0130	17880 (E Asia)
0030-0730	17715 & 21740 (Pacific)
0030-0800	11880 & 17795 (Pacific)
0030-0830	15240 (Pacific)
0030-0900	11720 (Pacific)
0030-1200	15160 (Pacific)
0100-0500	21525 (E Asia)
0400-0500	Sa/Su 17750, Sa/Su 17880 & Sa/Su 21525 (E Asia)
0400-0700	17670 (E Asia)
0500-0700	17750 & 17880 (E Asia)
0500-0800	21525 (E Asia)
0630-0830	6020 (Pacific)
0630-1300	6060 (Pacific & **W North Am**)
0800-0900	6080, 7240 & 9710 (Pacific)
0800-2130	5995 (Pacific), 9580 (Pacific & **N America**)
0830-0900	6020 (Pacific)
0900-1000	13605 & 15170 (E Asia)
1100-1200	13605 & 15170 (E Asia)
1100-1230	6080 & 9710 (Pacific)
1100-1300	6020 (Pacific)
1100-2100	7240 (Pacific)
1300-1530	11800 (Pacific & **N America**), 11800 (E Asia)
1430-2130	6060 (Pacific & **W North Am**)
1600-2100	13605 (Pacific)
1600-2130	6080 & 11910 (Pacific)
1900-2400	11720 (Pacific)
2100-2400	11880 (Pacific)
2130-2330	9540 (Pacific)
2200-2330	11855 (Pacific)
2200-2400	15160 & 17795 (Pacific)
2200-0730	15320 & 15365 (Pacific)

AUSTRIA
RADIO AUSTRIA INTERNATIONAL
0130-0200	9875 & 13730 (**N America**)
0330-0400	9870 (C America), 13730 (**N America**)
0530-0600	**6015** (**N America**), 6155 & 13730 (Europe), 15410 & 21490 (Mideast)
0630-0700	**6015** (**N America**)
0730-0800	6155 & 13730 (Europe), 15410 & 21490 (Mideast)
0830-0900	6155 & 13730 (Europe), 15450 & 21490 (Australasia)
1030-1100	15450 & 21490 (Australasia)
1130-1200	6155 (Europe), 11780 (E Asia), 13730 (Europe & **E North Am**), 15450 & 17730 (E Asia)
1330-1400	11780, 15450 & 17730 (E Asia)
1430-1500	6155 & 13730 (Europe)
1530-1600	13730 (Europe)
1830-1905	5945 & 6155 (Europe), 12010 (Mideast)
2130-2200	5945 & 6155 (Europe), 9870 (W Europe)

BANGLADESH
RADIO BANGLADESH—(Europe)
1200-1230	15200
1745-1900	9578, 12030

BELGIUM
BELGISCHE RADIO & TV
0030-0055	9930 (**E North Am**)

0630-0655	5910 (Europe)
0730-0755	5910 (Europe), 11695 (Europe & Australasia)
1000-1025	M-Sa 9905 & M-Sa 13675 (Europe)
1230-1255	Su 17555 (**N America**), Su 21810 (**E North Am**)
1400-1425	M-Sa 17555 (**N America**), M-Sa 21810 (**E North Am**)
1900-1925	5910 & 9905 (Europe)
2100-2125	5910 (Europe)
2200-2225	5910 & 9905 (Europe)

BRAZIL
RADIO NACIONAL

1200-1320	11745/15445 (**N America** & C America)
1800-1920	15265 (Europe)

BULGARIA
RADIO SOFIA

0000-0045	11660 (Europe & **E North Am**), 11720 & 15330 (**E North Am**)
0100-0145	9700 & 11720 (**E North Am**)
0300-0430	9850 & 15160 (Europe)
0300-0530	11720 (Europe)
0400-0530	11765 (Europe)
1100-1230	11630 (Europe)
1730-1900	9700, 11720, 15330 & 17780 (Europe)
1830-2000	6035, 9560, 9700, 11680 & 11720 (Europe)
1945-2030	17780 (Europe)
2045-2130	9560 & 11680 (Europe)
2145-2315	11660 (Europe & **E North Am**), 11720 & 15330 (**E North Am**)
2245-0015	9595 (C America), 9700 (**E North Am**), 11660 & 11680 (**N America**), 11720 (**E North Am**)

CANADA
CBC NORTHERN SERVICE—(**E North Am**)

0000-0300	Su 9625
0200-0300	Tu-Sa 9625
0300-0310	M 9625
0330-0610	M 9625
0400-0610	Su 9625
0500-0610	Tu-Sa 9625
1200-1255	M-F 9625
1200-1505	Sa 9625
1200-1700	Su 9625
1700-1805	Sa 9625
1800-2400	Su 9625
2200-2225	M-F 9625
2240-2330	M-F 9625

CFRX-CFRB, Toronto ON

24h	6070 (**E North Am**)

CFVP-CFCN, Calgary AB

24h	6030 (**W North Am**)

CHNX-CHNS, Halifax NS

24h	6130 (**E North Am**)

CIQX-CIQC, Montréal PQ

24h	6005 (**E North Am**)

CKFX-CKWX, Vancouver BC

24h	6080 (**W North Am**)

CKZN-CBN, St. John's NF

0930-0500	6160 (**E North Am**)

CKZU-CBU, Vancouver BC

24h	6160 (**W North Am**)

RADIO CANADA INTL

0000-0030	Tu-Sa 13670 (**E North Am**)
0000-0130	5960 & 9755 (**E North Am**)
0030-0100	Su/M 5960 & Su/M 9755 (**E North Am**)
0100-0200	Su/M 9755 & Su/M 11845 (C America)
0130-0200	Su/M 5960 & Su/M 9755 (**E North Am**)
0200-0300	Tu-Sa 9755 & Tu-Sa 11845 (C America)
0400-0430	**6150** (Europe), **9505** (Mideast), **9650**, **9670** & **11905** (Europe), **11925**, **15275** & **15445** (Mideast)
0515-0600	M-F **6050**, M-F 6150, M-F **7295** & M-F 9750 (Europe)
0615-0700	M-F **6050**, M-F 6150, M-F **7155** & M-F 9760 (Europe), M-F **11905** (Mideast)
1200-1300	M-F 11855 (**E North Am**), M-F 17820 (C America)
1200-1400	M-F 9635 (**E North Am**)
1300-1400	M-F 11855 (**E North Am**), M-F 17820 (C America)
1300-1600	Su 11955 (**E North Am**), Su 17820 (C America)
1330-1400	**6095**, **6150**, **9535**, **9700** & **11795** (E Asia)
1400-1700	Su 11955 (**E North Am**), Su 17820 (C America)
1415-1430	**11935**, M-Sa 15305, **15315**, **15325**, M-Sa 17795, **17820** & 21545 (Europe)
1515-1530	**9555** (Europe), **11915** (E Europe), **11935**, M-Sa 13650, M-Sa 15315, **15325**, M-Sa 17820 & 21545 (Europe)
1600-1630	**11935**, 15305, **15325**, 17820 & 21545 (Europe)
1700-1730	**5995**, **7235**, 13650, 15325, 17820 & 21545 (Europe)
1900-1930	**7235** (Europe)
1900-2000	21675 (Europe)
1900-2030	**5995** (Europe)
1900-2130	13650 (Europe)
1900-2200	15325 & 17875 (Europe)
1930-2000	**9670** (Europe)
2000-2015	13650 & 15140 (Europe)
2000-2030	**7235** (Europe)
2000-2100	11945 & 15140 (Europe)
2030-2100	**6010** & **7230** (Europe)
2100-2130	**5995** & **7235** (Europe)
2200-2230	5960 (**E North Am**), **5995** & **7180** (Europe), 9755 & 11905 (**E North Am**), 13650 (Europe), 13670 (**E North Am**)
2200-2300	9760 & 11945 (Europe)
2300-2330	9755 (**E North Am** & C America), 11730 & 13670 (C America)
2330-2400	5960, 9755 & M-F 13670 (**E North Am**)

CHINA (PR)
RADIO BEIJING

0000-0100	**9770**, **11715** (**N America**)
0300-0400	**9690** (**N America** & C America), **9770** & **11715** (**N America**)
0400-0500	11680/11695 (**W North Am**)
0400-0600	**11840** (**N America**)
0900-1100	11755, 15440 & 17710 (Australasia)

1200-1300	9665/15210 (**E North Am** & C America)
1200-1400	11600/15440 (Pacific), 15450 (Australasia)
1300-1500	11855 (**W North Am**)
1400-1600	7405 (**W North Am**)
1900-2000	6955 (N Africa)
1900-2100	9440 & 11515 (Mideast & N Africa)
2000-2100	9785 (Mideast)
<u>2000-2200</u>	9920 & 11500 (<u>Europe</u>)
<u>2200-2230</u>	**3985** (<u>Europe</u>)
<u>2200-2300</u>	**7170/9740** (<u>Europe</u>)

CHINA (TAIWAN)
VOICE OF FREE CHINA

0200-0300	**5950** (**E North Am**), **11740** (C America)
0200-0400	**9680** (**W North Am**), 9765 (Australasia), 15345 (E Asia)
0300-0400	**5950** (**E North Am** & C America)
0700-0800	**5950** (C America)
<u>2200-2300</u>	**9853, 11580, 17750** & **21720** (<u>Europe</u>)

COSTA RICA
ADVENTIST WORLD R—(C America)

1100-1230	9725, 11870
1230-1300	Su-F 9725, Su-F 11870
2300-0100	9725, 11870

RADIO FOR PEACE INTERNATIONAL

0100-0700	7375 (C America), 13630 (USB) & 15030 (**N America**)
0700-0730	W/Th/Sa-M 7375 (C America), W/Th/Sa-M 13630 & W/Th/Sa-M 15030 (**N America**)
0730-0800	7375 (C America), 13630 (USB) & 15030 (**N America**)
0900-1500	7375 (C America), 13630 (USB) & 15030 (**N America**)
1500-1530	W/Th/Sa-M 7375 (C America), W/Th/Sa-M 13630 (USB) & W/Th/Sa-M 15030 (**N America**)
1530-1600	7375 (C America), 13630 (USB) & 15030 (**N America**)
1700-2300	7375 (C America), 13630 (USB) & 15030 (**N America**)
1900-2300	21465 (**N America**)
2300-2330	W/Th/Sa-M 7375 (C America), W/Th/Sa-M 13630, W/Th/Sa-M 15030 (USB) & W/Th/Sa-M 21465 (**N America**)
2330-2400	7375 (C America), 13630 (USB), 15030 & 21465 (**N America**)

CROATIA
CROATIAN RADIO

0000-0015	**7315** (**E North Am**)
0500-0515	**7315** (**E North Am**), **9495** (**Americas**)
<u>0700-0715</u>	M-Sa 6210, M-Sa 7240, M-Sa 9830 & M-Sa 13830 (<u>Europe</u>), M-Sa 21480
<u>0900-0915</u>	M-Sa 6210, M-Sa 7240, M-Sa 9830 & M-Sa 13830 (<u>Europe</u>), M-Sa 21480
<u>1300-1315</u>	6210, 7240, 9830 & 13830 (<u>Europe</u>), 21480
<u>2200-2215</u>	6210, 7240, 9830 & 13830 (<u>Europe</u>), 21480

CUBA
RADIO HABANA CUBA

0000-0500	11950/11970 (**E North Am**)
0200-0430	13710/13700 (**E North Am**)
0400-0500	6180 & 11760 (C America)
0600-0800	11760 (**W North Am**)

CZECHOSLOVAKIA
RADIO CZECHOSLOVAKIA

0000-0030	7345 (**N America**), 9540 & 9580 (**E North Am**), 11990 (**N America**)
0100-0130	5930 & 7345 (**N America**), 9540 & 9580 (**E North Am**)
0300-0330	5930 & 7345 (**N America**), 9540 & 9810 (**E North Am**), 11990 (**N America**)
0400-0430	5930 & 7345 (**N America**), 9540 & 9810 (**E North Am**), 11990, 13715 & 15355 (**N America**)
<u>0600-0630</u>	11990 (<u>Europe</u>)
<u>0700-0730</u>	6055, 7345 & 9505 (<u>Europe</u>)
0730-0800	17725 & 21705 (Australasia)
<u>1030-1100</u>	11990 (<u>Europe</u>), 15355 (<u>W Europe</u>)
<u>1130-1200</u>	6055, 7345 & 9505 (<u>Europe</u>)
<u>1800-1830</u>	5930, 6055, 7345 & 9605 (<u>Europe</u>)
<u>1930-2000</u>	6055 & 7345 (<u>Europe</u>)
<u>2100-2130</u>	5930, 6055, 7345 & 9605 (<u>Europe</u>)
<u>2200-2230</u>	5930, 6055, 7345 & 9605 (<u>Europe</u>)

ECUADOR
HCJB-VOICE OF THE ANDES

<u>**0030-0430**</u>	9745 & 15155 (**N America** & C America), 21455 (USB) (<u>Europe</u> & Pacific)
0500-0700	11925 (**N America** & C America)
<u>0500-1600</u>	21455 (USB) (<u>Europe</u> & Pacific)
<u>0700-0830</u>	11730 & 15270 (<u>Europe</u>)
0730-1130	9745 (Australasia), 11925 (Australasia & Pacific)
1130-1430	15115 (**Americas**)
1130-1600	11925 & 17890 (**N America** & C America)
<u>1630-1700</u>	Su-F 21480 (Mideast), 21455 (USB) (<u>Europe</u> & Pacific), 21480 (Mideast)
<u>1700-1745</u>	21480 (Mideast), 21455 (USB) (<u>Europe</u> & Pacific), 21480 (Mideast)
<u>1745-1800</u>	M-F 21480 (Mideast), 21455 (USB) (<u>Europe</u> & Pacific), 21480 (Mideast)
<u>1900-2000</u>	15270 & 17790 (<u>Europe</u>), 21455 (USB) (<u>Europe</u>)
<u>2130-2200</u>	15270 & 17790 (<u>Europe</u>), 21455 (USB) (<u>Europe</u>)

EGYPT
RADIO CAIRO

0200-0330	9475 & 11865 (**N America**)
<u>2115-2245</u>	9900 (<u>Europe</u>)

ESTONIA
RADIO ESTONIA—(Europe)

<u>1620-1630</u>	M-F 5925
<u>2130-2200</u>	M-F 5925

FINLAND
RADIO FINLAND

0130-0150	11755 & 15185 (**N America**)
0230-0250	9560 & 11755 (**N America**)
<u>0520-0530</u>	9665 (<u>E Europe</u>), 11755 (<u>Europe</u>), 15440 (Mideast)

0620-0630	6120 & 11755 (Europe), 15440 (Mideast)
0645-0700	11755 (Europe)
0745-0800	6120, 9560 & 11755 (Europe)
0830-0900	15355 (E Asia)
0900-0925	17800 & 21550 (Australasia)
0930-1000	15245 & 17800 (E Asia)
1230-1250	M-F 15400 (**N America**)
1330-1355	M-F 15400 & M-F 17880 (**N America**)
1405-1430	11755 (Europe), 11820 (E Europe), Sa/Su 15400 (**N America**), 15440 (Mideast), Sa/Su 17880 (**N America**)
1430-1500	15400 & 17880 (**N America**)
1505-1530	6120 (Europe), 9730 (E Europe), 11755 (Europe), 15440 & 21550 (Mideast)
1830-1900	9730 (W Europe), 11755 (Europe), 15440 (W Europe)
1930-2000	6120 (Europe), 9730 (W Europe), 11755 (Europe)
2130-2155	11755 (Europe), 15440 (W Europe)
2230-2255	6120 (Europe), 9730 (W Europe), 11755 (E Asia)

FRANCE
RADIO FRANCE INTERNATIONALE
1230-1300	9805, 11670, 15155 & 15195 (E Europe), 15365 (**E North Am**), 21645 (C America)
1400-1500	**4130** (E Asia), 17650 (Mideast)
1600-1700	6175 (Europe & N Africa), 11705 (N Africa), 15530 (Mideast)

GEORGIA
RADIO GEORGIA—(Europe)
0530-0600	11805, 12050
2030-2100	11760
2130-2200	11760

GERMANY
DEUTSCHE WELLE
0100-0150	**6040** & 6055 (**N America**), 6085 & 6145 (**N America** & C America), 9565 (**E North Am** & C America), 9610 (C America), 9640 &11810 (**E North Am**), 11865 (**N America** & C America), 13610 (C America), 13770 (**N America**), **15105** (**E North Am** & C America)
0300-0350	6055 (**N America**), **6085** (**N America** & C America), 6120 (**N America**), 9535 (**Americas**), **9545** (**N America** & C America), 9640 (**E North Am**), **9700** (**N America** & C America), 9705 (C America), 9770 (**Americas**), 118 10 & 11890 (**N America**), 13610 (C America), 13770 (**N America**), **15205** (**E North Am** & C America)
0400-0450	6130 (**N America**), 6130 (C America), 7275 (Europe), 9665 & 13610 (C America), 13770 (Mideast)
0500-0550	5960, 6045, 6055, 6120, 6130, 9515 & **9670** (**N America**), 9690 (C America), 11705 & 11925 (**N America**), 13610 (C America), 13790 (**N America**)
0900-0950	**6160** (C America & Australasia), **11915** & 17780 (Australasia), 17780 (E Asia), **17820** (Australasia), 21465 (E Asia), 21465, 21650 & 21680 (Australasia), 21680 (E Asia)
1500-1550	17735 (Mideast)
1900-1950	11905 & 13780 (Mideast)
2100-2150	6185, **9670** & 9765 (Australasia), 9765 (E Asia), **11785** (Australasia), 13780 (E Asia), 15360 (Australasia)

GREECE
FONI TIS HELLADAS
0135-0145	9395, 9420 & 11645 (**N America**)
0335-0345	9395, 9420 & 11645 (**N America**)
0835-0845	15650, 17525, 17535 & 17550 (Australasia)
1035-1050	15650 & 17535 (E Asia)
1235-1245	15550, 15630, 15650, 17515 & 17525 (**N America** & Europe)
1530-1540	11645, 15550, 15630 & 17525 (**N America** & Europe)
2000-2015	7450, 9395 & 11645 (Europe)

GUAM
ADVENTIST WORLD RADIO
0200-0300	Sa/Su 13720 (E Asia)

KTWR-TRANS WORLD RADIO
0900-1000	11805 (Australasia)

HOLLAND
RADIO NEDERLAND
0030-0125	6020 (**E North Am**), 6165 (**N America**), **11835** (**E North Am**)
0330-0425	**6165** & **9590** (**W North Am**)
0730-0825	**9630** (Australasia)
0730-1025	**11895** (Australasia)
0930-1025	**9720** (Australasia)
1230-1325	5955 (Europe)

HUNGARY
RADIO BUDAPEST
0200-0300	15220 (**N America**)
0300-0400	6110, 9835 & 11910 (**N America**)
2200-2300	6110, 9835 & 11910 (Europe)

INDIA
ALL INDIA RADIO
1000-1100	15050 (E Asia), 17387 (Australasia), 17895 & 21735 (E Asia)
1745-1945	7412 (W Europe), 9950 (N Africa), 11620 (W Europe), 11860 (N Africa)
2045-2230	7412 (Europe), 9910 (Australasia), 9950 (Europe), 11620 (W Europe), 11715 & 15265 (Australasia)

INDONESIA
VOICE OF INDONESIA
0100-0200	11752 (Asia & Pacific)
0800-0900	11752 (Asia & Pacific)
2000-2100	11752 (Europe)

IRAN
VOICE OF THE ISLAMIC REPUBLIC
0030-0130	9022 (**Americas**), 9720 & 15260 (**N America** & C America)

1030-1130	7115, 11715, 11930 & 11940 (Mideast)
1130-1230	9525, 9685 & 11745 (Mideast)
<u>1930-2030</u>	6140 & 9022 (<u>Europe</u>)
2330-0030	11930 (C America)

IRAQ
RADIO IRAQ INTERNATIONAL
<u>1400-1700</u>	15250 & 15400 (<u>Europe</u> & Mideast)
<u>1800-1930</u>	15210 (<u>Europe</u>)
<u>1900-2030</u>	13680 (<u>Europe</u>)
<u>1945-2000</u>	15210 (<u>Europe</u>)
<u>2045-2100</u>	13680 (<u>Europe</u>)

ISRAEL
KOL ISRAEL
<u>0500-0515</u>	11588 (<u>W Europe</u> & **E North Am**)
<u>1100-1130</u>	17543 (<u>W Europe</u>)
<u>1300-1325</u>	Su-Th 15640 (<u>W Europe</u>), Su-Th 15650 (Australasia), Su-Th 17575 (<u>W Europe</u> & **E North Am**), Su-Th 17590 (E Europe)
<u>1400-1430</u>	Su-Th 11587 & Su-Th 11605 (<u>W Europe</u>), Su-Th 15640 (<u>W Europe</u> & **E North Am**), Su-Th 15650 (Australasia), Su-Th 17575 (**E North Am**), Su-Th 17590 (E Europe)
<u>1700-1715</u>	15590 (W Europe)
<u>1800-1815</u>	11587 (<u>W Europe</u>), 11675 (<u>E Europe</u>), 15640 (<u>W Europe</u> & **E North Am**)
<u>1900-1930</u>	15640 & 17575 (<u>W Europe</u> & **E North Am**), 17575 (**E North Am**)
<u>2000-2030</u>	7465, 9435 & 11587 (<u>W Europe</u> & **E North Am**), 11605 (C America), 11675 (<u>E Europe</u>)
<u>2030-2100</u>	15100 (<u>E Europe</u>)
<u>2130-2200</u>	15100 (<u>E Europe</u>), 15590 (W Europe), 15640 (C America)
<u>2230-2300</u>	7465 (<u>W Europe</u> & **E North Am**), 9435 (C America), 11587 & 11605 (<u>W Europe</u> & **E North Am**), 11675 (E Europe)

ITALY
ADVENTIST WORLD R—(Europe)
<u>0830-0900</u>	7230
<u>1130-1200</u>	7230

EUROPEAN CHRISTIAN R—(Europe)
<u>0700-0715</u>	Su 6210
<u>0745-0800</u>	Su 6210

ITALIAN RADIO RELAY—(Europe)
<u>0500-0600</u>	Su 9815
<u>0600-0800</u>	M-F 9815
<u>0800-0815</u>	Sa 9815
<u>0815-0930</u>	Sa/Su 9815
<u>0930-1000</u>	Sa 9815
<u>1030-1400</u>	Su 9815
<u>1400-1500</u>	Sa/Su 9815
<u>1500-1600</u>	9815
<u>2030-2200</u>	9815

RTV ITALIANA/RAI
<u>0100-0120</u>	9575 (**E North Am**), 11800 (**E North Am** & C America)
<u>0425-0440</u>	5990 & 7275 (<u>Europe</u>, N Africa & Mideast), 9575 (<u>Europe</u>, Mideast & N Africa)
<u>1935-1955</u>	7275, 9710 & 11800 (<u>Europe</u>)

<u>2025-2045</u>	7235 (<u>E Europe</u> & Mideast), 9575 & 11800 (Mideast)
2200-2225	5990, 9710, 11800 & 15330 (E Asia)
<u>2230-0500</u>	6060 (<u>Europe</u>, Mideast & N Africa)

JAPAN
RADIO JAPAN/NHK
<u>0100-0200</u>	5960 (**E North Am** & C America), 15195 & 17835 (E Asia)
<u>0300-0330</u>	15325 (C America), 17825 (**W North Am** & C America), 21610 (Pacific)
<u>0300-0400</u>	5960 (**E North Am** & C America), 11870 (**W North Am**), 15230 (E Asia)
<u>0500-0600</u>	6035 (<u>Europe</u> & N Africa), **7280** (<u>Europe</u>), **9695** (<u>Europe</u> & N Africa), **9770** (<u>Europe</u>), 11870 (**W North Am**), 15230 (Pacific & **N America**), 17765 (E Asia), 17825 (**W North Am** & C America), 17860 & 17890 (Australasia)
<u>0700-0800</u>	5970 (<u>Europe</u>), **6025** & **9670** (<u>Europe</u> & N Africa), **9770**, 15170 & 15250 (<u>Europe</u>), 17765 (E Asia), 17860 & 17890 (Australasia), **21575** (<u>Europe</u> & N Africa)
0900-1000	11840 (E Asia), 15270, 17860 & 17890 (Australasia)
<u>1100-1200</u>	6120 (**N America**), 11840 (E Asia)
<u>1400-1600</u>	9505 & 11865 (Pacific & **W North Am**)
<u>1700-1800</u>	7140 (E Asia), 9505 & 11865 (Pacific & **W North Am**), 15210 & 15345 (Mideast)
<u>1900-1930</u>	9505 (Pacific & **W North Am**), 9640 & 11850 (Australasia), 11865 (Pacific & **W North Am**)
<u>2100-2200</u>	11735 (<u>Europe</u> & N Africa), 11815 (E Asia), 17890 (Australasia)
<u>2300-2400</u>	6025 (<u>Europe</u>), 6160 (<u>Europe</u> & N Africa), 11815 & 15195 (E Asia)

KAZAKHSTAN
RADIO ALMA-ATA
0030-0100	5915 & 6135 (Asia)
1430-1500	7255 (E Asia)
1530-1600	5915 & 6135 (Asia)
1930-2000	**3955**, 4400, 5035, 5260, 5960, 5970, 9505, 11825, 15215, 15270, 15315, 15360, 15385, 17605, 17715, 17730, 17765 & **21490** (Omnidirectional)
2130-2200	**3955**, 4400, 5035, 5260, 5960, 5970, 9505, 11825, 15215, 15270, 15315, 15360, 15385, 17605, 17715, 17730, 17765 & **21490** (Omnidirectional)
2330-2400	7255 (E Asia)

KOREA (DPR)
RADIO PYONGYANG
0000-0050	13760 & 15115 (C America)
0700-0750	15340 (E Asia)
1100-1150	6576, 9977 & 11335 (C America)
<u>1300-1350</u>	9325 (<u>Europe</u>), 9345 (<u>Europe</u> & Mideast)
<u>1500-1550</u>	9325 (<u>Europe</u>), 9640 (Mideast), 11705 (<u>Europe</u>)

1700-1750	9325 (Europe), 9640 (Mideast), 11705 (Europe)
2000-2050	6576 (Europe), 9345 (Europe & Mideast), 9640 (Mideast)
2300-2350	11700 & 13650 (C America)

KOREA (REPUBLIC)
RADIO KOREA
0030-0130	15575 (**E North Am**)
0045-0100	7275 (E Asia)
0600-0700	7275 (E Asia), 11810 (**E North Am**), 15170 (**W North Am**)
0800-0900	7550 & 13670 (Europe)
1030-1100	**11715 (N America)**
1100-1200	15575 (Mideast)
1130-1200	**9650 (N America)**
1215-1315	**9750 (E North Am)**
1545-1600	7275 (E Asia)
1600-1700	5975 (E Asia), 9870 (Mideast)
1900-2000	6135 (E Asia)
2145-2245	6480 (Europe), 7550 (Mideast), 15575 (Europe)

KUWAIT
RADIO KUWAIT
| **1800-2100** | 13620 (Europe & **E North Am**) |

LATVIA
RADIO RIGA INTL—(Europe)
0700-0730	Su 5935
1830-1900	Sa 5935
2130-2140	M-F 5935

LEBANON
KING OF HOPE—(Mideast)
| 0700-1100 | 6280 |
| 1400-1700 | 6280 |
WINGS OF HOPE—(Europe)
| 0700-1100 | 11530 |
| 1400-2400 | 11530 |

LITHUANIA
RADIO VILNIUS
0000-0030	**7400 (E North Am)**, 9710 (Europe), **10344** (E Asia), **17605** & **17690 (W North Am)**
2230-2300	9710 (Europe)
2300-2330	**13645** & **15580 (W North Am)**

LUXEMBOURG
RADIO LUXEMBOURG
| **24h** | 15350 (**E North Am**) |

MALAYSIA
VOICE OF MALAYSIA
| 0555-0825 | 15295 (Australasia) |

MALTA
VO MEDITERRANEAN—(Europe, N Africa & Mideast)
| 0600-0700 | 9765 |
| 1400-1500 | 11925 |

MOLDOVA
RADIO MOLDOVA INTERNATIONAL (Projected)
0130-0200	11675 & 11730 (**N America**)
1200-1230	15430 & 17800 (Europe)
1830-1900	13640 & 15315 (Europe)

MONACO
TRANS WORLD RADIO—(W Europe)
0635-0835	9480
0735-0935	7240
0835-0850	Su-F 9480
0850-0915	Su 9480
0935-0950	Su-F 7240
0950-1015	Su 9480

MONGOLIA
RADIO ULAANBAATAR
0910-0940	11850 (Australasia), W/Th/Sa-M 12015 (E Asia & Australasia), 12015 (Australasia)
1200-1230	W/Th/Sa-M 11850 (E Asia)
1445-1515	M-Sa 9795 & M-Sa 13780 (E Asia)
1940-2010	11850 & 12050 (Europe)

MOROCCO
RTV MAROCAINE—(Europe)
1530-1700	M-F 17595
1700-1800	Sa 17815
1900-2000	Su 11920

NETHERLANDS ANTILLES
TRANS WORLD RADIO
| **0300-0400** | 9535 & 11930 (**N America**) |
| **1100-1300** | 11815 (**E North Am**), 15345 (**N America**) |

NEW ZEALAND
R NEW ZEALAND INTL—(Pacific)
0700-1210	9700
1205-1655	9510
1655-1850	Su-F 9675
1750-2200	Su-F 15120
1850-2140	Su-F 11735
2200-0800	17770

NORTHERN MARIANA IS
KFBS-FAR EAST BC
| 1930-2000 | 9465 (E Europe) |

NORWAY
RADIO NORWAY INTERNATIONAL
0000-0030	Sa/Su 9645 (**W North Am**), Su/M 15165 (**E North Am** & C America)
0100-0130	Su/M 9565 (**W North Am**), Su/M 9615 (**E North Am** & C America)
0200-0230	Su/M 9565 (**W North Am**), Su/M 11930 (**N America**)
0400-0430	Su/M 9560 (**N America**), Su/M 9650 (**W North Am**), Su/M 11865 (**W North Am** & Pacific)
1200-1230	Sa/Su 17860 & Sa/Su 21705 (Australasia)
1300-1330	Sa/Su 9590, Sa/Su 15270 & Sa/Su 25730 (Europe)
1600-1630	Sa/Su 11875, Sa/Su 15230 & Sa/Su 17720 (Mideast)
1700-1730	Sa/Su 9655 (Europe)
1900-1930	Sa/Su 17730 (Australasia), Sa/Su 17860 (E Asia & Australasia)
2100-2130	Sa/Su 15180, Sa/Su 17845 & Sa/Su 21705 (Australasia)
2300-2330	Sa/Su 11795 (**E North Am** & C America)

PAKISTAN
RADIO PAKISTAN

0800-0845	17870 & 21520 (Europe)
1100-1120	17870 & 21520 (Europe)
1600-1630	13665 (Mideast), 15605, 17555 & 21580 (Mideast & N Africa)
1700-1800	7305, 9370, 11570 & 15550 (Europe)

PALAU
KHBN-VOICE OF HOPE—(E Asia)

0300-0800	11900, 11980

PHILIPPINES
RADYO PILIPINAS

0230-0330	21580 (E Asia)

POLAND
POLISH RADIO—(Europe)

1300-1355	6135, 7145, 9525, 11815
1600-1655	7285, 9525, 11840
1800-1855	7145, 9525
1930-2025	7145, 9525
2030-2125	6095, 6135, 7145, 7270, 9525

PORTUGAL
RADIO PORTUGAL INTERNATIONAL

0230-0300	Tu-Sa 9570 (**E North Am**), Tu-Sa 9705 (**N America**)
0845-0900	Sa/Su 9615 (Europe)
1600-1630	M-F 15425 (Mideast)
2000-2030	M-F 11740 (Europe)

ROMANIA
RADIO ROMANIA INTERNATIONAL

0200-0300	5990 (C America), 6155, 9510, 9570, 11830 & 11940 (**Americas**)
0400-0430	5990 (C America), 6155, 9510, 9570, 11830 & 11940 (**Americas**)
0635-0645	7225, 9665, 11940 & 15365 (Europe)
0645-0715	11810 & 11940 (Australasia), 15335 (Asia & Australasia), 17720, 17805 & 21665 (Australasia)
1300-1400	11940, 15365 & 17720 (Europe), 17850 (W Europe)
1430-1530	15335 (Mideast)
1730-1800	11790 (Europe)
1900-2000	5990, 6105, 7145, 7195, 9690, 9750 & 11940 (Europe)
2100-2200	5955, 5990, 6105, 7145, 7195, 9690, 9750 & 11940 (Europe)

RUSSIA
ADVENTIST WORLD RADIO

0430-0500	15125 (Europe)
0700-0800	11855 (Asia)
1600-1630	15125 (Europe)
1900-2000	9835 (E Asia)

RADIO MOSCOW INTERNATIONAL

0030-0800	17825 (E Asia & Australasia)
0230-0500	9470 (**E North Am**)
0300-0800	7270 (**W North Am**)
0400-0800	9505 (**W North Am**)
0700-1600	11705 (Europe)
0730-1600	13705/13710 (Europe)
1430-0900	15420 (E Asia & Australasia)
1600-2100	17695 (**E North Am**)
1630-2000	11630 (Europe)

1800-2300	17655 (**E North Am**)
1830-0600	12050 (**W North Am**)
1930-0400	15425 (**W North Am**)
2000-2400	9480 (E Asia)
2100-0300	7115 (**E North Am**)
2100-0700	7150 (**E North Am**)
2130-0900	17720 (**W North Am**)
2230-0900	17890/21790 (E Asia & Australasia)
2230-1000	21690 (E Asia & Australasia)

RADIO GALAXY—(Europe)

1900-2200	11880
2000-2300	9880

SAUDI ARABIA
BS OF THE KINGDOM

1600-2100	9705 (Europe), 9720 (E Europe)

SOUTH AFRICA
RADIO RSA

0200-0400	7270 (Africa & **N America**)
0300-0500	5960 (Africa & **N America**)
0400-0500	15230 (Africa & **N America**)
0600-0700	15220 (Africa & **N America**)

RADIO ORION

2300-0300	3320/4810 (Africa, **N America** & Europe)

SPAIN
RADIO EXTERIOR DE ESPANA

0000-0200	9530 (**N America** & C America)
0500-0600	9530 (**N America** & C America)
1900-2000	6130 (Mideast), 9685 & 9875 (Europe)
2100-2200	9875 (Europe)

SRI LANKA
SRI LANKA BROADCASTING CORP

0445-0515	9720 & 15425 (**W North Am**)
1030-1130	11835 (Australasia), 15120 (E Asia)
2000-2130	9720 (E Asia), 15120 (Mideast)
2330-2400	15425 (**N America**)

SWEDEN
RADIO SWEDEN

0200-0230	9695 (**N America**), 11705 (**E North Am** & C America)
1330-1400	21625 (Australasia)
1600-1630	15270 (Mideast), 17870 (**N America**), 21500 (**E North Am** & C America)
2130-2230	6065 (Europe), 9655 (Europe & N Africa), 11730 (Australasia)
2330-2400	6065 (Europe)

SWITZERLAND
RED CROSS BC SVC—(Europe & N Africa)

1100-1130	Either first or last Su of month 7210
1700-1730	Either first or last M of month 7210

SWISS RADIO INTERNATIONAL

0000-0030	6135 (**N America** & C America), 9650 (C America), **17730** (C America & **W North Am**)
0200-0230	6135 (**N America** & C America), 9650 (C America), 9885 & 12035 (**E North Am** & C America)
0400-0430	6135 (**N America** & C America), 9885 & 12035 (**N America**), 13635 (**N America** & C America)
0500-0530	3985 (Europe), 6165 & 9535 (Europe & N Africa)

0600-0630	21770 (Mideast)
0700-0730	3985 (Europe), 6165 & 9535 (Europe & N Africa)
0900-0930	9560, 13685, 17670 & 21770 (Australasia)
1100-1130	13635 (Australasia), 15505 (E Asia & Australasia), 17670 (Australasia)
1200-1230	6165, 9535 & 12030 (Europe & N Africa)
1300-1330	**7480** & 13635 (E Asia)
1500-1530	13635, 15505, 17670 & 21770 (Mideast)
1700-1730	13635 & 15430 (Mideast)
1800-1815	9885 (E Europe)

SYRIA
SYRIAN BROADCASTING SERVICE
2005-2105	12085 & 15095 (Europe)
2110-2210	12085 (**N America**), 15095 (Australasia)

THAILAND
RADIO THAILAND—(Asia)
0500-0600	9655, 11905
1130-1230	9655, 11905
2300-0430	9655, 11905

TURKEY
VOICE OF TURKEY
0400-0450	9445 (**E North Am**)
1330-1400	9675 (Mideast)
2100-2150	9445 (Europe)
2300-2350	7185 (Mideast), 9445 (**E North Am**), 11895 (Europe)

UKRAINE
RADIO UKRAINE
0000-0100	7195 (W Europe), 7250 & 9635 (Europe), 11520, 11790 & 12000 (**E North Am**), 12040 (C America), 120 60 & 12330 (**E North Am**), **13645 (W North Am**), 15355 (**E North Am**), 15570 (Europe & Atlantic), **15580 (W North Am**)
0100-0200	4825 (Europe), 7240 (W Europe & N Africa), 7400, 9860 & 9870 (**E North Am**), **10344** (E Asia), **17605** & **17690 (W North Am**)
2100-2200	7250, 9600, 9635 & 9865 (Europe), 15135 (**E North Am**), 15570 (Europe & Atlantic)
2100-2300	5960 (Europe)
2200-2300	6020 (Europe), 7380 (Europe & **E North Am**), 9785 (Europe & N Africa)

UNITED ARAB EMIRATES
UAE RADIO, ABU DHABI
2200-2400	7215, 9605, 11965 & 13605 (**E North Am**), 15305 & 17855 (**E North Am** & C America)

UAE RADIO, DUBAI
0330-0400	11945 & 13675 (**E North Am** & C America), 15400 & 15435 (**E North Am**)
0530-0600	15435 (Australasia), 17830 (E Asia), 21700 (Australasia)
1030-1110	13675 (Europe), 15320 (N Africa), 15435 & 21605 (Europe)
1330-1400	13675 (Europe), 15320 (N Africa), 15435 & 21605 (Europe)
1600-1640	11795 & 13675 (Europe), 15320 (N Africa), 21605 (Europe)

UNITED KINGDOM
BBC
0000-0045	**9570** (E Asia)
0000-0200	**6180** (E Europe)
0000-0330	7325 (C America)
0000-0430	9915 (**Americas**)
0030-0045	**15280** & **17830** (E Asia)
0030-0145	**5965** (E Europe)
0030-0230	**9590** (C America)
0100-0300	Su **15280** & Su **21715** (E Asia)
0100-0330	**17790** (E Asia)
0200-0300	7325 & 9410 (E Europe)
0200-0330	**7135** & **9670** (Mideast)
0200-0815	6195 (Europe)
0300-0400	**6180** (Europe), 7120 (E Europe), 12095 (Europe), **15575** (Mideast)
0300-0430	7230 (E Europe)
0300-0730	3955 (Europe)
0300-0815	**11760** & **15310** (Mideast)
0300-0915	**15280** (E Asia)
0300-1030	**21715** (E Asia)
0300-2315	9410 (Europe)
0330-0430	**6175** (**E North Am**), 12095 (**N America**)
0400-0730	**6180** (Europe), **15575** (Mideast)
0400-0900	12095 (Europe)
0430-0730	**5975** (C America)
0500-0815	**9640** (C America)
0600-0730	**15575** (Europe), **15575** (N Africa)
0600-0615	7180 (Australasia)
0800-0915	**11955** (Australasia)
0600-1000	**15360** (E Asia), **17830** (Australasia)
0800-2030	15070 (Europe & N Africa)
0700-0915	7325 (Europe)
0700-1200	9760 (Europe)
0730-0815	5975 (W Europe & N Africa)
0730-0900	Sa/Su **15575** (Mideast)
0800-0900	Sa/Su **9660** (Europe), 17705 (N Africa)
0800-1515	17640 (Europe & N Africa)
0815-0945	Su 5975 (W Europe & N Africa)
0900-1000	**11765** (E Asia)
0900-1400	**11760** (Mideast)
0900-1515	**9660** (Europe), **15575** (Mideast)
0900-1530	9750 (Europe)
0900-1615	17705 (N Africa)
0900-1830	**15310** (Mideast)
0900-2315	12095 (Europe & N Africa)
0915-1000	**7180** & **11955** (E Asia)
0945-1400	5975 (W Europe & N Africa)
1030-1200	Su 9760 (Europe)
1030-1515	**9740** (Asia & Australasia)
1100-1130	**5965** (**E North Am**)
1100-1400	**15220** (**E North Am**)
1100-1430	6195 (C America)
1100-1745	**9515** (**E North Am**)
1200-1615	9760 (Europe)
1300-1500	**11820** (E Asia)
1300-1615	**7180** (E Asia)
1400-1615	**17840** (Americas)
1400-1745	**15260** (N America)
1500-2315	6195 (Europe)
1515-1700	**7215** (Asia)
1530-1615	9750 (Europe)

1700-2200	**6180** (Europe)
1700-2315	3955 (Europe)
1715-1830	**7160** (Mideast)
1800-2200	**11955** (Australasia)
1830-2030	**9740** (Mideast)
1900-2030	**7160** (Mideast)
2000-2200	7325 (Europe)
2000-2315	**15340** (Australasia)
2000-0430	**5975 (Americas)**
2030-2200	3975 (Europe)
2030-2315	15070 (W Europe & N Africa)
2100-2200	**7180** (E Asia)
2100-0030	**9590** (**E North Am**), 15070 (**E North Am** & C America)
2200-2400	**9915 (Americas)**
2200-0030	**11955** (E Asia & Australasia)
2200-0200	7325 (E Europe)
2200-0330	12095 (**N America** & C America)
2200-0430	7325 (**N America** & C America)
2300-2400	**9570** (E Asia)
2300-0045	**11945, 15280** & **17830** (E Asia)
2300-0330	**6175** (**E North Am**)

BRITISH FORCES BS—(Mideast)

0330-0430	6840
1300-1500	15670
1700-2300	6840

USA

CHRISTIAN SCIENCE MONITOR WS

0000-0100	Sa/Su **17865** (E Asia)
0000-0115	M 7395 (**E North Am** & C America)
0000-0155	Tu-Sa 7395 (**E North Am** & C America)
0100-0155	Su 7395 (**E North Am** & C America), Sa **17865** (E Asia)
0200-0300	9455 (**W North Am** & C America), Sa/Su **17865** (E Asia)
0300-0315	M 9455 (**W North Am** & C America)
0300-0355	Tu-F 9455 (**W North Am** & C America), Su **17865** (E Asia)
0400-0500	9455 (**W North Am**), **17780** (E Asia)
0400-0515	M 9870 & M 13760 (C America)
0400-0555	Tu-F 9870 & Tu-F 13760 (C America)
0500-0515	M 9455 (**W North Am**)
0500-0555	Tu-F 9455 (**W North Am**), Sa/Su 9870 & Sa/Su 13760 (C America), M-Sa **17780** (E Asia)
0600-0700	9455 (**W North Am**), M-F 9870 (C America)
0600-0755	M-F 9840 (Europe), **17780** (E Asia)
0700-0755	M-F 9455 (**W North Am**), Su 9840 (Europe), 9870 (C America)
0800-0900	13615 & M-F **15665** (Australasia), **17555** (E Asia)
0800-0955	M-F 9840 & M-F 11705 (Europe)
0900-0955	Su 9840 & Su 11705 (Europe), M-F 13615 & **15665** (Australasia), Su-F **17555** (E Asia)
1000-1100	**9495** (**E North Am**)
1000-1155	**17555** (E Asia)
1100-1155	M-F 9495 (**E North Am**)
1200-1300	M-F **9425** (Australasia), 9495 (**E North Am**), Sa/Su 15665 (Europe), M-F **15665** (Australasia), Sa/Su 17510 (Europe)
1200-1355	M-F 13760 (C America)
1300-1355	**9425** (Australasia), M-F 9495 (**E**

	North Am), Sa/Su 13760 (C America), **15665** (Australasia)
1400-1500	Sa/Su 13710 (**E North Am** & C America), M-F 13760 (**W North Am** & C America), Sa/Su 15665 (**E North Am** & C America), Sa 15665, Su 15665, Sa 17510 & Su 17510 (Europe)
1400-1555	**9530** (E Asia), M-F 15665 & M-F 17510 (Europe)
1500-1555	13760 (**W North Am** & C America)
1600-1715	Su 17555 (**W North Am** & C America)
1600-1755	**11580** (E Asia), Sa/Su 13710 & Sa/Su 15665 (**E North Am** & C America)
1700-1755	Sa 17555 (**W North Am** & C America)
1800-1900	Su-F **9430** & Su-F **13840** (Australasia)
1800-1915	Su 15665 & Su 17510 (**E North Am** & Europe), Su 17555 (**W North Am** & C America)
1800-1955	Su-F **9495** (Europe & Mideast), M-F 15665 (**E North Am** & Europe), Su-F **15665** (Europe & Mideast), M-F 17510 (**E North Am** & Europe)
1900-1955	**9430** (Australasia), Sa **9495** (Europe & Mideast), **13840** (Australasia), Sa 15665 (**E North Am** & Europe), Sa **15665** (Europe & Mideast), Sa 17510 (**E North Am** & Europe), Sa 17555 (**W North Am** & C America)
2000-2100	Su-F **13840** (Australasia)
2000-2115	Su 13770 (Europe & Mideast), Su 15665 (**E North Am** & Europe), Su 15665 (Europe & Mideast), Su 17510 (**E North Am** & Europe)
2000-2155	**9455** (E Asia), M-F 13770 (Europe & Mideast), M-F 15665 (**E North Am**), M-F 15665 (Europe & Mideast), M-F 17510 (**E North Am** & Europe)
2100-2155	**13840** (Australasia)
2200-2300	9465 (**E North Am** & C America)
2200-2315	Su 13770 & Su 15665 (Europe)
2200-2355	M-F 13770 (Europe), **15405** (E Asia), M-F 15665 (Europe)
2300-2315	Su 9465 (**E North Am** & C America)

KCBI—(**N America**, projected)

0230-1400	9815
1400-0230	15375

KGEI-VOICE OF FRIENDSHIP

2200-2230	Su 15280 (C America)

KJES—(**N America**)

0700-0900	M-F 15385
0900-1000	M-F 9510
1400-1600	M-F 11715
1800-1900	M-F 9510
2000-2100	M-F 9510

KNLS-NEW LIFE STN—(E Asia)

0800-0900	7365
1300-1400	7355, 9660/11580

KTBN—(**E North Am**)

0000-1600	7510
1600-2400	15590

KVOH-VOICE OF HOPE—(**W North Am** & C America)

0000-0330	Tu-Sa 17775
0400-0800	9785

1800-1900	Su 17775
1900-2100	Sa/Su 17775
2100-2200	Su 17775

VOA

0000-0100	11695 (C America)
0000-0200	5995, 6130, 7405, 9455, 9775, 11580, 15120 & 15205 (C America)
0100-0300	7651 (Europe), **9740** (Mideast)
0200-0230	Tu-Sa 5995, Tu-Sa 7405, Tu-Sa 9775, Tu-Sa 11580, Tu-Sa 15120 & Tu-Sa 15205 (C America)
0300-0700	9575 & 15752 (N Africa)
0400-0500	**15205** (Mideast)
0400-0600	**7200** (Europe)
0400-0700	**5995** (E Europe), **6040** & **6140** (Europe), 6873 & **7170** (N Africa), **11965** (Mideast)
0430-0700	**3980** (Europe)
0500-0600	**9670** (Europe), **9700** (N Africa)
0500-0700	11825 & 15205 (Mideast)
0530-0700	**6060** (E Europe)
0600-0700	**6005** & **6095** (N Africa), **7325** (Europe), **11805** (N Africa), 11915 & 11925 (Europe)
0800-1100	**11735, 11740, 15160, 15195, 21455** & **21570** (Mideast)
1000-1200	5985 (Pacific & Australasia), 9590 (C America), **11720** (E Asia & Australasia), 11915 & 15120 (C America)
1000-1500	**15425** (Pacific)
1100-1400	**15155** (E Asia)
1100-1500	**9760** (E Asia)
1200-1330	**11715** (E Asia & Australasia)
1400-1500	**15160** (E Asia), **15205** (Mideast)
1400-1800	**9645** (E Asia)
1500-1700	**15205** (Europe)
1500-1800	**15255** (Mideast)
1500-2200	**9700** (Mideast), **15205** (E Europe), 19379 (Europe)
1600-2200	19262 (N Africa)
1630-1700	6180 (E Europe), 9760 (Europe), **11855** & **15245** (E Europe), **17735** (E Europe & Mideast)
1630-2200	**6040** (Europe)
1700-1800	**11855** (E Asia)
1700-2200	**9760** (Europe), **15205** (N Africa, Mideast & E Europe)
1800-2000	**3980** (Europe)
1900-2000	**9525** & **11870** (E Asia & Australasia), **15180** (Pacific)
2000-2100	18275 (N Africa)
2100-2200	**11870** (E Asia & Australasia)
2100-2400	**11960** (Mideast)
2100-0100	**15185** (Pacific), **17735** (E Asia & Australasia)
2200-2400	**6095, 6160, 9530, 11895, 11905, 15215** & **15255** (Mideast), **15305** (E Asia & Australasia), **15445, 17810** & **17885** (Mideast)
2200-0100	**15290** & **17820** (E Asia)

WEWN (Projected—various languages)

0000-0100	17890 (E Asia)
0200-0300	9985 (Europe & Mideast)
0300-0500	7520 (Europe)
0500-1000	7465 (Europe)
0800-1600	9870 (**W North Am** & C America)
1300-1700	11735 (**W North Am** & C America)
1300-1800	18930 (Europe), 21670 (N Africa)

1600-2400	13615 (**W North Am** & C America)
1800-2000	13710 (Europe)
2000-2200	7540 (Europe), 11970 (Europe & N Africa)
2000-2400	13710 (C America)
2200-0800	7540 (**W North Am** & C America)
2200-1000	5825 (Europe)

WINB-WORLD INTL BC—(Europe & N Africa)

1600-1700	15295
1700-1730	M-Sa 15295
1730-1800	Su-F 15295
1800-2100	15295
2100-2245	15185
2245-2330	15145
2330-2345	Th/Sa-Tu 15145

WJCR-JESUS CHRIST RADIO

24h	7460 & 7490 (**E North Am**), 15660 (**N America**)

WMLK—(Europe, Mideast & **N America**)

0400-0900	Su-F 9465
1700-2200	Su-F 9465

WORLD HARVEST RADIO

0000-0100	Su/M 9495 (C America)
0100-0400	7315 (**E North Am**), M 9495 (C America)
0400-0500	9495 (C America)
0500-0600	Su 7315 (**E North Am**), Su 9495 (C America)
0600-0800	9495 (C America)
0600-1100	7315 (**E North Am**)
0800-1100	7355 (C America)
1100-1300	Su 11790 (C America)
1100-1600	9465 (**E North Am**)
1300-1400	11790 (C America)
1400-1600	15105 (C America)
1600-1700	Su 15105 (C America)
1600-2100	13760 (**E North Am** & W Europe)
1700-1800	15105 (C America)
1800-2100	17830 (C America)
2100-2200	M-Sa 13760 (**E North Am** & W Europe), M-Sa 17830 (C America)
2200-2300	17830 (C America)
2200-2400	13760 (**E North Am** & W Europe)
2300-2400	Sa/Su 9495 (C America)

WRNO WORLDWIDE—(**E North Am**)

1400-1600	Su 15420
1500-2300	15420
2300-0100	7355

WWCR—(**E North Am** & Europe)

0000-0100	15690
0000-1200	7435
0100-0200	12160/13815
0100-1300	5920
1000-1200	15690
1100-1600	12160/13815
1200-2215	15690
1400-2200	17535
2200-0100	12160/13815
2215-2245	W-Su 15690

WYFR-FAMILY RADIO

0000-0045	5985 (**E North Am**)
0100-0200	9505 (**W North Am**)
0100-0245	15440 (C America)
0100-0445	6085 (**E North Am**)
0200-0445	9505 (**W North Am**)
0500-0600	9850 & 11580 (Europe)
0500-0700	5935 (**W North Am**), 11915 (Europe)
0500-0745	11725 (Europe)

Kim Shippey, Executive Producer and International Advisor of the Christian Science Monitor World Service, is heard worldwide each weekday.

0600-0745	7355 & 9680 (Europe)
1000-1400	5950 (**E North Am**)
1100-1200	11830 (**W North Am**)
1100-1245	7355 (**W North Am**)
1200-1445	6015 (**W North Am**)
1200-1700	11680 (**W North Am**), 17750 & 17760 (C America)
1300-1400	13695 (**E North Am**)
1300-1445	9705 (**W North Am**)
1500-1700	11705 & 15215 (**W North Am**)
1600-1700	15355 & 21615 (Europe)
1700-1900	21500 (Europe)
1900-1945	16355 (Europe)

1900-2145	21615 (Europe)
2000-2200	7355 & 15566 (Europe)
2200-2245	11915 (Europe)

VATICAN STATE
VATICAN RADIO

0250-0315	6095 (**N America** & C America), 7305 (**E North Am** & C America), 9605 (**N America** & C America), 11620 (**E North Am** & C America)
0600-0620	6245 (Europe)
0600-0630	7250 (W Europe)
0730-0745	M-Sa 6245 (Europe), M-Sa 7250 (Europe, Mideast & N Africa), M-Sa 9645 (E Europe), M-Sa 15210 (Mideast)
1120-1130	M-Sa 6245 (Europe), M-Sa 7250 (Europe, N Africa & Mideast), M-Sa 9645 (W Europe), M-Sa 15210 (Mideast)
1345-1405	11830 & 15090 (Australasia)
1345-1415	17525 (Australasia)
1600-1700	Su 15090 (Australasia)
1715-1730	6245 (Europe), 7250 (Europe, N Africa & Mideast)
2050-2110	5882 (Europe), 7250 (W Europe)
2245-2315	7305 (E Asia), 9600 & 11830 (Australasia), 15090 (E Asia & Australasia)

VIETNAM
VOICE OF VIETNAM

1230-1300	9840, 12018 & 15009 (E Asia & **Americas**)
1800-1830	9840, 12018 & 15009 (Europe)
1900-1930	9840, 12018 & 15009 (Europe)
2030-2100	9840, 12018 & 15009 (Europe)
2330-2400	9840, 12018 & 15009 (E Asia & **Americas**)

YUGOSLAVIA
RADIO YUGOSLAVIA

0030-0100	11870 (**E North Am**)
0130-0200	9580 (**E North Am**), 11870 (**W North Am**)
0230-0300	9580 (**W North Am**)
1930-2000	6100 & 7200 (Europe, N Africa & Mideast)
2200-2230	6100 & 7200 (Europe, N Africa & Mideast)

Voices From Home

For some, the offerings in English on world band radio are merely icing on the cake. Their real interest is in listening to programs aimed at national compatriots. Voices from home.

"Home" may be a place of family origin, or perhaps it's a favorite country you once visited or lived in. Vacationers and business travelers also tune in to keep in touch with events at home. For yet others, it is the perfect way to keep limber in a second tongue.

Schedules Prepared for Entire Year

To be as helpful as possible throughout the year, *Passport's* schedules consist not just of observed activity, but also that which we have creatively opined will take place during the entire year. This latter information is original from us, and therefore, of course, will not be so exact as factual information.

Following are frequencies for the most popular stations that are likely to be heard beyond their national borders. Some you'll hear, some you won't—which being which depending, among other things, on your location and receiving equipment. Keep in mind that the stations in this "Voices from Home" section often come in weaker than those in English, so better receiving equipment may be required. Those in bold tend to come in most strongly, as they are from relay transmitters close to the listening audience.

Reception Sometimes Best Outside Prime Time

Stations in "Voices from Home," unlike those in English, sometimes come in best—or only—outside the usual prime early-evening listening hours. Choice late-afternoon and evening frequencies are usually found in the world band segments between 5800 and 12160 kHz, sometimes even 3900-17900 kHz. But earlier in the day try 9250-21785 kHz, sometimes even 5800-26095 kHz. See *World Band Spectrum* in the Glossary at the back of the book for how to tune for best results.

Times and days of the week are given in World Time, explained in the *Passport* Glossary. Midyear, many programs are heard an hour earlier, whereas some in the southern hemisphere are heard an hour later. For transmission times and target zones, please refer to The Blue Pages.

ALGERIA
"VOICE OF PALESTINE"
Arabic 6145, 6160, 7145, 11715, 15205, 15215 kHz
RTV ALGERIENNE
French 7245, 9509, 9685, 15160, 17745 kHz
Arabic 6145, 6160, 7145, 7245, 9535, 11715, 15205, 15215 kHz

ARGENTINA—Spanish
RADIO ARGENTINA-RAE
11710, 15345 kHz
RADIO NACIONAL
6060, 9690, 11710, 15345 kHz

ARMENIA—Armenian
ARMENIAN RADIO
4040, 4810, 6065, **7175** kHz
RADIO YEREVAN
4040, 4810, 4990, 6065, 7390, **7400**, **7440**, 9450, 9480, **9750**, **11675**, 11920, 11980, 12050, 12060, 12065, **13645** , 15130, **15580**, **17605**, 17660, **17690** kHz

AUSTRIA—German
RADIO AUSTRIA INTERNATIONAL
5945, **6015**, 6155, 9870, 9875, 11780, 12010, 13730, 15410, 15450, 17730, 21490 kHz

BAHRAIN—Arabic
RADIO BAHRAIN
9746 kHz

BELGIUM
BELGISCHE RADIO & TV
French 5910, 9905, 9930, 11695, 13655, 13675, 15515, 17550, 17555, 21810 kHz
Dutch 5910, 9905, 9930, 11695, 13655, 13675, 13710, 15515, 17550, 17555, 21810, 21815 kHz

BRAZIL—Portuguese
RADIO CLUBE DO PARA
4885 kHz
RADIO CULTURA DO PARA
5045 kHz
RADIO DIFUSORA ACREANA
4885 kHz
R NACIONAL DA AMAZONIA
6180, 11780 kHz
RADIO ANHANGUERA
4915, 6080, 11830 kHz
RADIO BARE
4895 kHz
RADIO CULTURA
6170, 9615, 17815 kHz
RADIO NACIONAL
15265, 17750 kHz

CANADA—French
CANADIAN BROADCASTING CORP
9625 kHz
RADIO CANADA INTERNATIONAL
5960, **5995**, **6025**, **6050**, 6120, 6150, **7155**, **7230**, **7235**, **7295**, 9535, 9650, **9670**, **9740**, 9750, 9 755, 9760, **11705**, 11730, **11775**, **11790**, 11845, 11855, 11880, **11905**, **11925**, 11940, 11945, 13650, 13670, 13720, 15140, 15150, 15235, 15260, 15325, 15390, 15425, 17820, **17840**, 17875, 21675 kHz

CHINA (PR)—Standard Chinese
CENTRAL PEOPLES BROADCASTING SVC
6750, 6790, 6840, 6890, 7440, 7504, 7516, 7620, 7770, 7935, 9064, 9080, 9170, 9290, 9380, 9455, 9755, 9775, 9800, 10010, 10260, 11000, 11040, 11100, 11330, 11610, 11630, 11740, 11935, 12120, 15390, 15500, 15550, 15710, 15880, 17605, 17700 kHz
RADIO BEIJING
6165, 6810, 6825, 6974, 7190, 7335, 7350, 7590, 7660, 7700, 7800, 9440, 9480, **9690**, **9770**, 9820, 9945, 11445, 11650, 11685, 11695, **11695**, **11715**, **11790**, 11910, 11945, 12015, 12055, 15100, **15170**, 15180, 15215, 15260, 15430, 15435, 15455 kHz

CHINA (TAIWAN)—Chinese
BROADCASTING CORP OF CHINA
5950, 7295, 9280, 9610, 9765, 11725, **11740**, **11775**, 11845, **11855**, 11885, 15125, 15270, **15440** kHz
VOICE OF FREE CHINA
5950, 7130, 7445, **9680**, 9730, 9765, 9845, 9955, 11745, 11825, 11860, 11915, **15130**, **15215**, 15270, 15345, 15370, 17720, **17750**, **17805**, **17845**, **21720** kHz

CLANDESTINE (M EAST)—Persian
"IRAN'S FLAG OF FREEDOM RADIO"
9250, 9355, 11470, 15100, 15565, 15620, 15640 kHz
"RADIO AZADI"
9400, 15615, 15650 kHz

COLOMBIA—Spanish
CARACOL COLOMBIA
5075, 5095, 6075, 6150 kHz
CARACOL VILLAVICENCIO
5955 kHz
LA VOZ DEL LLANO
6116 kHz
LA VOZ DEL CINARUCO
4865 kHz
LA VOZ DEL RIO ARAUCA
4895 kHz
RADIO NACIONAL
11822, 17865 kHz

CROATIA—Croatian
CROATIAN RADIO
6210, 7240, 7315, 9465, 9495, 9530, 13830, 16105, 21480 kHz

CUBA—Spanish
RADIO HABANA CUBA
6060, 6180, **9515**, 9550, **9590**, 9620, 11760, 11875, **11920**, 13710/13700, 15105, 15230, 15260, 15340, **15350**, **17710**, 17750, 17770, **21670** kHz
RADIO REBELDE
3366, 5025 kHz

DENMARK—Danish
DANMARKS RADIO (Via Radio Norway)
5965, **7165**, **7210**, **7215**, **9550**, **9560**, **9565**, **9590**, **9615**, **9640**, **9645**, **9650**, **9655**, **11720**, **11735**, **11740**, **11775**, **11795**, **11805**, **11850**, **11860**, **11865**, **11870**, **11875**, **11930**, **15165**, **15175**, **15180**, **15195**, **15220**, **15230**, **15270**, **15330**,

15355, 17710, 17720, 17730, 17740, 17755,
17785, 17795, 17805, 17815, 17845, 17860,
17865, 21595, 21705, 21710, 25730 kHz

DOMINICAN REPUBLIC—Spanish
RADIO BARAHONA
  4930 kHz
RADIO N-103
  4800 kHz
RADIO SANTIAGO
  9878 kHz

ECUADOR—Spanish
HCJB-VOICE OF THE ANDES
  6050, 6080, 9765, 11910, 11960, 15140, 15270,
  17790, 17875, 21455 USB, 21480 kHz
RADIO CENTINELA DEL SUR
  4890/4899 kHz
RADIO NACIONAL
  15350 kHz
RADIO NACIONAL PROGRESO
  5060 kHz
RADIO NACIONAL ESPEJO
  4679.5/4635 kHz
RADIO QUITO
  4920 kHz

EGYPT—Arabic
RADIO CAIRO
  9620, 9670, 9700, 9755, 9770, 9800, 9850, 9900,
  11665, 11785, 11980, 12050, 15115, 15220,
  15285, 15435, 17670, 17745, 17770, 17 800 kHz

FINLAND—Finnish/Swedish
RADIO FINLAND
  6120, 9560, 9665, 9730, 11755, 11820, 15185,
  15245, 15355, 15400, 15440, 17800, 17880,
  21550 kHz

FRANCE—French
RADIO FRANCE INTERNATIONALE
  3965, **4890**, 5945, 5990, 5995, 6040, 6045, 6175,
  7120, 7135, 7160, 7175, 7195, 7280, 9550, 9605,
  9650, 9715, 9745, 9790, 9800, 9805, 9830,
  11660, 11670, **11680, 11685**, 11695, 11700,
  11705, 11790, 11800, 11845, 11850, **11890**,
  11965, 11995, 12005, **12025**, 12035, 15135,
  15155, 15180, 15190, 15195, **15215, 15275**,
  15285, 15300, 15315, 15360, 15365, 15405,
  15425, 15435, 15460, 15485, 15530, **17575**,
  17620, 17650, **17690**, 17695, **17705, 17710**,
  17720, 17775, 17785, 17795, 17800, 17845,
  17850, **17860, 21520**, 21530, 21535, 21580,
  21620, 21 645, 21685, **21765**, 25820 kHz

FRENCH POLYNESIA
RFO-TAHITI
  French 6135, 9750, 11827, 15171 kHz
  Tahitian 6135, 9750, 11827, 15171 kHz

GABON—French
AFRIQUE NUMERO UN
  9580, 15475, 17630 kHz
RTV GABONAISE
  4777, 7270 kHz

GERMANY—German
BAYERISCHER RUNDFUNK
  6085 kHz

DEUTSCHE WELLE
  3995, 6075, **6085**, 6100, 6115, 6145, 6180, 6185,
  7110, 7130, 7140, 7185, 7225, **7250, 7270**, 7275,
  7315, 7340, 9545, 9605, 9640, 9650, 9665, **9690**,
  9700, 9715, 9730, 9735, 9755, **9885, 11655**,
  11730, 11735, 11765, 11785, 11795, 11810,
  11865, **11915**, 11950, **11965**, 11970, 13610,
  13690, 13780, 13790, 15105, 15135, 15145,
  15245, 15250, 15270, 15275, 15320, 15350,
  15390, **15410**, 15510, **15560**, 17560, 17710,
  17715, 17755, **17810**, 17820, 17830, 17845,
  17860, 21540, 21560, **21570**, 21600, **21640**,
  21680, 25740 kHz
RADIO BREMEN
  6190 kHz
RIAS
  6005 kHz
SENDER FREIES BERLIN-SFB
  6190 kHz
SUDDEUTSCHER RUNDFUNK
  6030 kHz
SUDWESTFUNK
  7265 kHz

GREECE—Greek
FONI TIS HELLADAS
  7450, 9395, 9420, 9425, 9535, 11645, 12105,
  15550, 15630, 15650, 17515, 17525, 17535,
  17550, 17715 kHz
RADIOFONIKOS STATHMOS MAKEDONIAS
  7430, 9935, 11595 kHz

GUINEA—French
RTV GUINEENNE
  6155, 7125, 9650 kHz

HOLLAND—Dutch
RADIO NEDERLAND
  5955, 6020, **6165**, 7130, **7285, 9590, 9630**, 9715,
  9720, 9855, 9860, 9895, **11655**, 11710, 11715,
  11730, **11825, 11890, 11895**, 11935, 11950,
  11955, 13700, 13770, **15120, 15155, 15315**,
  15560, 17580, **17605**, 17895, 21480, 21530,
  21685, 25940 kHz

HUNGARY—Hungarian
RADIO BUDAPEST
  6025, 6110, 7220, 9835, 11910, 15160,
  15220 kHz
RADIO KOSSUTH
  6025 kHz

IRAN—Persian
VOICE OF THE ISLAMIC REPUBLIC
  4985, 5995, 11790, 15084 kHz

IRAQ—Arabic
RADIO IRAQ INTERNATIONAL
  11830, 13680, 15150, 15210, 15320, 15340,
  15455, 17740 kHz
REPUBLIC OF IRAQ RADIO
  3980, 4600/4750, 7350, 9725, 11740, 11755,
  15150, 15600, 17720, 17940 kHz

ISRAEL—Hebrew
KOL ISRAEL
  Easy Hebrew 11587, 11675, 17590 kHz
  Yiddish 9435, 11587, 11805, 11675, 15590,
  15640, 17575, 17590 kHz

RASHUTH HASHIDUR
   Hebrew 9388, 11588, 13753, 15615, 17543 kHz

ITALY—Italian
   RTV ITALIANA/RAI
      3995, 5990, 6060, 7175, 7235, 7275, 7290, 9515,
      9575, 9710, 11800, 11905, 15245, 15330, 15385,
      17780, 17795, 17800, 21515, 2153 5, 21560,
      21690 kHz

JAPAN—Japanese
   NIPPON HOSO KYOKAI
      3970, 6005, 6130, 6175, 6190, 9535, 9550 kHz
   RADIO JAPAN/NHK
      5960, 5970, 6025, 6030, 6120, 6160, 6185, 7140,
      7210, 9505, 9535, 9580, 9640, **9645, 9670, 9675,**
      9685, 9695, 9770, 11735, 11815, 11840, 11850,
      11865, 11870, 11875, 15195, **15210,** 15230,
      15250, 15280, 15320, **15325, 15345, 15350,**
      15430, 17765, 17810, **17820,** 17825, 17835,
      17845, 17860, 17890, **21575,** 21610, **21635,**
      21640, 21700 kHz
   RADIO TAMPA
      3925, 3945, 6055, 6115, 9595, 9760 kHz

JORDAN—Arabic
   RADIO JORDAN
      7155, 9560, 9830, 11810, 11940, 11955, 15435
      kHz

KOREA (DPR)—Korean
   KOREAN CENTRAL BROADCASTING SVC
      6100, 9665, 11680 kHz
   RADIO PYONGYANG
      6125, 6540, 6576, 7200, 7250, 9325, 9345, 9505,
      9640, 9835, 9977, 11700, 11705, 11735, 11905,
      13760, 15115, 15180, 15230, 17765 kHz

KOREA (REPUBLIC)—Korean
   KOREAN BROADCASTING SYSTEM
      3930, 6015, 6135, 9525 kHz
   RADIO KOREA
      5975, 6135, **6145,** 6480, 7275, 7550, 9570, 9640,
      9650, 9870, 11725, 11740, 11810, 13670, 15170,
      15575 kHz

KUWAIT—Arabic
   RADIO KUWAIT
      6055, 11990, 15345, 15495, 15505, 21675 kHz

LIBYA—Arabic
   RADIO JAMAHIRIYA
      6185, 9600, 15235, 15415, 15435, 17725 kHz

LITHUANIA—Lithuanian
   LITHUANIAN RADIO
      6010, 9675, 9710 kHz
   RADIO VILNIUS
      7400, 9675, 9710, **13645, 15485, 15580, 17605,**
      17690 kHz

MALI—French
   RTV MALIENNE
      4783, 4835, 5995, 7110, 7285, 9635, 11960 kHz

MAURITANIA—Arabic
   ORT DE MAURITANIE
      4845, 9610 kHz

MEXICO—Spanish
   RADIO EDUCACION
      6185 kHz
   OTHERS (Heard near or in Mexico)
      5982, 6010, 6017, 6045, 6105, 6115, 9546, 9555,
      9600, 9680 kHz

MOROCCO
   RADIO MEDI UN
      French/Arabic 9575 kHz
   RTV MAROCAINE
      French 11920, 17595, 17815 kHz
      Arabic 15105, 15330, 15335, 15345, 15360,
      17815 kHz

NORWAY—Norwegian
   RADIO NORWAY INTERNATIONAL
      5965, 7165, 7210, 7215, 9550, 9560, 9565, 9590,
      9615, 9640, 9645, 9650, 9655, 11720, 11735,
      11740, 11775, 11795, 11805, 11850, 11860,
      11865, 11870, 11875, 11930, 15165, 15175,
      15180, 15195, 15220, 15230, 15270, 15330,
      15355, 17710, 17720, 17730, 17740, 17755,
      17785, 17795, 17805, 1 7815, 17845, 17860,
      17865, 21595, 21705, 21710, 25730 kHz

OMAN—Arabic
   RADIO OMAN
      6085, 7270, 9735, 11745, 11840, 11890, 17735 kHz

PARAGUAY—Spanish
   RADIO ENCARNACION
      11940 kHz
   RADIO NACIONAL
      9735 kHz

PERU—Spanish
   RADIO CORA
      4915 kHz
   RADIO UNION
      6115 kHz

POLAND—Polish
   POLISH RADIO WARSAW
      6095, 6135, 7145, 7270, 7285, 9525, 9540 kHz

PORTUGAL—Portuguese
   RADIO PORTUGAL INTERNATIONAL
      6130, 9570, 9600, 9615, 9635, 9705, 9740,

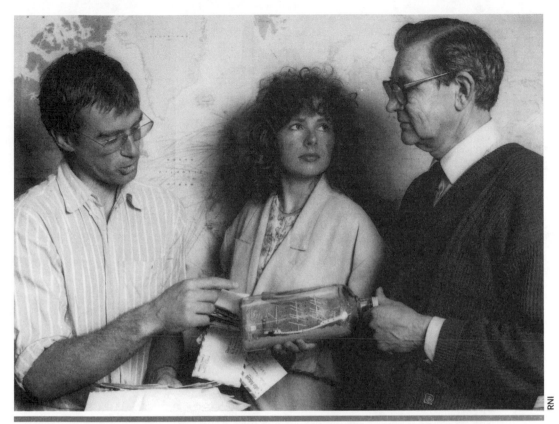

Radio Norway International's Arne Bakke, Janne Gro Rygg and Einar Lie, with bottle, appear to have found why boats can take so long to deliver mail. You can hear their Norwegian-language listener request show, *Postkassa*, each Saturday.

11740, 11750, 11800, 11840, 15140, 15225, 15250, 15285, 15425, 21515, 21655, 21700 kHz
RADIO RENASCENCA
9600 kHz

RUSSIA—Russian
RADIO ALA
3995, 5040, 6015, 6025, 6155, 7315, 7370, 7400, 11685, 11925, 11965, 12030, 15255 kHz
RADIO MOSCOW—DS-1
5910, 5940, 6000, 7160, 7165, 7240, 7355, 7400, 9450, 9490, 9605, 9775, 9780, 9835, 11780, 11825, 11840, 11870, 12000, 12060, 1 2070, 13760, 13820, 15460, 15490 kHz
RADIO MOSCOW—DS-2
5920, 7200, 7235, 7340, 7490, 9570, 9590, 9640, 9645, 9790, 9810, 11850, 11880 kHz
RADIO MOSCOW—Mayak
6190, 7240, 9180, 9470, 11900, 13695 kHz
RADIO PAMYAT
6145, 7230, 12040, 12060 kHz
RADIO POLIS
6045 kHz
RUSSIA'S RADIO (RADIO ROSSII)
6065, 7120, 7180, 7220, 7315, 7340, 7355, 7420, 9585, 9820, 11990 kHz
VOICE OF RUSSIA (GOLOS ROSSII)

SAUDI ARABIA—Arabic
BROADCASTING SVC OF THE KINGDOM
6000, 6020, 7150, 7210, 7220, 7250, 7275, 7280, 9570, 9580, 9705, 9720, 9870, 9885, 11685, 11780, 11935, 11950, 15140, 15170, 1 5240, 15435, 21495, 21505, 21665 kHz

SENEGAL—French
ORT DU SENEGAL
4890, 7170 kHz

SOUTH AFRICA
R SUID AFRICA/R ORION
3320/4810 kHz

SPAIN—Spanish
RADIO EXTERIOR DE ESPANA
4130, **5250**, 5970, 6020, 6055, 6125, 6130, 6140, 7105, 9530, 9580, 9620, 9650, 9685, 9745, 9765, 11730, 11790, 11880, 11 890, **11910**, 11920, 11945, 12035, 15110, 15395, 15445, 17715, 17755, 17845, 17890 kHz

SWEDEN—Swedish
RADIO SWEDEN
6065, 9620, 9655, 9670, 9695, 11705, 11730, 15230, 15240, 15245, 15270, 15390, 17870, 21500, 21625 kHz

SWITZERLAND
RED CROSS BROADCASTING SVC
French 7210 kHz
German 7210 kHz
SWISS RADIO INTERNATIONAL
French 3985, 6135, 6165, **7480**, 9535, 9560,
9650, 9810, 9885, **11690**, 12030, 12035, 13635,
13685, 15430, 15505, 15525, 15 570, 17565,
17635, 17670, 21770 kHz
German 3985, 6135, 6165, **7480**, 9535, 9560,
9650, 9810, 9885, **11690**, 12035, 13635, 13685,
15430, 15505, 15525, 15570, 17565, 17635,
17670, **17730**, 21770 kHz
Italian 3985, 6135, 6165, **7480**, 9535, 9560,
9885, 12035, 13635, 15430, 15505, 15525,
17635, 17670, **17730**, 21770 kHz

SYRIA—Arabic
SYRIAN BROADCASTING SERVICE
9950, 12085, 15095 kHz

TOGO
RTV TOGOLAISE
5047 kHz

TUNISIA—Arabic
RTV TUNISIENNE
7475, 11550, 12005, 15450, 17500, 21535 kHz

TURKEY—Turkish
VOICE OF TURKEY
5980, 6140, 9445, 9460, 9665, 9685, 11775,
11895, 11925, 11955, 15160, 15220, 15325,
15350, 15405 kHz

UKRAINE—Ukrainian
RADIO UKRAINE
4825, 5960, 6010, 6020, 6050, 6080, 6090, 7195,
7240, 7250, 7330, 7340, 7380, 7400, 9470, 9560,
9600, 9635, 9640, 9785, 9810, 9 860, 9865,
9870, **10344**, 11520, 11690, 11705, 11720,
11780, 11790, 11805, 11825, 11840, 11980,
12000, 12040, 12060, 12330, **13645**, 15135,
15195, 1535 5, 15375, 15455, 15495, 15525,
15570, **15580**, 15585, 15595, **17605**, **17690**,
17745 kHz
UKRAINIAN RADIO
4825, 5960, 5980, 6020, 6030, 6070, 6140, 6145,
6165, 6195, 7195, 7240, 7250, 7400, 9470, 9560,
9620, 9635, 9640, 9810, 9870, 11520, 11705,

11765, 11780, 11790, 11805, 11810, 11825,
11840, 11870, 11980, 12000, 12040, 12060,
12330, 13795, 15135, 15195, 15375, 15385,
15455, 15485, 1 5495, 15525, 15570, 15585,
15595, 17605, 17645, 17745, 17780, 17790,
17810, 21460, 21800 kHz

UNITED ARAB EMIRATES—Arabic
UAE RADIO
7215, 9605, 9695, 9780, 11795, 11815, 11945,
11965, 11985, 13605, 13675, 15265, 15305,
15315, 15320, 15400, 15435, 17830, 17855,
21510, 21515, 21605, 21700, 21735, 25690 kHz

UNITED KINGDOM
BBC WORLD SERVICE
Arabic **6030**, 6110, **7140**, 7320, 9825, 11680,
11730, **11740**, 13660, 15180, **15235**, 15245,
15575, **15590**, 17715, **17785** kHz
Persian **5975**, **9590** kHz

URUGUAY—Spanish
RADIO EL ESPECTADOR
11835.7 kHz

VENEZUELA—Spanish
ECOS DEL TORBES
4980, 9640 kHz
RADIO CONTINENTAL
4940 kHz
RADIO FRONTERA
4761 kHz
RADIO NACIONAL
9540 kHz
RADIO RUMBOS
4970, 9660 kHz
RADIO TACHIRA
4830 kHz
RADIO VALERA
4840 kHz

VIETNAM—Vietnamese
VOICE OF VIETNAM
5924, 6450, 9840, 10059, 12018, 15009 kHz

YUGOSLAVIA—Serbian
RADIO BEOGRAD
7200 kHz
RADIO YUGOSLAVIA
6100, 11870 kHz

Addresses Plus

Station Addresses...Plus Local Times for Each Country, Toll-Free Telephone Numbers, Free Gifts, Goodies for Sale, Who to Contact, Return Postage Requirements and Fax Numbers

How to order a Central American T-shirt? Who sells Pacific Island discs? Want to say something nice about a program just heard? What's the best hotel in La Paz, Bolivia?

Letters and faxes are often a station's only link with its listeners. This means that dozens—even hundreds—of broadcasters around the world are eager to hear from you . . . and be generous in return.

Free Collectibles

To advertise their presence and stimulate listener correspondence, some stations give out souvenirs and tourist literature, as well as the usual complimentary program schedules. These goodies include brochures on national or regional history, exotic calendars (usually around year's end), offbeat magazines and newspapers, attractive verification postcards, costume jewelry pins, colorful pennants, T-shirts from places most people have never heard of, stickers and decals, key chains—even, on rare occasion, recordings, weird coins, stamps . . . and, in one case, a doorknob hanger.

If you want a souvenir, speak up or be passed up. Specify politely what you'd like; in this section of *Passport*, we detail what was available last time we checked. Too, it helps to send along a little souvenir of your own: an autographed photo of your family, a bumper sticker from a local station or business, a local tourist brochure or postcard with a note of explanation—even a stick of chewing gum. Pocket calendars and Hallmark Date Books, free from local merchants around year's end, are also effective. Too, if you're not a stamp collector yourself, you can enclose interesting stamps taken from envelopes of other stations that have replied to you.

Of course, especially with photos, keep in mind the religious and cultural sensibilities of the recipient. And, whenever possible, provide constructive, sincere comments on their programs—these are especially welcomed by stations.

By the Buy

World band stations traditionally have taken the mandarin perspective on earning a profit, and simply given away token items. However, a growing number—such as the Christian Science Monitor, BBC World Service and Radio New Zealand International— sell a wide variety of goods by mail, both as a service to listeners and to help offset operating costs. These offerings are detailed in this section.

Many of these products can't be found anywhere else, and are delightful. But there are pitfalls. Americans should remember when buying clothing from other countries to order big, as sizes elsewhere tend to be smaller. Of course, it works in reverse if you're not an American and you're ordering from the United States or Canada. If in doubt, send a life-sized paper cutout of the desired article of clothing in your size. Payment in U.S. dollars is usually okay, provided it's in cash, but charge cards are less chancy. Be sure to take the usual precautions when sending currency or other funds through the mail.

Tourist Tips Not in Your Baedeker

If you're traveling abroad, here's a little-known secret: World band stations are sometimes willing to provide helpful information to prospective visitors. When writing, especially to smaller stations, appeal to their civic pride and treat them like kindly uncles you're seeking a favor from. After all, catering to tourist inquiries is hardly a requirement of operating most radio stations. (This section mentions which stations provide tourist literature as a matter of course.)

This approach has its limits, especially among that small coterie of central African stations that regards Westerners as sheep to be fleeced. But when it clicks, you can be treated to exceptional information on local cultures, sites, restaurants, places to stay, and events that are nowhere to be found within the pages of any guide book. This is especially true of domestic radio stations, whose primary audiences are in their own backyards—and who know just about all there is to know about those backyards.

Stations and Listeners Help Each Other

Long ago, when world band radio was something of an experiment, stations were anxious for feedback from listeners on how well their signals were coming in. By way of saying "thanks," stations would reply with a letter or postcard verifying that the station the listener reported hearing was, in fact, their station.

These verification cards and letters quickly became collectors' items and today are still sought out by some. Indeed, historic verification correspondence is preserved at the Smithsonian Institution in Washington, as well as the Committee to Preserve Radio Verifications (30 Eastern Ave., Lexington MA

02173 USA)—both of which welcome additions to their collections.

A number of stations still seek out this sort of information, but many are more interested in feedback on how well you liked their programs. Too, nearly all are interested in immediate feedback, such as by fax, when something technical has suddenly gone wrong—a transmitter drifting off frequency, for example, or poor modulation.

Journalists also appreciate tips on stories relevant to their countries. For example, should a Swedish-American community decide to hold a Swedish cultural festival, this might be of interest to Radio Sweden's New York bureau. Equally, if you're a student or journalist doing research on nationalism in the Balkans, you might profit from contact with the various countries' broadcasters in that region.

Some stations, to their considerable credit, are dedicated to helping the poor, hungry, ill and others on the margins of existence. These sorts of legitimate charitable activities we know of, and that need listener financial support, are cited within this section. We very much welcome further information and documentation.

How to Visit Stations

Many public and religious stations are delighted to have firsthand visits from listeners, who otherwise may be separated from them by land and sea. Complimentary tours of studios are often given on weekdays by professional guides or other station personnel. A few friendly stations also give separate guided tours of their transmission facilities.

Most commercial stations are not set up to give formal tours. Yet, many are delighted to meet informally with listeners. For example, individual radio enthusiasts from North America, Germany and Japan have been known to fly thousands of miles to embark on pilgrimages to stations in such out-of-the-way places as the Andes mountains or Amazon rain forest.

These visits can have unexpected consequences. According to Tiare Publications' Gerry Dexter, one enthusiast dropped by to visit a small Latin American station notorious for not responding to listeners' correspondence. While in the men's room, he found several years' worth of unanswered letters in a huge stack . . . being used in lieu of the customary paper roll.

For that reason, in this section the wheat is separated from the chaff. Only stations known or likely to respond to listener correspondence are included.

In general, it's a good idea to write in advance if you wish to tour a public or religious station. Courtesy dictates the same treatment for commercial stations, but with some smaller stations it works best simply to appear, like Lassie, unannounced at the door.

Gift giving? If you're visiting a large international broadcaster outside Africa or Japan, forget it. In Moslem countries avoid cross-gender gift giving, which may be misunderstood. But if you're the guest of a smaller or private station, or one in Africa or Japan, a simple, noncontroversial memento—restaurant T-shirt, sports team cap, or other souvenir from where you live or work—can go a long way towards sealing a relationship. Present your gift openly, without ostentation, for best results. Of course, never give money.

Remember, you're a guest, not a customer. You represent your nation's culture and people. Act accordingly, and you will be remembered accordingly.

Will Writing Get You Into Trouble?

No, not these days—at least not in most democratic countries, although in 1992 it was reported that Canadian authorities had been opening registered mail to Radio Damascus.

Use common sense. If you aspire to be Director of the CIA, don't write sealed letters to Cuba, Libya, Iraq, clandestine stations and such. If in doubt, use a postcard—cheaper, too.

Listeners who have written certain stations, notably in West Africa, sometimes find themselves receiving correspondence from "students" or allegedly devout Christians seeking goods, money or sponsorship to emigrate to Western countries. Some are so brazen they will actually specify the brand names and model numbers of the items they want!

Women, it seems, are favored targets. *Passport* reader Izzie Slaughter, for example, reports a Gambian correspondent proposing their arranging a marriage of convenience so he could become a United States citizen; requests for money from various Nigerian men; and an offer from a gentleman in Ghana for her to participate in a peculiar "gift exchange."

More recently, suspicious solicitations to aid "sick children" and the like have appeared from Lithuania (see) and other countries of the former USSR.

There are hassles in world band—not many, but they're there. Use your usual protective instincts and you'll be okay.

Addresses, Fax and Toll-Free Numbers

Here they are—addresses, fax and toll-free numbers for all stations known to be responding, even if only occasionally, to listener correspondence. If someone is responsible for listener correspondence, that name is given. Otherwise, simply address your correspondence to the station itself.

Fax *Savoir Faire*

Faxing (an abbreviation, not an acronym, and therefore "fax," not "FAX") has become the most democratic and successful electronic equivalent to the traditional mailbox. Still, it's not quite the same thing. For example, station personnel tend to go into a slow burn when someone ties up their fax machine with unsolicited reception reports, requests for freebies and the like. If you're hoping to seduce a station into a reply, stick to the postal system for such routine correspondence.

On the other hand, stations do appreciate material, such as listeners' questions, that can be used over the air. Also, immediate feedback on programs can be helpful to producers and announcers. Faxed technical feedback may be useful, but only if it is truly newsworthy, such as to report something amiss, during a crisis or for a special transmission.

Remember that under these circumstances the station may want to get back to you. Try to give them a callback number that's answered by a fax "beep"—not "hello"—and don't ask them to call first, because they won't.

Paying the Postman

Most major stations that reply do so for free. However, many smaller organizations expect, or at least hope for, reimbursement for postage costs. Most effective, especially for

Latin American and Indonesian stations, is to enclose return postage; that is, unused (mint) stamps from the *station's* country. These are available from Plum's Airmail Postage, 12 Glenn Road, Flemington NJ 08822 USA (send $1 or a self-addressed, stamped envelope for details); DX Stamp Service, 7661 Roder Parkway, Ontario NY 14519 USA (ditto); DX-QSL Associates, 434 Blair Road NW, Vienna VA 22180 USA; and some local private stamp dealers. Unused Brazilian international stamps (10 stamps, good for 10 replies, for $2 or 11 IRCs) are also available from Antonio Ribeiro da Motta, Caixa Postal 949, São José dos Campos— SP, Brazil.

One way to help ensure your return postage will be used for the intended purpose is to affix it onto a preaddressed return airmail envelope (self-addressed stamped envelope, or SASE). However, if the envelope is too small the contents may have to be folded to fit in.

You can also prompt reluctant stations by donating one U.S. dollar, preferably hidden from prying eyes by a piece of foil-covered carbon paper or the like—registration helps, too. Additionally, International Reply Coupons (IRCs), which recipients may exchange locally for air or surface stamps, are available at many post offices worldwide. Thing is, they're relatively costly, aren't all that effective, and aren't accepted by postal authorities in all countries.

Tips for Best Results

When writing, remember to make your letter interesting and helpful from the recipient's point of view, and friendly without being excessively personal or forward. Well-thought-out comments on specific programs are almost always appreciated. If you must use a foreign-language form letter as the basis for your communication, individualize it for each occasion either by writing or typing it out, or by making use of a word processor.

Writing in the broadcaster's tongue is always a plus—this section of *Passport* indicates when it is a requirement—but English is usually the next best bet. Remember, when writing Spanish-speaking countries, that what gringos think of as the "last name" is actually written as the middle name. Thus Antonio Vargas García, which also can be written as Antonio Vargas G., refers to Sr.

Vargas; so your salutation should read, *Estimado Sr. Vargas*.

What's that "García" doing there, then? That's *mamita's* father's family name. Latinos more or less solved the problem of gender fairness in names long before the Anglos.

But, wait—what about Portuguese, used by all those stations in Brazil? Same concept, but in reverse. Mama's father's family name is in the middle, and the "real" last name is where we're used to it, at the end.

In Chinese the "last" name comes first. However, when writing in English, Chinese names are sometimes reversed for the benefit of *low faan*—foreigners. Use your judgment. For example, "Li" is a common Chinese last name, so if you see "Li Dan," it's "Mr. Li." But if it's "Dan Li," he's already one step ahead of you, and it's still "Mr. Li". If in doubt, fall back on the ever-safe "Dear Sir" or "Dear Madam."

Less widely known is that the same can also occur in Hungarian. For example, "Bartók Béla" for Béla Bartók.

Be patient—replies usually take weeks, sometimes months. Slow responders, those that tend to take six months or more to reply, are cited in this section, as are erratic repliers.

World Time in Relation to Each Country

Local times are given in terms of hours' difference from World Time, formally known as Coordinated Universal Time (UTC), Greenwich Mean Time (GMT) and Zulu time (Z).

For example, Algeria is World Time +1; that is, one hour later than World Time. So, if World Time is 1200, the local time in Algeria is 1300 (1:00 PM). On the other hand, México City is World Time –6; that is, six hours earlier than World Time. If World Time is 1200, in México City it's 6:00 AM. And so it goes for each country in this section. Times in (parentheses) are for the middle of the year—roughly April-October.

These nominal times are almost always the actual times, as well. Yet, there are exceptions. Take China, for example, where the actual time nationwide is World Time +8 ("Beijing Time"), but in one region, Xinjiang, it's officially +6 ("Urümqi Time"). The responsible Chinese official explains:

Passport: "How long has the [+6 Urümqi] zone existed?"

Official: "It's always been there, but the trains, buses and airlines use Beijing Time. They would be impossible to manage otherwise. (Ponders for a moment.) And all the government offices. They have to work with the rest of the country. (Pauses again.) Also, the countryside people don't really pay much attention to anyone's time. Their day begins and ends with the sun."

Passport: "Who's left?"

Official: "The man who made the rule."

For more information on World Time, see the Glossary, and the World Time box within "Getting Started with World Band Radio."

Spotted Something New?

The staff and friends of International Broadcasting Services, scattered about the globe, strive year-round to gather and prepare material for *Passport*. In addition to having unearthed and sifted through tens of thousands of items of data, they have made countless judgment calls based on decades of experience in world band radio. Still, we don't uncover everything, we don't always call it right, and the passage of time invariably brings about a decline in the accuracy of what's on the page.

Has something changed since we went to press? A missing detail? Please let us know! Your update information, especially photocopies of material received from stations, is very much welcomed and appreciated at the IBS Editorial Office, Box 300, Penn's Park, PA 18943 USA, fax +1 (215) 598 3794.

Keeping Current

This section of *Passport* is usually more than adequate for the needs of world band listeners and DXers. For passionate radiophiles, however, it helps to supplement this with freshly breaking news on the small, faint stations they seek to hear. The best solution is the DX newsletter.

Continuing information on addresses and schedules of rarely heard broadcasters worldwide is available each week via the authoritative *Número Uno* (Box 54, Caledonia NY 14423 USA), a superb newsletter sent to no more than a couple of dozen professionals and experienced station chasers worldwide who have been invited into membership.

Another timely newsletter, *Fine Tuning*, is available each week to anyone in any country who wishes to subscribe. For a sample, send $1 and a self-addressed envelope to Mitch Sams, Managing Editor, Fine Tuning, 779 Galilea Court, Blue Springs MO 64014 USA.

Valuable information on the stations of Latin America is found in the monthly *Radio Nuevo Mundo* newsletter (5-6-6 Nukui-kita, Koganei-shi, Tokyo 184, Japan). As with *NU*, *Radio Nuevo Mundo* is available only to a small group of seasoned experts invited into membership, but a somewhat smaller newsletter, *Onda Corta*, is available to one and all from Casilla 2868, 1000-Buenos Aires, Argentina.

Specialized information on Russian stations is available from the monthly *DX Moscow* newsletter (6 IRCs or $3 from A. Klepov, ul. Tvardovskogo, d. 23, kv. 365, Moscow 123458, Russia); and the periodic *DXing ex-USSR* bulletin (5 IRCs or $3 from A. Osipov, Kazanskaya 4-87, St. Petersburg 195213, Russia). However, before sending currency or IRCs to Russia see "Warning" under "Russia" within this section.

Our thanks to John Herkimer, Editor and Publisher of *NU*, Don Jensen, Editor Emeritus of *NU*, Tetsuya Hirahara, Overseas Charge Secretary of *Radio Nuevo Mundo*, and the members of *NU* and *Radio Nuevo Mundo*—as well as pioneering Russian editors Anatoly Klepov and Alexey Osipov—for their kind cooperation in the preparation of this section of *Passport/93*.

Using Passport's Addresses PLUS Section

- All stations known to reply to correspondence from listeners are included.
- Additionally, stations that have not replied to listener correspondence in the recent past, but which we feel may yet reply, are included.
- Proper mailing addresses are given, which may differ from stations' physical locations; e.g., as given in the Blue Pages. This is because correspondence is not always accepted or properly handled at the physical location.
- Private organizations that lease air time, but which possess no world band transmitters of their own, may be reached via the station over which they have been heard.

- Unless otherwise indicated:
  - Stations reply regularly within six months to most listeners' letters in English.
  - Stations provide, upon request, free station schedules and souvenir verification postcards or letters.
  - Stations do not require compensation for postage costs incurred in replying to you. Where compensation is required, we provide details as to what to send.
- Local times are given in difference from World Time (UTC). Times in (parentheses) are for the middle of the year—around April-October.

AFGHANISTAN World Time +4:30
RADIO AFGHANISTAN, P.O. Box 544, Kabul, Afghanistan.
ALBANIA World Time +1
RADIO TIRANA, Radiotelevisione Shqiptar, International Service, Rrug Ismail Qemali, Tirana, Albania. Contact: Micho Zima, Director. Free tourist literature, stickers, Albanian stamps, pins and other souvenirs. Sells Albanian audio and video cassettes.
ALGERIA World Time +1
RADIO ALGIERS INTERNATIONAL—same details as "Radiodiffusion-Télévision Algerienne," below.
RADIODIFFUSION-TELEVISION ALGERIENNE (ENRS), 21 Boulevard des Martyrs, Algiers, Algeria. Contact: L. Zaghlami; (technical) Direction des Services Techniques. Replies irregularly. French or Arabic preferred, but English accepted.
ANGOLA World Time +1
A VOZ DA RESISTENCIA DO GALO NEGRO (Voice of the Resistence of the Black Cockerel), Free Angola Information Service, P.O. Box 65463, Washington DC 20035 USA (physical address is 1350 Connecticut Avenue NW, Suite 907, Washington DC 20036); or 1850 K Street NW, Suite 370, Washington DC 20006 USA. Contact: (Connecticut Avenue) Jaime de Azevedo Vila Santa, Director of Information; (K Street) Jardo Muekalia. Pro-UNITA, supported by South Africa and the United States.
RADIO NACIONAL DE ANGOLA, Cx. Postal 1329, Luanda, Angola. Fax: +244 (2) 391 234. Contact: Bernardino Costa, Public Opinion Office; Sra. Luiza Fancony, Diretora de Programas; Lourdes de Almeida, Chefe de Secção; or Cesar A.B. da Silva, Diretor Geral. Replies occasionally to correspondence, preferably in Portuguese. $1, return postage or 2 IRCs most helpful.
EMISSORA PROVINCIAL DE BENGUELA, Cx. Postal 19, Benguela, Angola. Contact: Simão Martíns Cuto, Responsavel Administrativo; or Celestino da Silva Mota, Diretor. $1 or return postage required. Replies irregularly.
EMISSORA PROVINCIAL DE BIE (when operating), C.P. 33, Kuito, Bié, Angola. Contact: José Cordeiro Chimo, O Diretor. Replies occasionally to correspondence in Portuguese.
EMISSORA PROVINCIAL DE MOXICO, Cx. Postal 74, Luena, Angola. Contact: Paulo Cahilo, Diretor. $1 or return postage required. Replies to correspondence in Portuguese.
Other *EMISSORA PROVINCIAL* stations—same address, etc., as Radio Nacional, above.
ANTARCTICA World Time +13 McMurdo; -2 (-3 midyear) Base Esperanza
AMERICAN FORCES ANTARCTIC NETWORK (AFAN) MCMURDO, U.S. Navy Communication Station COMNAVSUPPOR-ANTARCTICA, McMurdo Station, FPO San Francisco CA 96601 USA.
RADIO NACIONAL ARCANGEL SAN GABRIEL—LRA 36, Base Antártica Esperanza (Tierra de San Martín), 9411 Territorio Antártico Argentino, Argentina. Contact: (nontechnical) Elizabeth Beltrán de Gallegos, Programación y Locución; (technical) Cristian Omar Guida, Técnica Operación. Return postage required. Replies irregularly to correspondence in Spanish. If no reply, try sending your correspondence (don't write station name on envelope) and 2 IRCs to the helpful Gabriel Iván Barrera, Casilla 2868, 1000-Buenos Aires, Argentina; fax +54 (1) 322-3351. Station is usually off the air for summer vacation from roughly January through February.

ANTIGUA World Time -4
BBC WORLD SERVICE—CARIBBEAN RELAY STATION, P.O. Box 1203, St. John's, Antigua. Contact: (technical) G. Hoef, Manager. Nontechnical correspondence should be sent to the BBC World Service in London (see).
DEUTSCHE WELLE—ANTIGUA—same address and contact as BBC World Service, above. Nontechnical correspondence should be sent to the Deutsche Welle in Germany (see).
ARGENTINA World Time -2 (-3 midyear); with exceptions that include the following: -3 Neuquén; -3 (-4 midyear) Córdoba, Entre Ríos, Jujuy, La Pampa, La Rioja, Mendoza, San Juan, San Luis, Santa Fe, Santiago del Estero and Tucumán
RADIODIFUSION ARGENTINA AL EXTERIOR—RAE, C.C. 555 Correo Central, 1000-Buenos Aires, Argentina. Fax: +54 (1) 325 9433. Contact: (nontechnical) J. Anthony Middleton, Head of the English Team, or Marcela G.R. Campos, Directora; (technical) Gabriel Iván Barrera, DX Editor; or Patricia Menéndez. Free paper pennant. Return postage or $1 appreciated.
RADIO CONTINENTAL, Rivadavia 835, 1002-Buenos Aires, Argentina. Contact: Julio A. Valles. Stickers and tourist literature; $1 or return postage required. Replies to correspondence in Spanish.
RADIO MALARGÜE, Esquivel Aldao 350, 5613-Malargüé, Argentina. Prefers correspondence in Spanish.
RADIO NACIONAL, BUENOS AIRES—LRA1/LRA31, Maipú 555, 1000-Buenos Aires, Argentina.
RADIO NACIONAL, MENDOZA—LRA6/LRA34 (when operating, once transmitter parts are obtained), Emilio Civit, 460, 5500-Mendoza, Argentina. Contact: Lic. Jorge Parvanoff.
ARMENIA World Time +4 (+5 midyear)
ARMENIAN RADIO—see "Radio Yerevan" for details.
RADIO YEREVAN, 5 Mravian Street, 375025 Yerevan, Armenia. Contact: V. Voskanian, Deputy Editor-in-Chief; R. Abalian, Editor-in-Chief; or Olga Iroshina. Replies slowly, but not quite so tardily as suggested by letters recently received from the station bearing "1962" postmarks in lieu of "1992."
ASCENSION ISLAND World Time exactly
BBC WORLD SERVICE—ATLANTIC RELAY STATION, English Bay, Ascension Island. Fax: +247 6117. Contact: (technical) Andrew Marsden, Transmitter Engineer. Nontechnical correspondence should be sent to the BBC World Service in London (see).
VOICE OF AMERICA—ASCENSION RELAY STATION—same details as "BBC World Service," above. Nontechnical correspondence should be directed to the regular VOA address (see "USA").
AUSTRALIA World Time +11 (+10 midyear) Victoria (VIC), Queensland (QLD), New South Wales and Tasmania; +10:30 (+9:30 midyear) South Australia; +9:30 Northern Territory (NT); +8 Western Australia (WA)
AUSTRALIAN BROADCASTING CORPORATION—ABC BRISBANE, GPO Box 9994, GPO Brisbane QLD 4001, Australia. Fax: +61 (7) 377 5442. Contact: John Kalinowski, Manager Network Services; (technical) Thomas A. Rowan, VK4BR, Transmission Manager. Free stickers, "Travellers Guide to ABC Radio." 3 IRCs or return postage helpful.
AUSTRALIAN BROADCASTING CORPORATION—ABC DARWIN, ABC Box 9994, GPO Darwin NT 0801, Australia. Fax: +61 (89) 433 125. Contact: Sue Camilleri, Officer Producer. Free stickers. Free "Travellers Guide to ABC Radio." 3 IRCs or return postage helpful.
AUSTRALIAN BROADCASTING CORPORATION—ABC PERTH, ABC Box 9994, GPO Perth WA 6001, Australia. Fax: +61 (9) 220 2919. Contact: (technical) Gary Matthews, Head of Broadcast and Technical Department (Radio). Free stickers and "Travellers Guide to ABC Radio." 3 IRCs or return postage helpful.
CAAMA RADIO—ABC, Central Australian Aboriginal Media Association, Bush Radio Service, P.O. Box 2924, Alice Springs NT 0871, Australia. Fax: +61 (89) 555-219. Contact: Barbara Richards; or Rae Allen, Regional Programme Manager. Free stickers. 2 IRCs or return postage helpful.
RADIO AUSTRALIA—ABC
Main Office: P.O. Box 755, Glen Waverley VIC 3150, Australia. Fax: (nontechnical) +61 (3) 881 2346; (technical) +61 (3) 881 2377. Contact: (nontechnical) Sue Duckworth, Acting Correspondence Officer; (technical) Nigel Holmes, Acting Frequency Manager, Frequency Management Unit. Free calendars and tourist literature. Books, tape recordings and T-shirts are available for sale. Contact: Business Development Manager.

Radio Austria International provides uncommon insight into Central Europe and violence-ridden Eastern Europe. English staffers include Patricia Maadi (near phone), Murray Hall, David Ward, Eugene Hartzell, Ann Dubsky, David Hermges and Elizabeth Blane.

New York Bureau, Nontechnical: 1 Rockefeller Plaza, Suite 1700, New York NY 10020 USA. Fax: +1 (212) 247 2095. Contact: Maggie Jones, Manager.

London Bureau, Nontechnical: 54 Portland Place, London W1N 4DY, United Kingdom. Fax: +44 (71) 323 0059. Contact: Alan Stephenson, Manager.

Bangkok Bureau, Nontechnical: 209 Soi Hutayana Off Soi Suanplu, South Sathorn Road, Bangkok 10120, Thailand. Fax: +66 (2) 287 2040. Contact: Nicholas Stuart.

RADIO RUM JUNGLE—ABC, Top Aboriginal Bush Association, P.O. Batchelor NT 0845, Australia. Fax: +61 (89) 760 270. Contact: Mae-Mae Morrison, Announcer; Andrew Joshua, Chairman; or George Butler. 3 IRCs or return postage helpful.

AUSTRIA World Time +1 (+2 midyear)

RADIO AUSTRIA INTERNATIONAL, A-1136 Vienna, Austria. Fax: +43 (1) 87 878 3630. Contact: (nontechnical) Prof. Paul Lendvai, Director; (technical) David Hermges, Producer, Austrian Shortwave Panorama. Free stickers, pennants and calendars.

AZERBAIJAN World Time +4 (+5 midyear)

AZERBAIJANI RADIO—see "Radio Baku" for details.

RADIO BAKU, ul. M. Guzeina 1, 370011 Baku, Azerbaijan. $1 or return postage helpful. Replies occasionally.

BAHRAIN World Time +3

RADIO BAHRAIN, Broadcasting & Television, Ministry of Information, P.O. Box 702, Al Manāmah, Bahrain. Contact: A. Suliman (for Director of Broadcasting). $1 or IRC required. Replies irregularly.

BANGLADESH World Time +6

RADIO BANGLADESH

Nontechnical correspondence: External Services, P.O. Box No. 2204, Dhaka, Bangladesh. Contact: Masudul Hasan, Deputy Director.

Technical correspondence: National Broadcasting Authority, NBA House, 121 Kazi Nazrul Islam Avenue, Dhaka 1000, Bangladesh. Contact: Mohammed Noor Al-Islam, Station Engineer (Research Wing); or Kazi Rafique.

BELGIUM World Time +1 (+2 midyear)

BELGISCHE RADIO EN TELEVISIE, P.O. Box 26, B-1000 Brussels, Belgium. Fax: +32 (2) 734 7804. Free pennants, stickers and Listeners' Club magazine. Replies sometimes take a while.

BELIZE World Time –6

BELIZE RADIO ONE, Broadcasting Corporation of Belize, Albert Catouse Building, P.O. Box 89, Belize City, Belize. Fax: +501 (2) 75040. Contact: (technical) E.R. Rosado, Chief Engineer.

BENIN World Time +1

OFFICE DE RADIODIFFUSION ET TELEVISION DU BENIN, La Voix de la Révolution, B.P. 366, Cotonou, Bénin; this address is for Cotonou and Parakou stations, alike. Contact: (Cotonou) Damien Zinsou Ala Hassa, or Leonce Goohouede; (Radio Parakou, nontechnical) J. de Matha, Le Chef de la Station, or (Radio Parakou, technical) Léon Donou, Le Chef des Services Techniques. Return postage, $1, return postage or IRC required. Replies irregularly and slowly to correspondence in French.

BHUTAN World Time +6

BHUTAN BROADCASTING SERVICE

Station: P.O. Box 101, Thimphu, Bhutan. Fax: +228 (975) 22533. 2 IRCs, return postage or $1 required. Replies extremely irregularly, correspondence to the U.N. Mission (see following) may be more fruitful.

United Nations Mission: Permanent Mission of the Kingdom of Bhutan to the United Nations, Two United Nations Plaza, 27th Floor, New York NY 10017 USA. Fax: +1 (212) 826-2998. Contact: Kunzang C. Namgyel, Third Secretary; Sonam Yangchen, Attaché; Leki Wangmo, Second Secretary; or Hari K. Chhetri, Second Secretary.

BOLIVIA World Time –4

LA VOZ DEL TROPICO, "Radiodifusora CVU," Casilla 2494, Cochabamba, Bolivia. Contact: Eduardo Avila Alberdi, Director; or Carlos Pocho Hochmann, Locutor. Return postage or $1 required. Replies occasionally to correspondence in Spanish.

RADIO ABAROA, Casilla 136, Riberalta, Bení, Bolivia. Contact: René Arias Pacheco, Director. Return postage or $1 required. Replies irregularly to correspondence in Spanish.

RADIO ANIMAS, Chocaya, Animas, Potosí, Bolivia. Return postage or $1 required. Replies irregularly to correspondence in Spanish.

RADIO CENTENARIO, LA NUEVA, Casilla 818, Santa Cruz de la Sierra, Bolivia. Contact: Pedro Salces Ruíz, Director. Return postage or $1 required. Replies to correspondence in Spanish.

RADIO COSMOS, Casilla 5303, Cochabamba, Bolivia. Contact: Laureano Rojas, Jr., Administrativo. $1 or return postage required. Replies irregularly to correspondence in Spanish.

RADIODIFUSORA MINERIA, Casilla 247, Oruro, Bolivia. Contact: Dr. José Carlos Gómez Espinoza, Gerente y Director General. Return postage or $1 required. Replies irregularly to correspondence in Spanish.

RADIO DOS DE FEBRERO (when operating), Vacadiez 400, Rurrenabaque, Bení, Bolivia. Contact: John Arce. Replies occasionally to correspondence in Spanish.

RADIO ECO, Av. Brasil, Correo Central, Reyes, Bení, Bolivia. Contact: Carlos Espinoza Gonzales Cortez, Director-Gerente; or Rolmán Medina Méndez. Free station literature. $1 or return postage required, and financial contributions solicited for the owner's physiotherapy incurred as a result of a pool accident. Replies irregularly to correspondence in Spanish.

RADIO EL MUNDO, Casilla 1984, Santa Cruz de la Sierra, Bolivia. Contact: Freddy Banegas Carrasco, Gerente. Free stickers. $1 or return postage required. Replies irregularly to correspondence in Spanish.

RADIO FIDES, Casilla 9143, La Paz, Bolivia. Contact: Roxana Beltrán C. Replies occasionally to correspondence in Spanish.

RADIO FRONTERA, Casilla 179, Cobija, Pando, Bolivia. Replies to correspondence in Spanish.

RADIO GALAXIA, Guayaramerín, Bení, Bolivia. Contact: Dorián Arias, Gerente; or Jeber Hitachi Banegas, Director. Return postage or $1 required. Replies to correspondence in Spanish.

RADIO HITACHI, Casilla 400, Correo Central, Guayaramerín, Bení, Bolivia; if no response, try Calle Sucre 20, Guayaramerín, Bení, Bolivia. Return postage of $1 required. Has replied in the past to correspondence in Spanish, but as of late correspondence has sometimes been returned as "addressee unknown."

RADIO ILLIMANI, Calle Ayacucho 467, 2° piso, La Paz, Bolivia. Contact: Sra. Gladys de Zamora, Administradora. $1 required, and your letter should be registered and include a tourist brochure or postcard from where you live. Replies irregularly to friendly correspondence in Spanish.

RADIO JUAN XXIII, San Ignacio de Velasco, Santa Cruz, Bolivia. Contact: Fdo. Manuel Picazo Torres, Director. Return postage or $1 required. Replies occasionally to correspondence in Spanish.

RADIO LA CRUZ DEL SUR, Casilla 1408, La Paz, Bolivia. Contact: Pastor Rodolfo Moya Jiménez, Director. Pennant for $1 or return postage. Replies slowly to correspondence in Spanish.

RADIO LA PERLA DEL ACRE, Cobija del Acre, Pando, Bolivia. Return postage or $1 required. Replies irregularly to correspondence in Spanish.

RADIO LIBERTAD, Avenida Sánchez Lima 2266, La Paz, Bolivia. Carmiña Ortiz H., Jefe de Publicidad y Relaciones Públicas. Fax: +591 (2) 391 995. Free pennants and stickers. Return postage or $1 required. Replies fairly regularly to correspondence in Spanish.

RADIO MAMORE, 25 de Mayo, Guayaramerín, Bení, Bolivia. Contact: Carlos Pinedo Suárez, Director General; or Carlos Lucio Montán E., Director-Proprietario. Return postage or $1 required. Replies irregularly to correspondence in Spanish.

RADIO MOVIMA, Calle Baptista No. 24, Santa Ana de Yacuma, Bení, Bolivia. Contact: Rubén Serrano López, Director. Return postage or $1 required. Replies irregularly to correspondence in Spanish.

RADIO NACIONAL DE HUANUNI, Casilla 681, Oruro, Bolivia. Contact: Rafael Linneo Morales, Director-General; or Alfredo Murillo, Director. Return postage or $1 required. Replies irregularly to correspondence in Spanish.

RADIO PADILLA, Padilla, Chuquisaca, Bolivia. Contact: Moisés Palma Salazar, Director. Return postage or $1 required. Replies to correspondence in Spanish.

RADIO PAITITI, Casilla 321, Guayaramerín, Bení, Bolivia. Contact: Armando Mollinedo Bacarreza, Director. Return postage or $1 required. Replies irregularly to correspondence in Spanish.

RADIO PANAMERICANA, C.P. 503, La Paz, Bolivia. Daniel Sánchez Rocha, Director. Replies irregularly, with correspondence in Spanish preferred. $1 or 2 IRCs helpful.

RADIO PERLA DEL ORIENTE, Roboré, Chiquitos, Santa Cruz de la Sierra, Bolivia. Heard requesting reception reports in Spanish.

RADIO PIO DOCE, Casilla 434, Llallagua, Potosí, Bolivia. Contact: Pbro. Roberto Durette, OMI, Director General. Return postage helpful. Replies occasionally to correspondence in Spanish.

RADIO SAN GABRIEL, Casilla 4792, La Paz, Bolivia. Contact: Hno. José Canut Saurat, franciscano, Director Gerente. $1 or return postage helpful. Free book on station, calendars and *La Voz del Pueblo Aymara* magazine. Replies fairly regularly to correspondence in Spanish.

RADIO SAN MIGUEL, Casilla 102, Riberalta, Bení, Bolivia. Contact: Héctor Salas Takaná, Director. Return postage or $1 required. Replies irregularly to correspondence in Spanish.

RADIO SANTA ANA, Cobija 285 esquina Bolívar, Santa Ana, Bení, Bolivia. Contact: Mario Roberto Suárez, Director. Return postage or $1 required. Replies irregularly to correspondence in Spanish.

RADIO SANTA CRUZ, Emisora del Instituto Radiofónico Fe y Alegría (IRFA), Casilla 672, Santa Cruz de la Sierra, Bolivia. Contact: Alvaro Puente C., S.J., Sub-Director; or Victor Blajot, S.J., Director General de INFACRUZ. Free pennants. Return postage required. Correspondence in Spanish preferred.

RADIO SANTA ROSA, Correo Central, Santa Rosa de Yacuma, Bení, Bolivia. Replies irregularly to correspondence in Spanish. $1 or 2 IRCs helpful.

RADIO TRINIDAD, Trinidad, Bení, Bolivia.

RADIO 20 DE SETIEMBRE (if operating), Bermejo, Tarija, Bolivia. Return postage or $1 required. Replies irregularly to correspondence in Spanish.

BOTSWANA World Time +2

RADIO BOTSWANA, Private Bag 0060, Gaborone, Botswana. Fax: +267 (31) 357 138. Contact: (nontechnical) Monica Mphusu, Producer, "Dedication Corner/Help Line"; (technical) Ted Makgekenene, Chief Engineer; or Kingsley Reebang. Return postage, $1 or 2 IRCs required. Replies slowly and irregularly.

VOICE OF AMERICA/VOA—BOTSWANA RELAY STATION
Transmitter Site: Voice of America, Botswana Relay Station, Moepeng Hill, Selebi-Phikwe, Botswana. Contact: William Connally, Station Manager. This address for technical correspondence only. Nontechnical correspondence should be directed to the regular VOA address (see "USA").

Frequency and Monitoring Office:, Voice of America, 330 Independence Avenue, S.W., Washington DC 20540 USA. Fax: +1 (202) 619 1781. Contact: Daniel Ferguson, Botswana QSL Desk, VOA/EOFF:Frequency Management & Monitoring Division. The Botswana Desk is for technical correspondence only. Nontechnical correspondence should be directed to the regular VOA address (see "USA").

BRAZIL World Time –1 (–2 midyear) Atlantic Islands; –2 (–3 midyear) Eastern, including Brasília and Rio de Janeiro; –3 (–4 midyear) Western; –4 (–5 midyear) Acre
Note: For Brazilian return postage, see introduction to this article.

RADIO ALVORADA—LONDRINA, Rua Sen. Souza Naves 9, 9 Andar, 86015 Londrina, Paraná, Brazil. Contact: Padre José Guidoreni, Diretor. Pennants for $1 or return postage. Replies to correspondence in Portuguese.

RADIO ALVORADA—PARINTINS, Travessa Leopoldo Neves 503, 69150 Parintins, Amazonas, Brazil. Contact: Raimunda Ribeira da Motta, Diretora. Return postage required. Replies occasionally to correspondence in Portuguese.

RADIO ANHANGUERA—GOIANIA, C.P. 13, 74001 Goiânia, Goiás, Brazil. Contact: Rossana F. da Silva. Return postage required. Replies to correspondence in Portuguese.

RADIO APARECIDA, C.P. 14664, 03698 São Paulo SP, Brazil. Contact: Padre Cabral; Cassiano Macedo; or Antonio C. Moreira, Diretor-Geral. Return postage or $1 required. Replies occasionally to correspondence in Portuguese.

RADIO BANDEIRANTES, C.P. 372, Rua Radiantes 13, Morumbí, 05699 São Paulo SP, Brazil. Contact: Salomão Esper, Superintendente. Free stickers and canceled Brazilian stamps. $1 or return postage required. Replies to correspondence in Portuguese.

RADIO BRASIL TROPICAL, Rua Joaquim Murtinho 1456, Palácio da Rádio, 78015 Cuiabá, Mato Grosso, Brazil. Contact: K. Santos. Free stickers. $1 required. Replies to correspondence in Portuguese.

RADIO CABOCLA (when operating), Rua 4 Casa 9, Conjunto dos Secretarios, 69000 Manaus, Amazonas, Brazil. Contact: Francisco Puga, Diretor-Geral. Return postage required. Replies occasionally to correspondence in Portuguese.

RADIO CAIARI, C.P. 104, 78901 Pôrto Velho, Rondônia, Brazil. Contact: Carlos Alberto Diniz Martins, Diretor-Geral. Free stickers. Return postage helpful. Replies irregularly to correspondence in Portuguese.

RADIO CANCAO NOVA, Estrada Particular alto de Bela Vista s/n, 12630 Cachoeira Paulista, São Paulo SP, Brazil. Contact: José Cardoso de O. Neto, Diretor, Depto. Radiodifusão; or Jorge Hartmann, Director. Free stickers, pennants and station brochure. $1 helpful. Replies at times to correspondence in Portuguese.

RADIO CAPIXABA, C.P. 509, 29001 Vitória, Espírito Santo, Brazil. Contact: Jairo Gouvea Maia, Diretor. Replies occasionally to correspondence in Portuguese.

RADIO CBN, Rua das Palmeiras 315, 01226 São Paulo SP, Brazil. Contact: Celso A. de Freitas. Return postage or $1 helpful. Replies irregularly to correspondence in Portuguese.

RADIO CLUBE DO PARA, C.P. 533, 66001 Belém, Pará, Brazil. Contact: Edyr Paiva Proença, Diretor-Geral. Return postage required. Replies irregularly to correspondence in Portuguese.

RADIO CULTURA DO PARA, Avenida Almirante Barroso 735, 66065 Belém, Pará, Brazil. Contact: Ronald Pastor; or Augusto

Proença, Diretor. Return postage required. Replies irregularly to correspondence in Portuguese.

RADIO CULTURA SAO PAULO, Rua Cenno Sbrighi 378, 05099 São Paulo SP, Brazil. Contact: Thais de Almeida Dias, Chefe de Produção e Programação; Sra. María Luíza Amaral Kfouri, Chefe de Produção; or José Munhoz, Coordenador. $1 or return postage required. Replies slowly to correspondence in Portuguese.

RADIO DIFUSORA AQUIDAUANA, C.P. 18, 79200 Aquidauana, Mato Grosso do Sul, Brazil. Contact: Primaz Aldo Bertoni, Diretor. Free tourist literature and used Brazilian stamps. $1 or return postage required. This station sometimes identifies during the program day as "Nova Difusora," but its sign-off announcement gives the official name as "Radio Difusora, Aquidauana."

RADIO DIFUSORA CACERES, C.P. 297, 78700 Cáceres, Mato Grosso, Brazil. Contact: Sra. Maridalva Amaral Vignardi. $1 or return postage required. Replies occasionally to correspondence in Portuguese.

RADIO DIFUSORA DE LONDRINA, C.P. 1870, 86010 Londrina, Paraná, Brazil. Contact: Walter Roberto Manganoli, Gerente. $1 or return postage helpful. Replies irregularly to correspondence in Portuguese.

RADIO DIFUSORA DO AMAZONAS, C.P. 311, 69001 Manaus, Amazonas, Brazil. Contact: J. Joaquim Marinho, Diretor.

RADIO DIFUSORA DO MARANHAO, C.P. 152, 65001 São Luíz, Maranhão, Brazil. Contact: Alonso Augusto Duque, BA, Presidente. Return postage required. Replies occasionally to correspondence in Portuguese.

RADIO DIFUSORA JATAI, C.P. 33 (or Rua José Carvalhos Bastos 542), 76801 Jataí, Goiás, Brazil. Contact: Zacarias Faleiros, Diretor.

RADIO DIFUSORA MACAPA, C.P. 2929, 68901 Macapá, Amapá, Brazil. Contact: Francisco de Paulo Silva Santos. $1 or return postage required. Replies irregularly to correspondence in Portuguese.

RADIO DIFUSORA RORAIMA, Rua Capitão Ene Garcez 830, 69300 Boa Vista, Roraima, Brazil. Contact: Geraldo França, Diretor-Geral; or Francisco Alves Vieira. Return postage required. Replies occasionally to correspondence in Portuguese.

RADIO EDUCACAO RURAL—CAMPO GRANDE, C.P. 261, 79100 Campo Grande, Mato Grosso do Sul, Brazil. Contact: Ailton Guerra, Gerente; or Diácono Tomás Schwamborn. $1 or return postage required. Replies to correspondence in Portuguese.

RADIO EDUCACAO RURAL—COARI, Praça São Sebastião 228, 69460 Coari, Amazonas, Brazil. Contact: Joaquim Florencio Coelho, Diretor Administrador da Comunidad Salgueiro. $1 or return postage helpful. Replies irregularly to correspondence in Portuguese.

RADIO EDUCADORA DE BRAGANCA, Rua Barão do Rio Branco 1151, 68600 Bragança, Brazil. Contact: José Rosendo de S. Neto. $1 or return postage required. Replies to correspondence in Portuguese.

RADIO EDUCADORA CARIRI, C.P. 57, 63101 Crato, Ceará, Brazil. Contact: Padre Gonçalo Farias Filho, Diretor Gerente. Return postage or $1 helpful. Replies irregularly to correspondence in Portuguese.

RADIO EDUCADORA DA BAHIA, Centro de Rádio, Rua Pedro Gama 413/E, Alto Sobradinho Federação, 40000 Salvador, Bahia, Brazil. Contact: Antonio Luis Almada, Coordenador do Radio; Elza Correa Ramos; or Walter Sequieros R. Tanure. $1 or return postage required. Replies irregularly to correspondence in Portuguese.

RADIO 8 DE SETEMBRO, C.P. 8, 13691, Descalvado, Sáo Paulo, Brazil. Contact: Adonias Gomes. Replies to corrrespondence in Portuguese.

RADIO EMISSORA ARUANA, C.P. 214, 78601 Barra do Garças, Mato Grosso, Brazil. Contact: Neusa da Costa Ataide. $1 required. Replies slowly and rarely to correspondence in Portuguese.

RADIO GAZETA (when operating), Avenida Paulista 900, 01310 São Paulo SP, Brazil. Contact: Ing. Aníbal Horta Figueiredo.

RADIO GUARUJA, C.P. 45, 88001 Florianópolis, Santa Catarina, Brazil. Contact: Acy Cabral Tieve, Diretor; or Rosa Michels de Souza. Return postage required. Replies irregularly to correspondence in Portuguese.

RADIO GAUCHA, Avenida Ipiranga 1075, Azenha, 90060 Pôrto Alegre, Rio Grande do Sul, Brazil. Replies occasionally to correspondence in Portuguese.

RADIO GLOBO, Rua das Palmeiras 315, 01226 São Paulo SP, Brazil. Contact: Ademar Dutra, Locutor, "Programa Ademar Dutra." Replies to correspondence in Portuguese.

RADIO INCONFIDENCIA, C.P. 1027, 30001 Belo Horizonte, Minas Gerais, Brazil. Contact: Isaias Lansky, Diretor; or Manuel E. de Lima Torres. $1 or return postage helpful.

RADIO INTEGRACAO, Rua Alagoas 270, lotes 8 e 9, 69980 Cruzeiro do Sul, Acre, Brazil. Contact: Claudio Onofre Ferreiro. Return postage required. Replies to correspondence in Portuguese.

RADIO IPB AM, Rua Itajaí 433, Barrio Antonio Vendas, 79050 Campo Grande, Mato Grosso do Sul, Brazil. Contact: Kelly Cristina Rodrigues da Silva, Secretária. Return postage required. Replies to correspondence in Portuguese.

RADIO MARAJOARA, Travessa Campos Sales 370, Centro, 66015 Belém, Pará, Brazil. Contact: Elizete Ma dos Santos Pamplona, Diretora Geral. Return postage required. Replies irregularly to correspondence in Portuguese.

RADIO NACIONAL DA AMAZONIA, Radiobras, C.P. 08840, 70323 Brasília DF, Brazil. Contact: Luís Antonio Alves, Diretor. Free stickers.

RADIO NOVAS DE PAZ, C.P. 22, 80001 Curitiba, Paraná, Brazil. Contact: João Falavinha Ienze, Gerente. $1 or return postage required. Replies irregularly to correspondence in Portuguese.

RADIO PIONEIRA DE TERESINA, 24 de Janeiro 150, 64000 Teresina, Piauí, Brazil. Contact: Luíz Eduardo Bastos; or Tony Batista, Diretor. $1 or return postage required. Replies slowly to correspondence in Portuguese.

RADIO PORTAL DA AMAZONIA, Rua Tenente Alcides Duarte de Souza, 533 Bº Duque de Caxias, 78010 Cuiabá, Mato Grosso, Brazil; also, C.P. 277, 78001 Cuiabá, Mato Grosso, Brazil. Contact: Arnaldo Medina. Return postage required. Replies occasionally to correspondence in Portuguese.

RADIO PROGRESSO, Estrada do Belmont s/n, Bº Nacional, 78000 Pôrto Velho, Rondônia, Brazil. Contact: Angela Xavier, Diretora-Geral. Return postage required. Replies occasionally to correspondence in Portuguese.

RADIO PROGRESSO DO ACRE, 69900 Rio Branco, Acre, Brazil. Contact: José Alves Pereira Neto, Diretor-Presidente. Return postage or $1 required. Replies occasionally to correspondence in Portuguese.

RADIO RECORD, C.P. 7920, 04084 São Paulo SP, Brazil. Contact: Mario Luíz Catto. Return postage or $1 required. Replies occasionally to correspondence in Portuguese.

RADIO SENTINELA, Travessa Ruy Barbosa 142 , 68250 Obidos, Pará, Brazil. Contact: Max Hamoy. Return postage required. Replies occasionally to correspondence in Portuguese.

RADIO TRANSAMERICA, C.P. 6084, 90031 Pôrto Alegre, Rio Grande do Sul, Brazil; or C.P. 551, 97100 Santa María, Rio Grande do Sul, Brazil. Contact: Marlene P. Nunes, Secretária. Return postage required. Replies to correspondence in Portuguese.

RADIO TUPI, Rua Nadir Dias Figueiredo 1329, 02110 São Paulo SP, Brazil. Contact: Elia Soares. Return postage required. Replies occasionally to correspondence in Portuguese.

RADIO UNIVERSO, C.P. 7133, 80001 Curitiba, Paraná, Brazil. Contact: Luíz Andreu Rúbio, Diretor. Replies occasionally to correspondence in Portuguese.

BULGARIA World Time +2 (+3 midyear)

RADIO HORIZONT—Same details as Radio Sofia, below.

RADIO SOFIA, 4 Dragan Tsankov Blvd., 1040 Sofia, Bulgaria. Fax: +359 (2) 662 215. Contact: Iva Delcheva; Kristina Mihailova, In Charge of Listeners' Letters, English Section; or Nadezhda Gecheva, Listeners' Letters Department. Free stickers and pennants. Bronze Diploma for correspondents meeting certain requirements. Replies regularly, but sometimes slowly.

BURKINA FASO World Time exactly

RADIODIFFUSION-TELEVISION BURKINA, B.P. 7029, Ouagadougou, Burkina Faso. Contact: Raphael L. Onadia. Replies irregularly to correspondence in French. IRC or return postage helpful.

BURMA—see "Myanmar."

BURUNDI World Time +2

LA VOIX DE LA REVOLUTION, B.P. 1900, Bujumbura, Burundi. Contact: Gregoire Barampumba, English News Announcer. $1 required.

BYELARUS World Time +2 (+3 midyear)

BYELARUSSIAN RADIO—see "Radiostantsiya Byelarus" for details.

GRODNO RADIO—see "Radiostantsiya Byelarus" for details.

MAHILEV RADIO—see "Radiostantsiya Byelarus" for details.

RADIO MENSK—see "Radiostantsiya Byelarus" for details.

RADIOSTANTSIYA BYELARUS—ul. Krasnaya 4, 220807 Mensk, Byelarus. Fax: 262 041. Free Byelarus stamps.

CAMBODIA   World Time +7

RADIO PHNOM PENH, Overseas Service, English Section, Phnom Penh, Cambodia (Kampuchea). Contact: Miss Hem Bory, English Announcer. Free pennants and Cambodian stamps. Replies irregularly and slowly. Do not include stamps, currency, IRCs or dutiable items in envelope. Registered letters stand a much better chance of getting through.

CAMEROON   World Time +1

Note: Any CRTV outlet is likely to be verified by contacting by registered mail, in English or French with $2 enclosed, James Achanyi-Fontem, Head of Programming, CRTV, B.P. 986, Douala, Cameroon.

CAMEROON RADIO TELEVISION CORPORATION (CRTV)—BAFOUSSAM, B.P. 970, Bafoussam (Ouest), Cameroon. Contact: Ndam Seidou. IRC or return postage required. Replies irregularly in French to correspondence in English or French.

CAMEROON RADIO TELEVISION CORPORATION (CRTV)—BERTOUA, B.P. 230, Bertoua (Eastern), Cameroon. Rarely replies to correspondence, preferably in French. $1 required.

CAMEROON RADIO TELEVISION CORPORATION (CRTV)—BUEA, P.M.B., Buea (Sud-Ouest), Cameroon. 3 IRCs, $1 or return postage required.

CAMEROON RADIO TELEVISION CORPORATION (CRTV)—DOUALA, B.P. 986, Douala (Littoral), Cameroon. Contact: Landry Piamy. 3 IRCs or $1 required.

CAMEROON RADIO TELEVISION CORPORATION (CRTV)—GAROUA, B.P. 103, Garoua (Nord/Adamawa), Cameroon. Contact: Kadeche Manguele. 3 IRCs or return postage required. Replies irregularly and slowly to correspondence in French.

CAMEROON RADIO TELEVISION CORPORATION (CRTV)—YAOUNDE, B.P. 1634, Yaoundé (Centre-Sud), Cameroon. Contact: Florent Etoya Eily, Le Directeur-Général. $1 required. Replies slowly to correspondence in French.

CANADA   World Time –3:30 (–2:30 midyear) Newfoundland; –4 (–3 midyear) Atlantic; –5 (–4 midyear) Eastern, including Quebec and Ontario; –6 (–5 midyear) Central; –7 (–6 midyear) Mountain; –8 (–7 midyear) Pacific, including Yukon

CANADIAN FORCES NETWORK RADIO

Studio Address: Jammstraße 9, W-7630 Lahr, Germany. Fax: +49 (7821) 21 235. Contact: Jean Choquette, VE2KL/DA1CV, Manager Technical Operations.

Transmission Offices: see "Radio Canada International," below.

CBC NORTHERN QUEBEC SHORTWAVE SERVICE—same address as Radio Canada International. Free doorknob hanger.

CFRX-CFRB

Main Address: 2 St. Clair Avenue West, Toronto ON, M4V 1L6 Canada. Fax: +1 (416) 323 6830. Contact: (technical) David Simon, Engineer. Free station history sheet. Replies are sometimes slow in coming. Reception reports should be sent to verification address, below.

Verification Address: ODXA, P.O. Box 161, Station A, Willowdale ON, M2N 5S8 Canada. Contact: Stephen Canney.

CFVP-CFCN, Broadcast House, P.O. Box 7060, Stn. E, Calgary AB, T3C 3L9 Canada. Fax: (general and technical) +1 (403) 240 5801; (news) +1 (403) 246 7099. Contact: (technical) John H. Bruins, Chief Engineer, Radio.

CHNX-CHNS, P.O. Box 400, Halifax NS, B3J 2R2 Canada. Fax: +1 (902) 422-5330. Contact: (technical) Kurt J. Arsenault, Chief Engineer. Return postage or $1 helpful. Replies irregularly.

CIQX-CIQC, Radio Montréal, Mount Royal Broadcasting, Inc., 1200 McGill College Avenue, Suite 300, Montréal PQ, H3B 4G7 Canada. Fax: +1 (514) 393 4659. Contact: André Chevalier, Program Director.

CKFX-CKWX, 2440 Ash Street, Vancouver BC, V5Z 4J6 Canada. Fax: +1 (604) 873 0877. Contact: Vijay Chanbra, Engineer.

CKZN-CBN, CBC, P.O. Box 12010, Station "A", St. John's NF, A1B 3T8 Canada. Fax: +1 (709) 737 4280. Contact: (technical) Charles Kempf; or Shawn R. Williams, Regional Engineer. Free folder with British perspective on Newfoundland's history.

CKZU-CBU, CBC, P.O. Box 4600, Vancouver BC, V6B 4A2 Canada. Fax: +1 (604) 662 6350. Contact: Dave Newbury.

RADIO CANADA INTERNATIONAL

Main Office: P.O. Box 6000, Montréal PQ, H3C 3A8 Canada. Fax: +1 (514) 284 0891. Free stickers, pennants and other station souvenirs. Canadian compact discs sold worldwide except North America, from International Sales, CBC Records, P.O. Box 500, Station "A", Toronto ON, M5W 1E6 Canada (VISA/MC), fax +1 (416) 975 3482; and within the United States from CBC/Allegro,

3434 SE Milwaukie Avenue, Portland OR 97202 USA, fax (503) 232 9504, toll-free telephone (800) 288-2007 (VISA/MC).

Transmission Office: (technical) P.O. Box 6000, Montréal PQ, H3C 3A8 Canada. Fax: +1 (514) 284 9550. Contact: Jacques Bouliane, Frequency Manager and Assistant to the Chief Engineer. This office only for informing about transmitter-related problems (interference, modulation quality, etc.), especially by fax. Verifications not given out at this office; requests for verification should be sent to the main office, above.

Washington Bureau, Nontechnical: CBC, Suite 500, National Press Building, 529 14th Street NW, Washington DC 20045 USA. Fax: +1 (202) 783 9321.

London Bureau, Nontechnical: CBC, 43 Great Titchfield Street, London W1, England. Fax: +44 (71) 631 3095.

Paris Bureau, Nontechnical: CBC, 17 avenue Matignon, F-75008 Paris, France.

CENTRAL AFRICAN REPUBLIC   World Time +1

RADIODIFFUSION-TELEVISION CENTRAFRICAINE, B.P. 940, Bangui, Central African Republic. Contact: (technical) Jacques Mbilo, Le Directeur des Services Techniques; or Michèl Bata, Services Techniques. Replies on rare occasion to correspondence in French; return postage required.

CHAD   World Time +1

RADIODIFFUSION NATIONALE TCHADIENNE—N'DJAMENA, B.P. 892, N'Djamena, Chad. Contact: Djimadoum Ngoka Kilamian. 2 IRCs or return postage required. Replies slowly to correspondence in French.

RADIO DIFFUSION NATIONALE TCHADIENNE—RADIO ABECHE, B.P. 105, Abéché, Ouaddai, Chad. Return postage helpful. Replies rarely to correspondence in French.

RADIODIFFUSION NATIONALE TCHADIENNE—RADIO MOUNDOU, B.P. 122, Moundou, Logone, Chad. Contact: Jacques Maimos, Le Chef de la Station Régionale de Radio Moundou.

CHILE   World Time –3 (–4 midyear)

RADIO ESPERANZA, Casilla 830, Temuco, Chile. Contact: Lorena M. Oyarce Arriagada. Free pennants, stickers, bookmarks and tourist information. $1 or return postage required. Replies, usually quite slowly, to correspondence in Spanish.

RADIO NACIONAL—when operating, such as for special sports events, use the following address, but don't write "Radio Nacional" on the envelope: Carlos Toledo Verdugo, Casilla 296, San Fernando, VI Region, Chile. Free souvenirs. 3 IRCs required. Replies to correspondence in Spanish. This station's transmitters are currently up for sale.

RADIO SANTA MARIA, Casilla 1, Coyhaique, Chile. Contact: Pedro Andrade Vera, Dpto. DX. $1 or return postage required. Replies to correspondence in Spanish.

RADIO TRIUNFAL EVANGELICA, Costanera Sur 7209, Comuna de Cerro Navia, Santiago, Chile. Contact: Fernando González Segura, Obispo de la Misión Pentecostal Fundamentalista. 2 IRCs required. Replies to correspondence in Spanish.

RADIO UNIVERSIDAD DE CONCEPCION, Miguel Claro 161, Providencia, Santiago, Chile. Contact: Jefe, Departamento Técnico. Replies to correspondence in Spanish, but station is essentially inaudible beyond a few hundred kilometers.

CHINA (PR)   World Time +8; still nominally +6 ("Urumqi Time") in the Xinjiang Uighur Autonomous Region, but in practice +8 is observed there, as well

Note: Radio Beijing, the Central People's Broadcasting Station and certain regional outlets reply regularly to listeners' letters in a variety of languages. If a Chinese regional station does not respond to your correspondence within four months—and many will not, unless your letter is in Chinese or the regional dialect—try writing them c/o Radio Beijing.

CENTRAL PEOPLE'S BROADCASTING STATION (CPBS), Zhongyang Renmin Guangbo Diantai, P.O. Box 4501, Beijing, People's Republic of China. Free stickers. Return postage helpful.

CHINA HUAYI BROADCASTING COMPANY, P.O. Box 251, Fuzhou City, Fujian 350001, People's Republic of China.

CHINA INTERNATIONAL RADIO STATION, Box 565, Beijing, People's Republic of China; or Box 11036, General Post Office, Hong Kong. Prefers correspondence in Chinese (Mandarin), Cantonese, Hakka, Chaozhou or Amoy.

FUJIAN PEOPLE'S BROADCASTING STATION, Fuzhou, Fujian, People's Republic of China. $1 helpful. Replies occasionally and usually slowly.

GANSU PEOPLE'S BROADCASTING STATION, Lanzhou, People's Republic of China. Contact: Li Mei. IRC helpful.

GUANGXI PEOPLE'S BROADCASTING STATION, No. 12 Min Zu Avenue, Nanning, Guangxi 530022, People's Republic of China. Contact: Song Yue, Staffer; or Li Hai Li, Staffer. Free stickers and handmade papercuts. IRC helpful. Replies irregularly.

HEILONGJIANG PEOPLE'S BROADCASTING STATION, No. 115 Zhongshan Road, Harbin City, Heilongjiang, People's Republic of China. $1 or return postage helpful.

HONGHE PEOPLE'S BROADCASTING STATION, Honghe, Yunnan, People's Republic of China.

HUBEI PEOPLE'S BROADCASTING STATION, No. 563 Jie Fang Avenue, Wuhan, Hubei, People's Republic of China.

JIANGXI PEOPLE'S BROADCASTING STATION, Nanchang, Jiangxi, People's Republic of China. Contact: Tang Ji Sheng, Editor, Chief Editor's Office. Free gold/red pins. Replies irregularly; Mr. Tang enjoys music, literature and stamps, so enclosing a small memento along these lines should help assure a speedy reply.

NEI MONGGOL (INNER MONGOLIA) PEOPLE'S BROADCASTING STATION, Hohhot, Nei Monggol Zizhiqu, People's Republic of China. Contact: Zhang Xiang-Quen, Secretary. Replies irregularly.

QINGHAI PEOPLE'S BROADCASTING STATION, Xining, Qinghai, People's Republic of China. $1 helpful.

RADIO BEIJING
Main Office: No. 2 Fuxingmenwai, Beijing 100866, People's Republic of China. Fax: +86 (1) 801 3175. Contact: (nontechnical or technical) Chen Lifang, Fan Fuquang or Qi Guilin, Audience Relations, English Department; or Producer, "Listeners' Letterbox"; (technical) Ge Hongzhang, Frequency Manager; Free bi-monthly The Messenger magazine, stickers, desk calendars, pins, hair ornaments and such small souvenirs as handmade papercuts. Two-volume, 820-page set of Day-to-Day Chinese language-lesson books for $15, including postage worldwide; contact Li Yi, English Department.
Washington Bureau, Nontechnical. 2401 Calvert Street NW, Washington DC 20008 USA. Fax: +1 (202) 387 0459, but call +1 (202) 387-6860 first so fax machine can be switched on. Contact: Chao Xie or Denong Chen.
Paris Bureau, Nontechnical: 7 rue Charles Lecocq, F-75015 Paris, France.

SICHUAN PEOPLE'S BROADCASTING STATION, Chengdu, Sichuan, People's Republic of China. Replies occasionally.

VOICE OF JINLING, P.O. Box 268, Nanjing, Jiangsu, People's Republic of China. Fax: +86 (25) 413 235. Free stickers and calendars, plus Chinese-language color station brochure and information on the Nanjing Technology Import & Export Corporation. Replies to correspondence in Chinese and to simple correspondence in English. $1 or return postage helpful.

VOICE OF PUJIANG, P.O. Box 3064, Shanghai, People's Republic of China. Contact: Jiang Bimiao, Editor & Reporter.

VOICE OF THE STRAIT, People's Liberation Army Broadcasting Centre, P.O. Box 187, Fuzhou, Fujian, People's Republic of China. Replies very irregularly.

WENZHOU PEOPLE'S BROADCASTING STATION, Wenzhou, People's Republic of China.

XILINGOL PEOPLE'S BROADCASTING STATION, Xilinhot, Xilingol, People's Republic of China.

XINJIANG PEOPLE'S BROADCASTING STATION, Urümqi, Xinjiang, People's Republic of China. Contact: Guo Ying. Free tourist booklet.

XIZANG PEOPLE'S BROADCASTING STATION, Lhasa, Xizang (Tibet), People's Republic of China. Contact: Lobsang Chonphel, Announcer.

YUNNAN PEOPLE'S BROADCASTING STATION, Kunming, Yunnan, People's Republic of China. Contact: F.K. Fan. Free Chinese-language brochure on Yunnan Province. $1 or return postage helpful. Replies occasionally.

CHINA (TAIWAN)   World Time +8
CENTRAL BROADCASTING SYSTEM (CBS), 55 Pei An Road, Taipei, Taiwan, Republic of China. Contact: Lee Ming, Deputy Director. Free stickers.

VOICE OF ASIA, P.O. Box 880, Kaohsiung, Taiwan, Republic of China. Free stickers.

VOICE OF FREE CHINA, P.O. Box 24-38, Taipei, Taiwan, Republic of China. Fax: +886 (2) 751 9277. Contact: (nontechnical) Daniel Dong, Chief, Listeners' Service Section, Department of International Service; (technical) Tai-Lau Ying. Free stickers, Voice of Free China Journal, annual diary, "Let's Learn Chinese" language-learning course materials, booklets and other publica-

tions, and Taiwanese stamps. Station offers listeners a free frisbee if they return the "Request Card" sent to them by the station.

CLANDESTINE—see "Disestablishmentarian and Clandestine."

COLOMBIA   World Time –5 (–4 midyear during El Niño years)
Note: Colombia, the country, is always spelled with two o's. It is never written as "Columbia."

CARACOL BOGOTA
Nontechnical: Radio Reloj, Apartado Aéreo 8700, Bogotá, Colombia. Contact: Ruth Vásquez; or Ricardo Alarcón G., Director-General. Free stickers. Return postage or $1 required. Replies infrequently and slowly to correspondence in Spanish.
Technical: DX Caracol, Apartado Aéreo 9291, Bogotá, Colombia. Fax: +57 (1) 268 1582. Replies to correspondence in Spanish.

ECOS CELESTIALES, Apartado Aéreo 8447, Medellín, Colombia. Return postage or $1 required. Replies occasionally to correspondence in Spanish. This station does not appear to be licensed by the Colombian authorities.

ECOS DEL ATRATO, Apartado Aéreo 78, Quibdó, Chocó, Colombia. Contact: Oscar Echeverri Mosquera, Director; or Julia Ma Cuesta L. Return postage or $1 required. Replies rarely to correspondence in Spanish.

ECOS DEL COMBEIMA, Parque Murillo Toto No. 3-29, piso 3, Ibagué, Tolima, Colombia. Contact: Jesús Erney Torres, Cronista. Return postage or $1 helpful. Replies irregularly to correspondence in Spanish.

EMISORA ARMONIAS DEL CAQUETA, Florencia, Caquetá, Colombia. Contact: P. Alvaro Serna Alzate, Director. Replies rarely to correspondence in Spanish; return postage required.

LA VOZ DEL CINARUCO, Calle 19 No. 19-62, Arauca, Colombia. Contact: Efrahim Valera, Director. Pennants for return postage. Replies rarely to correspondence in Spanish; return postage required.

LA VOZ DEL GUAINIA, Calle 6 con Carretera 3, Puerto Inírida, Guainía, Colombia. Contact: Ancizar Gómez Arzimendi, Director. Return postage or $1 required. Replies occasionally to correspondence in Spanish.

LA VOZ DEL GUAVIARE, Carretera 3, Calle 2, San José del Guaviare, Colombia. Contact: José Harley Ramírez Sánchez, Locutor. Free stickers and Colombian stamps. $1 or return postage required. Replies, rarely, to correspondence in Spanish.

LA VOZ DEL RIO ARAUCA, Apartado Aéreo 16555, Bogotá, Colombia. Contact: Guillermo Pulido, Gerente. Free stickers. $1 or return postage required; return postage on a preaddressed airmail envelope even better. Replies occasionally to correspondence in Spanish; persist.

LA VOZ DE LOS CENTAUROS, Apartado Aéreo 2472, Villavicencio, Meta, Colombia. Contact: Carlos Torres Leyva, Gerencia; or Cielo de Corredor, Administradora. Return postage required. Replies to correspondence in Spanish.

ONDAS DEL META, Apartado Aéreo 2196, Villavicencio, Meta, Colombia. Contact: Yolanda Plazas de Lozada, Administradora. Return postage required. Replies irregularly and slowly to correspondence in Spanish.

ONDAS DEL ORTEGUAZA, Calle 16, No. 12-48, piso 2, Florencia, Caquetá, Colombia. Contact: Sra. Dani Yasmín Anturi Durán, Secretaria; or C.P. Norberto Plaza Vargas, Subgerente. Free stickers, IRC, return postage or $1 required. Replies occasionally to correspondence in Spanish.

RADIODIFUSORA NACIONAL DE COLOMBIA, CAN, Apartado Aéreo 94321, Bogotá, Colombia. Contact: (English) Juan Carlos Pardo or Jaime Molina, "Colombia DX"; (Spanish) Adriana Giraldo Cifuentes, Directora. Tends to reply a bit slowly.

RADIO MELODIA, Calle 61, No. 3B-05, Bogotá, Colombia. Contact: Gerardo Páez Mejía, Vicepresidente; or Elvira Mejía de Páez, Gerente General. Stickers and pennants for $1 or return postage. Replies, rarely, to correspondence in Spanish.

RADIO SANTA FE, Calle 57, No. 17-48, Bogotá, Colombia. Fax: (certain working hours only) +57 (1) 249 60 95. Contact: María Luisa Bernal Mahe, Gerente. Free stickers. IRC, $1 or return postage required. Replies to correspondence in Spanish.

COMOROS   World Time +4
RADIO COMORO, B.P. 250, Moroni, Grande Comore, Comoros. Contact: Ali Hamoi Hissani; or Antufi Mohamed Bacar, Le Directeur de Programme. Return postage required. Replies very rarely to correspondence in French.

CONGO   World Time +1
RADIO CONGO, Radiodiffusion-Télévision Congolaise, B.P. 2241, Brazzaville, Congo. Contact: Antoine Mgongo, Rédacteur en

chef; or Albert Fayette Mikano, Directeur. $1 required. Replies irregularly to letters in French sent via registered mail.

COOK ISLANDS   World Time –10

RADIO COOK ISLANDS, P.O. Box 126, Avarua, Rarotonga. Fax: +686 21907. Contact: (nontechnical) Tauraki Rongo Raea; (technical) Orango Tango, Assistant Chief Engineer. Has replied extremely irregularly since 1985. $1 or return postage required, plus creative token gift helpful.

COSTA RICA   World Time –6

ADVENTIST WORLD RADIO, THE VOICE OF HOPE, TIAWR, Radio Lira Internacional, Radiodifusora Adventista, Apartado 1177, 4050 Alajuela, Costa Rica. Fax +506 (41) 1282. Contact: David L. Gregory, General Manager; Juan Ochoa, Senior Administrator; or William Gomez, Producer, "Su Correo Amigo." Free stickers, calendars, Costa Rican stamps, pennants and religious printed matter. $1, IRC or return postage helpful, with $0.50 in unused U.S. stamps being acceptable. Also, see "USA."

FARO DEL CARIBE

Main Office: TIFC, Apartado 2710, 1000 San José, Costa Rica. Contact: Juan Jacinto Ochoa F., Administrador; Free stickers. $1 or IRCs helpful.

U.S. Office, Nontechnical: P.O. Box 620485, Orlando FL 32862 USA. Contact: Lim Ortiz.

RADIO CASINO, Apartado 287, 7301 Puerto Limón, Costa Rica. Contact: (technical) Ing. Jorge Pardo, Director Técnico.

RADIO FOR PEACE INTERNATIONAL

Main Office: University for Peace, Apartado 88, Santa Ana, Costa Rica. Fax: +506 (49) 1929. Contact: (nontechnical) Debra Latham, General Manager; (nontechnical or technical) James L. Latham, Station Manager; (technical) Bentley Born. Replies sometimes slow in coming because of the mail. Free stickers, sample *Vista* newsletter and sociopolitical literature; quarterly *Vista* newsletter for $35 annual membership; station T-shirt $15 (VISA/MC). Actively solicits listener contributions. $1, 3 IRCs or return postage required.

U.S. Office, Nontechnical: World Peace University, P.O. Box 10869, Eugene OR 97440 USA. Fax: +1 (503) 741 1279. Contact: Dr. Richard Schneider, Chancellor. Newsletter and T-shirt as above.

German Bureau: Postfach 110 226, W-3400 Göttingen, Germany. Contact: Harald Kuhl, Produzent, "DX-Magazin."

RADIO RELOJ, Sistema Radiofónico H.B., Apartado 341, 1000 San José, Costa Rica. Contact: Roger Barahona, Gerente; or Francisco Barahona Gómez. $1 required.

RADIO UNIVERSIDAD DE COSTA RICA, Ciudad Universitaria Rodrigo Facio, 1000 San José, Costa Rica. Contact: Marco González.

COTE D'IVOIRE   World Time exactly

AFRIQUE NUMERO UN—see "Gabon" for details of this station, which hopes to add transmissions, reportedly at 500 kW, from Côte d'Ivoire in early 1993.

CROATIA   World Time +1 (+2 midyear)

CROATIAN RADIO, STUDIO ZAGREB

Main Office: Hrvatska Radio-Televizija (HRT), Studio Zagreb, P.O. Box 1000 (or Odasiljaci i veze, Radnicka c. 22) (or Jurišiçeva 4), 41000 Zagreb, Croatia. Fax: +38 (41) 451 145 or +38 (41) 451 060. Free Croatian stamps. Sells subscriptions to *Croatian Voice*. $1 helpful. Replies regularly, although sometimes slowly.

Washington Bureau, Nontechnical: Croatian-American Association, 1912 Sunderland Place NW, Washington DC 20036 USA. Fax: +1 (202) 429–5545. Contact: Bob Schneider, Director.

HRVATSKA RADIO TELEVIZIJA—see "Croatian Radio, Studio Zagreb," above, for details.

"RADIO FREE CROATIA"—see "WHRI, USA," for address.

CUBA   World Time –5 (–4 midyear)

RADIO HABANA CUBA

Nontechnical: P.O. Box 7026, Havana, Cuba. Contact: (nontechnical) Rolando Peláez, Head of Correspondence; Mike La Guardia, Senior Editor; Milagro Hernández Cuba, General Director; (technical) Arnie Coro, Director of DX Programming. Free wallet and wall calendars, pennants, stickers, keychains and pins. DX Listeners' Club. Replies slowly to correspondence from the United States, which has no diplomatic relations with Cuba, because of circuitous mail service, usually via Canada.

Technical: P.O. Box 6240, Havana, Cuba.

RADIO REBELDE, Apartado 6277, Havana 6, Cuba. Contact: Noemí Cairo Marín, Secretaria, Relaciones Públicas; or Jorge Luis Mas Zabala, Director, Relaciones Públicas.

CYPRUS   World Time +2

Greek Sector

BBC WORLD SERVICE—EAST MEDITERRANEAN RELAY, P.O. Box 219, Limassol, Cyprus. Nontechnical correspondence should be sent to the BBC World Service in London (see).

CYPRUS BROADCASTING CORPORATION, Broadcasting House, P.O. Box 4824, Nicosia, Cyprus. Fax: +357 (2) 314 050. Replies occasionally, sometimes slowly. IRC or $1 helpful.

Turkish Sector

RADIO BAYRAK, Bayrak Radio & T.V. Corporation, P.O. Box 417, Lefkosa, Mersin 10, Turkey. Fax: +90 (5) 208 1991. Contact: (technical) A. Ziya Dincer, Technical Director. Replies occasionally.

CZECHOSLOVAKIA   World Time +1 (+2 midyear)

RADIO CZECHOSLOVAKIA, External Programs Department, Vinohradská 12, 120 99 Prague 2, Czechoslovakia. Fax: +42 (2) 232 1020. Contact: Jan Valeška, Head of English Section; Lenka Adamová, "Mailbag"; or L. Kubik. Free stickers, pennants and calendars; free Radio Czechoslovakia Monitor Club "DX Diploma" for regular correspondents. Samples of *Welcome to Czechoslovakia* and *Czechoslovak Life* available upon request from Orbis, Vinohradská 46, 120 41 Prague 2, Czechoslovakia.

DENMARK   World Time +1 (+2 midyear)

DANMARKS RADIO

Main Office, Nontechnical: Radiohuset, DK-1999 Frederiksberg C, Denmark. Danish-language 24-hour telephone tape recording for schedule information +45 (3) 536-3270 (Americas, Europe, Africa), +45 (3) 536-3090 (elsewhere). Fax: +45 (3) 139 8040. Contact: Lulu Vittrup. $1-2 required, and enclosing local souvenirs helpful. Free stickers. Replies occasionally to friendly correspondence in English, particularly to those who point out they are of Danish ancestry, but regularly to correspondence in Danish. As of June 1, 1989, has not issued verifications from this office.

Norwegian Office, Technical: Details of reception quality are best sent to the Engineering Department of Radio Norway International (see), which operates the transmitters used for Radio Denmark.

Washington News Bureau, Nontechnical: 3001 Q Street NW, Washington DC 20007 USA. Fax: +1 (202) 342 2463.

DISESTABLISHMENTARIAN AND CLANDESTINE   (via unlicensed transmitters or as programs by disestablishmentarian groups over licensed stations)

Note 1:   Disestablishmentarian and clandestine organizational activities, including addresses and broadcasting schedules, are unusually subject to abrupt change or termination. Being operated by anti-establishment political and/or military organizations, these groups tend to be suspicious of outsiders' motives. Thus, they are most likely to reply to correspondence from those who write in the station's native tongue, and who are perceived to be at least somewhat favorably disposed to their cause. Most will provide, upon request, printed matter in their native tongue on their cause.

Note 2:   According to WWCR, at least one exile program, "Radio Khalistan," has been taken off the air by them at the behest of the U.S. Department of State after an official complaint by India. This precedent, if repeated often enough, could diminish the number of such broadcasts via licensed U.S. private stations. However, numerous protests by the Cuban government to the United Nations, the International Telecommunication Union and representatives of the U.S. Department of State have thus far not succeeded in bringing about the termination of broadcasts from Radio Martí or Radio Miami Internacional.

"AL KUDS RADIO," Palestinian Arab Broadcasting, P.O. Box 10412, Tripoli, Libya; or P.O. Box 5092, Damascus, Syria. Pro-Palestinian, anti-Israeli government. ("Al Kuds ash Sherif" is an Arab name for Jerusalem). Rarely replies except to correspondence in Arabic.

"ALTERNATIVA"—see "Radio Miami Internacional, USA," for address. Contact: Orlando Gutiérrez, Executive Producer. Anti-Castro, anti-communist; privately supported by the Directorio Revolucionario Democrático Cubano.

A VOZ DA RESISTENCIA DO GALO NEGRO (Voice of the Resistence of the Black Cockerel)—see "Angola."

"ESPERANZA"—see "Radio Miami Internacional, USA," for address. Contact: Julio Esterino, Program Director. Anti-Castro, anti-communist; privately supported by Los Municipios de Cuba en el Exilio.

"FORUM REVOLUCIONARIO"—see "Radio Miami Internacional, USA," for address. Anti-Castro, anti-communist; privately supported by the Forum Revolucionario Democratico Cubano.

"IRAN'S FLAG OF FREEDOM RADIO," P.O. Box 19740, Irving CA 92714 USA; Postfach 05559B, W-2000 Hamburg, Germany; Post Boks 103, DK-2670 Greve Strand, Denmark; or 20 rue de Concorcet, F-75009 Paris, France. Five-minute news in Farsi from station's organizers may be heard by telephone: (USA) +1 (818) 792-4726; (U.K.) +44 (71) 376-1611. Contact: (USA) Reza Farhadi; (elsewhere) Sazeman Darferesh Kaviani; M. Ganji, Secretary General; or M.K. Fathi. Anti-Iranian government, pro-monarchist station of the Suzmani Darashta Kaviane group; supported by CIA and Egyptian government.

"LA VOZ DE ALPHA 66"—see "Radio Miami Internacional, USA," for address. Contact: Diego Medina, Producer. Anti-Castro, anti-communist; privately supported by the Alpha 66 organization.

"LA VOZ DE LA FUNDACION," P.O. Box 440069, Miami FL 33144 USA. Contact: Ninoska Pérez Castellón, Executive Producer; (technical) Mariela Ferretti. Free stickers. Anti-Castro, anti-communist; privately supported by the Cuban American National Foundation.

"LA VOZ DEL CID," Apartado de Correo 8130, 1000 San José, Costa Rica; or 10021 SW 37th Terrace, Miami FL 33165 USA; or Apartado Postal 51403, Sabana Grande 1050, Caracas, Venezuela. Contact: Francisco Fernández. Anti-Castro, anti-communist; privately supported by Cuba Independiente y Democrática.

"LA VOZ DEL MOVIMIENTO 30 DE NOVIEMBRE"—see "Radio Miami Internacional, USA," for address. Anti-Castro, anti-communist; privately supported by the Movimiento 30 de Noviembre.

"LA VOZ DE LOS MEDICOS CUBANOS LIBRES"—see "Radio Miami Internacional, USA," for address. Anti-Castro, anti-communist; privately supported by the PACHA organization.

"LA VOZ DE TRIBUNA LIBRE"—see "Radio Miami Internacional, USA," for address. Contact: José Pérez Linares, Director. Anti-Castro, anti-communist; privately supported by the Alianza Cubana.

"LA VOZ POPULAR," Arcoios, P.O. Box 835, Seattle WA 98111 USA; Apartado 19619, México City D.F. 03910, Mexico; or Network in Solidarity with the People of Guatemala, 930 "F" Street NW, Suite 720, Washington DC 20004 USA.

"NATIONAL VANGUARD RADIO," P.O. Box 90, Hillsboro WV 24946 USA. $1 for catalog of books and tapes. Program, possibly replacing "Voice of To-Morrow," of the neo-Nazi National Alliance. Via facilities of WRNO.

"PUEBLO LIBRE"—see "Radio Miami Internacional, USA," for address. Anti-Castro, anti-communist; privately supported by the Junta Patriótica Cubana.

"RADIO AZADI IRAN" ("Radio Liberty of Iran"), 17 Boulevard Raspail, F-75007 Paris, France. Anti-Iranian government, formerly pro-Bakhtiar; supported by CIA and Egyptian government.

"RADIO CONCIENCIA"—see "Radio Miami Internacional, USA," for address. Contact: Ramón Sánchez, Director. Anti-Castro, anti-communist; privately supported by the Comisión Nacional Cubana.

"RADIO FREE AMERICA"
Network: Sun Radio Network, 2857 Executive Drive, Clearwater FL 34622 USA. Contact: Tom Valentine, Host. Sells tapes of past broadcasts for $9. Aired via WWCR, succeeds *Liberty Lobby* program aired two decades ago.
Sponsoring Organization: Liberty Lobby, 300 Independence Avenue SE, Washington DC 20003 USA. Fax: +1 (202) 546 3626. Contact: Don Markey, Public Affairs Associate. *Spotlight* newspaper for $36/year; sells books at various prices. Anti-Bilderberg/Trilateralist organization described by itself as populist; described by PBS' *Frontline* as "the largest anti-semitic group in the country."

"RADIO FREE BOUGAINVILLE," 2 Griffith Avenue, Roseville NSW 2069, Australia. Fax: +61 (2) 417 1066. Contact: Sam Voron, Australian Director. $5, AUS$5 or 5 IRCs required.

"RADIO FREE CROATIA," P.O. Box 25481, Chicago IL 60625 USA. Contact: Ivica Metzger, Chicago Media Workshop. Supportive of Croatian independence. This address for nontechnical correspondence only; technical correspondence should be sent to "Croatian Radio—Studio Zagreb" (see "Croatia").

"RADIO LIBERTY OF IRAN"—see "Radio Azadi Iran," above.

"RADIO MOJAHEDIN OF AFGHANISTAN" (if operating), P.O. Box 204, Peshawar, Pakistan. Pro-Islamic fighters.

"RADIO OF THE IRAQI REPUBLIC FROM BAGHDAD, VOICE OF THE IRAQI PEOPLE" ("Idha'at al-Jamahiriya al-Iraqiya min Baghdad, Saut al-Sha'b al-Iraqi"), Broadcasting Service of the Kingdom of Saudi Arabia, P.O. Box 61718, Riyadh 11575, Saudi Arabia. Contact: Suliman A. Al-Samnan, Director of Frequency Management. Anti-Saddam Hussein "black" clandestine sup-

ported by CIA, British intelligence and, surprisingly openly, Saudi Arabia. The name of this station has changed periodically since its inception during the Gulf crisis.

"RADIO PERIODICO PANAMERICANO"—see "Radio Miami Internacional, USA," for address. Contact: René L. Díaz, Program Director. Moderately anti-Castro and anti-communist; privately supported by Caribe Infopress and allied with the Plataforma Democrática Cubana.

"RADIO PERIODICO SEMANAL DE LOS COORDINADORES SOCIAL DEMOCRATA DE CUBA"—see "Un Solo Pueblo," below.

"RADIO 16TH OF DECEMBER"—see "Radio Miami Internacional, USA," for address. Wants to restore the former Aristide government back to power in Haiti.

"RADIO VOLUNTAD DEMOCRATICA"—see "Radio Miami Internacional, USA," for address. Contact: Dr. Antonio de Varona, Jefe. Anti-Castro, anti-communist; privately supported by the Partido Revolucionario Cubano Auténtico.

"RUMBO A LA LIBERTAD"—see "Radio Miami Internacional, USA," for address. Contact: Rafael Cabezas, Brigade President. Anti-Castro, anti-communist; privately supported by the Brigada 2506, consisting of veterans of the Bay of Pigs.

"UN SOLO PUEBLO"—see "Radio Miami Internacional, USA," for address. Anti-Castro, anti-communist; privately supported by the Coordinadora Social Democrata.

"VOICE OF CHINA," Democratization of China, P.O. Box 11663, Berkeley CA 94701 USA; Foundation for China in the 21st Century, P.O. Box 11696, Berkeley CA 94701 USA; or P.O. Box 79218, Monkok, Hong Kong. Fax: +1 (510) 843 4370. Contact: Bangtai Xu, Director. Mainly "overseas Chinese students" interested in the democratisation of China. Financial support from the Foundation for China in the 21st Century. Have "picked up the mission" of the earlier Voice of June 4th, but have no organizational relationship with it. Transmits via the facilities of the Central Broadcasting System, Taiwan (see), which also may be contacted.

"VOICE OF KASHMIR FREEDOM," P.O. Box 102, Muzaffarabad, Azad Kashmir, Pakistan. Favors Azad Kashmiri independence from India; pro-Moslem.

"VOICE OF NATIONAL SALVATION" ("Gugugui Sori Pangsong"), Front for National Salvation, Kankoku Minzoku Minshu Tensen, 1-2-1 Hirakawa-machi, Chiyota-ku, Tokyo, Japan. Free newspaper. Pro-North Korea, pro-Korean unification; supported by North Korean government. On the air since 1967, but not under the same name.

"VOICE OF PALESTINE" ("Sautah-Filistine"), Office of the Permanent Observer for Palestine to the United Nations, 115 East 65th Street, New York NY 10021 USA. Contact: Dr. Nasser Al-Kidwa, Permanent Observer to the United Nations. Fax: +1 (212) 517 2377. Radio organ of the main, pro-Arafat, faction of the Palestine Liberation Organization (PLO). This is the oldest clandestine program/station on the air using the same name, having been heard via the facilities of RTV Algerienne and other stations since at least 1972.

"VOICE OF TO-MORROW" (when and if operating), P.O. Box 314, Clackamas OR 97015 USA. Contact: Michael Rosetti. Return postage helpful. Replies irregular and sometimes slow in coming. Neo-Nazi National Alliance. May have been replaced by "National Vanguard Radio" (see above).

"VOICE OF THE BROAD MASSES OF ERITREA"—see "Ethiopia."

"VOICE OF THE COMMUNIST PARTY OF IRAN"—see "Voice of the Iranian Revolution," below, for details.

"VOICE OF THE FREE SAHARA" ("La Voz del Sahara Libre, La Vox del Pueblo Sahel"), Sahara Libre, Frente Polisario, B.P. 10, El Mouradia, Algiers, Algeria; or Sahara Libre, Ambassade de la République Arabe Saraui Démocratique, 1 Av. Franklin Roosevelt, 16000 Algiers, Algeria; or B.P. 10, Al-Mouradia, Algiers, Algeria. Fax: +213 747 933. Contact: Mohamed Lamin Abdesalem; Mahafud Zein or Sneiba Lehbib. Free stickers, booklets, cards, maps, paper flags and calendars. 2 IRCs helpful. Pro-Polisario Front; supported by Algerian government.

"VOICE OF THE GREAT NATIONAL UNION FRONT OF CAMBODIA," 212 E. 47th Street #24G, New York NY 10017 USA; or Permanent Mission of Democratic Kampuchea to the United Nations, 747 3rd Avenue, 8th Floor, New York NY 10017 USA. Khmer Rouge station.

"VOICE OF THE IRAQI PEOPLE"—see "Radio of the Iraqi Republic from Baghdad, Voice of the Iraqi People," above.

"VOICE OF THE KHMER" ("Samleng Khmer"), P.O. Box 22-25, Ramindra Post Office, Bangkok 10 220, Thailand. Contact: Pol

Ham, Chief Editor. Return postage required. Replies irregularly. Station of the Khmer Nationalist Forces, which consist of two groups: the Khmer People's National Liberation Front, and the National United Front for an Independent, Neutral, Peaceful and Cooperative Cambodia; nominally noncommunist and anti-Vietnamese.

DJIBOUTI World Time +3

RADIODIFFUSION-TELEVISION DE DJIBOUTI, B.P. 97, Djibouti. Return postage helpful. Correspondence in French preferred.

DOMINICAN REPUBLIC World Time –4

LA N-103/RADIO NORTE, Apartado Postal 320, Santiago, Dominican Republic. Contact: Antonio Pérez, Dueño; or Héctor Castillo, Gerente.

RADIO AMANECER INTERNACIONAL, Apartado Postal 1500, Santo Domingo, Dominican Republic. Contact: (nontechnical) Pastor Alexis Muñoz D., Director; or Rosa O. Alcantara, Secretaria; (technical) Ing. Sócrates Domínguez. $1 or return postage required. Replies slowly to correspondence in Spanish.

RADIO BARAHONA, Apartado 201, Barahona, Dominican Republic; or Gustavo Mejía Ricart No. 293, Apto. 2-B, Ens. Quisqueya, Santo Domingo, Dominican Republic. Contact: (nontechnical) Rodolfo Z. Lama Jaar, Administrador; (technical) Ing. Roberto Lama Sajour, Administrador General. Free stickers. Letters should be sent via registered mail. $1 or return postage helpful. Replies to correspondence in Spanish.

RADIO SANTIAGO, Apartado 282, Santiago, Dominican Republic.

ECUADOR World Time –5; –6 Galapagos

Note: According to HCJB's "DX Party Line," during periods of drought, such as caused by "El Niño," electricity rationing causes periods in which transmitters cannot operate, as well as spikes which occasionally damage transmitters. Accordingly, Ecuadorian stations tend to be somewhat irregular during drought conditions.

ECOS DEL ORIENTE, 11 de Febrero y Mariscal Sucre, Lago Agrio, Sucumbios, Ecuador. Contact: Elsa Irene Velástegui, Secretaria. Sometimes includes free 20 sucre note (Ecuadorian currency) with reply. $1 or return postage required. Replies, often slowly, to correspondence in Spanish.

EMISORAS GRAN COLOMBIA (when operating), Casilla 2246 (Calle Guayaquil), Quito, Pichincha, Ecuador. Contact: (nontechnical) Lic. César Farah, Director General; (technical) Matilde Castro Vda. de Cevallos, Presidenta. Return postage or $1 required. Replies to correspondence in Spanish.

ESCUELAS RADIOFONICAS POPULARES DEL ECUADOR, Casilla 4755, Riobamba, Ecuador. Fax: +593 (2) 961 625. Contact: Juan Pérez Sarmiento, Director Ejecutivo; or Patricio Muñoz Jacome, Director Ejecutivo de ERPE. Return postage helpful. Replies to correspondence in Spanish.

HCJB, VOICE OF THE ANDES

Main Office: Casilla 17-17-691, Quito, Pichincha, Ecuador. Fax: +593 (2) 447 263. Contact: (nontechnical or technical) Ken MacHarg, Host, Saludos Amigos (letterbox); (technical) G. Volkhardt, Director of Broadcasting; or Wolfgang Brinkmann, Frequency Manager. Free religious brochures, calendars and pennants. ANDEX International listeners' club bulletin. *Catch the Vision* book for $8, postpaid. IRC or unused U.S., Canadian or Ecuadorian stamps required for airmail reply.

U.S. Office: International Headquarters, World Radio Missionary Fellowship, Inc., P.O. Box 39800, Colorado Springs CO 80949 USA. Fax: +1 (719) 590 9801. Contact: Richard D. Jacquin, Manager. Various items sold via U.S. address—catalog available.

Canadian Office: 6981 Millcreek Drive, Unit 23, Mississauga ON, L5N 6B8 Canada.

U.K. Office: 131 Grattan Road, Bradford, West Yorkshire BD1 2HS, United Kingdom. Contact: Bill Rapley, Producer.

Australian Office: G.P.O. Box 691, Melbourne, VIC 3001, Australia.

LA VOZ DE LOS CARAS (when not off during drought), Casilla 628, Bahía de Caráquez, Manabi, Ecuador. Contact: Prof. Eduardo Rodríguez Coll, Director de Programación. $1 or return postage required. Replies occasionally and slowly to correspondence in Spanish.

LA VOZ DE SAQUISILI—RADIO LIBERTADOR (when not off during drought), Casilla 669, Saquisilí, Ecuador. Contact: Srta. Carmen Mena Corrales. Return postage required. Replies irregularly and slowly to correspondence in Spanish.

LA VOZ DEL NAPO, Misión Josefina, Tena, Napo, Ecuador. Contact: Ramiro Cubrero, Director. Free pennants and stickers. $1 or return postage required. Replies occasionally to correspondence in Spanish.

LA VOZ DEL UPANO, Vicariato Apostólico de Méndez, Misión Salesiana, 10 de Agosto s/n, Macas, Ecuador. Contact: Sor Luz Benigna Torres; Ramiro Cabrera; or Sor Dolores M. Palacios C., Directora. Free stickers, pennants and calendars. On one occasion, not necessarily to be repeated, sent tape of Ecuadorian folk music for $2. Otherwise, $1 required. Replies to correspondence in Spanish.

ONDAS QUEVEDENAS, 12ma. Calle 207, Quevedo, Ecuador. Contact: Sra. Maruja Jaramillo, Gerente; or Humberto Alvarado P., Director-Dueño. Return postage required. Replies irregularly to correspondence in Spanish.

RADIO BAHA'I, Instituto Baha'í, Calle Quito 7-12, Otavalo, Ecuador. Contact: Sra. Nooshin Burwell, Coordinadora. Return postage helpful. This station of the Baha'í faith replies irregularly.

RADIO CATOLICA, Apartado Postal 17-24-00006, Santo Domingo de los Colorados, Pichincha, Ecuador. Contact: Nancy Moncada, Secretaria RCSD; or Padre Cesareo Tiestos L., Sch.P, Director. Free pennants. Return postage or $1 helpful. Replies to correspondence in Spanish.

RADIO CATOLICA NACIONAL, Av. América 1830 y Mercadillo, Quito, Pichincha, Ecuador. Contact: Monseñor Antonio Arregui Y., Director-General; or Yolanda Gorzón Molina, Secretaria; or John Siguenza, Director Adjunto. Free stickers. Return postage required. Replies to correspondence in Spanish.

RADIO CENTRO (when not off during drought), Casilla 18-01-0574, Ambato, Tungurahua, Ecuador. Contact: (nontechnical) Luis A. Gamboa T., Director-Gerente; (technical) Sócrates Domínguez, Ingeniero. Free stickers and sometimes free newspaper. Return postage or $1 required. Replies occasionally to correspondence in Spanish.

RADIO CENTINELA DEL SUR, Casilla 196, Loja, Ecuador. Return postage of $1 helpful, as are cancelled non-Ecuadorian stamps. Replies occasionally to correspondence in Spanish.

RADIODIFUSORA CULTURAL, LA VOZ DEL NAPO—see "La Voz del Napo," above.

RADIODIFUSORA NACIONAL DEL ECUADOR, c/o DX Party Line, HCJB, Casilla 691, Quito, Pichincha, Ecuador. Contact: Gustavo Cevallos, Director; or Eduardo Rodríguez, Productor, "Cartas para los Ecuatorianos Ausentes." IRC or $1 required.

RADIO FEDERACION, Casilla 1422, Quito, Pichincha, Ecuador. Contact: Prof. Albino M. Utitiaj P., Director de Medios. Return postage or $1 required. Replies irregularly to correspondence in Spanish.

RADIO INTEROCEANICA, Santa Rosa de Quijos, Cantón El Chaco, Provincia de Napo, Ecuador. Contact: Byron Medina, Gerente; or Ing. Olaf Hegmuir. $1 or return postage required, and donations appreciated (station owned by Swedish Covenant Church). Replies slowly to correspondence in Spanish or Swedish.

RADIO JESUS DEL GRAN PODER, Casilla de Correo 133, Quito, Pichincha, Ecuador. Contact: Padre Jorge Enríquez. Free pennants and religious material. Return postage required. Replies irregularly to correspondence in Spanish.

RADIO LUZ Y VIDA, Casilla 222, Loja, Ecuador. Contact: Srta. Jolly Pardo. Replies irregularly to correspondence in Spanish.

RADIO NACIONAL ESPEJO (when not off during drought), Casilla 352, Quito, Pichincha, Ecuador. Contact: Marco Caceido, Gerente; or Mercedes B. de Caceido, Secretaria. Replies to correspondence in Spanish.

RADIO NACIONAL PROGRESO (when not off during drought), Sistema de Emisoras Progreso, Casilla V, Loja, Ecuador. Contact: José Guaman Guajala, Director del programa Círculo Dominical. Replies irregularly to correspondence in Spanish, particularly for feedback on "Círculo Dominical" program aired Sundays between 1100-1300. Free pennants.

RADIO PASTAZA (if shortwave transmitter repaired and relicensed), Casilla 728, El Puyo, Pastaza, Ecuador. Contact: Galo Amores, Gerente. Return postage or $1 required. Replies irregularly to correspondence in Spanish. As the station manager is also head of the local taxi drivers' union, printed matter, photos or discussion of this topic may help elicit a response.

RADIO POPULAR INDEPENDIENTE, Av. Loja 2408, Cuenca, Azuay, Ecuador. Contact: Sra. Manena de Villavicencio, Secretaria. Return postage or $1 required. Replies occasionally to correspondence in Spanish.

RADIO QUITO, "El Comercio," Casilla 57, Quito, Pichincha, Ecuador. Contact: Gonzalo Ruíz Alvarez, Gerente; or José Almeida, Subgerente. Pennants. Return postage required. Replies slowly, but regularly.

RADIO RIO TARQUI, Casilla 877, Cuenca, Azuay, Ecuador. Contact: Boris Cornejo. Replies irregularly to correspondence in Spanish.

EGYPT World Time +2 (UTC +3 midyear)
RADIO CAIRO

Nontechnical: P.O. Box 566, Cairo, Egypt. Contact: Sahar Khalil, Director of English Service. Free stickers, calendars and *External Services of Radio Cairo* book. Free individually tutored Arabic-language lessons with loaned textbooks from Arabic by Radio, Radio Cairo, P.O. Box 325, Cairo, Egypt. Arabic-language religious, cultural and language-learning audio and video tapes from the Egyptian Radio and Television Union sold via Sono Cairo Audio-Video, P.O. Box 2017, Cairo, Egypt; when ordering video tapes, inquire to ensure they function on the television standard (NTSC, PAL or SECAM) in your country. Replies regularly, but sometimes slowly.

Technical: P.O. Box 1186, Cairo, Egypt. Contact: Nivene W. Laurence, Engineer; or Hamdy Abdel Hallem, Director of Propagation; or Fathi El Bayoumi, Chief Engineer. Comments and suggestions on audio quality and level welcomed.

EL SALVADOR World Time –6
RADIO VENCEREMOS

Main Office: San Salvador, El Salvador. Contact: (nontechnical) Carlos Henríquez Gonsalves ("Camarada Santiago"), Director; (technical) "El Cieguito." $1 helpful.

North American Office: El Salvador Media Project, 335 West 38th Street, New York NY 10018 USA. Contact: Anita Ocampo. $1 required.

German Office: SRV Pres Bureau, Scharnhorstr. 6, 5000 Cologne 60, Germany. $1 or DM2.00 required.

ENGLAND—see "UNITED KINGDOM"

EQUATORIAL GUINEA World Time +1

RADIO AFRICA 2000, Embajada de España, Cooperación Española, Malabo, Isla Bioko, Equatorial Guinea. Contact: Concha Chamorro; or Teodora Silochi Thompson, Secretaría, who likes to correspond with people in other countries. Replies to correspondence in Spanish.

RADIO AFRICA

Transmission Office: Same details as "Radio Nacional Bata," below.

U.S. Office: Pierce International Communications, 10201 Torre Avenue, Suite 320, Cupertino CA 95014 USA. Fax: +1 (408) 252 6855. Contact: Carmen Jung or James Manero. $1 or return postage required.

RADIO EAST AFRICA—same details as "Radio Africa," above.

RADIO NACIONAL BATA, Apartado 749, Bata, Río Muni, Equatorial Guinea. Spanish preferred. Also, see U.S. Office under "Radio Africa," above.

RADIO NACIONAL MALABO, Apartado 195, Malabo, Isla Bioko, Equatorial Guinea. Contact: (nontechnical) Román Manuel Mane Abaga, Jefe de Programación; (technical) Hermenegildo Moliko Chele, Jefe Servicios Técnicos de Radio y Televisión. $1 or return postage required. Replies irregularly to correspondence in Spanish.

ESTONIA World Time +2 (+3 midyear)

ESTONIAN RADIO (Eesti Raadio)—same details as "Radio Estonia," below, except replace "External Service, The Estonian Broadcasting Company" with "Eesti Raadio."

RADIO ESTONIA, External Service, The Estonian Broadcasting Company, Gonsiori 21, EE-0100 Tallinn, Estonia. Fax: (via Russian circuit) +7 (0142) 43 44 57. Contact: Silja Orusalu, Editor, I.C.A. Department; Harry Tiido; or Elena Rogova. Free pennants. $1 required. Replies occasionally.

ETHIOPIA World Time +3

VOICE OF ETHIOPIA: P.O. Box 654 (External Service), or P.O. Box 1020 (Domestic Service)—both in Addis Ababa, Ethiopia. A very poor replier to correspondence in recent years, but with the new political structure this could change.

VOICE OF THE BROAD MASSES OF ERITREA (Dimisi Hafash), EPLF National Guidance, Information Department, Radio Branch, P.O. Box 872, Asmera, Eritrea, Ethiopia; EPLF National Guidance, Information Department, Radio Branch, P.O. Box 2571, Addis Ababa, Ethiopia; Eritrean Relief Committee, 475 Riverside Drive, Suite 907, New York NY 10015 USA; or EPLF National Guidance, Information Department, Radio Branch, Sahel Eritrea, P.O. Box 891, Port Sudan, Sudan; or EPLF Desk for Nordic Countries, Torsplan 3, 1 tr, S-113 64 Stockholm, Sweden. Fax (Stockholm) +46 (8) 322 337. Contact: (Eritrea) Ghebreab Ghebremedhin; (Ethiopia and Sudan) Mehreteab Tesfagiorgis. Return postage or $1 helpful. Free information on history of station, Ethiopian People's Liberation Front and Eritrea.

FINLAND World Time +2 (+3 midyear)
YLE/RADIO FINLAND

Main Office, Nontechnical: Radio and TV Centre, Box 10, SF-00241 Helsinki, Finland. Fax: +358 (0) 148 1169. Contact: Riitta Raukko, International Information; Juhani Niinistö, Head of External Broadcasting; or Kate Moore and Teri Schultz, "Air Mail." Free stickers, tourist and other magazines. *Finnish by Radio* textbook and *Nuntii Latini* Latin-language book apparently available for purchase.

Main Office, Technical: Broadcasting House, P.O. Box 95, SF-00251 Helsinki, Finland. Contact: Kari Ilmonen, Head of International Technical Affairs. Replies to correspondence, but doesn't provide verification data.

U.S. Office: P.O. Box 462, Windsor CT 06095 USA. 24-hour toll-free telephone for schedule: (toll-free, U.S. only) (800) 221-9539; (elsewhere in North America) (203) 688-5540.

FRANCE World Time +1 (+2 midyear)
RADIO FRANCE INTERNATIONALE (RFI)

Main Office: B.P. 9516, F-75016 Paris Cedex 16, France. Fax: +33 (1) 45 24 39 13 or +33 (1) 42 30 30 71. Three minutes of tape-delayed RFI news in English audible 24 hours by telephoning the Washington (USA) number of +1 (202) 944-6075. Fax: (general information and English programs) +33 (1) 45 24 39 13; (non-English programs) +33 (1) 42 30 44 81. Contact: (English programs) Simon Najovits, Chief, English Department; (other programs) Denis Louche, Directeur du développement et de la communication; André Larquié, Président; or J.P. Charbonnier, Producer, "Lettres des Auditeurs"; (technical) M. Raymond Pincon, Producer, "Le Courrier Technique." Free souvenir keychains, pins, pencils, T-shirts and stickers have been received by some—especially when visiting the headquarters at 116 avenue du Président Kennedy, in the chichi 16th Arrondissement. Can provide supplementary materials for "Dites-moi tout" French-language course; write to the attention of Mme. Chantal de Grandpre, "Dites-moi tout."

Transmission Office: (technical) Télédiffusion de France, 21-27 rue Barbès, F-92542 Montrouge, France. Fax: +33 (1) 49 65 19 11. Contact: Daniel Bochent, Chef du service ondes décamétriques; or, for the most significant matters only, Xavier Gouyou Beauchamps, Président. This office only for informing about transmitter-related problems (interference, modulation quality, etc.), especially by fax. Verifications not given out at this office; requests for verification should be sent to the main office, above.

New York News Bureau, Nontechnical: 1290 Avenue of the Americas, New York NY 10019. Fax: +1 (212) 541 4309. Contact: Bruno Albin, reporter.

San Francisco Office, Schedules: 2654 17th Avenue, San Francisco CA 94116 USA. Contact: George Poppin. This address only provides RFI schedules to listeners. All other correspondence should be sent directly to Paris.

FRENCH GUIANA World Time –3

SOCIETE NATIONALE DE RADIO TELEVISION FRANCAISE D'OUTRE-MER—RFO GUYANE, Cayenne, French Guiana. Free stickers. Replies occasionally and sometimes slowly; correspondence in French preferred, but English often okay.

FRENCH POLYNESIA World Time –10 Tahiti

SOCIETE NATIONALE DE RADIO TELEVISION FRANCAISE D'OUTRE-MER—RFO TAHITI, B.P. 125, Papeete, Tahiti, French Polynesia. Fax: +689 413 155. Contact: (technical or nontechnical) León Siquin, Services Techniques. Free stickers, tourist brochures and broadcast-coverage map. 3 IRCs, return postage, 5 francs or $1 helpful, but not mandatory. M. Siquin and his teenage sons Xavier and Philippe, all friendly and fluent in English, collect pins from radio/TV stations, memorabilia from the Chicago Bulls basketball team and other souvenirs of American pop culture; these make more appropriate enclosures than the usual postage-reimbursement items.

GABON World Time +1

ADVENTIST WORLD RADIO, THE VOICE OF HOPE (via Afrique Numéro Un), P.O. Box 1751, Abidjan 08, Côte d'Ivoire. Contact: Daniel Grisier, Director. Free religious printed matter. Also, see "USA."

AFRIQUE NUMERO UN, B.P. 1, Libreville, Gabon. Fax: +241 742 133. Contact: (nontechnical) Gaston Didace Singangoye; (technical) Mme. Marguerite Bayimbi, Le Directeur [sic] Technique.

Free calendars and bumper stickers. $1, 2 IRCs or return postage helpful. Replies very slowly.

GEORGIA World Time +4 (+5 midyear)
GEORGIAN RADIO, TV-Radio Tbilisi, ul. Rostava 68, Tbilisi 380 015, Republic of Georgia. Contact: (external service) Helena Apkhadze, Foreign Editor; (domestic service) Lia Uumlaelsa, Manager. Replies occasionally and slowly.

GERMANY World Time +1 (+2 midyear)
BAYERISCHER RUNDFUNK, Rundfunkplatz 1, W-8000 Munich, Germany. Fax: +49 (89) 590 001. Free stickers and 250-page program schedule book.
CANADIAN FORCES NETWORK RADIO—see "Canada."
DEUTSCHE WELLE, THE VOICE OF GERMANY
Main Office: Postfach 10 04 44, W-5000 Cologne 1, Germany. Fax: +49 (221) 389 3000; +49 (221) 389 4155; or (Public Relations) +49 (221) 389 2047. Contact: (nontechnical) Ernst Peterssen, Head of Audience Research and Listeners' Mail; (technical) Peter Senger, Head, Radio Frequency Department. Free stickers, key chains, pens, *Deutsche—Warum Nicht?* language-course book, *Germany—A European Country and its People* book, and the excellent *tune-in* magazine. Local Deutsche Welle Listeners' Clubs in selected countries.
Brussels Bureau: International Press Center, 1 Boulevard Charlemagne, B-1040 Brussels, Belgium.
Tokyo Bureau: C.P.O. Box 132, Tokyo 100-91, Japan.
RADIO IN THE AMERICAN SECTOR (RIAS), Kufsteinerstr. 69, W-1000 Berlin 62, Germany. Fax: +49 (30) 850 3390. Contact: Martina Klich. $1 or return postage required. Free stickers, postcards and *RIAS Yearbook*.
RADIO BREMEN, Bürgemeister-Spittaallee 45, W-2800 Bremen 33, Germany. Fax: +49 (421) 246 1010. Free stickers and shortwave guidebook.
SENDER FREIES BERLIN, Nordostdeutscher Rundfunk, Masurenallee 14, W-1000 Berlin 19, Germany. Fax: +49 (30) 301 5062. Free stickers and frequency publication.
SÜDDEUTSCHER RUNDFUNK, Postfach 106040, W-7000 Stuttgart 1, Germany. Fax: +49 (711) 288 2600. Free stickers.
SÜDWESTFUNK, Postfach 820, W-7570 Baden-Baden, Germany. Fax: +49 (7221) 922 010. Contact: (technical) Prof. Dr. Krank, Technical Director.

GHANA World Time exactly
RADIO GHANA, Ghana Broadcasting Corporation, P.O. Box 1633, Accra, Ghana. Contact: (nontechnical) Maud Blankson-Mills, Head, Audience Research; G.A. Sam; or Victor Markin, Producer, English Section. Mr. Markin is interested in reception reports as well as feedback on the program he produces, "Health Update"; (technical) E. Heneath, Propagation Department. IRC, return postage or $1 helpful.

GREECE World Time +2 (+3 midyear)
FONI TIS HELLADAS
Nontechnical: ERT A.E., ERA-E Program, Voice of Greece, Mesogion 432 Str., Aghia Paraskevi, GR-153 42 Athens, Greece. Fax: (specify "5th Program" on cover sheet) +301 (1) 655 0943 or +301 (1) 686 8305. Contact: Kosta Valetas, Director, Programs for Abroad; or Demetri Vafaas. Free tourist literature.
Technical: ERT 5th Program, Direction of Engineering, P.O. Box 60019, GR-153 10 Aghia Paraskevi Attikis, Athens, Greece. Fax: +301 (1) 639 0652.
RADIOPHONIKOS STATHMOS MAKEDONIAS
Nontechnical: Odos Yeorghikis Scholis 129, GR-546 39 Thessaloniki, Greece.
Technical: ERT S.A., Subdirection of Technical Support, P.O. Box 11312, GR-541 10 Thessaloniki, Greece. Contact: Tassos A. Glias, Telecommunications Engineer.
VOICE OF AMERICA—Does not welcome direct correspondence at its Greek facilities in Kaválla and Rhodes. See "USA" for acceptable VOA address and related information.

GUAM World Time +10
ADVENTIST WORLD RADIO, THE VOICE OF HOPE—KSDA
Main Office, General Programs: P.O. Box 7500, Agat, Guam 96928 USA. Fax: +671 565 2983. Contact: Mrs. Andrea Steele, Editor; or Chris Cary, Producer, "Listener Mailbox"; (technical) Engineer. Free pennants, stickers, postcards, quarterly *AWR-Asiawaves* newsletter and religious printed matter. Also, see "USA."
"DX-Asiawaves" Program: ARDXC, Box 227, Box Hill 3128 VIC, Australia.
Hong Kong Office: AWR Asia, P.O. Box 310, Hong Kong.

TRANS WORLD RADIO—KTWR
Main Office: P.O. Box CC, Agana, Guam 96910 USA. Also, see "USA." Free stickers.
Australian Office: G.P.O. Box 602D, Melbourne 3001, Australia.
Singapore Bureau, Nontechnical: 134-136 Braddel Road, Singapore.

GUATEMALA World Time –6 (–5 midyear)
ADVENTIST WORLD RADIO, THE VOICE OF HOPE—UNION RADIO, Radiodifusora Adventista, Apartado de Correo 35-C, Guatemala, Guatemala. Contact: Lizbeth de Morán; Nora Lissette Vásquez R.; or M.J. Castaneda, Sec. Free tourist and religious literature, and Guatemalan stamps. Return postage, 3 IRCs or $1 helpful. Correspondence in Spanish preferred. Also, see "USA."
RADIO CULTURAL—TGNA, Apartado de Correo 601, Guatemala, Guatemala. Contact: Wayne Berger, Chief Engineer. Free religious printed matter. Return postage or $1 appreciated.
LA VOZ DE ATITLAN—TGDS, Santiago Atitlán, Guatemala. Contact: Juan Ajtzip Alvorado, Director. Free 25th anniversary (1992) pennants, while they last. Return postage required. Replies to correspondence in Spanish.
LA VOZ DE NAHUALA, Nahualá, Sololá, Guatemala. Contact: (technical) Juan Fidel Lepe Juárez, Técnico Auxiliar. Return postage required. Correspondence in Spanish preferred.
RADIO BUENAS NUEVAS, 13020 San Sebastián, Huehuetenango, Guatemala. Contact: Israel Rodas Mérida, Gerente. $1 or return postage helpful. Free religious and station information in Spanish. Replies to correspondence in Spanish.
RADIO CHORTIS, Centro Social, 20004 Jocotán, Chiquimula, Guatemala. Contact: Padre Juan María Boxus, Director. $1 or return postage required. Replies irregularly to correspondence in Spanish.
RADIO K'EKCHI—TGVC, K'ekchi Baptist Association, 16015 Fray Bartolomé de las Casas, Alta Verapaz, Guatemala. Contact: Gilberto Sun Xicol, Gerente; or Carlos Díaz Araújo, Director; or David Daniel, Media Consultant. Free paper pennant. $1 or return postage required. Replies to correspondence in Spanish.
RADIO MAM, Acu'Mam, Cabricán, Quetzaltenango, Guatemala. Contact: José Benito Escalante Ramos, Director. $1 or return postage required. Replies irregularly to correspondence in Spanish.
RADIO MAYA DE BARILLAS—TGBA, 13026 Barillas, Huehuetenango, Guatemala. Contact: Juan Baltazar, Gerente. Free pennants and pins. $1 or return postage required. Replies occasionally to correspondence in Spanish.
RADIO TEZULUTLAN, Apartado de Correo 19, 16901 Cobán, Guatemala. Contact: Alberto P.A. Macz, Director; or Hno. Antonio Jacobs, Director Ejecutivo. $1 or return postage required. Replies to correspondence in Spanish.

GUINEA World Time exactly
RADIODIFFUSION-TELEVISION GUINEENNE, B.P. 391, Conakry, Guinea. Contact: (nontechnical) Yaoussou Diaby, Journaliste Sportif; (technical) Mbaye Gagne, Chef de Studio; Alpha Sylla, Directeur, Sofoniya I Centre de Transmission; or Direction des Services Techniques. Return postage or $1 required. Replies very irregularly to correspondence in French.

GUYANA World Time –3
VOICE OF GUYANA, Guyana Broadcasting Corporation, P.O. Box 10760, Georgetown, Guyana. Contact: (technical) Roy Marshall, Senior Technician; or S. Goodman, Chief Engineer. $1 or IRC helpful. Sending a spare sticker from another station helps assure a reply.

HAITI World Time –5 (–4 midyear)
RADIO 4VEH
Main Office: B.P. 1, Cap-Haïtien, Haiti. Contact: (nontechnical) Gaudin Charles, Director; (technical) Mardy Picazo, Development Engineer, or Jean Van Dervort, Verification Secretary. Return postage, IRC or $1 required.
U.S. Office, Nontechnical: Oriental Missionary Society International, Inc., Box A, Greenwood IN 46142 USA. Contact: Robert Erny, Vice President of Field Operations.

HOLLAND (THE NETHERLANDS) World Time +1 (+2 midyear)
RADIO NEDERLAND WERELDOMROEP
Main Office: Postbus 222, NL-1200 JG Hilversum, Holland. Fax: +31 (35) 72 43 52 or +31 (35) 181 12. Contact (RNW): (nontechnical) J.C. Veltcamp Helbach, Director of Public Relations; or Jonathan Marks, Head, English Department; (technical) ing. Hans Bakhuizen, Frequency Bureau; or Martine Jolly. Free

RNW stickers, newsletter and booklets. Free "Happy Station" (Sunday program) calendars and stickers.

Canadian Office: P.O. Box 247, West Hill ON, M1E 4R5 Canada.

HONDURAS   World Time –6

LA VOZ DE LA MOSQUITIA, Puerto Lempira, Región Mosquitia, Honduras. Contact: Sra. Wilkinson.

LA VOZ EVANGELICA—HRVC

Main Office: Apartado Postal 3252, Tegucigalpa, D.C., Honduras. Contact: Orfa Esther Durón Mendoza, Secretaria. Free stickers and pennants. 3 IRCs or $1 required.

U.S. Office: Conservative Baptist Home Mission Society, Box 828, Wheaton IL 60187 USA. Fax: +1 (708) 653 4936. Contact: Jill Smith.

RADIO LUZ Y VIDA—HRPC, Apartado 303, San Pedro Sula, Honduras. Fax: +504 57 0394. Contact: C. Paul Easley, Director; or, to have your letter read over the air, "English Friendship Program." Return postage or $1 appreciated.

SANI RADIO, Apartado 113, La Ceiba, Honduras. Contact: Jacinto Molina G., Director; or Mario S. Corzo. Return postage or $1 required.

HONG KONG   World Time +8

BBC WORLD SERVICE—HONG KONG RELAY, Flat B, 24 Beacon Hill Road, Kowloon Tong, Kowloon, Hong Kong. Contact: (technical) Phillip Sandell, Resident Engineer. Nontechnical correspondence should be sent to the BBC World Service in London (see).

RADIO TELEVISION HONG KONG, C.P.O. Box 70200, Kowloon, Hong Kong. Fax: +852 (3) 380 279. Contact: (technical) W.K. Li, for Director of Broadcasting. May broadcast weather reports every even two years, usually around late April, on 3940 kHz for the South China Yacht Sea Race.

HUNGARY   World Time +1 (+2 midyear)

RADIO BUDAPEST, Bródy Sándor utca 5-7, H-1800 Budapest, Hungary. Fax: +86 (1) 801 3175. Contact: Charles Coutts, Len Scott, Ilona Kiss or Anton Réger. Free pennants, stickers and T-shirts, while they last.

ICELAND   World Time exactly

RIKISUTVARPID, Efstaleiti 1, 150 Reykjavík, Iceland. Fax: +354 (1) 693 010. Free stickers.

INDIA   World Time +5:30

ALL INDIA RADIO—BOMBAY, P.O. Box 13034, Bombay-400 020, India. Contact: Sarla Mirchandani, Programme Executive, for Station Director. Return postage helpful.

ALL INDIA RADIO—DELHI, Jamnagar House, Shahjahan Road, New Delhi-110 011, Delhi, India. $1 helpful.

ALL INDIA RADIO—EXTERNAL SERVICES DIVISION, Parliament Street, P.O. Box 500, New Delhi-110 001, Delhi, India. Contact: (nontechnical) Director of External Services; or Audience Relations Officer; (technical) S.A.S. Abidi, Assistant Director Engineering (F.A.). Free monthly *India Calling* magazine and stickers. Except for stations listed below, correspondence to domestic stations is more likely to be responded to if it is sent via the External Services Division; request that your letter be forwarded to the appropriate domestic station.

ALL INDIA RADIO—GORAKHPUR, Post Bag 26, Town Hall, Gorakhpur-273 001, Uttar Pradesh, India. Contact: (technical) V.K. Sharma, Superintendent Engineer.

ALL INDIA RADIO—GUWAHATI, P.O. Box 28, Chandmari, Guwahati-781 003, Assam, India. N.C. Jain, Assistant Station Engineer.

ALL INDIA RADIO—JAMMU—Technical: See "All India Radio—External Services Division," above. Contact: S.A.S. Abidi, Assistant Director Engineering (F.A.).

ALL INDIA RADIO—KOHIMA, Kohima-797 001, Nagaland, India. Contact: (technical) G.C. Tyagi, Superintending Engineer. Return postage, $1 or IRC helpful.

ALL INDIA RADIO—KURSEONG, Mehta Club Building, Kurseong-734 203, Darjeeling, West Bengal, India. Contact: Madan Lei, Assistant Director of Engineering.

ALL INDIA RADIO—PORT BLAIR, Dilanipur, Port Blair-744 102, South Andaman, Andaman & Nicobar Islands, Union Territory, India. Contact: (technical) Yuvraj Bajaj, Station Engineer. Registering letter appears to be useful.

INDONESIA   World Time +7 Western: Waktu Indonesia Bagian Barat (Jawa, Sumatera); +8 Central: Waktu Indonesia Bagian Tengal (Bali, Kalimantan, Sulawesi, Nusa Tenggara); +9 Eastern: Waktu Indonesia Bagian Timur (Irian Jaya, Maluku)

Note: Except where otherwise indicated, Indonesian stations, especially those of the Radio Republik Indonesia (RRI) network,

will reply to at least some correspondence in English. However, correspondence in Indonesian is more likely to ensure a reply.

ELKIRA RADIO, Kotak Pos No. 199, JAT, Jakarta 13001, Indonesia. This "amatir" station is unlicensed.

RADIO ARISTA, Jalan Timbangan No. 25., Rt. 005/RW01, Kelurahan Kembangan, Jakarta Barat 10610, Indonesia. This "amatir" station is unlicensed.

RADIO GEMA PESONA MUDA, c/o Wisma Pondok Gede, Jakarta Selatan, Indonesia. This "amatir" station is unlicensed.

RADIO PEMERINTAH DAERAH TK II—RPD BENGKALIS, Kotak Pos 0123, Bengkalis, Riau, Indonesia. Contact: Meiriqal, SMHK. Return postage required. Replies occasionally to correspondence in Indonesian.

RADIO PEMERINTAH DAERAH KABUPATEN TK II—RPDK BERAU, Jalan SA Maulana, Tanjungredeb, Kalimantan Timur, Indonesia. Contact: Kus Syariman.

RADIO PEMERINTAH DAERAH KABUPATEN TK II—RPDK BIMA, Jalan Achmad Yani No. 1, Bima (Raba), Sumbawa, Nusa Tenggara Barat, Indonesia. Free stickers. Return postage required. Replies irregularly to correspondence in Indonesian.

RADIO PEMERINTAH DAERAH KABUPATEN TK II—RPDK BUOL-TOLITOLI, Jalan Mohamed Ismail Bantilan No. 4, Tolitoli 94511, Sulawesi, Indonesia. Contact: Said Rasjid, Kepala Studio. Return postage required. Replies extremely irregularly to correspondence in Indonesian.

RADIO PEMERINTAH DAERAH KABUPATEN TK II—RPDK ENDE, Jalan Panglima Sudirman, Ende, Flores, Nusa Tenggara Timor, Indonesia. Contact: (technical) Thomas Keropong, YC9LHD. Return postage required.

RADIO PEMERINTAH DAERAH KABUPATEN TK II—RPDK BIMA, Jalan A. Yani Atau, Sukarno Hatta No. 2, Nusa Tenggara Barat (NTB), Kode Pos 84116, Indonesia. Contact: (technical) Mr. Chairil, Technisi RKPD Dati. II. Free stickers. Replies slowly and irregularly to correspondence in Indonesian; return postage required.

RADIO PEMERINTAH DAERAH KABUPATEN TK II—RPDK LUWU, Kantor Deppen Kabupaten Luwu, Jalan Diponegoro 5, Palopo, Sulawesi Selatan, Indonesia. Contact: Arman Mailangkay.

RADIO PEMERINTAH DAERAH KABUPATEN TK II—RPDK MANGGARAI, Ruteng, Flores, Nusa Tenggara Timur, Indonesia. Contact: Simon Saleh, B.A. Return postage required.

RADIO PEMERINTAH DAERAH KABUPATEN TK II—RPDK SAMBAS, Jalan M. Sushawary, Sambas, Kalimantan Barat, Indonesia.

RADIO PEMERINTAH DAERAH KABUPATEN TK II—RPDK TAPANULI SELATAN, Kotak Pos No. 9, Padang-Sidempuan, Sumatera Utara, Indonesia. Return postage required.

RADIO PEMERINTAH KABUPATEN DAERAH TK II—RPKD BELITUNG, Jalan A. Yani, Tanjungpandan 33412, Belitung, Indonesia. Contact: Drs H. Fadjri Nashir B., Kepala Stasiun. Free tourist brochure. 1 IRC helpful.

RADIO PRIMADONA, Jalan Bintaro Permai Raya No. 5, Jakarta Selatan, Indonesia. This "amatir" station is unlicensed.

RADIO REPUBLIK INDONESIA—RRI BANDA ACEH, Kotak Pos No. 112, Banda Aceh, Aceh, Indonesia. Contact: S.H. Rosa Kim. Return postage helpful.

RADIO REPUBLIK INDONESIA—RRI BANDUNG, Stasiun Regional 1, Kotak Pos No. 1055, Bandung 40010, Jawa Barat, Indonesia. Contact: Kepala, Beni Koesbani. Return postage or IRC helpful.

RADIO REPUBLIK INDONESIA—RRI BANJARMASIN, Stasiun Nusantara 111, Kotak Pos No. 117, Banjarmasin 70234, Kalimantan Selatan, Indonesia. Contact: Jul Chaidir, Stasiun Kepala. Return postage or IRCs helpful.

RADIO REPUBLIK INDONESIA—RRI BENGKULU, Stasiun Regional 1, Kotak Pos No. 13 Kawat, Kotamadya Bengkulu, Indonesia. Contact: Drs H. Hamdan Syahbeni, Head of RRI Bengkulu. Free picture postcards, decals and tourist literature. Return postage or 2 IRCs helpful.

RADIO REPUBLIK INDONESIA—RRI BUKITTINGGI, Stasiun Regional 1 Bukittinggi, Jalan Prof. Muhammad Yamin No. 199, Kuning, Bukittinggi, Sumatera Barat, Indonesia. Contact: Mr. Effendi, Sekretaris. Return postage helpful.

RADIO REPUBLIK INDONESIA—RRI CIREBON, Jalan Brigjen. Dharsono/By Pass, Cirebon, Jawa Barat, Indonesia. Contact: Ahmad Sugiarto, Kepala Ceksi Siaran. Return postage helpful.

RADIO REPUBLIK INDONESIA—RRI DILI, Jalan Kaikoli, Dili, Timor, Indonesia. Contact: Paul J. Amalo, Kepala Stasiun. Return postage or $1 helpful.

RADIO REPUBLIK INDONESIA—RRI FAK FAK, Jalan Kapten P. Tendean, Kotak Pos No. 54, Fak-Fak 98601, Irian Jaya, Indonesia. Contact: A. Rachman Syukur, Kepala Stasiun; or Aloys Ngotra. Return postage required. Replies occasionally.

RADIO REPUBLIK INDONESIA—RRI GORONTALO, Jalan Jendral Sudirman, Gorontalo, Sulawesi Utara, Indonesia. Contact: Saleh S. Thalib. Return postage helpful. Replies occasionally, preferably to correspondence in Indonesian.

RADIO REPUBLIK INDONESIA—RRI JAKARTA, Stasiun Nasional Jakarta, Kotak Pos No. 356, Jakarta, Jawa Barat, Indonesia. Contact: Drs R. Baskara, Stasiun Kepala. Return postage helpful. Replies irregularly.

RADIO REPUBLIK INDONESIA—RRI JAMBI, Jalan Jendral A. Yani No. 5, Telanaipura, Jambi 36122, Propinsi Jambi, Indonesia. Contact: Marlis Ramali, Manager. Return postage helpful.

RADIO REPUBLIK INDONESIA—RRI JAYAPURA, Jalan Tasangkapura No. 23, Jayapura, Irian Jaya, Indonesia. Contact: Harry Liborang, Direktorat Radio. Return postage helpful.

RADIO REPUBLIK INDONESIA—RRI KENDARI, Kotak Pos No. 7, Kendari, Sulawesi Tenggara, Indonesia. Contact: H. Sjahbuddin BA. Return postage required. Replies slowly to correspondence in Indonesian.

RADIO REPUBLIK INDONESIA—RRI KUPANG, Jalan Tompello No. 8, Kupang, Timor, Indonesia. Contact: Daud Yusaf Maro, Kepala Seksi Siaran; or Alfonsus Soetarno, BA. Return postage helpful.

RADIO REPUBLIK INDONESIA—RRI MADIUN, Jalan Mayjend Panjaitan No. 10, Madiun, Jawa Timur, Indonesia. Contact: Imam Soeprapto, Kepala Seksi Siaran. Return postage helpful.

RADIO REPUBLIK INDONESIA—RRI MALANG, Kotak Pos No. 78, Malang 65112, Jawa Timur, Indonesia. Contact: Ml. Mawahib, Kepala Seksi Siaran; or Dra Hartati Soekemi, Mengetahui.

RADIO REPUBLIK INDONESIA—RRI MANADO, Jalan TNI 6 Radio No. 1, No. 12, Manado 95124 Sulawesi Utara, Indonesia. Contact: Costher H. Gultony. Return postage required. Replies occasionally to correspondence in Indonesian.

RADIO REPUBLIK INDONESIA—RRI MANOKWARI, Regional II, Jalan Merdeka No. 68, Manokwari, Irian Jaya, Indonesia. Contact: Nurdin Mokoginta, P.J. Kepala Stasiun. Return postage helpful.

RADIO REPUBLIK INDONESIA—RRI MATARAM, Stasiun Regional I Mataram, Jalan Langko No. 83, Mataram 83114, Nusa Tenggara Barat, Indonesia. Contact: Mr. Soekino, Kepala, Direktorat Radio. Return postage required. With sufficient return postage or small token gift, sometimes sends tourist information and Batik print. Replies to correspondence in Indonesian.

RADIO REPUBLIK INDONESIA—RRI MEDAN, Jalan Letkol Martinus Lubis No. 5, Medan 20232, Sumatera, Indonesia. Contact: Kepala Stasiun, Ujamalul Abidin Ass. Free stickers. Return postage required. Replies to correspondence in Indonesian.

RADIO REPUBLIK INDONESIA—RRI MERAUKE, Statiun Regional 1, Kotak Pos No. 11, Merauke, Irian Jaya, Indonesia. Contact: (nontechnical) Achmad Ruskaya B.A. Kepala Stasiun, or John Manuputty, Kepala Subseksi Pemancar; (technical) Daf'an Kubangun, Kepala Seksi Tehnik. Return postage helpful.

RADIO REPUBLIK INDONESIA—RRI NABIRE, Kotak Pos No. 11, Nabire 98801, Irian Jaya, Indonesia. Contact: Ismail Saya, Head of Broadcasting Section. Occasional free picture postcards. Return postage or IRCs helpful.

RADIO REPUBLIK INDONESIA—RRI PADANG, Kotak Pos No. 77, Padang, Sumatera Barat, Indonesia. Contact: Syair Siak, Kepala Stasiun. Return postage helpful.

RADIO REPUBLIK INDONESIA—RRI PALANGKARAYA, Jalan Husni Thamrin No. 1, Palangkaraya, Kalimantan Tengah, Indonesia. Contact: Drs Amiruddin; Gumer Kamis; or Soedarsono, Kepala Stasiun. Return postage helpful. Correspondence in Indonesian preferred.

RADIO REPUBLIK INDONESIA—RRI PALEMBANG, Jalan Radio No. 2, Km. 4, Palembang, Sumatera Selatan, Indonesia. Contact: Drs Abdul Roshim; or Iskandar Suradilaga, B.A. Kepala Stasiun. Return postage helpful.

RADIO REPUBLIK INDONESIA—RRI PALU, Jalan R.A. Kartini, Palu, Sulawesi (Tg. Karang), Indonesia. Contact: Akson Boole; or M. Hasjim, Head of Programming. Return postage required. Replies slowly to correspondence in Indonesian.

RADIO REPUBLIK INDONESIA—RRI PEKANBARU, Jalan Jend Sudirman No. 440, Tromolpos 51, Pekanbaru, Riau, Indonesia. Contact: Zainal Abbas. Return postage helpful.

RADIO REPUBLIK INDONESIA—RRI PONTIANAK, Kotak Pos No. 6, Pontianak, Kalimantan Barat, Indonesia. Contact: Supomo Hadisaputro, Kepala Seksi Siaran; or Muchlis Marzuki B.A. Return postage helpful.

RADIO REPUBLIK INDONESIA—RRI PURWOKERTO, Stasiun Regional II, Kotak Pos No. 5, Purwokerto 53116, Jawa Tengah, Indonesia. Contact: Yon Maryono, Stasiun Kepala. Return postage helpful.

RADIO REPUBLIK INDONESIA—RRI SEMARANG, Kotak Pos No. 74, Semarang Jateng, Jawa Tengah, Indonesia. Contact: Djarwanto, SH. Return postage helpful.

RADIO REPUBLIK INDONESIA—RRI SAMARINDA, Kotak Pos No. 45, Samarinda, Kalimantan Timur 75001, Indonesia. Contact: Siti Thomah, Kepala Seksi Siaran. Return postage helpful.

RADIO REPUBLIK INDONESIA—RRI SERUI, Jalan Pattimura, Serui, Irian Jaya, Indonesia. Contact: Agus Raunsai, Kepala Stasiun. Replies occasionally to correspondence in Indonesian. IRC or return postage helpful.

RADIO REPUBLIK INDONESIA—RRI SIBOLGA, Jalan Ade Irma Suryani, Nasution No. 5, Sibolga, Sumatera Utara, Indonesia. Return postage required. Replies occasionally to correspondence in Indonesian.

RADIO REPUBLIK INDONESIA—RRI SORONG, Jalan Jendral Achmad Yani, Klademak II, Sorong, Irian Jaya, Indonesia. Contact: Mrs. Tien Widarsanto. Return postage helpful.

RADIO REPUBLIK INDONESIA—RRI SUMENEP, Jalan Urip Sumoharjo No. 26, Sumenep, Madura, Jawa Timur, Indonesia. Return postage helpful.

RADIO REPUBLIK INDONESIA—RRI SURABAYA, Stasiun Regional 1, Kotak Pos No. 239, Surabaya 60271, Jawa Timur, Indonesia. Fax: +62 (31) 42351. Contact: Zainal Abbas, Kepala Stasiun; Drs Agus Widjaja, Kepala Subseksi Programa Siaran; or Ny Koen Tarjadi. Return postage or IRCs helpful.

RADIO REPUBLIK INDONESIA—RRI SURAKARTA, Kotak Pos No. 40, Surakarta 57133, Jawa Tengah, Indonesia. Contact: Ton Martono, Head of Broadcasting. Return postage helpful.

RADIO REPUBLIK INDONESIA—RRI TANJUNGKARANG, Kotak Pos No. 24, Pahoman, Bandar Lampung, Indonesia. Contact: Hi Hanafie Umar. Return postage helpful. Replies in Indonesian to correspondence in English or Indonesian.

RADIO REPUBLIK INDONESIA—RRI TANJUNG PINANG, Jalan St. Abdel Rachman No. 1, Tanjung Pinang, Riau, Indonesia. Return postage helpful.

RADIO REPUBLIK INDONESIA—RRI TERNATE, Jalan Kedaton, Ternate (Ternate), Maluku, Indonesia. Contact: (technical) Rusdy Bachmid, Head of Engineering. Return postage helpful.

RADIO REPUBLIK INDONESIA—RRI UJUNG PANDANG, RRI Nusantara IV, Kotak Pos No. 103, Ujung Pandang, Sulawesi Selatan, Indonesia. Contact: Drs H. Harmyn Husein, Kepala Stasiun; or H. Kamaruddin Alkaf. Return postage, $1 or IRCs helpful. Replies irregularly and sometimes slowly.

RADIO REPUBLIK INDONESIA—RRI WAMENA, RRI Regional II, Kotak Pos No. 10, Wamena, Irian Jaya 99501, Indonesia. Contact: Yoswa Kumurawak, Penjab Subseksi Pemancar. Return postage helpful.

RADIO REPUBLIK INDONESIA—RRI YOGYAKARTA, Jalan Amat Jazuli 4, Tromol Pos 18, Yogyakarta, Jawa Tengah, Indonesia. IRC, return postage or $1 helpful. Replies occasionally to correspondence in Indonesian or English.

RADIO RIBUBUNG SUBANG, Komplex AURI, Subang, Jawa Barat, Indonesia.

RADIO SUARA KASIH AGUNG, Jalan Trikora No. 30, Dok V, Jayapura, Irian Jaya, Indonesia. Contact: Mrs. Setiyono Hadi. This "amatir" station is unlicensed.

RADIO SUARA KENCANA BROADCASTING SYSTEM, Jalan Yos Sudarso Timur, Gombong, Jawa Tengah, Indonesia. This "amatir" station is unlicensed.

RADIO SUARA MITRA, Jalan Haji Lut, Gang Kresem No. 15, Cigudak, Tangerang, Jawa Barat, Indonesia. This "amatir" station is unlicensed.

VOICE OF INDONESIA, Kotak Pos No. 157, Jakarta, Indonesia.

IRAN World Time +3:30 (+4:30 midyear)

VOICE OF THE ISLAMIC REPUBLIC OF IRAN, IRIB External Services, P.O. Box 3333, Tehran, Iran. Fax: +98 (21) 291 095. Contact: Hamid Yasamin, Public Affairs; or Hameed Barimani, Producer, "Listeners Special." Free seven-volume set of books on Islam, magazines, calendars, book markers, tourist literature and postcards.

IRAQ World Time +3 (+4 midyear)

RADIO IRAQ INTERNATIONAL (Idha'at al-Iraq al-Duwaliyah)

Main Office: P.O. Box 8145, Baghdad, Iraq. Contact: Muzaffar Abdal-Al, Director.

India Address: P.O. Box 3044, New Delhi 110003, India.

RADIO OF IRAQ, CALL OF THE KINFOLK (Idha'at al-Iraq, Nida' al-Ahl)—same details as "Radio Iraq International," above.

IRELAND   World Time Exactly (+1 midyear)

Community Radio, Radio Dublin International, P.O. Box 2077, 4 St. Vincent Street West, Dublin 8, Ireland. Contact: (nontechnical) Jane Cooke; (technical) Eamon Cooke, Director; or Joe Doyle, Producer, "DX Show." 12-page station history $2 postpaid. Cottage and 11.5 acres of rural land for $140,000. Free stickers and calendar. $1 required. Replies irregularly. This station is as yet unlicensed.

ISRAEL   World Time +2 (+3 midyear)

KOL ISRAEL, ISRAEL RADIO, THE VOICE OF ISRAEL

Main Office: P.O. Box 1082, 91 010 Jerusalem, Israel. Fax: +972 (2) 253 282. Contact: (nontechnical) Sara Manobla, Head of English Service; Yishai Eldar, Senior Editor, English Service; Rosalyn Gelcer, Editor, "Calling All Listeners"; or Moshe Sela, Director of Western Broadcasts; (technical) Ben Dalfen, Editor, "DX Corner." Free quarterly *Kol Israel* magazine, *Israel and the Arab States* booklet of maps, station booklets and stickers, "Ulpan of the Air" Hebrew-language lesson scripts, pennants and other small souvenirs, and various political, religious, tourist, immigration and language publications.

Transmission Office: (technical) Engineering & Planning Division, TV & Radio Broadcasting Section, Bezeq, P.O. Box 29555, 61 290 Tel Aviv, Israel. Fax: +972 (3) 510 0696 or +972 (3) 515 1232. Contact: Marian Kaminski, Head of AM Radio Broadcasting. This address only for pointing out transmitter-related problems (interference, modulation quality, network mixups, etc.), especially by fax. Verifications not given out at this office; requests for verification should be sent to Ben Dalfen at the main office, above.

San Francisco Office, Schedules: 2654 17th Avenue, San Francisco CA 94116 USA. Contact: George Poppin. This address only provides Kol Israel schedules to listeners. All other correspondence should be sent to the main office in Jerusalem.

ITALY   World Time +1 (+2 midyear)

ADVENTIST WORLD RADIO, THE VOICE OF HOPE, C.P. 383, I-47100 Forlì, Italy. Fax: +39 (543) 768 198. Contact: Paolo Benini, Director; Lina Lega, Secretary; Roger Graves, Producer, "Update"; or Stefano Losio, Producer, "DX News" in Italian. Free stickers, pennants and religious printed matter. 2 IRCs, $1 or return postage required. Also, see "USA."

EUROPEAN CHRISTIAN RADIO, Postfach 500, A-2345 Brunn, Austria. Fax: +39 (2) 29 51 74 63. Contact: John Adams, Director. $1 or 2 IRCs required.

ITALIAN RADIO RELAY SERVICE, IRRS-Shortwave, Nexus IBA, P.O. Box 10980, I-20110 Milan MI, Italy. Fax: +39 (2) 706 38151. Contact: (nontechnical) Alfredo E. Cotroneo, President & Producer of "Hello There"; (technical) Anna S. Boschetti, Verification Manager. Free station literature. 2 IRCs or $1 helpful.

RADIO EUROPE, via Davanzati 8, I-20158 Milan MI, Italy. Fax: +39 (2) 670 4900. Contact: Dario Monferini, Director.

RTV ITALIANA/RAI

External Service, Nontechnical: Radio Roma, Casella Postale 320, Centro Corrispondenza, I-00100 Rome, Italy. Contact: Giorgio Brovelli, Director, Direzione Servizi Giornalistici e Programmi per L'Estero (DPA). Free magazines. Can provide supplementary materials for Italian-language course aired over RAI's Italian-language (sic) external service.

External Service, Technical: RAI, Radiotelevisione Italiana, Supporto Tecnico, Progettazione Alta Frequenza, Onda Corta (PAOC), Viale Mazzini 14, I-00195 Rome, Italy. Contact: Maria Luisa I.

Radio Uno Domestic Service, Caltanissetta Relay: Radio Uno, Via Cerda 19, I-90139 Palermo, Sicily, Italy. $1 required.

RAI New York Office, Nontechnical: RAI/Radio Division, 21st floor, 1350 Avenue of the Americas, New York NY 10019 USA. Fax: +1 (212) 765 1956. RAI caps, aprons and tote bags for sale at Boutique RAI, c/o the New York address.

VOICE OF EUROPE, P.O. Box 26, I-33170 Pordenone, Italy. IRC or $1 helpful. Fax: +39 (6) 488 0196.

JAPAN   World Time +9

NHK OSAKA, 3-43 Bamba-cho, Higashi-ku, Osaka 540, Japan. Fax: +81 (6) 941 0612. Contact: (technical) Technical Bureau. IRC or $1 helpful.

NHK SAPPORO, 1 Ohdori Nisha, Chuo-ku, Sapporo 060, Japan. Fax: +81 (11) 232 5951.

NHK TOKYO/SHOBU-KUKI, JOAK, 2-2-1 Jinnan, Shibuya-ku,

Tokyo 150-01, Japan. Fax: +81 (480) 85 1508. Contact: Hisao Kakinuma, Transmission Technical Center. IRC or $1 helpful. Replies occasionally. Letters should be sent via registered mail.

RADIO JAPAN/NHK

Main Office: 2-2-1 Jinnan, Shibuya-ku, Tokyo 150-01, Japan. Fax: +81 (33) 481 1350 or +81 (33) 481 1413 Contact: (nontechnical) Ian McFarland, Producer; (technical) Hiromi Ito, Producer, "Media Roundup"; or Kinitashi Hishikawa, Verification Secretary. Free station newsletter, stickers, compasses, rulers, note holders, "Let's Learn/Practice Japanese" language-course materials and—if you really rate—large, beautiful wall calendars. Quizzes with prizes over "Media Roundup."

Washington Bureau, Nontechnical: NHK, 2030 M Street NW, Washington DC 20554 USA. Fax: +1 (202) 828 4571.

Singapore Bureau, nontechnical: NHK, 1 Scotts Road #15-06, Singapore. Fax: +65 737 5251.

RADIO TAMPA/NSB (until around 1997, when scheduled to cease)

Main Office: 9-15 Akasaka 1-chome, Minato-ku, Tokyo 107, Japan. Fax: +81 (3) 3583 9062. Contact: M. Teshima. Free stickers and Japanese stamps. $1 or IRC helpful.

New York News Bureau, Nontechnical: 1325 Avenue of the Americas #2403, New York NY 10019 USA. Fax: +1 (212) 261 6449. Contact: Noboru Fukui, reporter.

JORDAN   World Time +2 (+3 midyear)

RADIO JORDAN, Radio of the Hashemite Kingdom of Jordan, P.O. Box 909, Amman, Jordan. Fax: +962 (6) 788 115. Contact: Jawad Zada, Director of English Service; Qasral Mushatta; or R. Alkhas, Director. Replies irregularly and slowly, but does not verify reception reports.

KAZAKHSTAN   World Time +6 (+7 midyear)

KAZAKH RADIO—see "Radio Alma-Ata" for details.

RADIO ALMA-ATA WORLD SERVICE, Zheltoksan Str. 175A, Alma-Ata 480013, Kazakhstan. Contact: Mr. Gulnar.

KENYA   World Time +3

KENYA BROADCASTING CORPORATION, P.O. Box 30456, Nairobi, Kenya. Fax: +254 (2) 220 675. Contact: (nontechnical) Managing Director; (technical) Augustine Kenyanjior Gochui, or Manager Technical Services. IRC required. Replies irregularly.

KIRIBATI   World Time +13

RADIO KIRIBATI, P.O. Box 78, Bairiki, Tarawa Atoll, Republic of Kiribati. Fax: +686 21096. Contact: Atiota Bauro, Program Organiser; Otiri Laboia; Tomasi Kei Tauru, Manager; T. Fakaofo, Technical Staff; or Moia Tetoa, Producer, "Kaoti Ami Iango," a program devoted to listeners views; (technical) Trakaogo, Engineer-in-Charge. Cassettes of local songs available for purchase. $1 or return postage required for a reply. (IRCs not accepted.)

KOREA (DPR)   World Time +9

RADIO PYONGYANG, Pyongyang Broadcasting Station, Ministry of Posts and Telecommunications, External Service, Pyongyang, Democratic People's Republic of Korea (not "North Korea"). Free Great Leader book, book for German speakers to learn Korean, sundry other publications, pennants, calendars, artistic prints and pins. Do not include dutiable items in your envelope. Replies are irregular, as mail from countries not having diplomatic relations with North Korea is sent via circuitous routes and apparently does not always arrive. Indeed, some listeners who have not obtained replies have received, instead, what appears to be bogus ("black propaganda") correspondence from alleged North Korean dissidents at Radio Pyongyang. This correspondence, mailed from Japan, appears to originate from South Korean sources, which tends to verify that at least some correspondence to Radio Pyongyang is not getting to North Korea. Nevertheless, this station appears to be replying increasingly often to mail sent from the United States and other countries with which North Korea has no diplomatic relations.

KOREA (REPUBLIC)   World Time +9

RADIO KOREA

Main Office: Overseas Service, Korean Broadcasting System, 18 Yoido-dong, Youngdungpo-ku, Seoul 150-790, Republic of Korea. Contact: Che Hong-Pyo, Director of English Section. Free stickers, calendars, *Let's Learn Korean* book and a wide variety of other small souvenirs.

Washington bureau, Nontechnical: National Press Building, Suite 1076, 529 14th Street NW, Washington DC 20045 USA. Fax: +1 (202) 662 7347.

KUWAIT   World Time +3 (+4 midyear)

RADIO KUWAIT, P.O. Box 397, 13004 Safat, Kuwait. Fax: +965 241 5946. Contact: Manager, External Service.

KYRGYZSTAN   World Time +5

KYRGYZ RADIO, Kyrgyz TV and Radio Center, Prospekt Moloday Gvardil 63, Bishkek 720 300, Kyrgyzstan. Contact: A.I. Vitshkov or E.M. Abdukarimov.

LAOS   World Time +7

LAO NATIONAL RADIO, LUANG PRABANG ("Sathani Withayu Kachaisiang Khueng Luang Prabang"), Luang Prabang, Laos; or P.O. Box 310, Vientiane, Laos. Return postage required (IRCs not accepted). Replies slowly and very rarely. Best bet is to write in Laotian or French directly to Luang Prabang, where the transmitter is located.

LAO NATIONAL RADIO, VIENTIANE, B.P. 310, Vientiane, Laos.

LATVIA   World Time +2 (+3 midyear)

LATVIAN RADIO, Latvijas Radio, Zakusalas Krastmala 3, Riga 226 018, Latvia. Replies to nontechnical correspondence in Latvian. Does not issue verification replies.

RADIO RIGA INTERNATIONAL, P.O. Box 266, Riga 226 018, Latvia. Contact: R. Visnere, Mailbag Editor, English Department. Free stickers and pennants. Unlike Latvian Radio, preceding, Radio Riga International verifies regularly.

LEBANON   World Time +2 (+3 midyear)

HCJB (via King/Wings of Hope)—see "Ecuador" for details.

KING OF HOPE, WINGS OF HOPE, P.O. Box 77, 10292 Metulla, Israel; or P.O. Box 3379, Limassol, Cyprus. Contact: Isaac Gronberg, Director; Mark Christian; or Pete Reilly. Free stickers. Also, see "KVOH—High Adventure Radio, USA."

VOICE OF LEBANON (when operating), P.O. Box 165271, Al-Ashrafiyah, Beirut, Lebanon. $1 required. Replies extremely irregularly to correspondence in Arabic.

LESOTHO   World Time +2

Radio Lesotho, P.O. Box 552, Maseru 100, Lesotho. Fax: +266 310 003.

LIBERIA   World Time exactly

ELBC, Liberian Broadcasting System, P.O. Box 594, 1000 Monrovia, Liberia. Contact: Noah A. Bordolo, Sr., Deputy Director General, Broadcasting.

ELWA

Main Office: (when operating), P.O. Box 192, 1000 Monrovia, Liberia. Contact: (technical) Dwight, EL2W. Also, see "Northern Mariana Islands."

U.S. Office: SIM, P.O. Box 7900, Charlotte NC 28241 USA. Donations to replace destroyed transmitters welcomed.

VOICE OF AMERICA—Facility in Monrovia has been destroyed by civil unrest and is not expected to be reactivated for some time.

LIBYA   World Time +1

RADIO JAMAHIRIYA

Main Office: P.O. Box 4677 (or P.O. Box 4396), Tripoli, Libya. Contact: R. Cachia. Arabic preferred.

Malta Office: European Branch Office, P.O. Box 17, Hamrun, Malta. This office replies more consistently than does the main office.

LITHUANIA   World Time +2 (+3 midyear)

Warning—Mail theft: Lithuanian officials warn that money or other items of any value whatsoever are routinely being stolen within the Lithuanian postal system. Authorities are taking steps to alleviate this problem, but for the time being nothing of value should be entrusted to the postal system. To help ensure your letter from abroad won't disappear—these are often stolen on the assumption they might contain money—either correspond by postcard or fax, or don't seal your envelope tightly.

Warning—Fake "Charities": An alleged charity, "Informacinis Klubas" (IK) of Vilnius, has been soliciting funds from American and European world band listeners and others for "sick children." Informed sources report that this solicitation is a scam, and other such scams may be in the works. Should you wish to aid needy Lithuanian children, there are at least two legitimate charities very much in need of your assistance: Lithuanian Catholic Religious Aid, 351 Highland Boulevard, Brooklyn NY 11207 USA, fax +1 (718) 827 6696 (newsletter available to contributors); or SOS Children, P.O. Box 497, South Boston MA 02127 USA.

LITHUANIAN RADIO—see "Radio Vilnius" for details.

RADIOCENTRAS, Spauda, P.O. Box 1792, LT-2019 Vilnius, Lithuania. Fax: +7 (0122) 22 01 72. Contact: Rimantas Pleikys, Manager. 2 IRCs or return postage required, but 1 IRC or $1 has been shown to suffice.

RADIO VILNIUS, Lietuvos Radijas, Konarskio 49, LT-2674 Vilnius, Lithuania. Fax: +7 (0122) 66 05 26. Contact: Rasa Lukaite, "Letterbox"; Edvinas Butkus, Editor-in-Chief; or Ilonia Rukiene, Head of English Department. Free stickers, pennants, Lithuanian

stamps and other souvenirs. Radio Vilnius' Listeners' Club may be reached by writing Mary Sabatini, 24 Sherman Terrace #4, Madison WI 53704 USA.

LUXEMBOURG   World Time +1 (+2 midyear)

RADIO LUXEMBOURG

Main Office: 45 Boulevard Pierre Frieden, L-2850 Kirchberg, Luxembourg. Fax: +352 421 422 756. Contact: M. Vaas, Chief, English Service. Free T-shirts and a wide variety of different stickers, plus a set of photo cards depicting their English-speaking announcers.

London Bureau, Nontechnical: 38 Hertford Street, London W1Y 8BA, United Kingdom.

Paris Bureau, Nontechnical: 22 rue Bayard, F-75008 Paris, France. Fax: +33 (1) 40 70 42 72 or +33 (1) 40 70 44 11.

MADAGASCAR   World Time +3

RADIO MADAGASIKARA, B.P. 1202, Antananarivo, Madagascar. Contact: Mlle. Rakotoniaina Soa Herimanitia, Secrétaire de Direction, a young lady who collects stamps. $1 required, and enclosing used stamps from various countries may help. Replies very rarely and slowly, preferably to friendly philatelist gentlemen who correspond in French.

RADIO NEDERLAND WERELDOMREOP—MADAGASCAR RELAY, B.P. 404, Antananarivo, Madagascar. Contact: (technical) J.A. Ratobimiarana, Chief Engineer. Nontechnical correspondence should be sent to Radio Nederland Wereldomreop in Holland (see).

MALAWI   World Time +2

MALAWI BROADCASTING CORPORATION, P.O. Box 30133, Chichiri, Blantyre 3, Malawi. Fax: +265 671 353. Contact: Henry R. Chirwa, Head of Production; or T.J. Sineta. Return postage or $1 helpful.

MALAYSIA   World Time +8

RADIO MALAYSIA, KAJANG, RTM, Angkasapuri, Bukit Putra, 50614 Kuala Lumpur, Peninsular Malaysia, Malaysia. Contact (Radio 4): Santokh Sing Gill, Controller, Radio 4. Return postage required.

RADIO MALAYSIA, KOTA KINABALU, RTM, 88614 Kota Kinabalu, Sabah, Malaysia. Contact: Benedict Janil, Director of Broadcasting; or Hasbullah Latiff. Return postage required.

RADIO MALAYSIA, SARAWAK (KUCHING), RTM, Broadcasting House, Jalan Satok, Kuching, Sarawak, Malaysia. Return postage helpful.

RADIO MALAYSIA, SARAWAK (MIRI), RTM, Miri, Sarawak, Malaysia. $1 or return postage helpful.

RADIO MALAYSIA, SARAWAK (SIBU), RTM, Jabatan Penyiaran, Bangunan Penyiaran, 96009 Sibu, Sarawak, Malaysia. Contact: Clement Stia, Divisional Controller, Broadcasting Department. $1 or return postage required. Replies irregularly and slowly.

VOICE OF MALAYSIA, Suara Malaysia, P.O. Box 11272-KL, 50740 Kuala Lumpur, Malaysia. Fax: +60 (3) 230 4735. Contact: (technical) Lin Chew, Director of Engineering. 2 IRCs or return postage helpful. Replies slowly and irregularly.

MALI   World Time exactly

RADIODIFFUSION TELEVISION MALIENNE, B.P. 171, Bamako, Mali. $1 or IRC helpful. Replies slowly and irregularly to correspondence in French.

MALTA   World Time +1 (+2 midyear)

VOICE OF THE MEDITERRANEAN, P.O. Box 143, Valletta, Malta. Fax: +356 241 501. Contact: Richard Vella Laurenti, Managing Director. IRC helpful. Sometimes replies slowly. Station is a joint venture of the Libyan and Maltese governments.

MAURITANIA   World Time exactly

OFFICE DE RADIODIFFUSION-TELEVISION DE MAURITANIE, B.P. 200, Nouakchott, Mauritania. Contact: Lemrabott Boukhary. Return postage or $1 required. Rarely replies.

MEXICO   World Time −6 Central, including México; −7 Mountain; −8 (−7 midyear) Pacific

LA HORA EXACTA—XEQK, IMER, Margaritas 18, Col. Florida, México, D.F. 01030, Mexico. Contact: Gerardo Romero.

LA VOZ DE VERACRUZ—XEFT, Apartado Postal 21, 91700-4H. Veracruz, Ver., Mexico. Contact: C.P. Miguel Rodríguez Sáez, Sub-Director; or Lic. Juan de Dios Rodríguez Díaz, Director-Gerente. Likely to reply to correspondence in Spanish. Free tourist guide to Vera Cruz. Return postage, IRC or $1 probably helpful.

RADIO EDUCACION—XEPPM, Angel Urraza 662, México, D.F. 03100, Mexico. Contact: (technical) Ing. Gustavo Carreño López, Subdirector, Dpto. Técnico; or Lic. Luis Ernesto Pi Orozco.

Replies slowly to correspondence in Spanish. Free station photo. Return postage or $1 required.

RADIO HUAYACOCOTLA—XEJN, Apartado Postal No. 13, 92600 Huayacocotla, Veracruz, Mexico. Return postage or $1 helpful. Replies irregularly to correspondence in Spanish.

RADIO MIL—XEOI, NRM, Insurgentes Sur 1870, Col. Florida, México, D.F. 01030, Mexico. Contact: Guillermo Salas Vargas, Presidente; or Zoila Quintanar Flores. Free stickers. $1 or return postage required.

RADIO UNIVERSIDAD/UNAM—XEUDS, Apartado Postal No. 1817, Hermosillo, Sonora 83000, Mexico. Contact: A. Merino M., Director. Free tourist literature. $1 or return postage required. Replies irregularly to correspondence in Spanish.

RADIO XEQQ, LA VOZ DE LA AMERICA LATINA, Sistema Radiópolis, Ayuntamiento 52, México D.F. 06070, Mexico; or Ejército Nacional No. 579 (6to piso), 11520 México, D.F., Mexico. Contact: (nontechnical) Sra. Martha Aguilar Sandoval; (technical) Ing. Miguel Angel Barrientos, Director Técnico de Plantas Transmisoras. Free pennants. $1, IRC or return postage required. Replies fairly regularly to correspondence in Spanish.

RADIO XEUJ, Apartado Postal No. 62, Linares, Nuevo León, Mexico. Contact: Marielo Becerra Gonzales. Replies very irregularly to correspondence in Spanish.

RADIO XEUW, Ocampo 119, 91700 Veracruz, Mexico. Contact: Ing. Baltazar Pazos de la Torre, Director General. Free pennants. Return postage required. Replies occasionally to correspondence in Spanish.

TUS PANTERAS—XEQM, Apartado Postal No. 217, 97000 Mérida, Yucatán, Mexico. Contact: Arturo Iglesias Villalobos. Replies irregularly to correspondence in Spanish.

MOLDOVA World Time +2 (+3 midyear)
Note: A Radio Moldova International Service on world band—in English, French, Spanish and possibly other languages—is being considered.

MONACO World Time +1 (+2 midyear)
RADIO MONTE CARLO
Main Office: B.P. 128, Monte Carlo, Monaco. Fax: +33 (93) 159 448. Contact: Bernard Poizat, Service Diffusion; or Caroline Wilson, Director of Communication. Free stickers.
Paris Office: 12 rue Magellan, F-75008 Paris, France. Fax: +33 (14) 500 9245.
TRANS WORLD RADIO
Station: B.P. 349, MC-98007 Monte Carlo, Monaco. Fax: +33 (93) 301 470. Contact: Jeanne Olson. Free paper pennant. IRC or $1 helpful. Also, see "USA."
European Office: P.O. Box 2020, NL-1200 CA Hilversum, Holland.

MONGOLIA World Time +8
RADIO ULAANBAATAR, English Department, External Services. C.P.O. Box 365, Ulaanbaatar, Mongolia. Contact: (nontechnical) Mr. Bayasa, Mail Editor; (technical) Ganhuu, Chief of Technical Department. Free pennants, newspapers and Mongolian stamps.

MOROCCO World Time exactly
RADIO MEDI UN
Main Office: B.P. 2055, Tangier, Morocco. 2 IRCs helpful. Free stickers. Correspondence in French preferred.
Paris Bureau, Nontechnical: 78 avenue Raymond Poincaré, F-75016 Paris, France. Correspondence in French preferred.
RTV MAROCAINE, 1 rue el-Brihi, Rabat, Morocco. +212 (7) 76 20 10. Contact: Mohammed Jamal Eddine Tanane, Public Affairs; or N. Read.
VOICE OF AMERICA—Does not welcome direct correspondence at its Moroccan facilities. See "USA" for acceptable VOA address and related information. Ten 500 kW transmitters, currently being installed at a second site in Morocco—Tangier is the initial site—are expected to be on the air sometime in the future.

MOZAMBIQUE World Time +2
RADIO MOCAMBIQUE, C.P. 2000, Maputo, Mozambique. Contact: Manuel Tomé, Diretor-Geral. Return postage, $1 or 2 IRCs required. Replies to correspondence in Portuguese.

MYANMAR (BURMA) World Time +6:30
RADIO MYANMAR
Station: GPO Box 1432, Yangon, Myanmar. Currently does not reply directly to correspondence, but this could change as political events evolve. See following.
Washington Embassy: Embassy of the Union of Myanmar, 2300 S Street NW, Washington DC 20008 USA. Fax: +1 (202) 332 9046. Contact: Daw Kyi Kyi Sein, Third Secretary. This address currently replies on behalf of Radio Myanmar.

NAMIBIA World Time +2
RADIO NAMIBIA/NBC, P.O. Box 321, Windhoek 9000, Namibia. Contact: P. Schachtschneider, Manager, Transmitter Maintenance. Free stickers.

NEPAL World Time +5:45
RADIO NEPAL, P.O. Box 634, Singha Durbar, Kathmandu, Nepal. Contact: (technical) Ram S. Karki, Divisional Engineer.

NETHERLANDS ANTILLES World Time –4
TRANS WORLD RADIO
Main Office: Bonaire, Netherlands Antilles. Also, see "USA." Fax: +599 (7) 8808. Contact: (nontechnical) McDaniel Phillips, Program Manager; (technical) Charles K. Roswell, Producer, "Bonaire Wavelengths," and Frequency Coordinator; Dave Butler, Chief Engineer; or Sally Rork, Verification Manager. Free calendars, pennants, religious material and hurricane tracking charts. Also, see "USA."
Canadian Office: P.O. Box 310, London ON, N6A 4W1 Canada. Fax: +1 (519) 672 6512. Contact: Keith Johnson, Eastern Canadian Representative.

NEW ZEALAND World Time +13 (+12 midyear)
RADIO NEW ZEALAND INTERNATIONAL, Broadcast House, P.O. Box 2092, Wellington, New Zealand. Fax: +64 (4) 474 1433. Contact: (nontechnical) Rudi Hill, Manager; (nontechnical or technical) Tony King, Producer, "Mailbox"; (technical) Adrian Sainsbury, Frequency Manager. Free flyer about station, paper pennants, Maori Tiki good-luck charms, map of New Zealand and tourist literature. English/Maori T-shirts for US$20; an interesting variety of CD recordings, including Pacific island music, also at $20 each (cassettes $15); plus books and other merchandise (VISA/MC). Free "Radio Reply" catalog of available RNZ program cassettes. Occasionally gives two-week tours of New Zealand for foreign listeners for $3,000 or so, including international air travel. 3 IRCs required.
PRINT DISABLED RADIO—ZLXA, P.O. Box 360, Levin 5500, New Zealand. Fax: +64 (6) 368 0151. Contact: Allen J. Little, Station Director; Ron Harper; Ash Bell; or Jim Meecham ZLZ BHF, Producer, "CQ Pacific, Radio about Radio." Free brochure. $1, return postage or 3 IRCs appreciated.

NICARAGUA World Time –6
RADIO MISKUT, Correo Central (Bragman's Bluff), Puerto Cabezas, Nicaragua. Contact: Evaristo Mercado Pérez, Director. $1 helpful. Replies slowly and irregularly to correspondence in Spanish.
RADIO NICARAGUA (when operating), Apartado Postal No. 3170, Managua, Nicaragua. Contact: Frank Arana, Gerente.
RADIO RICA, Apartado Postal No. 38, Sucursal 14 de Septiembre, Managua, Nicaragua. Contact: Digna Bendaña B., Directora. Free black T-shirts. $1 required. Correspondence in Spanish preferred.

NIGER World Time +1
LA VOIX DU SAHEL, O.R.T.N., B.P. 361, Niamey, Niger. Fax: +227 72 35 48. Contact: Yacouba Alwali; (nontechnical) Oumar Tiello, Directeur; or Mounkaïla Inazadan, Producer, "Inter Jeunes Variétés"; (technical) Afo Sourou Victor. $1 helpful. Correspondence in French preferred. Correspondence by males with this station may result in requests for certain unusual types of magazines.

NIGERIA World Time +1
Warning—Confidence Artists: Correspondence with Nigerian stations may result in requests from skilled confidence artists for money, free electronic or other products, publications or immigration sponsorship.
RADIO NIGERIA—ENUGU, P.M.B. 1051, Enugu (Anambra), Nigeria. Contact: L. Nnamuchi. 2 IRCs, return postage or $1 required. Replies slowly.
RADIO NIGERIA—KADUNA, P.O. Box 250, Kaduna (Kaduna), Nigeria. Contact: Yusuf Garba. $1 or return postage required. Replies slowly.
RADIO NIGERIA—LAGOS, P.M.B. 12504, Ikoyi, Lagos, Nigeria. Contact: Babatunde Olalekan Raji, Monitoring Unit. 2 IRCs or return postage helpful. Replies slowly and irregularly.
VOICE OF NIGERIA, P.M.B. 4003 Falomo, Ikoyi, Lagos, Nigeria. Contact: (nontechnical) Alhaji Lawal Saulawa, Director of Programming; (technical) J.O. Kroni, Engineering Services. 2 IRCs or return postage helpful.

NORTHERN MARIANA ISLANDS World Time +10
CHRISTIAN SCIENCE MONITOR WORLD SERVICE—KHBI, P.O. Box 1387, Saipan, MP 96950 USA; or write to Boston address (see "USA"). Fax: +670 234 6515. Contact: Doming Villar, Station Manager; or M. Khoury. Free stickers. Return postage appreciated if writing to Saipan; no return postage when writing to Boston.

ELWA—see "KFBS Saipan," below, and "ELWA, Liberia" for details.

KFBS SAIPAN
Main Office: P.O. Box 209, Saipan, Mariana Islands CM 96950 USA. Fax: +670 (322) 3060. Contact: Robert Springer or Ana I. Kapilec. Replies sometimes take months.
California Office: Far East Broadcasting Company, Inc., Box 1, 15700 Imperial Highway, La Mirada CA 90637 USA. Fax: +1 (213) 943 0160. Contact: Jim Bowman.

NORWAY World Time +1 (+2 midyear)
RADIO NORWAY INTERNATIONAL
Main Office: Utgitt av Utenlandssendingen/NRK N-0340 Oslo, Norway. Norwegian-language 24-hour telephone tape recording for schedule information +47 (2) 45-80-08 (Americas, Europe, Africa), +47 (2) 45-80-09 (elsewhere). Fax: +47 (2) 45 71 34 or +47 (2) 60 57 19. Contact: (nontechnical) Sverre Fredheim, Head of External Broadcasting; or Grundel Krauss Dahl, Producer, "Listeners Corner." (technical) Olav Grimdalen, Frequency Manager. Free stickers and flags.
Singapore Bureau, Nontechnical: NRK, 325 River Valley Road #01-04, Singapore.

OMAN World Time +4
BBC WORLD SERVICE—EASTERN RELAY STATION, P.O. Box 3716, Ruwi Post Office, Muscat, Oman. Contact: (technical) David P. Bones, Senior Transmitter Engineer; or Dave Plater, Senior Transmitter Engineer. Nontechnical correspondence should be sent to the BBC World Service in London (see).
RADIO OMAN, P.O. Box 600, Muscat, Oman. Fax: +968 602 831. Contact: Rashid Haroon or A. Al-Sawafi. Replies irregularly, and responses can take anywhere from two weeks to two years; but $1, return postage or 3 IRCs helpful.

PAKISTAN World Time +5
AZAD KASHMIR RADIO, Muzaffarabad, Azad Kashmir, Pakistan. Contact: (technical) M. Sajjad Ali Siddiqui, Director of Engineering. Registered mail helpful. Rarely replies to correspondence.
PAKISTAN BROADCASTING CORPORATION—same address, fax and contact as "Radio Pakistan," below.
RADIO PAKISTAN, External Services, Pakistan Broadcasting Corporation Headquarters, Broadcasting House, Constitution Avenue, Islamabad, Pakistan. Fax: +92 (51) 811 861. Contact: (technical) Anwer Inayet Khan, Senior Broadcast Engineer, Room No. 324, Frequency Management Cell. Free stickers, pennants and "Pakistan Calling" magazine.

PALAU World Time +9
VOICE OF HOPE/KHBN, High Adventure Radio—Asia, P.O. Box 66, Koror, Palau PW 96940, Pacific Islands (USA). Fax: +1 (680) 488 2163. Contact: (technical) Paul Swartzendruber, Chief Engineer. Solicits funds for transmitter roof repair. Also, see "USA."

PAPUA NEW GUINEA World Time +10
NATIONAL BROADCASTING COMMISSION OF PAPUA NEW GUINEA (when operating), P.O. Box 1359, Boroko, Papua New Guinea. Contact: Bob Kabewa, Sr. Technical Officer; G. Nakau; or Downey Fova, Producer, "What Do You Think?" 2 IRCs or return postage helpful. Replies irregularly.
RADIO CENTRAL, P.O. Box 1359, Boroko, NCD, Papua New Guinea. Contact: Steven Gamini, Station Manager; or Amos Langit, Technician. $1, 2 IRCs or return postage helpful. Replies irregularly.
RADIO EASTERN HIGHLANDS, P.O. Box 311, Goroka, EHP, Papua New Guinea. Fax: +675 722 841. Contact: Paia Ottawa, Technician; or Kiri Nige. $1 or return postage required. Replies irregularly.
RADIO EAST NEW BRITAIN, P.O. Box 393, Rabaul, ENBP, Papua New Guinea. Fax: +675 923 254. Contact: Esekia Mael, Station Manager. Return postage required. Replies slowly.
RADIO EAST SEPIK, P.O. Box 65, Wewak, E.S.P., Papua New Guinea. Fax: +675 862 405. Contact: Luke Umbo, Station Manager.
RADIO ENGA, P.O. Box 196, Wabag, Enga, Papua New Guinea. Fax: +675 571 069. Contact: (technical) Felix Tumun K., Station Technician; (nontechnical or technical) John Lyein Kur, Station Manager.
RADIO GULF (when operating), P.O. Box 36, Kerema, Gulf, Papua New Guinea. Contact: Mailau Daniel, Station Manager.
RADIO MADANG, P.O. Box 2138, Yomba, Madang, Papua New Guinea. Fax: +675 822 360. Contact: Simon Tiori, Station Manager; D. Boaging, Assistant Manager; or Lloyd Guvil, Technician.
RADIO MANUS, P.O. Box 505, Lorengau, Manus, Papua New

Guinea. Fax: +675 409 079. Contact: Eluan Sereman, Station Manager; or John P. Mandrakamu.
RADIO MILNE BAY, P.O. Box 111, Alotau, Milne Bay, Papua New Guinea. Contact: Trevor Webumo, Assistant Manager; Simon Muraga, Station Manager; or Philip Maik, Technician.
RADIO MOROBE, P.O. Box 1262, Lae, Morobe, Papua New Guinea. Fax: 426 423. Contact: Aloysius R. Nase, Station Manager.
RADIO NEW IRELAND, P.O. Box 140, Kavieng, New Ireland, Papua New Guinea. Fax: +675 941 489. Contact: Otto A. Malatana, Station Manager. Return postage or $1 helpful.
RADIO NORTHERN, Voice of Oro, P.O. Box 137, Popondetta, Oro, Papua New Guinea. Contact: Misael Pendaia, Station Manager. Return postage required.
RADIO NORTH SOLOMONS, P.O. Box 393, Rabaul, ENBP, Papua New Guinea. Fax: +675 923 254. Contact: Aloysius L. Rumina, Station Manager. Replies irregularly.
RADIO SANDAUN, P.O. Box 37, Vanimo, West Sepik, Papua New Guinea. Fax: +675 871 305. Contact: Gabriel Deckwalen, Station Manager. $1 helpful.
RADIO SIMBU, P.O. Box 228, Kundiawa, Chimbu, Papua New Guinea. Fax: +675 751 012. Contact: (technical) Gabriel Paiao, Station Technician. Free two-Kina banknote.
RADIO SOUTHERN HIGHLANDS, P.O. Box 104, Mendi, SHP, Papua New Guinea. Fax: +675 591 017. Contact: Andrew Meles, Station Manager; or Jay Emma, Producer, "Listeners Choice - Thinking of You." $1 or return postage helpful; or donate a wall poster of a rock band, singer or American landscape.
RADIO WESTERN, P.O. Box 23, Daru, Western Province, Papua New Guinea. Contact: Robin Wainetti, Station Manager; or Samson Tobel, Technician. $1 or return postage required. Replies irregularly.
RADIO WESTERN HIGHLANDS, P.O. Box 311, Mount Hagen, WHP, Papua New Guinea. Fax: 521 279. Contact: Esau Okole, Technician. $1 or return postage helpful. Replies occasionally.
RADIO WEST NEW BRITAIN, P.O. Box 412, Kimbe, WNBP, Papua New Guinea. Fax: +675 935 600. Contact: Valuka Lowa, Provincial Station Manager. Return postage required.

PARAGUAY World Time –3 (–4 midyear)
RADIO NACIONAL, Calle Montevideo, esq. Estrella, Asunción, Paraguay. Contact: (technical) Carlos Montaner, Director Técnico; or Filemón G. Argüello M. $1 or return postage required. Replies, sometimes slowly, to correspondence in Spanish. Registration of correspondence helps assure receipt.

PERU World Time –5 year-round at nearly all locations; the few exceptions are –4 (–5 midyear)
Note: Internal unrest and terrorism, widespread cholera, a tottering economy, and devestating earthquakes all combine to make Peruvian broadcasting a perilous affair. Obtaining replies from Peruvian stations thus calls for creativity, tact, patience—and the proper use of Spanish, not form letters and the like. There are nearly 150 world band stations operating from Perú on any given day. While virtually all of these may be reached simply by using as the address the station's city, as given in the Blue Pages, the following are the only stations known to be replying—even if only occasionally—to correspondence from abroad.
LA VOZ DE LA SELVA—see "Radio La Voz de la Selva."
LA VOZ DE CELENDÍN—see "Radio La Voz de Celendín."
ONDAS DEL SUR ORIENTE, Correo Central, Quillabamba, Cusco, Perú. Contact: Roberto Challco Cusi Huallpa, Periodista. $1 helpful. Replies occasionally to corresondence in Spanish.
RADIO ALTURA, Apartado de Correo 140, Cerro de Pasco, Pasco, Perú. Contact: Oswaldo de la Cruz Vásquez, Gerente-General. Replies to correspondence in Spanish.
RADIO ANCASH, Apartado de Correo 210, Huáraz. Perú. Contact: Armando Moreno Romero, Gerente-General; or Dante Moreno Neglia, Gerente de Programación. $1 required. Replies to correspondence in Spanish.
RADIO ANDAHUAYLAS S.A., Jr. Ayacucho No. 248, Andahuaylas, Apurímac, Perú. Contact: Sr. Daniel Andréu C., Gerente. $1 required. Replies irregularly to correspondence in Spanish.
RADIO ATALAYA, Teniente Mejía y Calle Iquitos s/n, Atalaya, Depto. de Ucayali, Perú. Replies irregularly to correspondence in Spanish.
RADIO ATLANTIDA, Apartado de Correo 786, Iquitos, Loreto, Perú. Contact: Pablo Rojas Bardales. $1 or return postage required. Replies irregularly to correspondence in Spanish.
RADIO CORA, Compañía Radiofónica Lima, S.A., Paseo de la República 144, Centro Cívico, Oficina 5, Lima 1, Perú. Fax: +51

(14) 336 134. Contact: (nontechnical and technical) Juan Ramírez Lazo, Director Gerente; (technical) Ing. Roger Antonio Roldán Mercedes. Free stickers. 2 IRCs or $1 required. Replies slowly to most correspondence in Spanish.

RADIO CUZCO, Apartado de Correo 251, Cusco, Perú. Contact: Raúl Siu Almonte, Gerente. $1 or return postage required. Replies irregularly to correspondence in Spanish. Note that station name continues to be spelled with a "z", even though the city and provincial names have been changed by decree to be spelled with an "s".

RADIO DEL PACIFICO, Apartado de Correo 4236, Lima 1, Perú. Contact: J. Petronio Allauca, Secretario, Depto. de Relaciones Públicas. $1 or return postage required. Replies occasionally to correspondence in Spanish.

RADIO ESTACION "C," Apartado de Correo 210, Moyobamba, San Martín, Perú.

RADIO FRECUENCIA LIDER, Jirón Jorge Chávez 416, Bambamarca, Cajamarca, Perú. Contact: Valentín Peralta Díaz, Gerente; or Oscar Lino Peralta, Director. Replies occasionally to correspondence in Spanish.

RADIO GRAN PAJATEN, Jirón Amazonas 710, Celendín, Cajamarca, Perú. Replies occasionally to correspondence in Spanish.

RADIO HORIZONTE, Jirón Próceres 745, Urb. Latina José L. Ortiz, Chiclayo, Lambayeque, Perú. Contact: Juan Vargas Rojas, Director de Publicidad. Replies occasionally to correspondence in Spanish. $1 required.

RADIO IMAGEN, Apartado de Correo 42, Tarapoto, San Martín, Perú. Contact: Jaime Ríos Tapullima, Gerente General. Replies irregularly to correspondence in Spanish. $1 or return postage helpful.

RADIO INCA, Jirón Manco Cápac 275, Baños del Inca, Cajamarca, Perú. Contact: Enrique Ocas Sánchez, Director. May reply to correspondence in Spanish.

RADIO JUANJI, Juanjuí, San Martín, Perú. Replies occasionally to correspondence in Spanish.

RADIO LA HORA, Apartado de Correo 540, Cusco, Perú. Contact: Edmundo Montesinos G., Gerente-General. Return postage required. Replies occasionally to correspondence in Spanish.

RADIO LA MERCED, (Tongol) Congoyo, San Miguel, Cajamarca, Perú. $1 or return postage required. Replies irregularly to correspondence in Spanish.

RADIO LA VOZ DE CELENDIN, Jirón Unión 311 y Plaza de Armas, Celendín, Cajamarca, Perú. Contact: Fernando Vásquez Castro, Gerente. Replies occasionally to correspondence in Spanish.

RADIO LA VOZ DE LA SELVA, Apartado de Correo 207, Iquitos, Loreto, Perú. Contact: Mery Blas Rojas. May reply occasionally to correspondence in Spanish.

RADIO LIRCAY, Jirón Libertad 188, Lircay, Angaraes, Huancavelica, Peru. Contact: Gilmar Zorilla Llancari, DJ. Replies rarely to correspondence in Spanish.

RADIO LOS ANDES, Pasaje Damián Nicolau s/n, Huamachuco, Perú. Contact: Pasio J. Cárdenas Valverde, Gerente-General. Return postage required. Replies occasionally to correspondence in Spanish.

RADIO NORANDINA, Jirón Pardo 579, Celendín, Cajamarca, Perú. Contact: (nontechnical) Misael Alcántara Guevara, Gerente y Jefe de Contabilidad; (technical) Roberto Alcántara G. Free calendar. $1 required. Donations (registered mail best) sought for the Committee for Good Health for Children, headed by Sr. Alcántara, which is active in saving the lives of hungry youngsters in poverty-stricken Cajamarca Province. Replies irregularly to casual or technical correspondence in Spanish, but regularly to Children's Committee donors and helpful correspondence in Spanish.

RADIO NUEVO CONTINENTE, Jirón Amazonas 660, Cajamarca, Perú. Contact: Eduardo Cabrera Urteaga, Gerente. May reply to correspondence in Spanish.

RADIO ONDAS DEL MAYO, Jirón Huallaga 350, Nuevo Cajamarca, San Martín, Perú. Contact: Víctor Huaras Rojas, Locutor.

RADIO ORIENTE, Av. Progreso 112, Yurimaguas, Loreto, Perú. Contact: Prof. Ricardo Arevaldo Flores, Director-Gerente; or Juan Antonio López-Manzanares Mascunana, Director de Redacción y Programación. $1 or return postage required. Replies occasionally to correspondence in Spanish.

RADIO ORIGENES, Avenida Augusto B. Leguía 126, Huancavelica, Peru. Replies occasionally to correspondence in Spanish.

RADIO POMABAMBA, Pomabamba, Ancash, Perú. $1 or return postage required. Replies occasionally to correspondence in Spanish.

RADIO QUILLABAMBA, Centro de los Medios de la Comunicación Social, Quillabamba, La Convención, Cusco, Perú. Replies very irregularly to correspondence in Spanish.

RADIO SAN ANTONIO DE PADUA, Difusora Mariana, Arequipa, Arequipa, Perú. $1 or return postage required. Replies irregularly to correspondence in Spanish.

RADIO SAN JUAN, Jirón Pumacahua 528, Caraz, Ancash, Perú. Contact: Víctor Morales. $1 or return postage helpful. Replies occasionally to correspondence in Spanish.

RADIO SAN MARTIN, Jirón Progreso 225, Tarapoto, San Martín, Perú. Contact: José Roberto Chong, Gerente-General. Return postage required. Replies occasionally to correspondence in Spanish.

RADIO SAN MIGUEL, Av. Huayna Cápac 146, Huánchac, Cusco, Perú. Replies to correspondence in Spanish.

RADIO SAN NICOLAS, Rodríguez de Mendoza, Lambayeque, Perú. Contact: Juan José Grandez Santillán, Director. $1 required. Replies to correspondence in Spanish.

RADIO SANTA MONICA, Calle Mariscal Cáceres No. 453, Santa Mónica, Santiago de Chuco, La Libertad, Perú. Contact: Faustino Leonidas Rodríguez Rebaza, Gerente. Free pennants and music cassettes. $1 required. Replies occasionally to correspondence in Spanish.

RADIO SATELITE E.U.C., Jirón Cutervo No. 570, Cajamarca, Santa Cruz, Perú. Contact: Sabino Llamas Chávez, Gerente. Free tourist brochure. $1 or return postage required. Replies irregularly to correspondence in Spanish.

RADIO TACNA, Casilla de Correo 370, Tacna, Perú. Contact: Yolanda Vda. de Cáceres, Directora; or Alfonso Cáceres, Director Técnico. $1 or return postage required. Replies irregularly to correspondence in Spanish.

RADIO TARAPOTO, Alegría Arias de Morey 334, Tarapoto, Perú. Replies occasionally to correspondence in Spanish.

RADIO TARMA, Casilla de Correo 167, Tarma, Perú. Contact: Mario Monteverde Pomareda, Gerente General. Sometimes sends 100 Inti banknote in return when $1 enclosed. $1 or return postage required. Replies irregularly to correspondence in Spanish.

RADIO TINGO MARIA, Av. Raymondi 592, Casilla de Correo 25, Tingo María, Huánuco, Perú. Contact: Gina A. de la Cruz Ricalde, Administradora; or Ricardo Abad Vásquez, Gerente. Free brochures. $1 required. Replies slowly to correspondence in Spanish.

RADIO TROPICAL S.A., Casilla de Correo 31, Tarapoto, Perú. Contact: Luis F. Mori, Gerente. Free pennant and station history booklet. Return postage required. Replies occasionally to correspondence in Spanish.

RADIO UNION, Apartado 6205, Lima 1, Perú. Contact: Juan Carlos Sologuren, Dpto. de Administración, who collects stamps. Free satin pennants and stickers. IRC required, and enclosing used or new stamps from various countries is especially appreciated. Replies irregularly to correspondence and tape recordings, especially from young women, with Spanish preferred.

RADIO VILLA RICA, Apartado 92, Huancavelica, Peru. Contact: Fidel Hilario Huamani, Locutor/Operador y Responsable de Correspondencia. $3 reportedly required, which is excessive. Replies occasionally to correspondence in Spanish.

PHILIPPINES   World Time +8

Note: Philippine stations sometimes send publications with lists of Philippine young ladies seeking "pen pal" courtships.

FAR EAST BROADCASTING COMPANY—FEBC RADIO INTERNATIONAL

Main Office: O/EARS, Box 2041, Valenzuela, Metro Manila, Philippines. Fax: +63 (2) 818 5988.

Contact: (nontechnical) Jane J. Colley; Alida Landman; or Peter McIntire, Director, Overseas English Department; (technical) Sanda Tun, Verification Secretary; or Danny F. Flores, Operator/Technician. Free FEBC magazine. Offers religious audio cassettes. 3 IRCs required for airmail reply.

Tokyo Bureau, Nontechnical: CPO Box 1055, Tokyo, Japan.

Singapore Bureau, Nontechnical: 20 Maxwell Road #03-01, Singapore. Fax: +65 222 1805.

RADYO PILIPINAS, Philippine Broadcasting Service, Sgt. Esquerra Avenue, 1103 Quezon City, Metro Manila, Philippines. Fax: +63 (2) 969 672. Contact: (nontechnical) Evelyn Salvador Agato, Producer, Office of the Press Secretary; or Elvie Catacutan, Co-Producer, with Evelyn S. Agato of "Kumusta ka, Kaibigan and

Listeners and Friends"; (technical) Mike Pangilinan, Engineer. Free postcards.

RADIO VERITAS ASIA, P.O. Box 939, Manila, Philippines. Fax: +63 (2) 907 436. Contact: Cleofe R. Labindao, Audience Relations Officer. Free station brochure.

VOICE OF AMERICA—Does not welcome direct correspondence at its Philippines facilities in Poro or Tinang. See "USA" for acceptable VOA address and related information.

PIRATE

Pirate radio stations are usually one-person operations airing home-brew entertainment and/or iconoclastic viewpoints. In order to avoid detection by the authorities, they tend to appear irregularly, with little concern for the niceties of conventional program scheduling. Most are found just above 6200 kHz, chiefly in Europe on Sundays; and just above 7375 kHz (notably 7415 kHz), mainly evenings in North America. These *sub rosa* stations and their addresses are subject to unusually abrupt change or termination, sometimes as a result of forays by radio authorities. Two worthy sources of current addresses and other information on pirate radio activity are: The *Pirate Radio Directory* (George Zeller, Tiare Publications), an excellent annual reference available from radio specialty stores; and A*C*E, Box 11201, Shawnee Mission KS 66207 USA, a club which publishes a periodical for serious pirate radio enthusiasts.

POLAND   World Time +1 (+2 midyear)

POLISH RADIO WARSAW, External Service, P.O. Box 46, 00-950 Warsaw, Poland. Fax: +48 (22) 445 280 or +48 (22) 447 307. Contact: Jacek Detco, Editor of English Section; María Goc, Editor of English Section; or Miroslaw Luboú, Deputy Director. Free stickers. DX Listeners' Club. A new Swiss 250 kW transmitter is being installed in Poland, possibly for a new station. Polish Radio Warsaw might have at least some access to this to improve reception.

PORTUGAL   World Time +1 (+2 midyear); Azores World Time –1 (World Time midyear)

IBRA RADIO

Swedish Office: International Broadcasting Association, Box 396, S-105 36 Stockholm, Sweden. Fax: +46 (8) 579 029. Free pennants and stickers, plus green-on-white IBRA T-shirt available. IBRA Radio is heard as a program over various radio stations, including Radio Trans Europe, Portugal; the Voice of Hope, Lebanon; and Trans World Radio, Monaco.

Canadian Office: P.O. Box 444, Niagara Falls ON, L2E 6T8 Canada.

RADIO PORTUGAL INTERNACIONAL, RDP-Internacional, Rua de São Marçal 1-B, 1200 Lisbon, Portugal. Fax: +351 (1) 347 44 75. Contact: (nontechnical) Carminda Días da Silva; (technical) Winnie Almeida, DX Producer/Host, English Section. Free stickers, paper pennants and calendars.

RADIO RENASCENCA, Rua Capelo 5, 1294 Lisbon, Portugal. Fax: +351 (1) 342 2658. Contact: C. Pabil, Director-Manager.

RADIO TRANS EUROPE, 6th Floor, Rua Braamcamp 84, 1200 Lisbon, Portugal.

SERVICO INTERNACIONAL DE RADIO PORTUGAL—Portuguese identification for "Radio Portugal International," above.

VOICE OF ORTHODOXY (program via Radio Trans Europe), B.P. 416-08, F-75366 Paris Cedex 08, France. Contact: Valentin Korelsky, General Secretary.

QATAR   World Time +3

QATAR BROADCASTING SERVICE, P.O. Box 3939, Doha, Qatar. Contact: Jassem Mohamed Al-Qattan, Head of Public Relations. Rarely replies, but return postage helpful.

ROMANIA   World Time +2 (+3 midyear)

RADIO ROMANIA INTERNATIONAL, 60-62 General Berthelot Street, P.O. Box 111, 70749 Bucharest, Romania. Contact: Frederica Dochinoiu, Head of the English Department. Free stickers, pins, pennants, Romanian stamps, coasters and other small souvenirs. Can provide supplementary materials for "Romanian by Radio" course. Listeners' Club. Replies somewhat slowly.

RUSSIA   (Times given for republics, oblasts and krays):

• World Time +2 (+3 midyear) Kaliningradskaya;
• World Time +3 (+4 midyear) Arkhangel'skaya (incl. Nenetskiy), Astrakhanskaya, Belgorodskaya, Bryanskaya, Ivanovskaya, Kaluzhskaya, Karelia, Kirovskaya, Komi, Kostromskaya, Kurskaya, Lipetskaya, Moscovskaya, Murmanskaya, Nizhegorodskaya, Novgorodskaya, Orlovskaya, Penzenskaya, Pskovskaya,

Riazanskaya, Samarskaya, Sankt-Peterburgskaya, Smolenskaya, Tambovskaya, Tulskaya, Tverskaya, Vladimirskaya, Vologodskaya, Volgogradskaya, Voronezhskaya, Yaroslavskaya;

• World Time +4 (+5 midyear) Checheno-Ingushia, Chuvashia, Dagestan, Kabardino-Balkaria, Kalmykia, Krasnodarskiy, Mari-Yel, Mordovia, Severnaya Osetia, Stavropolskiy, Tatarstan, Udmurtia;
• World Time +5 (+6 midyear) Bashkortostan, Chelyabinskaya, Kurganskaya, Orenburgskaya, Permskaya, Yekaterinburgskaya, Tyumenskaya;
• World Time +6 (+7 midyear) Omskaya;
• World Time +7 (+8 midyear) Altayskaya, Kemerovskaya, Krasnoyarskiy (incl. Evenkiyskiy), Novosibirskaya, Tomskaya, Tuva;
• World Time +8 (+9 midyear) Buryatia, Irkutskaya;
• World Time +9 (+10 midyear) Amurskaya, Chitinskaya, Sakha (West);
• World Time +10 (+11 midyear) Khabarovskiy, Primorskiy, Sakha (Center), Yevreyskaya;
• World Time +11 (+12 midyear) Magadanskaya (exc. Chukotskiy), Sakha (East), Sakhalinskaya;
• World Time +12 (+13 midyear) Chukotskiy, Kamchatskaya;
• World Time +13 (+14 midyear) all points east of longtitude 172.30 E.

Warning—Mail Theft: For the time being, airmail correspondence, especially containing funds or IRCs, from North America and Japan to Russian stations is unlikely to arrive safely even if sent by registered mail, as such mail enters via the Moscow Airport, gateway to the world's most notorious nest of mail thieves. However, funds sent from Europe, North America and Japan via surface mail, enter via St. Petersburg, and thus stand a decent chance of arriving safely. Currently, surface and air mail from overseas both take about the same time—one month—to arrive.

Translation Service: Your correspondence and reception reports in English may be translated into Russian and forwarded to the appropriate Russian station by sending your material plus 2 IRCs or $1 (see preceding warning) to Anatoly Klepov, ul. Tvardovskogo, d. 23, kv. 365, Moscow 123 458, Russia.

ADVENTIST WORLD RADIO, THE VOICE OF HOPE

Main Office: AWR-Russia Media Centre, P.O. Box 170, 300000 Tula, Tulskaya Oblast, Russia.

European Office: AWR-Europe, C.P. 383, I-47100 Forlì, Italy. Fax: +39 (543) 768 198. Contact: Roger Graves, Producer; Paolo Benini, Director; or Lina Lega, Secretary. Free stickers, pennants and religious printed matter. 2 IRCs, $1 or return postage required.

Hong Kong Office: AWR, P.O. Box 310, Hong Kong. Free quarterly *AWR-Asiawaves* newsletter and religious printed matter.

ARKHANGEL'SK RADIO, Dom Radio, ul. Popova 2, Arkhangel'sk, 163000, Arkhangel'skaya Oblast, Russia; or U1PR, Valentin G. Kalasnikov, ul. Suvorov 2, kv. 16, Arkhangel'sk, Arkhangel'skaya Oblast, Russia. Replies irregularly to correspondence in Russian.

BURYAT RADIO, Dom Radio, ul. Erbanova 7, 670000 Ulan-Ude, Republic of Buryatia, Russia. Contact: Z.A. Telin or L.S. Shikhanova.

CHITA RADIO, Box 45, 672090 Chita, Chitinskaya Oblast, Russia. Contact: (technical) V.A. Klimov, Engineer; or A.A. Anufriyev.

CHRISTIAN RADIO STATION ALPHA AND OMEGA, Izdatelstvo "Protestant," Mukomolskyproezd.d.1, kor.2, 123290 Moscow, Russia.

FAR EAST CHRISTIAN BROADCASTING, FEBC-Russia, Box 2128, 680020 Khabarovsk, Khavarovskiy Kray, Russia.

GOLOS ROSSII (Voice of Russia), ul. Pyatnitskaya 25, 113326 Moscow, Russia. Fax: +7 (095) 233 6449 or +7 (095) 973 2000.

KABARDINO-BALKAR RADIO, ul. Nogmova 38, Nalchik 360000, Russia.

KAMCHATKA RADIO, RTV Center, Dom Radio, ul. Sovietskaya 62-G, 683000 Petropavlovsk-Kamchatskiy, Kamchatskaya Oblast, Russia. Contact: A. Borodin, Chief OTK; or V.I. Aibabin. Replies in Russian to correspondence in Russian or English.

KHABAROVSK RADIO, RTV Center, ul. Lenina 71, 680013 Khabarovsk, Khabarovskiy Kray, Russia; or Dom Radio, pl. Slavy, 682632 Khabarovsk, Khabarovskiy Kray, Russia. Contact: (technical) V.N. Kononov, Glavnyy Inzhener.

KHANTY-MANSIYSK RADIO, Dom Radio, ul. Lenina 21, 626200 Khanty-Mansiysk, Tyumenskaya Oblast, Russia. Contact: (technical) Vladimir Sokolov, Engineer.

KRASNOYARSK RADIO, RTV Center, Sovietskaya 128, 660017 Krasnoyarsk, Krasnoyarskiy Kray, Russia. Contact: Valeriy Korotchenko; or Anatoliy A. Potehin, RA0AKE. Replies in Russian to correspondence in English or Russian. Return postage helpful.

MAGADAN RADIO, RTV Center, ul. Kommuny 8/12, 685013 Magadan, Magadanskaya Oblast, Russia. Contact: Viktor Loktionov; or V.G. Kuznetsov. Return postage helpful. May reply to correspondence in Russian.

MARIY RADIO, ul. Krasnoarmejskaya 76-a, Yoshkar-Ola 424031, Russia.

MURMANSK RADIO, per. Rusanova 7, 183767 Murmansk, Murmanskaya Oblast, Russia; or RTV Center, Sopka Varnichaya, 183042 Murmansk, Murmanskaya Oblast, Russia.

NEW WAVE RADIO STATION (Radiostantsiya Novaya Volna) (independent program aired via Radio Moscow's First Program and Golos Rossii), ul. Akademika Koroleva 19, 127427 Moscow, Russia. Fax: +7 (095) 215 0847. Contact: Vladimir Razin, Editor-in-Chief.

PRIMORSK RADIO, RTV Center, ul. Uborevieha 20A, 690000 Vladivostok, Primorskiy Kray, Russia. Contact: A.G. Giryuk. Return postage helpful.

RADIO ALA, P.O. Box 159, 124047 Moscow, Russia. Fax: +7 (095) 233 7842. Contact: Alexander Leonovich Astafjev, Director; Sergei Vostchekov, Newscaster; Natalja Demina; or Anatoli Kirev, Announcer.

RADIO ALEF (joint project of Radio Moscow and Yiddish Child's Organization.), Pyatnitskaya ul., 25, 113326 Moscow, Russia.

RADIO AUM SHINRIKYO ("Evangelion tis Vasilias," Gospel of the Kingdom), 3-8-11 Miyamae, Suginami-ku, Tokyo 168, Japan. Fax: +81 (3) 5370 1604. Contact: Shoko Ashara. Replies to listener technical and other correspondence in Japanese and English. Free *The Teaching of the Truth* and other books by Shoko Ashara. Transmitted via facilities of Radio Moscow International.

RADIO GALAXY (Radiostantsiya Galaktika), P.O. Box 7, 117418 Moscow, Russia. Fax: +7 (095) 230 2828.

RADIO MOSCOW (domestic service), ul. Akademika Koroleva 19, 127427 Moscow, Russia. Fax: +7 (095) 215 0847. Correspondence in Russian preferred, but English increasingly accepted.

RADIO MOSCOW INTERNATIONAL (typically identifies simply as "Radio Moscow"), TV & Radio Agency "Astra," ul. Pyatnitskaya 25, 113326 Moscow, Russia. Fax: +7 (095) 230 2828. Contact (World Service in English): (Listeners' questions to be answered on the air) Joe Adamov; (all other listener correspondence) Valentina Knjasewa; (administrative correspondence) Iouri Minaev, Director. Free stickers, calendars, "Russian by Radio" supplementary materials, booklets and cookbooks.

RADIO N—contact via "Radiostudiya Dvizheniye."

RADIO POLIS (Radio Pole), P.O. Box 90, St. Petersburg, Sankt-Peterburgskaya Oblast, Russia.

RADIO RADONEZH, ul.Pyatnitskaya, 25, 113326 Moscow, Russia.

RADIO ROSSII—see "Russia's Radio," below.

RADIO SAMARA, ul. Sovietscoj Army 205, Samara, Samarskaya Oblast, Russia.

RADIO SHARK, Prospekt Oktyabrya 56/1, 450054 Ufa, Bashkortostan, Russia. Contact: Anatskiy Sergey, Director.

RADIO SNC (Radio Stas Namin Center), ul. Krymskiy Val 9, 117049 Moscow, Russia. Fax: +7 (095) 237 3435.

RADIOSTANTSIYA ATLANTIKA (program of Radio Riga and Murmansk Radio, aired via Golo Rossii), per. Rusanova 7 "A", 183767 Murmansk, Russia.

RADIOSTANTSIYA PAMYAT (Memory Radio Station), P.O. Box 23, 113535 Moscow, Russia; or Mirolyubov, ul. Valovaya, d.32, kv.4, 113054 Moscow, Russia. Contact: (nontechnical) Dimitrly Vasilyev, Leader; (technical) Yuri Mirolyukov, Radio Operator. Audio cassettes of broadcasts available for five rubles or $2. Correspondence in Russian preferred.

RADIOSTANTSIYA RADONEZH (Radonezh Orthodox Radio Station), Studio 158, ul. Pyatnitskaya 25, 113326 Moscow, Russia. Contact: Anton Parshin, Announcer.

RADIOSTANTSIYA VEDO, P.O. Box 1940, 400123 Volgograd, Volgogradskaya Oblast, Russia. Contact: Andrei Bogdanov. Correspondence in Russian preferred, but French and English also acceptable.

RADIOSTANTSIYA YAKUTSK, ul. Semena Dezhneva, 75/2, Radiocenter, 677000 Yakutsk, Russia.

RADIOSTUDIYA DVIZHENIYE (Traffic Radio Studio, program aired by Radio N), Radio Company of the Union of Journalists, Poste Restante, Main Post Office, 620000 Yekaterinburg, Yekaterinburgskaya Oblast, Russia; or ul. Turgeneva 13, Komnata 119, 13-u etazh, 620219 Yekaterinburg, Yekaterinburgskaya Oblast, Russia. Contact: Sergei Biryukov. Likely to prefer correspondence in Russian.

RADIO TIKHIY OKEAN (program of Primorsk Radio aired via Golos Rossii), RTV Center, ul. Uborevieha 20A, 690000 Vladivostok, Primorskiy Kray, Russia.

RADIO TREK, P.O. Box 932, 620063 Yekaterinburg, Russia.

RADIO YUNOST (Radio Youth, a program of Radio Moscow)—see "Radio Moscow."

RUSSIA'S RADIO (Radio Rossii), Room 121, 5-R Ulitsa, 19/21 Yamskogo Polya, Moscow 125124, Russia. Fax: +7 (095) 250 0105. Contact: Sergei Yerofeyev, Director of International Operations; or Sergei Davidov, Director. Free English-language information sheet.

SAKHALIN RADIO, Dom Radio, ul. Komsomolskaya 209, 693000 Yuzhno-Sakhalinsk, Sakhalin Is., Sakhalinskaya Oblast, Russia. Contact: V. Belyaev, Chairman of Sakhalinsk RTV Committee.

TATAR RADIO, RTV Center, ul. M. Gorkova 15, 420015 Kazan', Republic of Tatarstan, Russia. May reply to correspondence in Russian. Return postage helpful.

TYUMEN' RADIO, RTV Center, ul. Permyakova 6, 625013 Tyumen', Tyumenskaya Oblast, Russia. Contact: (technical) V.D. Kizerov, Engineer, Technical Center. May reply to correspondence in Russian. Return postage helpful.

VOICE OF RUSSIA—see "Golos Rossii."

YAKUT RADIO, Dom Radio, 48 Ordzhonikdze Street, 677892 Yakutsk, Sakha (Yakutia) Republic, Russia. Fax: +7 (095) 230 2919. Contact: (nontechnical) Alexandra Borisova; Lia Sharoborina, Advertising Editor; or Albina Danilova, Producer, "Your Letters"; (technical) Sergei Bobnev, Technical Director. Russian books available for $15. C60 audio cassettes available for $10. Free station stickers and original Yakutian souvenirs. Replies to correspondence in English.

RWANDA   World Time +2

RADIO RWANDA, B.P. 83, Kigali, Rwanda. Fax: +250 (7) 6185. Contact: Marcel Singirankabo; or Etienne Ntirugirisonu. $1 required. Rarely replies, slowly, with correspondence in French preferred.

SAO TOME E PRINCIPE   World Time exactly

VOICE OF AMERICA—future new site, post-1993, for the Voice of America, using 100 kW transmitters. See "USA" for address and other details.

SAUDI ARABIA   World Time +3

BROADCASTING SERVICE OF THE KINGDOM OF SAUDI ARABIA, P.O. Box 61718, Riyadh 11575, Saudi Arabia. Contact: (technical) Suliman A. Al-Samnan, Director of Frequency Management; or A. Shah. Free travel information and book on Saudi history. Sometimes replies slowly.

RADIO ISLAM FROM HOLY MECCA (Idha'at Islam min Mecca al-Mukarama)—same details as "Broadcasting Service of the Kingdom of Saudi Arabia," above.

SENEGAL   World Time exactly

OFFICE DE RADIODIFFUSION-TELEVISION DU SENEGAL, B.P. 1765, Dakar, Senegal. Contact: Joseph Nesseim. Free stickers and Senegalese stamps. Return postage, $1 or 2 IRCs required; as Mr. Nesseim collects stamps, unusual stamps may be even more appreciated. Replies to correspondence in French.

SEYCHELLES   World Time +4

BBC WORLD SERVICE—INDIAN OCEAN RELAY STATION, P.O. Box 448, Victoria, Mahé, Seychelles; or Grand Anse, Mahé, Seychelles. Fax: +248 78500. Contact: (technical) Peter Lee, Resident Engineer; or Peter J. Loveday, Station Manager. Nontechnical correspondence should be sent to the BBC World Service in London (see).

FAR EAST BROADCASTING ASSOCIATION—FEBA RADIO
Main Office: P.O. Box 234, Mahé, Seychelles. Fax: +248 25171. Contact: (nontechnical) Roger Foyle, Audience Relations Counsellor; (technical) Mary Asba, Verification Secretary. Free stickers and station information sheet. $1 or one IRC helpful.
Canadian Office: Box 2233, Vancouver BC, Canada.

SIERRA LEONE   World Time exactly

SIERRA LEONE BROADCASTING SERVICE, New England, Freetown, Sierra Leone. Contact: (technical) Emmanuel B. Ehirim, Project Engineer.

SINGAPORE   World Time +8

BBC WORLD SERVICE—FAR EASTERN RELAY STATION, P.O. Box 434, 26 Olive Road, Singapore. Fax: +65 669 0834. Contact: (technical) Far East Resident Engineer. Nontechnical correspondence should be sent to the BBC World Service in London (see).

SINGAPORE BROADCASTING CORPORATION, P.O. Box 60, Singapore 9128, Singapore. Fax: +65 253 8808. Contact: Lillian

Tan, Public Relations Division. Free stickers. Do not include currency in envelope.

SOLOMON ISLANDS   World Time +11

SOLOMON ISLANDS BROADCASTING CORPORATION, P.O. Box 654, Honiara, Solomon Islands. Fax: +677 23159. Contact: (technical) Chief Engineer. IRC or $1 helpful.

SOMALIA   World Time +3

RADIO MOGADISHU, Ministry of Information, Private Postbag, Mogadishu, Somalia. Contact: Mohamed Aden Hirsi, Director; or Dr. Abdel-Qadir Muhammad Mursal, Director, Media Department. Replies irregularly. Letters should be via registered mail.

"Somaliland"

Note: "Somaliland," claimed as a independent nation, is diplomatically recognized only as part of Somalia.

RADIO HARGEISA, P.O. Box 14, Hargeisa, Somaliland, Somalia. Sulayman Abdel-Rahman, announcer. Most likely to respond to correspondence in Somali or Arabic.

SOUTH AFRICA   World Time +2

RADIO RSA, P.O. Box 91313, Auckland Park 2006, Republic of South Africa. Fax: (nontechnical) +27 (11) 714 4956 or +27 (11) 714 6377; (technical) +27 (11) 714 5812. Contact: (nontechnical) G.A. Wynne, Manager of English Service; (technical) Lucienne Libotte, Technology Operations. Free stickers.

SOUTH AFRICAN BROADCASTING CORPORATION, P.O. Box 91312, Auckland Park 2006, South Africa. Fax: (nontechnical) +27 (11) 714 5055; (technical) +27 (11) 714 3106.
Contact: *Radio Five:* Helena Boshoff, Public Relations Officer; *Radio Oranje:* Hennie Klopper, Announcer; or Christo Olivier; *Radio Orion:* Public Relations Officer. Free stickers.

SPAIN   World Time +1 (+2 midyear)

RADIO EXTERIOR DE ESPANA

Main Office: Apartado 156.202, E-28080 Madrid, Spain. Fax: +34 (1) 261 6388. Contact: Pilar Salvador M., Relaciones con la Audiencia. Free stickers, calendars and pennants.

Washington News Bureau, Nontechnical: National Press Building, 529 14th Street NW, Washington DC 20045 USA.

SRI LANKA   World Time +5:30

RADIO JAPAN/NHK, c/o SLBC, P.O. Box 574, Torrington Square, Colombo 7, Sri Lanka. Nontechnical correspondence should be sent to the Radio Japan address in Japan.

SRI LANKA BROADCASTING CORPORATION, P.O. Box 574, Colombo 7, Sri Lanka. Fax: +94 (1) 695 488. Contact: H. Jerando, Director of Audience Research; Lal Herath, Deputy Director General of Broadcasting; or Icumar Ratnayake, Controller, "Mailbag Program." Color magazine available celebrating 25 years of broadcasting for US$20. Has tended to reply irregularly, but this seems to have improved as of late.

TRANS WORLD RADIO

Transmitter: P.O. Box 364, 91 Wijerama Mawatha, Colombo 7, Sri Lanka. Fax: +94 (1) 685 245. Contact: (technical) Robert Schultz. Anticipates world band transmissions to begin by 1993. Initial power is expected to be 12.5 kW, rising to 100 kW by 1994 or thereabouts.

Studio: P.O. Box 4407, L-15, Green Park, New Delhi-110 016, India. Fax: +91 (11) 686 8049.

VOICE OF AMERICA—SRI LANKA RELAY STATION, P.O. Box 574, Colombo 7, Sri Lanka. Fax: +94 (1) 695 488. Contact: David Sites, VOA Manager.

SUDAN   World Time +2

NATIONAL UNITY RADIO—see "Sudan National Broadcasting Corporation," below, for details.

SUDAN NATIONAL BROADCASTING CORPORATION, P.O. Box 572, Omdurman, Sudan. Contact: (technical) Abbas Sidig, Director General, Engineering and Technical Affairs; or Adil Didahammed, Engineering Department. Replies very irregularly.

SURINAME   World Time –3

RADIO APINTIE, Postbus 595, Paramaribo, Suriname. Contact: Ch. E. Vervuurt, Director. Rarely replies.

SWAZILAND   World Time +2

SWAZILAND COMMERCIAL RADIO

Nontechnical Correspondence: P.O. Box 23114, Joubert Park 2044, South Africa. Contact: Rob Vickers, Manager Religion. IRC helpful. Replies irregularly.

Technical Correspondence: P.O. Box 99, Amsterdam 2375, South Africa. Contact: G.A. Doult, Chief Engineer.

TRANS WORLD RADIO, P.O. Box 64, Manzini, Swaziland. Fax: +268 55333. Contact: L. Stavropoulos or Carol J. Tatlow. Free stickers. $1, return postage or IRC required. Also, see "USA."

SWEDEN   World Time +1 (+2 midyear)

RADIO SWEDEN

Main Office: S-105 10 Stockholm, Sweden. Fax: (general) +46 (8) 667 62 83; (polling to receive schedule) +46 8 667 37 01. Contact: (nontechnical) Alan Prix, Host, "In Touch with Stockholm" (include your telephone number); Martha Rose Ugirst; Lilian von Arnold; Inga Holmberg, Assistant to the Director; or Hans Wachholz, Director; (technical) Rolf Beckman, Head, Technical Department. Free stickers. "Moose Gustafsson" T-shirts for $17 or £10.

New York News Bureau, Nontechnical: 12 W. 37th Street, 7th Floor, New York NY 10018 USA. Fax: +1 (212) 594 6413. Contact: Elizabeth Johansson or Ann Hedengren.

SWITZERLAND   World Time +1 (+2 midyear)

RED CROSS BROADCASTING SERVICE, Département de la Communication, CICR/ICRC, 19 Avenue de la Paix, CH-1202 Geneva, Switzerland. Fax: +41 (22) 734 8280. Contact: Elisabeth Copson or Patrick Piper, "Red Crossroads"; or Carlos Bauverd, Chef, Division de la Presse. Free stickers, wall calendar and station information. IRC appreciated.

SWISS RADIO INTERNATIONAL

Main Office: SBC, P.O. Box, CH-3000 Berne 15, Switzerland. Fax: +41 (31) 43 95 44 or +41 (31) 43 95 69. Contact: (nontechnical) Roy Oppenheim, Director; or Walter Fankhauser, Press and Public Relations Officer; (technical) Bob Zanotti, DX Editor; (radioteletype) Monika Lüthi, Manager of RTTY Transmissions. Free station flyers. SRI compact discs of Swiss music available, presumably for sale.

Washington News Bureau, Nontechnical: 2030 M Street NW, Washington DC 20554 USA. Christophe Erbea, reporter.

SYRIA   World Time +2 (+3 midyear)

RADIO DAMASCUS, Syrian Radio & Television, Ommayad Square, Damascus, Syria. Free stickers, paper pennants and *The Syria Times* newspaper. Contact: AFAF, Director General. Replies can be highly erratic, but as of late have been more regular, if sometimes slow.

TAHITI—see "French Polynesia."

TAJIKISTAN   World Time +6

RADIO DUSHANBE,' ul. Chapayev 25, Dushanbe 734 015, Tajikistan. Correspondence in Russian preferred.

RADIO PAY-I 'AJAM, Radio House, 31 Chapayev Street, 734015 Dushanbe, Tajikistan.

TAJIK RADIO—see "Radio Dushanbe" for details.

TANZANIA   World Time +3

RADIO TANZANIA, Director of Broadcasting, P.O. Box 9191, Dar Es Salaam, Tanzania. Fax: +255 (51) 29416. Contact: (nontechnical) Controller of Programs; or Ahmed Jongo, Producer, "Your Answer"; (technical) Head of Research & Planning. Replies to correspondence in English.

VOICE OF TANZANIA ZANZIBAR, P.O. Box 1178, Zanzibar, Tanzania. Contact: (technical) Nassor M. Suleiman, Maintenance Engineer. Return postage helpful.

THAILAND   World Time +7

RADIO THAILAND, External Service, Bangkok 10200, Thailand. Contact: Bupha Laemluang, Chief of External Services. Free pennants. Replies irregularly, especially to those who persist.

VOICE OF AMERICA—New facility to go on the air about February 1993, with transmitters of 500 kW. See "USA" for address and related information.

TOGO   World Time exactly

RADIO LOME, Lomé, Togo. Return postage, $1 or 2 IRCs helpful.

TONGA   World Time +13

TONGA BROADCASTING COMMISSION (when facilities, damaged by a cyclone, are repaired), A3Z, P.O. Box 36, Nuku'alofa, Tonga. Fax: +676 22670. Contact: (nontechnical) Tavake Fusimalohi, General Manager; (technical) M. Indiran, Chief Engineer.

TUNISIA   World Time +1

RADIODIFFUSION TELEVISION TUNISIENNE, Radio Sfax, 71 Avenue de la Liberté, Tunis, Tunisia. Contact: Mongai Caffai, Director General; Mohamed Abdelkafi, Director; or Smaoui Sadok, Chief Engineer. Replies irregularly and slowly to correspondence in French or Arabic.

TURKEY   World Time +2 (+3 midyear)

TURKISH POLICE RADIO, T.C. Içiçleri Bakanligi, Emniyet Genel Müdürlügü, Ankara, Turkey. Contact: Station Director. Tourist literature for return postage. Replies irregularly.

TURKISH RADIO-TELEVISION CORPORATION—VOICE OF TURKEY

Main Office, Nontechnical: P.K. 333, 06.443 Yenisehir Ankara, Turkey. Fax: +90 (4) 435 3816. Contact: (English) Osman Erkan, Host, "Letterbox"; Semra Eren, Head of English Department; (other foreign languages) Rafet Esit, Head of Foreign Language Programming; (Turkish and other languages) Savas Kirati, Managing Director. Free stickers, pennants and tourist literature.

Main Office, Technical: P.K. 333, 06.443 Yenisehir Ankara, Turkey. Fax: +90 (4) 490 1733. Contact: A. Akad Cukurova, Deputy Director General, Engineering.

San Francisco Office, Schedules: 2654 17th Avenue, San Francisco CA 94116 USA. Contact: George Poppin. This address only provides TRT schedules to listeners. All other correspondence should be sent directly to Ankara.

VOICE OF METEOROLOGY, T.C. Tarim Bakanligi, Devlet Meteoroloji Isleri, Genel Mudurlugu, P.K. 401, Ankara, Turkey. Contact: Faysal Geyik, Director General of the Turkish State Meteorological Service. Free tourish literature. Return postage helpful.

TURKMENISTAN World Time +5

TURKMEN RADIO, Kurortnaya 111, Ashkhabad 744 024, Turkmenistan. Contact: K. Karayev.

UGANDA World Time +3

RADIO UGANDA, P.O. Box 7142, Kampala, Uganda. Fax: +256 (41) 256 888. Contact: Kikulwe Rashid Harolin or A.K. Mlamizo. $1 or return postage required. Replies infrequently and slowly.

UKRAINE World Time +2 (+3 midyear)

Warning—Mail Theft: For the time being, letters to Ukrainian stations, especially containing funds or IRCs, are most likely to arrive safely if sent by registered mail.

RADIO UKRAINE INTERNATIONAL, ul. Kreshchatik 26, 252001 Kiev, Ukraine. Free stickers and Ukrainian stamps. Replies slowly and, as of late, irregularly, perhaps because of deteriorating mail service.

RADIO NEZALEZHNIST, ul. Vatutina 6, 290005 Lvov, Ukraine.

UKRAINIAN RADIO—see "Radio Ukraine International" for details.

UNITED ARAB EMIRATES World Time +4

CAPITAL RADIO—see "UAE Radio from Abu Dhabi," below, for details.

UAE RADIO IN DUBAI, P.O. Box 1695, Dubai, United Arab Emirates. Fax: +971 (4) 374 111 or +971 (4) 370 975. Contact: (technical) K.F. Fenner, Chief Engineer—Radio; or Ahmed Al Muhaideb. Free pennants.

UAE RADIO FROM ABU DHABI, Ministry of Information & Culture, P.O. Box 63, Abu Dhabi, United Arab Emirates. Fax: +971 (2) 451 155. Contact: (nontechnical) Ahmed A. Shouly, Controller General; or Abdul Hadi Mubarak, Producer, "Live Program"; (technical) Ibrahim Rashid, Technical Department.

UNITED KINGDOM World Time exactly (+1 midyear)

BBC WORLD SERVICE

Main Office: P.O. Box 76, Bush House, Strand, London WC2B 4PH, United Kingdom. Fax: ("Write On" listeners' letters program) +44 (71) 497 0287; (general information) +44 (71) 240 8760; (World Service Shop) +44 (71) 379 6640; (technical) +44 (71) 240 8926. Contact: ("Write On") Paddy Feeny, Presenter. Free sample of excellent monthly *London Calling* magazine, which also may be subscribed to for $20, £12, CAN$25 or AUS$25 per year. Numerous audio/video (PAL/VHS only for video) recordings, publications (including *Passport to World Band Radio*), portable world band radios, T-shirts, sweatshirts and other BBC souvenirs available by mail from BBC World Service Shop, at the above London address (VISA/MC/AX/Access). Tapes of BBC programs from BBC Topical Tapes, also at the above London address. World band schedules and weekly *WBI* newsletter for £350 plus air postage per year; audio and teletype feeds for news agencies; and world broadcasting program summaries for researchers; all from BBC Monitoring, Caversham Park, Reading RG4 8TZ, United Kingdom. *BBC English* magazine, to aid in learning English, from BBC English, P.O. Box 96, Cambridge, United Kingdom. Also, see "Antigua," "Ascension Island," "Oman," "Seychelles" and "Singapore," which are where technical correspondence concerning these BBC relay transmissions should be sent if you seek a reply with full verification data, as no such data are provided via the London address.

New York Office: 630 Fifth Avenue, New York NY 10020 USA. Fax: +1 (212) 245 0565. Contact: (nontechnical) Heather Maclean, World Service Affairs.

Ottawa Office: P.O. Box 1555, Station "B", Ottawa ON, K1P 5R5 Canada.

Paris Office: 155 rue du Faubourg St. Honoré, F-75008 Paris, France. Fax: +33 (1) 45 63 67 12.

Berlin Office: Savingnyplatz 6, W-1000 Berlin 12, Germany.

Tokyo Office: P.O. Box 29, Kopjimachi, Tokyo, Japan.

Singapore Office: P.O. Box 434, Maxwell Road Post Office, Singapore 9008, Singapore. Fax: +65 253 8131.

Australian Office: Suite 101, 80 William Street, East Sydney, NSW 2011, Australia. Fax: 61 (2) 361 0853. Contact: (nontechnical) Michelle Rowland; or Marilyn Eccles, Information Desk.

BRITISH FORCES BROADCASTING SERVICE, Bridge House, North Wharf Road, London W2 1LA, United Kingdom. Fax: +44 (71) 706 1582. Contact: Richard Astbury, Station Manager. Free station brochure.

UNITED NATIONS

UNITED NATIONS RADIO/UNESCO (aired via various stations throughout the world, such as Radio Myanmar, IRRS/Italy, All India Radio and RFPI/Costa Rica), United Nations, UN Plaza, New York NY 10017 USA; or write the station over which UN Radio was heard. Contact: Sylvester E. Rowe, Chief, Electronic Magazine and Features Service; Ayman El-Amir, Chief, Radio Section, Department of Public Information; or Carmen Blandon, Secretary. Free UN stickers, T-shirts, pennants, stamps and *UN Frequency* publication.

URUGUAY World Time –2 (–3 midyear)

EL ESPECTADOR, Río Branco 1483, 11100 Montevideo, Uruguay.

LA VOZ DE ARTIGAS, Av. Lecueder 483, 55000 Artigas, Uruguay.

RADIO INTEGRACION AMERICANA, Soriano 1287, 11100 Montevideo, Uruguay. Contact: Andrea Cruz. $1 or return postage required. Replies irregularly to correspondence in Spanish.

RADIO MONTE CARLO, Av. 18 de Julio 1224, 11100 Montevideo, Uruguay. Contact: Ana Ferreira de Errázquin, Secretaria, Departmento de Prensa de la Cooperativa de Radioemisoras. Correspondence in Spanish preferred.

RADIO ORIENTAL—Same as Radio Monte Carlo, above.

International radio's number one sportscaster, Paddy Feeny, also presents *Write On*, which airs listeners' letters each weekend over the BBC World Service.

Finnish radio authority Simo Soininen visits with Jeff White, General Manager of Radio Miami Internacional. Both are avid collectors of radio memorabilia.

SODRE
Nontechnical: Casilla 1412, 11000 Montevideo, Uruguay.
Technical: DX Club del Uruguay, Casilla 801, 11000 Montevideo, Uruguay. Contact: Daniel Muñoz Faccioli; or A. Souto.
USA World Time –4 Atlantic, including Puerto Rico and Virgin Islands; –5 (–4 midyear) Eastern, excluding Indiana; –5 Indiana, except northwest and southwest portions; –6 (–5 midyear) Central, including northwest and southwest Indiana; –7 (–6 midyear) Mountain, except Arizona; –7 Arizona; –8 (–7 midyear) Pacific; –9 (–10 midyear) Alaska, except Aleutian Islands; –10 (–11 midyear) Aleutian Islands; –10 Hawaii; –11 Samoa
ADVENTIST WORLD RADIO, THE VOICE OF HOPE, International Headquarters, 12501 Old Columbia Pike, Silver Spring MD 20904 USA. Fax: +1 (301) 680 6090. Contact: (nontechnical) Walter R.L. Scragg, Director; (technical) Tulio R. Haylock, Technical Director. Free religious printed matter, pennants and other small souvenirs. IRC or $1 appreciated. Technical correspondence is best sent to the country where the transmitter is located—Costa Rica, Gabon, Guam, Italy, or Russia.
CHRISTIAN SCIENCE MONITOR, SHORTWAVE WORLD SERVICE, WCNS/WSHB/KHBI, P.O. Box 860, Boston MA 02123 USA; toll-free telephone (U.S. only) (800) 225-7090 [+1 (617) 450-2929 outside U.S.], extension 2060 (24-hour for schedules) or 2929 (Shortwave Helpline). Contact: Margaret D. Girard, Shortwave Helpline; Kate Dearborn, Director of Radio; Monty Haas, Host, "Letterbox"; or Dave Casanave, Producer, "Letterbox." Free stickers and information on Christian Science religion. *Christian Science Monitor* newspaper and full line of Christian Science books, Sangean and other world band radios, plus *Passport to World Band Radio* available from 1 Norway Street, Boston MA 02115 USA; toll-free telephone for the public and bookstores (U.S only) (800) 877-8400. *Science and Health* book available for $17 postpaid from Science & Health, P.O. Box 1875, Boston MA 02117 USA. When ordering please specify the language version you require; English, Spanish, German or Portuguese. Also, see "Northern Mariana Islands."
CHRISTIAN SCIENCE MONITOR, SHORTWAVE WORLD SERVICE/WCSN, P.O. Box 130, Costigan ME 04423 USA. Fax: +1 (207) 732 4741. Contact: (technical) Ken Fox, Engineer; or Robert Stressel, Station Manager. This address for technical feedback on Maine transmissions only; other inquiries should be directed to the usual Boston address.
CHRISTIAN SCIENCE MONITOR, SHORTWAVE WORLD SERVICE/WSHB, Rt. 2, Box 107A, Pineland SC 29934 USA. Fax: +1 (803) 625 5559. Contact: (technical) Michael R. Batchelor, Systems/Operations Engineer; C. Ed Evans, Senior Station Manager; or Judy P. Cooke. This address for technical feedback on South Carolina transmissions only; other inquiries should be directed to the usual Boston address.
KGEI—VOICE OF FRIENDSHIP, 1400 Radio Road, Redwood City CA 94065 USA. Fax: +1 (415) 591-0233. Contact: Jesús C. Elizondo. Free religious literature.
KJES, The Lord's Ranch, Star Route 300, Mesquite NM 88048 USA.
KNLS—NEW LIFE STATION
Operations Center: P.O. Box 681706, Franklin TN 37068 USA (letters sent to the Alaska transmitter site are usually forwarded to Franklin). Fax: +1 (615) 371 8791. Contact: Wesley Jones, Manager, Follow-Up Department; or Beverly Jones, Follow-Up Department. Free pennants, stickers, Russian language religious tapes and literature, and English-language learning course materials for Russian speakers. Swaps cancelled stamps from different countries to help listeners round out their stamp collections. Return postage helpful.
Transmitter Site: P.O. Box 473, Anchor Point AK 99556 USA. Contact: (nontechnical or technical) Mike Osborne, Production Manager; (technical) Kevin Chambers, Engineer.
Administrative Office: P.O. Box 3857, Abilene TX 79604 USA. Fax: +1 (915) 676 5663.
Tokyo Office: P.O. Box 27, Tachikawa, Tokyo 190, Japan. Fax: +81 (425) 34 0062.
KTBN—TRINITY BROADCASTING NETWORK, P.O. Box A, Santa Ana CA 92711 USA. Fax: +1 (714) 731 4196. Contact: Ben Miller, WB5TLZ. Monthly TBN newsletter. Religious merchandise sold. Return postage helpful.
KVOH—HIGH ADVENTURE RADIO
Main Office: P.O. Box 93937, Los Angeles CA 90093 USA. Fax:

+1 (805) 520 7823. Contact: (nontechnical) John Tayloe, International Program Director; or Patrick C. Kowalick, On-Air Minister; (technical) Dr. Don Myers, Chief Engineer. Free stickers, *Voice of Hope* book, "High Adventure Ministries" pamphlet and sample "Voice of Hope" broadcast tape. Also, see "Lebanon." Replies as time permits.
Canadian Office, Nontechnical: Box 425, Station "E", Toronto, M6H 4E3 Canada. Contact: Don McLaughlin, Director.
London Office, Nontechnical: BM Box 2575, London WC1N 3XX, United Kingdom. Contact: Paul Ogle, Director.
Singapore Office: Orchard Point, P.O. Box 796, 9123 Singapore.
KWHR—planned sister station of WHRI (see). Expects to be on the air from Hawaii by the end of 1993.
RADIO FREE AFGHANISTAN—see "RFE-RL," below, for details.
RADIO MARTI—see "Voice of America," below, for details, but contact: Mike Pallone.
RADIO MIAMI INTERNACIONAL, P.O. Box 526852, Miami FL 33152 USA. Fax: +1 (305) 477 3639. Contact: Jeff White, General Manager. This organization, which plans to set up its own station in the near future, currently acts as a broker for anti-Castro programs aired via U.S. stations WHRI and WRNO. Technical correspondence may be sent either to RMI or to the station over which the program was heard.
Venezuelan Office: Apartado 6028, Caracas 1010, Venezuela. Contact: Héctor Silva.
RFE-RL
Main Office: Oettingenstrasse. 67 AM Englischen Garten, D-8000 Munich 22, Germany. Fax: (general) +49 (89) 2102 3308; (Public Affairs) +49 (89) 2102 3322. Contact: (nontechnical) Terry B. Shroeder, Director, Public Affairs, Mail Box 5; or Melissa Fleming, Public Affairs Specialist, Mail Box 5.
Washington Office, Nontechnical: 1201 Connecticut Avenue NW, 11th floor, Washington DC 20036 USA. Fax: +1 (202) 457 6974.
New York Office: 1775 Broadway, New York NY 10019 USA. Fax: +1 (212) 397 5380. Contact: (*RFE Research Report*) Irina Klionsky; (technical) David Walcutt, Engineering. Annual subscription to *RFE Research Report* $150, $75 for students.
London Bureau, Nontechnical: 2 South Audley Street, London W1, United Kingdom.
TRANS WORLD RADIO, International Headquarters, P.O. Box 700, Cary NC 27512 USA. Fax: +1 (919) 460 9598. Contact: (nontechnical) Donna Moss, Public Affairs. Free "Towers to Eternity" publication. Technical correspondence should be sent directly to the country where the transmitter is located—Guam, Monaco, Netherlands Antilles or Swaziland.
VOICE OF AMERICA/VOA—ALL TRANSMITTER LOCATIONS
Main Office, Nontechnical: 330 Independence Avenue SW, Washington DC 20547 USA. Fax: (general information) +1 (202) 376 1066; or (Public Liaison) +1 (202) 485 8241. Contact: Marie Ciliberti, Audience Mail, Room 6-759. Free key chains, *The Constitution of the United States* book, sundry booklets on the United States, stickers and other items to listeners with addresses *outside* the United States. Free "Music Time in Africa" calendar, to non-U.S. addresses only, from Rita Rochelle, Africa Division, Room 1622. If you're an American and miffed because you can't receive these goodies from the VOA, don't blame the station—they're only following the law.
Main Office, Technical: 330 Independence Avenue SW, Washington DC 20547 USA. Contact: Irene Green, Verification Officer.
Frequency and Monitoring Office, Technical: VOA:EOFF:Frequency Management & Monitoring Division, 330 Independence Avenue SW, Washington DC 20547 USA. Fax: +1 (202) 619 1781. Contact: Dan Ferguson. Also, see "Botswana" and "Sri Lanka."
Portuguese Office: Apartado 4258, Lisbon 1700, Portugal.
VOICE OF AMERICA/VOA CINCINNATI—BETHANY RELAY STATION, P.O. Box 227, Mason OH 45040 USA. Fax: +1 (513) 777 4736. Contact: (technical) John Vodenik, WB9AUJ, Engineer. Nontechnical correspondence should be sent to the VOA address in Washington.
VOICE OF AMERICA/VOA—DELANO RELAY STATION, Rt. 1, Box 1350, Delano CA 93215 USA. Fax: +1 (805) 725 6511. Contact: (technical) Jim O'Neill, Engineer. Nontechnical correspondence should be sent to the VOA address in Washington.
VOICE OF AMERICA/VOA—GREENVILLE RELAY STATION, P.O. Box 1826, Greenville NC 27834 USA. Fax: +1 (919) 752 5959. Contact: (technical) Dennis Brewer, Deputy Manager. Nontechnical correspondence should be sent to the VOA address in Washington.

VOICE OF THE OAS, Organization of American States, 17th St. & Constitution Avenue NW, Washington DC 20006 USA. Fax: +1 (202) 458 3930. Contact: Mario Martínez, Co-director; or Carlos Flores, Co-director.
WCSN—see "Christian Science Monitor," above.
WEWN (scheduled to begin operation 12/92), Eternal Word Network, P.O. Box 380247, Birmingham AL 35238 USA. Fax: +1 (205) 672 9988. Contact: Bob German, Manager. Plans to sell religious publications, as well as possibly T-shirts, world band radios and related items. IRC or return postage requested.
WHRI—WORLD HARVEST RADIO, P.O. Box 12, South Bend IN 46624 USA. Fax: +1 (219) 291 9043. Contact: (nontechnical) Robert Willinger; (technical) James Holycross, Engineer. Return postage appreciated. Carries programs from various expatriate political organizations, such as Cuban nationalist groups; these may be contacted via WHRI. "Radio Free Croatia" may be contacted directly at 3611 Wood Street, Chicago IL 60609 USA.
WINB, P.O. Box 88, Red Lion PA 17356 USA. Fax: +1 (717) 244 9316. Contact: John Thomas; or John W. Norris, Jr., Manager. Return postage helpful outside United States.
WJCR, P.O. Box 91, Upton KY 42784 USA. Contact: Pastor Don Powell, President; Gerri Powell; or Trish Powell. Free religious printed matter. Return postage appreciated. Actively solicits listener contributions.
WMLK—ASSEMBLIES OF YAHWEH, P.O. Box C, Bethel PA 19507 USA. Contact: Elder Jacob O. Mayer, Manager. Free stickers and religious material. Replies slowly, but enclosing return postage or IRCs helps speed things up.
WRNO, Box 100, New Orleans LA 70181 USA; or 4539 I-10 Service Road North, Metairie LA 70006 USA. Fax: +1 (504) 889 0602. Contact: Joseph Mark Costello III, General Manager. Free stickers. Free tourist literature for correspondence, including return postage, addressed to WRNO World Band Radio, c/o Lt. Gov. Paul Hardy, Louisiana Office of Tourism, P.O. Box 44243, Baton Rouge LA 70804 USA.
WSHB—see "Christian Science Monitor," above.
WWCR—WORLD WIDE CHRISTIAN RADIO, F.W. Robbert Broadcasting Co., 1300 WWCR Avenue, Nashville TN 37218 USA. Contact: Adam W. Lock, Sr., WA2JAL/4, Program Director; George McClintock, General Manager; or Jay Litton, Public Affairs. Toll-free telephone (U.S. only): (800) 238-5576. Free stickers. Tends to reply slowly; return postage helpful. Is considering further expansion of its transmission facilities. Carries various programs that call themselves "Radio" this or that, such as Allan Weiner's "Radio New York International" (toll-free U.S. on-air telephone 800/326-2957) from organizations lacking their own broadcasting facilities; these organizations may be contacted via WWCR. "For the People" should be contacted direct at its Telford Hotel, 3 River Street, White Springs FL 32096 USA; fax +1 (904) 397-4149.
WWV, Frequency-Time Broadcast Services Section, Time and Frequency Division, NIST, Mail Station 847, 325 Broadway, Boulder CO 80303 USA. Fax: +1 (303) 497 3371. Contact: (technical) James C. Maxton, Engineer-in-Charge; or John B. Milton. Free Special Publication 432 "NIST Time & Frequency Services" pamphlet.
WWVH, NIST, P.O. Box 417, Kekaha, Kauai HI 96752 USA. Fax: +1 (808) 335 4747. Contact: (technical) Noboru Hironaka, Engineer-in-Charge. Free Special Publication 432 "NIST Time & Frequency Services" pamphlet.
WYFR—FAMILY RADIO
Nontechnical: Family Stations, Inc., 290 Hegenberger Road, Oakland CA 94621 USA. Toll-free telephone (U.S. only) (800) 534-1495. Fax: +1 (415) 562 1023. Contact: Thomas A. Schaff, Shortwave Program Manager. Free stickers and pocket diaries.
Technical: WYFR/Family Radio, 10400 NW 240th Street, Okeechobee FL 34972 USA. Fax: +1 (813) 763 8867. Contact: Dan Elyea, Engineering Manager.
UZBEKISTAN World Time +5
RADIO TASHKENT, 49 Khorezm Street, Tashkent 700 047, Uzbekistan. Contact: V. Danchev, Correspondence Section; G. Babadjanova, Chief Director of Programmes; or Florida Perevertailo, Producer, "At Listeners' Request and Others." Free pennants, badges, wallet calendars and postcards. Books in English by Uzbek writers are apparently available for purchase.
UZBEK RADIO—see "Radio Tashkent" for details.
VANUATU World Time +12 (+11 midyear)
RADIO VANUATU, Information & Public Relations, P.M.B. 049, Port Vila, Vanuatu. Fax: 678 22026 (no direct dial as yet). Contact: (technical) K.J. Page, Principal Engineer.

VATICAN CITY STATE World Time +1 (+2 midyear)
VATICAN RADIO, 00120 Vatican City, Vatican State. Fax: +39 (6) 698 3237. Contact: Fr. Federico Lombardi, S.J., Program Manager; or Fr. Pasquale Borgomeo, S.J., Director General. Free station stickers and pennants. Compact disc musical recordings for $13 each from sales office, Freq. s.r.l.—Edizioni Fonografiche, Via Volturno 80, Edilnord/Portici 1, I-20047 Brugherio MI, Italy.

VENEZUELA World Time –4
Note: Although widely heard, Venezuelan stations are not always the best in responding to listeners' correspondence. Friendly, personalized correspondence in Spanish (Spanish is typically a "must"), with $1 or return postage and some photos or other mementos enclosed, appears to work best in eliciting a reply.
ECOS DEL TORBES, Apartado 152, San Cristóbal 5001, Táchira, Venezuela. Contact: (nontechnical) Gregorio González Lovera, Presidente; (technical) Ing. Iván Escobar S., Jefe Técnico.
RADIO CONTINENTAL, Apartado 202, Barinas 5201, Venezuela. Contact: (nontechnical) Angel M. Pérez, Director; (technical) Ing. Santiago San Gil G. $1, return postage or 2 IRCs required. Free small souvenirs. Replies occasionally to correspondence in Spanish.
RADIO CONTINENTE, Apartado 866, Caracas 1010, Venezuela. May reply to correspondence in Spanish.
RADIO FRONTERA, Edificio Radio, San Antonio del Táchira, Táchira, Venezuela. Contact: N. Marchena, Director. May reply to correspondence in Spanish. $1 or return postage suggested. If no reply, try with $1 via Sr. Contín at Radio Mara, below.
RADIO LOS ANDES, Apartado 40, Mérida, Venezuela. May reply to correspondence in Spanish. $1 or return postage suggested.
RADIO MARA, Calle Los Lirios No. 1219, Urbanización Miraflores, Cabimas 4013, Zulia, Venezuela. Contact: Antonio J. Contín E. $1 required. Replies occasionally.
RADIO MARACAIBO, Calle 67 No. 24-88, Maracaibo, Venezuela. Contact: Máximo Flores Velázquez, Director-Gerente. $1 or return postage required. Replies to correspondence in Spanish. If no reply, try with $1 via Sr. Contín at Radio Mara, above.
RADIO NACIONAL DE VENEZUELA, RNV
Main Office: Apartado 3979, Caracas 1050, Venezuela. Contact: Martin G. Delfin, English News Director. Free 50th anniversary stickers, while they last, and other small souvenirs. Lone Star exile Marty Delfin, a former TV newscaster, hails from San Antonio and UT/Austin, Texas. If no response, try Apartado 50700, Caracas 1050, Venezuela.
Miami Postal Address: Jet Cargo International, M-7, P.O. Box 020010, Miami FL 33102 USA. Contact: Martin G. Delfin, English News Director.
RADIO RUMBOS, Apartado 2618, Caracas 1010A, Venezuela. Contact: (technical) YV5UU. $1 or IRC required. Replies occasionally to correspondence in Spanish.
RADIO TACHIRA, Apartado 152, San Cristóbal 5001, Táchira, Venezuela. Contact: Eleázar Silva M., Gerente.
RADIO TURISMO (when operating), Apartado 12, Valera, Trujillo, Venezuela. Rarely replies to correspondence in Spanish. If no reply, try with $1 via Sr. Contín at Radio Mara, above.
RADIO VALERA, Av. 10 No. 9-31, Valera, Trujillo, Venezuela. If no reply, try with $1 via Sr. Contín at Radio Mara, above.

VIETNAM World Time +7
BAC THAI BROADCASTING SERVICE—contact via "Voice of Vietnam, Overseas Service," below.
LAI CHAU BROADCASTING SERVICE—contact via "Voice of Vietnam, Overseas Service," below.
LAM DONG BROADCASTING SERVICE, Da Lat, Vietnam. Contact: Hoang Van Trung. Replies slowly to correspondence in Vietnamese.
SON LA BROADCASTING SERVICE, Son La, Vietnam. Contact: Nguyen Hang, Director. Replies slowly to correspondence in Vietnamese.

VOICE OF VIETNAM, Domestic Service—contact via "Voice of Vietnam, Overseas Service," below.
VOICE OF VIETNAM, Overseas Service, 58 Quan Su Street, Hanoi, Vietnam; or (technical) Office of Radio Reception Quality, Central Department of Radio and Television Broadcast Engineering, Vietnam General Corporation of Posts and Telecommunications, Hanoi, Vietnam. Contact (Overseas Service): Dao Dinh Tuan, Director of External Broadcasting. Free pennant and Vietnamese stamps. $1 helpful, but IRCs apparently of no use. Replies slowly.
YEN BAI BROADCASTING STATION—contact via "Voice of Vietnam, Overseas Service," above.

YEMEN World Time +3
REPUBLIC OF YEMEN RADIO, Ministry of Information, San'a, Yemen. Contact: (nontechnical correspondence in English) English Service; (technical) Abdullah Farhan, Technical Director.

YUGOSLAVIA World Time +1 (+2 midyear)
RADIO BEOGRAD, Hilendarska 2/IV, YU-11000 Belgrade, Serbia, Yugoslavia. Fax: +38 (11) 332 014. Contact: (technical) B. Miletic, Operations Manager of HF Broadcasting.
RADIO YUGOSLAVIA, P.O. Box 200, Hilendarska 2/IV, YU-11000 Belgrade, Serbia, Yugoslavia. Fax: +38 (11) 332 014. Contact: (nontechnical) Aleksandar Georgiev; (technical) B. Miletic, Operations Manager of HF Broadcasting, Technical Department. Free pennants and pins. $1 helpful. Responses are now relatively fast, friendly and reliable.

ZAIRE World Time +1 Western, including Kinshasa; +2 Eastern
LA VOIX DU ZAIRE—KINSHASA, B.P. 3171, Kinshasa-Gombe, Zaïre. Contact: Ayimpam Mwan-a-ngo, Directeur des Programmes, Radio. Letters should be sent via registered mail. $1 or 3 IRCs helpful. Correspondence in French preferred.
LA VOIX DU ZAIRE—KISANGANI, B.P. 1745, Kisangani, Zaïre. Contact: (nontechnical) Lumeto lue Lumeto, Le Directeur Regional de l'O.Z.R.T.; (technical) Lukusa Kowumayi Branly, Technician. $1 or 2 IRCs required. Correspondence in French preferred. Replies to North American listeners sometimes are mailed via the Oakland, California, post office.
RADIO LUBUMBASHI, LA VOIX DU ZAIRE, B.P. 7296, Lubumbashi, Zaïre. Contact: Senga Lokavu, Le Chef du Service de l'Audiovisuel; or Bébé Beshelemu, Le Directeur Regional de l'O.Z.R.T; or Mulenga Kanso, Le Chef du Service Logistique. Letters should be sent via registered mail. $1 or 3 IRCs helpful. Correspondence in French preferred.

ZAMBIA World Time +2
RADIO ZAMBIA, Broadcasting House, P.O. Box 50015, Lusaka, Zambia. Fax: +260 (1) 254013. Contact: (nontechnical) Emmanuel Chayi, Acting Director-General; (technical) W. Lukozu, Project Engineer. $1 required, and postal correspondence should be sent via registered mail. Replies slowly and irregularly.

Credits: Craig Tyson; also Tony Jones, Lawrence Magne, Numero Uno and Radio Nuevo Mundo; with special thanks to Abdelkader Abbadi, DXing ex-USSR, DX Moscow/Anatoly Klepov, Gabriel Iván Barrera, Antonio Ribeiro da Motta, Gordon Darling, Lon Kinley, Marie Lamb, Toshimichi Ohtake, David Pfeiffer, George Poppin and Harlan Seyfer.

The Blue Pages

Channel-by-Channel Guide to World Band Schedules

There are hundreds of channels of news, music and entertainment available on world band radio, with some being shared by several stations. With so much to choose from, it can take some doing just to figure out what is out there.

Schedules at a Glance

Ordinary listings of what's on world band radio are unwieldy, as there are thousands of items of data. That's why *Passport* includes these quick-access Blue Pages. Now, everything—stations, times, languages, targets and more—can be found at a glance. If an abbreviation or something else is not clear, the Glossary at the back of the book explains it. There is also a handy key to languages and symbols at the bottom of each pair of Blue Pages.

For example, if you're in North America listening to 6175 kHz at 2300 World Time, you'll see that the BBC World Service is broadcast in English to this area at that hour. The transmitter is located in Canada and operates at a power of 250 kW.

To be as helpful as possible throughout the year, *Passport's* schedules consist not just of observed activity, but also that which we have creatively opined will take place during the entire year. This latter information is original from us, and therefore, of course, will not be so exact as factual information.

World Band Stations Heard Beyond Intended Target

With several hundred stations on the air at the same time, many on the same channels, you can't begin to hear all—or even most. Nevertheless, you can hear some stations even though they're not targeted at your part of the world. Tune around the airwaves, using the Blue Pages as your guide, and you'll discover more variety than ever.

World Time

Times and days of the week are given in World Time, explained in the *Passport* Glossary. Midyear, many programs are heard an hour earlier, whereas some in the southern hemisphere are heard an hour later.

Guide to Blue Pages Format

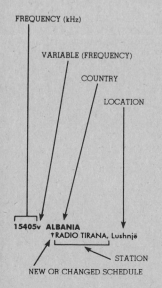
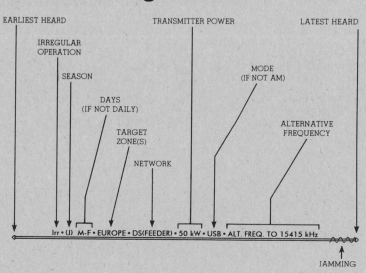

FREQUENCY (kHz)

VARIABLE (FREQUENCY)

COUNTRY

LOCATION

EARLIEST HEARD

IRREGULAR OPERATION

SEASON

DAYS (IF NOT DAILY)

TARGET ZONE(S)

NETWORK

TRANSMITTER POWER

MODE (IF NOT AM)

ALTERNATIVE FREQUENCY

LATEST HEARD

15405v ALBANIA
↑RADIO TIRANA, Lushnjë

STATION

NEW OR CHANGED SCHEDULE

Irr • (J) M-F • EUROPE • DS(FEEDER) • 50 kW • USB • ALT. FREQ. TO 15415 kHz

JAMMING

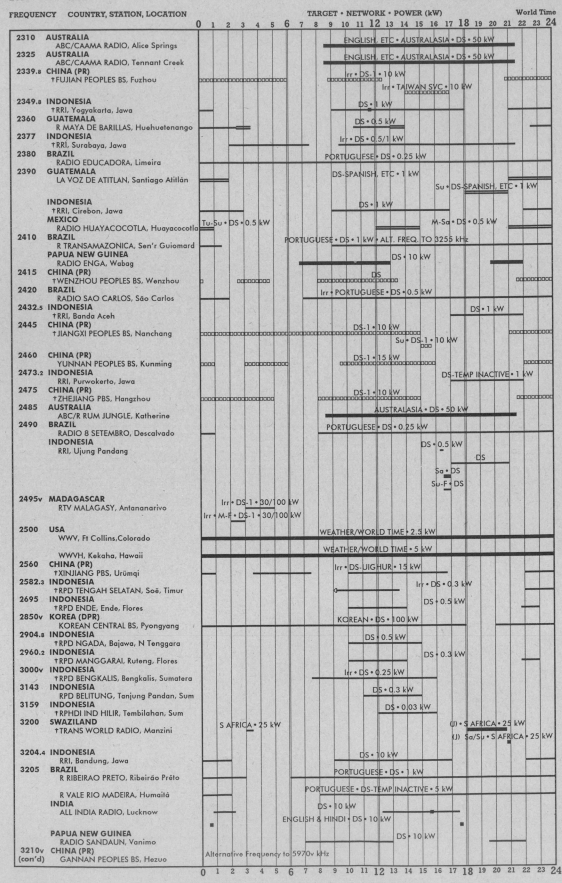

FREQUENCY   COUNTRY, STATION, LOCATION   TARGET • NETWORK • POWER (kW)   World Time

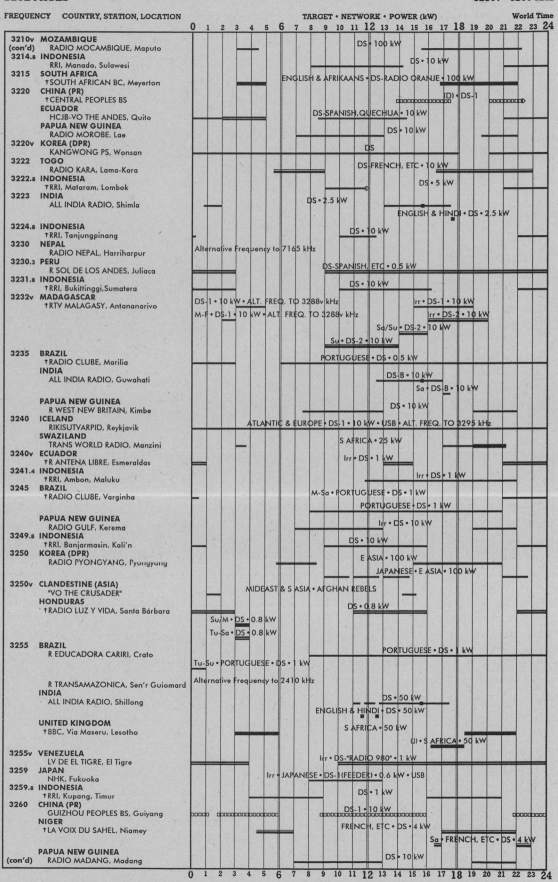

FREQUENCY	COUNTRY, STATION, LOCATION	Details
3210v (con'd)	MOZAMBIQUE — RADIO MOCAMBIQUE, Maputo	DS • 100 kW
3214.8	INDONESIA — RRI, Manado, Sulawesi	DS • 10 kW
3215	SOUTH AFRICA — †SOUTH AFRICAN BC, Meyerton	ENGLISH & AFRIKAANS • DS-RADIO ORANJE • 100 kW
3220	CHINA (PR) — †CENTRAL PEOPLES BS	(D) • DS-1
	ECUADOR — HCJB-VO THE ANDES, Quito	DS-SPANISH, QUECHUA • 10 kW
	PAPUA NEW GUINEA — RADIO MOROBE, Lae	DS • 10 kW
3220v	KOREA (DPR) — KANGWONG PS, Wonsan	DS
3222	TOGO — RADIO KARA, Lama-Kara	DS-FRENCH, ETC • 10 kW
3222.8	INDONESIA — †RRI, Mataram, Lombok	DS • 5 kW
3223	INDIA — ALL INDIA RADIO, Shimla	DS • 2.5 kW; ENGLISH & HINDI • DS • 2.5 kW
3224.8	INDONESIA — †RRI, Tanjungpinang	DS • 10 kW
3230	NEPAL — RADIO NEPAL, Harriharpur	Alternative Frequency to 7165 kHz
3230.3	PERU — R SOL DE LOS ANDES, Juliaca	DS-SPANISH, ETC • 0.5 kW
3231.8	INDONESIA — †RRI, Bukittinggi, Sumatera	DS • 10 kW
3232v	MADAGASCAR — †RTV MALAGASY, Antananarivo	DS-1 • 10 kW • ALT. FREQ. TO 3288v kHz; Irr • DS-1 • 10 kW; M-F • DS-1 • 10 kW • ALT. FREQ. TO 3288v kHz; Irr • DS-2 • 10 kW; Sa/Su • DS-2 • 10 kW; Su • DS-2 • 10 kW
3235	BRAZIL — †RADIO CLUBE, Marilia	PORTUGUESE • DS • 0.5 kW
	INDIA — ALL INDIA RADIO, Guwahati	DS-B • 10 kW; Sa • DS-B • 10 kW
	PAPUA NEW GUINEA — R WEST NEW BRITAIN, Kimbe	DS • 10 kW
3240	ICELAND — RIKISUTVARPID, Reykjavik	ATLANTIC & EUROPE • DS-1 • 10 kW • USB • ALT. FREQ. TO 3295 kHz
	SWAZILAND — TRANS WORLD RADIO, Manzini	S AFRICA • 25 kW
3240v	ECUADOR — †R ANTENA LIBRE, Esmeraldas	Irr • DS • 1 kW
3241.4	INDONESIA — †RRI, Ambon, Maluku	Irr • DS • 1 kW
3245	BRAZIL — †RADIO CLUBE, Varginha	M-Sa • PORTUGUESE • DS • 1 kW; PORTUGUESE • DS • 1 kW
	PAPUA NEW GUINEA — RADIO GULF, Kerema	Irr • DS • 10 kW
3249.8	INDONESIA — †RRI, Banjarmasin, Kali'n	DS • 10 kW
3250	KOREA (DPR) — RADIO PYONGYANG, Pyongyang	E ASIA • 100 kW; JAPANESE • E ASIA • 100 kW
3250v	CLANDESTINE (ASIA) — "VO THE CRUSADER"	MIDEAST & S ASIA • AFGHAN REBELS
	HONDURAS — †RADIO LUZ Y VIDA, Santa Bárbara	DS • 0.8 kW; Su/M • DS • 0.8 kW; Tu-Sa • DS • 0.8 kW
3255	BRAZIL — R EDUCADORA CARIRI, Crato	PORTUGUESE • DS • 1 kW; Tu-Su • PORTUGUESE • DS • 1 kW
	R TRANSAMAZONICA, Sen'r Guiomard	Alternative Frequency to 2410 kHz
	INDIA — ALL INDIA RADIO, Shillong	DS • 50 kW; ENGLISH & HINDI • DS • 50 kW
	UNITED KINGDOM — †BBC, Via Maseru, Lesotho	S AFRICA • 50 kW; (J) • S AFRICA • 50 kW
3255v	VENEZUELA — LV DE EL TIGRE, El Tigre	Irr • DS-"RADIO 980" • 1 kW
3259	JAPAN — NHK, Fukuoka	Irr • JAPANESE • DS-1 (FEEDER) • 0.6 kW • USB
3259.8	INDONESIA — †RRI, Kupang, Timur	DS • 1 kW
3260	CHINA (PR) — GUIZHOU PEOPLES BS, Guiyang	DS-1 • 10 kW
	NIGER — †LA VOIX DU SAHEL, Niamey	FRENCH, ETC • DS • 4 kW; Sa • FRENCH, ETC • DS • 4 kW
(con'd)	PAPUA NEW GUINEA — RADIO MADANG, Madang	DS • 10 kW

ENGLISH ▬▬   ARABIC ⧖⧖⧖   CHINESE □□□   FRENCH ▬▬   GERMAN ▬▬   RUSSIAN ═══   SPANISH ▬▬   OTHER ▬▬

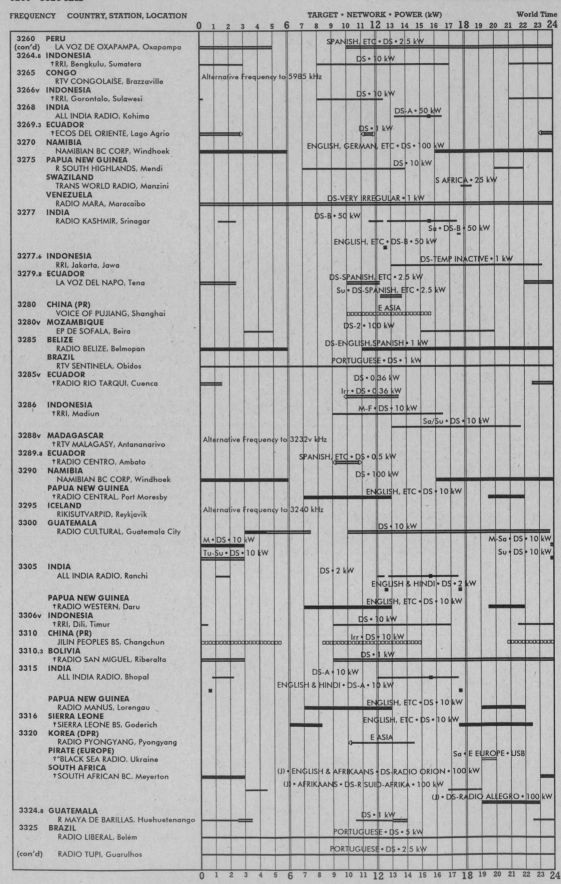

FREQUENCY   COUNTRY, STATION, LOCATION

TARGET • NETWORK • POWER (kW)

World Time

0 1 2 3 4 5 6 7 8 9 10 11 12 13 14 15 16 17 18 19 20 21 22 23 24

3260 **PERU**
(con'd)   LA VOZ DE OXAPAMPA, Oxapampa — SPANISH, ETC • DS • 2.5 kW

3264.8 **INDONESIA**
  †RRI, Bengkulu, Sumatera — DS • 10 kW

3265 **CONGO**
  RTV CONGOLAISE, Brazzaville — Alternative Frequency to 5985 kHz

3266v **INDONESIA**
  †RRI, Gorontalo, Sulawesi — DS • 10 kW

3268 **INDIA**
  ALL INDIA RADIO, Kohima — DS-A • 50 kW

3269.3 **ECUADOR**
  †ECOS DEL ORIENTE, Lago Agrio — DS • 1 kW

3270 **NAMIBIA**
  NAMIBIAN BC CORP, Windhoek — ENGLISH, GERMAN, ETC • DS • 100 kW

3275 **PAPUA NEW GUINEA**
  R SOUTH HIGHLANDS, Mendi — DS • 10 kW
SWAZILAND
  TRANS WORLD RADIO, Manzini — S AFRICA • 25 kW
VENEZUELA
  RADIO MARA, Maracaibo — DS-VERY IRREGULAR • 1 kW

3277 **INDIA**
  RADIO KASHMIR, Srinagar — DS-B • 50 kW
  Sa • DS-B • 50 kW
  ENGLISH, ETC • DS-B • 50 kW

3277.6 **INDONESIA**
  RRI, Jakarta, Jawa — DS-TEMP INACTIVE • 1 kW

3279.8 **ECUADOR**
  LA VOZ DEL NAPO, Tena — DS-SPANISH, ETC • 2.5 kW
  Su • DS-SPANISH, ETC • 2.5 kW

3280 **CHINA (PR)**
  VOICE OF PUJIANG, Shanghai — E ASIA

3280v **MOZAMBIQUE**
  EP DE SOFALA, Beira — DS-2 • 100 kW

3285 **BELIZE**
  RADIO BELIZE, Belmopan — DS-ENGLISH, SPANISH • 1 kW
BRAZIL
  RTV SENTINELA, Obidos — PORTUGUESE • DS • 1 kW

3285v **ECUADOR**
  †RADIO RIO TARQUI, Cuenca — DS • 0.36 kW
  Irr • DS • 0.36 kW

3286 **INDONESIA**
  †RRI, Madiun — M-F • DS • 10 kW
  Sa/Su • DS • 10 kW

3288v **MADAGASCAR**
  †RTV MALAGASY, Antananarivo — Alternative Frequency to 3232v kHz

3289.8 **ECUADOR**
  †RADIO CENTRO, Ambato — SPANISH, ETC • DS • 0.5 kW

3290 **NAMIBIA**
  NAMIBIAN BC CORP, Windhoek — DS • 100 kW
PAPUA NEW GUINEA
  †RADIO CENTRAL, Port Moresby — ENGLISH, ETC • DS • 10 kW

3295 **ICELAND**
  RIKISUTVARPID, Reykjavik — Alternative Frequency to 3240 kHz

3300 **GUATEMALA**
  RADIO CULTURAL, Guatemala City — DS • 10 kW
  M • DS • 10 kW
  M-Sa • DS • 10 kW
  Tu-Su • DS • 10 kW
  Su • DS • 10 kW

3305 **INDIA**
  ALL INDIA RADIO, Ranchi — DS • 2 kW
  ENGLISH & HINDI • DS • 2 kW
PAPUA NEW GUINEA
  †RADIO WESTERN, Daru — ENGLISH, ETC • DS • 10 kW

3306v **INDONESIA**
  †RRI, Dili, Timur — DS • 10 kW

3310 **CHINA (PR)**
  JILIN PEOPLES BS, Changchun — Irr • DS • 10 kW

3310.3 **BOLIVIA**
  †RADIO SAN MIGUEL, Riberalta — DS • 1 kW

3315 **INDIA**
  ALL INDIA RADIO, Bhopal — DS-A • 10 kW
  ENGLISH & HINDI • DS-A • 10 kW
PAPUA NEW GUINEA
  RADIO MANUS, Lorengau — ENGLISH, ETC • DS • 10 kW

3316 **SIERRA LEONE**
  †SIERRA LEONE BS, Goderich — ENGLISH, ETC • DS • 10 kW

3320 **KOREA (DPR)**
  RADIO PYONGYANG, Pyongyang — E ASIA
PIRATE (EUROPE)
  †"BLACK SEA RADIO, Ukraine — Sa • E EUROPE • USB
SOUTH AFRICA
  †SOUTH AFRICAN BC, Meyerton — (J) • ENGLISH & AFRIKAANS • DS-RADIO ORION • 100 kW
  (J) • AFRIKAANS • DS-R SUID-AFRIKA • 100 kW
  (J) • DS-RADIO ALLEGRO • 100 kW

3324.8 **GUATEMALA**
  R MAYA DE BARILLAS, Huehuetenango — DS • 1 kW

3325 **BRAZIL**
  RADIO LIBERAL, Belém — PORTUGUESE • DS • 5 kW

(con'd)   RADIO TUPI, Guarulhos — PORTUGUESE • DS • 2.5 kW

0 1 2 3 4 5 6 7 8 9 10 11 12 13 14 15 16 17 18 19 20 21 22 23 24

SUMMER ONLY (J)   WINTER ONLY (D)   JAMMING / OR /\   EARLIEST HEARD ◁   LATEST HEARD ▷   NEW OR CHANGED FOR 1993 †

FREQUENCY   COUNTRY, STATION, LOCATION

TARGET • NETWORK • POWER (kW)

World Time

0 1 2 3 4 5 6 7 8 9 10 11 12 13 14 15 16 17 18 19 20 21 22 23 24

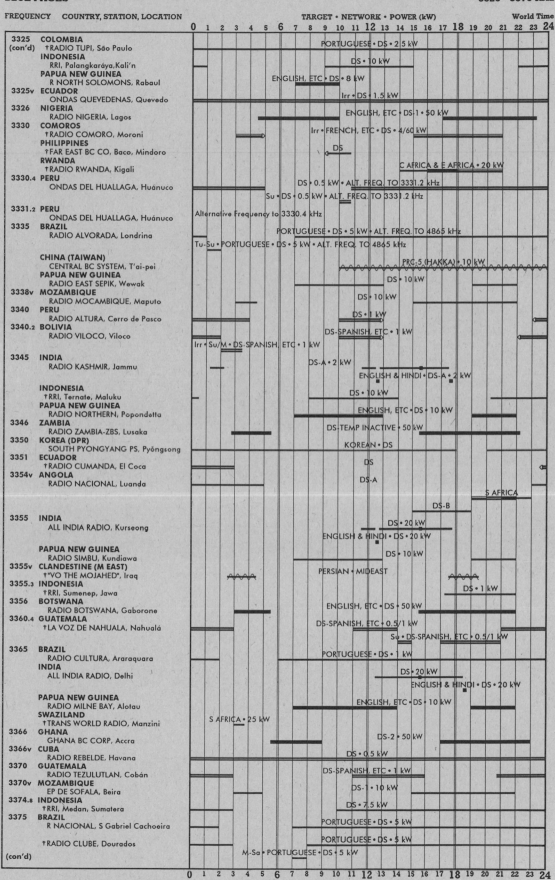

Frequency	Country, Station, Location	Details
3325 (con'd)	COLOMBIA — †RADIO TUPI, São Paulo	PORTUGUESE • DS • 2.5 kW
	INDONESIA — RRI, Palangkaráya, Kali'n	DS • 10 kW
	PAPUA NEW GUINEA — R NORTH SOLOMONS, Rabaul	ENGLISH, ETC • DS • 8 kW
3325v	ECUADOR — ONDAS QUEVEDENAS, Quevedo	Irr • DS • 1.5 kW
3326	NIGERIA — RADIO NIGERIA, Lagos	ENGLISH, ETC • DS-1 • 50 kW
3330	COMOROS — †RADIO COMORO, Moroni	Irr • FRENCH, ETC • DS • 4/60 kW
	PHILIPPINES — †FAR EAST BC CO, Baco, Mindoro	DS
	RWANDA — †RADIO RWANDA, Kigali	C AFRICA & E AFRICA • 20 kW
3330.4	PERU — ONDAS DEL HUALLAGA, Huánuco	DS • 0.5 kW • ALT. FREQ. TO 3331.2 kHz / Su • DS • 0.5 kW • ALT. FREQ. TO 3331.2 kHz
3331.2	PERU — ONDAS DEL HUALLAGA, Huánuco	Alternative Frequency to 3330.4 kHz
3335	BRAZIL — RADIO ALVORADA, Londrina	PORTUGUESE • DS • 5 kW • ALT. FREQ. TO 4865 kHz / Tu-Su • PORTUGUESE • DS • 5 kW • ALT. FREQ. TO 4865 kHz
	CHINA (TAIWAN) — CENTRAL BC SYSTEM, T'ai-pei	PRC-5 (HAKKA) • 10 kW
	PAPUA NEW GUINEA — RADIO EAST SEPIK, Wewak	DS • 10 kW
3338v	MOZAMBIQUE — RADIO MOCAMBIQUE, Maputo	DS • 10 kW
3340	PERU — RADIO ALTURA, Cerro de Pasco	DS • 1 kW
3340.2	BOLIVIA — RADIO VILOCO, Viloco	DS-SPANISH, ETC • 1 kW / Irr • Su/M • DS-SPANISH, ETC • 1 kW
3345	INDIA — RADIO KASHMIR, Jammu	DS-A • 2 kW / ENGLISH & HINDI • DS-A • 2 kW
	INDONESIA — †RRI, Ternate, Maluku	DS • 10 kW
	PAPUA NEW GUINEA — RADIO NORTHERN, Popondetta	ENGLISH, ETC • DS • 10 kW
3346	ZAMBIA — RADIO ZAMBIA-ZBS, Lusaka	DS • TEMP INACTIVE • 50 kW
3350	KOREA (DPR) — SOUTH PYONGYANG PS, Pyŏngsong	KOREAN • DS
3351	ECUADOR — †RADIO CUMANDA, El Coca	DS
3354v	ANGOLA — RADIO NACIONAL, Luanda	DS-A / S AFRICA / DS-B
3355	INDIA — ALL INDIA RADIO, Kurseong	DS • 20 kW / ENGLISH & HINDI • DS • 20 kW
	PAPUA NEW GUINEA — RADIO SIMBU, Kundiawa	DS • 10 kW
3355v	CLANDESTINE (M EAST) — †"VO THE MOJAHED", Iraq	PERSIAN • MIDEAST
3355.3	INDONESIA — †RRI, Sumenep, Jawa	DS • 1 kW
3356	BOTSWANA — RADIO BOTSWANA, Gaborone	ENGLISH, ETC • DS • 50 kW
3360.4	GUATEMALA — †LA VOZ DE NAHUALA, Nahualá	DS-SPANISH, ETC • 0.5/1 kW / Su • DS-SPANISH, ETC • 0.5/1 kW
3365	BRAZIL — RADIO CULTURA, Araraquara	PORTUGUESE • DS • 1 kW
	INDIA — ALL INDIA RADIO, Delhi	DS • 20 kW / ENGLISH & HINDI • DS • 20 kW
	PAPUA NEW GUINEA — RADIO MILNE BAY, Alotau	ENGLISH, ETC • DS • 10 kW
	SWAZILAND — †TRANS WORLD RADIO, Manzini	S AFRICA • 25 kW
3366	GHANA — GHANA BC CORP, Accra	DS-2 • 50 kW
3366v	CUBA — RADIO REBELDE, Havana	DS • 0.5 kW
3370	GUATEMALA — RADIO TEZULUTLAN, Cobán	DS-SPANISH, ETC • 1 kW
3370v	MOZAMBIQUE — EP DE SOFALA, Beira	DS-1 • 10 kW
3374.8	INDONESIA — †RRI, Medan, Sumatera	DS • 7.5 kW
3375	BRAZIL — R NACIONAL, S Gabriel Cachoeira	PORTUGUESE • DS • 5 kW
	†RADIO CLUBE, Dourados	PORTUGUESE • DS • 5 kW / M-Sa • PORTUGUESE • DS • 5 kW
(con'd)		

0 1 2 3 4 5 6 7 8 9 10 11 12 13 14 15 16 17 18 19 20 21 22 23 24

ENGLISH ▬   ARABIC ▨   CHINESE ▫▫▫   FRENCH ▭   GERMAN ▬   RUSSIAN ▬   SPANISH ▭   OTHER ▬

FREQUENCY   COUNTRY, STATION, LOCATION   TARGET • NETWORK • POWER (kW)   World Time

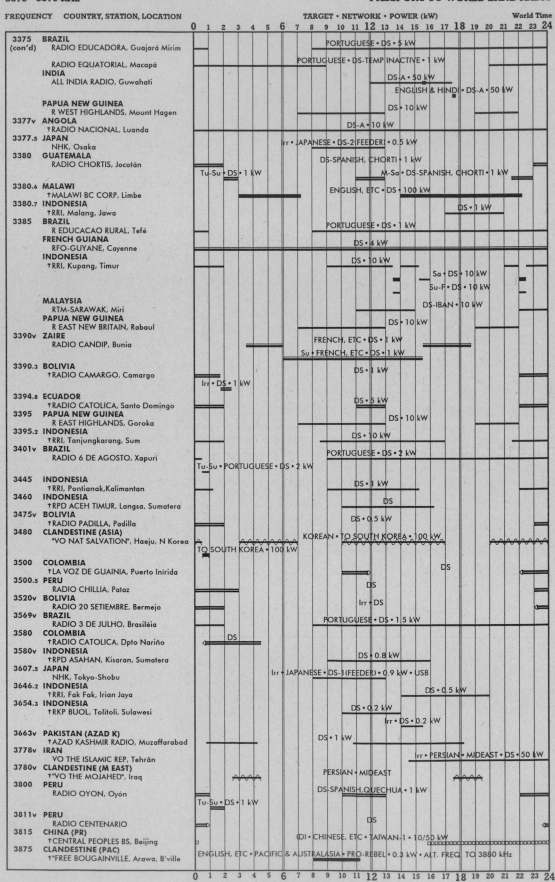

Frequency	Country, Station, Location	Notes
3375 (con'd)	**BRAZIL** RADIO EDUCADORA, Guajará Mirim	PORTUGUESE • DS • 5 kW
	RADIO EQUATORIAL, Macapá	PORTUGUESE • DS-TEMP INACTIVE • 1 kW
	INDIA ALL INDIA RADIO, Guwahati	DS-A • 50 kW / ENGLISH & HINDI • DS-A • 50 kW
	PAPUA NEW GUINEA R WEST HIGHLANDS, Mount Hagen	DS • 10 kW
3377v	**ANGOLA** †RADIO NACIONAL, Luanda	DS-A • 10 kW
3377.5	**JAPAN** NHK, Osaka	Irr • JAPANESE • DS-2 (FEEDER) • 0.5 kW
3380	**GUATEMALA** RADIO CHORTIS, Jocotán	DS-SPANISH, CHORTI • 1 kW / Tu-Su • DS • 1 kW / M-Sa • DS-SPANISH, CHORTI • 1 kW
3380.6	**MALAWI** †MALAWI BC CORP, Limbe	ENGLISH, ETC • DS • 100 kW
3380.7	**INDONESIA** †RRI, Malang, Jawa	DS • 1 kW
3385	**BRAZIL** R EDUCACAO RURAL, Tefé	PORTUGUESE • DS • 1 kW
	FRENCH GUIANA RFO-GUYANE, Cayenne	DS • 4 kW
	INDONESIA †RRI, Kupang, Timur	DS • 10 kW / Sa • DS • 10 kW / Su-F • DS • 10 kW
	MALAYSIA RTM-SARAWAK, Miri	DS-IBAN • 10 kW
	PAPUA NEW GUINEA R EAST NEW BRITAIN, Rabaul	DS • 10 kW
3390v	**ZAIRE** RADIO CANDIP, Bunia	FRENCH, ETC • DS • 1 kW / Su • FRENCH, ETC • DS • 1 kW
3390.3	**BOLIVIA** †RADIO CAMARGO, Camargo	DS • 1 kW / Irr • DS • 1 kW
3394.8	**ECUADOR** †RADIO CATOLICA, Santo Domingo	DS • 5 kW
3395	**PAPUA NEW GUINEA** R EAST HIGHLANDS, Goroka	DS • 10 kW
3395.2	**INDONESIA** †RRI, Tanjungkarang, Sum	DS • 10 kW
3401v	**BRAZIL** RADIO 6 DE AGOSTO, Xapurí	PORTUGUESE • DS • 2 kW / Tu-Su • PORTUGUESE • DS • 2 kW
3445	**INDONESIA** †RRI, Pontianak, Kalimantan	DS • 1 kW
3460	**INDONESIA** †RPD ACEH TIMUR, Langsa, Sumatera	DS
3475v	**BOLIVIA** †RADIO PADILLA, Padilla	DS • 0.5 kW
3480	**CLANDESTINE (ASIA)** "VO NAT SALVATION", Haeju, N Korea	KOREAN • TO SOUTH KOREA • 100 kW / TO SOUTH KOREA • 100 kW
3500	**COLOMBIA** †LA VOZ DE GUAINIA, Puerto Inírida	DS
3500.5	**PERU** RADIO CHILLIA, Pataz	DS
3520v	**BOLIVIA** RADIO 20 SETIEMBRE, Bermejo	Irr • DS
3569v	**BRAZIL** RADIO 3 DE JULHO, Brasiléia	PORTUGUESE • DS • 1.5 kW
3580	**COLOMBIA** †RADIO CATOLICA, Dpto Nariño	DS
3580v	**INDONESIA** †RPD ASAHAN, Kisaran, Sumatera	DS • 0.8 kW
3607.5	**JAPAN** NHK, Tokyo-Shobu	Irr • JAPANESE • DS-1 (FEEDER) • 0.9 kW • USB
3646.2	**INDONESIA** †RRI, Fak Fak, Irian Jaya	DS • 0.5 kW
3654.3	**INDONESIA** †RKP BUOL, Tolitoli, Sulawesi	DS • 0.2 kW / Irr • DS • 0.2 kW
3663v	**PAKISTAN (AZAD K)** †AZAD KASHMIR RADIO, Muzaffarabad	DS • 1 kW
3778v	**IRAN** VO THE ISLAMIC REP, Tehrän	Irr • PERSIAN • MIDEAST • DS • 50 kW
3780v	**CLANDESTINE (M EAST)** †"VO THE MOJAHED", Iraq	PERSIAN • MIDEAST
3800	**PERU** RADIO OYON, Oyón	DS-SPANISH, QUECHUA • 1 kW / Tu-Su • DS • 1 kW
3811v	**PERU** RADIO CENTENARIO	DS
3815	**CHINA (PR)** †CENTRAL PEOPLES BS, Beijing	(D) • CHINESE, ETC • TAIWAN-1 • 10/50 kW
3875	**CLANDESTINE (PAC)** †"FREE BOUGAINVILLE", Arawa, B'ville	ENGLISH, ETC • PACIFIC & AUSTRALASIA • PRO-REBEL • 0.3 kW • ALT. FREQ. TO 3880 kHz

SUMMER ONLY (J)   WINTER ONLY (D)   JAMMING / OR ∧   EARLIEST HEARD ◁   LATEST HEARD ▷   NEW OR CHANGED FOR 1993 †

FREQUENCY   COUNTRY, STATION, LOCATION   TARGET • NETWORK • POWER (kW)   World Time

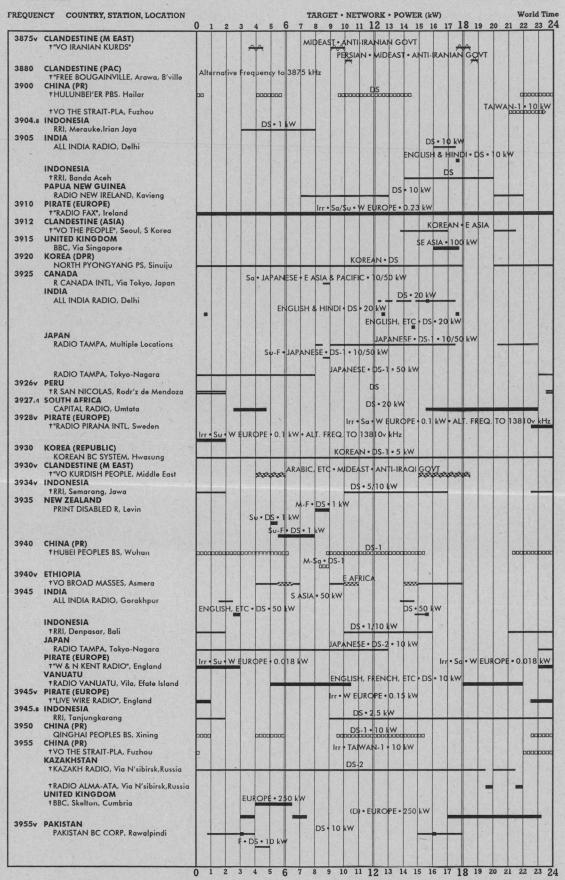

FREQUENCY	COUNTRY, STATION, LOCATION	TARGET • NETWORK • POWER (kW)
3875v	CLANDESTINE (M EAST)	MIDEAST • ANTI-IRANIAN GOVT
	†"VO IRANIAN KURDS"	PERSIAN • MIDEAST • ANTI-IRANIAN GOVT
3880	CLANDESTINE (PAC)	Alternative Frequency to 3875 kHz
	†"FREE BOUGAINVILLE, Arawa, B'ville	
3900	CHINA (PR)	DS
	†HULUNBEI'ER PBS. Hailar	
	†VO THE STRAIT-PLA, Fuzhou	TAIWAN-1 • 10 kW
3904.8	INDONESIA	DS • 1 kW
	RRI, Merauke, Irian Jaya	
3905	INDIA	DS • 10 kW
	ALL INDIA RADIO, Delhi	ENGLISH & HINDI • DS • 10 kW
	INDONESIA	DS
	†RRI, Banda Aceh	
	PAPUA NEW GUINEA	DS • 10 kW
	RADIO NEW IRELAND, Kavieng	
3910	PIRATE (EUROPE)	Irr • Sa/Su • W EUROPE • 0.23 kW
	†"RADIO FAX", Ireland	
3912	CLANDESTINE (ASIA)	KOREAN • E ASIA
	†"VO THE PEOPLE", Seoul, S Korea	
3915	UNITED KINGDOM	SE ASIA • 100 kW
	BBC, Via Singapore	
3920	KOREA (DPR)	KOREAN • DS
	NORTH PYONGYANG PS, Sinuiju	
3925	CANADA	Sa • JAPANESE • E ASIA & PACIFIC • 10/50 kW
	R CANADA INTL, Via Tokyo, Japan	
	INDIA	DS • 20 kW
	ALL INDIA RADIO, Delhi	ENGLISH & HINDI • DS • 20 kW
		ENGLISH, ETC • DS • 20 kW
	JAPAN	JAPANESE • DS-1 • 10/50 kW
	RADIO TAMPA, Multiple Locations	Su-F • JAPANESE • DS-1 • 10/50 kW
	RADIO TAMPA, Tokyo-Nagara	JAPANESE • DS-1 • 50 kW
3926v	PERU	DS
	†R SAN NICOLAS, Rodr'z de Mendoza	
3927.1	SOUTH AFRICA	DS • 20 kW
	CAPITAL RADIO, Umtata	
3928v	PIRATE (EUROPE)	Irr • Sa • W EUROPE • 0.1 kW • ALT. FREQ. TO 13810v kHz
	†"RADIO PIRANA INTL, Sweden	Irr • Su • W EUROPE • 0.1 kW • ALT. FREQ. TO 13810v kHz
3930	KOREA (REPUBLIC)	KOREAN • DS-1 • 5 kW
	KOREAN BC SYSTEM, Hwasung	
3930v	CLANDESTINE (M EAST)	ARABIC, ETC • MIDEAST • ANTI-IRAQI GOVT
	†"VO KURDISH PEOPLE, Middle East	
3934v	INDONESIA	DS • 5/10 kW
	†RRI, Semarang, Jawa	
3935	NEW ZEALAND	M-F • DS • 1 kW
	PRINT DISABLED R, Levin	Su • DS • 1 kW
		Su-F • DS • 1 kW
3940	CHINA (PR)	DS-1
	†HUBEI PEOPLES BS, Wuhan	
		M-Sa • DS-1
3940v	ETHIOPIA	E AFRICA
	†VO BROAD MASSES, Asmera	
3945	INDIA	S ASIA • 50 kW
	ALL INDIA RADIO, Gorakhpur	ENGLISH, ETC • DS • 50 kW DS • 50 kW
	INDONESIA	DS • 1/10 kW
	†RRI, Denpasar, Bali	
	JAPAN	JAPANESE • DS-2 • 10 kW
	RADIO TAMPA, Tokyo-Nagara	
	PIRATE (EUROPE)	Irr • Su • W EUROPE • 0.018 kW Irr • Sa • W EUROPE • 0.018 kW
	†"W & N KENT RADIO", England	
	VANUATU	ENGLISH, FRENCH, ETC • DS • 10 kW
	†RADIO VANUATU, Vila, Efate Island	
3945v	PIRATE (EUROPE)	Irr • W EUROPE • 0.15 kW
	†"LIVE WIRE RADIO", England	
3945.8	INDONESIA	DS • 2.5 kW
	RRI, Tanjungkarang	
3950	CHINA (PR)	DS-1 • 10 kW
	QINGHAI PEOPLES BS, Xining	
3955	CHINA (PR)	Irr • TAIWAN-1 • 10 kW
	†VO THE STRAIT-PLA, Fuzhou	
	KAZAKHSTAN	DS-2
	†KAZAKH RADIO, Via N'sibirsk, Russia	
	†RADIO ALMA-ATA, Via N'sibirsk, Russia	
	UNITED KINGDOM	EUROPE • 250 kW
	†BBC, Skelton, Cumbria	(D) • EUROPE • 250 kW
3955v	PAKISTAN	DS • 10 kW
	PAKISTAN BC CORP, Rawalpindi	F • DS • 10 kW

ENGLISH ▬▬   ARABIC ⩘⩘   CHINESE □□□   FRENCH ▬▬   GERMAN ▬▬   RUSSIAN ══   SPANISH ▬▬   OTHER ▬

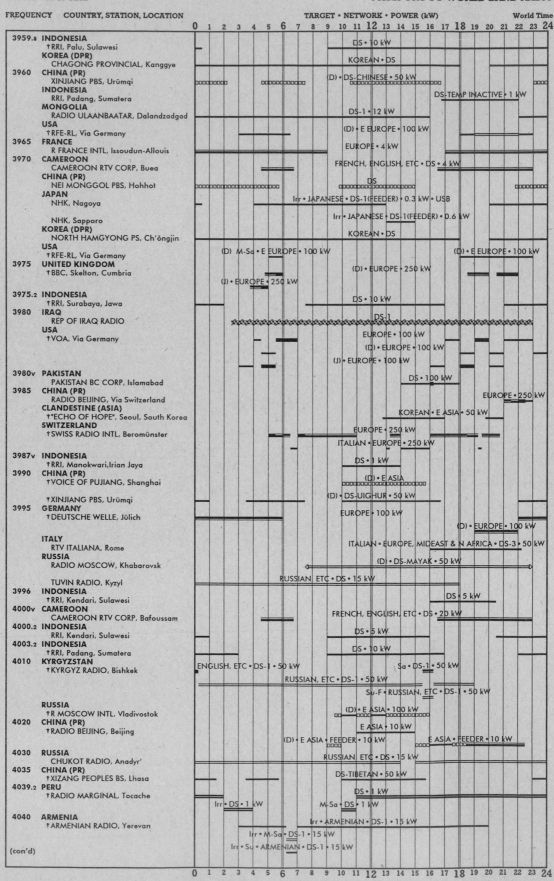

FREQUENCY   COUNTRY, STATION, LOCATION   TARGET • NETWORK • POWER (kW)   World Time
                                                0 1 2 3 4 5 6 7 8 9 10 11 12 13 14 15 16 17 18 19 20 21 22 23 24

3959.8 INDONESIA
        †RRI, Palu, Sulawesi — DS • 10 kW
        KOREA (DPR)
        CHAGONG PROVINCIAL, Kanggye — KOREAN • DS
3960   CHINA (PR)
        XINJIANG PBS, Urümqi — (D) • DS-CHINESE • 50 kW
        INDONESIA
        RRI, Padang, Sumatera — DS-TEMP INACTIVE • 1 kW
        MONGOLIA
        RADIO ULAANBAATAR, Dalandzadgad — DS-1 • 12 kW
        USA
        †RFE-RL, Via Germany — (D) • E EUROPE • 100 kW
3965   FRANCE
        R FRANCE INTL, Issoudun-Allouis — EUROPE • 4 kW
3970   CAMEROON
        CAMEROON RTV CORP, Buea — FRENCH, ENGLISH, ETC • DS • 4 kW
        CHINA (PR)
        NEI MONGGOL PBS, Hohhot — DS
        JAPAN
        NHK, Nagoya — Irr • JAPANESE • DS-1(FEEDER) 0.3 kW • USB
        NHK, Sapporo — Irr • JAPANESE • DS-1(FEEDER) • 0.6 kW
        KOREA (DPR)
        NORTH HAMGYONG PS, Ch'ŏngjin — KOREAN • DS
        USA
        †RFE-RL, Via Germany — (D) M-Sa • E EUROPE • 100 kW   (D) • E EUROPE • 100 kW
3975   UNITED KINGDOM
        †BBC, Skelton, Cumbria — (D) • EUROPE • 250 kW
                                 (J) • EUROPE • 250 kW
3975.2 INDONESIA
        †RRI, Surabaya, Jawa — DS • 10 kW
3980   IRAQ
        REP OF IRAQ RADIO — DS-1
        USA
        †VOA, Via Germany — EUROPE • 100 kW
                            (D) • EUROPE • 100 kW
                            (J) • EUROPE • 100 kW
3980v   PAKISTAN
        PAKISTAN BC CORP, Islamabad — DS • 100 kW
3985   CHINA (PR)
        RADIO BEIJING, Via Switzerland — EUROPE • 250 kW
        CLANDESTINE (ASIA)
        †"ECHO OF HOPE", Seoul, South Korea — KOREAN • E ASIA • 50 kW
        SWITZERLAND
        †SWISS RADIO INTL, Beromünster — EUROPE • 250 kW
                                         ITALIAN • EUROPE • 250 kW
3987v   INDONESIA
        †RRI, Manokwari,Irian Jaya — DS • 1 kW
3990   CHINA (PR)
        †VOICE OF PUJIANG, Shanghai — (D) • E ASIA
        †XINJIANG PBS, Urümqi — (D) • DS-UIGHUR • 50 kW
3995   GERMANY
        †DEUTSCHE WELLE, Jülich — EUROPE • 100 kW
                                  (D) • EUROPE • 100 kW
        ITALY
        RTV ITALIANA, Rome — ITALIAN • EUROPE, MIDEAST & N AFRICA • DS-3 • 50 kW
        RUSSIA
        RADIO MOSCOW, Khabarovsk — (D) • DS-MAYAK • 50 kW
        TUVIN RADIO, Kyzyl — RUSSIAN, ETC • DS • 15 kW
3996   INDONESIA
        †RRI, Kendari, Sulawesi — DS • 5 kW
4000v   CAMEROON
        CAMEROON RTV CORP, Bafoussam — FRENCH, ENGLISH, ETC • DS • 20 kW
4000.2 INDONESIA
        RRI, Kendari, Sulawesi — DS • 5 kW
4003.2 INDONESIA
        †RRI, Padang, Sumatera — DS • 10 kW
4010   KYRGYZSTAN
        †KYRGYZ RADIO, Bishkek — ENGLISH, ETC • DS-1 • 50 kW   Sa • DS-1 • 50 kW
                                 RUSSIAN, ETC • DS-1 • 50 kW
                                 Su-F • RUSSIAN, ETC • DS-1 • 50 kW
        RUSSIA
        †R MOSCOW INTL, Vladivostok — (D) • E ASIA • 100 kW
4020   CHINA (PR)
        †RADIO BEIJING, Beijing — E ASIA • 10 kW
                                 (D) • E ASIA • FEEDER • 10 kW   E ASIA • FEEDER • 10 kW
4030   RUSSIA
        CHUKOT RADIO, Anadyr' — RUSSIAN, ETC • DS • 15 kW
4035   CHINA (PR)
        †XIZANG PEOPLES BS, Lhasa — DS-TIBETAN • 50 kW
4039.2 PERU
        †RADIO MARGINAL, Tocache — DS • 1 kW
                                   Irr • DS • 1 kW   M-Sa • DS • 1 kW
4040   ARMENIA
        †ARMENIAN RADIO, Yerevan — Irr • ARMENIAN • DS-1 • 15 kW
                                   Irr • M-Sa • DS-1 • 15 kW
                                   Irr • Su • ARMENIAN • DS-1 • 15 kW
(con'd)

                                                0 1 2 3 4 5 6 7 8 9 10 11 12 13 14 15 16 17 18 19 20 21 22 23 24

FREQUENCY	COUNTRY, STATION, LOCATION	TARGET • NETWORK • POWER (kW) / World Time

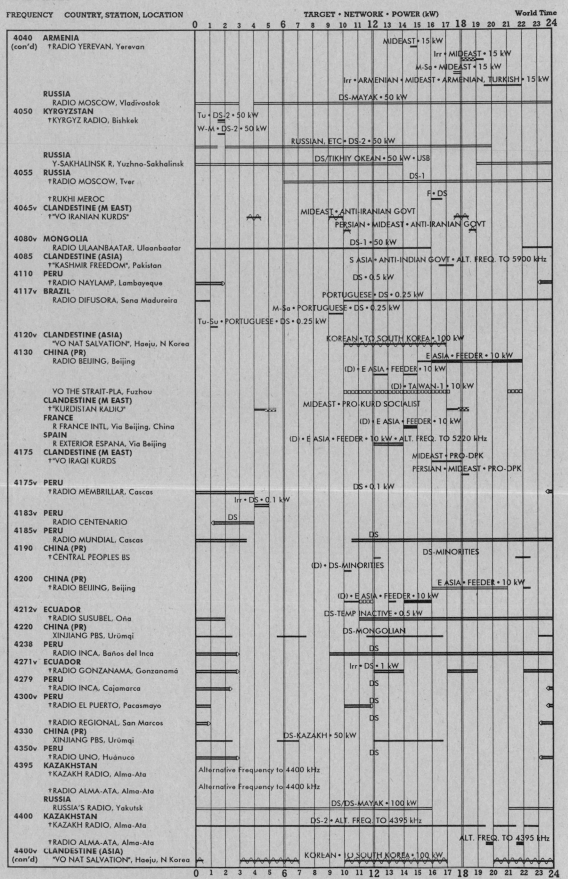

```
4040        ARMENIA
(con'd)     †RADIO YEREVAN, Yerevan                    MIDEAST • 15 kW
                                                          Irr • MIDEAST • 15 kW
                                                        M-Sa • MIDEAST • 15 kW
                                              Irr • ARMENIAN • MIDEAST • ARMENIAN, TURKISH • 15 kW

            RUSSIA
            RADIO MOSCOW, Vladivostok                  DS-MAYAK • 50 kW
4050        KYRGYZSTAN
            †KYRGYZ RADIO, Bishkek            Tu • DS-2 • 50 kW
                                              W-M • DS-2 • 50 kW
                                                        RUSSIAN, ETC • DS-2 • 50 kW

            RUSSIA
            Y-SAKHALINSK R, Yuzhno-Sakhalinsk          DS/TIKHIY OKEAN • 50 kW • USB
4055        RUSSIA
            †RADIO MOSCOW, Tver                         DS-1

            †RUKHI MEROC                                F • DS
4065v       CLANDESTINE (M EAST)
            †"VO IRANIAN KURDS"             MIDEAST • ANTI-IRANIAN GOVT
                                           PERSIAN • MIDEAST • ANTI-IRANIAN GOVT

4080v       MONGOLIA
            RADIO ULAANBAATAR, Ulaanbaatar             DS-1 • 50 kW
4085        CLANDESTINE (ASIA)            S ASIA • ANTI-INDIAN GOVT • ALT. FREQ. TO 5900 kHz
            †"KASHMIR FREEDOM", Pakistan
4110        PERU
            †RADIO NAYLAMP, Lambayeque                 DS • 0.5 kW
4117v       BRAZIL
            RADIO DIFUSORA, Sena Madureira    PORTUGUESE • DS • 0.25 kW
                                           M-Sa • PORTUGUESE • DS • 0.25 kW
                                        Tu-Su • PORTUGUESE • DS • 0.25 kW

4120v       CLANDESTINE (ASIA)            KOREAN • TO SOUTH KOREA • 100 kW
            "VO NAT SALVATION", Haeju, N Korea
4130        CHINA (PR)                                 E ASIA • FEEDER • 10 kW
            RADIO BEIJING, Beijing          (D) • E ASIA • FEEDER • 10 kW
                                                      (D) • TAIWAN-1 • 10 kW
            VO THE STRAIT-PLA, Fuzhou
            CLANDESTINE (M EAST)         MIDEAST • PRO-KURD SOCIALIST
            †"KURDISTAN RADIO"
            FRANCE                          (D) • E ASIA • FEEDER • 10 kW
            R FRANCE INTL, Via Beijing, China
            SPAIN                    (D) • E ASIA • FEEDER • 10 kW • ALT. FREQ. TO 5220 kHz
            R EXTERIOR ESPANA, Via Beijing, China
4175        CLANDESTINE (M EAST)                 MIDEAST • PRO-DPK
            †"VO IRAQI KURDS                       PERSIAN • MIDEAST • PRO-DPK

4175v       PERU
            †RADIO MEMBRILLAR, Cascas              DS • 0.1 kW
                                        Irr • DS • 0.1 kW
4183v       PERU
            RADIO CENTENARIO             DS
4185v       PERU
            RADIO MUNDIAL, Cascas                     DS
4190        CHINA (PR)                                 DS-MINORITIES
            †CENTRAL PEOPLES BS          (D) • DS-MINORITIES

4200        CHINA (PR)                                 E ASIA • FEEDER • 10 kW
            †RADIO BEIJING, Beijing       (D) • E ASIA • FEEDER • 10 kW

4212v       ECUADOR                       DS-TEMP INACTIVE • 0.5 kW
            †RADIO SUSUBEL, Oña
4220        CHINA (PR)                    DS-MONGOLIAN
            XINJIANG PBS, Urümqi
4238        PERU                                        DS
            RADIO INCA, Baños del Inca
4271v       ECUADOR                       Irr • DS • 1 kW
            †RADIO GONZANAMA, Gonzanamá
4279        PERU                                        DS
            †RADIO INCA, Cajamarca
4300v       PERU                                        DS
            †RADIO EL PUERTO, Pacasmayo
                                                        DS
            †RADIO REGIONAL, San Marcos
4330        CHINA (PR)                    DS-KAZAKH • 50 kW
            XINJIANG PBS, Urümqi
4350v       PERU                                        DS
            †RADIO UNO, Huánuco
4395        KAZAKHSTAN
            †KAZAKH RADIO, Alma-Ata     Alternative Frequency to 4400 kHz

            †RADIO ALMA-ATA, Alma-Ata   Alternative Frequency to 4400 kHz
            RUSSIA
            RUSSIA'S RADIO, Yakutsk                     DS/DS-MAYAK • 100 kW
4400        KAZAKHSTAN
            †KAZAKH RADIO, Alma-Ata        DS-2 • ALT. FREQ. TO 4395 kHz

            †RADIO ALMA-ATA, Alma-Ata                          ALT. FREQ. TO 4395 kHz
4400v       CLANDESTINE (ASIA)            KOREAN • TO SOUTH KOREA • 100 kW
(con'd)     "VO NAT SALVATION", Haeju, N Korea
```

ENGLISH ■■■   ARABIC ⌇⌇⌇   CHINESE □□□   FRENCH ══   GERMAN ▬▬   RUSSIAN ══   SPANISH ■■   OTHER ▬

FREQUENCY　　COUNTRY, STATION, LOCATION　　　　　　　TARGET • NETWORK • POWER (kW)　　　World Time

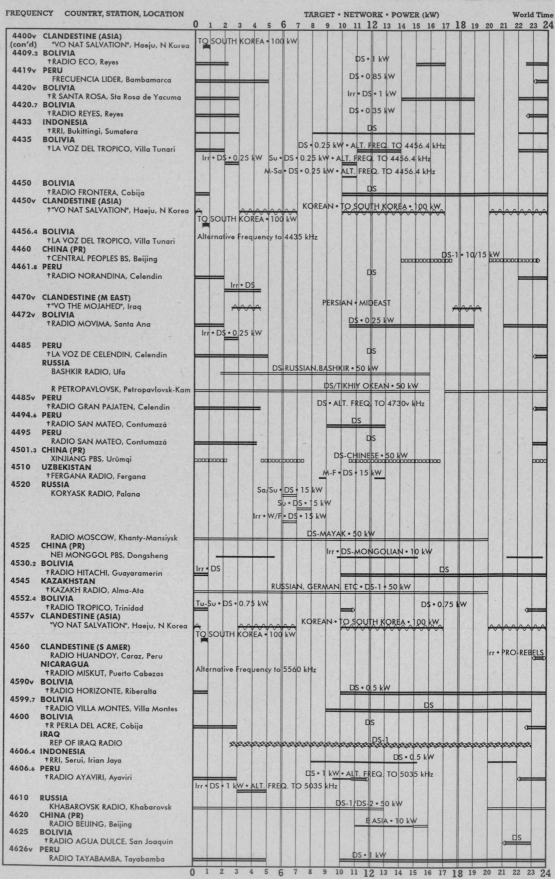

4400v　CLANDESTINE (ASIA)
(con'd)　　"VO NAT SALVATION", Haeju, N Korea
4409.2　BOLIVIA
　　　†RADIO ECO, Reyes
4419v　PERU
　　　FRECUENCIA LIDER, Bambamarca
4420v　BOLIVIA
　　　†R SANTA ROSA, Sta Rosa de Yacuma
4420.7　BOLIVIA
　　　†RADIO REYES, Reyes
4433　INDONESIA
　　　†RRI, Bukittingi, Sumatera
4435　BOLIVIA
　　　†LA VOZ DEL TROPICO, Villa Tunari

4450　BOLIVIA
　　　†RADIO FRONTERA, Cobija
4450v　CLANDESTINE (ASIA)
　　　†"VO NAT SALVATION", Haeju, N Korea

4456.4　BOLIVIA
　　　†LA VOZ DEL TROPICO, Villa Tunari
4460　CHINA (PR)
　　　†CENTRAL PEOPLES BS, Beijing
4461.8　PERU
　　　†RADIO NORANDINA, Celendin

4470v　CLANDESTINE (M EAST)
　　　†"VO THE MOJAHED", Iraq
4472v　BOLIVIA
　　　†RADIO MOVIMA, Santa Ana

4485　PERU
　　　†LA VOZ DE CELENDIN, Celendin
　　　RUSSIA
　　　　BASHKIR RADIO, Ufa
　　　R PETROPAVLOVSK, Petropavlovsk-Kam
4485v　PERU
　　　†RADIO GRAN PAJATEN, Celendin
4494.6　PERU
　　　RADIO SAN MATEO, Contumazá
4495　PERU
　　　RADIO SAN MATEO, Contumazá
4501.3　CHINA (PR)
　　　XINJIANG PBS, Urümqi
4510　UZBEKISTAN
　　　†FERGANA RADIO, Fergana
4520　RUSSIA
　　　KORYASK RADIO, Palana

　　　RADIO MOSCOW, Khanty-Mansiysk
4525　CHINA (PR)
　　　NEI MONGGOL PBS, Dongsheng
4530.2　BOLIVIA
　　　†RADIO HITACHI, Guayaramerín
4545　KAZAKHSTAN
　　　†KAZAKH RADIO, Alma-Ata
4552.4　BOLIVIA
　　　†RADIO TROPICO, Trinidad
4557v　CLANDESTINE (ASIA)
　　　"VO NAT SALVATION", Haeju, N Korea

4560　CLANDESTINE (S AMER)
　　　RADIO HUANDOY, Caraz, Peru
　　　NICARAGUA
　　　†RADIO MISKUT, Puerto Cabezas
4590v　BOLIVIA
　　　†RADIO HORIZONTE, Riberalta
4599.7　BOLIVIA
　　　†RADIO VILLA MONTES, Villa Montes
4600　BOLIVIA
　　　†R PERLA DEL ACRE, Cobija
　　　IRAQ
　　　REP OF IRAQ RADIO
4606.4　INDONESIA
　　　†RRI, Serui, Irian Jaya
4606.6　PERU
　　　†RADIO AYAVIRI, Ayaviri

4610　RUSSIA
　　　KHABAROVSK RADIO, Khabarovsk
4620　CHINA (PR)
　　　RADIO BEIJING, Beijing
4625　BOLIVIA
　　　†RADIO AGUA DULCE, San Joaquín
4626v　PERU
　　　RADIO TAYABAMBA, Tayabamba

Chart annotations:
- TO SOUTH KOREA • 100 kW
- DS • 1 kW
- DS • 0.85 kW
- Irr • DS • 1 kW
- DS • 0.35 kW
- DS
- DS • 0.25 kW • ALT. FREQ. TO 4456.4 kHz
- Irr • DS • 0.25 kW · Su • DS • 0.25 kW • ALT. FREQ. TO 4456.4 kHz
- M-Sa • DS • 0.25 kW • ALT. FREQ. TO 4456.4 kHz
- DS
- KOREAN • TO SOUTH KOREA • 100 kW
- TO SOUTH KOREA • 100 kW
- Alternative Frequency to 4435 kHz
- DS-1 • 10/15 kW
- DS
- Irr • DS
- PERSIAN • MIDEAST
- DS • 0.25 kW
- Irr • DS • 0.25 kW
- DS
- DS-RUSSIAN, BASHKIR • 50 kW
- DS/TIKHIY OKEAN • 50 kW
- DS • ALT. FREQ. TO 4730v kHz
- DS
- DS
- DS-CHINESE • 50 kW
- M-F • DS • 15 kW
- Sa/Su • DS • 15 kW
- Su • DS • 15 kW
- Irr • W/F • DS • 15 kW
- DS-MAYAK • 50 kW
- Irr • DS-MONGOLIAN • 10 kW
- Irr • DS / DS
- RUSSIAN, GERMAN, ETC • DS-1 • 50 kW
- Tu-Su • DS • 0.75 kW / DS • 0.75 kW
- KOREAN • TO SOUTH KOREA • 100 kW
- TO SOUTH KOREA • 100 kW
- Irr • PRO-REBELS
- Alternative Frequency to 5560 kHz
- DS • 0.5 kW
- DS
- DS
- DS-1
- DS • 0.5 kW
- DS • 1 kW • ALT. FREQ. TO 5035 kHz
- Irr • DS • 1 kW • ALT. FREQ. TO 5035 kHz
- DS-1/DS-2 • 50 kW
- E ASIA • 10 kW
- DS
- DS • 1 kW

SUMMER ONLY (J)　　WINTER ONLY (D)　　JAMMING / OR ∧　　EARLIEST HEARD ◁　　LATEST HEARD ▷　　NEW OR CHANGED FOR 1993 †

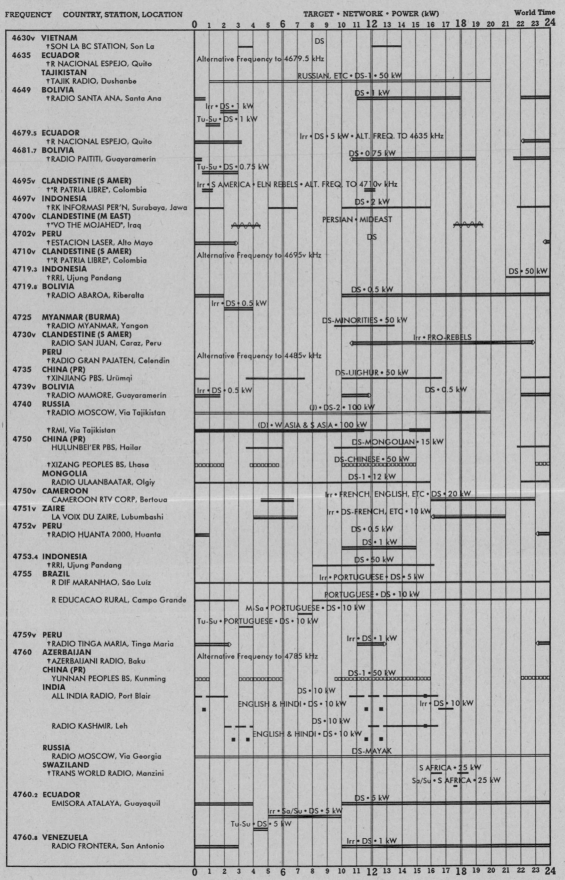

FREQUENCY   COUNTRY, STATION, LOCATION   TARGET • NETWORK • POWER (kW)   World Time

FREQUENCY	COUNTRY, STATION, LOCATION	Notes
4630v	VIETNAM †SON LA BC STATION, Son La	DS
4635	ECUADOR †R NACIONAL ESPEJO, Quito	Alternative Frequency to 4679.5 kHz
	TAJIKISTAN †TAJIK RADIO, Dushanbe	RUSSIAN, ETC • DS-1 • 50 kW
4649	BOLIVIA †RADIO SANTA ANA, Santa Ana	DS • 1 kW; Irr • DS • 1 kW; Tu-Su • DS • 1 kW
4679.5	ECUADOR †R NACIONAL ESPEJO, Quito	Irr • DS • 5 kW • ALT. FREQ. TO 4635 kHz
4681.7	BOLIVIA †RADIO PAITITI, Guayaramerin	DS • 0.75 kW; Tu-Su • DS • 0.75 kW
4695v	CLANDESTINE (S AMER) †"R PATRIA LIBRE", Colombia	Irr • S AMERICA • ELN REBELS • ALT. FREQ. TO 4710v kHz
4697v	INDONESIA †RK INFORMASI PER'N, Surabaya, Jawa	DS • 2 kW
4700v	CLANDESTINE (M EAST) †"VO THE MOJAHED", Iraq	PERSIAN • MIDEAST
4702v	PERU †ESTACION LASER, Alto Mayo	DS
4710v	CLANDESTINE (S AMER) †"R PATRIA LIBRE", Colombia	Alternative Frequency to 4695v kHz
4719.3	INDONESIA †RRI, Ujung Pandang	DS • 50 kW
4719.8	BOLIVIA †RADIO ABAROA, Riberalta	DS • 0.5 kW; Irr • DS • 0.5 kW
4725	MYANMAR (BURMA) †RADIO MYANMAR, Yangon	DS-MINORITIES • 50 kW
4730v	CLANDESTINE (S AMER) RADIO SAN JUAN, Caraz, Peru	Irr • PRO-REBELS
	PERU †RADIO GRAN PAJATEN, Celendin	Alternative Frequency to 4485v kHz
4735	CHINA (PR) †XINJIANG PBS, Urümqi	DS-UIGHUR • 50 kW
4739v	BOLIVIA †RADIO MAMORE, Guayaramerin	Irr • DS • 0.5 kW; DS • 0.5 kW
4740	RUSSIA †RADIO MOSCOW, Via Tajikistan	(J) • DS-2 • 100 kW
	†RMI, Via Tajikistan	(D) • W ASIA & S ASIA • 100 kW
4750	CHINA (PR) HULUNBEI'ER PBS, Hailar	DS-MONGOLIAN • 15 kW
	†XIZANG PEOPLES BS, Lhasa	DS-CHINESE • 50 kW
	MONGOLIA RADIO ULAANBAATAR, Olgiy	DS-1 • 12 kW
4750v	CAMEROON CAMEROON RTV CORP, Bertoua	Irr • FRENCH, ENGLISH, ETC • DS • 20 kW
4751v	ZAIRE LA VOIX DU ZAIRE, Lubumbashi	Irr • DS-FRENCH, ETC • 10 kW
4752v	PERU †RADIO HUANTA 2000, Huanta	DS • 0.5 kW; DS • 1 kW
4753.4	INDONESIA †RRI, Ujung Pandang	DS • 50 kW
4755	BRAZIL R DIF MARANHAO, São Luíz	Irr • PORTUGUESE • DS • 5 kW
	R EDUCACAO RURAL, Campo Grande	PORTUGUESE • DS • 10 kW; M-Sa • PORTUGUESE • DS • 10 kW; Tu-Su • PORTUGUESE • DS • 10 kW
4759v	PERU †RADIO TINGA MARIA, Tinga Maria	Irr • DS • 1 kW
4760	AZERBAIJAN †AZERBAIJANI RADIO, Baku	Alternative Frequency to 4785 kHz
	CHINA (PR) YUNNAN PEOPLES BS, Kunming	DS-1 • 50 kW
	INDIA ALL INDIA RADIO, Port Blair	DS • 10 kW; ENGLISH & HINDI • DS • 10 kW; Irr • DS • 10 kW
	RADIO KASHMIR, Leh	DS • 10 kW; ENGLISH & HINDI • DS • 10 kW
	RUSSIA RADIO MOSCOW, Via Georgia	DS-MAYAK
	SWAZILAND †TRANS WORLD RADIO, Manzini	S AFRICA • 25 kW; Sa/Su • S AFRICA • 25 kW
4760.2	ECUADOR EMISORA ATALAYA, Guayaquil	DS • 5 kW; Irr • Sa/Su • DS • 5 kW; Tu-Su • DS • 5 kW
4760.8	VENEZUELA RADIO FRONTERA, San Antonio	Irr • DS • 1 kW

ENGLISH ▬▬   ARABIC ×××   CHINESE □□□   FRENCH ═══   GERMAN ▬▬   RUSSIAN ══   SPANISH ▬▬   OTHER ▬▬

FREQUENCY   COUNTRY, STATION, LOCATION   TARGET • NETWORK • POWER (kW)   World Time

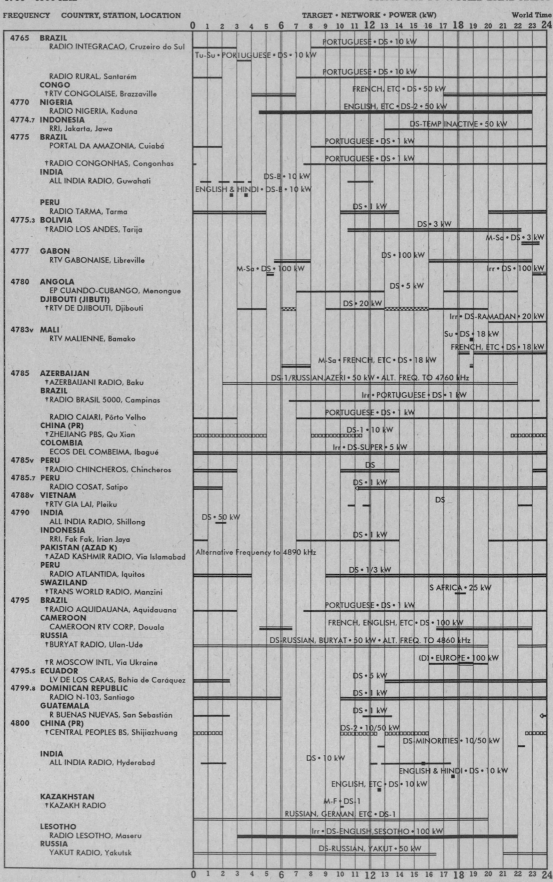

FREQUENCY	COUNTRY, STATION, LOCATION	TARGET • NETWORK • POWER (kW)
4765	**BRAZIL** RADIO INTEGRACAO, Cruzeiro do Sul	PORTUGUESE • DS • 10 kW Tu-Su • PORTUGUESE • DS • 10 kW
	RADIO RURAL, Santarém	PORTUGUESE • DS • 10 kW
	CONGO †RTV CONGOLAISE, Brazzaville	FRENCH, ETC • DS • 50 kW
4770	**NIGERIA** RADIO NIGERIA, Kaduna	ENGLISH, ETC • DS-2 • 50 kW
4774.7	**INDONESIA** RRI, Jakarta, Jawa	DS-TEMP INACTIVE • 50 kW
4775	**BRAZIL** PORTAL DA AMAZONIA, Cuiabá	PORTUGUESE • DS • 1 kW
	†RADIO CONGONHAS, Congonhas	PORTUGUESE • DS • 1 kW
	INDIA ALL INDIA RADIO, Guwahati	DS-B • 10 kW ENGLISH & HINDI • DS-B • 10 kW
	PERU RADIO TARMA, Tarma	DS • 1 kW
4775.3	**BOLIVIA** †RADIO LOS ANDES, Tarija	DS • 3 kW M-Sa • DS • 3 kW
4777	**GABON** RTV GABONAISE, Libreville	DS • 100 kW M-Sa • DS • 100 kW Irr • DS • 100 kW
4780	**ANGOLA** EP CUANDO-CUBANGO, Menongue	DS • 5 kW
	DJIBOUTI (JIBUTI) †RTV DE DJIBOUTI, Djibouti	DS • 20 kW Irr • DS-RAMADAN • 20 kW
4783v	**MALI** RTV MALIENNE, Bamako	Su • DS • 18 kW FRENCH, ETC • DS • 18 kW M-Sa • FRENCH, ETC • DS • 18 kW
4785	**AZERBAIJAN** †AZERBAIJANI RADIO, Baku	DS-1/RUSSIAN, AZERI • 50 kW • ALT. FREQ. TO 4760 kHz
	BRAZIL †RADIO BRASIL 5000, Campinas	Irr • PORTUGUESE • DS • 1 kW
	RADIO CAIARI, Pôrto Velho	PORTUGUESE • DS • 1 kW
	CHINA (PR) †ZHEJIANG PBS, Qu Xian	DS-1 • 10 kW
	COLOMBIA ECOS DEL COMBEIMA, Ibagué	Irr • DS-SUPER • 5 kW
4785v	**PERU** †RADIO CHINCHEROS, Chincheros	DS
4785.7	**PERU** RADIO COSAT, Satipo	DS • 1 kW
4788v	**VIETNAM** †RTV GIA LAI, Pleiku	DS
4790	**INDIA** ALL INDIA RADIO, Shillong	DS • 50 kW
	INDONESIA RRI, Fak Fak, Irian Jaya	DS • 1 kW
	PAKISTAN (AZAD K) †AZAD KASHMIR RADIO, Via Islamabad	Alternative Frequency to 4890 kHz
	PERU RADIO ATLANTIDA, Iquitos	DS • 1/3 kW
	SWAZILAND †TRANS WORLD RADIO, Manzini	S AFRICA • 25 kW
4795	**BRAZIL** †RADIO AQUIDAUANA, Aquidauana	PORTUGUESE • DS • 1 kW
	CAMEROON CAMEROON RTV CORP, Douala	FRENCH, ENGLISH, ETC • DS • 100 kW
	RUSSIA †BURYAT RADIO, Ulan-Ude	DS-RUSSIAN, BURYAT • 50 kW • ALT. FREQ. TO 4860 kHz
	†R MOSCOW INTL, Via Ukraine	(D) • EUROPE • 100 kW
4795.5	**ECUADOR** LV DE LOS CARAS, Bahía de Caráquez	DS • 5 kW
4799.8	**DOMINICAN REPUBLIC** RADIO N-103, Santiago	DS • 1 kW
	GUATEMALA R BUENAS NUEVAS, San Sebastián	DS • 1 kW
4800	**CHINA (PR)** †CENTRAL PEOPLES BS, Shijiazhuang	DS-2 • 10/50 kW DS-MINORITIES • 10/50 kW
	INDIA ALL INDIA RADIO, Hyderabad	DS • 10 kW ENGLISH & HINDI • DS • 10 kW ENGLISH, ETC • DS • 10 kW
	KAZAKHSTAN †KAZAKH RADIO	M-F • DS-1 RUSSIAN, GERMAN, ETC • DS-1
	LESOTHO RADIO LESOTHO, Maseru	Irr • DS-ENGLISH, SESOTHO • 100 kW
	RUSSIA YAKUT RADIO, Yakutsk	DS-RUSSIAN, YAKUT • 50 kW

SUMMER ONLY (J)   WINTER ONLY (D)   JAMMING / OR ∧   EARLIEST HEARD ◁   LATEST HEARD ▷   NEW OR CHANGED FOR 1993 †

FREQUENCY   COUNTRY, STATION, LOCATION

TARGET • NETWORK • POWER (kW)

World Time

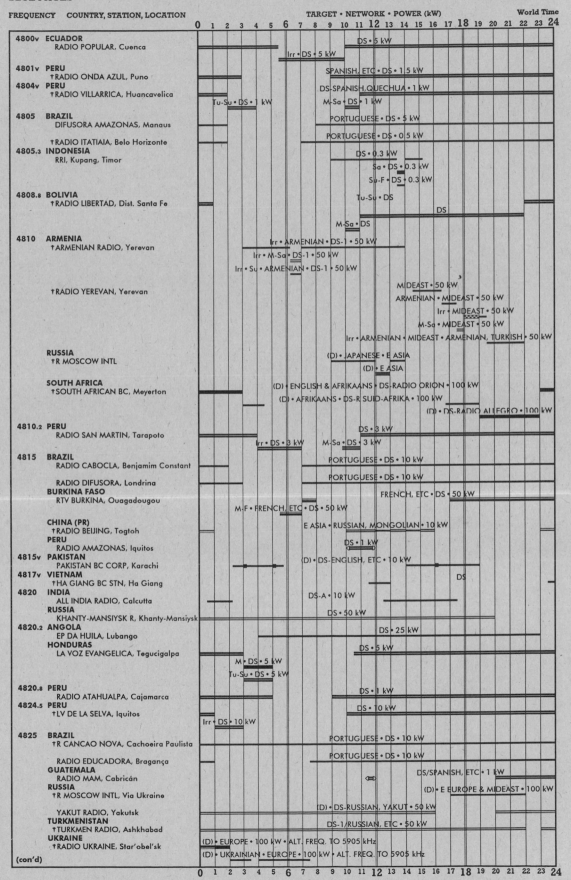

FREQUENCY	COUNTRY, STATION, LOCATION	TARGET • NETWORK • POWER (kW)
4800v	ECUADOR RADIO POPULAR, Cuenca	DS • 5 kW / Irr • DS • 5 kW
4801v	PERU †RADIO ONDA AZUL, Puno	SPANISH, ETC • DS • 1.5 kW
4804v	PERU †RADIO VILLARRICA, Huancavelica	DS-SPANISH, QUECHUA • 1 kW / Tu-Su • DS • 1 kW / M-Sa • DS • 1 kW
4805	BRAZIL DIFUSORA AMAZONAS, Manaus	PORTUGUESE • DS • 5 kW
	†RADIO ITATIAIA, Belo Horizonte	PORTUGUESE • DS • 0.5 kW
4805.3	INDONESIA RRI, Kupang, Timor	DS • 0.3 kW / Sa • DS • 0.3 kW / Su-F • DS • 0.3 kW
4808.8	BOLIVIA †RADIO LIBERTAD, Dist. Santa Fe	Tu-Su • DS / DS / M-Sa • DS
4810	ARMENIA †ARMENIAN RADIO, Yerevan	Irr • ARMENIAN • DS-1 • 50 kW / Irr • M-Sa • DS-1 • 50 kW / Irr • Su • ARMENIAN • DS-1 • 50 kW
	†RADIO YEREVAN, Yerevan	MIDEAST • 50 kW / ARMENIAN • MIDEAST • 50 kW / Irr • MIDEAST • 50 kW / M-Sa • MIDEAST • 50 kW / Irr • ARMENIAN • MIDEAST • ARMENIAN, TURKISH • 50 kW
	RUSSIA †R MOSCOW INTL	(D) • JAPANESE • E ASIA / (D) • E ASIA
	SOUTH AFRICA †SOUTH AFRICAN BC, Meyerton	(D) • ENGLISH & AFRIKAANS • DS-RADIO ORION • 100 kW / (D) • AFRIKAANS • DS-R SUID-AFRIKA • 100 kW / (D) • DS-RADIO ALLEGRO • 100 kW
4810.2	PERU RADIO SAN MARTIN, Tarapoto	DS • 3 kW / Irr • DS • 3 kW / M-Sa • DS • 3 kW
4815	BRAZIL RADIO CABOCLA, Benjamim Constant	PORTUGUESE • DS • 10 kW
	RADIO DIFUSORA, Londrina	PORTUGUESE • DS • 10 kW
	BURKINA FASO RTV BURKINA, Ouagadougou	FRENCH, ETC • DS • 50 kW / M-F • FRENCH, ETC • DS • 50 kW
	CHINA (PR) †RADIO BEIJING, Togtoh	E ASIA • RUSSIAN, MONGOLIAN • 10 kW
	PERU RADIO AMAZONAS, Iquitos	DS • 1 kW
4815v	PAKISTAN PAKISTAN BC CORP, Karachi	(D) • DS-ENGLISH, ETC • 10 kW
4817v	VIETNAM †HA GIANG BC STN, Ha Giang	DS
4820	INDIA ALL INDIA RADIO, Calcutta	DS-A • 10 kW
	RUSSIA KHANTY-MANSIYSK R, Khanty-Mansiysk	DS • 50 kW
4820.2	ANGOLA EP DA HUILA, Lubango	DS • 25 kW
	HONDURAS LA VOZ EVANGELICA, Tegucigalpa	DS • 5 kW / M • DS • 5 kW / Tu-Su • DS • 5 kW
4820.8	PERU RADIO ATAHUALPA, Cajamarca	DS • 1 kW
4824.5	PERU †LV DE LA SELVA, Iquitos	DS • 10 kW / Irr • DS • 10 kW
4825	BRAZIL †R CANCAO NOVA, Cachoeira Paulista	PORTUGUESE • DS • 10 kW
	RADIO EDUCADORA, Bragança	PORTUGUESE • DS • 10 kW
	GUATEMALA RADIO MAM, Cabricán	DS/SPANISH, ETC • 1 kW
	RUSSIA †R MOSCOW INTL, Via Ukraine	(D) • E EUROPE & MIDEAST • 100 kW
	YAKUT RADIO, Yakutsk	(D) • DS-RUSSIAN, YAKUT • 50 kW
	TURKMENISTAN †TURKMEN RADIO, Ashkhabad	DS-1/RUSSIAN, ETC • 50 kW
	UKRAINE †RADIO UKRAINE, Star'obel'sk	(D) • EUROPE • 100 kW • ALT. FREQ. TO 5905 kHz / (D) • UKRAINIAN • EUROPE • 100 kW • ALT. FREQ. TO 5905 kHz

(con'd)

FREQUENCY   COUNTRY, STATION, LOCATION   TARGET • NETWORK • POWER (kW)   World Time

0 1 2 3 4 5 6 7 8 9 10 11 12 13 14 15 16 17 18 19 20 21 22 23 24

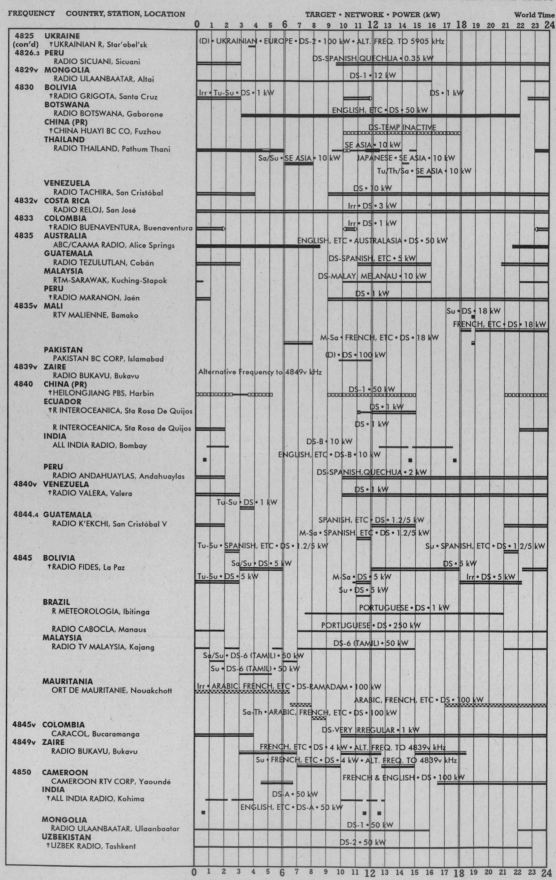

Frequency	Country, Station, Location	Details
4825 (con'd)	**UKRAINE** †UKRAINIAN R, Star'obel'sk	(D) • UKRAINIAN • EUROPE • DS-2 • 100 kW • ALT. FREQ. TO 5905 kHz
4826.3	**PERU** RADIO SICUANI, Sicuani	DS-SPANISH, QUECHUA • 0.35 kW
4829v	**MONGOLIA** RADIO ULAANBAATAR, Altai	DS-1 • 12 kW
4830	**BOLIVIA** †RADIO GRIGOTA, Santa Cruz	Irr • Tu-Su • DS • 1 kW DS • 1 kW
	BOTSWANA RADIO BOTSWANA, Gaborone	ENGLISH, ETC • DS • 50 kW
	CHINA (PR) †CHINA HUAYI BC CO, Fuzhou	DS-TEMP INACTIVE
	THAILAND RADIO THAILAND, Pathum Thani	SE ASIA • 10 kW Sa/Su • SE ASIA • 10 kW JAPANESE • SE ASIA • 10 kW Tu/Th/Sa • SE ASIA • 10 kW
	VENEZUELA RADIO TACHIRA, San Cristóbal	DS • 10 kW
4832v	**COSTA RICA** RADIO RELOJ, San José	Irr • DS • 3 kW
4833	**COLOMBIA** †RADIO BUENAVENTURA, Buenaventura	Irr • DS • 1 kW
4835	**AUSTRALIA** ABC/CAAMA RADIO, Alice Springs	ENGLISH, ETC • AUSTRALASIA • DS • 50 kW
	GUATEMALA RADIO TEZULUTLAN, Cobán	DS-SPANISH, ETC • 5 kW
	MALAYSIA RTM-SARAWAK, Kuching-Stapok	DS-MALAY, MELANAU • 10 kW
	PERU †RADIO MARANON, Jaén	DS • 1 kW
4835v	**MALI** RTV MALIENNE, Bamako	Su • DS • 18 kW FRENCH, ETC • DS • 18 kW M-Sa • FRENCH, ETC • DS • 18 kW
	PAKISTAN PAKISTAN BC CORP, Islamabad	(D) • DS • 100 kW
4839v	**ZAIRE** RADIO BUKAVU, Bukavu	Alternative Frequency to 4849v kHz
4840	**CHINA (PR)** †HEILONGJIANG PBS, Harbin	DS-1 • 50 kW
	ECUADOR †R INTEROCEANICA, Sta Rosa De Quijos	DS • 1 kW
	R INTEROCEANICA, Sta Rosa de Quijos	DS • 1 kW
	INDIA ALL INDIA RADIO, Bombay	DS-B • 10 kW ENGLISH, ETC • DS-B • 10 kW
	PERU RADIO ANDAHUAYLAS, Andahuaylas	DS-SPANISH, QUECHUA • 2 kW
4840v	**VENEZUELA** †RADIO VALERA, Valera	DS • 1 kW Tu-Su • DS • 1 kW
4844.4	**GUATEMALA** RADIO K'EKCHI, San Cristóbal V	SPANISH, ETC • DS • 1.2/5 kW M-Sa • SPANISH, ETC • DS • 1.2/5 kW Tu-Su • SPANISH, ETC • DS • 1.2/5 kW Su • SPANISH, ETC • DS • 1.2/5 kW
4845	**BOLIVIA** †RADIO FIDES, La Paz	Sa/Su • DS • 5 kW DS • 5 kW Tu-Su • DS • 5 kW M-Sa • DS • 5 kW Irr • DS • 5 kW Su • DS • 5 kW
	BRAZIL R METEOROLOGIA, Ibitinga	PORTUGUESE • DS • 1 kW
	RADIO CABOCLA, Manaus	PORTUGUESE • DS • 250 kW
	MALAYSIA RADIO TV MALAYSIA, Kajang	DS-6 (TAMIL) • 50 kW Sa/Su • DS-6 (TAMIL) • 50 kW Su • DS-6 (TAMIL) • 50 kW
	MAURITANIA ORT DE MAURITANIE, Nouakchott	Irr • ARABIC, FRENCH, ETC • DS-RAMADAM • 100 kW ARABIC, FRENCH, ETC • DS • 100 kW Sa-Th • ARABIC, FRENCH, ETC • DS • 100 kW
4845v	**COLOMBIA** CARACOL, Bucaramanga	DS-VERY IRREGULAR • 1 kW
4849v	**ZAIRE** RADIO BUKAVU, Bukavu	FRENCH, ETC • DS • 4 kW • ALT. FREQ. TO 4839v kHz Su • FRENCH, ETC • DS • 4 kW • ALT. FREQ. TO 4839v kHz
4850	**CAMEROON** CAMEROON RTV CORP, Yaoundé	FRENCH & ENGLISH • DS • 100 kW
	INDIA †ALL INDIA RADIO, Kohima	DS-A • 50 kW ENGLISH, ETC • DS-A • 50 kW
	MONGOLIA RADIO ULAANBAATAR, Ulaanbaatar	DS-1 • 50 kW
	UZBEKISTAN †UZBEK RADIO, Tashkent	DS-2 • 50 kW

0 1 2 3 4 5 6 7 8 9 10 11 12 13 14 15 16 17 18 19 20 21 22 23 24

SUMMER ONLY (J)   WINTER ONLY (D)   JAMMING / OR ∧   EARLIEST HEARD ◁   LATEST HEARD ▷   NEW OR CHANGED FOR 1993 †

FREQUENCY   COUNTRY, STATION, LOCATION   TARGET • NETWORK • POWER (kW)   World Time

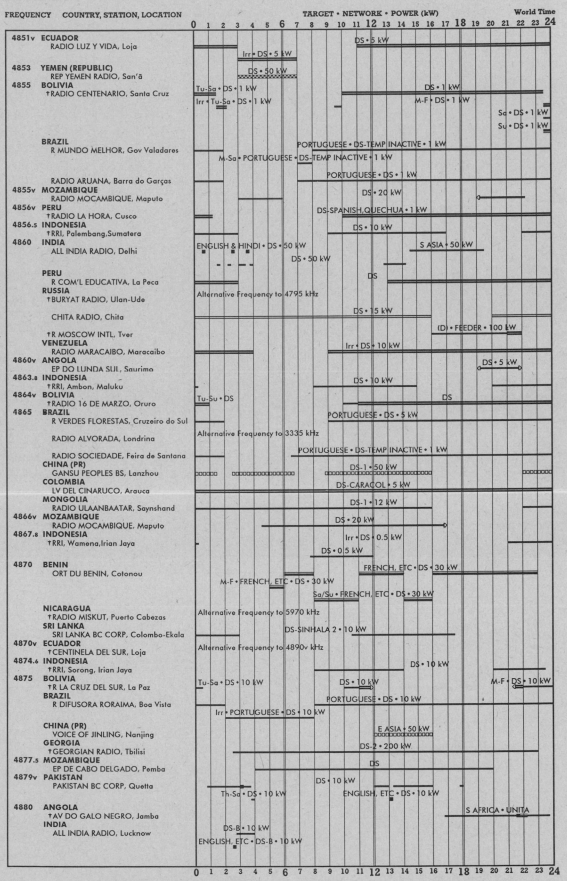

Frequency	Country, Station, Location	Details
4851v	**ECUADOR** — RADIO LUZ Y VIDA, Loja	DS • 5 kW; Irr • DS • 5 kW
4853	**YEMEN (REPUBLIC)** — REP YEMEN RADIO, San'ā	DS • 50 kW
4855	**BOLIVIA** — †RADIO CENTENARIO, Santa Cruz	Tu-Sa • DS • 1 kW; Irr • Tu-Sa • DS • 1 kW; DS • 1 kW; M-F • DS • 1 kW; Sa • DS • 1 kW; Su • DS • 1 kW
	BRAZIL — R MUNDO MELHOR, Gov Valadares	PORTUGUESE • DS-TEMP INACTIVE • 1 kW; M-Sa • PORTUGUESE • DS-TEMP INACTIVE • 1 kW
	RADIO ARUANA, Barra do Garças	PORTUGUESE • DS • 1 kW
4855v	**MOZAMBIQUE** — RADIO MOCAMBIQUE, Maputo	DS • 20 kW
4856v	**PERU** — †RADIO LA HORA, Cusco	DS-SPANISH, QUECHUA • 1 kW
4856.5	**INDONESIA** — †RRI, Palembang, Sumatera	DS • 10 kW
4860	**INDIA** — ALL INDIA RADIO, Delhi	ENGLISH & HINDI • DS • 50 kW; S ASIA • 50 kW; DS • 50 kW
	PERU — R COM'L EDUCATIVA, La Peca	DS
	RUSSIA — †BURYAT RADIO, Ulan-Ude	Alternative Frequency to 4795 kHz
	CHITA RADIO, Chita	DS • 15 kW
	†R MOSCOW INTL, Tver	(D) • FEEDER • 100 kW
	VENEZUELA — RADIO MARACAIBO, Maracaibo	Irr • DS • 10 kW
4860v	**ANGOLA** — EP DO LUNDA SUL, Saurimo	DS • 5 kW
4863.8	**INDONESIA** — †RRI, Ambon, Maluku	DS • 10 kW
4864v	**BOLIVIA** — †RADIO 16 DE MARZO, Oruro	Tu-Su • DS; DS
4865	**BRAZIL** — R VERDES FLORESTAS, Cruzeiro do Sul	PORTUGUESE • DS • 5 kW
	RADIO ALVORADA, Londrina	Alternative Frequency to 3335 kHz
	RADIO SOCIEDADE, Feira de Santana	PORTUGUESE • DS-TEMP INACTIVE • 1 kW
	CHINA (PR) — GANSU PEOPLES BS, Lanzhou	DS-1 • 50 kW
	COLOMBIA — LV DEL CINARUCO, Arauca	DS-CARACOL • 5 kW
	MONGOLIA — RADIO ULAANBAATAR, Saynshand	DS-1 • 12 kW
4866v	**MOZAMBIQUE** — RADIO MOCAMBIQUE, Maputo	DS • 20 kW
4867.8	**INDONESIA** — †RRI, Wamena, Irian Jaya	Irr • DS • 0.5 kW; DS • 0.5 kW
4870	**BENIN** — ORT DU BENIN, Cotonou	FRENCH, ETC • DS • 30 kW; M-F • FRENCH, ETC • DS • 30 kW; Sa/Su • FRENCH, ETC • DS • 30 kW
	NICARAGUA — †RADIO MISKUT, Puerto Cabezas	Alternative Frequency to 5970 kHz
	SRI LANKA — SRI LANKA BC CORP, Colombo-Ekala	DS-SINHALA 2 • 10 kW
4870v	**ECUADOR** — †CENTINELA DEL SUR, Loja	Alternative Frequency to 4890v kHz
4874.6	**INDONESIA** — †RRI, Sorong, Irian Jaya	DS • 10 kW
4875	**BOLIVIA** — †R LA CRUZ DEL SUR, La Paz	Tu-Sa • DS • 10 kW; DS • 10 kW; M-F • DS • 10 kW
	BRAZIL — R DIFUSORA RORAIMA, Boa Vista	PORTUGUESE • DS • 10 kW; Irr • PORTUGUESE • DS • 10 kW
	CHINA (PR) — VOICE OF JINLING, Nanjing	E ASIA • 50 kW
	GEORGIA — †GEORGIAN RADIO, Tbilisi	DS-2 • 200 kW
4877.5	**MOZAMBIQUE** — EP DE CABO DELGADO, Pemba	DS
4879v	**PAKISTAN** — PAKISTAN BC CORP, Quetta	DS • 10 kW; Th-Sa • DS • 10 kW; ENGLISH, ETC • DS • 10 kW
4880	**ANGOLA** — †AV DO GALO NEGRO, Jamba	S AFRICA • UNITA
	INDIA — ALL INDIA RADIO, Lucknow	DS-B • 10 kW; ENGLISH, ETC • DS-B • 10 kW

ENGLISH ▬   ARABIC ▧▧▧   CHINESE ▫▫▫   FRENCH ▭▭   GERMAN ▬▬   RUSSIAN ═   SPANISH ▭▭   OTHER —

FREQUENCY   COUNTRY, STATION, LOCATION

TARGET • NETWORK • POWER (kW)

World Time

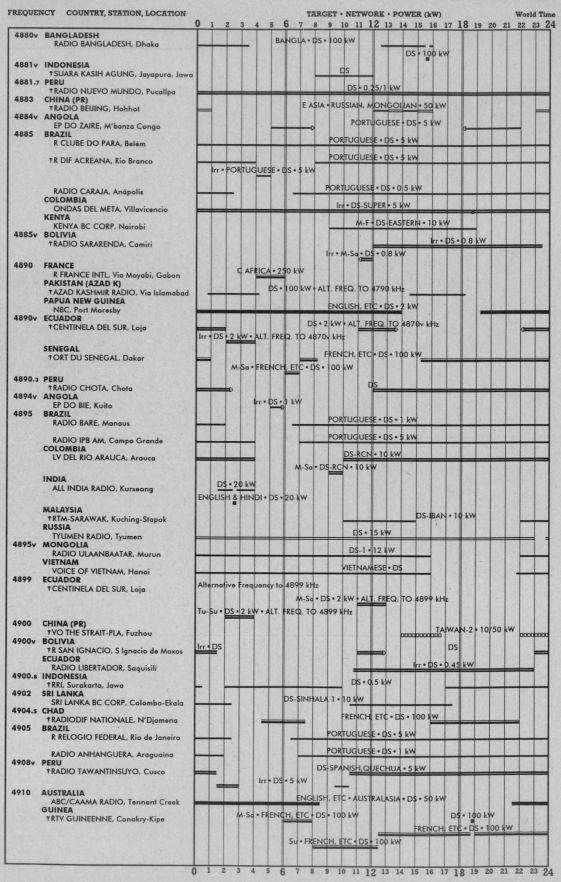

FREQUENCY	COUNTRY, STATION, LOCATION	TARGET • NETWORK • POWER (kW)
4880v	**BANGLADESH**	
	RADIO BANGLADESH, Dhaka	BANGLA • DS • 100 kW
		DS • 100 kW
4881v	**INDONESIA**	
	†SUARA KASIH AGUNG, Jayapura, Jawa	DS
4881.7	**PERU**	
	†RADIO NUEVO MUNDO, Pucallpa	DS • 0.25/1 kW
4883	**CHINA (PR)**	
	†RADIO BEIJING, Hohhot	E ASIA • RUSSIAN, MONGOLIAN • 50 kW
4884v	**ANGOLA**	
	EP DO ZAIRE, M'banza Congo	PORTUGUESE • DS • 5 kW
4885	**BRAZIL**	
	R CLUBE DO PARA, Belém	PORTUGUESE • DS • 5 kW
	†R DIF ACREANA, Rio Branco	PORTUGUESE • DS • 5 kW
		Irr • PORTUGUESE • DS • 5 kW
	RADIO CARAJA, Anápolis	PORTUGUESE • DS • 0.5 kW
	COLOMBIA	
	ONDAS DEL META, Villavicencio	Irr • DS-SUPER • 5 kW
	KENYA	
	KENYA BC CORP, Nairobi	M-F • DS-EASTERN • 10 kW
4885v	**BOLIVIA**	
	†RADIO SARARENDA, Camiri	Irr • DS • 0.8 kW
		Irr • M-Sa • DS • 0.8 kW
4890	**FRANCE**	
	R FRANCE INTL, Via Moyabi, Gabon	C AFRICA • 250 kW
	PAKISTAN (AZAD K)	
	†AZAD KASHMIR RADIO, Via Islamabad	DS • 100 kW • ALT. FREQ. TO 4790 kHz
	PAPUA NEW GUINEA	
	NBC, Port Moresby	ENGLISH, ETC • DS • 2 kW
4890v	**ECUADOR**	
	†CENTINELA DEL SUR, Loja	DS • 2 kW • ALT. FREQ. TO 4870v kHz
		Irr • DS • 2 kW • ALT. FREQ. TO 4870v kHz
	SENEGAL	
	†ORT DU SENEGAL, Dakar	FRENCH, ETC • DS • 100 kW
		M-Sa • FRENCH, ETC • DS • 100 kW
4890.3	**PERU**	
	†RADIO CHOTA, Chota	DS
4894v	**ANGOLA**	
	EP DO BIE, Kuito	Irr • DS • 1 kW
4895	**BRAZIL**	
	RADIO BARE, Manaus	PORTUGUESE • DS • 1 kW
	RADIO IPB AM, Campo Grande	PORTUGUESE • DS • 5 kW
	COLOMBIA	
	LV DEL RIO ARAUCA, Arauca	DS-RCN • 10 kW
		M-Sa • DS-RCN • 10 kW
	INDIA	
	ALL INDIA RADIO, Kurseong	DS • 20 kW
		ENGLISH & HINDI • DS • 20 kW
	MALAYSIA	
	†RTM-SARAWAK, Kuching-Stapok	DS-IBAN • 10 kW
	RUSSIA	
	TYUMEN RADIO, Tyumen	DS • 15 kW
4895v	**MONGOLIA**	
	RADIO ULAANBAATAR, Murun	DS-1 • 12 kW
	VIETNAM	
	VOICE OF VIETNAM, Hanoi	VIETNAMESE • DS
4899	**ECUADOR**	
	†CENTINELA DEL SUR, Loja	Alternative Frequency to 4899 kHz
		M-Sa • DS • 2 kW • ALT. FREQ. TO 4899 kHz
		Tu-Su • DS • 2 kW • ALT. FREQ. TO 4899 kHz
4900	**CHINA (PR)**	
	†VO THE STRAIT-PLA, Fuzhou	TAIWAN-2 • 10/50 kW
4900v	**BOLIVIA**	
	†R SAN IGNACIO, S Ignacio de Moxos	Irr • DS
		DS
	ECUADOR	
	RADIO LIBERTADOR, Saquisilí	Irr • DS • 0.45 kW
4900.8	**INDONESIA**	
	†RRI, Surakarta, Jawa	DS • 0.5 kW
4902	**SRI LANKA**	
	SRI LANKA BC CORP, Colombo-Ekala	DS-SINHALA 1 • 10 kW
4904.5	**CHAD**	
	†RADIODIF NATIONALE, N'Djamena	FRENCH, ETC • DS • 100 kW
4905	**BRAZIL**	
	R RELOGIO FEDERAL, Rio de Janeiro	PORTUGUESE • DS • 5 kW
	RADIO ANHANGUERA, Araguaína	PORTUGUESE • DS • 1 kW
4908v	**PERU**	
	†RADIO TAWANTINSUYO, Cusco	DS-SPANISH, QUECHUA • 5 kW
		Irr • DS • 5 kW
4910	**AUSTRALIA**	
	ABC/CAAMA RADIO, Tennant Creek	ENGLISH, ETC • AUSTRALASIA • DS • 50 kW
	GUINEA	
	†RTV GUINEENNE, Conakry-Kipe	M-Sa • FRENCH, ETC • DS • 100 kW
		DS • 100 kW
		FRENCH, ETC • DS • 100 kW
		Su • FRENCH, ETC • DS • 100 kW

FREQUENCY   COUNTRY, STATION, LOCATION

TARGET • NETWORK • POWER (kW)   World Time

0 1 2 3 4 5 6 7 8 9 10 11 12 13 14 15 16 17 18 19 20 21 22 23 24

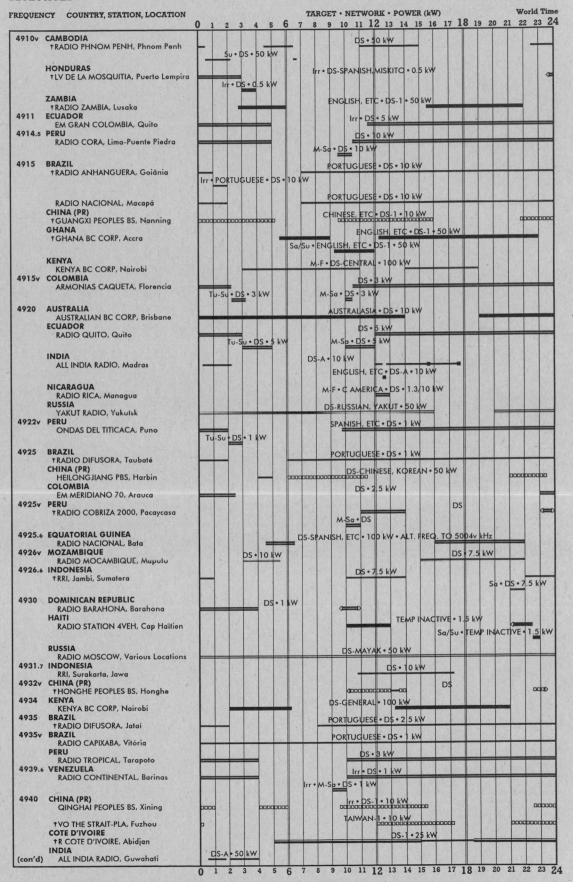

Frequency	Country, Station, Location	Notes
4910v	**CAMBODIA**	DS • 50 kW
	†RADIO PHNOM PENH, Phnom Penh	Su • DS • 50 kW
	HONDURAS	Irr • DS-SPANISH,MISKITO • 0.5 kW
	†LV DE LA MOSQUITIA, Puerto Lempira	Irr • DS • 0.5 kW
	ZAMBIA	ENGLISH, ETC • DS-1 • 50 kW
	†RADIO ZAMBIA, Lusaka	
4911	**ECUADOR**	Irr • DS • 5 kW
	EM GRAN COLOMBIA, Quito	
4914.5	**PERU**	DS • 10 kW
	RADIO CORA, Lima-Puente Piedra	M-Sa • DS • 10 kW
4915	**BRAZIL**	PORTUGUESE • DS • 10 kW
	†RADIO ANHANGUERA, Goiânia	Irr • PORTUGUESE • DS • 10 kW
	RADIO NACIONAL, Macapá	PORTUGUESE • DS • 10 kW
	CHINA (PR)	CHINESE, ETC • DS-1 • 10 kW
	†GUANGXI PEOPLES BS, Nanning	
	GHANA	ENGLISH, ETC • DS-1 • 50 kW
	†GHANA BC CORP, Accra	Sa/Su • ENGLISH, ETC • DS-1 • 50 kW
	KENYA	M-F • DS-CENTRAL • 100 kW
	KENYA BC CORP, Nairobi	
4915v	**COLOMBIA**	DS • 3 kW
	ARMONIAS CAQUETA, Florencia	Tu-Su • DS • 3 kW M-Sa • DS • 3 kW
4920	**AUSTRALIA**	AUSTRALASIA • DS • 10 kW
	AUSTRALIAN BC CORP, Brisbane	
	ECUADOR	DS • 5 kW
	RADIO QUITO, Quito	Tu-Su • DS • 5 kW M-Sa • DS • 5 kW
	INDIA	DS-A • 10 kW
	ALL INDIA RADIO, Madras	ENGLISH, ETC • DS-A • 10 kW
	NICARAGUA	M-F • C AMERICA • DS • 1.3/10 kW
	RADIO RICA, Managua	
	RUSSIA	DS-RUSSIAN, YAKUT • 50 kW
	YAKUT RADIO, Yukutsk	
4922v	**PERU**	SPANISH, ETC • DS • 1 kW
	ONDAS DEL TITICACA, Puno	Tu-Su • DS • 1 kW
4925	**BRAZIL**	PORTUGUESE • DS • 1 kW
	†RADIO DIFUSORA, Taubaté	
	CHINA (PR)	DS-CHINESE, KOREAN • 50 kW
	HEILONGJIANG PBS, Harbin	
	COLOMBIA	DS • 2.5 kW
	EM MERIDIANO 70, Arauca	
4925v	**PERU**	DS
	†RADIO COBRIZA 2000, Pacaycasa	M-Sa • DS
4925.6	**EQUATORIAL GUINEA**	DS-SPANISH, ETC • 100 kW • ALT. FREQ. TO 5004v kHz
	RADIO NACIONAL, Bata	
4926v	**MOZAMBIQUE**	DS • 10 kW DS • 7.5 kW
	RADIO MOCAMBIQUE, Maputo	
4926.6	**INDONESIA**	DS • 7.5 kW
	†RRI, Jambi, Sumatera	Sa • DS • 7.5 kW
4930	**DOMINICAN REPUBLIC**	DS • 1 kW
	RADIO BARAHONA, Barahona	
	HAITI	TEMP INACTIVE • 1.5 kW
	RADIO STATION 4VEH, Cap Haïtien	Sa/Su • TEMP INACTIVE • 1.5 kW
	RUSSIA	DS-MAYAK • 50 kW
	RADIO MOSCOW, Various Locations	
4931.7	**INDONESIA**	DS • 10 kW
	RRI, Surakarta, Jawa	
4932v	**CHINA (PR)**	DS
	†HONGHE PEOPLES BS, Honghe	
4934	**KENYA**	DS-GENERAL • 100 kW
	KENYA BC CORP, Nairobi	
4935	**BRAZIL**	PORTUGUESE • DS • 2.5 kW
	†RADIO DIFUSORA, Jataí	
4935v	**BRAZIL**	PORTUGUESE • DS • 1 kW
	RADIO CAPIXABA, Vitória	
	PERU	DS • 3 kW
	RADIO TROPICAL, Tarapoto	
4939.6	**VENEZUELA**	Irr • DS • 1 kW
	RADIO CONTINENTAL, Barinas	Irr • M-Sa • DS • 1 kW
4940	**CHINA (PR)**	Irr • DS-1 • 10 kW
	QINGHAI PEOPLES BS, Xining	TAIWAN-1 • 10 kW
	†VO THE STRAIT-PLA, Fuzhou	
	COTE D'IVOIRE	DS-1 • 25 kW
	†R COTE D'IVOIRE, Abidjan	
(con'd)	**INDIA**	DS-A • 50 kW
	ALL INDIA RADIO, Guwahati	

0 1 2 3 4 5 6 7 8 9 10 11 12 13 14 15 16 17 18 19 20 21 22 23 24

ENGLISH ▬▬   ARABIC ▨▨   CHINESE □□□   FRENCH ▬▬   GERMAN ▬▬   RUSSIAN ═══   SPANISH ▬▬   OTHER ▬

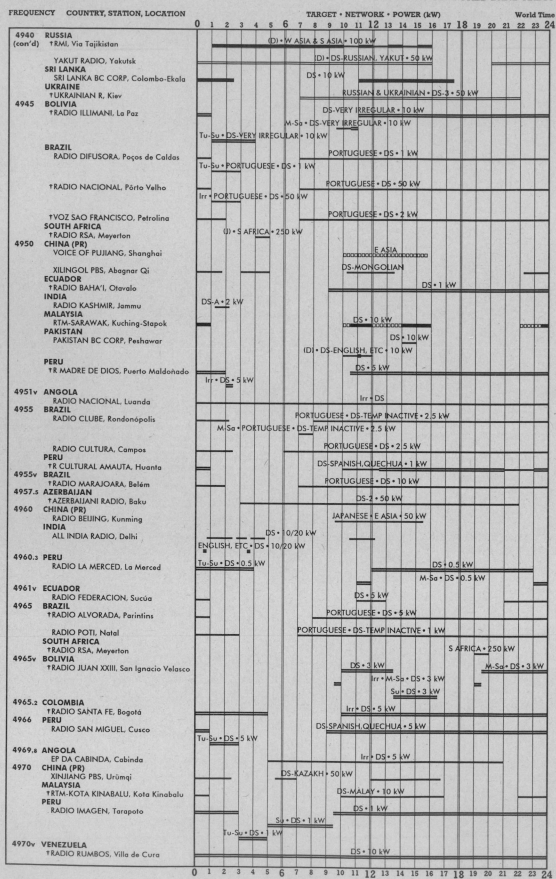

FREQUENCY COUNTRY, STATION, LOCATION

TARGET • NETWORK • POWER (kW)   World Time

FREQUENCY	COUNTRY, STATION, LOCATION	Notes
4940 (con'd)	RUSSIA †RMI, Via Tajikistan	(D) • W ASIA & S ASIA • 100 kW
	YAKUT RADIO, Yakutsk	(D) • DS-RUSSIAN, YAKUT • 50 kW
	SRI LANKA SRI LANKA BC CORP, Colombo-Ekala	DS • 10 kW
	UKRAINE †UKRAINIAN R, Kiev	RUSSIAN & UKRAINIAN • DS-3 • 50 kW
4945	BOLIVIA †RADIO ILLIMANI, La Paz	DS-VERY IRREGULAR • 10 kW / M-Sa • DS-VERY IRREGULAR • 10 kW / Tu-Su • DS-VERY IRREGULAR • 10 kW
	BRAZIL RADIO DIFUSORA, Poços de Caldas	PORTUGUESE • DS • 1 kW / Tu-Su • PORTUGUESE • DS • 1 kW
	†RADIO NACIONAL, Pôrto Velho	PORTUGUESE • DS • 50 kW / Irr • PORTUGUESE • DS • 50 kW
	†VOZ SAO FRANCISCO, Petrolina	PORTUGUESE • DS • 2 kW
	SOUTH AFRICA †RADIO RSA, Meyerton	(J) • S AFRICA • 250 kW
4950	CHINA (PR) VOICE OF PUJIANG, Shanghai	E ASIA
	XILINGOL PBS, Abagnar Qi	DS-MONGOLIAN
	ECUADOR †RADIO BAHA'I, Otavalo	DS • 1 kW
	INDIA RADIO KASHMIR, Jammu	DS-A • 2 kW
	MALAYSIA RTM-SARAWAK, Kuching-Stapok	DS • 10 kW
	PAKISTAN PAKISTAN BC CORP, Peshawar	DS • 10 kW / (D) • DS-ENGLISH, ETC • 10 kW
	PERU †R MADRE DE DIOS, Puerto Maldonado	DS • 5 kW / Irr • DS • 5 kW
4951v	ANGOLA RADIO NACIONAL, Luanda	Irr • DS
4955	BRAZIL RADIO CLUBE, Rondonópolis	PORTUGUESE • DS-TEMP INACTIVE • 2.5 kW / M-Sa • PORTUGUESE • DS-TEMP INACTIVE • 2.5 kW
	RADIO CULTURA, Campos	PORTUGUESE • DS • 2.5 kW
	PERU †R CULTURAL AMAUTA, Huanta	DS-SPANISH, QUECHUA • 1 kW
4955v	BRAZIL †RADIO MARAJOARA, Belém	PORTUGUESE • DS • 10 kW
4957.5	AZERBAIJAN †AZERBAIJANI RADIO, Baku	DS-2 • 50 kW
4960	CHINA (PR) RADIO BEIJING, Kunming	JAPANESE • E ASIA • 50 kW
	INDIA ALL INDIA RADIO, Delhi	DS • 10/20 kW / ENGLISH, ETC • DS • 10/20 kW
4960.3	PERU RADIO LA MERCED, La Merced	Tu-Su • DS • 0.5 kW / DS • 0.5 kW / M-Sa • DS • 0.5 kW
4961v	ECUADOR RADIO FEDERACION, Sucúa	DS • 5 kW
4965	BRAZIL †RADIO ALVORADA, Parintins	PORTUGUESE • DS • 5 kW
	RADIO POTI, Natal	PORTUGUESE • DS-TEMP INACTIVE • 1 kW
	SOUTH AFRICA †RADIO RSA, Meyerton	S AFRICA • 250 kW
4965v	BOLIVIA †RADIO JUAN XXIII, San Ignacio Velasco	DS • 3 kW / M-Sa • DS • 3 kW / Irr • M-Sa • DS • 3 kW / Su • DS • 3 kW
4965.2	COLOMBIA †RADIO SANTA FE, Bogotá	Irr • DS • 5 kW
4966	PERU RADIO SAN MIGUEL, Cusco	DS-SPANISH, QUECHUA • 5 kW / Tu-Su • DS • 5 kW
4969.8	ANGOLA EP DA CABINDA, Cabinda	Irr • DS • 5 kW
4970	CHINA (PR) XINJIANG PBS, Urümqi	DS-KAZAKH • 50 kW
	MALAYSIA †RTM-KOTA KINABALU, Kota Kinabalu	DS-MALAY • 10 kW
	PERU RADIO IMAGEN, Tarapoto	DS • 1 kW / Su • DS • 1 kW / Tu-Su • DS • 1 kW
4970v	VENEZUELA †RADIO RUMBOS, Villa de Cura	DS • 10 kW

SUMMER ONLY (J)   WINTER ONLY (D)   JAMMING / OR ∧   EARLIEST HEARD ◁   LATEST HEARD ▷   NEW OR CHANGED FOR 1993 †

FREQUENCY   COUNTRY, STATION, LOCATION   TARGET • NETWORK • POWER (kW)   World Time

0 1 2 3 4 5 6 7 8 9 10 11 12 13 14 15 16 17 18 19 20 21 22 23 24

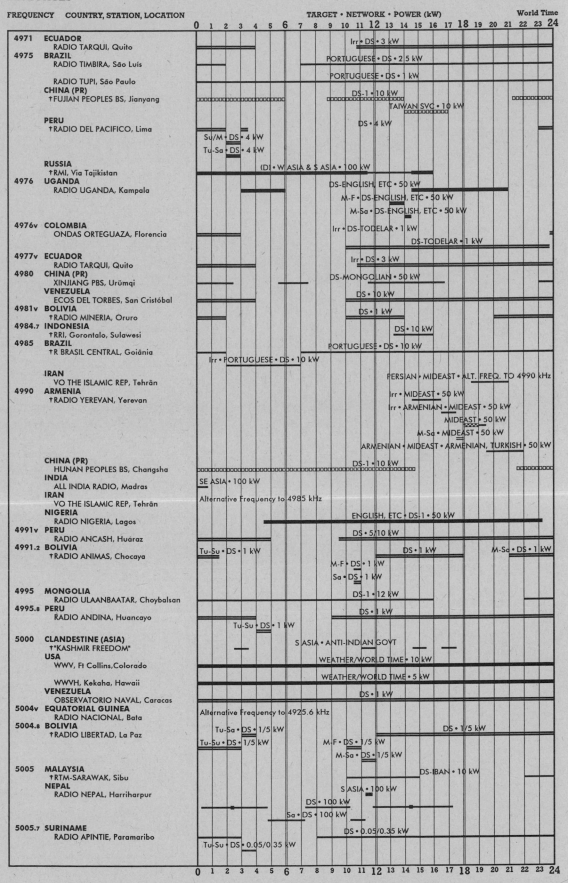

4971 ECUADOR
RADIO TARQUI, Quito — Irr • DS • 3 kW

4975 BRAZIL
RADIO TIMBIRA, São Luís — PORTUGUESE • DS • 2.5 kW

RADIO TUPI, São Paulo — PORTUGUESE • DS • 1 kW

CHINA (PR)
†FUJIAN PEOPLES BS, Jianyang — DS-1 • 10 kW / TAIWAN SVC • 10 kW

PERU
†RADIO DEL PACIFICO, Lima — DS • 4 kW
Su/M • DS • 4 kW
Tu-Sa • DS • 4 kW

RUSSIA
†RMI, Via Tajikistan — (D) • W ASIA & S ASIA • 100 kW

4976 UGANDA
RADIO UGANDA, Kampala — DS-ENGLISH, ETC • 50 kW
M-F • DS-ENGLISH, ETC • 50 kW
M-Sa • DS-ENGLISH, ETC • 50 kW

4976v COLOMBIA
ONDAS ORTEGUAZA, Florencia — Irr • DS-TODELAR • 1 kW
DS-TODELAR • 1 kW

4977v ECUADOR
RADIO TARQUI, Quito — Irr • DS • 3 kW

4980 CHINA (PR)
XINJIANG PBS, Urümqi — DS-MONGOLIAN • 50 kW
VENEZUELA
ECOS DEL TORBES, San Cristóbal — DS • 10 kW

4981v BOLIVIA
†RADIO MINERIA, Oruro — DS • 1 kW

4984.7 INDONESIA
†RRI, Gorontalo, Sulawesi — DS • 10 kW

4985 BRAZIL
†R BRASIL CENTRAL, Goiânia — PORTUGUESE • DS • 10 kW
Irr • PORTUGUESE • DS • 10 kW

IRAN
VO THE ISLAMIC REP, Tehrän — PERSIAN • MIDEAST • ALT. FREQ. TO 4990 kHz

4990 ARMENIA
†RADIO YEREVAN, Yerevan — Irr • MIDEAST • 50 kW
Irr • ARMENIAN • MIDEAST • 50 kW
MIDEAST • 50 kW
M-Sa • MIDEAST • 50 kW
ARMENIAN • MIDEAST • ARMENIAN, TURKISH • 50 kW

CHINA (PR)
HUNAN PEOPLES BS, Changsha — DS-1 • 10 kW
INDIA
ALL INDIA RADIO, Madras — SE ASIA • 100 kW
IRAN
VO THE ISLAMIC REP, Tehrän — Alternative Frequency to 4985 kHz
NIGERIA
RADIO NIGERIA, Lagos — ENGLISH, ETC • DS-1 • 50 kW

4991v PERU
RADIO ANCASH, Huáraz — DS • 5/10 kW

4991.2 BOLIVIA
†RADIO ANIMAS, Chocaya — Tu-Su • DS • 1 kW / DS • 1 kW / M-Sa • DS • 1 kW
M-F • DS • 1 kW
Sa • DS • 1 kW

4995 MONGOLIA
RADIO ULAANBAATAR, Choybalsan — DS-1 • 12 kW

4995.8 PERU
RADIO ANDINA, Huancayo — DS • 1 kW
Tu-Su • DS • 1 kW

5000 CLANDESTINE (ASIA)
†"KASHMIR FREEDOM" — S ASIA • ANTI-INDIAN GOVT
USA
WWV, Ft Collins, Colorado — WEATHER/WORLD TIME • 10 kW

WWVH, Kekaha, Hawaii — WEATHER/WORLD TIME • 5 kW
VENEZUELA
OBSERVATORIO NAVAL, Caracas — DS • 1 kW

5004v EQUATORIAL GUINEA
RADIO NACIONAL, Bata — Alternative Frequency to 4925.6 kHz

5004.8 BOLIVIA
†RADIO LIBERTAD, La Paz — Tu-Sa • DS • 1/5 kW / DS • 1/5 kW
Tu-Su • DS • 1/5 kW
M-F • DS • 1/5 kW
M-Sa • DS • 1/5 kW

5005 MALAYSIA
†RTM-SARAWAK, Sibu — DS-IBAN • 10 kW
NEPAL
RADIO NEPAL, Harriharpur — S ASIA • 100 kW
DS • 100 kW
Sa • DS • 100 kW

5005.7 SURINAME
RADIO APINTIE, Paramaribo — DS • 0.05/0.35 kW
Tu-Su • DS • 0.05/0.35 kW

0 1 2 3 4 5 6 7 8 9 10 11 12 13 14 15 16 17 18 19 20 21 22 23 24

ENGLISH ▬   ARABIC ▧▧▧   CHINESE ▦▦▦   FRENCH ▭   GERMAN ▬   RUSSIAN ═   SPANISH ▬   OTHER ▬

FREQUENCY　　COUNTRY, STATION, LOCATION　　　　　TARGET • NETWORK • POWER (kW)　　　　World Time

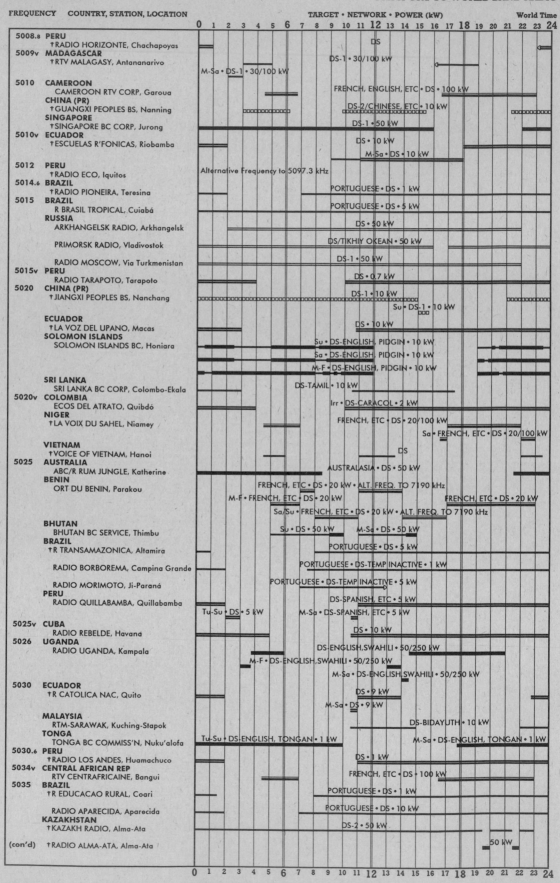

Frequency	Country, Station, Location	Notes
5008.8	**PERU**	
	†RADIO HORIZONTE, Chachapoyas	DS
5009v	**MADAGASCAR**	
	†RTV MALAGASY, Antananarivo	DS-1 • 30/100 kW / M-Sa • DS-1 • 30/100 kW
5010	**CAMEROON**	
	CAMEROON RTV CORP, Garoua	FRENCH, ENGLISH, ETC • DS • 100 kW
	CHINA (PR)	
	†GUANGXI PEOPLES BS, Nanning	DS-2/CHINESE, ETC • 10 kW
	SINGAPORE	
	†SINGAPORE BC CORP, Jurong	DS-1 • 50 kW
5010v	**ECUADOR**	
	†ESCUELAS R'FONICAS, Riobamba	DS • 10 kW / M-Sa • DS 10 kW
5012	**PERU**	
	†RADIO ECO, Iquitos	Alternative Frequency to 5097.3 kHz
5014.6	**BRAZIL**	
	†RADIO PIONEIRA, Teresina	PORTUGUESE • DS • 1 kW
5015	**BRAZIL**	
	R BRASIL TROPICAL, Cuiabá	PORTUGUESE • DS • 5 kW
	RUSSIA	
	ARKHANGELSK RADIO, Arkhangelsk	DS • 50 kW
	PRIMORSK RADIO, Vladivostok	DS/TIKHIY OKEAN • 50 kW
	RADIO MOSCOW, Via Turkmenistan	DS-1 • 50 kW
5015v	**PERU**	
	RADIO TARAPOTO, Tarapoto	DS • 0.7 kW
5020	**CHINA (PR)**	
	†JIANGXI PEOPLES BS, Nanchang	DS-1 • 10 kW / Su • DS-1 • 10 kW
	ECUADOR	
	†LA VOZ DEL UPANO, Macas	DS • 10 kW
	SOLOMON ISLANDS	
	SOLOMON ISLANDS BC, Honiara	Su • DS-ENGLISH, PIDGIN • 10 kW / Sa • DS-ENGLISH, PIDGIN • 10 kW / M-F • DS-ENGLISH, PIDGIN • 10 kW
	SRI LANKA	
	SRI LANKA BC CORP, Colombo-Ekala	DS-TAMIL • 10 kW
5020v	**COLOMBIA**	
	ECOS DEL ATRATO, Quibdó	Irr • DS-CARACOL • 2 kW
	NIGER	
	†LA VOIX DU SAHEL, Niamey	FRENCH, ETC • DS • 20/100 kW / Sa • FRENCH, ETC • DS • 20/100 kW
	VIETNAM	
	†VOICE OF VIETNAM, Hanoi	DS
5025	**AUSTRALIA**	
	ABC/R RUM JUNGLE, Katherine	AUSTRALASIA • DS • 50 kW
	BENIN	
	ORT DU BENIN, Parakou	FRENCH, ETC • DS • 20 kW • ALT. FREQ. TO 7190 kHz / M-F • FRENCH, ETC • DS • 20 kW / FRENCH, ETC • DS • 20 kW / Sa/Su • FRENCH, ETC • DS • 20 kW • ALT. FREQ. TO 7190 kHz
	BHUTAN	
	BHUTAN BC SERVICE, Thimbu	Su • DS 50 kW / M-Sa • DS • 50 kW
	BRAZIL	
	†R TRANSAMAZONICA, Altamira	PORTUGUESE • DS • 5 kW
	RADIO BORBOREMA, Campina Grande	PORTUGUESE • DS-TEMP INACTIVE • 1 kW
	RADIO MORIMOTO, Ji-Paraná	PORTUGUESE • DS-TEMP INACTIVE • 5 kW
	PERU	
	RADIO QUILLABAMBA, Quillabamba	DS-SPANISH, ETC • 5 kW / Tu-Su • DS • 5 kW / M-Sa • DS-SPANISH, ETC • 5 kW
5025v	**CUBA**	
	RADIO REBELDE, Havana	DS • 10 kW
5026	**UGANDA**	
	RADIO UGANDA, Kampala	DS-ENGLISH, SWAHILI • 50/250 kW / M-F • DS-ENGLISH, SWAHILI • 50/250 kW / M-Sa • DS-ENGLISH, SWAHILI • 50/250 kW
5030	**ECUADOR**	
	†R CATOLICA NAC, Quito	DS • 9 kW / M-Sa • DS • 9 kW
	MALAYSIA	
	RTM-SARAWAK, Kuching-Stapok	DS-BIDAYUTH • 10 kW
	TONGA	
	TONGA BC COMMISS'N, Nuku'alofa	Tu-Su • DS-ENGLISH, TONGAN • 1 kW / M-Sa • DS-ENGLISH, TONGAN • 1 kW
5030.6	**PERU**	
	†RADIO LOS ANDES, Huamachuco	DS • 1 kW
5034v	**CENTRAL AFRICAN REP**	
	RTV CENTRAFRICAINE, Bangui	FRENCH, ETC • DS • 100 kW
5035	**BRAZIL**	
	†R EDUCACAO RURAL, Coari	PORTUGUESE • DS • 1 kW
	RADIO APARECIDA, Aparecida	PORTUGUESE • DS • 10 kW
	KAZAKHSTAN	
	†KAZAKH RADIO, Alma-Ata	DS-2 • 50 kW
(con'd)	†RADIO ALMA-ATA, Alma-Ata	50 kW

FREQUENCY	COUNTRY, STATION, LOCATION	TARGET • NETWORK • POWER (kW)	World Time

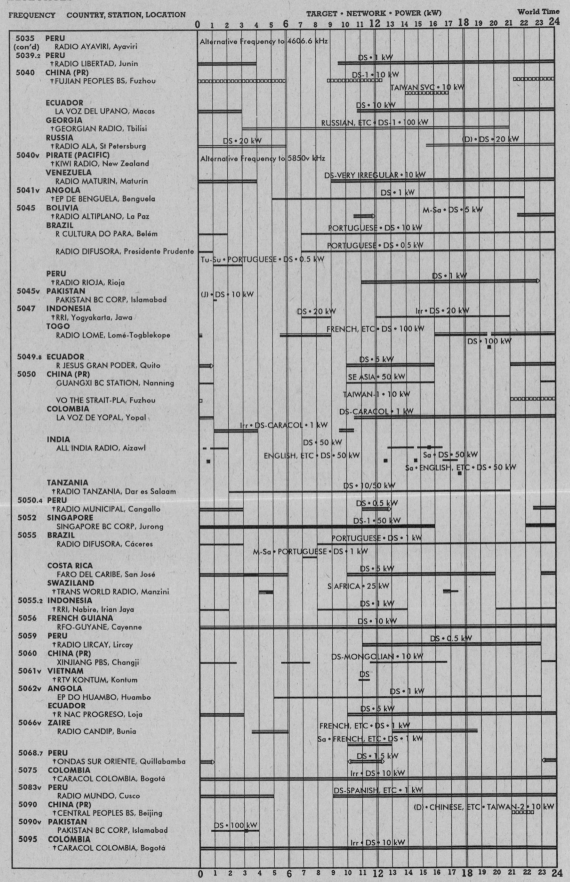

5035 (con'd)	**PERU** RADIO AYAVIRI, Ayaviri	Alternative Frequency to 4606.6 kHz
5039.2	**PERU** †RADIO LIBERTAD, Junín	DS • 1 kW
5040	**CHINA (PR)** †FUJIAN PEOPLES BS, Fuzhou	DS-1 • 10 kW / TAIWAN SVC • 10 kW
	ECUADOR LA VOZ DEL UPANO, Macas	DS • 10 kW
	GEORGIA †GEORGIAN RADIO, Tbilisi	RUSSIAN, ETC • DS-1 • 100 kW
	RUSSIA †RADIO ALA, St Petersburg	DS • 20 kW / (D) • DS • 20 kW
5040v	**PIRATE (PACIFIC)** †KIWI RADIO, New Zealand	Alternative Frequency to 5850v kHz
	VENEZUELA RADIO MATURIN, Maturín	DS-VERY IRREGULAR • 10 kW
5041v	**ANGOLA** †EP DE BENGUELA, Benguela	DS • 1 kW
5045	**BOLIVIA** †RADIO ALTIPLANO, La Paz	M-Sa • DS • 5 kW
	BRAZIL R CULTURA DO PARA, Belém	PORTUGUESE • DS • 10 kW
	RADIO DIFUSORA, Presidente Prudente	PORTUGUESE • DS • 0.5 kW / Tu-Su • PORTUGUESE • DS • 0.5 kW
	PERU †RADIO RIOJA, Rioja	DS • 1 kW
5045v	**PAKISTAN** PAKISTAN BC CORP, Islamabad	(J) • DS • 10 kW
5047	**INDONESIA** †RRI, Yogyakarta, Jawa	DS • 20 kW / Irr • DS • 20 kW
	TOGO RADIO LOME, Lomé-Togblekope	FRENCH, ETC • DS • 100 kW / DS • 100 kW
5049.8	**ECUADOR** R JESUS GRAN PODER, Quito	DS • 5 kW
5050	**CHINA (PR)** GUANGXI BC STATION, Nanning	SE ASIA • 50 kW
	VO THE STRAIT-PLA, Fuzhou	TAIWAN-1 • 10 kW
	COLOMBIA LA VOZ DE YOPAL, Yopal	DS-CARACOL • 1 kW / Irr • DS-CARACOL • 1 kW
	INDIA ALL INDIA RADIO, Aizawl	DS • 50 kW / ENGLISH, ETC • DS • 50 kW / Sa • DS • 50 kW / Sa • ENGLISH, ETC • DS • 50 kW
	TANZANIA †RADIO TANZANIA, Dar es Salaam	DS • 10/50 kW
5050.4	**PERU** †RADIO MUNICIPAL, Cangallo	DS • 0.5 kW
5052	**SINGAPORE** SINGAPORE BC CORP, Jurong	DS-1 • 50 kW
5055	**BRAZIL** RADIO DIFUSORA, Cáceres	PORTUGUESE • DS • 1 kW / M-Sa • PORTUGUESE • DS • 1 kW
	COSTA RICA FARO DEL CARIBE, San José	DS • 5 kW
	SWAZILAND †TRANS WORLD RADIO, Manzini	S AFRICA • 25 kW
5055.2	**INDONESIA** †RRI, Nabire, Irian Jaya	DS • 1 kW
5056	**FRENCH GUIANA** RFO-GUYANE, Cayenne	DS • 10 kW
5059	**PERU** †RADIO LIRCAY, Lircay	DS • 0.5 kW
5060	**CHINA (PR)** XINJIANG PBS, Changji	DS-MONGOLIAN • 10 kW
5061v	**VIETNAM** †RTV KONTUM, Kontum	DS
5062v	**ANGOLA** EP DO HUAMBO, Huambo	DS • 1 kW
	ECUADOR †R NAC PROGRESO, Loja	DS • 5 kW
5066v	**ZAIRE** RADIO CANDIP, Bunia	FRENCH, ETC • DS • 1 kW / Sa • FRENCH, ETC • DS • 1 kW
5068.7	**PERU** †ONDAS SUR ORIENTE, Quillabamba	DS • 1.5 kW
5075	**COLOMBIA** †CARACOL COLOMBIA, Bogotá	Irr • DS • 10 kW
5083v	**PERU** RADIO MUNDO, Cusco	DS-SPANISH, ETC • 1 kW
5090	**CHINA (PR)** †CENTRAL PEOPLES BS, Beijing	(D) • CHINESE, ETC • TAIWAN-2 • 10 kW
5090v	**PAKISTAN** PAKISTAN BC CORP, Islamabad	DS • 100 kW
5095	**COLOMBIA** †CARACOL COLOMBIA, Bogotá	Irr • DS • 10 kW

ENGLISH ▬ ARABIC ⧆ CHINESE ▫▫▫ FRENCH ═ GERMAN ▬ RUSSIAN ＝ SPANISH ▭ OTHER ▬

FREQUENCY	COUNTRY, STATION, LOCATION

TARGET • NETWORK • POWER (kW)

World Time

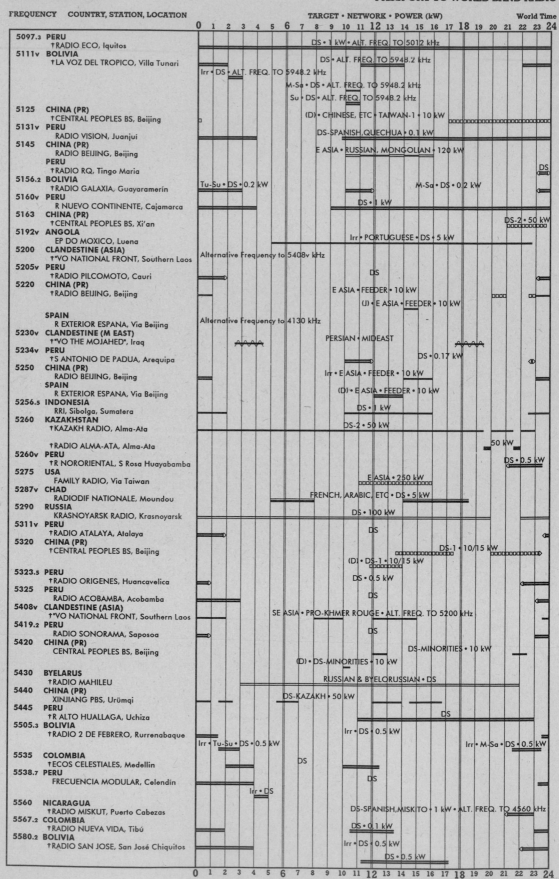

Frequency	Country / Station	Details
5097.3	**PERU** †RADIO ECO, Iquitos	DS • 1 kW • ALT. FREQ. TO 5012 kHz
5111v	**BOLIVIA** †LA VOZ DEL TROPICO, Villa Tunari	DS • ALT. FREQ. TO 5948.2 kHz / Irr • DS • ALT. FREQ. TO 5948.2 kHz / M-Sa • DS • ALT. FREQ. TO 5948.2 kHz / Su • DS • ALT. FREQ. TO 5948.2 kHz
5125	**CHINA (PR)** †CENTRAL PEOPLES BS, Beijing	(D) • CHINESE, ETC • TAIWAN-1 • 10 kW
5131v	**PERU** RADIO VISION, Juanjuí	DS-SPANISH,QUECHUA • 0.1 kW
5145	**CHINA (PR)** RADIO BEIJING, Beijing	E ASIA • RUSSIAN, MONGOLIAN • 120 kW
	PERU †RADIO RQ, Tingo Maria	DS
5156.2	**BOLIVIA** †RADIO GALAXIA, Guayaramerín	Tu-Su • DS • 0.2 kW / M-Sa • DS • 0.2 kW
5160v	**PERU** R NUEVO CONTINENTE, Cajamarca	DS • 1 kW
5163	**CHINA (PR)** †CENTRAL PEOPLES BS, Xi'an	DS-2 • 50 kW
5192v	**ANGOLA** EP DO MOXICO, Luena	Irr • PORTUGUESE • DS • 5 kW
5200	**CLANDESTINE (ASIA)** †"VO NATIONAL FRONT, Southern Laos	Alternative Frequency to 5408v kHz
5205v	**PERU** †RADIO PILCOMOTO, Cauri	DS
5220	**CHINA (PR)** †RADIO BEIJING, Beijing	E ASIA • FEEDER • 10 kW / (J) • E ASIA • FEEDER • 10 kW
	SPAIN R EXTERIOR ESPANA, Via Beijing	Alternative Frequency to 4130 kHz
5230v	**CLANDESTINE (M EAST)** †"VO THE MOJAHED", Iraq	PERSIAN • MIDEAST
5234v	**PERU** †S ANTONIO DE PADUA, Arequipa	DS • 0.17 kW
5250	**CHINA (PR)** RADIO BEIJING, Beijing	Irr • E ASIA • FEEDER • 10 kW
	SPAIN R EXTERIOR ESPANA, Via Beijing	(D) • E ASIA • FEEDER • 10 kW
5256.5	**INDONESIA** RRI, Sibolga, Sumatera	DS • 1 kW
5260	**KAZAKHSTAN** †KAZAKH RADIO, Alma-Ata	DS-2 • 50 kW
	†RADIO ALMA-ATA, Alma-Ata	50 kW
5260v	**PERU** †R NORORIENTAL, S Rosa Huayabamba	DS • 0.5 kW
5275	**USA** FAMILY RADIO, Via Taiwan	E ASIA • 250 kW
5287v	**CHAD** RADIODIF NATIONALE, Moundou	FRENCH, ARABIC, ETC • DS • 5 kW
5290	**RUSSIA** KRASNOYARSK RADIO, Krasnoyarsk	DS • 100 kW
5311v	**PERU** †RADIO ATALAYA, Atalaya	DS
5320	**CHINA (PR)** †CENTRAL PEOPLES BS, Beijing	DS-1 • 10/15 kW / (D) • DS-1 • 10/15 kW
5323.5	**PERU** †RADIO ORIGENES, Huancavelica	DS • 0.5 kW
5325	**PERU** RADIO ACOBAMBA, Acobamba	DS
5408v	**CLANDESTINE (ASIA)** †"VO NATIONAL FRONT, Southern Laos	SE ASIA • PRO-KHMER ROUGE • ALT. FREQ. TO 5200 kHz
5419.2	**PERU** RADIO SONORAMA, Saposoa	DS
5420	**CHINA (PR)** CENTRAL PEOPLES BS, Beijing	DS-MINORITIES • 10 kW / (D) • DS-MINORITIES • 10 kW
5430	**BYELARUS** †RADIO MAHILEU	RUSSIAN & BYELORUSSIAN • DS
5440	**CHINA (PR)** XINJIANG PBS, Urümqi	DS-KAZAKH • 50 kW
5445	**PERU** †R ALTO HUALLAGA, Uchiza	DS
5505.3	**BOLIVIA** †RADIO 2 DE FEBRERO, Rurrenabaque	Irr • DS • 0.5 kW / Irr • Tu-Su • DS • 0.5 kW / Irr • M-Sa • DS • 0.5 kW
5535	**COLOMBIA** †ECOS CELESTIALES, Medellin	DS
5538.7	**PERU** FRECUENCIA MODULAR, Celendín	DS / Irr • DS
5560	**NICARAGUA** †RADIO MISKUT, Puerto Cabezas	DS-SPANISH,MISKITO • 1 kW • ALT. FREQ. TO 4560 kHz
5567.2	**COLOMBIA** †RADIO NUEVA VIDA, Tibú	DS • 0.1 kW
5580.2	**BOLIVIA** †RADIO SAN JOSE, San José Chiquitos	Irr • DS • 0.5 kW / DS • 0.5 kW

FREQUENCY   COUNTRY, STATION, LOCATION

TARGET • NETWORK • POWER (kW)

World Time
0 1 2 3 4 5 6 7 8 9 10 11 12 13 14 15 16 17 18 19 20 21 22 23 24

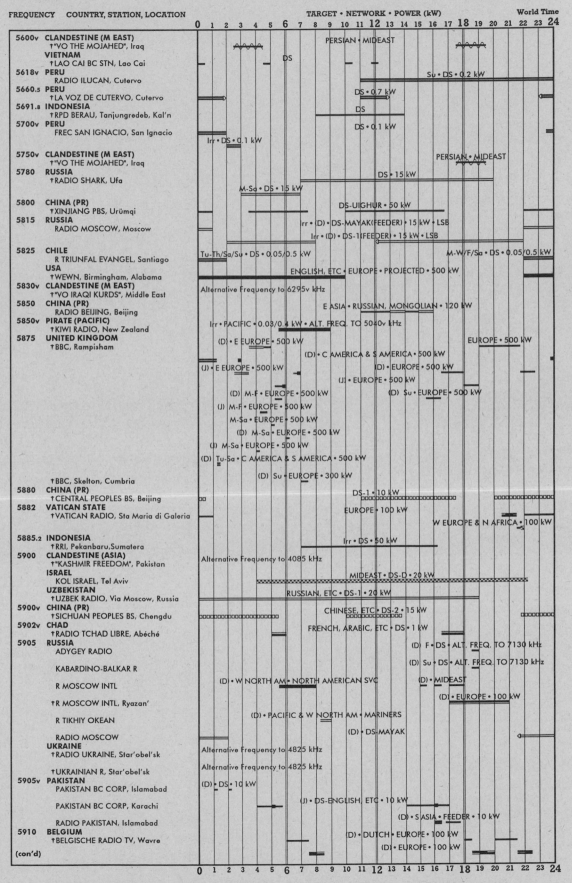

Frequency	Country, Station, Location	Notes
5600v	CLANDESTINE (M EAST) †"VO THE MOJAHED", Iraq	PERSIAN • MIDEAST
	VIETNAM †LAO CAI BC STN, Lao Cai	DS
5618v	PERU RADIO ILUCAN, Cutervo	Su • DS • 0.2 kW
5660.5	PERU †LA VOZ DE CUTERVO, Cutervo	DS • 0.7 kW
5691.8	INDONESIA †RPD BERAU, Tanjungredeb, Kal'n	DS
5700v	PERU FREC SAN IGNACIO, San Ignacio	DS • 0.1 kW / Irr • DS • 0.1 kW
5750v	CLANDESTINE (M EAST) †"VO THE MOJAHED", Iraq	PERSIAN • MIDEAST
5780	RUSSIA †RADIO SHARK, Ufa	DS • 15 kW / M-Sa • DS • 15 kW
5800	CHINA (PR) †XINJIANG PBS, Urümqi	DS-UIGHUR • 50 kW
5815	RUSSIA RADIO MOSCOW, Moscow	Irr • (D) • DS-MAYAK(FEEDER) • 15 kW • LSB / Irr • (D) • DS-1 (FEEDER) • 15 kW • LSB
5825	CHILE R TRIUNFAL EVANGEL, Santiago	Tu-Th/Sa/Su • DS • 0.05/0.5 kW M-W/F/Sa • DS • 0.05/0.5 kW
	USA †WEWN, Birmingham, Alabama	ENGLISH, ETC • EUROPE • PROJECTED • 500 kW
5830v	CLANDESTINE (M EAST) †"VO IRAQI KURDS", Middle East	Alternative Frequency to 6295v kHz
5850	CHINA (PR) RADIO BEIJING, Beijing	E ASIA • RUSSIAN, MONGOLIAN • 120 kW
5850v	PIRATE (PACIFIC) †KIWI RADIO, New Zealand	Irr • PACIFIC • 0.03/0.4 kW • ALT. FREQ. TO 5040v kHz
5875	UNITED KINGDOM †BBC, Rampisham	(D) • E EUROPE • 500 kW EUROPE • 500 kW / (D) • C AMERICA & S AMERICA • 500 kW / (J) • E EUROPE • 500 kW / (D) • EUROPE • 500 kW / (J) • EUROPE • 500 kW / (D) M-F • EUROPE • 500 kW / (D) Su • EUROPE • 500 kW / (J) M-F • EUROPE • 500 kW / M-Sa • EUROPE • 500 kW / (D) M-Sa • EUROPE • 500 kW / (J) M-Sa • EUROPE • 500 kW / (D) Tu-Sa • C AMERICA & S AMERICA • 500 kW
	†BBC, Skelton, Cumbria	(D) Su • EUROPE • 300 kW
5880	CHINA (PR) †CENTRAL PEOPLES BS, Beijing	DS-1 • 10 kW
5882	VATICAN STATE †VATICAN RADIO, Sta Maria di Galeria	EUROPE • 100 kW W EUROPE & N AFRICA • 100 kW
5885.2	INDONESIA †RRI, Pekanbaru, Sumatera	Irr • DS • 50 kW
5900	CLANDESTINE (ASIA) †"KASHMIR FREEDOM", Pakistan	Alternative Frequency to 4085 kHz
	ISRAEL KOL ISRAEL, Tel Aviv	MIDEAST • DS-D • 20 kW
	UZBEKISTAN †UZBEK RADIO, Via Moscow, Russia	RUSSIAN, ETC • DS-1 • 20 kW
5900v	CHINA (PR) †SICHUAN PEOPLES BS, Chengdu	CHINESE, ETC • DS-2 • 15 kW
5902v	CHAD †RADIO TCHAD LIBRE, Abéché	FRENCH, ARABIC, ETC • DS • 1 kW
5905	RUSSIA ADYGEY RADIO	(D) F • DS • ALT. FREQ. TO 7130 kHz
	KABARDINO-BALKAR R	(D) Su • DS • ALT. FREQ. TO 7130 kHz
	R MOSCOW INTL	(D) • W NORTH AM • NORTH AMERICAN SVC (D) • MIDEAST
	†R MOSCOW INTL, Ryazan'	(D) • EUROPE • 100 kW
	R TIKHIY OKEAN	(D) • PACIFIC & W NORTH AM • MARINERS
	RADIO MOSCOW	(D) • DS-MAYAK
	UKRAINE †RADIO UKRAINE, Star'obel'sk	Alternative Frequency to 4825 kHz
	†UKRAINIAN R, Star'obel'sk	Alternative Frequency to 4825 kHz
5905v	PAKISTAN PAKISTAN BC CORP, Islamabad	(D) • DS • 10 kW
	PAKISTAN BC CORP, Karachi	(J) • DS-ENGLISH, ETC • 10 kW
	RADIO PAKISTAN, Islamabad	(D) • S ASIA • FEEDER • 10 kW
5910	BELGIUM †BELGISCHE RADIO TV, Wavre	(D) • DUTCH • EUROPE • 100 kW / (D) • EUROPE • 100 kW
(con'd)		

0 1 2 3 4 5 6 7 8 9 10 11 12 13 14 15 16 17 18 19 20 21 22 23 24

ENGLISH ▬ ARABIC ▧ CHINESE □□□ FRENCH ═ GERMAN ▬ RUSSIAN ══ SPANISH ▬ OTHER ─

FREQUENCY   COUNTRY, STATION, LOCATION   TARGET • NETWORK • POWER (kW)   World Time

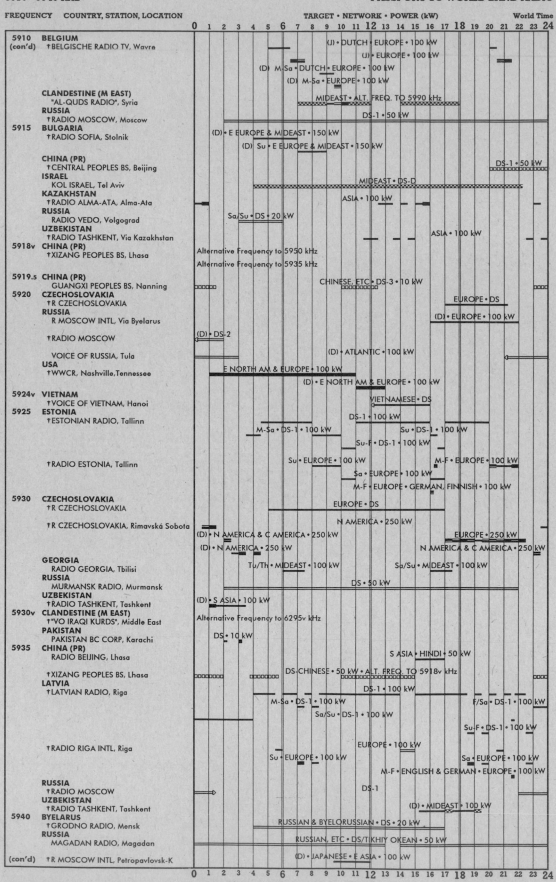

0 1 2 3 4 5 6 7 8 9 10 11 12 13 14 15 16 17 18 19 20 21 22 23 24

5910 **BELGIUM**
(con'd)   †BELGISCHE RADIO TV, Wavre
                                               (J) • DUTCH • EUROPE • 100 kW
                                               (J) • EUROPE • 100 kW
                                        (D) M-Sa • DUTCH • EUROPE • 100 kW
                                           (D) M-Sa • EUROPE • 100 kW

          CLANDESTINE (M EAST)
          "AL-QUDS RADIO", Syria
                                           MIDEAST • ALT. FREQ. TO 5990 kHz
          RUSSIA
          †RADIO MOSCOW, Moscow
                                                 DS-1 • 50 kW
5915 **BULGARIA**
          †RADIO SOFIA, Stolnik
                        (D) • E EUROPE & MIDEAST • 150 kW
                            (D) Su • E EUROPE & MIDEAST • 150 kW

          CHINA (PR)
          †CENTRAL PEOPLES BS, Beijing
                                                                    DS-1 • 50 kW
          ISRAEL
          KOL ISRAEL, Tel Aviv
                                               MIDEAST • DS-D
          KAZAKHSTAN
          †RADIO ALMA-ATA, Alma-Ata
                                          ASIA • 100 kW
          RUSSIA
          RADIO VEDO, Volgograd
                        Sa/Su • DS • 20 kW
          UZBEKISTAN
          †RADIO TASHKENT, Via Kazakhstan
                                                  ASIA • 100 kW
5918v **CHINA (PR)**
          †XIZANG PEOPLES BS, Lhasa
                      Alternative Frequency to 5950 kHz
                      Alternative Frequency to 5935 kHz

5919.5 **CHINA (PR)**
          GUANGXI PEOPLES BS, Nanning
                                       CHINESE, ETC • DS-3 • 10 kW
5920 **CZECHOSLOVAKIA**
          †R CZECHOSLOVAKIA
                                                          EUROPE • DS
          RUSSIA
          R MOSCOW INTL, Via Byelarus
                                                 (D) • EUROPE • 100 kW

          †RADIO MOSCOW
                      (D) • DS-2

          VOICE OF RUSSIA, Tula
                                           (D) • ATLANTIC • 100 kW
          USA
          †WWCR, Nashville,Tennessee
                      E NORTH AM & EUROPE • 100 kW
                                          (D) • E NORTH AM & EUROPE • 100 kW

5924v **VIETNAM**
          †VOICE OF VIETNAM, Hanoi
                                               VIETNAMESE • DS
5925 **ESTONIA**
          †ESTONIAN RADIO, Tallinn
                                               DS-1 • 100 kW
                        M-Sa • DS-1 • 100 kW   Su • DS-1 • 100 kW
                                          Su-F • DS-1 • 100 kW

          †RADIO ESTONIA, Tallinn
                              Su • EUROPE • 100 kW   M-F • EUROPE • 100 kW
                                          Sa • EUROPE • 100 kW
                                          M-F • EUROPE • GERMAN, FINNISH • 100 kW

5930 **CZECHOSLOVAKIA**
          †R CZECHOSLOVAKIA
                                               EUROPE • DS

          †R CZECHOSLOVAKIA, Rimavská Sobota
                                               N AMERICA • 250 kW
                      (D) • N AMERICA & C AMERICA • 250 kW   EUROPE • 250 kW
                      (D) • N AMERICA • 250 kW   N AMERICA & C AMERICA • 250 kW
          GEORGIA
          RADIO GEORGIA, Tbilisi
                        Tu/Th • MIDEAST • 100 kW   Sa/Su • MIDEAST • 100 kW
          RUSSIA
          MURMANSK RADIO, Murmansk
                                               DS • 50 kW
          UZBEKISTAN
          †RADIO TASHKENT, Tashkent
                      (D) • S ASIA • 100 kW
5930v **CLANDESTINE (M EAST)**
          †"VO IRAQI KURDS", Middle East
                      Alternative Frequency to 6295v kHz
          PAKISTAN
          PAKISTAN BC CORP, Karachi
                      DS • 10 kW
5935 **CHINA (PR)**
          RADIO BEIJING, Lhasa
                                               S ASIA • HINDI • 50 kW

          †XIZANG PEOPLES BS, Lhasa
                      DS-CHINESE • 50 kW • ALT. FREQ. TO 5918v kHz
          LATVIA
          †LATVIAN RADIO, Riga
                                               DS-1 • 100 kW
                        M-Sa • DS-1 • 100 kW   F/Sa • DS-1 • 100 kW
                        Sa/Su • DS-1 • 100 kW
                                          Su-F • DS-1 • 100 kW

          †RADIO RIGA INTL, Riga
                                          EUROPE • 100 kW
                        Su • EUROPE • 100 kW   Sa • EUROPE • 100 kW
                                          M-F • ENGLISH & GERMAN • EUROPE • 100 kW

          RUSSIA
          †RADIO MOSCOW
                                               DS-1
          UZBEKISTAN
          †RADIO TASHKENT, Tashkent
                                          (D) • MIDEAST • 100 kW
5940 **BYELARUS**
          †GRODNO RADIO, Mensk
                      RUSSIAN & BYELORUSSIAN • DS • 20 kW
          RUSSIA
          MAGADAN RADIO, Magadan
                      RUSSIAN, ETC • DS/TIKHIY OKEAN • 50 kW

(con'd)   †R MOSCOW INTL, Petropavlovsk-K
                      (D) • JAPANESE • E ASIA • 100 kW

0 1 2 3 4 5 6 7 8 9 10 11 12 13 14 15 16 17 18 19 20 21 22 23 24

SUMMER ONLY (J)   WINTER ONLY (D)   JAMMING / OR ∧   EARLIEST HEARD ◁   LATEST HEARD ▷   NEW OR CHANGED FOR 1993 †

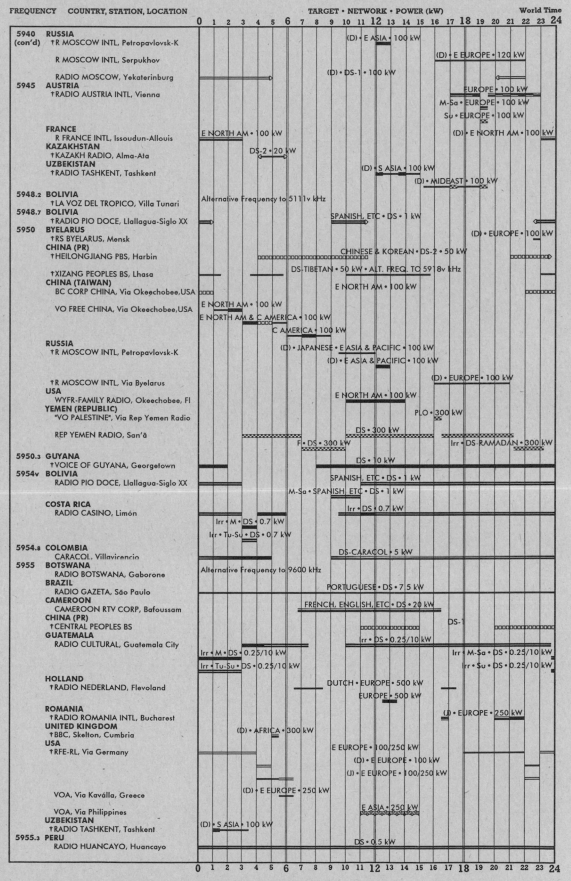

FREQUENCY   COUNTRY, STATION, LOCATION   TARGET • NETWORK • POWER (kW)   World Time

5940 (con'd)	**RUSSIA**
	†R MOSCOW INTL, Petropavlovsk-K — (D) • E ASIA • 100 kW
	R MOSCOW INTL, Serpukhov — (D) • E EUROPE • 120 kW
	RADIO MOSCOW, Yekaterinburg — (D) • DS-1 • 100 kW
5945	**AUSTRIA**
	†RADIO AUSTRIA INTL, Vienna — EUROPE • 100 kW / M-Sa • EUROPE • 100 kW / Su • EUROPE • 100 kW
	FRANCE
	R FRANCE INTL, Issoudun-Allouis — E NORTH AM • 100 kW / (D) • E NORTH AM • 100 kW
	KAZAKHSTAN
	†KAZAKH RADIO, Alma-Ata — DS-2 • 20 kW
	UZBEKISTAN
	†RADIO TASHKENT, Tashkent — (D) • S ASIA • 100 kW / (D) • MIDEAST • 100 kW
5948.2	**BOLIVIA**
	†LA VOZ DEL TROPICO, Villa Tunari — Alternative Frequency to 5111v kHz
5948.7	**BOLIVIA**
	†RADIO PIO DOCE, Llallagua-Siglo XX — SPANISH, ETC • DS • 1 kW
5950	**BYELARUS**
	†RS BYELARUS, Mensk — (D) • EUROPE • 100 kW
	CHINA (PR)
	†HEILONGJIANG PBS, Harbin — CHINESE & KOREAN • DS-2 • 50 kW
	†XIZANG PEOPLES BS, Lhasa — DS-TIBETAN • 50 kW • ALT. FREQ. TO 5918v kHz
	CHINA (TAIWAN)
	BC CORP CHINA, Via Okeechobee, USA — E NORTH AM • 100 kW
	VO FREE CHINA, Via Okeechobee, USA — E NORTH AM • 100 kW / E NORTH AM & C AMERICA • 100 kW / C AMERICA • 100 kW
	RUSSIA
	†R MOSCOW INTL, Petropavlovsk-K — (D) • JAPANESE • E ASIA & PACIFIC • 100 kW / (D) • E ASIA & PACIFIC • 100 kW
	†R MOSCOW INTL, Via Byelarus — (D) • EUROPE • 100 kW
	USA
	WYFR-FAMILY RADIO, Okeechobee, Fl — E NORTH AM • 100 kW
	YEMEN (REPUBLIC)
	"VO PALESTINE", Via Rep Yemen Radio — PLO • 300 kW
	REP YEMEN RADIO, San'ā — DS • 300 kW / F • DS • 300 kW / Irr • DS-RAMADAN • 300 kW
5950.3	**GUYANA**
	†VOICE OF GUYANA, Georgetown — DS • 10 kW
5954v	**BOLIVIA**
	RADIO PIO DOCE, Llallagua-Siglo XX — SPANISH, ETC • DS • 1 kW / M-Sa • SPANISH, ETC • DS • 1 kW
	COSTA RICA
	RADIO CASINO, Limón — Irr • DS • 0.7 kW / Irr • M • DS • 0.7 kW / Irr • Tu-Su • DS • 0.7 kW
5954.8	**COLOMBIA**
	CARACOL, Villavicencio — DS-CARACOL • 5 kW
5955	**BOTSWANA**
	RADIO BOTSWANA, Gaborone — Alternative Frequency to 9600 kHz
	BRAZIL
	RADIO GAZETA, São Paulo — PORTUGUESE • DS • 7.5 kW
	CAMEROON
	CAMEROON RTV CORP, Bafoussam — FRENCH, ENGLISH, ETC • DS • 20 kW
	CHINA (PR)
	†CENTRAL PEOPLES BS — DS-1
	GUATEMALA
	RADIO CULTURAL, Guatemala City — Irr • DS • 0.25/10 kW / Irr • M • DS • 0.25/10 kW / Irr • M-Sa • DS • 0.25/10 kW / Irr • Tu-Su • DS • 0.25/10 kW / Irr • Su • DS • 0.25/10 kW
	HOLLAND
	†RADIO NEDERLAND, Flevoland — DUTCH • EUROPE • 500 kW / EUROPE • 500 kW
	ROMANIA
	†RADIO ROMANIA INTL, Bucharest — (J) • EUROPE • 250 kW
	UNITED KINGDOM
	†BBC, Skelton, Cumbria — (D) • AFRICA • 300 kW
	USA
	†RFE-RL, Via Germany — E EUROPE • 100/250 kW / (D) • E EUROPE • 100 kW / (J) • E EUROPE • 100/250 kW
	VOA, Via Kaválla, Greece — (D) • E EUROPE • 250 kW
	VOA, Via Philippines — E ASIA • 250 kW
	UZBEKISTAN
	†RADIO TASHKENT, Tashkent — (D) • S ASIA • 100 kW
5955.3	**PERU**
	RADIO HUANCAYO, Huancayo — DS • 0.5 kW

0 1 2 3 4 5 6 7 8 9 10 11 12 13 14 15 16 17 18 19 20 21 22 23 24

ENGLISH ▬   ARABIC ⧆   CHINESE ☐☐☐   FRENCH ══   GERMAN ▬   RUSSIAN ──   SPANISH ▬▬   OTHER ──

FREQUENCY   COUNTRY, STATION, LOCATION   TARGET • NETWORK • POWER (kW)   World Time

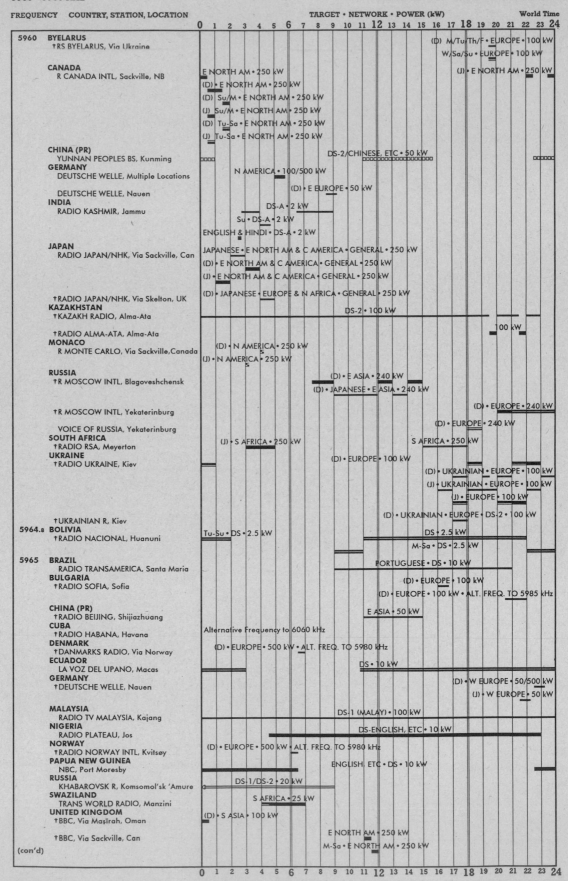

FREQUENCY	COUNTRY, STATION, LOCATION	TARGET • NETWORK • POWER (kW)
5960	**BYELARUS**	
	†RS BYELARUS, Via Ukraine	(D) • M/Tu/Th/F • EUROPE • 100 kW
		W/Sa/Su • EUROPE • 100 kW
	CANADA	
	R CANADA INTL, Sackville, NB	E NORTH AM • 250 kW
		(J) • E NORTH AM • 250 kW
		(D) • E NORTH AM • 250 kW
		(D) • Su/M • E NORTH AM • 250 kW
		(J) • Su/M • E NORTH AM • 250 kW
		(D) • Tu-Sa • E NORTH AM • 250 kW
		(J) • Tu-Sa • E NORTH AM • 250 kW
	CHINA (PR)	
	YUNNAN PEOPLES BS, Kunming	DS-2/CHINESE, ETC • 50 kW
	GERMANY	
	DEUTSCHE WELLE, Multiple Locations	N AMERICA • 100/500 kW
	DEUTSCHE WELLE, Nauen	(D) • E EUROPE • 50 kW
	INDIA	
	RADIO KASHMIR, Jammu	DS-A • 2 kW
		Su • DS-A • 2 kW
		ENGLISH & HINDI • DS-A • 2 kW
	JAPAN	
	RADIO JAPAN/NHK, Via Sackville, Can	JAPANESE • E NORTH AM & C AMERICA • GENERAL • 250 kW
		(D) • E NORTH AM & C AMERICA • GENERAL • 250 kW
		(J) • E NORTH AM & C AMERICA • GENERAL • 250 kW
	†RADIO JAPAN/NHK, Via Skelton, UK	(D) • JAPANESE • EUROPE & N AFRICA • GENERAL • 250 kW
	KAZAKHSTAN	
	†KAZAKH RADIO, Alma-Ata	DS-2 • 100 kW
	†RADIO ALMA-ATA, Alma-Ata	100 kW
	MONACO	
	R MONTE CARLO, Via Sackville, Canada	(D) • N AMERICA • 250 kW
		(J) • N AMERICA • 250 kW
	RUSSIA	
	†R MOSCOW INTL, Blagoveshchensk	(D) • E ASIA • 240 kW
		(D) • JAPANESE • E ASIA • 240 kW
	†R MOSCOW INTL, Yekaterinburg	(D) • EUROPE • 240 kW
	VOICE OF RUSSIA, Yekaterinburg	(D) • EUROPE • 240 kW
	SOUTH AFRICA	
	†RADIO RSA, Meyerton	(J) • S AFRICA • 250 kW
		S AFRICA • 250 kW
	UKRAINE	
	†RADIO UKRAINE, Kiev	(D) • EUROPE • 100 kW
		(D) • UKRAINIAN • EUROPE • 100 kW
		(J) • UKRAINIAN • EUROPE • 100 kW
		(J) • EUROPE • 100 kW
	†UKRAINIAN R, Kiev	(D) • UKRAINIAN • EUROPE • DS-2 • 100 kW
5964.8	**BOLIVIA**	
	†RADIO NACIONAL, Huanuni	Tu-Su • DS • 2.5 kW
		DS • 2.5 kW
		M-Sa • DS • 2.5 kW
5965	**BRAZIL**	
	RADIO TRANSAMERICA, Santa Maria	PORTUGUESE • DS • 10 kW
	BULGARIA	
	†RADIO SOFIA, Sofia	(D) • EUROPE • 100 kW
		(D) • EUROPE • 100 kW • ALT. FREQ. TO 5985 kHz
	CHINA (PR)	
	†RADIO BEIJING, Shijiazhuang	E ASIA • 50 kW
	CUBA	
	†RADIO HABANA, Havana	Alternative Frequency to 6060 kHz
	DENMARK	
	†DANMARKS RADIO, Via Norway	(D) • EUROPE • 500 kW • ALT. FREQ. TO 5980 kHz
	ECUADOR	
	LA VOZ DEL UPANO, Macas	DS • 10 kW
	GERMANY	
	†DEUTSCHE WELLE, Nauen	(D) • W EUROPE • 50/500 kW
		(J) • W EUROPE • 50 kW
	MALAYSIA	
	RADIO TV MALAYSIA, Kajang	DS-1 (MALAY) • 100 kW
	NIGERIA	
	RADIO PLATEAU, Jos	DS-ENGLISH, ETC • 10 kW
	NORWAY	
	†RADIO NORWAY INTL, Kvitsøy	(D) • EUROPE • 500 kW • ALT. FREQ. TO 5980 kHz
	PAPUA NEW GUINEA	
	NBC, Port Moresby	ENGLISH ETC • DS • 10 kW
	RUSSIA	
	KHABAROVSK R, Komsomol'sk 'Amure	DS-1/DS-2 • 20 kW
	SWAZILAND	
	TRANS WORLD RADIO, Manzini	S AFRICA • 25 kW
	UNITED KINGDOM	
	†BBC, Via Maşīrah, Oman	(D) • S ASIA • 100 kW
	†BBC, Via Sackville, Can	E NORTH AM • 250 kW
		M-Sa • E NORTH AM • 250 kW
(con'd)		

World Time: 0 1 2 3 4 5 6 7 8 9 10 11 12 13 14 15 16 17 18 19 20 21 22 23 24

SUMMER ONLY (J)   WINTER ONLY (D)   JAMMING / OR ∧   EARLIEST HEARD ◁   LATEST HEARD ▷   NEW OR CHANGED FOR 1993 †

| FREQUENCY | COUNTRY, STATION, LOCATION | TARGET • NETWORK • POWER (kW) | World Time |

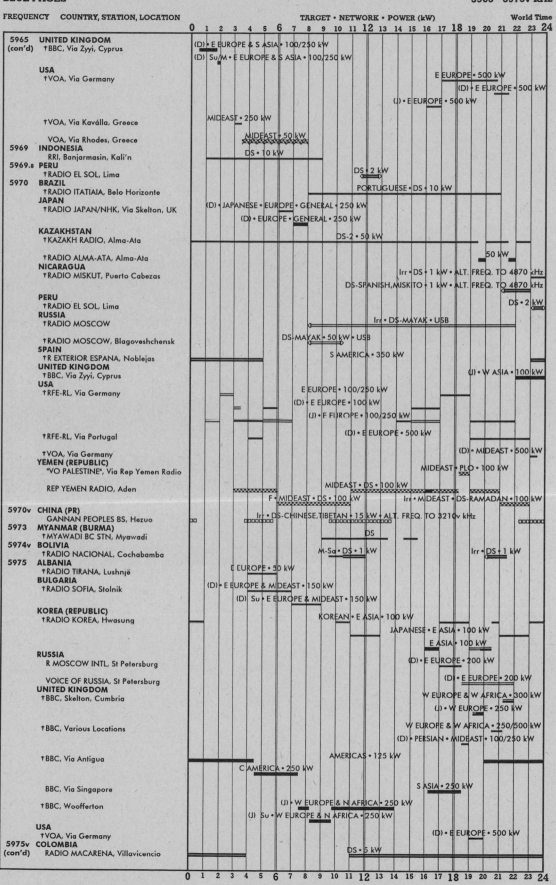

5965 (con'd) — UNITED KINGDOM
†BBC, Via Zyyi, Cyprus — (D) • E EUROPE & S ASIA • 100/250 kW
(D) • Su/M • E EUROPE & S ASIA • 100/250 kW

USA
†VOA, Via Germany — E EUROPE • 500 kW
(D) • E EUROPE • 500 kW
(J) • E EUROPE • 500 kW

†VOA, Via Kaválla, Greece — MIDEAST • 250 kW

VOA, Via Rhodes, Greece — MIDEAST • 50 kW

5969 INDONESIA
RRI, Banjarmasin, Kali'n — DS • 10 kW

5969.8 PERU
†RADIO EL SOL, Lima — DS • 2 kW

5970 BRAZIL
†RADIO ITATIAIA, Belo Horizonte — PORTUGUESE • DS • 10 kW

JAPAN
†RADIO JAPAN/NHK, Via Skelton, UK — (D) • JAPANESE • EUROPE • GENERAL • 250 kW
(D) • EUROPE • GENERAL • 250 kW

KAZAKHSTAN
†KAZAKH RADIO, Alma-Ata — DS-2 • 50 kW

†RADIO ALMA-ATA, Alma-Ata — 50 kW

NICARAGUA
†RADIO MISKUT, Puerto Cabezas — Irr • DS • 1 kW • ALT. FREQ. TO 4870 kHz
DS-SPANISH, MISKITO • 1 kW • ALT. FREQ. TO 4870 kHz

PERU
†RADIO EL SOL, Lima — DS • 2 kW

RUSSIA
†RADIO MOSCOW — Irr • DS-MAYAK • USB

†RADIO MOSCOW, Blagoveshchensk — DS-MAYAK • 50 kW • USB

SPAIN
†R EXTERIOR ESPANA, Noblejas — S AMERICA • 350 kW

UNITED KINGDOM
†BBC, Via Zyyi, Cyprus — (J) • W ASIA • 100 kW

USA
†RFE-RL, Via Germany — E EUROPE • 100/250 kW
(D) • E EUROPE • 100 kW
(J) • E EUROPE • 100/250 kW

†RFE-RL, Via Portugal — (D) • E EUROPE • 500 kW

†VOA, Via Germany — (D) • MIDEAST • 500 kW

YEMEN (REPUBLIC)
"VO PALESTINE", Via Rep Yemen Radio — MIDEAST • PLO • 100 kW

REP YEMEN RADIO, Aden — MIDEAST • DS • 100 kW
F • MIDEAST • DS • 100 kW   Irr • MIDEAST • DS-RAMADAN • 100 kW

5970v CHINA (PR)
GANNAN PEOPLES BS, Hezuo — Irr • DS-CHINESE, TIBETAN • 15 kW • ALT. FREQ. TO 3210v kHz

5973 MYANMAR (BURMA)
†MYAWADI BC STN, Myawadi — DS

5974v BOLIVIA
†RADIO NACIONAL, Cochabamba — M-Sa • DS • 1 kW   Irr • DS • 1 kW

5975 ALBANIA
†RADIO TIRANA, Lushnjë — E EUROPE • 50 kW

BULGARIA
†RADIO SOFIA, Stolnik — (D) • E EUROPE & MIDEAST • 150 kW
(D) • Su • E EUROPE & MIDEAST • 150 kW

KOREA (REPUBLIC)
†RADIO KOREA, Hwasung — KOREAN • E ASIA • 100 kW
JAPANESE • E ASIA • 100 kW
E ASIA • 100 kW

RUSSIA
R MOSCOW INTL, St Petersburg — (D) • E EUROPE • 200 kW

VOICE OF RUSSIA, St Petersburg — (D) • E EUROPE • 200 kW

UNITED KINGDOM
†BBC, Skelton, Cumbria — W EUROPE & W AFRICA • 300 kW
(J) • W EUROPE • 250 kW

†BBC, Various Locations — W EUROPE & W AFRICA • 250/500 kW
(D) • PERSIAN • MIDEAST • 100/250 kW

†BBC, Via Antigua — AMERICAS • 125 kW
C AMERICA • 250 kW

BBC, Via Singapore — S ASIA • 250 kW

†BBC, Woofferton — (J) • W EUROPE & N AFRICA • 250 kW
(J) • Su • W EUROPE & N AFRICA • 250 kW

USA
†VOA, Via Germany — (D) • E EUROPE • 500 kW

5975v COLOMBIA (con'd)
RADIO MACARENA, Villavicencio — DS • 5 kW

| 0 1 2 3 4 5 6 7 8 9 10 11 12 13 14 15 16 17 18 19 20 21 22 23 24 |

ENGLISH ▬ ARABIC ᘏ CHINESE ▭▭▭ FRENCH ▬ GERMAN ▬ RUSSIAN ▭ SPANISH ▬ OTHER ▬

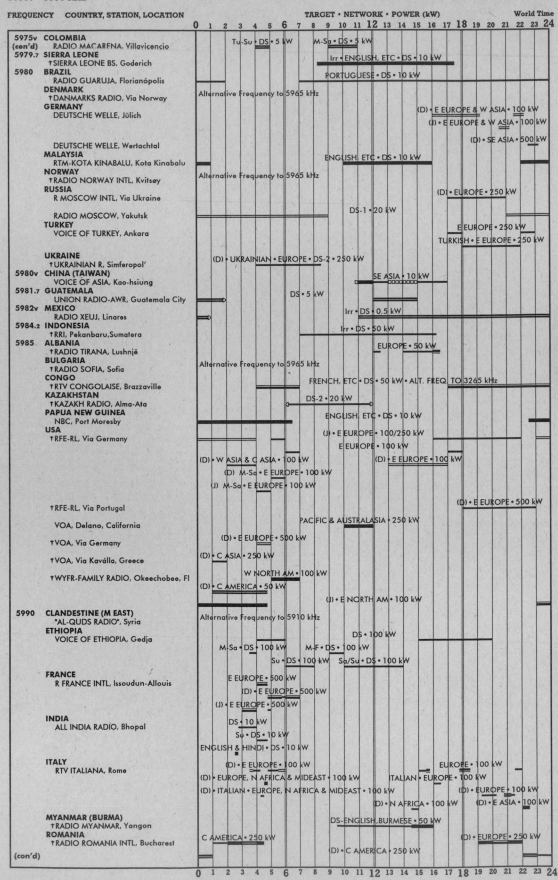

FREQUENCY · COUNTRY, STATION, LOCATION · TARGET • NETWORK • POWER (kW) · World Time

5975v (con'd) COLOMBIA — RADIO MACARENA, Villavicencio	Tu-Su • DS • 5 kW / M-Sa • DS • 5 kW
5979.7 SIERRA LEONE — †SIERRA LEONE BS, Goderich	Irr • ENGLISH, ETC • DS • 10 kW
5980 BRAZIL — RADIO GUARUJA, Florianópolis	PORTUGUESE • DS • 10 kW
DENMARK — †DANMARKS RADIO, Via Norway	Alternative Frequency to 5965 kHz
GERMANY — DEUTSCHE WELLE, Jülich	(D) • E EUROPE & W ASIA • 100 kW / (J) • E EUROPE & W ASIA • 100 kW / (D) • SE ASIA • 500 kW
DEUTSCHE WELLE, Wertachtal	
MALAYSIA — RTM-KOTA KINABALU, Kota Kinabalu	ENGLISH, ETC • DS • 10 kW
NORWAY — †RADIO NORWAY INTL, Kvitsøy	Alternative Frequency to 5965 kHz
RUSSIA — R MOSCOW INTL, Via Ukraine	(D) • EUROPE • 250 kW
RADIO MOSCOW, Yakutsk	DS-1 • 20 kW
TURKEY — VOICE OF TURKEY, Ankara	E EUROPE • 250 kW / TURKISH • E EUROPE • 250 kW
UKRAINE — †UKRAINIAN R, Simferopol'	(D) • UKRAINIAN • EUROPE • DS-2 • 250 kW
5980v CHINA (TAIWAN) — VOICE OF ASIA, Kao-hsiung	SE ASIA • 10 kW
5981.7 GUATEMALA — UNION RADIO-AWR, Guatemala City	DS • 5 kW
5982v MEXICO — RADIO XEUJ, Linares	Irr • DS • 0.5 kW
5984.2 INDONESIA — †RRI, Pekanbaru, Sumatera	Irr • DS • 50 kW
5985 ALBANIA — †RADIO TIRANA, Lushnjë	EUROPE • 50 kW
BULGARIA — †RADIO SOFIA, Sofia	Alternative Frequency to 5965 kHz
CONGO — †RTV CONGOLAISE, Brazzaville	FRENCH, ETC • DS • 50 kW • ALT. FREQ. TO 3265 kHz
KAZAKHSTAN — †KAZAKH RADIO, Alma-Ata	DS-2 • 20 kW
PAPUA NEW GUINEA — NBC, Port Moresby	ENGLISH, ETC • DS • 10 kW
USA — †RFE-RL, Via Germany	(J) • E EUROPE • 100/250 kW / E EUROPE • 100 kW / (D) • W ASIA & C ASIA • 100 kW / (D) • E EUROPE • 100 kW / (D) M-Sa • E EUROPE • 100 kW / (J) M-Sa • E EUROPE • 100 kW
†RFE-RL, Via Portugal	(D) • E EUROPE • 500 kW
VOA, Delano, California	PACIFIC & AUSTRALASIA • 250 kW
†VOA, Via Germany	(D) • E EUROPE • 500 kW
†VOA, Via Kaválla, Greece	(D) • C ASIA • 250 kW
†WYFR-FAMILY RADIO, Okeechobee, Fl	W NORTH AM • 100 kW / (D) • C AMERICA • 50 kW / (J) • E NORTH AM • 100 kW
5990 CLANDESTINE (M EAST) — "AL-QUDS RADIO", Syria	Alternative Frequency to 5910 kHz
ETHIOPIA — VOICE OF ETHIOPIA, Gedja	DS • 100 kW / M-Sa • DS • 100 kW / M-F • DS • 100 kW / Su • DS • 100 kW / Sa/Su • DS • 100 kW
FRANCE — R FRANCE INTL, Issoudun-Allouis	E EUROPE • 500 kW / (D) • E EUROPE • 500 kW / (J) • E EUROPE • 500 kW
INDIA — ALL INDIA RADIO, Bhopal	DS • 10 kW / Su • DS • 10 kW / ENGLISH & HINDI • DS • 10 kW
ITALY — RTV ITALIANA, Rome	(D) • E EUROPE • 100 kW / EUROPE • 100 kW / (D) • EUROPE, N AFRICA & MIDEAST • 100 kW / ITALIAN • EUROPE • 100 kW / (D) • ITALIAN • EUROPE, N AFRICA & MIDEAST • 100 kW / (D) • EUROPE • 100 kW / (D) • N AFRICA • 100 kW / (D) • E ASIA • 100 kW
MYANMAR (BURMA) — †RADIO MYANMAR, Yangon	DS-ENGLISH, BURMESE • 50 kW
ROMANIA — †RADIO ROMANIA INTL, Bucharest	C AMERICA • 250 kW / (D) • EUROPE • 250 kW / (D) • C AMERICA • 250 kW
(con'd)	

FREQUENCY   COUNTRY, STATION, LOCATION   TARGET • NETWORK • POWER (kW)   World Time

0 1 2 3 4 5 6 7 8 9 10 11 12 13 14 15 16 17 18 19 20 21 22 23 24

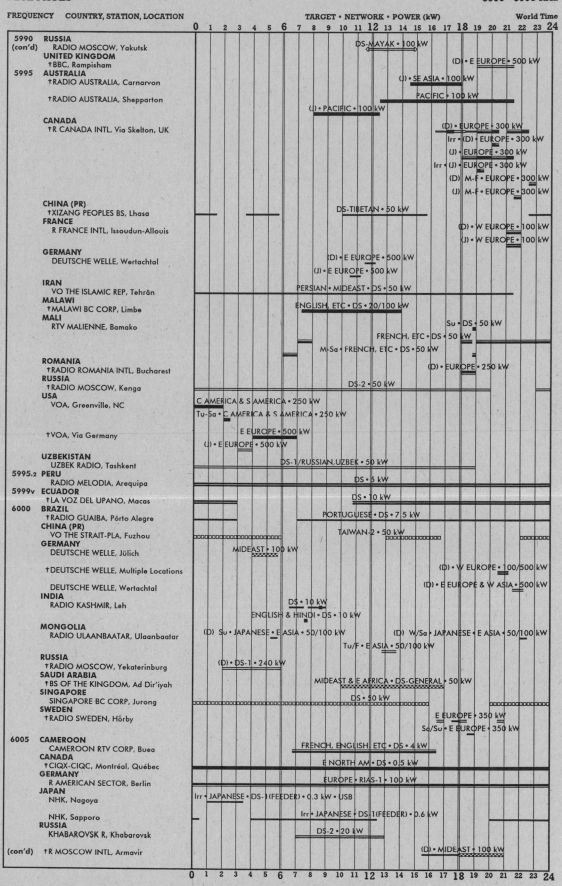

Frequency	Country, Station, Location	Target • Network • Power
5990 (con'd)	RUSSIA	
	RADIO MOSCOW, Yakutsk	DS-MAYAK • 100 kW
	UNITED KINGDOM	
	†BBC, Rampisham	(D) • E EUROPE • 500 kW
5995	AUSTRALIA	
	†RADIO AUSTRALIA, Carnarvon	(J) • SE ASIA • 100 kW
	†RADIO AUSTRALIA, Shepparton	PACIFIC • 100 kW
		(J) • PACIFIC • 100 kW
	CANADA	
	†R CANADA INTL, Via Skelton, UK	(D) • EUROPE • 300 kW
		Irr • (D) • EUROPE • 300 kW
		(J) • EUROPE • 300 kW
		Irr • (J) • EUROPE • 300 kW
		(D) • M-F • EUROPE • 300 kW
		(J) • M-F • EUROPE • 300 kW
	CHINA (PR)	
	†XIZANG PEOPLES BS, Lhasa	DS-TIBETAN • 50 kW
	FRANCE	
	R FRANCE INTL, Issoudun-Allouis	(D) • W EUROPE • 100 kW
		(J) • W EUROPE • 100 kW
	GERMANY	
	DEUTSCHE WELLE, Wertachtal	(D) • E EUROPE • 500 kW
		(J) • E EUROPE • 500 kW
	IRAN	
	VO THE ISLAMIC REP, Tehrān	PERSIAN • MIDEAST • DS • 50 kW
	MALAWI	
	†MALAWI BC CORP, Limbe	ENGLISH, ETC • DS • 20/100 kW
	MALI	
	RTV MALIENNE, Bamako	Su • DS • 50 kW
		FRENCH, ETC • DS • 50 kW
		M-Sa • FRENCH, ETC • DS • 50 kW
	ROMANIA	
	†RADIO ROMANIA INTL, Bucharest	(D) • EUROPE • 250 kW
	RUSSIA	
	†RADIO MOSCOW, Kenga	DS-2 • 50 kW
	USA	
	VOA, Greenville, NC	C AMERICA & S AMERICA • 250 kW
		Tu-Sa • C AMERICA & S AMERICA • 250 kW
		E EUROPE • 500 kW
	†VOA, Via Germany	(J) • E EUROPE • 500 kW
	UZBEKISTAN	
	UZBEK RADIO, Tashkent	DS-1/RUSSIAN, UZBEK • 50 kW
5995.2	PERU	
	RADIO MELODIA, Arequipa	DS • 5 kW
5999v	ECUADOR	
	†LA VOZ DEL UPANO, Macas	DS • 10 kW
6000	BRAZIL	
	†RADIO GUAIBA, Pôrto Alegre	PORTUGUESE • DS • 7.5 kW
	CHINA (PR)	
	VO THE STRAIT-PLA, Fuzhou	TAIWAN-2 • 50 kW
	GERMANY	
	DEUTSCHE WELLE, Jülich	MIDEAST • 100 kW
	†DEUTSCHE WELLE, Multiple Locations	(D) • W EUROPE • 100/500 kW
	DEUTSCHE WELLE, Wertachtal	(D) • E EUROPE & W ASIA • 500 kW
	INDIA	
	RADIO KASHMIR, Leh	DS • 10 kW
		ENGLISH & HINDI • DS • 10 kW
	MONGOLIA	
	RADIO ULAANBAATAR, Ulaanbaatar	(D) Su • JAPANESE • E ASIA • 50/100 kW
		(D) W/Sa • JAPANESE • E ASIA • 50/100 kW
		Tu/F • E ASIA • 50/100 kW
	RUSSIA	
	†RADIO MOSCOW, Yekaterinburg	(D) • DS-1 • 240 kW
	SAUDI ARABIA	
	†BS OF THE KINGDOM, Ad Dir'iyah	MIDEAST & E AFRICA • DS-GENERAL • 50 kW
	SINGAPORE	
	SINGAPORE BC CORP, Jurong	DS • 50 kW
	SWEDEN	
	†RADIO SWEDEN, Hörby	E EUROPE • 350 kW
		Sa/Su • E EUROPE • 350 kW
6005	CAMEROON	
	CAMEROON RTV CORP, Buea	FRENCH, ENGLISH, ETC • DS • 4 kW
	CANADA	
	†CIQX-CIQC, Montréal, Québec	E NORTH AM • DS • 0.5 kW
	GERMANY	
	R AMERICAN SECTOR, Berlin	EUROPE • RIAS-1 • 100 kW
	JAPAN	
	NHK, Nagoya	Irr • JAPANESE • DS-1 (FEEDER) • 0.3 kW • USB
	NHK, Sapporo	Irr • JAPANESE • DS-1 (FEEDER) • 0.6 kW
	RUSSIA	
	KHABAROVSK R, Khabarovsk	DS-2 • 20 kW
(con'd)	†R MOSCOW INTL, Armavir	(D) • MIDEAST • 100 kW

0 1 2 3 4 5 6 7 8 9 10 11 12 13 14 15 16 17 18 19 20 21 22 23 24

ENGLISH ▬   ARABIC ▩   CHINESE ▭▭▭   FRENCH ▬   GERMAN ▬   RUSSIAN ▬   SPANISH ▬   OTHER ▬

| FREQUENCY | COUNTRY, STATION, LOCATION | TARGET • NETWORK • POWER (kW) | World Time |

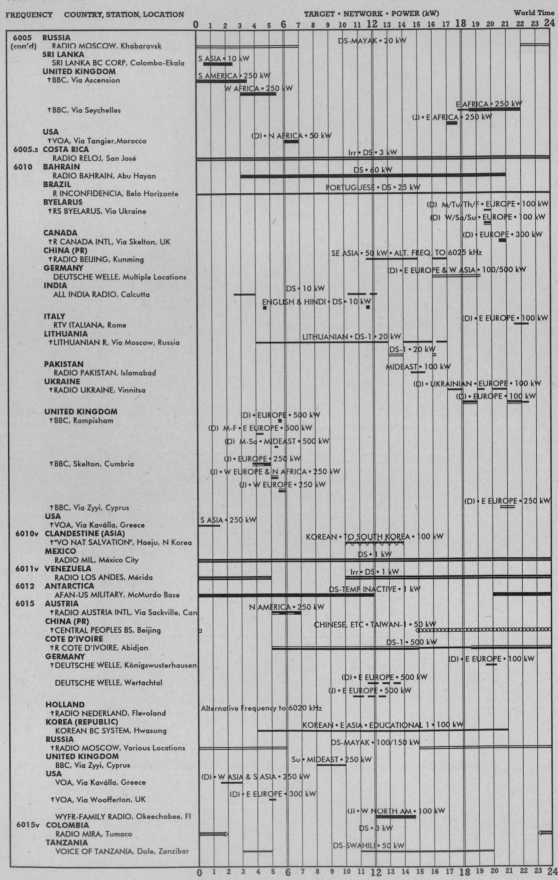

6005 (con'd) **RUSSIA** — RADIO MOSCOW, Khabarovsk — DS-MAYAK • 20 kW

SRI LANKA — SRI LANKA BC CORP, Colombo-Ekala — S ASIA • 10 kW

UNITED KINGDOM — †BBC, Via Ascension — S AMERICA • 250 kW / W AFRICA • 250 kW

†BBC, Via Seychelles — E AFRICA • 250 kW / (J) • E AFRICA • 250 kW

USA — †VOA, Via Tangier, Morocco — (D) • N AFRICA • 50 kW

6005.5 **COSTA RICA** — RADIO RELOJ, San José — Irr • DS • 3 kW

6010 **BAHRAIN** — RADIO BAHRAIN, Abu Hayan — DS • 60 kW

BRAZIL — R INCONFIDENCIA, Belo Horizonte — PORTUGUESE • DS • 25 kW

BYELARUS — †RS BYELARUS, Via Ukraine — (D) M/Tu/Th/F • EUROPE • 100 kW / (D) W/Sa/Su • EUROPE • 100 kW

CANADA — †R CANADA INTL, Via Skelton, UK — (D) • EUROPE • 300 kW

CHINA (PR) — †RADIO BEIJING, Kunming — SE ASIA • 50 kW • ALT. FREQ. TO 6025 kHz

GERMANY — DEUTSCHE WELLE, Multiple Locations — (D) • E EUROPE & W ASIA • 100/500 kW

INDIA — ALL INDIA RADIO, Calcutta — DS • 10 kW / ENGLISH & HINDI • DS • 10 kW

ITALY — RTV ITALIANA, Rome — (D) • E EUROPE • 100 kW

LITHUANIA — †LITHUANIAN R, Via Moscow, Russia — LITHUANIAN • DS-1 • 20 kW / DS-1 • 20 kW

PAKISTAN — RADIO PAKISTAN, Islamabad — MIDEAST • 100 kW

UKRAINE — †RADIO UKRAINE, Vinnitsa — (D) • UKRAINIAN • EUROPE • 100 kW / (D) • EUROPE • 100 kW

UNITED KINGDOM — †BBC, Rampisham — (D) • EUROPE • 500 kW / (D) M-F • E EUROPE • 500 kW / (D) M-Sa • MIDEAST • 500 kW

†BBC, Skelton, Cumbria — (J) • EUROPE • 250 kW / (J) • W EUROPE & N AFRICA • 250 kW / (J) • W EUROPE • 250 kW

†BBC, Via Zyyi, Cyprus — (D) • E EUROPE • 250 kW

USA — †VOA, Via Kaválla, Greece — S ASIA • 250 kW

6010v **CLANDESTINE (ASIA)** — †"VO NAT SALVATION", Haeju, N Korea — KOREAN • TO SOUTH KOREA • 100 kW

MEXICO — RADIO MIL, México City — DS • 1 kW

6011v **VENEZUELA** — RADIO LOS ANDES, Mérida — Irr • DS • 1 kW

6012 **ANTARCTICA** — AFAN-US MILITARY, McMurdo Base — DS-TEMP INACTIVE • 1 kW

6015 **AUSTRIA** — †RADIO AUSTRIA INTL, Via Sackville, Can — N AMERICA • 250 kW

CHINA (PR) — †CENTRAL PEOPLES BS, Beijing — CHINESE, ETC • TAIWAN-1 • 50 kW

COTE D'IVOIRE — †R COTE D'IVOIRE, Abidjan — DS-1 • 500 kW

GERMANY — †DEUTSCHE WELLE, Königswusterhausen — (D) • E EUROPE • 100 kW

DEUTSCHE WELLE, Wertachtal — (D) • E EUROPE • 500 kW / (J) • E EUROPE • 500 kW

HOLLAND — †RADIO NEDERLAND, Flevoland — Alternative Frequency to 6020 kHz

KOREA (REPUBLIC) — KOREAN BC SYSTEM, Hwasung — KOREAN • E ASIA • EDUCATIONAL 1 • 100 kW

RUSSIA — †RADIO MOSCOW, Various Locations — DS-MAYAK • 100/150 kW

UNITED KINGDOM — BBC, Via Zyyi, Cyprus — Su • MIDEAST • 250 kW

USA — VOA, Via Kaválla, Greece — (D) • W ASIA & S ASIA • 250 kW

†VOA, Via Woofferton, UK — (D) • E EUROPE • 300 kW

WYFR-FAMILY RADIO, Okeechobee, Fl — (J) • W NORTH AM • 100 kW

6015v **COLOMBIA** — RADIO MIRA, Tumaco — DS • 3 kW

TANZANIA — VOICE OF TANZANIA, Dole, Zanzibar — DS-SWAHILI • 50 kW

FREQUENCY	COUNTRY, STATION, LOCATION	TARGET • NETWORK • POWER (kW) — World Time

Scale: 0 1 2 3 4 5 6 7 8 9 10 11 12 13 14 15 16 17 18 19 20 21 22 23 24

Frequency	Country / Station / Location	Schedule details
6016v	**BOLIVIA** †RADIO EL MUNDO, Santa Cruz	Su • DS • 10 kW; DS • 10 kW; Irr • Tu-Sa • DS • 10 kW; Tu-Su • DS • 10 kW
6017v	**MEXICO** RADIO XEUW, Veracruz	Irr • DS • 0.25 kW
6020	**AUSTRALIA** †RADIO AUSTRALIA, Shepparton	PACIFIC • 100 kW; (J) • PACIFIC • 100 kW
	BRAZIL RADIO GAUCHA, Pôrto Alegre	PORTUGUESE • DS • 7.5 kW; Irr • PORTUGUESE • DS • 7.5 kW
	HOLLAND †RADIO NEDERLAND, Flevoland	C AMERICA • 500 kW; E NORTH AM • 500 kW; DUTCH • E NORTH AM • 500 kW; W EUROPE • 500 kW; DUTCH • W EUROPE • 500 kW; W EUROPE • 500 kW • ALT. FREQ. TO 6015 kHz
	†RADIO NEDERLAND, Via Madagascar	DUTCH • S AFRICA • 300 kW; S AFRICA • 300 kW
	†RADIO NEDERLAND, Via Neth Antilles	DUTCH • C AMERICA • 300 kW; C AMERICA • 300 kW
	INDIA ALL INDIA RADIO, Shimla	DS • 2.5 kW; ENGLISH & HINDI • DS • 2.5 kW
	RUSSIA VOICE OF RUSSIA, Khabarovsk	(D) • E ASIA & PACIFIC • 50 kW
	SAUDI ARABIA BS OF THE KINGDOM, Jiddah	MIDEAST & E AFRICA • DS-2 • 50 kW
	SPAIN †R EXTERIOR ESPANA, Noblejas	EUROPE • 350 kW; M-F • EUROPE • 350 kW
	SWAZILAND TRANS WORLD RADIO, Manzini	S AFRICA • 25 kW
	UKRAINE †UKRAINIAN R, Kiev	UKRAINIAN • DS-2 • 20 kW; (J) • UKRAINIAN • DS-2 • 20/100 kW
6025	**BOLIVIA** †RADIO ILLIMANI, La Paz	DS • 10 kW; Tu-Su • DS • 10 kW; M-Sa • DS • 10 kW
	CANADA †R CANADA INTL, Via Skelton, UK	(D) • MIDEAST • 250 kW
	CHINA (PR) †RADIO BEIJING, Kunming	Alternative Frequency to 6010 kHz
	DOMINICAN REPUBLIC RADIO AMANECER, Santo Domingo	DS • 1 kW
	GERMANY DEUTSCHE WELLE, Via Cyclops, Malta	N AFRICA • 250 kW
	HUNGARY RADIO BUDAPEST, Diósd	N AMERICA • 100 kW; M • N AMERICA • 100 kW
	†RADIO KOSSUTH, Székésfehérvár	EUROPE • DS • 100 kW
	JAPAN †RADIO JAPAN/NHK, Via Skelton, UK	(D) • JAPANESE • EUROPE & N AFRICA • GENERAL • 250 kW; EUROPE • 250 kW; (D) • EUROPE & N AFRICA • GENERAL • 250 kW; JAPANESE • EUROPE • GENERAL • 250 kW; (J) • JAPANESE • EUROPE • GENERAL • 250 kW; (J) • EUROPE • GENERAL • 250 kW
	MALAYSIA RADIO TV MALAYSIA, Kajang	DS-5 • 100 kW; Sa/Su • DS-5 • 100 kW
	NIGERIA FEDERAL RADIO CORP, Enugu	ENGLISH, ETC • DS • 10 kW
	PARAGUAY RADIO NACIONAL, Asunción	SPANISH, ETC • DS-TEMP INACTIVE • 0.6/2 kW
6025v	**MOZAMBIQUE** EP DE SOFALA, Beira	DS • 10 kW
6029.6	**CHILE** RADIO SANTA MARIA, Coihaique	DS • 10 kW; Tu-Su • DS • 10 kW; M-Sa • DS • 10 kW
6030	**ALBANIA** †RADIO TIRANA, Lushnjë	E EUROPE • 50 kW
	BRAZIL RADIO GLOBO, Rio de Janeiro	Irr • PORTUGUESE • DS • 10 kW
	CANADA CFVP-CFCN, Calgary, Alberta	W NORTH AM • DS • 0.1 kW
	CYPRUS †CYPRUS BC CORP, Zyyi	(D) • F-Su • EUROPE • 250 kW
	GERMANY SUDDEUTSCHER RFUNK, Mühlacker	EUROPE • DS-1 • 20 kW
	JAPAN †RADIO JAPAN/NHK, Via Skelton, UK	(D) • JAPANESE • EUROPE • GENERAL • 250 kW
	PHILIPPINES FEBC RADIO INTL, Bocaue	SE ASIA • 50 kW
(con'd)	**UKRAINE** †UKRAINIAN R, Multiple Locations	(D) • UKRAINIAN • DS-2 • 20 kW

Scale: 0 1 2 3 4 5 6 7 8 9 10 11 12 13 14 15 16 17 18 19 20 21 22 23 24

ENGLISH ▬▬   ARABIC ▨▨   CHINESE □□□   FRENCH ▬▬   GERMAN ▬▬   RUSSIAN ══   SPANISH ▬▬   OTHER ▬

FREQUENCY   COUNTRY, STATION, LOCATION   TARGET • NETWORK • POWER (kW)   World Time

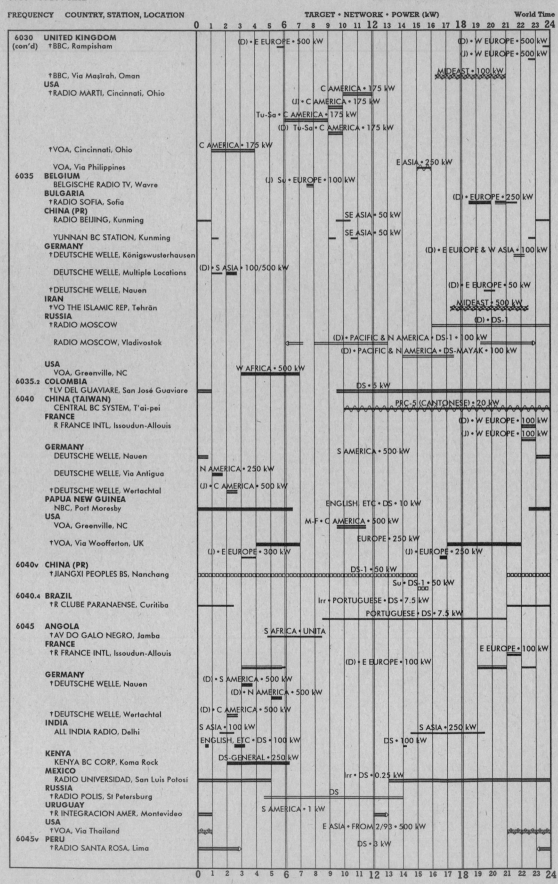

0 1 2 3 4 5 6 7 8 9 10 11 12 13 14 15 16 17 18 19 20 21 22 23 24

6030 UNITED KINGDOM
(con'd) †BBC, Rampisham
- (D) • E EUROPE • 500 kW
- (D) • W EUROPE • 500 kW
- (J) • W EUROPE • 500 kW

†BBC, Via Maşīrah, Oman
- MIDEAST • 100 kW

USA
†RADIO MARTI, Cincinnati, Ohio
- C AMERICA • 175 kW
- (J) • C AMERICA • 175 kW
- Tu-Sa • C AMERICA • 175 kW
- (D) • Tu-Sa • C AMERICA • 175 kW

†VOA, Cincinnati, Ohio
- C AMERICA • 175 kW

VOA, Via Philippines
- E ASIA • 250 kW

6035 BELGIUM
BELGISCHE RADIO TV, Wavre
- (J) • Su • EUROPE • 100 kW

BULGARIA
†RADIO SOFIA, Sofia
- (D) • EUROPE • 250 kW

CHINA (PR)
RADIO BEIJING, Kunming
- SE ASIA • 50 kW

YUNNAN BC STATION, Kunming
- SE ASIA • 50 kW

GERMANY
†DEUTSCHE WELLE, Königswusterhausen
- (D) • E EUROPE & W ASIA • 100 kW

DEUTSCHE WELLE, Multiple Locations
- (D) • S ASIA • 100/500 kW

†DEUTSCHE WELLE, Nauen
- (D) • E EUROPE • 50 kW

IRAN
†VO THE ISLAMIC REP, Tehrān
- MIDEAST • 500 kW

RUSSIA
†RADIO MOSCOW
- (D) • DS-1

RADIO MOSCOW, Vladivostok
- (D) • PACIFIC & N AMERICA • DS-1 • 100 kW
- (D) • PACIFIC & N AMERICA • DS-MAYAK • 100 kW

USA
VOA, Greenville, NC
- W AFRICA • 500 kW

6035.2 COLOMBIA
†LV DEL GUAVIARE, San José Guaviare
- DS • 5 kW

6040 CHINA (TAIWAN)
CENTRAL BC SYSTEM, T'ai-pei
- PRC-5 (CANTONESE) • 20 kW

FRANCE
R FRANCE INTL, Issoudun-Allouis
- (D) • W EUROPE • 100 kW
- (J) • W EUROPE • 100 kW

GERMANY
DEUTSCHE WELLE, Nauen
- S AMERICA • 500 kW

DEUTSCHE WELLE, Via Antigua
- N AMERICA • 250 kW
- (J) • C AMERICA • 500 kW

†DEUTSCHE WELLE, Wertachtal

PAPUA NEW GUINEA
NBC, Port Moresby
- ENGLISH, ETC • DS • 10 kW

USA
VOA, Greenville, NC
- M-F • C AMERICA • 500 kW

†VOA, Via Woofferton, UK
- EUROPE • 250 kW
- (J) • E EUROPE • 300 kW
- (J) • EUROPE • 250 kW

6040v CHINA (PR)
†JIANGXI PEOPLES BS, Nanchang
- DS-1 • 50 kW
- Su • DS-1 • 50 kW

6040.4 BRAZIL
†R CLUBE PARANAENSE, Curitiba
- Irr • PORTUGUESE • DS • 7.5 kW
- PORTUGUESE • DS • 7.5 kW

6045 ANGOLA
†AV DO GALO NEGRO, Jamba
- S AFRICA • UNITA

FRANCE
†R FRANCE INTL, Issoudun-Allouis
- E EUROPE • 100 kW
- (D) • E EUROPE • 100 kW

GERMANY
†DEUTSCHE WELLE, Nauen
- (D) • S AMERICA • 500 kW
- (D) • N AMERICA • 500 kW

†DEUTSCHE WELLE, Wertachtal
- (D) • C AMERICA • 500 kW

INDIA
ALL INDIA RADIO, Delhi
- S ASIA • 100 kW
- S ASIA • 250 kW
- ENGLISH, ETC • DS • 100 kW
- DS • 100 kW

KENYA
KENYA BC CORP, Koma Rock
- DS-GENERAL • 250 kW

MEXICO
RADIO UNIVERSIDAD, San Luis Potosí
- Irr • DS • 0.25 kW

RUSSIA
†RADIO POLIS, St Petersburg
- DS

URUGUAY
†R INTEGRACION AMER, Montevideo
- S AMERICA • 1 kW

USA
†VOA, Via Thailand
- E ASIA • FROM 2/93 • 500 kW

6045v PERU
†RADIO SANTA ROSA, Lima
- DS • 3 kW

0 1 2 3 4 5 6 7 8 9 10 11 12 13 14 15 16 17 18 19 20 21 22 23 24

SUMMER ONLY (J)   WINTER ONLY (D)   JAMMING / OR ∧   EARLIEST HEARD ◁   LATEST HEARD ▷   NEW OR CHANGED FOR 1993 †

FREQUENCY	COUNTRY, STATION, LOCATION	TARGET • NETWORK • POWER (kW) World Time

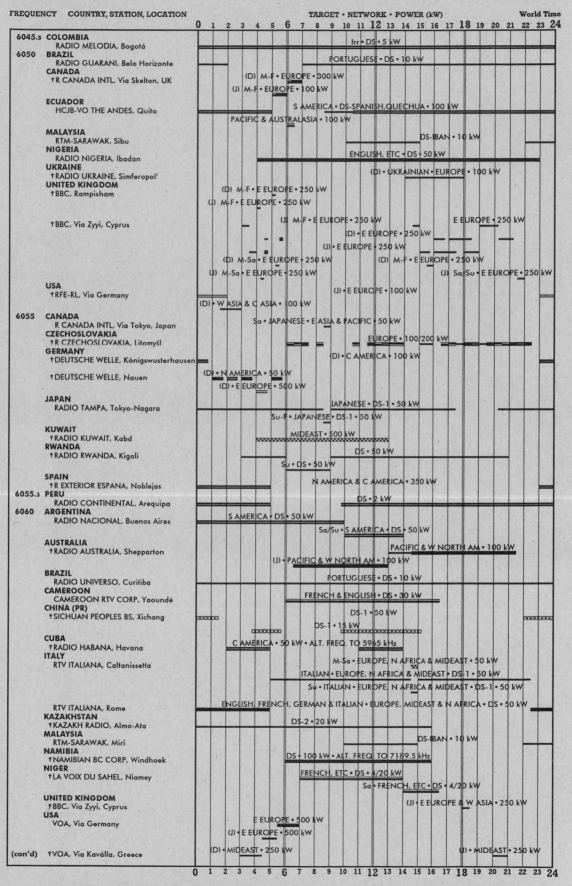

6045.5 COLOMBIA
        RADIO MELODIA, Bogotá — Irr • DS • 5 kW

6050 BRAZIL
        RADIO GUARANI, Belo Horizonte — PORTUGUESE • DS • 10 kW
      CANADA
        †R CANADA INTL, Via Skelton, UK — (D) M-F • EUROPE • 300 kW / (J) M-F • EUROPE • 100 kW
      ECUADOR
        HCJB-VO THE ANDES, Quito — S AMERICA • DS-SPANISH, QUECHUA • 100 kW / PACIFIC & AUSTRALASIA • 100 kW
      MALAYSIA
        RTM-SARAWAK, Sibu — DS-IBAN • 10 kW
      NIGERIA
        RADIO NIGERIA, Ibadan — ENGLISH, ETC • DS • 50 kW
      UKRAINE
        †RADIO UKRAINE, Simferopol' — (D) • UKRAINIAN • EUROPE • 100 kW
      UNITED KINGDOM
        †BBC, Rampisham — (D) M-F • E EUROPE • 250 kW / (J) M-F • E EUROPE • 250 kW
        †BBC, Via Zyyi, Cyprus — (J) M-F • E EUROPE • 250 kW / E EUROPE • 250 kW / (D) • E EUROPE • 250 kW / (J) • E EUROPE • 250 kW / (D) M-Sa • E EUROPE • 250 kW / (D) M-F • E EUROPE • 250 kW / (J) M-Sa • E EUROPE • 250 kW / (J) Sa/Su • E EUROPE • 250 kW
      USA
        †RFE-RL, Via Germany — (J) • E EUROPE • 100 kW / (D) • W ASIA & C ASIA • 100 kW

6055 CANADA
        R CANADA INTL, Via Tokyo, Japan — Sa • JAPANESE • E ASIA & PACIFIC • 50 kW
      CZECHOSLOVAKIA
        †R CZECHOSLOVAKIA, Litomyšl — EUROPE • 100/200 kW
      GERMANY
        †DEUTSCHE WELLE, Königswusterhausen — (D) • C AMERICA • 100 kW
        †DEUTSCHE WELLE, Nauen — (D) • N AMERICA • 50 kW / (D) • E EUROPE • 500 kW
      JAPAN
        RADIO TAMPA, Tokyo-Nagara — JAPANESE • DS-1 • 50 kW / Su-F • JAPANESE • DS-1 • 50 kW
      KUWAIT
        †RADIO KUWAIT, Kabd — MIDEAST • 500 kW
      RWANDA
        †RADIO RWANDA, Kigali — DS • 50 kW / Su • DS • 50 kW
      SPAIN
        †R EXTERIOR ESPANA, Noblejas — N AMERICA & C AMERICA • 350 kW

6055.3 PERU
        RADIO CONTINENTAL, Arequipa — DS • 2 kW

6060 ARGENTINA
        RADIO NACIONAL, Buenos Aires — S AMERICA • DS • 50 kW / Sa/Su • S AMERICA • DS • 50 kW
      AUSTRALIA
        †RADIO AUSTRALIA, Shepparton — PACIFIC & W NORTH AM • 100 kW / (J) • PACIFIC & W NORTH AM • 100 kW
      BRAZIL
        RADIO UNIVERSO, Curitiba — PORTUGUESE • DS • 10 kW
      CAMEROON
        CAMEROON RTV CORP, Yaoundé — FRENCH & ENGLISH • DS • 30 kW
      CHINA (PR)
        †SICHUAN PEOPLES BS, Xichang — DS-1 • 50 kW / DS-1 • 15 kW
      CUBA
        †RADIO HABANA, Havana — C AMERICA • 50 kW • ALT. FREQ. TO 5965 kHz
      ITALY
        RTV ITALIANA, Caltanissetta — M-Sa • EUROPE, N AFRICA & MIDEAST • 50 kW / ITALIAN • EUROPE, N AFRICA & MIDEAST • DS-1 • 50 kW / Su • ITALIAN • EUROPE, N AFRICA & MIDEAST • DS-1 • 50 kW
        RTV ITALIANA, Rome — ENGLISH, FRENCH, GERMAN & ITALIAN • EUROPE, MIDEAST & N AFRICA • DS • 50 kW
      KAZAKHSTAN
        †KAZAKH RADIO, Alma-Ata — DS-2 • 20 kW
      MALAYSIA
        RTM-SARAWAK, Miri — DS-IBAN • 10 kW
      NAMIBIA
        †NAMIBIAN BC CORP, Windhoek — DS • 100 kW • ALT. FREQ TO 7189.5 kHz
      NIGER
        †LA VOIX DU SAHEL, Niamey — FRENCH, ETC • DS • 4/20 kW / Sa • FRENCH, ETC • DS • 4/20 kW
      UNITED KINGDOM
        †BBC, Via Zyyi, Cyprus — (J) • E EUROPE & W ASIA • 250 kW
      USA
        VOA, Via Germany — E EUROPE • 500 kW / (J) • E EUROPE • 500 kW

(con'd) †VOA, Via Kaválla, Greece — (D) • MIDEAST • 250 kW / (J) • MIDEAST • 250 kW

ENGLISH ▬▬   ARABIC ⨯⨯⨯   CHINESE □□□   FRENCH ▬▬▬   GERMAN ▬▬   RUSSIAN ▬▬   SPANISH ▬▬   OTHER ▬▬

FREQUENCY   COUNTRY, STATION, LOCATION   TARGET • NETWORK • POWER (kW)   World Time

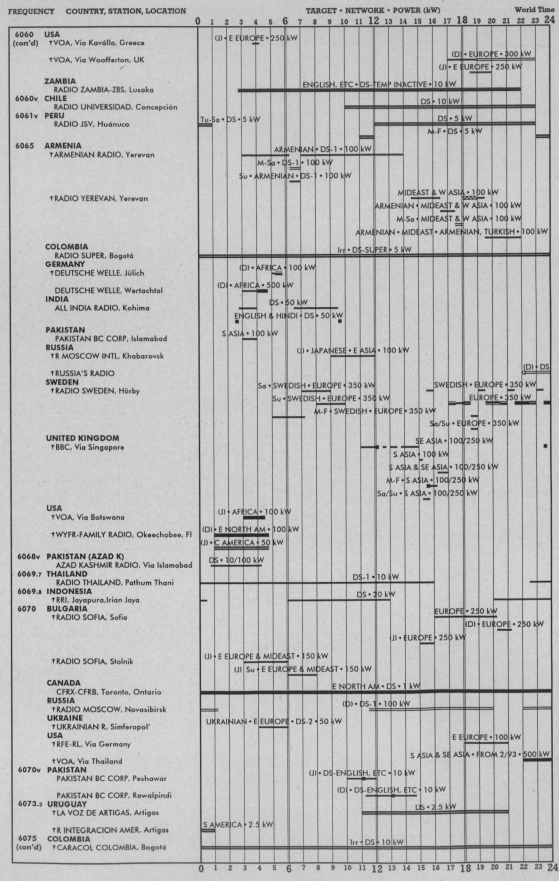

FREQUENCY	COUNTRY, STATION, LOCATION	TARGET • NETWORK • POWER (kW)
6060 (con'd)	USA †VOA, Via Kaválla, Greece	(J) • E EUROPE • 250 kW
	†VOA, Via Woofferton, UK	(D) • EUROPE • 300 kW / (J) • E EUROPE • 250 kW
	ZAMBIA RADIO ZAMBIA-ZBS, Lusaka	ENGLISH, ETC • DS-TEMP INACTIVE • 10 kW
6060v	CHILE RADIO UNIVERSIDAD, Concepción	DS • 10 kW
6061v	PERU RADIO JSV, Huánuco	Tu-Sa • DS • 5 kW / DS • 5 kW / M-F • DS • 5 kW
6065	ARMENIA †ARMENIAN RADIO, Yerevan	ARMENIAN • DS-1 • 100 kW / M-Sa • DS-1 • 100 kW / Su • ARMENIAN • DS-1 • 100 kW
	†RADIO YEREVAN, Yerevan	MIDEAST & W ASIA • 100 kW / ARMENIAN • MIDEAST & W ASIA • 100 kW / M-Sa • MIDEAST & W ASIA • 100 kW / ARMENIAN • MIDEAST • ARMENIAN, TURKISH • 100 kW
	COLOMBIA RADIO SUPER, Bogotá	Irr • DS-SUPER • 5 kW
	GERMANY †DEUTSCHE WELLE, Jülich	(D) • AFRICA • 100 kW
	DEUTSCHE WELLE, Wertachtal	(D) • AFRICA • 500 kW
	INDIA ALL INDIA RADIO, Kohima	DS • 50 kW / ENGLISH & HINDI • DS • 50 kW
	PAKISTAN PAKISTAN BC CORP, Islamabad	S ASIA • 100 kW
	RUSSIA †R MOSCOW INTL, Khabarovsk	(J) • JAPANESE • E ASIA • 100 kW
	†RUSSIA'S RADIO	(D) • DS
	SWEDEN †RADIO SWEDEN, Hörby	Sa • SWEDISH • EUROPE • 350 kW / Su • SWEDISH • EUROPE • 350 kW / M-F • SWEDISH • EUROPE • 350 kW / SWEDISH • EUROPE • 350 kW / EUROPE • 350 kW / Sa/Su • EUROPE • 350 kW
	UNITED KINGDOM †BBC, Via Singapore	SE ASIA • 100/250 kW / S ASIA • 100 kW / S ASIA & SE ASIA • 100/250 kW / M-F • S ASIA • 100/250 kW / Sa/Su • S ASIA • 100/250 kW
	USA †VOA, Via Botswana	(J) • AFRICA • 100 kW
	†WYFR-FAMILY RADIO, Okeechobee, Fl	(D) • E NORTH AM • 100 kW / (J) • C AMERICA • 50 kW
6068v	PAKISTAN (AZAD K) AZAD KASHMIR RADIO, Via Islamabad	DS • 10/100 kW
6069.7	THAILAND RADIO THAILAND, Pathum Thani	DS-1 • 10 kW
6069.8	INDONESIA †RRI, Jayapura, Irian Jaya	DS • 20 kW
6070	BULGARIA †RADIO SOFIA, Sofia	EUROPE • 250 kW / (D) • EUROPE • 250 kW / (J) • EUROPE • 250 kW
	†RADIO SOFIA, Stolnik	(J) • E EUROPE & MIDEAST • 150 kW / (J) Su • E EUROPE & MIDEAST • 150 kW
	CANADA CFRX-CFRB, Toronto, Ontario	E NORTH AM • DS • 1 kW
	RUSSIA †RADIO MOSCOW, Novosibirsk	(D) • DS-1 • 100 kW
	UKRAINE †UKRAINIAN R, Simferopol'	UKRAINIAN • E EUROPE • DS-2 • 50 kW
	USA †RFE-RL, Via Germany	E EUROPE • 100 kW
	†VOA, Via Thailand	S ASIA & SE ASIA • FROM 2/93 • 500 kW
6070v	PAKISTAN PAKISTAN BC CORP, Peshawar	(J) • DS-ENGLISH, ETC • 10 kW
	PAKISTAN BC CORP, Rawalpindi	(D) • DS-ENGLISH, ETC • 10 kW
6073.3	URUGUAY †LA VOZ DE ARTIGAS, Artigas	DS • 2.5 kW
	†R INTEGRACION AMER, Artigas	S AMERICA • 2.5 kW
6075 (con'd)	COLOMBIA †CARACOL COLOMBIA, Bogotá	Irr • DS • 10 kW

SUMMER ONLY (J)   WINTER ONLY (D)   JAMMING / OR /\   EARLIEST HEARD ◁   LATEST HEARD ▷   NEW OR CHANGED FOR 1993 †

FREQUENCY   COUNTRY, STATION, LOCATION   TARGET • NETWORK • POWER (kW)   World Time

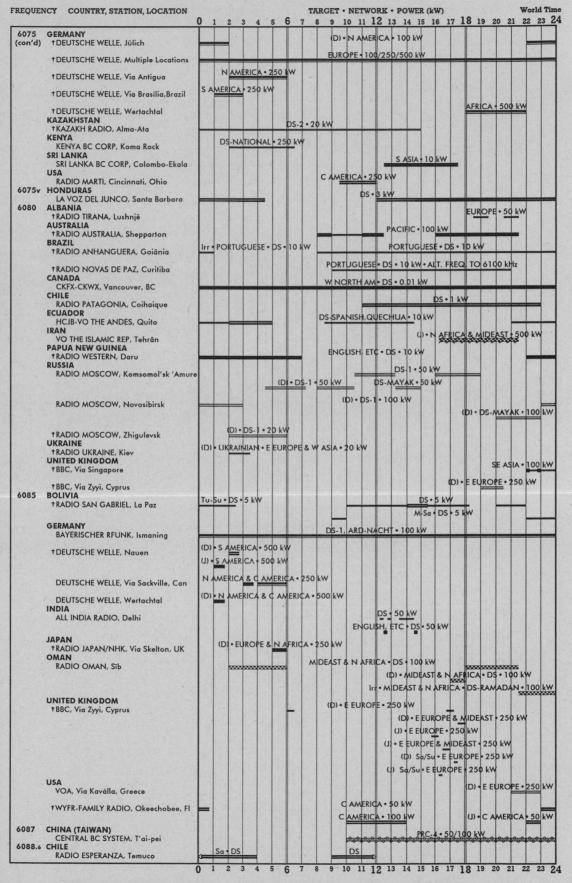

FREQUENCY	COUNTRY, STATION, LOCATION	TARGET • NETWORK • POWER (kW)
6075 (con'd)	**GERMANY** †DEUTSCHE WELLE, Jülich	(D) • N AMERICA • 100 kW
	†DEUTSCHE WELLE, Multiple Locations	EUROPE • 100/250/500 kW
	†DEUTSCHE WELLE, Via Antigua	N AMERICA • 250 kW
	†DEUTSCHE WELLE, Via Brasília, Brazil	S AMERICA • 250 kW
	†DEUTSCHE WELLE, Wertachtal	AFRICA • 500 kW
	KAZAKHSTAN †KAZAKH RADIO, Alma-Ata	DS-2 • 20 kW
	KENYA KENYA BC CORP, Koma Rock	DS-NATIONAL • 250 kW
	SRI LANKA SRI LANKA BC CORP, Colombo-Ekala	S ASIA • 10 kW
	USA RADIO MARTI, Cincinnati, Ohio	C AMERICA • 250 kW
6075v	**HONDURAS** LA VOZ DEL JUNCO, Santa Barbara	DS • 3 kW
6080	**ALBANIA** †RADIO TIRANA, Lushnjë	EUROPE • 50 kW
	AUSTRALIA †RADIO AUSTRALIA, Shepparton	PACIFIC • 100 kW
	BRAZIL †RADIO ANHANGUERA, Goiânia	Irr • PORTUGUESE • DS • 10 kW PORTUGUESE • DS • 10 kW
	†RADIO NOVAS DE PAZ, Curitiba	PORTUGUESE • DS • 10 kW • ALT. FREQ. TO 6100 kHz
	CANADA CKFX-CKWX, Vancouver, BC	W NORTH AM • DS • 0.01 kW
	CHILE RADIO PATAGONIA, Coihaique	DS • 1 kW
	ECUADOR HCJB-VO THE ANDES, Quito	DS-SPANISH, QUECHUA • 10 kW
	IRAN VO THE ISLAMIC REP, Tehrān	(J) • N AFRICA & MIDEAST • 500 kW
	PAPUA NEW GUINEA †RADIO WESTERN, Daru	ENGLISH, ETC • DS • 10 kW
	RUSSIA RADIO MOSCOW, Komsomol'sk 'Amure	DS-1 • 50 kW (D) • DS-1 • 50 kW DS-MAYAK • 50 kW
	RADIO MOSCOW, Novosibirsk	(D) • DS-1 • 100 kW (D) • DS-MAYAK • 100 kW
	†RADIO MOSCOW, Zhigulevsk	(D) • DS-1 • 20 kW
	UKRAINE †RADIO UKRAINE, Kiev	(D) • UKRAINIAN • E EUROPE & W ASIA • 20 kW
	UNITED KINGDOM †BBC, Via Singapore	SE ASIA • 100 kW
	†BBC, Via Zyyi, Cyprus	(D) • E EUROPE • 250 kW
6085	**BOLIVIA** †RADIO SAN GABRIEL, La Paz	Tu-Su • DS • 5 kW DS • 5 kW M-Sa • DS • 5 kW
	GERMANY BAYERISCHER RFUNK, Ismaning	DS-1, ARD-NACHT • 100 kW
	†DEUTSCHE WELLE, Nauen	(D) • S AMERICA • 500 kW (J) • S AMERICA • 500 kW
	DEUTSCHE WELLE, Via Sackville, Can	N AMERICA & C AMERICA • 250 kW
	DEUTSCHE WELLE, Wertachtal	(D) • N AMERICA & C AMERICA • 500 kW
	INDIA ALL INDIA RADIO, Delhi	DS • 50 kW ENGLISH, ETC • DS • 50 kW
	JAPAN †RADIO JAPAN/NHK, Via Skelton, UK	(D) • EUROPE & N AFRICA • 250 kW
	OMAN RADIO OMAN, Sib	MIDEAST & N AFRICA • DS • 100 kW (D) • MIDEAST & N AFRICA • DS • 100 kW Irr • MIDEAST & N AFRICA • DS-RAMADAN • 100 kW
	UNITED KINGDOM †BBC, Via Zyyi, Cyprus	(D) • E EUROPE • 250 kW (D) • E EUROPE & MIDEAST • 250 kW (J) • E EUROPE • 250 kW (J) • E EUROPE & MIDEAST • 250 kW (D) Sa/Su • E EUROPE • 250 kW (J) Sa/Su • E EUROPE • 250 kW
	USA VOA, Via Kaválla, Greece	(D) • E EUROPE • 250 kW
	†WYFR-FAMILY RADIO, Okeechobee, Fl	C AMERICA • 50 kW C AMERICA • 100 kW (J) • C AMERICA • 50 kW
6087	**CHINA (TAIWAN)** CENTRAL BC SYSTEM, T'ai-pei	PRC-4 • 50/100 kW
6088.6	**CHILE** RADIO ESPERANZA, Temuco	Sa • DS DS

ENGLISH ▬   ARABIC ⌇⌇⌇   CHINESE □□□   FRENCH ▬▬   GERMAN ▬▬   RUSSIAN ══   SPANISH ▬▬   OTHER ▬

FREQUENCY	COUNTRY, STATION, LOCATION	TARGET • NETWORK • POWER (kW)	World Time

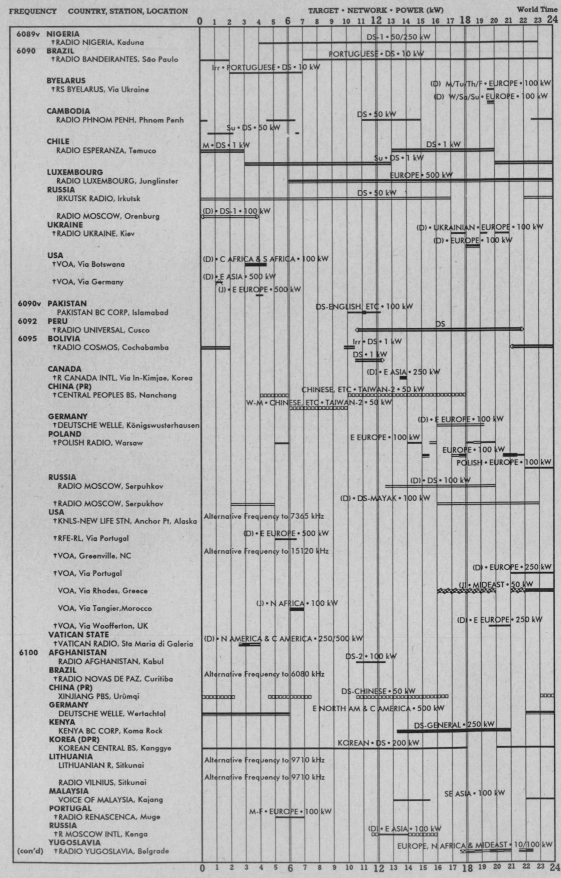

		TARGET • NETWORK • POWER (kW)
6089v	**NIGERIA** †RADIO NIGERIA, Kaduna	DS-1 • 50/250 kW
6090	**BRAZIL** †RADIO BANDEIRANTES, São Paulo	PORTUGUESE • DS • 10 kW
		Irr • PORTUGUESE • DS • 10 kW
	BYELARUS †RS BYELARUS, Via Ukraine	(D) M/Tu/Th/F • EUROPE • 100 kW
		(D) W/Sa/Su • EUROPE • 100 kW
	CAMBODIA RADIO PHNOM PENH, Phnom Penh	DS • 50 kW
		Su • DS • 50 kW
	CHILE RADIO ESPERANZA, Temuco	M • DS • 1 kW ... DS • 1 kW
		Su • DS • 1 kW
	LUXEMBOURG RADIO LUXEMBOURG, Junglinster	EUROPE • 500 kW
	RUSSIA IRKUTSK RADIO, Irkutsk	DS • 50 kW
	RADIO MOSCOW, Orenburg	(D) • DS-1 • 100 kW
	UKRAINE †RADIO UKRAINE, Kiev	(D) • UKRAINIAN • EUROPE • 100 kW
		(D) • EUROPE • 100 kW
	USA †VOA, Via Botswana	(D) • C AFRICA & S AFRICA • 100 kW
	†VOA, Via Germany	(D) • E ASIA • 500 kW
		(J) • E EUROPE • 500 kW
6090v	**PAKISTAN** PAKISTAN BC CORP, Islamabad	DS-ENGLISH, ETC • 100 kW
6092	**PERU** †RADIO UNIVERSAL, Cusco	DS
6095	**BOLIVIA** †RADIO COSMOS, Cochabamba	Irr • DS • 1 kW
		DS • 1 kW
	CANADA †R CANADA INTL, Via In-Kimjae, Korea	(D) • E ASIA • 250 kW
	CHINA (PR) †CENTRAL PEOPLES BS, Nanchang	CHINESE, ETC • TAIWAN-2 • 50 kW
		W-M • CHINESE, ETC • TAIWAN-2 • 50 kW
	GERMANY †DEUTSCHE WELLE, Königswusterhausen	(D) • E EUROPE • 100 kW
	POLAND †POLISH RADIO, Warsaw	E EUROPE • 100 kW
		EUROPE • 100 kW
		POLISH • EUROPE • 100 kW
	RUSSIA RADIO MOSCOW, Serpuhkov	(D) • DS • 100 kW
	†RADIO MOSCOW, Serpukhov	(D) • DS-MAYAK • 100 kW
	USA †KNLS-NEW LIFE STN, Anchor Pt, Alaska	Alternative Frequency to 7365 kHz
	†RFE-RL, Via Portugal	(D) • E EUROPE • 500 kW
	†VOA, Greenville, NC	Alternative Frequency to 15120 kHz
	†VOA, Via Portugal	(D) • EUROPE • 250 kW
	VOA, Via Rhodes, Greece	(J) • MIDEAST • 50 kW
	VOA, Via Tangier, Morocco	(J) • N AFRICA • 100 kW
	†VOA, Via Woofferton, UK	(D) • E EUROPE • 250 kW
	VATICAN STATE †VATICAN RADIO, Sta Maria di Galeria	(D) • N AMERICA & C AMERICA • 250/500 kW
6100	**AFGHANISTAN** RADIO AFGHANISTAN, Kabul	DS-2 • 100 kW
	BRAZIL †RADIO NOVAS DE PAZ, Curitiba	Alternative Frequency to 6080 kHz
	CHINA (PR) XINJIANG PBS, Urümqi	DS-CHINESE • 50 kW
	GERMANY DEUTSCHE WELLE, Wertachtal	E NORTH AM & C AMERICA • 500 kW
	KENYA KENYA BC CORP, Koma Rock	DS-GENERAL • 250 kW
	KOREA (DPR) KOREAN CENTRAL BS, Kanggye	KOREAN • DS • 200 kW
	LITHUANIA LITHUANIAN R, Sitkunai	Alternative Frequency to 9710 kHz
	RADIO VILNIUS, Sitkunai	Alternative Frequency to 9710 kHz
	MALAYSIA VOICE OF MALAYSIA, Kajang	SE ASIA • 100 kW
	PORTUGAL †RADIO RENASCENCA, Muge	M-F • EUROPE • 100 kW
	RUSSIA †R MOSCOW INTL, Kenga	(D) • E ASIA • 100 kW
	YUGOSLAVIA	
(con'd)	†RADIO YUGOSLAVIA, Belgrade	EUROPE, N AFRICA & MIDEAST • 10/100 kW

SUMMER ONLY (J)   WINTER ONLY (D)   JAMMING / OR ⋀   EARLIEST HEARD ◁   LATEST HEARD ▷   NEW OR CHANGED FOR 1993 †

FREQUENCY   COUNTRY, STATION, LOCATION   TARGET • NETWORK • POWER (kW)   World Time

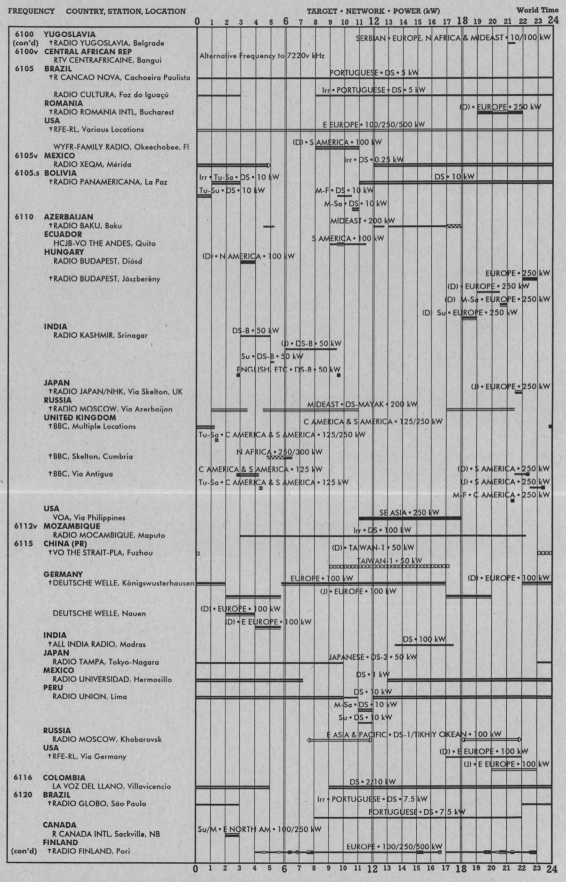

0 1 2 3 4 5 6 7 8 9 10 11 12 13 14 15 16 17 18 19 20 21 22 23 24

Freq	Country / Station / Location	Details
6100 (con'd)	YUGOSLAVIA — †RADIO YUGOSLAVIA, Belgrade	SERBIAN • EUROPE, N AFRICA & MIDEAST • 10/100 kW
6100v	CENTRAL AFRICAN REP — RTV CENTRAFRICAINE, Bangui	Alternative Frequency to 7220v kHz
6105	BRAZIL — †R CANCAO NOVA, Cachoeira Paulista	PORTUGUESE • DS • 5 kW
	RADIO CULTURA, Foz do Iguaçu	Irr • PORTUGUESE • DS • 5 kW
	ROMANIA — †RADIO ROMANIA INTL, Bucharest	(D) • EUROPE • 250 kW
	USA — †RFE-RL, Various Locations	E EUROPE • 100/250/500 kW
	WYFR-FAMILY RADIO, Okeechobee, Fl	(D) • S AMERICA • 100 kW
6105v	MEXICO — RADIO XEQM, Mérida	Irr • DS • 0.25 kW
6105.5	BOLIVIA — †RADIO PANAMERICANA, La Paz	Irr • Tu-Sa • DS • 10 kW / DS • 10 kW / Tu-Su • DS • 10 kW / M-F • DS • 10 kW / M-Sa • DS • 10 kW
6110	AZERBAIJAN — †RADIO BAKU, Baku	MIDEAST • 200 kW
	ECUADOR — HCJB-VO THE ANDES, Quito	S AMERICA • 100 kW
	HUNGARY — RADIO BUDAPEST, Diósd	(D) • N AMERICA • 100 kW
	†RADIO BUDAPEST, Jászberény	EUROPE • 250 kW / (D) • EUROPE • 250 kW / (D) M-Sa • EUROPE • 250 kW / (D) Su • EUROPE • 250 kW
	INDIA — RADIO KASHMIR, Srinagar	DS-B • 50 kW / (J) • DS-B • 50 kW / Su • DS-B • 50 kW / ENGLISH, ETC • DS-B • 50 kW
	JAPAN — †RADIO JAPAN/NHK, Via Skelton, UK	(J) • EUROPE • 250 kW
	RUSSIA — †RADIO MOSCOW, Via Azerbaijan	MIDEAST • DS-MAYAK • 200 kW
	UNITED KINGDOM — †BBC, Multiple Locations	C AMERICA & S AMERICA • 125/250 kW / Tu-Sa • C AMERICA & S AMERICA • 125/250 kW
	†BBC, Skelton, Cumbria	N AFRICA • 250/300 kW
	†BBC, Via Antigua	C AMERICA & S AMERICA • 125 kW / Tu-Sa • C AMERICA & S AMERICA • 125 kW / (D) • S AMERICA • 250 kW / (J) • S AMERICA • 250 kW / M-F • C AMERICA • 250 kW
	USA — VOA, Via Philippines	SE ASIA • 250 kW
6112v	MOZAMBIQUE — RADIO MOCAMBIQUE, Maputo	Irr • DS • 100 kW
6115	CHINA (PR) — †VO THE STRAIT-PLA, Fuzhou	(D) • TAIWAN-1 • 50 kW / TAIWAN-1 • 50 kW
	GERMANY — †DEUTSCHE WELLE, Königswusterhausen	EUROPE • 100 kW / (D) • EUROPE • 100 kW / (J) • EUROPE • 100 kW
	DEUTSCHE WELLE, Nauen	(D) • EUROPE • 100 kW / (D) • E EUROPE • 100 kW
	INDIA — †ALL INDIA RADIO, Madras	DS • 100 kW
	JAPAN — RADIO TAMPA, Tokyo-Nagara	JAPANESE • DS-2 • 50 kW
	MEXICO — RADIO UNIVERSIDAD, Hermosillo	DS • 1 kW
	PERU — RADIO UNION, Lima	DS • 10 kW / M-Sa • DS • 10 kW / Su • DS • 10 kW
	RUSSIA — RADIO MOSCOW, Khabarovsk	E ASIA & PACIFIC • DS-1/TIKHIY OKEAN • 100 kW
	USA — †RFE-RL, Via Germany	(D) • E EUROPE • 100 kW / (J) • E EUROPE • 100 kW
6116	COLOMBIA — LA VOZ DEL LLANO, Villavicencio	DS • 2/10 kW
6120	BRAZIL — †RADIO GLOBO, São Paulo	Irr • PORTUGUESE • DS • 7.5 kW / PORTUGUESE • DS • 7.5 kW
	CANADA — R CANADA INTL, Sackville, NB	Su/M • E NORTH AM • 100/250 kW
(con'd)	FINLAND — †RADIO FINLAND, Pori	EUROPE • 100/250/500 kW

0 1 2 3 4 5 6 7 8 9 10 11 12 13 14 15 16 17 18 19 20 21 22 23 24

ENGLISH ▬   ARABIC ⌇⌇⌇   CHINESE □□□   FRENCH ═   GERMAN ▬   RUSSIAN ══   SPANISH ══   OTHER ▬

FREQUENCY   COUNTRY, STATION, LOCATION   TARGET • NETWORK • POWER (kW)   World Time

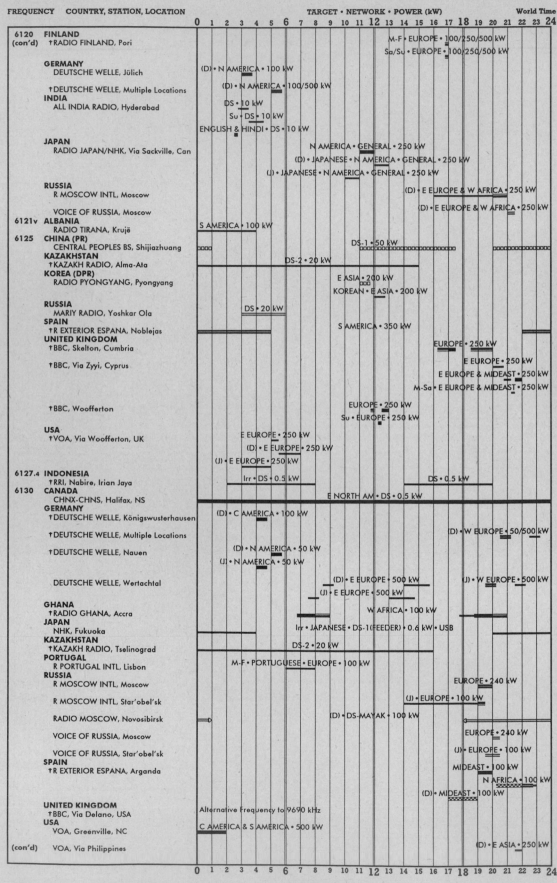

Schedule entries (World Time 0–24):

6120 (con'd) FINLAND
- †RADIO FINLAND, Pori — M-F • EUROPE • 100/250/500 kW; Sa/Su • EUROPE • 100/250/500 kW

GERMANY
- DEUTSCHE WELLE, Jülich — (D) • N AMERICA • 100 kW
- †DEUTSCHE WELLE, Multiple Locations — (D) • N AMERICA • 100/500 kW

INDIA
- ALL INDIA RADIO, Hyderabad — DS • 10 kW; Su • DS • 10 kW; ENGLISH & HINDI • DS • 10 kW

JAPAN
- RADIO JAPAN/NHK, Via Sackville, Can — N AMERICA • GENERAL • 250 kW; (D) • JAPANESE • N AMERICA • GENERAL • 250 kW; (J) • JAPANESE • N AMERICA • GENERAL • 250 kW

RUSSIA
- R MOSCOW INTL, Moscow — (D) • E EUROPE & W AFRICA • 250 kW
- VOICE OF RUSSIA, Moscow — (D) • E EUROPE & W AFRICA • 250 kW

6121v ALBANIA
- RADIO TIRANA, Krujë — S AMERICA • 100 kW

6125 CHINA (PR)
- CENTRAL PEOPLES BS, Shijiazhuang — DS-1 • 50 kW

KAZAKHSTAN
- †KAZAKH RADIO, Alma-Ata — DS-2 • 20 kW

KOREA (DPR)
- RADIO PYONGYANG, Pyongyang — E ASIA • 200 kW; KOREAN • E ASIA • 200 kW

RUSSIA
- MARIY RADIO, Yoshkar Ola — DS • 20 kW

SPAIN
- †R EXTERIOR ESPANA, Noblejas — S AMERICA • 350 kW

UNITED KINGDOM
- †BBC, Skelton, Cumbria — EUROPE • 250 kW
- †BBC, Via Zyyi, Cyprus — E EUROPE • 250 kW; E EUROPE & MIDEAST • 250 kW; M-Sa • E EUROPE & MIDEAST • 250 kW
- †BBC, Woofferton — EUROPE • 250 kW; Su • EUROPE • 250 kW

USA
- †VOA, Via Woofferton, UK — E EUROPE • 250 kW; (D) • E EUROPE • 250 kW; (J) • E EUROPE • 250 kW

6127.4 INDONESIA
- †RRI, Nabire, Irian Jaya — Irr • DS • 0.5 kW; DS • 0.5 kW

6130 CANADA
- CHNX-CHNS, Halifax, NS — E NORTH AM • DS • 0.5 kW

GERMANY
- †DEUTSCHE WELLE, Königswusterhausen — (D) • C AMERICA • 100 kW
- †DEUTSCHE WELLE, Multiple Locations — (D) • W EUROPE • 50/500 kW
- †DEUTSCHE WELLE, Nauen — (D) • N AMERICA • 50 kW; (J) • N AMERICA • 50 kW
- DEUTSCHE WELLE, Wertachtal — (D) • E EUROPE • 500 kW; (J) • E EUROPE • 500 kW; (J) • W EUROPE • 500 kW

GHANA
- †RADIO GHANA, Accra — W AFRICA • 100 kW

JAPAN
- NHK, Fukuoka — Irr • JAPANESE • DS-1 (FEEDER) • 0.6 kW • USB

KAZAKHSTAN
- †KAZAKH RADIO, Tselinograd — DS-2 • 20 kW

PORTUGAL
- R PORTUGAL INTL, Lisbon — M-F • PORTUGUESE • EUROPE • 100 kW

RUSSIA
- R MOSCOW INTL, Moscow — EUROPE • 240 kW
- R MOSCOW INTL, Star'obel'sk — (J) • EUROPE • 100 kW
- RADIO MOSCOW, Novosibirsk — (D) • DS-MAYAK • 100 kW
- VOICE OF RUSSIA, Moscow — EUROPE • 240 kW
- VOICE OF RUSSIA, Star'obel'sk — (J) • EUROPE • 100 kW

SPAIN
- †R EXTERIOR ESPANA, Arganda — MIDEAST • 100 kW; N AFRICA • 100 kW; (D) • MIDEAST • 100 kW

UNITED KINGDOM
- †BBC, Via Delano, USA — Alternative Frequency to 9690 kHz

USA
- VOA, Greenville, NC — C AMERICA & S AMERICA • 500 kW

(con'd)
- VOA, Via Philippines — (D) • E ASIA • 250 kW

SUMMER ONLY (J)   WINTER ONLY (D)   JAMMING / OR ∧   EARLIEST HEARD ◁   LATEST HEARD ▷   NEW OR CHANGED FOR 1993 †

FREQUENCY   COUNTRY, STATION, LOCATION   TARGET • NETWORK • POWER (kW)   World Time

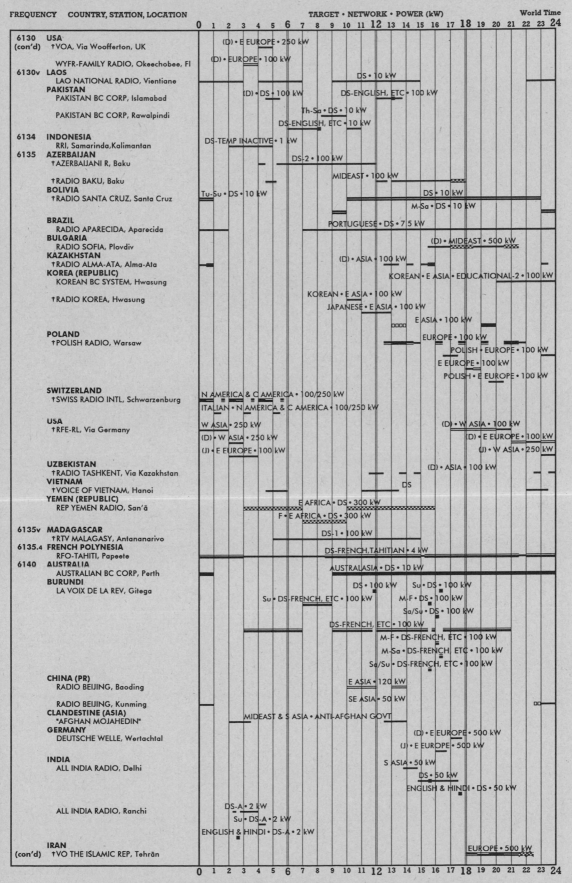

Frequency	Country, Station, Location	Target • Network • Power
6130 (con'd)	USA	
	†VOA, Via Woofferton, UK	(D) • E EUROPE • 250 kW
	WYFR-FAMILY RADIO, Okeechobee, Fl	(D) • EUROPE • 100 kW
6130v	LAOS	
	LAO NATIONAL RADIO, Vientiane	DS • 10 kW
	PAKISTAN	
	PAKISTAN BC CORP, Islamabad	(D) • DS • 100 kW DS-ENGLISH, ETC • 100 kW
	PAKISTAN BC CORP, Rawalpindi	Th-Sa • DS • 10 kW DS-ENGLISH, ETC • 10 kW
6134	INDONESIA	
	RRI, Samarinda, Kalimantan	DS-TEMP INACTIVE • 1 kW
6135	AZERBAIJAN	
	†AZERBAIJANI R, Baku	DS-2 • 100 kW
	†RADIO BAKU, Baku	MIDEAST • 100 kW
	BOLIVIA	
	†RADIO SANTA CRUZ, Santa Cruz	Tu-Su • DS • 10 kW DS • 10 kW M-Sa • DS • 10 kW
	BRAZIL	
	RADIO APARECIDA, Aparecida	PORTUGUESE • DS • 7.5 kW
	BULGARIA	
	RADIO SOFIA, Plovdiv	(D) • MIDEAST • 500 kW
	KAZAKHSTAN	
	†RADIO ALMA-ATA, Alma-Ata	(D) • ASIA • 100 kW
	KOREA (REPUBLIC)	
	KOREAN BC SYSTEM, Hwasung	KOREAN • E ASIA • EDUCATIONAL-2 • 100 kW
	†RADIO KOREA, Hwasung	KOREAN • E ASIA • 100 kW JAPANESE • E ASIA • 100 kW E ASIA • 100 kW
	POLAND	
	†POLISH RADIO, Warsaw	EUROPE • 100 kW POLISH • EUROPE • 100 kW E EUROPE • 100 kW POLISH • E EUROPE • 100 kW
	SWITZERLAND	
	†SWISS RADIO INTL, Schwarzenburg	N AMERICA & C AMERICA • 100/250 kW ITALIAN • N AMERICA & C AMERICA • 100/250 kW
	USA	
	†RFE-RL, Via Germany	W ASIA • 250 kW (D) • W ASIA • 100 kW (D) • W ASIA • 250 kW (D) • E EUROPE • 100 kW (J) • E EUROPE • 100 kW (J) • W ASIA • 250 kW
	UZBEKISTAN	
	†RADIO TASHKENT, Via Kazakhstan	(D) • ASIA • 100 kW
	VIETNAM	
	†VOICE OF VIETNAM, Hanoi	DS
	YEMEN (REPUBLIC)	
	REP YEMEN RADIO, San'ā	E AFRICA • DS • 300 kW F • E AFRICA • DS • 300 kW
6135v	MADAGASCAR	
	†RTV MALAGASY, Antananarivo	DS-1 • 100 kW
6135.4	FRENCH POLYNESIA	
	RFO-TAHITI, Papeete	DS-FRENCH, TAHITIAN • 4 kW
6140	AUSTRALIA	
	AUSTRALIAN BC CORP, Perth	AUSTRALASIA • DS • 10 kW
	BURUNDI	
	LA VOIX DE LA REV, Gitega	DS • 100 kW Su • DS • 100 kW Su • DS-FRENCH, ETC • 100 kW M-F • DS • 100 kW Sa/Su • DS • 100 kW DS-FRENCH, ETC • 100 kW M-F • DS-FRENCH, ETC • 100 kW M-Sa • DS-FRENCH, ETC • 100 kW Sa/Su • DS-FRENCH, ETC • 100 kW
	CHINA (PR)	
	RADIO BEIJING, Baoding	E ASIA • 120 kW
	RADIO BEIJING, Kunming	SE ASIA • 50 kW
	CLANDESTINE (ASIA)	
	"AFGHAN MOJAHEDIN"	MIDEAST & S ASIA • ANTI-AFGHAN GOVT
	GERMANY	
	DEUTSCHE WELLE, Wertachtal	(D) • E EUROPE • 500 kW (J) • E EUROPE • 500 kW
	INDIA	
	ALL INDIA RADIO, Delhi	S ASIA • 50 kW DS • 50 kW ENGLISH & HINDI • DS • 50 kW
	ALL INDIA RADIO, Ranchi	DS-A • 2 kW Su • DS-A • 2 kW ENGLISH & HINDI • DS-A • 2 kW
6140 (con'd)	IRAN	
	†VO THE ISLAMIC REP, Tehrān	EUROPE • 500 kW

ENGLISH ▬   ARABIC ▨   CHINESE ▭   FRENCH ═   GERMAN ▬   RUSSIAN ═   SPANISH ▬   OTHER ▬

| FREQUENCY | COUNTRY, STATION, LOCATION | TARGET • NETWORK • POWER (kW) | World Time |

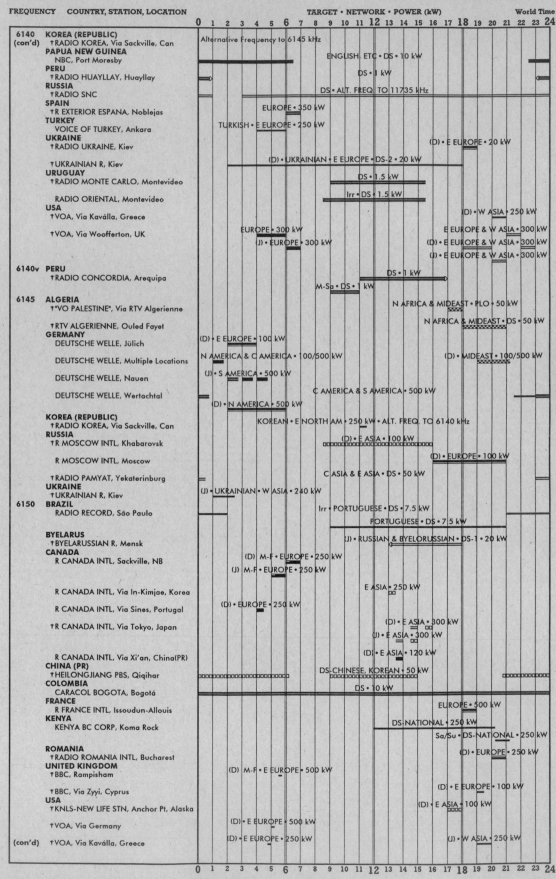

0 1 2 3 4 5 6 7 8 9 10 11 12 13 14 15 16 17 18 19 20 21 22 23 24

6140
(con'd) **KOREA (REPUBLIC)**
   ↑RADIO KOREA, Via Sackville, Can — Alternative Frequency to 6145 kHz
PAPUA NEW GUINEA
   NBC, Port Moresby — ENGLISH, ETC • DS • 10 kW
PERU
   ↑RADIO HUAYLLAY, Huayllay — DS • 1 kW
RUSSIA
   ↑RADIO SNC — DS • ALT. FREQ. TO 11735 kHz
SPAIN
   ↑R EXTERIOR ESPANA, Noblejas — EUROPE • 350 kW
TURKEY
   VOICE OF TURKEY, Ankara — TURKISH • E EUROPE • 250 kW
UKRAINE
   ↑RADIO UKRAINE, Kiev — (D) • E EUROPE • 20 kW

   ↑UKRAINIAN R, Kiev — (D) • UKRAINIAN • E EUROPE • DS-2 • 20 kW
URUGUAY
   ↑RADIO MONTE CARLO, Montevideo — DS • 1.5 kW

   RADIO ORIENTAL, Montevideo — Irr • DS • 1.5 kW
USA
   ↑VOA, Via Kaválla, Greece — (D) • W ASIA • 250 kW

   ↑VOA, Via Woofferton, UK — EUROPE • 300 kW / E EUROPE & W ASIA • 300 kW
   (J) • EUROPE • 300 kW / (D) • E EUROPE & W ASIA • 300 kW
   (J) • E EUROPE & W ASIA • 300 kW

6140v **PERU**
   ↑RADIO CONCORDIA, Arequipa — DS • 1 kW
   M-Sa • DS • 1 kW

6145 **ALGERIA**
   ↑"VO PALESTINE", Via RTV Algerienne — N AFRICA & MIDEAST • PLO • 50 kW

   ↑RTV ALGERIENNE, Ouled Fayet — N AFRICA & MIDEAST • DS • 50 kW
GERMANY
   DEUTSCHE WELLE, Jülich — (D) • E EUROPE • 100 kW

   DEUTSCHE WELLE, Multiple Locations — N AMERICA & C AMERICA • 100/500 kW / (D) • MIDEAST • 100/500 kW

   DEUTSCHE WELLE, Nauen — (J) • S AMERICA • 500 kW

   DEUTSCHE WELLE, Wertachtal — C AMERICA & S AMERICA • 500 kW

   (D) • N AMERICA • 500 kW
KOREA (REPUBLIC)
   ↑RADIO KOREA, Via Sackville, Can — KOREAN • E NORTH AM • 250 kW • ALT. FREQ. TO 6140 kHz
RUSSIA
   ↑R MOSCOW INTL, Khabarovsk — (D) • E ASIA • 100 kW

   R MOSCOW INTL, Moscow — (D) • EUROPE • 100 kW

   ↑RADIO PAMYAT, Yekaterinburg — C ASIA & E ASIA • DS • 50 kW
UKRAINE
   ↑UKRAINIAN R, Kiev — (J) • UKRAINIAN • W ASIA • 240 kW
6150 **BRAZIL**
   RADIO RECORD, São Paulo — Irr • PORTUGUESE • DS • 7.5 kW
   PORTUGUESE • DS • 7.5 kW

BYELARUS
   ↑BYELARUSSIAN R, Mensk — (J) • RUSSIAN & BYELORUSSIAN • DS-1 • 20 kW
CANADA
   R CANADA INTL, Sackville, NB — (D) M-F • EUROPE • 250 kW
   (J) M-F • EUROPE • 250 kW

   R CANADA INTL, Via In-Kimjae, Korea — E ASIA • 250 kW

   R CANADA INTL, Via Sines, Portugal — (D) • EUROPE • 250 kW

   ↑R CANADA INTL, Via Tokyo, Japan — (D) • E ASIA • 300 kW
   (J) • E ASIA • 300 kW

   R CANADA INTL, Via Xi'an, China(PR) — (D) • E ASIA • 120 kW
CHINA (PR)
   ↑HEILONGJIANG PBS, Qiqihar — DS-CHINESE, KOREAN • 50 kW
COLOMBIA
   CARACOL BOGOTA, Bogotá — DS • 10 kW
FRANCE
   R FRANCE INTL, Issoudun-Allouis — EUROPE • 500 kW
KENYA
   KENYA BC CORP, Koma Rock — DS-NATIONAL • 250 kW
   Sa/Su • DS-NATIONAL • 250 kW

ROMANIA
   ↑RADIO ROMANIA INTL, Bucharest — (D) • EUROPE • 250 kW
UNITED KINGDOM
   ↑BBC, Rampisham — (D) M-F • E EUROPE • 500 kW

   ↑BBC, Via Zyyi, Cyprus — (D) • E EUROPE • 100 kW
USA
   ↑KNLS-NEW LIFE STN, Anchor Pt, Alaska — (D) • E ASIA • 100 kW

   ↑VOA, Via Germany — (D) • E EUROPE • 500 kW

(con'd) ↑VOA, Via Kaválla, Greece — (D) • E EUROPE • 250 kW / (J) • W ASIA • 250 kW

0 1 2 3 4 5 6 7 8 9 10 11 12 13 14 15 16 17 18 19 20 21 22 23 24

SUMMER ONLY (J)   WINTER ONLY (D)   JAMMING / OR ∧   EARLIEST HEARD ◁   LATEST HEARD ▷   NEW OR CHANGED FOR 1993 ↑

FREQUENCY   COUNTRY, STATION, LOCATION

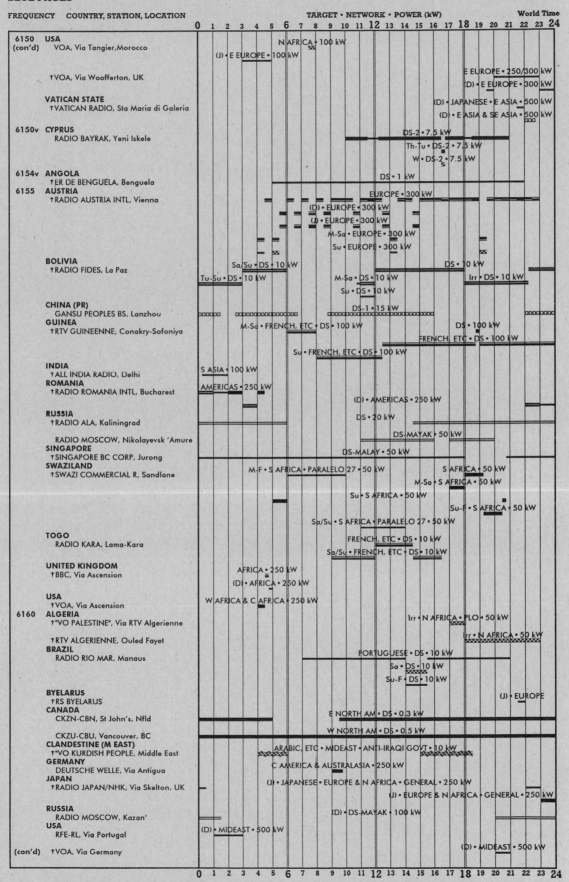

0 1 2 3 4 5 6 7 8 9 10 11 12 13 14 15 16 17 18 19 20 21 22 23 24

6150 **USA**
(con'd)   VOA, Via Tangier, Morocco — N AFRICA • 100 kW / (J) • E EUROPE • 100 kW

†VOA, Via Woofferton, UK — E EUROPE • 250/300 kW / (D) • E EUROPE • 300 kW

VATICAN STATE
†VATICAN RADIO, Sta Maria di Galeria — (D) • JAPANESE • E ASIA • 500 kW / (D) • E ASIA & SE ASIA • 500 kW

6150v **CYPRUS**
RADIO BAYRAK, Yeni Iskele — DS-2 • 7.5 kW / Th-Tu • DS-2 • 7.5 kW / W • DS-2 • 7.5 kW

6154v **ANGOLA**
†ER DE BENGUELA, Benguela — DS • 1 kW
6155 **AUSTRIA**
†RADIO AUSTRIA INTL, Vienna — EUROPE • 300 kW / (D) • EUROPE • 300 kW / (J) • EUROPE • 300 kW / M-Sa • EUROPE • 300 kW / Su • EUROPE • 300 kW

BOLIVIA
†RADIO FIDES, La Paz — Sa/Su • DS • 10 kW / DS • 10 kW / Tu-Su • DS • 10 kW / M-Sa • DS • 10 kW / Irr • DS • 10 kW / Su • DS • 10 kW

CHINA (PR)
GANSU PEOPLES BS, Lanzhou — DS-1 • 15 kW
GUINEA
†RTV GUINEENNE, Conakry-Sofoniya — M-Sa • FRENCH, ETC • DS • 100 kW / FRENCH, ETC • DS • 100 kW / Su • FRENCH, ETC • DS • 100 kW

INDIA
†ALL INDIA RADIO, Delhi — S ASIA • 100 kW
ROMANIA
†RADIO ROMANIA INTL, Bucharest — AMERICAS • 250 kW / (D) • AMERICAS • 250 kW

RUSSIA
†RADIO ALA, Kaliningrad — DS • 20 kW

RADIO MOSCOW, Nikolayevsk 'Amure — DS-MAYAK • 50 kW
SINGAPORE
†SINGAPORE BC CORP, Jurong — DS-MALAY • 50 kW
SWAZILAND
†SWAZI COMMERCIAL R, Sandlane — M-F • S AFRICA • PARALELO 27 • 50 kW / S AFRICA • 50 kW / M-Sa • S AFRICA • 50 kW / Su • S AFRICA • 50 kW / Su-F • S AFRICA • 50 kW / Sa/Su • S AFRICA • PARALELO 27 • 50 kW

TOGO
RADIO KARA, Lama-Kara — FRENCH, ETC • DS • 10 kW / Sa/Su • FRENCH, ETC • DS • 10 kW

UNITED KINGDOM
†BBC, Via Ascension — AFRICA • 250 kW / (D) • AFRICA • 250 kW

USA
†VOA, Via Ascension — W AFRICA & C AFRICA • 250 kW
6160 **ALGERIA**
†"VO PALESTINE", Via RTV Algerienne — Irr • N AFRICA • PLO • 50 kW / Irr • N AFRICA • 50 kW

†RTV ALGERIENNE, Ouled Fayet
BRAZIL
RADIO RIO MAR, Manaus — PORTUGUESE • DS • 10 kW / Sa • DS • 10 kW / Su-F • DS • 10 kW

BYELARUS
†RS BYELARUS — (J) • EUROPE
CANADA
CKZN-CBN, St John's, Nfld — E NORTH AM • DS • 0.3 kW

CKZU-CBU, Vancouver, BC — W NORTH AM • DS • 0.5 kW
CLANDESTINE (M EAST)
†"VO KURDISH PEOPLE", Middle East — ARABIC, ETC • MIDEAST • ANTI-IRAQI GOVT • 10 kW
GERMANY
DEUTSCHE WELLE, Via Antigua — C AMERICA & AUSTRALASIA • 250 kW
JAPAN
†RADIO JAPAN/NHK, Via Skelton, UK — (J) • JAPANESE • EUROPE & N AFRICA • GENERAL • 250 kW / (J) • EUROPE & N AFRICA • GENERAL • 250 kW

RUSSIA
RADIO MOSCOW, Kazan' — (D) • DS-MAYAK • 100 kW
USA
RFE-RL, Via Portugal — (D) • MIDEAST • 500 kW

(con'd)   †VOA, Via Germany — (D) • MIDEAST • 500 kW

0 1 2 3 4 5 6 7 8 9 10 11 12 13 14 15 16 17 18 19 20 21 22 23 24

FREQUENCY   COUNTRY, STATION, LOCATION   TARGET • NETWORK • POWER (kW)   World Time

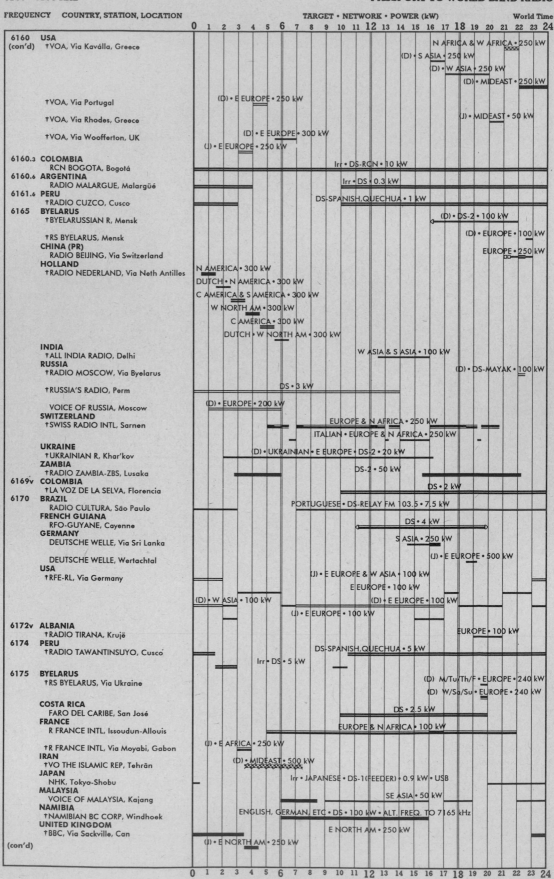

FREQUENCY	COUNTRY, STATION, LOCATION	TARGET • NETWORK • POWER (kW)
6160 (con'd)	USA †VOA, Via Kaválla, Greece	N AFRICA & W AFRICA • 250 kW / (D) • S ASIA • 250 kW / (D) • W ASIA • 250 kW / (D) • MIDEAST • 250 kW
	†VOA, Via Portugal	(D) • E EUROPE • 250 kW
	†VOA, Via Rhodes, Greece	(J) • MIDEAST • 50 kW
	†VOA, Via Woofferton, UK	(D) • E EUROPE • 300 kW
		(J) • E EUROPE • 250 kW
6160.3	COLOMBIA RCN BOGOTA, Bogotá	Irr • DS-RCN • 10 kW
6160.6	ARGENTINA RADIO MALARGUE, Malargüé	Irr • DS • 0.3 kW
6161.6	PERU †RADIO CUZCO, Cusco	DS-SPANISH, QUECHUA • 1 kW
6165	BYELARUS †BYELARUSSIAN R, Mensk	(D) • DS-2 • 100 kW
	†RS BYELARUS, Mensk	(D) • EUROPE • 100 kW
	CHINA (PR) RADIO BEIJING, Via Switzerland	EUROPE • 250 kW
	HOLLAND †RADIO NEDERLAND, Via Neth Antilles	N AMERICA • 300 kW
		DUTCH • N AMERICA • 300 kW
		C AMERICA & S AMERICA • 300 kW
		W NORTH AM • 300 kW
		C AMERICA • 300 kW
		DUTCH • W NORTH AM • 300 kW
	INDIA †ALL INDIA RADIO, Delhi	W ASIA & S ASIA • 100 kW
	RUSSIA †RADIO MOSCOW, Via Byelarus	(D) • DS-MAYAK • 100 kW
	†RUSSIA'S RADIO, Perm	DS • 3 kW
	VOICE OF RUSSIA, Moscow	(D) • EUROPE • 200 kW
	SWITZERLAND †SWISS RADIO INTL, Sarnen	EUROPE & N AFRICA • 250 kW
		ITALIAN • EUROPE & N AFRICA • 250 kW
	UKRAINE †UKRAINIAN R, Khar'kov	(D) • UKRAINIAN • E EUROPE • DS-2 • 20 kW
	ZAMBIA †RADIO ZAMBIA-ZBS, Lusaka	DS-2 • 50 kW
6169v	COLOMBIA †LA VOZ DE LA SELVA, Florencia	DS • 2 kW
6170	BRAZIL RADIO CULTURA, São Paulo	PORTUGUESE • DS-RELAY FM 103.5 • 7.5 kW
	FRENCH GUIANA RFO-GUYANE, Cayenne	DS • 4 kW
	GERMANY DEUTSCHE WELLE, Via Sri Lanka	S ASIA • 250 kW
	DEUTSCHE WELLE, Wertachtal	(J) • E EUROPE • 500 kW
	USA †RFE-RL, Via Germany	(J) • E EUROPE & W ASIA • 100 kW
		E EUROPE • 100 kW
		(D) • W ASIA • 100 kW / (D) • E EUROPE • 100 kW
		(J) • E EUROPE • 100 kW
6172v	ALBANIA †RADIO TIRANA, Krujë	EUROPE • 100 kW
6174	PERU †RADIO TAWANTINSUYO, Cusco	DS-SPANISH, QUECHUA • 5 kW
		Irr • DS • 5 kW
6175	BYELARUS †RS BYELARUS, Via Ukraine	(D) • M/Tu/Th/F • EUROPE • 240 kW
		(D) • W/Sa/Su • EUROPE • 240 kW
	COSTA RICA FARO DEL CARIBE, San José	DS • 2.5 kW
	FRANCE R FRANCE INTL, Issoudun-Allouis	EUROPE & N AFRICA • 100 kW
	†R FRANCE INTL, Via Moyabi, Gabon	(J) • E AFRICA • 250 kW
	IRAN †VO THE ISLAMIC REP, Tehrān	(D) • MIDEAST • 500 kW
	JAPAN NHK, Tokyo-Shobu	Irr • JAPANESE • DS-1 (FEEDER) • 0.9 kW • USB
	MALAYSIA VOICE OF MALAYSIA, Kajang	SE ASIA • 50 kW
	NAMIBIA †NAMIBIAN BC CORP, Windhoek	ENGLISH, GERMAN, ETC • DS • 100 kW • ALT. FREQ. TO 7165 kHz
	UNITED KINGDOM †BBC, Via Sackville, Can	E NORTH AM • 250 kW
(con'd)		(J) • E NORTH AM • 250 kW

SUMMER ONLY (J)   WINTER ONLY (D)   JAMMING / OR ∧   EARLIEST HEARD ◁   LATEST HEARD ▷   NEW OR CHANGED FOR 1993 †

FREQUENCY   COUNTRY, STATION, LOCATION   TARGET • NETWORK • POWER (kW)   World Time

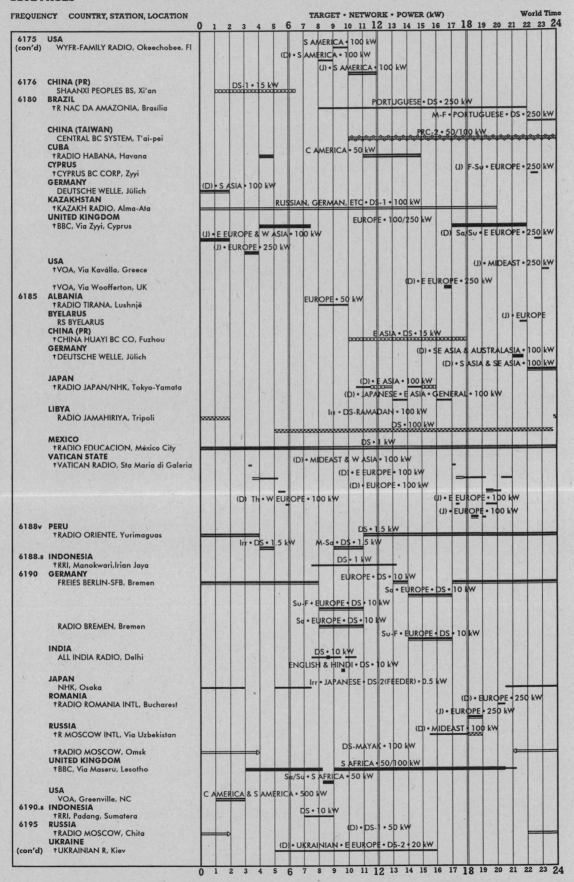

FREQUENCY	COUNTRY, STATION, LOCATION	TARGET • NETWORK • POWER (kW)
6175 (con'd)	**USA** WYFR-FAMILY RADIO, Okeechobee, Fl	S AMERICA • 100 kW; (D) • S AMERICA • 100 kW; (J) • S AMERICA • 100 kW
6176	**CHINA (PR)** SHAANXI PEOPLES BS, Xi'an	DS-1 • 15 kW
6180	**BRAZIL** ↑R NAC DA AMAZONIA, Brasilia	PORTUGUESE • DS 250 kW; M-F • PORTUGUESE • DS 250 kW
	CHINA (TAIWAN) CENTRAL BC SYSTEM, T'ai-pei	PRC-2 • 50/100 kW
	CUBA ↑RADIO HABANA, Havana	C AMERICA • 50 kW
	CYPRUS ↑CYPRUS BC CORP, Zyyi	(J) F-Su • EUROPE • 250 kW
	GERMANY DEUTSCHE WELLE, Jülich	(D) • S ASIA • 100 kW
	KAZAKHSTAN ↑KAZAKH RADIO, Alma-Ata	RUSSIAN, GERMAN, ETC • DS-1 • 100 kW
	UNITED KINGDOM ↑BBC, Via Zyyi, Cyprus	EUROPE • 100/250 kW; (J) • E EUROPE & W ASIA • 100 kW; (D) Sa/Su • E EUROPE • 250 kW; (J) • EUROPE • 250 kW
	USA ↑VOA, Via Kaválla, Greece	(J) • MIDEAST • 250 kW
	↑VOA, Via Woofferton, UK	(D) • E EUROPE • 250 kW
6185	**ALBANIA** ↑RADIO TIRANA, Lushnjë	EUROPE • 50 kW
	BYELARUS RS BYELARUS	(J) • EUROPE
	CHINA (PR) ↑CHINA HUAYI BC CO, Fuzhou	E ASIA • DS • 15 kW
	GERMANY ↑DEUTSCHE WELLE, Jülich	(D) • SE ASIA & AUSTRALASIA • 100 kW; (D) • S ASIA & SE ASIA • 100 kW
	JAPAN ↑RADIO JAPAN/NHK, Tokyo-Yamata	(D) • E ASIA • 100 kW; (D) • JAPANESE • E ASIA • GENERAL • 100 kW
	LIBYA RADIO JAMAHIRIYA, Tripoli	Irr • DS-RAMADAN • 100 kW; DS • 100 kW
	MEXICO ↑RADIO EDUCACION, México City	DS • 1 kW
	VATICAN STATE ↑VATICAN RADIO, Sta Maria di Galeria	(D) • MIDEAST & W ASIA • 100 kW; (D) • E EUROPE • 100 kW; (D) • EUROPE • 100 kW; (D) Th • W EUROPE • 100 kW; (J) • E EUROPE • 100 kW; (J) • EUROPE • 100 kW
6188v	**PERU** ↑RADIO ORIENTE, Yurimaguas	DS • 1.5 kW; Irr • DS • 1.5 kW; M-Sa • DS • 1.5 kW
6188.8	**INDONESIA** ↑RRI, Manokwari, Irian Jaya	DS • 1 kW
6190	**GERMANY** FREIES BERLIN-SFB, Bremen	EUROPE • DS • 10 kW; Sa • EUROPE • DS • 10 kW; Su-F • EUROPE • DS • 10 kW
	RADIO BREMEN, Bremen	Sa • EUROPE • DS • 10 kW; Su-F • EUROPE • DS • 10 kW
	INDIA ALL INDIA RADIO, Delhi	DS • 10 kW; ENGLISH & HINDI • DS • 10 kW
	JAPAN NHK, Osaka	Irr • JAPANESE • DS-2(FEEDER) • 0.5 kW
	ROMANIA ↑RADIO ROMANIA INTL, Bucharest	(D) • EUROPE • 250 kW; (J) • EUROPE • 250 kW
	RUSSIA ↑R MOSCOW INTL, Via Uzbekistan	(D) • MIDEAST • 100 kW
	↑RADIO MOSCOW, Omsk	DS-MAYAK • 100 kW
	UNITED KINGDOM ↑BBC, Via Maseru, Lesotho	S AFRICA • 50/100 kW; Sa/Su • S AFRICA • 50 kW
	USA VOA, Greenville, NC	C AMERICA & S AMERICA • 500 kW
6190.8	**INDONESIA** ↑RRI, Padang, Sumatera	DS • 10 kW
6195	**RUSSIA** ↑RADIO MOSCOW, Chita	(D) • DS-1 • 50 kW
	UKRAINE ↑UKRAINIAN R, Kiev	(D) • UKRAINIAN • E EUROPE • DS-2 • 20 kW
(con'd)		

ENGLISH ▬   ARABIC ≋   CHINESE ☐☐☐   FRENCH ═   GERMAN ▬   RUSSIAN ══   SPANISH ▬   OTHER ─

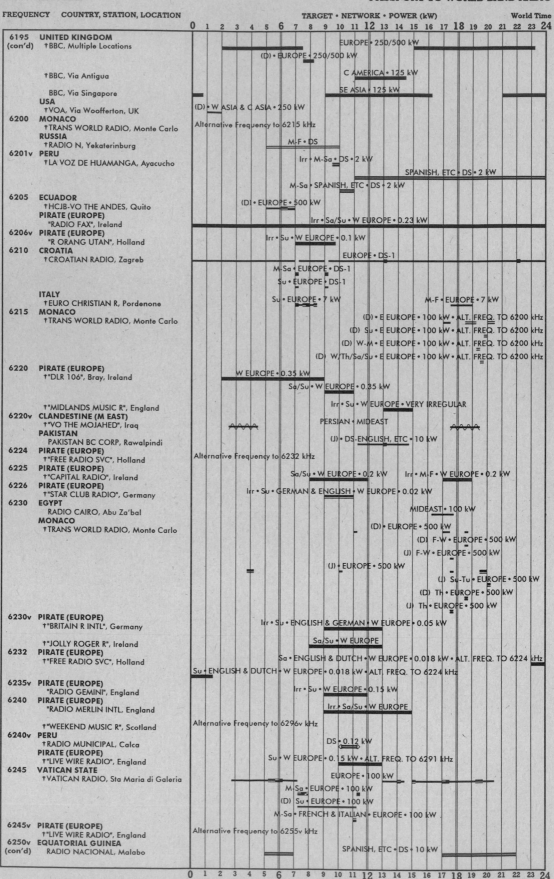

FREQUENCY	COUNTRY, STATION, LOCATION	TARGET • NETWORK • POWER (kW)	World Time

6195 (con'd) **UNITED KINGDOM**
†BBC, Multiple Locations — EUROPE • 250/500 kW
(D) • EUROPE • 250/500 kW

†BBC, Via Antigua — C AMERICA • 125 kW

BBC, Via Singapore — SE ASIA • 125 kW

USA
†VOA, Via Woofferton, UK — (D) • W ASIA & C ASIA • 250 kW

6200 MONACO
†TRANS WORLD RADIO, Monte Carlo — Alternative Frequency to 6215 kHz

RUSSIA
†RADIO N, Yekaterinburg — M-F • DS

6201v PERU
†LA VOZ DE HUAMANGA, Ayacucho — Irr • M-Sa • DS • 2 kW
SPANISH, ETC • DS • 2 kW
M-Sa • SPANISH, ETC • DS • 2 kW

6205 ECUADOR
†HCJB-VO THE ANDES, Quito — (D) • EUROPE • 500 kW

PIRATE (EUROPE)
"RADIO FAX", Ireland — Irr • Sa/Su • W EUROPE • 0.23 kW

6206v PIRATE (EUROPE)
"R ORANG UTAN", Holland — Irr • Su • W EUROPE • 0.1 kW

6210 CROATIA
†CROATIAN RADIO, Zagreb — EUROPE • DS-1
M-Sa • EUROPE • DS-1
Su • EUROPE • DS-1

ITALY
†EURO CHRISTIAN R, Pordenone — Su • EUROPE • 7 kW   M-F • EUROPE • 7 kW

6215 MONACO
†TRANS WORLD RADIO, Monte Carlo — (D) • E EUROPE • 100 kW • ALT. FREQ. TO 6200 kHz
(D) Su • E EUROPE • 100 kW • ALT. FREQ. TO 6200 kHz
(D) W-M • E EUROPE • 100 kW • ALT. FREQ. TO 6200 kHz
(D) W/Th/Sa/Su • E EUROPE • 100 kW • ALT. FREQ. TO 6200 kHz

6220 PIRATE (EUROPE)
†"DLR 106", Bray, Ireland — W EUROPE • 0.35 kW
Sa/Su • W EUROPE • 0.35 kW

†"MIDLANDS MUSIC R", England — Irr • Su • W EUROPE • VERY IRREGULAR

6220v CLANDESTINE (M EAST)
†"VO THE MOJAHED", Iraq — PERSIAN • MIDEAST

PAKISTAN
PAKISTAN BC CORP, Rawalpindi — (J) • DS-ENGLISH, ETC • 10 kW

6224 PIRATE (EUROPE)
†"FREE RADIO SVC", Holland — Alternative Frequency to 6232 kHz

6225 PIRATE (EUROPE)
†"CAPITAL RADIO", Ireland — Sa/Su • W EUROPE • 0.2 kW   Irr • M-F • W EUROPE • 0.2 kW

6226 PIRATE (EUROPE)
†"STAR CLUB RADIO", Germany — Irr • Su • GERMAN & ENGLISH • W EUROPE • 0.02 kW

6230 EGYPT
RADIO CAIRO, Abu Za'bal — MIDEAST • 100 kW

MONACO
†TRANS WORLD RADIO, Monte Carlo — (D) • EUROPE • 500 kW
(D) F-W • EUROPE • 500 kW
(J) F-W • EUROPE • 500 kW
(J) • EUROPE • 500 kW
(J) Su-Tu • EUROPE • 500 kW
(D) Th • EUROPE • 500 kW
(J) Th • EUROPE • 500 kW

6230v PIRATE (EUROPE)
†"BRITAIN R INTL", Germany — Irr • Su • ENGLISH & GERMAN • W EUROPE • 0.05 kW

†"JOLLY ROGER R", Ireland — Sa/Su • W EUROPE

6232 PIRATE (EUROPE)
†"FREE RADIO SVC", Holland — Sa • ENGLISH & DUTCH • W EUROPE • 0.018 kW • ALT. FREQ. TO 6224 kHz
Su • ENGLISH & DUTCH • W EUROPE • 0.018 kW • ALT. FREQ. TO 6224 kHz

6235v PIRATE (EUROPE)
"RADIO GEMINI", England — Irr • Su • W EUROPE • 0.15 kW

6240 PIRATE (EUROPE)
"RADIO MERLIN INTL, England — Irr • Sa/Su • W EUROPE

†"WEEKEND MUSIC R", Scotland — Alternative Frequency to 6296v kHz

6240v PERU
†RADIO MUNICIPAL, Calca — DS • 0.12 kW

PIRATE (EUROPE)
†"LIVE WIRE RADIO", England — Su • W EUROPE • 0.15 kW • ALT. FREQ. TO 6291 kHz

6245 VATICAN STATE
†VATICAN RADIO, Sta Maria di Galeria — EUROPE • 100 kW
M-Sa • EUROPE • 100 kW
(D) Su • EUROPE • 100 kW
M-Sa • FRENCH & ITALIAN • EUROPE • 100 kW

6245v PIRATE (EUROPE)
†"LIVE WIRE RADIO", England — Alternative Frequency to 6255v kHz

6250v EQUATORIAL GUINEA
(con'd) RADIO NACIONAL, Malabo — SPANISH, ETC • DS • 10 kW

FREQUENCY   COUNTRY, STATION, LOCATION

TARGET • NETWORK • POWER (kW)   World Time

0 1 2 3 4 5 6 7 8 9 10 11 12 13 14 15 16 17 18 19 20 21 22 23 24

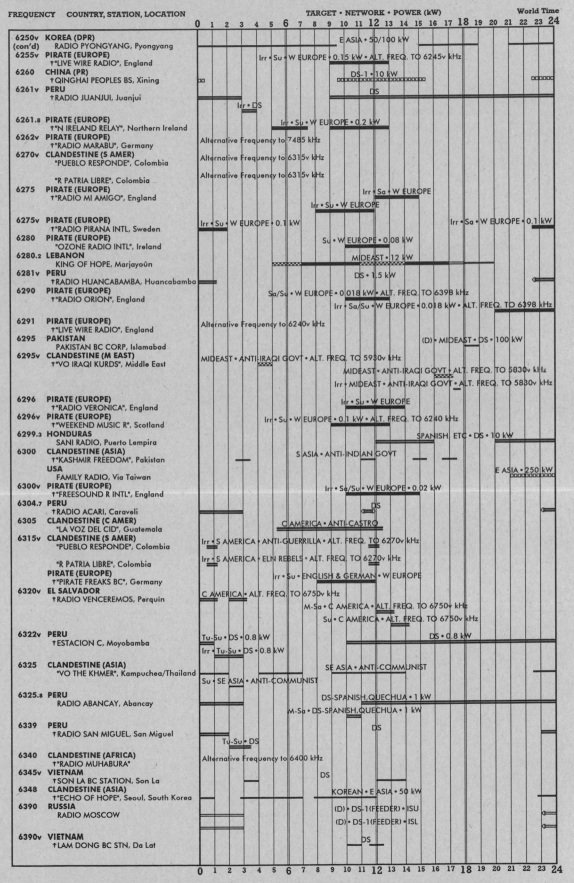

Frequency	Country, Station, Location	Target • Network • Power (kW)
6250v (con'd)	KOREA (DPR) RADIO PYONGYANG, Pyongyang	E ASIA • 50/100 kW
6255v	PIRATE (EUROPE) †"LIVE WIRE RADIO", England	Irr • Su • W EUROPE • 0.15 kW • ALT. FREQ. TO 6245v kHz
6260	CHINA (PR) †QINGHAI PEOPLES BS, Xining	DS-1 • 10 kW
6261v	PERU †RADIO JUANJUI, Juanjui	DS / Irr • DS
6261.8	PIRATE (EUROPE) †"N IRELAND RELAY", Northern Ireland	Irr • Su • W EUROPE • 0.2 kW
6262v	PIRATE (EUROPE) †"RADIO MARABU", Germany	Alternative Frequency to 7485 kHz
6270v	CLANDESTINE (S AMER) "PUEBLO RESPONDE", Colombia	Alternative Frequency to 6315v kHz
	"R PATRIA LIBRE", Colombia	Alternative Frequency to 6315v kHz
6275	PIRATE (EUROPE) †"RADIO MI AMIGO", England	Irr • Sa • W EUROPE / Irr • Su • W EUROPE
6275v	PIRATE (EUROPE) †"RADIO PIRANA INTL", Sweden	Irr • Su • W EUROPE • 0.1 kW Irr • Sa • W EUROPE • 0.1 kW
6280	PIRATE (EUROPE) "OZONE RADIO INTL", Ireland	Su • W EUROPE • 0.08 kW
6280.2	LEBANON KING OF HOPE, Marjayoûn	MIDEAST • 12 kW
6281v	PERU †RADIO HUANCABAMBA, Huancabamba	DS • 1.5 kW
6290	PIRATE (EUROPE) †"RADIO ORION", England	Sa/Su • W EUROPE • 0.018 kW • ALT. FREQ. TO 6398 kHz / Irr • Sa/Su • W EUROPE • 0.018 kW • ALT. FREQ. TO 6398 kHz
6291	PIRATE (EUROPE) †"LIVE WIRE RADIO", England	Alternative Frequency to 6240v kHz
6295	PAKISTAN PAKISTAN BC CORP, Islamabad	(D) • MIDEAST • DS • 100 kW
6295v	CLANDESTINE (M EAST) †"VO IRAQI KURDS", Middle East	MIDEAST • ANTI-IRAQI GOVT • ALT. FREQ. TO 5930v kHz / MIDEAST • ANTI-IRAQI GOVT • ALT. FREQ. TO 5830v kHz / Irr • MIDEAST • ANTI-IRAQI GOVT • ALT. FREQ. TO 5830v kHz
6296	PIRATE (EUROPE) †"RADIO VERONICA", England	Irr • Su • W EUROPE
6296v	PIRATE (EUROPE) †"WEEKEND MUSIC R", Scotland	Irr • Su • W EUROPE • 0.1 kW • ALT. FREQ. TO 6240 kHz
6299.3	HONDURAS SANI RADIO, Puerto Lempira	SPANISH, ETC • DS • 10 kW
6300	CLANDESTINE (ASIA) †"KASHMIR FREEDOM", Pakistan	S ASIA • ANTI-INDIAN GOVT
	USA FAMILY RADIO, Via Taiwan	E ASIA • 250 kW
6300v	PIRATE (EUROPE) †"FREESOUND R INTL", England	Irr • Sa/Su • W EUROPE • 0.02 kW
6304.7	PERU †RADIO ACARI, Caraveli	DS
6305	CLANDESTINE (C AMER) "LA VOZ DEL CID", Guatemala	C AMERICA • ANTI-CASTRO
6315v	CLANDESTINE (S AMER) "PUEBLO RESPONDE", Colombia	Irr • S AMERICA • ANTI-GUERRILLA • ALT. FREQ. TO 6270v kHz
	"R PATRIA LIBRE", Colombia	Irr • S AMERICA • ELN REBELS • ALT. FREQ. TO 6270v kHz
	PIRATE (EUROPE) †"PIRATE FREAKS BC", Germany	Irr • Su • ENGLISH & GERMAN • W EUROPE
6320v	EL SALVADOR †RADIO VENCEREMOS, Perquin	C AMERICA • ALT. FREQ. TO 6750v kHz / M-Sa • C AMERICA • ALT. FREQ. TO 6750v kHz / Su • C AMERICA • ALT. FREQ. TO 6750v kHz
6322v	PERU †ESTACION C, Moyobamba	Tu-Su • DS • 0.8 kW DS • 0.8 kW / Irr • Tu-Su • DS • 0.8 kW
6325	CLANDESTINE (ASIA) "VO THE KHMER", Kampuchea/Thailand	SE ASIA • ANTI-COMMUNIST / Su • SE ASIA • ANTI-COMMUNIST
6325.8	PERU RADIO ABANCAY, Abancay	DS-SPANISH, QUECHUA • 1 kW / M-Sa • DS-SPANISH, QUECHUA • 1 kW
6339	PERU †RADIO SAN MIGUEL, San Miguel	DS / Tu-Su • DS
6340	CLANDESTINE (AFRICA) †"RADIO MUHABURA"	Alternative Frequency to 6400 kHz
6345v	VIETNAM †SON LA BC STATION, Son La	DS
6348	CLANDESTINE (ASIA) †"ECHO OF HOPE", Seoul, South Korea	KOREAN • E ASIA • 50 kW
6390	RUSSIA RADIO MOSCOW	(D) • DS-1 (FEEDER) • ISU / (D) • DS-1 (FEEDER) • ISL
6390v	VIETNAM †LAM DONG BC STN, Da Lat	DS

0 1 2 3 4 5 6 7 8 9 10 11 12 13 14 15 16 17 18 19 20 21 22 23 24

ENGLISH ▬▬   ARABIC ≋≋   CHINESE □□□   FRENCH ══   GERMAN ▬▬   RUSSIAN ══   SPANISH ▬▬   OTHER ──

FREQUENCY   COUNTRY, STATION, LOCATION   TARGET • NETWORK • POWER (kW)   World Time

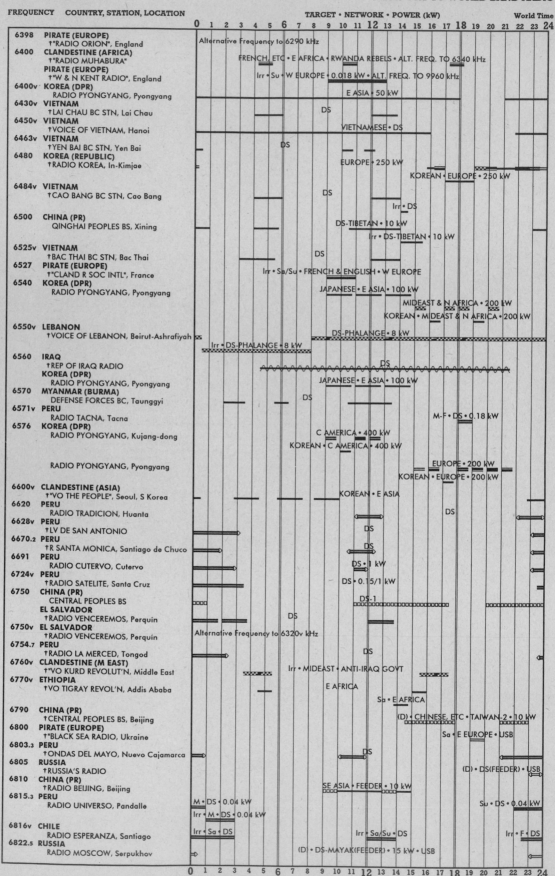

Frequency	Country, Station, Location	Target • Network • Power (kW)
6398	PIRATE (EUROPE) †"RADIO ORION", England	Alternative Frequency to 6290 kHz
6400	CLANDESTINE (AFRICA) †"RADIO MUHABURA"	FRENCH, ETC • E AFRICA • RWANDA REBELS • ALT. FREQ. TO 6340 kHz
	PIRATE (EUROPE) †"W & N KENT RADIO", England	Irr • Su • W EUROPE • 0.018 kW • ALT. FREQ. TO 9960 kHz
6400v	KOREA (DPR) RADIO PYONGYANG, Pyongyang	E ASIA • 50 kW
6430v	VIETNAM †LAI CHAU BC STN, Lai Chau	DS
6450v	VIETNAM †VOICE OF VIETNAM, Hanoi	VIETNAMESE • DS
6463v	VIETNAM †YEN BAI BC STN, Yen Bai	DS
6480	KOREA (REPUBLIC) †RADIO KOREA, In-Kimjae	EUROPE • 250 kW / KOREAN • EUROPE • 250 kW
6484v	VIETNAM †CAO BANG BC STN, Cao Bang	DS / Irr • DS
6500	CHINA (PR) QINGHAI PEOPLES BS, Xining	DS-TIBETAN • 10 kW / Irr • DS-TIBETAN • 10 kW
6525v	VIETNAM †BAC THAI BC STN, Bac Thai	DS
6527	PIRATE (EUROPE) †"CLAND R SOC INTL", France	Irr • Sa/Su • FRENCH & ENGLISH • W EUROPE
6540	KOREA (DPR) RADIO PYONGYANG, Pyongyang	JAPANESE • E ASIA • 100 kW / MIDEAST & N AFRICA • 200 kW / KOREAN • MIDEAST & N AFRICA • 200 kW
6550v	LEBANON †VOICE OF LEBANON, Beirut-Ashrafiyah	DS-PHALANGE • 8 kW / Irr • DS-PHALANGE • 8 kW
6560	IRAQ †REP OF IRAQ RADIO	DS
	KOREA (DPR) RADIO PYONGYANG, Pyongyang	JAPANESE • E ASIA • 100 kW
6570	MYANMAR (BURMA) DEFENSE FORCES BC, Taunggyi	DS
6571v	PERU RADIO TACNA, Tacna	M-F • DS • 0.18 kW
6576	KOREA (DPR) RADIO PYONGYANG, Kujang-dong	C AMERICA • 400 kW / KOREAN • C AMERICA • 400 kW
	RADIO PYONGYANG, Pyongyang	EUROPE • 200 kW / KOREAN • EUROPE • 200 kW
6600v	CLANDESTINE (ASIA) †"VO THE PEOPLE", Seoul, S Korea	KOREAN • E ASIA
6620	PERU RADIO TRADICION, Huanta	DS
6628v	PERU †LV DE SAN ANTONIO	DS
6670.2	PERU †R SANTA MONICA, Santiago de Chuco	DS
6691	PERU RADIO CUTERVO, Cutervo	DS • 1 kW
6724v	PERU †RADIO SATELITE, Santa Cruz	DS • 0.15/1 kW
6750	CHINA (PR) CENTRAL PEOPLES BS	DS-1
	EL SALVADOR †RADIO VENCEREMOS, Perquin	DS
6750v	EL SALVADOR †RADIO VENCEREMOS, Perquin	Alternative Frequency to 6320v kHz
6754.7	PERU †RADIO LA MERCED, Tongod	DS
6760v	CLANDESTINE (M EAST) †"VO KURD REVOLUT'N, Middle East	Irr • MIDEAST • ANTI-IRAQ GOVT
6770v	ETHIOPIA †VO TIGRAY REVOL'N, Addis Ababa	E AFRICA / Sa • E AFRICA
6790	CHINA (PR) †CENTRAL PEOPLES BS, Beijing	(D) • CHINESE, ETC • TAIWAN-2 • 10 kW
6800	PIRATE (EUROPE) †"BLACK SEA RADIO, Ukraine	Sa • E EUROPE • USB
6803.3	PERU †ONDAS DEL MAYO, Nuevo Cajamarca	DS
6805	RUSSIA †RUSSIA'S RADIO	(D) • DS(FEEDER) • USB
6810	CHINA (PR) †RADIO BEIJING, Beijing	SE ASIA • FEEDER • 10 kW
6815.3	PERU RADIO UNIVERSO, Pandalle	M • DS • 0.04 kW / Irr • M • DS • 0.04 kW / Su • DS • 0.04 kW
6816v	CHILE RADIO ESPERANZA, Santiago	Irr • Sa • DS / Irr • Sa/Su • DS / Irr • F • DS
6822.5	RUSSIA RADIO MOSCOW, Serpukhov	(D) • DS-MAYAK(FEEDER) • 15 kW • USB

World Time scale: 0 1 2 3 4 5 6 7 8 9 10 11 12 13 14 15 16 17 18 19 20 21 22 23 24

SUMMER ONLY (J)   WINTER ONLY (D)   JAMMING / OR ∧   EARLIEST HEARD ◁   LATEST HEARD ▷   NEW OR CHANGED FOR 1993 †

FREQUENCY   COUNTRY, STATION, LOCATION   TARGET • NETWORK • POWER (kW)   World Time

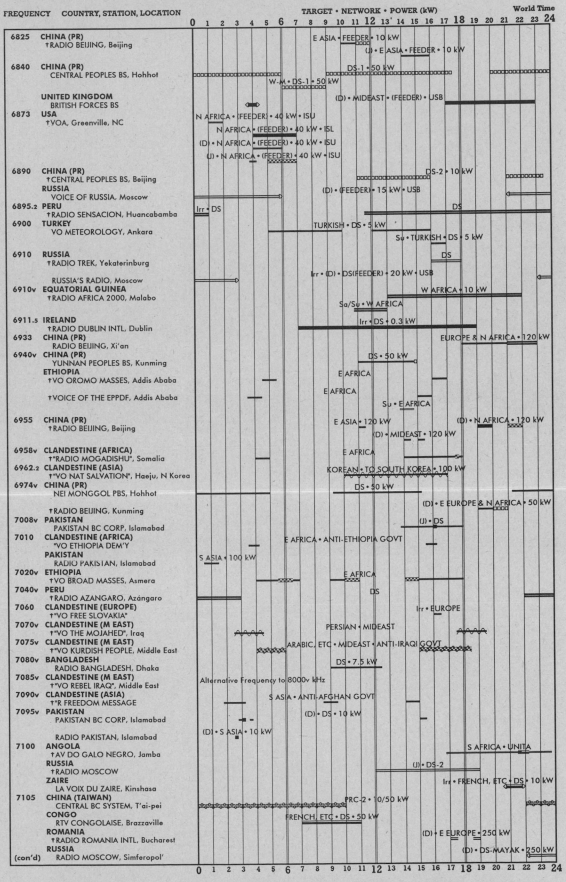

Frequency	Country, Station, Location	Target • Network • Power
6825	CHINA (PR) †RADIO BEIJING, Beijing	E ASIA • FEEDER • 10 kW / (J) • E ASIA • FEEDER • 10 kW
6840	CHINA (PR) CENTRAL PEOPLES BS, Hohhot	DS-1 • 50 kW / W-M • DS-1 • 50 kW
	UNITED KINGDOM BRITISH FORCES BS	(D) • MIDEAST • (FEEDER) • USB
6873	USA †VOA, Greenville, NC	N AFRICA • (FEEDER) • 40 kW • ISU / N AFRICA • (FEEDER) • 40 kW • ISL / (D) • N AFRICA • (FEEDER) • 40 kW • ISU / (J) • N AFRICA • (FEEDER) • 40 kW • ISU
6890	CHINA (PR) †CENTRAL PEOPLES BS, Beijing	DS-2 • 10 kW
	RUSSIA VOICE OF RUSSIA, Moscow	(D) • (FEEDER) • 15 kW • USB
6895.2	PERU †RADIO SENSACION, Huancabamba	Irr • DS / DS
6900	TURKEY VO METEOROLOGY, Ankara	TURKISH • DS • 5 kW / Su • TURKISH • DS • 5 kW
6910	RUSSIA †RADIO TREK, Yekaterinburg	DS
	RUSSIA'S RADIO, Moscow	Irr • (D) • DS(FEEDER) • 20 kW • USB
6910v	EQUATORIAL GUINEA †RADIO AFRICA 2000, Malabo	W AFRICA • 10 kW / Sa/Su • W AFRICA
6911.5	IRELAND †RADIO DUBLIN INTL, Dublin	Irr • DS • 0.3 kW
6933	CHINA (PR) RADIO BEIJING, Xi'an	EUROPE & N AFRICA • 120 kW
6940v	CHINA (PR) YUNNAN PEOPLES BS, Kunming	DS • 50 kW
	ETHIOPIA †VO OROMO MASSES, Addis Ababa	E AFRICA
	†VOICE OF THE EPPDF, Addis Ababa	E AFRICA / Su • E AFRICA
6955	CHINA (PR) †RADIO BEIJING, Beijing	E ASIA • 120 kW / (D) • MIDEAST • 120 kW / (D) • N AFRICA • 120 kW
6958v	CLANDESTINE (AFRICA) †"RADIO MOGADISHU", Somalia	E AFRICA
6962.2	CLANDESTINE (ASIA) †"VO NAT SALVATION", Haeju, N Korea	KOREAN • TO SOUTH KOREA • 100 kW
6974v	CHINA (PR) NEI MONGGOL PBS, Hohhot	DS • 50 kW
	†RADIO BEIJING, Kunming	(D) • E EUROPE & N AFRICA • 50 kW
7008v	PAKISTAN PAKISTAN BC CORP, Islamabad	(J) • DS
7010	CLANDESTINE (AFRICA) "VO ETHIOPIA DEM'Y	E AFRICA • ANTI-ETHIOPIA GOVT
	PAKISTAN RADIO PAKISTAN, Islamabad	S ASIA • 100 kW
7020v	ETHIOPIA †VO BROAD MASSES, Asmera	E AFRICA
7040v	PERU †RADIO AZANGARO, Azángaro	DS
7060	CLANDESTINE (EUROPE) †"VO FREE SLOVAKIA"	Irr • EUROPE
7070v	CLANDESTINE (M EAST) †"VO THE MOJAHED", Iraq	PERSIAN • MIDEAST
7075v	CLANDESTINE (M EAST) †"VO KURDISH PEOPLE", Middle East	ARABIC, ETC • MIDEAST • ANTI-IRAQI GOVT
7080v	BANGLADESH RADIO BANGLADESH, Dhaka	DS • 7.5 kW
7085v	CLANDESTINE (M EAST) †"VO REBEL IRAQ", Middle East	Alternative Frequency to 8000v kHz
7090v	CLANDESTINE (ASIA) †"R FREEDOM MESSAGE"	S ASIA • ANTI-AFGHAN GOVT
7095v	PAKISTAN PAKISTAN BC CORP, Islamabad	(D) • DS • 10 kW
	RADIO PAKISTAN, Islamabad	(D) • S ASIA • 10 kW
7100	ANGOLA †AV DO GALO NEGRO, Jamba	S AFRICA • UNITA
	RUSSIA †RADIO MOSCOW	(J) • DS-2
	ZAIRE LA VOIX DU ZAIRE, Kinshasa	Irr • FRENCH, ETC • DS • 10 kW
7105	CHINA (TAIWAN) CENTRAL BC SYSTEM, T'ai-pei	PRC-2 • 10/50 kW
	CONGO RTV CONGOLAISE, Brazzaville	FRENCH, ETC • DS • 50 kW
	ROMANIA †RADIO ROMANIA INTL, Bucharest	(D) • E EUROPE • 250 kW
	RUSSIA	(D) • DS-MAYAK • 250 kW
(con'd)	RADIO MOSCOW, Simferopol'	

ENGLISH ▬   ARABIC ⧆   CHINESE □□□   FRENCH ▬   GERMAN ▬   RUSSIAN ═   SPANISH ▬   OTHER ▬

7105–7115 kHz

PASSPORT TO WORLD BAND RADIO

FREQUENCY   COUNTRY, STATION, LOCATION

TARGET • NETWORK • POWER (kW)   World Time

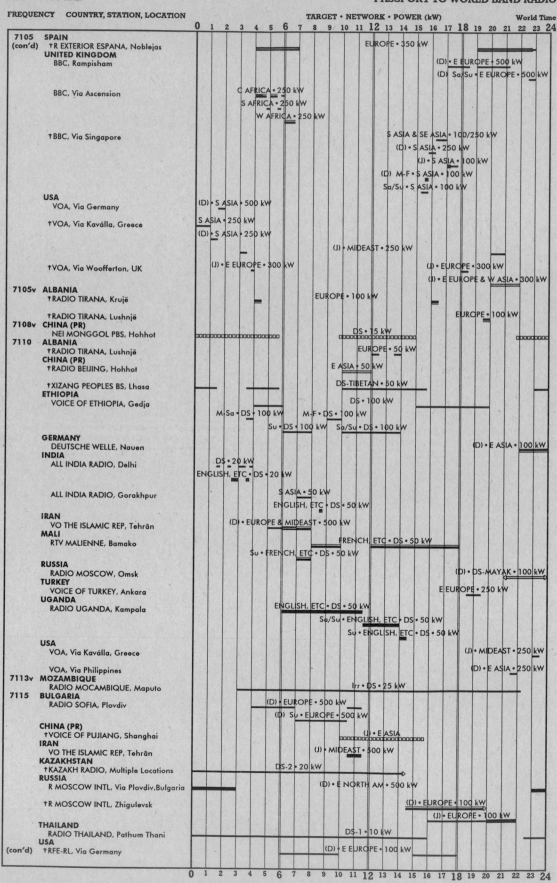

SUMMER ONLY (J)   WINTER ONLY (D)   JAMMING / OR ∧   EARLIEST HEARD ◁   LATEST HEARD ▷   NEW OR CHANGED FOR 1993 †

FREQUENCY   COUNTRY, STATION, LOCATION

TARGET • NETWORK • POWER (kW)

World Time

0 1 2 3 4 5 6 7 8 9 10 11 12 13 14 15 16 17 18 19 20 21 22 23 24

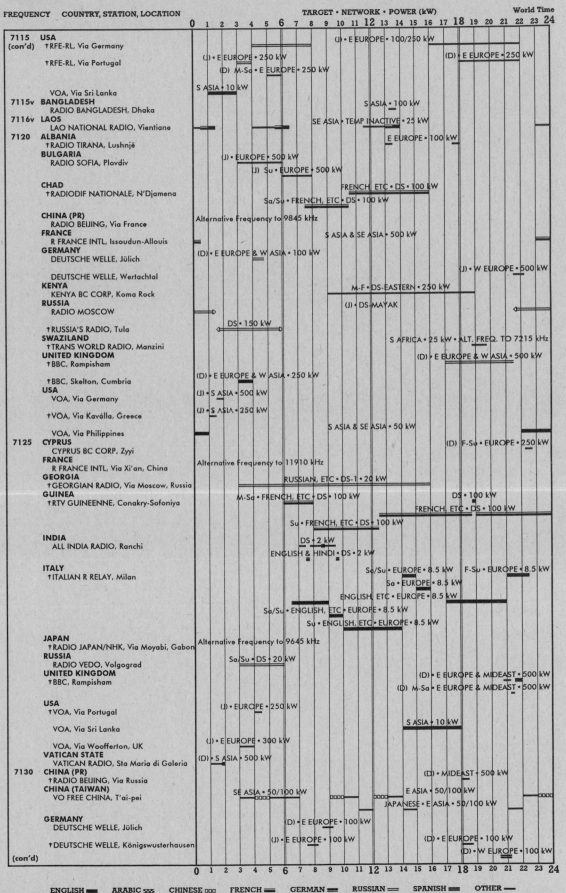

Frequency	Country, Station, Location	Target • Network • Power
7115 (con'd)	USA ↑RFE-RL, Via Germany	(J) • E EUROPE • 100/250 kW
		(J) • E EUROPE • 250 kW
		(D) • E EUROPE • 250 kW
	↑RFE-RL, Via Portugal	(D) M-Sa • E EUROPE • 250 kW
	VOA, Via Sri Lanka	S ASIA • 10 kW
7115v	BANGLADESH RADIO BANGLADESH, Dhaka	S ASIA • 100 kW
7116v	LAOS LAO NATIONAL RADIO, Vientiane	SE ASIA • TEMP INACTIVE • 25 kW
7120	ALBANIA ↑RADIO TIRANA, Lushnjë	E EUROPE • 100 kW
	BULGARIA RADIO SOFIA, Plovdiv	(J) • EUROPE • 500 kW
		(J) Su • EUROPE • 500 kW
	CHAD ↑RADIODIF NATIONALE, N'Djamena	FRENCH, ETC • DS • 100 kW
		Sa/Su • FRENCH, ETC • DS • 100 kW
	CHINA (PR) RADIO BEIJING, Via France	Alternative Frequency to 9845 kHz
	FRANCE R FRANCE INTL, Issoudun-Allouis	S ASIA & SE ASIA • 500 kW
	GERMANY DEUTSCHE WELLE, Jülich	(D) • E EUROPE & W ASIA • 100 kW
	DEUTSCHE WELLE, Wertachtal	(J) • W EUROPE • 500 kW
	KENYA KENYA BC CORP, Koma Rock	M-F • DS-EASTERN • 250 kW
	RUSSIA RADIO MOSCOW	(J) • DS-MAYAK
	↑RUSSIA'S RADIO, Tula	DS • 150 kW
	SWAZILAND ↑TRANS WORLD RADIO, Manzini	S AFRICA • 25 kW • ALT. FREQ. TO 7215 kHz
	UNITED KINGDOM ↑BBC, Rampisham	(D) • E EUROPE & W ASIA • 500 kW
	↑BBC, Skelton, Cumbria	(D) • E EUROPE & W ASIA • 250 kW
	USA VOA, Via Germany	(J) • S ASIA • 500 kW
	↑VOA, Via Kaválla, Greece	(J) • S ASIA • 250 kW
	VOA, Via Philippines	S ASIA & SE ASIA • 50 kW
7125	CYPRUS CYPRUS BC CORP, Zyyi	(D) F-Su • EUROPE • 250 kW
	FRANCE R FRANCE INTL, Via Xi'an, China	Alternative Frequency to 11910 kHz
	GEORGIA ↑GEORGIAN RADIO, Via Moscow, Russia	RUSSIAN, ETC • DS-1 • 20 kW
	GUINEA ↑RTV GUINEENNE, Conakry-Sofoniya	M-Sa • FRENCH, ETC • DS • 100 kW
		DS • 100 kW
		FRENCH, ETC • DS • 100 kW
		Su • FRENCH, ETC • DS • 100 kW
	INDIA ALL INDIA RADIO, Ranchi	DS • 2 kW
		ENGLISH & HINDI • DS • 2 kW
	ITALY ↑ITALIAN R RELAY, Milan	Sa/Su • EUROPE • 8.5 kW
		F-Su • EUROPE • 8.5 kW
		Sa • EUROPE • 8.5 kW
		ENGLISH, ETC • EUROPE • 8.5 kW
		Sa/Su • ENGLISH, ETC • EUROPE • 8.5 kW
		Su • ENGLISH, ETC • EUROPE • 8.5 kW
	JAPAN ↑RADIO JAPAN/NHK, Via Moyabi, Gabon	Alternative Frequency to 9645 kHz
	RUSSIA RADIO VEDO, Volgograd	Sa/Su • DS • 20 kW
	UNITED KINGDOM ↑BBC, Rampisham	(D) • E EUROPE & MIDEAST • 500 kW
		(D) M-Sa • E EUROPE & MIDEAST • 500 kW
	USA ↑VOA, Via Portugal	(J) • EUROPE • 250 kW
	VOA, Via Sri Lanka	S ASIA • 10 kW
	VOA, Via Woofferton, UK	(J) • E EUROPE • 300 kW
	VATICAN STATE VATICAN RADIO, Sta Maria di Galeria	(D) • S ASIA • 500 kW
7130	CHINA (PR) ↑RADIO BEIJING, Via Russia	(D) • MIDEAST • 500 kW
	CHINA (TAIWAN) VO FREE CHINA, T'ai-pei	SE ASIA • 50/100 kW
		E ASIA • 50/100 kW
		JAPANESE • E ASIA • 50/100 kW
	GERMANY DEUTSCHE WELLE, Jülich	(D) • E EUROPE • 100 kW
	↑DEUTSCHE WELLE, Königswusterhausen	(J) • E EUROPE • 100 kW
		(D) • E EUROPE • 100 kW
		(D) • W EUROPE • 100 kW
(con'd)		

0 1 2 3 4 5 6 7 8 9 10 11 12 13 14 15 16 17 18 19 20 21 22 23 24

ENGLISH ▬   ARABIC ▧   CHINESE ▭▭▭   FRENCH ═   GERMAN ▬▬   RUSSIAN ══   SPANISH ▬   OTHER ▬

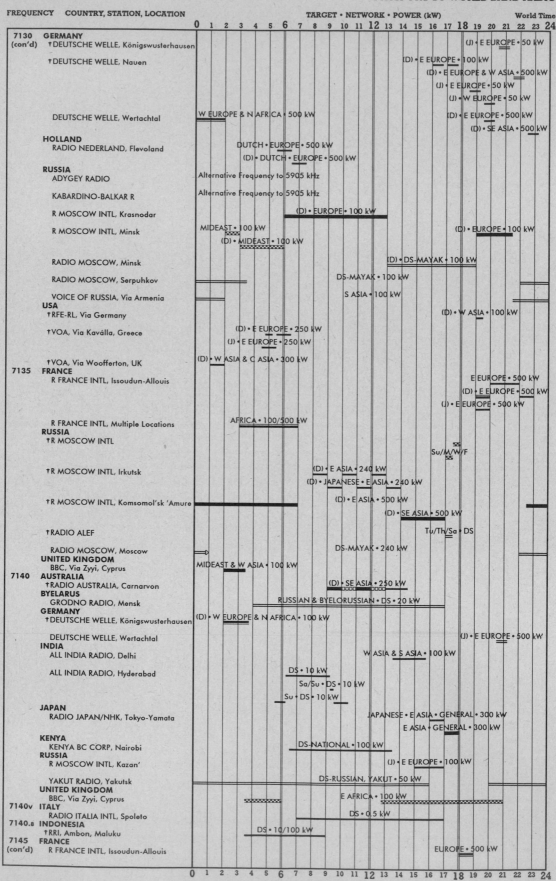

FREQUENCY   COUNTRY, STATION, LOCATION

TARGET • NETWORK • POWER (kW)

World Time

7130	GERMANY	
(con'd)	†DEUTSCHE WELLE, Königswusterhausen	(J) • E EUROPE • 50 kW
	†DEUTSCHE WELLE, Nauen	(D) • E EUROPE • 100 kW
		(D) • E EUROPE & W ASIA • 500 kW
		(J) • E EUROPE • 50 kW
		(J) • W EUROPE • 50 kW
	DEUTSCHE WELLE, Wertachtal	W EUROPE & N AFRICA • 500 kW
		(D) • E EUROPE • 500 kW
		(D) • SE ASIA • 500 kW
	HOLLAND	
	RADIO NEDERLAND, Flevoland	DUTCH • EUROPE • 500 kW
		(D) • DUTCH • EUROPE • 500 kW
	RUSSIA	
	ADYGEY RADIO	Alternative Frequency to 5905 kHz
	KABARDINO-BALKAR R	Alternative Frequency to 5905 kHz
	R MOSCOW INTL, Krasnodar	(D) • EUROPE • 100 kW
	R MOSCOW INTL, Minsk	MIDEAST • 100 kW
		(D) • MIDEAST • 100 kW
		(D) • EUROPE • 100 kW
	RADIO MOSCOW, Minsk	(D) • DS-MAYAK • 100 kW
	RADIO MOSCOW, Serpuhkov	DS-MAYAK • 100 kW
	VOICE OF RUSSIA, Via Armenia	S ASIA • 100 kW
	USA	
	†RFE-RL, Via Germany	(D) • W ASIA • 100 kW
	†VOA, Via Kaválla, Greece	(D) • E EUROPE • 250 kW
		(J) • E EUROPE • 250 kW
	†VOA, Via Woofferton, UK	(D) • W ASIA & C ASIA • 300 kW
7135	FRANCE	
	R FRANCE INTL, Issoudun-Allouis	E EUROPE • 500 kW
		(D) • E EUROPE • 500 kW
		(J) • E EUROPE • 500 kW
	R FRANCE INTL, Multiple Locations	AFRICA • 100/500 kW
	RUSSIA	
	†R MOSCOW INTL	Su/M/W/F
	†R MOSCOW INTL, Irkutsk	(D) • E ASIA • 240 kW
		(D) • JAPANESE • E ASIA • 240 kW
	†R MOSCOW INTL, Komsomol'sk 'Amure	(D) • E ASIA • 500 kW
		(D) • SE ASIA • 500 kW
	†RADIO ALEF	Tu/Th/Sa • DS
	RADIO MOSCOW, Moscow	DS-MAYAK • 240 kW
	UNITED KINGDOM	
	BBC, Via Zyyi, Cyprus	MIDEAST & W ASIA • 100 kW
7140	AUSTRALIA	
	†RADIO AUSTRALIA, Carnarvon	(D) • SE ASIA • 250 kW
	BYELARUS	
	GRODNO RADIO, Mensk	RUSSIAN & BYELORUSSIAN • DS • 20 kW
	GERMANY	
	†DEUTSCHE WELLE, Königswusterhausen	(D) • W EUROPE & N AFRICA • 100 kW
	DEUTSCHE WELLE, Wertachtal	(J) • E EUROPE • 500 kW
	INDIA	
	ALL INDIA RADIO, Delhi	W ASIA & S ASIA • 100 kW
	ALL INDIA RADIO, Hyderabad	DS • 10 kW
		Sa/Su • DS • 10 kW
		Su • DS • 10 kW
	JAPAN	
	RADIO JAPAN/NHK, Tokyo-Yamata	JAPANESE • E ASIA • GENERAL • 300 kW
		E ASIA • GENERAL • 300 kW
	KENYA	
	KENYA BC CORP, Nairobi	DS-NATIONAL • 100 kW
	RUSSIA	
	R MOSCOW INTL, Kazan'	(J) • E EUROPE • 100 kW
	YAKUT RADIO, Yakutsk	DS-RUSSIAN, YAKUT • 50 kW
	UNITED KINGDOM	
	BBC, Via Zyyi, Cyprus	E AFRICA • 100 kW
7140v	ITALY	
	RADIO ITALIA INTL, Spoleto	DS • 0.5 kW
7140.8	INDONESIA	
	†RRI, Ambon, Maluku	DS • 10/100 kW
7145	FRANCE	
(con'd)	R FRANCE INTL, Issoudun-Allouis	EUROPE • 500 kW

FREQUENCY   COUNTRY, STATION, LOCATION

TARGET • NETWORK • POWER (kW)

World Time

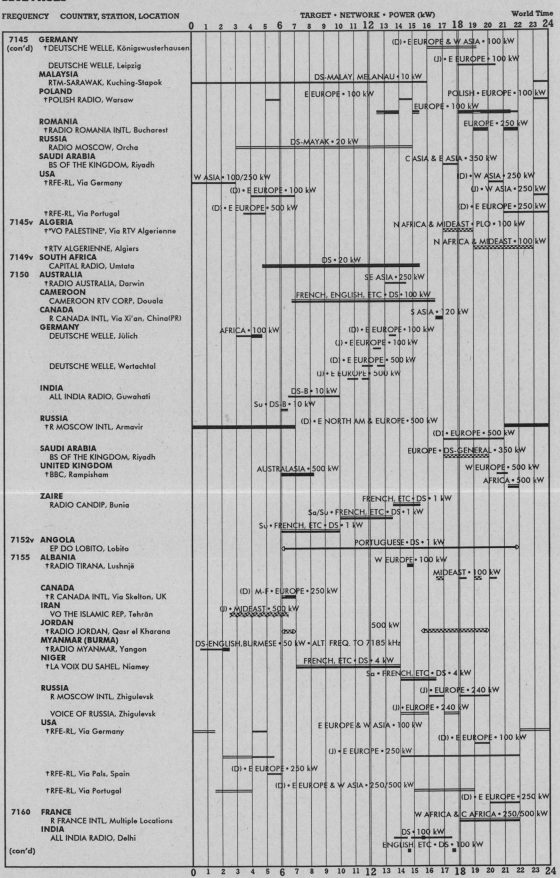

FREQUENCY	COUNTRY, STATION, LOCATION	TARGET • NETWORK • POWER (kW)
7145 (con'd)	GERMANY †DEUTSCHE WELLE, Königswusterhausen	(D) • E EUROPE & W ASIA • 100 kW
		(J) • E EUROPE • 100 kW
	DEUTSCHE WELLE, Leipzig	
	MALAYSIA RTM-SARAWAK, Kuching-Stapok	DS-MALAY, MELANAU • 10 kW
	POLAND †POLISH RADIO, Warsaw	E EUROPE • 100 kW POLISH • EUROPE • 100 kW
		EUROPE • 100 kW
	ROMANIA †RADIO ROMANIA INTL, Bucharest	EUROPE • 250 kW
	RUSSIA RADIO MOSCOW, Orcha	DS-MAYAK • 20 kW
	SAUDI ARABIA BS OF THE KINGDOM, Riyadh	C ASIA & E ASIA • 350 kW
	USA †RFE-RL, Via Germany	W ASIA • 100/250 kW (D) • W ASIA • 250 kW
		(D) • E EUROPE • 100 kW (J) • W ASIA • 250 kW
	†RFE-RL, Via Portugal	(D) • E EUROPE • 500 kW (D) • E EUROPE • 250 kW
7145v	ALGERIA †"VO PALESTINE", Via RTV Algerienne	N AFRICA & MIDEAST • PLO • 100 kW
	†RTV ALGERIENNE, Algiers	N AFRICA & MIDEAST • 100 kW
7149v	SOUTH AFRICA CAPITAL RADIO, Umtata	DS • 20 kW
7150	AUSTRALIA †RADIO AUSTRALIA, Darwin	SE ASIA • 250 kW
	CAMEROON CAMEROON RTV CORP, Douala	FRENCH, ENGLISH, ETC • DS • 100 kW
	CANADA R CANADA INTL, Via Xi'an, China(PR)	S ASIA • 120 kW
	GERMANY DEUTSCHE WELLE, Jülich	AFRICA • 100 kW (D) • E EUROPE • 100 kW
		(J) • E EUROPE • 100 kW
	DEUTSCHE WELLE, Wertachtal	(D) • E EUROPE • 500 kW
		(J) • E EUROPE • 500 kW
	INDIA ALL INDIA RADIO, Guwahati	DS-B • 10 kW
		Su • DS-B • 10 kW
	RUSSIA †R MOSCOW INTL, Armavir	(D) • E NORTH AM & EUROPE • 500 kW
		(D) • EUROPE • 500 kW
	SAUDI ARABIA BS OF THE KINGDOM, Riyadh	EUROPE • DS-GENERAL • 350 kW
	UNITED KINGDOM †BBC, Rampisham	AUSTRALASIA • 500 kW W EUROPE • 500 kW
		AFRICA • 500 kW
	ZAIRE RADIO CANDIP, Bunia	FRENCH, ETC • DS • 1 kW
		Sa/Su • FRENCH, ETC • DS • 1 kW
		Su • FRENCH, ETC • DS • 1 kW
7152v	ANGOLA EP DO LOBITO, Lobito	PORTUGUESE • DS • 1 kW
7155	ALBANIA †RADIO TIRANA, Lushnjë	W EUROPE • 100 kW
		MIDEAST • 100 kW
	CANADA †R CANADA INTL, Via Skelton, UK	(D) M-F • EUROPE • 250 kW
	IRAN VO THE ISLAMIC REP, Tehrān	(J) • MIDEAST • 500 kW
	JORDAN †RADIO JORDAN, Qasr el Kharana	500 kW
	MYANMAR (BURMA) †RADIO MYANMAR, Yangon	DS-ENGLISH, BURMESE • 50 kW • ALT FREQ. TO 7185 kHz
	NIGER †LA VOIX DU SAHEL, Niamey	FRENCH, ETC • DS • 4 kW
		Sa • FRENCH, ETC • DS • 4 kW
	RUSSIA R MOSCOW INTL, Zhigulevsk	(J) • EUROPE • 240 kW
	VOICE OF RUSSIA, Zhigulevsk	(J) • EUROPE • 240 kW
	USA †RFE-RL, Via Germany	E EUROPE & W ASIA • 100 kW
		(D) • E EUROPE • 100 kW
		(J) • E EUROPE • 250 kW
	†RFE-RL, Via Pals, Spain	(D) • E EUROPE • 250 kW
	†RFE-RL, Via Portugal	(D) • E EUROPE & W ASIA • 250/500 kW
		(D) • E EUROPE • 250 kW
7160	FRANCE R FRANCE INTL, Multiple Locations	W AFRICA & C AFRICA • 250/500 kW
	INDIA ALL INDIA RADIO, Delhi	DS • 100 kW
		ENGLISH, ETC • DS • 100 kW
(con'd)		

FREQUENCY   COUNTRY, STATION, LOCATION

TARGET • NETWORK • POWER (kW)   World Time

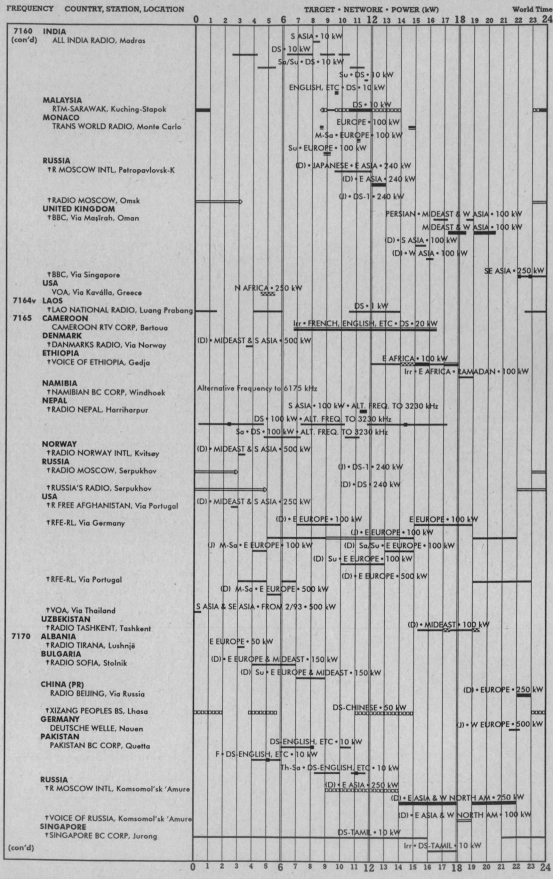

FREQUENCY	COUNTRY, STATION, LOCATION	TARGET • NETWORK • POWER (kW)
7160 (con'd)	INDIA — ALL INDIA RADIO, Madras	S ASIA • 10 kW / DS • 10 kW / Sa/Su • DS • 10 kW / Su • DS • 10 kW / ENGLISH, ETC • DS • 10 kW
	MALAYSIA — RTM-SARAWAK, Kuching-Stapok	DS • 10 kW
	MONACO — TRANS WORLD RADIO, Monte Carlo	EUROPE • 100 kW / M-Sa • EUROPE • 100 kW / Su • EUROPE • 100 kW
	RUSSIA — †R MOSCOW INTL, Petropavlovsk-K	(D) • JAPANESE • E ASIA • 240 kW / (D) • E ASIA • 240 kW / (J) • DS-1 • 240 kW
	†RADIO MOSCOW, Omsk	
	UNITED KINGDOM — †BBC, Via Maṣīrah, Oman	PERSIAN • MIDEAST & W ASIA • 100 kW / MIDEAST & W ASIA • 100 kW / (D) • S ASIA • 100 kW / (D) • W ASIA • 100 kW
	†BBC, Via Singapore	SE ASIA • 250 kW
	USA — VOA, Via Kaválla, Greece	N AFRICA • 250 kW
7164v	LAOS — †LAO NATIONAL RADIO, Luang Prabang	DS • 1 kW
7165	CAMEROON — CAMEROON RTV CORP, Bertoua	Irr • FRENCH, ENGLISH, ETC • DS • 20 kW
	DENMARK — †DANMARKS RADIO, Via Norway	(D) • MIDEAST & S ASIA • 500 kW
	ETHIOPIA — †VOICE OF ETHIOPIA, Gedja	E AFRICA • 100 kW / Irr • E AFRICA • RAMADAN • 100 kW
	NAMIBIA — †NAMIBIAN BC CORP, Windhoek	Alternative Frequency to 6175 kHz
	NEPAL — †RADIO NEPAL, Harriharpur	S ASIA • 100 kW • ALT. FREQ. TO 3230 kHz / DS • 100 kW • ALT. FREQ. TO 3230 kHz / Sa • DS • 100 kW • ALT. FREQ. TO 3230 kHz
	NORWAY — †RADIO NORWAY INTL, Kvitsøy	(D) • MIDEAST & S ASIA • 500 kW
	RUSSIA — †RADIO MOSCOW, Serpukhov	(J) • DS-1 • 240 kW
	†RUSSIA'S RADIO, Serpukhov	(D) • DS • 240 kW
	USA — †R FREE AFGHANISTAN, Via Portugal	(D) • MIDEAST & S ASIA • 250 kW
	†RFE-RL, Via Germany	(D) • E EUROPE • 100 kW / E EUROPE • 100 kW / (J) • E EUROPE • 100 kW / (J) M-Sa • E EUROPE • 100 kW / (D) Sa/Su • E EUROPE • 100 kW / (D) Su • E EUROPE • 100 kW / (D) • E EUROPE • 500 kW
	†RFE-RL, Via Portugal	(D) M-Sa • E EUROPE • 500 kW
	†VOA, Via Thailand	S ASIA & SE ASIA • FROM 2/93 • 500 kW
	UZBEKISTAN — †RADIO TASHKENT, Tashkent	(D) • MIDEAST • 100 kW
7170	ALBANIA — †RADIO TIRANA, Lushnjë	E EUROPE • 50 kW
	BULGARIA — †RADIO SOFIA, Stolnik	(D) • E EUROPE & MIDEAST • 150 kW / (D) Su • E EUROPE & MIDEAST • 150 kW
	CHINA (PR) — RADIO BEIJING, Via Russia	(D) • EUROPE • 250 kW
	†XIZANG PEOPLES BS, Lhasa	DS-CHINESE • 50 kW
	GERMANY — DEUTSCHE WELLE, Nauen	(J) • W EUROPE • 500 kW
	PAKISTAN — PAKISTAN BC CORP, Quetta	DS-ENGLISH, ETC • 10 kW / F • DS-ENGLISH, ETC • 10 kW / Th-Sa • DS-ENGLISH, ETC • 10 kW
	RUSSIA — †R MOSCOW INTL, Komsomol'sk 'Amure	(D) • E ASIA • 250 kW / (D) • E ASIA & W NORTH AM • 250 kW
	†VOICE OF RUSSIA, Komsomol'sk 'Amure	(D) • E ASIA & W NORTH AM • 100 kW
	SINGAPORE — †SINGAPORE BC CORP, Jurong	DS-TAMIL • 10 kW / Irr • DS-TAMIL • 10 kW
(con'd)		

FREQUENCY   COUNTRY, STATION, LOCATION

TARGET • NETWORK • POWER (kW)

World Time

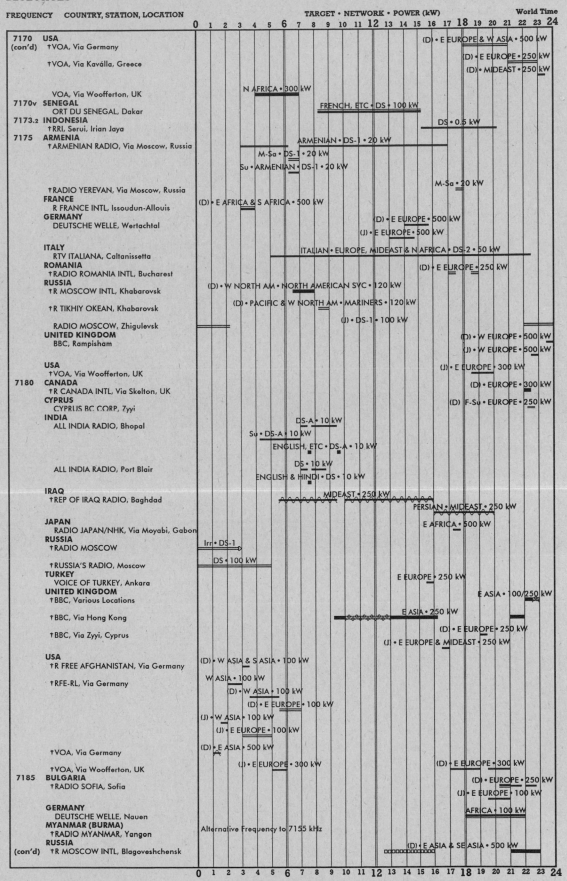

FREQUENCY	COUNTRY, STATION, LOCATION	Schedule (World Time 0–24)
7170 (con'd)	**USA** †VOA, Via Germany	(D) • E EUROPE & W ASIA • 500 kW
	†VOA, Via Kaválla, Greece	(D) • E EUROPE • 250 kW / (D) • MIDEAST • 250 kW
	VOA, Via Woofferton, UK	N AFRICA • 300 kW
7170v	**SENEGAL** ORT DU SENEGAL, Dakar	FRENCH, ETC • DS • 100 kW
7173.2	**INDONESIA** †RRI, Serui, Irian Jaya	DS • 0.5 kW
7175	**ARMENIA** †ARMENIAN RADIO, Via Moscow, Russia	ARMENIAN • DS-1 • 20 kW / M-Sa • DS-1 • 20 kW / Su • ARMENIAN • DS-1 • 20 kW
	†RADIO YEREVAN, Via Moscow, Russia	M-Sa • 20 kW
	FRANCE R FRANCE INTL, Issoudun-Allouis	(D) • E AFRICA & S AFRICA • 500 kW
	GERMANY DEUTSCHE WELLE, Wertachtal	(D) • E EUROPE • 500 kW / (J) • E EUROPE • 500 kW
	ITALY RTV ITALIANA, Caltanissetta	ITALIAN • EUROPE, MIDEAST & N AFRICA • DS-2 • 50 kW
	ROMANIA †RADIO ROMANIA INTL, Bucharest	(D) • E EUROPE • 250 kW
	RUSSIA †R MOSCOW INTL, Khabarovsk	(D) • W NORTH AM • NORTH AMERICAN SVC • 120 kW
	†R TIKHIY OKEAN, Khabarovsk	(D) • PACIFIC & W NORTH AM • MARINERS • 120 kW
	RADIO MOSCOW, Zhigulevsk	(J) • DS-1 • 100 kW
	UNITED KINGDOM BBC, Rampisham	(D) • W EUROPE • 500 kW / (J) • W EUROPE • 500 kW
	USA †VOA, Via Woofferton, UK	(J) • E EUROPE • 300 kW
7180	**CANADA** †R CANADA INTL, Via Skelton, UK	(D) • EUROPE • 300 kW
	CYPRUS CYPRUS BC CORP, Zyyi	(D) • F-Su • EUROPE • 250 kW
	INDIA ALL INDIA RADIO, Bhopal	DS-A • 10 kW / Su • DS-A • 10 kW / ENGLISH, ETC • DS-A • 10 kW
	ALL INDIA RADIO, Port Blair	DS • 10 kW / ENGLISH & HINDI • DS • 10 kW
	IRAQ †REP OF IRAQ RADIO, Baghdad	MIDEAST • 250 kW / PERSIAN • MIDEAST • 250 kW
	JAPAN RADIO JAPAN/NHK, Via Moyabi, Gabon	E AFRICA • 500 kW
	RUSSIA †RADIO MOSCOW	Irr • DS-1
	†RUSSIA'S RADIO, Moscow	DS • 100 kW
	TURKEY VOICE OF TURKEY, Ankara	E EUROPE • 250 kW
	UNITED KINGDOM †BBC, Various Locations	E ASIA • 100/250 kW
	†BBC, Via Hong Kong	E ASIA • 250 kW
	†BBC, Via Zyyi, Cyprus	(D) • E EUROPE • 250 kW / (J) • E EUROPE & MIDEAST • 250 kW
	USA †R FREE AFGHANISTAN, Via Germany	(D) • W ASIA & S ASIA • 100 kW
	†RFE-RL, Via Germany	W ASIA • 100 kW / (D) • W ASIA • 100 kW / (D) • E EUROPE • 100 kW / (J) • W ASIA • 100 kW / (J) • E EUROPE • 100 kW
	†VOA, Via Germany	(D) • E ASIA • 500 kW
	†VOA, Via Woofferton, UK	(J) • E EUROPE • 300 kW
7185	**BULGARIA** †RADIO SOFIA, Sofia	(D) • EUROPE • 250 kW / (J) • E EUROPE • 100 kW
	GERMANY DEUTSCHE WELLE, Nauen	AFRICA • 100 kW
	MYANMAR (BURMA) †RADIO MYANMAR, Yangon	Alternative Frequency to 7155 kHz
(con'd)	**RUSSIA** †R MOSCOW INTL, Blagoveshchensk	(D) • E ASIA & SE ASIA • 500 kW

ENGLISH ▬   ARABIC ∞   CHINESE □□□   FRENCH ═   GERMAN ▭   RUSSIAN ═   SPANISH ▭   OTHER ▬

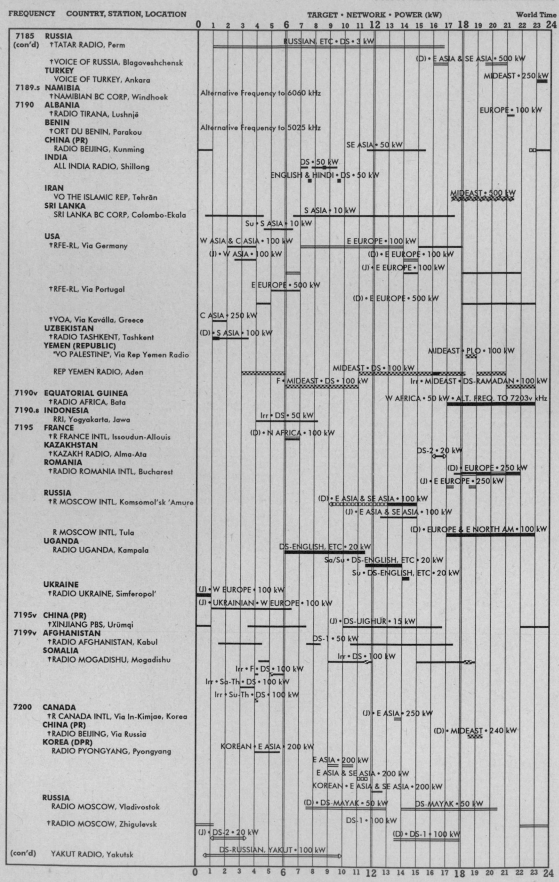

FREQUENCY   COUNTRY, STATION, LOCATION   TARGET • NETWORK • POWER (kW)   World Time

0 1 2 3 4 5 6 7 8 9 10 11 12 13 14 15 16 17 18 19 20 21 22 23 24

7185   RUSSIA
(con'd) †TATAR RADIO, Perm   RUSSIAN, ETC • DS • 3 kW

         †VOICE OF RUSSIA, Blagoveshchensk   (D) • E ASIA & SE ASIA • 500 kW
TURKEY
         VOICE OF TURKEY, Ankara   MIDEAST • 250 kW
7189.5 NAMIBIA
         †NAMIBIAN BC CORP, Windhoek   Alternative Frequency to 6060 kHz
7190   ALBANIA
         †RADIO TIRANA, Lushnjë   EUROPE • 100 kW
        BENIN
         †ORT DU BENIN, Parakou   Alternative Frequency to 5025 kHz
        CHINA (PR)
         RADIO BEIJING, Kunming   SE ASIA • 50 kW
        INDIA
         ALL INDIA RADIO, Shillong   DS • 50 kW
                                              ENGLISH & HINDI • DS • 50 kW
        IRAN
         VO THE ISLAMIC REP, Tehrān   MIDEAST • 500 kW
        SRI LANKA
         SRI LANKA BC CORP, Colombo-Ekala   S ASIA • 10 kW
                                            Su • S ASIA • 10 kW
        USA
         †RFE-RL, Via Germany   W ASIA & C ASIA • 100 kW   E EUROPE • 100 kW
                                         (J) • W ASIA • 100 kW   (D) • E EUROPE • 100 kW
                                                                        (J) • E EUROPE • 100 kW

         †RFE-RL, Via Portugal   E EUROPE • 500 kW   (D) • E EUROPE • 500 kW

         †VOA, Via Kaválla, Greece   C ASIA • 250 kW
        UZBEKISTAN
         †RADIO TASHKENT, Tashkent   (D) • S ASIA • 100 kW
        YEMEN (REPUBLIC)
         "VO PALESTINE", Via Rep Yemen Radio   MIDEAST • PLO • 100 kW

         REP YEMEN RADIO, Aden   MIDEAST • DS • 100 kW
                                            F • MIDEAST • DS • 100 kW   Irr • MIDEAST • DS-RAMADAN • 100 kW
7190v   EQUATORIAL GUINEA
         †RADIO AFRICA, Bata   W AFRICA • 50 kW • ALT. FREQ. TO 7203v kHz
7190.8 INDONESIA
         RRI, Yogyakarta, Jawa   Irr • DS • 50 kW
7195   FRANCE
         †R FRANCE INTL, Issoudun-Allouis (D) • N AFRICA • 100 kW
        KAZAKHSTAN
         †KAZAKH RADIO, Alma-Ata   DS-2 • 20 kW
        ROMANIA
         †RADIO ROMANIA INTL, Bucharest   (D) • EUROPE • 250 kW
                                                             (J) • E EUROPE • 250 kW
        RUSSIA
         †R MOSCOW INTL, Komsomol'sk 'Amure   (D) • E ASIA & SE ASIA • 100 kW
                                                     (J) • E ASIA & SE ASIA • 100 kW

         R MOSCOW INTL, Tula   (D) • EUROPE & E NORTH AM • 100 kW
        UGANDA
         RADIO UGANDA, Kampala   DS-ENGLISH, ETC • 20 kW
                                                    Sa/Su • DS-ENGLISH, ETC • 20 kW
                                                    Su • DS-ENGLISH, ETC • 20 kW
        UKRAINE
         †RADIO UKRAINE, Simferopol'   (J) • W EUROPE • 100 kW
                                         (J) • UKRAINIAN • W EUROPE • 100 kW
7195v   CHINA (PR)
         †XINJIANG PBS, Urümqi   (J) • DS-UIGHUR • 15 kW
7199v   AFGHANISTAN
         †RADIO AFGHANISTAN, Kabul   DS-1 • 50 kW
        SOMALIA
         †RADIO MOGADISHU, Mogadishu   Irr • DS • 100 kW
                                          Irr • F • DS • 100 kW
                                       Irr • Sa-Th • DS • 100 kW
                                       Irr • Su-Th • DS • 100 kW

7200   CANADA
         †R CANADA INTL, Via In-Kimjae, Korea   (J) • E ASIA • 250 kW
        CHINA (PR)
         †RADIO BEIJING, Via Russia   (D) • MIDEAST • 240 kW
        KOREA (DPR)
         RADIO PYONGYANG, Pyongyang   KOREAN • E ASIA • 200 kW
                                                    E ASIA • 200 kW
                                                    E ASIA & SE ASIA • 200 kW
                                                    KOREAN • E ASIA & SE ASIA • 200 kW
        RUSSIA
         RADIO MOSCOW, Vladivostok   (D) • DS-MAYAK • 50 kW   DS-MAYAK • 50 kW

         †RADIO MOSCOW, Zhigulevsk   DS-1 • 100 kW
                                         (J) • DS-2 • 20 kW
                                                             (D) • DS-1 • 100 kW
(con'd) YAKUT RADIO, Yakutsk   DS-RUSSIAN, YAKUT • 100 kW

0 1 2 3 4 5 6 7 8 9 10 11 12 13 14 15 16 17 18 19 20 21 22 23 24

SUMMER ONLY (J)   WINTER ONLY (D)   JAMMING / OR ∧   EARLIEST HEARD ◁   LATEST HEARD ▷   NEW OR CHANGED FOR 1993 †

FREQUENCY   COUNTRY, STATION, LOCATION   TARGET • NETWORK • POWER (kW)   World Time

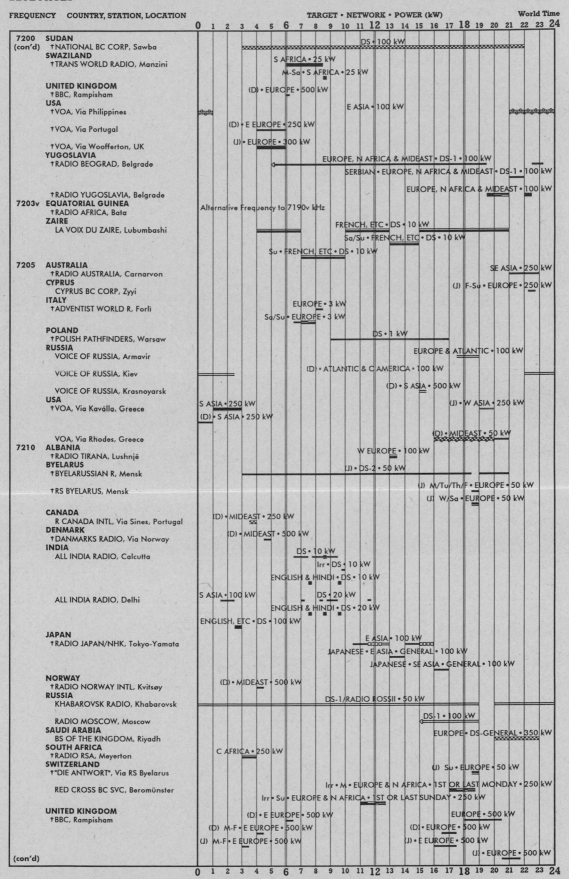

Freq	Country / Station / Location	Schedule notes
7200 (con'd)	**SUDAN** †NATIONAL BC CORP, Sawba	DS • 100 kW
	SWAZILAND †TRANS WORLD RADIO, Manzini	S AFRICA • 25 kW / M-Sa • S AFRICA • 25 kW
	UNITED KINGDOM †BBC, Rampisham	(D) • EUROPE • 500 kW
	USA †VOA, Via Philippines	E ASIA • 100 kW
	†VOA, Via Portugal	(D) • E EUROPE • 250 kW
	†VOA, Via Woofferton, UK	(J) • EUROPE • 300 kW
	YUGOSLAVIA †RADIO BEOGRAD, Belgrade	EUROPE, N AFRICA & MIDEAST • DS-1 • 100 kW / SERBIAN • EUROPE, N AFRICA & MIDEAST • DS-1 • 100 kW
	†RADIO YUGOSLAVIA, Belgrade	EUROPE, N AFRICA & MIDEAST • 100 kW
7203v	**EQUATORIAL GUINEA** †RADIO AFRICA, Bata	Alternative Frequency to 7190v kHz
	ZAIRE LA VOIX DU ZAIRE, Lubumbashi	FRENCH, ETC • DS • 10 kW / Sa/Su • FRENCH, ETC • DS • 10 kW / Su • FRENCH, ETC • DS • 10 kW
7205	**AUSTRALIA** †RADIO AUSTRALIA, Carnarvon	SE ASIA • 250 kW
	CYPRUS CYPRUS BC CORP, Zyyi	(J) F-Su • EUROPE • 250 kW
	ITALY †ADVENTIST WORLD R, Forlì	EUROPE • 3 kW / Sa/Su • EUROPE • 3 kW
	POLAND †POLISH PATHFINDERS, Warsaw	DS • 1 kW
	RUSSIA VOICE OF RUSSIA, Armavir	EUROPE & ATLANTIC • 100 kW
	VOICE OF RUSSIA, Kiev	(D) • ATLANTIC & C AMERICA • 100 kW
	VOICE OF RUSSIA, Krasnoyarsk	(D) • S ASIA • 500 kW
	USA †VOA, Via Kaválla, Greece	S ASIA • 250 kW / (D) • S ASIA • 250 kW / (J) • W ASIA • 250 kW
	VOA, Via Rhodes, Greece	(D) • MIDEAST • 50 kW
7210	**ALBANIA** †RADIO TIRANA, Lushnjë	W EUROPE • 100 kW
	BYELARUS †BYELARUSSIAN R, Mensk	(J) • DS-2 • 50 kW
	†RS BYELARUS, Mensk	(J) M/Tu/Th/F • EUROPE • 50 kW / (J) W/Sa • EUROPE • 50 kW
	CANADA R CANADA INTL, Via Sines, Portugal	(D) • MIDEAST • 250 kW
	DENMARK †DANMARKS RADIO, Via Norway	(D) • MIDEAST • 500 kW
	INDIA ALL INDIA RADIO, Calcutta	DS • 10 kW / Irr • DS • 10 kW / ENGLISH & HINDI • DS • 10 kW
	ALL INDIA RADIO, Delhi	S ASIA • 100 kW / DS • 20 kW / ENGLISH & HINDI • DS • 20 kW / ENGLISH, ETC • DS • 100 kW
	JAPAN †RADIO JAPAN/NHK, Tokyo-Yamata	E ASIA • 100 kW / JAPANESE • E ASIA • GENERAL • 100 kW / JAPANESE • SE ASIA • GENERAL • 100 kW
	NORWAY †RADIO NORWAY INTL, Kvitsøy	(D) • MIDEAST • 500 kW
	RUSSIA KHABAROVSK RADIO, Khabarovsk	DS-1/RADIO ROSSII • 50 kW
	RADIO MOSCOW, Moscow	DS-1 • 100 kW
	SAUDI ARABIA BS OF THE KINGDOM, Riyadh	EUROPE • DS-GENERAL • 350 kW
	SOUTH AFRICA †RADIO RSA, Meyerton	C AFRICA • 250 kW
	SWITZERLAND †"DIE ANTWORT", Via RS Byelarus	(J) Su • EUROPE • 50 kW / Irr • M • EUROPE & N AFRICA • 1ST OR LAST MONDAY • 250 kW
	RED CROSS BC SVC, Beromünster	Irr • Su • EUROPE & N AFRICA • 1ST OR LAST SUNDAY • 250 kW
	UNITED KINGDOM †BBC, Rampisham	(D) • E EUROPE • 500 kW / EUROPE • 500 kW / (D) M-F • E EUROPE • 500 kW / (D) • EUROPE • 500 kW / (J) M-F • E EUROPE • 500 kW / (J) • E EUROPE • 500 kW / (J) • EUROPE • 500 kW

(con'd)

ENGLISH ▬   ARABIC ▨   CHINESE □□□   FRENCH ▬   GERMAN ▬   RUSSIAN ═   SPANISH ▬   OTHER ▬

| FREQUENCY | COUNTRY, STATION, LOCATION | TARGET • NETWORK • POWER (kW) | World Time |

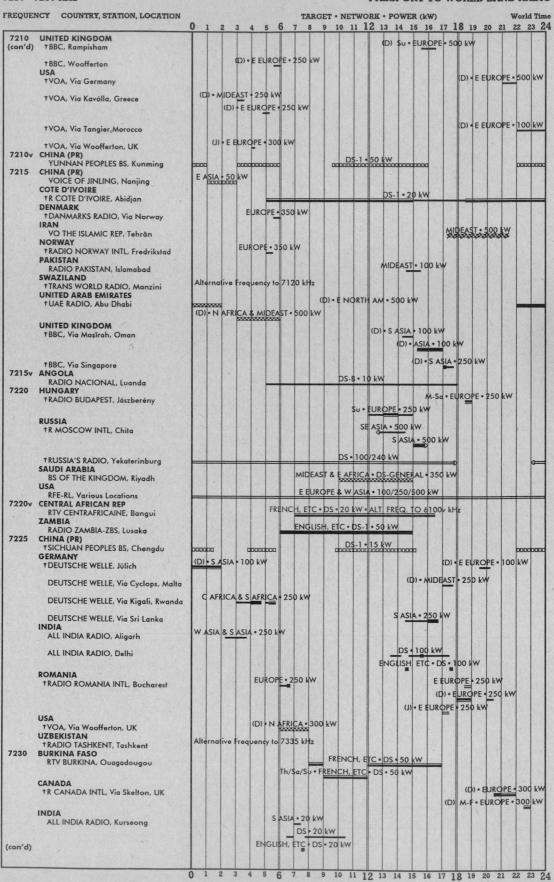

FREQUENCY	COUNTRY, STATION, LOCATION	TARGET • NETWORK • POWER (kW)
7210 (con'd)	UNITED KINGDOM	
	†BBC, Rampisham	(D) Su • EUROPE • 500 kW
	†BBC, Woofferton	(D) • E EUROPE • 250 kW
	USA	
	†VOA, Via Germany	(D) • E EUROPE • 500 kW
	†VOA, Via Kaválla, Greece	(D) • MIDEAST • 250 kW / (D) • E EUROPE • 250 kW
	†VOA, Via Tangier, Morocco	(D) • E EUROPE • 100 kW
	†VOA, Via Woofferton, UK	(J) • E EUROPE • 300 kW
7210v	CHINA (PR)	
	YUNNAN PEOPLES BS, Kunming	DS-1 • 50 kW
7215	CHINA (PR)	
	VOICE OF JINLING, Nanjing	E ASIA • 50 kW
	COTE D'IVOIRE	
	†R COTE D'IVOIRE, Abidjan	DS-1 • 20 kW
	DENMARK	
	†DANMARKS RADIO, Via Norway	EUROPE • 350 kW
	IRAN	
	VO THE ISLAMIC REP, Tehrān	MIDEAST • 500 kW
	NORWAY	
	†RADIO NORWAY INTL, Fredrikstad	EUROPE • 350 kW
	PAKISTAN	
	RADIO PAKISTAN, Islamabad	MIDEAST • 100 kW
	SWAZILAND	
	†TRANS WORLD RADIO, Manzini	Alternative Frequency to 7120 kHz
	UNITED ARAB EMIRATES	
	†UAE RADIO, Abu Dhabi	(D) • E NORTH AM • 500 kW / (D) • N AFRICA & MIDEAST • 500 kW
	UNITED KINGDOM	
	†BBC, Via Maşīrah, Oman	(D) • S ASIA • 100 kW / (D) • ASIA • 100 kW
	†BBC, Via Singapore	(D) • S ASIA • 250 kW
7215v	ANGOLA	
	RADIO NACIONAL, Luanda	DS-B • 10 kW
7220	HUNGARY	
	†RADIO BUDAPEST, Jászberény	M-Sa • EUROPE • 250 kW / Su • EUROPE • 250 kW
	RUSSIA	
	†R MOSCOW INTL, Chita	SE ASIA • 500 kW / S ASIA • 500 kW
	†RUSSIA'S RADIO, Yekaterinburg	DS • 100/240 kW
	SAUDI ARABIA	
	BS OF THE KINGDOM, Riyadh	MIDEAST & E AFRICA • DS-GENERAL • 350 kW
	USA	
	RFE-RL, Various Locations	E EUROPE & W ASIA • 100/250/500 kW
7220v	CENTRAL AFRICAN REP	
	RTV CENTRAFRICAINE, Bangui	FRENCH, ETC • DS • 20 kW • ALT. FREQ. TO 6100v kHz
	ZAMBIA	
	RADIO ZAMBIA-ZBS, Lusaka	ENGLISH, ETC • DS-1 • 50 kW
7225	CHINA (PR)	
	†SICHUAN PEOPLES BS, Chengdu	DS-1 • 15 kW
	GERMANY	
	†DEUTSCHE WELLE, Jülich	(D) • S ASIA • 100 kW / (D) • E EUROPE • 100 kW
	DEUTSCHE WELLE, Via Cyclops, Malta	(D) • MIDEAST • 250 kW
	DEUTSCHE WELLE, Via Kigali, Rwanda	C AFRICA & S AFRICA • 250 kW
	DEUTSCHE WELLE, Via Sri Lanka	S ASIA • 250 kW
	INDIA	
	ALL INDIA RADIO, Aligarh	W ASIA & S ASIA • 250 kW
	ALL INDIA RADIO, Delhi	DS • 100 kW / ENGLISH, ETC • DS • 100 kW
	ROMANIA	
	†RADIO ROMANIA INTL, Bucharest	EUROPE • 250 kW / E EUROPE • 250 kW / (D) • EUROPE • 250 kW / (J) • E EUROPE • 250 kW
	USA	
	†VOA, Via Woofferton, UK	(D) • N AFRICA • 300 kW
	UZBEKISTAN	
	†RADIO TASHKENT, Tashkent	Alternative Frequency to 7335 kHz
7230	BURKINA FASO	
	RTV BURKINA, Ouagadougou	FRENCH, ETC • DS • 50 kW / Th/Sa/Su • FRENCH, ETC • DS • 50 kW
	CANADA	
	†R CANADA INTL, Via Skelton, UK	(D) • EUROPE • 300 kW / (D) M-F • EUROPE • 300 kW
	INDIA	
	ALL INDIA RADIO, Kurseong	S ASIA • 20 kW / DS • 20 kW / ENGLISH, ETC • DS • 20 kW
(con'd)		

FREQUENCY   COUNTRY, STATION, LOCATION

TARGET • NETWORK • POWER (kW)

World Time

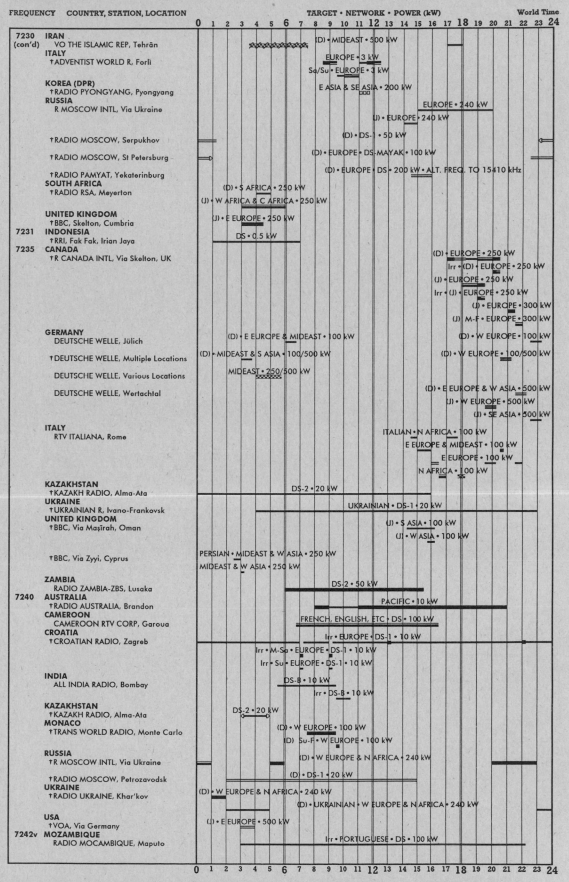

7230 (con'd)	IRAN	
	VO THE ISLAMIC REP, Tehrān	(D) • MIDEAST • 500 kW
	ITALY	
	†ADVENTIST WORLD R, Forlì	EUROPE • 3 kW / Sa/Su • EUROPE • 3 kW
	KOREA (DPR)	
	†RADIO PYONGYANG, Pyongyang	E ASIA & SE ASIA • 200 kW
	RUSSIA	
	R MOSCOW INTL, Via Ukraine	EUROPE • 240 kW / (J) • EUROPE • 240 kW
	†RADIO MOSCOW, Serpukhov	(D) • DS-1 • 50 kW
	†RADIO MOSCOW, St Petersburg	(D) • EUROPE • DS-MAYAK • 100 kW
	†RADIO PAMYAT, Yekaterinburg	(D) • EUROPE • DS • 200 kW • ALT. FREQ. TO 15410 kHz
	SOUTH AFRICA	
	†RADIO RSA, Meyerton	(D) • S AFRICA • 250 kW / (J) • W AFRICA & C AFRICA • 250 kW
	UNITED KINGDOM	
	†BBC, Skelton, Cumbria	(J) • E EUROPE • 250 kW
7231	INDONESIA	
	†RRI, Fak Fak, Irian Jaya	DS • 0.5 kW
7235	CANADA	
	†R CANADA INTL, Via Skelton, UK	(D) • EUROPE • 250 kW / Irr • (D) • EUROPE • 250 kW / (J) • EUROPE • 250 kW / Irr • (J) • EUROPE • 250 kW / (J) • EUROPE • 300 kW / (J) • M-F • EUROPE • 300 kW
	GERMANY	
	DEUTSCHE WELLE, Jülich	(D) • E EUROPE & MIDEAST • 100 kW / (D) • W EUROPE • 100 kW
	†DEUTSCHE WELLE, Multiple Locations	(D) • MIDEAST & S ASIA • 100/500 kW / (D) • W EUROPE • 100/500 kW
	DEUTSCHE WELLE, Various Locations	MIDEAST • 250/500 kW
	DEUTSCHE WELLE, Wertachtal	(D) • E EUROPE & W ASIA • 500 kW / (J) • W EUROPE • 500 kW / (J) • SE ASIA • 500 kW
	ITALY	
	RTV ITALIANA, Rome	ITALIAN • N AFRICA • 100 kW / E EUROPE & MIDEAST • 100 kW / E EUROPE • 100 kW / N AFRICA • 100 kW
	KAZAKHSTAN	
	†KAZAKH RADIO, Alma-Ata	DS-2 • 20 kW
	UKRAINE	
	†UKRAINIAN R, Ivano-Frankovsk	UKRAINIAN • DS-1 • 20 kW
	UNITED KINGDOM	
	†BBC, Via Maşīrah, Oman	(J) • S ASIA • 100 kW / (J) • W ASIA • 100 kW
	†BBC, Via Zyyi, Cyprus	PERSIAN • MIDEAST & W ASIA • 250 kW / MIDEAST & W ASIA • 250 kW
	ZAMBIA	
	RADIO ZAMBIA-ZBS, Lusaka	DS-2 • 50 kW
7240	AUSTRALIA	
	†RADIO AUSTRALIA, Brandon	PACIFIC • 10 kW
	CAMEROON	
	CAMEROON RTV CORP, Garoua	FRENCH, ENGLISH, ETC • DS • 100 kW
	CROATIA	
	†CROATIAN RADIO, Zagreb	Irr • EUROPE • DS-1 • 10 kW / Irr • M-Sa • EUROPE • DS-1 • 10 kW / Irr • Su • EUROPE • DS-1 • 10 kW
	INDIA	
	ALL INDIA RADIO, Bombay	DS-B • 10 kW / Irr • DS-B • 10 kW
	KAZAKHSTAN	
	†KAZAKH RADIO, Alma-Ata	DS-2 • 20 kW
	MONACO	
	†TRANS WORLD RADIO, Monte Carlo	(D) • W EUROPE • 100 kW / (D) • Su-F • W EUROPE • 100 kW
	RUSSIA	
	†R MOSCOW INTL, Via Ukraine	(D) • W EUROPE & N AFRICA • 240 kW
	†RADIO MOSCOW, Petrozavodsk	(D) • DS-1 • 20 kW
	UKRAINE	
	†RADIO UKRAINE, Khar'kov	(D) • W EUROPE & N AFRICA • 240 kW / (D) • UKRAINIAN • W EUROPE & N AFRICA • 240 kW
	USA	
	†VOA, Via Germany	(J) • E EUROPE • 500 kW
7242v	MOZAMBIQUE	
	RADIO MOCAMBIQUE, Maputo	Irr • PORTUGUESE • DS • 100 kW

ENGLISH ▬▬   ARABIC ⨯⨯⨯   CHINESE □□□   FRENCH ═══   GERMAN ▬▬   RUSSIAN ══   SPANISH ══   OTHER ▬

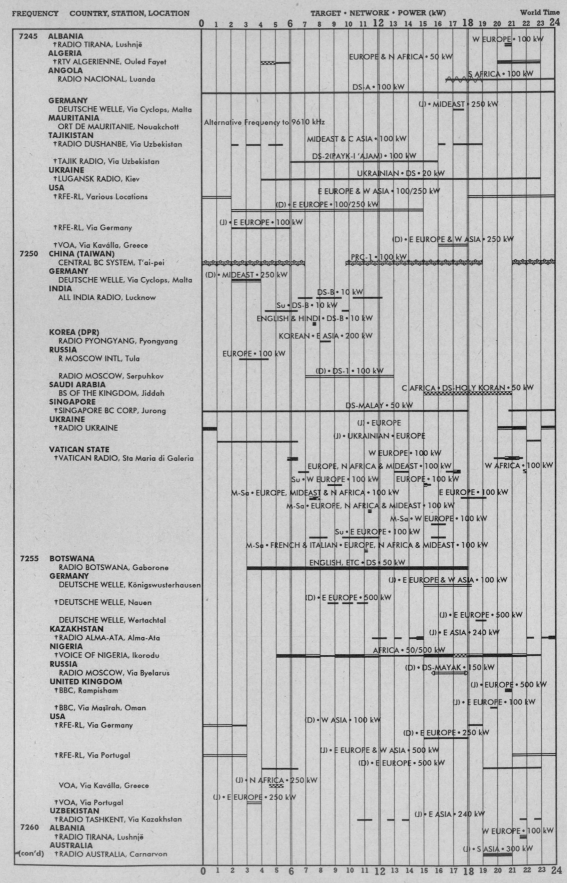

The broadcast schedule chart lists the following entries:

7245 ALBANIA — †RADIO TIRANA, Lushnjë — W EUROPE • 100 kW

ALGERIA — †RTV ALGERIENNE, Ouled Fayet — EUROPE & N AFRICA • 50 kW

ANGOLA — RADIO NACIONAL, Luanda — S AFRICA • 100 kW; DS-A • 100 kW

GERMANY — DEUTSCHE WELLE, Via Cyclops, Malta — (J) • MIDEAST • 250 kW

MAURITANIA — ORT DE MAURITANIE, Nouakchott — Alternative Frequency to 9610 kHz

TAJIKISTAN — †RADIO DUSHANBE, Via Uzbekistan — MIDEAST & C ASIA • 100 kW

†TAJIK RADIO, Via Uzbekistan — DS-2(PAYK-I 'AJAM) • 100 kW

UKRAINE — †LUGANSK RADIO, Kiev — UKRAINIAN • DS • 20 kW

USA — †RFE-RL, Various Locations — E EUROPE & W ASIA • 100/250 kW; (D) • E EUROPE • 100/250 kW

†RFE-RL, Via Germany — (J) • E EUROPE • 100 kW

†VOA, Via Kaválla, Greece — (D) • E EUROPE & W ASIA • 250 kW

7250 CHINA (TAIWAN) — CENTRAL BC SYSTEM, T'ai-pei — PRC-1 • 100 kW

GERMANY — DEUTSCHE WELLE, Via Cyclops, Malta — (D) • MIDEAST • 250 kW

INDIA — ALL INDIA RADIO, Lucknow — DS-B • 10 kW; Su • DS-B • 10 kW; ENGLISH & HINDI • DS-B • 10 kW

KOREA (DPR) — RADIO PYONGYANG, Pyongyang — KOREAN • E ASIA • 200 kW

RUSSIA — R MOSCOW INTL, Tula — EUROPE • 100 kW

RADIO MOSCOW, Serpuhkov — (D) • DS-1 • 100 kW

SAUDI ARABIA — BS OF THE KINGDOM, Jiddah — C AFRICA • DS-HOLY KORAN • 50 kW

SINGAPORE — †SINGAPORE BC CORP, Jurong — DS-MALAY • 50 kW

UKRAINE — †RADIO UKRAINE — (J) • EUROPE; (J) • UKRAINIAN • EUROPE

VATICAN STATE — †VATICAN RADIO, Sta Maria di Galeria — W EUROPE • 100 kW; EUROPE, N AFRICA & MIDEAST • 100 kW; W AFRICA • 100 kW; Su • W EUROPE • 100 kW; EUROPE • 100 kW; M-Sa • EUROPE, MIDEAST & N AFRICA • 100 kW; E EUROPE • 100 kW; M-Sa • EUROPE, N AFRICA & MIDEAST • 100 kW; M-Sa • W EUROPE • 100 kW; Su • E EUROPE • 100 kW; M-Sa • FRENCH & ITALIAN • EUROPE, N AFRICA & MIDEAST • 100 kW

7255 BOTSWANA — RADIO BOTSWANA, Gaborone — ENGLISH, ETC • DS • 50 kW

GERMANY — DEUTSCHE WELLE, Königswusterhausen — (J) • E EUROPE & W ASIA • 100 kW

†DEUTSCHE WELLE, Nauen — (D) • E EUROPE • 500 kW

DEUTSCHE WELLE, Wertachtal — (J) • E EUROPE • 500 kW

KAZAKHSTAN — †RADIO ALMA-ATA, Alma-Ata — (J) • E ASIA • 240 kW

NIGERIA — †VOICE OF NIGERIA, Ikorodu — AFRICA • 50/500 kW

RUSSIA — RADIO MOSCOW, Via Byelarus — (D) • DS-MAYAK • 150 kW

UNITED KINGDOM — †BBC, Rampisham — (J) • EUROPE • 500 kW

†BBC, Via Maşīrah, Oman — (J) • E EUROPE • 100 kW

USA — †RFE-RL, Via Germany — (D) • W ASIA • 100 kW; (D) • E EUROPE • 250 kW

†RFE-RL, Via Portugal — (J) • E EUROPE & W ASIA • 500 kW; (D) • E EUROPE • 500 kW

VOA, Via Kaválla, Greece — (J) • N AFRICA • 250 kW

†VOA, Via Portugal — (J) • E EUROPE • 250 kW

UZBEKISTAN — †RADIO TASHKENT, Via Kazakhstan — (J) • E ASIA • 240 kW

7260 ALBANIA — †RADIO TIRANA, Lushnjë — W EUROPE • 100 kW

AUSTRALIA — (con'd) †RADIO AUSTRALIA, Carnarvon — (J) • S ASIA • 300 kW

FREQUENCY   COUNTRY, STATION, LOCATION

TARGET • NETWORK • POWER (kW)

World Time

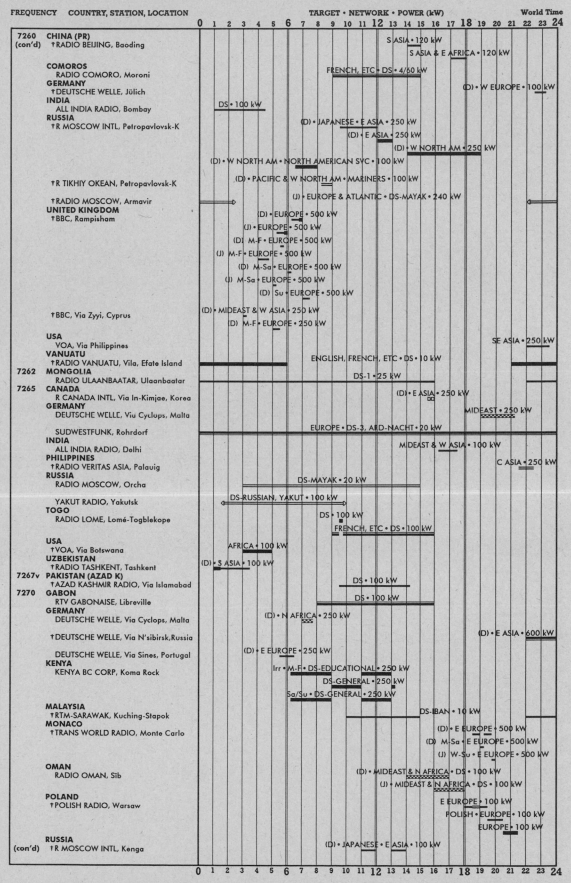

Freq	Country / Station / Location	Schedule
7260 (con'd)	**CHINA (PR)** †RADIO BEIJING, Baoding	S ASIA • 120 kW; S ASIA & E AFRICA • 120 kW
	COMOROS RADIO COMORO, Moroni	FRENCH, ETC • DS • 4/60 kW
	GERMANY †DEUTSCHE WELLE, Jülich	(D) • W EUROPE • 100 kW
	INDIA ALL INDIA RADIO, Bombay	DS • 100 kW
	RUSSIA †R MOSCOW INTL, Petropavlovsk-K	(D) • JAPANESE • E ASIA • 250 kW; (D) • E ASIA • 250 kW; (D) • W NORTH AM • 250 kW; (D) • W NORTH AM • NORTH AMERICAN SVC • 100 kW
	†R TIKHIY OKEAN, Petropavlovsk-K	(D) • PACIFIC & W NORTH AM • MARINERS • 100 kW
	†RADIO MOSCOW, Armavir	(J) • EUROPE & ATLANTIC • DS-MAYAK • 240 kW
	UNITED KINGDOM †BBC, Rampisham	(D) • EUROPE • 500 kW; (J) • EUROPE • 500 kW; (D) M-F • EUROPE • 500 kW; (J) M-F • EUROPE • 500 kW; (D) M-Sa • EUROPE • 500 kW; (J) M-Sa • EUROPE • 500 kW; (D) Su • EUROPE • 500 kW
	†BBC, Via Zyyi, Cyprus	(D) • MIDEAST & W ASIA • 250 kW; (D) M-F • EUROPE • 250 kW
	USA VOA, Via Philippines	SE ASIA • 250 kW
	VANUATU †RADIO VANUATU, Vila, Efate Island	ENGLISH, FRENCH, ETC • DS • 10 kW
7262	**MONGOLIA** RADIO ULAANBAATAR, Ulaanbaatar	DS-1 • 25 kW
7265	**CANADA** R CANADA INTL, Via In-Kimjae, Korea	(D) • E ASIA • 250 kW
	GERMANY DEUTSCHE WELLE, Via Cyclops, Malta	MIDEAST • 250 kW
	SUDWESTFUNK, Rohrdorf	EUROPE • DS-3, ARD-NACHT • 20 kW
	INDIA ALL INDIA RADIO, Delhi	MIDEAST & W ASIA • 100 kW
	PHILIPPINES †RADIO VERITAS ASIA, Palauig	C ASIA • 250 kW
	RUSSIA RADIO MOSCOW, Orcha	DS-MAYAK • 20 kW
	YAKUT RADIO, Yakutsk	DS-RUSSIAN, YAKUT • 100 kW
	TOGO RADIO LOME, Lomé-Togblekope	DS • 100 kW; FRENCH, ETC • DS • 100 kW
	USA †VOA, Via Botswana	AFRICA • 100 kW
	UZBEKISTAN †RADIO TASHKENT, Tashkent	(D) • S ASIA • 100 kW
7267v	**PAKISTAN (AZAD K)** †AZAD KASHMIR RADIO, Via Islamabad	DS • 100 kW
7270	**GABON** RTV GABONAISE, Libreville	DS • 100 kW
	GERMANY DEUTSCHE WELLE, Via Cyclops, Malta	(D) • N AFRICA • 250 kW
	†DEUTSCHE WELLE, Via N'sibirsk, Russia	(D) • E ASIA • 600 kW
	DEUTSCHE WELLE, Via Sines, Portugal	(D) • E EUROPE • 250 kW
	KENYA KENYA BC CORP, Koma Rock	Irr • M-F • DS-EDUCATIONAL • 250 kW; DS-GENERAL • 250 kW; Sa/Su • DS-GENERAL • 250 kW
	MALAYSIA †RTM-SARAWAK, Kuching-Stapok	DS-IBAN • 10 kW
	MONACO †TRANS WORLD RADIO, Monte Carlo	(D) • E EUROPE • 500 kW; (D) M-Sa • E EUROPE • 500 kW; (J) W-Su • E EUROPE • 500 kW
	OMAN RADIO OMAN, Sīb	(D) • MIDEAST & N AFRICA • DS • 100 kW; (J) • MIDEAST & N AFRICA • DS • 100 kW
	POLAND †POLISH RADIO, Warsaw	E EUROPE • 100 kW; POLISH • EUROPE • 100 kW; EUROPE • 100 kW
(con'd)	**RUSSIA** †R MOSCOW INTL, Kenga	(D) • JAPANESE • E ASIA • 100 kW

ENGLISH ▬ ARABIC ▨ CHINESE ▫▫▫ FRENCH ══ GERMAN ▬▬ RUSSIAN ═══ SPANISH ▬▬ OTHER ▬

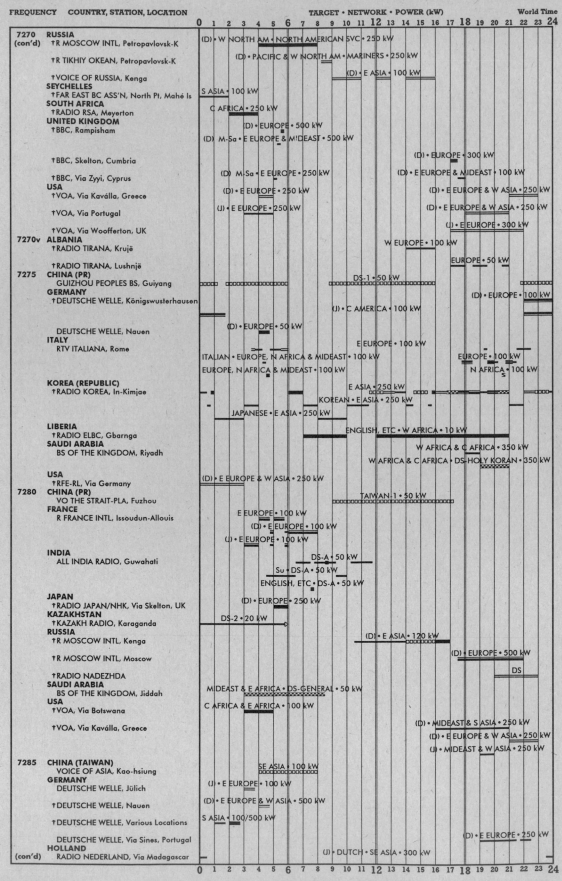

7270 RUSSIA
(con'd) †R MOSCOW INTL, Petropavlovsk-K   (D) • W NORTH AM • NORTH AMERICAN SVC • 250 kW

†R TIKHIY OKEAN, Petropavlovsk-K   (D) • PACIFIC & W NORTH AM • MARINERS • 250 kW

†VOICE OF RUSSIA, Kenga   (D) • E ASIA • 100 kW
SEYCHELLES
†FAR EAST BC ASS'N, North Pt, Mahé Is   S ASIA • 100 kW
SOUTH AFRICA
†RADIO RSA, Meyerton   C AFRICA • 250 kW
UNITED KINGDOM
†BBC, Rampisham   (D) • EUROPE • 500 kW
(D) M-Sa • E EUROPE & MIDEAST • 500 kW

†BBC, Skelton, Cumbria   (D) • EUROPE • 300 kW

†BBC, Via Zyyi, Cyprus   (D) M-Sa • E EUROPE • 250 kW   (D) • E EUROPE & MIDEAST • 100 kW
USA
†VOA, Via Kaválla, Greece   (D) • E EUROPE • 250 kW   (D) • E EUROPE & W ASIA • 250 kW

†VOA, Via Portugal   (J) • E EUROPE • 250 kW   (D) • E EUROPE & W ASIA • 250 kW

†VOA, Via Woofferton, UK   (J) • E EUROPE • 300 kW
7270v ALBANIA
†RADIO TIRANA, Krujë   W EUROPE • 100 kW

†RADIO TIRANA, Lushnjë   EUROPE • 50 kW
7275 CHINA (PR)
GUIZHOU PEOPLES BS, Guiyang   DS-1 • 50 kW
GERMANY
†DEUTSCHE WELLE, Königswusterhausen   (D) • EUROPE • 100 kW
(J) • C AMERICA • 100 kW

DEUTSCHE WELLE, Nauen   (D) • EUROPE • 50 kW
ITALY
RTV ITALIANA, Rome   E EUROPE • 100 kW
ITALIAN • EUROPE, N AFRICA & MIDEAST • 100 kW   EUROPE • 100 kW
EUROPE, N AFRICA & MIDEAST • 100 kW   N AFRICA • 100 kW

KOREA (REPUBLIC)
†RADIO KOREA, In-Kimjae   E ASIA • 250 kW
KOREAN • E ASIA • 250 kW
JAPANESE • E ASIA • 250 kW

LIBERIA
†RADIO ELBC, Gbarnga   ENGLISH, ETC • W AFRICA • 10 kW
SAUDI ARABIA
BS OF THE KINGDOM, Riyadh   W AFRICA & C AFRICA • 350 kW
W AFRICA & C AFRICA • DS-HOLY KORAN • 350 kW

USA
†RFE-RL, Via Germany   (D) • E EUROPE & W ASIA • 250 kW
7280 CHINA (PR)
VO THE STRAIT-PLA, Fuzhou   TAIWAN-1 • 50 kW
FRANCE
R FRANCE INTL, Issoudun-Allouis   E EUROPE • 100 kW
(D) • E EUROPE • 100 kW
(J) • E EUROPE • 100 kW

INDIA
ALL INDIA RADIO, Guwahati   DS-A • 50 kW
Su • DS-A • 50 kW
ENGLISH, ETC • DS-A • 50 kW

JAPAN
†RADIO JAPAN/NHK, Via Skelton, UK   (D) • EUROPE • 250 kW
KAZAKHSTAN
†KAZAKH RADIO, Karaganda   DS-2 • 20 kW
RUSSIA
†R MOSCOW INTL, Kenga   (D) • E ASIA • 120 kW

†R MOSCOW INTL, Moscow   (D) • EUROPE • 500 kW

†RADIO NADEZHDA   DS
SAUDI ARABIA
BS OF THE KINGDOM, Jiddah   MIDEAST & E AFRICA • DS-GENERAL • 50 kW
USA
†VOA, Via Botswana   C AFRICA & E AFRICA • 100 kW

†VOA, Via Kaválla, Greece   (D) • MIDEAST & S ASIA • 250 kW
(D) • E EUROPE & W ASIA • 250 kW
(J) • MIDEAST & W ASIA • 250 kW

7285 CHINA (TAIWAN)
VOICE OF ASIA, Kao-hsiung   SE ASIA • 100 kW
GERMANY
DEUTSCHE WELLE, Jülich   (J) • E EUROPE • 100 kW

†DEUTSCHE WELLE, Nauen   (D) • E EUROPE & W ASIA • 500 kW

†DEUTSCHE WELLE, Various Locations   S ASIA • 100/500 kW

DEUTSCHE WELLE, Via Sines, Portugal   (D) • E EUROPE • 250 kW
HOLLAND
(con'd) RADIO NEDERLAND, Via Madagascar   (J) • DUTCH • SE ASIA • 300 kW

FREQUENCY   COUNTRY, STATION, LOCATION   TARGET • NETWORK • POWER (kW)   World Time

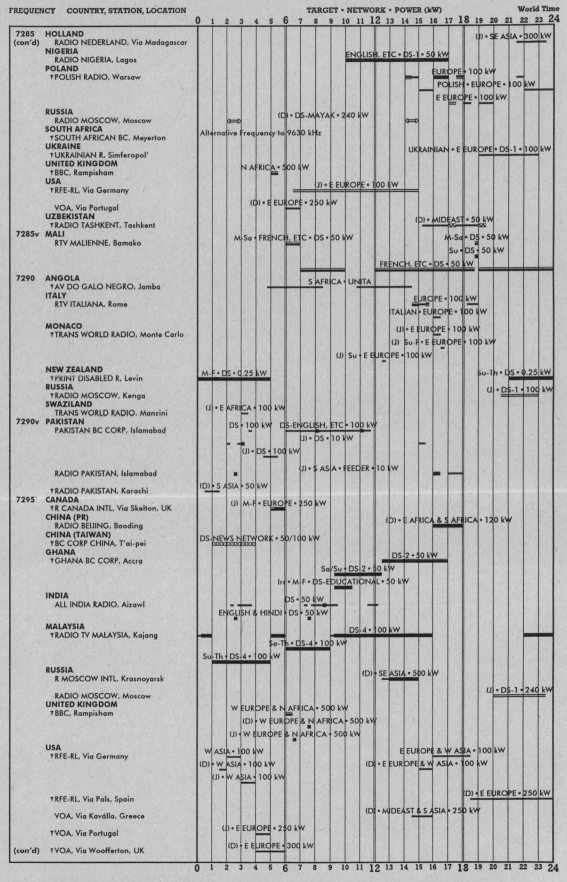

FREQUENCY	COUNTRY, STATION, LOCATION	TARGET • NETWORK • POWER (kW)
7285 (con'd)	HOLLAND RADIO NEDERLAND, Via Madagascar	(J) • SE ASIA • 300 kW
	NIGERIA RADIO NIGERIA, Lagos	ENGLISH, ETC • DS-1 • 50 kW
	POLAND †POLISH RADIO, Warsaw	EUROPE • 100 kW POLISH • EUROPE • 100 kW E EUROPE • 100 kW
	RUSSIA RADIO MOSCOW, Moscow	(D) • DS-MAYAK • 240 kW
	SOUTH AFRICA †SOUTH AFRICAN BC, Meyerton	Alternative Frequency to 9630 kHz
	UKRAINE †UKRAINIAN R, Simferopol'	UKRAINIAN • E EUROPE • DS-1 • 100 kW
	UNITED KINGDOM †BBC, Rampisham	N AFRICA • 500 kW
	USA †RFE-RL, Via Germany	(J) • E EUROPE • 100 kW
	VOA, Via Portugal	(D) • E EUROPE • 250 kW
	UZBEKISTAN †RADIO TASHKENT, Tashkent	(D) • MIDEAST • 50 kW
7285v	MALI RTV MALIENNE, Bamako	M-Sa • FRENCH, ETC • DS • 50 kW M-Sa • DS • 50 kW Su • DS • 50 kW FRENCH, ETC • DS • 50 kW
7290	ANGOLA †AV DO GALO NEGRO, Jamba	S AFRICA • UNITA
	ITALY RTV ITALIANA, Rome	EUROPE • 100 kW ITALIAN • EUROPE • 100 kW
	MONACO †TRANS WORLD RADIO, Monte Carlo	(J) • E EUROPE • 100 kW (J) Su-F • E EUROPE • 100 kW (J) Su • E EUROPE • 100 kW
	NEW ZEALAND †PRINT DISABLED R, Levin	M-F • DS • 0.25 kW Su-Th • DS • 0.25 kW
	RUSSIA †RADIO MOSCOW, Kenga	(J) • DS-1 • 100 kW
	SWAZILAND TRANS WORLD RADIO, Manzini	(J) • E AFRICA • 100 kW
7290v	PAKISTAN PAKISTAN BC CORP, Islamabad	DS • 100 kW DS-ENGLISH, ETC • 100 kW (J) • DS • 10 kW (J) • DS • 100 kW
	RADIO PAKISTAN, Islamabad	(J) • S ASIA • FEEDER • 10 kW
	†RADIO PAKISTAN, Karachi	(D) • S ASIA • 50 kW
7295	CANADA †R CANADA INTL, Via Skelton, UK	(J) M-F • EUROPE • 250 kW
	CHINA (PR) RADIO BEIJING, Baoding	(D) • E AFRICA & S AFRICA • 120 kW
	CHINA (TAIWAN) †BC CORP CHINA, T'ai-pei	DS-NEWS NETWORK • 50/100 kW
	GHANA †GHANA BC CORP, Accra	DS-2 • 50 kW Sa/Su • DS-2 • 50 kW Irr • M-F • DS-EDUCATIONAL • 50 kW
	INDIA ALL INDIA RADIO, Aizawl	DS • 50 kW ENGLISH & HINDI • DS • 50 kW
	MALAYSIA †RADIO TV MALAYSIA, Kajang	DS-4 • 100 kW Sa-Th • DS-4 • 100 kW Su-Th • DS-4 • 100 kW
	RUSSIA R MOSCOW INTL, Krasnoyarsk	(D) • SE ASIA • 500 kW
	RADIO MOSCOW, Moscow	(J) • DS-1 • 240 kW
	UNITED KINGDOM †BBC, Rampisham	W EUROPE & N AFRICA • 500 kW (D) • W EUROPE & N AFRICA • 500 kW (J) • W EUROPE & N AFRICA • 500 kW
	USA †RFE-RL, Via Germany	W ASIA • 100 kW E EUROPE & W ASIA • 100 kW (D) • W ASIA • 100 kW (D) • E EUROPE & W ASIA • 100 kW (J) • W ASIA • 100 kW
	†RFE-RL, Via Pals, Spain	(D) • E EUROPE • 250 kW
	VOA, Via Kaválla, Greece	(D) • MIDEAST & S ASIA • 250 kW
	†VOA, Via Portugal	(J) • E EUROPE • 250 kW
(con'd)	†VOA, Via Woofferton, UK	(D) • E EUROPE • 300 kW

ENGLISH ▬▬   ARABIC ≋≋≋   CHINESE □□□   FRENCH ══   GERMAN ▬▬   RUSSIAN ══   SPANISH ══   OTHER ▬▬

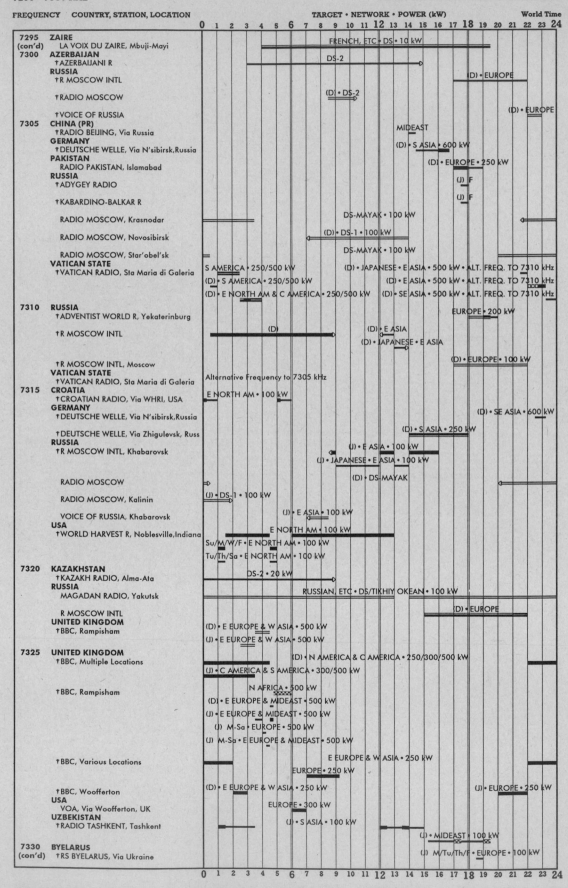

FREQUENCY	COUNTRY, STATION, LOCATION	TARGET • NETWORK • POWER (kW) / World Time

7295
(con'd) **ZAIRE**
  LA VOIX DU ZAIRE, Mbuji-Mayi — FRENCH, ETC • DS • 10 kW

7300 **AZERBAIJAN**
  †AZERBAIJANI R — DS-2

RUSSIA
  †R MOSCOW INTL — (D) • EUROPE

  †RADIO MOSCOW — (D) • DS-2

  †VOICE OF RUSSIA — (D) • EUROPE

7305 **CHINA (PR)**
  †RADIO BEIJING, Via Russia — MIDEAST

GERMANY
  †DEUTSCHE WELLE, Via N'sibirsk, Russia — (D) • S ASIA • 600 kW

PAKISTAN
  RADIO PAKISTAN, Islamabad — (D) • EUROPE • 250 kW

RUSSIA
  †ADYGEY RADIO — (J) F

  †KABARDINO-BALKAR R — (J) F

  RADIO MOSCOW, Krasnodar — DS-MAYAK • 100 kW

  RADIO MOSCOW, Novosibirsk — (D) • DS-1 • 100 kW

  RADIO MOSCOW, Star'obel'sk — DS-MAYAK • 100 kW

VATICAN STATE
  †VATICAN RADIO, Sta Maria di Galeria — S AMERICA • 250/500 kW / (D) • JAPANESE • E ASIA • 500 kW • ALT. FREQ. TO 7310 kHz
  (D) • S AMERICA • 250/500 kW / (D) • E ASIA • 500 kW • ALT. FREQ. TO 7310 kHz
  (D) • E NORTH AM & C AMERICA • 250/500 kW / (D) • SE ASIA • 500 kW • ALT. FREQ. TO 7310 kHz

7310 **RUSSIA**
  †ADVENTIST WORLD R, Yekaterinburg — EUROPE • 200 kW

  †R MOSCOW INTL — (D) / (D) • E ASIA / (D) • JAPANESE • E ASIA

  †R MOSCOW INTL, Moscow — (D) • EUROPE • 100 kW

VATICAN STATE
  †VATICAN RADIO, Sta Maria di Galeria — Alternative Frequency to 7305 kHz

7315 **CROATIA**
  †CROATIAN RADIO, Via WHRI, USA — E NORTH AM • 100 kW

GERMANY
  †DEUTSCHE WELLE, Via N'sibirsk, Russia — (D) • SE ASIA • 600 kW

  †DEUTSCHE WELLE, Via Zhigulevsk, Russ — (D) • S ASIA • 250 kW

RUSSIA
  †R MOSCOW INTL, Khabarovsk — (J) • E ASIA • 100 kW / (J) • JAPANESE • E ASIA • 100 kW

  RADIO MOSCOW — (D) • DS-MAYAK

  RADIO MOSCOW, Kalinin — (J) • DS-1 • 100 kW

  VOICE OF RUSSIA, Khabarovsk — (J) • E ASIA • 100 kW

USA
  †WORLD HARVEST R, Noblesville, Indiana — E NORTH AM • 100 kW
  Su/M/W/F • E NORTH AM • 100 kW
  Tu/Th/Sa • E NORTH AM • 100 kW

7320 **KAZAKHSTAN**
  †KAZAKH RADIO, Alma-Ata — DS-2 • 20 kW

RUSSIA
  MAGADAN RADIO, Yakutsk — RUSSIAN, ETC • DS/TIKHIY OKEAN • 100 kW

  R MOSCOW INTL — (D) • EUROPE

UNITED KINGDOM
  †BBC, Rampisham — (D) • E EUROPE & W ASIA • 500 kW
  (J) • E EUROPE & W ASIA • 500 kW

7325 **UNITED KINGDOM**
  †BBC, Multiple Locations — (D) • N AMERICA & C AMERICA • 250/300/500 kW
  (J) • C AMERICA & S AMERICA • 300/500 kW

  †BBC, Rampisham — N AFRICA • 500 kW
  (D) • E EUROPE & MIDEAST • 500 kW
  (J) • E EUROPE & MIDEAST • 500 kW
  (J) M-Sa • EUROPE • 500 kW
  (J) M-Sa • E EUROPE & MIDEAST • 500 kW

  †BBC, Various Locations — E EUROPE & W ASIA • 250 kW
  EUROPE • 250 kW

  †BBC, Woofferton — (D) • E EUROPE & W ASIA • 250 kW / (J) • EUROPE • 250 kW

USA
  VOA, Via Woofferton, UK — EUROPE • 300 kW

UZBEKISTAN
  †RADIO TASHKENT, Tashkent — (J) • S ASIA • 100 kW / (J) • MIDEAST • 100 kW

7330 **BYELARUS**
(con'd) †RS BYELARUS, Via Ukraine — (J) M/Tu/Th/F • EUROPE • 100 kW

SUMMER ONLY (J)   WINTER ONLY (D)   JAMMING / OR ∧   EARLIEST HEARD ◁   LATEST HEARD ▷   NEW OR CHANGED FOR 1993 †

FREQUENCY   COUNTRY, STATION, LOCATION   TARGET • NETWORK • POWER (kW)   World Time

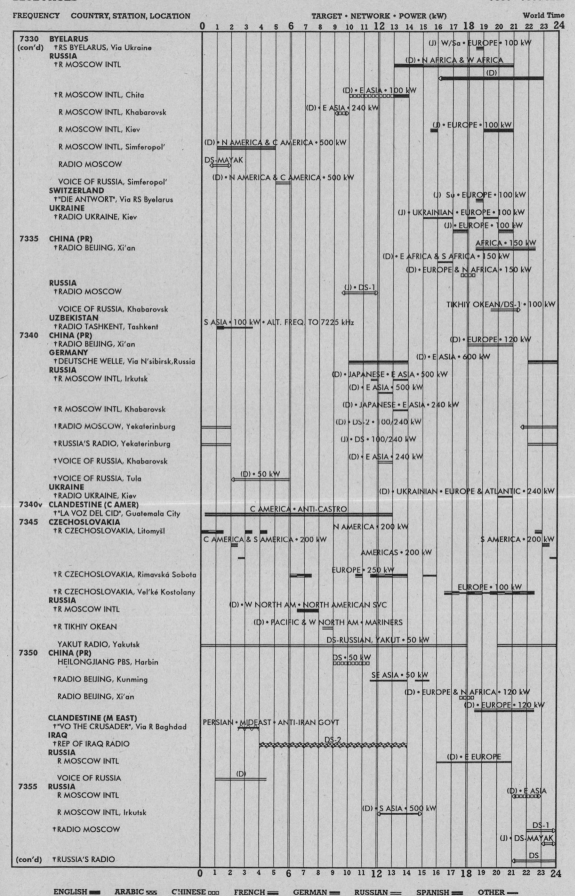

Frequency	Country, Station, Location	Target • Network • Power
7330 (con'd)	BYELARUS †RS BYELARUS, Via Ukraine	(J) W/Sa • EUROPE • 100 kW
	RUSSIA †R MOSCOW INTL	(D) • N AFRICA & W AFRICA ; (D)
	†R MOSCOW INTL, Chita	(D) • E ASIA • 100 kW
	R MOSCOW INTL, Khabarovsk	(D) • E ASIA • 240 kW
	R MOSCOW INTL, Kiev	(J) • EUROPE • 100 kW
	R MOSCOW INTL, Simferopol'	(D) • N AMERICA & C AMERICA • 500 kW
	RADIO MOSCOW	DS-MAYAK
	VOICE OF RUSSIA, Simferopol'	(D) • N AMERICA & C AMERICA • 500 kW
	SWITZERLAND †"DIE ANTWORT", Via RS Byelarus	(J) • Su • EUROPE • 100 kW
	UKRAINE †RADIO UKRAINE, Kiev	(J) • UKRAINIAN • EUROPE • 100 kW ; (J) • EUROPE • 100 kW
7335	CHINA (PR) †RADIO BEIJING, Xi'an	AFRICA • 150 kW ; (D) • E AFRICA & S AFRICA • 150 kW ; (D) • EUROPE & N AFRICA • 150 kW
	RUSSIA †RADIO MOSCOW	(J) • DS-1
	VOICE OF RUSSIA, Khabarovsk	TIKHIY OKEAN/DS-1 • 100 kW
	UZBEKISTAN †RADIO TASHKENT, Tashkent	S ASIA • 100 kW • ALT. FREQ. TO 7225 kHz
7340	CHINA (PR) †RADIO BEIJING, Xi'an	(D) • EUROPE • 120 kW
	GERMANY †DEUTSCHE WELLE, Via N'sibirsk, Russia	(D) • E ASIA • 600 kW
	RUSSIA †R MOSCOW INTL, Irkutsk	(D) • JAPANESE • E ASIA • 500 kW ; (D) • E ASIA • 500 kW
	†R MOSCOW INTL, Khabarovsk	(D) • JAPANESE • E ASIA • 240 kW
	†RADIO MOSCOW, Yekaterinburg	(D) • DS-2 • 100/240 kW
	†RUSSIA'S RADIO, Yekaterinburg	(J) • DS 100/240 kW
	†VOICE OF RUSSIA, Khabarovsk	(D) • E ASIA • 240 kW
	†VOICE OF RUSSIA, Tula	(D) • 50 kW
	UKRAINE †RADIO UKRAINE, Kiev	(D) • UKRAINIAN • EUROPE & ATLANTIC • 240 kW
7340v	CLANDESTINE (C AMER) †"LA VOZ DEL CID", Guatemala City	C AMERICA • ANTI-CASTRO
7345	CZECHOSLOVAKIA †R CZECHOSLOVAKIA, Litomyšl	N AMERICA • 200 kW ; C AMERICA & S AMERICA • 200 kW ; AMERICAS • 200 kW ; S AMERICA • 200 kW
	†R CZECHOSLOVAKIA, Rimavská Sobota	EUROPE • 250 kW
	†R CZECHOSLOVAKIA, Vel'ké Kostolany	EUROPE • 100 kW
	RUSSIA †R MOSCOW INTL	(D) • W NORTH AM • NORTH AMERICAN SVC
	†R TIKHIY OKEAN	(D) • PACIFIC & W NORTH AM • MARINERS
	YAKUT RADIO, Yakutsk	DS-RUSSIAN, YAKUT • 50 kW
7350	CHINA (PR) HEILONGJIANG PBS, Harbin	DS • 50 kW
	†RADIO BEIJING, Kunming	SE ASIA • 50 kW
	RADIO BEIJING, Xi'an	(D) • EUROPE & N AFRICA • 120 kW ; (D) • EUROPE • 120 kW
	CLANDESTINE (M EAST) †"VO THE CRUSADER", Via R Baghdad	PERSIAN • MIDEAST • ANTI-IRAN GOVT
	IRAQ †REP OF IRAQ RADIO	DS-2
	RUSSIA R MOSCOW INTL	(D) • E EUROPE
	VOICE OF RUSSIA	(D)
7355	RUSSIA R MOSCOW INTL	(D) • E ASIA
	R MOSCOW INTL, Irkutsk	(D) • S ASIA • 500 kW
	†RADIO MOSCOW	DS-1 ; (J) • DS-MAYAK ; DS
(con'd)	†RUSSIA'S RADIO	

ENGLISH ▬ ARABIC ≋ CHINESE ▭▭ FRENCH ▭ GERMAN ▬ RUSSIAN ═ SPANISH ▬ OTHER ▬

FREQUENCY   COUNTRY, STATION, LOCATION   TARGET • NETWORK • POWER (kW)   World Time

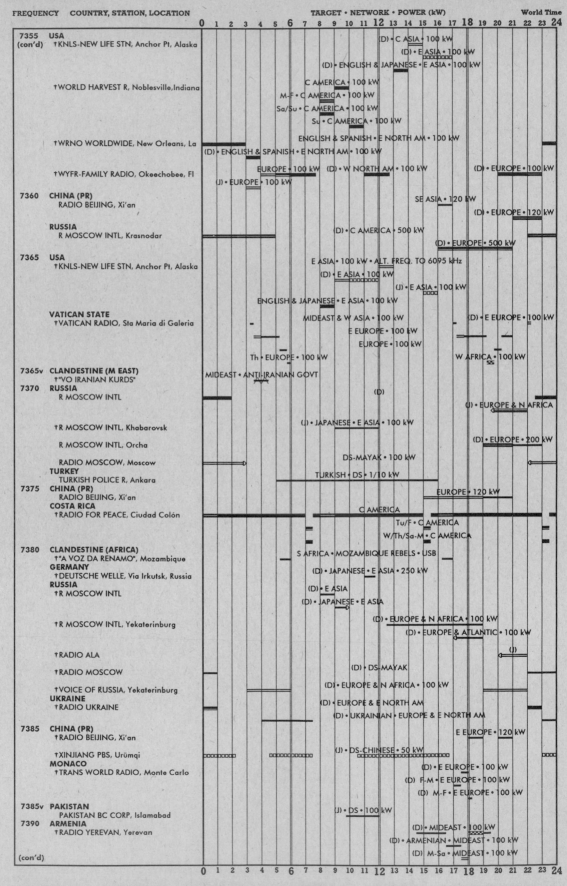

Frequency	Country, Station, Location	Broadcast details
7355 (con'd)	**USA** †KNLS-NEW LIFE STN, Anchor Pt, Alaska	(D) • C ASIA • 100 kW; (D) • E ASIA • 100 kW; (D) • ENGLISH & JAPANESE • E ASIA • 100 kW
	†WORLD HARVEST R, Noblesville, Indiana	C AMERICA • 100 kW; M-F • C AMERICA • 100 kW; Sa/Su • C AMERICA • 100 kW; Su • C AMERICA • 100 kW
	†WRNO WORLDWIDE, New Orleans, La	ENGLISH & SPANISH • E NORTH AM • 100 kW; (D) • ENGLISH & SPANISH • E NORTH AM • 100 kW
	†WYFR-FAMILY RADIO, Okeechobee, Fl	EUROPE • 100 kW; (D) • W NORTH AM • 100 kW; (D) • EUROPE • 100 kW; (J) • EUROPE • 100 kW
7360	**CHINA (PR)** RADIO BEIJING, Xi'an	SE ASIA • 120 kW; (D) • EUROPE • 120 kW
	RUSSIA R MOSCOW INTL, Krasnodar	(D) • C AMERICA • 500 kW; (D) • EUROPE • 500 kW
7365	**USA** †KNLS-NEW LIFE STN, Anchor Pt, Alaska	E ASIA • 100 kW • ALT. FREQ. TO 6095 kHz; (D) • E ASIA • 100 kW; (J) • E ASIA • 100 kW; ENGLISH & JAPANESE • E ASIA • 100 kW
	VATICAN STATE †VATICAN RADIO, Sta Maria di Galeria	MIDEAST & W ASIA • 100 kW; (D) • E EUROPE • 100 kW; E EUROPE • 100 kW; EUROPE • 100 kW; Th • EUROPE • 100 kW; W AFRICA • 100 kW
7365v	**CLANDESTINE (M EAST)** †"VO IRANIAN KURDS"	MIDEAST • ANTI-IRANIAN GOVT
7370	**RUSSIA** R MOSCOW INTL	(D); (J) • EUROPE & N AFRICA
	†R MOSCOW INTL, Khabarovsk	(J) • JAPANESE • E ASIA • 100 kW
	R MOSCOW INTL, Orcha	(D) • EUROPE • 200 kW
	RADIO MOSCOW, Moscow	DS-MAYAK • 100 kW
	TURKEY TURKISH POLICE R, Ankara	TURKISH • DS • 1/10 kW
7375	**CHINA (PR)** RADIO BEIJING, Xi'an	EUROPE • 120 kW
	COSTA RICA †RADIO FOR PEACE, Ciudad Colón	C AMERICA; Tu/F • C AMERICA; W/Th/Sa-M • C AMERICA
7380	**CLANDESTINE (AFRICA)** †"A VOZ DA RENAMO", Mozambique	S AFRICA • MOZAMBIQUE REBELS • USB
	GERMANY †DEUTSCHE WELLE, Via Irkutsk, Russia	(D) • JAPANESE • E ASIA • 250 kW
	RUSSIA †R MOSCOW INTL	(D) • E ASIA; (D) • JAPANESE • E ASIA
	†R MOSCOW INTL, Yekaterinburg	(D) • EUROPE & N AFRICA • 100 kW; (D) • EUROPE & ATLANTIC • 100 kW
	†RADIO ALA	(J)
	†RADIO MOSCOW	(D) • DS-MAYAK
	†VOICE OF RUSSIA, Yekaterinburg	(D) • EUROPE & N AFRICA • 100 kW
	UKRAINE †RADIO UKRAINE	(D) • EUROPE & E NORTH AM; (D) • UKRAINIAN • EUROPE & E NORTH AM
7385	**CHINA (PR)** †RADIO BEIJING, Xi'an	E EUROPE • 120 kW
	†XINJIANG PBS, Urümqi	(J) • DS-CHINESE • 50 kW
	MONACO †TRANS WORLD RADIO, Monte Carlo	(D) • E EUROPE • 100 kW; (D) F-M • E EUROPE • 100 kW; (D) M-F • E EUROPE • 100 kW
7385v	**PAKISTAN** PAKISTAN BC CORP, Islamabad	(J) • DS • 100 kW
7390	**ARMENIA** †RADIO YEREVAN, Yerevan	(D) • MIDEAST • 100 kW; (D) • ARMENIAN • MIDEAST • 100 kW; (D) M-Sa • MIDEAST • 100 kW

(con'd)

SUMMER ONLY (J)   WINTER ONLY (D)   JAMMING / OR ∧   EARLIEST HEARD ◁   LATEST HEARD ▷   NEW OR CHANGED FOR 1993 †

| FREQUENCY | COUNTRY, STATION, LOCATION | TARGET • NETWORK • POWER (kW) | World Time |

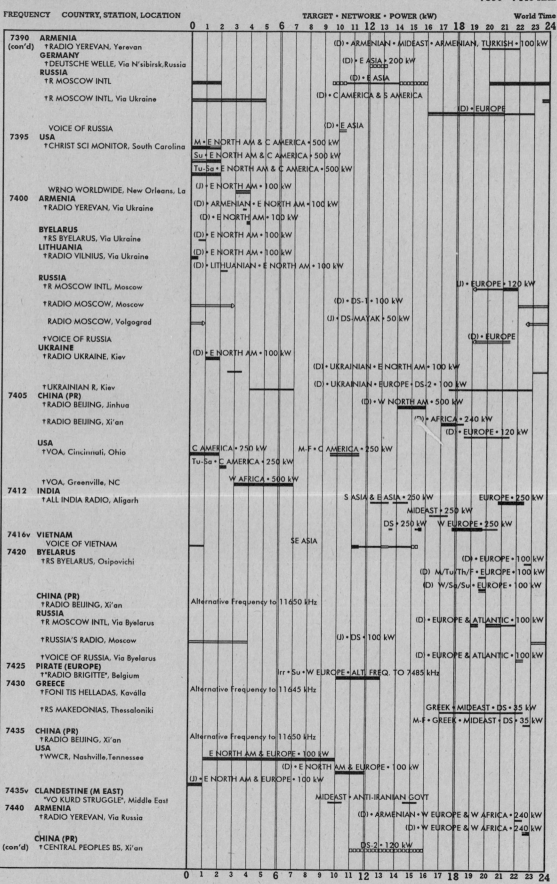

7390 ARMENIA
(con'd) †RADIO YEREVAN, Yerevan — (D) • ARMENIAN • MIDEAST • ARMENIAN, TURKISH • 100 kW
GERMANY
†DEUTSCHE WELLE, Via N'sibirsk, Russia — (D) E ASIA • 200 kW
RUSSIA
†R MOSCOW INTL — (D) • E ASIA
†R MOSCOW INTL, Via Ukraine — (D) • C AMERICA & S AMERICA
— (D) • EUROPE
VOICE OF RUSSIA — (D) • E ASIA

7395 USA
†CHRIST SCI MONITOR, South Carolina — M • E NORTH AM & C AMERICA • 500 kW
— Su • E NORTH AM & C AMERICA • 500 kW
— Tu-Sa • E NORTH AM & C AMERICA • 500 kW
WRNO WORLDWIDE, New Orleans, La — (J) • E NORTH AM • 100 kW

7400 ARMENIA
†RADIO YEREVAN, Via Ukraine — (D) • ARMENIAN • E NORTH AM • 100 kW
— (D) • E NORTH AM • 100 kW
BYELARUS
†RS BYELARUS, Via Ukraine — (D) • E NORTH AM • 100 kW
LITHUANIA
†RADIO VILNIUS, Via Ukraine — (D) • E NORTH AM • 100 kW
— (D) • LITHUANIAN • E NORTH AM • 100 kW
RUSSIA
†R MOSCOW INTL, Moscow — (J) • EUROPE • 120 kW
†RADIO MOSCOW, Moscow — (D) • DS-1 • 100 kW
RADIO MOSCOW, Volgograd — (J) • DS-MAYAK • 50 kW
†VOICE OF RUSSIA — (D) • EUROPE
UKRAINE
†RADIO UKRAINE, Kiev — (D) • E NORTH AM • 100 kW
— (D) • UKRAINIAN • E NORTH AM • 100 kW
†UKRAINIAN R, Kiev — (D) • UKRAINIAN • EUROPE • DS-2 • 100 kW

7405 CHINA (PR)
†RADIO BEIJING, Jinhua — (D) • W NORTH AM • 500 kW
†RADIO BEIJING, Xi'an — (D) • AFRICA • 240 kW
— (D) • EUROPE • 120 kW
USA
†VOA, Cincinnati, Ohio — C AMERICA • 250 kW — M-F • C AMERICA • 250 kW
— Tu-Sa • C AMERICA • 250 kW
†VOA, Greenville, NC — W AFRICA • 500 kW

7412 INDIA
†ALL INDIA RADIO, Aligarh — S ASIA & E ASIA • 250 kW — EUROPE • 250 kW
— MIDEAST • 250 kW
— DS • 250 kW — W EUROPE • 250 kW

7416v VIETNAM
VOICE OF VIETNAM — SE ASIA

7420 BYELARUS
†RS BYELARUS, Osipovichi — (D) • EUROPE • 100 kW
— (D) • M/Tu/Th/F • EUROPE • 100 kW
— (D) • W/Sa/Su • EUROPE • 100 kW
CHINA (PR)
†RADIO BEIJING, Xi'an — Alternative Frequency to 11650 kHz
RUSSIA
†R MOSCOW INTL, Via Byelarus — (D) • EUROPE & ATLANTIC • 100 kW
†RUSSIA'S RADIO, Moscow — (J) • DS • 100 kW
†VOICE OF RUSSIA, Via Byelarus — (D) • EUROPE & ATLANTIC • 100 kW

7425 PIRATE (EUROPE)
†"RADIO BRIGITTE", Belgium — Irr • Su • W EUROPE • ALT. FREQ. TO 7485 kHz

7430 GREECE
†FONI TIS HELLADAS, Kaválla — Alternative Frequency to 11645 kHz
†RS MAKEDONIAS, Thessaloniki — GREEK • MIDEAST • DS • 35 kW
— M-F • GREEK • MIDEAST • DS • 35 kW

7435 CHINA (PR)
†RADIO BEIJING, Xi'an — Alternative Frequency to 11650 kHz
USA
†WWCR, Nashville, Tennessee — E NORTH AM & EUROPE • 100 kW
— (D) • E NORTH AM & EUROPE • 100 kW
— (J) • E NORTH AM & EUROPE • 100 kW

7435v CLANDESTINE (M EAST)
"VO KURD STRUGGLE", Middle East — MIDEAST • ANTI-IRANIAN GOVT

7440 ARMENIA
†RADIO YEREVAN, Via Russia — (D) • ARMENIAN • W EUROPE & W AFRICA • 240 kW
— (D) • W EUROPE & W AFRICA • 240 kW
CHINA (PR)
(con'd) †CENTRAL PEOPLES BS, Xi'an — DS-2 • 120 kW

ENGLISH ▬ ARABIC ⧨⧨⧨ CHINESE □□□ FRENCH ▬ GERMAN ▬ RUSSIAN ══ SPANISH ▬ OTHER ▬

FREQUENCY	COUNTRY, STATION, LOCATION	TARGET • NETWORK • POWER (kW)

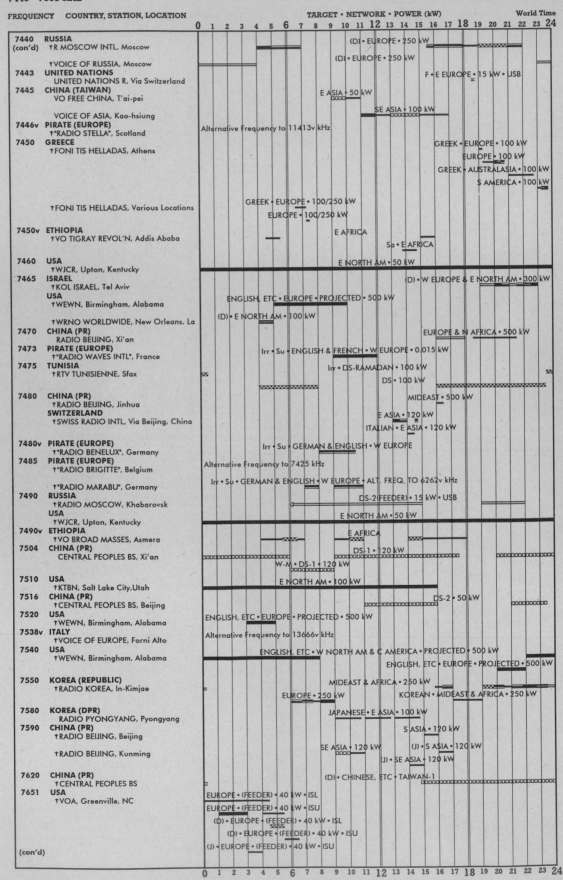

FREQUENCY	COUNTRY, STATION, LOCATION
7440 (con'd)	RUSSIA
	†R MOSCOW INTL, Moscow — (D) • EUROPE • 250 kW
	†VOICE OF RUSSIA, Moscow — (D) • EUROPE • 250 kW
7443	UNITED NATIONS
	UNITED NATIONS R, Via Switzerland — F • E EUROPE • 15 kW • USB
7445	CHINA (TAIWAN)
	VO FREE CHINA, T'ai-pei — E ASIA • 50 kW
	VOICE OF ASIA, Kao-hsiung — SE ASIA • 100 kW
7446v	PIRATE (EUROPE)
	†"RADIO STELLA", Scotland — Alternative Frequency to 11413v kHz
7450	GREECE
	†FONI TIS HELLADAS, Athens — GREEK • EUROPE • 100 kW
	— EUROPE • 100 kW
	— GREEK • AUSTRALASIA • 100 kW
	— S AMERICA • 100 kW
	†FONI TIS HELLADAS, Various Locations — GREEK • EUROPE • 100/250 kW
	— EUROPE • 100/250 kW
7450v	ETHIOPIA
	†VO TIGRAY REVOL'N, Addis Ababa — E AFRICA
	— Sa • E AFRICA
7460	USA
	†WJCR, Upton, Kentucky — E NORTH AM • 50 kW
7465	ISRAEL
	†KOL ISRAEL, Tel Aviv — (D) • W EUROPE & E NORTH AM • 300 kW
	USA
	†WEWN, Birmingham, Alabama — ENGLISH, ETC • EUROPE • PROJECTED • 500 kW
	†WRNO WORLDWIDE, New Orleans, La — (D) • E NORTH AM • 100 kW
7470	CHINA (PR)
	RADIO BEIJING, Xi'an — EUROPE & N AFRICA • 500 kW
7473	PIRATE (EUROPE)
	†"RADIO WAVES INTL", France — Irr • Su • ENGLISH & FRENCH • W EUROPE • 0.015 kW
7475	TUNISIA
	†RTV TUNISIENNE, Sfax — Irr • DS-RAMADAN • 100 kW
	— DS • 100 kW
7480	CHINA (PR)
	†RADIO BEIJING, Jinhua — MIDEAST • 500 kW
	SWITZERLAND
	†SWISS RADIO INTL, Via Beijing, China — E ASIA • 120 kW
	— ITALIAN • E ASIA • 120 kW
7480v	PIRATE (EUROPE)
	†"RADIO BENELUX", Germany — Irr • Su • GERMAN & ENGLISH • W EUROPE
7485	PIRATE (EUROPE)
	†"RADIO BRIGITTE", Belgium — Alternative Frequency to 7425 kHz
	†"RADIO MARABU", Germany — Irr • Su • GERMAN & ENGLISH • W EUROPE • ALT. FREQ. TO 6262v kHz
7490	RUSSIA
	†RADIO MOSCOW, Khabarovsk — DS-2 (FEEDER) • 15 kW • USB
	USA
	†WJCR, Upton, Kentucky — E NORTH AM • 50 kW
7490v	ETHIOPIA
	†VO BROAD MASSES, Asmera — E AFRICA
7504	CHINA (PR)
	CENTRAL PEOPLES BS, Xi'an — DS-1 • 120 kW
	— W-M • DS-1 • 120 kW
7510	USA
	†KTBN, Salt Lake City, Utah — E NORTH AM • 100 kW
7516	CHINA (PR)
	†CENTRAL PEOPLES BS, Beijing — DS-2 • 50 kW
7520	USA
	†WEWN, Birmingham, Alabama — ENGLISH, ETC • EUROPE • PROJECTED • 500 kW
7538v	ITALY
	†VOICE OF EUROPE, Forni Alto — Alternative Frequency to 13666v kHz
7540	USA
	†WEWN, Birmingham, Alabama — ENGLISH, ETC • W NORTH AM & C AMERICA • PROJECTED • 500 kW
	— ENGLISH, ETC • EUROPE • PROJECTED • 500 kW
7550	KOREA (REPUBLIC)
	†RADIO KOREA, In-Kimjae — MIDEAST & AFRICA • 250 kW
	— EUROPE • 250 kW
	— KOREAN • MIDEAST & AFRICA • 250 kW
7580	KOREA (DPR)
	RADIO PYONGYANG, Pyongyang — JAPANESE • E ASIA • 100 kW
7590	CHINA (PR)
	†RADIO BEIJING, Beijing — S ASIA • 120 kW
	†RADIO BEIJING, Kunming — SE ASIA • 120 kW
	— (J) • S ASIA • 120 kW
	— (J) • SE ASIA • 120 kW
7620	CHINA (PR)
	†CENTRAL PEOPLES BS — (D) • CHINESE, ETC • TAIWAN-1
7651	USA
	†VOA, Greenville, NC — EUROPE • (FEEDER) • 40 kW • ISL
	— EUROPE • (FEEDER) • 40 kW • ISU
	— (D) • EUROPE • (FEEDER) • 40 kW • ISL
	— (D) • EUROPE • (FEEDER) • 40 kW • ISU
	— (J) • EUROPE • (FEEDER) • 40 kW • ISU
(con'd)	

FREQUENCY COUNTRY, STATION, LOCATION   TARGET • NETWORK • POWER (kW)   World Time

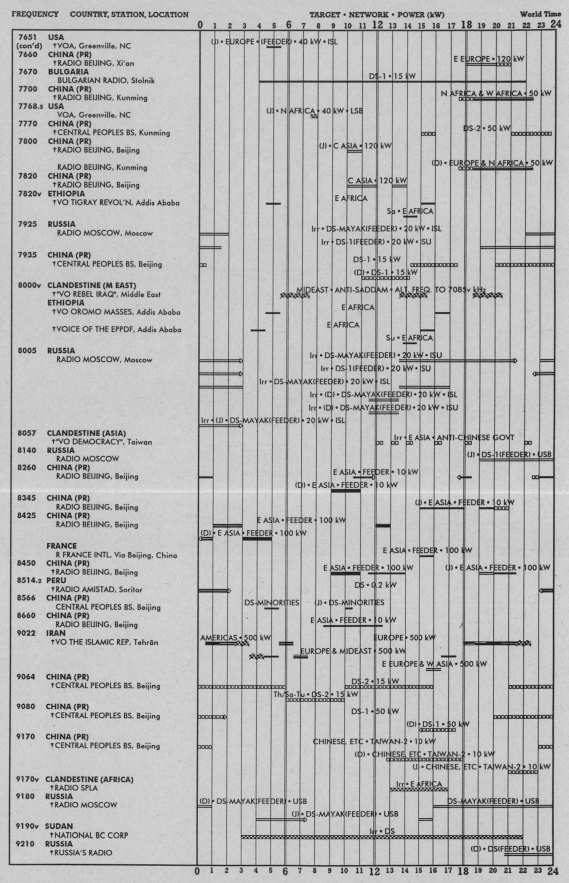

FREQUENCY	COUNTRY, STATION, LOCATION	TARGET • NETWORK • POWER (kW)
7651 (con'd)	USA · †VOA, Greenville, NC	(J) • EUROPE • (FEEDER) • 40 kW • ISL
7660	CHINA (PR) · †RADIO BEIJING, Xi'an	E EUROPE • 120 kW
7670	BULGARIA · BULGARIAN RADIO, Stolnik	DS-1 • 15 kW
7700	CHINA (PR) · †RADIO BEIJING, Kunming	N AFRICA & W AFRICA • 50 kW
7768.5	USA · VOA, Greenville, NC	(J) • N AFRICA • 40 kW • LSB
7770	CHINA (PR) · †CENTRAL PEOPLES BS, Kunming	DS-2 • 50 kW
7800	CHINA (PR) · †RADIO BEIJING, Beijing	(J) • C ASIA • 120 kW
	RADIO BEIJING, Kunming	(D) • EUROPE & N AFRICA • 50 kW
7820	CHINA (PR) · †RADIO BEIJING, Beijing	C ASIA • 120 kW
7820v	ETHIOPIA · †VO TIGRAY REVOL'N, Addis Ababa	E AFRICA — Sa • E AFRICA
7925	RUSSIA · RADIO MOSCOW, Moscow	Irr • DS-MAYAK(FEEDER) • 20 kW • ISL / Irr • DS-1(FEEDER) • 20 kW • ISU
7935	CHINA (PR) · †CENTRAL PEOPLES BS, Beijing	DS-1 • 15 kW / (D) • DS-1 • 15 kW
8000v	CLANDESTINE (M EAST) · †"VO REBEL IRAQ", Middle East	MIDEAST • ANTI-SADDAM • ALT. FREQ. TO 7085v kHz
	ETHIOPIA · †VO OROMO MASSES, Addis Ababa	E AFRICA
	†VOICE OF THE EPPDF, Addis Ababa	E AFRICA — Su • E AFRICA
8005	RUSSIA · RADIO MOSCOW, Moscow	Irr • DS-MAYAK(FEEDER) • 20 kW • ISU / Irr • DS-1(FEEDER) • 20 kW • ISU / Irr • DS-MAYAK(FEEDER) • 20 kW • ISL / Irr • (D) • DS-MAYAK(FEEDER) • 20 kW • ISL / Irr • (D) • DS-MAYAK(FEEDER) • 20 kW • ISU / Irr • (J) • DS-MAYAK(FEEDER) • 20 kW • ISL
8057	CLANDESTINE (ASIA) · †"VO DEMOCRACY", Taiwan	Irr • E ASIA • ANTI-CHINESE GOVT
8140	RUSSIA · RADIO MOSCOW	(J) • DS-1(FEEDER) • USB
8260	CHINA (PR) · RADIO BEIJING, Beijing	E ASIA • FEEDER • 10 kW / (D) • E ASIA • FEEDER • 10 kW
8345	CHINA (PR) · RADIO BEIJING, Beijing	(J) • E ASIA • FEEDER • 10 kW
8425	CHINA (PR) · RADIO BEIJING, Beijing	E ASIA • FEEDER • 100 kW / (D) • E ASIA • FEEDER • 100 kW
	FRANCE · R FRANCE INTL, Via Beijing, China	E ASIA • FEEDER • 100 kW
8450	CHINA (PR) · †RADIO BEIJING, Beijing	E ASIA • FEEDER • 100 kW / (J) • E ASIA • FEEDER • 100 kW
8514.2	PERU · †RADIO AMISTAD, Soritor	DS • 0.2 kW
8566	CHINA (PR) · CENTRAL PEOPLES BS, Beijing	DS-MINORITIES / (J) • DS-MINORITIES
8660	CHINA (PR) · RADIO BEIJING, Beijing	E ASIA • FEEDER • 10 kW
9022	IRAN · †VO THE ISLAMIC REP, Tehrān	AMERICAS • 500 kW / EUROPE • 500 kW / EUROPE & MIDEAST • 500 kW / E EUROPE & W ASIA • 500 kW
9064	CHINA (PR) · †CENTRAL PEOPLES BS, Beijing	DS-2 • 15 kW / Th/Sa-Tu • DS-2 • 15 kW
9080	CHINA (PR) · †CENTRAL PEOPLES BS, Beijing	DS-1 • 50 kW / (D) • DS-1 • 50 kW
9170	CHINA (PR) · †CENTRAL PEOPLES BS, Beijing	CHINESE, ETC • TAIWAN-2 • 10 kW / (D) • CHINESE, ETC • TAIWAN-2 • 10 kW / (J) • CHINESE, ETC • TAIWAN-2 • 10 kW
9170v	CLANDESTINE (AFRICA) · †RADIO SPLA	Irr • E AFRICA
9180	RUSSIA · †RADIO MOSCOW	(D) • DS-MAYAK(FEEDER) • USB / (J) • DS-MAYAK(FEEDER) • USB / DS-MAYAK(FEEDER) • USB
9190v	SUDAN · †NATIONAL BC CORP	Irr • DS
9210	RUSSIA · †RUSSIA'S RADIO	(D) • DS(FEEDER) • USB

World Time: 0 1 2 3 4 5 6 7 8 9 10 11 12 13 14 15 16 17 18 19 20 21 22 23 24

ENGLISH ▬ ARABIC ⨯⨯⨯ CHINESE □□□ FRENCH ▬▬ GERMAN ▬ RUSSIAN ▬ SPANISH ▬ OTHER ▬

FREQUENCY   COUNTRY, STATION, LOCATION   TARGET • NETWORK • POWER (kW)   World Time

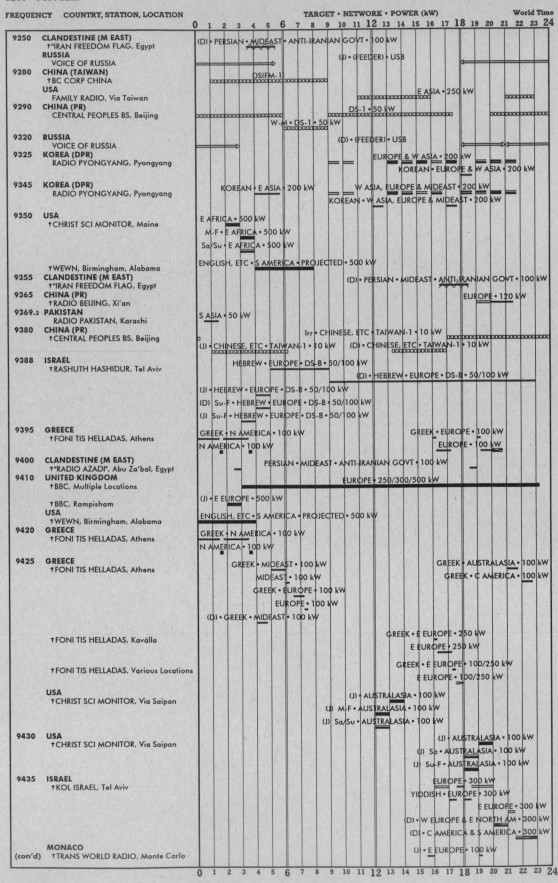

FREQUENCY	COUNTRY, STATION, LOCATION	TARGET • NETWORK • POWER (kW)
9250	CLANDESTINE (M EAST) †"IRAN FREEDOM FLAG, Egypt	(D) • PERSIAN • MIDEAST • ANTI-IRANIAN GOVT • 100 kW
	RUSSIA VOICE OF RUSSIA	(J) • (FEEDER) • USB
9280	CHINA (TAIWAN) †BC CORP CHINA	DS(FM-1)
	USA FAMILY RADIO, Via Taiwan	E ASIA • 250 kW
9290	CHINA (PR) CENTRAL PEOPLES BS, Beijing	DS-1 • 50 kW W-M • DS-1 • 50 kW
9320	RUSSIA VOICE OF RUSSIA	(D) • (FEEDER) • USB
9325	KOREA (DPR) RADIO PYONGYANG, Pyongyang	EUROPE & W ASIA • 200 kW KOREAN • EUROPE & W ASIA • 200 kW
9345	KOREA (DPR) RADIO PYONGYANG, Pyongyang	KOREAN • E ASIA • 200 kW W ASIA, EUROPE & MIDEAST • 200 kW KOREAN • W ASIA, EUROPE & MIDEAST • 200 kW
9350	USA †CHRIST SCI MONITOR, Maine	E AFRICA • 500 kW M-F • E AFRICA • 500 kW Sa/Su • E AFRICA • 500 kW
	†WEWN, Birmingham, Alabama	ENGLISH, ETC • S AMERICA • PROJECTED • 500 kW
9355	CLANDESTINE (M EAST) †"IRAN FREEDOM FLAG, Egypt	(D) • PERSIAN • MIDEAST • ANTI-IRANIAN GOVT • 100 kW
9365	CHINA (PR) †RADIO BEIJING, Xi'an	EUROPE • 120 kW
9369.3	PAKISTAN RADIO PAKISTAN, Karachi	S ASIA • 50 kW
9380	CHINA (PR) †CENTRAL PEOPLES BS, Beijing	Irr • CHINESE, ETC • TAIWAN-1 • 10 kW (J) • CHINESE, ETC • TAIWAN-1 • 10 kW (D) • CHINESE, ETC • TAIWAN-1 • 10 kW
9388	ISRAEL †RASHUTH HASHIDUR, Tel Aviv	HEBREW • EUROPE • DS-B • 50/100 kW (D) • HEBREW • EUROPE • DS-B • 50/100 kW (J) • HEBREW • EUROPE • DS-B • 50/100 kW (D) Su-F • HEBREW • EUROPE • DS-B • 50/100 kW (J) Su-F • HEBREW • EUROPE • DS-B • 50/100 kW
9395	GREECE †FONI TIS HELLADAS, Athens	GREEK • N AMERICA • 100 kW N AMERICA • 100 kW GREEK • EUROPE • 100 kW EUROPE • 100 kW
9400	CLANDESTINE (M EAST) †"RADIO AZADI", Abu Za'bal, Egypt	PERSIAN • MIDEAST • ANTI-IRANIAN GOVT • 100 kW
9410	UNITED KINGDOM †BBC, Multiple Locations	EUROPE • 250/300/500 kW
	†BBC, Rampisham	(J) • E EUROPE • 500 kW
	USA †WEWN, Birmingham, Alabama	ENGLISH, ETC • S AMERICA • PROJECTED • 500 kW
9420	GREECE †FONI TIS HELLADAS, Athens	GREEK • N AMERICA • 100 kW N AMERICA • 100 kW
9425	GREECE †FONI TIS HELLADAS, Athens	GREEK • MIDEAST • 100 kW MIDEAST • 100 kW GREEK • EUROPE • 100 kW EUROPE • 100 kW (D) • GREEK • MIDEAST • 100 kW GREEK • AUSTRALASIA • 100 kW GREEK • C AMERICA • 100 kW
	†FONI TIS HELLADAS, Kaválla	GREEK • E EUROPE • 250 kW E EUROPE • 250 kW
	†FONI TIS HELLADAS, Various Locations	GREEK • E EUROPE • 100/250 kW E EUROPE • 100/250 kW
	USA †CHRIST SCI MONITOR, Via Saipan	(J) • AUSTRALASIA • 100 kW (J) M-F • AUSTRALASIA • 100 kW (J) Sa/Su • AUSTRALASIA • 100 kW
9430	USA †CHRIST SCI MONITOR, Via Saipan	(J) • AUSTRALASIA • 100 kW (J) Sa • AUSTRALASIA • 100 kW (J) Su-F • AUSTRALASIA • 100 kW
9435	ISRAEL †KOL ISRAEL, Tel Aviv	EUROPE • 300 kW YIDDISH • EUROPE • 300 kW E EUROPE • 300 kW (D) • W EUROPE & E NORTH AM • 300 kW (D) • C AMERICA & S AMERICA • 300 kW
(con'd)	MONACO †TRANS WORLD RADIO, Monte Carlo	(J) • E EUROPE • 100 kW

SUMMER ONLY (J)   WINTER ONLY (D)   JAMMING / OR ⋀   EARLIEST HEARD ◁   LATEST HEARD ▷   NEW OR CHANGED FOR 1993 †

FREQUENCY	COUNTRY, STATION, LOCATION	TARGET • NETWORK • POWER (kW)
9435 (con'd)	MONACO †TRANS WORLD RADIO, Monte Carlo	(J) M-F • E EUROPE • 100 kW
9440	CHINA (PR) †RADIO BEIJING, Beijing	SE ASIA • 120 kW; MIDEAST • 120 kW
	RADIO BEIJING, Xi'an	SE ASIA • 120 kW
9445	TURKEY VOICE OF TURKEY, Ankara	TURKISH • E NORTH AM • 500 kW; EUROPE • 250 kW; E NORTH AM • 500 kW
9450	ARMENIA †RADIO YEREVAN, Yerevan	(J) • ARMENIAN • EUROPE; (J) • EUROPE
	RUSSIA †R MOSCOW INTL, Moscow	(D) • W AFRICA • 240 kW
	†R MOSCOW INTL, Novosibirsk	(D) • E ASIA • 250 kW
	†RADIO MOSCOW, Novosibirsk	(J) • DS-1 • 50 kW
	†RADIO RADONEZH, Moscow	Alternative Frequency to 9865 kHz
	†RS ALPHA & OMEGA, Moscow	Alternative Frequency to 9865 kHz
	VOICE OF RUSSIA	(D) • E ASIA
	VOICE OF RUSSIA, Moscow	W AFRICA & ATLANTIC • 240 kW
9455	CHINA (PR) †CENTRAL PEOPLES BS, Kunming	(J) • CHINESE, ETC • TAIWAN-1 • 50 kW; CHINESE, ETC • TAIWAN-1 • 50 kW
	USA †CHRIST SCI MONITOR, South Carolina	W NORTH AM & C AMERICA • 500 kW; W NORTH AM • 500 kW; M • W NORTH AM & C AMERICA • 500 kW; M • W NORTH AM • 500 kW; M-F • W NORTH AM • 500 kW; M-F • S AMERICA • 500 kW; Sa/Su • W NORTH AM & C AMERICA • 500 kW; Sa/Su • W NORTH AM • 500 kW; Sa/Su • S AMERICA • 500 kW; Tu-F • W NORTH AM & C AMERICA • 500 kW; Tu-F • W NORTH AM • 500 kW
	†CHRIST SCI MONITOR, Via Saipan	E ASIA • 100 kW
	VOA, Greenville, NC	C AMERICA & S AMERICA • 500 kW; (D) • C AMERICA & S AMERICA • 500 kW; (J) • C AMERICA & S AMERICA • 500 kW
9460	TURKEY †VOICE OF TURKEY, Ankara	TURKISH • EUROPE • 500 kW
9465	CROATIA †CROATIAN RADIO, Via WHRI, USA	E NORTH AM • 100 kW
	NORTHERN MARIANA IS †KFBS-FAR EAST BC, Saipan Island	E EUROPE & W ASIA • 100 kW; F-Tu • E EUROPE & W ASIA • 100 kW; Sa • E EUROPE & W ASIA • 100 kW; Su-F • E EUROPE & W ASIA • 100 kW; W/Th • E EUROPE & W ASIA • 100 kW
	USA †CHRIST SCI MONITOR, South Carolina	E NORTH AM & C AMERICA • 500 kW; Sa • E NORTH AM & C AMERICA • 500 kW; Su • E NORTH AM & C AMERICA • 500 kW
	FAMILY RADIO, Via Taiwan	E ASIA • 250 kW
	†VOA, Delano, California	C AMERICA & S AMERICA • 250 kW; M-F • S AMERICA • 250 kW
	†WMLK, Bethel, Pa	Su-F • EUROPE, MIDEAST & N AMERICA • 50 kW
	†WORLD HARVEST R, Noblesville, Indiana	E NORTH AM • 100 kW
9470	RUSSIA †R MOSCOW INTL	(J) • E NORTH AM
	†R MOSCOW INTL, Simbirsk	(D) • S AMERICA • 100 kW; (J) • EUROPE • 100 kW
	†RADIO MOSCOW, Irkutsk	DS-MAYAK(FEEDER) • 15 kW • USB
	UKRAINE †RADIO UKRAINE	(D) • EUROPE; (D) • UKRAINIAN • EUROPE
	†UKRAINIAN R	(D) • UKRAINIAN • EUROPE

World Time 0–24

ENGLISH ▬ ARABIC ▭ CHINESE ▫▫▫ FRENCH ═ GERMAN ═ RUSSIAN ═ SPANISH ═ OTHER —

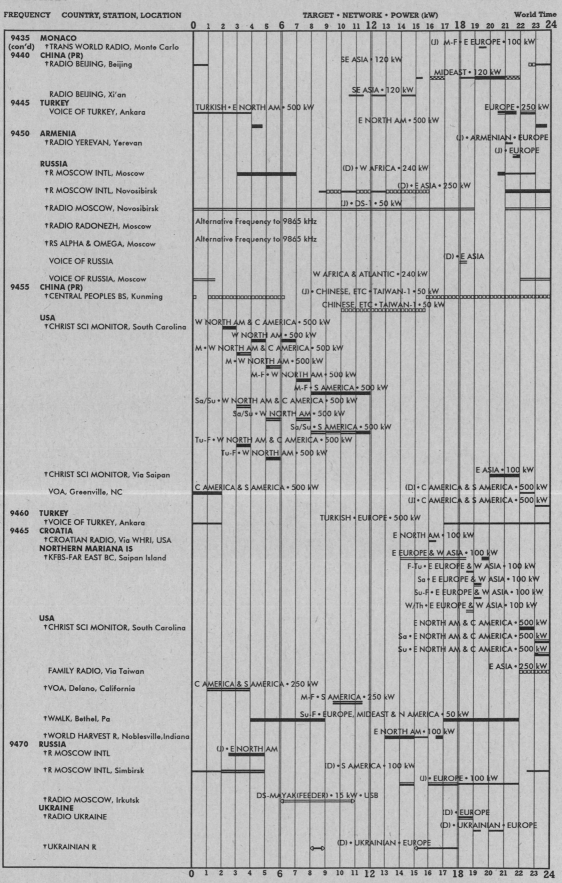

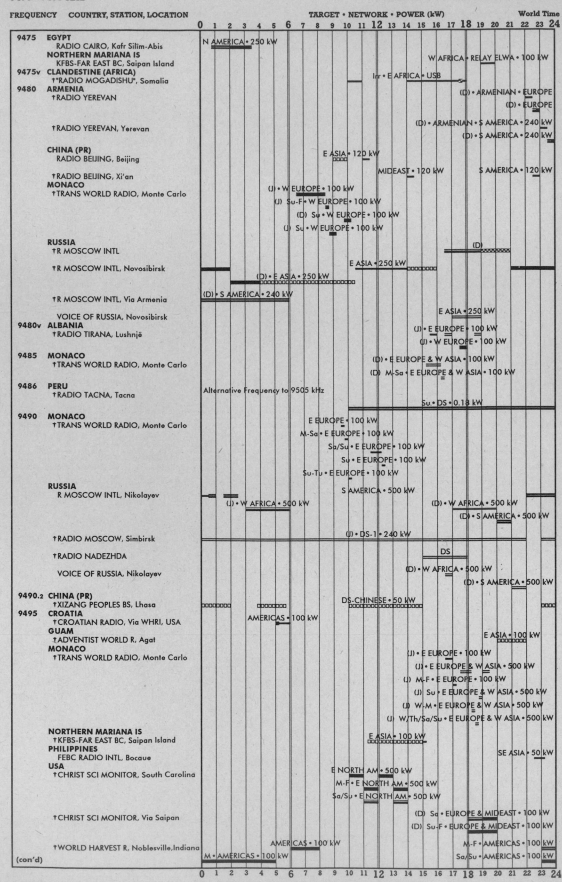

FREQUENCY   COUNTRY, STATION, LOCATION

TARGET • NETWORK • POWER (kW)

World Time

0 1 2 3 4 5 6 7 8 9 10 11 12 13 14 15 16 17 18 19 20 21 22 23 24

9475   EGYPT
           RADIO CAIRO, Kafr Silim-Abis — N AMERICA • 250 kW
        NORTHERN MARIANA IS
           KFBS-FAR EAST BC, Saipan Island — W AFRICA • RELAY ELWA • 100 kW
9475v   CLANDESTINE (AFRICA)
           †"RADIO MOGADISHU", Somalia — Irr • E AFRICA • USB
9480   ARMENIA
           †RADIO YEREVAN — (D) • ARMENIAN • EUROPE
                              (D) • EUROPE
           †RADIO YEREVAN, Yerevan — (D) • ARMENIAN • S AMERICA • 240 kW
                                       (D) • S AMERICA • 240 kW
        CHINA (PR)
           RADIO BEIJING, Beijing — E ASIA • 120 kW
           †RADIO BEIJING, Xi'an — MIDEAST • 120 kW   S AMERICA • 120 kW
        MONACO
           †TRANS WORLD RADIO, Monte Carlo — (J) • W EUROPE • 100 kW
                                              (J) Su-F • W EUROPE • 100 kW
                                              (D) Su • W EUROPE • 100 kW
                                              (J) Su • W EUROPE • 100 kW
        RUSSIA
           †R MOSCOW INTL — (D)
           †R MOSCOW INTL, Novosibirsk — E ASIA • 250 kW
                                          (D) • E ASIA • 250 kW
           †R MOSCOW INTL, Via Armenia — (D) • S AMERICA • 240 kW
           VOICE OF RUSSIA, Novosibirsk — E ASIA • 250 kW
9480v   ALBANIA
           †RADIO TIRANA, Lushnjë — (J) • E EUROPE • 100 kW
                                     (J) • W EUROPE • 100 kW
9485   MONACO
           †TRANS WORLD RADIO, Monte Carlo — (D) • E EUROPE & W ASIA • 100 kW
                                              (D) M-Sa • E EUROPE & W ASIA • 100 kW
9486   PERU
           †RADIO TACNA, Tacna — Alternative Frequency to 9505 kHz   Su • DS • 0.18 kW
9490   MONACO
           †TRANS WORLD RADIO, Monte Carlo — E EUROPE • 100 kW
                                              M-Sa • E EUROPE • 100 kW
                                              Sa/Su • E EUROPE • 100 kW
                                              Su • E EUROPE • 100 kW
                                              Su-Tu • E EUROPE • 100 kW
        RUSSIA
           R MOSCOW INTL, Nikolayev — S AMERICA • 500 kW
                                       (J) • W AFRICA • 500 kW   (D) • W AFRICA • 500 kW
                                                                   (D) • S AMERICA • 500 kW
           †RADIO MOSCOW, Simbirsk — (J) • DS-1 • 240 kW
           †RADIO NADEZHDA — DS
           VOICE OF RUSSIA, Nikolayev — (D) • W AFRICA • 500 kW
                                         (D) • S AMERICA • 500 kW
9490.2 CHINA (PR)
           †XIZANG PEOPLES BS, Lhasa — DS-CHINESE • 50 kW
9495   CROATIA
           †CROATIAN RADIO, Via WHRI, USA — AMERICAS • 100 kW
        GUAM
           †ADVENTIST WORLD R, Agat — E ASIA • 100 kW
        MONACO
           †TRANS WORLD RADIO, Monte Carlo — (J) • E EUROPE • 100 kW
                                              (J) • E EUROPE & W ASIA • 500 kW
                                              (J) M-F • E EUROPE • 100 kW
                                              (J) Su • E EUROPE & W ASIA • 500 kW
                                              (J) W-M • E EUROPE & W ASIA • 500 kW
                                              (J) W/Th/Sa/Su • E EUROPE & W ASIA • 500 kW
        NORTHERN MARIANA IS
           †KFBS-FAR EAST BC, Saipan Island — E ASIA • 100 kW
        PHILIPPINES
           FEBC RADIO INTL, Bocaue — SE ASIA • 50 kW
        USA
           †CHRIST SCI MONITOR, South Carolina — E NORTH AM • 500 kW
                                                  M-F • E NORTH AM • 500 kW
                                                  Sa/Su • E NORTH AM • 500 kW
           †CHRIST SCI MONITOR, Via Saipan — (D) Sa • EUROPE & MIDEAST • 100 kW
                                              (D) Su-F • EUROPE & MIDEAST • 100 kW
           †WORLD HARVEST R, Noblesville, Indiana — AMERICAS • 100 kW   M-F • AMERICAS • 100 kW
(con'd)   M • AMERICAS • 100 kW   Sa/Su • AMERICAS • 100 kW

0 1 2 3 4 5 6 7 8 9 10 11 12 13 14 15 16 17 18 19 20 21 22 23 24

| FREQUENCY | COUNTRY, STATION, LOCATION | TARGET • NETWORK • POWER (kW) | World Time |

Frequency	Country, Station, Location	Schedule
9495 (con'd)	**USA** †WORLD HARVEST R, Noblesville, Indiana	Tu-Su • AMERICAS • 100 kW
9500	**ALBANIA** †RADIO TIRANA, Lushnjë	(J) • E EUROPE • 100 kW
		(J) • W EUROPE • 100 kW
	RUSSIA R MOSCOW INTL, Armavir	MIDEAST & E AFRICA • 100 kW
	RADIO MOSCOW	DS-1
	VOICE OF RUSSIA, Armavir	MIDEAST & E AFRICA • 100 kW
	SWAZILAND †TRANS WORLD RADIO, Manzini	Alternative Frequency to 9620 kHz
	VATICAN STATE †VATICAN RADIO, Sta Maria di Galeria	E EUROPE • 500 kW
9505	**AUSTRALIA** †RADIO AUSTRALIA, Carnarvon	SE ASIA • 100 kW
	BRAZIL RADIO RECORD, São Paulo	Irr • PORTUGUESE • DS • 7.5 kW
		PORTUGUESE • DS • 7.5 kW
	CANADA R CANADA INTL, Via Germany	(D) • MIDEAST • 500 kW
	†R CANADA INTL, Via Skelton, UK	(D) • MIDEAST • 250 kW
	CHINA (PR) †VO THE STRAIT-PLA, Fuzhou	TAIWAN-2 • 50 kW
	CUBA †RADIO HABANA, Havana	Alternative Frequency to 9550 kHz
	CZECHOSLOVAKIA †R CZECHOSLOVAKIA, Vel'ké Kostolany	EUROPE • 100 kW
	JAPAN RADIO JAPAN/NHK, Tokyo-Yamata	(D) • JAPANESE • PACIFIC & W NORTH AM • GENERAL • 300 kW
		(D) • PACIFIC & W NORTH AM • GENERAL • 300 kW
	KAZAKHSTAN †KAZAKH RADIO, Alma-Ata	DS-2 • 100 kW
	†RADIO ALMA-ATA, Alma-Ata	100 kW
	KOREA (DPR) †RADIO PYONGYANG, Pyongyang	JAPANESE • E ASIA • 200 kW
		KOREAN • E ASIA • 200 kW
	PERU †RADIO TACNA, Tacna	Tu-Su • DS • 0.18 kW DS • 0.18 kW • ALT. FREQ. TO 9486 kHz
	RUSSIA †R MOSCOW INTL, Komsomol'sk 'Amure	(D) • W NORTH AM • NORTH AMERICAN SVC • 100 kW
	USA †RFE-RL, Via Germany	(J) • E EUROPE • 100 kW E EUROPE • 100 kW
	†RFE-RL, Via Pals, Spain	W ASIA • 250 kW
	†RFE-RL, Via Portugal	E EUROPE • 250/500 kW
		(D) • E EUROPE • 250/500 kW
		(J) • E EUROPE • 500 kW
	VOA, Via Philippines	SE ASIA • 100 kW
	†VOA, Via Tangier, Morocco	(J) • E EUROPE • 100 kW
	WYFR-FAMILY RADIO, Okeechobee, Fl	W NORTH AM • 100 kW
		(D) • W NORTH AM • 100 kW
9509v	**ALGERIA** †RTV ALGERIENNE, Ouled Fayet	EUROPE & N AFRICA • 50 kW
9510	**AUSTRALIA** †RADIO AUSTRALIA, Carnarvon	(J) • SE ASIA • 250 kW
	GERMANY †DEUTSCHE WELLE, Via Sri Lanka	(D) • MIDEAST • 250 kW
	NEW ZEALAND †R NEW ZEALAND INTL, Rangitaiki	Irr • PACIFIC • SPORTS • 100 kW
	ROMANIA †RADIO ROMANIA INTL, Bucharest	AMERICAS • 250 kW
		EUROPE • 250 kW
		(D) • EUROPE • 250 kW
		(D) • AMERICAS • 250 kW
	SWAZILAND †TRANS WORLD RADIO, Manzini	S AFRICA • 25 kW • ALT. FREQ. TO 9520 kHz
		S AFRICA • 100 kW • ALT. FREQ. TO 9520 kHz
		Sa/Su • S AFRICA • 100 kW • ALT. FREQ. TO 9520 kHz
	UNITED KINGDOM †BBC, Rampisham	(J) • E EUROPE • 500 kW
	USA †KJES, Vado, New Mexico	M-F • N AMERICA • 1 kW
	†VOA, Via Philippines	SE ASIA • 50/250 kW
9515	**BRAZIL** †R NOVAS DE PAZ, Curitiba	PORTUGUESE • DS • 10 kW
	GERMANY DEUTSCHE WELLE, Jülich	(J) • W EUROPE • 100 kW
(con'd)	†DEUTSCHE WELLE, Nauen	(D) • S AMERICA • 500 kW

0 1 2 3 4 5 6 7 8 9 10 11 12 13 14 15 16 17 18 19 20 21 22 23 24

ENGLISH ▬ ARABIC ▨ CHINESE ▫▫▫ FRENCH ▬ GERMAN ▬ RUSSIAN ═ SPANISH ▬ OTHER ▬

FREQUENCY   COUNTRY, STATION, LOCATION

TARGET • NETWORK • POWER (kW)   World Time

0 1 2 3 4 5 6 7 8 9 10 11 12 13 14 15 16 17 18 19 20 21 22 23 24

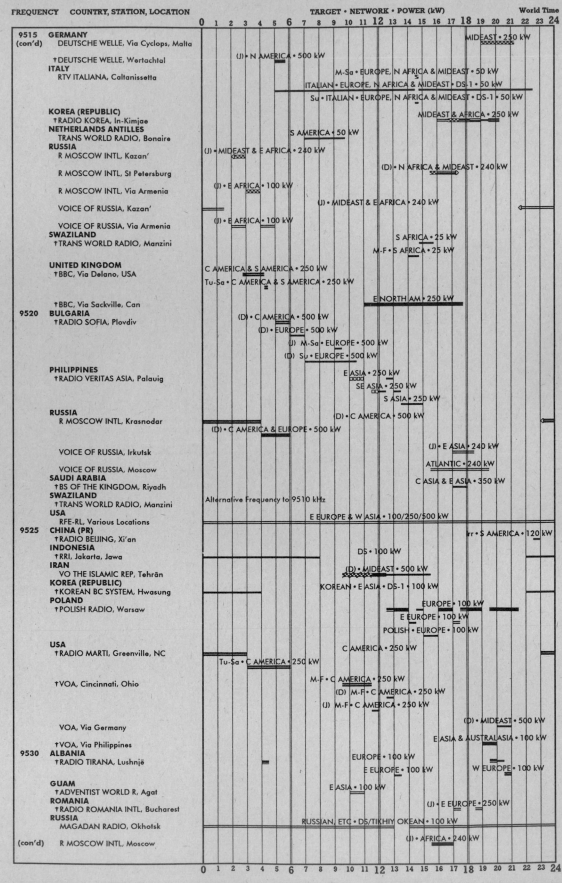

9515 **GERMANY**
(con'd)   DEUTSCHE WELLE, Via Cyclops, Malta   MIDEAST • 250 kW
        (J) • N AMERICA • 500 kW
    †DEUTSCHE WELLE, Wertachtal
    ITALY   M-Sa • EUROPE, N AFRICA & MIDEAST • 50 kW
    RTV ITALIANA, Caltanissetta   ITALIAN • EUROPE, N AFRICA & MIDEAST • DS-1 • 50 kW
        Su • ITALIAN • EUROPE, N AFRICA & MIDEAST • DS-1 • 50 kW

    KOREA (REPUBLIC)   MIDEAST & AFRICA • 250 kW
    †RADIO KOREA, In-Kimjae
    NETHERLANDS ANTILLES
    TRANS WORLD RADIO, Bonaire   S AMERICA • 50 kW
    RUSSIA
    R MOSCOW INTL, Kazan' (J) • MIDEAST & E AFRICA • 240 kW

    R MOSCOW INTL, St Petersburg   (D) • N AFRICA & MIDEAST • 240 kW

    R MOSCOW INTL, Via Armenia (J) • E AFRICA • 100 kW

    VOICE OF RUSSIA, Kazan'   (J) • MIDEAST & E AFRICA • 240 kW

    VOICE OF RUSSIA, Via Armenia (J) • E AFRICA • 100 kW
    SWAZILAND   S AFRICA • 25 kW
    †TRANS WORLD RADIO, Manzini M-F • S AFRICA • 25 kW

    UNITED KINGDOM   C AMERICA & S AMERICA • 250 kW
    †BBC, Via Delano, USA Tu-Sa • C AMERICA & S AMERICA • 250 kW

    †BBC, Via Sackville, Can   E NORTH AM • 250 kW
9520 **BULGARIA**   (D) • C AMERICA • 500 kW
    †RADIO SOFIA, Plovdiv   (D) • EUROPE • 500 kW
        (J) M-Sa • EUROPE • 500 kW
        (D) Su • EUROPE • 500 kW

    PHILIPPINES   E ASIA • 250 kW
    †RADIO VERITAS ASIA, Palauig SE ASIA • 250 kW
        S ASIA • 250 kW

    RUSSIA   (D) • C AMERICA • 500 kW
    R MOSCOW INTL, Krasnodar (D) • C AMERICA & EUROPE • 500 kW

    VOICE OF RUSSIA, Irkutsk   (J) • E ASIA • 240 kW

    VOICE OF RUSSIA, Moscow   ATLANTIC • 240 kW
    SAUDI ARABIA   C ASIA & E ASIA • 350 kW
    †BS OF THE KINGDOM, Riyadh
    SWAZILAND
    †TRANS WORLD RADIO, Manzini Alternative Frequency to 9510 kHz
    USA
    RFE-RL, Various Locations E EUROPE & W ASIA • 100/250/500 kW
9525 **CHINA (PR)**   Irr • S AMERICA • 120 kW
    †RADIO BEIJING, Xi'an
    INDONESIA   DS • 100 kW
    †RRI, Jakarta, Jawa
    IRAN   (D) • MIDEAST • 500 kW
    VO THE ISLAMIC REP, Tehrān
    KOREA (REPUBLIC) KOREAN • E ASIA • DS-1 • 100 kW
    †KOREAN BC SYSTEM, Hwasung
    POLAND   EUROPE • 100 kW
    †POLISH RADIO, Warsaw E EUROPE • 100 kW
        POLISH • EUROPE • 100 kW

    USA   C AMERICA • 250 kW
    †RADIO MARTI, Greenville, NC Tu-Sa • C AMERICA • 250 kW

    †VOA, Cincinnati, Ohio M-F • C AMERICA • 250 kW
        (D) M-F • C AMERICA • 250 kW
        (J) M-F • C AMERICA • 250 kW

    VOA, Via Germany   (D) • MIDEAST • 500 kW

    †VOA, Via Philippines   E ASIA & AUSTRALASIA • 100 kW
9530 **ALBANIA**   EUROPE • 100 kW
    †RADIO TIRANA, Lushnjë E EUROPE • 100 kW   W EUROPE • 100 kW

    GUAM   E ASIA • 100 kW
    †ADVENTIST WORLD R, Agat
    ROMANIA   (J) • E EUROPE • 250 kW
    †RADIO ROMANIA INTL, Bucharest
    RUSSIA
    MAGADAN RADIO, Okhotsk RUSSIAN, ETC • DS/TIKHIY OKEAN • 100 kW

(con'd)   R MOSCOW INTL, Moscow (J) • AFRICA • 240 kW

0 1 2 3 4 5 6 7 8 9 10 11 12 13 14 15 16 17 18 19 20 21 22 23 24

FREQUENCY   COUNTRY, STATION, LOCATION TARGET • NETWORK • POWER (kW) World Time

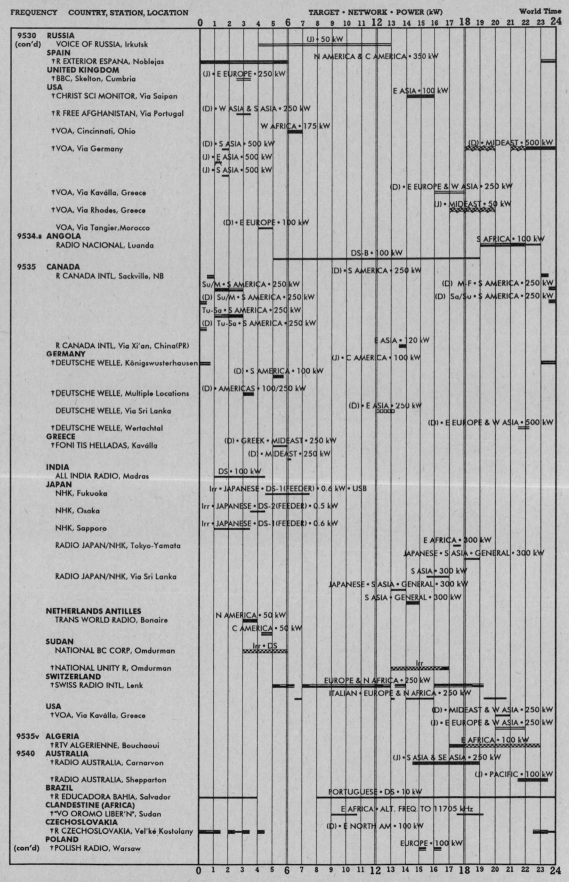

9530 **RUSSIA**		
(con'd)	VOICE OF RUSSIA, Irkutsk	(J) • 50 kW
	SPAIN	
	†R EXTERIOR ESPANA, Noblejas	N AMERICA & C AMERICA • 350 kW
	UNITED KINGDOM	
	†BBC, Skelton, Cumbria	(J) • E EUROPE • 250 kW
	USA	
	†CHRIST SCI MONITOR, Via Saipan	E ASIA • 100 kW
	†R FREE AFGHANISTAN, Via Portugal	(D) • W ASIA & S ASIA • 250 kW
	†VOA, Cincinnati, Ohio	W AFRICA • 175 kW
	†VOA, Via Germany	(D) • S ASIA • 500 kW / (D) • MIDEAST • 500 kW
		(J) • E ASIA • 500 kW
		(J) • S ASIA • 500 kW
	†VOA, Via Kaválla, Greece	(D) • E EUROPE & W ASIA • 250 kW
	†VOA, Via Rhodes, Greece	(J) • MIDEAST • 50 kW
	VOA, Via Tangier, Morocco	(D) • E EUROPE • 100 kW
9534.8	**ANGOLA**	
	RADIO NACIONAL, Luanda	S AFRICA • 100 kW / DS-B • 100 kW
9535	**CANADA**	
	R CANADA INTL, Sackville, NB	(D) • S AMERICA • 250 kW
		Su/M • S AMERICA • 250 kW / (D) M-F • S AMERICA • 250 kW
		(D) Su/M • S AMERICA • 250 kW / (D) Sa/Su • S AMERICA • 250 kW
		Tu-Sa • S AMERICA • 250 kW
		(D) Tu-Sa • S AMERICA • 250 kW
	R CANADA INTL, Via Xi'an, China(PR)	E ASIA • 120 kW
	GERMANY	
	†DEUTSCHE WELLE, Königswusterhausen	(J) • C AMERICA • 100 kW
		(D) • S AMERICA • 100 kW
	†DEUTSCHE WELLE, Multiple Locations	(D) • AMERICAS • 100/250 kW
	DEUTSCHE WELLE, Via Sri Lanka	(D) • E ASIA • 250 kW
	†DEUTSCHE WELLE, Wertachtal	(D) • E EUROPE & W ASIA • 500 kW
	GREECE	
	†FONI TIS HELLADAS, Kaválla	(D) • GREEK • MIDEAST • 250 kW
		(D) • MIDEAST • 250 kW
	INDIA	
	ALL INDIA RADIO, Madras	DS • 100 kW
	JAPAN	
	NHK, Fukuoka	Irr • JAPANESE • DS-1 (FEEDER) • 0.6 kW • USB
	NHK, Osaka	Irr • JAPANESE • DS-2 (FEEDER) • 0.5 kW
	NHK, Sapporo	Irr • JAPANESE • DS-1 (FEEDER) • 0.6 kW
	RADIO JAPAN/NHK, Tokyo-Yamata	E AFRICA • 300 kW
		JAPANESE • S ASIA • GENERAL • 300 kW
	RADIO JAPAN/NHK, Via Sri Lanka	S ASIA • 300 kW
		JAPANESE • S ASIA • GENERAL • 300 kW
		S ASIA • GENERAL • 300 kW
	NETHERLANDS ANTILLES	
	TRANS WORLD RADIO, Bonaire	N AMERICA • 50 kW
		C AMERICA • 50 kW
	SUDAN	
	NATIONAL BC CORP, Omdurman	Irr • DS
	†NATIONAL UNITY R, Omdurman	Irr
	SWITZERLAND	
	†SWISS RADIO INTL, Lenk	EUROPE & N AFRICA • 250 kW
		ITALIAN • EUROPE & N AFRICA • 250 kW
	USA	
	†VOA, Via Kaválla, Greece	(D) • MIDEAST & W ASIA • 250 kW
		(J) • E EUROPE & W ASIA • 250 kW
9535v	**ALGERIA**	
	†RTV ALGERIENNE, Bouchaoui	E AFRICA • 100 kW
9540	**AUSTRALIA**	
	†RADIO AUSTRALIA, Carnarvon	(J) • S ASIA & SE ASIA • 250 kW
	†RADIO AUSTRALIA, Shepparton	(J) • PACIFIC • 100 kW
	BRAZIL	
	†R EDUCADORA BAHIA, Salvador	PORTUGUESE • DS • 10 kW
	CLANDESTINE (AFRICA)	
	†"VO OROMO LIBER'N", Sudan	E AFRICA • ALT. FREQ. TO 11705 kHz
	CZECHOSLOVAKIA	
	†R CZECHOSLOVAKIA, Vel'ké Kostolany	(D) • E NORTH AM • 100 kW
	POLAND	
(con'd)	†POLISH RADIO, Warsaw	EUROPE • 100 kW

ENGLISH ▬ ARABIC ≋ CHINESE ▭▭▭ FRENCH ═ GERMAN ▬ RUSSIAN ═ SPANISH ▬ OTHER ▬

FREQUENCY   COUNTRY, STATION, LOCATION   TARGET • NETWORK • POWER (kW)   World Time

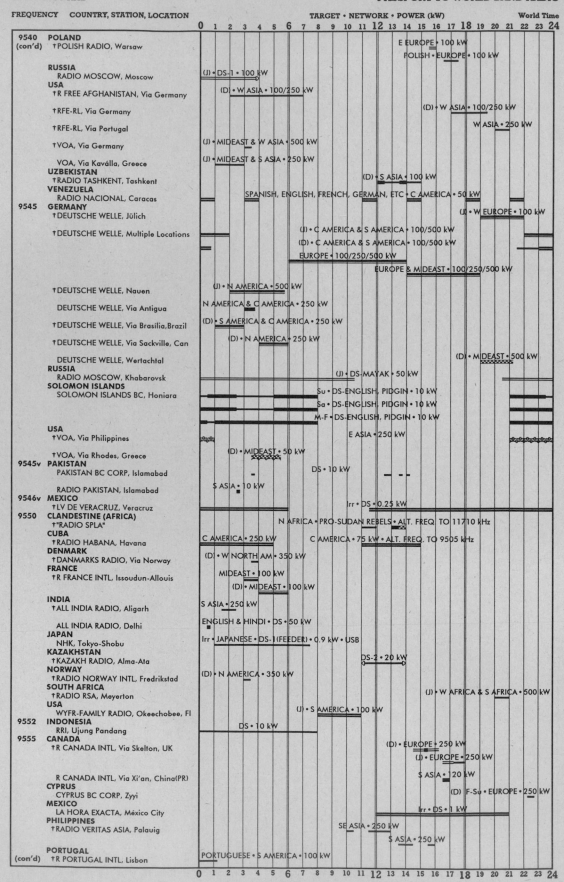

0 1 2 3 4 5 6 7 8 9 10 11 12 13 14 15 16 17 18 19 20 21 22 23 24

Frequency	Country, Station, Location	Target • Network • Power
9540 (con'd)	**POLAND** †POLISH RADIO, Warsaw	E EUROPE • 100 kW / POLISH • EUROPE • 100 kW
	RUSSIA RADIO MOSCOW, Moscow	(J) • DS-1 • 100 kW
	USA †R FREE AFGHANISTAN, Via Germany	(D) • W ASIA • 100/250 kW
	†RFE-RL, Via Germany	(D) • W ASIA • 100/250 kW
	†RFE-RL, Via Portugal	W ASIA • 250 kW
	†VOA, Via Germany	(J) • MIDEAST & W ASIA • 500 kW
	VOA, Via Kaválla, Greece	(J) • MIDEAST & S ASIA • 250 kW
	UZBEKISTAN †RADIO TASHKENT, Tashkent	(D) • S ASIA • 100 kW
	VENEZUELA RADIO NACIONAL, Caracas	SPANISH, ENGLISH, FRENCH, GERMAN, ETC • C AMERICA • 50 kW
9545	**GERMANY** †DEUTSCHE WELLE, Jülich	(J) • W EUROPE • 100 kW
	†DEUTSCHE WELLE, Multiple Locations	(J) • C AMERICA & S AMERICA • 100/500 kW / (D) • C AMERICA & S AMERICA • 100/500 kW / EUROPE • 100/250/500 kW / EUROPE & MIDEAST • 100/250/500 kW
	†DEUTSCHE WELLE, Nauen	(J) • N AMERICA • 500 kW
	DEUTSCHE WELLE, Via Antigua	N AMERICA & C AMERICA • 250 kW
	†DEUTSCHE WELLE, Via Brasilia, Brazil	(D) • S AMERICA & C AMERICA • 250 kW
	†DEUTSCHE WELLE, Via Sackville, Can	(D) • N AMERICA • 250 kW
	DEUTSCHE WELLE, Wertachtal	(D) • MIDEAST • 500 kW
	RUSSIA RADIO MOSCOW, Khabarovsk	(J) • DS-MAYAK • 50 kW
	SOLOMON ISLANDS SOLOMON ISLANDS BC, Honiara	Su • DS-ENGLISH, PIDGIN • 10 kW / Sa • DS-ENGLISH, PIDGIN • 10 kW / M-F • DS-ENGLISH, PIDGIN • 10 kW
	USA †VOA, Via Philippines	E ASIA • 250 kW
9545v	†VOA, Via Rhodes, Greece	(D) • MIDEAST • 50 kW
	PAKISTAN PAKISTAN BC CORP, Islamabad	DS • 10 kW
	RADIO PAKISTAN, Islamabad	S ASIA • 10 kW
9546v	**MEXICO** †LV DE VERACRUZ, Veracruz	Irr • DS • 0.25 kW
9550	**CLANDESTINE (AFRICA)** †"RADIO SPLA"	N AFRICA • PRO-SUDAN REBELS • ALT. FREQ. TO 11710 kHz
	CUBA †RADIO HABANA, Havana	C AMERICA • 250 kW / C AMERICA • 75 kW • ALT. FREQ. TO 9505 kHz
	DENMARK †DANMARKS RADIO, Via Norway	(D) • W NORTH AM • 350 kW
	FRANCE †R FRANCE INTL, Issoudun-Allouis	MIDEAST • 100 kW / (D) • MIDEAST • 100 kW
	INDIA †ALL INDIA RADIO, Aligarh	S ASIA • 250 kW
	ALL INDIA RADIO, Delhi	ENGLISH & HINDI • DS • 50 kW
	JAPAN NHK, Tokyo-Shobu	Irr • JAPANESE • DS-1 (FEEDER) • 0.9 kW • USB
	KAZAKHSTAN †KAZAKH RADIO, Alma-Ata	DS-2 • 20 kW
	NORWAY †RADIO NORWAY INTL, Fredrikstad	(D) • N AMERICA • 350 kW
	SOUTH AFRICA †RADIO RSA, Meyerton	(J) • W AFRICA & S AFRICA • 500 kW
	USA WYFR-FAMILY RADIO, Okeechobee, Fl	(J) • S AMERICA • 100 kW
9552	**INDONESIA** RRI, Ujung Pandang	DS • 10 kW
9555	**CANADA** †R CANADA INTL, Via Skelton, UK	(D) • EUROPE • 250 kW / (J) • EUROPE • 250 kW
	R CANADA INTL, Via Xi'an, China(PR)	S ASIA • 120 kW
	CYPRUS CYPRUS BC CORP, Zyyi	(D) • F-Su • EUROPE • 250 kW
	MEXICO LA HORA EXACTA, México City	Irr • DS • 1 kW
	PHILIPPINES †RADIO VERITAS ASIA, Palauig	SE ASIA • 250 kW / S ASIA • 250 kW
(con'd)	**PORTUGAL** †R PORTUGAL INTL, Lisbon	PORTUGUESE • S AMERICA • 100 kW

0 1 2 3 4 5 6 7 8 9 10 11 12 13 14 15 16 17 18 19 20 21 22 23 24

SUMMER ONLY (J)   WINTER ONLY (D)   JAMMING / OR ∧   EARLIEST HEARD ◁   LATEST HEARD ▷   NEW OR CHANGED FOR 1993 †

FREQUENCY   COUNTRY, STATION, LOCATION

TARGET • NETWORK • POWER (kW)

World Time

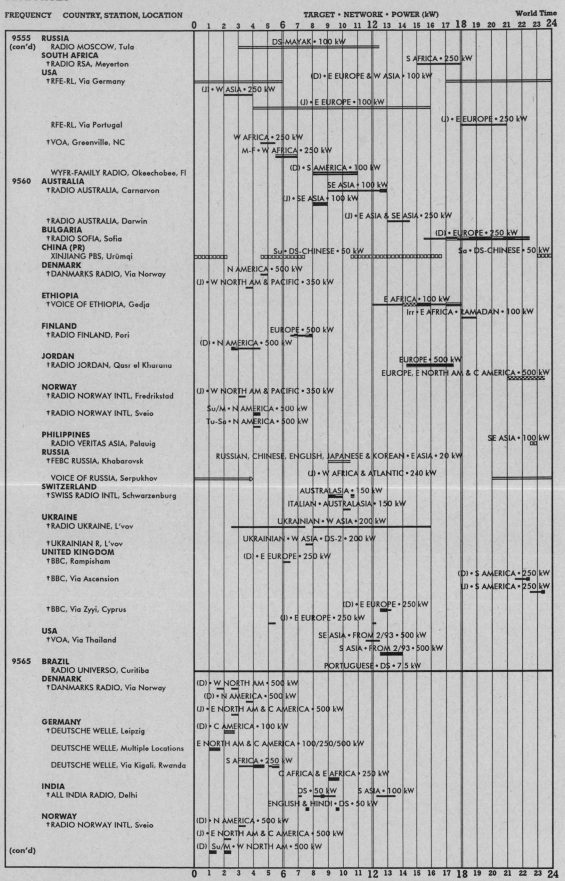

0 1 2 3 4 5 6 7 8 9 10 11 12 13 14 15 16 17 18 19 20 21 22 23 24

9555 RUSSIA
(con'd)   RADIO MOSCOW, Tula — DS-MAYAK • 100 kW
SOUTH AFRICA
   †RADIO RSA, Meyerton — S AFRICA • 250 kW
USA
   †RFE-RL, Via Germany — (D) • E EUROPE & W ASIA • 100 kW
   (J) • W ASIA • 250 kW
   (J) • E EUROPE • 100 kW

   RFE-RL, Via Portugal — (J) • E EUROPE • 250 kW
   †VOA, Greenville, NC — W AFRICA • 250 kW
   M-F • W AFRICA • 250 kW

   WYFR-FAMILY RADIO, Okeechobee, Fl — (D) • S AMERICA • 100 kW
9560 AUSTRALIA
   †RADIO AUSTRALIA, Carnarvon — SE ASIA • 100 kW
   (J) • SE ASIA • 100 kW

   †RADIO AUSTRALIA, Darwin — (J) • E ASIA & SE ASIA • 250 kW
BULGARIA
   †RADIO SOFIA, Sofia — (D) • EUROPE • 250 kW
CHINA (PR)
   XINJIANG PBS, Urümqi — Su • DS-CHINESE • 50 kW   Sa • DS-CHINESE • 50 kW
DENMARK
   †DANMARKS RADIO, Via Norway — N AMERICA • 500 kW
   (J) • W NORTH AM & PACIFIC • 350 kW
ETHIOPIA
   †VOICE OF ETHIOPIA, Gedja — E AFRICA • 100 kW
   Irr • E AFRICA • RAMADAN • 100 kW
FINLAND
   †RADIO FINLAND, Pori — EUROPE • 500 kW
   (D) • N AMERICA • 500 kW
JORDAN
   †RADIO JORDAN, Qasr el Kharana — EUROPE • 500 kW
   EUROPE, E NORTH AM & C AMERICA • 500 kW
NORWAY
   †RADIO NORWAY INTL, Fredrikstad — (J) • W NORTH AM & PACIFIC • 350 kW
   †RADIO NORWAY INTL, Sveio — Su/M • N AMERICA • 500 kW
   Tu-Sa • N AMERICA • 500 kW
PHILIPPINES
   RADIO VERITAS ASIA, Palauig — SE ASIA • 100 kW
RUSSIA
   †FEBC RUSSIA, Khabarovsk — RUSSIAN, CHINESE, ENGLISH, JAPANESE & KOREAN • E ASIA • 20 kW
   VOICE OF RUSSIA, Serpukhov — (J) • W AFRICA & ATLANTIC • 240 kW
SWITZERLAND
   †SWISS RADIO INTL, Schwarzenburg — AUSTRALASIA • 150 kW
   ITALIAN • AUSTRALASIA • 150 kW
UKRAINE
   †RADIO UKRAINE, L'vov — UKRAINIAN • W ASIA • 200 kW
   †UKRAINIAN R, L'vov — UKRAINIAN • W ASIA • DS-2 • 200 kW
UNITED KINGDOM
   †BBC, Rampisham — (D) • E EUROPE • 250 kW
   †BBC, Via Ascension — (D) • S AMERICA • 250 kW
   (J) • S AMERICA • 250 kW
   †BBC, Via Zyyi, Cyprus — (D) • E EUROPE • 250 kW
   (J) • E EUROPE • 250 kW
USA
   †VOA, Via Thailand — SE ASIA • FROM 2/93 • 500 kW
   S ASIA • FROM 2/93 • 500 kW
9565 BRAZIL
   RADIO UNIVERSO, Curitiba — PORTUGUESE • DS • 7.5 kW
DENMARK
   †DANMARKS RADIO, Via Norway — (D) • W NORTH AM • 500 kW
   (D) • N AMERICA • 500 kW
   (J) • E NORTH AM & C AMERICA • 500 kW
GERMANY
   †DEUTSCHE WELLE, Leipzig — (D) • C AMERICA • 100 kW
   DEUTSCHE WELLE, Multiple Locations — E NORTH AM & C AMERICA • 100/250/500 kW
   DEUTSCHE WELLE, Via Kigali, Rwanda — S AFRICA • 250 kW
   C AFRICA & E AFRICA • 250 kW
INDIA
   †ALL INDIA RADIO, Delhi — DS • 50 kW   S ASIA • 100 kW
   ENGLISH & HINDI • DS • 50 kW
NORWAY
   †RADIO NORWAY INTL, Sveio — (D) • N AMERICA • 500 kW
   (J) • E NORTH AM & C AMERICA • 500 kW
   (D) Su/M • W NORTH AM • 500 kW

(con'd)

0 1 2 3 4 5 6 7 8 9 10 11 12 13 14 15 16 17 18 19 20 21 22 23 24

ENGLISH ▬   ARABIC ⌇⌇⌇   CHINESE ▫▫▫   FRENCH ▭▭   GERMAN ▬   RUSSIAN ══   SPANISH ▬   OTHER ▬

| FREQUENCY | COUNTRY, STATION, LOCATION | TARGET • NETWORK • POWER (kW) | World Time |

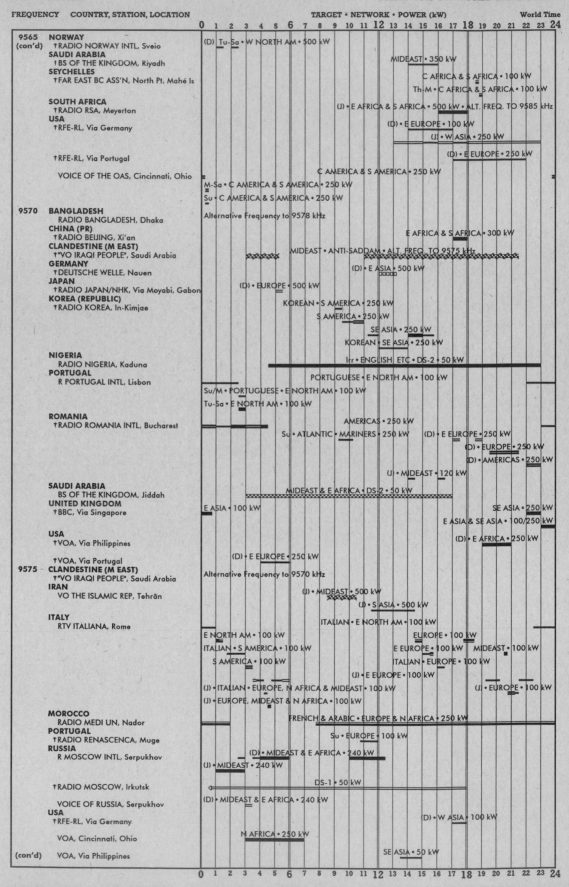

9565 NORWAY
(con'd) †RADIO NORWAY INTL, Sveio — (D) • Tu-Sa • W NORTH AM • 500 kW
SAUDI ARABIA
†BS OF THE KINGDOM, Riyadh — MIDEAST • 350 kW
SEYCHELLES
†FAR EAST BC ASS'N, North Pt, Mahé Is — C AFRICA & S AFRICA • 100 kW / Th-M • C AFRICA & S AFRICA • 100 kW
SOUTH AFRICA
†RADIO RSA, Meyerton — (J) • E AFRICA & S AFRICA • 500 kW • ALT. FREQ. TO 9585 kHz
USA
†RFE-RL, Via Germany — (D) • E EUROPE • 100 kW / (J) • W ASIA • 250 kW
†RFE-RL, Via Portugal — (D) • E EUROPE • 250 kW
VOICE OF THE OAS, Cincinnati, Ohio — C AMERICA & S AMERICA • 250 kW / M-Sa • C AMERICA & S AMERICA • 250 kW / Su • C AMERICA & S AMERICA • 250 kW

9570 BANGLADESH
RADIO BANGLADESH, Dhaka — Alternative Frequency to 9578 kHz
CHINA (PR)
†RADIO BEIJING, Xi'an — E AFRICA & S AFRICA • 300 kW
CLANDESTINE (M EAST)
†"VO IRAQI PEOPLE", Saudi Arabia — MIDEAST • ANTI-SADDAM • ALT. FREQ. TO 9575 kHz
GERMANY
†DEUTSCHE WELLE, Nauen — (D) • E ASIA • 500 kW
JAPAN
†RADIO JAPAN/NHK, Via Moyabi, Gabon — (D) • EUROPE • 500 kW
KOREA (REPUBLIC)
†RADIO KOREA, In-Kimjae — KOREAN • S AMERICA • 250 kW / S AMERICA • 250 kW / SE ASIA • 250 kW / KOREAN • SE ASIA • 250 kW
NIGERIA
RADIO NIGERIA, Kaduna — Irr • ENGLISH, ETC • DS-2 • 50 kW
PORTUGAL
R PORTUGAL INTL, Lisbon — PORTUGUESE • E NORTH AM • 100 kW / Su/M • PORTUGUESE • E NORTH AM • 100 kW / Tu-Sa • E NORTH AM • 100 kW
ROMANIA
†RADIO ROMANIA INTL, Bucharest — AMERICAS • 250 kW / Su • ATLANTIC MARINERS • 250 kW / (D) • E EUROPE • 250 kW / (D) • EUROPE • 250 kW / (D) • AMERICAS • 250 kW / (J) • MIDEAST • 120 kW
SAUDI ARABIA
BS OF THE KINGDOM, Jiddah — MIDEAST & E AFRICA • DS-2 • 50 kW
UNITED KINGDOM
†BBC, Via Singapore — E ASIA • 100 kW / SE ASIA • 250 kW / E ASIA & SE ASIA • 100/250 kW
USA
†VOA, Via Philippines — (D) • E AFRICA • 250 kW
†VOA, Via Portugal — (D) • E EUROPE • 250 kW

9575 CLANDESTINE (M EAST)
†"VO IRAQI PEOPLE", Saudi Arabia — Alternative Frequency to 9570 kHz
IRAN
VO THE ISLAMIC REP, Tehrān — (J) • MIDEAST • 500 kW / (J) • S ASIA • 500 kW
ITALY
RTV ITALIANA, Rome — ITALIAN • E NORTH AM • 100 kW / E NORTH AM • 100 kW / EUROPE • 100 kW / ITALIAN • S AMERICA • 100 kW / E EUROPE • 100 kW / MIDEAST • 100 kW / S AMERICA • 100 kW / ITALIAN • EUROPE • 100 kW / (J) • E EUROPE • 100 kW / (J) • ITALIAN • EUROPE, N AFRICA & MIDEAST • 100 kW / (J) • EUROPE • 100 kW / (J) • EUROPE, MIDEAST & N AFRICA • 100 kW
MOROCCO
RADIO MEDI UN, Nador — FRENCH & ARABIC • EUROPE & N AFRICA • 250 kW
PORTUGAL
†RADIO RENASCENCA, Muge — Su • EUROPE • 100 kW
RUSSIA
R MOSCOW INTL, Serpukhov — (D) • MIDEAST & E AFRICA • 240 kW / (J) • MIDEAST • 240 kW
†RADIO MOSCOW, Irkutsk — DS-1 • 50 kW
VOICE OF RUSSIA, Serpukhov — (D) • MIDEAST & E AFRICA • 240 kW
USA
†RFE-RL, Via Germany — (D) • W ASIA • 100 kW
VOA, Cincinnati, Ohio — N AFRICA • 250 kW
(con'd) VOA, Via Philippines — SE ASIA • 50 kW

SUMMER ONLY (J)   WINTER ONLY (D)   JAMMING / OR ∧   EARLIEST HEARD ◁   LATEST HEARD ▷   NEW OR CHANGED FOR 1993 †

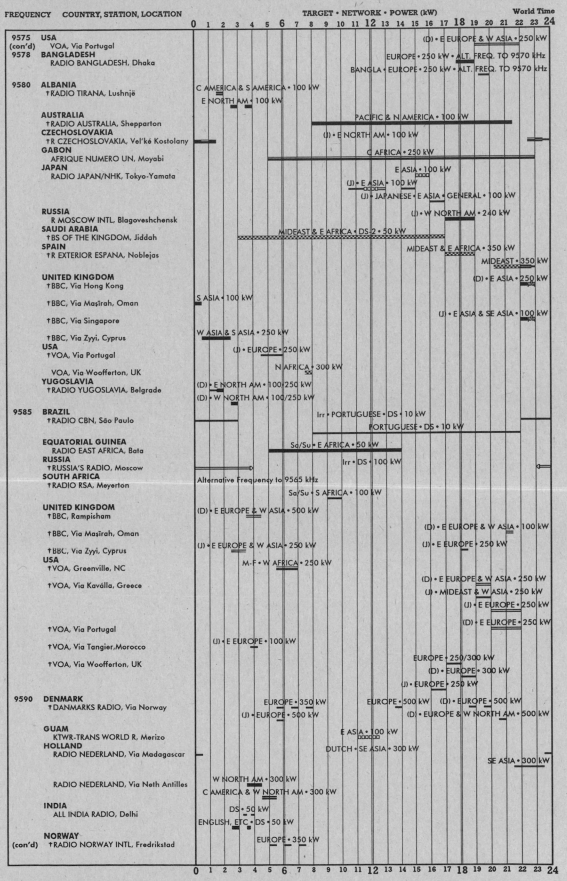

FREQUENCY   COUNTRY, STATION, LOCATION

TARGET • NETWORK • POWER (kW)

World Time

0 1 2 3 4 5 6 7 8 9 10 11 12 13 14 15 16 17 18 19 20 21 22 23 24

9575 (con'd)	USA
	VOA, Via Portugal — (D) • E EUROPE & W ASIA • 250 kW
9578	BANGLADESH
	RADIO BANGLADESH, Dhaka — EUROPE • 250 kW • ALT. FREQ. TO 9570 kHz
	BANGLA • EUROPE • 250 kW • ALT. FREQ. TO 9570 kHz
9580	ALBANIA
	†RADIO TIRANA, Lushnjë — C AMERICA & S AMERICA • 100 kW / E NORTH AM • 100 kW
	AUSTRALIA
	†RADIO AUSTRALIA, Shepparton — PACIFIC & N AMERICA • 100 kW
	CZECHOSLOVAKIA
	†R CZECHOSLOVAKIA, Vel'ké Kostolany — (J) • E NORTH AM • 100 kW
	GABON
	AFRIQUE NUMERO UN, Moyabi — C AFRICA • 250 kW
	JAPAN
	RADIO JAPAN/NHK, Tokyo-Yamata — E ASIA • 100 kW / (J) • E ASIA • 100 kW / (J) • JAPANESE • E ASIA • GENERAL • 100 kW
	RUSSIA
	R MOSCOW INTL, Blagoveshchensk — (J) • W NORTH AM • 240 kW
	SAUDI ARABIA
	†BS OF THE KINGDOM, Jiddah — MIDEAST & E AFRICA • DS-2 • 50 kW
	SPAIN
	†R EXTERIOR ESPANA, Noblejas — MIDEAST & E AFRICA • 350 kW / MIDEAST • 350 kW
	UNITED KINGDOM
	†BBC, Via Hong Kong — (D) • E ASIA • 250 kW
	†BBC, Via Maşîrah, Oman — S ASIA • 100 kW
	†BBC, Via Singapore — (J) • E ASIA & SE ASIA • 100 kW
	†BBC, Via Zyyi, Cyprus — W ASIA & S ASIA • 250 kW
	USA
	†VOA, Via Portugal — (J) • EUROPE • 250 kW
	VOA, Via Woofferton, UK — N AFRICA • 300 kW
	YUGOSLAVIA
	†RADIO YUGOSLAVIA, Belgrade — (D) • E NORTH AM • 100/250 kW / (D) • W NORTH AM • 100/250 kW
9585	BRAZIL
	†RADIO CBN, São Paulo — Irr • PORTUGUESE • DS • 10 kW / PORTUGUESE • DS • 10 kW
	EQUATORIAL GUINEA
	RADIO EAST AFRICA, Bata — Sa/Su • E AFRICA • 50 kW
	RUSSIA
	†RUSSIA'S RADIO, Moscow — Irr • DS • 100 kW
	SOUTH AFRICA
	†RADIO RSA, Meyerton — Alternative Frequency to 9565 kHz / Sa/Su • S AFRICA • 100 kW
	UNITED KINGDOM
	†BBC, Rampisham — (D) • E EUROPE & W ASIA • 500 kW
	†BBC, Via Maşîrah, Oman — (D) • E EUROPE & W ASIA • 100 kW
	†BBC, Via Zyyi, Cyprus — (J) • E EUROPE & W ASIA • 250 kW / (J) • E EUROPE • 250 kW
	USA
	†VOA, Greenville, NC — M-F • W AFRICA • 250 kW
	†VOA, Via Kaválla, Greece — (D) • E EUROPE & W ASIA • 250 kW / (J) • MIDEAST & W ASIA • 250 kW / (J) • E EUROPE • 250 kW / (D) • E EUROPE • 250 kW
	†VOA, Via Portugal — (J) • E EUROPE • 100 kW
	†VOA, Via Tangier, Morocco — EUROPE • 250/300 kW
	†VOA, Via Woofferton, UK — (D) • EUROPE • 300 kW / (J) • EUROPE • 250 kW
9590	DENMARK
	†DANMARKS RADIO, Via Norway — EUROPE • 350 kW / EUROPE • 500 kW / (D) • EUROPE • 500 kW / (J) • EUROPE • 500 kW / (D) • EUROPE & W NORTH AM • 500 kW
	GUAM
	KTWR-TRANS WORLD R, Merizo — E ASIA • 100 kW
	HOLLAND
	RADIO NEDERLAND, Via Madagascar — DUTCH • SE ASIA • 300 kW / SE ASIA • 300 kW
	RADIO NEDERLAND, Via Neth Antilles — W NORTH AM • 300 kW / C AMERICA & W NORTH AM • 300 kW
	INDIA
	ALL INDIA RADIO, Delhi — DS • 50 kW / ENGLISH, ETC • DS • 50 kW
	NORWAY
(con'd)	†RADIO NORWAY INTL, Fredrikstad — EUROPE • 350 kW

0 1 2 3 4 5 6 7 8 9 10 11 12 13 14 15 16 17 18 19 20 21 22 23 24

ENGLISH ▬▬   ARABIC ▨▨   CHINESE ▢▢▢   FRENCH ▭▭   GERMAN ▬▬   RUSSIAN ▬▬   SPANISH ▬▬   OTHER ▬▬

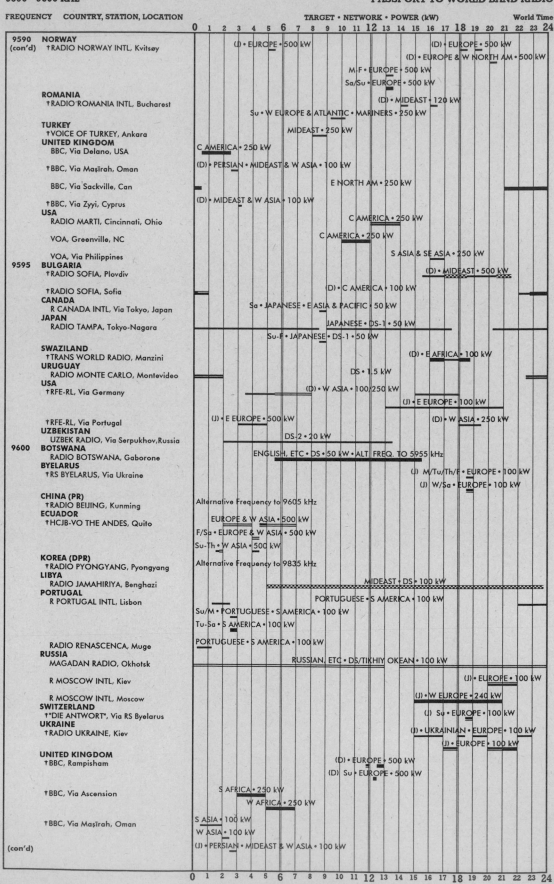

FREQUENCY   COUNTRY, STATION, LOCATION

TARGET • NETWORK • POWER (kW)

World Time

FREQUENCY	COUNTRY, STATION, LOCATION	TARGET • NETWORK • POWER (kW)
9590 (con'd)	**NORWAY** †RADIO NORWAY INTL, Kvitsøy	(J) • EUROPE • 500 kW / (D) • EUROPE • 500 kW / (D) • EUROPE & W NORTH AM • 500 kW / M-F • EUROPE • 500 kW / Sa/Su • EUROPE • 500 kW
	ROMANIA †RADIO ROMANIA INTL, Bucharest	(D) • MIDEAST • 120 kW / Su • W EUROPE & ATLANTIC • MARINERS • 250 kW
	TURKEY †VOICE OF TURKEY, Ankara	MIDEAST • 250 kW
	UNITED KINGDOM BBC, Via Delano, USA	C AMERICA • 250 kW
	†BBC, Via Maşīrah, Oman	(D) • PERSIAN • MIDEAST & W ASIA • 100 kW
	BBC, Via Sackville, Can	E NORTH AM • 250 kW
	†BBC, Via Zyyi, Cyprus	(D) • MIDEAST & W ASIA • 100 kW
	USA RADIO MARTI, Cincinnati, Ohio	C AMERICA • 250 kW
	VOA, Greenville, NC	C AMERICA • 250 kW
	VOA, Via Philippines	S ASIA & SE ASIA • 250 kW
9595	**BULGARIA** †RADIO SOFIA, Plovdiv	(D) • MIDEAST • 500 kW
	†RADIO SOFIA, Sofia	(D) • C AMERICA • 100 kW
	CANADA R CANADA INTL, Via Tokyo, Japan	Sa • JAPANESE • E ASIA & PACIFIC • 50 kW
	JAPAN RADIO TAMPA, Tokyo-Nagara	JAPANESE • DS-1 • 50 kW / Su-F • JAPANESE • DS-1 • 50 kW
	SWAZILAND †TRANS WORLD RADIO, Manzini	(D) • E AFRICA • 100 kW
	URUGUAY RADIO MONTE CARLO, Montevideo	DS • 1.5 kW
	USA †RFE-RL, Via Germany	(D) • W ASIA • 100/250 kW / (J) • E EUROPE • 100 kW
	†RFE-RL, Via Portugal	(J) • E EUROPE • 500 kW / (D) • W ASIA • 250 kW
	UZBEKISTAN UZBEK RADIO, Via Serpukhov,Russia	DS-2 • 20 kW
9600	**BOTSWANA** RADIO BOTSWANA, Gaborone	ENGLISH, ETC • DS • 50 kW • ALT FREQ. TO 5955 kHz
	BYELARUS †RS BYELARUS, Via Ukraine	(J) M/Tu/Th/F • EUROPE • 100 kW / (J) W/Sa • EUROPE • 100 kW
	CHINA (PR) †RADIO BEIJING, Kunming	Alternative Frequency to 9605 kHz
	ECUADOR †HCJB-VO THE ANDES, Quito	EUROPE & W ASIA • 500 kW / F/Sa • EUROPE & W ASIA • 500 kW / Su-Th • W ASIA • 500 kW
	KOREA (DPR) †RADIO PYONGYANG, Pyongyang	Alternative Frequency to 9835 kHz
	LIBYA RADIO JAMAHIRIYA, Benghazi	MIDEAST • DS • 100 kW
	PORTUGAL R PORTUGAL INTL, Lisbon	PORTUGUESE • S AMERICA • 100 kW / Su/M • PORTUGUESE • S AMERICA • 100 kW / Tu-Sa • S AMERICA • 100 kW
	RADIO RENASCENCA, Muge	PORTUGUESE • S AMERICA • 100 kW
	RUSSIA MAGADAN RADIO, Okhotsk	RUSSIAN, ETC • DS/TIKHIY OKEAN • 100 kW
	R MOSCOW INTL, Kiev	(J) • EUROPE • 100 kW
	R MOSCOW INTL, Moscow	(J) • W EUROPE • 240 kW
	SWITZERLAND †"DIE ANTWORT", Via RS Byelarus	(J) Su • EUROPE • 100 kW
	UKRAINE †RADIO UKRAINE, Kiev	(J) • UKRAINIAN • EUROPE • 100 kW / (J) • EUROPE • 100 kW
	UNITED KINGDOM †BBC, Rampisham	(D) • EUROPE • 500 kW / (D) Su • EUROPE • 500 kW
	†BBC, Via Ascension	S AFRICA • 250 kW / W AFRICA • 250 kW
	†BBC, Via Maşīrah, Oman	S ASIA • 100 kW / W ASIA • 100 kW / (J) • PERSIAN • MIDEAST & W ASIA • 100 kW
(con'd)		

FREQUENCY   COUNTRY, STATION, LOCATION

TARGET • NETWORK • POWER (kW)

World Time

0 1 2 3 4 5 6 7 8 9 10 11 12 13 14 15 16 17 18 19 20 21 22 23 24

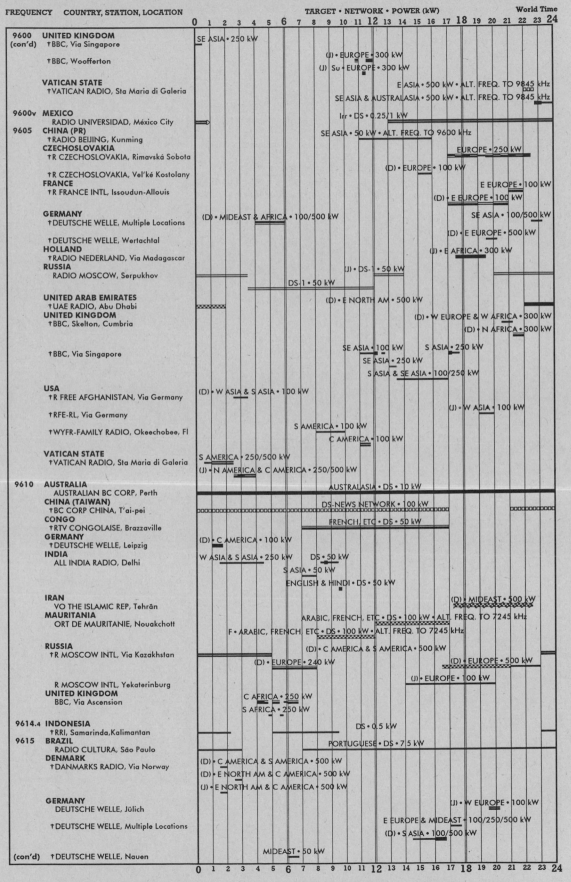

9600	UNITED KINGDOM	
(con'd)	†BBC, Via Singapore	SE ASIA • 250 kW
	†BBC, Woofferton	(J) • EUROPE • 300 kW
		(J) • Su • EUROPE • 300 kW
	VATICAN STATE	
	†VATICAN RADIO, Sta Maria di Galeria	E ASIA • 500 kW • ALT. FREQ. TO 9845 kHz
		SE ASIA & AUSTRALASIA • 500 kW • ALT. FREQ. TO 9845 kHz
9600v	MEXICO	
	RADIO UNIVERSIDAD, México City	Irr • DS • 0.25/1 kW
9605	CHINA (PR)	
	†RADIO BEIJING, Kunming	SE ASIA • 50 kW • ALT. FREQ. TO 9600 kHz
	CZECHOSLOVAKIA	
	†R CZECHOSLOVAKIA, Rimavská Sobota	EUROPE • 250 kW
		(D) • EUROPE • 100 kW
	†R CZECHOSLOVAKIA, Vel'ké Kostolany	E EUROPE • 100 kW
	FRANCE	
	†R FRANCE INTL, Issoudun-Allouis	(D) • E EUROPE • 100 kW
	GERMANY	
	†DEUTSCHE WELLE, Multiple Locations	(D) • MIDEAST & AFRICA • 100/500 kW
		SE ASIA • 100/500 kW
	†DEUTSCHE WELLE, Wertachtal	(D) • E EUROPE • 500 kW
	HOLLAND	
	†RADIO NEDERLAND, Via Madagascar	(J) • E AFRICA • 300 kW
	RUSSIA	
	RADIO MOSCOW, Serpukhov	(J) • DS-1 • 50 kW
		DS-1 • 50 kW
	UNITED ARAB EMIRATES	
	†UAE RADIO, Abu Dhabi	(D) • E NORTH AM • 500 kW
	UNITED KINGDOM	
	†BBC, Skelton, Cumbria	(D) • W EUROPE & W AFRICA • 300 kW
		(D) • N AFRICA • 300 kW
	†BBC, Via Singapore	SE ASIA • 100 kW S ASIA • 250 kW
		SE ASIA • 250 kW
		S ASIA & SE ASIA • 100/250 kW
	USA	
	†R FREE AFGHANISTAN, Via Germany	(D) • W ASIA & S ASIA • 100 kW
	†RFE-RL, Via Germany	(J) • W ASIA • 100 kW
	†WYFR-FAMILY RADIO, Okeechobee, Fl	S AMERICA • 100 kW
		C AMERICA • 100 kW
	VATICAN STATE	
	†VATICAN RADIO, Sta Maria di Galeria	S AMERICA • 250/500 kW
		(J) • N AMERICA & C AMERICA • 250/500 kW
9610	AUSTRALIA	
	AUSTRALIAN BC CORP, Perth	AUSTRALASIA • DS • 10 kW
	CHINA (TAIWAN)	
	†BC CORP CHINA, T'ai-pei	DS-NEWS NETWORK • 100 kW
	CONGO	
	†RTV CONGOLAISE, Brazzaville	FRENCH, ETC • DS • 50 kW
	GERMANY	
	†DEUTSCHE WELLE, Leipzig	(D) • C AMERICA • 100 kW
	INDIA	
	ALL INDIA RADIO, Delhi	W ASIA & S ASIA • 250 kW DS • 50 kW
		S ASIA • 50 kW
		ENGLISH & HINDI • DS • 50 kW
	IRAN	
	VO THE ISLAMIC REP, Tehrān	(D) • MIDEAST • 500 kW
	MAURITANIA	
	ORT DE MAURITANIE, Nouakchott	ARABIC, FRENCH, ETC • DS • 100 kW • ALT. FREQ. TO 7245 kHz
		F • ARABIC, FRENCH, ETC • DS • 100 kW • ALT. FREQ. TO 7245 kHz
	RUSSIA	
	†R MOSCOW INTL, Via Kazakhstan	(D) • C AMERICA & S AMERICA • 500 kW
		(D) • EUROPE • 240 kW (D) • EUROPE • 500 kW
		(J) • EUROPE • 100 kW
	R MOSCOW INTL, Yekaterinburg	
	UNITED KINGDOM	
	BBC, Via Ascension	C AFRICA • 250 kW
		S AFRICA • 250 kW
9614.4	INDONESIA	
	†RRI, Samarinda, Kalimantan	DS • 0.5 kW
9615	BRAZIL	
	RADIO CULTURA, São Paulo	PORTUGUESE • DS • 7.5 kW
	DENMARK	
	†DANMARKS RADIO, Via Norway	(D) • C AMERICA & S AMERICA • 500 kW
		(D) • E NORTH AM & C AMERICA • 500 kW
		(J) • E NORTH AM & C AMERICA • 500 kW
	GERMANY	
	DEUTSCHE WELLE, Jülich	(J) • W EUROPE • 100 kW
		E EUROPE & MIDEAST • 100/250/500 kW
	†DEUTSCHE WELLE, Multiple Locations	(D) • S ASIA • 100/500 kW
(con'd)	†DEUTSCHE WELLE, Nauen	MIDEAST • 50 kW

0 1 2 3 4 5 6 7 8 9 10 11 12 13 14 15 16 17 18 19 20 21 22 23 24

ENGLISH ▬   ARABIC ▨   CHINESE ▫▫▫   FRENCH ▬   GERMAN ▬   RUSSIAN ═   SPANISH ▬   OTHER ▬

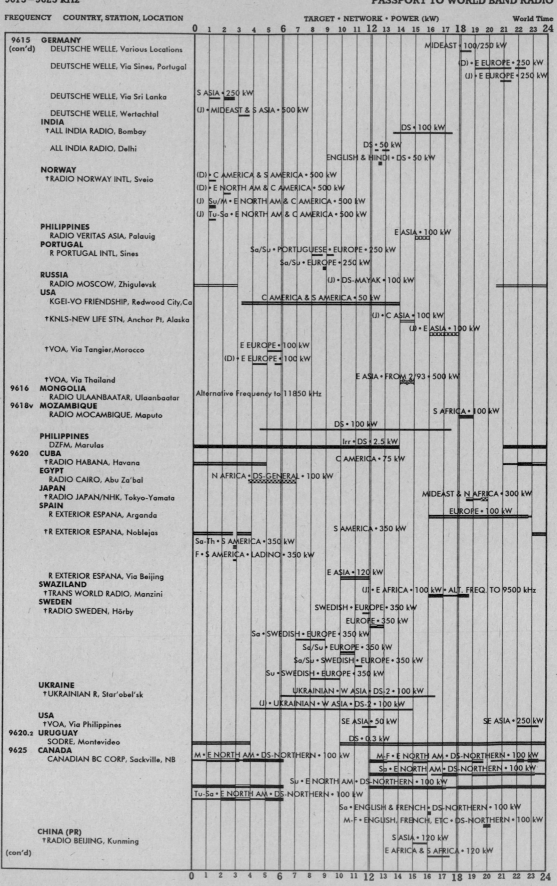

FREQUENCY | COUNTRY, STATION, LOCATION | TARGET • NETWORK • POWER (kW) | World Time

FREQUENCY	COUNTRY, STATION, LOCATION	TARGET • NETWORK • POWER (kW)
9615 (con'd)	**GERMANY** DEUTSCHE WELLE, Various Locations	MIDEAST • 100/250 kW
	DEUTSCHE WELLE, Via Sines, Portugal	(D) • E EUROPE • 250 kW / (J) • E EUROPE • 250 kW
	DEUTSCHE WELLE, Via Sri Lanka	S ASIA • 250 kW
	DEUTSCHE WELLE, Wertachtal	(J) • MIDEAST & S ASIA • 500 kW
	INDIA †ALL INDIA RADIO, Bombay	DS • 100 kW
	ALL INDIA RADIO, Delhi	DS • 50 kW / ENGLISH & HINDI • DS • 50 kW
	NORWAY †RADIO NORWAY INTL, Sveio	(D) • C AMERICA & S AMERICA • 500 kW / (D) • E NORTH AM & C AMERICA • 500 kW / (J) Su/M • E NORTH AM & C AMERICA • 500 kW / (J) Tu-Sa • E NORTH AM & C AMERICA • 500 kW
	PHILIPPINES RADIO VERITAS ASIA, Palauig	E ASIA • 100 kW
	PORTUGAL R PORTUGAL INTL, Sines	Sa/Su • PORTUGUESE • EUROPE • 250 kW / Sa/Su • EUROPE • 250 kW
	RUSSIA RADIO MOSCOW, Zhigulevsk	(J) • DS-MAYAK • 100 kW
	USA KGEI-VO FRIENDSHIP, Redwood City, Ca	C AMERICA & S AMERICA • 50 kW
	†KNLS-NEW LIFE STN, Anchor Pt, Alaska	(J) • C ASIA • 100 kW / (J) • E ASIA • 100 kW
	†VOA, Via Tangier, Morocco	E EUROPE • 100 kW / (D) • E EUROPE • 100 kW
	†VOA, Via Thailand	E ASIA • FROM 2/93 • 500 kW
9616	**MONGOLIA** RADIO ULAANBAATAR, Ulaanbaatar	Alternative Frequency to 11850 kHz
9618v	**MOZAMBIQUE** RADIO MOCAMBIQUE, Maputo	S AFRICA • 100 kW / DS • 100 kW
	PHILIPPINES DZFM, Marulas	Irr • DS • 2.5 kW
9620	**CUBA** †RADIO HABANA, Havana	C AMERICA • 75 kW
	EGYPT RADIO CAIRO, Abu Za'bal	N AFRICA • DS-GENERAL • 100 kW
	JAPAN †RADIO JAPAN/NHK, Tokyo-Yamata	MIDEAST & N AFRICA • 300 kW
	SPAIN R EXTERIOR ESPANA, Arganda	EUROPE • 100 kW
	†R EXTERIOR ESPANA, Noblejas	S AMERICA • 350 kW / Sa-Th • S AMERICA • 350 kW / F • S AMERICA • LADINO • 350 kW
	R EXTERIOR ESPANA, Via Beijing	E ASIA • 120 kW
	SWAZILAND †TRANS WORLD RADIO, Manzini	(J) • E AFRICA • 100 kW • ALT. FREQ. TO 9500 kHz
	SWEDEN †RADIO SWEDEN, Hörby	SWEDISH • EUROPE • 350 kW / EUROPE • 350 kW / Sa • SWEDISH • EUROPE • 350 kW / Sa/Su • EUROPE • 350 kW / Sa/Su • SWEDISH • EUROPE • 350 kW / Su • SWEDISH • EUROPE • 350 kW
	UKRAINE †UKRAINIAN R, Star'obel'sk	UKRAINIAN • W ASIA • DS-2 • 100 kW / (J) • UKRAINIAN • W ASIA • DS-2 • 100 kW
	USA †VOA, Via Philippines	SE ASIA • 50 kW / SE ASIA • 250 kW
9620.2	**URUGUAY** SODRE, Montevideo	DS • 0.3 kW
9625	**CANADA** CANADIAN BC CORP, Sackville, NB	M • E NORTH AM • DS-NORTHERN • 100 kW / M-F • E NORTH AM • DS-NORTHERN • 100 kW / Sa • E NORTH AM • DS-NORTHERN • 100 kW / Su • E NORTH AM • DS-NORTHERN • 100 kW / Tu-Sa • E NORTH AM • DS-NORTHERN • 100 kW / Sa • ENGLISH & FRENCH • DS-NORTHERN • 100 kW / M-F • ENGLISH, FRENCH, ETC • DS-NORTHERN • 100 kW
	CHINA (PR) †RADIO BEIJING, Kunming	S ASIA • 120 kW / E AFRICA & S AFRICA • 120 kW
(con'd)		

SUMMER ONLY (J)   WINTER ONLY (D)   JAMMING / OR ∧   EARLIEST HEARD ◁   LATEST HEARD ▷   NEW OR CHANGED FOR 1993 †

FREQUENCY   COUNTRY, STATION, LOCATION   TARGET • NETWORK • POWER (kW)   World Time

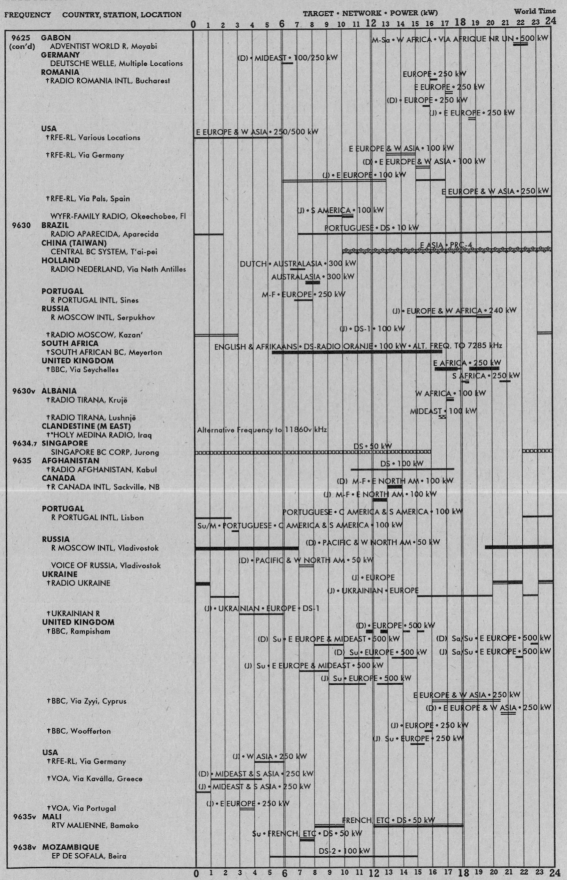

FREQUENCY	COUNTRY, STATION, LOCATION	TARGET • NETWORK • POWER (kW)
9625 (con'd)	**GABON** ADVENTIST WORLD R, Moyabi	M-Sa • W AFRICA • VIA AFRIQUE NR UN • 500 kW
	GERMANY DEUTSCHE WELLE, Multiple Locations	(D) • MIDEAST • 100/250 kW
	ROMANIA †RADIO ROMANIA INTL, Bucharest	EUROPE • 250 kW / E EUROPE • 250 kW / (D) • EUROPE • 250 kW / (J) • E EUROPE • 250 kW
	USA †RFE-RL, Various Locations	E EUROPE & W ASIA • 250/500 kW
	†RFE-RL, Via Germany	E EUROPE & W ASIA • 100 kW / (D) • E EUROPE & W ASIA • 100 kW / (J) • E EUROPE • 100 kW / E EUROPE & W ASIA • 250 kW
	†RFE-RL, Via Pals, Spain	
	WYFR-FAMILY RADIO, Okeechobee, Fl	(J) • S AMERICA • 100 kW
9630	**BRAZIL** RADIO APARECIDA, Aparecida	PORTUGUESE • DS • 10 kW
	CHINA (TAIWAN) CENTRAL BC SYSTEM, T'ai-pei	E ASIA • PRC-4
	HOLLAND RADIO NEDERLAND, Via Neth Antilles	DUTCH • AUSTRALASIA • 300 kW / AUSTRALASIA • 300 kW
	PORTUGAL R PORTUGAL INTL, Sines	M-F • EUROPE • 250 kW
	RUSSIA R MOSCOW INTL, Serpukhov	(J) • EUROPE & W AFRICA • 240 kW
	†RADIO MOSCOW, Kazan'	(J) • DS-1 • 100 kW
	SOUTH AFRICA †SOUTH AFRICAN BC, Meyerton	ENGLISH & AFRIKAANS • DS-RADIO ORANJE • 100 kW • ALT. FREQ. TO 7285 kHz
	UNITED KINGDOM †BBC, Via Seychelles	E AFRICA • 250 kW / S AFRICA • 250 kW
9630v	**ALBANIA** †RADIO TIRANA, Krujë	W AFRICA • 100 kW
	†RADIO TIRANA, Lushnjë	MIDEAST • 100 kW
	CLANDESTINE (M EAST) †"HOLY MEDINA RADIO, Iraq	Alternative Frequency to 11860v kHz
9634.7	**SINGAPORE** SINGAPORE BC CORP, Jurong	DS • 50 kW
9635	**AFGHANISTAN** †RADIO AFGHANISTAN, Kabul	DS • 100 kW
	CANADA †R CANADA INTL, Sackville, NB	(D) • M-F • E NORTH AM • 100 kW / (J) • M-F • E NORTH AM • 100 kW
	PORTUGAL R PORTUGAL INTL, Lisbon	PORTUGUESE • C AMERICA & S AMERICA • 100 kW / Su/M • PORTUGUESE • C AMERICA & S AMERICA • 100 kW
	RUSSIA R MOSCOW INTL, Vladivostok	(D) • PACIFIC & W NORTH AM • 50 kW
	VOICE OF RUSSIA, Vladivostok	(D) • PACIFIC & W NORTH AM • 50 kW
	UKRAINE †RADIO UKRAINE	(J) • EUROPE / (J) • UKRAINIAN • EUROPE
	†UKRAINIAN R	(J) • UKRAINIAN • EUROPE • DS-1
	UNITED KINGDOM †BBC, Rampisham	(D) • EUROPE • 500 kW / (D) Su • E EUROPE & MIDEAST • 500 kW / (D) Sa/Su • E EUROPE • 500 kW / (D) Su • EUROPE • 500 kW / (J) Sa/Su • E EUROPE • 500 kW / (J) Su • E EUROPE & MIDEAST • 500 kW / (J) Su • EUROPE • 500 kW
	†BBC, Via Zyyi, Cyprus	E EUROPE & W ASIA • 250 kW / (D) • E EUROPE & W ASIA • 250 kW
	†BBC, Woofferton	(J) • EUROPE • 250 kW / (J) Su • EUROPE • 250 kW
	USA †RFE-RL, Via Germany	(J) • W ASIA • 250 kW
	†VOA, Via Kaválla, Greece	(D) • MIDEAST & S ASIA • 250 kW / (J) • MIDEAST & S ASIA • 250 kW
	†VOA, Via Portugal	(J) • E EUROPE • 250 kW
9635v	**MALI** RTV MALIENNE, Bamako	FRENCH, ETC • DS • 50 kW / Su • FRENCH, ETC • DS • 50 kW
9638v	**MOZAMBIQUE** EP DE SOFALA, Beira	DS-2 • 100 kW

ENGLISH ▬   ARABIC ▨▨▨   CHINESE □□□   FRENCH ═══   GERMAN ▬▬   RUSSIAN ══   SPANISH ▬▬   OTHER ▬

FREQUENCY   COUNTRY, STATION, LOCATION

TARGET • NETWORK • POWER (kW)   World Time

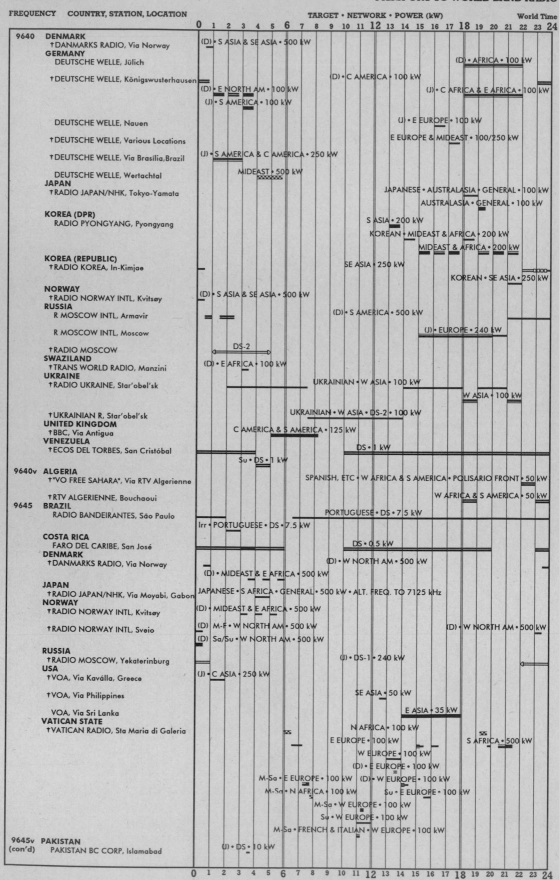

9640	**DENMARK**	
	†DANMARKS RADIO, Via Norway	(D) • S ASIA & SE ASIA • 500 kW
	GERMANY	
	DEUTSCHE WELLE, Jülich	(D) • AFRICA • 100 kW
		(D) • C AMERICA • 100 kW
	†DEUTSCHE WELLE, Königswusterhausen	(D) • E NORTH AM • 100 kW
		(J) • C AFRICA & E AFRICA • 100 kW
		(J) • S AMERICA • 100 kW
	DEUTSCHE WELLE, Nauen	(J) • E EUROPE • 100 kW
	†DEUTSCHE WELLE, Various Locations	E EUROPE & MIDEAST • 100/250 kW
	†DEUTSCHE WELLE, Via Brasília, Brazil	(J) • S AMERICA & C AMERICA • 250 kW
	DEUTSCHE WELLE, Wertachtal	MIDEAST • 500 kW
	JAPAN	
	†RADIO JAPAN/NHK, Tokyo-Yamata	JAPANESE • AUSTRALASIA • GENERAL • 100 kW
		AUSTRALASIA • GENERAL • 100 kW
	KOREA (DPR)	
	RADIO PYONGYANG, Pyongyang	S ASIA • 200 kW
		KOREAN • MIDEAST & AFRICA • 200 kW
		MIDEAST & AFRICA • 200 kW
	KOREA (REPUBLIC)	
	†RADIO KOREA, In-Kimjae	SE ASIA • 250 kW
		KOREAN • SE ASIA • 250 kW
	NORWAY	
	†RADIO NORWAY INTL, Kvitsøy	(D) • S ASIA & SE ASIA • 500 kW
	RUSSIA	
	R MOSCOW INTL, Armavir	(D) • S AMERICA • 500 kW
	R MOSCOW INTL, Moscow	(J) • EUROPE • 240 kW
	†RADIO MOSCOW	DS-2
	SWAZILAND	
	†TRANS WORLD RADIO, Manzini	(D) • E AFRICA • 100 kW
	UKRAINE	
	†RADIO UKRAINE, Star'obel'sk	UKRAINIAN • W ASIA • 100 kW
		W ASIA • 100 kW
	†UKRAINIAN R, Star'obel'sk	UKRAINIAN • W ASIA • DS-2 • 100 kW
	UNITED KINGDOM	
	†BBC, Via Antigua	C AMERICA & S AMERICA • 125 kW
	VENEZUELA	
	†ECOS DEL TORBES, San Cristóbal	DS • 1 kW
		Su • DS • 1 kW
9640v	**ALGERIA**	
	†"VO FREE SAHARA", Via RTV Algerienne	SPANISH, ETC • W AFRICA & S AMERICA • POLISARIO FRONT • 50 kW
	†RTV ALGERIENNE, Bouchaoui	W AFRICA & S AMERICA • 50 kW
9645	**BRAZIL**	
	RADIO BANDEIRANTES, São Paulo	PORTUGUESE • DS • 7.5 kW
		Irr • PORTUGUESE • DS • 7.5 kW
	COSTA RICA	
	FARO DEL CARIBE, San José	DS • 0.5 kW
	DENMARK	
	†DANMARKS RADIO, Via Norway	(D) • W NORTH AM • 500 kW
		(D) • MIDEAST & E AFRICA • 500 kW
	JAPAN	
	†RADIO JAPAN/NHK, Via Moyabi, Gabon	JAPANESE • S AFRICA • GENERAL • 500 kW • ALT. FREQ. TO 7125 kHz
	NORWAY	
	†RADIO NORWAY INTL, Kvitsøy	(D) • MIDEAST & E AFRICA • 500 kW
	†RADIO NORWAY INTL, Sveio	(D) • M-F • W NORTH AM • 500 kW
		(D) • W NORTH AM • 500 kW
		(D) • Sa/Su • W NORTH AM • 500 kW
	RUSSIA	
	†RADIO MOSCOW, Yekaterinburg	(J) • DS-1 • 240 kW
	USA	
	†VOA, Via Kaválla, Greece	(J) • C ASIA • 250 kW
	†VOA, Via Philippines	SE ASIA • 50 kW
	VOA, Via Sri Lanka	E ASIA • 35 kW
	VATICAN STATE	
	†VATICAN RADIO, Sta Maria di Galeria	N AFRICA • 100 kW
		E EUROPE • 100 kW
		S AFRICA • 500 kW
		W EUROPE • 100 kW
		(D) • E EUROPE • 100 kW
		M-Sa • E EUROPE • 100 kW (D) • W EUROPE • 100 kW
		M-Sa • N AFRICA • 100 kW Su • E EUROPE • 100 kW
		M-Sa • W EUROPE • 100 kW
		Su • W EUROPE • 100 kW
		M-Sa • FRENCH & ITALIAN • W EUROPE • 100 kW
9645v (con'd)	**PAKISTAN**	
	PAKISTAN BC CORP, Islamabad	(J) • DS • 10 kW

FREQUENCY   COUNTRY, STATION, LOCATION   TARGET • NETWORK • POWER (kW)   World Time

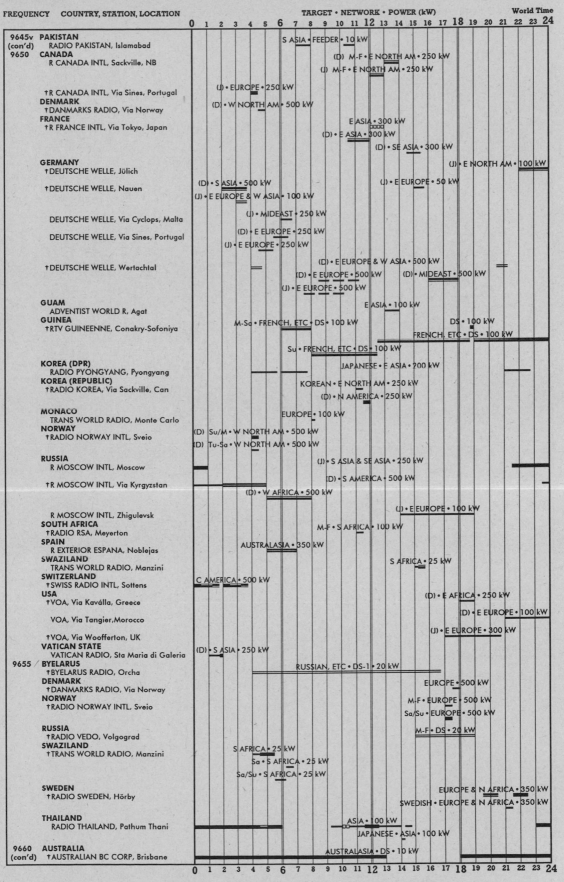

Frequency	Country / Station / Location	Transmission details
9645v (con'd)	**PAKISTAN** RADIO PAKISTAN, Islamabad	S ASIA • FEEDER • 10 kW
9650	**CANADA** R CANADA INTL, Sackville, NB	(D) M-F • E NORTH AM • 250 kW
		(J) M-F • E NORTH AM • 250 kW
	†R CANADA INTL, Via Sines, Portugal	(J) • EUROPE • 250 kW
	DENMARK †DANMARKS RADIO, Via Norway	(D) • W NORTH AM • 500 kW
	FRANCE †R FRANCE INTL, Via Tokyo, Japan	E ASIA • 300 kW
		(D) • E ASIA • 300 kW
		(D) • SE ASIA • 300 kW
	GERMANY †DEUTSCHE WELLE, Jülich	(J) • E NORTH AM • 100 kW
	†DEUTSCHE WELLE, Nauen	(D) • S ASIA • 500 kW
		(J) • E EUROPE • 50 kW
		(J) • E EUROPE & W ASIA • 100 kW
	DEUTSCHE WELLE, Via Cyclops, Malta	(J) • MIDEAST • 250 kW
	DEUTSCHE WELLE, Via Sines, Portugal	(D) • E EUROPE • 250 kW
		(J) • E EUROPE • 250 kW
	†DEUTSCHE WELLE, Wertachtal	(D) • E EUROPE & W ASIA • 500 kW
		(D) • E EUROPE • 500 kW (D) • MIDEAST • 500 kW
		(J) • E EUROPE • 500 kW
	GUAM ADVENTIST WORLD R, Agat	E ASIA • 100 kW
	GUINEA †RTV GUINEENNE, Conakry-Sofoniya	M-Sa • FRENCH, ETC • DS • 100 kW DS • 100 kW
		FRENCH, ETC • DS • 100 kW
		Su • FRENCH, ETC • DS • 100 kW
	KOREA (DPR) RADIO PYONGYANG, Pyongyang	JAPANESE • E ASIA • 200 kW
	KOREA (REPUBLIC) †RADIO KOREA, Via Sackville, Can	KOREAN • E NORTH AM • 250 kW
		(D) • N AMERICA • 250 kW
	MONACO TRANS WORLD RADIO, Monte Carlo	EUROPE • 100 kW
	NORWAY †RADIO NORWAY INTL, Sveio	(D) Su/M • W NORTH AM • 500 kW
		(D) Tu-Sa • W NORTH AM • 500 kW
	RUSSIA R MOSCOW INTL, Moscow	(J) • S ASIA & SE ASIA • 250 kW
	†R MOSCOW INTL, Via Kyrgyzstan	(D) • S AMERICA • 500 kW
		(D) • W AFRICA • 500 kW
	R MOSCOW INTL, Zhigulevsk	(J) • E EUROPE • 100 kW
	SOUTH AFRICA †RADIO RSA, Meyerton	M-F • S AFRICA • 100 kW
	SPAIN R EXTERIOR ESPANA, Noblejas	AUSTRALASIA • 350 kW
	SWAZILAND TRANS WORLD RADIO, Manzini	S AFRICA • 25 kW
	SWITZERLAND †SWISS RADIO INTL, Sottens	C AMERICA • 500 kW
	USA †VOA, Via Kaválla, Greece	(D) • E AFRICA • 250 kW
	VOA, Via Tangier, Morocco	(D) • E EUROPE • 100 kW
	†VOA, Via Woofferton, UK	(J) • E EUROPE • 300 kW
	VATICAN STATE VATICAN RADIO, Sta Maria di Galeria	(D) • S ASIA • 250 kW
9655	**BYELARUS** †BYELARUS RADIO, Orcha	RUSSIAN, ETC • DS-1 • 20 kW
	DENMARK †DANMARKS RADIO, Via Norway	EUROPE • 500 kW
	NORWAY †RADIO NORWAY INTL, Sveio	M-F • EUROPE • 500 kW
		Sa/Su • EUROPE • 500 kW
	RUSSIA †RADIO VEDO, Volgograd	M-F • DS • 20 kW
	SWAZILAND †TRANS WORLD RADIO, Manzini	S AFRICA • 25 kW
		Sa • S AFRICA • 25 kW
		Sa/Su • S AFRICA • 25 kW
	SWEDEN †RADIO SWEDEN, Hörby	EUROPE & N AFRICA • 350 kW
		SWEDISH • EUROPE & N AFRICA • 350 kW
	THAILAND RADIO THAILAND, Pathum Thani	ASIA • 100 kW
		JAPANESE • ASIA • 100 kW
9660 (con'd)	**AUSTRALIA** †AUSTRALIAN BC CORP, Brisbane	AUSTRALASIA • DS • 10 kW

ENGLISH ▬▬   ARABIC ≋≋   CHINESE □□□   FRENCH ══   GERMAN ▭▭   RUSSIAN ══   SPANISH ══   OTHER ──

FREQUENCY   COUNTRY, STATION, LOCATION

TARGET • NETWORK • POWER (kW)

World Time

0 1 2 3 4 5 6 7 8 9 10 11 12 13 14 15 16 17 18 19 20 21 22 23 24

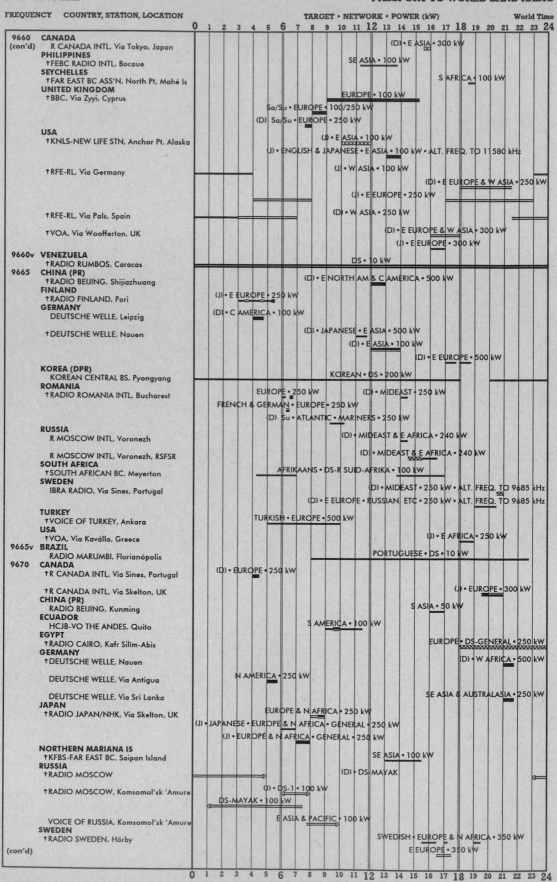

FREQUENCY	COUNTRY, STATION, LOCATION	TARGET • NETWORK • POWER (kW)
9660 (con'd)	**CANADA**	
	R CANADA INTL, Via Tokyo, Japan	(D) • E ASIA • 300 kW
	PHILIPPINES	
	†FEBC RADIO INTL, Bocaue	SE ASIA • 100 kW
	SEYCHELLES	
	†FAR EAST BC ASS'N, North Pt, Mahé Is	S AFRICA • 100 kW
	UNITED KINGDOM	
	†BBC, Via Zyyi, Cyprus	EUROPE • 100 kW
		Sa/Su • EUROPE • 100/250 kW
		(D) Sa/Su • EUROPE • 250 kW
	USA	
	†KNLS-NEW LIFE STN, Anchor Pt, Alaska	(J) • E ASIA • 100 kW
		(J) • ENGLISH & JAPANESE • E ASIA • 100 kW • ALT. FREQ. TO 11580 kHz
	†RFE-RL, Via Germany	(J) • W ASIA • 100 kW
		(D) • E EUROPE & W ASIA • 250 kW
		(J) • E EUROPE • 250 kW
	†RFE-RL, Via Pals, Spain	(D) • W ASIA • 250 kW
	†VOA, Via Woofferton, UK	(D) • E EUROPE & W ASIA • 300 kW
		(J) • E EUROPE • 300 kW
9660v	**VENEZUELA**	
	†RADIO RUMBOS, Caracas	DS • 10 kW
9665	**CHINA (PR)**	
	†RADIO BEIJING, Shijiazhuang	(D) • E NORTH AM & C AMERICA • 500 kW
	FINLAND	
	†RADIO FINLAND, Pori	(J) • E EUROPE • 250 kW
	GERMANY	
	DEUTSCHE WELLE, Leipzig	(D) • C AMERICA • 100 kW
	†DEUTSCHE WELLE, Nauen	(D) • JAPANESE • E ASIA • 500 kW
		(D) • E ASIA • 100 kW
		(D) • E EUROPE • 500 kW
	KOREA (DPR)	
	KOREAN CENTRAL BS, Pyongyang	KOREAN • DS • 200 kW
	ROMANIA	
	†RADIO ROMANIA INTL, Bucharest	EUROPE • 250 kW
		(D) • MIDEAST • 250 kW
		FRENCH & GERMAN • EUROPE • 250 kW
		(D) Su • ATLANTIC • MARINERS • 250 kW
	RUSSIA	
	R MOSCOW INTL, Voronezh	(D) • MIDEAST & E AFRICA • 240 kW
	R MOSCOW INTL, Voronezh, RSFSR	(D) • MIDEAST & E AFRICA • 240 kW
	SOUTH AFRICA	
	†SOUTH AFRICAN BC, Meyerton	AFRIKAANS • DS-R SUID-AFRIKA • 100 kW
	SWEDEN	
	IBRA RADIO, Via Sines, Portugal	(D) • MIDEAST • 250 kW • ALT. FREQ. TO 9685 kHz
		(D) • E EUROPE • RUSSIAN, ETC • 250 kW • ALT. FREQ. TO 9685 kHz
	TURKEY	
	†VOICE OF TURKEY, Ankara	TURKISH • EUROPE • 500 kW
	USA	
	†VOA, Via Kaválla, Greece	(J) • E AFRICA • 250 kW
9665v	**BRAZIL**	
	RADIO MARUMBI, Florianópolis	PORTUGUESE • DS • 10 kW
9670	**CANADA**	
	†R CANADA INTL, Via Sines, Portugal	(D) • EUROPE • 250 kW
	†R CANADA INTL, Via Skelton, UK	(J) • EUROPE • 300 kW
	CHINA (PR)	
	RADIO BEIJING, Kunming	S ASIA • 50 kW
	ECUADOR	
	HCJB-VO THE ANDES, Quito	S AMERICA • 100 kW
	EGYPT	
	†RADIO CAIRO, Kafr Silim-Abis	EUROPE • DS-GENERAL • 250 kW
	GERMANY	
	†DEUTSCHE WELLE, Nauen	(D) • W AFRICA • 500 kW
	DEUTSCHE WELLE, Via Antigua	N AMERICA • 250 kW
	DEUTSCHE WELLE, Via Sri Lanka	SE ASIA & AUSTRALASIA • 250 kW
	JAPAN	
	†RADIO JAPAN/NHK, Via Skelton, UK	EUROPE & N AFRICA • 250 kW
		(J) • JAPANESE • EUROPE & N AFRICA • GENERAL • 250 kW
		(J) • EUROPE & N AFRICA • GENERAL • 250 kW
	NORTHERN MARIANA IS	
	†KFBS-FAR EAST BC, Saipan Island	SE ASIA • 100 kW
	RUSSIA	
	†RADIO MOSCOW	(D) • DS-MAYAK
	†RADIO MOSCOW, Komsomol'sk 'Amure	(J) • DS-1 • 100 kW
		DS-MAYAK • 100 kW
	VOICE OF RUSSIA, Komsomol'sk 'Amure	E ASIA & PACIFIC • 100 kW
	SWEDEN	
	†RADIO SWEDEN, Hörby	SWEDISH • EUROPE & N AFRICA • 350 kW
		E EUROPE • 350 kW
(con'd)		

0 1 2 3 4 5 6 7 8 9 10 11 12 13 14 15 16 17 18 19 20 21 22 23 24

SUMMER ONLY (J)   WINTER ONLY (D)   JAMMING / OR ∧   EARLIEST HEARD ◁   LATEST HEARD ▷   NEW OR CHANGED FOR 1993 †

FREQUENCY   COUNTRY, STATION, LOCATION   TARGET • NETWORK • POWER (kW)   World Time

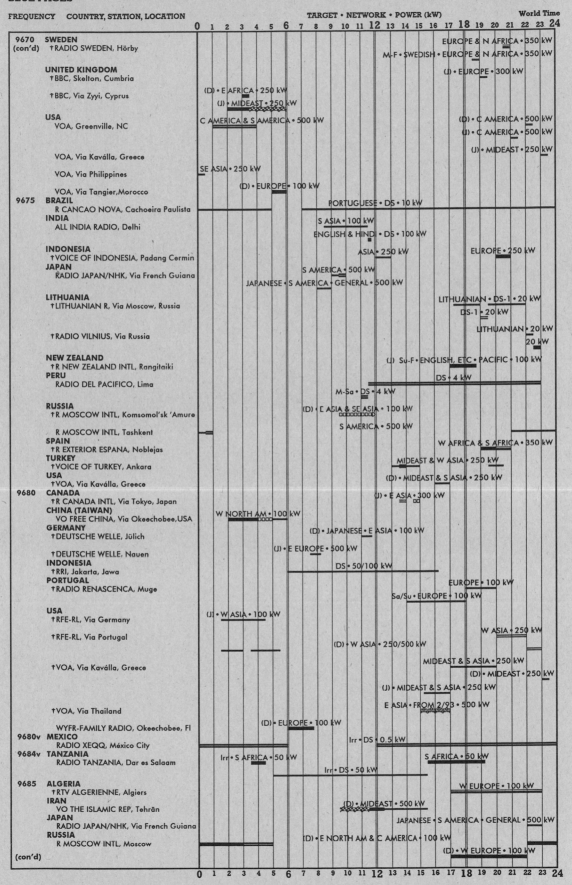

FREQUENCY	COUNTRY, STATION, LOCATION	TARGET • NETWORK • POWER (kW)
9670 (con'd)	**SWEDEN** †RADIO SWEDEN, Hörby	EUROPE & N AFRICA • 350 kW / M-F • SWEDISH • EUROPE & N AFRICA • 350 kW
	UNITED KINGDOM †BBC, Skelton, Cumbria	(J) • EUROPE • 300 kW
	†BBC, Via Zyyi, Cyprus	(D) • E AFRICA • 250 kW / (J) • MIDEAST • 250 kW
	USA VOA, Greenville, NC	C AMERICA & S AMERICA • 500 kW / (D) • C AMERICA • 500 kW / (J) • C AMERICA • 500 kW
	VOA, Via Kaválla, Greece	(J) • MIDEAST • 250 kW
	VOA, Via Philippines	SE ASIA • 250 kW
	VOA, Via Tangier, Morocco	(D) • EUROPE • 100 kW
9675	**BRAZIL** R CANCAO NOVA, Cachoeira Paulista	PORTUGUESE • DS • 10 kW
	INDIA ALL INDIA RADIO, Delhi	S ASIA • 100 kW / ENGLISH & HIND • DS • 100 kW
	INDONESIA †VOICE OF INDONESIA, Padang Cermin	ASIA • 250 kW / EUROPE • 250 kW
	JAPAN RADIO JAPAN/NHK, Via French Guiana	S AMERICA • 500 kW / JAPANESE • S AMERICA • GENERAL • 500 kW
	LITHUANIA †LITHUANIAN R, Via Moscow, Russia	LITHUANIAN • DS-1 • 20 kW / DS-1 • 20 kW
	†RADIO VILNIUS, Via Russia	LITHUANIAN • 20 kW / 20 kW
	NEW ZEALAND †R NEW ZEALAND INTL, Rangitaiki	(J) Su-F • ENGLISH, ETC • PACIFIC • 100 kW
	PERU RADIO DEL PACIFICO, Lima	DS • 4 kW / M-Sa • DS • 4 kW
	RUSSIA †R MOSCOW INTL, Komsomol'sk 'Amure	(D) • C ASIA & SE ASIA • 100 kW / S AMERICA • 500 kW
	R MOSCOW INTL, Tashkent	
	SPAIN †R EXTERIOR ESPANA, Noblejas	W AFRICA & S AFRICA • 350 kW
	TURKEY †VOICE OF TURKEY, Ankara	MIDEAST & W ASIA • 250 kW
	USA †VOA, Via Kaválla, Greece	(D) • MIDEAST & S ASIA • 250 kW
9680	**CANADA** †R CANADA INTL, Via Tokyo, Japan	(J) • E ASIA • 300 kW
	CHINA (TAIWAN) VO FREE CHINA, Via Okeechobee, USA	W NORTH AM • 100 kW
	GERMANY †DEUTSCHE WELLE, Jülich	(D) • JAPANESE • E ASIA • 100 kW
	†DEUTSCHE WELLE, Nauen	(J) • E EUROPE • 500 kW
	INDONESIA †RRI, Jakarta, Jawa	DS • 50/100 kW
	PORTUGAL †RADIO RENASCENCA, Muge	EUROPE • 100 kW / Sa/Su • EUROPE • 100 kW
	USA †RFE-RL, Via Germany	(J) • W ASIA • 100 kW
	†RFE-RL, Via Portugal	W ASIA • 250 kW / (D) • W ASIA • 250/500 kW
	†VOA, Via Kaválla, Greece	MIDEAST & S ASIA • 250 kW / (D) • MIDEAST • 250 kW / (J) • MIDEAST & S ASIA • 250 kW
	†VOA, Via Thailand	E ASIA • FROM 2/93 • 500 kW
	WYFR-FAMILY RADIO, Okeechobee, Fl	(D) • EUROPE • 100 kW
9680v	**MEXICO** RADIO XEQQ, México City	Irr • DS • 0.5 kW
9684v	**TANZANIA** RADIO TANZANIA, Dar es Salaam	Irr • S AFRICA • 50 kW / S AFRICA • 50 kW / Irr • DS • 50 kW
9685	**ALGERIA** †RTV ALGERIENNE, Algiers	W EUROPE • 100 kW
	IRAN VO THE ISLAMIC REP, Tehrān	(D) • MIDEAST • 500 kW
	JAPAN RADIO JAPAN/NHK, Via French Guiana	JAPANESE • S AMERICA • GENERAL • 500 kW
	RUSSIA R MOSCOW INTL, Moscow	(D) • E NORTH AM & C AMERICA • 100 kW / (D) • W EUROPE • 100 kW
(con'd)		

ENGLISH ▬▬   ARABIC ⨯⨯⨯   CHINESE □□□   FRENCH ▬   GERMAN ═══   RUSSIAN ══   SPANISH ▬▬   OTHER ▬

FREQUENCY   COUNTRY, STATION, LOCATION   TARGET • NETWORK • POWER (kW)   World Time

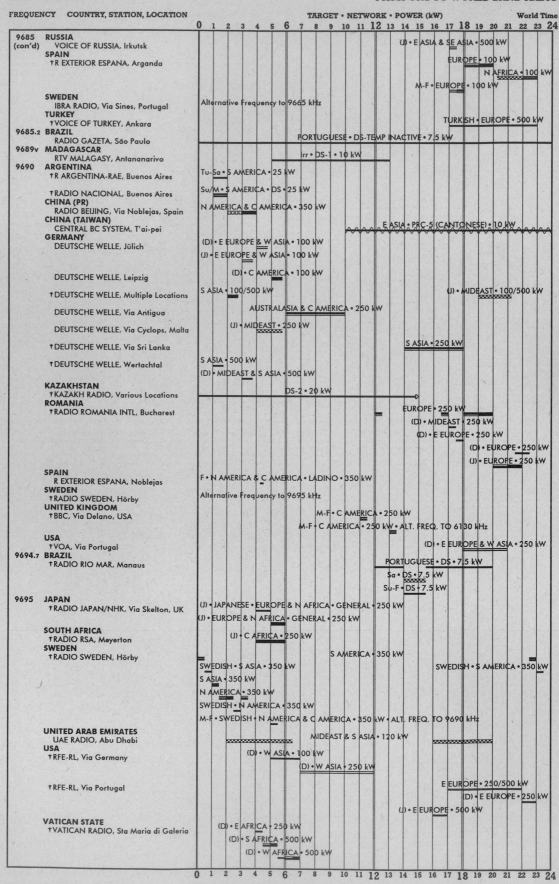

0 1 2 3 4 5 6 7 8 9 10 11 12 13 14 15 16 17 18 19 20 21 22 23 24

9685 RUSSIA
(con'd)   VOICE OF RUSSIA, Irkutsk — (J) • E ASIA & SE ASIA • 500 kW
SPAIN
    †R EXTERIOR ESPANA, Arganda — EUROPE • 100 kW / N AFRICA • 100 kW / M-F • EUROPE • 100 kW
SWEDEN
    IBRA RADIO, Via Sines, Portugal — Alternative Frequency to 9665 kHz
TURKEY
    †VOICE OF TURKEY, Ankara — TURKISH • EUROPE • 500 kW
9685.2 BRAZIL
    RADIO GAZETA, São Paulo — PORTUGUESE • DS-TEMP INACTIVE • 7.5 kW
9689v MADAGASCAR
    RTV MALAGASY, Antananarivo — Irr • DS-1 • 10 kW
9690 ARGENTINA
    †R ARGENTINA-RAE, Buenos Aires — Tu-Sa • S AMERICA • 25 kW
    †RADIO NACIONAL, Buenos Aires — Su/M • S AMERICA • DS • 25 kW
CHINA (PR)
    RADIO BEIJING, Via Noblejas, Spain — N AMERICA & C AMERICA • 350 kW
CHINA (TAIWAN)
    CENTRAL BC SYSTEM, T'ai-pei — E ASIA • PRC-5 (CANTONESE) • 10 kW
GERMANY
    DEUTSCHE WELLE, Jülich — (D) • E EUROPE & W ASIA • 100 kW / (J) • E EUROPE & W ASIA • 100 kW
    DEUTSCHE WELLE, Leipzig — (D) • C AMERICA • 100 kW
    †DEUTSCHE WELLE, Multiple Locations — S ASIA • 100/500 kW / (J) • MIDEAST • 100/500 kW
    DEUTSCHE WELLE, Via Antigua — AUSTRALASIA & C AMERICA • 250 kW
    DEUTSCHE WELLE, Via Cyclops, Malta — (J) • MIDEAST • 250 kW
    †DEUTSCHE WELLE, Via Sri Lanka — S ASIA • 250 kW
    †DEUTSCHE WELLE, Wertachtal — S ASIA • 500 kW / (D) • MIDEAST & S ASIA • 500 kW
KAZAKHSTAN
    †KAZAKH RADIO, Various Locations — DS-2 • 20 kW
ROMANIA
    †RADIO ROMANIA INTL, Bucharest — EUROPE • 250 kW / (D) • MIDEAST • 250 kW / (D) • E EUROPE • 250 kW / (D) • EUROPE • 250 kW / (J) • EUROPE • 250 kW
SPAIN
    R EXTERIOR ESPANA, Noblejas — F • N AMERICA & C AMERICA • LADINO • 350 kW
SWEDEN
    †RADIO SWEDEN, Hörby — Alternative Frequency to 9695 kHz
UNITED KINGDOM
    †BBC, Via Delano, USA — M-F • C AMERICA • 250 kW / M-F • C AMERICA • 250 kW • ALT. FREQ. TO 6130 kHz
USA
    †VOA, Via Portugal — (D) • E EUROPE & W ASIA • 250 kW
9694.7 BRAZIL
    †RADIO RIO MAR, Manaus — PORTUGUESE • DS • 7.5 kW / Sa • DS • 7.5 kW / Su-F • DS • 7.5 kW
9695 JAPAN
    †RADIO JAPAN/NHK, Via Skelton, UK — (J) • JAPANESE • EUROPE & N AFRICA • GENERAL • 250 kW / (J) • EUROPE & N AFRICA • GENERAL • 250 kW
SOUTH AFRICA
    †RADIO RSA, Meyerton — (J) • C AFRICA • 250 kW
SWEDEN
    †RADIO SWEDEN, Hörby — S AMERICA • 350 kW / SWEDISH • S ASIA • 350 kW / SWEDISH • S AMERICA • 350 kW / S ASIA • 350 kW / N AMERICA • 350 kW / SWEDISH • N AMERICA • 350 kW / M-F • SWEDISH • N AMERICA & C AMERICA • 350 kW • ALT. FREQ. TO 9690 kHz
UNITED ARAB EMIRATES
    UAE RADIO, Abu Dhabi — MIDEAST & S ASIA • 120 kW
USA
    †RFE-RL, Via Germany — (D) • W ASIA • 100 kW / (D) • W ASIA • 250 kW
    †RFE-RL, Via Portugal — E EUROPE • 250/500 kW / (D) • E EUROPE • 250 kW / (J) • E EUROPE • 500 kW
VATICAN STATE
    †VATICAN RADIO, Sta Maria di Galeria — (D) • E AFRICA • 250 kW / (D) • S AFRICA • 500 kW / (D) • W AFRICA • 500 kW

0 1 2 3 4 5 6 7 8 9 10 11 12 13 14 15 16 17 18 19 20 21 22 23 24

SUMMER ONLY (J)   WINTER ONLY (D)   JAMMING / OR ∧   EARLIEST HEARD ◁   LATEST HEARD ▷   NEW OR CHANGED FOR 1993 †

FREQUENCY	COUNTRY, STATION, LOCATION	TARGET • NETWORK • POWER (kW)	World Time

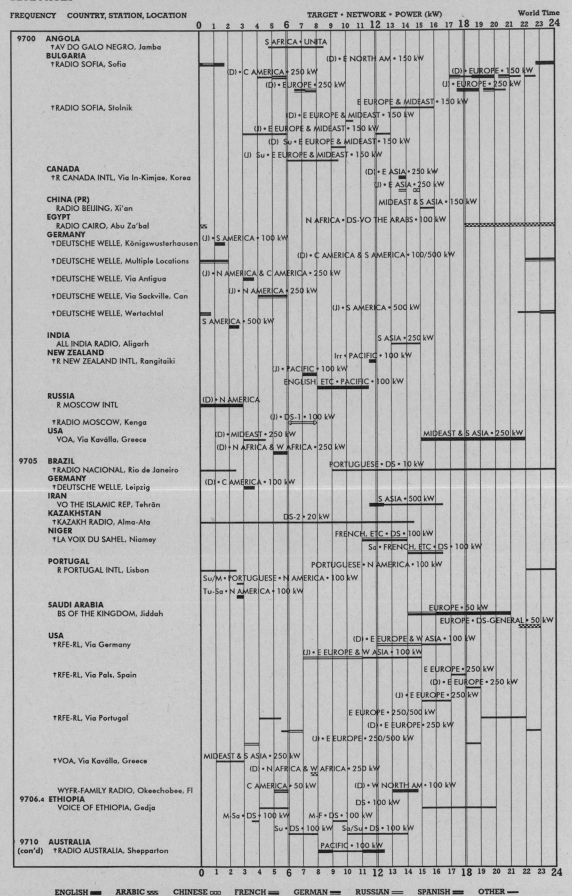

9700 ANGOLA
†AV DO GALO NEGRO, Jamba — S AFRICA • UNITA

BULGARIA
†RADIO SOFIA, Sofia — (D) • E NORTH AM • 150 kW; (D) • C AMERICA • 250 kW; (D) • EUROPE • 150 kW; (D) • EUROPE • 250 kW; (J) • EUROPE • 250 kW

†RADIO SOFIA, Stolnik — E EUROPE & MIDEAST • 150 kW; (D) • E EUROPE & MIDEAST • 150 kW; (J) • E EUROPE & MIDEAST • 150 kW; (D) • Su • E EUROPE & MIDEAST • 150 kW; (J) • Su • E EUROPE & MIDEAST • 150 kW

CANADA
†R CANADA INTL, Via In-Kimjae, Korea — (D) • E ASIA • 250 kW; (J) • E ASIA • 250 kW

CHINA (PR)
RADIO BEIJING, Xi'an — MIDEAST & S ASIA • 150 kW

EGYPT
RADIO CAIRO, Abu Za'bal — N AFRICA • DS-VO THE ARABS • 100 kW

GERMANY
†DEUTSCHE WELLE, Königswusterhausen — (J) • S AMERICA • 100 kW

†DEUTSCHE WELLE, Multiple Locations — (D) • C AMERICA & S AMERICA • 100/500 kW

†DEUTSCHE WELLE, Via Antigua — (J) • N AMERICA & C AMERICA • 250 kW

†DEUTSCHE WELLE, Via Sackville, Can — (J) • N AMERICA • 250 kW

†DEUTSCHE WELLE, Wertachtal — (J) • S AMERICA • 500 kW; S AMERICA • 500 kW

INDIA
ALL INDIA RADIO, Aligarh — S ASIA • 250 kW

NEW ZEALAND
†R NEW ZEALAND INTL, Rangitaiki — Irr • PACIFIC • 100 kW; (J) • PACIFIC • 100 kW; ENGLISH, ETC • PACIFIC • 100 kW

RUSSIA
R MOSCOW INTL — (D) • N AMERICA

†RADIO MOSCOW, Kenga — (J) • DS-1 • 100 kW

USA
VOA, Via Kaválla, Greece — (D) • MIDEAST • 250 kW; MIDEAST & S ASIA • 250 kW; (D) • N AFRICA & W AFRICA • 250 kW

9705 BRAZIL
†RADIO NACIONAL, Rio de Janeiro — PORTUGUESE • DS • 10 kW

GERMANY
†DEUTSCHE WELLE, Leipzig — (D) • C AMERICA • 100 kW

IRAN
VO THE ISLAMIC REP, Tehrān — S ASIA • 500 kW

KAZAKHSTAN
†KAZAKH RADIO, Alma-Ata — DS-2 • 20 kW

NIGER
†LA VOIX DU SAHEL, Niamey — FRENCH, ETC • DS • 100 kW; Sa • FRENCH, ETC • DS • 100 kW

PORTUGAL
R PORTUGAL INTL, Lisbon — PORTUGUESE • N AMERICA • 100 kW; Su/M • PORTUGUESE • N AMERICA • 100 kW; Tu-Sa • N AMERICA • 100 kW

SAUDI ARABIA
BS OF THE KINGDOM, Jiddah — EUROPE • 50 kW; EUROPE • DS-GENERAL • 50 kW

USA
†RFE-RL, Via Germany — (D) • E EUROPE & W ASIA • 100 kW; (J) • E EUROPE & W ASIA • 100 kW

†RFE-RL, Via Pals, Spain — E EUROPE • 250 kW; (D) • E EUROPE • 250 kW; (J) • E EUROPE • 250 kW

†RFE-RL, Via Portugal — E EUROPE • 250/500 kW; (D) • E EUROPE • 250 kW; (J) • E EUROPE • 250/500 kW

†VOA, Via Kaválla, Greece — MIDEAST & S ASIA • 250 kW; (D) • N AFRICA & W AFRICA • 250 kW

WYFR-FAMILY RADIO, Okeechobee, Fl — C AMERICA • 50 kW; (D) • W NORTH AM • 100 kW

9706.4 ETHIOPIA
VOICE OF ETHIOPIA, Gedja — DS • 100 kW; M-Sa • DS • 100 kW; M-F • DS • 100 kW; Su • DS • 100 kW; Sa/Su • DS • 100 kW

9710 AUSTRALIA
(con'd) †RADIO AUSTRALIA, Shepparton — PACIFIC • 100 kW

ENGLISH ▬ ARABIC ⋙ CHINESE □□□ FRENCH ═ GERMAN ▬ RUSSIAN ═ SPANISH ▬ OTHER ─

FREQUENCY　　COUNTRY, STATION, LOCATION　　　　　　　　TARGET • NETWORK • POWER (kW)　　　World Time

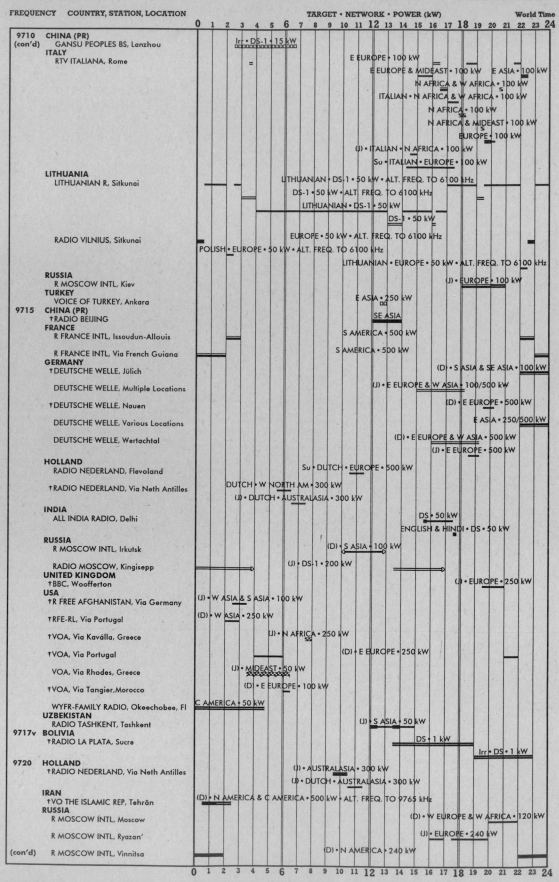

9710 (con'd) CHINA (PR)
GANSU PEOPLES BS, Lanzhou — Irr • DS-1 • 15 kW

ITALY
RTV ITALIANA, Rome
- E EUROPE • 100 kW
- E EUROPE & MIDEAST • 100 kW　E ASIA • 100 kW
- N AFRICA & W AFRICA • 100 kW
- ITALIAN • N AFRICA & W AFRICA • 100 kW
- N AFRICA • 100 kW
- N AFRICA & MIDEAST • 100 kW
- EUROPE • 100 kW
- (J) • ITALIAN • N AFRICA • 100 kW
- Su • ITALIAN • EUROPE • 100 kW

LITHUANIA
LITHUANIAN R, Sitkunai
- LITHUANIAN • DS-1 • 50 kW • ALT. FREQ. TO 6100 kHz
- DS-1 • 50 kW • ALT. FREQ. TO 6100 kHz
- LITHUANIAN • DS-1 • 50 kW
- DS-1 • 50 kW

RADIO VILNIUS, Sitkunai
- EUROPE • 50 kW • ALT. FREQ. TO 6100 kHz
- POLISH • EUROPE • 50 kW • ALT. FREQ. TO 6100 kHz
- LITHUANIAN • EUROPE • 50 kW • ALT. FREQ. TO 6100 kHz

RUSSIA
R MOSCOW INTL, Kiev — (J) • EUROPE • 100 kW

TURKEY
VOICE OF TURKEY, Ankara — E ASIA • 250 kW

9715 CHINA (PR)
†RADIO BEIJING — SE ASIA

FRANCE
R FRANCE INTL, Issoudun-Allouis — S AMERICA • 500 kW
R FRANCE INTL, Via French Guiana — S AMERICA • 500 kW

GERMANY
†DEUTSCHE WELLE, Jülich — (D) • S ASIA & SE ASIA • 100 kW
DEUTSCHE WELLE, Multiple Locations — (J) • E EUROPE & W ASIA • 100/500 kW
†DEUTSCHE WELLE, Nauen — (D) • E EUROPE • 500 kW
DEUTSCHE WELLE, Various Locations — E ASIA • 250/500 kW
DEUTSCHE WELLE, Wertachtal — (D) • E EUROPE & W ASIA • 500 kW / (J) • E EUROPE • 500 kW

HOLLAND
RADIO NEDERLAND, Flevoland — Su • DUTCH • EUROPE • 500 kW
†RADIO NEDERLAND, Via Neth Antilles — DUTCH • W NORTH AM • 300 kW / (J) • DUTCH • AUSTRALASIA • 300 kW

INDIA
ALL INDIA RADIO, Delhi — DS • 50 kW / ENGLISH & HINDI • DS • 50 kW

RUSSIA
R MOSCOW INTL, Irkutsk — (D) • S ASIA • 100 kW
RADIO MOSCOW, Kingisepp — (J) • DS-1 • 200 kW

UNITED KINGDOM
†BBC, Woofferton — (J) • EUROPE • 250 kW

USA
†R FREE AFGHANISTAN, Via Germany — (J) • W ASIA & S ASIA • 100 kW
†RFE-RL, Via Portugal — (D) • W ASIA • 250 kW
†VOA, Via Kaválla, Greece — (J) • N AFRICA • 250 kW
†VOA, Via Portugal — (D) • E EUROPE • 250 kW
VOA, Via Rhodes, Greece — (J) • MIDEAST • 50 kW
†VOA, Via Tangier, Morocco — (D) • E EUROPE • 100 kW
WYFR-FAMILY RADIO, Okeechobee, Fl — C AMERICA • 50 kW

UZBEKISTAN
RADIO TASHKENT, Tashkent — (J) • S ASIA • 50 kW

9717v BOLIVIA
†RADIO LA PLATA, Sucre — DS • 1 kW / Irr • DS • 1 kW

9720 HOLLAND
†RADIO NEDERLAND, Via Neth Antilles — (J) • AUSTRALASIA • 300 kW / (J) • DUTCH • AUSTRALASIA • 300 kW

IRAN
†VO THE ISLAMIC REP, Tehrān — (D) • N AMERICA & C AMERICA • 500 kW • ALT. FREQ. TO 9765 kHz

RUSSIA
R MOSCOW INTL, Moscow — (D) • W EUROPE & W AFRICA • 120 kW
R MOSCOW INTL, Ryazan' — (J) • EUROPE • 240 kW
(con'd) R MOSCOW INTL, Vinnitsa — (D) • N AMERICA • 240 kW

FREQUENCY   COUNTRY, STATION, LOCATION TARGET • NETWORK • POWER (kW)   World Time

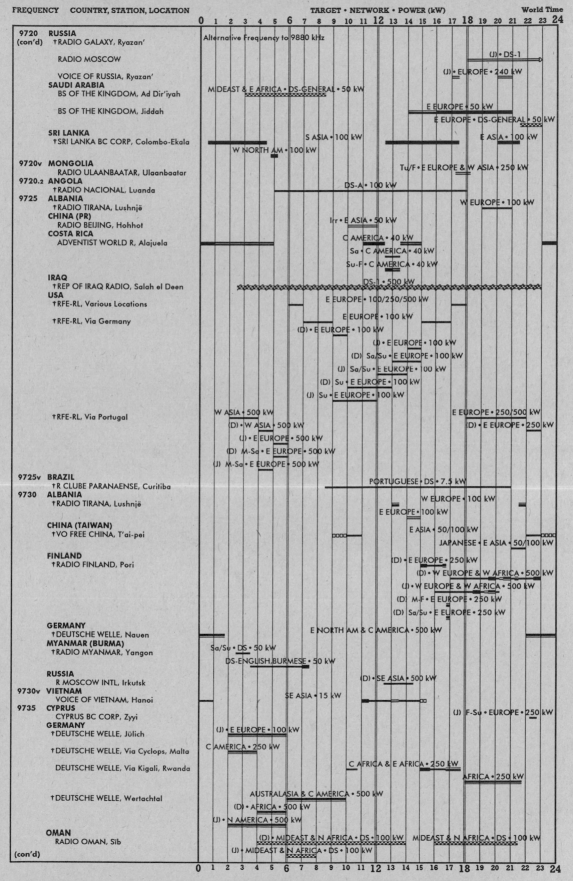

| 0 1 2 3 4 5 6 7 8 9 10 11 12 13 14 15 16 17 18 19 20 21 22 23 24 |

9720 RUSSIA
(con'd) †RADIO GALAXY, Ryazan'
Alternative Frequency to 9880 kHz

RADIO MOSCOW
(J) • DS-1

VOICE OF RUSSIA, Ryazan'
(J) • EUROPE • 240 kW

SAUDI ARABIA
BS OF THE KINGDOM, Ad Dir'iyah
MIDEAST & E AFRICA • DS-GENERAL • 50 kW

BS OF THE KINGDOM, Jiddah
E EUROPE • 50 kW
E EUROPE • DS-GENERAL • 50 kW

SRI LANKA
†SRI LANKA BC CORP, Colombo-Ekala
S ASIA • 100 kW   E ASIA • 100 kW
W NORTH AM • 100 kW

9720v MONGOLIA
RADIO ULAANBAATAR, Ulaanbaatar
Tu/F • E EUROPE & W ASIA • 250 kW

9720.2 ANGOLA
†RADIO NACIONAL, Luanda
DS-A • 100 kW

9725 ALBANIA
†RADIO TIRANA, Lushnjë
W EUROPE • 100 kW

CHINA (PR)
RADIO BEIJING, Hohhot
Irr • E ASIA • 50 kW

COSTA RICA
ADVENTIST WORLD R, Alajuela
C AMERICA • 40 kW
Sa • C AMERICA • 40 kW
Su-F • C AMERICA • 40 kW

IRAQ
†REP OF IRAQ RADIO, Salah el Deen
DS-1 • 500 kW

USA
†RFE-RL, Various Locations
E EUROPE • 100/250/500 kW

†RFE-RL, Via Germany
E EUROPE • 100 kW
(D) • E EUROPE • 100 kW
(J) • E EUROPE • 100 kW
(D) Sa/Su • E EUROPE • 100 kW
(J) Sa/Su • E EUROPE • 100 kW
(D) Su • E EUROPE • 100 kW
(J) Su • E EUROPE • 100 kW

†RFE-RL, Via Portugal
W ASIA • 500 kW   E EUROPE • 250/500 kW
(D) • W ASIA • 500 kW   (D) • E EUROPE • 250 kW
(J) • E EUROPE • 500 kW
(D) M-Sa • E EUROPE • 500 kW
(J) M-Sa • E EUROPE • 500 kW

9725v BRAZIL
†R CLUBE PARANAENSE, Curitiba
PORTUGUESE • DS • 7.5 kW

9730 ALBANIA
†RADIO TIRANA, Lushnjë
W EUROPE • 100 kW
E EUROPE • 100 kW

CHINA (TAIWAN)
†VO FREE CHINA, T'ai-pei
E ASIA • 50/100 kW
JAPANESE • E ASIA • 50/100 kW

FINLAND
†RADIO FINLAND, Pori
(D) • E EUROPE • 250 kW
(D) • W EUROPE & W AFRICA • 500 kW
(J) • W EUROPE & W AFRICA • 500 kW
(D) M-F • E EUROPE • 250 kW
(D) Sa/Su • E EUROPE • 250 kW

GERMANY
†DEUTSCHE WELLE, Nauen
E NORTH AM & C AMERICA • 500 kW

MYANMAR (BURMA)
†RADIO MYANMAR, Yangon
Sa/Su • DS • 50 kW
DS-ENGLISH, BURMESE • 50 kW

RUSSIA
R MOSCOW INTL, Irkutsk
(D) • SE ASIA • 500 kW

9730v VIETNAM
VOICE OF VIETNAM, Hanoi
SE ASIA • 15 kW

9735 CYPRUS
CYPRUS BC CORP, Zyyi
(J) F-Su • EUROPE • 250 kW

GERMANY
†DEUTSCHE WELLE, Jülich
(J) • E EUROPE • 100 kW
C AMERICA • 250 kW

†DEUTSCHE WELLE, Via Cyclops, Malta
C AFRICA & E AFRICA • 250 kW

DEUTSCHE WELLE, Via Kigali, Rwanda
AFRICA • 250 kW

†DEUTSCHE WELLE, Wertachtal
AUSTRALASIA & C AMERICA • 500 kW
(D) • AFRICA • 500 kW
(J) • N AMERICA • 500 kW

OMAN
RADIO OMAN, Sīb
(D) • MIDEAST & N AFRICA • DS • 100 kW   MIDEAST & N AFRICA • DS • 100 kW
(J) • MIDEAST & N AFRICA • DS • 100 kW

(con'd)

| 0 1 2 3 4 5 6 7 8 9 10 11 12 13 14 15 16 17 18 19 20 21 22 23 24 |

ENGLISH ▬   ARABIC ≋   CHINESE ▭▭▭   FRENCH ▥   GERMAN ▬   RUSSIAN ▤   SPANISH ▦   OTHER ▬

FREQUENCY	COUNTRY, STATION, LOCATION	TARGET • NETWORK • POWER (kW) — World Time

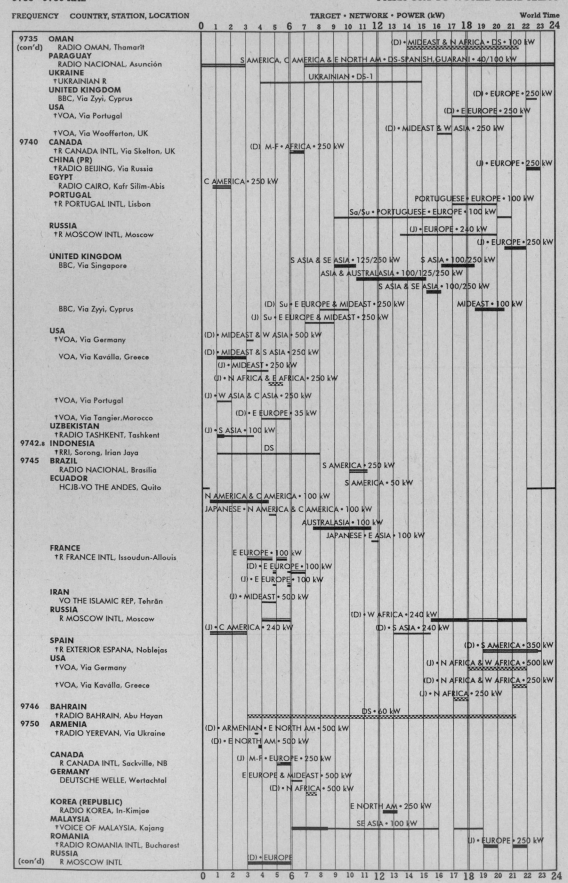

9735 **OMAN**
(con'd)   RADIO OMAN, Thamarīt — (D) • MIDEAST & N AFRICA • DS • 100 kW
PARAGUAY
   RADIO NACIONAL, Asunción — S AMERICA, C AMERICA & E NORTH AM • DS-SPANISH, GUARANI • 40/100 kW
UKRAINE
   †UKRAINIAN R — UKRAINIAN • DS-1
UNITED KINGDOM
   BBC, Via Zyyi, Cyprus — (D) • EUROPE • 250 kW
USA
   †VOA, Via Portugal — (D) • E EUROPE • 250 kW

   †VOA, Via Woofferton, UK — (D) • MIDEAST & W ASIA • 250 kW
9740 **CANADA**
   †R CANADA INTL, Via Skelton, UK — (D) M-F • AFRICA • 250 kW
CHINA (PR)
   †RADIO BEIJING, Via Russia — (J) • EUROPE • 250 kW
EGYPT
   RADIO CAIRO, Kafr Silīm-Abis — C AMERICA • 250 kW
PORTUGAL
   †R PORTUGAL INTL, Lisbon — PORTUGUESE • EUROPE • 100 kW
   — Sa/Su • PORTUGUESE • EUROPE • 100 kW
RUSSIA
   †R MOSCOW INTL, Moscow — (J) • EUROPE • 240 kW
   — (J) • EUROPE • 250 kW
UNITED KINGDOM
   BBC, Via Singapore — S ASIA & SE ASIA • 125/250 kW   S ASIA • 100/250 kW
   — ASIA & AUSTRALASIA • 100/125/250 kW
   — S ASIA & SE ASIA • 100/250 kW

   BBC, Via Zyyi, Cyprus — (D) Su • E EUROPE & MIDEAST • 250 kW   MIDEAST • 100 kW
   — (J) Su • E EUROPE & MIDEAST • 250 kW
USA
   †VOA, Via Germany — (D) • MIDEAST & W ASIA • 500 kW
   VOA, Via Kaválla, Greece — (D) • MIDEAST & S ASIA • 250 kW
   — (J) • MIDEAST • 250 kW
   — (J) • N AFRICA & E AFRICA • 250 kW
   †VOA, Via Portugal — (J) • W ASIA & C ASIA • 250 kW
   †VOA, Via Tangier, Morocco — (D) • E EUROPE • 35 kW
UZBEKISTAN
   †RADIO TASHKENT, Tashkent — (J) • S ASIA • 100 kW
9742.8 INDONESIA
   †RRI, Sorong, Irian Jaya — DS
9745 **BRAZIL**
   RADIO NACIONAL, Brasília — S AMERICA • 250 kW
ECUADOR
   HCJB-VO THE ANDES, Quito — S AMERICA • 50 kW
   — N AMERICA & C AMERICA • 100 kW
   — JAPANESE • N AMERICA & C AMERICA • 100 kW
   — AUSTRALASIA • 100 kW
   — JAPANESE • E ASIA • 100 kW
FRANCE
   †R FRANCE INTL, Issoudun-Allouis — E EUROPE • 100 kW
   — (D) • E EUROPE • 100 kW
   — (J) • E EUROPE • 100 kW
IRAN
   VO THE ISLAMIC REP, Tehrān — (J) • MIDEAST • 500 kW
RUSSIA
   R MOSCOW INTL, Moscow — (D) • W AFRICA • 240 kW
   — (J) • C AMERICA • 240 kW   (D) • S ASIA • 240 kW
SPAIN
   †R EXTERIOR ESPAÑA, Noblejas — (D) • S AMERICA • 350 kW
USA
   †VOA, Via Germany — (J) • N AFRICA & W AFRICA • 500 kW
   †VOA, Via Kaválla, Greece — (D) • N AFRICA & W AFRICA • 250 kW
   — (J) • N AFRICA • 250 kW
9746 **BAHRAIN**
   †RADIO BAHRAIN, Abu Hayan — DS • 60 kW
9750 **ARMENIA**
   †RADIO YEREVAN, Via Ukraine — (D) • ARMENIAN • E NORTH AM • 500 kW
   — (D) • E NORTH AM • 500 kW
CANADA
   R CANADA INTL, Sackville, NB — (J) M-F • EUROPE • 250 kW
GERMANY
   DEUTSCHE WELLE, Wertachtal — E EUROPE & MIDEAST • 500 kW
   — (D) • N AFRICA • 500 kW
KOREA (REPUBLIC)
   RADIO KOREA, In-Kimjae — E NORTH AM • 250 kW
MALAYSIA
   †VOICE OF MALAYSIA, Kajang — SE ASIA • 100 kW
ROMANIA
   †RADIO ROMANIA INTL, Bucharest — (J) • EUROPE • 250 kW
RUSSIA
(con'd)   R MOSCOW INTL — (D) • EUROPE

FREQUENCY   COUNTRY, STATION, LOCATION   TARGET • NETWORK • POWER (kW)   World Time

0 1 2 3 4 5 6 7 8 9 10 11 12 13 14 15 16 17 18 19 20 21 22 23 24

9750 UNITED KINGDOM
(con'd) †BBC, Rampisham
(J) • E EUROPE & MIDEAST • 500 kW
(J) M-F • E EUROPE • 500 kW
(J) M-Sa • E EUROPE & MIDEAST • 500 kW

†BBC, Skelton, Cumbria
EUROPE • 250 kW
(D) • EUROPE • 250 kW
(J) • EUROPE • 250 kW

†BBC, Various Locations
EUROPE • 250 kW

†BBC, Via Maşīrah, Oman
E EUROPE & W ASIA • 100 kW
(D) • E EUROPE & W ASIA • 100 kW
(J) • E EUROPE & W ASIA • 100 kW

†BBC, Via Zyyi, Cyprus
(D) • E EUROPE & W ASIA • 250 kW   (D) • E EUROPE & W ASIA • 100 kW
(D) • EUROPE • 250 kW

USA
†RFE-RL, Via Portugal
E EUROPE & W ASIA • 250 kW
(D) • E EUROPE & W ASIA • 250 kW

9750v FRENCH POLYNESIA
RFO-TAHITI, Papeete
DS-FRENCH, TAHITIAN • 4 kW
9755 CANADA
†R CANADA INTL, Sackville, NB
E NORTH AM • 250 kW   E NORTH AM & C AMERICA • 100/250 kW
(D) • E NORTH AM • 250 kW   (J) • E NORTH AM • 250 kW
Su/M • E NORTH AM • 250 kW   (D) M-F • C AMERICA & S AMERICA • 250 kW
(D) • Su/M • E NORTH AM • 250 kW
(J) • Su/M • E NORTH AM • 250 kW
(J) • Su/M • C AMERICA & S AMERICA • 250 kW
Tu-Sa • C AMERICA & S AMERICA • 250 kW
(D) • Tu-Sa • E NORTH AM • 250 kW
(J) • Tu-Sa • E NORTH AM • 250 kW
(J) • Tu-Sa • C AMERICA & S AMERICA • 250 kW

CHINA (PR)
CENTRAL PEOPLES BS, Baoji
DS-2 • 50 kW
EGYPT
†RADIO CAIRO, Cairo-Mokattam
N AFRICA & MIDEAST • DS-KORAN • 100 kW
GERMANY
DEUTSCHE WELLE, Königswusterhausen
(D) • AFRICA • 100 kW
MONACO
R MONTE CARLO, Via Sackville, Canada
(D) • N AMERICA • 250 kW
(J) • N AMERICA • 250 kW

USA
VOA, Via Philippines
E ASIA • 250 kW
UZBEKISTAN
†RADIO TASHKENT, Tashkent
Alternative Frequency to 11975 kHz
VATICAN STATE
†VATICAN RADIO, Sta Maria di Galeria
(D) • MIDEAST & W ASIA • 100 kW
(D) • E EUROPE & W ASIA • 100 kW
(J) • MIDEAST & W ASIA • 100 kW • ALT. FREQ. TO 11640 kHz
(J) • E EUROPE & W ASIA • 100 kW • ALT. FREQ. TO 11640 kHz
(J) • E EUROPE • 250 kW
(J) • EUROPE • 250 kW   (J) • MIDEAST & W ASIA • 100 kW
(D) Su • E EUROPE • 100 kW   (J) • E EUROPE & W ASIA • 100 kW
(J) Su • E EUROPE • 100 kW
(J) Th • EUROPE • 250 kW

9760 ALBANIA
†RADIO TIRANA, Lushnjë
E NORTH AM • 100 kW   W EUROPE • 100 kW
CANADA
R CANADA INTL, Sackville, NB
(D) M-F • EUROPE • 250 kW   (D) • EUROPE • 250 kW
CUBA
†RADIO HABANA, Via Tula, Russia
(D) • W AFRICA & C AFRICA • 100 kW
JAPAN
RADIO TAMPA, Tokyo-Nagara
JAPANESE • DS-2 • 50 kW
RUSSIA
†RADIO MOSCOW, Kenga
(J) • DS-1 • 100 kW
UNITED KINGDOM
†BBC, Skelton, Cumbria
(J) • EUROPE • 250 kW   EUROPE • 250 kW
(D) • EUROPE • 250 kW
(D) Su • EUROPE • 250 kW

†BBC, Various Locations
EUROPE • 250/500 kW
(J) • EUROPE • 250/500 kW

†BBC, Woofferton
(J) M-F • EUROPE • 250 kW
(J) M-Sa • EUROPE • 250 kW

USA
†VOA, Via Kaválla, Greece
(J) • MIDEAST • 250 kW

(con'd) †VOA, Via Philippines
E ASIA & SE ASIA • 250 kW

0 1 2 3 4 5 6 7 8 9 10 11 12 13 14 15 16 17 18 19 20 21 22 23 24

ENGLISH ▬   ARABIC ⧓⧓⧓   CHINESE □□□   FRENCH ▭▭   GERMAN ▬▬   RUSSIAN ══   SPANISH ▬▬   OTHER ──

FREQUENCY   COUNTRY, STATION, LOCATION   TARGET • NETWORK • POWER (kW)   World Time
0 1 2 3 4 5 6 7 8 9 10 11 12 13 14 15 16 17 18 19 20 21 22 23 24

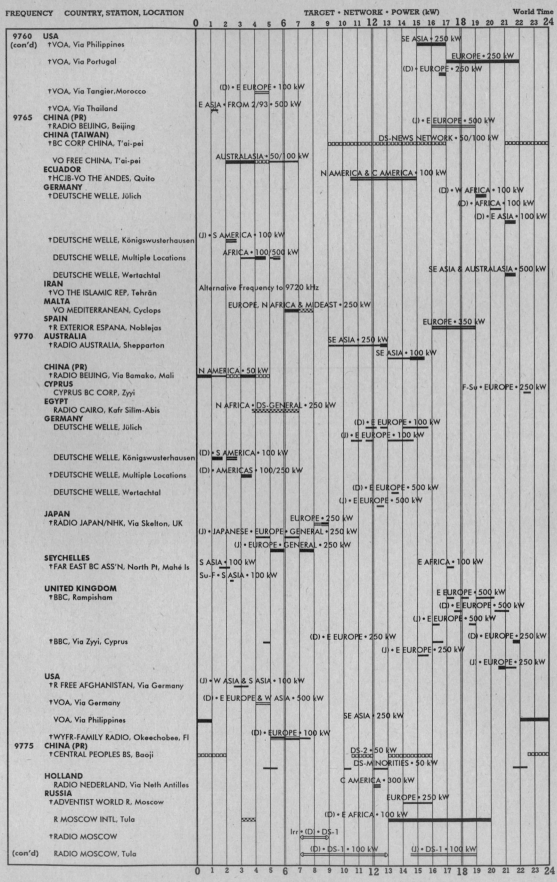

9760 USA
(con'd) †VOA, Via Philippines — SE ASIA • 250 kW
         †VOA, Via Portugal — EUROPE • 250 kW / (D) • EUROPE • 250 kW
         †VOA, Via Tangier, Morocco — (D) • E EUROPE • 100 kW
         †VOA, Via Thailand — E ASIA • FROM 2/93 • 500 kW
9765 CHINA (PR)
         †RADIO BEIJING, Beijing — (J) • E EUROPE • 500 kW
      CHINA (TAIWAN)
         †BC CORP CHINA, T'ai-pei — DS-NEWS NETWORK • 50/100 kW
         VO FREE CHINA, T'ai-pei — AUSTRALASIA • 50/100 kW
      ECUADOR
         †HCJB-VO THE ANDES, Quito — N AMERICA & C AMERICA • 100 kW
      GERMANY
         †DEUTSCHE WELLE, Jülich — (D) • W AFRICA • 100 kW / (D) • AFRICA • 100 kW / (D) • E ASIA • 100 kW
         †DEUTSCHE WELLE, Königswusterhausen — (J) • S AMERICA • 100 kW
         DEUTSCHE WELLE, Multiple Locations — AFRICA • 100/500 kW
         DEUTSCHE WELLE, Wertachtal — SE ASIA & AUSTRALASIA • 500 kW
      IRAN
         †VO THE ISLAMIC REP, Tehrān — Alternative Frequency to 9720 kHz
      MALTA
         VO MEDITERRANEAN, Cyclops — EUROPE, N AFRICA & MIDEAST • 250 kW
      SPAIN
         †R EXTERIOR ESPANA, Noblejas — EUROPE • 350 kW
9770 AUSTRALIA
         †RADIO AUSTRALIA, Shepparton — SE ASIA • 250 kW / SE ASIA • 100 kW
      CHINA (PR)
         †RADIO BEIJING, Via Bamako, Mali — N AMERICA • 50 kW
      CYPRUS
         CYPRUS BC CORP, Zyyi — F-Su • EUROPE • 250 kW
      EGYPT
         RADIO CAIRO, Kafr Silim-Abis — N AFRICA • DS-GENERAL • 250 kW
      GERMANY
         DEUTSCHE WELLE, Jülich — (D) • E EUROPE • 100 kW / (J) • E EUROPE • 100 kW
         DEUTSCHE WELLE, Königswusterhausen — (D) • S AMERICA • 100 kW
         †DEUTSCHE WELLE, Multiple Locations — (D) • AMERICAS • 100/250 kW
         DEUTSCHE WELLE, Wertachtal — (D) • E EUROPE • 500 kW / (J) • E EUROPE • 500 kW
      JAPAN
         †RADIO JAPAN/NHK, Via Skelton, UK — EUROPE • 250 kW / (J) • JAPANESE • EUROPE • GENERAL • 250 kW / (J) • EUROPE • GENERAL • 250 kW
      SEYCHELLES
         †FAR EAST BC ASS'N, North Pt, Mahé Is — S ASIA • 100 kW / E AFRICA • 100 kW / Su-F • S ASIA • 100 kW
      UNITED KINGDOM
         †BBC, Rampisham — E EUROPE • 500 kW / (D) • E EUROPE • 500 kW / (J) • E EUROPE • 500 kW
         †BBC, Via Zyyi, Cyprus — (D) • E EUROPE • 250 kW / (D) • EUROPE • 250 kW / (J) • E EUROPE • 250 kW / (J) • EUROPE • 250 kW
      USA
         †R FREE AFGHANISTAN, Via Germany — (J) • W ASIA & S ASIA • 100 kW
         †VOA, Via Germany — (D) • E EUROPE & W ASIA • 500 kW
         VOA, Via Philippines — SE ASIA • 250 kW
         †WYFR-FAMILY RADIO, Okeechobee, Fl — (D) • EUROPE • 100 kW
9775 CHINA (PR)
         †CENTRAL PEOPLES BS, Baoji — DS-2 • 50 kW / DS-MINORITIES • 50 kW
      HOLLAND
         RADIO NEDERLAND, Via Neth Antilles — C AMERICA • 300 kW
      RUSSIA
         †ADVENTIST WORLD R, Moscow — EUROPE • 250 kW
         R MOSCOW INTL, Tula — (D) • E AFRICA • 100 kW
         †RADIO MOSCOW — Irr • (D) • DS-1
(con'd) RADIO MOSCOW, Tula — (D) • DS-1 • 100 kW / (J) • DS-1 • 100 kW

0 1 2 3 4 5 6 7 8 9 10 11 12 13 14 15 16 17 18 19 20 21 22 23 24

SUMMER ONLY (J)   WINTER ONLY (D)   JAMMING / OR ∧   EARLIEST HEARD ◁   LATEST HEARD ▷   NEW OR CHANGED FOR 1993 †

FREQUENCY　COUNTRY, STATION, LOCATION　　　TARGET • NETWORK • POWER (kW)　　　World Time

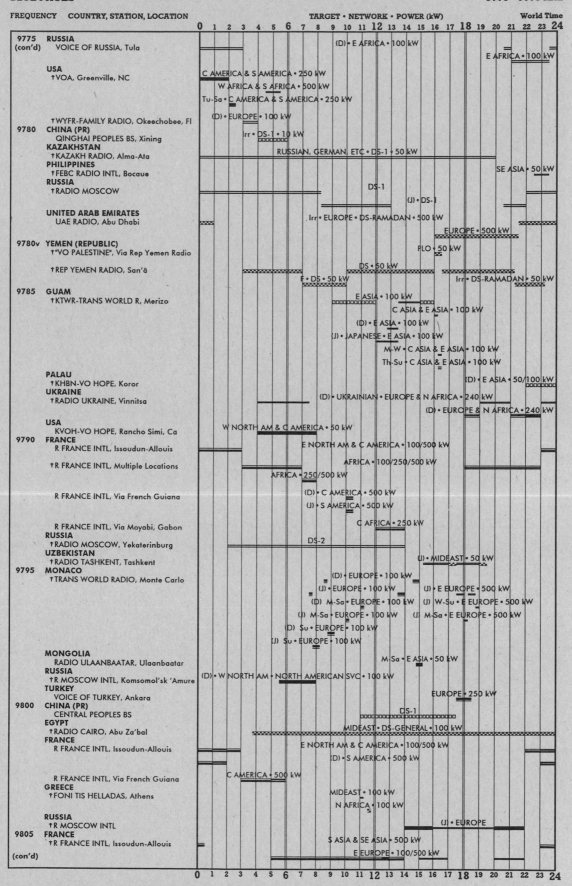

Frequency	Country, Station, Location	Target • Network • Power (kW)
9775 (con'd)	**RUSSIA**　VOICE OF RUSSIA, Tula	(D) • E AFRICA • 100 kW;　E AFRICA • 100 kW
	USA　†VOA, Greenville, NC	C AMERICA & S AMERICA • 250 kW;　W AFRICA & S AFRICA • 500 kW;　Tu-Sa • C AMERICA & S AMERICA • 250 kW
	†WYFR-FAMILY RADIO, Okeechobee, Fl	(D) • EUROPE • 100 kW
9780	**CHINA (PR)**　QINGHAI PEOPLES BS, Xining	Irr • DS-1 • 10 kW
	KAZAKHSTAN　†KAZAKH RADIO, Alma-Ata	RUSSIAN, GERMAN, ETC • DS-1 • 50 kW
	PHILIPPINES　†FEBC RADIO INTL, Bocaue	SE ASIA • 50 kW
	RUSSIA　†RADIO MOSCOW	DS-1;　(J) • DS-1
	UNITED ARAB EMIRATES　UAE RADIO, Abu Dhabi	Irr • EUROPE • DS-RAMADAN • 500 kW;　EUROPE • 500 kW
9780v	**YEMEN (REPUBLIC)**　†"VO PALESTINE", Via Rep Yemen Radio	FLO • 50 kW
	†REP YEMEN RADIO, San'ā	DS • 50 kW;　F • DS • 50 kW;　Irr • DS-RAMADAN • 50 kW
9785	**GUAM**　†KTWR-TRANS WORLD R, Merizo	E ASIA • 100 kW;　C ASIA & E ASIA • 100 kW;　(D) • E ASIA • 100 kW;　(J) • JAPANESE • E ASIA • 100 kW;　M-W • C ASIA & E ASIA • 100 kW;　Th-Su • C ASIA & E ASIA • 100 kW
	PALAU　†KHBN-VO HOPE, Koror	(D) • E ASIA • 50/100 kW
	UKRAINE　†RADIO UKRAINE, Vinnitsa	(D) • UKRAINIAN • EUROPE & N AFRICA • 240 kW;　(D) • EUROPE & N AFRICA • 240 kW
	USA　KVOH-VO HOPE, Rancho Simi, Ca	W NORTH AM & C AMERICA • 50 kW
9790	**FRANCE**　R FRANCE INTL, Issoudun-Allouis	E NORTH AM & C AMERICA • 100/500 kW
	†R FRANCE INTL, Multiple Locations	AFRICA • 100/250/500 kW
		AFRICA • 250/500 kW
	R FRANCE INTL, Via French Guiana	(D) • C AMERICA • 500 kW;　(J) • S AMERICA • 500 kW
	R FRANCE INTL, Via Moyabi, Gabon	C AFRICA • 250 kW
	RUSSIA　†RADIO MOSCOW, Yekaterinburg	DS-2
	UZBEKISTAN　†RADIO TASHKENT, Tashkent	(J) • MIDEAST • 50 kW
9795	**MONACO**　†TRANS WORLD RADIO, Monte Carlo	(D) • EUROPE • 100 kW;　(J) • EUROPE • 100 kW;　(J) • E EUROPE • 500 kW;　(D) M-Sa • EUROPE • 100 kW;　(J) W-Su • E EUROPE • 500 kW;　(J) M-Sa • EUROPE • 100 kW;　(J) M-Sa • E EUROPE • 500 kW;　(D) Su • EUROPE • 100 kW;　(J) Su • EUROPE • 100 kW;　M-Sa • E ASIA • 50 kW
	MONGOLIA　RADIO ULAANBAATAR, Ulaanbaatar	
	RUSSIA　†R MOSCOW INTL, Komsomol'sk 'Amure	(D) • W NORTH AM • NORTH AMERICAN SVC • 100 kW
	TURKEY　VOICE OF TURKEY, Ankara	EUROPE • 250 kW
9800	**CHINA (PR)**　CENTRAL PEOPLES BS	DS-1
	EGYPT　†RADIO CAIRO, Abu Za'bal	MIDEAST • DS-GENERAL • 100 kW
	FRANCE　R FRANCE INTL, Issoudun-Allouis	E NORTH AM & C AMERICA • 100/500 kW;　(D) • S AMERICA • 500 kW
	R FRANCE INTL, Via French Guiana	C AMERICA • 500 kW
	GREECE　†FONI TIS HELLADAS, Athens	MIDEAST • 100 kW;　N AFRICA • 100 kW
	RUSSIA　†R MOSCOW INTL	(J) • EUROPE
9805	**FRANCE**　†R FRANCE INTL, Issoudun-Allouis	S ASIA & SE ASIA • 500 kW;　E EUROPE • 100/500 kW
(con'd)		

ENGLISH ▬　ARABIC ▨　CHINESE ▫▫▫　FRENCH ▬　GERMAN ▬　RUSSIAN ═　SPANISH ▬　OTHER ▬

FREQUENCY   COUNTRY, STATION, LOCATION

TARGET • NETWORK • POWER (kW)

World Time

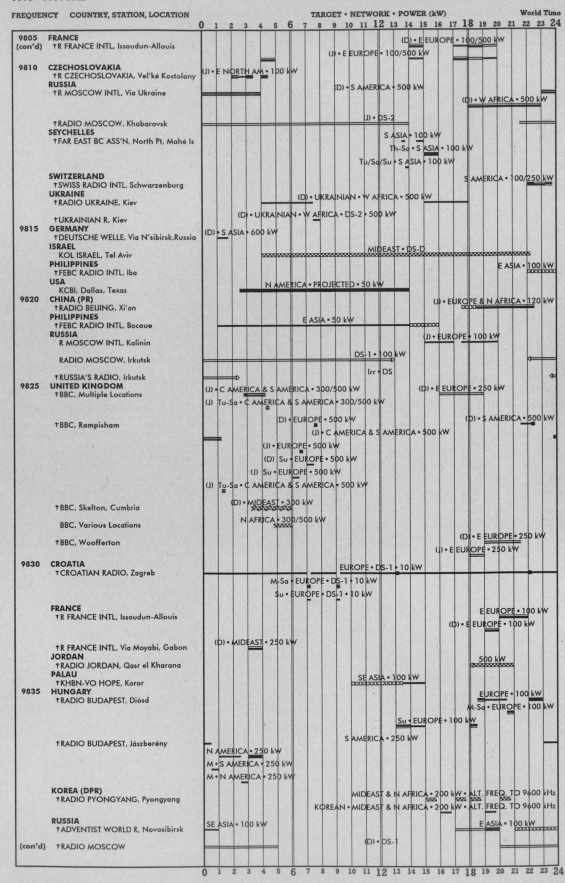

FREQUENCY	COUNTRY, STATION, LOCATION	TARGET • NETWORK • POWER (kW)
9805 (con'd)	FRANCE †R FRANCE INTL, Issoudun-Allouis	(D) • E EUROPE • 100/500 kW · (J) • E EUROPE • 100/500 kW
9810	CZECHOSLOVAKIA †R CZECHOSLOVAKIA, Vel'ké Kostolany	(J) • E NORTH AM • 100 kW
	RUSSIA †R MOSCOW INTL, Via Ukraine	(D) • S AMERICA • 500 kW · (D) • W AFRICA • 500 kW
	†RADIO MOSCOW, Khabarovsk	(J) • DS-2
	SEYCHELLES †FAR EAST BC ASS'N, North Pt, Mahé Is	S ASIA • 100 kW · Th-Sa • S ASIA • 100 kW · Tu/Sa/Su • S ASIA • 100 kW
	SWITZERLAND †SWISS RADIO INTL, Schwarzenburg	S AMERICA • 100/250 kW
	UKRAINE †RADIO UKRAINE, Kiev	(D) • UKRAINIAN • W AFRICA • 500 kW
	†UKRAINIAN R, Kiev	(D) • UKRAINIAN • W AFRICA • DS-2 • 500 kW
9815	GERMANY †DEUTSCHE WELLE, Via N'sibirsk, Russia	(D) • S ASIA • 600 kW
	ISRAEL KOL ISRAEL, Tel Aviv	MIDEAST • DS-D
	PHILIPPINES †FEBC RADIO INTL, Iba	E ASIA • 100 kW
	USA KCBI, Dallas, Texas	N AMERICA • PROJECTED • 50 kW
9820	CHINA (PR) †RADIO BEIJING, Xi'an	(J) • EUROPE & N AFRICA • 120 kW
	PHILIPPINES †FEBC RADIO INTL, Bocaue	E ASIA • 50 kW
	RUSSIA R MOSCOW INTL, Kalinin	(J) • EUROPE • 100 kW
	RADIO MOSCOW, Irkutsk	DS-1 • 100 kW
	†RUSSIA'S RADIO, Irkutsk	Irr • DS
9825	UNITED KINGDOM †BBC, Multiple Locations	(J) • C AMERICA & S AMERICA • 300/500 kW · (J) Tu-Sa • C AMERICA & S AMERICA • 300/500 kW · (D) • E EUROPE • 250 kW
	†BBC, Rampisham	(D) • EUROPE • 500 kW · (J) • C AMERICA & S AMERICA • 500 kW · (D) • S AMERICA • 500 kW · (J) • EUROPE • 500 kW · (D) Su • EUROPE • 500 kW · (J) Su • EUROPE • 500 kW · (J) Tu-Sa • C AMERICA & S AMERICA • 500 kW
	†BBC, Skelton, Cumbria	(D) • MIDEAST • 300 kW
	BBC, Various Locations	N AFRICA • 300/500 kW
	†BBC, Woofferton	(D) • E EUROPE • 250 kW · (J) • E EUROPE • 250 kW
9830	CROATIA †CROATIAN RADIO, Zagreb	EUROPE • DS-1 • 10 kW · M-Sa • EUROPE • DS-1 • 10 kW · Su • EUROPE • DS-1 • 10 kW
	FRANCE †R FRANCE INTL, Issoudun-Allouis	E EUROPE • 100 kW · (D) • E EUROPE • 100 kW
	†R FRANCE INTL, Via Moyabi, Gabon	(D) • MIDEAST • 250 kW
	JORDAN †RADIO JORDAN, Qasr el Kharana	500 kW
	PALAU †KHBN-VO HOPE, Koror	SE ASIA • 100 kW
9835	HUNGARY †RADIO BUDAPEST, Diósd	EUROPE • 100 kW · M-Sa • EUROPE • 100 kW · Su • EUROPE • 100 kW
	†RADIO BUDAPEST, Jászberény	S AMERICA • 250 kW · N AMERICA • 250 kW · M • S AMERICA • 250 kW · M • N AMERICA • 250 kW
	KOREA (DPR) †RADIO PYONGYANG, Pyongyang	MIDEAST & N AFRICA • 200 kW • ALT. FREQ. TO 9600 kHz · KOREAN • MIDEAST & N AFRICA • 200 kW • ALT. FREQ. TO 9600 kHz
	RUSSIA †ADVENTIST WORLD R, Novosibirsk	SE ASIA • 100 kW · E ASIA • 100 kW
(con'd)	†RADIO MOSCOW	(D) • DS-1

FREQUENCY   COUNTRY, STATION, LOCATION   TARGET • NETWORK • POWER (kW)   World Time

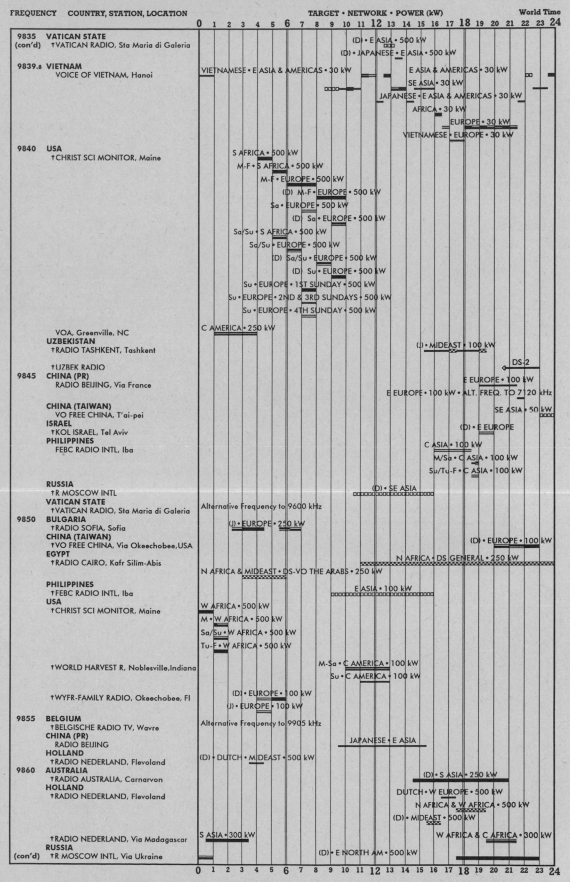

FREQUENCY	COUNTRY, STATION, LOCATION	TARGET • NETWORK • POWER (kW)
9835 (con'd)	VATICAN STATE †VATICAN RADIO, Sta Maria di Galeria	(D) • E ASIA • 500 kW; (D) • JAPANESE • E ASIA • 500 kW
9839.8	VIETNAM VOICE OF VIETNAM, Hanoi	VIETNAMESE • E ASIA & AMERICAS • 30 kW; E ASIA & AMERICAS • 30 kW; SE ASIA • 30 kW; JAPANESE • E ASIA & AMERICAS • 30 kW; AFRICA • 30 kW; EUROPE • 30 kW; VIETNAMESE • EUROPE • 30 kW
9840	USA †CHRIST SCI MONITOR, Maine	S AFRICA • 500 kW; M-F • S AFRICA • 500 kW; M-F • EUROPE • 500 kW; (D) M-F • EUROPE • 500 kW; Sa • EUROPE • 500 kW; (D) Sa • EUROPE • 500 kW; Sa/Su • S AFRICA • 500 kW; Sa/Su • EUROPE • 500 kW; (D) Sa/Su • EUROPE • 500 kW; (D) Su • EUROPE • 500 kW; Su • EUROPE • 1ST SUNDAY • 500 kW; Su • EUROPE • 2ND & 3RD SUNDAYS • 500 kW; Su • EUROPE • 4TH SUNDAY • 500 kW
	VOA, Greenville, NC	C AMERICA • 250 kW
	UZBEKISTAN †RADIO TASHKENT, Tashkent	(J) • MIDEAST • 100 kW
	†UZBEK RADIO	DS-2
9845	CHINA (PR) RADIO BEIJING, Via France	E EUROPE • 100 kW; E EUROPE • 100 kW • ALT. FREQ. TO 7120 kHz
	CHINA (TAIWAN) VO FREE CHINA, T'ai-pei	SE ASIA • 50 kW
	ISRAEL †KOL ISRAEL, Tel Aviv	(D) • E EUROPE
	PHILIPPINES FEBC RADIO INTL, Iba	C ASIA • 100 kW; M/Sa • C ASIA • 100 kW; Su/Tu-F • C ASIA • 100 kW
	RUSSIA †R MOSCOW INTL	(D) • SE ASIA
	VATICAN STATE †VATICAN RADIO, Sta Maria di Galeria	Alternative Frequency to 9600 kHz
9850	BULGARIA †RADIO SOFIA, Sofia	(J) • EUROPE • 250 kW
	CHINA (TAIWAN) †VO FREE CHINA, Via Okeechobee, USA	(D) • EUROPE • 100 kW
	EGYPT †RADIO CAIRO, Kafr Silīm-Abis	N AFRICA • DS GENERAL • 250 kW; N AFRICA & MIDEAST • DS-VO THE ARABS • 250 kW
	PHILIPPINES †FEBC RADIO INTL, Iba	E ASIA • 100 kW
	USA †CHRIST SCI MONITOR, Maine	W AFRICA • 500 kW; M • W AFRICA • 500 kW; Sa/Su • W AFRICA • 500 kW; Tu-F • W AFRICA • 500 kW
	†WORLD HARVEST R, Noblesville, Indiana	M-Sa • C AMERICA • 100 kW; Su • C AMERICA • 100 kW
	†WYFR-FAMILY RADIO, Okeechobee, Fl	(D) • EUROPE • 100 kW; (J) • EUROPE • 100 kW
9855	BELGIUM †BELGISCHE RADIO TV, Wavre	Alternative Frequency to 9905 kHz
	CHINA (PR) RADIO BEIJING	JAPANESE • E ASIA
	HOLLAND †RADIO NEDERLAND, Flevoland	(D) • DUTCH • MIDEAST • 500 kW
9860	AUSTRALIA †RADIO AUSTRALIA, Carnarvon	(D) • S ASIA • 250 kW
	HOLLAND †RADIO NEDERLAND, Flevoland	DUTCH • W EUROPE • 500 kW; N AFRICA & W AFRICA • 500 kW; (D) • MIDEAST • 500 kW
	†RADIO NEDERLAND, Via Madagascar	S ASIA • 300 kW; W AFRICA & C AFRICA • 300 kW
(con'd)	RUSSIA †R MOSCOW INTL, Via Ukraine	(D) • E NORTH AM • 500 kW

ENGLISH ▬ ARABIC ▧ CHINESE ▫▫▫ FRENCH ▭ GERMAN ▬ RUSSIAN ═ SPANISH ▬ OTHER ▬

FREQUENCY   COUNTRY, STATION, LOCATION   TARGET • NETWORK • POWER (kW)   World Time

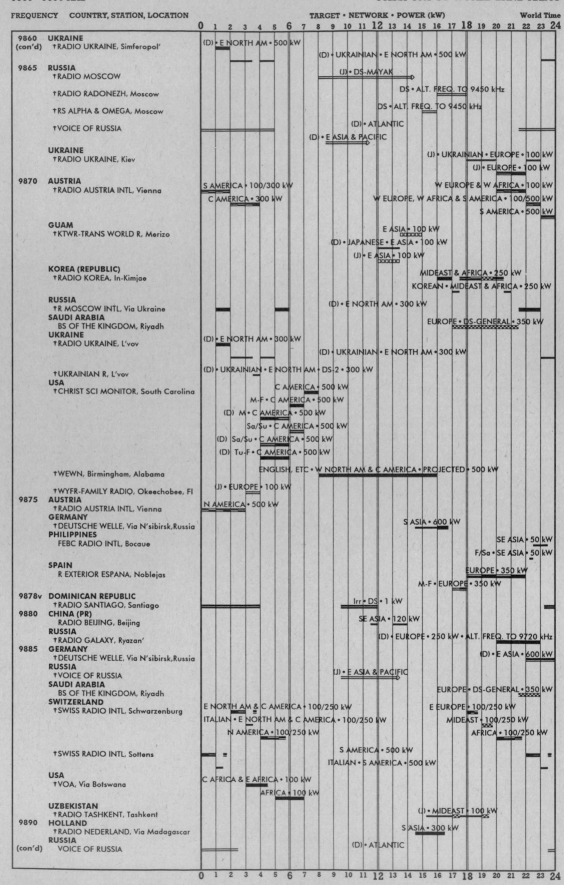

FREQUENCY	COUNTRY, STATION, LOCATION	Schedule
9860 (con'd)	**UKRAINE** †RADIO UKRAINE, Simferopol'	(D) • E NORTH AM • 500 kW; (D) • UKRAINIAN • E NORTH AM • 500 kW
9865	**RUSSIA** †RADIO MOSCOW	(J) • DS-MAYAK
	†RADIO RADONEZH, Moscow	DS • ALT. FREQ. TO 9450 kHz
	†RS ALPHA & OMEGA, Moscow	DS • ALT. FREQ. TO 9450 kHz
	†VOICE OF RUSSIA	(D) • ATLANTIC; (D) • E ASIA & PACIFIC
	UKRAINE †RADIO UKRAINE, Kiev	(J) • UKRAINIAN • EUROPE • 100 kW; (J) • EUROPE • 100 kW
9870	**AUSTRIA** †RADIO AUSTRIA INTL, Vienna	S AMERICA • 100/300 kW; C AMERICA • 300 kW; W EUROPE & W AFRICA • 100 kW; W EUROPE, W AFRICA & S AMERICA • 100/500 kW; S AMERICA • 500 kW
	GUAM †KTWR-TRANS WORLD R, Merizo	E ASIA • 100 kW; (D) • JAPANESE • E ASIA • 100 kW; (J) • E ASIA • 100 kW
	KOREA (REPUBLIC) †RADIO KOREA, In-Kimjae	MIDEAST & AFRICA • 250 kW; KOREAN • MIDEAST & AFRICA • 250 kW
	RUSSIA †R MOSCOW INTL, Via Ukraine	(D) • E NORTH AM • 300 kW
	SAUDI ARABIA BS OF THE KINGDOM, Riyadh	EUROPE • DS-GENERAL • 350 kW
	UKRAINE †RADIO UKRAINE, L'vov	(D) • E NORTH AM • 300 kW; (D) • UKRAINIAN • E NORTH AM • 300 kW
	†UKRAINIAN R, L'vov	(D) • UKRAINIAN • E NORTH AM • DS-2 • 300 kW
	USA †CHRIST SCI MONITOR, South Carolina	C AMERICA • 500 kW; M-F • C AMERICA • 500 kW; (D) M • C AMERICA • 500 kW; Sa/Su • C AMERICA • 500 kW; (D) Sa/Su • C AMERICA • 500 kW; (D) Tu-F • C AMERICA • 500 kW
	†WEWN, Birmingham, Alabama	ENGLISH, ETC • W NORTH AM & C AMERICA • PROJECTED • 500 kW
	†WYFR-FAMILY RADIO, Okeechobee, Fl	(J) • EUROPE • 100 kW
9875	**AUSTRIA** †RADIO AUSTRIA INTL, Vienna	N AMERICA • 500 kW
	GERMANY †DEUTSCHE WELLE, Via N'sibirsk, Russia	S ASIA • 600 kW
	PHILIPPINES FEBC RADIO INTL, Bocaue	SE ASIA • 50 kW; F/Sa • SE ASIA • 50 kW
	SPAIN R EXTERIOR ESPANA, Noblejas	EUROPE • 350 kW; M-F • EUROPE • 350 kW
9878v	**DOMINICAN REPUBLIC** †RADIO SANTIAGO, Santiago	Irr • DS • 1 kW
9880	**CHINA (PR)** RADIO BEIJING, Beijing	SE ASIA • 120 kW
	RUSSIA †RADIO GALAXY, Ryazan'	(D) • EUROPE • 250 kW • ALT. FREQ. TO 9720 kHz
9885	**GERMANY** †DEUTSCHE WELLE, Via N'sibirsk, Russia	(D) • E ASIA • 600 kW
	RUSSIA †VOICE OF RUSSIA	(J) • E ASIA & PACIFIC
	SAUDI ARABIA BS OF THE KINGDOM, Riyadh	EUROPE • DS-GENERAL • 350 kW
	SWITZERLAND †SWISS RADIO INTL, Schwarzenburg	E NORTH AM & C AMERICA • 100/250 kW; ITALIAN • E NORTH AM & C AMERICA • 100/250 kW; N AMERICA • 100/250 kW; E EUROPE • 100/250 kW; MIDEAST • 100/250 kW; AFRICA • 100/250 kW
	†SWISS RADIO INTL, Sottens	S AMERICA • 500 kW; ITALIAN • S AMERICA • 500 kW
	USA †VOA, Via Botswana	C AFRICA & E AFRICA • 100 kW; AFRICA • 100 kW
	UZBEKISTAN †RADIO TASHKENT, Tashkent	(J) • MIDEAST • 100 kW
9890	**HOLLAND** †RADIO NEDERLAND, Via Madagascar	S ASIA • 300 kW
(con'd)	**RUSSIA** VOICE OF RUSSIA	(D) • ATLANTIC

SUMMER ONLY (J)   WINTER ONLY (D)   JAMMING / OR ∧   EARLIEST HEARD ◁   LATEST HEARD ▷   NEW OR CHANGED FOR 1993 †

FREQUENCY   COUNTRY, STATION, LOCATION   TARGET • NETWORK • POWER (kW)   World Time

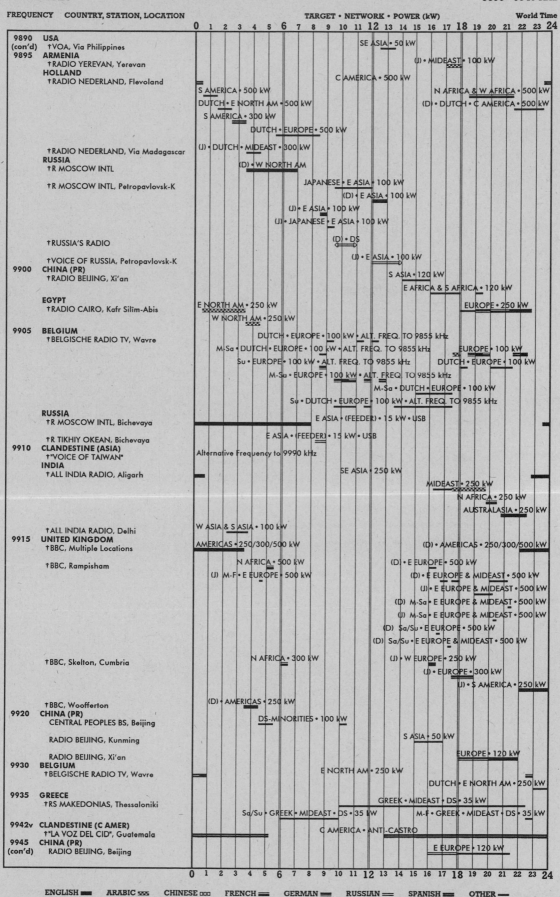

FREQUENCY	COUNTRY, STATION, LOCATION	TARGET • NETWORK • POWER (kW)
9890 (con'd)	USA †VOA, Via Philippines	SE ASIA • 50 kW
9895	ARMENIA †RADIO YEREVAN, Yerevan	(J) • MIDEAST • 100 kW
	HOLLAND †RADIO NEDERLAND, Flevoland	C AMERICA • 500 kW / S AMERICA • 500 kW / N AFRICA & W AFRICA • 500 kW / DUTCH • E NORTH AM • 500 kW / (D) • DUTCH • C AMERICA • 500 kW / S AMERICA • 300 kW / DUTCH • EUROPE • 500 kW
	†RADIO NEDERLAND, Via Madagascar	(J) • DUTCH • MIDEAST • 300 kW
	RUSSIA †R MOSCOW INTL	(D) • W NORTH AM
	†R MOSCOW INTL, Petropavlovsk-K	JAPANESE • E ASIA • 100 kW / (D) • E ASIA • 100 kW / (J) • E ASIA • 100 kW / (J) • JAPANESE • E ASIA • 100 kW
	†RUSSIA'S RADIO	(D) • DS
	†VOICE OF RUSSIA, Petropavlovsk-K	(J) • E ASIA • 100 kW
9900	CHINA (PR) †RADIO BEIJING, Xi'an	S ASIA • 120 kW / E AFRICA & S AFRICA • 120 kW
	EGYPT †RADIO CAIRO, Kafr Silim-Abis	E NORTH AM • 250 kW / EUROPE • 250 kW / W NORTH AM • 250 kW
9905	BELGIUM †BELGISCHE RADIO TV, Wavre	DUTCH • EUROPE • 100 kW • ALT. FREQ. TO 9855 kHz / M-Sa • DUTCH • EUROPE • 100 kW • ALT. FREQ. TO 9855 kHz / EUROPE • 100 kW / Su • EUROPE • 100 kW • ALT. FREQ. TO 9855 kHz / DUTCH • EUROPE • 100 kW / M-Sa • EUROPE • 100 kW • ALT. FREQ. TO 9855 kHz / M-Sa • DUTCH • EUROPE • 100 kW / Su • DUTCH • EUROPE • 100 kW • ALT. FREQ. TO 9855 kHz
	RUSSIA †R MOSCOW INTL, Bichevaya	E ASIA • (FEEDER) • 15 kW • USB
	†R TIKHIY OKEAN, Bichevaya	E ASIA • (FEEDER) • 15 kW • USB
9910	CLANDESTINE (ASIA) †"VOICE OF TAIWAN"	Alternative Frequency to 9990 kHz
	INDIA †ALL INDIA RADIO, Aligarh	SE ASIA • 250 kW / MIDEAST • 250 kW / N AFRICA • 250 kW / AUSTRALASIA • 250 kW
9915	†ALL INDIA RADIO, Delhi	W ASIA & S ASIA • 100 kW
	UNITED KINGDOM †BBC, Multiple Locations	AMERICAS • 250/300/500 kW / (D) • AMERICAS • 250/300/500 kW
	†BBC, Rampisham	N AFRICA • 500 kW / (D) • E EUROPE • 500 kW / (J) M-F • E EUROPE • 500 kW / (D) • E EUROPE & MIDEAST • 500 kW / (J) • E EUROPE & MIDEAST • 500 kW / (D) M-Sa • E EUROPE & MIDEAST • 500 kW / (J) M-Sa • E EUROPE & MIDEAST • 500 kW / (D) Sa/Su • E EUROPE • 500 kW / (D) Sa/Su • E EUROPE & MIDEAST • 500 kW
	†BBC, Skelton, Cumbria	N AFRICA • 300 kW / (J) • W EUROPE • 250 kW / (J) • EUROPE • 300 kW / (J) • S AMERICA • 250 kW
	†BBC, Woofferton	(D) • AMERICAS • 250 kW
9920	CHINA (PR) CENTRAL PEOPLES BS, Beijing	DS-MINORITIES • 100 kW
	RADIO BEIJING, Kunming	S ASIA • 50 kW
	RADIO BEIJING, Xi'an	EUROPE • 120 kW
9930	BELGIUM †BELGISCHE RADIO TV, Wavre	E NORTH AM • 250 kW / DUTCH • E NORTH AM • 250 kW
9935	GREECE †RS MAKEDONIAS, Thessaloniki	GREEK • MIDEAST • DS • 35 kW / Sa/Su • GREEK • MIDEAST • DS • 35 kW / M-F • GREEK • MIDEAST • DS • 35 kW
9942v	CLANDESTINE (C AMER) †"LA VOZ DEL CID", Guatemala	C AMERICA • ANTI-CASTRO
9945 (con'd)	CHINA (PR) RADIO BEIJING, Beijing	E EUROPE • 120 kW

ENGLISH ▬▬   ARABIC ≋≋≋   CHINESE □□□   FRENCH ▭▭   GERMAN ▬▬   RUSSIAN ══   SPANISH ▬▬   OTHER ▬▬

FREQUENCY   COUNTRY, STATION, LOCATION   TARGET • NETWORK • POWER (kW)   World Time

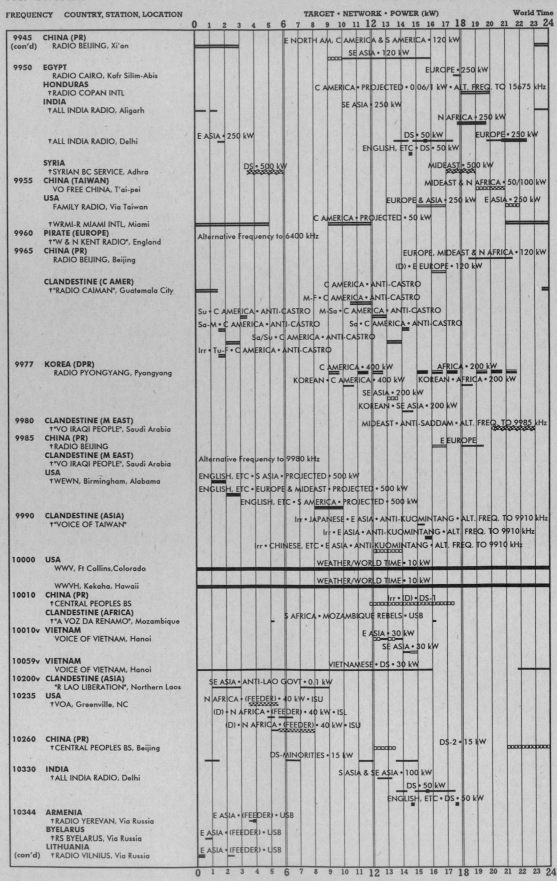

Frequency	Country, Station, Location	Target • Network • Power
9945 (con'd)	**CHINA (PR)** RADIO BEIJING, Xi'an	E NORTH AM, C AMERICA & S AMERICA • 120 kW; SE ASIA • 120 kW
9950	**EGYPT** RADIO CAIRO, Kafr Silim-Abis	EUROPE • 250 kW
	HONDURAS †RADIO COPAN INTL	C AMERICA • PROJECTED • 0.06/1 kW • ALT. FREQ. TO 15675 kHz
	INDIA †ALL INDIA RADIO, Aligarh	SE ASIA • 250 kW; N AFRICA • 250 kW
	†ALL INDIA RADIO, Delhi	E ASIA • 250 kW; DS • 50 kW; EUROPE • 250 kW; ENGLISH, ETC • DS • 50 kW
	SYRIA †SYRIAN BC SERVICE, Adhra	DS • 500 kW; MIDEAST • 500 kW
9955	**CHINA (TAIWAN)** VO FREE CHINA, T'ai-pei	MIDEAST & N AFRICA • 50/100 kW
	USA FAMILY RADIO, Via Taiwan	EUROPE & ASIA • 250 kW; E ASIA • 250 kW
	†WRMI-R MIAMI INTL, Miami	C AMERICA • PROJECTED • 50 kW
9960	**PIRATE (EUROPE)** †"W & N KENT RADIO", England	Alternative Frequency to 6400 kHz
9965	**CHINA (PR)** RADIO BEIJING, Beijing	EUROPE, MIDEAST & N AFRICA • 120 kW; (D) • E EUROPE • 120 kW
	CLANDESTINE (C AMER) †"RADIO CAIMAN", Guatemala City	C AMERICA • ANTI-CASTRO; M-F • C AMERICA • ANTI-CASTRO; Su • C AMERICA • ANTI-CASTRO; M-Sa • C AMERICA • ANTI-CASTRO; Sa-M • C AMERICA • ANTI-CASTRO; Sa • C AMERICA • ANTI-CASTRO; Sa/Su • C AMERICA • ANTI-CASTRO; Irr • Tu-F • C AMERICA • ANTI-CASTRO
9977	**KOREA (DPR)** RADIO PYONGYANG, Pyongyang	C AMERICA • 400 kW; AFRICA • 200 kW; KOREAN • C AMERICA • 400 kW; KOREAN • AFRICA • 200 kW; SE ASIA • 200 kW; KOREAN • SE ASIA • 200 kW
9980	**CLANDESTINE (M EAST)** †"VO IRAQI PEOPLE", Saudi Arabia	MIDEAST • ANTI-SADDAM • ALT. FREQ. TO 9985 kHz
9985	**CHINA (PR)** †RADIO BEIJING	E EUROPE
	CLANDESTINE (M EAST) †"VO IRAQI PEOPLE", Saudi Arabia	Alternative Frequency to 9980 kHz
	USA †WEWN, Birmingham, Alabama	ENGLISH, ETC • S ASIA • PROJECTED • 500 kW; ENGLISH, ETC • EUROPE & MIDEAST • PROJECTED • 500 kW; ENGLISH, ETC • S AMERICA • PROJECTED • 500 kW
9990	**CLANDESTINE (ASIA)** †"VOICE OF TAIWAN"	Irr • JAPANESE • E ASIA • ANTI-KUOMINTANG • ALT. FREQ. TO 9910 kHz; Irr • E ASIA • ANTI-KUOMINTANG • ALT. FREQ. TO 9910 kHz; Irr • CHINESE, ETC • E ASIA • ANTI-KUOMINTANG • ALT. FREQ. TO 9910 kHz
10000	**USA** WWV, Ft Collins, Colorado	WEATHER/WORLD TIME • 10 kW
	WWVH, Kekaha, Hawaii	WEATHER/WORLD TIME • 10 kW
10010	**CHINA (PR)** †CENTRAL PEOPLES BS	Irr • (D) • DS-1
	CLANDESTINE (AFRICA) †"A VOZ DA RENAMO", Mozambique	S AFRICA • MOZAMBIQUE REBELS • USB
10010v	**VIETNAM** VOICE OF VIETNAM, Hanoi	E ASIA • 30 kW; SE ASIA • 30 kW
10059v	**VIETNAM** VOICE OF VIETNAM, Hanoi	VIETNAMESE • DS • 30 kW
10200v	**CLANDESTINE (ASIA)** "R LAO LIBERATION", Northern Laos	SE ASIA • ANTI-LAO GOVT • 0.1 kW
10235	**USA** †VOA, Greenville, NC	N AFRICA • (FEEDER) • 40 kW • ISU; (D) • N AFRICA • (FEEDER) • 40 kW • ISL; (D) • N AFRICA • (FEEDER) • 40 kW • ISU
10260	**CHINA (PR)** †CENTRAL PEOPLES BS, Beijing	DS-2 • 15 kW; DS-MINORITIES • 15 kW
10330	**INDIA** †ALL INDIA RADIO, Delhi	S ASIA & SE ASIA • 100 kW; DS • 50 kW; ENGLISH, ETC • DS • 50 kW
10344	**ARMENIA** †RADIO YEREVAN, Via Russia	E ASIA • (FEEDER) • USB
	BYELARUS †RS BYELARUS, Via Russia	E ASIA • (FEEDER) • USB
	LITHUANIA †RADIO VILNIUS, Via Russia (con'd)	E ASIA • (FEEDER) • USB

SUMMER ONLY (J)   WINTER ONLY (D)   JAMMING / OR ∧   EARLIEST HEARD ◁   LATEST HEARD ▷   NEW OR CHANGED FOR 1993 †

FREQUENCY   COUNTRY, STATION, LOCATION   TARGET • NETWORK • POWER (kW)   World Time

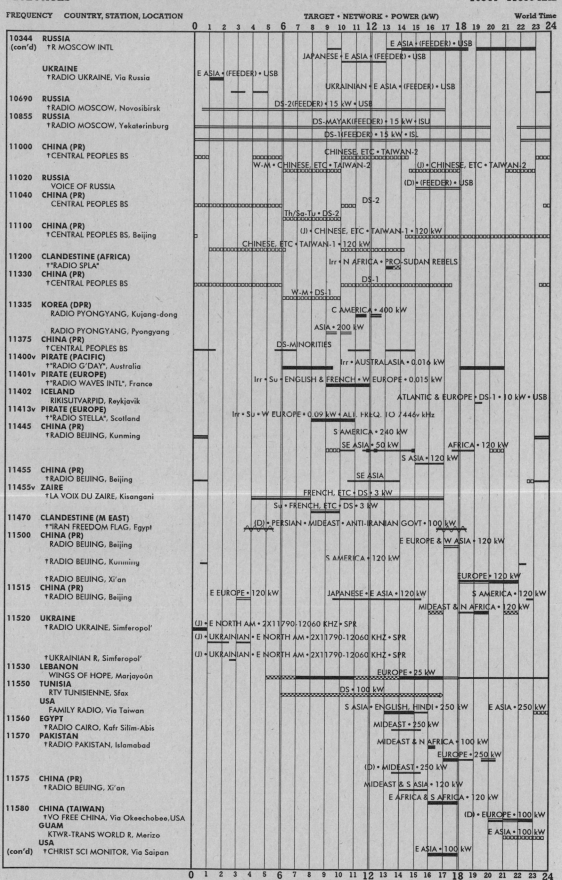

Frequency	Country, Station, Location	Target • Network • Power (kW)
10344 (con'd)	**RUSSIA** †R MOSCOW INTL	E ASIA • (FEEDER) • USB JAPANESE • E ASIA • (FEEDER) • USB
	UKRAINE †RADIO UKRAINE, Via Russia	E ASIA • (FEEDER) • USB UKRAINIAN • E ASIA • (FEEDER) • USB
10690	**RUSSIA** †RADIO MOSCOW, Novosibirsk	DS-2 (FEEDER) • 15 kW • USB
10855	**RUSSIA** †RADIO MOSCOW, Yekaterinburg	DS-MAYAK (FEEDER) • 15 kW • ISU DS-1 (FEEDER) • 15 kW • ISL
11000	**CHINA (PR)** †CENTRAL PEOPLES BS	CHINESE, ETC • TAIWAN-2 W-M • CHINESE, ETC • TAIWAN-2 (J) • CHINESE, ETC • TAIWAN-2
11020	**RUSSIA** VOICE OF RUSSIA	(D) • (FEEDER) • USB
11040	**CHINA (PR)** CENTRAL PEOPLES BS	DS-2 Th/Sa-Tu • DS-2
11100	**CHINA (PR)** †CENTRAL PEOPLES BS, Beijing	(J) • CHINESE, ETC • TAIWAN-1 • 120 kW CHINESE, ETC • TAIWAN-1 • 120 kW
11200	**CLANDESTINE (AFRICA)** †"RADIO SPLA"	Irr • N AFRICA • PRO-SUDAN REBELS
11330	**CHINA (PR)** †CENTRAL PEOPLES BS	DS-1 W-M • DS-1
11335	**KOREA (DPR)** RADIO PYONGYANG, Kujang-dong	C AMERICA • 400 kW
	RADIO PYONGYANG, Pyongyang	ASIA • 200 kW
11375	**CHINA (PR)** †CENTRAL PEOPLES BS	DS-MINORITIES
11400v	**PIRATE (PACIFIC)** †"RADIO G'DAY", Australia	Irr • AUSTRALASIA • 0.016 kW
11401v	**PIRATE (EUROPE)** †"RADIO WAVES INTL", France	Irr • Su • ENGLISH & FRENCH • W EUROPE • 0.015 kW
11402	**ICELAND** RIKISUTVARPID, Reykjavik	ATLANTIC & EUROPE • DS-1 • 10 kW • USB
11413v	**PIRATE (EUROPE)** †"RADIO STELLA", Scotland	Irr • Su • W EUROPE • 0.09 kW • ALT. FREQ. TO 7446v kHz
11445	**CHINA (PR)** †RADIO BEIJING, Kunming	S AMERICA • 240 kW SE ASIA • 50 kW AFRICA • 120 kW S ASIA • 120 kW
11455	**CHINA (PR)** †RADIO BEIJING, Beijing	SE ASIA
11455v	**ZAIRE** †LA VOIX DU ZAIRE, Kisangani	FRENCH, ETC • DS • 3 kW Su • FRENCH, ETC • DS • 3 kW
11470	**CLANDESTINE (M EAST)** †"IRAN FREEDOM FLAG, Egypt	(D) • PERSIAN • MIDEAST • ANTI-IRANIAN GOVT • 100 kW
11500	**CHINA (PR)** RADIO BEIJING, Beijing	E EUROPE & W ASIA • 120 kW
	†RADIO BEIJING, Kunming	S AMERICA • 120 kW
	†RADIO BEIJING, Xi'an	EUROPE • 120 kW
11515	**CHINA (PR)** †RADIO BEIJING, Beijing	E EUROPE • 120 kW JAPANESE • E ASIA • 120 kW S AMERICA • 120 kW MIDEAST & N AFRICA • 120 kW
11520	**UKRAINE** †RADIO UKRAINE, Simferopol'	(J) • E NORTH AM • 2X11790-12060 KHZ • SPR (J) • UKRAINIAN • E NORTH AM • 2X11790-12060 KHZ • SPR (J) • UKRAINIAN • E NORTH AM • 2X11790-12060 KHZ • SPR
	†UKRAINIAN R, Simferopol'	
11530	**LEBANON** WINGS OF HOPE, Marjayoûn	EUROPE • 25 kW
11550	**TUNISIA** RTV TUNISIENNE, Sfax	DS • 100 kW
	USA FAMILY RADIO, Via Taiwan	S ASIA • ENGLISH, HINDI • 250 kW E ASIA • 250 kW
11560	**EGYPT** †RADIO CAIRO, Kafr Silim-Abis	MIDEAST • 250 kW
11570	**PAKISTAN** †RADIO PAKISTAN, Islamabad	MIDEAST & N AFRICA • 100 kW EUROPE • 250 kW (D) • MIDEAST • 250 kW
11575	**CHINA (PR)** †RADIO BEIJING, Xi'an	MIDEAST & S ASIA • 120 kW E AFRICA & S AFRICA • 120 kW
11580	**CHINA (TAIWAN)** †VO FREE CHINA, Via Okeechobee, USA	(D) • EUROPE • 100 kW
	GUAM KTWR-TRANS WORLD R, Merizo	E ASIA • 100 kW
(con'd)	**USA** †CHRIST SCI MONITOR, Via Saipan	E ASIA • 100 kW

0 1 2 3 4 5 6 7 8 9 10 11 12 13 14 15 16 17 18 19 20 21 22 23 24

ENGLISH ▬   ARABIC ∽∽∽   CHINESE ▭▭▭   FRENCH ▬▬   GERMAN ▬▬   RUSSIAN ═══   SPANISH ▬▬   OTHER ▬

FREQUENCY　　COUNTRY, STATION, LOCATION　　　　　　　TARGET • NETWORK • POWER (kW)　　　　World Time

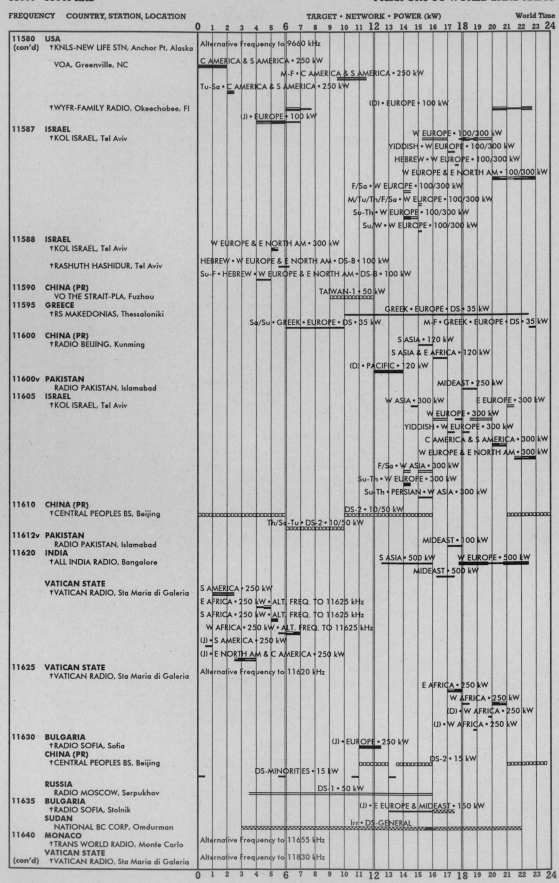

11580 (con'd)	**USA** †KNLS-NEW LIFE STN, Anchor Pt, Alaska — Alternative Frequency to 9660 kHz
	VOA, Greenville, NC — C AMERICA & S AMERICA • 250 kW M-F • C AMERICA & S AMERICA • 250 kW Tu-Sa • C AMERICA & S AMERICA • 250 kW
	†WYFR-FAMILY RADIO, Okeechobee, Fl — (D) • EUROPE • 100 kW (J) • EUROPE • 100 kW
11587	**ISRAEL** †KOL ISRAEL, Tel Aviv — W EUROPE • 100/300 kW YIDDISH • W EUROPE • 100/300 kW HEBREW • W EUROPE • 100/300 kW W EUROPE & E NORTH AM • 100/300 kW F/Sa • W EUROPE • 100/300 kW M/Tu/Th/F/Sa • W EUROPE • 100/300 kW Su-Th • W EUROPE • 100/300 kW Su/W • W EUROPE • 100/300 kW
11588	**ISRAEL** †KOL ISRAEL, Tel Aviv — W EUROPE & E NORTH AM • 300 kW
	†RASHUTH HASHIDUR, Tel Aviv — HEBREW • W EUROPE & E NORTH AM • DS-B • 100 kW Su-F • HEBREW • W EUROPE & E NORTH AM • DS-B • 100 kW
11590	**CHINA (PR)** VO THE STRAIT-PLA, Fuzhou — TAIWAN-1 • 50 kW
11595	**GREECE** †RS MAKEDONIAS, Thessaloniki — GREEK • EUROPE • DS • 35 kW Sa/Su • GREEK • EUROPE • DS • 35 kW　M-F • GREEK • EUROPE • DS • 35 kW
11600	**CHINA (PR)** †RADIO BEIJING, Kunming — S ASIA • 120 kW S ASIA & E AFRICA • 120 kW (D) • PACIFIC • 120 kW
11600v	**PAKISTAN** RADIO PAKISTAN, Islamabad — MIDEAST • 250 kW
11605	**ISRAEL** †KOL ISRAEL, Tel Aviv — W ASIA • 300 kW　　E EUROPE • 300 kW W EUROPE • 300 kW YIDDISH • W EUROPE • 300 kW C AMERICA & S AMERICA • 300 kW W EUROPE & E NORTH AM • 300 kW F/Sa • W ASIA • 300 kW Su-Th • W EUROPE • 300 kW Su-Th • PERSIAN • W ASIA • 300 kW
11610	**CHINA (PR)** †CENTRAL PEOPLES BS, Beijing — DS-2 • 10/50 kW Th/Sa-Tu • DS-2 • 10/50 kW
11612v	**PAKISTAN** RADIO PAKISTAN, Islamabad — MIDEAST • 100 kW
11620	**INDIA** †ALL INDIA RADIO, Bangalore — S ASIA • 500 kW　W EUROPE • 500 kW MIDEAST • 500 kW
	VATICAN STATE †VATICAN RADIO, Sta Maria di Galeria — S AMERICA • 250 kW E AFRICA • 250 kW • ALT. FREQ. TO 11625 kHz S AFRICA • 250 kW • ALT. FREQ. TO 11625 kHz W AFRICA • 250 kW • ALT. FREQ. TO 11625 kHz (J) • S AMERICA • 250 kW (J) • E NORTH AM & C AMERICA • 250 kW
11625	**VATICAN STATE** †VATICAN RADIO, Sta Maria di Galeria — Alternative Frequency to 11620 kHz E AFRICA • 250 kW W AFRICA • 250 kW (D) • W AFRICA • 250 kW (J) • W AFRICA • 250 kW
11630	**BULGARIA** †RADIO SOFIA, Sofia — (J) • EUROPE • 250 kW **CHINA (PR)** †CENTRAL PEOPLES BS, Beijing — DS-2 • 15 kW DS-MINORITIES • 15 kW
	RUSSIA RADIO MOSCOW, Serpukhov — DS-1 • 50 kW
11635	**BULGARIA** †RADIO SOFIA, Stolnik — (J) • E EUROPE & MIDEAST • 150 kW **SUDAN** NATIONAL BC CORP, Omdurman — Irr • DS-GENERAL
11640	**MONACO** †TRANS WORLD RADIO, Monte Carlo — Alternative Frequency to 11655 kHz
(con'd)	**VATICAN STATE** †VATICAN RADIO, Sta Maria di Galeria — Alternative Frequency to 11830 kHz

FREQUENCY	COUNTRY, STATION, LOCATION	TARGET • NETWORK • POWER (kW) World Time

0 1 2 3 4 5 6 7 8 9 10 11 12 13 14 15 16 17 18 19 20 21 22 23 24

11640 **VATICAN STATE**
(con'd) †VATICAN RADIO, Sta Maria di Galeria — Alternative Frequency to 9755 kHz

11645 **GREECE**
†FONI TIS HELLADAS, Athens
- MIDEAST • 100 kW   EUROPE • 100 kW
- N AFRICA • 100 kW   (D) • GREEK • S AFRICA • 100 kW
- GREEK • N AMERICA & EUROPE • 100 kW
- N AMERICA & EUROPE • 100 kW
- GREEK • EUROPE • 100 kW
- (D) • GREEK • C AFRICA • 100 kW
- (D) • GREEK • W ASIA • 100 kW
- (D) • S AFRICA • 100 kW
- (J) • GREEK • W ASIA • 100 kW

†FONI TIS HELLADAS, Kaválla
- GREEK • N AMERICA • 250 kW • ALT. FREQ. TO 7430 kHz   GREEK • AUSTRALASIA • 250 kW
- N AMERICA • 250 kW • ALT. FREQ. TO 7430 kHz   S AMERICA • 250 kW
- GREEK • MIDEAST • 250 kW

†FONI TIS HELLADAS, Various Locations
- GREEK • MIDEAST • 100/250 kW   GREEK • E EUROPE • 100/250 kW
- GREEK • EUROPE • 100/250 kW   E EUROPE • 100/250 kW
- EUROPE • 100/250 kW
- (J) • GREEK • EUROPE • 100/250 kW

11650 **CHINA (PR)**
RADIO BEIJING, Kunming
- SE ASIA • 50 kW

†RADIO BEIJING, Via French Guiana
- S AMERICA • 500 kW

†RADIO BEIJING, Xi'an
- S AMERICA • 120 kW • ALT. FREQ. TO 7435 kHz
- E EUROPE & N AFRICA • 120 kW • ALT. FREQ. TO 7420 kHz

GUAM
†KTWR-TRANS WORLD R, Merizo
- S ASIA • 100 kW   W AFRICA • 100 kW
- Su • S ASIA • 100 kW

NORTHERN MARIANA IS
KFBS-FAR EAST BC, Saipan Island
- E ASIA • 100 kW

PHILIPPINES
FEBC RADIO INTL, Bocaue
- SE ASIA • 50 kW
- F/Sa • SE ASIA • 50 kW

11655 **GERMANY**
†DEUTSCHE WELLE, Via Zhigulevsk, Russ
- (D) • S ASIA • 250 kW

HOLLAND
†RADIO NEDERLAND, Flevoland
- N AFRICA & E AFRICA • 500 kW

†RADIO NEDERLAND, Via Madagascar
- S ASIA • 300 kW   DUTCH • E AFRICA • 300 kW
- W AFRICA & C AFRICA • 300 kW

MONACO
†TRANS WORLD RADIO, Monte Carlo
- (J) • E EUROPE & W ASIA • 100/500 kW • ALT. FREQ. TO 11640 kHz
- (J) M-Sa • E EUROPE & W ASIA • 100/500 kW • ALT. FREQ. TO 11640 kHz

RUSSIA
RADIO MOSCOW, Via Byelarus
- DS-MAYAK • 20 kW

RADIO MOSCOW, Via Kazakhstan
- DS-MAYAK • 50 kW

11660 **BULGARIA**
BULGARIAN RADIO, Sofia
- EUROPE, N AFRICA & ATLANTIC • DS-1 • 250 kW
- (D) • EUROPE, N AFRICA & ATLANTIC • DS-1 • 250 kW
- (J) • EUROPE, N AFRICA & ATLANTIC • DS-1 • 250 kW

†RADIO SOFIA, Sofia
- (D) • N AMERICA • 250 kW
- (D) • C AMERICA & S AMERICA • 250 kW
- (J) • EUROPE & E NORTH AM • 250 kW
- (J) • EUROPE • 250 kW

CHINA (PR)
RADIO BEIJING, Kunming
- SE ASIA • 50 kW

FRANCE
R FRANCE INTL, Issoudun-Allouis
- S ASIA & SE ASIA • 500 kW
- M • ANTARCTICA • 100 kW

HOLLAND
RADIO NEDERLAND, Flevoland
- S AMERICA • 500 kW

RADIO NEDERLAND, Via Neth Antilles
- C AMERICA • 300 kW

RUSSIA
R MOSCOW INTL, Taldom
- S ASIA & SE ASIA • 500 kW

11665 **EGYPT**
RADIO CAIRO, Abu Za'bal
- C AFRICA & E AFRICA • DS-VO THE ARABS • 100 kW
- MIDEAST • DS-GENERAL • 100 kW

GUAM
KTWR-TRANS WORLD R, Merizo
- E ASIA • 100 kW

NORTHERN MARIANA IS
KFBS-FAR EAST BC, Saipan Island
- W ASIA • 100 kW
- M-F • E EUROPE & W ASIA • 100 kW
- Sa/Su • E EUROPE & W ASIA • 100 kW

RUSSIA
(con'd) R MOSCOW INTL
- (D) • W NORTH AM • USB

0 1 2 3 4 5 6 7 8 9 10 11 12 13 14 15 16 17 18 19 20 21 22 23 24

ENGLISH ▬   ARABIC ≋   CHINESE ▫▫▫   FRENCH ═   GERMAN ▬   RUSSIAN ═   SPANISH ▬   OTHER ▬

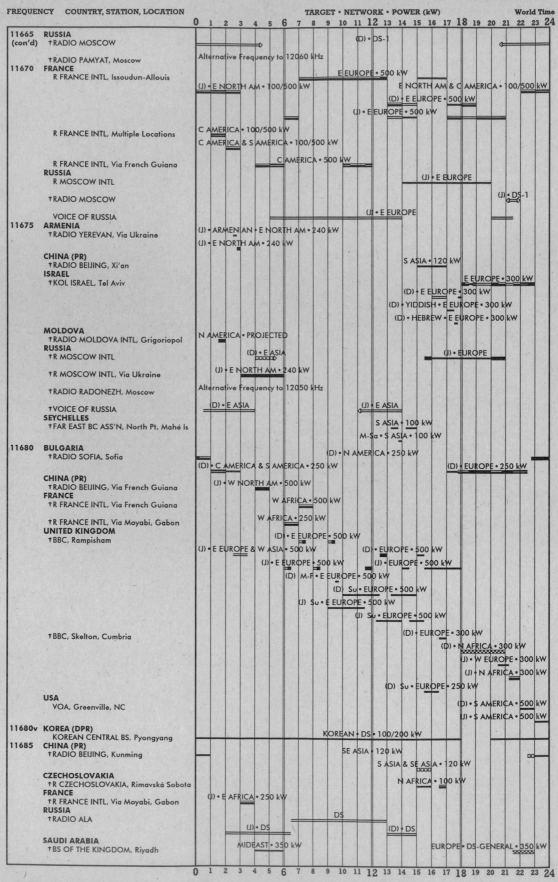

FREQUENCY	COUNTRY, STATION, LOCATION	TARGET • NETWORK • POWER (kW)

World Time
0 1 2 3 4 5 6 7 8 9 10 11 12 13 14 15 16 17 18 19 20 21 22 23 24

11665 **RUSSIA**
(con'd)   †RADIO MOSCOW — (D) • DS-1
            †RADIO PAMYAT, Moscow — Alternative Frequency to 12060 kHz
11670 **FRANCE**
            R FRANCE INTL, Issoudun-Allouis — E EUROPE • 500 kW
            (J) • E NORTH AM • 100/500 kW / E NORTH AM & C AMERICA • 100/500 kW
            (D) • E EUROPE • 500 kW
            (J) • E EUROPE • 500 kW
            R FRANCE INTL, Multiple Locations — C AMERICA • 100/500 kW
            C AMERICA & S AMERICA • 100/500 kW
            R FRANCE INTL, Via French Guiana — C AMERICA • 500 kW
         RUSSIA
            R MOSCOW INTL — (J) • E EUROPE
            †RADIO MOSCOW — (J) • DS-1
            VOICE OF RUSSIA — (J) • E EUROPE
11675 **ARMENIA**
            †RADIO YEREVAN, Via Ukraine — (J) • ARMENIAN • E NORTH AM • 240 kW
            (J) • E NORTH AM • 240 kW
         CHINA (PR)
            †RADIO BEIJING, Xi'an — S ASIA • 120 kW
         ISRAEL
            †KOL ISRAEL, Tel Aviv — E EUROPE • 300 kW
            (D) • E EUROPE • 300 kW
            (D) • YIDDISH • E EUROPE • 300 kW
            (D) • HEBREW • E EUROPE • 300 kW
         MOLDOVA
            †RADIO MOLDOVA INTL, Grigoriopol — N AMERICA • PROJECTED
         RUSSIA
            †R MOSCOW INTL — (D) • E ASIA
            (J) • EUROPE
            †R MOSCOW INTL, Via Ukraine — (J) • E NORTH AM • 240 kW
            †RADIO RADONEZH, Moscow — Alternative Frequency to 12050 kHz
            †VOICE OF RUSSIA — (D) • E ASIA / (J) • E ASIA
         SEYCHELLES
            †FAR EAST BC ASS'N, North Pt, Mahé Is — S ASIA • 100 kW
            M-Sa • S ASIA • 100 kW
11680 **BULGARIA**
            †RADIO SOFIA, Sofia — (D) • N AMERICA • 250 kW
            (D) • C AMERICA & S AMERICA • 250 kW / (D) • EUROPE • 250 kW
         CHINA (PR)
            †RADIO BEIJING, Via French Guiana — (J) • W NORTH AM • 500 kW
         FRANCE
            †R FRANCE INTL, Via French Guiana — W AFRICA • 500 kW
            †R FRANCE INTL, Via Moyabi, Gabon — W AFRICA • 250 kW
         UNITED KINGDOM
            †BBC, Rampisham — (D) • E EUROPE • 500 kW
            (J) • E EUROPE & W ASIA • 500 kW / (D) • EUROPE • 500 kW
            (J) • E EUROPE • 500 kW / (J) • EUROPE • 500 kW
            (D) • M-F • E EUROPE • 500 kW
            (D) • Su • EUROPE • 500 kW
            (J) • Su • E EUROPE • 500 kW
            (J) • Su • EUROPE • 500 kW
            †BBC, Skelton, Cumbria — (D) • EUROPE • 300 kW
            (D) • N AFRICA • 300 kW
            (J) • W EUROPE • 300 kW
            (J) • N AFRICA • 300 kW
            (D) • Su • EUROPE • 250 kW
         USA
            VOA, Greenville, NC — (D) • S AMERICA • 500 kW
            (J) • S AMERICA • 500 kW
11680v **KOREA (DPR)**
            KOREAN CENTRAL BS, Pyongyang — KOREAN • DS • 100/200 kW
11685 **CHINA (PR)**
            †RADIO BEIJING, Kunming — SE ASIA • 120 kW
            S ASIA & SE ASIA • 120 kW
         CZECHOSLOVAKIA
            †R CZECHOSLOVAKIA, Rimavská Sobota — N AFRICA • 100 kW
         FRANCE
            †R FRANCE INTL, Via Moyabi, Gabon — (J) • E AFRICA • 250 kW
         RUSSIA
            †RADIO ALA — DS
            (J) • DS / (D) • DS
         SAUDI ARABIA
            †BS OF THE KINGDOM, Riyadh — MIDEAST • 350 kW / EUROPE • DS-GENERAL • 350 kW

0 1 2 3 4 5 6 7 8 9 10 11 12 13 14 15 16 17 18 19 20 21 22 23 24

FREQUENCY   COUNTRY, STATION, LOCATION   TARGET • NETWORK • POWER (kW)   World Time

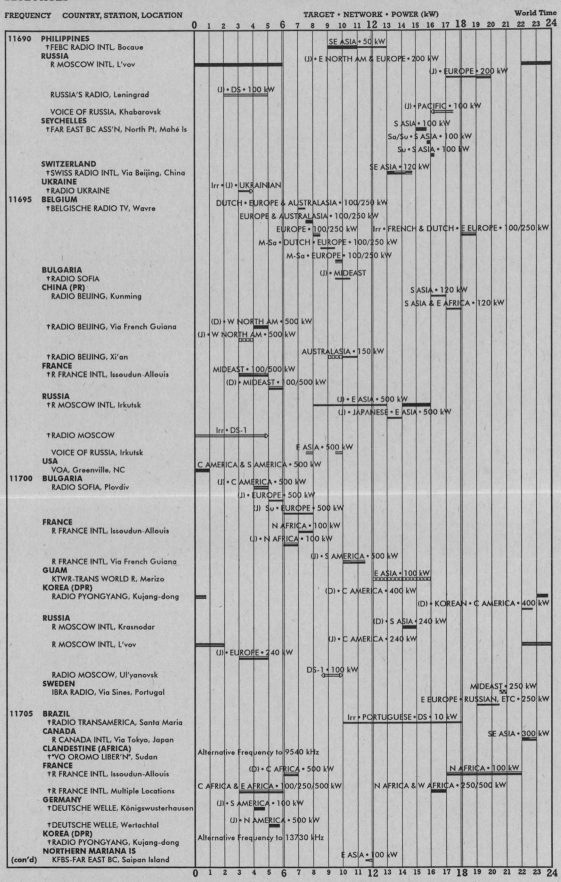

Frequency	Country, Station, Location	Schedule
11690	PHILIPPINES †FEBC RADIO INTL, Bocaue	SE ASIA • 50 kW
	RUSSIA R MOSCOW INTL, L'vov	(J) • E NORTH AM & EUROPE • 200 kW; (J) • EUROPE • 200 kW
	RUSSIA'S RADIO, Leningrad	(J) • DS • 100 kW
	VOICE OF RUSSIA, Khabarovsk	(J) • PACIFIC • 100 kW
	SEYCHELLES †FAR EAST BC ASS'N, North Pt, Mahé Is	S ASIA • 100 kW; Sa/Su • S ASIA • 100 kW; Su • S ASIA • 100 kW
	SWITZERLAND †SWISS RADIO INTL, Via Beijing, China	SE ASIA • 120 kW
	UKRAINE †RADIO UKRAINE	Irr • (J) • UKRAINIAN
11695	BELGIUM †BELGISCHE RADIO TV, Wavre	DUTCH • EUROPE & AUSTRALASIA • 100/250 kW; EUROPE & AUSTRALASIA • 100/250 kW; EUROPE • 100/250 kW; Irr • FRENCH & DUTCH • E EUROPE • 100/250 kW; M-Sa • DUTCH • EUROPE • 100/250 kW; M-Sa • EUROPE • 100/250 kW
	BULGARIA †RADIO SOFIA	(J) • MIDEAST
	CHINA (PR) RADIO BEIJING, Kunming	S ASIA • 120 kW; S ASIA & E AFRICA • 120 kW
	†RADIO BEIJING, Via French Guiana	(D) • W NORTH AM • 500 kW; (J) • W NORTH AM • 500 kW
	†RADIO BEIJING, Xi'an	AUSTRALASIA • 150 kW
	FRANCE †R FRANCE INTL, Issoudun-Allouis	MIDEAST • 100/500 kW; (D) • MIDEAST • 100/500 kW
	RUSSIA †R MOSCOW INTL, Irkutsk	(J) • E ASIA • 500 kW; (J) • JAPANESE • E ASIA • 500 kW
	†RADIO MOSCOW	Irr • DS-1
	VOICE OF RUSSIA, Irkutsk	E ASIA • 500 kW
	USA VOA, Greenville, NC	C AMERICA & S AMERICA • 500 kW
11700	BULGARIA RADIO SOFIA, Plovdiv	(J) • C AMERICA • 500 kW; (J) • EUROPE • 500 kW; (J) • Su • EUROPE • 500 kW
	FRANCE R FRANCE INTL, Issoudun-Allouis	N AFRICA • 100 kW; (J) • N AFRICA • 100 kW
	R FRANCE INTL, Via French Guiana	(J) • S AMERICA • 500 kW
	GUAM KTWR-TRANS WORLD R, Merizo	E ASIA • 100 kW
	KOREA (DPR) RADIO PYONGYANG, Kujang-dong	(D) • C AMERICA • 400 kW; (D) • KOREAN • C AMERICA • 400 kW
	RUSSIA R MOSCOW INTL, Krasnodar	(D) • S ASIA • 240 kW
	R MOSCOW INTL, L'vov	(J) • C AMERICA • 240 kW; (J) • EUROPE • 240 kW
	RADIO MOSCOW, Ul'yanovsk	DS-1 • 100 kW
	SWEDEN IBRA RADIO, Via Sines, Portugal	MIDEAST • 250 kW; E EUROPE • RUSSIAN, ETC • 250 kW
11705	BRAZIL †RADIO TRANSAMERICA, Santa Maria	Irr • PORTUGUESE • DS • 10 kW
	CANADA R CANADA INTL, Via Tokyo, Japan	SE ASIA • 300 kW
	CLANDESTINE (AFRICA) †"VO OROMO LIBER'N", Sudan	Alternative Frequency to 9540 kHz
	FRANCE †R FRANCE INTL, Issoudun-Allouis	(D) • C AFRICA • 500 kW; N AFRICA • 100 kW
	†R FRANCE INTL, Multiple Locations	C AFRICA & E AFRICA • 100/250/500 kW; N AFRICA & W AFRICA • 250/500 kW
	GERMANY †DEUTSCHE WELLE, Königswusterhausen	(J) • S AMERICA • 100 kW
	†DEUTSCHE WELLE, Wertachtal	(J) • N AMERICA • 500 kW
	KOREA (DPR) †RADIO PYONGYANG, Kujang-dong	Alternative Frequency to 13730 kHz
	NORTHERN MARIANA IS KFBS-FAR EAST BC, Saipan Island	E ASIA • 100 kW
(con'd)		

0 1 2 3 4 5 6 7 8 9 10 11 12 13 14 15 16 17 18 19 20 21 22 23 24

ENGLISH ▬   ARABIC ∾∾   CHINESE □□□   FRENCH ▬   GERMAN ▬   RUSSIAN ═   SPANISH ▬   OTHER ▬

| FREQUENCY | COUNTRY, STATION, LOCATION | TARGET • NETWORK • POWER (kW) | World Time |

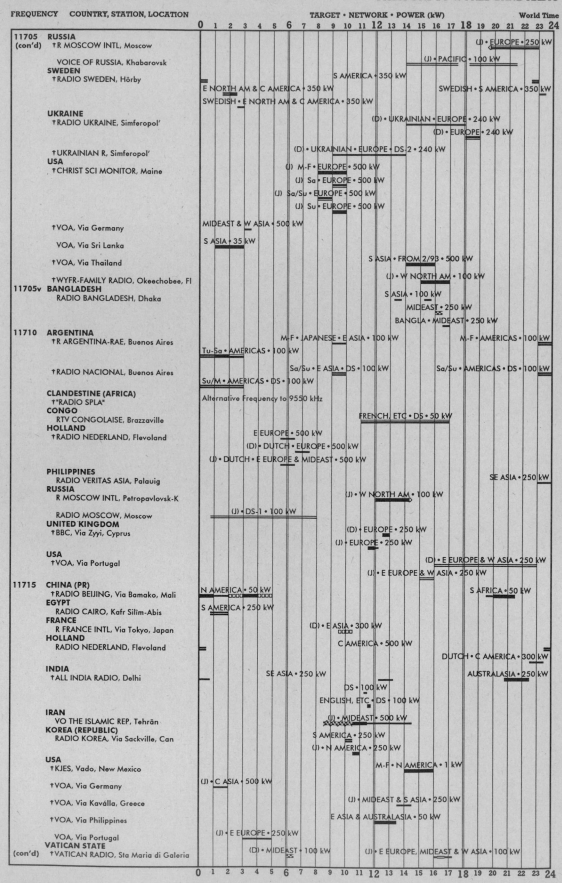

11705 **RUSSIA**
(con'd) †R MOSCOW INTL, Moscow — (J) • EUROPE • 250 kW

VOICE OF RUSSIA, Khabarovsk — (J) • PACIFIC • 100 kW
SWEDEN
†RADIO SWEDEN, Hörby — S AMERICA • 350 kW
— E NORTH AM & C AMERICA • 350 kW — SWEDISH • S AMERICA • 350 kW
— SWEDISH • E NORTH AM & C AMERICA • 350 kW

UKRAINE
†RADIO UKRAINE, Simferopol' — (D) • UKRAINIAN • EUROPE • 240 kW
— (D) • EUROPE • 240 kW

†UKRAINIAN R, Simferopol' — (D) • UKRAINIAN • EUROPE • DS-2 240 kW
USA
†CHRIST SCI MONITOR, Maine — (J) • M-F • EUROPE • 500 kW
— (J) • Sa • EUROPE • 500 kW
— (J) • Sa/Su • EUROPE • 500 kW
— (J) • Su • EUROPE • 500 kW

†VOA, Via Germany — MIDEAST & W ASIA • 500 kW

VOA, Via Sri Lanka — S ASIA • 35 kW

†VOA, Via Thailand — S ASIA • FROM 2/93 • 500 kW

†WYFR-FAMILY RADIO, Okeechobee, Fl — (J) • W NORTH AM • 100 kW
11705v **BANGLADESH**
RADIO BANGLADESH, Dhaka — S ASIA • 100 kW
— MIDEAST • 250 kW
— BANGLA • MIDEAST • 250 kW

11710 **ARGENTINA**
†R ARGENTINA-RAE, Buenos Aires — M-F • JAPANESE • E ASIA • 100 kW — M-F • AMERICAS • 100 kW
— Tu-Sa • AMERICAS • 100 kW

†RADIO NACIONAL, Buenos Aires — Sa/Su • E ASIA • DS • 100 kW — Sa/Su • AMERICAS • DS • 100 kW
— Su/M • AMERICAS • DS • 100 kW

CLANDESTINE (AFRICA)
†"RADIO SPLA" — Alternative Frequency to 9550 kHz
CONGO
RTV CONGOLAISE, Brazzaville — FRENCH, ETC • DS • 50 kW
HOLLAND
†RADIO NEDERLAND, Flevoland — E EUROPE • 500 kW
— (D) • DUTCH • EUROPE • 500 kW
— (J) • DUTCH • E EUROPE & MIDEAST • 500 kW

PHILIPPINES
RADIO VERITAS ASIA, Palauig — SE ASIA • 250 kW
RUSSIA
R MOSCOW INTL, Petropavlovsk-K — (J) • W NORTH AM • 100 kW

RADIO MOSCOW, Moscow — (J) • DS-1 • 100 kW
UNITED KINGDOM
†BBC, Via Zyyi, Cyprus — (D) • EUROPE • 250 kW
— (J) • EUROPE • 250 kW

USA
†VOA, Via Portugal — (D) • E EUROPE & W ASIA • 250 kW
— (J) • E EUROPE & W ASIA • 250 kW

11715 **CHINA (PR)**
†RADIO BEIJING, Via Bamako, Mali — N AMERICA • 50 kW — S AFRICA • 50 kW
EGYPT
RADIO CAIRO, Kafr Silim-Abis — S AMERICA • 250 kW
FRANCE
R FRANCE INTL, Via Tokyo, Japan — (D) • E ASIA • 300 kW
HOLLAND
RADIO NEDERLAND, Flevoland — C AMERICA • 500 kW
— DUTCH • C AMERICA • 300 kW

INDIA
†ALL INDIA RADIO, Delhi — SE ASIA • 250 kW — AUSTRALASIA • 250 kW
— DS • 100 kW
— ENGLISH, ETC • DS • 100 kW

IRAN
VO THE ISLAMIC REP, Tehrān — (J) • MIDEAST • 500 kW
KOREA (REPUBLIC)
RADIO KOREA, Via Sackville, Can — S AMERICA • 250 kW
— (J) • N AMERICA • 250 kW

USA
†KJES, Vado, New Mexico — M-F • N AMERICA • 1 kW

†VOA, Via Germany — (J) • C ASIA • 500 kW

†VOA, Via Kaválla, Greece — (J) • MIDEAST & S ASIA • 250 kW

†VOA, Via Philippines — E ASIA & AUSTRALASIA • 50 kW

VOA, Via Portugal — (J) • E EUROPE • 250 kW
VATICAN STATE
(con'd) †VATICAN RADIO, Sta Maria di Galeria — (D) • MIDEAST • 100 kW — (J) • E EUROPE, MIDEAST & W ASIA • 100 kW

SUMMER ONLY (J)   WINTER ONLY (D)   JAMMING / OR ∧   EARLIEST HEARD ◁   LATEST HEARD ▷   NEW OR CHANGED FOR 1993 †

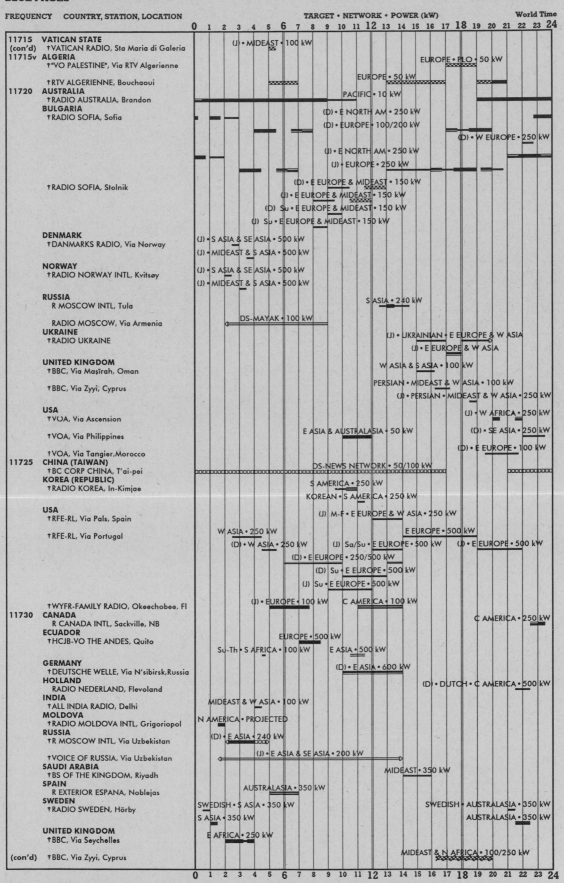

FREQUENCY   COUNTRY, STATION, LOCATION   TARGET • NETWORK • POWER (kW)   World Time

Frequency	Country, Station, Location	Target • Network • Power
11715 (con'd)	**VATICAN STATE** †VATICAN RADIO, Sta Maria di Galeria	(J) • MIDEAST • 100 kW
11715v	**ALGERIA** †"VO PALESTINE", Via RTV Algerienne	EUROPE • PLO • 50 kW
	†RTV ALGERIENNE, Bouchaoui	EUROPE • 50 kW
11720	**AUSTRALIA** †RADIO AUSTRALIA, Brandon	PACIFIC • 10 kW
	BULGARIA †RADIO SOFIA, Sofia	(D) • E NORTH AM • 250 kW
		(D) • EUROPE • 100/200 kW
		(D) • W EUROPE • 250 kW
		(J) • E NORTH AM • 250 kW
		(J) • EUROPE • 250 kW
	†RADIO SOFIA, Stolnik	(D) • E EUROPE & MIDEAST • 150 kW
		(J) • E EUROPE & MIDEAST • 150 kW
		(D) Su • E EUROPE & MIDEAST • 150 kW
		(J) Su • E EUROPE & MIDEAST • 150 kW
	DENMARK †DANMARKS RADIO, Via Norway	(J) • S ASIA & SE ASIA • 500 kW
		(J) • MIDEAST & S ASIA • 500 kW
	NORWAY †RADIO NORWAY INTL, Kvitsøy	(J) • S ASIA & SE ASIA • 500 kW
		(J) • MIDEAST & S ASIA • 500 kW
	RUSSIA R MOSCOW INTL, Tula	S ASIA • 240 kW
	RADIO MOSCOW, Via Armenia	DS-MAYAK • 100 kW
	UKRAINE †RADIO UKRAINE	(J) • UKRAINIAN • E EUROPE & W ASIA
		(J) • E EUROPE & W ASIA
	UNITED KINGDOM †BBC, Via Maṣīrah, Oman	W ASIA & S ASIA • 100 kW
	†BBC, Via Zyyi, Cyprus	PERSIAN • MIDEAST & W ASIA • 100 kW
		(J) • PERSIAN • MIDEAST & W ASIA • 250 kW
	USA †VOA, Via Ascension	(J) • W AFRICA • 250 kW
	†VOA, Via Philippines	E ASIA & AUSTRALASIA • 50 kW
		(D) • SE ASIA • 250 kW
	†VOA, Via Tangier, Morocco	(D) • E EUROPE • 100 kW
11725	**CHINA (TAIWAN)** †BC CORP CHINA, T'ai-pei	DS-NEWS NETWORK • 50/100 kW
	KOREA (REPUBLIC) †RADIO KOREA, In-Kimjae	S AMERICA • 250 kW
		KOREAN • S AMERICA • 250 kW
	USA †RFE-RL, Via Pals, Spain	(J) • M-F • E EUROPE & W ASIA • 250 kW
	†RFE-RL, Via Portugal	W ASIA • 250 kW
		E EUROPE • 500 kW
		(D) • W ASIA • 250 kW
		(J) Sa/Su • E EUROPE • 500 kW
		(J) • E EUROPE • 500 kW
		(D) • E EUROPE • 250/500 kW
		(D) Su • E EUROPE • 500 kW
		(J) Su • E EUROPE • 500 kW
	†WYFR-FAMILY RADIO, Okeechobee, Fl	(J) • EUROPE • 100 kW
		C AMERICA • 100 kW
11730	**CANADA** R CANADA INTL, Sackville, NB	C AMERICA • 250 kW
	ECUADOR †HCJB-VO THE ANDES, Quito	EUROPE • 500 kW
		Su-Th • S AFRICA • 100 kW
		E ASIA • 500 kW
	GERMANY †DEUTSCHE WELLE, Via N'sibirsk, Russia	(D) • E ASIA • 600 kW
	HOLLAND RADIO NEDERLAND, Flevoland	(D) • DUTCH • C AMERICA • 500 kW
	INDIA †ALL INDIA RADIO, Delhi	MIDEAST & W ASIA • 100 kW
	MOLDOVA †RADIO MOLDOVA INTL, Grigoriopol	N AMERICA • PROJECTED
	RUSSIA †R MOSCOW INTL, Via Uzbekistan	(D) • E ASIA • 240 kW
	†VOICE OF RUSSIA, Via Uzbekistan	(J) • E ASIA & SE ASIA • 200 kW
	SAUDI ARABIA †BS OF THE KINGDOM, Riyadh	MIDEAST • 350 kW
	SPAIN R EXTERIOR ESPANA, Noblejas	AUSTRALASIA • 350 kW
	SWEDEN †RADIO SWEDEN, Hörby	SWEDISH • S ASIA • 350 kW
		SWEDISH • AUSTRALASIA • 350 kW
		S ASIA • 350 kW
		AUSTRALASIA • 350 kW
	UNITED KINGDOM †BBC, Via Seychelles	E AFRICA • 250 kW
(con'd)	†BBC, Via Zyyi, Cyprus	MIDEAST & N AFRICA • 100/250 kW

0 1 2 3 4 5 6 7 8 9 10 11 12 13 14 15 16 17 18 19 20 21 22 23 24

ENGLISH ▬▬   ARABIC ▨▨   CHINESE ▯▯▯   FRENCH ▬▬   GERMAN ▬▬   RUSSIAN ══   SPANISH ▬▬   OTHER —

FREQUENCY	COUNTRY, STATION, LOCATION	TARGET • NETWORK • POWER (kW)	World Time

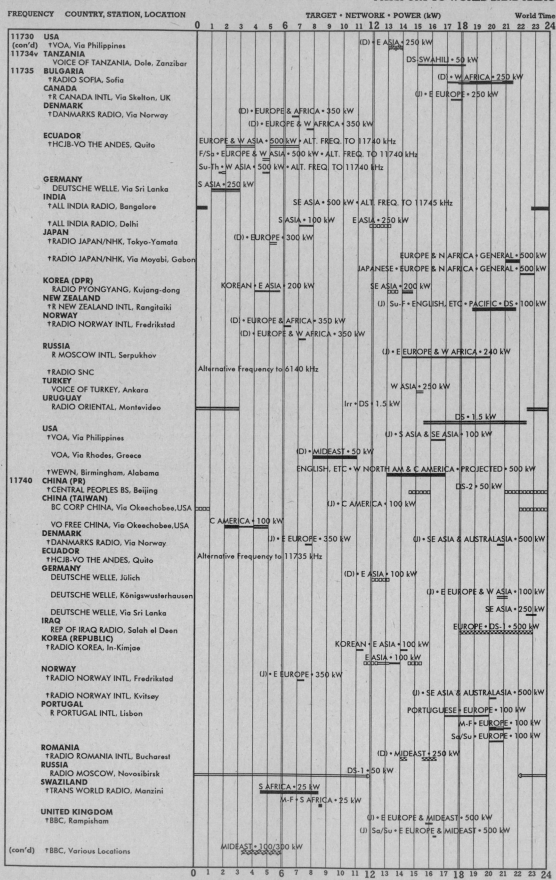

11730 (con'd)	USA †VOA, Via Philippines	(D) • E ASIA • 250 kW
11734v	TANZANIA VOICE OF TANZANIA, Dole, Zanzibar	DS • SWAHILI • 50 kW
11735	BULGARIA †RADIO SOFIA, Sofia	(D) • W AFRICA • 250 kW
	CANADA †R CANADA INTL, Via Skelton, UK	(J) • E EUROPE • 250 kW
	DENMARK †DANMARKS RADIO, Via Norway	(D) • EUROPE & AFRICA • 350 kW (D) • EUROPE & W AFRICA • 350 kW
	ECUADOR †HCJB-VO THE ANDES, Quito	EUROPE & W ASIA • 500 kW • ALT. FREQ. TO 11740 kHz F/Sa • EUROPE & W ASIA • 500 kW • ALT. FREQ. TO 11740 kHz Su-Th • W ASIA • 500 kW • ALT. FREQ. TO 11740 kHz
	GERMANY DEUTSCHE WELLE, Via Sri Lanka	S ASIA • 250 kW
	INDIA †ALL INDIA RADIO, Bangalore	SE ASIA • 500 kW • ALT. FREQ. TO 11745 kHz
	†ALL INDIA RADIO, Delhi	S ASIA • 100 kW E ASIA • 250 kW
	JAPAN †RADIO JAPAN/NHK, Tokyo-Yamata	(D) • EUROPE • 300 kW
	†RADIO JAPAN/NHK, Via Moyabi, Gabon	EUROPE & N AFRICA • GENERAL • 500 kW JAPANESE • EUROPE & N AFRICA • GENERAL • 500 kW
	KOREA (DPR) RADIO PYONGYANG, Kujang-dong	KOREAN • E ASIA • 200 kW SE ASIA • 200 kW
	NEW ZEALAND †R NEW ZEALAND INTL, Rangitaiki	(J) Su-F • ENGLISH, ETC • PACIFIC • DS • 100 kW
	NORWAY †RADIO NORWAY INTL, Fredrikstad	(D) • EUROPE & AFRICA • 350 kW (D) • EUROPE & W AFRICA • 350 kW
	RUSSIA R MOSCOW INTL, Serpukhov	(J) • E EUROPE & W AFRICA • 240 kW
	†RADIO SNC	Alternative Frequency to 6140 kHz
	TURKEY VOICE OF TURKEY, Ankara	W ASIA • 250 kW
	URUGUAY RADIO ORIENTAL, Montevideo	Irr • DS • 1.5 kW DS • 1.5 kW
	USA †VOA, Via Philippines	(J) • S ASIA & SE ASIA • 100 kW
	VOA, Via Rhodes, Greece	(D) • MIDEAST • 50 kW
	†WEWN, Birmingham, Alabama	ENGLISH, ETC • W NORTH AM & C AMERICA • PROJECTED • 500 kW
11740	CHINA (PR) †CENTRAL PEOPLES BS, Beijing	DS-2 • 50 kW
	CHINA (TAIWAN) BC CORP CHINA, Via Okeechobee, USA	(J) • C AMERICA • 100 kW
	VO FREE CHINA, Via Okeechobee, USA	C AMERICA • 100 kW
	DENMARK †DANMARKS RADIO, Via Norway	(J) • E EUROPE • 350 kW (J) • SE ASIA & AUSTRALASIA • 500 kW
	ECUADOR †HCJB-VO THE ANDES, Quito	Alternative Frequency to 11735 kHz
	GERMANY DEUTSCHE WELLE, Jülich	(D) • E ASIA • 100 kW
	DEUTSCHE WELLE, Königswusterhausen	(J) • E EUROPE & W ASIA • 100 kW
	DEUTSCHE WELLE, Via Sri Lanka	SE ASIA • 250 kW
	IRAQ REP OF IRAQ RADIO, Salah el Deen	EUROPE • DS-1 • 500 kW
	KOREA (REPUBLIC) †RADIO KOREA, In-Kimjae	KOREAN • E ASIA • 100 kW E ASIA • 100 kW
	NORWAY †RADIO NORWAY INTL, Fredrikstad	(J) • E EUROPE • 350 kW
	†RADIO NORWAY INTL, Kvitsøy	(J) • SE ASIA & AUSTRALASIA • 500 kW
	PORTUGAL R PORTUGAL INTL, Lisbon	PORTUGUESE • EUROPE • 100 kW M-F • EUROPE • 100 kW Sa/Su • EUROPE • 100 kW
	ROMANIA †RADIO ROMANIA INTL, Bucharest	(D) • MIDEAST • 250 kW
	RUSSIA RADIO MOSCOW, Novosibirsk	DS-1 • 50 kW
	SWAZILAND †TRANS WORLD RADIO, Manzini	S AFRICA • 25 kW M-F • S AFRICA • 25 kW
	UNITED KINGDOM †BBC, Rampisham	(J) • E EUROPE & MIDEAST • 500 kW (J) Sa/Su • E EUROPE & MIDEAST • 500 kW
(con'd)	†BBC, Various Locations	MIDEAST • 100/300 kW

FREQUENCY	COUNTRY, STATION, LOCATION	TARGET • NETWORK • POWER (kW) World Time 0–24
11740 (con'd)	**UNITED KINGDOM** †BBC, Via Maşīrah, Oman	PERSIAN • MIDEAST & W ASIA • 100 kW
		MIDEAST & W ASIA • 100 kW
	†BBC, Woofferton	(J) • E EUROPE • 250 kW
		(J) Sa/Su • E EUROPE • 250 kW
	USA †VOA, Via Kaválla, Greece	E AFRICA • 250 kW
		(D) • E EUROPE & W ASIA • 250 kW
		(D) • MIDEAST • 250 kW
	†VOA, Via Philippines	(D) • E ASIA • 250 kW
	VOA, Via Rhodes, Greece	(J) • MIDEAST • 50 kW
	VATICAN STATE †VATICAN RADIO, Sta Maria di Galeria	E EUROPE • 100 kW
		MIDEAST • 250 kW
		W EUROPE • 100 kW
		Su • E EUROPE • 100 kW
		Su • W EUROPE • 100 kW
11745	**ALBANIA** †RADIO TIRANA, Lushnjë	E NORTH AM • 100 kW
	BRAZIL †RADIO NACIONAL, Brasília	N AMERICA & C AMERICA • 250 kW • ALT. FREQ. TO 15445 kHz
	CHINA (PR) †RADIO BEIJING, Beijing	E EUROPE & W ASIA • 120 kW
		S AMERICA • 120 kW
	CHINA (TAIWAN) VO FREE CHINA, T'ai-pei	SE ASIA • 50/100 kW
		E ASIA • 50/100 kW
		JAPANESE • E ASIA • 50/100 kW
	GERMANY †DEUTSCHE WELLE, Wertachtal	E EUROPE & MIDEAST • 500 kW
	INDIA †ALL INDIA RADIO, Bangalore	Alternative Frequency to 11735 kHz
	IRAN VO THE ISLAMIC REP, Tehrān	(D) • MIDEAST • 500 kW
	OMAN RADIO OMAN, Sīb	(J) • MIDEAST • DS • 100 kW
	RUSSIA R MOSCOW INTL, Minsk	W AFRICA • 240 kW
		(J) • W AFRICA • 240 kW
	R MOSCOW INTL, Vinnitsa	(D) • W EUROPE & W AFRICA • 100 kW
	VOICE OF RUSSIA, Minsk	(J) • W AFRICA • 240 kW
	VOICE OF RUSSIA, Vinnitsa	(D) • W EUROPE & W AFRICA • 100 kW
11750	**AUSTRALIA** †RADIO AUSTRALIA, Shepparton	(D) • SE ASIA • 100 kW
	PORTUGAL †R PORTUGAL INTL, Lisbon	M-F • PORTUGUESE • E AFRICA & S AFRICA • 100 kW
	RUSSIA RADIO MOSCOW, Kazan'	DS-1 • 100 kW
	UNITED KINGDOM †BBC, Rampisham	(J) • E EUROPE • 500 kW
	†BBC, Skelton, Cumbria	(D) • E EUROPE & MIDEAST • 250 kW
		(D) Sa/Su • E EUROPE & MIDEAST • 250 kW
	BBC, Via Ascension	S AMERICA • 250 kW
	†BBC, Via Maşīrah, Oman	S ASIA • 100 kW
	†BBC, Via Singapore	S ASIA & SE ASIA • 100/250 kW
		(J) • S ASIA • 250 kW
		E ASIA • 100 kW
		S ASIA • 250 kW
	USA VOA, Via Philippines	(D) • E ASIA • 250 kW
	†VOA, Via Portugal	(J) • E EUROPE • 250 kW
	†VOA, Via Tangier, Morocco	(D) • E EUROPE • 100 kW
11752v	**INDONESIA** VOICE OF INDONESIA, Jakarta, Jawa	ASIA & PACIFIC • 100 kW
		EUROPE • 100 kW
		JAPANESE • ASIA & PACIFIC • 100 kW
11755	**CHINA (PR)** RADIO BEIJING, Beijing	E EUROPE & W ASIA • 120 kW
		AUSTRALASIA • 240 kW
	FINLAND †RADIO FINLAND, Pori	(D) • N AMERICA • 500 kW
		(D) • E ASIA • 500 kW
		(D) • MIDEAST & E AFRICA • 500 kW
		(D) M-F • EUROPE • 500 kW
		(D) • EUROPE • 250/500 kW
		(J) • N AMERICA • 500 kW
		(J) M-F • EUROPE • 500 kW
		(J) • MIDEAST • 500 kW
		(D) Sa/Su • EUROPE • 500 kW
		(J) • EUROPE • 500 kW
		(J) Sa/Su • EUROPE • 500 kW
(con'd)	**IRAQ** REP OF IRAQ RADIO, Salah el Deen	EUROPE • DS-1 • 500 kW

ENGLISH ▬ ARABIC ▨ CHINESE ▫▫▫ FRENCH ═ GERMAN ═ RUSSIAN ═ SPANISH ═ OTHER —

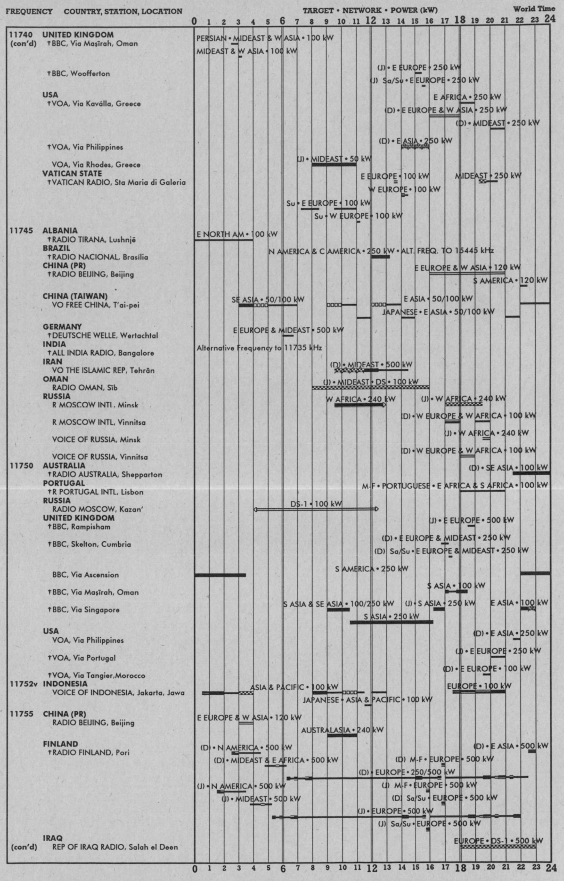

FREQUENCY	COUNTRY, STATION, LOCATION	TARGET • NETWORK • POWER (kW)	World Time

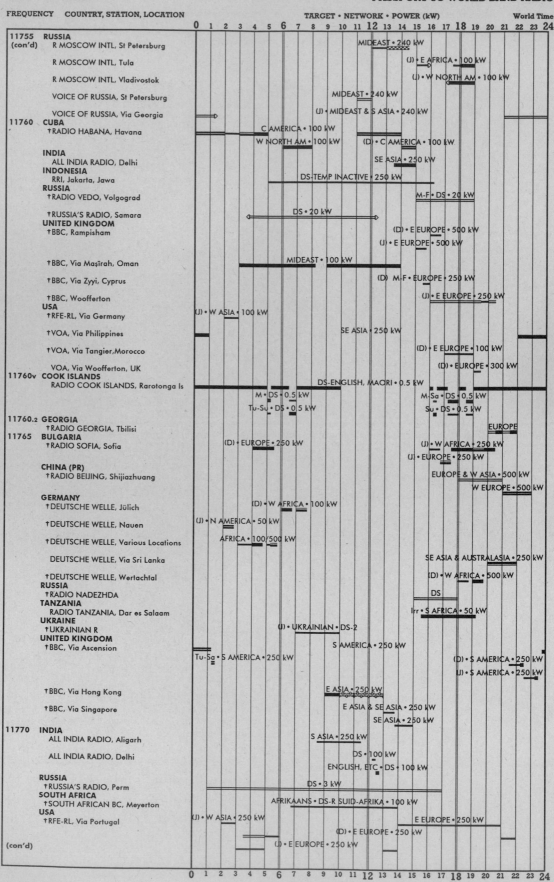

11755 RUSSIA
(con'd) R MOSCOW INTL, St Petersburg — MIDEAST • 240 kW
R MOSCOW INTL, Tula — (J) • E AFRICA • 100 kW
R MOSCOW INTL, Vladivostok — (J) • W NORTH AM • 100 kW
VOICE OF RUSSIA, St Petersburg — MIDEAST • 240 kW
VOICE OF RUSSIA, Via Georgia — (J) • MIDEAST & S ASIA • 240 kW

11760 CUBA
†RADIO HABANA, Havana — C AMERICA • 100 kW / W NORTH AM • 100 kW / (D) • C AMERICA • 100 kW

INDIA
ALL INDIA RADIO, Delhi — SE ASIA • 250 kW
INDONESIA
RRI, Jakarta, Jawa — DS • TEMP INACTIVE • 250 kW
RUSSIA
†RADIO VEDO, Volgograd — M-F • DS • 20 kW
†RUSSIA'S RADIO, Samara — DS • 20 kW
UNITED KINGDOM
†BBC, Rampisham — (D) • E EUROPE • 500 kW / (J) • E EUROPE • 500 kW
†BBC, Via Maşīrah, Oman — MIDEAST • 100 kW
†BBC, Via Zyyi, Cyprus — (D) M-F • EUROPE • 250 kW
†BBC, Woofferton — (J) • E EUROPE • 250 kW
USA
†RFE-RL, Via Germany — (J) • W ASIA • 100 kW
†VOA, Via Philippines — SE ASIA • 250 kW
†VOA, Via Tangier, Morocco — (D) • E EUROPE • 100 kW
VOA, Via Woofferton, UK — (D) • EUROPE • 300 kW

11760v COOK ISLANDS
RADIO COOK ISLANDS, Rarotonga Is — DS-ENGLISH, MAORI • 0.5 kW
M • DS • 0.5 kW / M-Sa • DS • 0.5 kW
Tu-Su • DS • 0.5 kW / Su • DS • 0.5 kW

11760.2 GEORGIA
†RADIO GEORGIA, Tbilisi — EUROPE
11765 BULGARIA
†RADIO SOFIA, Sofia — (D) • EUROPE • 250 kW / (J) • W AFRICA • 250 kW / (J) • EUROPE • 250 kW

CHINA (PR)
†RADIO BEIJING, Shijiazhuang — EUROPE & W ASIA • 500 kW / W EUROPE • 500 kW

GERMANY
†DEUTSCHE WELLE, Jülich — (D) • W AFRICA • 100 kW
†DEUTSCHE WELLE, Nauen — (J) • N AMERICA • 50 kW
†DEUTSCHE WELLE, Various Locations — AFRICA • 100/500 kW
DEUTSCHE WELLE, Via Sri Lanka — SE ASIA & AUSTRALASIA • 250 kW
†DEUTSCHE WELLE, Wertachtal — (D) • W AFRICA • 500 kW
RUSSIA
†RADIO NADEZHDA — DS
TANZANIA
RADIO TANZANIA, Dar es Salaam — Irr • S AFRICA • 50 kW
UKRAINE
†UKRAINIAN R — (J) • UKRAINIAN • DS-2
UNITED KINGDOM
†BBC, Via Ascension — S AMERICA • 250 kW / Tu-Sa • S AMERICA • 250 kW / (D) • S AMERICA • 250 kW / (J) • S AMERICA • 250 kW
†BBC, Via Hong Kong — E ASIA • 250 kW
†BBC, Via Singapore — E ASIA & SE ASIA • 250 kW / SE ASIA • 250 kW

11770 INDIA
ALL INDIA RADIO, Aligarh — S ASIA • 250 kW
ALL INDIA RADIO, Delhi — DS • 100 kW / ENGLISH, ETC • DS • 100 kW
RUSSIA
†RUSSIA'S RADIO, Perm — DS • 3 kW
SOUTH AFRICA
†SOUTH AFRICAN BC, Meyerton — AFRIKAANS • DS-R SUID-AFRIKA • 100 kW
USA
†RFE-RL, Via Portugal — (J) • W ASIA • 250 kW / E EUROPE • 250 kW / (D) • E EUROPE • 250 kW

(con'd) — (J) • E EUROPE • 250 kW

| FREQUENCY | COUNTRY, STATION, LOCATION | TARGET • NETWORK • POWER (kW) | World Time |

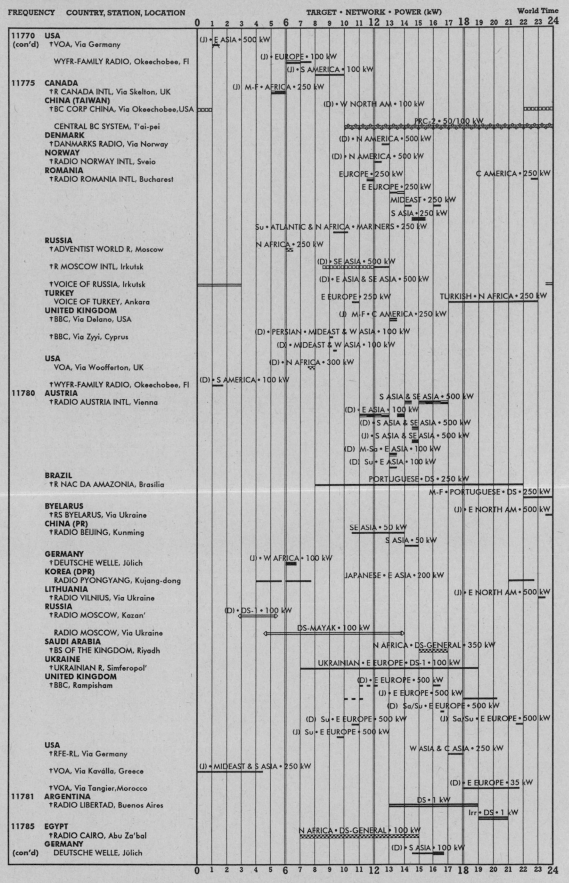

FREQUENCY　　COUNTRY, STATION, LOCATION　　　　　TARGET • NETWORK • POWER (kW)　　　World Time

0　1　2　3　4　5　6　7　8　9　10　11　12　13　14　15　16　17　18　19　20　21　22　23　24

11770 USA
(con'd)　†VOA, Via Germany　　　(J) • E ASIA • 500 kW

　　　　(J) • EUROPE • 100 kW
　　WYFR-FAMILY RADIO, Okeechobee, Fl
　　　　(J) • S AMERICA • 100 kW

11775 CANADA
　†R CANADA INTL, Via Skelton, UK　　(J) M-F • AFRICA • 250 kW
CHINA (TAIWAN)
　†BC CORP CHINA, Via Okeechobee, USA　　(D) • W NORTH AM • 100 kW

　CENTRAL BC SYSTEM, T'ai-pei　　　PRC-2 • 50/100 kW
DENMARK
　†DANMARKS RADIO, Via Norway　　(D) • N AMERICA • 500 kW
NORWAY
　†RADIO NORWAY INTL, Sveio　　(D) • N AMERICA • 500 kW
ROMANIA
　†RADIO ROMANIA INTL, Bucharest　　EUROPE • 250 kW　　C AMERICA • 250 kW
　　　　E EUROPE • 250 kW
　　　　MIDEAST • 250 kW
　　　　S ASIA • 250 kW
　　Su • ATLANTIC & N AFRICA • MARINERS • 250 kW
RUSSIA
　†ADVENTIST WORLD R, Moscow　　N AFRICA • 250 kW

　†R MOSCOW INTL, Irkutsk　　(D) • SE ASIA • 500 kW

　†VOICE OF RUSSIA, Irkutsk　　(D) • E ASIA & SE ASIA • 500 kW
TURKEY
　VOICE OF TURKEY, Ankara　　E EUROPE • 250 kW　　TURKISH • N AFRICA • 250 kW
UNITED KINGDOM
　†BBC, Via Delano, USA　　(J) M-F • C AMERICA • 250 kW

　†BBC, Via Zyyi, Cyprus　　(D) • PERSIAN • MIDEAST & W ASIA • 100 kW
　　　　(D) • MIDEAST & W ASIA • 100 kW
USA
　VOA, Via Woofferton, UK　　(D) • N AFRICA • 300 kW

　†WYFR-FAMILY RADIO, Okeechobee, Fl　(D) • S AMERICA • 100 kW
11780 AUSTRIA
　†RADIO AUSTRIA INTL, Vienna　　S ASIA & SE ASIA • 500 kW
　　　　(D) • E ASIA • 100 kW
　　　　(D) • S ASIA & SE ASIA • 500 kW
　　　　(J) • S ASIA & SE ASIA • 500 kW
　　　　(D) M-Sa • E ASIA • 100 kW
　　　　(D) Su • E ASIA • 100 kW
BRAZIL
　†R NAC DA AMAZONIA, Brasilia　　PORTUGUESE • DS • 250 kW

　　　　M-F • PORTUGUESE • DS • 250 kW
BYELARUS
　†RS BYELARUS, Via Ukraine　　(J) • E NORTH AM • 500 kW
CHINA (PR)
　†RADIO BEIJING, Kunming　　SE ASIA • 50 kW
　　　　S ASIA • 50 kW
GERMANY
　†DEUTSCHE WELLE, Jülich　　(J) • W AFRICA • 100 kW
KOREA (DPR)
　RADIO PYONGYANG, Kujang-dong　　JAPANESE • E ASIA • 200 kW
LITHUANIA
　†RADIO VILNIUS, Via Ukraine　　(J) • E NORTH AM • 500 kW
RUSSIA
　†RADIO MOSCOW, Kazan'　　(D) • DS-1 • 100 kW

　RADIO MOSCOW, Via Ukraine　　DS-MAYAK • 100 kW
SAUDI ARABIA
　†BS OF THE KINGDOM, Riyadh　　N AFRICA • DS-GENERAL • 350 kW
UKRAINE
　†UKRAINIAN R, Simferopol'　　UKRAINIAN • E EUROPE • DS-1 • 100 kW
UNITED KINGDOM
　†BBC, Rampisham　　(D) • E EUROPE • 500 kW
　　　　(J) • E EUROPE • 500 kW
　　　　(D) Sa/Su • E EUROPE • 500 kW
　　(D) Su • E EUROPE • 500 kW　　(J) Sa/Su • E EUROPE • 500 kW
　　(J) Su • E EUROPE • 500 kW

USA
　†RFE-RL, Via Germany　　W ASIA & C ASIA • 250 kW

　†VOA, Via Kaválla, Greece　　(J) • MIDEAST & S ASIA • 250 kW

　†VOA, Via Tangier, Morocco　　(D) • E EUROPE • 35 kW
11781 ARGENTINA
　†RADIO LIBERTAD, Buenos Aires　　DS • 1 kW
　　　　Irr • DS • 1 kW

11785 EGYPT
　†RADIO CAIRO, Abu Za'bal　　N AFRICA • DS-GENERAL • 100 kW
GERMANY
(con'd)　DEUTSCHE WELLE, Jülich　　(D) • S ASIA • 100 kW

0　1　2　3　4　5　6　7　8　9　10　11　12　13　14　15　16　17　18　19　20　21　22　23　24

ENGLISH ▬　　ARABIC ⁓⁓⁓　　CHINESE □□□　　FRENCH ══　　GERMAN ▬▬　　RUSSIAN ══　　SPANISH ▬▬　　OTHER ──

FREQUENCY   COUNTRY, STATION, LOCATION

TARGET • NETWORK • POWER (kW)   World Time

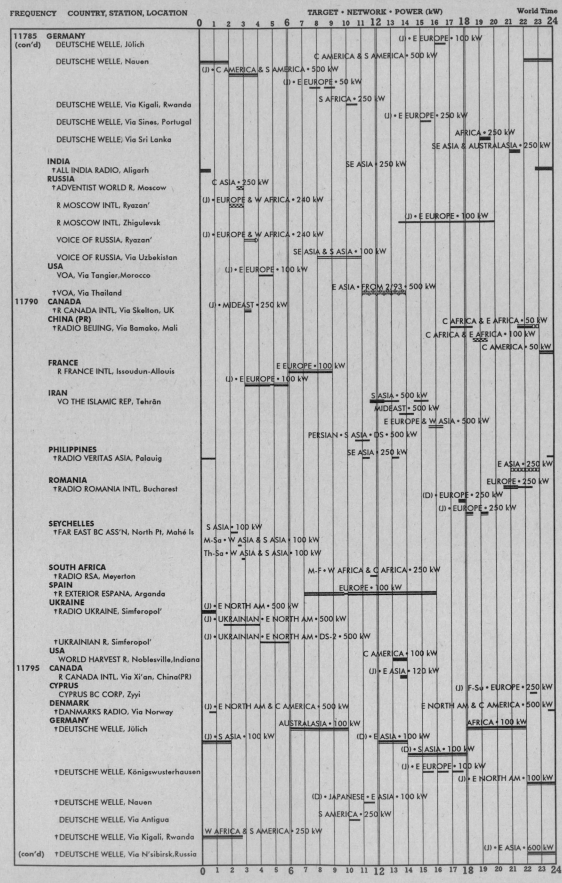

FREQUENCY	COUNTRY, STATION, LOCATION	TARGET • NETWORK • POWER (kW)
11785 (con'd)	GERMANY	
	DEUTSCHE WELLE, Jülich	(J) • E EUROPE • 100 kW
	DEUTSCHE WELLE, Nauen	C AMERICA & S AMERICA • 500 kW
		(J) • C AMERICA & S AMERICA • 500 kW
		(J) • E EUROPE • 50 kW
		S AFRICA • 250 kW
	DEUTSCHE WELLE, Via Kigali, Rwanda	
	DEUTSCHE WELLE, Via Sines, Portugal	(J) • E EUROPE • 250 kW
	DEUTSCHE WELLE, Via Sri Lanka	AFRICA • 250 kW
		SE ASIA & AUSTRALASIA • 250 kW
	INDIA	
	†ALL INDIA RADIO, Aligarh	SE ASIA • 250 kW
	RUSSIA	
	†ADVENTIST WORLD R, Moscow	C ASIA • 250 kW
	R MOSCOW INTL, Ryazan'	(J) • EUROPE & W AFRICA • 240 kW
	R MOSCOW INTL, Zhigulevsk	(J) • E EUROPE • 100 kW
	VOICE OF RUSSIA, Ryazan'	(J) • EUROPE & W AFRICA • 240 kW
	VOICE OF RUSSIA, Via Uzbekistan	SE ASIA & S ASIA • 100 kW
	USA	
	VOA, Via Tangier, Morocco	(J) • E EUROPE • 100 kW
	†VOA, Via Thailand	E ASIA • FROM 2/93 • 500 kW
11790	CANADA	
	†R CANADA INTL, Via Skelton, UK	(J) • MIDEAST • 250 kW
	CHINA (PR)	
	†RADIO BEIJING, Via Bamako, Mali	C AFRICA & E AFRICA • 50 kW
		C AFRICA & E AFRICA • 100 kW
		C AMERICA • 50 kW
	FRANCE	
	R FRANCE INTL, Issoudun-Allouis	E EUROPE • 100 kW
		(J) • E EUROPE • 100 kW
	IRAN	
	VO THE ISLAMIC REP, Tehrān	S ASIA • 500 kW
		MIDEAST • 500 kW
		E EUROPE & W ASIA • 500 kW
		PERSIAN • S ASIA • DS • 500 kW
	PHILIPPINES	
	†RADIO VERITAS ASIA, Palauig	SE ASIA • 250 kW
		E ASIA • 250 kW
	ROMANIA	
	†RADIO ROMANIA INTL, Bucharest	EUROPE • 250 kW
		(D) • EUROPE • 250 kW
		(J) • EUROPE • 250 kW
	SEYCHELLES	
	†FAR EAST BC ASS'N, North Pt, Mahé Is	S ASIA • 100 kW
		M-Sa • W ASIA & S ASIA • 100 kW
		Th-Sa • W ASIA & S ASIA • 100 kW
	SOUTH AFRICA	
	†RADIO RSA, Meyerton	M-F • W AFRICA & C AFRICA • 250 kW
	SPAIN	
	†R EXTERIOR ESPANA, Arganda	EUROPE • 100 kW
	UKRAINE	
	†RADIO UKRAINE, Simferopol'	(J) • E NORTH AM • 500 kW
		(J) • UKRAINIAN • E NORTH AM • 500 kW
	†UKRAINIAN R, Simferopol'	(J) • UKRAINIAN • E NORTH AM • DS-2 • 500 kW
	USA	
	WORLD HARVEST R, Noblesville, Indiana	C AMERICA • 100 kW
11795	CANADA	
	R CANADA INTL, Via Xi'an, China(PR)	(J) • E ASIA • 120 kW
	CYPRUS	
	CYPRUS BC CORP, Zyyi	(J) F-Su • EUROPE • 250 kW
	DENMARK	
	†DANMARKS RADIO, Via Norway	(J) • E NORTH AM & C AMERICA • 500 kW
		E NORTH AM & C AMERICA • 500 kW
	GERMANY	
	†DEUTSCHE WELLE, Jülich	AUSTRALASIA • 100 kW
		AFRICA • 100 kW
		(J) • S ASIA • 100 kW
		(D) • E ASIA • 100 kW
		(D) • S ASIA • 100 kW
	†DEUTSCHE WELLE, Königswusterhausen	(J) • E EUROPE • 100 kW
		(J) • E NORTH AM • 100 kW
	†DEUTSCHE WELLE, Nauen	(D) • JAPANESE • E ASIA • 100 kW
		S AMERICA • 250 kW
	DEUTSCHE WELLE, Via Antigua	W AFRICA & S AMERICA • 250 kW
	†DEUTSCHE WELLE, Via Kigali, Rwanda	
(con'd)	†DEUTSCHE WELLE, Via N'sibirsk, Russia	(J) • E ASIA • 600 kW

SUMMER ONLY (J)   WINTER ONLY (D)   JAMMING / OR ∧   EARLIEST HEARD ◁   LATEST HEARD ▷   NEW OR CHANGED FOR 1993 †

FREQUENCY   COUNTRY, STATION, LOCATION   TARGET • NETWORK • POWER (kW)   World Time

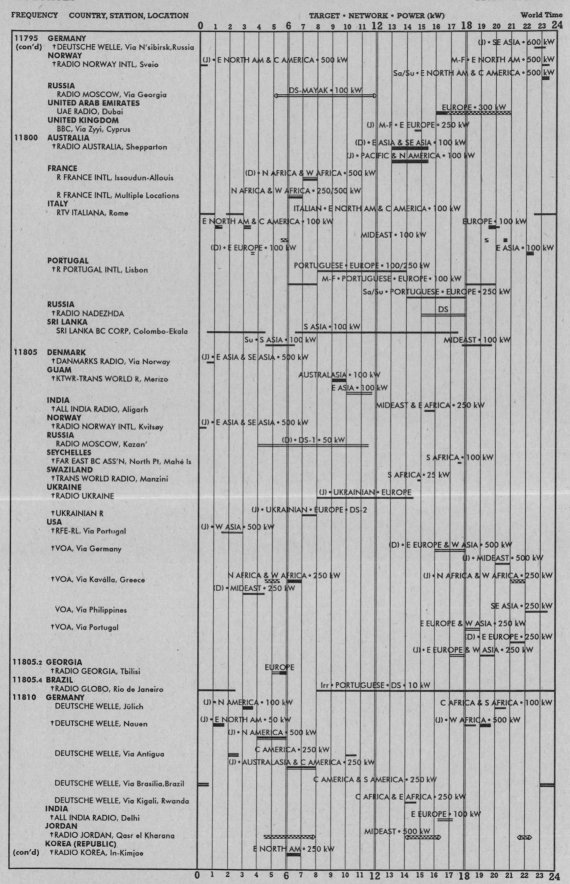

Frequency	Country, Station, Location	Target • Network • Power
11795 (con'd)	GERMANY †DEUTSCHE WELLE, Via N'sibirsk, Russia	(J) • SE ASIA • 600 kW
	NORWAY †RADIO NORWAY INTL, Sveio	(J) • E NORTH AM & C AMERICA • 500 kW; M-F • E NORTH AM • 500 kW; Sa/Su • E NORTH AM & C AMERICA • 500 kW
	RUSSIA RADIO MOSCOW, Via Georgia	DS-MAYAK • 100 kW
	UNITED ARAB EMIRATES UAE RADIO, Dubai	EUROPE • 300 kW
	UNITED KINGDOM BBC, Via Zyyi, Cyprus	(J) M-F • E EUROPE • 250 kW
11800	AUSTRALIA †RADIO AUSTRALIA, Shepparton	(D) • E ASIA & SE ASIA • 100 kW; (J) • PACIFIC & N AMERICA • 100 kW
	FRANCE R FRANCE INTL, Issoudun-Allouis	(D) • N AFRICA & W AFRICA • 500 kW
	R FRANCE INTL, Multiple Locations	N AFRICA & W AFRICA • 250/500 kW
	ITALY RTV ITALIANA, Rome	ITALIAN • E NORTH AM & C AMERICA • 100 kW; E NORTH AM & C AMERICA • 100 kW; EUROPE • 100 kW; MIDEAST • 100 kW; (D) • E EUROPE • 100 kW; E ASIA • 100 kW
	PORTUGAL †R PORTUGAL INTL, Lisbon	PORTUGUESE • EUROPE • 100/250 kW; M-F • PORTUGUESE • EUROPE • 100 kW; Sa/Su • PORTUGUESE • EUROPE • 250 kW
	RUSSIA †RADIO NADEZHDA	DS
	SRI LANKA SRI LANKA BC CORP, Colombo-Ekala	S ASIA • 100 kW; Su • S ASIA • 100 kW; MIDEAST • 100 kW
11805	DENMARK †DANMARKS RADIO, Via Norway	(J) • E ASIA & SE ASIA • 500 kW
	GUAM †KTWR-TRANS WORLD R, Merizo	AUSTRALASIA • 100 kW; E ASIA • 100 kW
	INDIA †ALL INDIA RADIO, Aligarh	MIDEAST & E AFRICA • 250 kW
	NORWAY †RADIO NORWAY INTL, Kvitsøy	(J) • E ASIA & SE ASIA • 500 kW
	RUSSIA RADIO MOSCOW, Kazan'	(D) • DS-1 • 50 kW
	SEYCHELLES †FAR EAST BC ASS'N, North Pt, Mahé Is	S AFRICA • 100 kW
	SWAZILAND †TRANS WORLD RADIO, Manzini	S AFRICA • 25 kW
	UKRAINE †RADIO UKRAINE	(J) • UKRAINIAN • EUROPE
	†UKRAINIAN R	(J) • UKRAINIAN • EUROPE • DS-2
	USA †RFE-RL, Via Portugal	(J) • W ASIA • 500 kW
	†VOA, Via Germany	(D) • E EUROPE & W ASIA • 500 kW; (J) • MIDEAST • 500 kW
	†VOA, Via Kaválla, Greece	N AFRICA & W AFRICA • 250 kW; (J) • N AFRICA & W AFRICA • 250 kW; (D) • MIDEAST • 250 kW
	VOA, Via Philippines	SE ASIA • 250 kW
	†VOA, Via Portugal	E EUROPE & W ASIA • 250 kW; (D) • E EUROPE • 250 kW; (J) • E EUROPE & W ASIA • 250 kW
11805.2	GEORGIA †RADIO GEORGIA, Tbilisi	EUROPE
11805.4	BRAZIL †RADIO GLOBO, Rio de Janeiro	Irr • PORTUGUESE • DS • 10 kW
11810	GERMANY DEUTSCHE WELLE, Jülich	(J) • N AMERICA • 100 kW; C AFRICA & S AFRICA • 100 kW
	†DEUTSCHE WELLE, Nauen	(J) • E NORTH AM • 50 kW; (J) • N AMERICA • 500 kW; (J) • W AFRICA • 500 kW
	DEUTSCHE WELLE, Via Antigua	C AMERICA • 250 kW; (J) • AUSTRALASIA & C AMERICA • 250 kW
	DEUTSCHE WELLE, Via Brasília, Brazil	C AMERICA & S AMERICA • 250 kW
	DEUTSCHE WELLE, Via Kigali, Rwanda	C AFRICA & E AFRICA • 250 kW
	INDIA †ALL INDIA RADIO, Delhi	E EUROPE • 100 kW
	JORDAN †RADIO JORDAN, Qasr el Kharana	MIDEAST • 500 kW
(con'd)	KOREA (REPUBLIC) †RADIO KOREA, In-Kimjae	E NORTH AM • 250 kW

ENGLISH ▬▬   ARABIC ∽∽∽   CHINESE □□□   FRENCH ▬▬   GERMAN ▬▬   RUSSIAN ▭▭   SPANISH ▬▬   OTHER ▬▬

FREQUENCY   COUNTRY, STATION, LOCATION   TARGET • NETWORK • POWER (kW)   World Time

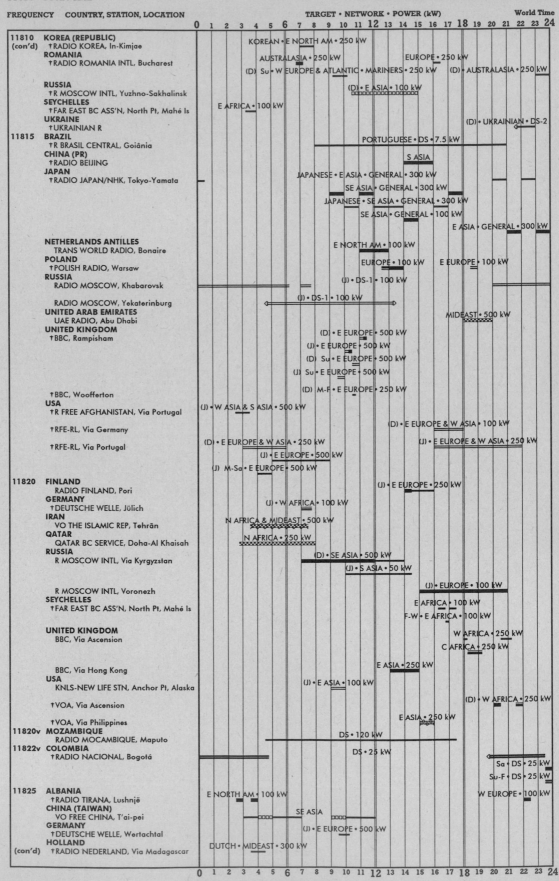

11810   **KOREA (REPUBLIC)**
(con'd)   †RADIO KOREA, In-Kimjae   KOREAN • E NORTH AM • 250 kW
     ROMANIA
     †RADIO ROMANIA INTL, Bucharest   AUSTRALASIA • 250 kW   EUROPE • 250 kW
       (D) Su • W EUROPE & ATLANTIC • MARINERS • 250 kW   (D) • AUSTRALASIA • 250 kW
     RUSSIA
     †R MOSCOW INTL, Yuzhno-Sakhalinsk   (D) • E ASIA • 100 kW
     SEYCHELLES
     †FAR EAST BC ASS'N, North Pt, Mahé Is   E AFRICA • 100 kW
     UKRAINE
     †UKRAINIAN R   (D) • UKRAINIAN • DS-2
11815   **BRAZIL**
     †R BRASIL CENTRAL, Goiânia   PORTUGUESE • DS • 7.5 kW
     CHINA (PR)
     †RADIO BEIJING   S ASIA
     JAPAN
     †RADIO JAPAN/NHK, Tokyo-Yamata   JAPANESE • E ASIA • GENERAL • 300 kW
       SE ASIA • GENERAL • 300 kW
       JAPANESE • SE ASIA • GENERAL • 300 kW
       SE ASIA • GENERAL • 100 kW
       E ASIA • GENERAL • 300 kW
     NETHERLANDS ANTILLES
     TRANS WORLD RADIO, Bonaire   E NORTH AM • 100 kW
     POLAND
     †POLISH RADIO, Warsaw   EUROPE • 100 kW   E EUROPE • 100 kW
     RUSSIA
     RADIO MOSCOW, Khabarovsk   (J) • DS-1 • 100 kW
     RADIO MOSCOW, Yekaterinburg   (J) • DS-1 • 100 kW
     UNITED ARAB EMIRATES
     UAE RADIO, Abu Dhabi   MIDEAST • 500 kW
     UNITED KINGDOM
     †BBC, Rampisham   (D) • E EUROPE • 500 kW
       (J) • E EUROPE • 500 kW
       (D) Su • E EUROPE • 500 kW
       (J) Su • E EUROPE • 500 kW
     †BBC, Woofferton   (D) M-F • E EUROPE • 250 kW
     USA
     †R FREE AFGHANISTAN, Via Portugal   (J) • W ASIA & S ASIA • 500 kW
     †RFE-RL, Via Germany   (D) • E EUROPE & W ASIA • 100 kW
     †RFE-RL, Via Portugal   (D) • E EUROPE & W ASIA • 250 kW   (J) • E EUROPE & W ASIA • 250 kW
       (J) • E EUROPE • 500 kW
       (J) M-Sa • E EUROPE • 500 kW
11820   **FINLAND**
     RADIO FINLAND, Pori   (J) • E EUROPE • 250 kW
     GERMANY
     †DEUTSCHE WELLE, Jülich   (J) • W AFRICA • 100 kW
     IRAN
     VO THE ISLAMIC REP, Tehrān   N AFRICA & MIDEAST • 500 kW
     QATAR
     QATAR BC SERVICE, Doha-Al Khaisah   N AFRICA • 250 kW
     RUSSIA
     R MOSCOW INTL, Via Kyrgyzstan   (D) • SE ASIA • 500 kW
       (J) • S ASIA • 50 kW
     R MOSCOW INTL, Voronezh   (J) • EUROPE • 100 kW
     SEYCHELLES
     †FAR EAST BC ASS'N, North Pt, Mahé Is   E AFRICA • 100 kW
       F-W • E AFRICA • 100 kW
     UNITED KINGDOM
     BBC, Via Ascension   W AFRICA • 250 kW
       C AFRICA • 250 kW
     BBC, Via Hong Kong   E ASIA • 250 kW
     USA
     KNLS-NEW LIFE STN, Anchor Pt, Alaska   (J) • E ASIA • 100 kW
     †VOA, Via Ascension   (D) • W AFRICA • 250 kW
     †VOA, Via Philippines   E ASIA • 250 kW
11820v **MOZAMBIQUE**
     RADIO MOCAMBIQUE, Maputo   DS • 120 kW
11822v **COLOMBIA**
     †RADIO NACIONAL, Bogotá   DS • 25 kW
       Sa • DS • 25 kW
       Su-F • DS • 25 kW
11825 **ALBANIA**
     †RADIO TIRANA, Lushnjë   E NORTH AM • 100 kW   W EUROPE • 100 kW
     CHINA (TAIWAN)
     VO FREE CHINA, T'ai-pei   SE ASIA
     GERMANY
     †DEUTSCHE WELLE, Wertachtal   (J) • E EUROPE • 500 kW
     HOLLAND
(con'd)   †RADIO NEDERLAND, Via Madagascar   DUTCH • MIDEAST • 300 kW

FREQUENCY   COUNTRY, STATION, LOCATION

TARGET • NETWORK • POWER (kW)

World Time

0 1 2 3 4 5 6 7 8 9 10 11 12 13 14 15 16 17 18 19 20 21 22 23 24

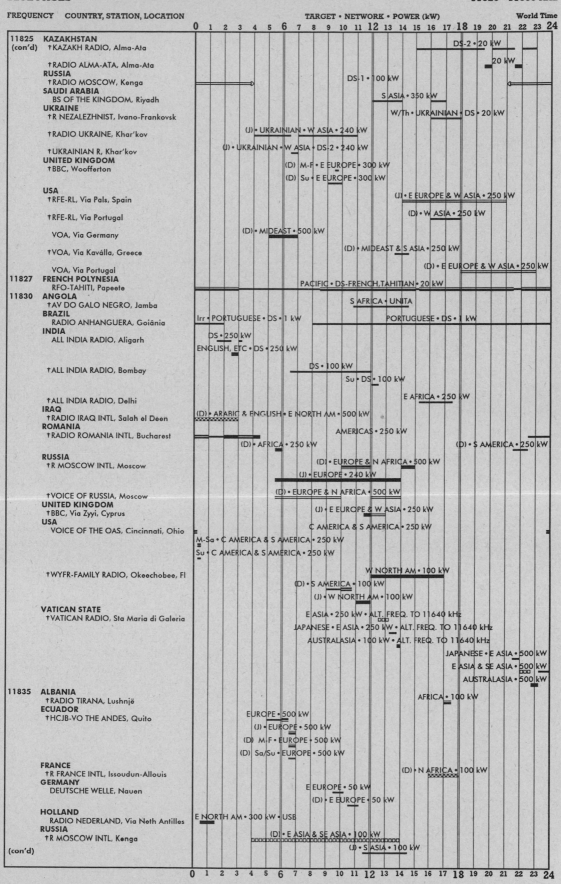

Frequency	Country, Station, Location	Target • Network • Power
11825 (con'd)	KAZAKHSTAN	
	†KAZAKH RADIO, Alma-Ata	DS-2 • 20 kW
	†RADIO ALMA-ATA, Alma-Ata	20 kW
	RUSSIA	
	†RADIO MOSCOW, Kenga	DS-1 • 100 kW
	SAUDI ARABIA	
	BS OF THE KINGDOM, Riyadh	S ASIA • 350 kW
	UKRAINE	
	†R NEZALEZHNIST, Ivano-Frankovsk	W/Th • UKRAINIAN • DS • 20 kW
	†RADIO UKRAINE, Khar'kov	(J) • UKRAINIAN • W ASIA • 240 kW
	†UKRAINIAN R, Khar'kov	(J) • UKRAINIAN • W ASIA • DS-2 • 240 kW
	UNITED KINGDOM	
	†BBC, Woofferton	(D) M-F • E EUROPE • 300 kW
		(D) Su • E EUROPE • 300 kW
	USA	
	†RFE-RL, Via Pals, Spain	(J) • E EUROPE & W ASIA • 250 kW
	†RFE-RL, Via Portugal	(D) • W ASIA • 250 kW
	VOA, Via Germany	(D) • MIDEAST • 500 kW
	†VOA, Via Kaválla, Greece	(D) • MIDEAST & S ASIA • 250 kW
	VOA, Via Portugal	(D) • E EUROPE & W ASIA • 250 kW
11827	FRENCH POLYNESIA	
	RFO-TAHITI, Papeete	PACIFIC • DS-FRENCH, TAHITIAN • 20 kW
11830	ANGOLA	
	†AV DO GALO NEGRO, Jamba	S AFRICA • UNITA
	BRAZIL	
	RADIO ANHANGUERA, Goiânia	Irr • PORTUGUESE • DS • 1 kW PORTUGUESE • DS • 1 kW
	INDIA	
	ALL INDIA RADIO, Aligarh	DS • 250 kW / ENGLISH, ETC • DS • 250 kW
	†ALL INDIA RADIO, Bombay	DS • 100 kW / Su • DS • 100 kW
	†ALL INDIA RADIO, Delhi	E AFRICA • 250 kW
	IRAQ	
	†RADIO IRAQ INTL, Salah el Deen	(D) • ARABIC & ENGLISH • E NORTH AM • 500 kW
	ROMANIA	
	†RADIO ROMANIA INTL, Bucharest	AMERICAS • 250 kW / (D) • AFRICA • 250 kW / (D) • S AMERICA • 250 kW
	RUSSIA	
	†R MOSCOW INTL, Moscow	(D) • EUROPE & N AFRICA • 500 kW / (J) • EUROPE • 240 kW
	†VOICE OF RUSSIA, Moscow	(D) • EUROPE & N AFRICA • 500 kW
	UNITED KINGDOM	
	†BBC, Via Zyyi, Cyprus	(J) • E EUROPE & W ASIA • 250 kW
	USA	
	VOICE OF THE OAS, Cincinnati, Ohio	C AMERICA & S AMERICA • 250 kW / M-Sa • C AMERICA & S AMERICA • 250 kW / Su • C AMERICA & S AMERICA • 250 kW
	†WYFR-FAMILY RADIO, Okeechobee, Fl	W NORTH AM • 100 kW / (D) • S AMERICA • 100 kW / (J) • W NORTH AM • 100 kW
	VATICAN STATE	
	†VATICAN RADIO, Sta Maria di Galeria	E ASIA • 250 kW • ALT. FREQ. TO 11640 kHz / JAPANESE • E ASIA • 250 kW • ALT. FREQ. TO 11640 kHz / AUSTRALASIA • 100 kW • ALT. FREQ. TO 11640 kHz / JAPANESE • E ASIA • 500 kW / E ASIA & SE ASIA • 500 kW / AUSTRALASIA • 500 kW
11835	ALBANIA	
	†RADIO TIRANA, Lushnjë	AFRICA • 100 kW
	ECUADOR	
	†HCJB-VO THE ANDES, Quito	EUROPE • 500 kW / (J) • EUROPE • 500 kW / (D) M-F • EUROPE • 500 kW / (D) Sa/Su • EUROPE • 500 kW
	FRANCE	
	†R FRANCE INTL, Issoudun-Allouis	(D) • N AFRICA • 100 kW
	GERMANY	
	DEUTSCHE WELLE, Nauen	E EUROPE • 50 kW / (D) • E EUROPE • 50 kW
	HOLLAND	
	RADIO NEDERLAND, Via Neth Antilles	E NORTH AM • 300 kW • USB
	RUSSIA	
	†R MOSCOW INTL, Kenga	(D) • E ASIA & SE ASIA • 100 kW / (J) • S ASIA • 100 kW
(con'd)		

0 1 2 3 4 5 6 7 8 9 10 11 12 13 14 15 16 17 18 19 20 21 22 23 24

ENGLISH ▬   ARABIC ∞∞∞   CHINESE □□□   FRENCH ▬   GERMAN ▬   RUSSIAN ═══   SPANISH ▬   OTHER ▬

FREQUENCY   COUNTRY, STATION, LOCATION

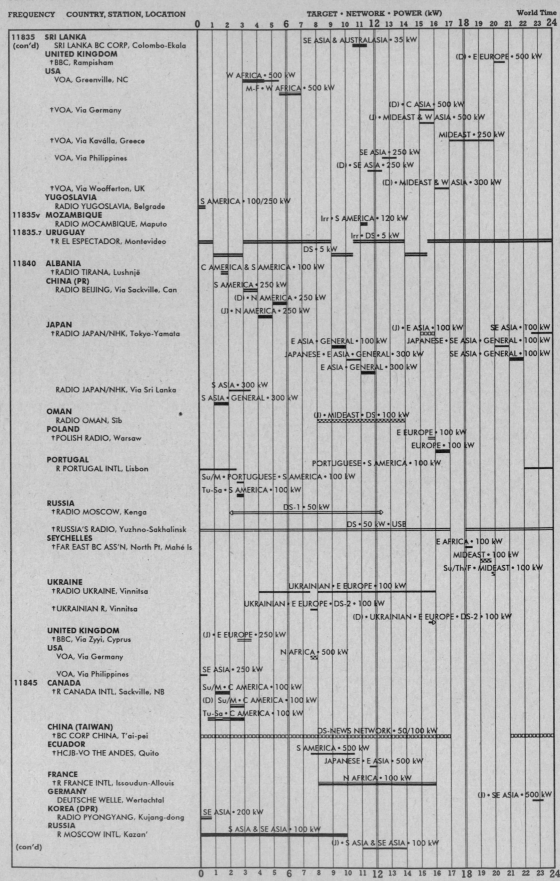

FREQUENCY	COUNTRY, STATION, LOCATION	TARGET • NETWORK • POWER (kW)
11835 (con'd)	SRI LANKA	
	SRI LANKA BC CORP, Colombo-Ekala	SE ASIA & AUSTRALASIA • 35 kW
	UNITED KINGDOM	
	†BBC, Rampisham	(D) • E EUROPE • 500 kW
	USA	
	VOA, Greenville, NC	W AFRICA • 500 kW
		M-F • W AFRICA • 500 kW
	†VOA, Via Germany	(D) • C ASIA • 500 kW
		(J) • MIDEAST & W ASIA • 500 kW
	†VOA, Via Kaválla, Greece	MIDEAST • 250 kW
	VOA, Via Philippines	SE ASIA • 250 kW
		(D) • SE ASIA • 250 kW
	†VOA, Via Woofferton, UK	(D) • MIDEAST & W ASIA • 300 kW
	YUGOSLAVIA	
	RADIO YUGOSLAVIA, Belgrade	S AMERICA • 100/250 kW
11835v	MOZAMBIQUE	
	RADIO MOCAMBIQUE, Maputo	Irr • S AMERICA • 120 kW
11835.7	URUGUAY	
	†R EL ESPECTADOR, Montevideo	Irr • DS • 5 kW
		DS • 5 kW
11840	ALBANIA	
	†RADIO TIRANA, Lushnjë	C AMERICA & S AMERICA • 100 kW
	CHINA (PR)	
	RADIO BEIJING, Via Sackville, Can	S AMERICA • 250 kW
		(D) • N AMERICA • 250 kW
		(J) • N AMERICA • 250 kW
	JAPAN	
	†RADIO JAPAN/NHK, Tokyo-Yamata	(J) • E ASIA • 100 kW / SE ASIA • 100 kW
		E ASIA • GENERAL • 100 kW / JAPANESE • SE ASIA • GENERAL • 100 kW
		JAPANESE • E ASIA • GENERAL • 300 kW / SE ASIA • GENERAL • 100 kW
		E ASIA • GENERAL • 300 kW
	RADIO JAPAN/NHK, Via Sri Lanka	S ASIA • 300 kW
		S ASIA • GENERAL • 300 kW
	OMAN	
	RADIO OMAN, Sīb	(J) • MIDEAST • DS • 100 kW
	POLAND	
	†POLISH RADIO, Warsaw	E EUROPE • 100 kW
		EUROPE • 100 kW
	PORTUGAL	
	R PORTUGAL INTL, Lisbon	PORTUGUESE • S AMERICA • 100 kW
		Su/M • PORTUGUESE • S AMERICA • 100 kW
		Tu-Sa • S AMERICA • 100 kW
	RUSSIA	
	†RADIO MOSCOW, Kenga	DS-1 • 50 kW
		DS • 50 kW • USB
	†RUSSIA'S RADIO, Yuzhno-Sakhalinsk	
	SEYCHELLES	
	†FAR EAST BC ASS'N, North Pt, Mahé Is	E AFRICA • 100 kW
		MIDEAST • 100 kW
		Su/Th/F • MIDEAST • 100 kW
	UKRAINE	
	†RADIO UKRAINE, Vinnitsa	UKRAINIAN • E EUROPE • 100 kW
	†UKRAINIAN R, Vinnitsa	UKRAINIAN • E EUROPE • DS-2 • 100 kW
		(D) • UKRAINIAN • E EUROPE • DS-2 • 100 kW
	UNITED KINGDOM	
	†BBC, Via Zyyi, Cyprus	(J) • E EUROPE • 250 kW
	USA	
	VOA, Via Germany	N AFRICA • 500 kW
	VOA, Via Philippines	SE ASIA • 250 kW
11845	CANADA	
	†R CANADA INTL, Sackville, NB	Su/M • C AMERICA • 100 kW
		(D) • Su/M • C AMERICA • 100 kW
		Tu-Sa • C AMERICA • 100 kW
	CHINA (TAIWAN)	
	†BC CORP CHINA, T'ai-pei	DS-NEWS NETWORK • 50/100 kW
	ECUADOR	
	†HCJB-VO THE ANDES, Quito	S AMERICA • 500 kW
		JAPANESE • E ASIA • 500 kW
	FRANCE	
	†R FRANCE INTL, Issoudun-Allouis	N AFRICA • 100 kW
	GERMANY	
	DEUTSCHE WELLE, Wertachtal	(J) • SE ASIA • 500 kW
	KOREA (DPR)	
	RADIO PYONGYANG, Kujang-dong	SE ASIA • 200 kW
	RUSSIA	
	R MOSCOW INTL, Kazan'	S ASIA & SE ASIA • 100 kW
(con'd)		(J) • S ASIA & SE ASIA • 100 kW

SUMMER ONLY (J)   WINTER ONLY (D)   JAMMING / OR /\   EARLIEST HEARD ◁   LATEST HEARD ▷   NEW OR CHANGED FOR 1993 †

BLUE PAGES   11845–11855 kHz

FREQUENCY   COUNTRY, STATION, LOCATION   TARGET • NETWORK • POWER (kW)   World Time

0 1 2 3 4 5 6 7 8 9 10 11 12 13 14 15 16 17 18 19 20 21 22 23 24

Frequency	Country, Station, Location	Target • Network • Power
11845 (con'd)	RUSSIA — VOICE OF RUSSIA, Kazan'	(J) • S ASIA & SE ASIA • 100 kW
	UNITED KINGDOM †BBC, Rampisham	(J) • E EUROPE • 500 kW
		(D) • E EUROPE & W ASIA • 100 kW
	†BBC, Via Maṣīrah, Oman	E EUROPE • 100/250 kW
	†BBC, Via Zyyi, Cyprus	(D) M-F • E EUROPE • 250 kW; (D) E EUROPE & W ASIA • 250 kW
		(J) M-F • E EUROPE • 250 kW; (J) • E EUROPE • 250 kW
		(J) Su • E EUROPE • 250 kW
	USA VOA, Via Kaválla, Greece	(D) • MIDEAST & S ASIA • 250 kW
	†VOA, Via Portugal	EUROPE • 250 kW
11850	CANADA R CANADA INTL, Sackville, NB	(D) M-F • C AMERICA • 250 kW
	DENMARK †DANMARKS RADIO, Via Norway	(D) • S AMERICA • 500 kW; (D) • W AFRICA • 500 kW
	FRANCE †R FRANCE INTL, Issoudun-Allouis	(D) • N AFRICA • 100 kW
	†R FRANCE INTL, Via Diósd, Hungary	(J) • N AFRICA • 100 kW
	GERMANY †DEUTSCHE WELLE, Nauen	(D) • N AFRICA • 500 kW
	†DEUTSCHE WELLE, Wertachtal	(D) • E EUROPE • 500 kW
	JAPAN RADIO JAPAN/NHK, Tokyo-Yamata	JAPANESE • AUSTRALASIA • GENERAL • 100 kW; AUSTRALASIA • GENERAL • 100 kW
	MONGOLIA RADIO ULAANBAATAR, Ulaanbaatar	E ASIA • 50 kW • ALT. FREQ. TO 9616 kHz; EUROPE • 250 kW
		AUSTRALASIA • 50 kW; Tu/F • JAPANESE • E ASIA • 250 kW
		M-Sa • E ASIA • 50 kW • ALT. FREQ. TO 9616 kHz
		Tu/F/Sa • JAPANESE • E ASIA • 50 kW • ALT. FREQ. TO 9616 kHz
		W/Th/Sa-M • E ASIA • 250 kW
	NORWAY †RADIO NORWAY INTL, Kvitsøy	(D) • S AMERICA • 500 kW
	†RADIO NORWAY INTL, Sveio	(D) • S AMERICA • 500 kW
	RUSSIA R MOSCOW INTL, Ryazan'	(J) • N AFRICA & MIDEAST • 240 kW
		MIDEAST & E AFRICA • 200 kW
		(J) • MIDEAST & E AFRICA • 240 kW
	†RADIO MOSCOW, Khabarovsk	(J) • DS-2 • 100 kW
	VOICE OF RUSSIA, Konevo	(D) • EUROPE • 240 kW
	UNITED KINGDOM †BBC, Various Locations	S ASIA • 100/250 kW
	†BBC, Via Maṣīrah, Oman	S ASIA • 100 kW; W ASIA & S ASIA • 100 kW
	†BBC, Via Singapore	SE ASIA • 250 kW; Sa/Su • SE ASIA • 250 kW
	†BBC, Via Zyyi, Cyprus	N AFRICA • 100/250 kW
	USA †VOA, Via Tangier, Morocco	W AFRICA • 35 kW; (J) • W AFRICA • 35 kW
11855	AUSTRALIA †RADIO AUSTRALIA, Carnarvon	(J) • SE ASIA • 250 kW
	†RADIO AUSTRALIA, Shepparton	(J) • SE ASIA & PACIFIC • 100 kW
	BRAZIL RADIO APARECIDA, Aparecida	PORTUGUESE • DS • 7.5 kW
	CANADA R CANADA INTL, Sackville, NB	(D) M-F • E NORTH AM • 250 kW; (J) M-F • E NORTH AM • 250 kW
		(D) Su • E NORTH AM • 100 kW; (J) Su • E NORTH AM • 100 kW
	CHINA (PR) †RADIO BEIJING, Jinhua	MIDEAST • 500 kW; MIDEAST & N AFRICA • 500 kW
		(J) • W NORTH AM • 500 kW
	CHINA (TAIWAN) †BC CORP CHINA, Via Okeechobee, USA	(J) • W NORTH AM • 100 kW; (D) • C AMERICA • 100 kW
	RUSSIA †ADVENTIST WORLD R, Novosibirsk	S ASIA • 100 kW; ASIA • 100 kW; SE ASIA • 100 kW
	USA †RFE-RL, Via Germany	W ASIA • 100 kW; (D) • W ASIA • 100 kW
(con'd)		

ENGLISH ■ ARABIC ≋ CHINESE □□□ FRENCH ▬ GERMAN ▬ RUSSIAN — SPANISH ▬ OTHER —

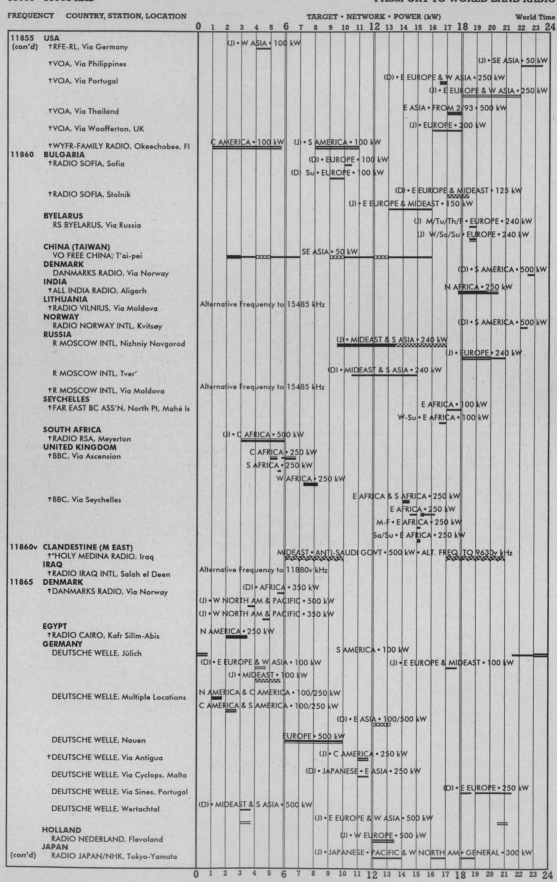

FREQUENCY   COUNTRY, STATION, LOCATION

TARGET • NETWORK • POWER (kW)   World Time

FREQUENCY	COUNTRY, STATION, LOCATION	TARGET • NETWORK • POWER (kW)
11855 (con'd)	USA	
	†RFE-RL, Via Germany	(J) • W ASIA • 100 kW
	†VOA, Via Philippines	(J) • SE ASIA • 50 kW
	†VOA, Via Portugal	(D) • E EUROPE & W ASIA • 250 kW / (J) • E EUROPE & W ASIA • 250 kW
	†VOA, Via Thailand	E ASIA • FROM 2/93 • 500 kW
	†VOA, Via Woofferton, UK	(J) • EUROPE • 300 kW
	†WYFR-FAMILY RADIO, Okeechobee, Fl	C AMERICA • 100 kW (J) • S AMERICA • 100 kW
11860	BULGARIA	
	†RADIO SOFIA, Sofia	(D) • EUROPE • 100 kW / (D) Su • EUROPE • 100 kW
	†RADIO SOFIA, Stolnik	(D) • E EUROPE & MIDEAST • 125 kW / (J) • E EUROPE & MIDEAST • 150 kW
	BYELARUS	
	RS BYELARUS, Via Russia	(J) • M/Tu/Th/F • EUROPE • 240 kW / (J) • W/Sa/Su • EUROPE • 240 kW
	CHINA (TAIWAN)	
	VO FREE CHINA, T'ai-pei	SE ASIA • 50 kW
	DENMARK	
	DANMARKS RADIO, Via Norway	(D) • S AMERICA • 500 kW
	INDIA	
	†ALL INDIA RADIO, Aligarh	N AFRICA • 250 kW
	LITHUANIA	
	†RADIO VILNIUS, Via Moldova	Alternative Frequency to 15485 kHz
	NORWAY	
	RADIO NORWAY INTL, Kvitsøy	(D) • S AMERICA • 500 kW
	RUSSIA	
	R MOSCOW INTL, Nizhniy Novgorod	(J) • MIDEAST & S ASIA • 240 kW / (J) • EUROPE • 240 kW
	R MOSCOW INTL, Tver'	(D) • MIDEAST & S ASIA • 240 kW
	†R MOSCOW INTL, Via Moldova	Alternative Frequency to 15485 kHz
	SEYCHELLES	
	†FAR EAST BC ASS'N, North Pt, Mahé Is	E AFRICA • 100 kW / W-Su • E AFRICA • 100 kW
	SOUTH AFRICA	
	†RADIO RSA, Meyerton	(J) • C AFRICA • 500 kW
	UNITED KINGDOM	
	†BBC, Via Ascension	C AFRICA • 250 kW / S AFRICA • 250 kW / W AFRICA • 250 kW
	†BBC, Via Seychelles	E AFRICA & S AFRICA • 250 kW / E AFRICA • 250 kW / M-F • E AFRICA • 250 kW / Sa/Su • E AFRICA • 250 kW
11860v	CLANDESTINE (M EAST)	
	†"HOLY MEDINA RADIO, Iraq	MIDEAST • ANTI-SAUDI GOVT • 500 kW • ALT. FREQ. TO 9630v kHz
	IRAQ	
	†RADIO IRAQ INTL, Salah el Deen	Alternative Frequency to 11880v kHz
11865	DENMARK	
	†DANMARKS RADIO, Via Norway	(D) • AFRICA • 350 kW / (J) • W NORTH AM & PACIFIC • 500 kW / (J) • W NORTH AM & PACIFIC • 350 kW
	EGYPT	
	†RADIO CAIRO, Kafr Silim-Abis	N AMERICA • 250 kW
	GERMANY	
	DEUTSCHE WELLE, Jülich	S AMERICA • 100 kW / (D) • E EUROPE & W ASIA • 100 kW / (J) • MIDEAST • 100 kW / (J) • E EUROPE & MIDEAST • 100 kW
	DEUTSCHE WELLE, Multiple Locations	N AMERICA & C AMERICA • 100/250 kW / C AMERICA & S AMERICA • 100/250 kW / (D) • E ASIA • 100/500 kW
	DEUTSCHE WELLE, Nauen	EUROPE • 500 kW
	†DEUTSCHE WELLE, Via Antigua	(J) • C AMERICA • 250 kW
	DEUTSCHE WELLE, Via Cyclops, Malta	(D) • JAPANESE • E ASIA • 250 kW
	DEUTSCHE WELLE, Via Sines, Portugal	(D) • E EUROPE • 250 kW
	DEUTSCHE WELLE, Wertachtal	(D) • MIDEAST & S ASIA • 500 kW / (J) • E EUROPE & W ASIA • 500 kW
	HOLLAND	
	RADIO NEDERLAND, Flevoland	(J) • W EUROPE • 500 kW
	JAPAN	
(con'd)	RADIO JAPAN/NHK, Tokyo-Yamata	(J) • JAPANESE • PACIFIC & W NORTH AM • GENERAL • 300 kW

FREQUENCY   COUNTRY, STATION, LOCATION   TARGET • NETWORK • POWER (kW)   World Time

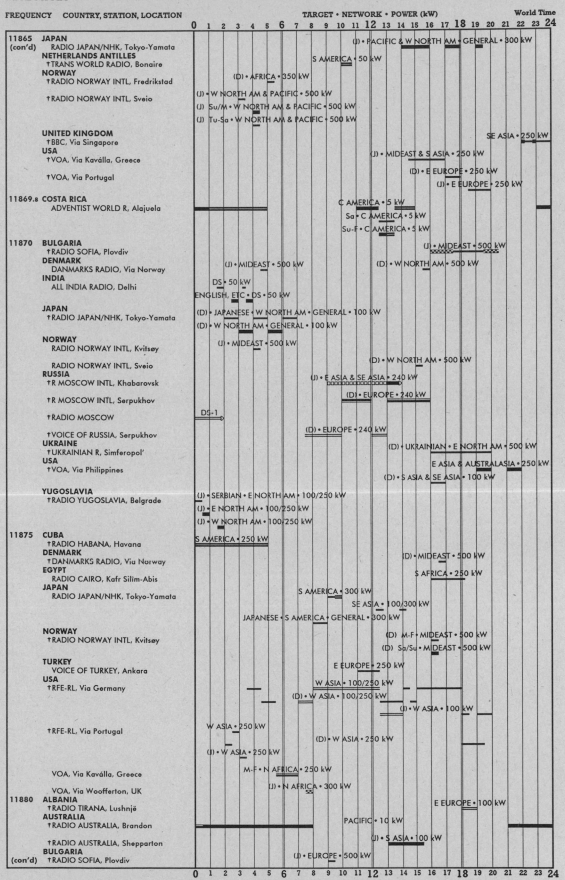

FREQUENCY	COUNTRY, STATION, LOCATION	TARGET • NETWORK • POWER (kW)
11865 (con'd)	JAPAN RADIO JAPAN/NHK, Tokyo-Yamata	(J) • PACIFIC & W NORTH AM • GENERAL • 300 kW
	NETHERLANDS ANTILLES †TRANS WORLD RADIO, Bonaire	S AMERICA • 50 kW
	NORWAY †RADIO NORWAY INTL, Fredrikstad	(D) • AFRICA • 350 kW
	†RADIO NORWAY INTL, Sveio	(J) • W NORTH AM & PACIFIC • 500 kW
		(J) • Su/M • W NORTH AM & PACIFIC • 500 kW
		(J) • Tu-Sa • W NORTH AM & PACIFIC • 500 kW
	UNITED KINGDOM †BBC, Via Singapore	SE ASIA • 250 kW
	USA †VOA, Via Kaválla, Greece	(J) • MIDEAST & S ASIA • 250 kW
		(D) • E EUROPE • 250 kW
	†VOA, Via Portugal	(J) • E EUROPE • 250 kW
11869.8	COSTA RICA ADVENTIST WORLD R, Alajuela	C AMERICA • 5 kW
		Sa • C AMERICA • 5 kW
		Su-F • C AMERICA • 5 kW
11870	BULGARIA †RADIO SOFIA, Plovdiv	(J) • MIDEAST • 500 kW
	DENMARK DANMARKS RADIO, Via Norway	(J) • MIDEAST • 500 kW (D) • W NORTH AM • 500 kW
	INDIA ALL INDIA RADIO, Delhi	DS • 50 kW / ENGLISH, ETC • DS • 50 kW
	JAPAN †RADIO JAPAN/NHK, Tokyo-Yamata	(D) • JAPANESE • W NORTH AM • GENERAL • 100 kW
		(D) • W NORTH AM • GENERAL • 100 kW
	NORWAY RADIO NORWAY INTL, Kvitsøy	(J) • MIDEAST • 500 kW
	RADIO NORWAY INTL, Sveio	(D) • W NORTH AM • 500 kW
	RUSSIA †R MOSCOW INTL, Khabarovsk	(J) • E ASIA & SE ASIA • 240 kW
	†R MOSCOW INTL, Serpukhov	(D) • EUROPE • 240 kW
	†RADIO MOSCOW	DS-1
	†VOICE OF RUSSIA, Serpukhov	(D) • EUROPE • 240 kW
	UKRAINE †UKRAINIAN R, Simferopol'	(D) • UKRAINIAN • E NORTH AM • 500 kW
	USA †VOA, Via Philippines	E ASIA & AUSTRALASIA • 250 kW
		(D) • S ASIA & SE ASIA • 100 kW
	YUGOSLAVIA †RADIO YUGOSLAVIA, Belgrade	(J) • SERBIAN • E NORTH AM • 100/250 kW
		(J) • E NORTH AM • 100/250 kW
		(J) • W NORTH AM • 100/250 kW
11875	CUBA †RADIO HABANA, Havana	S AMERICA • 250 kW
	DENMARK †DANMARKS RADIO, Via Norway	(D) • MIDEAST • 500 kW
	EGYPT RADIO CAIRO, Kafr Silim-Abis	S AFRICA • 250 kW
	JAPAN RADIO JAPAN/NHK, Tokyo-Yamata	S AMERICA • 300 kW
		SE ASIA • 100/300 kW
		JAPANESE • S AMERICA • GENERAL • 300 kW
	NORWAY †RADIO NORWAY INTL, Kvitsøy	(D) • M-F • MIDEAST • 500 kW
		(D) • Sa/Su • MIDEAST • 500 kW
	TURKEY VOICE OF TURKEY, Ankara	E EUROPE • 250 kW
	USA †RFE-RL, Via Germany	W ASIA • 100/250 kW
		(D) • W ASIA • 100/250 kW
		(J) • W ASIA • 100 kW
	†RFE-RL, Via Portugal	W ASIA • 250 kW
		(D) • W ASIA • 250 kW
		(J) • W ASIA • 250 kW
	VOA, Via Kaválla, Greece	M-F • N AFRICA • 250 kW
	VOA, Via Woofferton, UK	(J) • N AFRICA • 300 kW
11880	ALBANIA †RADIO TIRANA, Lushnjë	E EUROPE • 100 kW
	AUSTRALIA †RADIO AUSTRALIA, Brandon	PACIFIC • 10 kW
	†RADIO AUSTRALIA, Shepparton	(J) • S ASIA • 100 kW
(con'd)	BULGARIA †RADIO SOFIA, Plovdiv	(J) • EUROPE • 500 kW

ENGLISH ▬   ARABIC ⬙⬙⬙   CHINESE □□□   FRENCH ▬   GERMAN ▬   RUSSIAN ═   SPANISH ▬   OTHER ▬

FREQUENCY	COUNTRY, STATION, LOCATION	TARGET • NETWORK • POWER (kW)	World Time

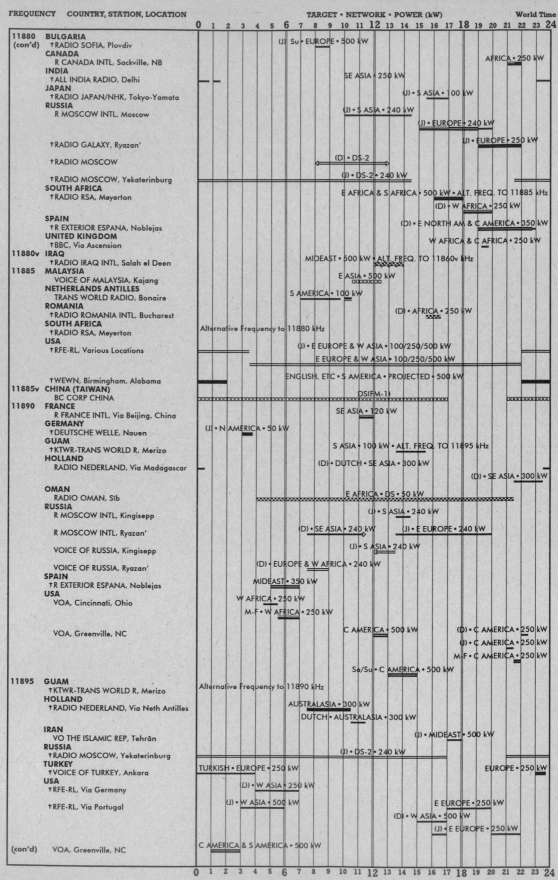

11880 BULGARIA
(con'd) †RADIO SOFIA, Plovdiv — (J) Su • EUROPE • 500 kW
CANADA
R CANADA INTL, Sackville, NB — AFRICA • 250 kW
INDIA
†ALL INDIA RADIO, Delhi — SE ASIA • 250 kW
JAPAN
†RADIO JAPAN/NHK, Tokyo-Yamata — (J) • S ASIA • 100 kW
RUSSIA
R MOSCOW INTL, Moscow — (J) • S ASIA • 240 kW / (J) • EUROPE • 240 kW
— (J) • EUROPE • 250 kW
†RADIO GALAXY, Ryazan' —
†RADIO MOSCOW — (D) • DS-2
†RADIO MOSCOW, Yekaterinburg — (J) • DS-2 • 240 kW
SOUTH AFRICA
†RADIO RSA, Meyerton — E AFRICA & S AFRICA • 500 kW • ALT. FREQ. TO 11885 kHz
— (D) • W AFRICA • 250 kW
SPAIN
†R EXTERIOR ESPANA, Noblejas — (D) • E NORTH AM & C AMERICA • 350 kW
UNITED KINGDOM
†BBC, Via Ascension — W AFRICA & C AFRICA • 250 kW
11880v IRAQ
†RADIO IRAQ INTL, Salah el Deen — MIDEAST • 500 kW • ALT. FREQ. TO 11860v kHz
11885 MALAYSIA
VOICE OF MALAYSIA, Kajang — E ASIA • 500 kW
NETHERLANDS ANTILLES
TRANS WORLD RADIO, Bonaire — S AMERICA • 100 kW
ROMANIA
†RADIO ROMANIA INTL, Bucharest — (D) • AFRICA • 250 kW
SOUTH AFRICA
†RADIO RSA, Meyerton — Alternative Frequency to 11880 kHz
USA
†RFE-RL, Various Locations — (J) • E EUROPE & W ASIA • 100/250/500 kW
— E EUROPE & W ASIA • 100/250/500 kW
†WEWN, Birmingham, Alabama — ENGLISH, ETC • S AMERICA • PROJECTED • 500 kW
11885v CHINA (TAIWAN)
BC CORP CHINA — DS(FM-1)
11890 FRANCE
R FRANCE INTL, Via Beijing, China — SE ASIA • 120 kW
GERMANY
†DEUTSCHE WELLE, Nauen — (J) • N AMERICA • 50 kW
GUAM
†KTWR-TRANS WORLD R, Merizo — S ASIA • 100 kW • ALT. FREQ. TO 11895 kHz
HOLLAND
RADIO NEDERLAND, Via Madagascar — (D) • DUTCH • SE ASIA • 300 kW
— (D) • SE ASIA • 300 kW
OMAN
RADIO OMAN, Sib — E AFRICA • DS • 50 kW
RUSSIA
R MOSCOW INTL, Kingisepp — (J) • S ASIA • 240 kW
R MOSCOW INTL, Ryazan' — (D) • SE ASIA • 240 kW / (J) • E EUROPE • 240 kW
VOICE OF RUSSIA, Kingisepp — (J) • S ASIA • 240 kW
VOICE OF RUSSIA, Ryazan' — (D) • EUROPE & W AFRICA • 240 kW
SPAIN
†R EXTERIOR ESPANA, Noblejas — MIDEAST • 350 kW
USA
VOA, Cincinnati, Ohio — W AFRICA • 250 kW
— M-F • W AFRICA • 250 kW
VOA, Greenville, NC — C AMERICA • 500 kW / (D) • C AMERICA • 250 kW
— (J) • C AMERICA • 250 kW
— M-F • C AMERICA • 250 kW
— Sa/Su • C AMERICA • 500 kW
11895 GUAM
†KTWR-TRANS WORLD R, Merizo — Alternative Frequency to 11890 kHz
HOLLAND
†RADIO NEDERLAND, Via Neth Antilles — AUSTRALASIA • 300 kW
— DUTCH • AUSTRALASIA • 300 kW
IRAN
VO THE ISLAMIC REP, Tehrān — (J) • MIDEAST • 500 kW
RUSSIA
†RADIO MOSCOW, Yekaterinburg — (J) • DS-2 • 240 kW
TURKEY
†VOICE OF TURKEY, Ankara — TURKISH • EUROPE • 250 kW / EUROPE • 250 kW
USA
†RFE-RL, Via Germany — (D) • W ASIA • 250 kW
†RFE-RL, Via Portugal — (J) • W ASIA • 500 kW / (D) • W ASIA • 500 kW
— (J) • E EUROPE • 250 kW
(con'd) VOA, Greenville, NC — C AMERICA & S AMERICA • 500 kW

FREQUENCY   COUNTRY, STATION, LOCATION   TARGET • NETWORK • POWER (kW)   World Time

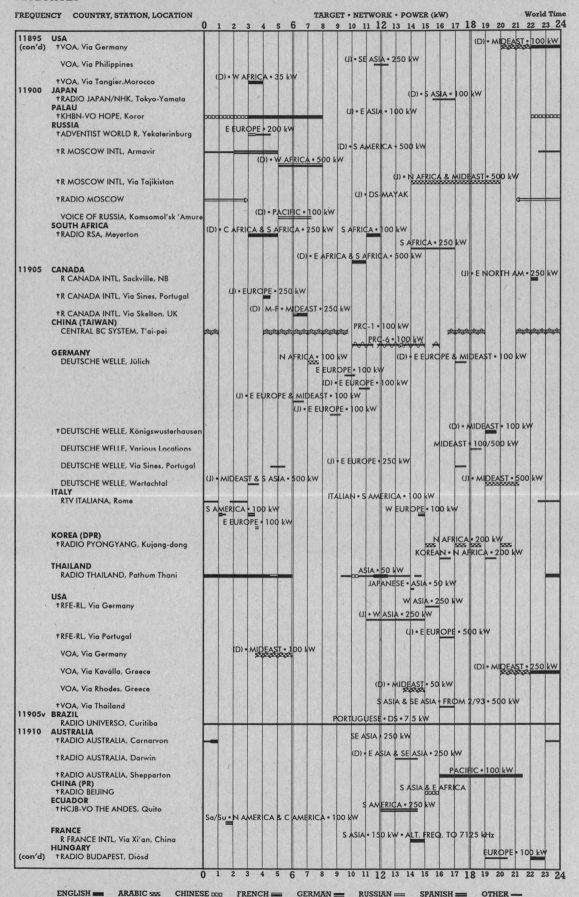

11895	USA	
(con'd)	†VOA, Via Germany	(D) • MIDEAST • 100 kW
	VOA, Via Philippines	(J) • SE ASIA • 250 kW
	†VOA, Via Tangier, Morocco	(D) • W AFRICA • 35 kW
11900	JAPAN	
	†RADIO JAPAN/NHK, Tokyo-Yamata	(D) • S ASIA • 100 kW
	PALAU	
	†KHBN-VO HOPE, Koror	(J) • E ASIA • 100 kW
	RUSSIA	
	†ADVENTIST WORLD R, Yekaterinburg	E EUROPE • 200 kW
		(D) • S AMERICA • 500 kW
	†R MOSCOW INTL, Armavir	(D) • W AFRICA • 500 kW
	†R MOSCOW INTL, Via Tajikistan	(J) • N AFRICA & MIDEAST • 500 kW
	†RADIO MOSCOW	(J) • DS-MAYAK
	VOICE OF RUSSIA, Komsomol'sk 'Amure	(D) • PACIFIC • 100 kW
	SOUTH AFRICA	
	†RADIO RSA, Meyerton	(D) • C AFRICA & S AFRICA • 250 kW S AFRICA • 100 kW
		S AFRICA • 250 kW
		(D) • E AFRICA & S AFRICA • 500 kW
11905	CANADA	
	R CANADA INTL, Sackville, NB	(J) • E NORTH AM • 250 kW
	†R CANADA INTL, Via Sines, Portugal	(J) • EUROPE • 250 kW
	†R CANADA INTL, Via Skelton, UK	(D) M-F • MIDEAST • 250 kW
	CHINA (TAIWAN)	
	CENTRAL BC SYSTEM, T'ai-pei	PRC-1 • 100 kW
		PRC-6 • 100 kW
	GERMANY	
	DEUTSCHE WELLE, Jülich	N AFRICA • 100 kW (D) • E EUROPE & MIDEAST • 100 kW
		E EUROPE • 100 kW
		(D) • E EUROPE • 100 kW
		(J) • E EUROPE & MIDEAST • 100 kW
		(J) • E EUROPE • 100 kW
	†DEUTSCHE WELLE, Königswusterhausen	(D) • MIDEAST • 100 kW
	DEUTSCHE WELLE, Various Locations	MIDEAST • 100/500 kW
	DEUTSCHE WELLE, Via Sines, Portugal	(J) • E EUROPE • 250 kW
	DEUTSCHE WELLE, Wertachtal	(J) • MIDEAST & S ASIA • 500 kW (J) • MIDEAST • 500 kW
	ITALY	
	RTV ITALIANA, Rome	ITALIAN • S AMERICA • 100 kW
		S AMERICA • 100 kW W EUROPE • 100 kW
		E EUROPE • 100 kW
	KOREA (DPR)	
	†RADIO PYONGYANG, Kujang-dong	N AFRICA • 200 kW
		KOREAN • N AFRICA • 200 kW
	THAILAND	
	RADIO THAILAND, Pathum Thani	ASIA • 50 kW
		JAPANESE • ASIA • 50 kW
	USA	
	†RFE-RL, Via Germany	W ASIA • 250 kW
		(J) • W ASIA • 250 kW
	†RFE-RL, Via Portugal	(J) • E EUROPE • 500 kW
	VOA, Via Germany	(D) • MIDEAST • 100 kW
	VOA, Via Kaválla, Greece	(D) • MIDEAST • 250 kW
	VOA, Via Rhodes, Greece	(D) • MIDEAST • 50 kW
	†VOA, Via Thailand	S ASIA & SE ASIA • FROM 2/93 • 500 kW
11905v	BRAZIL	
	RADIO UNIVERSO, Curitiba	PORTUGUESE • DS • 7.5 kW
11910	AUSTRALIA	
	†RADIO AUSTRALIA, Carnarvon	SE ASIA • 250 kW
	†RADIO AUSTRALIA, Darwin	(D) • E ASIA & SE ASIA • 250 kW
	†RADIO AUSTRALIA, Shepparton	PACIFIC • 100 kW
	CHINA (PR)	
	†RADIO BEIJING	S ASIA & E AFRICA
	ECUADOR	
	†HCJB-VO THE ANDES, Quito	S AMERICA • 250 kW
		Sa/Su • N AMERICA & C AMERICA • 100 kW
	FRANCE	
	R FRANCE INTL, Via Xi'an, China	S ASIA • 150 kW • ALT. FREQ. TO 7125 kHz
	HUNGARY	
(con'd)	†RADIO BUDAPEST, Diósd	EUROPE • 100 kW

ENGLISH ▬   ARABIC ⧓⧓⧓   CHINESE □□□   FRENCH ▬   GERMAN ▬   RUSSIAN ══   SPANISH ══   OTHER ▬

FREQUENCY	COUNTRY, STATION, LOCATION	TARGET • NETWORK • POWER (kW)	World Time

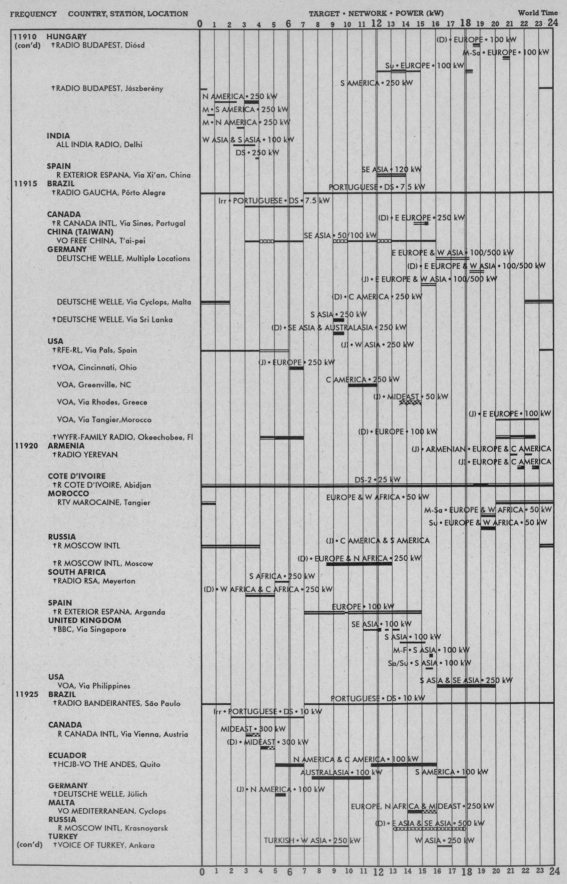

11910 (con'd)	**HUNGARY** †RADIO BUDAPEST, Diósd	(D) • EUROPE • 100 kW / M-Sa • EUROPE • 100 kW / Su • EUROPE • 100 kW / S AMERICA • 250 kW
	†RADIO BUDAPEST, Jászberény	N AMERICA • 250 kW / M • S AMERICA • 250 kW / M • N AMERICA • 250 kW
	INDIA ALL INDIA RADIO, Delhi	W ASIA & S ASIA • 100 kW / DS • 250 kW
	SPAIN R EXTERIOR ESPANA, Via Xi'an, China	SE ASIA • 120 kW
11915	**BRAZIL** †RADIO GAUCHA, Pôrto Alegre	PORTUGUESE • DS • 7.5 kW / Irr • PORTUGUESE • DS • 7.5 kW
	CANADA †R CANADA INTL, Via Sines, Portugal	(D) • E EUROPE • 250 kW
	CHINA (TAIWAN) VO FREE CHINA, T'ai-pei	SE ASIA • 50/100 kW
	GERMANY DEUTSCHE WELLE, Multiple Locations	E EUROPE & W ASIA • 100/500 kW / (D) • E EUROPE & W ASIA • 100/500 kW / (J) • E EUROPE & W ASIA • 100/500 kW
	DEUTSCHE WELLE, Via Cyclops, Malta	(D) • C AMERICA • 250 kW
	†DEUTSCHE WELLE, Via Sri Lanka	S ASIA • 250 kW / (D) • SE ASIA & AUSTRALASIA • 250 kW
	USA †RFE-RL, Via Pals, Spain	(J) • W ASIA • 250 kW
	†VOA, Cincinnati, Ohio	(J) • EUROPE • 250 kW
	VOA, Greenville, NC	C AMERICA • 250 kW
	VOA, Via Rhodes, Greece	(J) • MIDEAST • 50 kW
	VOA, Via Tangier, Morocco	(J) • E EUROPE • 100 kW
	†WYFR-FAMILY RADIO, Okeechobee, Fl	(D) • EUROPE • 100 kW
11920	**ARMENIA** †RADIO YEREVAN	(J) • ARMENIAN • EUROPE & C AMERICA / (J) • EUROPE & C AMERICA
	COTE D'IVOIRE †R COTE D'IVOIRE, Abidjan	DS-2 • 25 kW
	MOROCCO RTV MAROCAINE, Tangier	EUROPE & W AFRICA • 50 kW / M-Sa • EUROPE & W AFRICA • 50 kW / Su • EUROPE & W AFRICA • 50 kW
	RUSSIA †R MOSCOW INTL	(J) • C AMERICA & S AMERICA
	†R MOSCOW INTL, Moscow	(D) • EUROPE & N AFRICA • 250 kW
	SOUTH AFRICA †RADIO RSA, Meyerton	S AFRICA • 250 kW / (D) • W AFRICA & C AFRICA • 250 kW
	SPAIN †R EXTERIOR ESPANA, Arganda	EUROPE • 100 kW
	UNITED KINGDOM †BBC, Via Singapore	SE ASIA • 100 kW / S ASIA • 100 kW / M-F • S ASIA • 100 kW / Sa/Su • S ASIA • 100 kW / S ASIA & SE ASIA • 250 kW
	USA VOA, Via Philippines	
11925	**BRAZIL** †RADIO BANDEIRANTES, São Paulo	PORTUGUESE • DS • 10 kW / Irr • PORTUGUESE • DS • 10 kW
	CANADA R CANADA INTL, Via Vienna, Austria	MIDEAST • 300 kW / (D) • MIDEAST • 300 kW
	ECUADOR †HCJB-VO THE ANDES, Quito	N AMERICA & C AMERICA • 100 kW / AUSTRALASIA • 100 kW / S AMERICA • 100 kW
	GERMANY †DEUTSCHE WELLE, Jülich	(J) • N AMERICA • 100 kW
	MALTA VO MEDITERRANEAN, Cyclops	EUROPE, N AFRICA & MIDEAST • 250 kW
	RUSSIA R MOSCOW INTL, Krasnoyarsk	(D) • E ASIA & SE ASIA • 500 kW
(con'd)	**TURKEY** †VOICE OF TURKEY, Ankara	TURKISH • W ASIA • 250 kW / W ASIA • 250 kW

SUMMER ONLY (J)   WINTER ONLY (D)   JAMMING / OR ∧   EARLIEST HEARD ◁   LATEST HEARD ▷   NEW OR CHANGED FOR 1993 †

FREQUENCY   COUNTRY, STATION, LOCATION   TARGET • NETWORK • POWER (kW)   World Time

0 1 2 3 4 5 6 7 8 9 10 11 12 13 14 15 16 17 18 19 20 21 22 23 24

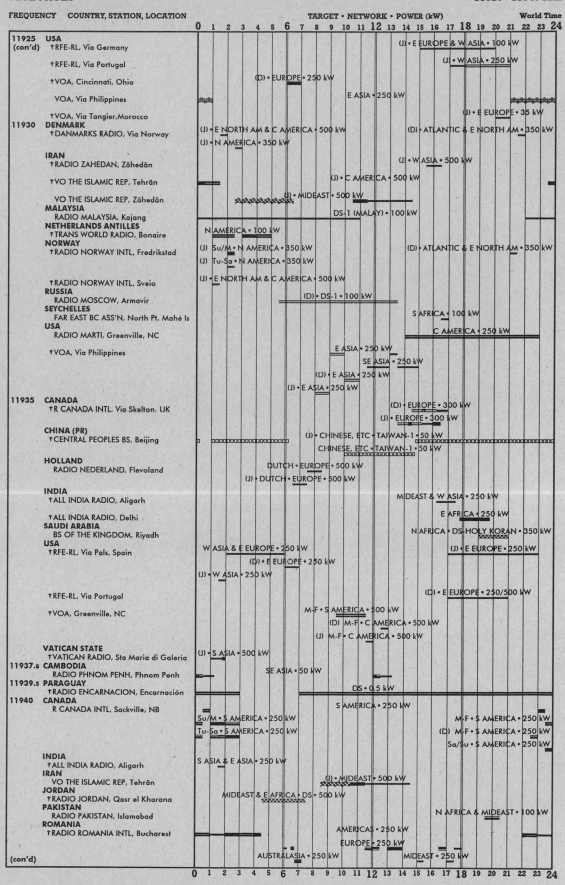

11925   **USA**
(con'd)   †RFE-RL, Via Germany   (J) • E EUROPE & W ASIA • 100 kW

     †RFE-RL, Via Portugal   (J) • W ASIA • 250 kW

     †VOA, Cincinnati, Ohio   (D) • EUROPE • 250 kW

     VOA, Via Philippines   E ASIA • 250 kW   (J) • E EUROPE

     †VOA, Via Tangier, Morocco   (J) • E EUROPE • 35 kW

11930   **DENMARK**
     †DANMARKS RADIO, Via Norway   (J) • E NORTH AM & C AMERICA • 500 kW   (D) • ATLANTIC & E NORTH AM • 350 kW
           (J) • N AMERICA • 350 kW

     IRAN
     †RADIO ZAHEDAN, Zāhedān   (J) • W ASIA • 500 kW

     †VO THE ISLAMIC REP, Tehrān   (J) • C AMERICA • 500 kW

     VO THE ISLAMIC REP, Zāhedān   (J) • MIDEAST • 500 kW
     MALAYSIA
     RADIO MALAYSIA, Kajang   DS-1 (MALAY) • 100 kW
     NETHERLANDS ANTILLES
     †TRANS WORLD RADIO, Bonaire   N AMERICA • 100 kW
     NORWAY
     †RADIO NORWAY INTL, Fredrikstad   (J) Su/M • N AMERICA • 350 kW   (D) • ATLANTIC & E NORTH AM • 350 kW
           (J) Tu-Sa • N AMERICA • 350 kW

     †RADIO NORWAY INTL, Sveio   (J) • E NORTH AM & C AMERICA • 500 kW
     RUSSIA
     RADIO MOSCOW, Armavir   (D) • DS-1 • 100 kW
     SEYCHELLES
     FAR EAST BC ASS'N, North Pt, Mahé Is   S AFRICA • 100 kW
     USA
     RADIO MARTI, Greenville, NC   C AMERICA • 250 kW

     †VOA, Via Philippines   E ASIA • 250 kW
           SE ASIA • 250 kW
           (D) • E ASIA • 250 kW
           (J) • E ASIA • 250 kW

11935   **CANADA**
     †R CANADA INTL, Via Skelton, UK   (D) • EUROPE • 300 kW
           (J) • EUROPE • 300 kW

     CHINA (PR)
     †CENTRAL PEOPLES BS, Beijing   (J) • CHINESE, ETC • TAIWAN-1 • 50 kW
           CHINESE, ETC • TAIWAN-1 • 50 kW

     HOLLAND
     RADIO NEDERLAND, Flevoland   DUTCH • EUROPE • 500 kW
           (J) • DUTCH • EUROPE • 500 kW

     INDIA
     †ALL INDIA RADIO, Aligarh   MIDEAST & W ASIA • 250 kW

     †ALL INDIA RADIO, Delhi   E AFRICA • 250 kW
     SAUDI ARABIA
     BS OF THE KINGDOM, Riyadh   N AFRICA • DS-HOLY KORAN • 350 kW
     USA
     †RFE-RL, Via Pals, Spain   W ASIA & E EUROPE • 250 kW   (J) • E EUROPE • 250 kW
           (D) • E EUROPE • 250 kW
           (J) • W ASIA • 250 kW

     †RFE-RL, Via Portugal   (D) • E EUROPE • 250/500 kW

     †VOA, Greenville, NC   M-F • S AMERICA • 500 kW
           (D) • M-F • C AMERICA • 500 kW
           (J) • M-F • C AMERICA • 500 kW

     VATICAN STATE
     †VATICAN RADIO, Sta Maria di Galeria   (J) • S ASIA • 500 kW
11937.8   **CAMBODIA**
     RADIO PHNOM PENH, Phnom Penh   SE ASIA • 50 kW
11939.5   **PARAGUAY**
     †RADIO ENCARNACION, Encarnación   DS • 0.5 kW
11940   **CANADA**
     R CANADA INTL, Sackville, NB   S AMERICA • 250 kW
     Su/M • S AMERICA • 250 kW   M-F • S AMERICA • 250 kW
     Tu-Sa • S AMERICA • 250 kW   (D) M-F • S AMERICA • 250 kW
           Sa/Su • S AMERICA • 250 kW

     INDIA
     †ALL INDIA RADIO, Aligarh   S ASIA & E ASIA • 250 kW
     IRAN
     VO THE ISLAMIC REP, Tehrān   (J) • MIDEAST • 500 kW
     JORDAN
     †RADIO JORDAN, Qasr el Kharana   MIDEAST & E AFRICA • DS • 500 kW
     PAKISTAN
     RADIO PAKISTAN, Islamabad   N AFRICA & MIDEAST • 100 kW
     ROMANIA
     †RADIO ROMANIA INTL, Bucharest   AMERICAS • 250 kW
           EUROPE • 250 kW

(con'd)   AUSTRALASIA • 250 kW   MIDEAST • 250 kW

0 1 2 3 4 5 6 7 8 9 10 11 12 13 14 15 16 17 18 19 20 21 22 23 24

ENGLISH ▬   ARABIC ≋   CHINESE ▫▫▫   FRENCH ▬   GERMAN ▬   RUSSIAN ▬   SPANISH ▬   OTHER ▬

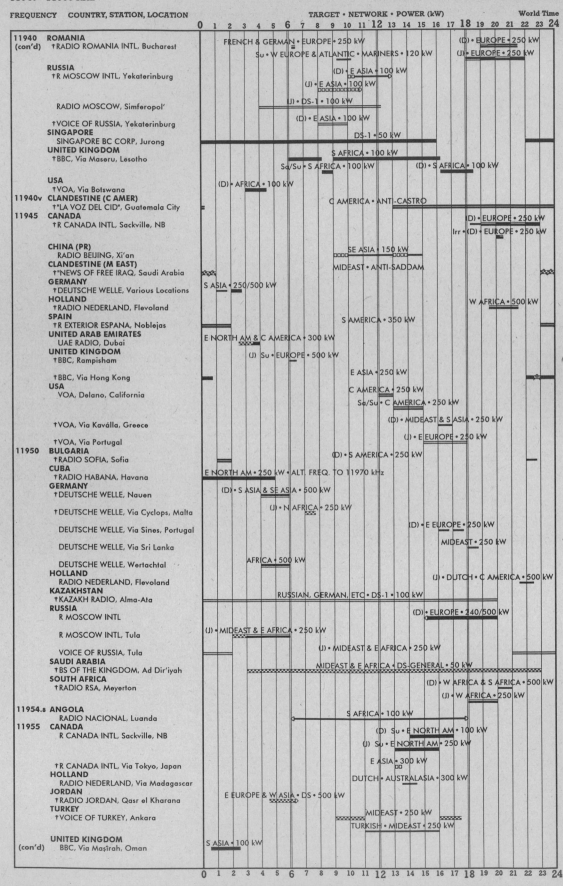

FREQUENCY	COUNTRY, STATION, LOCATION	TARGET • NETWORK • POWER (kW)	World Time

11940 ROMANIA
(con'd) †RADIO ROMANIA INTL, Bucharest — FRENCH & GERMAN • EUROPE • 250 kW — (D) • EUROPE • 250 kW — Su • W EUROPE & ATLANTIC • MARINERS • 120 kW — (J) • EUROPE • 250 kW

RUSSIA
†R MOSCOW INTL, Yekaterinburg — (D) • E ASIA • 100 kW — (J) • E ASIA • 100 kW

RADIO MOSCOW, Simferopol' — (J) • DS-1 • 100 kW

†VOICE OF RUSSIA, Yekaterinburg — (D) • E ASIA • 100 kW
SINGAPORE
SINGAPORE BC CORP, Jurong — DS-1 • 50 kW
UNITED KINGDOM
†BBC, Via Maseru, Lesotho — S AFRICA • 100 kW — Sa/Su • S AFRICA • 100 kW — (D) • S AFRICA • 100 kW

USA
†VOA, Via Botswana — (D) • AFRICA • 100 kW
11940v CLANDESTINE (C AMER)
†"LA VOZ DEL CID", Guatemala City — C AMERICA • ANTI-CASTRO
11945 CANADA
†R CANADA INTL, Sackville, NB — (D) • EUROPE • 250 kW — Irr • (D) • EUROPE • 250 kW

CHINA (PR)
RADIO BEIJING, Xi'an — SE ASIA • 150 kW
CLANDESTINE (M EAST)
†"NEWS OF FREE IRAQ", Saudi Arabia — MIDEAST • ANTI-SADDAM
GERMANY
†DEUTSCHE WELLE, Various Locations — S ASIA • 250/500 kW
HOLLAND
†RADIO NEDERLAND, Flevoland — W AFRICA • 500 kW
SPAIN
†R EXTERIOR ESPANA, Noblejas — S AMERICA • 350 kW
UNITED ARAB EMIRATES
UAE RADIO, Dubai — E NORTH AM & C AMERICA • 300 kW
UNITED KINGDOM
†BBC, Rampisham — (J) Su • EUROPE • 500 kW

†BBC, Via Hong Kong — E ASIA • 250 kW
USA
VOA, Delano, California — C AMERICA • 250 kW — Sa/Su • C AMERICA • 250 kW

†VOA, Via Kaválla, Greece — (D) • MIDEAST & S ASIA • 250 kW

†VOA, Via Portugal — (J) • E EUROPE • 250 kW
11950 BULGARIA
†RADIO SOFIA, Sofia — (D) • S AMERICA • 250 kW
CUBA
†RADIO HABANA, Havana — E NORTH AM • 250 kW • ALT. FREQ. TO 11970 kHz
GERMANY
†DEUTSCHE WELLE, Nauen — (D) • S ASIA & SE ASIA • 500 kW

†DEUTSCHE WELLE, Via Cyclops, Malta — (J) • N AFRICA • 250 kW

DEUTSCHE WELLE, Via Sines, Portugal — (D) • E EUROPE • 250 kW

DEUTSCHE WELLE, Via Sri Lanka — MIDEAST • 250 kW

DEUTSCHE WELLE, Wertachtal — AFRICA • 500 kW
HOLLAND
RADIO NEDERLAND, Flevoland — (J) • DUTCH • C AMERICA • 500 kW
KAZAKHSTAN
†KAZAKH RADIO, Alma-Ata — RUSSIAN, GERMAN, ETC • DS-1 • 100 kW
RUSSIA
R MOSCOW INTL — (D) • EUROPE • 240/500 kW

R MOSCOW INTL, Tula — (J) • MIDEAST & E AFRICA • 250 kW

VOICE OF RUSSIA, Tula — (J) • MIDEAST & E AFRICA • 250 kW
SAUDI ARABIA
†BS OF THE KINGDOM, Ad Dir'iyah — MIDEAST & E AFRICA • DS-GENERAL • 50 kW
SOUTH AFRICA
†RADIO RSA, Meyerton — (D) • W AFRICA & S AFRICA • 500 kW — (J) • W AFRICA • 250 kW

11954.8 ANGOLA
RADIO NACIONAL, Luanda — S AFRICA • 100 kW
11955 CANADA
R CANADA INTL, Sackville, NB — (D) Su • E NORTH AM • 100 kW — (J) Su • E NORTH AM • 250 kW

†R CANADA INTL, Via Tokyo, Japan — E ASIA • 300 kW
HOLLAND
RADIO NEDERLAND, Via Madagascar — DUTCH • AUSTRALASIA • 300 kW
JORDAN
†RADIO JORDAN, Qasr el Kharana — E EUROPE & W ASIA • DS • 500 kW
TURKEY
†VOICE OF TURKEY, Ankara — MIDEAST • 250 kW — TURKISH • MIDEAST • 250 kW

UNITED KINGDOM
(con'd) BBC, Via Maṣīrah, Oman — S ASIA • 100 kW

FREQUENCY   COUNTRY, STATION, LOCATION

TARGET • NETWORK • POWER (kW)

World Time

0 1 2 3 4 5 6 7 8 9 10 11 12 13 14 15 16 17 18 19 20 21 22 23 24

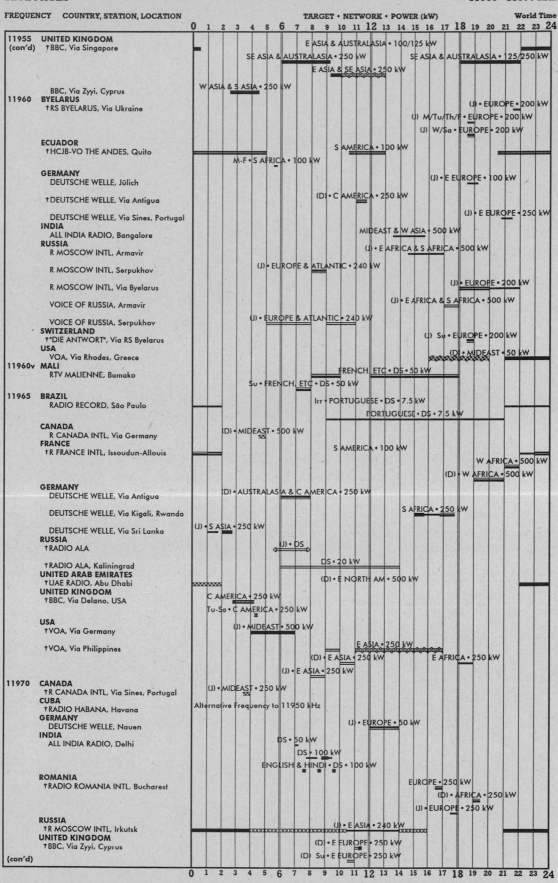

Frequency	Country, Station, Location	Target • Network • Power
11955 (con'd)	UNITED KINGDOM †BBC, Via Singapore	E ASIA & AUSTRALASIA • 100/125 kW; SE ASIA & AUSTRALASIA • 250 kW; SE ASIA & AUSTRALASIA • 125/250 kW; E ASIA & SE ASIA • 250 kW
	BBC, Via Zyyi, Cyprus	W ASIA & S ASIA • 250 kW
11960	BYELARUS †RS BYELARUS, Via Ukraine	(J) • EUROPE • 200 kW; (J) M/Tu/Th/F • EUROPE • 200 kW; (J) W/Sa • EUROPE • 200 kW
	ECUADOR †HCJB-VO THE ANDES, Quito	S AMERICA • 100 kW; M-F • S AFRICA • 100 kW
	GERMANY DEUTSCHE WELLE, Jülich	(J) • E EUROPE • 100 kW
	†DEUTSCHE WELLE, Via Antigua	(D) • C AMERICA • 250 kW
	DEUTSCHE WELLE, Via Sines, Portugal	(J) • E EUROPE • 250 kW
	INDIA ALL INDIA RADIO, Bangalore	MIDEAST & W ASIA • 500 kW
	RUSSIA R MOSCOW INTL, Armavir	(J) • E AFRICA & S AFRICA • 500 kW
	R MOSCOW INTL, Serpukhov	(J) • EUROPE & ATLANTIC • 240 kW
	R MOSCOW INTL, Via Byelarus	(J) • EUROPE • 200 kW
	VOICE OF RUSSIA, Armavir	(J) • E AFRICA & S AFRICA • 500 kW
	VOICE OF RUSSIA, Serpukhov	(J) • EUROPE & ATLANTIC • 240 kW
	SWITZERLAND †"DIE ANTWORT", Via RS Byelarus	(J) Su • EUROPE • 200 kW
	USA VOA, Via Rhodes, Greece	(D) • MIDEAST • 50 kW
11960v	MALI RTV MALIENNE, Bamako	FRENCH, ETC • DS • 50 kW; Su • FRENCH, ETC • DS • 50 kW
11965	BRAZIL RADIO RECORD, São Paulo	Irr • PORTUGUESE • DS • 7.5 kW; PORTUGUESE • DS • 7.5 kW
	CANADA R CANADA INTL, Via Germany	(D) • MIDEAST • 500 kW
	FRANCE †R FRANCE INTL, Issoudun-Allouis	S AMERICA • 100 kW; W AFRICA • 500 kW; (D) • W AFRICA • 500 kW
	GERMANY DEUTSCHE WELLE, Via Antigua	(D) • AUSTRALASIA & C AMERICA • 250 kW
	DEUTSCHE WELLE, Via Kigali, Rwanda	S AFRICA • 250 kW
	DEUTSCHE WELLE, Via Sri Lanka	(J) • S ASIA • 250 kW
	RUSSIA †RADIO ALA	(J) • DS
	†RADIO ALA, Kaliningrad	DS • 20 kW
	UNITED ARAB EMIRATES †UAE RADIO, Abu Dhabi	(D) • E NORTH AM • 500 kW
	UNITED KINGDOM †BBC, Via Delano, USA	C AMERICA • 250 kW; Tu-Sa • C AMERICA • 250 kW
	USA †VOA, Via Germany	(J) • MIDEAST • 500 kW
	†VOA, Via Philippines	E ASIA • 250 kW; (D) • E ASIA • 250 kW; E AFRICA • 250 kW; (J) • E ASIA • 250 kW
11970	CANADA †R CANADA INTL, Via Sines, Portugal	(J) • MIDEAST • 250 kW
	CUBA †RADIO HABANA, Havana	Alternative Frequency to 11950 kHz
	GERMANY DEUTSCHE WELLE, Nauen	(J) • EUROPE • 50 kW
	INDIA ALL INDIA RADIO, Delhi	DS • 50 kW; DS • 100 kW; ENGLISH & HINDI • DS • 100 kW
	ROMANIA †RADIO ROMANIA INTL, Bucharest	EUROPE • 250 kW; (D) • AFRICA • 250 kW; (J) • EUROPE • 250 kW
	RUSSIA †R MOSCOW INTL, Irkutsk	(J) • E ASIA • 240 kW
	UNITED KINGDOM †BBC, Via Zyyi, Cyprus	(D) • E EUROPE • 250 kW; (D) Su • E EUROPE • 250 kW
(con'd)		

0 1 2 3 4 5 6 7 8 9 10 11 12 13 14 15 16 17 18 19 20 21 22 23 24

ENGLISH ■■   ARABIC ∞∞   CHINESE □□□   FRENCH ══   GERMAN ══   RUSSIAN ══   SPANISH ══   OTHER ──

FREQUENCY	COUNTRY, STATION, LOCATION	TARGET • NETWORK • POWER (kW)	World Time

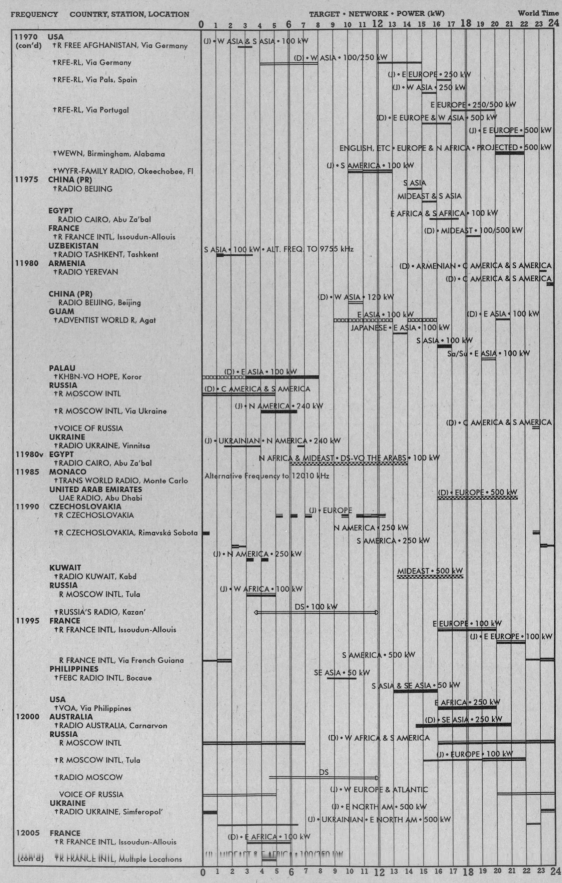

11970
(con'd) **USA**
    †R FREE AFGHANISTAN, Via Germany — (J) • W ASIA & S ASIA • 100 kW
    †RFE-RL, Via Germany — (D) • W ASIA • 100/250 kW
    †RFE-RL, Via Pals, Spain — (J) • E EUROPE • 250 kW / (J) • W ASIA • 250 kW
    †RFE-RL, Via Portugal — E EUROPE • 250/500 kW / (D) • E EUROPE & W ASIA • 500 kW / (J) • E EUROPE • 500 kW
    †WEWN, Birmingham, Alabama — ENGLISH, ETC • EUROPE & N AFRICA • PROJECTED • 500 kW
    †WYFR-FAMILY RADIO, Okeechobee, Fl — (J) • S AMERICA • 100 kW

11975 **CHINA (PR)**
    †RADIO BEIJING — S ASIA / MIDEAST & S ASIA

EGYPT
    RADIO CAIRO, Abu Za'bal — E AFRICA & S AFRICA • 100 kW
FRANCE
    †R FRANCE INTL, Issoudun-Allouis — (D) • MIDEAST • 100/500 kW
UZBEKISTAN
    †RADIO TASHKENT, Tashkent — S ASIA • 100 kW • ALT. FREQ. TO 9755 kHz
11980 **ARMENIA**
    †RADIO YEREVAN — (D) • ARMENIAN • C AMERICA & S AMERICA / (D) • C AMERICA & S AMERICA

CHINA (PR)
    RADIO BEIJING, Beijing — (D) • W ASIA • 120 kW
GUAM
    †ADVENTIST WORLD R, Agat — E ASIA • 100 kW / (D) • E ASIA • 100 kW / JAPANESE • E ASIA • 100 kW / S ASIA • 100 kW / Sa/Su • E ASIA • 100 kW

PALAU
    †KHBN-VO HOPE, Koror — (D) • E ASIA • 100 kW
RUSSIA
    †R MOSCOW INTL — (D) • C AMERICA & S AMERICA
    †R MOSCOW INTL, Via Ukraine — (J) • N AMERICA • 240 kW
    †VOICE OF RUSSIA — (D) • C AMERICA & S AMERICA
UKRAINE
    †RADIO UKRAINE, Vinnitsa — (J) • UKRAINIAN • N AMERICA • 240 kW
11980v **EGYPT**
    †RADIO CAIRO, Abu Za'bal — N AFRICA & MIDEAST • DS-VO THE ARABS • 100 kW
11985 **MONACO**
    †TRANS WORLD RADIO, Monte Carlo — Alternative Frequency to 12010 kHz
UNITED ARAB EMIRATES
    UAE RADIO, Abu Dhabi — (D) • EUROPE • 500 kW
11990 **CZECHOSLOVAKIA**
    †R CZECHOSLOVAKIA — (J) • EUROPE
    †R CZECHOSLOVAKIA, Rimavská Sobota — N AMERICA • 250 kW / S AMERICA • 250 kW / (J) • N AMERICA • 250 kW

KUWAIT
    †RADIO KUWAIT, Kabd — MIDEAST • 500 kW
RUSSIA
    R MOSCOW INTL, Tula — (J) • W AFRICA • 100 kW
    †RUSSIA'S RADIO, Kazan' — DS • 100 kW
11995 **FRANCE**
    †R FRANCE INTL, Issoudun-Allouis — E EUROPE • 100 kW / (J) • E EUROPE • 100 kW / S AMERICA • 500 kW
    R FRANCE INTL, Via French Guiana
PHILIPPINES
    †FEBC RADIO INTL, Bocaue — SE ASIA • 50 kW / S ASIA & SE ASIA • 50 kW

USA
    †VOA, Via Philippines — E AFRICA • 250 kW
12000 **AUSTRALIA**
    †RADIO AUSTRALIA, Carnarvon — (D) • SE ASIA • 250 kW
RUSSIA
    R MOSCOW INTL — (D) • W AFRICA & S AMERICA
    †R MOSCOW INTL, Tula — (J) • EUROPE • 100 kW
    †RADIO MOSCOW — DS
    VOICE OF RUSSIA — (J) • W EUROPE & ATLANTIC
UKRAINE
    †RADIO UKRAINE, Simferopol' — (J) • E NORTH AM • 500 kW / (J) • UKRAINIAN • E NORTH AM • 500 kW

12005 **FRANCE**
    †R FRANCE INTL, Issoudun-Allouis — (D) • E AFRICA • 100 kW
(con'd) †R FRANCE INTL, Multiple Locations — (J) • MIDEAST & E AFRICA • 100/250 kW

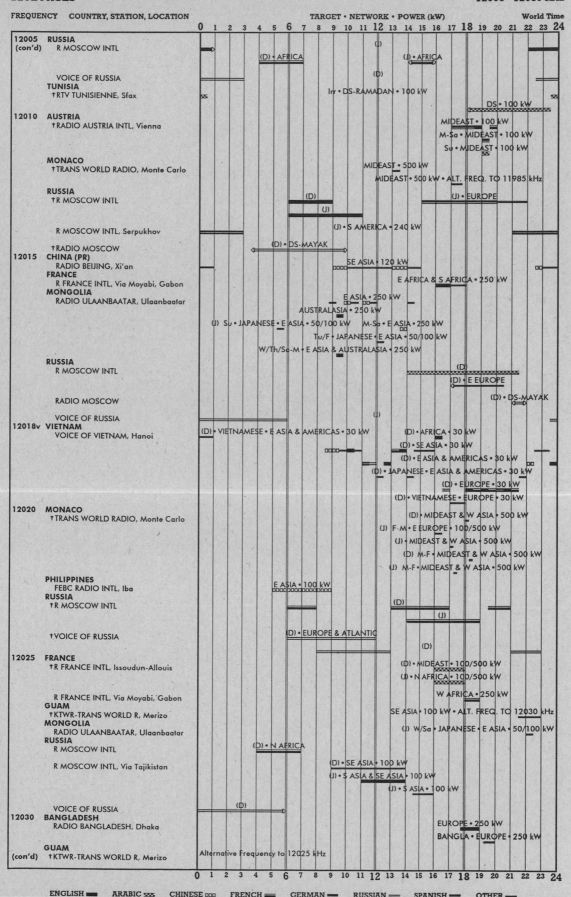

FREQUENCY	COUNTRY, STATION, LOCATION	TARGET • NETWORK • POWER (kW)
12005 (con'd)	RUSSIA R MOSCOW INTL	(J) (D) • AFRICA (J) • AFRICA (D)
	VOICE OF RUSSIA	
	TUNISIA †RTV TUNISIENNE, Sfax	Irr • DS-RAMADAN • 100 kW DS • 100 kW
12010	AUSTRIA †RADIO AUSTRIA INTL, Vienna	MIDEAST • 100 kW M-Sa • MIDEAST • 100 kW Su • MIDEAST • 100 kW
	MONACO †TRANS WORLD RADIO, Monte Carlo	MIDEAST • 500 kW MIDEAST • 500 kW • ALT. FREQ. TO 11985 kHz
	RUSSIA †R MOSCOW INTL	(D) (J) (J) • EUROPE
	R MOSCOW INTL, Serpukhov	(J) • S AMERICA • 240 kW
	†RADIO MOSCOW	(D) • DS-MAYAK
12015	CHINA (PR) RADIO BEIJING, Xi'an	SE ASIA • 120 kW
	FRANCE R FRANCE INTL, Via Moyabi, Gabon	E AFRICA & S AFRICA • 250 kW
	MONGOLIA RADIO ULAANBAATAR, Ulaanbaatar	E ASIA • 250 kW AUSTRALASIA • 250 kW (J) Su • JAPANESE • E ASIA • 50/100 kW M-Sa • E ASIA • 250 kW Tu/F • JAPANESE • E ASIA • 50/100 kW W/Th/Sa-M • E ASIA & AUSTRALASIA • 250 kW
	RUSSIA R MOSCOW INTL	(D) (D) • E EUROPE
	RADIO MOSCOW	(D) • DS-MAYAK
	VOICE OF RUSSIA	(J)
12018v	VIETNAM VOICE OF VIETNAM, Hanoi	(D) • VIETNAMESE • E ASIA & AMERICAS • 30 kW (D) • AFRICA • 30 kW (D) • SE ASIA • 30 kW (D) • E ASIA & AMERICAS • 30 kW (D) • JAPANESE • E ASIA & AMERICAS • 30 kW (D) • EUROPE • 30 kW (D) • VIETNAMESE • EUROPE • 30 kW
12020	MONACO †TRANS WORLD RADIO, Monte Carlo	(D) • MIDEAST & W ASIA • 500 kW (J) F-M • E EUROPE • 100/500 kW (J) • MIDEAST & W ASIA • 500 kW (D) M-F • MIDEAST & W ASIA • 500 kW (J) M-F • MIDEAST & W ASIA • 500 kW
	PHILIPPINES FEBC RADIO INTL, Iba	E ASIA • 100 kW
	RUSSIA †R MOSCOW INTL	(D) (J)
	†VOICE OF RUSSIA	(D) • EUROPE & ATLANTIC (D)
12025	FRANCE †R FRANCE INTL, Issoudun-Allouis	(D) • MIDEAST • 100/500 kW (J) • N AFRICA • 100/500 kW
	R FRANCE INTL, Via Moyabi, Gabon	W AFRICA • 250 kW
	GUAM †KTWR-TRANS WORLD R, Merizo	SE ASIA • 100 kW • ALT. FREQ. TO 12030 kHz
	MONGOLIA RADIO ULAANBAATAR, Ulaanbaatar	(J) W/Sa • JAPANESE • E ASIA • 50/100 kW
	RUSSIA R MOSCOW INTL	(D) • N AFRICA
	R MOSCOW INTL, Via Tajikistan	(D) • SE ASIA • 100 kW (J) • S ASIA & SE ASIA • 100 kW (J) • S ASIA • 100 kW
	VOICE OF RUSSIA	(D)
12030	BANGLADESH RADIO BANGLADESH, Dhaka	EUROPE • 250 kW BANGLA • EUROPE • 250 kW
(con'd)	GUAM †KTWR-TRANS WORLD R, Merizo	Alternative Frequency to 12025 kHz

FREQUENCY   COUNTRY, STATION, LOCATION

TARGET • NETWORK • POWER (kW)

World Time

0 1 2 3 4 5 6 7 8 9 10 11 12 13 14 15 16 17 18 19 20 21 22 23 24

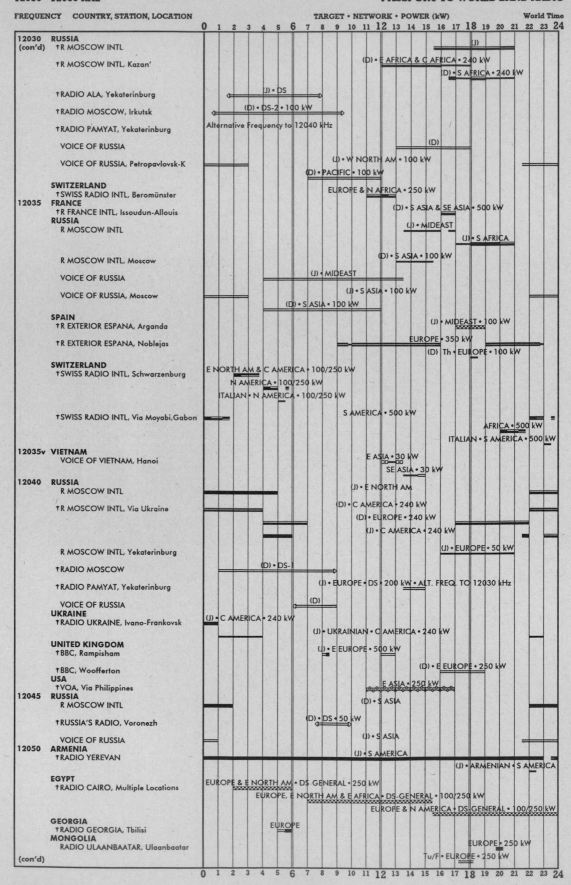

12030 RUSSIA
(con'd)   †R MOSCOW INTL
(J)

          †R MOSCOW INTL, Kazan'
(D) • E AFRICA & C AFRICA • 240 kW
(D) • S AFRICA • 240 kW

          †RADIO ALA, Yekaterinburg
(J) • DS

          †RADIO MOSCOW, Irkutsk
(D) • DS-2 • 100 kW

          †RADIO PAMYAT, Yekaterinburg
Alternative Frequency to 12040 kHz

          VOICE OF RUSSIA
(D)

          VOICE OF RUSSIA, Petropavlovsk-K
(J) • W NORTH AM • 100 kW
(D) • PACIFIC • 100 kW

SWITZERLAND
          †SWISS RADIO INTL, Beromünster
EUROPE & N AFRICA • 250 kW
12035 FRANCE
          †R FRANCE INTL, Issoudun-Allouis
(D) • S ASIA & SE ASIA • 500 kW
RUSSIA
          R MOSCOW INTL
(J) • MIDEAST
(J) • S AFRICA

          R MOSCOW INTL, Moscow
(D) • S ASIA • 100 kW

          VOICE OF RUSSIA
(J) • MIDEAST

          VOICE OF RUSSIA, Moscow
(J) • S ASIA • 100 kW
(D) • S ASIA • 100 kW

SPAIN
          †R EXTERIOR ESPANA, Arganda
(J) • MIDEAST • 100 kW

          †R EXTERIOR ESPANA, Noblejas
EUROPE • 350 kW
(D) • Th • EUROPE • 100 kW

SWITZERLAND
          †SWISS RADIO INTL, Schwarzenburg
E NORTH AM & C AMERICA • 100/250 kW
N AMERICA • 100/250 kW
ITALIAN • N AMERICA • 100/250 kW

          †SWISS RADIO INTL, Via Moyabi, Gabon
S AMERICA • 500 kW
AFRICA • 500 kW
ITALIAN • S AMERICA • 500 kW

12035v VIETNAM
          VOICE OF VIETNAM, Hanoi
E ASIA • 30 kW
SE ASIA • 30 kW

12040 RUSSIA
          R MOSCOW INTL
(J) • E NORTH AM

          †R MOSCOW INTL, Via Ukraine
(D) • C AMERICA • 240 kW
(D) • EUROPE • 240 kW
(J) • C AMERICA • 240 kW

          R MOSCOW INTL, Yekaterinburg
(J) • EUROPE • 50 kW

          †RADIO MOSCOW
(D) • DS-1

          †RADIO PAMYAT, Yekaterinburg
(J) • EUROPE • DS • 200 kW • ALT. FREQ. TO 12030 kHz

          VOICE OF RUSSIA
(D)
UKRAINE
          †RADIO UKRAINE, Ivano-Frankovsk
(J) • C AMERICA • 240 kW
(J) • UKRAINIAN • C AMERICA • 240 kW

UNITED KINGDOM
          †BBC, Rampisham
(J) • E EUROPE • 500 kW

          †BBC, Woofferton
(D) • E EUROPE • 250 kW
USA
          †VOA, Via Philippines
E ASIA • 250 kW
12045 RUSSIA
          R MOSCOW INTL
(D) • S ASIA

          †RUSSIA'S RADIO, Voronezh
(D) • DS • 50 kW

          VOICE OF RUSSIA
(J) • S ASIA
12050 ARMENIA
          †RADIO YEREVAN
(J) • S AMERICA
(J) • ARMENIAN • S AMERICA

EGYPT
          †RADIO CAIRO, Multiple Locations
EUROPE & E NORTH AM • DS-GENERAL • 250 kW
EUROPE, E NORTH AM & E AFRICA • DS-GENERAL • 100/250 kW
EUROPE & N AMERICA • DS-GENERAL • 100/250 kW

GEORGIA
          †RADIO GEORGIA, Tbilisi
EUROPE
MONGOLIA
          RADIO ULAANBAATAR, Ulaanbaatar
EUROPE • 250 kW
Tu/F • EUROPE • 250 kW
(con'd)

0 1 2 3 4 5 6 7 8 9 10 11 12 13 14 15 16 17 18 19 20 21 22 23 24

SUMMER ONLY (J)   WINTER ONLY (D)   JAMMING / OR ∧   EARLIEST HEARD ◁   LATEST HEARD ▷   NEW OR CHANGED FOR 1993 †

FREQUENCY   COUNTRY, STATION, LOCATION   TARGET • NETWORK • POWER (kW)   World Time

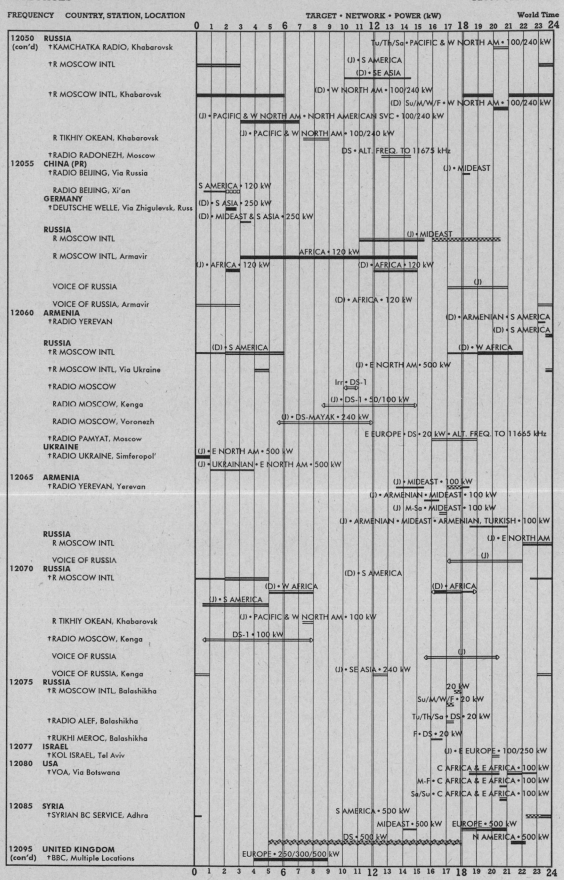

Frequency	Country, Station, Location	Target • Network • Power
12050 (con'd)	**RUSSIA** †KAMCHATKA RADIO, Khabarovsk	Tu/Th/Sa • PACIFIC & W NORTH AM • 100/240 kW
	†R MOSCOW INTL	(J) • S AMERICA / (D) • SE ASIA
	†R MOSCOW INTL, Khabarovsk	(D) • W NORTH AM • 100/240 kW / (D) • Su/M/W/F • W NORTH AM • 100/240 kW / (J) • PACIFIC & W NORTH AM • NORTH AMERICAN SVC • 100/240 kW
	R TIKHIY OKEAN, Khabarovsk	(J) • PACIFIC & W NORTH AM • 100/240 kW
	†RADIO RADONEZH, Moscow	DS • ALT. FREQ. TO 11675 kHz
12055	**CHINA (PR)** †RADIO BEIJING, Via Russia	(J) • MIDEAST
	RADIO BEIJING, Xi'an	S AMERICA • 120 kW
	GERMANY †DEUTSCHE WELLE, Via Zhigulevsk, Russ	(D) • S ASIA • 250 kW / (D) • MIDEAST & S ASIA • 250 kW
	RUSSIA R MOSCOW INTL	(J) • MIDEAST
	R MOSCOW INTL, Armavir	AFRICA • 120 kW / (J) • AFRICA • 120 kW / (D) • AFRICA • 120 kW
	VOICE OF RUSSIA	(J)
	VOICE OF RUSSIA, Armavir	(D) • AFRICA • 120 kW
12060	**ARMENIA** †RADIO YEREVAN	(D) • ARMENIAN • S AMERICA / (D) • S AMERICA
	RUSSIA †R MOSCOW INTL	(D) • S AMERICA / (D) • W AFRICA
	†R MOSCOW INTL, Via Ukraine	(J) • E NORTH AM • 500 kW
	†RADIO MOSCOW	Irr • DS-1
	RADIO MOSCOW, Kenga	(J) • DS-1 • 50/100 kW
	RADIO MOSCOW, Voronezh	(J) • DS-MAYAK • 240 kW
	†RADIO PAMYAT, Moscow	E EUROPE • DS • 20 kW • ALT. FREQ. TO 11665 kHz
	UKRAINE †RADIO UKRAINE, Simferopol'	(J) • E NORTH AM • 500 kW / (J) • UKRAINIAN • E NORTH AM • 500 kW
12065	**ARMENIA** †RADIO YEREVAN, Yerevan	(J) • MIDEAST • 100 kW / (J) • ARMENIAN • MIDEAST • 100 kW / (J) M-Sa • MIDEAST • 100 kW / (J) • ARMENIAN • MIDEAST • ARMENIAN, TURKISH • 100 kW
	RUSSIA R MOSCOW INTL	(J) • E NORTH AM
	VOICE OF RUSSIA	(J)
12070	**RUSSIA** †R MOSCOW INTL	(D) • S AMERICA / (D) • W AFRICA / (D) • AFRICA / (J) • S AMERICA
	R TIKHIY OKEAN, Khabarovsk	(J) • PACIFIC & W NORTH AM • 100 kW
	†RADIO MOSCOW, Kenga	DS-1 • 100 kW
	VOICE OF RUSSIA	(J)
	VOICE OF RUSSIA, Kenga	(J) • SE ASIA • 240 kW
12075	**RUSSIA** †R MOSCOW INTL, Balashikha	20 kW / Su/M/W/F • 20 kW
	†RADIO ALEF, Balashikha	Tu/Th/Sa • DS • 20 kW
	†RUKHI MEROC, Balashikha	F • DS • 20 kW
12077	**ISRAEL** †KOL ISRAEL, Tel Aviv	(J) • E EUROPE • 100/250 kW
12080	**USA** †VOA, Via Botswana	C AFRICA & E AFRICA • 100 kW / M-F • C AFRICA & E AFRICA • 100 kW / Sa/Su • C AFRICA & E AFRICA • 100 kW
12085	**SYRIA** †SYRIAN BC SERVICE, Adhra	S AMERICA • 500 kW / MIDEAST • 500 kW / EUROPE • 500 kW / DS • 500 kW / N AMERICA • 500 kW
12095 (con'd)	**UNITED KINGDOM** †BBC, Multiple Locations	EUROPE • 250/300/500 kW

ENGLISH ▬▬   ARABIC ≋≋≋   CHINESE □□□   FRENCH ▬▬   GERMAN ▬▬   RUSSIAN ══   SPANISH ▬▬   OTHER ──

| FREQUENCY | COUNTRY, STATION, LOCATION | TARGET • NETWORK • POWER (kW) | World Time |

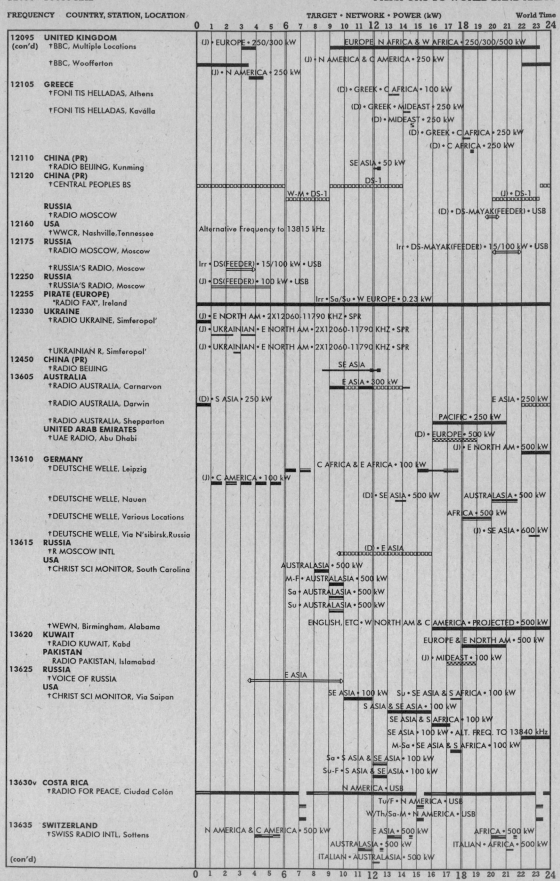

12095 (con'd)	UNITED KINGDOM †BBC, Multiple Locations	(J) • EUROPE • 250/300 kW EUROPE, N AFRICA & W AFRICA • 250/300/500 kW
	†BBC, Woofferton	(J) • N AMERICA & C AMERICA • 250 kW
		(J) • N AMERICA • 250 kW
12105	GREECE †FONI TIS HELLADAS, Athens	(D) • GREEK • C AFRICA • 100 kW
	†FONI TIS HELLADAS, Kaválla	(D) • GREEK • MIDEAST • 250 kW
		(D) • MIDEAST • 250 kW
		(D) • GREEK • C AFRICA • 250 kW
		(D) • C AFRICA • 250 kW
12110	CHINA (PR) †RADIO BEIJING, Kunming	SE ASIA • 50 kW
12120	CHINA (PR) †CENTRAL PEOPLES BS	DS-1
		W-M • DS-1 (J) • DS-1
	RUSSIA †RADIO MOSCOW	(D) • DS-MAYAK(FEEDER) • USB
12160	USA †WWCR, Nashville,Tennessee	Alternative Frequency to 13815 kHz
12175	RUSSIA †RADIO MOSCOW, Moscow	Irr • DS-MAYAK(FEEDER) • 15/100 kW • USB
	†RUSSIA'S RADIO, Moscow	Irr • DS(FEEDER) • 15/100 kW • USB
12250	RUSSIA †RUSSIA'S RADIO, Moscow	(J) • DS(FEEDER) • 100 kW • USB
12255	PIRATE (EUROPE) "RADIO FAX", Ireland	Irr • Sa/Su • W EUROPE • 0.23 kW
12330	UKRAINE †RADIO UKRAINE, Simferopol'	(J) • E NORTH AM • 2X12060-11790 KHZ • SPR
		(J) • UKRAINIAN • E NORTH AM • 2X12060-11790 KHZ • SPR
	†UKRAINIAN R, Simferopol'	(J) • UKRAINIAN • E NORTH AM • 2X12060-11790 KHZ • SPR
12450	CHINA (PR) †RADIO BEIJING	SE ASIA
13605	AUSTRALIA †RADIO AUSTRALIA, Carnarvon	E ASIA • 300 kW
	†RADIO AUSTRALIA, Darwin	(D) • S ASIA • 250 kW E ASIA • 250 kW
	†RADIO AUSTRALIA, Shepparton	PACIFIC • 250 kW
	UNITED ARAB EMIRATES †UAE RADIO, Abu Dhabi	(D) • EUROPE • 500 kW
		(J) • E NORTH AM • 500 kW
13610	GERMANY †DEUTSCHE WELLE, Leipzig	C AFRICA & E AFRICA • 100 kW
		(J) • C AMERICA • 100 kW
	†DEUTSCHE WELLE, Nauen	(D) • SE ASIA • 500 kW AUSTRALASIA • 500 kW
	†DEUTSCHE WELLE, Various Locations	AFRICA • 500 kW
	†DEUTSCHE WELLE, Via N'sibirsk,Russia	(J) • SE ASIA • 600 kW
13615	RUSSIA †R MOSCOW INTL	(D) • E ASIA
	USA †CHRIST SCI MONITOR, South Carolina	AUSTRALASIA • 500 kW
		M-F • AUSTRALASIA • 500 kW
		Sa • AUSTRALASIA • 500 kW
		Su • AUSTRALASIA • 500 kW
	†WEWN, Birmingham, Alabama	ENGLISH, ETC • W NORTH AM & C AMERICA • PROJECTED • 500 kW
13620	KUWAIT †RADIO KUWAIT, Kabd	EUROPE & E NORTH AM • 500 kW
	PAKISTAN RADIO PAKISTAN, Islamabad	(J) • MIDEAST • 100 kW
13625	RUSSIA †VOICE OF RUSSIA	E ASIA
	USA †CHRIST SCI MONITOR, Via Saipan	SE ASIA • 100 kW Su • SE ASIA & S AFRICA • 100 kW
		S ASIA & SE ASIA • 100 kW
		SE ASIA & S AFRICA • 100 kW
		SE ASIA • 100 kW • ALT. FREQ. TO 13840 kHz
		M-Sa • SE ASIA & S AFRICA • 100 kW
		Sa • S ASIA & SE ASIA • 100 kW
		Su-F • S ASIA & SE ASIA • 100 kW
13630v	COSTA RICA †RADIO FOR PEACE, Ciudad Colón	N AMERICA • USB
		Tu/F • N AMERICA • USB
		W/Th/Sa-M • N AMERICA • USB
13635	SWITZERLAND †SWISS RADIO INTL, Sottens	N AMERICA & C AMERICA • 500 kW E ASIA • 500 kW AFRICA • 500 kW
		AUSTRALASIA • 500 kW ITALIAN • AFRICA • 500 kW
		ITALIAN • AUSTRALASIA • 500 kW
(con'd)		

FREQUENCY	COUNTRY, STATION, LOCATION	TARGET • NETWORK • POWER (kW) — World Time

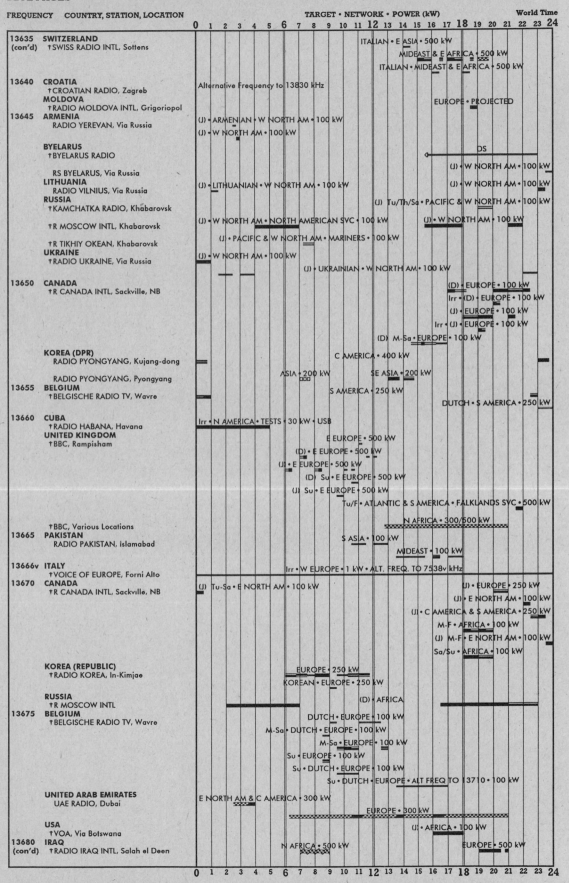

13635 SWITZERLAND
(con'd) †SWISS RADIO INTL, Sottens
- ITALIAN • E ASIA • 500 kW
- MIDEAST & E AFRICA • 500 kW
- ITALIAN • MIDEAST & E AFRICA • 500 kW

13640 CROATIA
†CROATIAN RADIO, Zagreb
- Alternative Frequency to 13830 kHz

MOLDOVA
†RADIO MOLDOVA INTL, Grigoriopol
- EUROPE • PROJECTED

13645 ARMENIA
RADIO YEREVAN, Via Russia
- (J) • ARMENIAN • W NORTH AM • 100 kW
- (J) • W NORTH AM • 100 kW

BYELARUS
†BYELARUS RADIO
- DS

RS BYELARUS, Via Russia
- (J) • W NORTH AM • 100 kW

LITHUANIA
RADIO VILNIUS, Via Russia
- (J) • LITHUANIAN • W NORTH AM • 100 kW
- (J) • W NORTH AM • 100 kW

RUSSIA
†KAMCHATKA RADIO, Khabarovsk
- (J) • Tu/Th/Sa • PACIFIC & W NORTH AM • 100 kW

†R MOSCOW INTL, Khabarovsk
- (J) • W NORTH AM • NORTH AMERICAN SVC • 100 kW
- (J) • W NORTH AM • 100 kW

†R TIKHIY OKEAN, Khabarovsk
- (J) • PACIFIC & W NORTH AM • MARINERS • 100 kW

UKRAINE
†RADIO UKRAINE, Via Russia
- (J) • W NORTH AM • 100 kW
- (J) • UKRAINIAN • W NORTH AM • 100 kW

13650 CANADA
†R CANADA INTL, Sackville, NB
- (D) • EUROPE • 100 kW
- Irr • (D) • EUROPE • 100 kW
- (J) • EUROPE • 100 kW
- Irr • (J) • EUROPE • 100 kW
- (D) M-Sa • EUROPE • 100 kW

KOREA (DPR)
RADIO PYONGYANG, Kujang-dong
- C AMERICA • 400 kW

RADIO PYONGYANG, Pyongyang
- ASIA • 200 kW
- SE ASIA • 200 kW

13655 BELGIUM
†BELGISCHE RADIO TV, Wavre
- S AMERICA • 250 kW
- DUTCH • S AMERICA • 250 kW

13660 CUBA
†RADIO HABANA, Havana
- Irr • N AMERICA • TESTS • 30 kW • USB

UNITED KINGDOM
†BBC, Rampisham
- E EUROPE • 500 kW
- (D) • E EUROPE • 500 kW
- (J) • E EUROPE • 500 kW
- (D) Su • E EUROPE • 500 kW
- (J) Su • E EUROPE • 500 kW
- Tu/F • ATLANTIC & S AMERICA • FALKLANDS SVC • 500 kW
- N AFRICA • 300/500 kW

†BBC, Various Locations

13665 PAKISTAN
RADIO PAKISTAN, Islamabad
- S ASIA • 100 kW
- MIDEAST • 100 kW

13666v ITALY
†VOICE OF EUROPE, Forni Alto
- Irr • W EUROPE • 1 kW • ALT. FREQ. TO 7538v kHz

13670 CANADA
†R CANADA INTL, Sackville, NB
- (J) Tu-Sa • E NORTH AM • 100 kW
- (J) • EUROPE • 250 kW
- (J) • E NORTH AM • 100 kW
- (J) • C AMERICA & S AMERICA • 250 kW
- M-F • AFRICA • 100 kW
- (J) M-F • E NORTH AM • 100 kW
- Sa/Su • AFRICA • 100 kW

KOREA (REPUBLIC)
†RADIO KOREA, In-Kimjae
- EUROPE • 250 kW
- KOREAN • EUROPE • 250 kW

RUSSIA
†R MOSCOW INTL
- (D) • AFRICA

13675 BELGIUM
†BELGISCHE RADIO TV, Wavre
- DUTCH • EUROPE • 100 kW
- M-Sa • DUTCH • EUROPE • 100 kW
- M-Sa • EUROPE • 100 kW
- Su • EUROPE • 100 kW
- Su • DUTCH • EUROPE • 100 kW
- Su • DUTCH • EUROPE • ALT FREQ TO 13710 • 100 kW

UNITED ARAB EMIRATES
UAE RADIO, Dubai
- E NORTH AM & C AMERICA • 300 kW
- EUROPE • 300 kW

USA
†VOA, Via Botswana
- (J) • AFRICA • 100 kW

13680 IRAQ
(con'd) †RADIO IRAQ INTL, Salah el Deen
- N AFRICA • 500 kW
- EUROPE • 500 kW

ENGLISH ▬ ARABIC ⧓ CHINESE ▭▭▭ FRENCH ▬ GERMAN ▬ RUSSIAN ═ SPANISH ▬ OTHER ▬

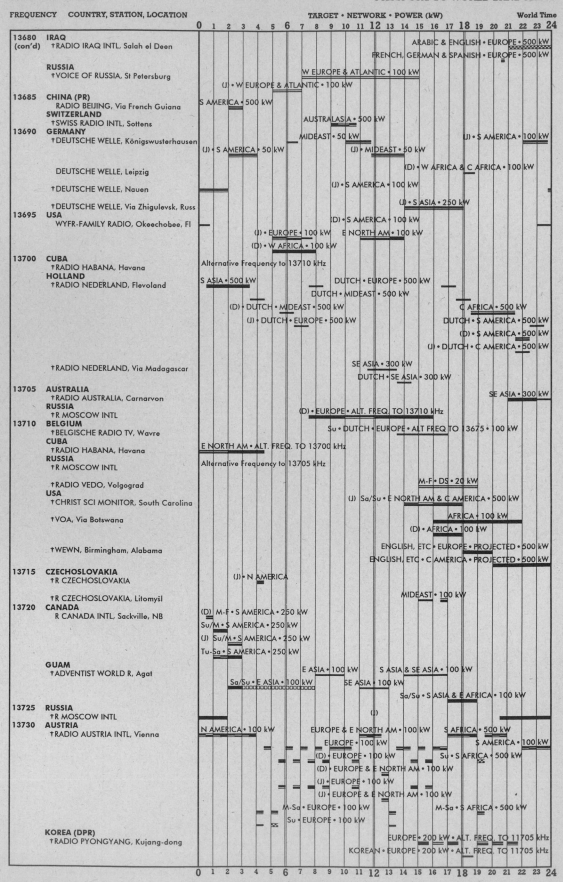

FREQUENCY	COUNTRY, STATION, LOCATION	TARGET • NETWORK • POWER (kW)

13680 IRAQ
(con'd) †RADIO IRAQ INTL, Salah el Deen — ARABIC & ENGLISH • EUROPE • 500 kW; FRENCH, GERMAN & SPANISH • EUROPE • 500 kW

RUSSIA
†VOICE OF RUSSIA, St Petersburg — W EUROPE & ATLANTIC • 100 kW; (J) • W EUROPE & ATLANTIC • 100 kW

13685 CHINA (PR)
RADIO BEIJING, Via French Guiana — S AMERICA • 500 kW

SWITZERLAND
†SWISS RADIO INTL, Sottens — AUSTRALASIA • 500 kW

13690 GERMANY
†DEUTSCHE WELLE, Königswusterhausen — MIDEAST • 50 kW; (J) • S AMERICA • 100 kW; (J) • S AMERICA • 50 kW; (J) • MIDEAST • 50 kW

DEUTSCHE WELLE, Leipzig — (D) • W AFRICA & C AFRICA • 100 kW

†DEUTSCHE WELLE, Nauen — (J) • S AMERICA • 100 kW

†DEUTSCHE WELLE, Via Zhigulevsk, Russ — (J) • S ASIA • 250 kW

13695 USA
WYFR-FAMILY RADIO, Okeechobee, Fl — (D) • S AMERICA • 100 kW; (J) • EUROPE • 100 kW; E NORTH AM • 100 kW; (D) • W AFRICA • 100 kW

13700 CUBA
†RADIO HABANA, Havana — Alternative Frequency to 13710 kHz

HOLLAND
†RADIO NEDERLAND, Flevoland — S ASIA • 500 kW; DUTCH • EUROPE • 500 kW; DUTCH • MIDEAST • 500 kW; (D) • DUTCH • MIDEAST • 500 kW; C AFRICA • 500 kW; (J) • DUTCH • EUROPE • 500 kW; DUTCH • S AMERICA • 500 kW; (D) • S AMERICA • 500 kW; (J) • DUTCH • C AMERICA • 500 kW

†RADIO NEDERLAND, Via Madagascar — SE ASIA • 300 kW; DUTCH • SE ASIA • 300 kW

13705 AUSTRALIA
†RADIO AUSTRALIA, Carnarvon — SE ASIA • 300 kW

RUSSIA
†R MOSCOW INTL — (D) • EUROPE • ALT. FREQ. TO 13710 kHz

13710 BELGIUM
†BELGISCHE RADIO TV, Wavre — Su • DUTCH • EUROPE • ALT FREQ TO 13675 • 100 kW

CUBA
†RADIO HABANA, Havana — E NORTH AM • ALT. FREQ. TO 13700 kHz

RUSSIA
†R MOSCOW INTL — Alternative Frequency to 13705 kHz

†RADIO VEDO, Volgograd — M-F • DS • 20 kW

USA
†CHRIST SCI MONITOR, South Carolina — (J) Sa/Su • E NORTH AM & C AMERICA • 500 kW

†VOA, Via Botswana — AFRICA • 100 kW; (D) • AFRICA • 100 kW

†WEWN, Birmingham, Alabama — ENGLISH, ETC • EUROPE • PROJECTED • 500 kW; ENGLISH, ETC • C AMERICA • PROJECTED • 500 kW

13715 CZECHOSLOVAKIA
†R CZECHOSLOVAKIA — (J) • N AMERICA

†R CZECHOSLOVAKIA, Litomyšl — MIDEAST • 100 kW

13720 CANADA
R CANADA INTL, Sackville, NB — (D) M-F • S AMERICA • 250 kW; Su/M • S AMERICA • 250 kW; (J) Su/M • S AMERICA • 250 kW; Tu-Sa • S AMERICA • 250 kW

GUAM
†ADVENTIST WORLD R, Agat — E ASIA • 100 kW; S ASIA & SE ASIA • 100 kW; Sa/Su • E ASIA • 100 kW; SE ASIA • 100 kW; Sa/Su • S ASIA & E AFRICA • 100 kW

13725 RUSSIA
†R MOSCOW INTL — (J)

13730 AUSTRIA
†RADIO AUSTRIA INTL, Vienna — N AMERICA • 100 kW; EUROPE & E NORTH AM • 100 kW; S AFRICA • 500 kW; EUROPE • 100 kW; S AMERICA • 100 kW; (D) • EUROPE • 100 kW; Su • S AFRICA • 500 kW; (D) • EUROPE & E NORTH AM • 100 kW; (J) • EUROPE • 100 kW; (J) • EUROPE & E NORTH AM • 100 kW; M-Sa • EUROPE • 100 kW; M-Sa • S AFRICA • 500 kW; Su • EUROPE • 100 kW

KOREA (DPR)
†RADIO PYONGYANG, Kujang-dong — EUROPE • 200 kW • ALT. FREQ. TO 11705 kHz; KOREAN • EUROPE • 200 kW • ALT. FREQ. TO 11705 kHz

FREQUENCY   COUNTRY, STATION, LOCATION

TARGET • NETWORK • POWER (kW)   World Time

0 1 2 3 4 5 6 7 8 9 10 11 12 13 14 15 16 17 18 19 20 21 22 23 24

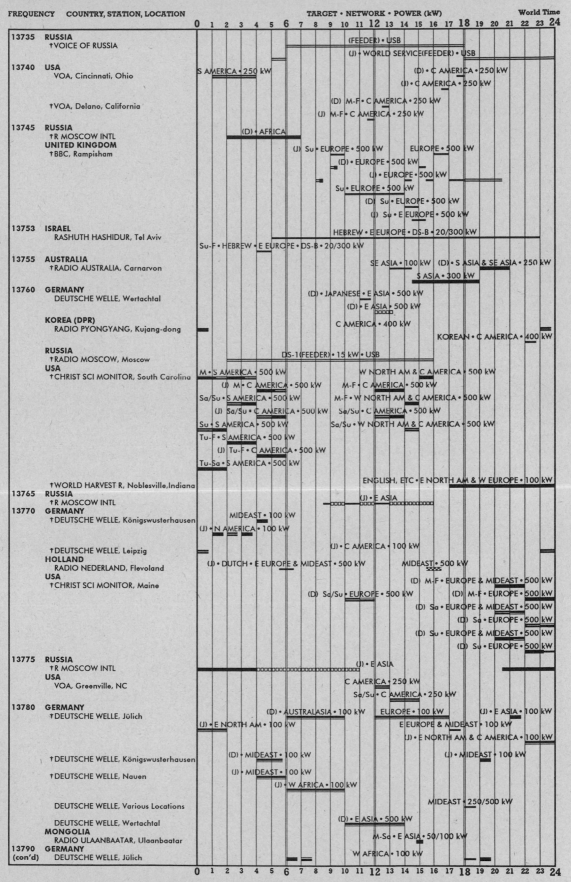

| 13735 | RUSSIA |
| | †VOICE OF RUSSIA |

(FEEDER) • USB

(J) • WORLD SERVICE(FEEDER) • USB

| 13740 | USA |
| | VOA, Cincinnati, Ohio |

S AMERICA • 250 kW

(D) • C AMERICA • 250 kW

(J) • C AMERICA • 250 kW

†VOA, Delano, California

(D) M-F • C AMERICA • 250 kW

(J) M-F • C AMERICA • 250 kW

13745	RUSSIA
	†R MOSCOW INTL
	UNITED KINGDOM
	†BBC, Rampisham

(D) • AFRICA

(J) Su • EUROPE • 500 kW   EUROPE • 500 kW

(D) • EUROPE • 500 kW

(J) • EUROPE • 500 kW

Su • EUROPE • 500 kW

(D) Su • EUROPE • 500 kW

(J) Su • E EUROPE • 500 kW

| 13753 | ISRAEL |
| | RASHUTH HASHIDUR, Tel Aviv |

HEBREW • E EUROPE • DS-B • 20/300 kW

Su-F • HEBREW • E EUROPE • DS-B • 20/300 kW

| 13755 | AUSTRALIA |
| | †RADIO AUSTRALIA, Carnarvon |

SE ASIA • 100 kW   (D) • S ASIA & SE ASIA • 250 kW

S ASIA • 300 kW

| 13760 | GERMANY |
| | DEUTSCHE WELLE, Wertachtal |

(D) • JAPANESE • E ASIA • 500 kW

(D) • E ASIA • 500 kW

| | KOREA (DPR) |
| | RADIO PYONGYANG, Kujang-dong |

C AMERICA • 400 kW

KOREAN • C AMERICA • 400 kW

	RUSSIA
	†RADIO MOSCOW, Moscow
	USA
	†CHRIST SCI MONITOR, South Carolina

DS-1(FEEDER) • 15 kW • USB

M • S AMERICA • 500 kW   W NORTH AM & C AMERICA • 500 kW

(J) M • C AMERICA • 500 kW   M-F • C AMERICA • 500 kW

Sa/Su • S AMERICA • 500 kW   M-F • W NORTH AM & C AMERICA • 500 kW

(J) Sa/Su • C AMERICA • 500 kW   Sa/Su • C AMERICA • 500 kW

Su • S AMERICA • 500 kW   Sa/Su • W NORTH AM & C AMERICA • 500 kW

Tu-F • S AMERICA • 500 kW

(J) Tu-F • C AMERICA • 500 kW

Tu-Sa • S AMERICA • 500 kW

| | †WORLD HARVEST R, Noblesville, Indiana |

ENGLISH, ETC • E NORTH AM & W EUROPE • 100 kW

| 13765 | RUSSIA |
| | †R MOSCOW INTL |

(J) • E ASIA

| 13770 | GERMANY |
| | †DEUTSCHE WELLE, Königswusterhausen |

MIDEAST • 100 kW

(J) • N AMERICA • 100 kW

	†DEUTSCHE WELLE, Leipzig
	HOLLAND
	RADIO NEDERLAND, Flevoland
	USA
	†CHRIST SCI MONITOR, Maine

(J) • C AMERICA • 100 kW

(J) • DUTCH • E EUROPE & MIDEAST • 500 kW   MIDEAST • 500 kW

(D) M-F • EUROPE & MIDEAST • 500 kW

(D) Sa/Su • EUROPE • 500 kW   (D) M-F • EUROPE • 500 kW

(D) Sa • EUROPE & MIDEAST • 500 kW

(D) Sa • EUROPE • 500 kW

(D) Su • EUROPE & MIDEAST • 500 kW

(D) Su • EUROPE • 500 kW

13775	RUSSIA
	†R MOSCOW INTL
	USA
	VOA, Greenville, NC

(J) • E ASIA

C AMERICA • 250 kW

Sa/Su • C AMERICA • 250 kW

| 13780 | GERMANY |
| | †DEUTSCHE WELLE, Jülich |

(D) • AUSTRALASIA • 100 kW   EUROPE • 100 kW   (J) • E ASIA • 100 kW

(J) • E NORTH AM • 100 kW   E EUROPE & MIDEAST • 100 kW

(J) • E NORTH AM & C AMERICA • 100 kW

| | †DEUTSCHE WELLE, Königswusterhausen |

(D) • MIDEAST • 100 kW   (J) • MIDEAST • 100 kW

| | †DEUTSCHE WELLE, Nauen |

(J) • MIDEAST • 100 kW

(J) • W AFRICA • 100 kW

| | DEUTSCHE WELLE, Various Locations |

MIDEAST • 250/500 kW

	DEUTSCHE WELLE, Wertachtal
	MONGOLIA
	RADIO ULAANBAATAR, Ulaanbaatar

(D) • E ASIA • 500 kW

M-Sa • E ASIA • 50/100 kW

| 13790 (con'd) | GERMANY |
| | DEUTSCHE WELLE, Jülich |

W AFRICA • 100 kW

0 1 2 3 4 5 6 7 8 9 10 11 12 13 14 15 16 17 18 19 20 21 22 23 24

ENGLISH ▬▬   ARABIC ⌇⌇⌇   CHINESE ▫▫▫   FRENCH ▬▬   GERMAN ▬▬   RUSSIAN ══   SPANISH ▬▬   OTHER ▬▬

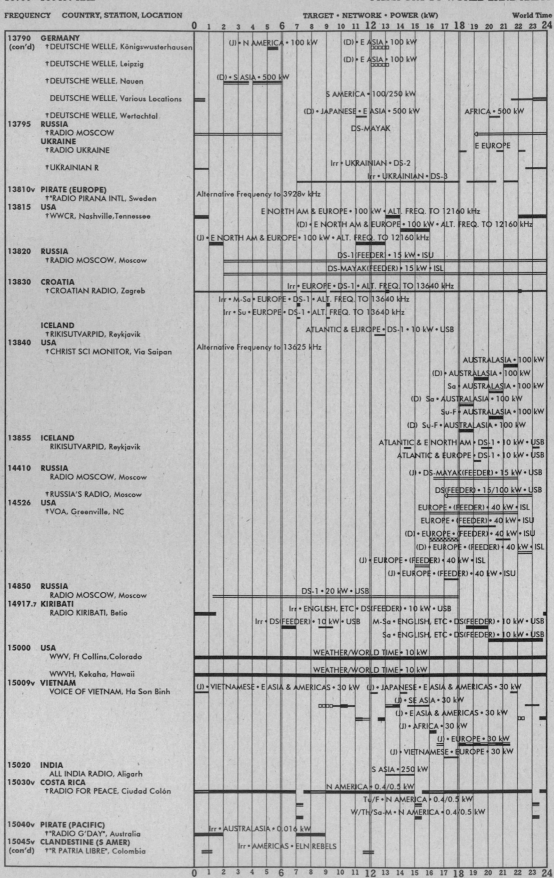

FREQUENCY   COUNTRY, STATION, LOCATION   TARGET • NETWORK • POWER (kW)   World Time

Freq	Country / Station / Location	Schedule notes
13790 (con'd)	GERMANY	
	†DEUTSCHE WELLE, Königswusterhausen	(J) • N AMERICA • 100 kW; (D) • E ASIA • 100 kW
	†DEUTSCHE WELLE, Leipzig	(D) • E ASIA • 100 kW
	†DEUTSCHE WELLE, Nauen	(D) • S ASIA • 500 kW
	DEUTSCHE WELLE, Various Locations	S AMERICA • 100/250 kW
	†DEUTSCHE WELLE, Wertachtal	(D) • JAPANESE • E ASIA • 500 kW; AFRICA • 500 kW
13795	RUSSIA	
	†RADIO MOSCOW	DS-MAYAK
	UKRAINE	
	†RADIO UKRAINE	E EUROPE
	†UKRAINIAN R	Irr • UKRAINIAN • DS-2; Irr • UKRAINIAN • DS-3
13810v	PIRATE (EUROPE)	
	†"RADIO PIRANA INTL, Sweden	Alternative Frequency to 3928v kHz
13815	USA	
	†WWCR, Nashville, Tennessee	E NORTH AM & EUROPE • 100 kW • ALT. FREQ. TO 12160 kHz; (D) • E NORTH AM & EUROPE • 100 kW • ALT. FREQ. TO 12160 kHz; (J) • E NORTH AM & EUROPE • 100 kW • ALT. FREQ. TO 12160 kHz
13820	RUSSIA	
	†RADIO MOSCOW, Moscow	DS-1 (FEEDER) • 15 kW • ISU; DS-MAYAK (FEEDER) • 15 kW • ISL
13830	CROATIA	
	†CROATIAN RADIO, Zagreb	Irr • EUROPE • DS-1 • ALT. FREQ. TO 13640 kHz; Irr • M-Sa • EUROPE • DS-1 • ALT. FREQ. TO 13640 kHz; Irr • Su • EUROPE • DS-1 • ALT. FREQ. TO 13640 kHz
	ICELAND	
	†RIKISUTVARPID, Reykjavik	ATLANTIC & EUROPE • DS-1 • 10 kW • USB
13840	USA	
	†CHRIST SCI MONITOR, Via Saipan	Alternative Frequency to 13625 kHz; AUSTRALASIA • 100 kW; (D) • AUSTRALASIA • 100 kW; Sa • AUSTRALASIA • 100 kW; (D) Sa • AUSTRALASIA • 100 kW; Su-F • AUSTRALASIA • 100 kW; (D) Su-F • AUSTRALASIA • 100 kW
13855	ICELAND	
	RIKISUTVARPID, Reykjavik	ATLANTIC & E NORTH AM • DS-1 • 10 kW • USB; ATLANTIC & EUROPE • DS-1 • 10 kW • USB
14410	RUSSIA	
	RADIO MOSCOW, Moscow	(J) • DS-MAYAK (FEEDER) • 15 kW • USB
	†RUSSIA'S RADIO, Moscow	DS (FEEDER) • 15/100 kW • USB
14526	USA	
	†VOA, Greenville, NC	EUROPE • (FEEDER) • 40 kW • ISL; EUROPE • (FEEDER) • 40 kW • ISU; (D) • EUROPE • (FEEDER) • 40 kW • ISU; (D) • EUROPE • (FEEDER) • 40 kW • ISL; (J) • EUROPE • (FEEDER) • 40 kW • ISL; (J) • EUROPE • (FEEDER) • 40 kW • ISU
14850	RUSSIA	
	RADIO MOSCOW, Moscow	DS-1 • 20 kW • USB
14917.7	KIRIBATI	
	RADIO KIRIBATI, Betio	Irr • ENGLISH, ETC • DS (FEEDER) • 10 kW • USB; Irr • DS (FEEDER) • 10 kW • USB; M-Sa • ENGLISH, ETC • DS (FEEDER) • 10 kW • USB; Sa • ENGLISH, ETC • DS (FEEDER) • 10 kW • USB
15000	USA	
	WWV, Ft Collins, Colorado	WEATHER/WORLD TIME • 10 kW
	WWVH, Kekaha, Hawaii	WEATHER/WORLD TIME • 10 kW
15009v	VIETNAM	
	VOICE OF VIETNAM, Ha Son Binh	(J) • VIETNAMESE • E ASIA & AMERICAS • 30 kW; (J) • JAPANESE • E ASIA & AMERICAS • 30 kW; (J) • SE ASIA • 30 kW; (J) • E ASIA & AMERICAS • 30 kW; (J) • AFRICA • 30 kW; (J) • EUROPE • 30 kW; (J) • VIETNAMESE • EUROPE • 30 kW
15020	INDIA	
	ALL INDIA RADIO, Aligarh	S ASIA • 250 kW
15030v	COSTA RICA	
	†RADIO FOR PEACE, Ciudad Colón	N AMERICA • 0.4/0.5 kW; Tu/F • N AMERICA • 0.4/0.5 kW; W/Th/Sa-M • N AMERICA • 0.4/0.5 kW
15040v	PIRATE (PACIFIC)	
	†"RADIO G'DAY", Australia	Irr • AUSTRALASIA • 0.016 kW
15045v (con'd)	CLANDESTINE (S AMER)	
	†"R PATRIA LIBRE", Colombia	Irr • AMERICAS • ELN REBELS

SUMMER ONLY (J)   WINTER ONLY (D)   JAMMING / OR ∧   EARLIEST HEARD ◁   LATEST HEARD ▷   NEW OR CHANGED FOR 1993 †

| FREQUENCY | COUNTRY, STATION, LOCATION | TARGET • NETWORK • POWER (kW) | World Time |

World Time scale: 0 1 2 3 4 5 6 7 8 9 10 11 12 13 14 15 16 17 18 19 20 21 22 23 24

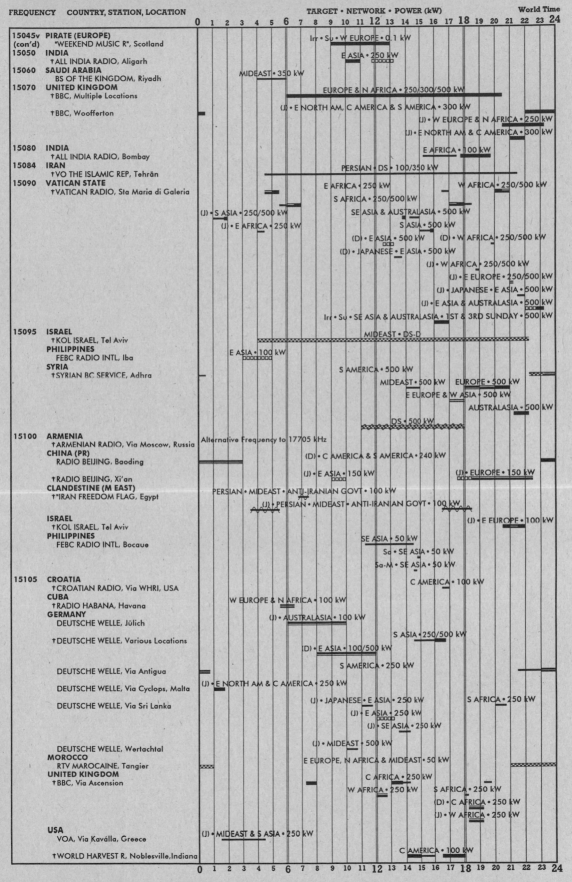

15045v **PIRATE (EUROPE)**
(con'd)   "WEEKEND MUSIC R", Scotland — Irr • Su • W EUROPE • 0.1 kW

15050 **INDIA**
  †ALL INDIA RADIO, Aligarh — E ASIA • 250 kW

15060 **SAUDI ARABIA**
  BS OF THE KINGDOM, Riyadh — MIDEAST • 350 kW

15070 **UNITED KINGDOM**
  †BBC, Multiple Locations — EUROPE & N AFRICA • 250/300/500 kW

  †BBC, Woofferton — (J) • E NORTH AM, C AMERICA & S AMERICA • 300 kW
  — (J) • W EUROPE & N AFRICA • 250 kW
  — (J) • E NORTH AM & C AMERICA • 300 kW

15080 **INDIA**
  †ALL INDIA RADIO, Bombay — E AFRICA • 100 kW

15084 **IRAN**
  †VO THE ISLAMIC REP, Tehrān — PERSIAN • DS • 100/350 kW

15090 **VATICAN STATE**
  †VATICAN RADIO, Sta Maria di Galeria
  — E AFRICA • 250 kW
  — W AFRICA • 250/500 kW
  — S AFRICA • 250/500 kW
  — (J) • S ASIA • 250/500 kW
  — SE ASIA & AUSTRALASIA • 500 kW
  — (J) • E AFRICA • 250 kW
  — S ASIA • 500 kW
  — (D) • E ASIA • 500 kW
  — (D) • W AFRICA • 250/500 kW
  — (D) • JAPANESE • E ASIA • 500 kW
  — (J) • W AFRICA • 250/500 kW
  — (J) • E EUROPE • 250/500 kW
  — (J) • JAPANESE • E ASIA • 500 kW
  — (J) • E ASIA & AUSTRALASIA • 500 kW
  — Irr • Su • SE ASIA & AUSTRALASIA • 1ST & 3RD SUNDAY • 500 kW

15095 **ISRAEL**
  †KOL ISRAEL, Tel Aviv — MIDEAST • DS-D
PHILIPPINES
  FEBC RADIO INTL, Iba — E ASIA • 100 kW
SYRIA
  †SYRIAN BC SERVICE, Adhra
  — S AMERICA • 500 kW
  — MIDEAST • 500 kW
  — EUROPE • 500 kW
  — E EUROPE & W ASIA • 500 kW
  — AUSTRALASIA • 500 kW
  — DS • 500 kW

15100 **ARMENIA**
  †ARMENIAN RADIO, Via Moscow, Russia — Alternative Frequency to 17705 kHz
CHINA (PR)
  RADIO BEIJING, Baoding — (D) • C AMERICA & S AMERICA • 240 kW
  †RADIO BEIJING, Xi'an
  — (J) • E ASIA • 150 kW
  — (J) • EUROPE • 150 kW
CLANDESTINE (M EAST)
  †"IRAN FREEDOM FLAG", Egypt
  — PERSIAN • MIDEAST • ANTI-IRANIAN GOVT • 100 kW
  — (J) • PERSIAN • MIDEAST • ANTI-IRANIAN GOVT • 100 kW
ISRAEL
  †KOL ISRAEL, Tel Aviv — (J) • E EUROPE • 100 kW
PHILIPPINES
  FEBC RADIO INTL, Bocaue
  — SE ASIA • 50 kW
  — Sa • SE ASIA • 50 kW
  — Sa-M • SE ASIA • 50 kW

15105 **CROATIA**
  †CROATIAN RADIO, Via WHRI, USA — C AMERICA • 100 kW
CUBA
  †RADIO HABANA, Havana — W EUROPE & N AFRICA • 100 kW
GERMANY
  DEUTSCHE WELLE, Jülich — (J) • AUSTRALASIA • 100 kW
  †DEUTSCHE WELLE, Various Locations
  — S ASIA • 250/500 kW
  — (D) • E ASIA • 100/500 kW
  DEUTSCHE WELLE, Via Antigua — S AMERICA • 250 kW
  DEUTSCHE WELLE, Via Cyclops, Malta — (J) • E NORTH AM & C AMERICA • 250 kW
  DEUTSCHE WELLE, Via Sri Lanka
  — (J) • JAPANESE • E ASIA • 250 kW
  — S AFRICA • 250 kW
  — (J) • E ASIA • 250 kW
  — (J) • SE ASIA • 250 kW
  DEUTSCHE WELLE, Wertachtal — (J) • MIDEAST • 500 kW
MOROCCO
  RTV MAROCAINE, Tangier — E EUROPE, N AFRICA & MIDEAST • 50 kW
UNITED KINGDOM
  †BBC, Via Ascension
  — C AFRICA • 250 kW
  — W AFRICA • 250 kW
  — S AFRICA • 250 kW
  — (D) • C AFRICA • 250 kW
  — (J) • W AFRICA • 250 kW
USA
  VOA, Via Kaválla, Greece — (J) • MIDEAST & S ASIA • 250 kW
  †WORLD HARVEST R, Noblesville, Indiana — C AMERICA • 100 kW

Bottom scale: 0 1 2 3 4 5 6 7 8 9 10 11 12 13 14 15 16 17 18 19 20 21 22 23 24

ENGLISH ▬▬ ARABIC ⋙ CHINESE ▫▫▫ FRENCH ▬▬ GERMAN ▬▬ RUSSIAN ═══ SPANISH ▬▬ OTHER ───

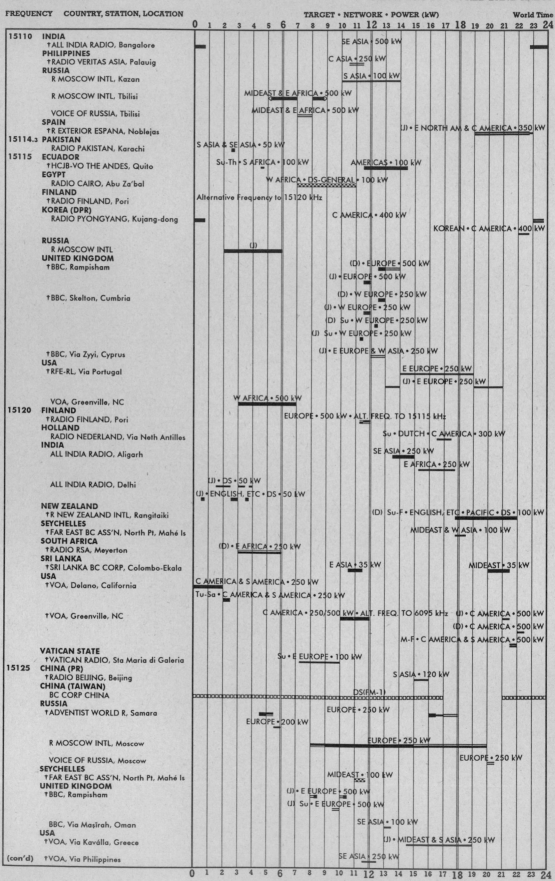

FREQUENCY   COUNTRY, STATION, LOCATION   TARGET • NETWORK • POWER (kW)   World Time

FREQUENCY	COUNTRY, STATION, LOCATION	TARGET • NETWORK • POWER (kW)
15110	INDIA †ALL INDIA RADIO, Bangalore	SE ASIA • 500 kW
	PHILIPPINES †RADIO VERITAS ASIA, Palauig	C ASIA • 250 kW
	RUSSIA R MOSCOW INTL, Kazan	S ASIA • 100 kW
	R MOSCOW INTL, Tbilisi	MIDEAST & E AFRICA • 500 kW
	VOICE OF RUSSIA, Tbilisi	MIDEAST & E AFRICA • 500 kW
	SPAIN †R EXTERIOR ESPANA, Noblejas	(J) • E NORTH AM & C AMERICA • 350 kW
15114.3	PAKISTAN RADIO PAKISTAN, Karachi	S ASIA & SE ASIA • 50 kW
15115	ECUADOR †HCJB-VO THE ANDES, Quito	Su-Th • S AFRICA • 100 kW AMERICAS • 100 kW
	EGYPT RADIO CAIRO, Abu Za'bal	W AFRICA • DS-GENERAL • 100 kW
	FINLAND †RADIO FINLAND, Pori	Alternative Frequency to 15120 kHz
	KOREA (DPR) RADIO PYONGYANG, Kujang-dong	C AMERICA • 400 kW KOREAN • C AMERICA • 400 kW
	RUSSIA R MOSCOW INTL	(J)
	UNITED KINGDOM †BBC, Rampisham	(D) • EUROPE • 500 kW (J) • EUROPE • 500 kW
	†BBC, Skelton, Cumbria	(D) • W EUROPE • 250 kW (J) • W EUROPE • 250 kW (D) Su • W EUROPE • 250 kW (J) Su • W EUROPE • 250 kW
	†BBC, Via Zyyi, Cyprus	(J) • E EUROPE & W ASIA • 250 kW
	USA †RFE-RL, Via Portugal	E EUROPE • 250 kW (J) • E EUROPE • 250 kW
	VOA, Greenville, NC	W AFRICA • 500 kW
15120	FINLAND †RADIO FINLAND, Pori	EUROPE • 500 kW • ALT. FREQ. TO 15115 kHz
	HOLLAND RADIO NEDERLAND, Via Neth Antilles	Su • DUTCH • C AMERICA • 300 kW
	INDIA ALL INDIA RADIO, Aligarh	SE ASIA • 250 kW E AFRICA • 250 kW
	ALL INDIA RADIO, Delhi	(J) • DS • 50 kW (J) • ENGLISH, ETC • DS • 50 kW
	NEW ZEALAND †R NEW ZEALAND INTL, Rangitaiki	(D) Su-F • ENGLISH, ETC • PACIFIC • DS • 100 kW
	SEYCHELLES †FAR EAST BC ASS'N, North Pt, Mahé Is	MIDEAST & W ASIA • 100 kW
	SOUTH AFRICA †RADIO RSA, Meyerton	(D) • E AFRICA • 250 kW
	SRI LANKA †SRI LANKA BC CORP, Colombo-Ekala	E ASIA • 35 kW MIDEAST • 35 kW
	USA †VOA, Delano, California	C AMERICA & S AMERICA • 250 kW Tu-Sa • C AMERICA & S AMERICA • 250 kW
	†VOA, Greenville, NC	C AMERICA • 250/500 kW • ALT. FREQ. TO 6095 kHz (J) • C AMERICA • 500 kW (D) • C AMERICA • 500 kW M-F • C AMERICA & S AMERICA • 500 kW
	VATICAN STATE †VATICAN RADIO, Sta Maria di Galeria	Su • E EUROPE • 100 kW
15125	CHINA (PR) †RADIO BEIJING, Beijing	S ASIA • 120 kW
	CHINA (TAIWAN) BC CORP CHINA	DS(FM-1)
	RUSSIA †ADVENTIST WORLD R, Samara	EUROPE • 250 kW EUROPE • 200 kW
	R MOSCOW INTL, Moscow	EUROPE • 250 kW
	VOICE OF RUSSIA, Moscow	EUROPE • 250 kW
	SEYCHELLES †FAR EAST BC ASS'N, North Pt, Mahé Is	MIDEAST • 100 kW
	UNITED KINGDOM †BBC, Rampisham	(J) • E EUROPE • 500 kW (J) Su • E EUROPE • 500 kW
	BBC, Via Maşirah, Oman	SE ASIA • 100 kW
	USA †VOA, Via Kaválla, Greece	(J) • MIDEAST & S ASIA • 250 kW
(con'd)	†VOA, Via Philippines	SE ASIA • 250 kW

SUMMER ONLY (J)   WINTER ONLY (D)   JAMMING / OR ∧   EARLIEST HEARD ◁   LATEST HEARD ▷   NEW OR CHANGED FOR 1993 †

FREQUENCY	COUNTRY, STATION, LOCATION	TARGET • NETWORK • POWER (kW)	World Time

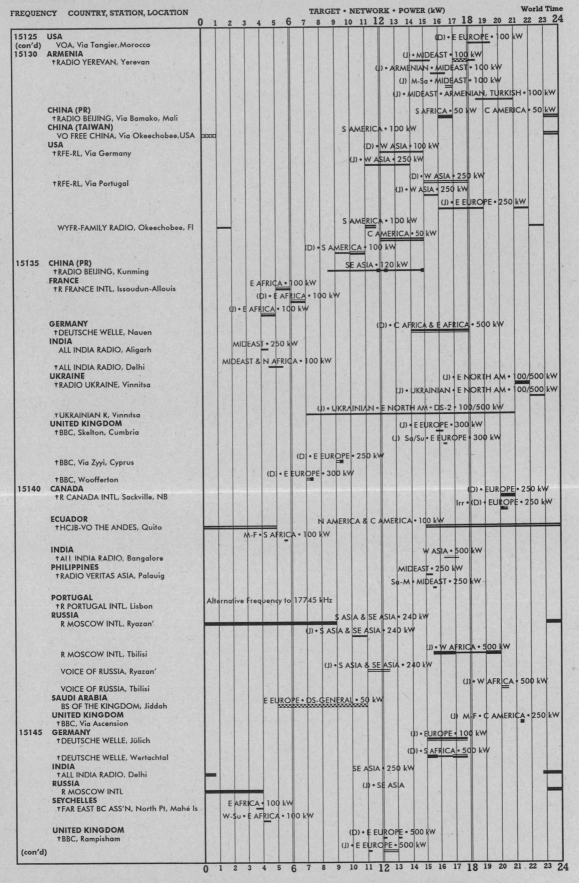

Frequency	Country / Station / Location	Target • Network • Power
15125 (con'd)	USA — VOA, Via Tangier, Morocco	(D) • E EUROPE • 100 kW
15130	ARMENIA — †RADIO YEREVAN, Yerevan	(J) • MIDEAST • 100 kW
		(J) • ARMENIAN • MIDEAST • 100 kW
		(J) • M-Sa • MIDEAST • 100 kW
		(J) • MIDEAST • ARMENIAN, TURKISH • 100 kW
	CHINA (PR) — †RADIO BEIJING, Via Bamako, Mali	S AFRICA • 50 kW C AMERICA • 50 kW
	CHINA (TAIWAN) — VO FREE CHINA, Via Okeechobee, USA	S AMERICA • 100 kW
	USA — †RFE-RL, Via Germany	(D) • W ASIA • 100 kW
		(J) • W ASIA • 250 kW
	†RFE-RL, Via Portugal	(D) • W ASIA • 250 kW
		(J) • W ASIA • 250 kW
		(J) • E EUROPE • 250 kW
	WYFR-FAMILY RADIO, Okeechobee, Fl	S AMERICA • 100 kW
		C AMERICA • 50 kW
		(D) • S AMERICA • 100 kW
15135	CHINA (PR) — †RADIO BEIJING, Kunming	SE ASIA • 120 kW
	FRANCE — †R FRANCE INTL, Issoudun-Allouis	E AFRICA • 100 kW
		(D) • E AFRICA • 100 kW
		(J) • E AFRICA • 100 kW
	GERMANY — †DEUTSCHE WELLE, Nauen	(D) • C AFRICA & E AFRICA • 500 kW
	INDIA — ALL INDIA RADIO, Aligarh	MIDEAST • 250 kW
	†ALL INDIA RADIO, Delhi	MIDEAST & N AFRICA • 100 kW
	UKRAINE — †RADIO UKRAINE, Vinnitsa	(J) • E NORTH AM • 100/500 kW
		(J) • UKRAINIAN • E NORTH AM • 100/500 kW
	†UKRAINIAN R, Vinnitsa	(J) • UKRAINIAN • E NORTH AM • DS-2 • 100/500 kW
	UNITED KINGDOM — †BBC, Skelton, Cumbria	(J) • E EUROPE • 300 kW
		(J) Sa/Su • E EUROPE • 300 kW
	†BBC, Via Zyyi, Cyprus	(D) • E EUROPE • 250 kW
	†BBC, Woofferton	(D) • E EUROPE • 300 kW
15140	CANADA — †R CANADA INTL, Sackville, NB	(D) • EUROPE • 250 kW
		Irr • (D) • EUROPE • 250 kW
	ECUADOR — †HCJB-VO THE ANDES, Quito	N AMERICA & C AMERICA • 100 kW
		M-F • S AFRICA • 100 kW
	INDIA — †ALL INDIA RADIO, Bangalore	W ASIA • 500 kW
	PHILIPPINES — †RADIO VERITAS ASIA, Palauig	MIDEAST • 250 kW
		Sa-M • MIDEAST • 250 kW
	PORTUGAL — †R PORTUGAL INTL, Lisbon	Alternative Frequency to 17745 kHz
	RUSSIA — R MOSCOW INTL, Ryazan'	S ASIA & SE ASIA • 240 kW
		(J) • S ASIA & SE ASIA • 240 kW
	R MOSCOW INTL, Tbilisi	(J) • W AFRICA • 500 kW
	VOICE OF RUSSIA, Ryazan'	(J) • S ASIA & SE ASIA • 240 kW
	VOICE OF RUSSIA, Tbilisi	(J) • W AFRICA • 500 kW
	SAUDI ARABIA — BS OF THE KINGDOM, Jiddah	E EUROPE • DS-GENERAL • 50 kW
	UNITED KINGDOM — †BBC, Via Ascension	(J) • M-F • C AMERICA • 250 kW
15145	GERMANY — †DEUTSCHE WELLE, Jülich	(J) • EUROPE • 100 kW
	†DEUTSCHE WELLE, Wertachtal	(D) • S AFRICA • 500 kW
	INDIA — †ALL INDIA RADIO, Delhi	SE ASIA • 250 kW
	RUSSIA — R MOSCOW INTL	(J) • SE ASIA
	SEYCHELLES — †FAR EAST BC ASS'N, North Pt, Mahé Is	E AFRICA • 100 kW
		W-Su • E AFRICA • 100 kW
	UNITED KINGDOM — †BBC, Rampisham	(D) • E EUROPE • 500 kW
		(J) • E EUROPE • 500 kW
(con'd)		

Time scale: 0 1 2 3 4 5 6 7 8 9 10 11 12 13 14 15 16 17 18 19 20 21 22 23 24

ENGLISH ▬   ARABIC ▨   CHINESE ▭▭▭   FRENCH ═   GERMAN ▬   RUSSIAN ═   SPANISH ▬   OTHER ─

FREQUENCY   COUNTRY, STATION, LOCATION

TARGET • NETWORK • POWER (kW)   World Time

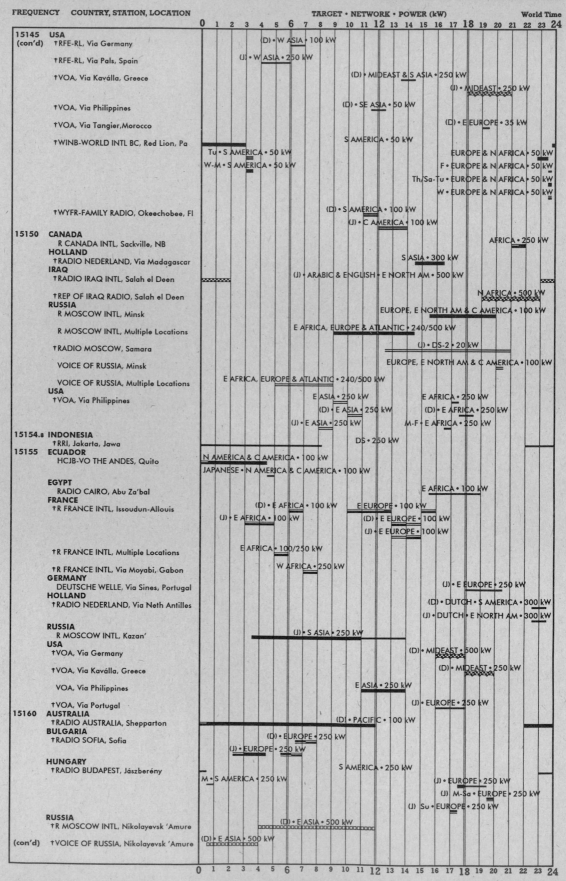

	0 1 2 3 4 5 6 7 8 9 10 11 12 13 14 15 16 17 18 19 20 21 22 23 24
15145 USA **(con'd)** †RFE-RL, Via Germany	(D) • W ASIA • 100 kW
†RFE-RL, Via Pals, Spain	(J) • W ASIA • 250 kW
†VOA, Via Kaválla, Greece	(D) • MIDEAST & S ASIA • 250 kW (J) • MIDEAST • 250 kW
†VOA, Via Philippines	(D) • SE ASIA • 50 kW
†VOA, Via Tangier, Morocco	(D) • E EUROPE • 35 kW
†WINB-WORLD INTL BC, Red Lion, Pa	S AMERICA • 50 kW Tu • S AMERICA • 50 kW W-M • S AMERICA • 50 kW EUROPE & N AFRICA • 50 kW F • EUROPE & N AFRICA • 50 kW Th/Sa-Tu • EUROPE & N AFRICA • 50 kW W • EUROPE & N AFRICA • 50 kW
†WYFR-FAMILY RADIO, Okeechobee, Fl	(D) • S AMERICA • 100 kW (J) • C AMERICA • 100 kW
15150 CANADA R CANADA INTL, Sackville, NB	AFRICA • 250 kW
HOLLAND †RADIO NEDERLAND, Via Madagascar	S ASIA • 300 kW
IRAQ †RADIO IRAQ INTL, Salah el Deen	(J) • ARABIC & ENGLISH • E NORTH AM • 500 kW
†REP OF IRAQ RADIO, Salah el Deen	N AFRICA • 500 kW
RUSSIA R MOSCOW INTL, Minsk	EUROPE, E NORTH AM & C AMERICA • 100 kW
R MOSCOW INTL, Multiple Locations	E AFRICA, EUROPE & ATLANTIC • 240/500 kW
†RADIO MOSCOW, Samara	(J) • DS-2 • 20 kW
VOICE OF RUSSIA, Minsk	EUROPE, E NORTH AM & C AMERICA • 100 kW
VOICE OF RUSSIA, Multiple Locations	E AFRICA, EUROPE & ATLANTIC • 240/500 kW
USA †VOA, Via Philippines	E ASIA • 250 kW E AFRICA • 250 kW (D) • E ASIA • 250 kW (D) • E AFRICA • 250 kW (J) • E ASIA • 250 kW M-F • E AFRICA • 250 kW
15154.8 INDONESIA †RRI, Jakarta, Jawa	DS • 250 kW
15155 ECUADOR HCJB-VO THE ANDES, Quito	N AMERICA & C AMERICA • 100 kW JAPANESE • N AMERICA & C AMERICA • 100 kW
EGYPT RADIO CAIRO, Abu Za'bal	E AFRICA • 100 kW
FRANCE †R FRANCE INTL, Issoudun-Allouis	(D) • E AFRICA • 100 kW E EUROPE • 100 kW (J) • E AFRICA • 100 kW (D) • E EUROPE • 100 kW (J) • E EUROPE • 100 kW
†R FRANCE INTL, Multiple Locations	E AFRICA • 100/250 kW
†R FRANCE INTL, Via Moyabi, Gabon	W AFRICA • 250 kW
GERMANY DEUTSCHE WELLE, Via Sines, Portugal	(J) • E EUROPE • 250 kW
HOLLAND †RADIO NEDERLAND, Via Neth Antilles	(D) • DUTCH • S AMERICA • 300 kW (J) • DUTCH • E NORTH AM • 300 kW
RUSSIA R MOSCOW INTL, Kazan'	(J) • S ASIA • 250 kW
USA †VOA, Via Germany	(D) • MIDEAST • 500 kW
†VOA, Via Kaválla, Greece	(D) • MIDEAST • 250 kW
VOA, Via Philippines	E ASIA • 250 kW
†VOA, Via Portugal	(J) • EUROPE • 250 kW
15160 AUSTRALIA †RADIO AUSTRALIA, Shepparton	(D) • PACIFIC • 100 kW
BULGARIA †RADIO SOFIA, Sofia	(D) • EUROPE • 250 kW (J) • EUROPE • 250 kW
HUNGARY †RADIO BUDAPEST, Jászberény	S AMERICA • 250 kW M • S AMERICA • 250 kW (J) • EUROPE • 250 kW (J) • M-Sa • EUROPE • 250 kW (J) Su • EUROPE • 250 kW
RUSSIA †R MOSCOW INTL, Nikolayevsk 'Amure	(D) • E ASIA • 500 kW
(con'd) †VOICE OF RUSSIA, Nikolayevsk 'Amure	(D) • E ASIA • 500 kW
	0 1 2 3 4 5 6 7 8 9 10 11 12 13 14 15 16 17 18 19 20 21 22 23 24

SUMMER ONLY (J)   WINTER ONLY (D)   JAMMING / OR ∧   EARLIEST HEARD ◁   LATEST HEARD ▷   NEW OR CHANGED FOR 1993 †

FREQUENCY   COUNTRY, STATION, LOCATION

TARGET • NETWORK • POWER (kW)   World Time

0 1 2 3 4 5 6 7 8 9 10 11 12 13 14 15 16 17 18 19 20 21 22 23 24

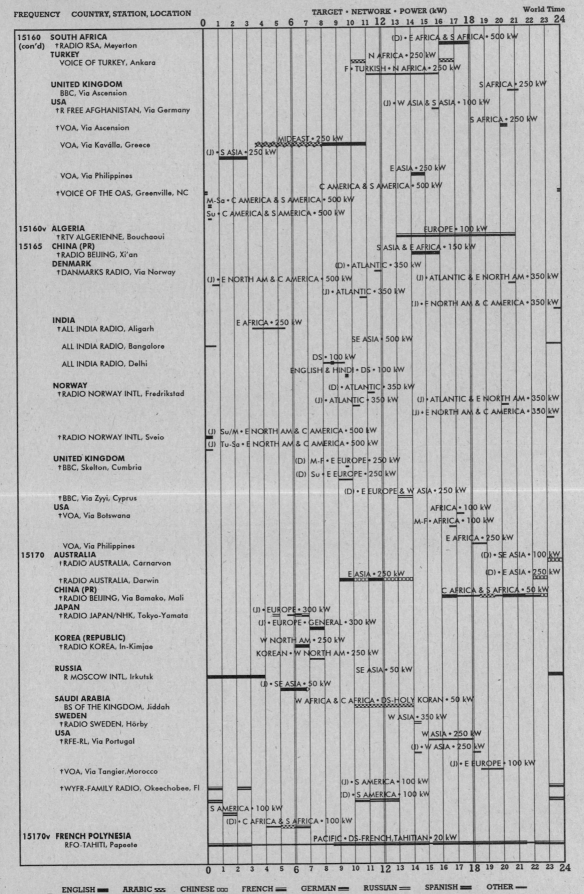

15160 (con'd)	SOUTH AFRICA †RADIO RSA, Meyerton	(D) • E AFRICA & S AFRICA • 500 kW
	TURKEY VOICE OF TURKEY, Ankara	N AFRICA • 250 kW / F • TURKISH • N AFRICA • 250 kW
	UNITED KINGDOM BBC, Via Ascension	S AFRICA • 250 kW
	USA †R FREE AFGHANISTAN, Via Germany	(J) • W ASIA & S ASIA • 100 kW
	†VOA, Via Ascension	S AFRICA • 250 kW
	VOA, Via Kaválla, Greece	MIDEAST • 250 kW / (J) • S ASIA • 250 kW
	VOA, Via Philippines	E ASIA • 250 kW
	†VOICE OF THE OAS, Greenville, NC	C AMERICA & S AMERICA • 500 kW / M-Sa • C AMERICA & S AMERICA • 500 kW / Su • C AMERICA & S AMERICA • 500 kW
15160v	ALGERIA †RTV ALGERIENNE, Bouchaoui	EUROPE • 100 kW
15165	CHINA (PR) †RADIO BEIJING, Xi'an	S ASIA & E AFRICA • 150 kW
	DENMARK †DANMARKS RADIO, Via Norway	(D) • ATLANTIC • 350 kW / (J) • E NORTH AM & C AMERICA • 500 kW / (J) • ATLANTIC, E NORTH AM • 350 kW / (J) • ATLANTIC • 350 kW / (J) • E NORTH AM & C AMERICA • 350 kW
	INDIA †ALL INDIA RADIO, Aligarh	E AFRICA • 250 kW
	ALL INDIA RADIO, Bangalore	SE ASIA • 500 kW
	ALL INDIA RADIO, Delhi	DS • 100 kW / ENGLISH & HINDI • DS • 100 kW
	NORWAY †RADIO NORWAY INTL, Fredrikstad	(D) • ATLANTIC • 350 kW / (J) • ATLANTIC • 350 kW / (J) • ATLANTIC & E NORTH AM • 350 kW / (J) • E NORTH AM & C AMERICA • 350 kW
	†RADIO NORWAY INTL, Sveio	(J) Su/M • E NORTH AM & C AMERICA • 500 kW / (J) Tu-Sa • E NORTH AM & C AMERICA • 500 kW
	UNITED KINGDOM †BBC, Skelton, Cumbria	(D) M-F • E EUROPE • 250 kW / (D) Su • E EUROPE • 250 kW
	†BBC, Via Zyyi, Cyprus	(D) • E EUROPE & W ASIA • 250 kW
	USA †VOA, Via Botswana	AFRICA • 100 kW / M-F • AFRICA • 100 kW / E AFRICA • 250 kW
	VOA, Via Philippines	
15170	AUSTRALIA †RADIO AUSTRALIA, Carnarvon	(D) • SE ASIA • 100 kW / (D) • E ASIA • 250 kW
	†RADIO AUSTRALIA, Darwin	E ASIA • 250 kW
	CHINA (PR) †RADIO BEIJING, Via Bamako, Mali	C AFRICA & S AFRICA • 50 kW
	JAPAN †RADIO JAPAN/NHK, Tokyo-Yamata	(J) • EUROPE • 300 kW / (J) • EUROPE • GENERAL • 300 kW
	KOREA (REPUBLIC) †RADIO KOREA, In-Kimjae	W NORTH AM • 250 kW / KOREAN • W NORTH AM • 250 kW
	RUSSIA R MOSCOW INTL, Irkutsk	SE ASIA • 50 kW / (J) • SE ASIA • 50 kW
	SAUDI ARABIA BS OF THE KINGDOM, Jiddah	W AFRICA & C AFRICA • DS-HOLY KORAN • 50 kW
	SWEDEN †RADIO SWEDEN, Hörby	W ASIA • 350 kW
	USA †RFE-RL, Via Portugal	W ASIA • 250 kW / (J) • W ASIA • 250 kW
	†VOA, Via Tangier, Morocco	(J) • E EUROPE • 100 kW
	†WYFR-FAMILY RADIO, Okeechobee, Fl	(J) • S AMERICA • 100 kW / (D) • S AMERICA • 100 kW / S AMERICA • 100 kW / (D) • C AFRICA & S AFRICA • 100 kW
15170v	FRENCH POLYNESIA RFO-TAHITI, Papeete	PACIFIC • DS-FRENCH, TAHITIAN • 20 kW

0 1 2 3 4 5 6 7 8 9 10 11 12 13 14 15 16 17 18 19 20 21 22 23 24

ENGLISH ▬▬   ARABIC ⋙   CHINESE □□□   FRENCH ▭▭   GERMAN ▬▬   RUSSIAN ══   SPANISH ▬▬   OTHER ▬

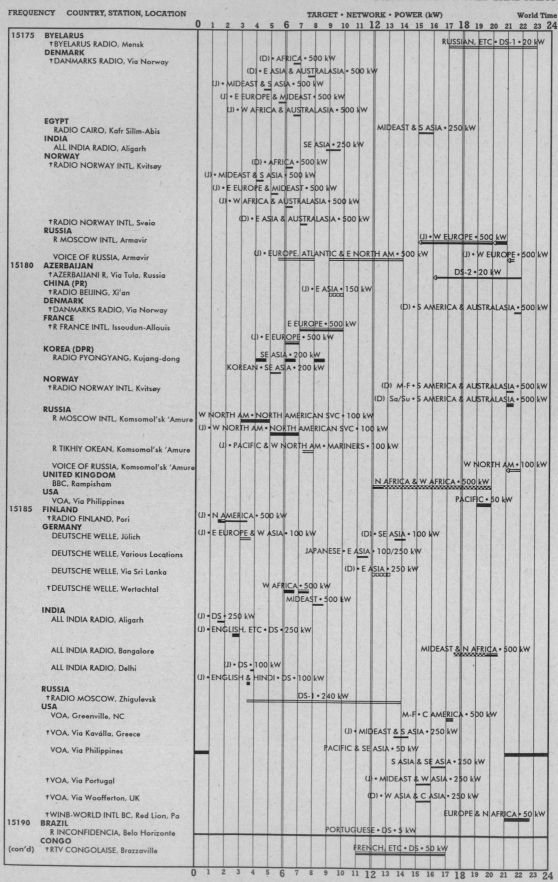

FREQUENCY   COUNTRY, STATION, LOCATION

TARGET • NETWORK • POWER (kW)   World Time

	Station	Target/Network/Power
15175	BYELARUS	
	†BYELARUS RADIO, Mensk	RUSSIAN, ETC • DS-1 • 20 kW
	DENMARK	
	†DANMARKS RADIO, Via Norway	(D) • AFRICA • 500 kW
		(D) • E ASIA & AUSTRALASIA • 500 kW
		(J) • MIDEAST & S ASIA • 500 kW
		(J) • E EUROPE & MIDEAST • 500 kW
		(J) • W AFRICA & AUSTRALASIA • 500 kW
	EGYPT	
	RADIO CAIRO, Kafr Silim-Abis	MIDEAST & S ASIA • 250 kW
	INDIA	
	ALL INDIA RADIO, Aligarh	SE ASIA • 250 kW
	NORWAY	
	†RADIO NORWAY INTL, Kvitsøy	(D) • AFRICA • 500 kW
		(J) • MIDEAST & S ASIA • 500 kW
		(J) • E EUROPE & MIDEAST • 500 kW
		(J) • W AFRICA & AUSTRALASIA • 500 kW
	†RADIO NORWAY INTL, Sveio	(D) • E ASIA & AUSTRALASIA • 500 kW
	RUSSIA	
	R MOSCOW INTL, Armavir	(J) • W EUROPE • 500 kW
	VOICE OF RUSSIA, Armavir	(J) • EUROPE, ATLANTIC & E NORTH AM • 500 kW (J) • W EUROPE • 500 kW
15180	AZERBAIJAN	
	†AZERBAIJANI R, Via Tula, Russia	DS-2 • 20 kW
	CHINA (PR)	
	†RADIO BEIJING, Xi'an	(J) • E ASIA • 150 kW
	DENMARK	
	†DANMARKS RADIO, Via Norway	(D) • S AMERICA & AUSTRALASIA • 500 kW
	FRANCE	
	†R FRANCE INTL, Issoudun-Allouis	E EUROPE • 500 kW
		(J) • E EUROPE • 500 kW
	KOREA (DPR)	
	RADIO PYONGYANG, Kujang-dong	SE ASIA • 200 kW
		KOREAN • SE ASIA • 200 kW
	NORWAY	
	†RADIO NORWAY INTL, Kvitsøy	(D) M-F • S AMERICA & AUSTRALASIA • 500 kW
		(D) Sa/Su • S AMERICA & AUSTRALASIA • 500 kW
	RUSSIA	
	R MOSCOW INTL, Komsomol'sk 'Amure	W NORTH AM • NORTH AMERICAN SVC • 100 kW
		(J) • W NORTH AM • NORTH AMERICAN SVC • 100 kW
	R TIKHIY OKEAN, Komsomol'sk 'Amure	(J) • PACIFIC & W NORTH AM • MARINERS • 100 kW
	VOICE OF RUSSIA, Komsomol'sk 'Amure	W NORTH AM • 100 kW
	UNITED KINGDOM	
	BBC, Rampisham	N AFRICA & W AFRICA • 500 kW
	USA	
	VOA, Via Philippines	PACIFIC • 50 kW
15185	FINLAND	
	†RADIO FINLAND, Pori	(J) • N AMERICA • 500 kW
	GERMANY	
	DEUTSCHE WELLE, Jülich	(J) • E EUROPE & W ASIA • 100 kW (D) • SE ASIA • 100 kW
	DEUTSCHE WELLE, Various Locations	JAPANESE • E ASIA • 100/250 kW
	DEUTSCHE WELLE, Via Sri Lanka	(D) • E ASIA • 250 kW
	†DEUTSCHE WELLE, Wertachtal	W AFRICA • 500 kW
		MIDEAST • 500 kW
	INDIA	
	ALL INDIA RADIO, Aligarh	(J) • DS • 250 kW
		(J) • ENGLISH, ETC • DS • 250 kW
	ALL INDIA RADIO, Bangalore	MIDEAST & N AFRICA • 500 kW
	ALL INDIA RADIO, Delhi	(J) • DS • 100 kW
		(J) • ENGLISH & HINDI • DS • 100 kW
	RUSSIA	
	†RADIO MOSCOW, Zhigulevsk	DS-1 • 240 kW
	USA	
	VOA, Greenville, NC	M-F • C AMERICA • 500 kW
	†VOA, Via Kaválla, Greece	(J) • MIDEAST & S ASIA • 250 kW
	VOA, Via Philippines	PACIFIC & SE ASIA • 50 kW
		S ASIA & SE ASIA • 250 kW
	†VOA, Via Portugal	(J) • MIDEAST & W ASIA • 250 kW
	†VOA, Via Woofferton, UK	(D) • W ASIA & C ASIA • 250 kW
	†WINB-WORLD INTL BC, Red Lion, Pa	EUROPE & N AFRICA • 50 kW
15190	BRAZIL	
	R INCONFIDENCIA, Belo Horizonte	PORTUGUESE • DS • 5 kW
	CONGO	
(con'd)	†RTV CONGOLAISE, Brazzaville	FRENCH, ETC • DS • 50 kW

FREQUENCY   COUNTRY, STATION, LOCATION

TARGET • NETWORK • POWER (kW)

World Time

0 1 2 3 4 5 6 7 8 9 10 11 12 13 14 15 16 17 18 19 20 21 22 23 24

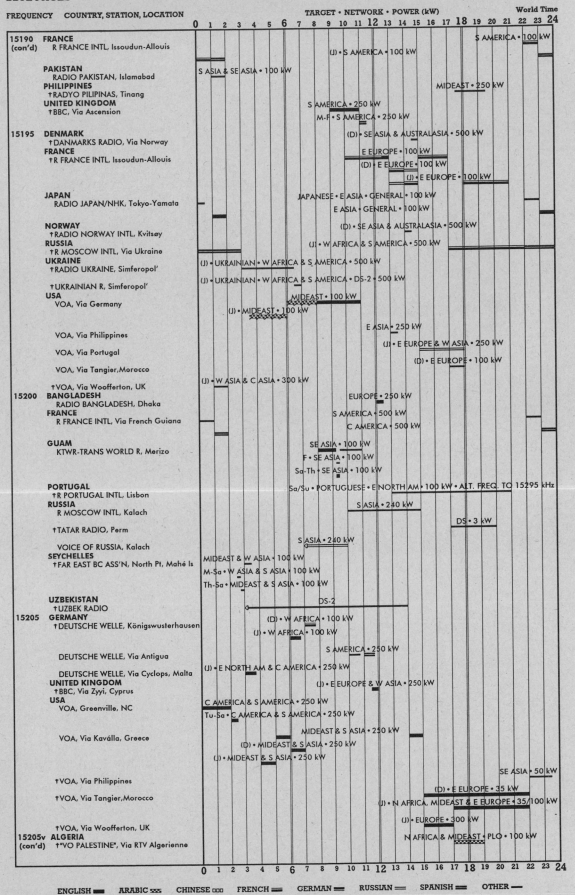

15190 **FRANCE**
(con'd)   R FRANCE INTL, Issoudun-Allouis
          S AMERICA • 100 kW

          (J) • S AMERICA • 100 kW

PAKISTAN
          RADIO PAKISTAN, Islamabad
          S ASIA & SE ASIA • 100 kW
PHILIPPINES
          †RADYO PILIPINAS, Tinang
          MIDEAST • 250 kW
UNITED KINGDOM
          †BBC, Via Ascension
          S AMERICA • 250 kW
          M-F • S AMERICA • 250 kW

15195 **DENMARK**
          †DANMARKS RADIO, Via Norway
          (D) • SE ASIA & AUSTRALASIA • 500 kW
FRANCE
          †R FRANCE INTL, Issoudun-Allouis
          E EUROPE • 100 kW
          (D) • E EUROPE • 100 kW
          (J) • E EUROPE • 100 kW

JAPAN
          RADIO JAPAN/NHK, Tokyo-Yamata
          JAPANESE • E ASIA • GENERAL • 100 kW
          E ASIA • GENERAL • 100 kW

NORWAY
          †RADIO NORWAY INTL, Kvitsøy
          (D) • SE ASIA & AUSTRALASIA • 500 kW
RUSSIA
          †R MOSCOW INTL, Via Ukraine
          (J) • W AFRICA & S AMERICA • 500 kW
UKRAINE
          †RADIO UKRAINE, Simferopol'
          (J) • UKRAINIAN • W AFRICA & S AMERICA • 500 kW

          †UKRAINIAN R, Simferopol'
          (J) • UKRAINIAN • W AFRICA & S AMERICA • DS-2 • 500 kW
USA
          VOA, Via Germany
          MIDEAST • 100 kW
          (J) • MIDEAST • 100 kW

          VOA, Via Philippines
          E ASIA • 250 kW

          VOA, Via Portugal
          (J) • E EUROPE & W ASIA • 250 kW

          VOA, Via Tangier, Morocco
          (D) • E EUROPE • 100 kW

          †VOA, Via Woofferton, UK
          (J) • W ASIA & C ASIA • 300 kW
15200 **BANGLADESH**
          RADIO BANGLADESH, Dhaka
          EUROPE • 250 kW
FRANCE
          R FRANCE INTL, Via French Guiana
          S AMERICA • 500 kW
          C AMERICA • 500 kW

GUAM
          KTWR-TRANS WORLD R, Merizo
          SE ASIA • 100 kW
          F • SE ASIA • 100 kW
          Sa-Th • SE ASIA • 100 kW

PORTUGAL
          †R PORTUGAL INTL, Lisbon
          Sa/Su • PORTUGUESE • E NORTH AM • 100 kW • ALT. FREQ. TO 15295 kHz
RUSSIA
          R MOSCOW INTL, Kalach
          S ASIA • 240 kW

          †TATAR RADIO, Perm
          DS • 3 kW

          VOICE OF RUSSIA, Kalach
          S ASIA • 240 kW
SEYCHELLES
          †FAR EAST BC ASS'N, North Pt, Mahé Is
          MIDEAST & W ASIA • 100 kW
          M-Sa • W ASIA & S ASIA • 100 kW
          Th-Sa • MIDEAST & S ASIA • 100 kW

UZBEKISTAN
          †UZBEK RADIO
          DS-2
15205 **GERMANY**
          †DEUTSCHE WELLE, Königswusterhausen
          (D) • W AFRICA • 100 kW
          (J) • W AFRICA • 100 kW

          DEUTSCHE WELLE, Via Antigua
          S AMERICA • 250 kW

          DEUTSCHE WELLE, Via Cyclops, Malta
          (J) • E NORTH AM & C AMERICA • 250 kW
UNITED KINGDOM
          †BBC, Via Zyyi, Cyprus
          (J) • E EUROPE & W ASIA • 250 kW
USA
          VOA, Greenville, NC
          C AMERICA & S AMERICA • 250 kW
          Tu-Sa • C AMERICA & S AMERICA • 250 kW

          VOA, Via Kaválla, Greece
          MIDEAST & S ASIA • 250 kW
          (D) • MIDEAST & S ASIA • 250 kW
          (J) • MIDEAST & S ASIA • 250 kW

          †VOA, Via Philippines
          SE ASIA • 50 kW

          †VOA, Via Tangier, Morocco
          (D) • E EUROPE • 35 kW
          (J) • N AFRICA, MIDEAST & E EUROPE • 35/100 kW

          †VOA, Via Woofferton, UK
          (J) • EUROPE • 300 kW
15205v **ALGERIA**
(con'd)   †"VO PALESTINE", Via RTV Algerienne
          N AFRICA & MIDEAST • PLO • 100 kW

0 1 2 3 4 5 6 7 8 9 10 11 12 13 14 15 16 17 18 19 20 21 22 23 24

ENGLISH ▬   ARABIC ▨▨▨   CHINESE □□□   FRENCH ▬▬   GERMAN ▬▬   RUSSIAN ══   SPANISH ══   OTHER ──

FREQUENCY   COUNTRY, STATION, LOCATION   TARGET • NETWORK • POWER (kW)   World Time

0 1 2 3 4 5 6 7 8 9 10 11 12 13 14 15 16 17 18 19 20 21 22 23 24

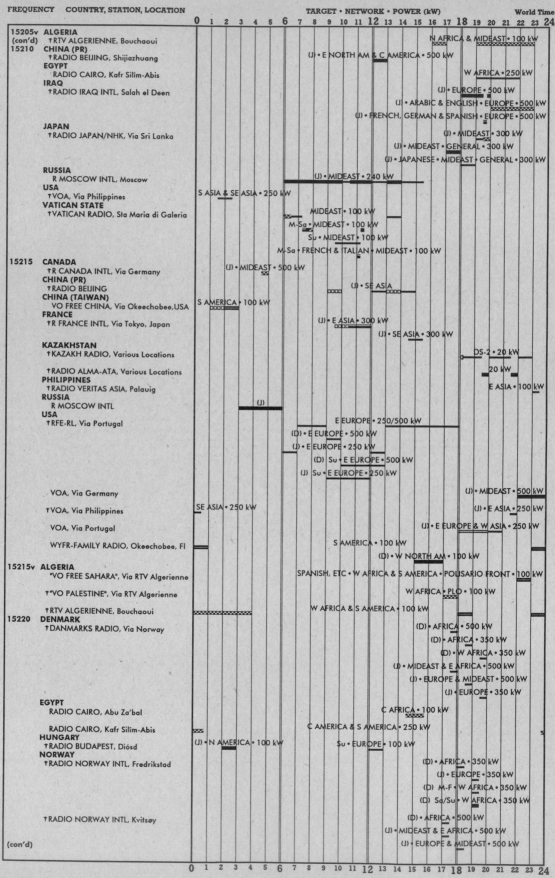

Frequency	Country / Station / Location	Schedule
15205v	**ALGERIA** (con'd) †RTV ALGERIENNE, Bouchaoui	N AFRICA & MIDEAST • 100 kW
15210	**CHINA (PR)** †RADIO BEIJING, Shijiazhuang	(J) • E NORTH AM & C AMERICA • 500 kW
	EGYPT RADIO CAIRO, Kafr Silim-Abis	W AFRICA • 250 kW
	IRAQ †RADIO IRAQ INTL, Salah el Deen	(J) • EUROPE • 500 kW
		(J) • ARABIC & ENGLISH • EUROPE • 500 kW
		(J) • FRENCH, GERMAN & SPANISH • EUROPE • 500 kW
	JAPAN †RADIO JAPAN/NHK, Via Sri Lanka	(J) • MIDEAST • 300 kW
		(J) • MIDEAST • GENERAL • 300 kW
		(J) • JAPANESE • MIDEAST • GENERAL • 300 kW
	RUSSIA R MOSCOW INTL, Moscow	(J) • MIDEAST • 240 kW
	USA †VOA, Via Philippines	S ASIA & SE ASIA • 250 kW
	VATICAN STATE †VATICAN RADIO, Sta Maria di Galeria	MIDEAST • 100 kW
		M-Sa • MIDEAST • 100 kW
		Su • MIDEAST • 100 kW
		M-Sa • FRENCH & ITALIAN • MIDEAST • 100 kW
15215	**CANADA** †R CANADA INTL, Via Germany	(J) • MIDEAST • 500 kW
	CHINA (PR) †RADIO BEIJING	(J) • SE ASIA
	CHINA (TAIWAN) VO FREE CHINA, Via Okeechobee, USA	S AMERICA • 100 kW
	FRANCE †R FRANCE INTL, Via Tokyo, Japan	(J) • E ASIA • 300 kW
		(J) • SE ASIA • 300 kW
	KAZAKHSTAN †KAZAKH RADIO, Various Locations	DS-2 • 20 kW
	†RADIO ALMA-ATA, Various Locations	20 kW
	PHILIPPINES †RADIO VERITAS ASIA, Palauig	E ASIA • 100 kW
	RUSSIA R MOSCOW INTL	(J)
	USA †RFE-RL, Via Portugal	E EUROPE • 250/500 kW
		(D) • E EUROPE • 500 kW
		(J) • E EUROPE • 250 kW
		(D) Su • E EUROPE • 500 kW
		(J) Su • E EUROPE • 250 kW
	VOA, Via Germany	(J) • MIDEAST • 500 kW
	†VOA, Via Philippines	SE ASIA • 250 kW / (J) • E ASIA • 250 kW
	VOA, Via Portugal	(J) • E EUROPE & W ASIA • 250 kW
	WYFR-FAMILY RADIO, Okeechobee, Fl	S AMERICA • 100 kW
		(D) • W NORTH AM • 100 kW
15215v	**ALGERIA** "VO FREE SAHARA", Via RTV Algerienne	SPANISH, ETC • W AFRICA & S AMERICA • POLISARIO FRONT • 100 kW
	†"VO PALESTINE", Via RTV Algerienne	W AFRICA • PLO • 100 kW
	†RTV ALGERIENNE, Bouchaoui	W AFRICA & S AMERICA • 100 kW
15220	**DENMARK** †DANMARKS RADIO, Via Norway	(D) • AFRICA • 500 kW
		(D) • AFRICA • 350 kW
		(D) • W AFRICA • 350 kW
		(J) • MIDEAST & E AFRICA • 500 kW
		(J) • EUROPE & MIDEAST • 500 kW
		(J) • EUROPE • 350 kW
	EGYPT RADIO CAIRO, Abu Za'bal	C AFRICA • 100 kW
	RADIO CAIRO, Kafr Silim-Abis	C AMERICA & S AMERICA • 250 kW
	HUNGARY †RADIO BUDAPEST, Diósd	(J) • N AMERICA • 100 kW / Su • EUROPE • 100 kW
	NORWAY †RADIO NORWAY INTL, Fredrikstad	(D) • AFRICA • 350 kW
		(J) • EUROPE • 350 kW
		(D) M-F • W AFRICA • 350 kW
		(D) Sa/Su • W AFRICA • 350 kW
	†RADIO NORWAY INTL, Kvitsøy	(D) • AFRICA • 500 kW
		(J) • MIDEAST & E AFRICA • 500 kW
	(con'd)	(J) • EUROPE & MIDEAST • 500 kW

0 1 2 3 4 5 6 7 8 9 10 11 12 13 14 15 16 17 18 19 20 21 22 23 24

SUMMER ONLY (J)   WINTER ONLY (D)   JAMMING / OR ∧   EARLIEST HEARD ◁   LATEST HEARD ▷   NEW OR CHANGED FOR 1993 †

FREQUENCY   COUNTRY, STATION, LOCATION   TARGET • NETWORK • POWER (kW)   World Time

```
                                                    0  1  2  3  4  5  6  7  8  9  10 11 12 13 14 15 16 17 18 19 20 21 22 23 24
```

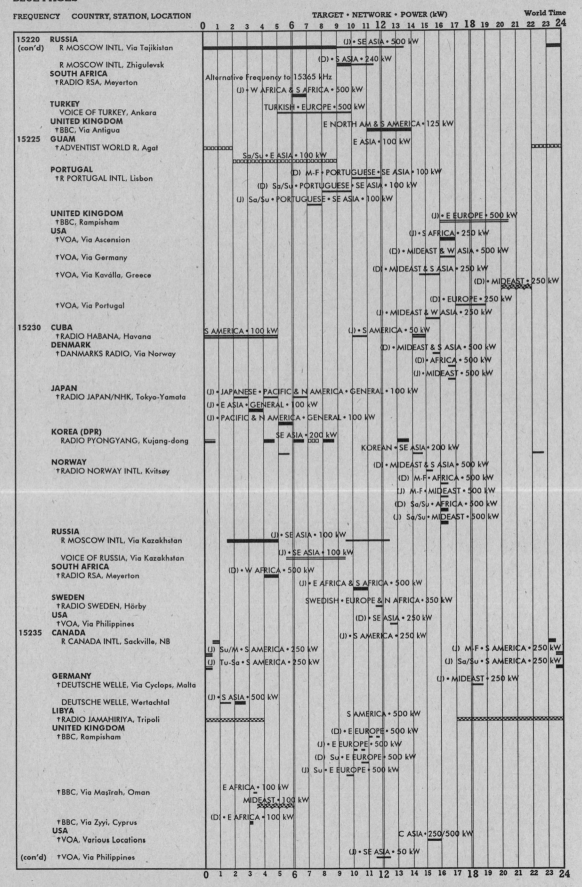

15220 **RUSSIA**
(con'd) R MOSCOW INTL, Via Tajikistan — (J) • SE ASIA • 500 kW

  R MOSCOW INTL, Zhigulevsk — (D) • S ASIA • 240 kW
SOUTH AFRICA
  †RADIO RSA, Meyerton — Alternative Frequency to 15365 kHz
  (J) • W AFRICA & S AFRICA • 500 kW

TURKEY
  VOICE OF TURKEY, Ankara — TURKISH • EUROPE • 500 kW
UNITED KINGDOM
  †BBC, Via Antigua — E NORTH AM & S AMERICA • 125 kW
15225 **GUAM**
  †ADVENTIST WORLD R, Agat — E ASIA • 100 kW
    Sa/Su • E ASIA • 100 kW

PORTUGAL
  †R PORTUGAL INTL, Lisbon — (D) M-F • PORTUGUESE • SE ASIA • 100 kW
    (D) Sa/Su • PORTUGUESE • SE ASIA • 100 kW
    (J) Sa/Su • PORTUGUESE • SE ASIA • 100 kW

UNITED KINGDOM
  †BBC, Rampisham — (J) • E EUROPE • 500 kW
USA
  †VOA, Via Ascension — (J) • S AFRICA • 250 kW
  †VOA, Via Germany — (D) • MIDEAST & W ASIA • 500 kW
  †VOA, Via Kaválla, Greece — (D) • MIDEAST & S ASIA • 250 kW
    (D) • MIDEAST • 250 kW
    (D) • EUROPE • 250 kW
  †VOA, Via Portugal — (J) • MIDEAST & W ASIA • 250 kW
15230 **CUBA**
  †RADIO HABANA, Havana — S AMERICA • 100 kW   (J) • S AMERICA • 50 kW
DENMARK
  †DANMARKS RADIO, Via Norway — (D) • MIDEAST & S ASIA • 500 kW
    (D) • AFRICA • 500 kW
    (J) • MIDEAST • 500 kW
JAPAN
  †RADIO JAPAN/NHK, Tokyo-Yamata — (J) • JAPANESE • PACIFIC & N AMERICA • GENERAL • 100 kW
    (J) • E ASIA • GENERAL • 100 kW
    (J) • PACIFIC & N AMERICA • GENERAL • 100 kW
KOREA (DPR)
  RADIO PYONGYANG, Kujang-dong — SE ASIA • 200 kW
    KOREAN • SE ASIA • 200 kW
NORWAY
  †RADIO NORWAY INTL, Kvitsøy — (D) • MIDEAST & S ASIA • 500 kW
    (D) M-F • AFRICA • 500 kW
    (J) M-F • MIDEAST • 500 kW
    (D) Sa/Su • AFRICA • 500 kW
    (J) Sa/Su • MIDEAST • 500 kW

RUSSIA
  R MOSCOW INTL, Via Kazakhstan — (J) • SE ASIA • 100 kW
  VOICE OF RUSSIA, Via Kazakhstan — (J) • SE ASIA • 100 kW
SOUTH AFRICA
  †RADIO RSA, Meyerton — (D) • W AFRICA • 500 kW
    (J) • E AFRICA & S AFRICA • 500 kW
SWEDEN
  †RADIO SWEDEN, Hörby — SWEDISH • EUROPE & N AFRICA • 350 kW
USA
  †VOA, Via Philippines — (D) • SE ASIA • 250 kW
15235 **CANADA**
  R CANADA INTL, Sackville, NB — (J) • S AMERICA • 250 kW
    (J) Su/M • S AMERICA • 250 kW   (J) M-F • S AMERICA • 250 kW
    (J) Tu-Sa • S AMERICA • 250 kW   (J) Sa/Su • S AMERICA • 250 kW
GERMANY
  †DEUTSCHE WELLE, Via Cyclops, Malta — (J) • MIDEAST • 250 kW
  DEUTSCHE WELLE, Wertachtal — (J) • S ASIA • 500 kW
LIBYA
  †RADIO JAMAHIRIYA, Tripoli — S AMERICA • 500 kW
UNITED KINGDOM
  †BBC, Rampisham — (D) • E EUROPE • 500 kW
    (J) • E EUROPE • 500 kW
    (D) Su • E EUROPE • 500 kW
    (J) Su • E EUROPE • 500 kW
  †BBC, Via Maşīrah, Oman — E AFRICA • 100 kW
    MIDEAST • 100 kW
  †BBC, Via Zyyi, Cyprus — (D) • E AFRICA • 100 kW
USA
  †VOA, Various Locations — C ASIA • 250/500 kW
(con'd) †VOA, Via Philippines — (J) • SE ASIA • 50 kW

```
                                                    0  1  2  3  4  5  6  7  8  9  10 11 12 13 14 15 16 17 18 19 20 21 22 23 24
```

ENGLISH ▬▬   ARABIC ⨯⨯⨯   CHINESE □□□   FRENCH ══   GERMAN ▬▬   RUSSIAN ══   SPANISH ▬▬   OTHER ▬▬

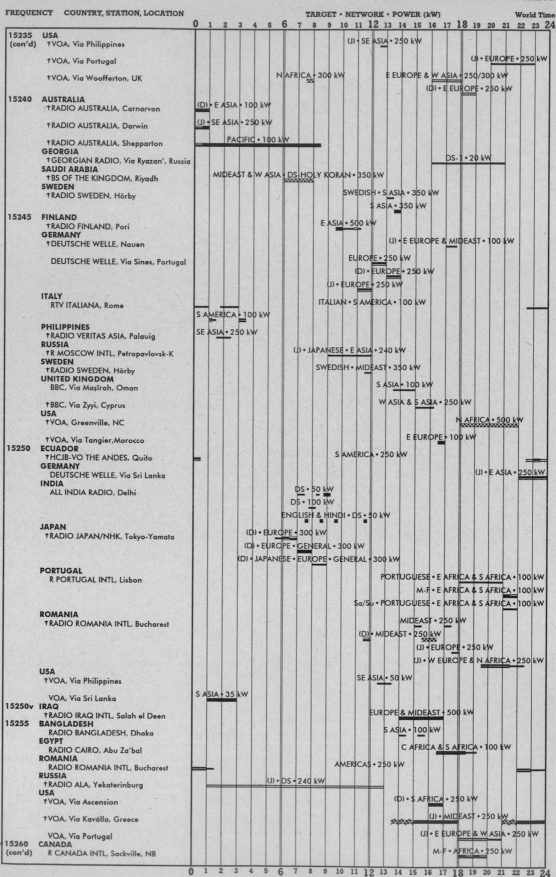

FREQUENCY   COUNTRY, STATION, LOCATION

TARGET • NETWORK • POWER (kW)   World Time

15235 (con'd)	USA	
	†VOA, Via Philippines	(J) • SE ASIA • 250 kW
	†VOA, Via Portugal	(J) • EUROPE • 250 kW
	†VOA, Via Woofferton, UK	N AFRICA • 300 kW E EUROPE & W ASIA • 250/300 kW
		(D) • E EUROPE • 250 kW
15240	AUSTRALIA	
	†RADIO AUSTRALIA, Carnarvon	(D) • E ASIA • 100 kW
	†RADIO AUSTRALIA, Darwin	(J) • SE ASIA • 250 kW
	†RADIO AUSTRALIA, Shepparton	PACIFIC • 100 kW
	GEORGIA	
	†GEORGIAN RADIO, Via Ryazan', Russia	DS-1 • 20 kW
	SAUDI ARABIA	
	†BS OF THE KINGDOM, Riyadh	MIDEAST & W ASIA • DS-HOLY KORAN • 350 kW
	SWEDEN	
	†RADIO SWEDEN, Hörby	SWEDISH • S ASIA • 350 kW
		S ASIA • 350 kW
15245	FINLAND	
	†RADIO FINLAND, Pori	E ASIA • 500 kW
	GERMANY	
	†DEUTSCHE WELLE, Nauen	(J) • E EUROPE & MIDEAST • 100 kW
	DEUTSCHE WELLE, Via Sines, Portugal	EUROPE • 250 kW
		(D) • EUROPE • 250 kW
		(J) • EUROPE • 250 kW
	ITALY	
	RTV ITALIANA, Rome	ITALIAN • S AMERICA • 100 kW
		S AMERICA • 100 kW
	PHILIPPINES	
	†RADIO VERITAS ASIA, Palauig	SE ASIA • 250 kW
	RUSSIA	
	†R MOSCOW INTL, Petropavlovsk-K	(J) • JAPANESE • E ASIA • 240 kW
	SWEDEN	
	†RADIO SWEDEN, Hörby	SWEDISH • MIDEAST • 350 kW
	UNITED KINGDOM	
	BBC, Via Maşīrah, Oman	S ASIA • 100 kW
	†BBC, Via Zyyi, Cyprus	W ASIA & S ASIA • 250 kW
	USA	
	†VOA, Greenville, NC	N AFRICA • 500 kW
	†VOA, Via Tangier, Morocco	E EUROPE • 100 kW
15250	ECUADOR	
	†HCJB-VO THE ANDES, Quito	S AMERICA • 250 kW
	GERMANY	
	DEUTSCHE WELLE, Via Sri Lanka	(J) • E ASIA • 250 kW
	INDIA	
	ALL INDIA RADIO, Delhi	DS • 50 kW
		DS • 100 kW
		ENGLISH & HINDI • DS • 50 kW
	JAPAN	
	†RADIO JAPAN/NHK, Tokyo-Yamata	(D) • EUROPE • 300 kW
		(D) • EUROPE • GENERAL • 300 kW
		(D) • JAPANESE • EUROPE • GENERAL • 300 kW
	PORTUGAL	
	R PORTUGAL INTL, Lisbon	PORTUGUESE • E AFRICA & S AFRICA • 100 kW
		M-F • E AFRICA & S AFRICA • 100 kW
		Sa/Su • PORTUGUESE • E AFRICA & S AFRICA • 100 kW
	ROMANIA	
	†RADIO ROMANIA INTL, Bucharest	MIDEAST • 250 kW
		(D) • MIDEAST • 250 kW
		(J) • EUROPE • 250 kW
		(J) • W EUROPE & N AFRICA • 250 kW
	USA	
	†VOA, Via Philippines	SE ASIA • 50 kW
	VOA, Via Sri Lanka	S ASIA • 35 kW
15250v	IRAQ	
	†RADIO IRAQ INTL, Salah el Deen	EUROPE & MIDEAST • 500 kW
15255	BANGLADESH	
	RADIO BANGLADESH, Dhaka	S ASIA • 100 kW
	EGYPT	
	RADIO CAIRO, Abu Za'bal	C AFRICA & S AFRICA • 100 kW
	ROMANIA	
	RADIO ROMANIA INTL, Bucharest	AMERICAS • 250 kW
	RUSSIA	
	†RADIO ALA, Yekaterinburg	(J) • DS • 240 kW
	USA	
	†VOA, Via Ascension	(D) • S AFRICA • 250 kW
	†VOA, Via Kaválla, Greece	(J) • MIDEAST • 250 kW
	VOA, Via Portugal	(J) • E EUROPE & W ASIA • 250 kW
15260 (con'd)	CANADA	
	R CANADA INTL, Sackville, NB	M-F • AFRICA • 250 kW

FREQUENCY   COUNTRY, STATION, LOCATION
TARGET • NETWORK • POWER (kW)
World Time

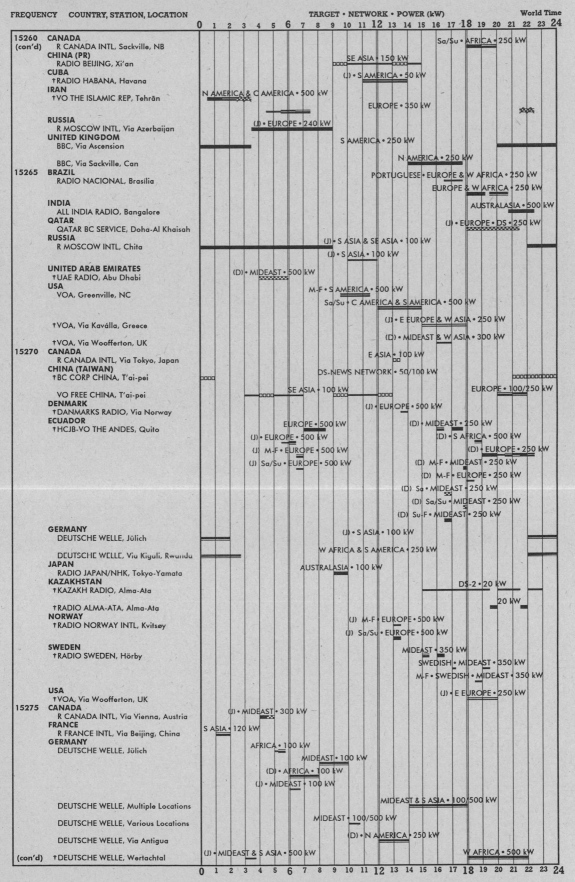

FREQUENCY	COUNTRY, STATION, LOCATION	TARGET • NETWORK • POWER (kW)
15260 (con'd)	CANADA — R CANADA INTL, Sackville, NB	Sa/Su • AFRICA • 250 kW
	CHINA (PR) — RADIO BEIJING, Xi'an	SE ASIA • 150 kW
	CUBA — †RADIO HABANA, Havana	(J) • S AMERICA • 50 kW
	IRAN — †VO THE ISLAMIC REP, Tehrān	N AMERICA & C AMERICA • 500 kW; EUROPE • 350 kW
	RUSSIA — R MOSCOW INTL, Via Azerbaijan	(J) • EUROPE • 240 kW
	UNITED KINGDOM — BBC, Via Ascension	S AMERICA • 250 kW
	BBC, Via Sackville, Can	N AMERICA • 250 kW
15265	BRAZIL — RADIO NACIONAL, Brasilia	PORTUGUESE • EUROPE & W AFRICA • 250 kW; EUROPE & W AFRICA • 250 kW
	INDIA — ALL INDIA RADIO, Bangalore	AUSTRALASIA • 500 kW
	QATAR — QATAR BC SERVICE, Doha-Al Khaisah	(J) • EUROPE • DS • 250 kW
	RUSSIA — R MOSCOW INTL, Chita	(J) • S ASIA & SE ASIA • 100 kW; (J) • S ASIA • 100 kW
	UNITED ARAB EMIRATES — †UAE RADIO, Abu Dhabi	(D) • MIDEAST • 500 kW
	USA — VOA, Greenville, NC	M-F • S AMERICA • 500 kW; Sa/Su • C AMERICA & S AMERICA • 500 kW
	†VOA, Via Kaválla, Greece	(J) • E EUROPE & W ASIA • 250 kW
	†VOA, Via Woofferton, UK	(D) • MIDEAST & W ASIA • 300 kW
15270	CANADA — R CANADA INTL, Via Tokyo, Japan	E ASIA • 100 kW
	CHINA (TAIWAN) — †BC CORP CHINA, T'ai-pei	DS-NEWS NETWORK • 50/100 kW
	VO FREE CHINA, T'ai-pei	SE ASIA • 100 kW; EUROPE • 100/250 kW
	DENMARK — †DANMARKS RADIO, Via Norway	(J) • EUROPE • 500 kW
	ECUADOR — †HCJB-VO THE ANDES, Quito	EUROPE • 500 kW; (D) • MIDEAST • 250 kW; (J) • EUROPE • 500 kW; (D) • S AFRICA • 500 kW; (J) • M-F • EUROPE • 500 kW; (D) • EUROPE • 250 kW; (J) • Sa/Su • EUROPE • 500 kW; (D) • M-F • MIDEAST • 250 kW; (D) • M-F • EUROPE • 250 kW; (D) • Sa • MIDEAST • 250 kW; (D) • Sa/Su • MIDEAST • 250 kW; (D) • Su-F • MIDEAST • 250 kW
	GERMANY — DEUTSCHE WELLE, Jülich	(J) • S ASIA • 100 kW
	DEUTSCHE WELLE, Via Kigali, Rwanda	W AFRICA & S AMERICA • 250 kW
	JAPAN — RADIO JAPAN/NHK, Tokyo-Yamata	AUSTRALASIA • 100 kW
	KAZAKHSTAN — †KAZAKH RADIO, Alma-Ata	DS-2 • 20 kW
	†RADIO ALMA-ATA, Alma-Ata	20 kW
	NORWAY — †RADIO NORWAY INTL, Kvitsøy	(J) • M-F • EUROPE • 500 kW; (J) • Sa/Su • EUROPE • 500 kW
	SWEDEN — †RADIO SWEDEN, Hörby	MIDEAST • 350 kW; SWEDISH • MIDEAST • 350 kW; M-F • SWEDISH • MIDEAST • 350 kW
	USA — †VOA, Via Woofferton, UK	(J) • E EUROPE • 250 kW
15275	CANADA — R CANADA INTL, Via Vienna, Austria	(J) • MIDEAST • 300 kW
	FRANCE — R FRANCE INTL, Via Beijing, China	S ASIA • 120 kW
	GERMANY — DEUTSCHE WELLE, Jülich	AFRICA • 100 kW; MIDEAST • 100 kW; (D) • AFRICA • 100 kW; (J) • MIDEAST • 100 kW
	DEUTSCHE WELLE, Multiple Locations	MIDEAST & S ASIA • 100/500 kW
	DEUTSCHE WELLE, Various Locations	MIDEAST • 100/500 kW
	DEUTSCHE WELLE, Via Antigua	(D) • N AMERICA • 250 kW
(con'd)	†DEUTSCHE WELLE, Wertachtal	(J) • MIDEAST & S ASIA • 500 kW; W AFRICA • 500 kW

ENGLISH ▬   ARABIC ⬚⬚⬚   CHINESE ▫▫▫   FRENCH ═══   GERMAN ▭▭▭   RUSSIAN ══   SPANISH ▬▬   OTHER ━

FREQUENCY   COUNTRY, STATION, LOCATION   TARGET • NETWORK • POWER (kW)   World Time

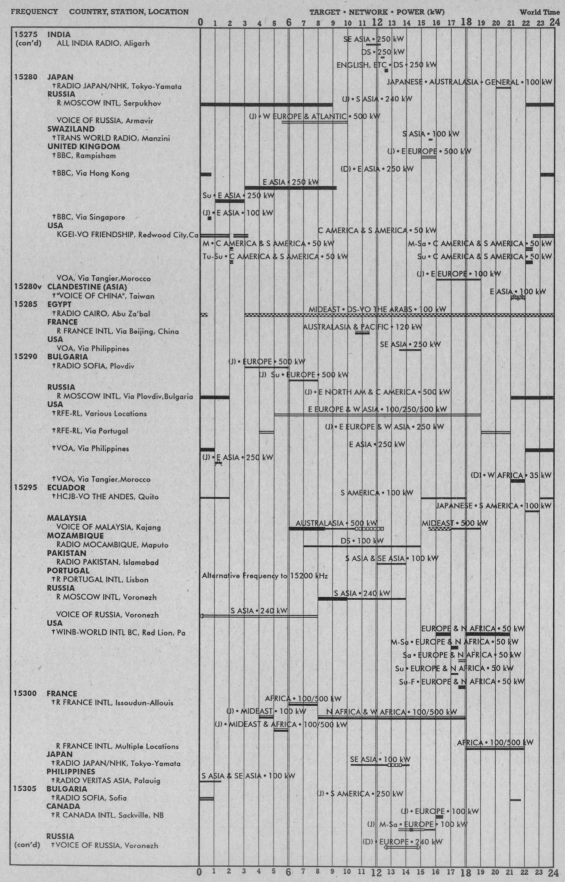

FREQUENCY	COUNTRY, STATION, LOCATION	TARGET • NETWORK • POWER (kW)
15275 (con'd)	**INDIA** ALL INDIA RADIO, Aligarh	SE ASIA • 250 kW / DS • 250 kW / ENGLISH, ETC • DS • 250 kW
15280	**JAPAN** †RADIO JAPAN/NHK, Tokyo-Yamata	JAPANESE • AUSTRALASIA • GENERAL • 100 kW
	RUSSIA R MOSCOW INTL, Serpukhov	(J) • S ASIA • 240 kW
	VOICE OF RUSSIA, Armavir	(J) • W EUROPE & ATLANTIC • 500 kW
	SWAZILAND †TRANS WORLD RADIO, Manzini	S ASIA • 100 kW
	UNITED KINGDOM †BBC, Rampisham	(J) • E EUROPE • 500 kW
	†BBC, Via Hong Kong	(D) • E ASIA • 250 kW
		E ASIA • 250 kW
		Su • E ASIA • 250 kW
	†BBC, Via Singapore	(J) • E ASIA • 100 kW
	USA KGEI-VO FRIENDSHIP, Redwood City, Ca	C AMERICA & S AMERICA • 50 kW
		M • C AMERICA & S AMERICA • 50 kW / M-Sa • C AMERICA & S AMERICA • 50 kW
		Tu-Su • C AMERICA & S AMERICA • 50 kW / Su • C AMERICA & S AMERICA • 50 kW
	VOA, Via Tangier, Morocco	(J) • E EUROPE • 100 kW
15280v	**CLANDESTINE (ASIA)** †"VOICE OF CHINA", Taiwan	E ASIA • 100 kW
15285	**EGYPT** †RADIO CAIRO, Abu Za'bal	MIDEAST • DS-VO THE ARABS • 100 kW
	FRANCE R FRANCE INTL, Via Beijing, China	AUSTRALASIA & PACIFIC • 120 kW
	USA VOA, Via Philippines	SE ASIA • 250 kW
15290	**BULGARIA** †RADIO SOFIA, Plovdiv	(J) • EUROPE • 500 kW
		(J) Su • EUROPE • 500 kW
	RUSSIA R MOSCOW INTL, Via Plovdiv, Bulgaria	(J) • E NORTH AM & C AMERICA • 500 kW
	USA †RFE-RL, Various Locations	E EUROPE & W ASIA • 100/250/500 kW
	†RFE-RL, Via Portugal	(J) • E EUROPE & W ASIA • 250 kW
	†VOA, Via Philippines	E ASIA • 250 kW
		(J) • E ASIA • 250 kW
	†VOA, Via Tangier, Morocco	(D) • W AFRICA • 35 kW
15295	**ECUADOR** †HCJB-VO THE ANDES, Quito	S AMERICA • 100 kW
		JAPANESE • S AMERICA • 100 kW
	MALAYSIA VOICE OF MALAYSIA, Kajang	AUSTRALASIA • 500 kW / MIDEAST • 500 kW
	MOZAMBIQUE RADIO MOCAMBIQUE, Maputo	DS • 100 kW
	PAKISTAN RADIO PAKISTAN, Islamabad	S ASIA & SE ASIA • 100 kW
	PORTUGAL †R PORTUGAL INTL, Lisbon	Alternative Frequency to 15200 kHz
	RUSSIA R MOSCOW INTL, Voronezh	S ASIA • 240 kW
	VOICE OF RUSSIA, Voronezh	S ASIA • 240 kW
	USA †WINB-WORLD INTL BC, Red Lion, Pa	EUROPE & N AFRICA • 50 kW
		M-Sa • EUROPE & N AFRICA • 50 kW
		Sa • EUROPE & N AFRICA • 50 kW
		Su • EUROPE & N AFRICA • 50 kW
		Su-F • EUROPE & N AFRICA • 50 kW
15300	**FRANCE** †R FRANCE INTL, Issoudun-Allouis	AFRICA • 100/500 kW
		(J) • MIDEAST • 100 kW / N AFRICA & W AFRICA • 100/500 kW
		(J) • MIDEAST & AFRICA • 100/500 kW
	R FRANCE INTL, Multiple Locations	AFRICA • 100/500 kW
	JAPAN †RADIO JAPAN/NHK, Tokyo-Yamata	SE ASIA • 100 kW
	PHILIPPINES †RADIO VERITAS ASIA, Palauig	S ASIA & SE ASIA • 100 kW
15305	**BULGARIA** †RADIO SOFIA, Sofia	(J) • S AMERICA • 250 kW
	CANADA †R CANADA INTL, Sackville, NB	(J) • EUROPE • 100 kW
		(J) M-Sa • EUROPE • 100 kW
(con'd)	**RUSSIA** †VOICE OF RUSSIA, Voronezh	(D) • EUROPE • 240 kW

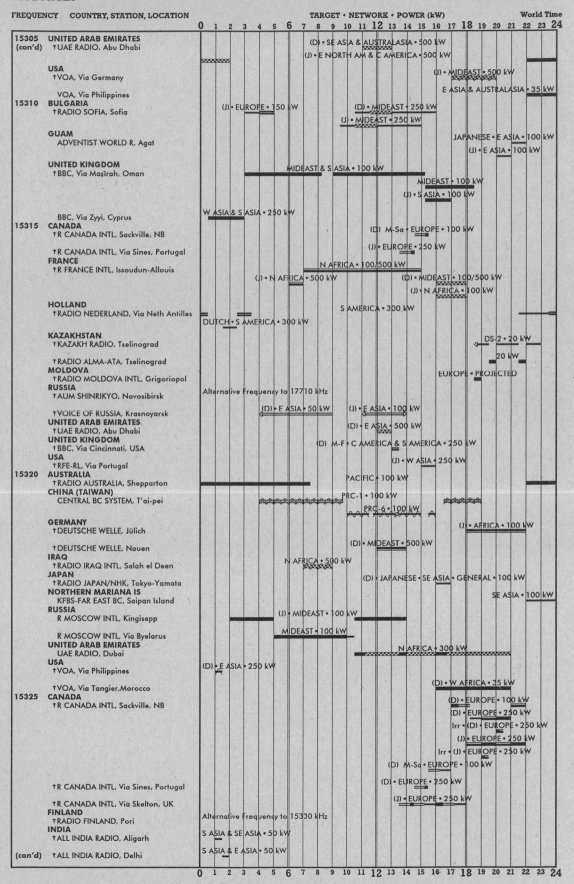

FREQUENCY   COUNTRY, STATION, LOCATION   TARGET • NETWORK • POWER (kW)   World Time

Frequency	Country, Station, Location	Target • Network • Power
15305 (con'd)	UNITED ARAB EMIRATES ↑UAE RADIO, Abu Dhabi	(D) • SE ASIA & AUSTRALASIA • 500 kW / (J) • E NORTH AM & C AMERICA • 500 kW
	USA ↑VOA, Via Germany	(J) • MIDEAST • 500 kW
	VOA, Via Philippines	E ASIA & AUSTRALASIA • 35 kW
15310	BULGARIA ↑RADIO SOFIA, Sofia	(J) • EUROPE • 150 kW / (D) • MIDEAST • 250 kW / (J) • MIDEAST • 250 kW
	GUAM ADVENTIST WORLD R, Agat	JAPANESE • E ASIA • 100 kW / (J) • E ASIA • 100 kW
	UNITED KINGDOM ↑BBC, Via Maṣīrah, Oman	MIDEAST & S ASIA • 100 kW / MIDEAST • 100 kW / (J) • S ASIA • 100 kW
	BBC, Via Zyyi, Cyprus	W ASIA & S ASIA • 250 kW
15315	CANADA ↑R CANADA INTL, Sackville, NB	(D) • M-Sa • EUROPE • 100 kW / (J) • EUROPE • 250 kW
	↑R CANADA INTL, Via Sines, Portugal	
	FRANCE ↑R FRANCE INTL, Issoudun-Allouis	N AFRICA • 100/500 kW / (J) • N AFRICA • 500 kW / (D) • MIDEAST • 100/500 kW / (J) • N AFRICA • 100 kW
	HOLLAND ↑RADIO NEDERLAND, Via Neth Antilles	S AMERICA • 300 kW / DUTCH • S AMERICA • 300 kW
	KAZAKHSTAN ↑KAZAKH RADIO, Tselinograd	DS-2 • 20 kW
	↑RADIO ALMA-ATA, Tselinograd	20 kW
	MOLDOVA ↑RADIO MOLDOVA INTL, Grigoriopol	EUROPE • PROJECTED
	RUSSIA ↑AUM SHINRIKYO, Novosibirsk	Alternative Frequency to 17710 kHz
	↑VOICE OF RUSSIA, Krasnoyarsk	(D) • E ASIA • 50 kW / (J) • E ASIA • 100 kW
	UNITED ARAB EMIRATES ↑UAE RADIO, Abu Dhabi	(D) • E ASIA • 500 kW
	UNITED KINGDOM ↑BBC, Via Cincinnati, USA	(D) • M-F • C AMERICA & S AMERICA • 250 kW
	USA ↑RFE-RL, Via Portugal	(J) • W ASIA • 250 kW
15320	AUSTRALIA ↑RADIO AUSTRALIA, Shepparton	PACIFIC • 100 kW
	CHINA (TAIWAN) CENTRAL BC SYSTEM, T'ai-pei	PRC-1 • 100 kW / PRC-6 • 100 kW
	GERMANY ↑DEUTSCHE WELLE, Jülich	(J) • AFRICA • 100 kW
	↑DEUTSCHE WELLE, Nauen	(D) • MIDEAST • 500 kW
	IRAQ ↑RADIO IRAQ INTL, Salah el Deen	N AFRICA • 500 kW
	JAPAN ↑RADIO JAPAN/NHK, Tokyo-Yamata	(D) • JAPANESE • SE ASIA • GENERAL • 100 kW
	NORTHERN MARIANA IS KFBS-FAR EAST BC, Saipan Island	SE ASIA • 100 kW
	RUSSIA R MOSCOW INTL, Kingisepp	(J) • MIDEAST • 100 kW
	R MOSCOW INTL, Via Byelarus	MIDEAST • 100 kW
	UNITED ARAB EMIRATES UAE RADIO, Dubai	N AFRICA • 300 kW
	USA ↑VOA, Via Philippines	(D) • E ASIA • 250 kW
	↑VOA, Via Tangier, Morocco	(D) • W AFRICA • 35 kW
15325	CANADA ↑R CANADA INTL, Sackville, NB	(D) • EUROPE • 100 kW / (D) • EUROPE • 250 kW / Irr • (D) • EUROPE • 250 kW / (J) • EUROPE • 250 kW / Irr • (J) • EUROPE • 250 kW / (D) • M-Sa • EUROPE • 100 kW
	↑R CANADA INTL, Via Sines, Portugal	(D) • EUROPE • 250 kW
	↑R CANADA INTL, Via Skelton, UK	(J) • EUROPE • 250 kW
	FINLAND ↑RADIO FINLAND, Pori	Alternative Frequency to 15330 kHz
	INDIA ↑ALL INDIA RADIO, Aligarh	S ASIA & SE ASIA • 50 kW
(con'd)	↑ALL INDIA RADIO, Delhi	S ASIA & E ASIA • 50 kW

World Time scale: 0 1 2 3 4 5 6 7 8 9 10 11 12 13 14 15 16 17 18 19 20 21 22 23 24

ENGLISH ▬   ARABIC ⧉   CHINESE ▭▭▭   FRENCH ▬▬   GERMAN ▬ ▬   RUSSIAN ═   SPANISH ▬▬   OTHER ▬

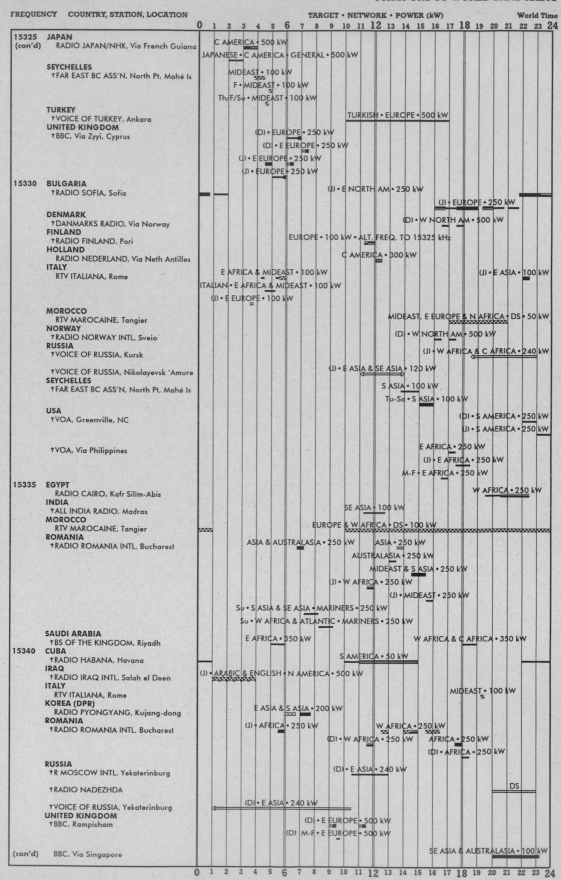

FREQUENCY   COUNTRY, STATION, LOCATION   TARGET • NETWORK • POWER (kW)   World Time

15325
(con'd)   JAPAN
  RADIO JAPAN/NHK, Via French Guiana — C AMERICA • 500 kW; JAPANESE • C AMERICA • GENERAL • 500 kW
SEYCHELLES
  †FAR EAST BC ASS'N, North Pt, Mahé Is — MIDEAST • 100 kW; F • MIDEAST • 100 kW; Th/F/Su • MIDEAST • 100 kW
TURKEY
  †VOICE OF TURKEY, Ankara — TURKISH • EUROPE • 500 kW
UNITED KINGDOM
  †BBC, Via Zyyi, Cyprus — (D) • EUROPE • 250 kW; (D) • E EUROPE • 250 kW; (J) • E EUROPE • 250 kW; (J) • EUROPE • 250 kW

15330   BULGARIA
  †RADIO SOFIA, Sofia — (J) • E NORTH AM • 250 kW; (J) • EUROPE • 250 kW
DENMARK
  †DANMARKS RADIO, Via Norway — (D) • W NORTH AM • 500 kW
FINLAND
  †RADIO FINLAND, Pori — EUROPE • 100 kW • ALT. FREQ. TO 15325 kHz
HOLLAND
  RADIO NEDERLAND, Via Neth Antilles — C AMERICA • 300 kW
ITALY
  RTV ITALIANA, Rome — E AFRICA & MIDEAST • 100 kW; (J) • E ASIA • 100 kW; ITALIAN • E AFRICA & MIDEAST • 100 kW; (J) • E EUROPE • 100 kW
MOROCCO
  RTV MAROCAINE, Tangier — MIDEAST, E EUROPE & N AFRICA • DS • 50 kW
NORWAY
  †RADIO NORWAY INTL, Sveio — (D) • W NORTH AM • 500 kW
RUSSIA
  †VOICE OF RUSSIA, Kursk — (J) • W AFRICA & C AFRICA • 240 kW
  †VOICE OF RUSSIA, Nikolayevsk 'Amure — (J) • E ASIA & SE ASIA • 120 kW
SEYCHELLES
  †FAR EAST BC ASS'N, North Pt, Mahé Is — S ASIA • 100 kW; Tu-Sa • S ASIA • 100 kW
USA
  †VOA, Greenville, NC — (D) • S AMERICA • 250 kW; (J) • S AMERICA • 250 kW
  †VOA, Via Philippines — E AFRICA • 250 kW; (J) • E AFRICA • 250 kW; M-F • E AFRICA • 250 kW

15335   EGYPT
  RADIO CAIRO, Kafr Silim-Abis — W AFRICA • 250 kW
INDIA
  †ALL INDIA RADIO, Madras — SE ASIA • 100 kW
MOROCCO
  RTV MAROCAINE, Tangier — EUROPE & W AFRICA • DS • 100 kW
ROMANIA
  †RADIO ROMANIA INTL, Bucharest — ASIA & AUSTRALASIA • 250 kW; ASIA • 250 kW; AUSTRALASIA • 250 kW; MIDEAST & S ASIA • 250 kW; (J) • W AFRICA • 250 kW; (J) • MIDEAST • 250 kW; Su • S ASIA & SE ASIA • MARINERS • 250 kW; Su • W AFRICA & ATLANTIC • MARINERS • 250 kW
SAUDI ARABIA
  †BS OF THE KINGDOM, Riyadh — E AFRICA • 350 kW; W AFRICA & C AFRICA • 350 kW
15340   CUBA
  †RADIO HABANA, Havana — S AMERICA • 50 kW
IRAQ
  †RADIO IRAQ INTL, Salah el Deen — (J) • ARABIC & ENGLISH • N AMERICA • 500 kW
ITALY
  RTV ITALIANA, Rome — MIDEAST • 100 kW
KOREA (DPR)
  RADIO PYONGYANG, Kujang-dong — E ASIA & S ASIA • 200 kW
ROMANIA
  †RADIO ROMANIA INTL, Bucharest — (J) • AFRICA • 250 kW; W AFRICA • 250 kW; (D) • W AFRICA • 250 kW; AFRICA • 250 kW; (D) • AFRICA • 250 kW
RUSSIA
  †R MOSCOW INTL, Yekaterinburg — (D) • E ASIA • 240 kW
  †RADIO NADEZHDA — DS
  †VOICE OF RUSSIA, Yekaterinburg — (D) • E ASIA • 240 kW
UNITED KINGDOM
  †BBC, Rampisham — (D) • E EUROPE • 500 kW; (D) M-F • E EUROPE • 500 kW
(con'd)   BBC, Via Singapore — SE ASIA & AUSTRALASIA • 100 kW

FREQUENCY	COUNTRY, STATION, LOCATION	TARGET • NETWORK • POWER (kW)	World Time

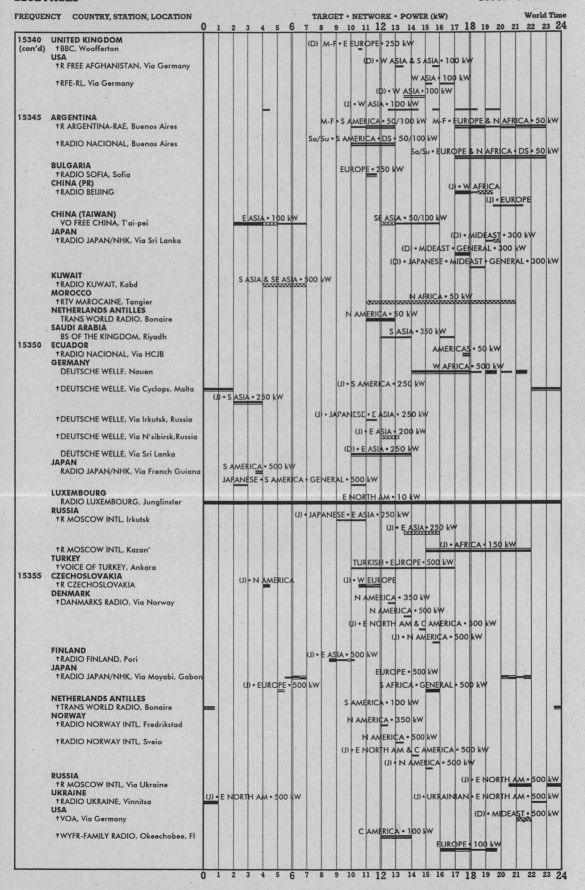

15340 (con'd)
UNITED KINGDOM
  †BBC, Woofferton — (D) • M-F • E EUROPE • 250 kW
USA
  †R FREE AFGHANISTAN, Via Germany — (D) • W ASIA & S ASIA • 100 kW
  †RFE-RL, Via Germany — W ASIA • 100 kW
  (D) • W ASIA • 100 kW
  (J) • W ASIA • 100 kW

15345
ARGENTINA
  †R ARGENTINA-RAE, Buenos Aires — M-F • S AMERICA • 50/100 kW   M-F • EUROPE & N AFRICA • 50 kW
  †RADIO NACIONAL, Buenos Aires — Sa/Su • S AMERICA • DS • 50/100 kW   Sa/Su • EUROPE & N AFRICA • DS • 50 kW
BULGARIA
  †RADIO SOFIA, Sofia — EUROPE • 250 kW
CHINA (PR)
  †RADIO BEIJING — (J) • W AFRICA   (J) • EUROPE
CHINA (TAIWAN)
  VO FREE CHINA, T'ai-pei — E ASIA • 100 kW   SE ASIA • 50/100 kW
JAPAN
  †RADIO JAPAN/NHK, Via Sri Lanka — (D) • MIDEAST • 300 kW
  (D) • MIDEAST • GENERAL • 300 kW
  (D) • JAPANESE • MIDEAST • GENERAL • 300 kW
KUWAIT
  †RADIO KUWAIT, Kabd — S ASIA & SE ASIA • 500 kW
MOROCCO
  †RTV MAROCAINE, Tangier — N AFRICA • 50 kW
NETHERLANDS ANTILLES
  †TRANS WORLD RADIO, Bonaire — N AMERICA • 50 kW
SAUDI ARABIA
  BS OF THE KINGDOM, Riyadh — S ASIA • 350 kW

15350
ECUADOR
  †RADIO NACIONAL, Via HCJB — AMERICAS • 50 kW
GERMANY
  DEUTSCHE WELLE, Nauen — W AFRICA • 500 kW
  †DEUTSCHE WELLE, Via Cyclops, Malta — (J) • S AMERICA • 250 kW
  (J) • S ASIA • 250 kW
  †DEUTSCHE WELLE, Via Irkutsk, Russia — (J) • JAPANESE • E ASIA • 250 kW
  †DEUTSCHE WELLE, Via N'sibirsk, Russia — (J) • E ASIA • 200 kW
  DEUTSCHE WELLE, Via Sri Lanka — (D) • E ASIA • 250 kW
JAPAN
  RADIO JAPAN/NHK, Via French Guiana — S AMERICA • 500 kW
  JAPANESE • S AMERICA • GENERAL • 500 kW
LUXEMBOURG
  RADIO LUXEMBOURG, Junglinster — E NORTH AM • 10 kW
RUSSIA
  †R MOSCOW INTL, Irkutsk — (J) • JAPANESE • E ASIA • 250 kW
  (J) • E ASIA • 250 kW
  †R MOSCOW INTL, Kazan' — (J) • AFRICA • 150 kW
TURKEY
  †VOICE OF TURKEY, Ankara — TURKISH • EUROPE • 500 kW

15355
CZECHOSLOVAKIA
  †R CZECHOSLOVAKIA — (J) • N AMERICA   (J) • W EUROPE
DENMARK
  †DANMARKS RADIO, Via Norway — N AMERICA • 350 kW
  N AMERICA • 500 kW
  (J) • E NORTH AM & C AMERICA • 500 kW
  (J) • N AMERICA • 500 kW
FINLAND
  †RADIO FINLAND, Pori — (J) • E ASIA • 500 kW
JAPAN
  †RADIO JAPAN/NHK, Via Moyabi, Gabon — EUROPE • 500 kW
  (J) • EUROPE • 500 kW   S AFRICA • GENERAL • 500 kW
NETHERLANDS ANTILLES
  †TRANS WORLD RADIO, Bonaire — S AMERICA • 100 kW
NORWAY
  †RADIO NORWAY INTL, Fredrikstad — N AMERICA • 350 kW
  †RADIO NORWAY INTL, Sveio — N AMERICA • 500 kW
  (J) • E NORTH AM & C AMERICA • 500 kW
  (J) • N AMERICA • 500 kW
RUSSIA
  †R MOSCOW INTL, Via Ukraine — (J) • E NORTH AM • 500 kW
UKRAINE
  †RADIO UKRAINE, Vinnitsa — (J) • E NORTH AM • 500 kW   (J) • UKRAINIAN • E NORTH AM • 500 kW
USA
  †VOA, Via Germany — (D) • MIDEAST • 500 kW
  †WYFR-FAMILY RADIO, Okeechobee, Fl — C AMERICA • 100 kW
  EUROPE • 100 kW

ENGLISH ▬ ARABIC ⋙ CHINESE ▭▭▭ FRENCH ══ GERMAN ▬▬ RUSSIAN ══ SPANISH ▬▬ OTHER ▬

FREQUENCY   COUNTRY, STATION, LOCATION   TARGET • NETWORK • POWER (kW)   World Time
                                          0 1 2 3 4 5 6 7 8 9 10 11 12 13 14 15 16 17 18 19 20 21 22 23 24

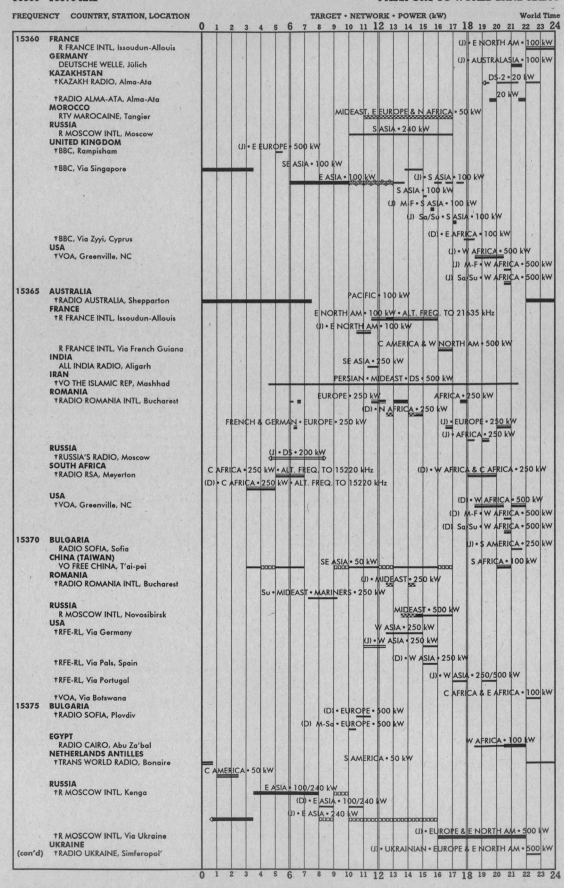

15360   **FRANCE**
              R FRANCE INTL, Issoudun-Allouis   (J) • E NORTH AM • 100 kW
              GERMANY
              DEUTSCHE WELLE, Jülich   (J) • AUSTRALASIA • 100 kW
              KAZAKHSTAN
              †KAZAKH RADIO, Alma-Ata   DS-2 • 20 kW
                                                                                           20 kW
              †RADIO ALMA-ATA, Alma-Ata
              MOROCCO
              RTV MAROCAINE, Tangier   MIDEAST, E EUROPE & N AFRICA • 50 kW
              RUSSIA
              R MOSCOW INTL, Moscow   S ASIA • 240 kW
              UNITED KINGDOM
              †BBC, Rampisham   (J) • E EUROPE • 500 kW

              †BBC, Via Singapore   SE ASIA • 100 kW
                                                            E ASIA • 100 kW
                                                                                 (J) • S ASIA • 100 kW
                                                                                 S ASIA • 100 kW
                                                                                 (J) • M-F • S ASIA • 100 kW
                                                                                 (J) Sa/Su • S ASIA • 100 kW

              †BBC, Via Zyyi, Cyprus   (D) • E AFRICA • 100 kW
              USA
              †VOA, Greenville, NC   (J) • W AFRICA • 500 kW
                                                                                 (J) • M-F • W AFRICA • 500 kW
                                                                                 (J) Sa/Su • W AFRICA • 500 kW

15365   **AUSTRALIA**
              †RADIO AUSTRALIA, Shepparton   PACIFIC • 100 kW
              FRANCE
              †R FRANCE INTL, Issoudun-Allouis   E NORTH AM • 100 kW • ALT. FREQ. TO 21635 kHz
                                                            (J) • E NORTH AM • 100 kW

              R FRANCE INTL, Via French Guiana   C AMERICA & W NORTH AM • 500 kW
              INDIA
              ALL INDIA RADIO, Aligarh   SE ASIA • 250 kW
              IRAN
              †VO THE ISLAMIC REP, Mashhad   PERSIAN • MIDEAST • DS • 500 kW
              ROMANIA
              †RADIO ROMANIA INTL, Bucharest   EUROPE • 250 kW   AFRICA • 250 kW
                                                                      (D) • N AFRICA • 250 kW
                                          FRENCH & GERMAN • EUROPE • 250 kW   (J) • EUROPE • 250 kW
                                                                                   (J) • AFRICA • 250 kW

              RUSSIA
              †RUSSIA'S RADIO, Moscow   (J) • DS • 200 kW
              SOUTH AFRICA
              †RADIO RSA, Meyerton   C AFRICA • 250 kW • ALT. FREQ. TO 15220 kHz   (D) • W AFRICA & C AFRICA • 250 kW
                                          (D) • C AFRICA • 250 kW • ALT. FREQ. TO 15220 kHz

              USA
              †VOA, Greenville, NC   (D) • W AFRICA • 500 kW
                                                                                 (D) • M-F • W AFRICA • 500 kW
                                                                                 (D) Sa/Su • W AFRICA • 500 kW

15370   **BULGARIA**
              RADIO SOFIA, Sofia   (J) • S AMERICA • 250 kW
              CHINA (TAIWAN)
              VO FREE CHINA, T'ai-pei   SE ASIA • 50 kW   S AFRICA • 100 kW
              ROMANIA
              †RADIO ROMANIA INTL, Bucharest   (J) • MIDEAST • 250 kW
                                          Su • MIDEAST • MARINERS • 250 kW

              RUSSIA
              R MOSCOW INTL, Novosibirsk   MIDEAST • 500 kW
              USA
              †RFE-RL, Via Germany   W ASIA • 250 kW
                                                            (J) • W ASIA • 250 kW

              †RFE-RL, Via Pals, Spain   (D) • W ASIA • 250 kW

              †RFE-RL, Via Portugal   (J) • W ASIA • 250/500 kW

              †VOA, Via Botswana   C AFRICA & E AFRICA • 100 kW
15375   **BULGARIA**
              †RADIO SOFIA, Plovdiv   (D) • EUROPE • 500 kW
                                                            (D) M-Sa • EUROPE • 500 kW

              EGYPT
              RADIO CAIRO, Abu Za'bal   W AFRICA • 100 kW
              NETHERLANDS ANTILLES
              †TRANS WORLD RADIO, Bonaire   S AMERICA • 50 kW
                                          C AMERICA • 50 kW

              RUSSIA
              †R MOSCOW INTL, Kenga   E ASIA • 100/240 kW
                                                            (D) • E ASIA • 100/240 kW
                                                            (J) • E ASIA • 240 kW

              †R MOSCOW INTL, Via Ukraine   (J) • EUROPE & E NORTH AM • 500 kW
              UKRAINE
(con'd)   †RADIO UKRAINE, Simferopol'   (J) • UKRAINIAN • EUROPE & E NORTH AM • 500 kW

                                          0 1 2 3 4 5 6 7 8 9 10 11 12 13 14 15 16 17 18 19 20 21 22 23 24

SUMMER ONLY (J)   WINTER ONLY (D)   JAMMING / OR ∧   EARLIEST HEARD ◁   LATEST HEARD ▷   NEW OR CHANGED FOR 1993 †

FREQUENCY   COUNTRY, STATION, LOCATION   TARGET • NETWORK • POWER (kW)   World Time

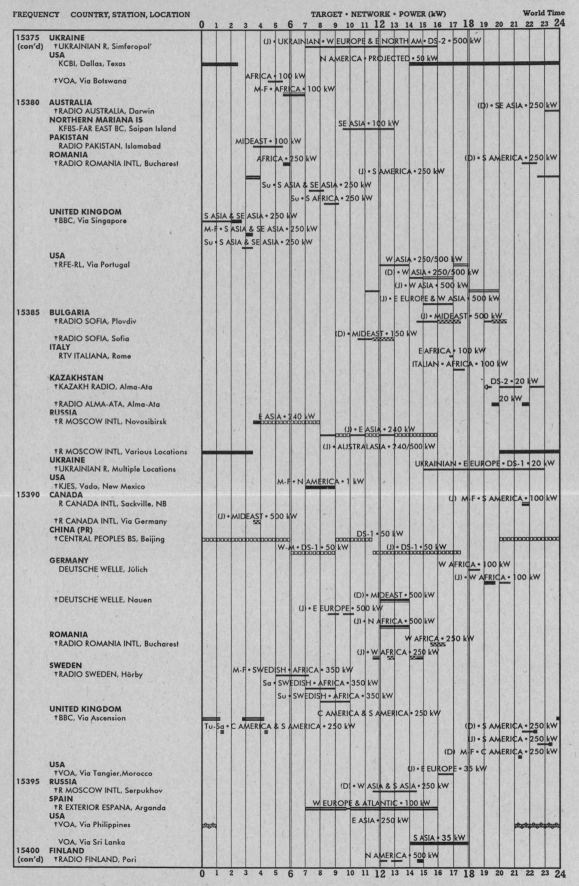

FREQUENCY	COUNTRY, STATION, LOCATION	TARGET • NETWORK • POWER
15375 (con'd)	**UKRAINE** †UKRAINIAN R, Simferopol'	(J) • UKRAINIAN • W EUROPE & E NORTH AM • DS-2 • 500 kW
	USA KCBI, Dallas, Texas	N AMERICA • PROJECTED • 50 kW
	†VOA, Via Botswana	AFRICA • 100 kW / M-F • AFRICA • 100 kW
15380	**AUSTRALIA** †RADIO AUSTRALIA, Darwin	(D) • SE ASIA • 250 kW
	NORTHERN MARIANA IS KFBS-FAR EAST BC, Saipan Island	SE ASIA • 100 kW
	PAKISTAN RADIO PAKISTAN, Islamabad	MIDEAST • 100 kW
	ROMANIA †RADIO ROMANIA INTL, Bucharest	AFRICA • 250 kW / (D) • S AMERICA • 250 kW / (J) • S AMERICA • 250 kW / Su • S ASIA & SE ASIA • 250 kW / Su • S AFRICA • 250 kW
	UNITED KINGDOM †BBC, Via Singapore	S ASIA & SE ASIA • 250 kW / M-F • S ASIA & SE ASIA • 250 kW / Su • S ASIA & SE ASIA • 250 kW
	USA †RFE-RL, Via Portugal	W ASIA • 250/500 kW / (D) • W ASIA • 250/500 kW / (J) • W ASIA • 500 kW / (J) • E EUROPE & W ASIA • 500 kW
15385	**BULGARIA** †RADIO SOFIA, Plovdiv	(J) • MIDEAST • 500 kW
	†RADIO SOFIA, Sofia	(D) • MIDEAST • 150 kW
	ITALY RTV ITALIANA, Rome	E AFRICA • 100 kW / ITALIAN • AFRICA • 100 kW
	KAZAKHSTAN †KAZAKH RADIO, Alma-Ata	DS-2 • 20 kW
	†RADIO ALMA-ATA, Alma-Ata	20 kW
	RUSSIA †R MOSCOW INTL, Novosibirsk	E ASIA • 240 kW / (J) • E ASIA • 240 kW
	†R MOSCOW INTL, Various Locations	(J) • AUSTRALASIA • 240/500 kW
	UKRAINE †UKRAINIAN R, Multiple Locations	UKRAINIAN • E EUROPE • DS-1 • 20 kW
	USA †KJES, Vado, New Mexico	M-F • N AMERICA • 1 kW
15390	**CANADA** R CANADA INTL, Sackville, NB	(J) • M-F • S AMERICA • 100 kW
	†R CANADA INTL, Via Germany	(J) • MIDEAST • 500 kW
	CHINA (PR) †CENTRAL PEOPLES BS, Beijing	DS-1 • 50 kW / W-M • DS-1 • 50 kW / (J) • DS-1 • 50 kW
	GERMANY DEUTSCHE WELLE, Jülich	W AFRICA • 100 kW / (J) • W AFRICA • 100 kW
	†DEUTSCHE WELLE, Nauen	(D) • MIDEAST • 500 kW / (J) • E EUROPE • 500 kW / (J) • N AFRICA • 500 kW
	ROMANIA †RADIO ROMANIA INTL, Bucharest	W AFRICA • 250 kW / (J) • W AFRICA • 250 kW
	SWEDEN †RADIO SWEDEN, Hörby	M-F • SWEDISH • AFRICA • 350 kW / Sa • SWEDISH • AFRICA • 350 kW / Su • SWEDISH • AFRICA • 350 kW
	UNITED KINGDOM †BBC, Via Ascension	C AMERICA & S AMERICA • 250 kW / Tu-Sa • C AMERICA & S AMERICA • 250 kW / (D) • S AMERICA • 250 kW / (J) • S AMERICA • 250 kW / (D) • M-F • C AMERICA • 250 kW
	USA †VOA, Via Tangier, Morocco	(J) • E EUROPE • 35 kW
15395	**RUSSIA** †R MOSCOW INTL, Serpukhov	(D) • W ASIA & S ASIA • 250 kW
	SPAIN †R EXTERIOR ESPANA, Arganda	W EUROPE & ATLANTIC • 100 kW
	USA †VOA, Via Philippines	E ASIA • 250 kW
	VOA, Via Sri Lanka	S ASIA • 35 kW
15400 (con'd)	**FINLAND** †RADIO FINLAND, Pori	N AMERICA • 500 kW

ENGLISH ▬▬   ARABIC ⧓⧓⧓   CHINESE □□□   FRENCH ▬▬   GERMAN ▬▬   RUSSIAN ══   SPANISH ▬▬   OTHER ——

FREQUENCY   COUNTRY, STATION, LOCATION   TARGET • NETWORK • POWER (kW)   World Time

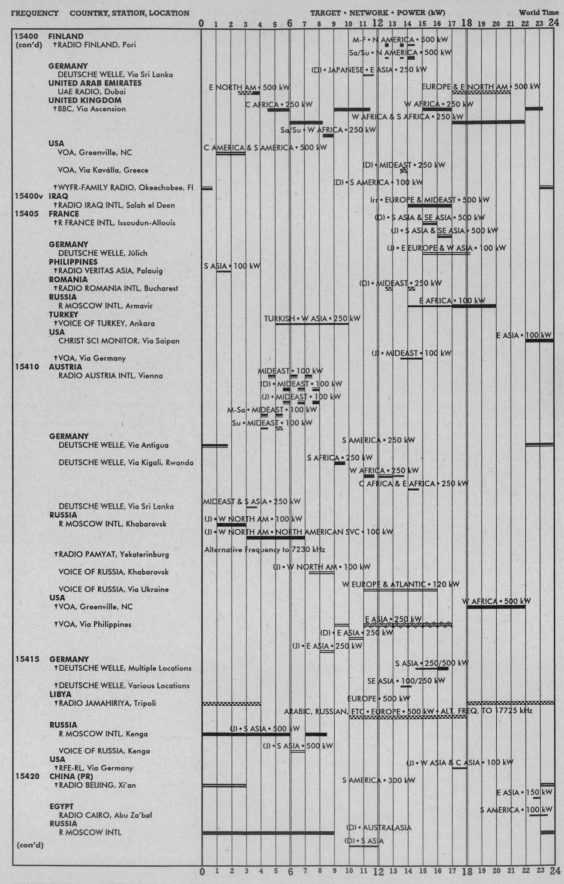

FREQUENCY	COUNTRY, STATION, LOCATION	TARGET • NETWORK • POWER (kW)
15400 (con'd)	**FINLAND** †RADIO FINLAND, Pori	M-F • N AMERICA • 500 kW / Sa/Su • N AMERICA • 500 kW
	GERMANY DEUTSCHE WELLE, Via Sri Lanka	(D) • JAPANESE • E ASIA • 250 kW
	UNITED ARAB EMIRATES UAE RADIO, Dubai	E NORTH AM • 500 kW / EUROPE & E NORTH AM • 500 kW
	UNITED KINGDOM †BBC, Via Ascension	C AFRICA • 250 kW / W AFRICA • 250 kW / W AFRICA & S AFRICA • 250 kW / Sa/Su • W AFRICA • 250 kW
	USA VOA, Greenville, NC	C AMERICA & S AMERICA • 500 kW
	VOA, Via Kaválla, Greece	(D) • MIDEAST • 250 kW
	†WYFR-FAMILY RADIO, Okeechobee, Fl	(D) • S AMERICA • 100 kW
15400v	**IRAQ** †RADIO IRAQ INTL, Salah el Deen	Irr • EUROPE & MIDEAST • 500 kW
15405	**FRANCE** †R FRANCE INTL, Issoudun-Allouis	(D) • S ASIA & SE ASIA • 500 kW / (J) • S ASIA & SE ASIA • 500 kW
	GERMANY DEUTSCHE WELLE, Jülich	(J) • E EUROPE & W ASIA • 100 kW
	PHILIPPINES †RADIO VERITAS ASIA, Palauig	S ASIA • 100 kW
	ROMANIA †RADIO ROMANIA INTL, Bucharest	(D) • MIDEAST • 250 kW
	RUSSIA R MOSCOW INTL, Armavir	E AFRICA • 100 kW
	TURKEY †VOICE OF TURKEY, Ankara	TURKISH • W ASIA • 250 kW
	USA CHRIST SCI MONITOR, Via Saipan	E ASIA • 100 kW
	†VOA, Via Germany	(J) • MIDEAST • 100 kW
15410	**AUSTRIA** RADIO AUSTRIA INTL, Vienna	MIDEAST • 100 kW / (D) • MIDEAST • 100 kW / (J) • MIDEAST • 100 kW / M-Sa • MIDEAST • 100 kW / Su • MIDEAST • 100 kW
	GERMANY DEUTSCHE WELLE, Via Antigua	S AMERICA • 250 kW
	DEUTSCHE WELLE, Via Kigali, Rwanda	S AFRICA • 250 kW / W AFRICA • 250 kW / C AFRICA & E AFRICA • 250 kW
	DEUTSCHE WELLE, Via Sri Lanka	MIDEAST & S ASIA • 250 kW
	RUSSIA R MOSCOW INTL, Khabarovsk	(J) • W NORTH AM • 100 kW / (J) • W NORTH AM • NORTH AMERICAN SVC • 100 kW
	†RADIO PAMYAT, Yekaterinburg	Alternative Frequency to 7230 kHz
	VOICE OF RUSSIA, Khabarovsk	(J) • W NORTH AM • 100 kW
	VOICE OF RUSSIA, Via Ukraine	W EUROPE & ATLANTIC • 120 kW
	USA †VOA, Greenville, NC	W AFRICA • 500 kW
	†VOA, Via Philippines	E ASIA • 250 kW / (D) • E ASIA • 250 kW / (J) • E ASIA • 250 kW
15415	**GERMANY** †DEUTSCHE WELLE, Multiple Locations	S ASIA • 250/500 kW
	†DEUTSCHE WELLE, Various Locations	SE ASIA • 100/250 kW
	LIBYA †RADIO JAMAHIRIYA, Tripoli	EUROPE • 500 kW / ARABIC, RUSSIAN, ETC • EUROPE • 500 kW • ALT. FREQ. TO 17725 kHz
	RUSSIA R MOSCOW INTL, Kenga	(J) • S ASIA • 500 kW
	VOICE OF RUSSIA, Kenga	(J) • S ASIA • 500 kW
	USA †RFE-RL, Via Germany	(J) • W ASIA & C ASIA • 100 kW
15420	**CHINA (PR)** †RADIO BEIJING, Xi'an	S AMERICA • 300 kW / E ASIA • 150 kW
	EGYPT RADIO CAIRO, Abu Za'bal	S AMERICA • 100 kW
	RUSSIA R MOSCOW INTL	(D) • AUSTRALASIA
(con'd)		(D) • S ASIA

FREQUENCY   COUNTRY, STATION, LOCATION   TARGET • NETWORK • POWER (kW)   World Time

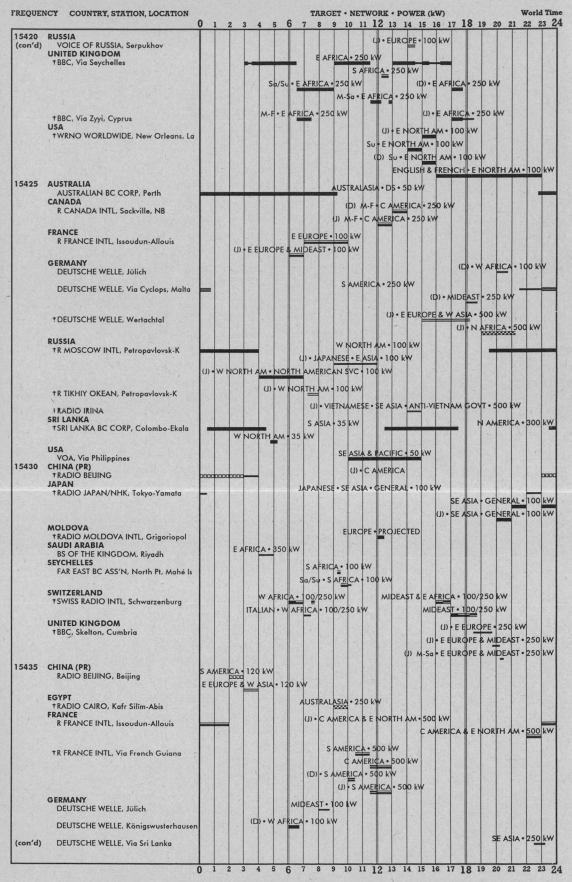

15420 **RUSSIA**	
(con'd) VOICE OF RUSSIA, Serpukhov	(J) • EUROPE • 100 kW
UNITED KINGDOM	
†BBC, Via Seychelles	E AFRICA • 250 kW
	S AFRICA • 250 kW
	Sa/Su • E AFRICA • 250 kW (D) • E AFRICA • 250 kW
	M-Sa • E AFRICA • 250 kW
†BBC, Via Zyyi, Cyprus	M-F • E AFRICA • 250 kW (J) • E AFRICA • 250 kW
USA	
†WRNO WORLDWIDE, New Orleans, La	(J) • E NORTH AM • 100 kW
	Su • E NORTH AM • 100 kW
	(D) Su • E NORTH AM • 100 kW
	ENGLISH & FRENCH • E NORTH AM • 100 kW
15425 **AUSTRALIA**	
AUSTRALIAN BC CORP, Perth	AUSTRALASIA • DS • 50 kW
CANADA	
R CANADA INTL, Sackville, NB	(D) M-F • C AMERICA • 250 kW
	(J) M-F • C AMERICA • 250 kW
FRANCE	
R FRANCE INTL, Issoudun-Allouis	E EUROPE • 100 kW
	(J) • E EUROPE & MIDEAST • 100 kW
GERMANY	
DEUTSCHE WELLE, Jülich	(D) • W AFRICA • 100 kW
	S AMERICA • 250 kW
DEUTSCHE WELLE, Via Cyclops, Malta	(D) • MIDEAST • 250 kW
†DEUTSCHE WELLE, Wertachtal	(J) • E EUROPE & W ASIA • 500 kW
	(J) • N AFRICA • 500 kW
RUSSIA	
†R MOSCOW INTL, Petropavlovsk-K	W NORTH AM • 100 kW
	(J) • JAPANESE • E ASIA • 100 kW
	(J) • W NORTH AM • NORTH AMERICAN SVC • 100 kW
†R TIKHIY OKEAN, Petropavlovsk-K	(J) • W NORTH AM • 100 kW
†RADIO IRINA	(J) • VIETNAMESE • SE ASIA • ANTI-VIETNAM GOVT • 500 kW
SRI LANKA	
†SRI LANKA BC CORP, Colombo-Ekala	S ASIA • 35 kW N AMERICA • 300 kW
	W NORTH AM • 35 kW
USA	
VOA, Via Philippines	SE ASIA & PACIFIC • 50 kW
15430 **CHINA (PR)**	
†RADIO BEIJING	(J) • C AMERICA
JAPAN	
†RADIO JAPAN/NHK, Tokyo-Yamata	JAPANESE • SE ASIA • GENERAL • 100 kW
	SE ASIA • GENERAL • 100 kW
	(J) • SE ASIA • GENERAL • 100 kW
MOLDOVA	
†RADIO MOLDOVA INTL, Grigoriopol	EUROPE • PROJECTED
SAUDI ARABIA	
BS OF THE KINGDOM, Riyadh	E AFRICA • 350 kW
SEYCHELLES	
FAR EAST BC ASS'N, North Pt, Mahé Is	S AFRICA • 100 kW
	Sa/Su • S AFRICA • 100 kW
SWITZERLAND	
†SWISS RADIO INTL, Schwarzenburg	W AFRICA • 100/250 kW MIDEAST & E AFRICA • 100/250 kW
	ITALIAN • W AFRICA • 100/250 kW MIDEAST • 100/250 kW
UNITED KINGDOM	
†BBC, Skelton, Cumbria	(J) • E EUROPE • 250 kW
	(J) • E EUROPE & MIDEAST • 250 kW
	(J) M-Sa • E EUROPE & MIDEAST • 250 kW
15435 **CHINA (PR)**	
RADIO BEIJING, Beijing	S AMERICA • 120 kW
	E EUROPE & W ASIA • 120 kW
EGYPT	
†RADIO CAIRO, Kafr Silim-Abis	AUSTRALASIA • 250 kW
FRANCE	
R FRANCE INTL, Issoudun-Allouis	(J) • C AMERICA & E NORTH AM • 500 kW
	C AMERICA & E NORTH AM • 500 kW
†R FRANCE INTL, Via French Guiana	S AMERICA • 500 kW
	C AMERICA • 500 kW
	(D) • S AMERICA • 500 kW
	(J) • S AMERICA • 500 kW
GERMANY	
DEUTSCHE WELLE, Jülich	MIDEAST • 100 kW
DEUTSCHE WELLE, Königswusterhausen	(D) • W AFRICA • 100 kW
(con'd) DEUTSCHE WELLE, Via Sri Lanka	SE ASIA • 250 kW

ENGLISH ▬▬   ARABIC ▨▨   CHINESE ▫▫▫   FRENCH ▬▬   GERMAN ▬▬   RUSSIAN ▬▬   SPANISH ▬▬   OTHER ▬▬

FREQUENCY   COUNTRY, STATION, LOCATION   TARGET • NETWORK • POWER (kW)   World Time

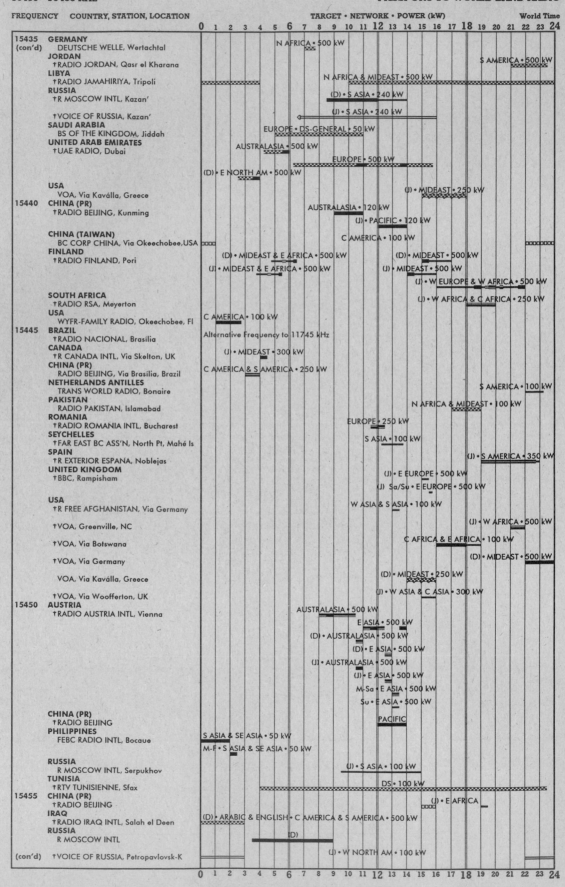

FREQUENCY	COUNTRY, STATION, LOCATION	TARGET • NETWORK • POWER (kW)
15435 (con'd)	**GERMANY** DEUTSCHE WELLE, Wertachtal	N AFRICA • 500 kW
	JORDAN †RADIO JORDAN, Qasr el Kharana	S AMERICA • 500 kW
	LIBYA †RADIO JAMAHIRIYA, Tripoli	N AFRICA & MIDEAST • 500 kW
	RUSSIA †R MOSCOW INTL, Kazan'	(D) • S ASIA • 240 kW
	†VOICE OF RUSSIA, Kazan'	(J) • S ASIA • 240 kW
	SAUDI ARABIA BS OF THE KINGDOM, Jiddah	EUROPE • DS-GENERAL • 50 kW
	UNITED ARAB EMIRATES †UAE RADIO, Dubai	AUSTRALASIA • 500 kW
		EUROPE • 500 kW
		(D) • E NORTH AM • 500 kW
	USA VOA, Via Kaválla, Greece	(J) • MIDEAST • 250 kW
15440	**CHINA (PR)** †RADIO BEIJING, Kunming	AUSTRALASIA • 120 kW
		(J) • PACIFIC • 120 kW
	CHINA (TAIWAN) BC CORP CHINA, Via Okeechobee, USA	C AMERICA • 100 kW
	FINLAND †RADIO FINLAND, Pori	(D) • MIDEAST & E AFRICA • 500 kW (D) • MIDEAST • 500 kW
		(J) • MIDEAST & E AFRICA • 500 kW (J) • MIDEAST • 500 kW
		(J) • W EUROPE & W AFRICA • 500 kW
	SOUTH AFRICA †RADIO RSA, Meyerton	(J) • W AFRICA & C AFRICA • 250 kW
	USA WYFR-FAMILY RADIO, Okeechobee, Fl	C AMERICA • 100 kW
15445	**BRAZIL** †RADIO NACIONAL, Brasília	Alternative Frequency to 11745 kHz
	CANADA †R CANADA INTL, Via Skelton, UK	(J) • MIDEAST • 300 kW
	CHINA (PR) RADIO BEIJING, Via Brasília, Brazil	C AMERICA & S AMERICA • 250 kW
	NETHERLANDS ANTILLES TRANS WORLD RADIO, Bonaire	S AMERICA • 100 kW
	PAKISTAN RADIO PAKISTAN, Islamabad	N AFRICA & MIDEAST • 100 kW
	ROMANIA †RADIO ROMANIA INTL, Bucharest	EUROPE • 250 kW
	SEYCHELLES †FAR EAST BC ASS'N, North Pt, Mahé Is	S ASIA • 100 kW
	SPAIN †R EXTERIOR ESPANA, Noblejas	(J) • S AMERICA • 350 kW
	UNITED KINGDOM †BBC, Rampisham	(J) • E EUROPE • 500 kW
		(J) Sa/Su • E EUROPE • 500 kW
	USA †R FREE AFGHANISTAN, Via Germany	W ASIA & S ASIA • 100 kW
	†VOA, Greenville, NC	(J) • W AFRICA • 500 kW
	†VOA, Via Botswana	C AFRICA & E AFRICA • 100 kW
	†VOA, Via Germany	(D) • MIDEAST • 500 kW
	VOA, Via Kaválla, Greece	(D) • MIDEAST • 250 kW
	†VOA, Via Woofferton, UK	(J) • W ASIA & C ASIA • 300 kW
15450	**AUSTRIA** †RADIO AUSTRIA INTL, Vienna	AUSTRALASIA • 500 kW
		E ASIA • 500 kW
		(D) • AUSTRALASIA • 500 kW
		(D) • E ASIA • 500 kW
		(J) • AUSTRALASIA • 500 kW
		(J) • E ASIA • 500 kW
		M-Sa • E ASIA • 500 kW
		Su • E ASIA • 500 kW
	CHINA (PR) †RADIO BEIJING	PACIFIC
	PHILIPPINES FEBC RADIO INTL, Bocaue	S ASIA & SE ASIA • 50 kW
		M-F • S ASIA & SE ASIA • 50 kW
	RUSSIA R MOSCOW INTL, Serpukhov	(J) • S ASIA • 100 kW
	TUNISIA †RTV TUNISIENNE, Sfax	DS • 100 kW
15455	**CHINA (PR)** †RADIO BEIJING	(J) • E AFRICA
	IRAQ †RADIO IRAQ INTL, Salah el Deen	(D) • ARABIC & ENGLISH • C AMERICA & S AMERICA • 500 kW
	RUSSIA R MOSCOW INTL	(D)
(con'd)	†VOICE OF RUSSIA, Petropavlovsk-K	(J) • W NORTH AM • 100 kW

SUMMER ONLY (J)   WINTER ONLY (D)   JAMMING / OR ∧   EARLIEST HEARD ◁   LATEST HEARD ▷   NEW OR CHANGED FOR 1993 †

FREQUENCY   COUNTRY, STATION, LOCATION   TARGET • NETWORK • POWER (kW)   World Time

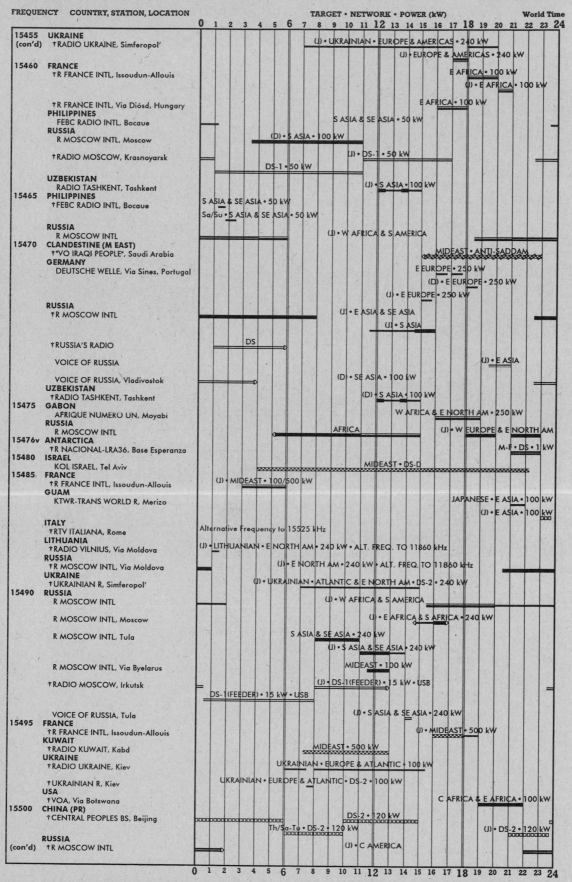

FREQUENCY	COUNTRY, STATION, LOCATION	TARGET • NETWORK • POWER
15455 (con'd)	UKRAINE †RADIO UKRAINE, Simferopol'	(J) • UKRAINIAN • EUROPE & AMERICAS • 240 kW; (J) • EUROPE & AMERICAS • 240 kW
15460	FRANCE †R FRANCE INTL, Issoudun-Allouis	E AFRICA • 100 kW; (J) • E AFRICA • 100 kW
	†R FRANCE INTL, Via Diósd, Hungary	E AFRICA • 100 kW
	PHILIPPINES FEBC RADIO INTL, Bocaue	S ASIA & SE ASIA • 50 kW
	RUSSIA R MOSCOW INTL, Moscow	(D) • S ASIA • 100 kW
	†RADIO MOSCOW, Krasnoyarsk	(J) • DS-1 • 50 kW
	UZBEKISTAN RADIO TASHKENT, Tashkent	DS-1 • 50 kW; (J) • S ASIA • 100 kW
15465	PHILIPPINES †FEBC RADIO INTL, Bocaue	S ASIA & SE ASIA • 50 kW; Sa/Su • S ASIA & SE ASIA • 50 kW
	RUSSIA R MOSCOW INTL	(J) • W AFRICA & S AMERICA
15470	CLANDESTINE (M EAST) †"VO IRAQI PEOPLE", Saudi Arabia	MIDEAST • ANTI-SADDAM
	GERMANY DEUTSCHE WELLE, Via Sines, Portugal	E EUROPE • 250 kW; (D) • E EUROPE • 250 kW; (J) • E EUROPE • 250 kW
	RUSSIA †R MOSCOW INTL	(J) • E ASIA & SE ASIA; (J) • S ASIA
	†RUSSIA'S RADIO	DS
	VOICE OF RUSSIA	(J) • E ASIA
	VOICE OF RUSSIA, Vladivostok	(D) • SE ASIA • 100 kW
	UZBEKISTAN †RADIO TASHKENT, Tashkent	(D) • S ASIA • 100 kW
15475	GABON AFRIQUE NUMERO UN, Moyabi	W AFRICA & E NORTH AM • 250 kW
	RUSSIA R MOSCOW INTL	AFRICA; (J) • W EUROPE & E NORTH AM
15476v	ANTARCTICA †R NACIONAL-LRA36, Base Esperanza	M-F • DS • 1 kW
15480	ISRAEL KOL ISRAEL, Tel Aviv	MIDEAST • DS-D
15485	FRANCE †R FRANCE INTL, Issoudun-Allouis	(J) • MIDEAST • 100/500 kW
	GUAM KTWR-TRANS WORLD R, Merizo	JAPANESE • E ASIA • 100 kW; (J) • E ASIA • 100 kW
	ITALY †RTV ITALIANA, Rome	Alternative Frequency to 15525 kHz
	LITHUANIA †RADIO VILNIUS, Via Moldova	(J) • LITHUANIAN • E NORTH AM • 240 kW • ALT. FREQ. TO 11860 kHz
	RUSSIA †R MOSCOW INTL, Via Moldova	(J) • E NORTH AM • 240 kW • ALT. FREQ. TO 11860 kHz
	UKRAINE †UKRAINIAN R, Simferopol'	(J) • UKRAINIAN • ATLANTIC & E NORTH AM • DS-2 • 240 kW
15490	RUSSIA R MOSCOW INTL	(J) • W AFRICA & S AMERICA
	R MOSCOW INTL, Moscow	(J) • E AFRICA & S AFRICA • 240 kW
	R MOSCOW INTL, Tula	S ASIA & SE ASIA • 240 kW; (J) • S ASIA & SE ASIA • 240 kW
	R MOSCOW INTL, Via Byelarus	MIDEAST • 100 kW
	†RADIO MOSCOW, Irkutsk	(J) • DS-1 (FEEDER) • 15 kW • USB; DS-1 (FEEDER) • 15 kW • USB
	VOICE OF RUSSIA, Tula	(J) • S ASIA & SE ASIA • 240 kW
15495	FRANCE †R FRANCE INTL, Issoudun-Allouis	(J) • MIDEAST • 500 kW
	KUWAIT †RADIO KUWAIT, Kabd	MIDEAST • 500 kW
	UKRAINE †RADIO UKRAINE, Kiev	UKRAINIAN • EUROPE & ATLANTIC • 100 kW
	†UKRAINIAN R, Kiev	UKRAINIAN • EUROPE & ATLANTIC • DS-2 • 100 kW
	USA †VOA, Via Botswana	C AFRICA & E AFRICA • 100 kW
15500	CHINA (PR) †CENTRAL PEOPLES BS, Beijing	DS-2 • 120 kW; Th/Sa-Tu • DS-2 • 120 kW; (J) • DS-2 • 120 kW
(con'd)	RUSSIA †R MOSCOW INTL	(J) • C AMERICA

ENGLISH ▬▬ ARABIC ⌇⌇⌇ CHINESE ▫▫▫ FRENCH ══ GERMAN ▬▬ RUSSIAN ▬▬ SPANISH ═══ OTHER ▬▬

FREQUENCY   COUNTRY, STATION, LOCATION

TARGET • NETWORK • POWER (kW)

World Time

0 1 2 3 4 5 6 7 8 9 10 11 12 13 14 15 16 17 18 19 20 21 22 23 24

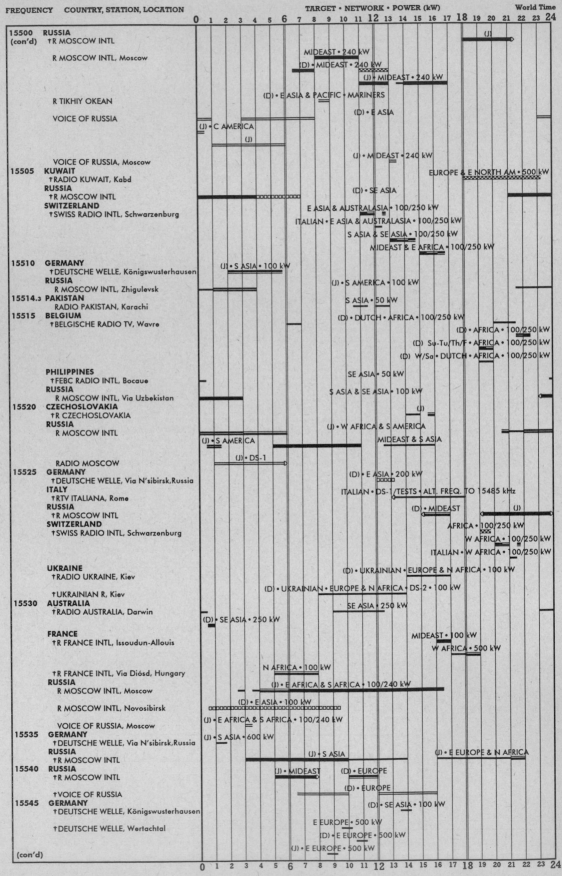

FREQUENCY	COUNTRY, STATION, LOCATION	TARGET • NETWORK • POWER (kW)
15500 (con'd)	RUSSIA †R MOSCOW INTL	(J)
	R MOSCOW INTL, Moscow	MIDEAST • 240 kW / (D) • MIDEAST • 240 kW / (J) MIDEAST • 240 kW
	R TIKHIY OKEAN	(D) • E ASIA & PACIFIC • MARINERS
	VOICE OF RUSSIA	(D) • E ASIA
		(J) • C AMERICA / (J)
	VOICE OF RUSSIA, Moscow	(J) • MIDEAST • 240 kW
15505	KUWAIT †RADIO KUWAIT, Kabd	EUROPE & E NORTH AM • 500 kW
	RUSSIA †R MOSCOW INTL	(D) • SE ASIA
	SWITZERLAND †SWISS RADIO INTL, Schwarzenburg	E ASIA & AUSTRALASIA • 100/250 kW / ITALIAN • E ASIA & AUSTRALASIA • 100/250 kW / S ASIA & SE ASIA • 100/250 kW / MIDEAST & E AFRICA • 100/250 kW
15510	GERMANY †DEUTSCHE WELLE, Königswusterhausen	(J) • S ASIA • 100 kW
	RUSSIA R MOSCOW INTL, Zhigulevsk	(J) • S AMERICA • 100 kW
15514.3	PAKISTAN RADIO PAKISTAN, Karachi	S ASIA • 50 kW
15515	BELGIUM †BELGISCHE RADIO TV, Wavre	(D) • DUTCH • AFRICA • 100/250 kW / (D) • AFRICA • 100/250 kW / (D) Su-Tu/Th/F • AFRICA • 100/250 kW / (D) W/Sa • DUTCH • AFRICA • 100/250 kW
	PHILIPPINES †FEBC RADIO INTL, Bocaue	SE ASIA • 50 kW
	RUSSIA R MOSCOW INTL, Via Uzbekistan	S ASIA & SE ASIA • 100 kW
15520	CZECHOSLOVAKIA †R CZECHOSLOVAKIA	(J)
	RUSSIA R MOSCOW INTL	(J) • W AFRICA & S AMERICA / (J) • S AMERICA / MIDEAST & S ASIA
	RADIO MOSCOW	(J) • DS-1
15525	GERMANY †DEUTSCHE WELLE, Via N'sibirsk, Russia	(D) • E ASIA • 200 kW
	ITALY †RTV ITALIANA, Rome	ITALIAN • DS-1 /TESTS • ALT. FREQ. TO 15485 kHz
	RUSSIA †R MOSCOW INTL	(D) • MIDEAST / (J)
	SWITZERLAND †SWISS RADIO INTL, Schwarzenburg	AFRICA • 100/250 kW / W AFRICA • 100/250 kW / ITALIAN • W AFRICA • 100/250 kW
	UKRAINE †RADIO UKRAINE, Kiev	(D) • UKRAINIAN • EUROPE & N AFRICA • 100 kW
	†UKRAINIAN R, Kiev	(D) • UKRAINIAN • EUROPE & N AFRICA • DS-2 • 100 kW
15530	AUSTRALIA †RADIO AUSTRALIA, Darwin	SE ASIA • 250 kW / (D) • SE ASIA • 250 kW
	FRANCE †R FRANCE INTL, Issoudun-Allouis	MIDEAST • 100 kW / W AFRICA • 500 kW
	†R FRANCE INTL, Via Diósd, Hungary	N AFRICA • 100 kW
	RUSSIA R MOSCOW INTL, Moscow	(J) • E AFRICA & S AFRICA • 100/240 kW
	R MOSCOW INTL, Novosibirsk	(D) • E ASIA • 100 kW
	VOICE OF RUSSIA, Moscow	(J) • E AFRICA & S AFRICA • 100/240 kW
15535	GERMANY †DEUTSCHE WELLE, Via N'sibirsk, Russia	(J) • S ASIA • 600 kW
	RUSSIA †R MOSCOW INTL	(J) • S ASIA / (J) • E EUROPE & N AFRICA
15540	RUSSIA †R MOSCOW INTL	(J) • MIDEAST / (D) • EUROPE
	†VOICE OF RUSSIA	(D) • EUROPE
15545	GERMANY †DEUTSCHE WELLE, Königswusterhausen	(D) • SE ASIA • 100 kW
	†DEUTSCHE WELLE, Wertachtal	E EUROPE • 500 kW / (D) • E EUROPE • 500 kW / (J) • E EUROPE • 500 kW
(con'd)		

0 1 2 3 4 5 6 7 8 9 10 11 12 13 14 15 16 17 18 19 20 21 22 23 24

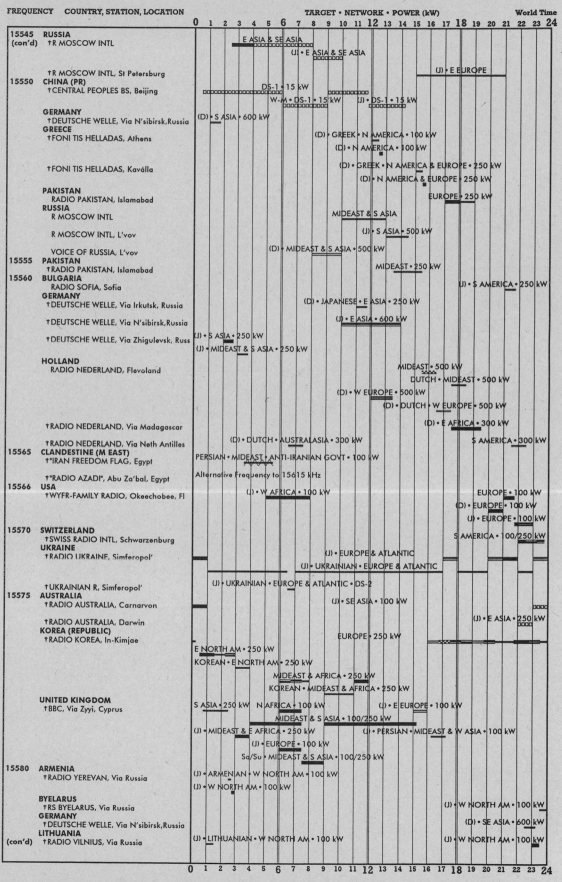

FREQUENCY	COUNTRY, STATION, LOCATION	TARGET • NETWORK • POWER (kW)	World Time

0 1 2 3 4 5 6 7 8 9 10 11 12 13 14 15 16 17 18 19 20 21 22 23 24

15545 RUSSIA
(con'd) †R MOSCOW INTL
E ASIA & SE ASIA
(J) • E ASIA & SE ASIA
(J) • E EUROPE

†R MOSCOW INTL, St Petersburg
15550 CHINA (PR)
†CENTRAL PEOPLES BS, Beijing
DS-1 • 15 kW
W-M • DS-1 • 15 kW   (J) • DS-1 • 15 kW

GERMANY
†DEUTSCHE WELLE, Via N'sibirsk, Russia
(D) • S ASIA • 600 kW
GREECE
†FONI TIS HELLADAS, Athens
(D) • GREEK • N AMERICA • 100 kW
(D) • N AMERICA • 100 kW

†FONI TIS HELLADAS, Kaválla
(D) • GREEK • N AMERICA & EUROPE • 250 kW
(D) • N AMERICA & EUROPE • 250 kW

PAKISTAN
RADIO PAKISTAN, Islamabad
EUROPE • 250 kW
RUSSIA
R MOSCOW INTL
MIDEAST & S ASIA
R MOSCOW INTL, L'vov
(J) • S ASIA • 500 kW

VOICE OF RUSSIA, L'vov
(D) • MIDEAST & S ASIA • 500 kW
15555 PAKISTAN
†RADIO PAKISTAN, Islamabad
MIDEAST • 250 kW
15560 BULGARIA
RADIO SOFIA, Sofia
(J) • S AMERICA • 250 kW
GERMANY
†DEUTSCHE WELLE, Via Irkutsk, Russia
(D) • JAPANESE • E ASIA • 250 kW

†DEUTSCHE WELLE, Via N'sibirsk, Russia
(J) • E ASIA • 600 kW

†DEUTSCHE WELLE, Via Zhigulevsk, Russ
(J) • S ASIA • 250 kW
(J) • MIDEAST & S ASIA • 250 kW

HOLLAND
RADIO NEDERLAND, Flevoland
MIDEAST • 500 kW
DUTCH • MIDEAST • 500 kW
(D) • W EUROPE • 500 kW
(D) • DUTCH • W EUROPE • 500 kW

†RADIO NEDERLAND, Via Madagascar
(D) • E AFRICA • 300 kW

†RADIO NEDERLAND, Via Neth Antilles
(D) • DUTCH • AUSTRALASIA • 300 kW
S AMERICA • 300 kW
15565 CLANDESTINE (M EAST)
†"IRAN FREEDOM FLAG", Egypt
PERSIAN • MIDEAST • ANTI-IRANIAN GOVT • 100 kW

†"RADIO AZADI", Abu Za'bal, Egypt
Alternative Frequency to 15615 kHz
15566 USA
†WYFR-FAMILY RADIO, Okeechobee, Fl
(J) • W AFRICA • 100 kW
EUROPE • 100 kW
(D) • EUROPE • 100 kW
(J) • EUROPE • 100 kW

15570 SWITZERLAND
†SWISS RADIO INTL, Schwarzenburg
S AMERICA • 100/250 kW
UKRAINE
†RADIO UKRAINE, Simferopol'
(J) • EUROPE & ATLANTIC
(J) • UKRAINIAN • EUROPE & ATLANTIC

†UKRAINIAN R, Simferopol'
(J) • UKRAINIAN • EUROPE & ATLANTIC • DS-2
15575 AUSTRALIA
†RADIO AUSTRALIA, Carnarvon
(J) • SE ASIA • 100 kW

†RADIO AUSTRALIA, Darwin
(J) • E ASIA • 250 kW
KOREA (REPUBLIC)
†RADIO KOREA, In-Kimjae
EUROPE • 250 kW
E NORTH AM • 250 kW
KOREAN • E NORTH AM • 250 kW
MIDEAST & AFRICA • 250 kW
KOREAN • MIDEAST & AFRICA • 250 kW

UNITED KINGDOM
†BBC, Via Zyyi, Cyprus
S ASIA • 250 kW   N AFRICA • 100 kW   (J) • E EUROPE • 100 kW
MIDEAST & S ASIA • 100/250 kW
(J) • MIDEAST & E AFRICA • 250 kW   (J) • PERSIAN • MIDEAST & W ASIA • 100 kW
(J) • EUROPE • 100 kW
Sa/Su • MIDEAST & S ASIA • 100/250 kW

15580 ARMENIA
†RADIO YEREVAN, Via Russia
(J) • ARMENIAN • W NORTH AM • 100 kW
(J) • W NORTH AM • 100 kW

BYELARUS
†RS BYELARUS, Via Russia
(J) • W NORTH AM • 100 kW
GERMANY
†DEUTSCHE WELLE, Via N'sibirsk, Russia
(D) • SE ASIA • 600 kW
LITHUANIA
(con'd) †RADIO VILNIUS, Via Russia
(J) • LITHUANIAN • W NORTH AM • 100 kW   (J) • W NORTH AM • 100 kW

0 1 2 3 4 5 6 7 8 9 10 11 12 13 14 15 16 17 18 19 20 21 22 23 24

ENGLISH ▬ ARABIC ⌇⌇ CHINESE ▢▢▢ FRENCH ▬▬ GERMAN ▬▬ RUSSIAN ══ SPANISH ▬▬ OTHER ▬

FREQUENCY   COUNTRY, STATION, LOCATION

TARGET • NETWORK • POWER (kW)   World Time

0 1 2 3 4 5 6 7 8 9 10 11 12 13 14 15 16 17 18 19 20 21 22 23 24

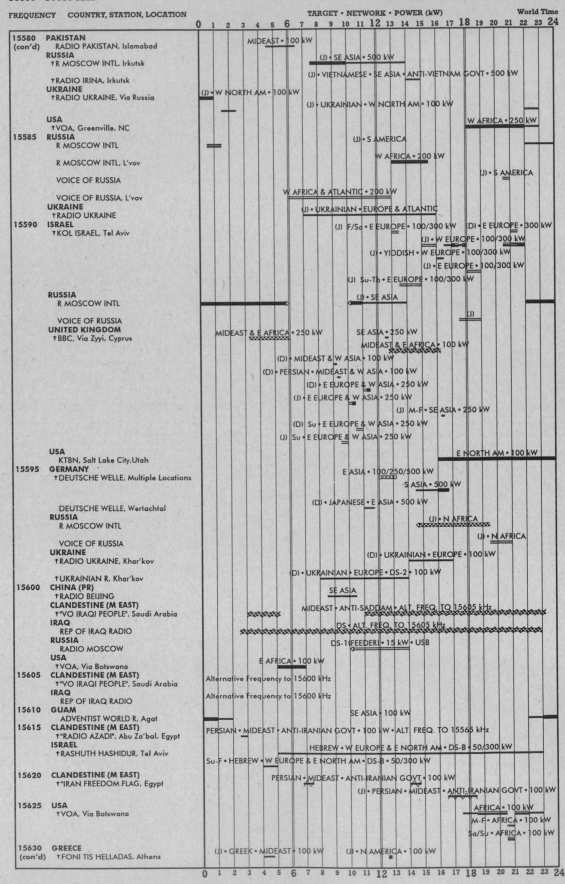

Frequency	Country, Station, Location	Target • Network • Power
15580 (con'd)	**PAKISTAN**	
	RADIO PAKISTAN, Islamabad	MIDEAST • 100 kW
	RUSSIA	
	†R MOSCOW INTL, Irkutsk	(J) • SE ASIA • 500 kW
	†RADIO IRINA, Irkutsk	(J) • VIETNAMESE • SE ASIA • ANTI-VIETNAM GOVT • 500 kW
	UKRAINE	
	†RADIO UKRAINE, Via Russia	(J) • W NORTH AM • 100 kW / (J) • UKRAINIAN • W NORTH AM • 100 kW
	USA	
	†VOA, Greenville, NC	W AFRICA • 250 kW
15585	**RUSSIA**	
	R MOSCOW INTL	(J) • S AMERICA
	R MOSCOW INTL, L'vov	W AFRICA • 200 kW
	VOICE OF RUSSIA	(J) • S AMERICA
	VOICE OF RUSSIA, L'vov	W AFRICA & ATLANTIC • 200 kW
	UKRAINE	
	†RADIO UKRAINE	(J) • UKRAINIAN • EUROPE & ATLANTIC
15590	**ISRAEL**	
	†KOL ISRAEL, Tel Aviv	(J) F/Sa • E EUROPE • 100/300 kW (D) • E EUROPE • 300 kW
		(J) • W EUROPE • 100/300 kW
		(J) • YIDDISH • W EUROPE • 100/300 kW
		(J) • E EUROPE • 100/300 kW
		(J) Su-Th • E EUROPE • 100/300 kW
	RUSSIA	
	R MOSCOW INTL	(J) • SE ASIA
	VOICE OF RUSSIA	(J)
	UNITED KINGDOM	
	†BBC, Via Zyyi, Cyprus	MIDEAST & E AFRICA • 250 kW SE ASIA • 250 kW
		MIDEAST & E AFRICA • 100 kW
		(D) • MIDEAST & W ASIA • 100 kW
		(D) • PERSIAN • MIDEAST & W ASIA • 100 kW
		(D) • E EUROPE & W ASIA • 250 kW
		(J) • E EUROPE & W ASIA • 250 kW
		(J) M-F • SE ASIA • 250 kW
		(D) Su • E EUROPE & W ASIA • 250 kW
		(J) Su • E EUROPE & W ASIA • 250 kW
	USA	
	KTBN, Salt Lake City, Utah	E NORTH AM • 100 kW
15595	**GERMANY**	
	†DEUTSCHE WELLE, Multiple Locations	E ASIA • 100/250/500 kW
		S ASIA • 500 kW
	DEUTSCHE WELLE, Wertachtal	(D) • JAPANESE • E ASIA • 500 kW
	RUSSIA	
	R MOSCOW INTL	(J) • N AFRICA
	VOICE OF RUSSIA	(J) • N AFRICA
	UKRAINE	
	†RADIO UKRAINE, Khar'kov	(D) • UKRAINIAN • EUROPE • 100 kW
	†UKRAINIAN R, Khar'kov	(D) • UKRAINIAN • EUROPE • DS-2 • 100 kW
15600	**CHINA (PR)**	
	†RADIO BEIJING	SE ASIA
	CLANDESTINE (M EAST)	
	†"VO IRAQI PEOPLE", Saudi Arabia	MIDEAST • ANTI-SADDAM • ALT. FREQ. TO 15605 kHz
	IRAQ	
	REP OF IRAQ RADIO	DS • ALT. FREQ. TO 15605 kHz
	RUSSIA	
	RADIO MOSCOW	DS-1 (FEEDER) • 15 kW • USB
	USA	
	†VOA, Via Botswana	E AFRICA • 100 kW
15605	**CLANDESTINE (M EAST)**	
	†"VO IRAQI PEOPLE", Saudi Arabia	Alternative Frequency to 15600 kHz
	IRAQ	
	REP OF IRAQ RADIO	Alternative Frequency to 15600 kHz
15610	**GUAM**	
	ADVENTIST WORLD R, Agat	SE ASIA • 100 kW
15615	**CLANDESTINE (M EAST)**	
	†"RADIO AZADI", Abu Za'bal, Egypt	PERSIAN • MIDEAST • ANTI-IRANIAN GOVT • 100 kW • ALT. FREQ. TO 15565 kHz
	ISRAEL	
	†RASHUTH HASHIDUR, Tel Aviv	HEBREW • W EUROPE & E NORTH AM • DS-B • 50/300 kW
		Su-F • HEBREW • W EUROPE & E NORTH AM • DS-B • 50/300 kW
15620	**CLANDESTINE (M EAST)**	
	†"IRAN FREEDOM FLAG", Egypt	PERSIAN • MIDEAST • ANTI-IRANIAN GOVT • 100 kW
		(J) • PERSIAN • MIDEAST • ANTI-IRANIAN GOVT • 100 kW
15625	**USA**	
	†VOA, Via Botswana	AFRICA • 100 kW
		M-F • AFRICA • 100 kW
		Sa/Su • AFRICA • 100 kW
15630 (con'd)	**GREECE**	
	†FONI TIS HELLADAS, Athens	(J) • GREEK • MIDEAST • 100 kW (J) • N AMERICA • 100 kW

0 1 2 3 4 5 6 7 8 9 10 11 12 13 14 15 16 17 18 19 20 21 22 23 24

SUMMER ONLY (J)   WINTER ONLY (D)   JAMMING / OR ∧   EARLIEST HEARD ◁   LATEST HEARD ▷   NEW OR CHANGED FOR 1993 †

FREQUENCY	COUNTRY, STATION, LOCATION	TARGET • NETWORK • POWER (kW) — World Time
15630 (con'd)	**GREECE** †FONI TIS HELLADAS, Athens	(J) • GREEK • N AMERICA • 100 kW
	†FONI TIS HELLADAS, Kaválla	(J) • GREEK • N AMERICA & EUROPE • 250 kW
		(J) • N AMERICA & EUROPE • 250 kW
	RUSSIA RUSSIA'S RADIO	DS(FEEDER) • USB
15640	**CLANDESTINE (M EAST)** †"IRAN FREEDOM FLAG", Egypt	(J) • PERSIAN • MIDEAST • ANTI-IRANIAN GOVT • 100 kW
	ISRAEL †KOL ISRAEL, Tel Aviv	(D) • MIDEAST & W ASIA • 300 kW
		(D) • PERSIAN • MIDEAST & W ASIA • 300 kW
		(D) • E EUROPE • 300 kW
		(D) • YIDDISH • E EUROPE • 300 kW
		(D) • W EUROPE & E NORTH AM • 300 kW
		(D) F/Sa • E EUROPE • 300 kW
		(J) F/Sa • W ASIA • 300 kW
		(J) • MIDEAST & W ASIA • 300 kW
		(J) • E EUROPE • 300 kW
		(J) • YIDDISH • E EUROPE • 300 kW
		(J) • AFRICA • 300 kW
		(J) • W EUROPE & E NORTH AM • 300 kW
		(J) • C AMERICA & S AMERICA • 300 kW
		(D) M-Th • MIDEAST • 300 kW
		(J) M-Th • MIDEAST • 300 kW
		(D) Su-Th • W EUROPE & E NORTH AM • 300 kW
		(J) Su-Th • W EUROPE • 300 kW
		(J) Su-Th • PERSIAN • MIDEAST & W ASIA • 300 kW
15650	**CLANDESTINE (M EAST)** †"RADIO AZADI", Abu Za'bal, Egypt	PERSIAN • MIDEAST • ANTI-IRANIAN GOVT • 100 kW
	GREECE †FONI TIS HELLADAS, Athens	GREEK • MIDEAST • 100 kW E EUROPE • 100 kW
		MIDEAST • 100 kW
		GREEK • ATLANTIC • 100 kW GREEK • E EUROPE • 100 kW
		GREEK • E ASIA • 100 kW
		E ASIA • 100 kW
		(D) • GREEK • AUSTRALASIA • 100 kW
		(D) • AUSTRALASIA • 100 kW
	†FONI TIS HELLADAS, Kaválla	GREEK • N AMERICA & EUROPE • 250 kW
		N AMERICA & EUROPE • 250 kW
		GREEK • C AFRICA • 250 kW
	ISRAEL †KOL ISRAEL, Tel Aviv	(D) F/Sa • ASIA • 300 kW
		(D) Su-Th • SE ASIA & AUSTRALASIA • 300 kW
		(J) Su-Th • SE ASIA & AUSTRALASIA • 300 kW
15660	**USA** †WJCR, Upton, Kentucky	N AMERICA • PROJECTED • 50 kW
15665	**USA** †CHRIST SCI MONITOR, Maine	(J) M-F • EUROPE • 500 kW
		(J) M-F • EUROPE & MIDEAST • 500 kW
		(J) Sa • EUROPE • 500 kW
		(J) Sa • EUROPE & MIDEAST • 500 kW
		(J) Sa/Su • EUROPE • 500 kW
		(J) Su • EUROPE • 500 kW
		(J) Su • EUROPE & MIDEAST • 500 kW
		(J) Sa • EUROPE • 1ST & 3RD SATURDAY • 500 kW
		(J) Sa • EUROPE • 2ND SATURDAY • 500 kW
		(J) Sa • EUROPE • 4TH SATURDAY • 500 kW
	†CHRIST SCI MONITOR, South Carolina	(D) M-F • E NORTH AM & EUROPE • 500 kW
		(D) M-F • E NORTH AM • 500 kW
		(D) Sa • E NORTH AM & EUROPE • 500 kW
		(D) Sa/Su • E NORTH AM & C AMERICA • 500 kW
		(D) Su • E NORTH AM & EUROPE • 500 kW
	†CHRIST SCI MONITOR, Via Saipan	AUSTRALASIA • 100 kW (J) Sa • EUROPE & MIDEAST • 100 kW
		(D) • AUSTRALASIA • 100 kW
		M-F • AUSTRALASIA • 100 kW (J) Su-F • EUROPE & MIDEAST • 100 kW
		(D) M-F • AUSTRALASIA • 100 kW
		Sa/Su • AUSTRALASIA • 100 kW
		(D) Sa/Su • AUSTRALASIA • 100 kW

World Time: 0 1 2 3 4 5 6 7 8 9 10 11 12 13 14 15 16 17 18 19 20 21 22 23 24

ENGLISH ▬ ARABIC ∾∾∾ CHINESE □□□ FRENCH ▬▬ GERMAN ▬ RUSSIAN ══ SPANISH ▬▬ OTHER ◁

| FREQUENCY | COUNTRY, STATION, LOCATION | TARGET • NETWORK • POWER (kW) | World Time |

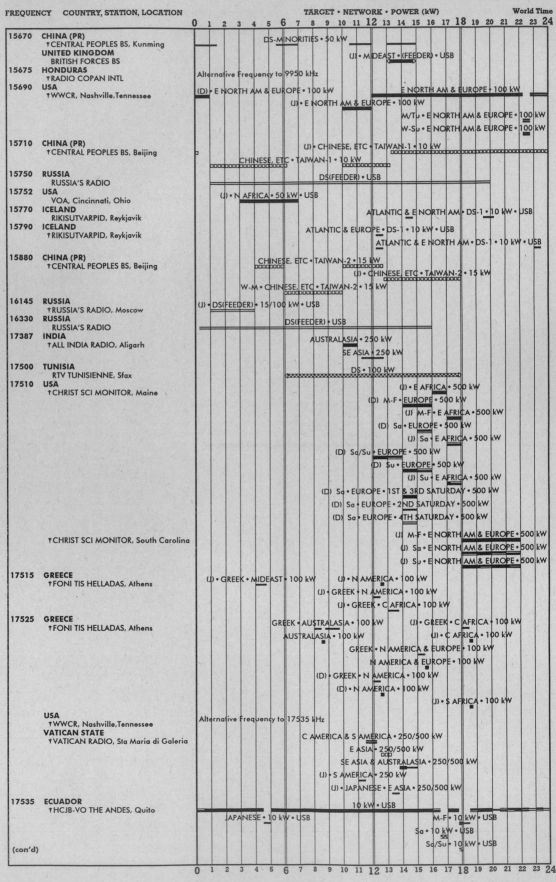

15670 CHINA (PR)
†CENTRAL PEOPLES BS, Kunming — DS-MINORITIES • 50 kW
UNITED KINGDOM
BRITISH FORCES BS — (J) • MIDEAST • (FEEDER) • USB
15675 HONDURAS
†RADIO COPAN INTL — Alternative Frequency to 9950 kHz
15690 USA
†WWCR, Nashville, Tennessee — (D) • E NORTH AM & EUROPE • 100 kW / E NORTH AM & EUROPE • 100 kW
(J) • E NORTH AM & EUROPE • 100 kW
M/Tu • E NORTH AM & EUROPE • 100 kW
W-Su • E NORTH AM & EUROPE • 100 kW
15710 CHINA (PR)
†CENTRAL PEOPLES BS, Beijing — (J) • CHINESE, ETC • TAIWAN-1 • 10 kW
CHINESE, ETC • TAIWAN-1 • 10 kW
15750 RUSSIA
RUSSIA'S RADIO — DS(FEEDER) • USB
15752 USA
VOA, Cincinnati, Ohio — (J) • N AFRICA • 50 kW • USB
15770 ICELAND
RIKISUTVARPID, Reykjavik — ATLANTIC & E NORTH AM • DS-1 • 10 kW • USB
15790 ICELAND
†RIKISUTVARPID, Reykjavik — ATLANTIC & EUROPE • DS-1 • 10 kW • USB
ATLANTIC & E NORTH AM • DS-1 • 10 kW • USB
15880 CHINA (PR)
†CENTRAL PEOPLES BS, Beijing — CHINESE, ETC • TAIWAN-2 • 15 kW
(J) • CHINESE, ETC • TAIWAN-2 • 15 kW
W-M • CHINESE, ETC • TAIWAN-2 • 15 kW
16145 RUSSIA
†RUSSIA'S RADIO, Moscow — (J) • DS(FEEDER) • 15/100 kW • USB
16330 RUSSIA
RUSSIA'S RADIO — DS(FEEDER) • USB
17387 INDIA
†ALL INDIA RADIO, Aligarh — AUSTRALASIA • 250 kW / SE ASIA • 250 kW
17500 TUNISIA
RTV TUNISIENNE, Sfax — DS • 100 kW
17510 USA
†CHRIST SCI MONITOR, Maine — (J) • E AFRICA • 500 kW
(D) M-F • EUROPE • 500 kW
(J) M-F • E AFRICA • 500 kW
(D) Sa • EUROPE • 500 kW
(J) Sa • E AFRICA • 500 kW
(D) Sa/Su • EUROPE • 500 kW
(D) Su • EUROPE • 500 kW
(J) Su • E AFRICA • 500 kW
(D) Sa • EUROPE • 1ST & 3RD SATURDAY • 500 kW
(D) Sa • EUROPE • 2ND SATURDAY • 500 kW
(D) Sa • EUROPE • 4TH SATURDAY • 500 kW
†CHRIST SCI MONITOR, South Carolina — (J) M-F • E NORTH AM & EUROPE • 500 kW
(J) Sa • E NORTH AM & EUROPE • 500 kW
(J) Su • E NORTH AM & EUROPE • 500 kW
17515 GREECE
†FONI TIS HELLADAS, Athens — (J) • GREEK • MIDEAST • 100 kW / (J) • N AMERICA • 100 kW
(J) • GREEK • N AMERICA • 100 kW
(J) • GREEK • C AFRICA • 100 kW
17525 GREECE
†FONI TIS HELLADAS, Athens — GREEK • AUSTRALASIA • 100 kW / (J) • GREEK • C AFRICA • 100 kW
AUSTRALASIA • 100 kW / (J) • C AFRICA • 100 kW
GREEK • N AMERICA & EUROPE • 100 kW
N AMERICA & EUROPE • 100 kW
(D) • GREEK • N AMERICA • 100 kW
(D) • N AMERICA • 100 kW
(J) • S AFRICA • 100 kW
USA
†WWCR, Nashville, Tennessee — Alternative Frequency to 17535 kHz
VATICAN STATE
†VATICAN RADIO, Sta Maria di Galeria — C AMERICA & S AMERICA • 250/500 kW
E ASIA • 250/500 kW
SE ASIA & AUSTRALASIA • 250/500 kW
(J) • S AMERICA • 250 kW
(J) • JAPANESE • E ASIA • 250/500 kW
17535 ECUADOR
†HCJB-VO THE ANDES, Quito — 10 kW • USB
JAPANESE • 10 kW • USB / M-F • 10 kW • USB
Sa • 10 kW • USB
Sa/Su • 10 kW • USB

(con'd)

SUMMER ONLY (J)   WINTER ONLY (D)   JAMMING / OR ∧   EARLIEST HEARD ◁   LATEST HEARD ▷   NEW OR CHANGED FOR 1993 †

FREQUENCY   COUNTRY, STATION, LOCATION   TARGET • NETWORK • POWER (kW)   World Time

0 1 2 3 4 5 6 7 8 9 10 11 12 13 14 15 16 17 18 19 20 21 22 23 24

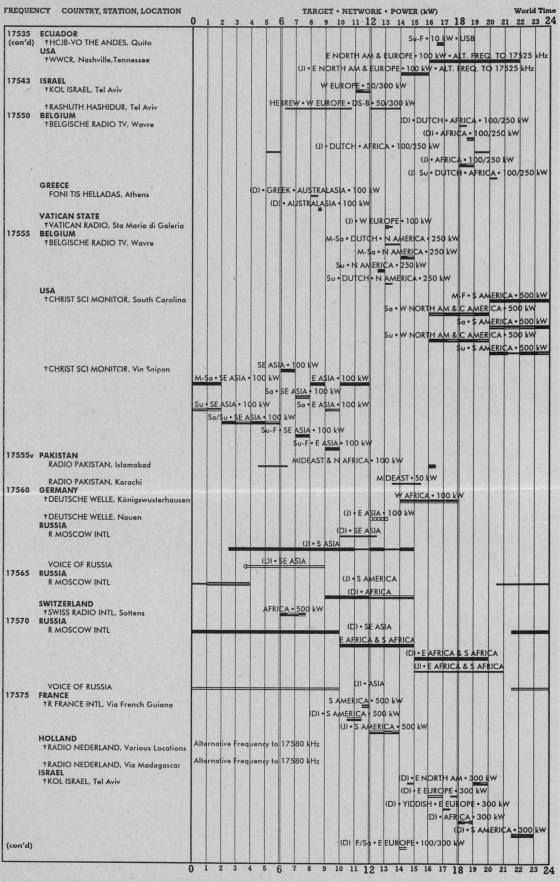

Frequency	Country, Station, Location	Target • Network • Power
17535 (con'd)	ECUADOR †HCJB-VO THE ANDES, Quito	Su-F • 10 kW • USB
	USA †WWCR, Nashville, Tennessee	E NORTH AM & EUROPE • 100 kW • ALT. FREQ. TO 17525 kHz / (J) • E NORTH AM & EUROPE • 100 kW • ALT. FREQ. TO 17525 kHz
17543	ISRAEL †KOL ISRAEL, Tel Aviv	W EUROPE • 50/300 kW
	†RASHUTH HASHIDUR, Tel Aviv	HEBREW • W EUROPE • DS-B • 50/300 kW
17550	BELGIUM †BELGISCHE RADIO TV, Wavre	(D) • DUTCH • AFRICA • 100/250 kW / (D) • AFRICA • 100/250 kW / (J) • DUTCH • AFRICA • 100/250 kW / (J) • AFRICA • 100/250 kW / (J) Su • DUTCH • AFRICA • 100/250 kW
	GREECE FONI TIS HELLADAS, Athens	(D) • GREEK • AUSTRALASIA • 100 kW / (D) • AUSTRALASIA • 100 kW
	VATICAN STATE †VATICAN RADIO, Sta Maria di Galeria	(J) • W EUROPE • 100 kW
17555	BELGIUM †BELGISCHE RADIO TV, Wavre	M-Sa • DUTCH • N AMERICA • 250 kW / M-Sa • N AMERICA • 250 kW / Su • N AMERICA • 250 kW / Su • DUTCH • N AMERICA • 250 kW
	USA †CHRIST SCI MONITOR, South Carolina	M-F • S AMERICA • 500 kW / Sa • W NORTH AM & C AMERICA • 500 kW / Sa • S AMERICA • 500 kW / Su • W NORTH AM & C AMERICA • 500 kW / Su • S AMERICA • 500 kW
	†CHRIST SCI MONITOR, Via Saipan	SE ASIA • 100 kW / M-Sa • SE ASIA • 100 kW / E ASIA • 100 kW / Sa • SE ASIA • 100 kW / Su • SE ASIA • 100 kW / Sa • E ASIA • 100 kW / Sa/Su • SE ASIA • 100 kW / Su-F • SE ASIA • 100 kW / Su-F • E ASIA • 100 kW
17555v	PAKISTAN RADIO PAKISTAN, Islamabad	MIDEAST & N AFRICA • 100 kW
	RADIO PAKISTAN, Karachi	MIDEAST • 50 kW
17560	GERMANY †DEUTSCHE WELLE, Königswusterhausen	W AFRICA • 100 kW
	†DEUTSCHE WELLE, Nauen	(J) • E ASIA • 100 kW
	RUSSIA R MOSCOW INTL	(D) • SE ASIA / (J) • S ASIA
	VOICE OF RUSSIA	(D) • SE ASIA
17565	RUSSIA R MOSCOW INTL	(J) • S AMERICA / (D) • AFRICA
	SWITZERLAND †SWISS RADIO INTL, Sottens	AFRICA • 500 kW
17570	RUSSIA R MOSCOW INTL	(D) • SE ASIA / E AFRICA & S AFRICA / (D) • E AFRICA & S AFRICA / (J) • E AFRICA & S AFRICA
	VOICE OF RUSSIA	(J) • ASIA
17575	FRANCE †R FRANCE INTL, Via French Guiana	S AMERICA • 500 kW / (D) • S AMERICA • 500 kW / (J) • S AMERICA • 500 kW
	HOLLAND †RADIO NEDERLAND, Various Locations	Alternative Frequency to 17580 kHz
	†RADIO NEDERLAND, Via Madagascar	Alternative Frequency to 17580 kHz
	ISRAEL †KOL ISRAEL, Tel Aviv	(D) • E NORTH AM • 300 kW / (D) • E EUROPE • 300 kW / (D) • YIDDISH • E EUROPE • 300 kW / (D) • AFRICA • 300 kW / (D) • S AMERICA • 300 kW / (D) F/Sa • E EUROPE • 100/300 kW

(con'd)

0 1 2 3 4 5 6 7 8 9 10 11 12 13 14 15 16 17 18 19 20 21 22 23 24

ENGLISH ▬   ARABIC ⬚⬚⬚   CHINESE ▫▫▫   FRENCH ▬   GERMAN ▬   RUSSIAN ═   SPANISH ▬   OTHER ▬

FREQUENCY   COUNTRY, STATION, LOCATION   TARGET • NETWORK • POWER (kW)   World Time

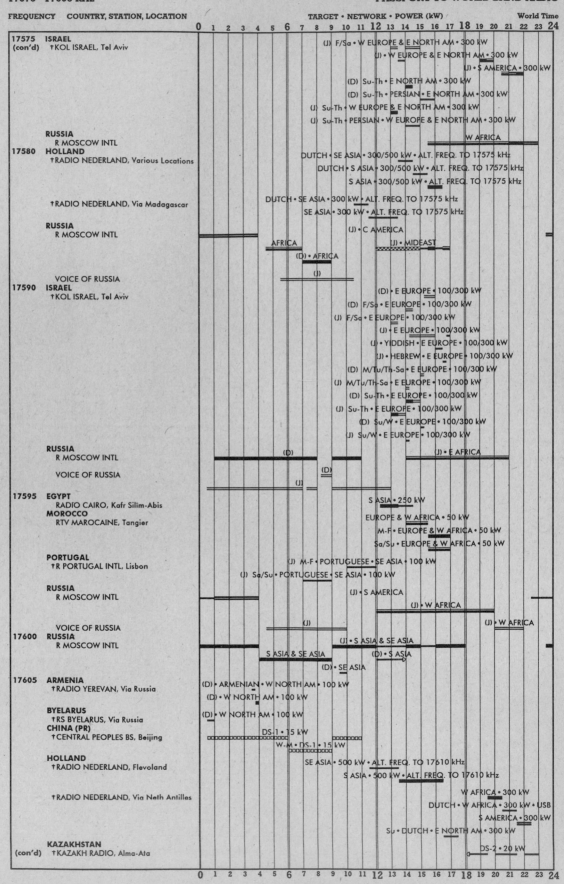

17575 **ISRAEL**
(con'd)   ↑KOL ISRAEL, Tel Aviv
           (J) F/Sa • W EUROPE & E NORTH AM • 300 kW
           (J) • W EUROPE & E NORTH AM • 300 kW
           (J) • S AMERICA • 300 kW
           (D) Su-Th • E NORTH AM • 300 kW
           (D) Su-Th • PERSIAN • E NORTH AM • 300 kW
           (J) Su-Th • W EUROPE & E NORTH AM • 300 kW
           (J) Su-Th • PERSIAN • W EUROPE & E NORTH AM • 300 kW

           RUSSIA
           R MOSCOW INTL
           W AFRICA
17580 **HOLLAND**
           ↑RADIO NEDERLAND, Various Locations
           DUTCH • SE ASIA • 300/500 kW • ALT. FREQ. TO 17575 kHz
           DUTCH • S ASIA • 300/500 kW • ALT. FREQ. TO 17575 kHz
           S ASIA • 300/500 kW • ALT. FREQ. TO 17575 kHz

           ↑RADIO NEDERLAND, Via Madagascar
           DUTCH • SE ASIA • 300 kW • ALT. FREQ. TO 17575 kHz
           SE ASIA • 300 kW • ALT. FREQ. TO 17575 kHz

           RUSSIA
           R MOSCOW INTL
           (J) • C AMERICA
           AFRICA   (J) • MIDEAST
           (D) • AFRICA

           VOICE OF RUSSIA
           (J)
17590 **ISRAEL**
           ↑KOL ISRAEL, Tel Aviv
           (D) • E EUROPE • 100/300 kW
           (D) F/Sa • E EUROPE • 100/300 kW
           (J) F/Sa • E EUROPE • 100/300 kW
           (J) • E EUROPE • 100/300 kW
           (J) • YIDDISH • E EUROPE • 100/300 kW
           (J) • HEBREW • E EUROPE • 100/300 kW
           (D) M/Tu/Th-Sa • E EUROPE • 100/300 kW
           (J) M/Tu/Th-Sa • E EUROPE • 100/300 kW
           (D) Su-Th • E EUROPE • 100/300 kW
           (J) Su-Th • E EUROPE • 100/300 kW
           (D) Su/W • E EUROPE • 100/300 kW
           (J) Su/W • E EUROPE • 100/300 kW

           RUSSIA
           R MOSCOW INTL
           (D)   (J) • E AFRICA

           VOICE OF RUSSIA
           (D)
           (J)
17595 **EGYPT**
           RADIO CAIRO, Kafr Silim-Abis
           S ASIA • 250 kW
           MOROCCO
           RTV MAROCAINE, Tangier
           EUROPE & W AFRICA • 50 kW
           M-F • EUROPE & W AFRICA • 50 kW
           Sa/Su • EUROPE & W AFRICA • 50 kW

           PORTUGAL
           ↑R PORTUGAL INTL, Lisbon
           (J) M-F • PORTUGUESE • SE ASIA • 100 kW
           (J) Sa/Su • PORTUGUESE • SE ASIA • 100 kW

           RUSSIA
           R MOSCOW INTL
           (J) • S AMERICA
           (J) • W AFRICA

           VOICE OF RUSSIA
           (J)   (J) • W AFRICA
17600 **RUSSIA**
           R MOSCOW INTL
           (J) • S ASIA & SE ASIA
           S ASIA & SE ASIA   (D) • S ASIA
           (D) • SE ASIA

17605 **ARMENIA**
           ↑RADIO YEREVAN, Via Russia
           (D) • ARMENIAN • W NORTH AM • 100 kW
           (D) • W NORTH AM • 100 kW

           BYELARUS
           ↑RS BYELARUS, Via Russia
           (D) • W NORTH AM • 100 kW
           CHINA (PR)
           ↑CENTRAL PEOPLES BS, Beijing
           DS-1 • 15 kW
           W-M • DS-1 • 15 kW

           HOLLAND
           ↑RADIO NEDERLAND, Flevoland
           SE ASIA • 500 kW • ALT. FREQ. TO 17610 kHz
           S ASIA • 500 kW • ALT. FREQ. TO 17610 kHz

           ↑RADIO NEDERLAND, Via Neth Antilles
           W AFRICA • 300 kW
           DUTCH • W AFRICA • 300 kW • USB
           S AMERICA • 300 kW
           Su • DUTCH • E NORTH AM • 300 kW

           KAZAKHSTAN
(con'd)   ↑KAZAKH RADIO, Alma-Ata
           DS-2 • 20 kW

SUMMER ONLY (J)   WINTER ONLY (D)   JAMMING / OR ⋀   EARLIEST HEARD ◁   LATEST HEARD ▷   NEW OR CHANGED FOR 1993 ↑

FREQUENCY   COUNTRY, STATION, LOCATION   TARGET • NETWORK • POWER (kW)   World Time

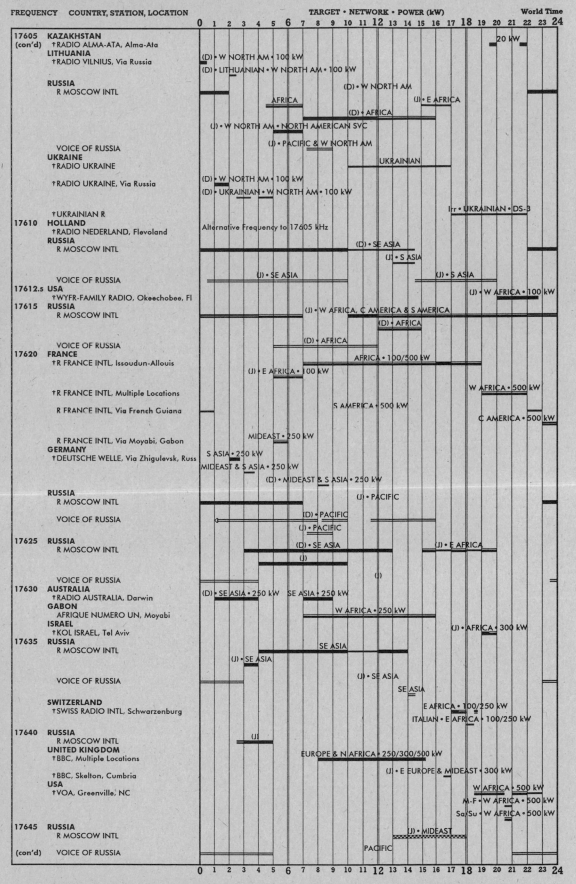

FREQUENCY	COUNTRY, STATION, LOCATION	TARGET • NETWORK • POWER (kW)
17605 (con'd)	KAZAKHSTAN †RADIO ALMA-ATA, Alma-Ata	20 kW
	LITHUANIA	(D) • W NORTH AM • 100 kW
	†RADIO VILNIUS, Via Russia	(D) • LITHUANIAN • W NORTH AM • 100 kW
	RUSSIA R MOSCOW INTL	(D) • W NORTH AM
		AFRICA
		(J) • E AFRICA
		(D) • AFRICA
		(J) • W NORTH AM • NORTH AMERICAN SVC
	VOICE OF RUSSIA	(J) • PACIFIC & W NORTH AM
	UKRAINE †RADIO UKRAINE	UKRAINIAN
	†RADIO UKRAINE, Via Russia	(D) • W NORTH AM • 100 kW
		(D) • UKRAINIAN • W NORTH AM • 100 kW
	†UKRAINIAN R	Irr • UKRAINIAN • DS-3
17610	HOLLAND †RADIO NEDERLAND, Flevoland	Alternative Frequency to 17605 kHz
	RUSSIA R MOSCOW INTL	(D) • SE ASIA
		(J) • S ASIA
	VOICE OF RUSSIA	(J) • SE ASIA
		(J) • S ASIA
17612.5	USA †WYFR-FAMILY RADIO, Okeechobee, Fl	(J) • W AFRICA • 100 kW
17615	RUSSIA R MOSCOW INTL	(J) • W AFRICA, C AMERICA & S AMERICA
		(D) • AFRICA
	VOICE OF RUSSIA	(D) • AFRICA
17620	FRANCE †R FRANCE INTL, Issoudun-Allouis	AFRICA • 100/500 kW
		(J) • E AFRICA • 100 kW
	†R FRANCE INTL, Multiple Locations	W AFRICA • 500 kW
	R FRANCE INTL, Via French Guiana	S AMERICA • 500 kW
		C AMERICA • 500 kW
	R FRANCE INTL, Via Moyabi, Gabon	MIDEAST • 250 kW
	GERMANY †DEUTSCHE WELLE, Via Zhigulevsk, Russ	S ASIA • 250 kW
		MIDEAST & S ASIA • 250 kW
		(D) • MIDEAST & S ASIA • 250 kW
	RUSSIA R MOSCOW INTL	(J) • PACIFIC
	VOICE OF RUSSIA	(D) • PACIFIC
		(J) • PACIFIC
17625	RUSSIA R MOSCOW INTL	(D) • SE ASIA
		(J) • E AFRICA
		(J)
	VOICE OF RUSSIA	(J)
17630	AUSTRALIA †RADIO AUSTRALIA, Darwin	(D) • SE ASIA • 250 kW SE ASIA • 250 kW
	GABON AFRIQUE NUMERO UN, Moyabi	W AFRICA • 250 kW
	ISRAEL †KOL ISRAEL, Tel Aviv	(J) • AFRICA • 300 kW
17635	RUSSIA R MOSCOW INTL	SE ASIA
		(J) • SE ASIA
	VOICE OF RUSSIA	(J) • SE ASIA
		SE ASIA
	SWITZERLAND †SWISS RADIO INTL, Schwarzenburg	E AFRICA • 100/250 kW
		ITALIAN • E AFRICA • 100/250 kW
17640	RUSSIA R MOSCOW INTL	(J)
	UNITED KINGDOM †BBC, Multiple Locations	EUROPE & N AFRICA • 250/300/500 kW
	†BBC, Skelton, Cumbria	(J) • E EUROPE & MIDEAST • 300 kW
	USA †VOA, Greenville, NC	W AFRICA • 500 kW
		M-F • W AFRICA • 500 kW
		Sa/Su • W AFRICA • 500 kW
17645	RUSSIA R MOSCOW INTL	(J) • MIDEAST
(con'd)	VOICE OF RUSSIA	PACIFIC

ENGLISH ▬▬   ARABIC ⨯⨯⨯   CHINESE □□□   FRENCH ══   GERMAN ▬▬   RUSSIAN ══   SPANISH ▬▬   OTHER ──

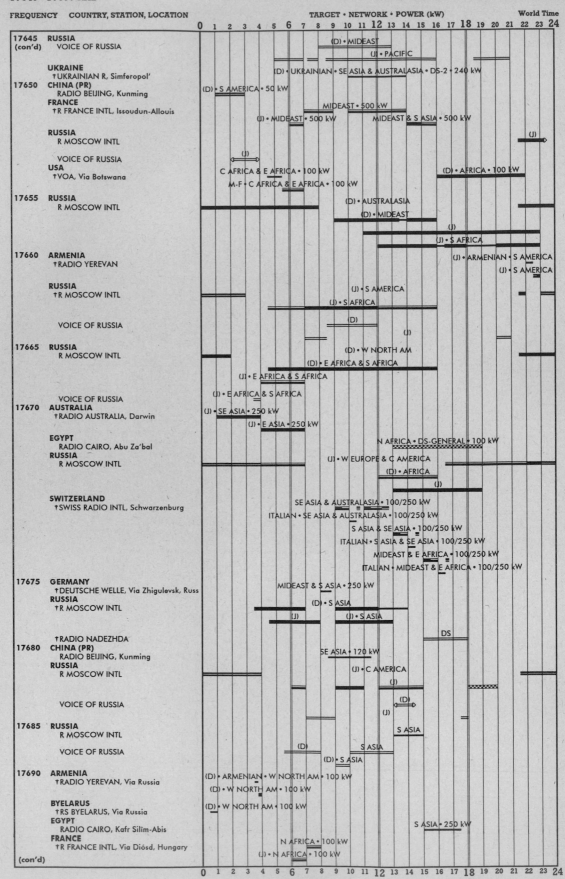

FREQUENCY   COUNTRY, STATION, LOCATION   TARGET • NETWORK • POWER (kW)   World Time

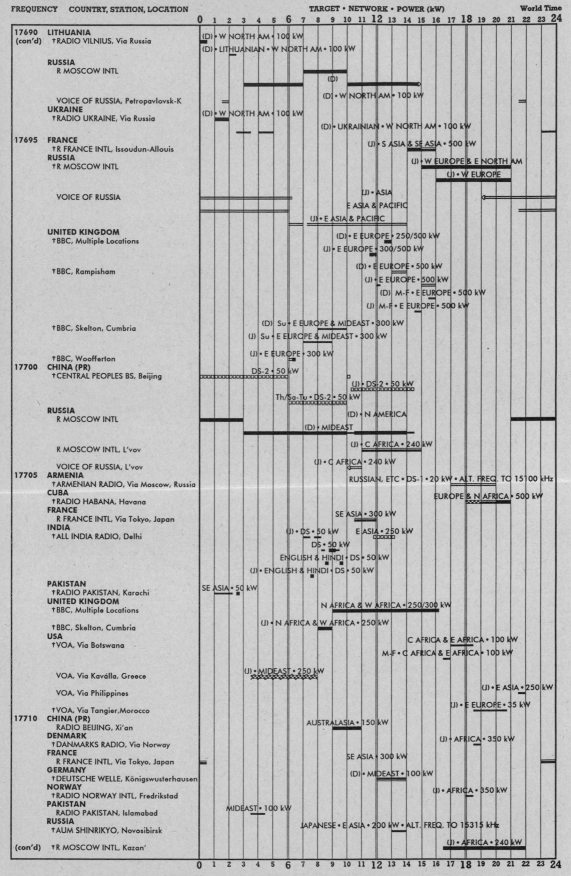

17690
(con'd) LITHUANIA
  †RADIO VILNIUS, Via Russia
    (D) • W NORTH AM • 100 kW
    (D) • LITHUANIAN • W NORTH AM • 100 kW

RUSSIA
  R MOSCOW INTL
    (D)

  VOICE OF RUSSIA, Petropavlovsk-K
    (D) • W NORTH AM • 100 kW
UKRAINE
  †RADIO UKRAINE, Via Russia
    (D) • W NORTH AM • 100 kW
    (D) • UKRAINIAN • W NORTH AM • 100 kW

17695 FRANCE
  †R FRANCE INTL, Issoudun-Allouis
    (J) • S ASIA & SE ASIA • 500 kW
RUSSIA
  †R MOSCOW INTL
    (J) • W EUROPE & E NORTH AM
    (J) • W EUROPE

  VOICE OF RUSSIA
    (J) • ASIA
    E ASIA & PACIFIC
    (J) • E ASIA & PACIFIC

UNITED KINGDOM
  †BBC, Multiple Locations
    (D) • E EUROPE • 250/500 kW
    (J) • E EUROPE • 300/500 kW

  †BBC, Rampisham
    (D) • E EUROPE • 500 kW
    (J) • E EUROPE • 500 kW
    (D) • M-F • E EUROPE • 500 kW
    (J) • M-F • E EUROPE • 500 kW

  †BBC, Skelton, Cumbria
    (D) Su • E EUROPE & MIDEAST • 300 kW
    (J) Su • E EUROPE & MIDEAST • 300 kW

  †BBC, Woofferton
    (J) • E EUROPE • 300 kW
17700 CHINA (PR)
  †CENTRAL PEOPLES BS, Beijing
    DS-2 • 50 kW
    (J) • DS-2 • 50 kW
    Th/Sa-Tu • DS-2 • 50 kW

RUSSIA
  R MOSCOW INTL
    (D) • N AMERICA
    (D) • MIDEAST

  R MOSCOW INTL, L'vov
    (J) • C AFRICA • 240 kW
  VOICE OF RUSSIA, L'vov
    (J) • C AFRICA • 240 kW
17705 ARMENIA
  †ARMENIAN RADIO, Via Moscow, Russia
    RUSSIAN, ETC • DS-1 • 20 kW • ALT. FREQ. TO 15100 kHz
CUBA
  †RADIO HABANA, Havana
    EUROPE & N AFRICA • 500 kW
FRANCE
  R FRANCE INTL, Via Tokyo, Japan
    SE ASIA • 300 kW
INDIA
  †ALL INDIA RADIO, Delhi
    (J) • DS • 50 kW   E ASIA • 250 kW
    DS • 50 kW
    ENGLISH & HINDI • DS • 50 kW
    (J) • ENGLISH & HINDI • DS • 50 kW

PAKISTAN
  †RADIO PAKISTAN, Karachi
    SE ASIA • 50 kW
UNITED KINGDOM
  †BBC, Multiple Locations
    N AFRICA & W AFRICA • 250/300 kW

  †BBC, Skelton, Cumbria
    (J) • N AFRICA & W AFRICA • 250 kW
USA
  †VOA, Via Botswana
    C AFRICA & E AFRICA • 100 kW
    M-F • C AFRICA & E AFRICA • 100 kW

  VOA, Via Kaválla, Greece
    (J) • MIDEAST • 250 kW
  VOA, Via Philippines
    (J) • E ASIA • 250 kW
  †VOA, Via Tangier, Morocco
    (J) • E EUROPE • 35 kW
17710 CHINA (PR)
  RADIO BEIJING, Xi'an
    AUSTRALASIA • 150 kW
DENMARK
  †DANMARKS RADIO, Via Norway
    (J) • AFRICA • 350 kW
FRANCE
  R FRANCE INTL, Via Tokyo, Japan
    SE ASIA • 300 kW
GERMANY
  †DEUTSCHE WELLE, Königswusterhausen
    (D) • MIDEAST • 100 kW
NORWAY
  †RADIO NORWAY INTL, Fredrikstad
    (J) • AFRICA • 350 kW
PAKISTAN
  RADIO PAKISTAN, Islamabad
    MIDEAST • 100 kW
RUSSIA
  †AUM SHINRIKYO, Novosibirsk
    JAPANESE • E ASIA • 200 kW • ALT. FREQ. TO 15315 kHz

(con'd) †R MOSCOW INTL, Kazan'
    (J) • AFRICA • 240 kW

ENGLISH ▬   ARABIC ⌇⌇⌇   CHINESE □□□   FRENCH ═══   GERMAN ▬▬   RUSSIAN ═══   SPANISH ▬▬   OTHER ───

FREQUENCY   COUNTRY, STATION, LOCATION   TARGET • NETWORK • POWER (kW)   World Time

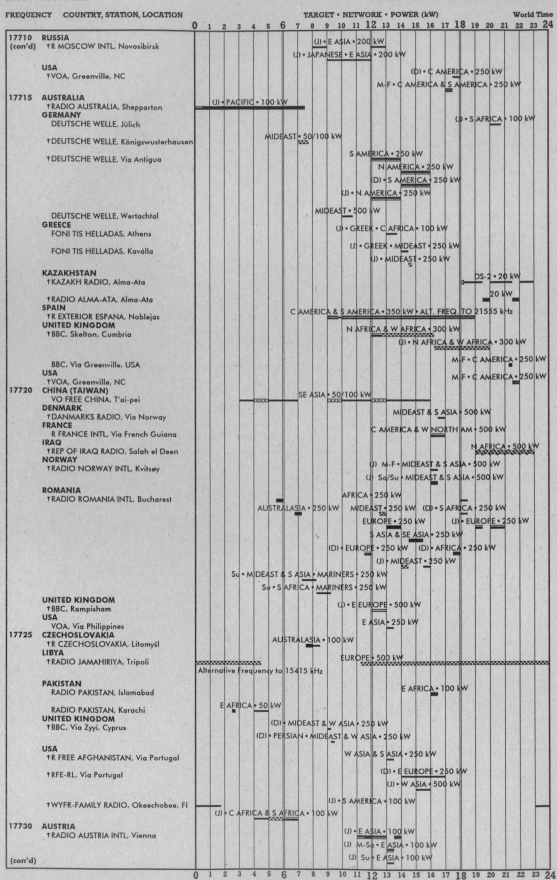

17710 **RUSSIA**
(con'd)   †R MOSCOW INTL, Novosibirsk — (J) • E ASIA • 200 kW
                                         (J) • JAPANESE • E ASIA • 200 kW

         USA
         †VOA, Greenville, NC — (D) • C AMERICA • 250 kW
                                M-F • C AMERICA & S AMERICA • 250 kW

17715 **AUSTRALIA**
         †RADIO AUSTRALIA, Shepparton — (J) • PACIFIC • 100 kW
         GERMANY
           DEUTSCHE WELLE, Jülich — (J) • S AFRICA • 100 kW

           †DEUTSCHE WELLE, Königswusterhausen — MIDEAST • 50/100 kW

           †DEUTSCHE WELLE, Via Antigua — S AMERICA • 250 kW
                                          N AMERICA • 250 kW
                                          (D) • S AMERICA • 250 kW
                                          (J) • N AMERICA • 250 kW

           DEUTSCHE WELLE, Wertachtal — MIDEAST • 500 kW
         GREECE
           FONI TIS HELLADAS, Athens — (J) • GREEK • C AFRICA • 100 kW

           FONI TIS HELLADAS, Kaválla — (J) • GREEK • MIDEAST • 250 kW
                                        (J) • MIDEAST • 250 kW

         KAZAKHSTAN
           †KAZAKH RADIO, Alma-Ata — DS-2 • 20 kW

           †RADIO ALMA-ATA, Alma-Ata — 20 kW
         SPAIN
           †R EXTERIOR ESPANA, Noblejas — C AMERICA & S AMERICA • 350 kW • ALT. FREQ. TO 21555 kHz
         UNITED KINGDOM
           †BBC, Skelton, Cumbria — N AFRICA & W AFRICA • 300 kW
                                    (J) • N AFRICA & W AFRICA • 300 kW

           BBC, Via Greenville, USA — M-F • C AMERICA • 250 kW
         USA
           †VOA, Greenville, NC — M-F • C AMERICA • 250 kW
17720 **CHINA (TAIWAN)**
           VO FREE CHINA, T'ai-pei — SE ASIA • 50/100 kW
         DENMARK
           †DANMARKS RADIO, Via Norway — MIDEAST & S ASIA • 500 kW
         FRANCE
           R FRANCE INTL, Via French Guiana — C AMERICA & W NORTH AM • 500 kW
         IRAQ
           †REP OF IRAQ RADIO, Salah el Deen — N AFRICA • 500 kW
         NORWAY
           †RADIO NORWAY INTL, Kvitsøy — (J) M-F • MIDEAST & S ASIA • 500 kW
                                         (J) Sa/Su • MIDEAST & S ASIA • 500 kW

         ROMANIA
           †RADIO ROMANIA INTL, Bucharest — AFRICA • 250 kW
                                  AUSTRALASIA • 250 kW   MIDEAST • 250 kW   (D) • S AFRICA • 250 kW
                                            EUROPE • 250 kW   (J) • EUROPE • 250 kW
                                            S ASIA & SE ASIA • 250 kW
                                  (D) • EUROPE • 250 kW   (D) • AFRICA • 250 kW
                                            (J) • MIDEAST • 250 kW
                                  Su • MIDEAST & S ASIA • MARINERS • 250 kW
                                  Su • S AFRICA • MARINERS • 250 kW

         UNITED KINGDOM
           †BBC, Rampisham — (J) • E EUROPE • 500 kW
         USA
           VOA, Via Philippines — E ASIA • 250 kW
17725 **CZECHOSLOVAKIA**
           †R CZECHOSLOVAKIA, Litomyšl — AUSTRALASIA • 100 kW
         LIBYA
           †RADIO JAMAHIRIYA, Tripoli — EUROPE • 500 kW
           Alternative Frequency to 15415 kHz

         PAKISTAN
           RADIO PAKISTAN, Islamabad — E AFRICA • 100 kW

           RADIO PAKISTAN, Karachi — E AFRICA • 50 kW
         UNITED KINGDOM
           †BBC, Via Zyyi, Cyprus — (D) • MIDEAST & W ASIA • 250 kW
                                    (D) • PERSIAN • MIDEAST & W ASIA • 250 kW

         USA
           †R FREE AFGHANISTAN, Via Portugal — W ASIA & S ASIA • 250 kW

           †RFE-RL, Via Portugal — (D) • E EUROPE • 250 kW
                                   (J) • W ASIA • 500 kW

           †WYFR-FAMILY RADIO, Okeechobee, Fl — (J) • S AMERICA • 100 kW
                                      (J) • C AFRICA & S AFRICA • 100 kW

17730 **AUSTRIA**
           †RADIO AUSTRIA INTL, Vienna — (J) • E ASIA • 100 kW
                                         (J) • M-Sa • E ASIA • 100 kW
                                         (J) Su • E ASIA • 100 kW

(con'd)

0 1 2 3 4 5 6 7 8 9 10 11 12 13 14 15 16 17 18 19 20 21 22 23 24

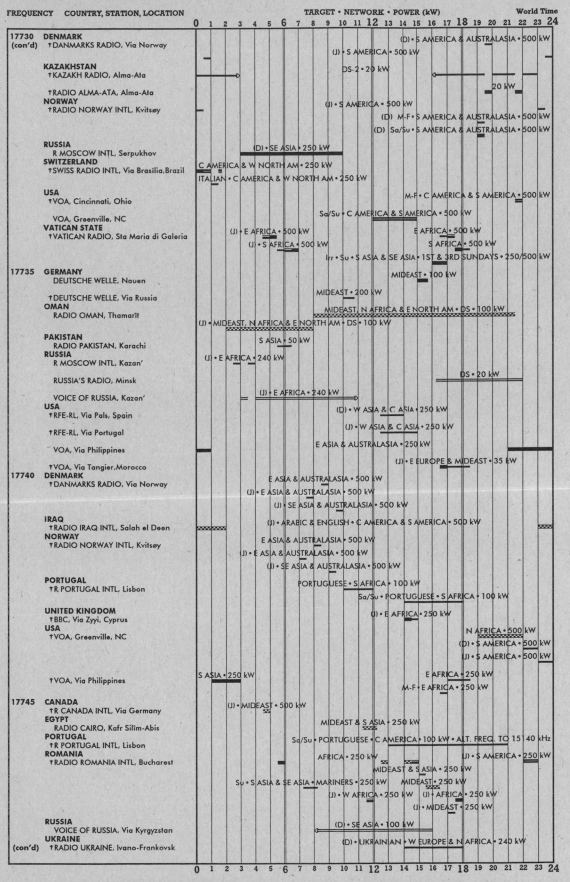

Frequency	Country, Station, Location	Target • Network • Power
17730 (con'd)	DENMARK †DANMARKS RADIO, Via Norway	(D) • S AMERICA & AUSTRALASIA • 500 kW (J) • S AMERICA • 500 kW
	KAZAKHSTAN †KAZAKH RADIO, Alma-Ata	DS-2 • 20 kW
	†RADIO ALMA-ATA, Alma-Ata NORWAY †RADIO NORWAY INTL, Kvitsøy	20 kW (J) • S AMERICA • 500 kW (D) • M-F • S AMERICA & AUSTRALASIA • 500 kW (D) • Sa/Su • S AMERICA & AUSTRALASIA • 500 kW
	RUSSIA R MOSCOW INTL, Serpukhov SWITZERLAND †SWISS RADIO INTL, Via Brasilia, Brazil	(D) • SE ASIA • 250 kW C AMERICA & W NORTH AM • 250 kW ITALIAN • C AMERICA & W NORTH AM • 250 kW
	USA †VOA, Cincinnati, Ohio VOA, Greenville, NC VATICAN STATE †VATICAN RADIO, Sta Maria di Galeria	M-F • C AMERICA & S AMERICA • 500 kW Sa/Su • C AMERICA & S AMERICA • 500 kW (J) • E AFRICA • 500 kW E AFRICA • 500 kW (J) • S AFRICA • 500 kW S AFRICA • 500 kW Irr • Su • S ASIA & SE ASIA • 1ST & 3RD SUNDAYS • 250/500 kW
17735	GERMANY DEUTSCHE WELLE, Nauen †DEUTSCHE WELLE, Via Russia OMAN RADIO OMAN, Thamarit	MIDEAST • 100 kW MIDEAST • 200 kW MIDEAST, N AFRICA & E NORTH AM • DS • 100 kW (J) • MIDEAST, N AFRICA & E NORTH AM • DS • 100 kW
	PAKISTAN RADIO PAKISTAN, Karachi RUSSIA R MOSCOW INTL, Kazan' RUSSIA'S RADIO, Minsk VOICE OF RUSSIA, Kazan' USA †RFE-RL, Via Pals, Spain †RFE-RL, Via Portugal VOA, Via Philippines †VOA, Via Tangier, Morocco	S ASIA • 50 kW (J) • E AFRICA • 240 kW DS • 20 kW (J) • E AFRICA • 240 kW (D) • W ASIA & C ASIA • 250 kW (J) • W ASIA & C ASIA • 250 kW E ASIA & AUSTRALASIA • 250 kW (J) • E EUROPE & MIDEAST • 35 kW
17740	DENMARK †DANMARKS RADIO, Via Norway	E ASIA & AUSTRALASIA • 500 kW (J) • E ASIA & AUSTRALASIA • 500 kW (J) • SE ASIA & AUSTRALASIA • 500 kW
	IRAQ †RADIO IRAQ INTL, Salah el Deen NORWAY †RADIO NORWAY INTL, Kvitsøy	(J) • ARABIC & ENGLISH • C AMERICA & S AMERICA • 500 kW E ASIA & AUSTRALASIA • 500 kW (J) • E ASIA & AUSTRALASIA • 500 kW (J) • SE ASIA & AUSTRALASIA • 500 kW
	PORTUGAL †R PORTUGAL INTL, Lisbon	PORTUGUESE • S AFRICA • 100 kW Sa/Su • PORTUGUESE • S AFRICA • 100 kW
	UNITED KINGDOM †BBC, Via Zyyi, Cyprus USA †VOA, Greenville, NC	(J) • E AFRICA • 250 kW N AFRICA • 500 kW (D) • S AMERICA • 500 kW (J) • S AMERICA • 500 kW
	†VOA, Via Philippines	S ASIA • 250 kW E AFRICA • 250 kW M-F • E AFRICA • 250 kW
17745	CANADA †R CANADA INTL, Via Germany EGYPT RADIO CAIRO, Kafr Silim-Abis PORTUGAL †R PORTUGAL INTL, Lisbon ROMANIA †RADIO ROMANIA INTL, Bucharest	(J) • MIDEAST • 500 kW MIDEAST & S ASIA • 250 kW Sa/Su • PORTUGUESE • C AMERICA • 100 kW • ALT. FREQ. TO 15140 kHz AFRICA • 250 kW (J) • S AMERICA • 250 kW MIDEAST & S ASIA • 250 kW Su • S ASIA & SE ASIA • MARINERS • 250 kW MIDEAST • 250 kW (J) • W AFRICA • 250 kW (J) • AFRICA • 250 kW (J) • MIDEAST • 250 kW
	RUSSIA VOICE OF RUSSIA, Via Kyrgyzstan UKRAINE	(D) • SE ASIA • 100 kW (D) • UKRAINIAN • W EUROPE & N AFRICA • 240 kW
(con'd)	†RADIO UKRAINE, Ivano-Frankovsk	

FREQUENCY   COUNTRY, STATION, LOCATION   TARGET • NETWORK • POWER (kW)   World Time

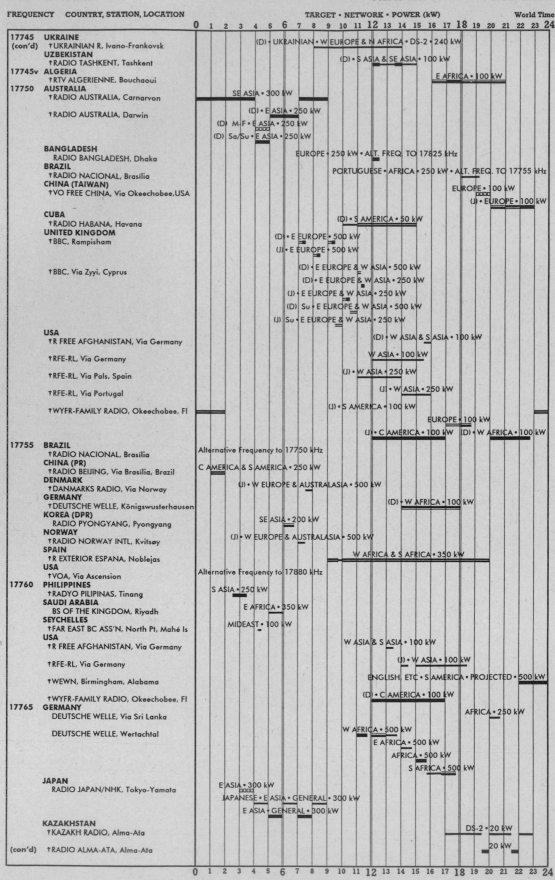

FREQUENCY	COUNTRY, STATION, LOCATION	TARGET • NETWORK • POWER (kW)
17745 (con'd)	**UKRAINE** †UKRAINIAN R, Ivano-Frankovsk	(D) • UKRAINIAN • W EUROPE & N AFRICA • DS-2 • 240 kW
	UZBEKISTAN †RADIO TASHKENT, Tashkent	(D) • S ASIA & SE ASIA • 100 kW
17745v	**ALGERIA** †RTV ALGERIENNE, Bouchaoui	E AFRICA • 100 kW
17750	**AUSTRALIA** †RADIO AUSTRALIA, Carnarvon	SE ASIA • 300 kW
	†RADIO AUSTRALIA, Darwin	(D) • E ASIA • 250 kW
		(D) • M-F • E ASIA • 250 kW
		(D) • Sa/Su • E ASIA • 250 kW
	BANGLADESH RADIO BANGLADESH, Dhaka	EUROPE • 250 kW • ALT. FREQ. TO 17825 kHz
	BRAZIL †RADIO NACIONAL, Brasilia	PORTUGUESE • AFRICA • 250 kW • ALT. FREQ. TO 17755 kHz
	CHINA (TAIWAN) †VO FREE CHINA, Via Okeechobee, USA	EUROPE • 100 kW
		(J) • EUROPE • 100 kW
	CUBA †RADIO HABANA, Havana	(D) • S AMERICA • 50 kW
	UNITED KINGDOM †BBC, Rampisham	(D) • E EUROPE • 500 kW
		(J) • E EUROPE • 500 kW
	†BBC, Via Zyyi, Cyprus	(D) • E EUROPE & W ASIA • 500 kW
		(D) • E EUROPE & W ASIA • 250 kW
		(J) • E EUROPE & W ASIA • 250 kW
		(D) • Su • E EUROPE & W ASIA • 500 kW
		(J) • Su • E EUROPE & W ASIA • 250 kW
	USA †R FREE AFGHANISTAN, Via Germany	(D) • W ASIA & S ASIA • 100 kW
	†RFE-RL, Via Germany	W ASIA • 100 kW
	†RFE-RL, Via Pals, Spain	(J) • W ASIA • 250 kW
	†RFE-RL, Via Portugal	(J) • W ASIA • 250 kW
	†WYFR-FAMILY RADIO, Okeechobee, Fl	(J) • S AMERICA • 100 kW
		EUROPE • 100 kW
		(J) • C AMERICA • 100 kW (D) • W AFRICA • 100 kW
17755	**BRAZIL** †RADIO NACIONAL, Brasilia	Alternative Frequency to 17750 kHz
	CHINA (PR) †RADIO BEIJING, Via Brasilia, Brazil	C AMERICA & S AMERICA • 250 kW
	DENMARK †DANMARKS RADIO, Via Norway	(J) • W EUROPE & AUSTRALASIA • 500 kW
	GERMANY †DEUTSCHE WELLE, Königswusterhausen	(D) • W AFRICA • 100 kW
	KOREA (DPR) RADIO PYONGYANG, Pyongyang	SE ASIA • 200 kW
	NORWAY †RADIO NORWAY INTL, Kvitsøy	(J) • W EUROPE & AUSTRALASIA • 500 kW
	SPAIN †R EXTERIOR ESPANA, Noblejas	W AFRICA & S AFRICA • 350 kW
	USA †VOA, Via Ascension	Alternative Frequency to 17880 kHz
17760	**PHILIPPINES** †RADYO PILIPINAS, Tinang	S ASIA • 250 kW
	SAUDI ARABIA BS OF THE KINGDOM, Riyadh	E AFRICA • 350 kW
	SEYCHELLES †FAR EAST BC ASS'N, North Pt, Mahé Is	MIDEAST • 100 kW
	USA †R FREE AFGHANISTAN, Via Germany	W ASIA & S ASIA • 100 kW
	†RFE-RL, Via Germany	(J) • W ASIA • 100 kW
	†WEWN, Birmingham, Alabama	ENGLISH, ETC • S AMERICA • PROJECTED • 500 kW
	†WYFR-FAMILY RADIO, Okeechobee, Fl	(D) • C AMERICA • 100 kW
17765	**GERMANY** DEUTSCHE WELLE, Via Sri Lanka	AFRICA • 250 kW
	DEUTSCHE WELLE, Wertachtal	W AFRICA • 500 kW
		E AFRICA • 500 kW
		AFRICA • 500 kW
		S AFRICA • 500 kW
	JAPAN RADIO JAPAN/NHK, Tokyo-Yamata	E ASIA • 300 kW
		JAPANESE • E ASIA • GENERAL • 300 kW
		E ASIA • GENERAL • 300 kW
	KAZAKHSTAN †KAZAKH RADIO, Alma-Ata	DS-2 • 20 kW
(con'd)	†RADIO ALMA-ATA, Alma-Ata	20 kW

SUMMER ONLY (J)   WINTER ONLY (D)   JAMMING / OR ∧   EARLIEST HEARD ◁   LATEST HEARD ▷   NEW OR CHANGED FOR 1993 †

FREQUENCY   COUNTRY, STATION, LOCATION

TARGET • NETWORK • POWER (kW)

World Time

0 1 2 3 4 5 6 7 8 9 10 11 12 13 14 15 16 17 18 19 20 21 22 23 24

Frequency	Country, Station, Location	Target • Network • Power
17765 (con'd)	**KOREA (DPR)** RADIO PYONGYANG, Pyongyang	SE ASIA • 200 kW; KOREAN • SE ASIA • 200 kW; E AFRICA • 200 kW
	RUSSIA R MOSCOW INTL, Armavir	(J) • S ASIA & SE ASIA • 500 kW
	R MOSCOW INTL, Tula	(D) • S ASIA & SE ASIA • 240 kW
	VOICE OF RUSSIA, Armavir	(J) • S ASIA & SE ASIA • 500 kW
	USA †VOA, Via Philippines	E ASIA • 250 kW
17770	**CUBA** †RADIO HABANA, Havana	MIDEAST • 100 kW; EUROPE & N AFRICA • 250 kW; Su • EUROPE & N AFRICA • 250 kW
	EGYPT RADIO CAIRO, Kafr Silim-Abis	S AMERICA • 250 kW; SE ASIA • 250 kW
	GERMANY DEUTSCHE WELLE, Nauen	(J) • SE ASIA • 100 kW
	NEW ZEALAND †R NEW ZEALAND INTL, Rangitaiki	ENGLISH, ETC • PACIFIC • DS • 100 kW; (D) • PACIFIC • DS • 100 kW
	QATAR QATAR BC SERVICE, Doha-Al Khaisah	(J) • EUROPE • 100/250 kW
	USA †VOA, Via Germany	(J) • MIDEAST & W ASIA • 500 kW
	†VOA, Via Tangier, Morocco	(J) • E EUROPE • 35 kW
17775	**FRANCE** R FRANCE INTL, Issoudun-Allouis	E AFRICA • MEDIAS FRANCE • 100 kW
	ROMANIA †RADIO ROMANIA INTL, Bucharest	(D) • W AFRICA • 250 kW
	RUSSIA R MOSCOW INTL, Via Kyrgyzstan	S ASIA & SE ASIA • 100 kW; (J) • E AFRICA • 500 kW; (J) • S ASIA & SE ASIA • 100 kW
	USA †KVOH-VO HOPE, Rancho Simi, Ca	Su/M • W NORTH AM & C AMERICA • 50 kW; Tu-Sa • W NORTH AM & C AMERICA • 50 kW; W NORTH AM & C AMERICA • 50 kW; M-F • W NORTH AM & C AMERICA • 50 kW; M-Sa • W NORTH AM & C AMERICA • 50 kW; Sa/Su • W NORTH AM & C AMERICA • 50 kW; Su • W NORTH AM & C AMERICA • 50 kW
17780	**BULGARIA** †RADIO SOFIA, Sofia	(D) • MIDEAST • 250 kW; (J) • MIDEAST • 250 kW; (J) • EUROPE • 250 kW
	GERMANY DEUTSCHE WELLE, Jülich	(D) • E ASIA • 100 kW
	†DEUTSCHE WELLE, Multiple Locations	(J) • JAPANESE • E ASIA • 250/500 kW
	DEUTSCHE WELLE, Via Sri Lanka	MIDEAST & S ASIA • 250 kW
	DEUTSCHE WELLE, Wertachtal	AUSTRALASIA • 500 kW
	ITALY RTV ITALIANA, Rome	E AFRICA • 100 kW; ITALIAN • E AFRICA • 100 kW; ITALIAN • E NORTH AM • 100 kW
	UKRAINE †UKRAINIAN R, Simferopol'	(D) • UKRAINIAN • E EUROPE • DS-2 • 100 kW
	UNITED KINGDOM †BBC, Rampisham	(J) • E EUROPE • 500 kW
	†BBC, Via Maşīrah, Oman	S ASIA & SE ASIA • 100 kW
	USA †CHRIST SCI MONITOR, Via Saipan	E ASIA • 100 kW; M-Sa • E ASIA • 100 kW; Su • E ASIA • 100 kW
	†VOA, Via Kaválla, Greece	(D) • C ASIA • 250 kW
	†VOA, Via Philippines	S ASIA & SE ASIA • 250 kW
17785	**DENMARK** †DANMARKS RADIO, Via Norway	C AMERICA & S AMERICA • 500 kW; (J) • E NORTH AM & C AMERICA • 500 kW
	FRANCE R FRANCE INTL, Issoudun-Allouis	W AFRICA • MEDIAS FRANCE • 500 kW; AFRICA • MEDIAS FRANCE • 500 kW
	INDIA ALL INDIA RADIO, Aligarh	MIDEAST • 250 kW
	JAPAN †RADIO JAPAN/NHK, Tokyo-Yamata	SE ASIA • 100 kW
(con'd)	**NORWAY** †RADIO NORWAY INTL, Sveio	C AMERICA & S AMERICA • 500 kW

0 1 2 3 4 5 6 7 8 9 10 11 12 13 14 15 16 17 18 19 20 21 22 23 24

ENGLISH ▬ ARABIC ≋ CHINESE ▫▫▫ FRENCH ═ GERMAN ▬ RUSSIAN ═ SPANISH ▬ OTHER ─

FREQUENCY   COUNTRY, STATION, LOCATION

TARGET • NETWORK • POWER (kW)

World Time

0 1 2 3 4 5 6 7 8 9 10 11 12 13 14 15 16 17 18 19 20 21 22 23 24

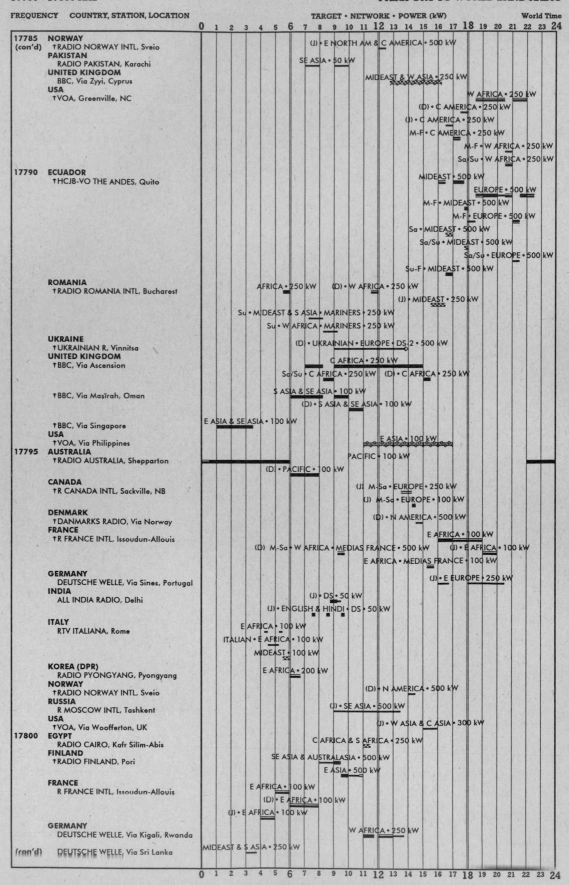

17785
(con'd) NORWAY
  †RADIO NORWAY INTL, Sveio — (J) • E NORTH AM & C AMERICA • 500 kW
PAKISTAN
  RADIO PAKISTAN, Karachi — SE ASIA • 50 kW
UNITED KINGDOM
  BBC, Via Zyyi, Cyprus — MIDEAST & W ASIA • 250 kW
USA
  †VOA, Greenville, NC — W AFRICA • 250 kW
   (D) • C AMERICA • 250 kW
   (J) • C AMERICA • 250 kW
   M-F • C AMERICA • 250 kW
   M-F • W AFRICA • 250 kW
   Sa/Su • W AFRICA • 250 kW

17790 ECUADOR
  †HCJB-VO THE ANDES, Quito — MIDEAST • 500 kW
   EUROPE • 500 kW
   M-F • MIDEAST • 500 kW
   M-F • EUROPE • 500 kW
   Sa • MIDEAST • 500 kW
   Sa/Su • MIDEAST • 500 kW
   Sa/Su • EUROPE • 500 kW
   Su-F • MIDEAST • 500 kW
ROMANIA
  †RADIO ROMANIA INTL, Bucharest — AFRICA • 250 kW
   (D) • W AFRICA • 250 kW
   (J) • MIDEAST • 250 kW
   Su • MIDEAST & S ASIA • MARINERS • 250 kW
   Su • W AFRICA • MARINERS • 250 kW
UKRAINE
  †UKRAINIAN R, Vinnitsa — (D) • UKRAINIAN • EUROPE • DS-2 • 500 kW
UNITED KINGDOM
  †BBC, Via Ascension — C AFRICA • 250 kW
   Sa/Su • C AFRICA • 250 kW   (D) • C AFRICA • 250 kW
  †BBC, Via Maṣīrah, Oman — S ASIA & SE ASIA • 100 kW
   (D) • S ASIA & SE ASIA • 100 kW
  †BBC, Via Singapore — E ASIA & SE ASIA • 100 kW
USA
  †VOA, Via Philippines — E ASIA • 100 kW
17795 AUSTRALIA
  †RADIO AUSTRALIA, Shepparton — PACIFIC • 100 kW
   (D) • PACIFIC • 100 kW
CANADA
  †R CANADA INTL, Sackville, NB — (J) M-Sa • EUROPE • 250 kW
   (J) M-Sa • EUROPE • 100 kW
DENMARK
  †DANMARKS RADIO, Via Norway — (D) • N AMERICA • 500 kW
FRANCE
  †R FRANCE INTL, Issoudun-Allouis — E AFRICA • 100 kW
   (D) M-Sa • W AFRICA • MEDIAS FRANCE • 500 kW   (J) • E AFRICA • 100 kW
   E AFRICA • MEDIAS FRANCE • 100 kW
GERMANY
  DEUTSCHE WELLE, Via Sines, Portugal — (J) • E EUROPE • 250 kW
INDIA
  ALL INDIA RADIO, Delhi — (J) • DS • 50 kW
   (J) • ENGLISH & HINDI • DS • 50 kW
ITALY
  RTV ITALIANA, Rome — E AFRICA • 100 kW
   ITALIAN • E AFRICA • 100 kW
   MIDEAST • 100 kW
KOREA (DPR)
  RADIO PYONGYANG, Pyongyang — E AFRICA • 200 kW
NORWAY
  †RADIO NORWAY INTL, Sveio — (D) • N AMERICA • 500 kW
RUSSIA
  R MOSCOW INTL, Tashkent — (J) • SE ASIA • 500 kW
USA
  †VOA, Via Woofferton, UK — (J) • W ASIA & C ASIA • 300 kW
17800 EGYPT
  RADIO CAIRO, Kafr Silim-Abis — C AFRICA & S AFRICA • 250 kW
FINLAND
  †RADIO FINLAND, Pori — SE ASIA & AUSTRALASIA • 500 kW
   E ASIA • 500 kW
FRANCE
  R FRANCE INTL, Issoudun-Allouis — E AFRICA • 100 kW
   (D) • E AFRICA • 100 kW
   (J) • E AFRICA • 100 kW
GERMANY
  DEUTSCHE WELLE, Via Kigali, Rwanda — W AFRICA • 250 kW
(con'd) DEUTSCHE WELLE, Via Sri Lanka — MIDEAST & S ASIA • 250 kW

0 1 2 3 4 5 6 7 8 9 10 11 12 13 14 15 16 17 18 19 20 21 22 23 24

SUMMER ONLY (J)   WINTER ONLY (D)   JAMMING / OR /\   EARLIEST HEARD ◁   LATEST HEARD ▷   NEW OR CHANGED FOR 1993 †

FREQUENCY   COUNTRY, STATION, LOCATION

TARGET • NETWORK • POWER (kW)

World Time

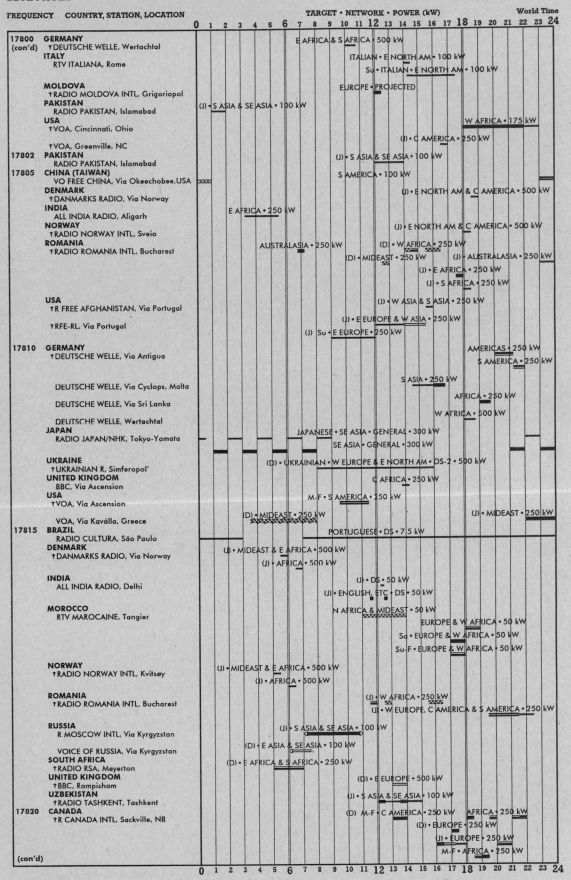

0 1 2 3 4 5 6 7 8 9 10 11 12 13 14 15 16 17 18 19 20 21 22 23 24

17800 (con'd)	GERMANY †DEUTSCHE WELLE, Wertachtal	E AFRICA & S AFRICA • 500 kW
	ITALY RTV ITALIANA, Rome	ITALIAN • E NORTH AM • 100 kW / Su • ITALIAN • E NORTH AM • 100 kW
	MOLDOVA †RADIO MOLDOVA INTL, Grigoriopol	EUROPE • PROJECTED
	PAKISTAN RADIO PAKISTAN, Islamabad	(J) • S ASIA & SE ASIA • 100 kW
	USA †VOA, Cincinnati, Ohio	W AFRICA • 175 kW
	†VOA, Greenville, NC	(J) • C AMERICA • 250 kW
17802	PAKISTAN RADIO PAKISTAN, Islamabad	(J) • S ASIA & SE ASIA • 100 kW
17805	CHINA (TAIWAN) VO FREE CHINA, Via Okeechobee, USA	S AMERICA • 100 kW
	DENMARK †DANMARKS RADIO, Via Norway	(J) • E NORTH AM & C AMERICA • 500 kW
	INDIA ALL INDIA RADIO, Aligarh	E AFRICA • 250 kW
	NORWAY †RADIO NORWAY INTL, Sveio	(J) • E NORTH AM & C AMERICA • 500 kW
	ROMANIA †RADIO ROMANIA INTL, Bucharest	AUSTRALASIA • 250 kW / (D) • W AFRICA • 250 kW / (D) • MIDEAST • 250 kW / (J) • AUSTRALASIA • 250 kW / (J) • E AFRICA • 250 kW / (J) • S AFRICA • 250 kW
	USA †R FREE AFGHANISTAN, Via Portugal	(J) • W ASIA & S ASIA • 250 kW
	†RFE-RL, Via Portugal	(J) • E EUROPE & W ASIA • 250 kW / (J) Su • E EUROPE • 250 kW
17810	GERMANY †DEUTSCHE WELLE, Via Antigua	AMERICAS • 250 kW / S AMERICA • 250 kW
	DEUTSCHE WELLE, Via Cyclops, Malta	S ASIA • 250 kW
	DEUTSCHE WELLE, Via Sri Lanka	AFRICA • 250 kW
	DEUTSCHE WELLE, Wertachtal	W AFRICA • 500 kW
	JAPAN RADIO JAPAN/NHK, Tokyo-Yamata	JAPANESE • SE ASIA • GENERAL • 300 kW / SE ASIA • GENERAL • 300 kW
	UKRAINE †UKRAINIAN R, Simferopol'	(D) • UKRAINIAN • W EUROPE & E NORTH AM • DS-2 • 500 kW
	UNITED KINGDOM BBC, Via Ascension	C AFRICA • 250 kW
	USA †VOA, Via Ascension	M-F • S AMERICA • 250 kW
	VOA, Via Kaválla, Greece	(D) • MIDEAST • 250 kW / (J) • MIDEAST • 250 kW
17815	BRAZIL RADIO CULTURA, São Paulo	PORTUGUESE • DS • 7.5 kW
	DENMARK †DANMARKS RADIO, Via Norway	(J) • MIDEAST & E AFRICA • 500 kW / (J) • AFRICA • 500 kW
	INDIA ALL INDIA RADIO, Delhi	(J) • DS • 50 kW / (J) • ENGLISH, ETC • DS • 50 kW
	MOROCCO RTV MAROCAINE, Tangier	N AFRICA & MIDEAST • 50 kW / EUROPE & W AFRICA • 50 kW / Sa • EUROPE & W AFRICA • 50 kW / Su-F • EUROPE & W AFRICA • 50 kW
	NORWAY †RADIO NORWAY INTL, Kvitsøy	(J) • MIDEAST & E AFRICA • 500 kW / (J) • AFRICA • 500 kW
	ROMANIA †RADIO ROMANIA INTL, Bucharest	(J) • W AFRICA • 250 kW / (J) • W EUROPE, C AMERICA & S AMERICA • 250 kW
	RUSSIA R MOSCOW INTL, Via Kyrgyzstan	(J) • S ASIA & SE ASIA • 100 kW
	VOICE OF RUSSIA, Via Kyrgyzstan	(D) • E ASIA & SE ASIA • 100 kW
	SOUTH AFRICA †RADIO RSA, Meyerton	(D) • E AFRICA & S AFRICA • 250 kW
	UNITED KINGDOM †BBC, Rampisham	(D) • E EUROPE • 500 kW
	UZBEKISTAN †RADIO TASHKENT, Tashkent	(J) • S ASIA & SE ASIA • 100 kW
17820	CANADA †R CANADA INTL, Sackville, NB	(D) M-F • C AMERICA • 250 kW / AFRICA • 250 kW / (D) • EUROPE • 250 kW / (J) • EUROPE • 250 kW / M-F • AFRICA • 250 kW

(con'd)

0 1 2 3 4 5 6 7 8 9 10 11 12 13 14 15 16 17 18 19 20 21 22 23 24

ENGLISH ▬   ARABIC ▨   CHINESE ▢▢▢   FRENCH ▭   GERMAN ▬   RUSSIAN ═   SPANISH ▬   OTHER ▬

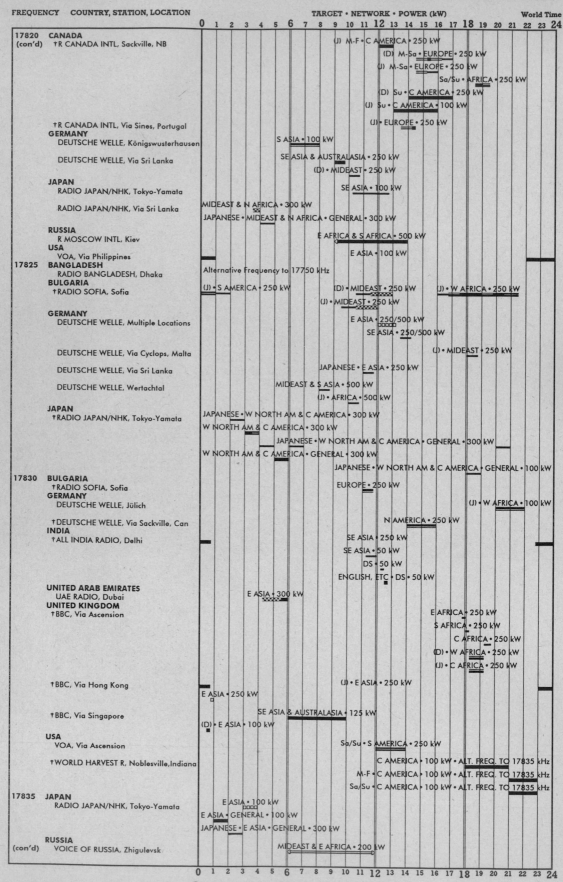

FREQUENCY   COUNTRY, STATION, LOCATION

TARGET • NETWORK • POWER (kW)   World Time

17820	CANADA	
(con'd)	†R CANADA INTL, Sackville, NB	(J) M-F • C AMERICA • 250 kW
		(D) M-Sa • EUROPE • 250 kW
		(J) M-Sa • EUROPE • 250 kW
		Sa/Su • AFRICA • 250 kW
		(D) Su • C AMERICA • 250 kW
		(J) Su • C AMERICA • 100 kW
	†R CANADA INTL, Via Sines, Portugal	(J) • EUROPE • 250 kW
	GERMANY	
	DEUTSCHE WELLE, Königswusterhausen	S ASIA • 100 kW
	DEUTSCHE WELLE, Via Sri Lanka	SE ASIA & AUSTRALASIA • 250 kW
		(D) • MIDEAST • 250 kW
	JAPAN	
	RADIO JAPAN/NHK, Tokyo-Yamata	SE ASIA • 100 kW
	RADIO JAPAN/NHK, Via Sri Lanka	MIDEAST & N AFRICA • 300 kW
		JAPANESE • MIDEAST & N AFRICA • GENERAL • 300 kW
	RUSSIA	
	R MOSCOW INTL, Kiev	E AFRICA & S AFRICA • 500 kW
	USA	
	VOA, Via Philippines	E ASIA • 100 kW
17825	BANGLADESH	
	RADIO BANGLADESH, Dhaka	Alternative Frequency to 17750 kHz
	BULGARIA	
	†RADIO SOFIA, Sofia	(J) • S AMERICA • 250 kW (D) • MIDEAST • 250 kW (J) • W AFRICA • 250 kW
		(J) • MIDEAST • 250 kW
	GERMANY	
	DEUTSCHE WELLE, Multiple Locations	E ASIA • 250/500 kW
		SE ASIA • 250/500 kW
	DEUTSCHE WELLE, Via Cyclops, Malta	(J) • MIDEAST • 250 kW
	DEUTSCHE WELLE, Via Sri Lanka	JAPANESE • E ASIA • 250 kW
	DEUTSCHE WELLE, Wertachtal	MIDEAST & S ASIA • 500 kW
		(J) • AFRICA • 500 kW
	JAPAN	
	†RADIO JAPAN/NHK, Tokyo-Yamata	JAPANESE • W NORTH AM & C AMERICA • 300 kW
		W NORTH AM & C AMERICA • 300 kW
		JAPANESE • W NORTH AM & C AMERICA • GENERAL • 300 kW
		W NORTH AM & C AMERICA • GENERAL • 300 kW
		JAPANESE • W NORTH AM & C AMERICA • GENERAL • 100 kW
17830	BULGARIA	
	†RADIO SOFIA, Sofia	EUROPE • 250 kW
	GERMANY	
	DEUTSCHE WELLE, Jülich	(J) • W AFRICA • 100 kW
	†DEUTSCHE WELLE, Via Sackville, Can	N AMERICA • 250 kW
	INDIA	
	†ALL INDIA RADIO, Delhi	SE ASIA • 250 kW
		SE ASIA • 50 kW
		DS • 50 kW
		ENGLISH, ETC • DS • 50 kW
	UNITED ARAB EMIRATES	
	UAE RADIO, Dubai	E ASIA • 300 kW
	UNITED KINGDOM	
	†BBC, Via Ascension	E AFRICA • 250 kW
		S AFRICA • 250 kW
		C AFRICA • 250 kW
		(D) • W AFRICA • 250 kW
		(J) • C AFRICA • 250 kW
	†BBC, Via Hong Kong	E ASIA • 250 kW (J) • E ASIA • 250 kW
	†BBC, Via Singapore	SE ASIA & AUSTRALASIA • 125 kW
		(D) • E ASIA • 100 kW
	USA	
	VOA, Via Ascension	Sa/Su • S AMERICA • 250 kW
	†WORLD HARVEST R, Noblesville, Indiana	C AMERICA • 100 kW • ALT. FREQ. TO 17835 kHz
		M-F • C AMERICA • 100 kW • ALT. FREQ. TO 17835 kHz
		Sa/Su • C AMERICA • 100 kW • ALT. FREQ. TO 17835 kHz
17835	JAPAN	
	RADIO JAPAN/NHK, Tokyo-Yamata	E ASIA • 100 kW
		E ASIA • GENERAL • 100 kW
		JAPANESE • E ASIA • GENERAL • 300 kW
	RUSSIA	
(con'd)	VOICE OF RUSSIA, Zhigulevsk	MIDEAST & E AFRICA • 200 kW

FREQUENCY   COUNTRY, STATION, LOCATION   TARGET • NETWORK • POWER (kW)   World Time

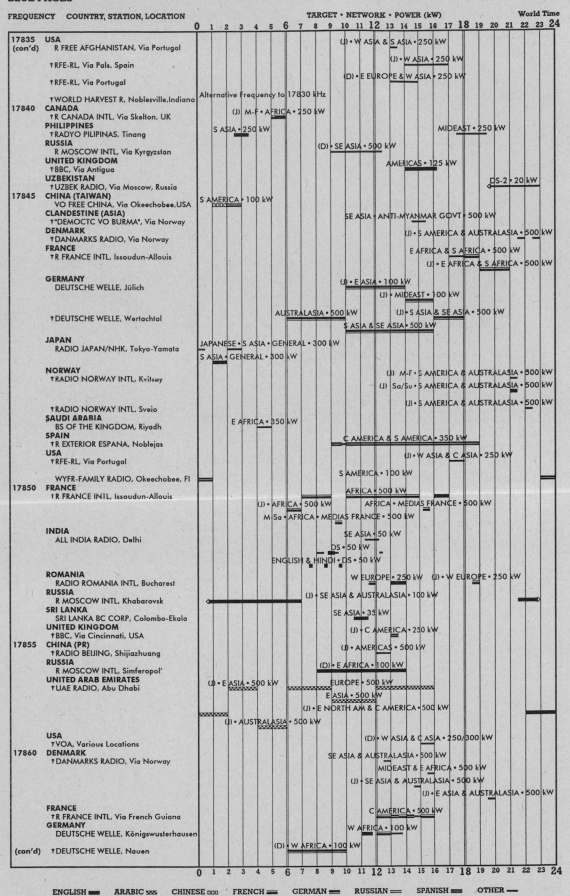

17835 (con'd)	USA
	R FREE AFGHANISTAN, Via Portugal — (J) • W ASIA & S ASIA • 250 kW
	†RFE-RL, Via Pals, Spain — (J) • W ASIA • 250 kW
	†RFE-RL, Via Portugal — (D) • E EUROPE & W ASIA • 250 kW
	†WORLD HARVEST R, Noblesville, Indiana — Alternative Frequency to 17830 kHz
17840	CANADA
	†R CANADA INTL, Via Skelton, UK — (J) M-F • AFRICA • 250 kW
	PHILIPPINES
	†RADYO PILIPINAS, Tinang — S ASIA • 250 kW MIDEAST • 250 kW
	RUSSIA
	R MOSCOW INTL, Via Kyrgyzstan — (D) • SE ASIA • 500 kW
	UNITED KINGDOM
	†BBC, Via Antigua — AMERICAS • 125 kW
	UZBEKISTAN
	†UZBEK RADIO, Via Moscow, Russia — DS-2 • 20 kW
17845	CHINA (TAIWAN)
	VO FREE CHINA, Via Okeechobee, USA — S AMERICA • 100 kW
	CLANDESTINE (ASIA)
	†"DEMOCTC VO BURMA", Via Norway — SE ASIA • ANTI-MYANMAR GOVT • 500 kW
	DENMARK
	†DANMARKS RADIO, Via Norway — (J) • S AMERICA & AUSTRALASIA • 500 kW
	FRANCE
	†R FRANCE INTL, Issoudun-Allouis — E AFRICA & S AFRICA • 500 kW
	— (J) • E AFRICA & S AFRICA • 500 kW
	GERMANY
	DEUTSCHE WELLE, Jülich — (J) • E ASIA • 100 kW
	— (J) • MIDEAST • 100 kW
	†DEUTSCHE WELLE, Wertachtal — AUSTRALASIA • 500 kW (J) • S ASIA & SE ASIA • 500 kW
	— S ASIA & SE ASIA • 500 kW
	JAPAN
	RADIO JAPAN/NHK, Tokyo-Yamata — JAPANESE • S ASIA • GENERAL • 300 kW
	— S ASIA • GENERAL • 300 kW
	NORWAY
	†RADIO NORWAY INTL, Kvitsøy — (J) M-F • S AMERICA & AUSTRALASIA • 500 kW
	— (J) Sa/Su • S AMERICA & AUSTRALASIA • 500 kW
	†RADIO NORWAY INTL, Sveio — (J) • S AMERICA & AUSTRALASIA • 500 kW
	SAUDI ARABIA
	BS OF THE KINGDOM, Riyadh — E AFRICA • 350 kW
	SPAIN
	†R EXTERIOR ESPANA, Noblejas — C AMERICA & S AMERICA • 350 kW
	USA
	†RFE-RL, Via Portugal — (J) • W ASIA & C ASIA • 250 kW
	WYFR-FAMILY RADIO, Okeechobee, Fl — S AMERICA • 100 kW
17850	FRANCE
	†R FRANCE INTL, Issoudun-Allouis — AFRICA • 500 kW
	— (J) • AFRICA • 500 kW AFRICA • MEDIAS FRANCE • 500 kW
	— M-Sa • AFRICA • MEDIAS FRANCE • 500 kW
	INDIA
	ALL INDIA RADIO, Delhi — SE ASIA • 50 kW
	— DS • 50 kW
	— ENGLISH & HINDI • DS • 50 kW
	ROMANIA
	RADIO ROMANIA INTL, Bucharest — W EUROPE • 250 kW (J) • W EUROPE • 250 kW
	RUSSIA
	R MOSCOW INTL, Khabarovsk — (J) • SE ASIA & AUSTRALASIA • 100 kW
	SRI LANKA
	SRI LANKA BC CORP, Colombo-Ekala — SE ASIA • 35 kW
	UNITED KINGDOM
	†BBC, Via Cincinnati, USA — (J) • C AMERICA • 250 kW
17855	CHINA (PR)
	†RADIO BEIJING, Shijiazhuang — (J) • AMERICAS • 500 kW
	RUSSIA
	R MOSCOW INTL, Simferopol' — (D) • E AFRICA • 100 kW
	UNITED ARAB EMIRATES
	†UAE RADIO, Abu Dhabi — (J) • E ASIA • 500 kW EUROPE • 500 kW
	— E ASIA • 500 kW
	— (J) • E NORTH AM & C AMERICA • 500 kW
	— (J) • AUSTRALASIA • 500 kW
	USA
	†VOA, Various Locations — (D) • W ASIA & C ASIA • 250/300 kW
17860	DENMARK
	†DANMARKS RADIO, Via Norway — SE ASIA & AUSTRALASIA • 500 kW
	— MIDEAST & E AFRICA • 500 kW
	— (J) • SE ASIA & AUSTRALASIA • 500 kW
	— (J) • E ASIA & AUSTRALASIA • 500 kW
	FRANCE
	†R FRANCE INTL, Via French Guiana — C AMERICA • 500 kW
	GERMANY
	DEUTSCHE WELLE, Königswusterhausen — W AFRICA • 100 kW
(con'd)	†DEUTSCHE WELLE, Nauen — (D) • W AFRICA • 100 kW

ENGLISH ▬▬   ARABIC ⸙⸙⸙   CHINESE □□□   FRENCH ▬   GERMAN ▬▬   RUSSIAN ══   SPANISH ▬▬   OTHER ▬

FREQUENCY   COUNTRY, STATION, LOCATION   TARGET • NETWORK • POWER (kW)   World Time

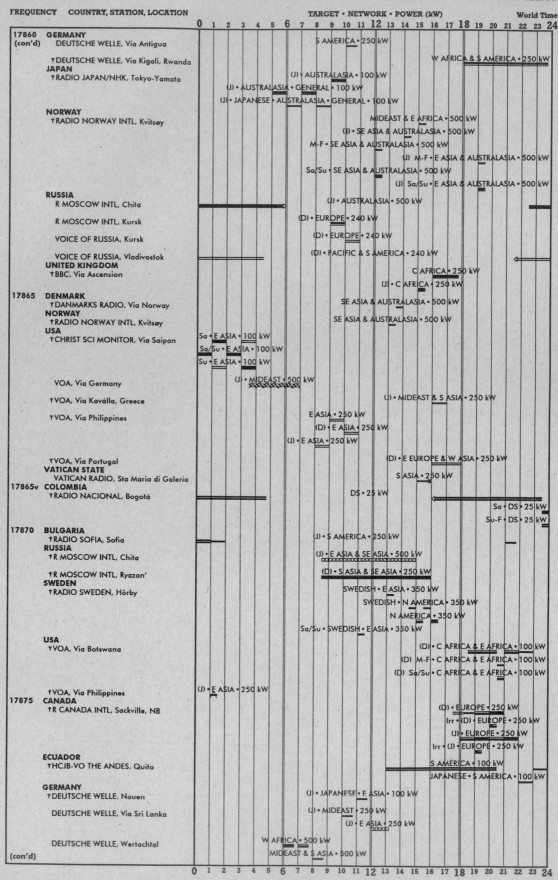

FREQUENCY	COUNTRY, STATION, LOCATION	TARGET • NETWORK • POWER (kW)
17860 (con'd)	GERMANY — DEUTSCHE WELLE, Via Antigua	S AMERICA • 250 kW
	†DEUTSCHE WELLE, Via Kigali, Rwanda	W AFRICA & S AMERICA • 250 kW
	JAPAN — †RADIO JAPAN/NHK, Tokyo-Yamata	(J) • AUSTRALASIA • 100 kW; (J) • AUSTRALASIA • GENERAL • 100 kW; (J) • JAPANESE • AUSTRALASIA • GENERAL • 100 kW
	NORWAY — †RADIO NORWAY INTL, Kvitsøy	MIDEAST & E AFRICA • 500 kW; (J) • SE ASIA & AUSTRALASIA • 500 kW; M-F • SE ASIA & AUSTRALASIA • 500 kW; (J) M-F • E ASIA & AUSTRALASIA • 500 kW; Sa/Su • SE ASIA & AUSTRALASIA • 500 kW; (J) Sa/Su • E ASIA & AUSTRALASIA • 500 kW
	RUSSIA — R MOSCOW INTL, Chita	(J) • AUSTRALASIA • 500 kW
	R MOSCOW INTL, Kursk	(D) • EUROPE • 240 kW
	VOICE OF RUSSIA, Kursk	(D) • EUROPE • 240 kW
	VOICE OF RUSSIA, Vladivostok	(D) • PACIFIC & S AMERICA • 240 kW
	UNITED KINGDOM — †BBC, Via Ascension	C AFRICA • 250 kW; (J) • C AFRICA • 250 kW
17865	DENMARK — †DANMARKS RADIO, Via Norway	SE ASIA & AUSTRALASIA • 500 kW
	NORWAY — †RADIO NORWAY INTL, Kvitsøy	SE ASIA & AUSTRALASIA • 500 kW
	USA — †CHRIST SCI MONITOR, Via Saipan	Sa • E ASIA • 100 kW; Sa/Su • E ASIA • 100 kW; Su • E ASIA • 100 kW
	VOA, Via Germany	(J) • MIDEAST • 500 kW
	†VOA, Via Kaválla, Greece	(J) • MIDEAST & S ASIA • 250 kW
	†VOA, Via Philippines	E ASIA • 250 kW; (D) • E ASIA • 250 kW; (J) • E ASIA • 250 kW
	†VOA, Via Portugal	(D) • E EUROPE & W ASIA • 250 kW
	VATICAN STATE — VATICAN RADIO, Sta Maria di Galeria	S ASIA • 250 kW
17865v	COLOMBIA — †RADIO NACIONAL, Bogotá	DS • 25 kW; Sa • DS • 25 kW; Su-F • DS • 25 kW
17870	BULGARIA — †RADIO SOFIA, Sofia	(J) • S AMERICA • 250 kW
	RUSSIA — †R MOSCOW INTL, Chita	(J) • E ASIA & SE ASIA • 500 kW
	†R MOSCOW INTL, Ryazan'	(D) • S ASIA & SE ASIA • 250 kW
	SWEDEN — †RADIO SWEDEN, Hörby	SWEDISH • E ASIA • 350 kW; SWEDISH • N AMERICA • 350 kW; N AMERICA • 350 kW; Sa/Su • SWEDISH • E ASIA • 350 kW
	USA — †VOA, Via Botswana	(D) • C AFRICA & E AFRICA • 100 kW; (D) M-F • C AFRICA & E AFRICA • 100 kW; (D) Sa/Su • C AFRICA & E AFRICA • 100 kW
	†VOA, Via Philippines	(J) • E ASIA • 250 kW
17875	CANADA — †R CANADA INTL, Sackville, NB	(D) • EUROPE • 250 kW; Irr • (D) • EUROPE • 250 kW; (J) • EUROPE • 250 kW; Irr • (J) • EUROPE • 250 kW
	ECUADOR — †HCJB-VO THE ANDES, Quito	S AMERICA • 100 kW; JAPANESE • S AMERICA • 100 kW
	GERMANY — †DEUTSCHE WELLE, Nauen	(J) • JAPANESE • E ASIA • 100 kW
	DEUTSCHE WELLE, Via Sri Lanka	(J) • MIDEAST • 250 kW; (J) • E ASIA • 250 kW
	DEUTSCHE WELLE, Wertachtal	W AFRICA • 500 kW; MIDEAST & S ASIA • 500 kW
(con'd)		

SUMMER ONLY (J)   WINTER ONLY (D)   JAMMING / OR ∧   EARLIEST HEARD ◁   LATEST HEARD ▷   NEW OR CHANGED FOR 1993 †

FREQUENCY   COUNTRY, STATION, LOCATION   TARGET • NETWORK • POWER (kW)   World Time

0 1 2 3 4 5 6 7 8 9 10 11 12 13 14 15 16 17 18 19 20 21 22 23 24

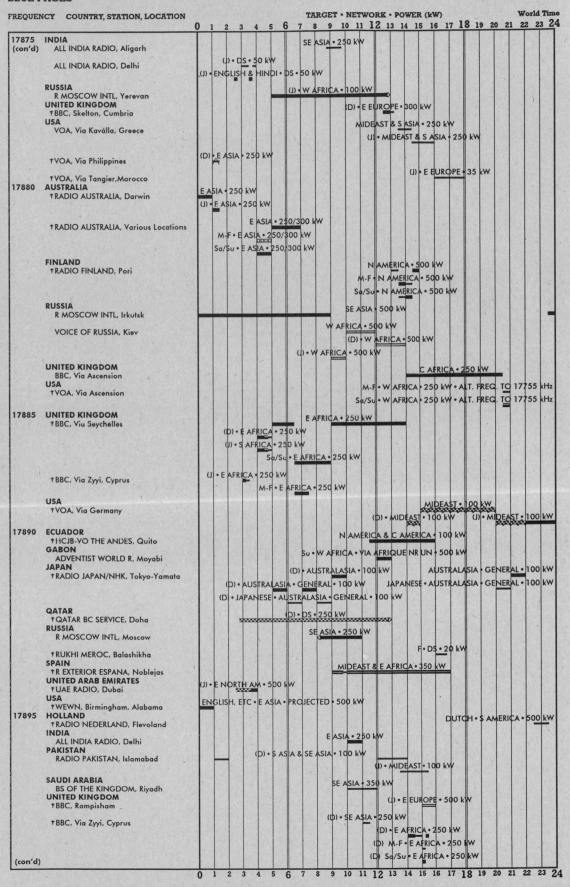

Frequency	Country, Station, Location	Target • Network • Power
17875 (con'd)	**INDIA** ALL INDIA RADIO, Aligarh	SE ASIA • 250 kW
	ALL INDIA RADIO, Delhi	(J) • DS • 50 kW
		(J) • ENGLISH & HINDI • DS • 50 kW
	RUSSIA R MOSCOW INTL, Yerevan	(J) • W AFRICA • 100 kW
	UNITED KINGDOM †BBC, Skelton, Cumbria	(D) • E EUROPE • 300 kW
	USA VOA, Via Kaválla, Greece	MIDEAST & S ASIA • 250 kW
		(J) • MIDEAST & S ASIA • 250 kW
	†VOA, Via Philippines	(D) • E ASIA • 250 kW
	†VOA, Via Tangier, Morocco	(J) • E EUROPE • 35 kW
17880	**AUSTRALIA** †RADIO AUSTRALIA, Darwin	E ASIA • 250 kW
		(J) • E ASIA • 250 kW
	†RADIO AUSTRALIA, Various Locations	E ASIA • 250/300 kW
		M-F • E ASIA • 250/300 kW
		Sa/Su • E ASIA • 250/300 kW
	FINLAND †RADIO FINLAND, Pori	N AMERICA • 500 kW
		M-F • N AMERICA • 500 kW
		Sa/Su • N AMERICA • 500 kW
	RUSSIA R MOSCOW INTL, Irkutsk	SE ASIA • 500 kW
	VOICE OF RUSSIA, Kiev	W AFRICA • 500 kW
		(D) • W AFRICA • 500 kW
		(J) • W AFRICA • 500 kW
	UNITED KINGDOM BBC, Via Ascension	C AFRICA • 250 kW
	USA †VOA, Via Ascension	M-F • W AFRICA • 250 kW • ALT. FREQ. TO 17755 kHz
		Sa/Su • W AFRICA • 250 kW • ALT. FREQ. TO 17755 kHz
17885	**UNITED KINGDOM** †BBC, Via Seychelles	E AFRICA • 250 kW
		(D) • E AFRICA • 250 kW
		(J) • S AFRICA • 250 kW
		Sa/Su • E AFRICA • 250 kW
	†BBC, Via Zyyi, Cyprus	(J) • E AFRICA • 250 kW
		M-F • E AFRICA • 250 kW
	USA †VOA, Via Germany	MIDEAST • 100 kW
		(D) • MIDEAST • 100 kW (J) • MIDEAST • 100 kW
17890	**ECUADOR** †HCJB-VO THE ANDES, Quito	N AMERICA & C AMERICA • 100 kW
	GABON ADVENTIST WORLD R, Moyabi	Su • W AFRICA • VIA AFRIQUE NR UN • 500 kW
	JAPAN †RADIO JAPAN/NHK, Tokyo-Yamata	(D) • AUSTRALASIA • 100 kW AUSTRALASIA • GENERAL • 100 kW
		(D) • AUSTRALASIA • GENERAL • 100 kW JAPANESE • AUSTRALASIA • GENERAL • 100 kW
		(D) • JAPANESE • AUSTRALASIA • GENERAL • 100 kW
	QATAR †QATAR BC SERVICE, Doha	(D) • DS • 250 kW
	RUSSIA R MOSCOW INTL, Moscow	SE ASIA • 250 kW
	†RUKHI MEROC, Balashikha	F • DS • 20 kW
	SPAIN †R EXTERIOR ESPANA, Noblejas	MIDEAST & E AFRICA • 350 kW
	UNITED ARAB EMIRATES †UAE RADIO, Dubai	(J) • E NORTH AM • 500 kW
	USA †WEWN, Birmingham, Alabama	ENGLISH, ETC • E ASIA • PROJECTED • 500 kW
17895	**HOLLAND** †RADIO NEDERLAND, Flevoland	DUTCH • S AMERICA • 500 kW
	INDIA ALL INDIA RADIO, Delhi	E ASIA • 250 kW
	PAKISTAN RADIO PAKISTAN, Islamabad	(D) • S ASIA & SE ASIA • 100 kW
		(J) • MIDEAST • 100 kW
	SAUDI ARABIA BS OF THE KINGDOM, Riyadh	SE ASIA • 350 kW
	UNITED KINGDOM †BBC, Rampisham	(J) • E EUROPE • 500 kW
	†BBC, Via Zyyi, Cyprus	(D) • SE ASIA • 250 kW
		(D) • E AFRICA • 250 kW
		(D) M-F • E AFRICA • 250 kW
		(D) Sa/Su • E AFRICA • 250 kW

(con'd)

0 1 2 3 4 5 6 7 8 9 10 11 12 13 14 15 16 17 18 19 20 21 22 23 24

ENGLISH ▬ ARABIC ⬝⬝⬝ CHINESE ⬝⬝⬝ FRENCH ▬ GERMAN ▬ RUSSIAN ═ SPANISH ▬ OTHER ▬

FREQUENCY   COUNTRY, STATION, LOCATION   TARGET • NETWORK • POWER (kW)   World Time

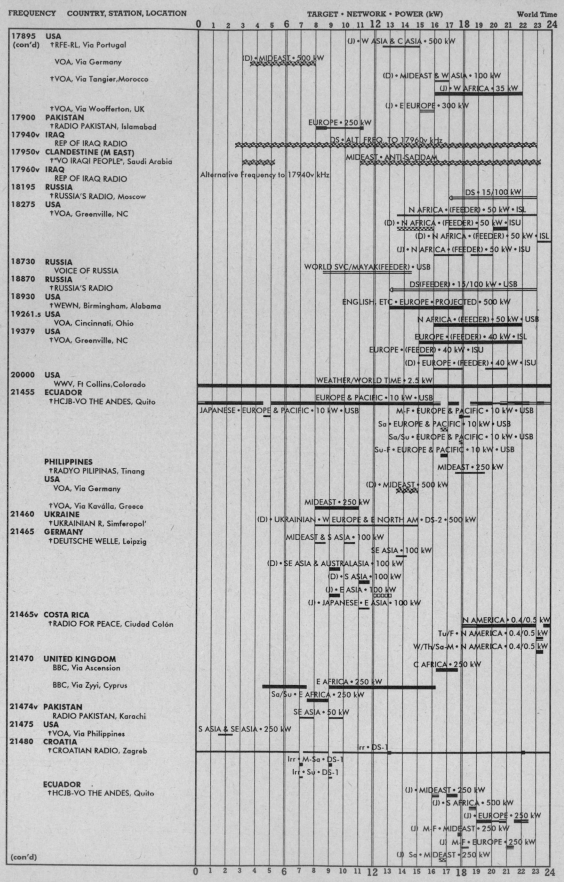

FREQUENCY	COUNTRY, STATION, LOCATION	TARGET • NETWORK • POWER (kW)
17895 (con'd)	USA †RFE-RL, Via Portugal	(J) • W ASIA & C ASIA • 500 kW
	VOA, Via Germany	(D) • MIDEAST • 500 kW
	†VOA, Via Tangier, Morocco	(D) • MIDEAST & W ASIA • 100 kW / (J) • W AFRICA • 35 kW
	†VOA, Via Woofferton, UK	(J) • E EUROPE • 300 kW
17900	PAKISTAN †RADIO PAKISTAN, Islamabad	EUROPE • 250 kW
17940v	IRAQ REP OF IRAQ RADIO	DS • ALT FREQ TO 17960v kHz
17950v	CLANDESTINE (M EAST) †"VO IRAQI PEOPLE", Saudi Arabia	MIDEAST • ANTI-SADDAM
17960v	IRAQ REP OF IRAQ RADIO	Alternative Frequency to 17940v kHz
18195	RUSSIA †RUSSIA'S RADIO, Moscow	DS • 15/100 kW
18275	USA †VOA, Greenville, NC	N AFRICA • (FEEDER) • 50 kW • ISL / (D) • N AFRICA • (FEEDER) • 50 kW • ISU / (D) • N AFRICA • (FEEDER) • 50 kW • ISL / (J) • N AFRICA • (FEEDER) • 50 kW • ISU
18730	RUSSIA VOICE OF RUSSIA	WORLD SVC/MAYAK(FEEDER) • USB
18870	RUSSIA †RUSSIA'S RADIO	DS(FEEDER) • 15/100 kW • USB
18930	USA †WEWN, Birmingham, Alabama	ENGLISH, ETC • EUROPE • PROJECTED • 500 kW
19261.5	USA VOA, Cincinnati, Ohio	N AFRICA • (FEEDER) • 50 kW • USB
19379	USA †VOA, Greenville, NC	EUROPE • (FEEDER) • 40 kW • ISL / EUROPE • (FEEDER) • 40 kW • ISU / (D) • EUROPE • (FEEDER) • 40 kW • ISU
20000	USA WWV, Ft Collins, Colorado	WEATHER/WORLD TIME • 2.5 kW
21455	ECUADOR †HCJB-VO THE ANDES, Quito	EUROPE & PACIFIC • 10 kW • USB / JAPANESE • EUROPE & PACIFIC • 10 kW • USB / M-F • EUROPE & PACIFIC • 10 kW • USB / Sa • EUROPE & PACIFIC • 10 kW • USB / Sa/Su • EUROPE & PACIFIC • 10 kW • USB / Su-F • EUROPE & PACIFIC • 10 kW • USB
	PHILIPPINES †RADYO PILIPINAS, Tinang	MIDEAST • 250 kW
	USA VOA, Via Germany	(D) • MIDEAST • 500 kW
	†VOA, Via Kaválla, Greece	MIDEAST • 250 kW
21460	UKRAINE †UKRAINIAN R, Simferopol'	(D) • UKRAINIAN • W EUROPE & E NORTH AM • DS-2 • 500 kW
21465	GERMANY †DEUTSCHE WELLE, Leipzig	MIDEAST & S ASIA • 100 kW / SE ASIA • 100 kW / (D) • SE ASIA & AUSTRALASIA • 100 kW / (D) • S ASIA • 100 kW / (J) • E ASIA • 100 kW / (J) • JAPANESE • E ASIA • 100 kW
21465v	COSTA RICA †RADIO FOR PEACE, Ciudad Colón	N AMERICA • 0.4/0.5 kW / Tu/F • N AMERICA • 0.4/0.5 kW / W/Th/Sa-M • N AMERICA • 0.4/0.5 kW
21470	UNITED KINGDOM BBC, Via Ascension	C AFRICA • 250 kW
	BBC, Via Zyyi, Cyprus	E AFRICA • 250 kW / Sa/Su • E AFRICA • 250 kW
21474v	PAKISTAN RADIO PAKISTAN, Karachi	SE ASIA • 50 kW
21475	USA †VOA, Via Philippines	S ASIA & SE ASIA • 250 kW
21480	CROATIA †CROATIAN RADIO, Zagreb	Irr • DS-1 / Irr • M-Sa • DS-1 / Irr • Su • DS-1
	ECUADOR †HCJB-VO THE ANDES, Quito	(J) • MIDEAST • 250 kW / (J) • S AFRICA • 500 kW / (J) • EUROPE • 250 kW / (J) • M-F • MIDEAST • 250 kW / (J) • M-F • EUROPE • 250 kW / (J) • Sa • MIDEAST • 250 kW

(con'd)

FREQUENCY　　COUNTRY, STATION, LOCATION　　　　TARGET • NETWORK • POWER (kW)　　　World Time

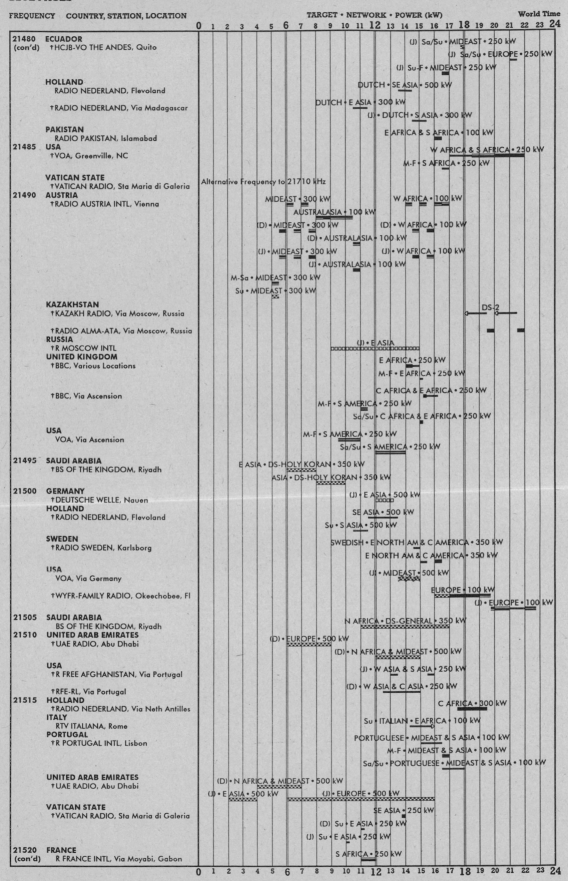

Frequency	Country, Station, Location	Target • Network • Power
21480 (con'd)	**ECUADOR** †HCJB-VO THE ANDES, Quito	(J) Sa/Su • MIDEAST • 250 kW; (J) Sa/Su • EUROPE • 250 kW; (J) Su-F • MIDEAST • 250 kW
	HOLLAND RADIO NEDERLAND, Flevoland	DUTCH • SE ASIA • 500 kW
	†RADIO NEDERLAND, Via Madagascar	DUTCH • E ASIA • 300 kW; (J) • DUTCH • S ASIA • 300 kW
	PAKISTAN RADIO PAKISTAN, Islamabad	E AFRICA & S AFRICA • 100 kW
21485	**USA** †VOA, Greenville, NC	W AFRICA & S AFRICA • 250 kW; M-F • S AFRICA • 250 kW
	VATICAN STATE †VATICAN RADIO, Sta Maria di Galeria	Alternative Frequency to 21710 kHz
21490	**AUSTRIA** †RADIO AUSTRIA INTL, Vienna	MIDEAST • 300 kW; AUSTRALASIA • 100 kW; W AFRICA • 100 kW; (D) • MIDEAST • 300 kW; (D) • W AFRICA • 100 kW; (D) • AUSTRALASIA • 100 kW; (J) • MIDEAST • 300 kW; (J) • W AFRICA • 100 kW; (J) • AUSTRALASIA • 100 kW; M-Sa • MIDEAST • 300 kW; Su • MIDEAST • 300 kW
	KAZAKHSTAN †KAZAKH RADIO, Via Moscow, Russia	DS-2
	†RADIO ALMA-ATA, Via Moscow, Russia	
	RUSSIA †R MOSCOW INTL	(J) • E ASIA
	UNITED KINGDOM †BBC, Various Locations	E AFRICA • 250 kW; M-F • E AFRICA • 250 kW; C AFRICA & E AFRICA • 250 kW
	†BBC, Via Ascension	M-F • S AMERICA • 250 kW; Sa/Su • C AFRICA & E AFRICA • 250 kW
	USA VOA, Via Ascension	M-F • S AMERICA • 250 kW; Sa/Su • S AMERICA • 250 kW
21495	**SAUDI ARABIA** †BS OF THE KINGDOM, Riyadh	E ASIA • DS-HOLY KORAN • 350 kW; ASIA • DS-HOLY KORAN • 350 kW
21500	**GERMANY** †DEUTSCHE WELLE, Nauen	(J) • E ASIA • 500 kW
	HOLLAND †RADIO NEDERLAND, Flevoland	SE ASIA • 500 kW; Su • S ASIA • 500 kW
	SWEDEN †RADIO SWEDEN, Karlsborg	SWEDISH • E NORTH AM & C AMERICA • 350 kW; E NORTH AM & C AMERICA • 350 kW
	USA VOA, Via Germany	(J) • MIDEAST • 500 kW
	†WYFR-FAMILY RADIO, Okeechobee, Fl	EUROPE • 100 kW; (J) • EUROPE • 100 kW
21505	**SAUDI ARABIA** BS OF THE KINGDOM, Riyadh	N AFRICA • DS-GENERAL • 350 kW
21510	**UNITED ARAB EMIRATES** †UAE RADIO, Abu Dhabi	(D) • EUROPE • 500 kW; (D) • N AFRICA & MIDEAST • 500 kW
	USA †R FREE AFGHANISTAN, Via Portugal	(J) • W ASIA & S ASIA • 250 kW
	†RFE-RL, Via Portugal	(D) • W ASIA & C ASIA • 250 kW
21515	**HOLLAND** †RADIO NEDERLAND, Via Neth Antilles	C AFRICA • 300 kW
	ITALY RTV ITALIANA, Rome	Su • ITALIAN • E AFRICA • 100 kW
	PORTUGAL †R PORTUGAL INTL, Lisbon	PORTUGUESE • MIDEAST & S ASIA • 100 kW; M-F • MIDEAST & S ASIA • 100 kW; Sa/Su • PORTUGUESE • MIDEAST & S ASIA • 100 kW
	UNITED ARAB EMIRATES †UAE RADIO, Abu Dhabi	(D) • N AFRICA & MIDEAST • 500 kW; (J) • E ASIA • 500 kW; (J) • EUROPE • 500 kW
	VATICAN STATE †VATICAN RADIO, Sta Maria di Galeria	SE ASIA • 250 kW; (D) Su • E ASIA • 250 kW; (J) Su • E ASIA • 250 kW
21520 (con'd)	**FRANCE** R FRANCE INTL, Via Moyabi, Gabon	S AFRICA • 250 kW

ENGLISH ▬　ARABIC ▨　CHINESE ▫▫▫　FRENCH ═　GERMAN ▬　RUSSIAN ═　SPANISH ▬　OTHER ▬

FREQUENCY	COUNTRY, STATION, LOCATION	TARGET • NETWORK • POWER (kW)	World Time

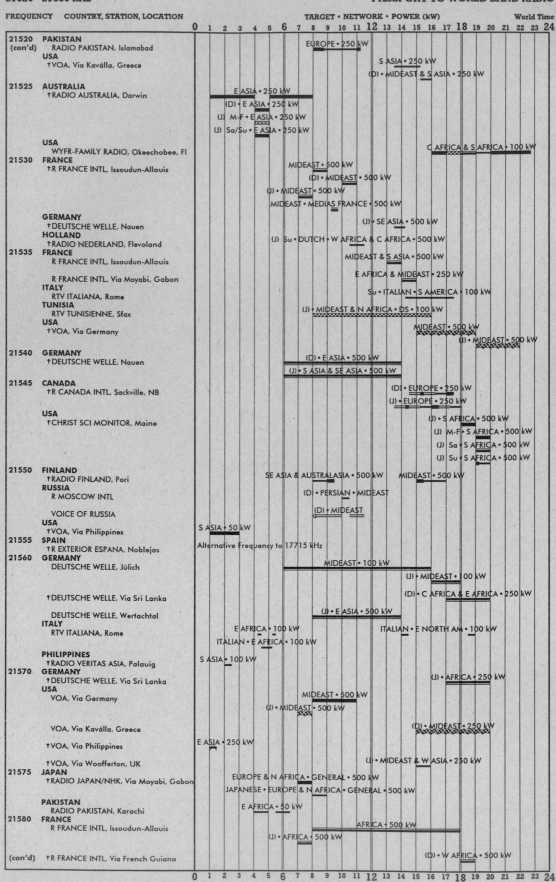

```
21520   PAKISTAN
(con'd)    RADIO PAKISTAN, Islamabad              EUROPE • 250 kW
        USA
           †VOA, Via Kaválla, Greece                          S ASIA • 250 kW
                                                  (D) • MIDEAST & S ASIA • 250 kW

21525   AUSTRALIA
           †RADIO AUSTRALIA, Darwin          E ASIA • 250 kW
                                          (D) • E ASIA • 250 kW
                                          (J) M-F • E ASIA • 250 kW
                                          (J) Sa/Su • E ASIA • 250 kW

        USA
           WYFR-FAMILY RADIO, Okeechobee, Fl          C AFRICA & S AFRICA • 100 kW
21530   FRANCE
           †R FRANCE INTL, Issoudun-Allouis     MIDEAST • 500 kW
                                             (D) • MIDEAST • 500 kW
                                        (J) • MIDEAST • 500 kW
                                        MIDEAST • MEDIAS FRANCE • 500 kW

        GERMANY
           †DEUTSCHE WELLE, Nauen                  (J) • SE ASIA • 500 kW
        HOLLAND
           †RADIO NEDERLAND, Flevoland    (J) Su • DUTCH • W AFRICA & C AFRICA • 500 kW
21535   FRANCE
           R FRANCE INTL, Issoudun-Allouis      MIDEAST & S ASIA • 500 kW

           R FRANCE INTL, Via Moyabi, Gabon       E AFRICA & MIDEAST • 250 kW
        ITALY
           RTV ITALIANA, Rome                  Su • ITALIAN • S AMERICA • 100 kW
        TUNISIA
           RTV TUNISIENNE, Sfax           (J) • MIDEAST & N AFRICA • DS • 100 kW
        USA
           †VOA, Via Germany                           MIDEAST • 500 kW
                                                  (J) • MIDEAST • 500 kW

21540   GERMANY
           †DEUTSCHE WELLE, Nauen              (D) • E ASIA • 500 kW
                                           (J) • S ASIA & SE ASIA • 500 kW

21545   CANADA
           †R CANADA INTL, Sackville, NB            (D) • EUROPE • 250 kW
                                                 (J) • EUROPE • 250 kW

        USA
           †CHRIST SCI MONITOR, Maine               (J) • S AFRICA • 500 kW
                                                (J) M-F • S AFRICA • 500 kW
                                                (J) Sa • S AFRICA • 500 kW
                                                (J) Su • S AFRICA • 500 kW

21550   FINLAND
           †RADIO FINLAND, Pori         SE ASIA & AUSTRALASIA • 500 kW    MIDEAST • 500 kW
        RUSSIA
           R MOSCOW INTL                   (D) • PERSIAN • MIDEAST

           VOICE OF RUSSIA                   (D) • MIDEAST
        USA
           †VOA, Via Philippines       S ASIA • 50 kW
21555   SPAIN
           †R EXTERIOR ESPANA, Noblejas   Alternative Frequency to 17715 kHz
21560   GERMANY
           DEUTSCHE WELLE, Jülich               MIDEAST • 100 kW

                                                    (J) • MIDEAST • 100 kW
           †DEUTSCHE WELLE, Via Sri Lanka       (D) • C AFRICA & E AFRICA • 250 kW

           DEUTSCHE WELLE, Wertachtal         (J) • E ASIA • 500 kW
        ITALY
           RTV ITALIANA, Rome          E AFRICA • 100 kW    ITALIAN • E NORTH AM • 100 kW
                                    ITALIAN • E AFRICA • 100 kW

        PHILIPPINES
           †RADIO VERITAS ASIA, Palauig   S ASIA • 100 kW
21570   GERMANY
           †DEUTSCHE WELLE, Via Sri Lanka              (J) • AFRICA • 250 kW
        USA
           VOA, Via Germany                   MIDEAST • 500 kW
                                        (J) • MIDEAST • 500 kW

           VOA, Via Kaválla, Greece              (D) • MIDEAST • 250 kW

           †VOA, Via Philippines      E ASIA • 250 kW

           †VOA, Via Woofferton, UK               (J) • MIDEAST & W ASIA • 250 kW
21575   JAPAN
           †RADIO JAPAN/NHK, Via Moyabi, Gabon   EUROPE & N AFRICA • GENERAL • 500 kW
                                        JAPANESE • EUROPE & N AFRICA • GENERAL • 500 kW

        PAKISTAN
           RADIO PAKISTAN, Karachi    E AFRICA • 50 kW
21580   FRANCE
           R FRANCE INTL, Issoudun-Allouis       AFRICA • 500 kW
                                          (J) • AFRICA • 500 kW

(con'd)   †R FRANCE INTL, Via French Guiana          (D) • W AFRICA • 500 kW
```

| | 0 1 2 3 4 5 6 7 8 9 10 11 12 13 14 15 16 17 18 19 20 21 22 23 24 |

FREQUENCY   COUNTRY, STATION, LOCATION   TARGET • NETWORK • POWER (kW)   World Time

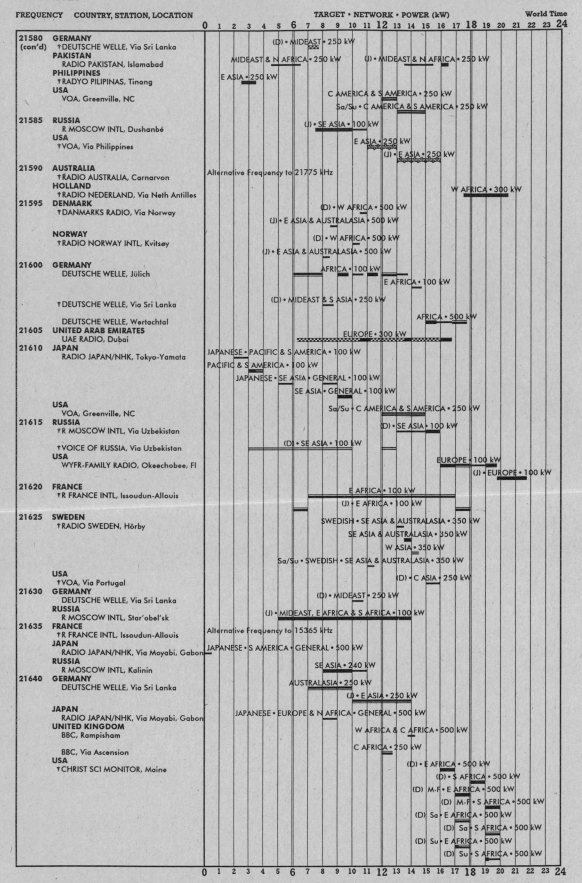

FREQUENCY	COUNTRY, STATION, LOCATION	TARGET • NETWORK • POWER (kW)
21580 (con'd)	GERMANY †DEUTSCHE WELLE, Via Sri Lanka	(D) • MIDEAST • 250 kW
	PAKISTAN RADIO PAKISTAN, Islamabad	MIDEAST & N AFRICA • 250 kW / (J) • MIDEAST & N AFRICA • 250 kW
	PHILIPPINES †RADYO PILIPINAS, Tinang	E ASIA • 250 kW
	USA VOA, Greenville, NC	C AMERICA & S AMERICA • 250 kW / Sa/Su • C AMERICA & S AMERICA • 250 kW
21585	RUSSIA R MOSCOW INTL, Dushanbé	(J) • SE ASIA • 100 kW
	USA †VOA, Via Philippines	E ASIA • 250 kW / (J) • E ASIA • 250 kW
21590	AUSTRALIA †RADIO AUSTRALIA, Carnarvon	Alternative Frequency to 21775 kHz
	HOLLAND †RADIO NEDERLAND, Via Neth Antilles	W AFRICA • 300 kW
21595	DENMARK †DANMARKS RADIO, Via Norway	(D) • W AFRICA • 500 kW / (J) • E ASIA & AUSTRALASIA • 500 kW
	NORWAY †RADIO NORWAY INTL, Kvitsøy	(D) • W AFRICA • 500 kW / (J) • E ASIA & AUSTRALASIA • 500 kW
21600	GERMANY DEUTSCHE WELLE, Jülich	AFRICA • 100 kW / E AFRICA • 100 kW
	†DEUTSCHE WELLE, Via Sri Lanka	(D) • MIDEAST & S ASIA • 250 kW
	DEUTSCHE WELLE, Wertachtal	AFRICA • 500 kW
21605	UNITED ARAB EMIRATES UAE RADIO, Dubai	EUROPE • 300 kW
21610	JAPAN RADIO JAPAN/NHK, Tokyo-Yamata	JAPANESE • PACIFIC & S AMERICA • 100 kW / PACIFIC & S AMERICA • 100 kW / JAPANESE • SE ASIA • GENERAL • 100 kW / SE ASIA • GENERAL • 100 kW
	USA VOA, Greenville, NC	Sa/Su • C AMERICA & S AMERICA • 250 kW
21615	RUSSIA †R MOSCOW INTL, Via Uzbekistan	(D) • SE ASIA • 100 kW
	†VOICE OF RUSSIA, Via Uzbekistan	(D) • SE ASIA • 100 kW
	USA WYFR-FAMILY RADIO, Okeechobee, Fl	EUROPE • 100 kW / (J) • EUROPE • 100 kW
21620	FRANCE †R FRANCE INTL, Issoudun-Allouis	E AFRICA • 100 kW / (J) • E AFRICA • 100 kW
21625	SWEDEN †RADIO SWEDEN, Hörby	SWEDISH • SE ASIA & AUSTRALASIA • 350 kW / SE ASIA & AUSTRALASIA • 350 kW / W ASIA • 350 kW / Sa/Su • SWEDISH • SE ASIA & AUSTRALASIA • 350 kW
	USA †VOA, Via Portugal	(D) • C ASIA • 250 kW
21630	GERMANY DEUTSCHE WELLE, Via Sri Lanka	(D) • MIDEAST • 250 kW
	RUSSIA R MOSCOW INTL, Star'obel'sk	(J) • MIDEAST, E AFRICA & S AFRICA • 100 kW
21635	FRANCE †R FRANCE INTL, Issoudun-Allouis	Alternative Frequency to 15365 kHz
	JAPAN RADIO JAPAN/NHK, Via Moyabi, Gabon	JAPANESE • S AMERICA • GENERAL • 500 kW
	RUSSIA R MOSCOW INTL, Kalinin	SE ASIA • 240 kW
21640	GERMANY DEUTSCHE WELLE, Via Sri Lanka	AUSTRALASIA • 250 kW / (J) • E ASIA • 250 kW
	JAPAN RADIO JAPAN/NHK, Via Moyabi, Gabon	JAPANESE • EUROPE & N AFRICA • GENERAL • 500 kW
	UNITED KINGDOM BBC, Rampisham	W AFRICA & C AFRICA • 500 kW
	BBC, Via Ascension	C AFRICA • 250 kW
	USA †CHRIST SCI MONITOR, Maine	(D) • E AFRICA • 500 kW / (D) • S AFRICA • 500 kW / (D) M-F • E AFRICA • 500 kW / (D) M-F • S AFRICA • 500 kW / (D) Sa • E AFRICA • 500 kW / (D) Sa • S AFRICA • 500 kW / (D) Su • E AFRICA • 500 kW / (D) Su • S AFRICA • 500 kW

ENGLISH ▬   ARABIC ▨   CHINESE ▦   FRENCH ▭   GERMAN ▬   RUSSIAN ═   SPANISH ▬   OTHER ─

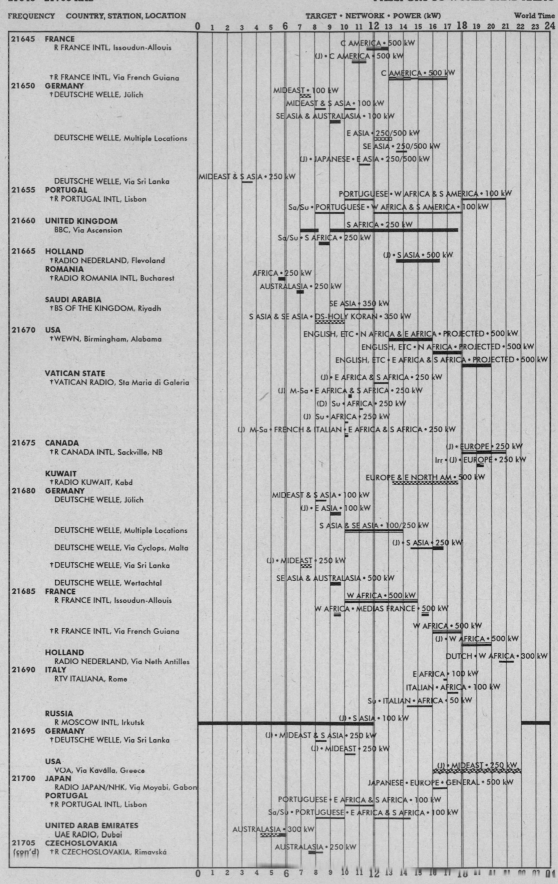

FREQUENCY   COUNTRY, STATION, LOCATION   TARGET • NETWORK • POWER (kW)   World Time

World Time scale: 0 1 2 3 4 5 6 7 8 9 10 11 12 13 14 15 16 17 18 19 20 21 22 23 24

Frequency	Country, Station, Location	Target • Network • Power (kW)
21645	**FRANCE** R FRANCE INTL, Issoudun-Allouis	C AMERICA • 500 kW
		(J) • C AMERICA • 500 kW
	†R FRANCE INTL, Via French Guiana	C AMERICA • 500 kW
21650	**GERMANY** †DEUTSCHE WELLE, Jülich	MIDEAST • 100 kW
		MIDEAST & S ASIA • 100 kW
		SE ASIA & AUSTRALASIA • 100 kW
	DEUTSCHE WELLE, Multiple Locations	E ASIA • 250/500 kW
		SE ASIA • 250/500 kW
		(J) • JAPANESE • E ASIA • 250/500 kW
	DEUTSCHE WELLE, Via Sri Lanka	MIDEAST & S ASIA • 250 kW
21655	**PORTUGAL** †R PORTUGAL INTL, Lisbon	PORTUGUESE • W AFRICA & S AMERICA • 100 kW
		Sa/Su • PORTUGUESE • W AFRICA & S AMERICA • 100 kW
21660	**UNITED KINGDOM** BBC, Via Ascension	S AFRICA • 250 kW
		Sa/Su • S AFRICA • 250 kW
21665	**HOLLAND** †RADIO NEDERLAND, Flevoland	(J) • S ASIA • 500 kW
	ROMANIA †RADIO ROMANIA INTL, Bucharest	AFRICA • 250 kW
		AUSTRALASIA • 250 kW
	SAUDI ARABIA †BS OF THE KINGDOM, Riyadh	SE ASIA • 350 kW
		S ASIA & SE ASIA • DS-HOLY KORAN • 350 kW
21670	**USA** †WEWN, Birmingham, Alabama	ENGLISH, ETC • N AFRICA & E AFRICA • PROJECTED • 500 kW
		ENGLISH, ETC • N AFRICA • PROJECTED • 500 kW
		ENGLISH, ETC • E AFRICA & S AFRICA • PROJECTED • 500 kW
	VATICAN STATE †VATICAN RADIO, Sta Maria di Galeria	(J) • E AFRICA & S AFRICA • 250 kW
		(J) M-Sa • E AFRICA & S AFRICA • 250 kW
		(D) Su • AFRICA • 250 kW
		(J) Su • AFRICA • 250 kW
		(J) M-Sa • FRENCH & ITALIAN • E AFRICA & S AFRICA • 250 kW
21675	**CANADA** †R CANADA INTL, Sackville, NB	(J) • EUROPE • 250 kW
		Irr • (J) • EUROPE • 250 kW
	KUWAIT †RADIO KUWAIT, Kabd	EUROPE & E NORTH AM • 500 kW
21680	**GERMANY** DEUTSCHE WELLE, Jülich	MIDEAST & S ASIA • 100 kW
		(J) • E ASIA • 100 kW
	DEUTSCHE WELLE, Multiple Locations	S ASIA & SE ASIA • 100/250 kW
	DEUTSCHE WELLE, Via Cyclops, Malta	(J) • S ASIA • 250 kW
	†DEUTSCHE WELLE, Via Sri Lanka	(J) • MIDEAST • 250 kW
	DEUTSCHE WELLE, Wertachtal	SE ASIA & AUSTRALASIA • 500 kW
21685	**FRANCE** R FRANCE INTL, Issoudun-Allouis	W AFRICA • 500 kW
		W AFRICA • MEDIAS FRANCE • 500 kW
	†R FRANCE INTL, Via French Guiana	W AFRICA • 500 kW
		(J) • W AFRICA • 500 kW
	HOLLAND RADIO NEDERLAND, Via Neth Antilles	DUTCH • W AFRICA • 300 kW
21690	**ITALY** RTV ITALIANA, Rome	E AFRICA • 100 kW
		ITALIAN • AFRICA • 100 kW
		Su • ITALIAN • AFRICA • 50 kW
	RUSSIA R MOSCOW INTL, Irkutsk	(J) • S ASIA • 100 kW
21695	**GERMANY** †DEUTSCHE WELLE, Via Sri Lanka	(J) • MIDEAST & S ASIA • 250 kW
		(J) • MIDEAST • 250 kW
	USA VOA, Via Kaválla, Greece	(J) • MIDEAST • 250 kW
21700	**JAPAN** RADIO JAPAN/NHK, Via Moyabi, Gabon	JAPANESE • EUROPE • GENERAL • 500 kW
	PORTUGAL †R PORTUGAL INTL, Lisbon	PORTUGUESE • E AFRICA & S AFRICA • 100 kW
		Sa/Su • PORTUGUESE • E AFRICA & S AFRICA • 100 kW
	UNITED ARAB EMIRATES UAE RADIO, Dubai	AUSTRALASIA • 300 kW
21705 (con'd)	**CZECHOSLOVAKIA** †R CZECHOSLOVAKIA, Rimavská	AUSTRALASIA • 250 kW

World Time scale: 0 1 2 3 4 5 6 7 8 9 10 11 12 13 14 15 16 17 18 19 20 21 22 23 24

SUMMER ONLY (J)   WINTER ONLY (D)   JAMMING / OR ∧   EARLIEST HEARD ◁   LATEST HEARD ▷   NEW OR CHANGED FOR 1993 †

FREQUENCY	COUNTRY, STATION, LOCATION	TARGET • NETWORK • POWER (kW)	World Time

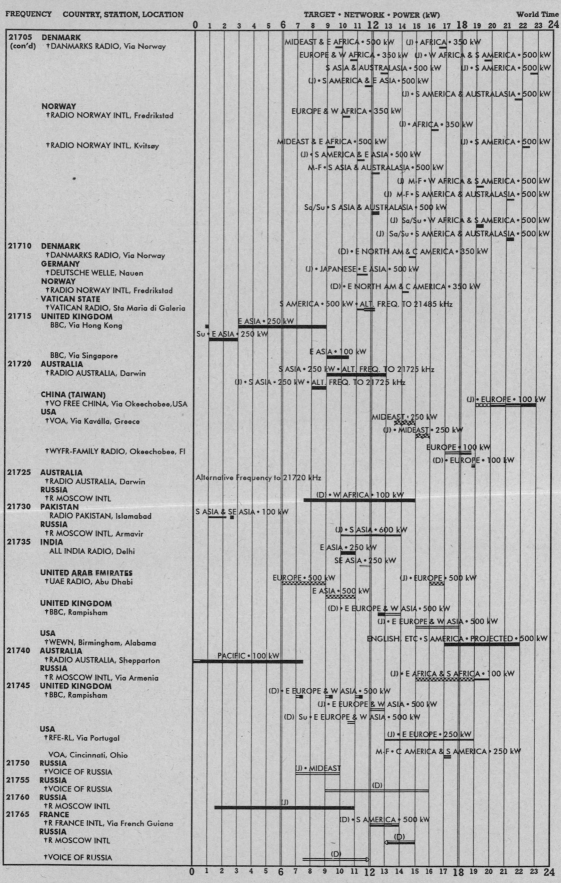

0 1 2 3 4 5 6 7 8 9 10 11 12 13 14 15 16 17 18 19 20 21 22 23 24

21705 DENMARK
(con'd) †DANMARKS RADIO, Via Norway
- MIDEAST & E AFRICA • 500 kW   (J) • AFRICA • 350 kW
- EUROPE & W AFRICA • 350 kW   (J) • W AFRICA & S AMERICA • 500 kW
- S ASIA & AUSTRALASIA • 500 kW   (J) • S AMERICA • 500 kW
- (J) • S AMERICA & E ASIA • 500 kW
- (J) • S AMERICA & AUSTRALASIA • 500 kW

NORWAY
†RADIO NORWAY INTL, Fredrikstad
- EUROPE & W AFRICA • 350 kW
- (J) • AFRICA • 350 kW

†RADIO NORWAY INTL, Kvitsøy
- MIDEAST & E AFRICA • 500 kW   (J) • S AMERICA • 500 kW
- (J) • S AMERICA & E ASIA • 500 kW
- M-F • S ASIA & AUSTRALASIA • 500 kW
- (J) M-F • W AFRICA & S AMERICA • 500 kW
- (J) M-F • S AMERICA & AUSTRALASIA • 500 kW
- Sa/Su • S ASIA & AUSTRALASIA • 500 kW
- (J) Sa/Su • W AFRICA & S AMERICA • 500 kW
- (J) Sa/Su • S AMERICA & AUSTRALASIA • 500 kW

21710 DENMARK
†DANMARKS RADIO, Via Norway
- (D) • E NORTH AM & C AMERICA • 350 kW

GERMANY
†DEUTSCHE WELLE, Nauen
- (J) • JAPANESE • E ASIA • 500 kW

NORWAY
†RADIO NORWAY INTL, Fredrikstad
- (D) • E NORTH AM & C AMERICA • 350 kW

VATICAN STATE
†VATICAN RADIO, Sta Maria di Galeria
- S AMERICA • 500 kW • ALT. FREQ. TO 21485 kHz

21715 UNITED KINGDOM
BBC, Via Hong Kong
- E ASIA • 250 kW
- Su • E ASIA • 250 kW

BBC, Via Singapore
- E ASIA • 100 kW

21720 AUSTRALIA
†RADIO AUSTRALIA, Darwin
- S ASIA • 250 kW • ALT. FREQ. TO 21725 kHz
- (J) • S ASIA • 250 kW • ALT. FREQ. TO 21725 kHz

CHINA (TAIWAN)
†VO FREE CHINA, Via Okeechobee, USA
- (J) • EUROPE • 100 kW

USA
†VOA, Via Kavála, Greece
- MIDEAST • 250 kW
- (J) • MIDEAST • 250 kW

†WYFR-FAMILY RADIO, Okeechobee, Fl
- EUROPE • 100 kW
- (D) • EUROPE • 100 kW

21725 AUSTRALIA
†RADIO AUSTRALIA, Darwin
- Alternative Frequency to 21720 kHz

RUSSIA
†R MOSCOW INTL
- (D) • W AFRICA • 100 kW

21730 PAKISTAN
RADIO PAKISTAN, Islamabad
- S ASIA & SE ASIA • 100 kW

RUSSIA
†R MOSCOW INTL, Armavir
- (J) • S ASIA • 600 kW

21735 INDIA
ALL INDIA RADIO, Delhi
- E ASIA • 250 kW
- SE ASIA • 250 kW

UNITED ARAB EMIRATES
†UAE RADIO, Abu Dhabi
- EUROPE • 500 kW   (J) • EUROPE • 500 kW
- E ASIA • 500 kW

UNITED KINGDOM
†BBC, Rampisham
- (D) • E EUROPE & W ASIA • 500 kW
- (J) • E EUROPE & W ASIA • 500 kW

USA
†WEWN, Birmingham, Alabama
- ENGLISH, ETC • S AMERICA • PROJECTED • 500 kW

21740 AUSTRALIA
†RADIO AUSTRALIA, Shepparton
- PACIFIC • 100 kW

RUSSIA
†R MOSCOW INTL, Via Armenia
- (J) • E AFRICA & S AFRICA • 100 kW

21745 UNITED KINGDOM
†BBC, Rampisham
- (D) • E EUROPE & W ASIA • 500 kW
- (J) • E EUROPE & W ASIA • 500 kW
- (D) Su • E EUROPE & W ASIA • 500 kW

USA
†RFE-RL, Via Portugal
- (J) • E EUROPE • 250 kW

VOA, Cincinnati, Ohio
- M-F • C AMERICA & S AMERICA • 250 kW

21750 RUSSIA
†VOICE OF RUSSIA
- (J) • MIDEAST

21755 RUSSIA
†VOICE OF RUSSIA
- (D)

21760 RUSSIA
†R MOSCOW INTL
- (J)

21765 FRANCE
†R FRANCE INTL, Via French Guiana
- (D) • S AMERICA • 500 kW

RUSSIA
†R MOSCOW INTL
- (D)

†VOICE OF RUSSIA
- (D)

0 1 2 3 4 5 6 7 8 9 10 11 12 13 14 15 16 17 18 19 20 21 22 23 24

ENGLISH ▬▬ ARABIC ⬚⬚⬚ CHINESE □□□ FRENCH ═══ GERMAN ▬▬ RUSSIAN ══ SPANISH ▬ OTHER ▬

FREQUENCY   COUNTRY, STATION, LOCATION   TARGET • NETWORK • POWER (kW)   World Time

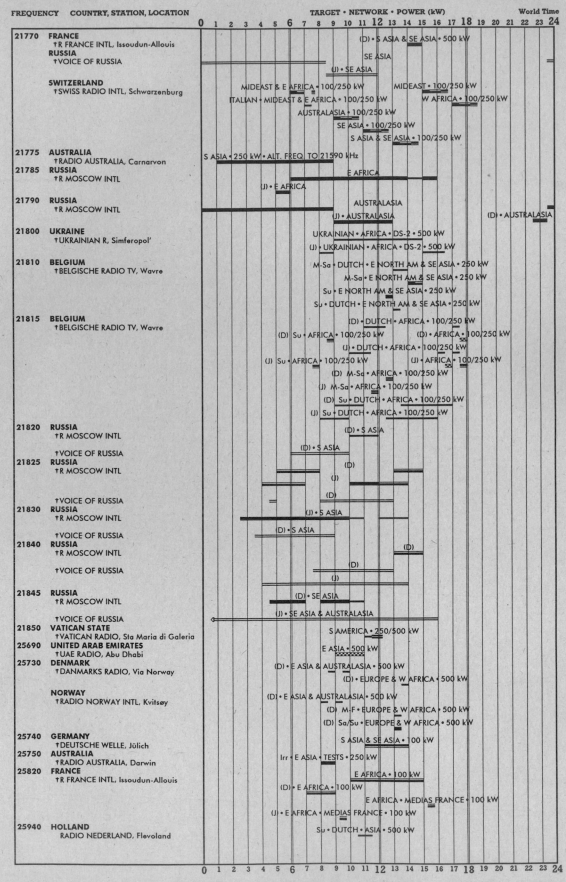

Frequency	Country, Station, Location	Target • Network • Power
21770	**FRANCE** †R FRANCE INTL, Issoudun-Allouis	(D) • S ASIA & SE ASIA • 500 kW
	RUSSIA †VOICE OF RUSSIA	SE ASIA / (J) • SE ASIA
	SWITZERLAND †SWISS RADIO INTL, Schwarzenburg	MIDEAST & E AFRICA • 100/250 kW / MIDEAST • 100/250 kW / ITALIAN • MIDEAST & E AFRICA • 100/250 kW / W AFRICA • 100/250 kW / AUSTRALASIA • 100/250 kW / SE ASIA • 100/250 kW / S ASIA & SE ASIA • 100/250 kW
21775	**AUSTRALIA** †RADIO AUSTRALIA, Carnarvon	S ASIA • 250 kW • ALT. FREQ. TO 21590 kHz
21785	**RUSSIA** †R MOSCOW INTL	E AFRICA / (J) • E AFRICA
21790	**RUSSIA** †R MOSCOW INTL	AUSTRALASIA / (J) • AUSTRALASIA / (D) • AUSTRALASIA
21800	**UKRAINE** †UKRAINIAN R, Simferopol'	UKRAINIAN • AFRICA • DS-2 • 500 kW / (J) • UKRAINIAN • AFRICA • DS-2 • 500 kW
21810	**BELGIUM** †BELGISCHE RADIO TV, Wavre	M-Sa • DUTCH • E NORTH AM & SE ASIA • 250 kW / M-Sa • E NORTH AM & SE ASIA • 250 kW / Su • E NORTH AM & SE ASIA • 250 kW / Su • DUTCH • E NORTH AM & SE ASIA • 250 kW
21815	**BELGIUM** †BELGISCHE RADIO TV, Wavre	(D) • DUTCH • AFRICA • 100/250 kW / (D) Su • AFRICA • 100/250 kW / (D) • AFRICA • 100/250 kW / (J) • DUTCH • AFRICA • 100/250 kW / (J) Su • AFRICA • 100/250 kW / (J) • AFRICA • 100/250 kW / (D) M-Sa • AFRICA • 100/250 kW / (J) M-Sa • AFRICA • 100/250 kW / (D) Su • DUTCH • AFRICA • 100/250 kW / (J) Su • DUTCH • AFRICA • 100/250 kW
21820	**RUSSIA** †R MOSCOW INTL	(D) • S ASIA
	†VOICE OF RUSSIA	(D) • S ASIA
21825	**RUSSIA** †R MOSCOW INTL	(D) / (J)
	†VOICE OF RUSSIA	(D)
21830	**RUSSIA** †R MOSCOW INTL	(J) • S ASIA
	†VOICE OF RUSSIA	(D) • S ASIA
21840	**RUSSIA** †R MOSCOW INTL	(D)
	†VOICE OF RUSSIA	(D) / (J)
21845	**RUSSIA** †R MOSCOW INTL	(D) • SE ASIA
	†VOICE OF RUSSIA	(J) • SE ASIA & AUSTRALASIA
21850	**VATICAN STATE** †VATICAN RADIO, Sta Maria di Galeria	S AMERICA • 250/500 kW
25690	**UNITED ARAB EMIRATES** †UAE RADIO, Abu Dhabi	E ASIA • 500 kW
25730	**DENMARK** †DANMARKS RADIO, Via Norway	(D) • E ASIA & AUSTRALASIA • 500 kW / (D) • EUROPE & W AFRICA • 500 kW
	NORWAY †RADIO NORWAY INTL, Kvitsøy	(D) • E ASIA & AUSTRALASIA • 500 kW / (D) M-F • EUROPE & W AFRICA • 500 kW / (D) Sa/Su • EUROPE & W AFRICA • 500 kW
25740	**GERMANY** †DEUTSCHE WELLE, Jülich	S ASIA & SE ASIA • 100 kW
25750	**AUSTRALIA** †RADIO AUSTRALIA, Darwin	Irr • E ASIA • TESTS • 250 kW
25820	**FRANCE** †R FRANCE INTL, Issoudun-Allouis	E AFRICA • 100 kW / (D) • E AFRICA • 100 kW / E AFRICA • MEDIAS FRANCE • 100 kW / (J) • E AFRICA • MEDIAS FRANCE • 100 kW
25940	**HOLLAND** RADIO NEDERLAND, Flevoland	Su • DUTCH • ASIA • 500 kW

Glossary

Terms and Abbreviations Used in World Band Radio

A variety of terms and abbreviations is used in world band radio. Some are specialized and need explanation; a few are foreign words that need translation; and yet others, are simply adaptations of common usage. Here, then is *Passport's* guide to what's what in world band terminology and abbreviations—including what each one means. For a through writeup on what determines how well a world band radio performs, please see the RDI White Paper, *How to Interpret Receiver Specifications and Lab Tests*.

Adjacent-Channel Rejection. *See* Selectivity.

AGC. *See* Automatic Gain Control.

Alt. Alternative frequency or channel. Frequency or channel that may be used unexpectedly in place of the regularly scheduled one.

Amateur Radio. *See* Hams.

AM Band. The local radio band, which currently runs from 520 to 1611 kHz (530–1705 kHz in the Western Hemisphere), within the Medium Frequency (MF) range of the radio spectrum. In many countries it is called the mediumwave (MW) band.

Analog Frequency Readout. Needle-and-dial tuning, greatly inferior to synthesized tuning for world band use. *See* Synthesizer.

Audio Quality, Audio Fidelity. *See* High Fidelity.

Automatic Gain Control (AGC). Smoothes out fluctuations in signal strength brought about by fading, a regular occurrence with world band signals.

AV. A Voz—Portuguese for "Voice of."

Bandwidth. The main variable to determine selectivity (*see*), bandwidth is the amount of radio signal at –6 dB a radio will let pass through, and thus be heard. With world band channel spacing at 5 kHz, the best single bandwidths are usually in the vicinity of 3 to 6 kHz. Better radios offer two or more selectable bandwidths: one of 5 to 7 kHz or so for when a station is in the clear, and one or more others between 2 to 4 kHz for when a station is hemmed in by other stations next to it. Proper selectivity is a key determinant of the aural quality of what you hear.

Baud. Rate by which radioteletype (*see*) is transmitted.

BC. Broadcasting, Broadcasting Company, Broadcasting Corporation.

Broadcast. A radio or TV transmission meant for the general public. *Compare* Utility Stations, Hams.

BS. Broadcasting Station, Broadcasting Service.

Cd. Ciudad—Spanish for "City."

Channel. An everyday term to indicate where a station is supposed to be located on the dial. World band channels are spaced exactly 5 kHz apart. Stations operating outside this norm are "off channel" (for these, *Passport* provides resolution to better than 1 kHz to aid in station identification).

Chugging. The sound made by some synthesized tuning systems when the tuning knob is turned. Called "chugging," as it is suggestive of the rhythmic "chug, chug" sound of a steam engine or chugalugging.

Cl. Club, Clube.

Cult. Cultura, Cultural.

(D). December. Heard winters only; not heard midyear.

Default. The setting a radio normally operates at, and to which it will eventually return.

Digital Frequency Display, Digital Tuning. *See* Synthesizer.

Domestic Service. *See* DS.

DS. Domestic Service—Broadcasting intended primarily for audiences in the broadcaster's home country. However, some domestic programs are relayed on world band to expatriates and other kinfolk abroad. *Compare* ES.

DXers. From an old telegraph term "to DX"; that is, to communicate over a great distance. Thus, DXers are those who specialize in finding distant or exotic stations. Few are considered to be regular DXers, but many others seek out DX stations every now and then, usually by bandscanning, which is facilitated by *Passport's* Blue Pages.

Dynamic Range. The ability of a receiver to handle weak signals in the presence of strong competing signals within the same world band segment (*see* World Band Spectrum). Sets with inferior dynamic range sometimes "overload," causing a mishmash of false signals mixed together up and down—and even beyond—the band segment being received.

Earliest Heard (or Latest Heard). See key at the bottom of each "Blue Page." If the *Passport* monitoring team cannot establish the definite sign-on (or sign-off) time of a station, the earliest (or latest) time that station could be traced is indicated, instead, by a triangular "flag." This means that the station almost certainly operates beyond the time shown by that "flag." It also means that, unless you live relatively close to the station, you're unlikely to be able to hear it beyond that "flagged" time.

ECSS. Exalted-carrier selectable sideband. *See* Synchronous Detector.

Ed, Educ. Educational , Educação, Educadora.

Em. Emissora, Emisora, Emissor, Emetteur—in effect, station in various languages.

Enhanced Fidelity. *See* High Fidelity.

EP. Emissor Provincial—Portuguese for "Provincial Station."

ER. Emissor Regional—Portuguese for "Regional Station."

Ergonomics. How handy and comfortable a set is to operate, especially hour after hour.

ES. External Service—Broadcasting intended primarily for audiences abroad. *Compare* DS.

External Service. *See* ES.

F. Friday.

Fax. *See* Radiofax.

Feeder. A utility station that transmits programs from the broadcaster's home country to a relay site some distance away. Although these specialized stations carry world band programming, they are not intended to be received by the general public. Many world band radios can process these quasi-broadcasts anyway. Feeders operate in lower sideband (LSB), upper sideband (USB) or independent sideband (termed ISL if heard on the lower side, ISU if heard on the upper side) modes. *See* Single Sideband, Utility Stations.

Frequency. The standard term to indicate where a station is located on the dial—regardless of whether it's "on-channel" or "off-channel" (*see* Channel). Measured in kilohertz (kHz) or Megahertz (MHz). Either measurement is equally valid, but to minimize confusion *Passport* designates frequencies only in kHz.

GMT. Greenwich Mean Time—*See* UTC.

Hams. Government-licensed amateur radio hobbyists who *transmit* to each other by radio, often by single sideband (*see*), for pleasure within special amateur bands. Many of these bands are within the shortwave spectrum (*see*). This is the same spectrum used by world band radio, but world band and ham radio are two very separate entities.

High Fidelity, Enhanced Fidelity. Radios with good audio performance and certain high-tech circuits can improve on the fidelity of world band reception. Among the newer fidelity-enhancing techniques is Synchronous Detection (*see*).

Image Rejection. A type of spurious-signal rejection (*see*).

Independent Sideband. *See* Single Sideband.

Interference. Sounds from other stations that are disturbing the one you're trying to hear. Worthy radios reduce interference by having good selectivity (*see*).

Ionosphere. *See* Propagation.

Irr. Irregular operation or hours of operation; i.e., schedule tends to be unpredictable.

ISB. Independent sideband. *See* Single Sideband.

ISL. Independent sideband, lower. *See* Feeder.

ISU. Independent sideband, upper. *See* Feeder.

(J). June. Heard midyear only; not heard winters.

Jamming. Deliberate interference to a transmission with the intent of discouraging listening.

kHz. Kilohertz, the most common unit for measuring where a station is on the world band dial. Formerly known as "kilocycles/second." 1,000 kilohertz equals one Megahertz.

kW. Kilowatt(s), the most common unit of measurement for transmitter power (*see*).

LCD. Liquid-crystal display. LCDs, if properly designed, are fairly easily seen in bright light, but require sidelighting under darker conditions. LCDs, being gray on gray, also tend to have mediocre contrast, and sometimes can be seen from only a certain angle or angles, but they consume nearly no battery power.

LED. Light-emitting diode. LEDs are very easily seen in the dark or in normal room light, but consume battery power and are hard to see in bright light.

Loc. Local.

Location. The physical location of a station's transmitter, which may be different from the studio location. Transmitter location is useful as a guide to reception quality. For example, if you're in Eastern North America and wish to listen to Radio Moscow International, a transmitter located in St. Petersburg will almost certainly provide better reception than one located in Siberia.

Longwave Band. The 148.5–283.5 kHz portion of the low-frequency (LF) radio spectrum used in Europe, the Near East, North Africa, Russia and Mongolia for domestic broadcasting. In general, these longwave signals, which have nothing to do with world band or shortwave signals, are not audible in other parts of the world.

LSB. Lower Sideband. *See* Feeder, Single Sideband.

LV. La Voix, La Voz—French and Spanish for "The Voice."

M. Monday.

Mediumwave Band, Mediumwave AM Band. *See* AM Band.

Memory(ies). *See* Preset.

Meters. An outdated unit of measurement used for individual world band segments of the shortwave spectrum. The frequency range covered by a given meters designation—also known as "wavelength"—can be gleaned from the following formula: frequency (kHz) = 299,792/meters. Thus, 49 meters comes out to a frequency of 6118 kHz—well within the range of frequencies included in that segment (*see* World Band Spectrum). Inversely, meters can be derived from the following: meters = 299,792/frequency (kHz).

MHz. Megahertz, a common unit to measure where a station is on the dial. Formerly known as "Megacycles/second." One Megahertz equals 1,000 kilohertz.

Mode. Method of transmission of radio signals. World band radio broadcasts are almost always in the AM mode, the same that's also used in the mediumwave AM band. The AM mode consists of three components: two "sidebands" and one "carrier." Each sideband contains the same programming as the other, and the carrier carries no programming, so a few stations are experimenting with the single-sideband (SSB) mode. SSB contains only one sideband, either the lower sideband (LSB) or upper sideband (USB), and no carrier. It requires special radio circuitry to be demodulated, or made intelligible. There are yet other modes used on shortwave, but usually not for world band. These include CW (Morse-type code), radiofax, RTTY (radioteletype) and narrow-band FM used by utility and ham stations. Narrow-band FM is not used for music, and is different from usual FM. *See* Single Sideband, ISB, ISL, ISU, LSB and USB.

N. New, Nueva, Nuevo, Nouvelle, Nacional, National, Nationale.

Nac. Spanish and Portuguese for "Nacional."

Nat, Natl. National, Nationale.

Other. Programs are in a language other than one of the world's primary languages.

Overloading. *See* Dynamic Range.

PBS. People's Broadcasting Station.

Power. Transmitter power *before* amplification by the antenna, expressed in kilowatts (kW). The present range of world band powers is 0.01 to 1,000 kW.

PR. People's Republic.

Preset. Allows you to select a station pre-stored in a radio's memory. The handiest presets require only one push of a button, as on a car radio.

Propagation. World band signals travel, like a basketball, up and down from the station to your radio. The "floor" below is the earth's surface, whereas the "player's hand" on high is the *ionosphere*, a gaseous layer that envelops the earth. While the earth's surface remains pretty much the same from day to day, the ionosphere—nature's own passive "satellite"—varies in how it propagates radio signals, depending on how much sunlight hits the "bounce points."

Thus, some world band segments do well mainly by day, whereas others are best by night. During winter there's less sunlight, so the "night bands" become unusually active, whereas the "day bands" become correspondingly less useful (see World Band Spectrum). Day-to-day changes in the sun's weather also cause short-term changes in world band radio reception; this explains why some days you can hear rare signals. Additionally, the 11-year sunspot cycle has a long-term effect on propagation.

PS. Provincial Station, Pangsong.

Pto. Puerto, Porto.

QSL. *See* Verification.

R. Radio, Radiodiffusion, Radiodifusora, Radiodifusão, Radiofonikos, Radiostantsiya, Radyo, Radyosu, and so forth.

Radiofax. Like ordinary fax-by-telephone, but by radio.

Radioteletype. Characters, but not illustrations, transmitted by radio. "Radio modem." *See* Baud.

Receiver. Synonym for a radio.

Reduced Carrier. *See* Single Sideband.

Reg. Regional.

Relay. A retransmission facility, shown in **bold** in "Worldwide Broadcasts in English" and "Voices from Home" in *Passport's* Worldscan section. Relay facilities are considered to be located outside the broadcaster's country. Being closer to the target audience, they usually provide superior reception. *See* Feeder.

Rep. Republic, République, República.

RN. *See* R and N.

RS. Radio Station, Radiostantsiya, Radiostudiya, Radiofonikos Stathmos.

RT, RTV. Radiodiffusion Télévision, Radio Télévision, and so forth.

RTTY. *See* Radioteletype.

S. San, Santa, Santo, São, Saint, Sainte. Also, South.

Sa. Saturday.

Scan, Scanning. Circuitry within a radio that allows it to band-scan or memory-scan automatically.

Selectivity. The ability of a radio to reject interference from signals on adjacent channels. Thus, also known as adjacent-channel rejection. A key variable in radio quality.

Sensitivity. The ability of a radio to receive weak signals. Also known as weak-signal sensitivity. Of special importance if you listening during the day, or if you're located in such parts of the world as Western North America and Australasia, where signals tend to be relatively weak.

Shortwave Spectrum. The shortwave spectrum—also known as the High Frequency (HF) spectrum—is, strictly speaking, that portion of the radio spectrum from 3-30 MHz (3,000-30,000 kHz). However, common usage places it from 2.3-30 MHz (2,000-30,000 kHz). World band operates on shortwave, but most of the shortwave spectrum is occupied by Hams (*see*) and Utility Stations (*see*)—*not* world band. Also, *see* World Band Spectrum.

Single Sideband, Independent Sideband. Spectrum- and power-conserving modes of transmission commonly used by utility stations and hams. Few broadcasters use these modes, but this may change early in the 21st century. Many world band radios are already capable of demodulating single-sideband transmissions, and some can even process independent-sideband transmissions. Certain single-sideband signals operate with reduced carrier, which allows them to be listened to, albeit with some distortion, on ordinary radios not equipped to demodulate single sideband. Properly designed synchronous detectors (*see*) prevent such distortion. *See* Feeder, Mode.

Site. *See* Location.

Slew Controls. Elevator-button-type up and down controls to tune a radio. On some radios with synthesized tuning, slewing is used in lieu of tuning by knob. Better is when slew controls are complemented by a tuning knob, which is more versatile.

SPR. Spurious (false) extra signal from a transmitter actually operating on another frequency.

Spurious-Signal Rejection. The ability of a radio receiver not to produce false, or "ghost," signals that might otherwise interfere with the clarity of the station you're trying to hear.

St, Sta, Sto. Abbreviations for words that mean "Saint."

Su. Sunday.

Synchronous Detector. World band radios are increasingly coming equipped with this high-tech circuit that greatly reduces fading distortion. Better synchronous detectors also allow for selectable sideband; that is, the ability to select the clearer of the two sidebands of a world band or other AM-mode signal. *See* Mode.

Synthesizer. Simple radios usually use archaic needle-and-dial tuning that makes it difficult to find a desired channel or to tell which station you are hearing, except by ear. Advanced models utilize a digital frequency *synthesizer* to tune in signals without your having to hunt and peck. Among other things, synthesizers allow for push-button tuning and presets, and display the exact frequency digitally—pluses that make tuning in the world considerably easier. Nearly a "must" feature.

Target. Where a transmission is beamed.

Th. Thursday.

Travel Power Lock. Control to disable the on/off switch to prevent a radio from switching on accidentally.

Transmitter Power. *See* Power.

Tu. Tuesday.

Universal Day. *See* UTC.

Universal Time. *See* UTC.

USB. Upper Sideband. *See* Feeder, Single Sideband.

UTC. Coordinated Universal Time, also known as World Time, Greenwich Mean Time and Zulu time. With nearly 170 countries on world band radio, if each announced its own local time you would need a calculator to figure it all out. To get around this, a single international time—UTC—is used. The difference between UTC and local time is detailed in the "Addresses PLUS" section of this *Passport*, or determined simply by listening to UTC announcements given on the hour by world band stations—or minute by minute by WWV and WWVH in the United States on such frequencies as 5000, 10000, 15000 and 20000 kHz. A 24-hour clock format is used, so "1800 UTC" means 6:00 PM UTC. If you're in, say, North America, Eastern Time is five hours behind UTC winters and four hours behind UTC summers, so 1800 UTC would be 1:00 PM EST or 2:00 PM EDT. The easiest solution is to use a 24-hour clock set to UTC. Many radios already have these built in, and UTC clocks are also available as accessories.

UTC also applies to the days of the week. So if it's 9:00 PM (21:00) Wednesday in New York during the winter, it's 0200 UTC *Thursday* World Day or Universal Day.

Utility Stations. Most signals within the shortwave spectrum are not world band stations. Rather, they are utility stations—radio telephones, ships at sea, aircraft and the like—that transmit point-to-point and are not intended to be heard by the general public. *Compare* Broadcast, Hams and Feeders.

v. Variable frequency; i.e., one that is unstable or drifting because of a transmitter malfunction.

Verification. A card or letter from a station verifying that a listener indeed heard that particular station.

Vo. Voice of.

W. Wednesday.

Wavelength. *See* Meters.

World Band Radio. Similar to regular mediumwave AM band and FM band radio, except that world band broadcasters can be heard over enormous distances and thus often carry news, music and entertainment programs created especially for audiences abroad. Some world band stations have audiences of over 100 million worldwide each day.

World Band Spectrum. The collected segments of the shortwave spectrum set aside by the International Telecommunication Union (ITU) for broadcasting. The ITU also allows some world band broadcasting to take place outside these sections. Official world band segments—along with, when appropriate, the "real world" segments [in brackets]—are detailed below, with general guides as to when reception should be best. Actual reception varies according to your location, station location, time of year, and other factors (*see* Propagation).

Rare, Faint Reception

*2 MHz (120 Meters):
2300–2498 kHz (Tropical domestic transmissions only)

Poor Reception Winter Nights

*3 MHz (90 Meters):
3200–3400 kHz (Tropical domestic transmissions only)

Fair-to-Good Reception Winter Nights except Americas

**4 MHz (75 Meters):
3900-3950 kHz (Asian & Pacific transmissions only)
3950-4000 kHz (European, African, Asian & Pacific transmissions only)

Weak-to-Fair Reception Winter Nights

*5 MHz (60 Meters):
4750–5060 kHz [4740–5100 kHz; to some extent 4000-4740 and 5100-5600 kHz] (Tropical domestic transmissions only)

Strong Night Reception, Some Day Reception

6 MHz (49 Meters):
5950–6200 kHz [5800–6305 kHz]
***7 MHz (41 Meters):
7100–7300 kHz [7100–7600 kHz] (No American-based transmissions below 7300 kHz)

Strong Night and Day Reception

9 MHz (31 Meters):
9500–9775 kHz [9350–10000 kHz; to some extent 9020-9350 kHz]

11 MHz (25 Meters):
11700–11975 kHz [11500–12160 kHz]

Strong Day Reception, Some Night Reception

*13 MHz (22 Meters):
[13600–13900 kHz]
15 MHz (19 Meters):
15100–15450 kHz [15000–15710 kHz]
17 MHz (16 Meters):
17700–17900 kHz [17500–17900 kHz]
21 MHz (13 Meters):
21450–21750 kHz [21450–21850 kHz]

Variable Day Reception

25 MHz (11 Meters):
25600–26100 kHz

World Day. *See* UTC.
World Time. *See* UTC.
WS. World Service.

*Shared with utility stations.
**Shared with American ham stations.
***7100-7300 kHz shared with American hams; 7300-7600 kHz shared with utility stations.

Printed in USA

Directory of Advertisers

Advertising Representative:
Mary Kroszner
IBS, Ltd.
Box 300
Penn's Park, PA 18943 USA
Telephone: 215/794-8252
Fax: 215/794-3396